2010
Principles of
Business Taxation

COORDINATING EDITOR

Linda M. Johnson, Ph.D., CPA
Accounting Professor (retired), and CEO, LNV Services, Inc.

AUTHORS

Alan D. Campbell, Ph.D., CPA

James Chapman, J.D., LL.M.

Janet Grange, J.D., CPA
Chicago State University

David Jaffe, J.D.

Linda M. Johnson, Ph.D., CPA
Accounting Professor (retired),
and CEO, LNV Services, Inc.

Mark Luscombe, J.D., LL.M., CPA

Gary L. Maydew, Ph.D, CPA
Iowa State University, Retired

Barry H. Williams, J.D., CPA
King's College

John P. Yuetter, Ph.D., CPA
Northeastern State University

SUSTAINABLE FORESTRY INITIATIVE

Certified Fiber Sourcing

www.sfiprogram.org

.CCH

a Wolters Kluwer business

Chicago

Editorial Staff

Lou Dagostino . . . . Production

This publication is designed to provide accurate and authoritative information in regard to the subject matter covered. It is sold with the understanding that the publisher is not engaged in rendering legal, accounting, or other professional service. If legal advice or other expert assistance is required, the services of a competent professional person should be sought.

ISBN 978-0-8080-2060-8

No claim is made to original government works; however, within this Product or Publication, the following are subject to CCH's copyright: (1) the gathering, compilation and arrangement of such government materials; (2) the magnetic translation and digital conversion of data, if applicable; (3) the historical, statutory and other notes and references; and (4) the commentary and other materials.

Printed in the United States of America

Preface

Most business students enrolled in the first federal income tax course at a four-year university do not pursue a career in tax. Moreover, upon graduation, more accounting majors are employed as auditors or corporate accountants than as tax practitioners. In fact, the vast majority of students who take the first tax course are not going to be tax practitioners at all. Thus, the big question is what is the best approach for the first tax course that can insure relevant and beneficial coverage for all students?

Traditional tax textbooks and undergraduate tax courses focus on individual income taxation and offer extensive coverage of personal items, such as who qualifies as a dependent, the rules regarding filing status, vacation homes, and qualifying for the earned income credit. Perhaps the rationale in this approach is that all students whether destined for tax practice or not can walk away with helpful information on individual income tax. Those students going into tax practice would have some basics to build on in future tax classes, and those who were not destined for tax practice could have some helpful information on their own financial future.

However, tax practice has changed and individual income tax preparation is no longer the major cornerstone of accounting services. Today, business tax planning and practice is more central to the modern accounting firm than individual tax compliance. The AICPA and others have posited for over a decade that a better starting point for teaching taxes is a business approach. Individual income taxation software has also taken much of the sting from individual income tax preparation, so the average business major is more likely to benefit from a good understanding of how business decisions, planning, and operations are affected by taxes than a crash course on the hundreds of tax rules that relate to their own individual taxes. Just as all business and finance majors are expected to understand the time value of money, basic tax considerations are now critical as well. Business decisions are based on the after-tax implications of decisions and the true cost of investment and risk.

Principles of Business Taxation focuses on the central concepts that build our tax framework and avoids many of the minor exceptions and details. This new text abandons minutia that not only affect a very small number of taxpayers, but also tend to change often. In this way there are no wasted motions. The book approaches the study of taxation from the perspective of the business person faced with business decisions that are inevitably affected by tax considerations. *Principles of Business Taxation* provides students with the necessary technical material to address common, everyday tax questions without feeling overwhelmed by the details. It accomplishes this by presenting the material in an easy-to-read and straight-forward manner. *Principles of Business Taxation* provides students who want to expand their technical knowledge with the skills to do so, by introducing them to tax research early in the book and then providing one research question in the homework for each subsequent chapter. This perspective leads to a very different coverage in this textbook—coverage that is useful for accounting, finance, and general business majors.

Using this approach, many items that pertain specifically to businesses usually not discussed in a traditional tax textbook are covered in this book. For example, *Principles of Business Taxation* emphasizes in each chapter the differences in how Generally Accepted Accounting Principles that students learn in their financial accounting courses and the tax laws they are learning in this course differ. This better prepares students to comprehend the need for the reconciliation between net income and taxable income on the corporate tax return and, more importantly, provides them with the foundation to perform this reconciliation before they enter their careers in auditing, accounting, or taxation. Although so many of the exclusions, deductions, and credits apply equally to individual and corporate taxpayers, this book focuses on the business perspective of these items. In some cases, this means covering an item not available to individuals (e.g., the dividends received deduction and the concept of earnings and profits and how it relates to corporate distributions). In other cases it means making the business, rather than the individual, aspects of the tax rules the primary focus of the topic.

While the focus is on concepts and how taxes affect business decisions, individual income taxation is not abandoned. After all, many core tax concepts apply to individuals as well as businesses, and the book is not shy in pointing out such application. As each topic is introduced and discussed, any differences that specifically apply to individuals are identified and discussed. For example, when charitable contributions are introduced, the general rules for deductibility are described, and then the limitations that apply to corporate and individual taxpayers are discussed separately. In addition, later in the book a special chapter that focuses on sole proprietorships includes an overview and summary of many of the tax rules that pertain specifically to individual taxpayers.

Also included in *Principles of Business Taxation* are two chapters on flow-through entities that tie together the underlying threads that have been introduced and discussed throughout the text. An overview of the rules for the formation and operation of, as well as the distributions from, flow-through entities are the primary focus of these last two chapters.

An advantage to this approach is that most of the students who take only one course in taxation will learn how businesses are taxed and, in turn, have a better appreciation for how taxes affect business decisions. Another advantage to this approach is that the topics dovetail into other business, finance, and accounting coursework.

Of course, we are fully aware that the vast majority of tax programs tend to stray from texts that move a little right or left of the traditional approaches. A perceived missing topic can often lead to a decision to stay with a traditional text rather than select a more streamlined approach. Fortunately, students using this book have access to a complete and comprehensive Fundamental Tax Topics library on CCH Study MATE, an online site that can be used to cover any and all fundamental tax topics. (A special card with access code is bound into this book.) In this way, we believe *Principles of Business Taxation* offers a tremendous opportunity for students of taxation to experience a course and text that truly offers the most useful approach for the future, and they can access these online courses for additional information that their instructor may deem helpful based on individual circumstances and objectives.

Your comments, criticisms, and questions are appreciated. We look forward to hearing from you.

Linda M. Johnson

March 2009

TABLE OF CONTENTS

PART I: OVERVIEW OF TAXES AND THE FEDERAL INCOME TAX SYSTEM

Chapter 1: Introduction to Taxation

Chapter 2: Understanding the Federal Tax Laws

Chapter 3: Tax Accounting

PART II: FEDERAL TAXATION OF BUSINESS INCOME AND DEDUCTIONS

Chapter 4: Federal Income Taxes and Gross Income

Chapter 5: Business Deductions: Ordinary and Necessary Business Expenses

Chapter 6: Business Deductions: Employment-Related Expenses

Chapter 7: Depreciation, Depletion, and Amortization

PART III: TRANSACTIONS INVOLVING BUSINESS PROPERTY

Chapter 8: Property Transactions: Realized and Recognized Gains and Losses

Chapter 9: Property Transactions: Character of Gain or Loss

PART IV: CALCULATING TAX LIABILITY AND TAXES OWED

Chapter 10: NOLs, AMT, and Other Business Taxes

Chapter 11: Tax Credits

PART V: BUSINESS ENTITY ISSUES

Chapter 12: Corporate Formation, Distributions, and Other Corporation-Related Tax Issues

Chapter 13: The Sole Proprietorship and Individual Tax Return

Chapter 14: Flow-Through Entities: Partnerships, LLPs, and LLCs

Chapter 15: Flow-Through Entities: S Corporations

Appendix

Finding Devices

PART I:

Overview of Taxes and the Federal Income Tax System

CHAPTER 1

Introduction to Taxation

Introduction to Taxation

LEARNING OBJECTIVES

1. Explain a government's need to tax.

2. List the various taxes U.S. residents and businesses pay and describe how the taxes are calculated.

3. Describe the factors governments take into consideration in deciding how to allocate the tax burden.

4. Explain why taxes are a transaction cost that should not be ignored when making decisions and why having a basic understanding of how the tax laws operate is important.

¶ 100 Introduction

But in this world nothing is certain but death and taxes. –Benjamin Franklin

This famous quote by Benjamin Franklin sums it up—there is just no way to avoid taxes. Sales taxes, property taxes, excise taxes, income taxes. It is hard to make it through the day without taxes affecting our lives. Thinking about taking on a second job to help pay your bills? Keep in mind that a portion of those extra earnings will go to the government to cover your payroll and income taxes. Have some money to invest? Depending on the type of investment you choose, you could end up sharing anywhere from zero percent to over 40 percent of the investment income with the government. Looking to buy a new car? The government could reimburse you up to $3,500 if you buy the right model at the right time of the year. Thinking about adopting a child? Depending on your income level, you can reduce your income taxes in 2009 by over $11,000 of the cost if the adoption is finalized by the end of the year. Heading to the grocery store? San Francisco debated a $.17 tax on grocery bags (not the groceries, just the bag itself).

So just how important are taxes to modern businesses? Major corporations employ dozens of tax specialists and pay tens of thousands of dollars each year for tax assistance from international and national accounting firms. Those accounting firms employ thousands of individuals who specialize in business taxation. Very few significant transactions occur in major corporations without their tax departments first analyzing them. For example, a business considering where to locate its new manufacturing facility will have cities, states, and even foreign countries lined up to discuss the tax incentives they can offer the company. Regardless of the aspect of business you plan to specialize in, eventually you will need to interact with the personnel in the tax department.

Therefore, it is essential that business students, and especially those majoring in accounting, have a basic understanding of how the tax laws operate.

This chapter describes the major role that taxes play when making decisions. It begins with a discussion of why governments tax and introduces some of the more common types of taxes that individuals and businesses frequently encounter. The chapter also discusses the various factors governments take into consideration when deciding whom and what to tax. It concludes with a discussion of why taxes are an important element to consider when making decisions.

¶ 101 Why Governments Must Tax

Taxes, after all, are dues that we pay for the privileges of membership in an organized society. –
Franklin D. Roosevelt

Why governments exist and the appropriate scope of government activities are philosophical and political questions. Within the United States, a broadly accepted role of government has been to protect the individual rights of citizens from threats within and outside its geographical boundaries. Accordingly, the federal government provides homeland security and national defense. Federal, state, and local governments all share responsibilities for enforcing laws protecting individual rights. Governments also fund the development of economic infrastructure, including roadways, water supply, and air traffic control. Modern governments also fund public services such as providing and maintaining schools, hospitals, and emergency response systems. They also provide benefits to the poor, elderly, and disabled. These are only a few of the many types of services that persons living in the United States have come to expect from the government. Still, the list is sufficient to illustrate that governments must spend tremendous amounts of cash to fund the goods and services they provide. Like any business, governments must generate revenues in order to pay for their expenditures. Taxes are the primary mechanism by which funds are transferred from the private sector (individuals and businesses) to the government.

¶ 102 Allocating the Tax Burden

The point to remember is that what the government gives it must first take away. –**John S. Coleman, address, Detroit Chamber of Commerce, 1956**

Although the need for revenues may be evident, the tax systems governments use to raise tax revenues are more complicated. To illustrate the dilemma governments face when deciding whom and what to tax, take as an example a neighborhood community where the residents have concerns about security. The community has voted to pay a security firm to patrol its streets between 10 p.m. and 6 a.m. each night, and now it must decide how to pay the $50,000 annual fee for these services. One option would be to divide the cost only among those in the community who want the security service. However, those who claim not to want the security service (perhaps to avoid paying for it) will still enjoy the benefits. Economists refer to this as a free-rider problem. In this case, the security service is a **public good**. A distinguishing characteristic of a public good is that there is no effective means of limiting the enjoyment of the good.

To avoid the free-rider problem, the community could divide the costs equally among all residences. This approach has the benefit of simplicity. Of course, this is not the only way to allocate the costs. For example, some community members might argue that residents with more expensive homes have more to gain from a security service and, therefore, should contribute more toward the costs. These members suggest that the cost should be spread among residences unequally, based on the assessed value of the homes. Although admittedly this approach would be more complicated, they believe it would be a much more equitable method of allocating the costs.

Now contrast the above situation with a community that wants to add a recreation center to the neighborhood. The community has agreed all homeowners would share in the cost of constructing the facility, and it is now in the process of deciding who should pay the annual costs of operating and maintaining the facility. Unlike the previous situation where providing security benefits the entire community, in this scenario, the community is able to control access to the facility and thus has the option of charging user fees to those who use it. However, the presence of a recreation center may make the community a more attractive place to live, which could cause property values to increase. Accordingly, the community needs to decide whether it would be appropriate to require only those who use the recreation center to bear the entire cost of maintaining it. These are the types of issues governments face when deciding whom and what to tax in order to raise revenues to fund government-provided goods and services.

When two parties enter into a transaction (including situations in which the government provides goods and services), the transaction may positively or negatively affect third parties. When the transaction affects persons or businesses unrelated to the transaction, economists refer to the situation as an **externality**. A negative externality results in a cost unwillingly borne by someone other than the parties involved in the transaction. An example of a negative externality is the pollution a factory generates during the manufacturing process. The costs neighboring residents and businesses bear in the form of poorer air quality, lower property values, etc., are a negative externality.

A positive externality, on the other hand, results when third parties derive benefits from the transaction. Public transportation is an example in which persons enter into transactions with the government to use a government-provided service. When individuals choose to use public transportation rather than drive their own vehicles, roadway congestion decreases and air quality improves. In addition, property values tend to be higher in areas that offer public transportation. Because public transportation provides benefits that extend beyond those who use it, governments generally charge a reduced user fee and find other ways to finance the remainder of the costs.

¶ 103 Deciding on a Tax Structure

When the government provides goods or services that are not public goods, it has the option of imposing a user fee on those who utilize the goods or services. Typically user fees are a flat amount. Examples of the government's use of user fees are the tollbooth charges drivers pay to use the Florida turnpike, entrance fees those who visit the Grand Canyon National Park pay, or the cost of postage for those who use the U.S. Postal Service to mail letters and packages.

If the amounts collected from user fees are not sufficient to cover the entire costs or if a public good is involved, the government raises the necessary revenues by imposing other taxes. This involves applying a tax rate to a tax base. Deciding on a **tax base** involves determining whom and what to tax. The tax base might be the amount of an employee's wages, the value of property, or the retail sales price of an item. However, many other tax bases could be used. Once the tax base has been established, it is multiplied by a tax rate to determine the amount of tax. Three types of tax rate structures are regressive, proportional, and progressive.

To illustrate the differences among these three tax rate structures, assume that a government needs to raise $12,000 in revenues from its residents. To keep things simple, the tax can be raised from two residents: Tom Johnson and Jane Smith. The government has decided that its tax base will be based on employee wages, and it now must decide upon a tax rate.

Under Proposal A, a tax rate of 7.65 percent would be imposed on the first $94,200 of employee wages. All wages in excess of that amount would be subject to a 1.45-percent tax. During the current year, Tom and Jane earn wages of $120,000 and $60,000, respectively. Their tax liabilities would be computed as follows.

Tom's tax liability under Proposal A

$94,200 × 7.65%	$ 7,206
($120,000 – $94,200) × 1.45%	374
	$ 7,580

Jane's tax liability under Proposal A
$60,000 × 7.65% $ 4,590

Total taxes raised ($7,580 + $4,590) $12,170

Under the tax structure in Proposal A, Tom would pay more taxes than Jane. However, Tom's $7,580 tax liability on his $120,000 tax base means that his average tax rate is only 6.32 percent ($7,580 ÷ $120,000), as compared to Jane's 7.65-percent average tax rate ($4,590 ÷ $60,000). By calculating the **average tax rate** (total tax liability ÷ the tax base) for each taxpayer, one can see what portion of each taxpayer's tax base is used to finance the tax burden. Although Tom would pay more tax than Jane, a smaller portion of his wages would be used to pay his share of the taxes. A tax structure in which the *average tax rate decreases as the tax base increases* is called a **regressive tax**.

Under Proposal B, a single tax rate of 6.75 percent would apply to all employee wages. A tax structure in which the *average tax rate stays constant as the tax base fluctuates* is called a **proportional tax**. This type of tax is also commonly called a **flat tax**.

Tom's tax liability under Proposal B
$120,000 × 6.75% $ 8,100

Jane's tax liability under Proposal B
$60,000 × 6.75% $ 4,050

Total taxes raised ($8,100 + $4,050) $12,150

Under Proposal C, the first $20,000 of wages would be taxed at two percent. Wages in excess of $20,000 but less than or equal to $40,000 would be taxed at four percent, wages in excess of $40,000 but less than or equal to $80,000 would be taxed at eight percent, and all wages in excess of $80,000 would be taxed at 12 percent. Under Proposal C, Tom and Jane's tax liabilities would be computed as follows.

Tom's tax liability under Proposal C
$20,000 × 2% $ 400
($40,000 – $20,000) × 4%   800
($80,000 – $40,000) × 8%   3,200
($120,000 – $80,000) × 12%   4,800
                                                       $ 9,200

Jane's tax liability under Proposal C
$20,000 × 2% $ 400
($40,000 – $20,000) × 4%   800
($60,000 – $40,000) × 8%   1,600
                                                       $ 2,800

Total taxes raised ($9,200 + $2,800) $12,000

Under Proposal C, Tom would not only pay more tax dollars than Jane would, but he would also pay a greater percentage of his gross wages in tax ($9,200 ÷ $120,000 = 7.67% versus Jane's $2,800 ÷ $60,000 = 4.67%). A tax structure where the *average tax rate increases as the tax base increases* is called a **progressive tax**.

Although each of these three proposals achieve the government's goal of raising the $12,000 of revenues needed to finance government operations, the distribution of the tax burden differs among the three tax rate structures. Thus, in addition to deciding upon a tax base, governments must also decide which tax rate structure to use. A proportional (flat) tax rate has the advantage of simplicity because each taxpayer is subject to the same single rate of tax. Although somewhat more complicated to calculate, a progressive tax allows governments to collect a greater portion of the tax liability from those who have higher tax bases. In the section that follows, the more commonly encountered taxes imposed by federal, state, and local governments in the United States are discussed. For each type of tax, pay special attention not only to the tax base employed but also to the tax rate structure used to calculate the tax. Governments use a variety of tax bases and rate schedules.

¶ 104 Major Types of Taxes

The federal government generates most of its revenues from income taxes and payroll taxes. In contrast, a main source of revenues for most local governments is property taxes; for state governments, sales taxes and income taxes are the main sources of revenues. Taxes affect everyday transactions. They directly affect the amount we pay for merchandise (sales tax) and certain items like gasoline, tobacco, and alcohol (excise taxes). They also reduce the amount employees take home from their paychecks (income taxes and payroll taxes) as well as affect the amount people pay to own property (property taxes). Businesses are affected by taxes when they hire employees (employment taxes), own property (property taxes), or generate profits (income taxes). Because taxes represent additional costs to individuals and businesses, they need to understand the various types of taxes they may encounter during the normal course of business. Although not every tax is discussed in this chapter, the more commonly encountered taxes are introduced.

.01 Property Taxes

State and local governments raise a significant portion of their revenues by collecting property taxes from property owners. For the twelve month period ending September 30, 2008, 31.6 percent of all state and local revenues came from property taxes.[1] Most property taxes are **ad valorem taxes**, which means the value of the property is used as the tax base. The tax rate used for computing property taxes is typically a single tax rate, making it a proportional or flat tax. In deciding what property to tax, governments realize that unless they can keep track of the owners of the property, low compliance will result. Thus, the most common property taxes are levied on real estate and personal property for which ownership records are kept.

Real estate taxes. The most common property tax the government collects is the annual tax imposed on owners of land and buildings. Since land and buildings are **real property,** this type of tax is commonly called a "real estate tax." Local (county) governments keep records of the owners of real property, thereby allowing them to collect real estate taxes with relatively low administrative and compliance costs. The tax base for real estate taxes is the property's value (or some percentage thereof). Since the true value of real property can only be ascertained upon its sale to an unrelated party, using value as a tax base requires that the real estate be periodically appraised. The appraisal process for real estate varies, but a commonly used method involves having a government worker

---

[1] U.S. Census Bureau. Federal, State, and Local Governments Table 1. National Totals of State and Local Tax Revenue, By Type of Tax. http://www.census.gov/govs/www/qtax.html Page last modified, September 26, 2008.

research recent sales of comparable property along with other relevant data to establish the property's value. The appraised value (or portion thereof) is then used to calculate the amount of property tax the real estate owners must pay. Many states calculate the real estate tax using a millage system. With a millage system the property tax rate is called the "millage rate" and is expressed in "mills." A mill is $1 per $1,000 of property value. So, for example, a millage rate of 15 mills would mean you would pay $1,500 per $100,000 of the property's taxable value.

Example 1: Stanford, Inc. operates a storefront in a county that imposes an annual real estate tax equal to one percent of the appraised value of the property. During 2008, Stanford's building was appraised at $300,000. Thus, its 2008 real estate taxes were $3,000 ($300,000 × 1%). During 2009, the building is appraised for $317,000, and accordingly, its real estate taxes for 2009 increase to $3,170 ($317,000 × 1%). If this tax had been expressed in "mills," the tax rate would have been stated as 10 mills representing a tax of $10 per $1,000 of appraised value.

 Spotlight: Over the years, real estate taxes have become less of a source of revenue for state governments, but they are still a primary source of revenue for local governments. Local governments, which include cities, counties, townships, and school districts, often use the revenues from real estate taxes to finance the construction and operation of public schools (kindergarten through 12th grade). Because real estate tends to appreciate over time, using value as the tax base allows governments to generate an increasing source of revenues without having to alter the tax rate.

Personal property taxes. Real property is not the only type of property subject to property taxes. Some states impose a tax on certain items of personal property. **Personal property** is all property other than real estate. Individuals can own real property for their own personal use, like personal residences or vacation homes. They can also own personal property that they use in their personal lives, like clothing, automobiles, and home furnishings. Businesses too can own both real and personal property. Office buildings, factories, and warehouses are examples of real property a business might own. Automobiles, office furniture, and machinery are examples of personal property used in a trade or business. It is important to distinguish between the general use of the term personal property and the specific use of that term as it relates to taxation. For tax purposes, personal property is any type of property that is not real estate.

Personal property can be tangible or intangible. Tangible property has physical characteristics; intangible property does not. Examples of **tangible personal property** include automobiles, jewelry, clothing, and equipment. States that impose a tax on tangible personal property generally tax property that taxpayers register with the state, like motor vehicles, boats, and aircraft. This allows the government to levy property taxes in conjunction with the annual registration or licensing of the property. Unlike real estate taxes, which are frequently used as a revenue source by local governments, personal property taxes are more likely to be assessed and collected by state governments.

Example 2: Under State of Florida statutes, anyone owning tangible personal property on January 1, who has a proprietorship, partnership, corporation, is a self-employed agent or a contractor, must file a tangible personal property return with the Property Appraiser by April 1 each year. Property owners who lease, lend, or rent property must also file. The appraised value of the tangible property is taxed at a millage rate established by the County in which the tangible property resides. As an example, if the tangible property had been appraised at $100,000 for 2008 and the millage rate imposed is 125 mills, the tax imposed upon the tangible property would be $1,250 ($100,000 × 125 mills (.125)).

Although it is not as common, some states impose a tax on intangible personal property. **Intangible property** has no physical characteristics; it includes copyrights, patents, goodwill, and other intangible assets frequently mentioned in financial accounting textbooks. For tax purposes, intangible personal property also includes stocks, bonds, mutual funds, and money market accounts. Since ascertaining the value of certain types of intangibles is easier than determining the value of other types of intangibles, states that impose an intangible personal property tax usually use as the tax base the current market value of stocks, bonds, mutual funds, and money market accounts the taxpayer owns.

Fair market value (FMV) is the price that a willing seller and a willing buyer would agree to with respect to the sale of property, provided neither party was compelled to enter into the transaction. In the case of intangible property like stocks, bonds, and mutual funds, market quotations are an acceptable measure of FMV, provided the quantity being valued is not so great as to significantly influence the market price as a result of the sale.

Example 3: Martin Vanderbilt lives in a state that imposes an intangibles tax on the value of stocks, bonds, mutual funds, and money market accounts as of January 1 of each year. The tax rate is $.50 for each $1,000 of intangibles valued in excess of $250,000. As of January 1, the value of Martin's intangible property is $700,000. Thus, Martin's intangible tax equals $225 ($700,000 – $250,000 – $450,000/$1,000 × $.50).

.02 Sales and Use Taxes

Sales tax is a broad-based tax on the consumption of goods and services. The federal government does not have a sales tax, but most state and local governments rely on sales taxes as a source of revenues. For the twelve month period ending September 30, 2008, general sales tax and gross receipts tax generated 24 percent of all state and local revenues.[2] Sales tax is added to the purchase price of goods and therefore it is levied on consumers but collected by the vendor, who is then responsible for remitting the tax amounts to the appropriate government agencies. Currently all states except Alaska, Delaware, Montana, New Hampshire, and Oregon impose a sales tax on the purchase of various goods. Although the sales tax rate is typically a flat rate, the rates vary not only from state to state, but also among various local governments.

The state of Florida provides for a state sales tax of six percent statewide and for a local government sales tax levied at the discretion of County government (referred to as a discretionary sales surtax). The discretionary sales surtax, also called a county tax, is imposed by many Florida counties and applies to most transactions subject to sales tax. A taxpayer responsible for the collection of tax must collect the discretionary sales surtax in addition to Florida's general sales tax of six percent. The discretionary sales surtax is based on the rate in the county where you deliver taxable goods or services. A few counties do not impose the surtax.

Example 4: Santiago Hardware Store operates in Alachua County, Florida. Based upon the Discretionary Sales Surtax for Alachua County, Santiago must collect the statewide six percent sales tax plus a County surtax of .25 percent. Based upon a taxable sale of $1,000, Santaigo would be required to collect $60 in state sales tax and $2.50 in surtax.

In addition to state and local sales taxes, some states impose an additional sales tax on certain items. For example, Minnesota has a 6.5-percent state sales tax, but it imposes a nine-percent sales tax on beer and liquor. Vermont's general sales tax is six percent, but it imposes a nine-percent sales tax on restaurant meals and hotel room rentals. New Hampshire does not have a sales tax, but it imposes an eight-percent tax on lodging and on meals served in restaurants.

Services are not usually subject to sales tax, and almost every state that imposes a sales tax exempts the purchase of prescription drugs. In many states, food is either exempt from sales tax or taxed at a significantly reduced rate. A few states exempt clothing from their tax base.

---

[2] *Id.*

Example 5: Karen's Entertainment Complex provides a wide variety of items for parties and entertainment including party favors, souvenirs and pony rides. The party favors and souvenirs that she sells are subject to sales tax, but the pony rides offered are exempt from sales tax. If the sales tax rate is six percent and Wayne purchased $500 in party favors and souvenirs and $1,000 in pony rides, he would have to pay $1,530 ($1,000 plus $500 plus the sales tax of $30 on the party favors and souvenirs).

Because sales tax rates vary from state to state, it is possible for residents of states with a higher sales tax to purchase their goods from states that have lower or no sales taxes. States combat this potential loss of revenues by levying a use tax. A **use tax** is a tax on the consumption, use, or storage of goods and services otherwise not subject to sales tax. Any goods purchased that are not subject to sales taxes because the transaction occurred outside of the state are likely to be subject to use taxes when brought back into the state for use, consumption, or storage. Accordingly, use taxes complement sales taxes by ensuring that the appropriate revenues are collected on all goods used, consumed, or stored in the state.

 Reason for the Rule: Use taxes ensure that states collect the appropriate sales taxes from residents who order merchandise from online companies. They also prevent residents from avoiding paying their state's full sales tax rate by making purchases in other states. For example, Tennessee's general sales tax rate is seven percent; Georgia's is four percent. If a Tennessee business purchases merchandise from a merchant in Georgia and pays a four-percent sales tax, the business then owes the Tennessee government a three-percent use tax. Use taxes not only raise state revenues but they also protect local merchants (who are required to collect the sales tax from their customers) from unfair competition from out-of-state merchants who do not charge the same rate of sales tax.

.03 Excise Taxes

An **excise tax** is a tax on the production or consumption of specific goods and services. Most excise taxes are assessed on a per-unit basis and are a source of revenue for all levels of government. For example, the federal government levies a $.39 excise tax on a pack of cigarettes. In addition to tobacco products, the federal government levies excise taxes on the sale of alcohol, gasoline, firearms, tires, telephone services, and air travel. It also imposes excise taxes on activities such as wagering or highway usage by trucks. Most states and many local governments levy excise taxes on gasoline, alcohol, and tobacco; however, the tax rates can vary greatly. For example, the state excise tax levied on a pack of cigarettes is $.07 in South Carolina but it is $2.46 in Rhode Island. Local taxes may range anywhere from $.01 to $1.50 a pack.

 Spotlight: Some local governments levy excise taxes on hotel occupancy and car rentals. These taxes are popular because they raise revenues to fund local services by taxing customers who typically live outside the local area.

Excise taxes are usually included in the price of the product. However, the tax can be levied on the producer of the product (for example, the refiner or importer of gasoline). When excise taxes are levied on the producer, the cost is usually passed forward to the retailer and then again to the consumer. Thus, regardless on whom the excise tax is levied, the consumer typically bears the economic burden of the excise tax. Many excise taxes are **indirect taxes** because they are levied on an intermediary who is not the one who ultimately bears the economic burden of the tax. In contrast, a **direct tax** is levied on the party who bears the economic burden of the tax. Sales taxes and property taxes are examples of direct taxes.

Example 6: Meredith Majors paid $2.45 a gallon for gasoline. Included in the purchase price were $.184 a gallon for federal excise tax and $.291 a gallon for state and local excises taxes. Thus, of the amount paid, $.475 was due to excise taxes, and just under $2 a gallon covered the retail sales price of the gasoline plus any sales tax imposed by the state and local governments.

 Spotlight: When an excise tax is imposed on a per-unit basis, the amount of revenue generated from excise taxes does not vary as the price for the good changes. Thus, to increase revenues from excise taxes, either the demand for the product or the tax rate must increase. Consumers have witnessed many states increasing the tax rate in recent years with excise taxes on tobacco products.

Severance taxes. A "severance tax" is an excise tax levied on the extraction of natural resources, like oil, gas, timber, ore, and coal. Common tax bases used to compute severance taxes are the value or number of units extracted. Severance taxes are a source of revenue for many state governments, as 39 states currently levy severance taxes on the extraction of at least one natural resource.

The Alaskan government levies a severance tax on oil and gas extracted in the state. Although the severance tax is levied on the oil companies, the additional cost is passed along and ultimately borne by consumers across the country. In 2007, the Alaskan government generated over $2.2 billion in revenue from severance taxes, which comprised more than 64 percent of the revenues collected that year.[3] As a result of the revenues generated from this tax, Alaska is the only state that does not levy either personal income taxes or state sales taxes. In fact, the amount of revenues the Alaskan government raises from excise taxes on oil and gas is so substantial that each spring the government mails out checks to its residents from the surplus of revenues.

.04 User Fees

A **user fee** is a tax the government charges those using government-provided goods and services. User fees are an appropriate form of taxation only when the government can control the use of the goods or services it provides. For example, the federal government provides and operates a postal delivery service. Since it is easy to identify the users of this service, the government can generate a portion of the revenues it needs to operate the U.S. Postal Service by charging postage each time the service is used. As previously discussed in the chapter, most governments impose user fees on persons who use their public transportation services as a way of financing part of the cost of providing the service. Other examples of governments' use of user fees include admission fees to museums and various government-provided performing art productions, like the ballet, opera, or symphony.

.05 Wealth Transfer Taxes

The federal government and several states tax the transfer of wealth either during a person's lifetime or at death. When the transfer occurs during a person's lifetime, the transfer is a gift, and any tax owed on the transfer is **gift tax**. Gift taxes are always levied on the transferor (donor). When the transfer occurs upon a person's death, the transfer is an inheritance and the tax owed is **estate tax** (when levied on the transferor) or an **inheritance tax** (when levied on the recipient).

The tax base for wealth transfer taxes is the FMV of the property transferred. In regard to real estate, a professional real estate appraisal can be used. Personal property appraisers can be useful in obtaining the value of tangible personal property. In the case of intangible property, like stocks,

---

[3] Judy Zello and Lisa Houlihan, "State Revenues Update," National Conference of State Legislatures (2008).

bonds, and mutual funds, market quotations are an acceptable measure of FMV, provided the quantity is not so great that it would significantly influence the market price if sold.

Federal gift tax. During a person's lifetime, the federal government taxes transfers of wealth. Attempting to tax all transfers between persons would be nearly impossible to administer because people customarily make gifts to one another on special occasions such as birthdays, holidays, graduations, and marriages. Thus, the tax laws specifically do not tax transfers up to a certain amount each year, and they allow unlimited transfers between spouses. As long as total transfers during the year to any one person (other than one's spouse) do not exceed this amount, the government does not require the transfers to be disclosed. During 2009, a person can transfer up to $13,000 to another individual without any federal gift tax consequences.

Example 7: Ted Walters and his wife Lynne have two children and five grandchildren. Ted can make unlimited transfers to Lynne without any gift tax consequences. He can also gift up to $13,000 to each of his children and grandchildren, thereby effectively transferring $91,000 ($13,000 × 7) of his wealth to other family members without reporting the gifts to the federal government. Likewise, Lynne can gift up to $13,000 to each of her seven descendants without any gift tax consequences.

Example 8: In January 2009, Frieda Smith gifts $13,000 to her best friend and then in October gifts the same friend property worth $200,000. Since Frieda's gifts to her friend during 2009 exceed $13,000, the $200,000 excess constitutes a taxable gift.

Persons who transfer amounts in excess of the annual exemption amount during a calendar year must report the gifts they make during the year to the federal government. A gift tax is imposed on all "taxable gifts" (gifts made to individuals in excess of the annual exclusion amount). The federal gift tax rates are progressive and, during 2009, range from 18 to 45 percent. As the amount of taxable gifts a person makes over one's lifetime accumulates, the tax rate assessed on taxable gifts increases. However, each person is currently allowed a reduction against his or her gift tax that is equivalent to a $1,000,000 lifetime exemption against taxable gifts. Accordingly, only taxable gifts in excess of the $1,000,000 lifetime exemption ever result in the actual payment to the federal government for gift taxes owed.

Example 9: Continuing with the previous example, Frieda's $200,000 taxable gift must be reported to the federal government. If this is the first year in which Frieda made any taxable gifts, she will not pay tax on the transfer. However, her $1,000,000 lifetime exemption for taxable gifts will be reduced to $800,000.

Federal estate tax. When a person dies, the value of all of the property owned at the time of death is referred to as the "decedent's estate." After reducing the value of the estate by amounts owed to creditors, certain expenses paid by the estate, and bequests made to the spouse and qualified charitable organizations, the remainder of the estate is added to the decedent's cumulative taxable gifts, and the entire amount of taxable wealth transfers is subject to estate tax. To avoid the need to file an estate tax return on a small estate, the federal government allows a reduction against the estate tax of an amount equivalent to $3.5 million of taxable wealth transfers for persons who die during 2009. Thus, for a decedent who has made taxable gifts during his or her lifetime, this $3.5 million estate exemption must be used to cover both taxable gifts and the decedent's taxable estate.

Example 10: Continuing with the previous example, Frieda dies in 2009 and leaves her entire estate (with a net worth of $5,000,000) to her son. The entire $5,000,000 plus the $200,000 taxable gift is subject to estate tax. However, once the $3,500,000 estate tax exemption is taken into consideration, only $1,700,000 ($5,200,000 − $3,500,000) of her estate is actually subject to federal estate tax.

State wealth transfer taxes. Only a handful of states tax transfers made during a person's lifetime. These states provide for annual and lifetime exemptions similar to those allowed by the federal government. Although the state gift tax rates are progressive, they are significantly lower than those imposed by the federal government. Currently 15 states levy an estate tax in addition to the federal estate taxes imposed on the decedent's estate, and 10 states impose an inheritance tax, which taxes beneficiaries on their inheritances. Among the states that impose wealth transfer taxes, all allow tax-free transfers to the decedent's spouse, and many have reduced tax rates on transfers to close family members.

 Spotlight: The state wealth transfer tax has been tied to the federal estate taxes in terms of the calculation of the tax due in certain states. For example, the Wisconsin estate tax is based upon the federal credit for state death taxes after December 31, 2007. Under federal law there will be no federal credit for state death taxes for deaths occurring in 2008 through 2010. Therefore, there is no Wisconsin estate tax for deaths occurring between January 1, 2008, and December 31, 2010. In the absence of a change in the federal or Wisconsin law, both the federal and Wisconsin estate tax will be restored for deaths occurring on or after January 1, 2011.

.06 Employment Taxes

There are two types of federal employment taxes: **FICA (Federal Insurance Contributions Act)** and **FUTA (Federal Unemployment Tax Act)**. FICA taxes consist of two parts: (1) social security taxes (also known as old-age, survivors, and disability insurance (OASDI)) and (2) Medicare taxes. FICA taxes are used to finance Medicare benefits paid to eligible beneficiaries and monthly payments made to the elderly and disabled. FUTA taxes, on the other hand, help finance the payment of unemployment benefits to those who have lost their jobs and are in the process of seeking gainful employment.

Social security and Medicare taxes. FICA tax is imposed on employees' wages at a combined 7.65-percent tax rate, which consists of a 6.2-percent tax for social security (OASDI) plus a 1.45-percent tax for Medicare. Both the employee and the employer pay FICA taxes. For 2009, the OASDI portion of the FICA tax applies only to the first $106,800 of an employee's wages. There is no limit on the amount of wages subject to the 1.45-percent Medicare tax. Thus, for the first $106,800 of an employee's wages, a total contribution of 15.3 percent (7.65 percent by the employee plus 7.65 percent by the employer) is made to the social security and Medicare systems. For wages in excess of $106,800, only a total rate of 2.9 percent is contributed to the Medicare system.

Example 11: Sara Jenkins's wages for 2009 are $50,000. From this amount, her employer withholds $3,100 for social security taxes ($50,000 × 6.2%) and $725 for Medicare taxes ($50,000 × 1.45%). Her employer matches these amounts and remits a total of $6,200 ($3,100 × 2) and $1,450 ($725 × 2), respectively to the Social Security Administration.

 Spotlight: In 2009, only the first $106,800 of an employee's wages is subject to the full 7.65-percent FICA tax rate. Wages in excess of this amount are subject to the 1.45-percent Medicare tax only. Therefore, as employees' wages exceed $106,800, the average tax rate decreases. For example, an employee with wages of $124,800 pays an average tax rate of 6.75 percent [($106,800 × 7.65%) + ($18,000 × 1.45%) = $8,129/$120,000)], which is less than the 7.65-percent rate paid on the first $106,800 of wages. Thus, for wages up to $106,800 in 2009, FICA is a flat tax. For all subsequent levels of income, it is regressive.

A self-employed business owner acts both as an employee and as an employer of the business. Therefore, these business owners, known as **sole proprietors**, are required to contribute both the employer and employee portions of FICA. When FICA tax is paid on the profits of a sole proprietorship, it is called a **self-employment tax**. For 2009, the self-employment tax rate is 15.3

percent on all *net earnings from self-employment* up to $106,800. After that, the self-employment tax rate drops to 2.9 percent.

Example 12: Judd Hampton operates his business as a sole proprietorship. During 2009, Judd's net earnings from self-employment were $45,000. Since that amount is less than $106,800, Judd's self-employment tax for 2009 is $6,885. The calculation of the amount is as follows:

Self-employment net earnings	$45,000
Tax rate on self-employment income	15.3%
Self-employment tax for 2009	$6,885

Example 13: Consider the same facts as in the previous example, except that Judd's 2009 net earnings from self-employment are $115,000. Since this amount exceeds $106,800 by $8,200, Judd's self-employment tax for 2009 is $16,578 [($106,800 × 15.3%) + ($8,200 × 2.9%)].

Employers' responsibility for withholding and contributing FICA taxes is discussed in Chapter 6. Self-employment taxes, including the calculation of net earnings from self-employment, are further discussed in Chapter 13.

Unemployment taxes. FUTA is a federal tax that was enacted so states could provide unemployed workers with a portion of their regular income during periods of temporary unemployment. Although FUTA taxes are imposed by the federal government, the amounts collected are distributed to the states, which then add the FUTA tax amounts to any unemployment tax amounts they collect. Unlike employment taxes, FUTA taxes are levied only on employers. In 2009, FUTA taxes will be assessed at a rate of 6.2 percent, which is reduced to an effective rate of .8 percent if the employer pays state unemployment tax on the wages and does so in a timely manner. The tax rate for the employer is then applied to the first $7,000 of an employee's wages paid during the year. Most states also impose unemployment taxes on employee wages. States may use a different maximum amount for employee wages that are subject to the state unemployment compensation tax than does the federal government. State tax rates range anywhere from zero percent to just over 10 percent. For example, the Pennsylvania unemployment compensation tax rates are based upon a standard tax rate adjusted for several factors including the amount of unemployment claims made by former employees. The standard unemployment compensation tax rates for 2009 in Pennsylvania range from 5.9632 percent to 9.9836 percent. In addition, the unemployment compensation tax rate is applied to the first $8,000 of employee's wages. An employer's responsibility for paying FUTA and state unemployment taxes is discussed further in Chapter 6.

Example 14: Jackson Industries operates a business in Pennsylvania where they employ several employees, all of whom make more than $10,000 per year. Pennsylvania has assigned Jackson an unemployment compensation tax rate of seven percent for 2009. Jackson filed timely all Pennsylvania unemployment compensation tax returns paying $560 ($8,000 × 7%) in state unemployment tax per employee for the 2009 tax year. In addition, Jackson will be liable for $56 ($7,000 × .8%) per employee in FUTA taxes for 2009. The FUTA rate of .8 percent applies because Jackson paid state unemployment taxes on all the wages on a timely basis.

 Reason for the Rule: Sole proprietors are required to pay unemployment taxes on their employees' wages, but they do not pay unemployment taxes on their business profits. Accordingly, sole proprietors are not eligible to receive unemployment benefits through their businesses.

.07 Federal Income Taxes

The federal government's primary source of revenues comes from income tax, which uses taxable income as its tax base. Simply put, **taxable income** is income that the government taxes minus any allowable deductions. The formula for computing taxable income is shown in Figure 1-1.

Figure 1-1 Taxable Income Formula

Income	$ xx,xxx
Less: Exclusions	(xx,xxx)
Gross Income	$ xx,xxx
Less: Deductions	(xx,xxx)
Taxable Income	$ xx,xxx

The tax laws define **income** broadly and suggest it includes all increases in wealth. Accordingly, a decrease in amounts a taxpayer owes causes wealth to increase; therefore, when a taxpayer's debt is forgiven, it constitutes "income" for purposes of computing taxable income. Along similar lines of reasoning, income would include appreciation in the value of property. However, mere appreciation in value is difficult to tax for several reasons, the most obvious being problems measuring the amount of appreciation. For most property, the true value can only be ascertained upon its sale to an unrelated party. In addition to the measurement issues, governments recognize that appreciation in value does not necessarily mean that the taxpayer has the resources available from which to pay the tax on the resulting income. Thus, the tax laws omit appreciation in value from income and instead operate under the **realization principle,** whereby income is realized only upon the disposal of property. The realization principle follows the **wherewithal-to-pay concept,** which recognizes that mere appreciation in value does not necessarily mean that the owner has the resources (wherewithal) to pay the tax associated with the appreciation. This wherewithal-to-pay is assured when the property is disposed of and the proceeds can be used to pay the necessary taxes.

In addition to the realization principle, the **capital recovery doctrine** ensures that when taxpayers dispose of property, the amount of proceeds that allows them to recover their investment in the property will not be taxed. Thus, only the excess of the proceeds over their investment is taxed. The capital recovery doctrine applies to all sales of property, including inventory. Therefore, only gross profit, computed as the excess of sales price over cost of goods sold, is included in income.

Despite the fact that the tax laws define income broadly, some income is exempt from taxation. Income that the government does not tax is called an **exclusion**. An example of an exclusion in the calculation of federal taxable income is the interest earned on investments in state and local government bonds (also called "municipal bonds"). Like corporate bonds, municipal bonds pay interest semiannually; however, the interest bondholders receive from municipal bonds is income that the federal government chooses not to tax. After exclusions are subtracted from total income, the amount remaining is known as **gross income**. Thus, gross income is all income that the government has decided to tax. The income tax laws are written such that all items of income are subject to tax unless a tax law exists that specifically states that they are not subject to tax. This is known as an **all-inclusive approach** to defining income. Therefore, in order to properly report the correct amounts of gross income on the federal tax return, it is necessary to study the tax laws to learn about all exclusions the government makes available to taxpayers. Gross income used in the calculation of federal taxable income is discussed in Chapter 4.

In addition to excluding certain types of income from tax, the federal government also allows most business expenditures to be deducted in arriving at taxable income. Ordinary and necessary expenses incurred in the operation of a business are allowed as a **deduction** to offset business income, as are losses on the sale of business and investment property. However, special rules may control the timing or the amount allowed as a deduction. Business deductions allowed in computing federal taxable income are the focus of Chapters 5, 6, and 7.

Once taxable income is computed, tax rates are applied to determine the taxpayer's tax liability. The federal government uses a progressive tax rate structure in which the average tax rate increases as taxable income increases. Corporate and individual income tax rates are discussed in Chapter 4 at ¶ 405. A progressive tax rate structure might look something like this:

Tax base over—	But not over—	Tax rate
$ 0	$ 10,000	1%
10,000	50,000	4%
50,000	100,000	8%
100,000		10%

Example 15: Jamie Rivers has taxable income of $150,000. Using the above tax rate schedule, Jamie computes the tax liability on her taxable income as follows.

$10,000 × 1%	$ 100
($50,000 – $10,000) × 4%	1,600
($100,000 – $50,000) × 8%	4,000
($150,000 – $100,000) × 10%	5,000
	$10,700

From tax liability, taxpayers subtract out tax credits, including prepayments, to arrive at the amount of taxes owed or refund due back from the government. Most **tax credits** are incentive-based items that taxpayers obtain by investing or participating in certain activities. Unlike deductions, which reduce taxable income, tax credits directly reduce tax liability. Accordingly, the tax savings derived from a $1 tax credit equals $1. The tax savings derived from a $1 deduction depends on the taxpayer's marginal tax rate. The **marginal tax rate** is the rate of tax that the taxpayer pays on the last dollar of income, or stated another way, the tax savings that a taxpayer derives by reducing taxable income by $1. If in Example 15 Jamie were to decrease her taxable income from $150,000 to $149,999, her tax liability would decrease by $.10. Therefore, Jamie's last dollar of taxable income is taxed at 10 percent, which is her marginal tax rate. Dollar-for-dollar, tax credits are always preferred to tax deductions. Tax credits are discussed in Chapter 11.

Example 16: Jamie Rivers from the previous example has the option of receiving a $1,000 deduction or a $1,000 credit. If Jamie chooses the deduction, her tax liability will be reduced by $100 ($1,000 × 10%). If she chooses the tax credit, her tax liability will be reduced by $1,000. Thus, all other things being equal, Jamie would prefer the $1,000 tax credit.

Tax credits can be refundable or nonrefundable. A **refundable tax credit** is one for which the credit not only reduces the taxpayer's tax liability but also results in a refund of any excess to the taxpayer when the credit exceeds the tax liability. A **nonrefundable tax credit** can only reduce the taxpayer's tax liability. Most tax credits are nonrefundable credits. A few personal tax credits available to individuals and a couple of business credits are refundable credits.

Example 17: Janice Hartman's tax liability is $1,300 and she reports a $2,000 tax credit on her tax return. If the tax credit is a nonrefundable credit, it will reduce her tax liability to $0. If it is a refundable credit, it will reduce her tax liability to $0 and she will be entitled to receive a $700 ($2,000 – $1,300) refund from the government.

Prepayments are amounts that the taxpayer has paid to the government during the year to cover the current year's tax liability. Employees prepay the government when they have amounts withheld from their paychecks during the year. Taxpayers that generate taxable income from sources other than wages are required to make quarterly estimated payments to the government to cover the corresponding tax liability. If the amount of prepayments the taxpayer makes during the year exceeds the amount left over after subtracting nonrefundable tax credits from tax liability, the excess is refundable. Thus, prepayments are considered a refundable tax credit. The calculation of taxes owed (refund due) is illustrated in Figure 1-2.

Figure 1-2 Calculation of Tax Owed or Refund Due

Tax liability	$ xx,xxx
Less: Nonrefundable tax credits	(xx,xxx)
Remaining tax liability (not less than $0)	$ xx,xxx
Less: Refundable tax credits, including prepayments	(xx,xxx)
Tax owed (refund due)	$ xx,xxx

Federal income tax is imposed on the taxable income of individuals and corporations (referred to as **C corporations**). When a business is operated as a sole proprietorship, the owner is personally responsible for the debts and activities of the business, and the profits from the business are taxed on the sole proprietor's personal income tax return. In contrast, profits from a C corporation are taxed on the corporation's income tax return and then again when distributed to shareholders in the form of a dividend. Although corporate profits may be taxed twice, one advantage of operating a business as a corporation is that the shareholders are not responsible for the liabilities of the business, a concept known as **limited liability**. Shareholders are only at risk for losing the amounts they have invested in the corporation (that is, amounts paid for their shares of stock). The treatment of corporate distributions and the impact of the double taxation of corporate profits are discussed in Chapter 12.

Businesses can also choose to operate as partnerships. A **partnership** is a business entity that must always have at least two owners (partners). Partnerships do not pay taxes, but they must file an annual tax return reporting the business's activities for the year. A partnership is a **flow-through entity,** which gets it name because throughout the year it gathers information about gross income, deductions, and credits generated during the year and at the end of the year it files a tax return and passes this information along to the partners. The partners then report on their own income tax returns their respective shares of income, deductions, and credits. Thus, one advantage of choosing to operate a business as a partnership is that the profits of the business are taxed directly to the owners. However, a disadvantage of operating a business as a partnership is that at least one partner must be personally liable for the debts of the partnership. The taxation of partnerships is discussed in Chapter 14.

An **S corporation** is a special type of business entity that shares features of both the corporate and partnership entities. Like the owners of a C corporation, the owners of an S corporation are shareholders, and as such, they are protected from the liabilities of the S corporation. However, S corporations are similar to partnerships in that they are flow-through entities whose profits are passed through (and taxed one time) to the shareholders. The advantage of operating as an S corporation should be obvious—the owners enjoy limited liability and a single layer of taxation. Like C corporations, S corporations can have just one shareholder, thereby making this business entity an attractive alternative to businesses with a sole owner. However, restrictions exist as to the number and type of shareholders an S corporation can have, which make it an entity choice only for certain smaller businesses. The taxation of S corporations is discussed in Chapter 15.

All states now allow businesses to operate as a **limited liability company (LLC)** or **limited liability partnership (LLP)**. Although state laws govern the rules of operation for LLCs and LLPs, the federal government allows these business entities to be taxed as partnerships. Accordingly, LLCs and LLPs are required to file an annual income tax return reporting the entity's activities for the year and to pass along to the owners their respective shares of income, deductions, and credits. The advantage of operating a business as an LLC or LLP is that while profits can be taxed a single time to the owners (similar to a partnership), the owners are sheltered from the general liabilities of the business (similar to a corporation). In addition, LLCs can have a single owner, making them attractive choices for businesses with a sole owner. Although some restrictions may apply to LLCs and LLPs, the restrictions are not as severe as those imposed on S corporations. LLCs provide their owners with more protection from liabilities of the business than LLPs; however, neither LLCs nor LLPs are required to have an owner that is personally responsible for the general liabilities of the business. For these reasons, LLCs and LLPs have become popular entity choices in recent years. LLCs and LLPs are discussed in Chapter 14.

Individual income tax. Many tax laws apply equally to all taxpayers; however, a few rules exist that apply solely to individual taxpayers. The tax laws that apply to individual taxpayers are the focus of Chapter 13; however, the business activities of a sole proprietorship are reported on the proprietor's individual income tax return, so it is important to understand the basics of the federal individual tax rules. Accordingly, this section summarizes some of the more basic features regarding the calculation of taxable income for individual taxpayers.

When individuals compute taxable income, deductions are separated into two categories: deductions for **adjusted gross income** (AGI) and deductions from AGI. Thus, the taxable income formula for individuals is expanded as shown in Figure 1-3.

Figure 1-3 Taxable Income Formula for Individual Taxpayers

Income	$ xx,xxx
Less: Exclusions	(xx,xxx)
Gross Income	$ xx,xxx
Less: Deductions for AGI	(xx,xxx)
Adjusted gross income (AGI)	$ xx,xxx
Less: Deductions from AGI	(xx,xxx)
Taxable Income	$ xx,xxx

The primary distinction between deductions *for* AGI and deductions *from* AGI is that the latter are primarily nonbusiness deductions. Expenditures that can be deducted for AGI include business deductions that are used to offset the business income from a sole proprietorship, rental expenses that are used to offset rental income reported by the landlord, and losses on the sale of business and investment property. In contrast, deductions taken from AGI involve expenditures that are much more personal in nature. For example, within the deductions from AGI, taxpayers are allowed two deductions: (1) the *greater of* a standard deduction or the taxpayer's itemized deductions, and (2) the taxpayer's personal and dependency exemptions.

Itemized deductions are the accumulation of various personal expenditures that the federal government allows individuals to offset against AGI. The most commonly deducted itemized deductions include charitable contributions, state and local income taxes or general sales taxes, home mortgage interest, and real estate taxes taxpayers pay in conjunction with owning a personal residence. Other itemized deductions include unreimbursed medical expenses in excess of 7.5 percent of the taxpayer's AGI and uninsured casualty and theft losses in excess of 10 percent AGI.

Unlike itemized deductions, which involve personal expenditures that taxpayers make during the year, the **standard deduction** is an amount that the federal government allows each individual taxpayer to deduct in lieu of deducting itemized deductions. The amount is based on the taxpayer's filing status (for example, single and married filing a joint return are two of five possible filing statuses). For 2009, the standard deduction for single taxpayers is $5,700; for married couples who file a joint return, the standard deduction is $11,400. Additional amounts are allowed if the taxpayer is blind or over age 64. Individuals deduct from AGI the *greater* of their itemized deductions or the standard deduction.

Example 18: Bruce Collins is unmarried. In 2009, Bruce's total itemized deductions are $2,400. Since this amount does not exceed the $5,700 standard deduction for single taxpayers in 2009, Bruce will subtract from AGI the $5,700 standard deduction in computing his 2009 taxable income.

Example 19: Tim and Diane Raines file a joint return. In 2009, the Raines have itemized deductions totaling $12,600. Since this amount exceeds the $11,400 standard deduction provided to married taxpayers in 2009, they will deduct $12,600 from AGI in computing their 2009 taxable income.

The second deduction from AGI is for the taxpayer's **personal and dependency exemptions.** For 2009, each exemption results in a $3,650 deduction in arriving at taxable income. Each taxpayer is entitled to one personal exemption; therefore, a married couple filing a joint tax return would be entitled to claim two personal exemptions. In addition to the personal exemption, individuals are allowed to take an exemption for each person who qualifies as their dependent. The taxpayer's minor children generally qualify as dependents, but others may qualify as well. Although the rules for who qualifies as a dependent are beyond the scope of this discussion, "dependents" are usually persons who either live with or are related to the taxpayer and for whom the taxpayer provides the majority of support during the year.

Corporate income taxes. The tax laws treat a C corporation as a tax-paying entity, separate and apart from its shareholders. As is true for individuals, the corporation's tax base is taxable income. Taxable income equals gross income minus all allowable deductions. A corporation's gross income is its gross profit (net sales minus cost of goods sold) plus other income earned, such as dividends, interest, rents, royalties, and gain from the sale of property other than inventory. From this amount, the corporation subtracts all deductions allowed by the law, such as depreciation, salaries, rent, property taxes, and loss on the sale of property. These deductions are similar to those allowed an individual taxpayer, except that all deductions are presumed to be business-related and a corporation is not entitled to a personal exemption. Taxes on corporate taxable income are determined through the use of a graduated progressive tax rate structure. See ¶ 405.01.

At the end of each fiscal year, all publicly-traded corporations are required to issue audited financial statements prepared in accordance with **generally accepted accounting principles (GAAP)**. The federal income tax laws are a compilation of the Internal Revenue Code, Treasury Regulations, IRS rulings, and case law. In many instances the tax laws used in computing federal taxable income and GAAP (used to compute net income) follow the same or similar rules. However, because different governing bodies are responsible for writing these two sets of rules, the calculation of taxable income may be different from the calculation of net income that is taught in financial accounting textbooks. As part of the annual tax filing process, larger C corporations are required to reconcile net income and taxable income, documenting where differences between the two exist. Accordingly, as the tax laws are presented throughout this textbook, any differences between the tax laws and financial accounting rules will be highlighted and discussed. Chapter 2 provides an overview of the various sources of the U.S. federal income tax laws.

 Spotlight: A recent IRS study of 30,430 corporate tax returns for the year 2004 revealed that the difference between taxable income and GAAP income was $131.7 billion. $81.6 billion of the difference was the result of timing differences and $50.1 billion reflected permanent differences.[4]

.08 State and Local Income Taxes

Most state governments impose an individual income tax, and many "piggyback" on the federal tax systems by modifying federal taxable income to compute their own versions of state taxable income. However, New Hampshire and Tennessee only tax interest and dividend income. Cities that impose an income tax typically use employees' wages as their tax base; however, some, like New York City, use a modified version of federal taxable income. Tax rates for state and local income taxes can be flat or progressive.

 Spotlight: In fiscal 2003, the city of Philadelphia generated over half of its revenues by imposing a "wage tax" on nonresidents' wages earned while working within the city limits as well as on all of the wages of its residents, regardless of where those wages were earned. Because all wages earned within the city limits are subject to the Philadelphia wage tax, visiting professional athletes are subject to the wage tax on the portion of their wages earned while playing their away games against Philadelphia's professional sports teams.

Although many states have a corporate income tax, some choose to levy a franchise tax on businesses. A **franchise tax** is an annual tax on the privilege of doing business in the state. It differs from an income tax in that the tax base is typically some combination of the value of the corporation's capital stock and its annual earnings. For example, Pennsylvania levies a franchise tax on corporations that do business in the state and uses the value of the corporation's allocable capital stock as its tax base. Texas also levies a franchise tax, but it uses the value of the corporation's allocable contributed capital and taxable earned surplus (defined as net income with a few adjustments) in computing its franchise tax. Although S corporations and LLCs are treated as flow-through entities for purposes of federal income tax, many states levy franchise taxes on these business entities.

---

[4] Charles Boynton, Portia DeFilippes, and Ellen Legel; "A First Look at 2004 Schedule M-3 Reporting by Large Corporations," *http://www.irs.gov/pub/irs-soi/06boynton.pdf*. Prepared for the 2006 IRS Research Conference.

¶ 105 The Makings of a "Good" Tax

Most everyone would agree that a good tax is one that is both equitable and efficient. An equitable tax system is one that fairly distributes the tax burden. An efficient tax is one that minimizes both the compliance costs to the taxpayer and the administrative costs to the government. Unfortunately, establishing a system of taxation that meets those criteria is more challenging than it may seem. One problem is the difficulty of arriving at a consensus as to what constitutes an equitable sharing of the tax burden. In addition, lawmakers have found that many factors that add to a tax system's fairness often increase its complexity, thereby adding to administrative and compliance costs.

.01 Make It Fair

An equitable tax is one that is *perceived* as being fair to all who are affected by the tax. However, perception is a subjective observation, and as such, it is virtually impossible for everyone to come to a consensus as to what constitutes a fair tax. An example earlier in the chapter illustrated this point. It involved a government that needed to raise $12,000 in revenues from its two residents: Tom Johnson and Jane Smith (see ¶ 103). The tax base was determined to be the employees' wages, and the government was in the process of considering three tax rate structures. The distribution of the tax burden under each tax rate structure is summarized below.

	Tax Liability		Tax Base		Average Tax Rate	
	Tom	Jane	Tom	Jane	Tom	Jane
Regressive	$7,580	$4,590	$120,000	$60,000	6.32%	7.65%
Proportional	$8,100	$4,050	$120,000	$60,000	6.75%	6.75%
Progressive	$9,200	$2,800	$120,000	$60,000	7.67%	4.67%

Because Tom's wages are more than Jane's, a tax that requires Jane to pay more taxes than Tom unarguably would be perceived as an unfair tax. Under each tax rate structure, Tom would pay more taxes than Jane, so one might initially conclude that any of these tax rate structures was an equitable way to distribute the $12,000 tax burden. However, under the regressive tax rate structure, Tom would pay considerably more taxes than Jane ($7,580 versus $4,590), but the amount represents a *smaller portion* of his wages (6.32% versus Jane's 7.65%). Thus, few would conclude that a regressive tax was an equitable way to distribute the tax burden.

Under a proportional tax, Tom and Jane would pay the same 6.75-percent rate of tax; under a progressive tax, Tom would pay a greater percentage of his gross wages in tax (7.67 percent versus 4.67 percent). Those who support the position that a proportional tax is the fairest tax might believe that Tom, who earns twice as much as Jane, should pay twice the amount of taxes Jane pays, and accordingly, he would be contributing his fair share toward the overall tax burden. On the other hand, those who feel that a progressive tax structure is more equitable may feel that as two single individuals, Tom and Jane have the same basic needs for food, shelter, clothing, etc. After they each finish paying for these basic needs, Tom should have more left over than Jane because his wages are double Jane's wages. Hence, Tom's ability to contribute to the tax system is greater than Jane's and therefore he should pay a greater portion of his wages in taxes. Regardless of which tax rate structure one believes to be more equitable, this example demonstrates that not everyone will perceive fairness the same way. Accordingly, governments attempting to enact a "fair" tax must recognize this fact.

.02 Make It Efficient

Inarguably, a good tax is one that minimizes compliance costs to the taxpayer and administrative costs to the government. The best way to accomplish this is to create a tax system in which the tax base is easy to identify and compute. A tax system with which taxpayers can comply with little personal effort would be preferred to one that requires extensive personal effort or requires the taxpayer to hire and pay for professional assistance. From an administrative standpoint, running a tax collection agency costs money. Inevitably, additional costs are incurred with a more complicated tax system. As we saw in the example involving Tom and Jane, the calculation of a flat tax is by far the easiest, but many believe that the more complicated progressive rate structure results in a more equitable distribution of the tax burden.

Too often, equity and efficiency are rivals when it comes to creating a tax system. Another example involves the role of the standard deduction and personal exemptions in the federal income tax system. The purpose behind these two deductions is to prevent lower-income taxpayers from having any taxable income. However, whenever exclusions, deductions, or credits are introduced into the tax system, the complexity of the system increases. Thus, any attempt to fairly allocate the tax burden usually sacrifices efficiency.

 Spotlight: In 2004, taxpayers paid approximately $243.9 million in their efforts to comply with the federal income tax system. This was just under $.25 for each $1 of federal revenue collected. It is estimated that taxpayers will spend over 6 billion hours complying with the federal income tax laws when filing their 2005 tax returns. This number of hours is equivalent to a workforce of 2,884,000 individuals working 40 hours per week for one year, which is staggering considering that number of people is larger than the populations of Dallas, Detroit, and Washington, D.C. combined. The number is also larger than the number of workers in the automotive, airline, computer manufacturing, and steel industries combined.[5]

¶ 106 Factors Taken Into Consideration When Creating a Tax

The art of taxation consists in so plucking the goose as to get the most feathers with the least hissing. –Jean Baptiste Colbert, French Economist and Minister of Finance under King Louis XIV of France (1619–1683)

Although raising revenues is the primary reason governments impose taxes, governments consider several factors when deciding whom and what to tax. The government must first decide whether it is possible to control usage of the goods or services. If so, then charging user fees would be feasible. However, when offering goods or services results in externalities, assessing user fees to cover the entire cost may not be appropriate. Public transportation is an example of a government-provided service for which usage can easily be controlled. As previously mentioned, when individuals use public transportation, roadways are less congested and air quality improves. Consequently, governments that provide public transportation generally charge a reduced user fee and find other means to finance the remainder of the costs.

To the extent that raising revenues through user fees is not feasible or appropriate, other factors are considered, including how to equitably spread the tax burden among taxpayers. Other issues may be contemplated as well. For example, many tax laws are enacted with the intention of eliciting certain types of behavior; others are enacted to redistribute wealth or to minimize administrative and compliance costs. Some tax laws are enacted purely for political reasons. Because it is often helpful to understand why a particular law was enacted, the various factors governments use in deciding how to allocate the tax burden are discussed below. As specific tax laws are presented throughout this textbook, these factors will be discussed in a boxed area called "Reason for the Rule."

---

[5] J. Scott Moody, Wendy P. Warcholik, and Scott A. Hodge, "The Rising Costs of Complying with the Federal Income Tax," *Tax Foundation Special Report*, no. 138 (December 2005).

.01 Equity Concerns

While no one likes paying taxes, taxpayers who believe that taxes are assessed and collected fairly to meet our nation's needs are more likely to comply with the tax laws. The Internal Revenue Service (IRS) estimates that a one-tenth of one percentage point (.1 percent) improvement in compliance would increase federal revenues by more than $1 billion annually.[6] In response, governments often strive to collect taxes from those who have the greatest ability to pay taxes. Common measures of a taxpayer's ability to pay are income or wealth. Among the three tax rate structures, the progressive tax rate structure best illustrates the **ability-to-pay concept.** With progressive tax rates, the taxpayer's average tax rate increases as the tax base increases. Accordingly, those with higher tax bases (presumably those in a better position to pay taxes) pay a greater percentage of their tax bases toward the overall tax burden.

Earlier in the chapter, the concept of marginal tax rate was introduced as a way of measuring the tax savings derived from deductions. Tax deductions become more valuable as the taxpayer's marginal tax rate increases. A $1,000 deduction to a taxpayer in the 15-percent tax bracket results in $150 of tax savings ($1,000 × 15%), whereas that same $1,000 deduction is worth $310 to a taxpayer in the 31-percent tax bracket ($1,000 x 31%). Since the tax rates increase as the tax base increases, deductions favor higher-income taxpayers under a progressive tax structure. Accordingly, governments that employ a progressive rate structure often enact tax laws that allow for tax credits rather than tax deductions, thereby providing the same tax savings to higher-and lower-income taxpayers.

When a proportional tax rate is used, other methods of addressing the ability to pay issue must be examined. Many state and local governments rely heavily on property taxes as a source of revenues. Since real estate taxes are *ad valorem,* real estate taxes increase as real estate values rise. Elderly persons tend to live on fixed incomes, and accordingly, often have more difficulty keeping up with increasing property taxes. Many state and local governments that impose taxes on real estate provide some mechanism in their tax systems that allows elderly homeowners to pay reduced real estate taxes.

For example, Nevada imposes an annual real estate tax on 35 percent of the FMV of real property, but it allows homeowners over age 61 who earn no more than $27,863 to receive tax rebates the amount of which may not exceed the amount of the accrued property tax paid by homeowner or $500, whichever is less. In Kentucky, homeowners over age 64 can exempt the first $31,400 of the assessed value of their homes from the property tax base for 2007 and 2008. Thus, a 70-year-old Kentucky homeowner with a home valued at $75,000 would only be subject to real estate taxes on an assessed value of $43,600 ($75,000 − $31,400), or 58 percent of its full market value ($43,600/$75,000). Compare this to a 70-year-old homeowner with a $200,000 home that would be subject to real estate taxes on an assessed value of $168,600 ($200,000 − $31,400), or 84 percent of its full market value ($168,600/$200,000). Kentucky's $31,400 exemption provides the greatest benefit to elderly residents with more modestly valued homes. These residents are presumably those less able to afford higher-priced homes, and they thus have less ability to pay taxes. It should be noted that when states enact special rules for certain taxpayers, the system can become more difficult to comprehend and administer, and consequently, efficiency may decrease.

Sales tax is also a proportional tax, and many state and local governments address the issue of ability to pay by exempting certain goods from sales tax or by imposing reduced tax rates on certain goods. The elderly often live on fixed incomes, but they are more likely to purchase prescription drugs. Hence, most every state and local government that imposes a sales tax exempts prescription drugs from the tax base. In addition, some states either exempt food and clothing or impose reduced tax rates on these items because they are considered necessities. For example, Pennsylvania imposes a six-percent sales tax on most goods, but it exempts food, clothing, textbooks, heating fuel, and prescription and nonprescription medications from its sales tax base. In Vermont,

---

[6] "IRS Moves to Ensure Fairness of Tax System: Research Program Works to Increase Compliance Program Effectiveness," Reduce Burdens on Taxpayers," IRS News Release, IR-2002-05, January 16, 2002.

where the state sales tax is also six percent, both prescription and nonprescription drugs are exempt from tax, but only clothing and shoes costing less than $110 are exempt from sales tax. These examples illustrate how various state governments have considered the issue of equity when enacting their tax laws. However, when they impose different rates on different goods, they introduce complexity and compromise efficiency.

.02 Social and Economic Considerations

If you want more of something, subsidize it; if you want less, tax it. –Unknown

In addition to enacting tax laws aimed at achieving an equitable distribution of the tax burden, governments frequently use taxes in an attempt to alter taxpayer behavior. This is typically done by providing tax incentives to taxpayers who make certain choices that they otherwise might not make.

Taxes used as a means to encourage certain activities. The federal government frequently enacts tax laws to elicit certain types of behavior. For example, some tax laws offer tax benefits to businesses that provide housing for low-income persons and families. By offering these tax incentives, the government hopes businesses will find low-income housing a worthwhile investment, thereby alleviating the government's need to construct and maintain such housing. To ensure that these businesses continue to offer low-income housing on a sustained basis, the low-income housing credit is taken over a 10-year period, and it is taken back if at any time during the first 15 years the percentage of low-income tenants falls below a specified level.

In 1996, the federal government enacted tax legislation allowing tax credits to businesses that employ certain groups of economically disadvantaged individuals, including welfare recipients, qualified ex-felons, and veterans. Normally employers are allowed a tax deduction for wages paid to their workers. The tax savings from this deduction depend on the employer's marginal tax rate. The work opportunity credit now allows employers to take a tax credit for a portion of the wages paid to qualified workers during their two years of employment (in the case of a qualified welfare recipient) or during their first year of employment (in the case of all other qualified workers). By offering a tax credit rather than a tax deduction for a portion of these employees' wages, businesses can generate greater tax savings by hiring specific workers who might otherwise have difficulty finding employment. This tax credit was enacted to encourage businesses to hire and retain workers from certain targeted groups. By allowing the credit to be taken over two years (in the case of a qualified welfare recipient) and by increasing the credit in the employee's second year, the tax law encourages businesses not only to hire, but also to retain, welfare recipients.

Example 20: Jacobs Enterprises is in the process of hiring a new worker. The worker will earn $16,000 during his first two years of employment. Jacobs's marginal tax rate is 25 percent. If Jacobs hires a qualified welfare recipient, it can take a work opportunity credit equal to 40 percent of the first $10,000 of the employee's first year wages and 50 percent of the first $10,000 of his second year wages. Any wages not taken as a credit would be deductible from gross income. If a qualified welfare recipient is hired at a salary of $16,000 per year, over the first two years of the worker's employment, Jacobs will be allowed to take a tax credit equal to $9,000 ($10,000 × 40% plus $10,000 × 50%). Jacobs will also be able to deduct the remaining $23,000 ($16,000 for two years minus $9,000) as a wage expense. The tax savings from this deduction equals $5,750 ($23,000 × 25%), and Jacobs's total taxes would be reduced by $14,750 ($9,000 + $5,750) during the worker's first two years of employment. Compare this to the total tax savings Jacobs would realize if the company hired a worker that was not from one of the targeted groups. In that case, Jacobs Enterprises could only deduct $8,000 ($16,000 deduction for wage expense × 2 years × 25%).

Another example of the federal government using income tax laws to encourage certain types of decisions involves hybrid automobiles. These automobiles generally cost a few thousand dollars more than their nonhybrid counterparts. For example, the Ford Escape Hybrid costs approximately $3,500 more than the Ford Escape XLT. Since hybrid cars are powered by a combination of gas and battery, they are more fuel efficient and emit less pollution than standard automobiles. Hybrid automobiles have been around since 1999; however, the additional costs associated with the purchase of a hybrid automobile typically outweigh the savings that would be realized from increased fuel efficiency. As a result, relatively few hybrid automobiles have been sold.

From 2002–2005, the federal government allowed taxpayers a $2,000 deduction from gross income in the year they purchased a hybrid automobile to help offset the higher costs associated with acquiring hybrid vehicles. The intent behind enacting this tax law was to encourage Americans to buy hybrid cars, thereby protecting the environment and decreasing dependence on oil from the Middle East. However, because the tax incentive was offered as a deduction, the actual tax savings ranged anywhere from $200 for taxpayers in the 10-percent tax bracket to almost $800 for those in the highest tax bracket. Although rising gasoline prices during 2005 increased demand for hybrid automobiles, they continue to comprise a small portion of new cars sold each year. In 2005, fewer than 200,000 new hybrid vehicles were sold in the United States, representing 1.2 percent of the total number of vehicles sold that year.[7]

For 2008, the federal government offered tax credits ranging anywhere from $400 to $3,400 to taxpayers that purchased hybrid automobiles. The exact amount depended upon a combination of the vehicle's fuel economy and its total expected lifetime fuel savings. By increasing the tax incentives in two ways from how it was structured prior to 2006—changing a deduction to a credit and increasing the amount now available to all taxpayers—the federal government hoped to encourage consumers to consider purchasing hybrid automobiles over standard models, with the intended results of decreasing demand for gasoline and improving air quality.

 Spotlight: The Internal Revenue Code also requires that the qualified hybrid motor vehicle credit begin to phase out after a manufacturer sells a specific quantity of qualifying vehicles. Toyota Motor Sales, U.S.A., Inc., manufacturer of Toyota and Lexus automobiles reached the 60,000 unit mark to initiate the phase out of the credit for their hybrid vehicles in the second quarter of 2006. Thus, Toyota and Lexus hybrids placed into service on or after October 1, 2006, will only qualify for 50 percent of the certified credit amount; hybrids placed in service on or after April 1, 2007, will only qualify for 25 percent of the certified credit amount; and hybrids placed in service on or after October 1, 2007, will be ineligible to claim any credit amount. The behavior that the government sought to encourage, utilizing hybrid automobiles, met the governments expectation and the limit placed upon the credit came into play. Currently, no domestic automobile manufacturer of certified hybrid motor vehicles has entered the phase out period.

Taxes used as a means to encourage growth in certain industries. The cost of business property whose usefulness extends beyond the current year must be deducted over a number of years. Examples include machinery, equipment, and buildings. The tax laws involved in the calculation of this deduction, known as "depreciation," have been used to stimulate capital investment and economic growth. Prior to 1981, the number of years over which the cost of an asset was deducted corresponded closely with the estimated useful life of the asset, which is similar to how depreciation is calculated in financial accounting. In 1981, Congress enacted the Accelerated Cost Recovery System (ACRS), for recovering capital costs using accelerated methods over predetermined recovery periods that were much shorter than the properties' useful lives. Under ACRS, automobiles were depreciated over three tax years; buildings were depreciated over 18 years. By allowing these assets to be written off over shorter periods, the government intended the tax savings from the depreciation deduction (equal to the amount of the deduction times the taxpayer's marginal tax rate) to be realized earlier, thereby accelerating cash flows into the earlier years. One of the principal reasons for enacting ACRS was to provide faster tax savings to businesses in an

---

[7] "Sales Continue to Speed Up," *News & Features,* Hybrid-cars.com (December 28, 2005).

attempt to stimulate capital formation and the growth of the economy.[8] In 1986, Congress enacted the Modified Accelerated Cost Recovery System (MACRS), which extended the depreciation periods for most depreciable assets, thereby slowing down the pace at which depreciation is deducted, but still allowing much shorter cost recovery periods than the actual useful lives of the assets. MACRS continues to be the depreciation system in effect today. The depreciation rules are discussed in Chapter 7.

The federal government also used the tax system to encourage businesses to acquire new property in the aftermath of the events of September 11, 2001. The provision allowed businesses to deduct "bonus" first-year depreciation on all purchases of new tangible personal property placed in service between September 11, 2001, and December 31, 2005. The remainder of the cost was depreciated using MACRS. By allowing larger tax deductions in the first year, businesses that purchased new machinery, equipment, and other tangible personal property were able to generate much greater tax savings (and greater cash back from their investments) in the first year than they would have without this provision.

Example 21: Kendell, Inc. purchased new machinery in 2005 for $800,000. Kendell is in the 35-percent tax bracket. By taking the bonus depreciation, Kendell was allowed to deduct 50 percent, or $400,000, of the cost of the machine in 2005 and to deduct the remaining $400,000 over the next eight years, starting in 2005. Because of the bonus depreciation provision, Kendell's 2005 taxes were reduced by $140,000 ($400,000 × 35%) plus the tax savings from the portion of the remaining $400,000 that was deducted in 2005 under MACRS. Without this provision, Kendell would have been required to deduct the $800,000 over the next eight years. Although the entire $800,000 would be deducted over an eight-year period in both scenarios, by allowing bonus depreciation in the first year, Kendall accelerated the timing of the deduction, thereby increasing cash flows in 2005. The cash savings could then be used to pay expenses, pay down debt, etc. Alternatively, the additional cash savings could be invested and could earn investment income for the company beginning in 2005.

In enacting the bonus depreciation rules, the federal government hoped that by providing businesses with the opportunity to accelerate the timing of the cash flows, demand for new tangible personal property would increase. In turn, job growth would ensue, as companies that manufacture these assets would need to increase their workforces to meet the increased demand.

Congress continues to view bonus depreciation as an important tool for stimulating the economy. The *American Recovery and Reinvestment Act of 2009*, signed into law in February 2009, extends bonus depreciation through 2010.

Taxes used as a means to encourage socially desirable behavior. Shortly after Hurricane Katrina, the federal government passed tax legislation that contained many provisions aimed at encouraging and rewarding certain behavior. For example, businesses that became inoperable due to the hurricane but continued to pay wages to their employees were allowed to take a tax credit equal to 40 percent of up to $6,000 of each employee's wages paid through the end of 2005. By offering this tax incentive, the government hoped businesses would continue to pay their employees while they looked for temporary employment. This action would then postpone or possibly avoid the need for those workers to file for unemployment benefits, thereby reducing state and federal governments' responsibilities to pay such benefits.

Another provision in this legislation allowed taxpayers an additional $500 exemption against taxable income for each qualified displaced Katrina person for whom they provided rent-free housing for a period lasting at least 60 consecutive days. This provision was intended to encourage and reward taxpayers who provided temporary housing to persons displaced by the hurricane.

---

[8] Staff of the Joint Committee on Taxation, 97th Cong., General Explanation of the Economic Recovery Tax Act of 1981, at 75–76 (Comm. Print 1981).

¶ 106.02

Another example of tax laws enacted to encourage socially desirable behavior involves the deduction allowed in arriving at taxable income for contributions made to qualified charities. In addition to encouraging and rewarding this behavior, the government attempts to enhance contributions to religious, charitable, educational, scientific, and literary organizations (among others) through its definition of what constitutes a qualified charity. These activities are deemed important to society, but they usually cannot be supported in the marketplace without at least some government assistance. Thus, to the extent that the tax laws encourage individuals and businesses to provide support for these activities, they help alleviate the government's responsibility to provide funding for the activities.

Example 22: Norton Industries is in the 35-percent tax bracket. Norton donates $1,000,000 to a qualified charity. This donation is deducted in arriving at Norton's taxable income and reduces its tax liability by $350,000 ($1,000,000 × 35%). Thus, of the $1 million donation, $650,000 ($1,000,000 – $350,000) came from Norton, and $350,000 came from the federal government. Even though the federal government is subsidizing $350,000 of the contribution, the charitable organization receives a $1,000,000 donation that the federal government might otherwise have been required to fund.

Taxes used as a means to discourage certain behavior. In addition to enacting tax laws that attempt to encourage certain types of decision-making behavior, the government may also enact tax laws that discourage certain types of behavior. For example, excise taxes on tobacco and alcohol are often referred to as "sin taxes," because of the negative connotation associated with the products being purchased. Governments use sin taxes to limit consumption of these goods. Although gasoline is not known as a sin tax, by increasing gasoline excise taxes (and therefore increasing the retail price of gasoline), the government encourages motorists to conserve fuel by carpooling, using public transportation, or purchasing more fuel-efficient vehicles.

In 1978, the federal government enacted a gas guzzler excise tax. This tax penalizes companies that manufacture passenger automobiles whose fuel economy is below 22.5 miles per gallon. The tax is imposed on manufacturers and importers of automobiles, but presumably some (if not all) of the tax is passed along to consumers through higher retail prices. Thus, the intent behind the gas guzzler tax is to discourage automakers from manufacturing and consumers from buying the less fuel-efficient automobiles.

San Francisco city officials considered a proposal that would charge grocery shoppers $.17 for every paper or plastic bag they took home. The $.17 user fee was determined based on the city's estimate of the costs it incurs to clean up and dispose of the thousands of plastic bags left on city streets during the year. Thus, San Francisco planned to pay for the entire cost of providing grocery bags by charging user fees. Those who were in favor of the bag tax cited environmental concerns, in particular, the number of trees cut down each year in the manufacture of grocery bags and the growing amount of plastic in the ocean that is choking marine life.[9] In commenting on the proposal, the San Francisco Commission vice-president said, "We're not trying to just charge a user fee; we're trying to make a change in behavior."[10] It appears that the Commission's plan has some merit, as in 2002 Ireland passed a $.22 per bag tax on plastic bags and found that within weeks, plastic bag use dropped 94 percent.[11]

As mentioned earlier in the chapter, the federal income tax system allows a deduction against business income of all ordinary and necessary expenses incurred in the regular course of a business. Accordingly, professional truck drivers may argue that speeding fines are an ordinary and necessary business expense in the trucking industry. The government, not wanting to reward this and similar types of behavior, specifically enacted tax laws that prohibit the deduction of expenses that are deemed to be in violation of public policy. Similar laws have been enacted to disallow the

---

[9] Traci Watson, "S.F. Considers 17-Cent Tax on Grocery Bags," *USA Today*, November 22, 2005.

[10] Wyatt Buchanan, "17-Cent Fee on Bags Okd by Environment Panel," *San Francisco Chronicle*, January 26, 2005.

[11] "With Tax, Plastic Bags Disappear in Ireland," *The New York Times*, Saturday, February 2, 2008.

deduction of bribes and kickbacks a business may make, even if they are incurred in the ordinary course of business.

 Spotlight: Every deduction the government allows to reduce taxable income reduces the taxpayer's tax liability by the amount of the deduction times the taxpayer's marginal tax rate. Therefore, by allowing a particular deduction, the government is subsidizing the expenditure. This, in turn, could be construed as the government endorsing any behavior that results in a tax deduction. For this reason, governments may enact tax laws that specifically disallow certain types of deductions.

.03 Redistribution of Wealth

The art of government consists of taking as much money as possible from one class of citizens to give to the other. –Voltaire

Some tax laws are enacted for the sole purpose of redistributing wealth from one group of taxpayers to another. The best example of this is wealth transfer taxes. Most property an individual owns at the time of his or her death has been previously taxed through any one of a number of means. All income earned was subject to income tax; most property was subject to sales tax at the time it was purchased. Less than two percent of the people who died in 2002 had estates large enough to pay any estate tax. Even though the estate tax comprises very little of the federal government's total revenues collected, and despite the fact that the tax laws surrounding the estate tax are extremely complicated, it nonetheless continues to exist and to serve as a means of redistributing wealth.

Other examples of the government's use of taxes to redistribute wealth involve the enactment of refundable personal tax credits. The tax laws allow a $1,000 tax credit for each child under the age of 17 claimed as a dependent on the taxpayer's income tax return. Because this credit is intended to help taxpayers with modest levels of income, the full credit is only available for taxpayers with an AGI below certain levels ($75,000 for unmarried taxpayers; $110,000 for married couples filing a joint return). However, when the amount of the child tax credit exceeds the taxpayer's tax liability, the excess may result in a refund. In such a case, not only does the taxpayer pay zero income taxes during the year, but he or she may also be entitled to a tax refund from the government. The funding for these refunds comes from other taxpayers, and the result is a redistribution of wealth.

Example 23: Nancy and David Clark are married and have two children, ages seven and nine. In 2009, the Clarks' taxable income is $16,500. Although taxes will be calculated on the $16,500 of taxable income, the Clarks will be allowed to reduce their taxes by $2,000 ($1,000 child tax credit for each child). If the amount of the credit exceeds the Clarks' tax liability, the excess may result in a refund.

Another tax credit the government makes available to lower-income taxpayers is the earned income credit (EIC). The EIC is a refundable credit that reduces the tax liabilities of low-income taxpayers and provides a tax refund for any excess credit. However, in order to generate any EIC, the taxpayer must report earned income on the tax return. Because only taxpayers with earned income qualify for this credit, not only is this tax provision used as a means of redistributing wealth, but it also encourages lower-income taxpayers to work so they can receive a refund from the federal government when they file their income tax returns.

Example 24: Samantha and Daniel Wright claim their two children as dependents. Because of the available deductions from AGI, the Wrights have zero taxable income and no income tax liability. However, because Samantha and Daniel both work and report earned income, they are entitled to a $1,420 EIC. Although the Wrights have no income tax liability, they will receive a $1,420 refund from the federal government when they file their tax return.

.04 Administrative Convenience

A tax law enacted to reduce either administrative or compliance costs is enacted for **administrative convenience**. As previously discussed in this chapter, the federal government does not require persons to file a gift tax return in 2009, provided that gifts to persons other than one's spouse do not exceed $13,000 per person. Subjecting every gift to a gift tax would be a difficult administrative task, and compliance would probably be very low. Allowing certain *de minimis* amounts of transfers between persons to occur each year without any tax or reporting consequences is one example of tax laws enacted for administrative convenience.

Another example of administrative convenience is the option given to taxpayers to deduct from taxable income the *greater of* the standard deduction or itemized deductions. Taxpayers who itemize report the total amounts spent for each type of expenditure; they are required to retain the receipts documenting their deductions for at least three years. The presence of the standard deduction allows taxpayers with limited amounts of itemized deductions to avoid having to keep track of these smaller expenditures, thereby minimizing their compliance costs as well as the government's administrative costs.

.05 Political Considerations

If you have been voting for politicians who promise to give you goodies at someone else's expense, then you have no right to complain when they take your money and give it to someone else, including themselves. –Thomas Sowell, syndicated columnist

Politicians strive to be re-elected; lobbyists strive to please their constituents. As a result, some tax laws are enacted solely because they are popular or for other political reasons. For example, tax laws have been enacted to provide tax breaks to specific industries. It was previously mentioned in this chapter that the excise taxes on a pack of cigarettes vary from state to state, ranging anywhere from $.07 a pack in South Carolina to $2.46 a pack in Rhode Island. In addition to seeking a source of revenues, governments impose excise taxes on tobacco products to discourage individuals from purchasing those products. Because the economy in tobacco-producing states depends heavily on the demand for tobacco products, imposing higher excise taxes on such products could hurt the state's economy. North Carolina, Kentucky, Tennessee, South Carolina, and Virginia are five of the largest tobacco-producing states in the United States. Therefore, it is not surprising that the excise taxes on a pack of cigarettes in those five states are among the seven lowest in the nation.

The elderly comprise a large percentage of voters, and consequently, it is not unusual to find tax breaks throughout the various tax systems to accommodate elderly taxpayers. Most local governments that impose real estate taxes allow a reduced tax base to elderly homeowners. The federal government allows taxpayers over age 64 an additional standard deduction when computing their taxable income, and state and local governments exempt prescription drugs from their tax bases for sales tax purposes. However, anytime a special exemption, deduction, or credit is incorporated into the tax laws, complexity is introduced into the tax system. Consequently, most special provisions that have been added to the tax laws for political reasons have contributed to their complexity and have reduced the efficiency of the U.S. tax system.

Sometimes tax laws are passed because of their popularity. Hotel occupancy taxes and rental car "surcharges" have become popular taxes for local governments. They provide local governments with a source of revenue, and the tax is usually levied on persons who do not live (and do not have a vote) in the community. Severance taxes are also a very popular means of increasing state revenues because the costs incurred by businesses that extract natural resources from the state are passed along to consumers in other states.

¶ 107 The Importance of Studying Federal Income Tax Laws

Taxes are transaction costs that must be considered when making business decisions. Since most sources of revenue a business generates will be subject to tax, only a portion of each dollar earned is retained by the business. Similarly, any expenditure a business makes that qualifies as a deduction results in less taxes owed. The taxpayer's marginal tax rate is used in determining the amount of the transaction costs when revenues and expenditures are involved. When determining a taxpayer's marginal tax rate, it is important to consider taxes imposed by all levels of government, not just the federal government.

Example 25: Speedy Services, Inc. operates in a state that imposes a flat 7.3-percent tax on taxable income. Speedy is in the 35-percent tax bracket for federal income tax purposes. Thus, when determining the tax savings from an additional dollar of deduction or the cost for an additional dollar of revenue, Speedy's marginal tax rate is 39.75 percent (35% + (7.3% × (100% − 35%)).

Tax credits also often arise from expenditures; however, $1 of tax credit results in $1 of tax savings. Accordingly, the tax consequences of receiving income or making expenditures must be considered in order to make the best possible decisions.

Example 26: In Example 20, Jacobs Enterprises (whose marginal tax rate was 25 percent) had the opportunity to save $14,750 in taxes ($9,000 tax credit plus $5,750 from deducting $23,000 as wage expense) over a two-year period by hiring a qualified welfare recipient. If Jacobs hires someone who is not a qualified welfare recipient, it will deduct the $32,000 of wages paid during the first two years, but the corresponding tax savings would be only $8,000 ($32,000 × 25%). Accordingly, the cash savings of hiring a person who is a qualified welfare recipient over one who is not would be $6,750 ($14,750 − $8,000) over a two-year period.

Some tax laws do not alter the amount of the deduction, but instead accelerate the timing of the deduction. Although in the end, the same amount will be deducted, deductions that can be taken in earlier years (as opposed to later years) result in less taxes paid today. Those accelerated tax savings constitute cash flows that can be invested today to generate additional cash flows in future years. Alternatively, the accelerated cash flows can be used to pay the company's current expenditures, thereby eliminating the need to find other sources from which to pay for those costs. Through tax planning, taxpayers can arrange their affairs to minimize taxes. However, proper tax planning involves a thorough understanding of the tax laws. U.S. Supreme Court Justice Learned Hand once said,

> Over and over again courts have said that there is nothing sinister in arranging one's affairs so as to make taxes as low as possible. Everybody does so, rich or poor, and do right, for nobody has any public duty to pay more taxes than the law demands. Taxes are enforced exaction, not voluntary contributions.

Tax avoidance is the art of using existing tax laws to pay the least amount of tax legally possible. **Tax evasion**, on the other hand, involves paying less than the full amount of taxes rightly owed to the government, whether through intentional disregard of the tax laws, through willful neglect, or for any other reason. Practicing tax avoidance is not illegal. It fact, it should be every taxpayer's goal when it comes to paying taxes.

> *Whereas tax planning was once an exclusive game for the rich, it is now the pursuit of everybody except the foolish.* –Charles Adams

As discussed in this chapter, the federal income tax laws allow businesses to deduct a wide array of expenditures related to the generation of business revenues. They also allow many types of income to be exempt from taxation and provide opportunities to generate tax credits that reduce taxes. Understanding which types of income the government taxes and which types of expenditures can be used to reduce taxable income (or perhaps tax liability) is essential in making the best business decisions. This book provides the foundation for understanding how the federal government taxes income its residents and businesses earn. As a Morgan Stanley advertisement once read, "You must pay taxes. But there's no law that says you gotta leave a tip."

Planning Pointer: Businesses need to consider all types of taxes when making decisions. This textbook focuses on the tax laws that are pertinent to the federal income tax system, which is one of the primary taxing bodies that businesses encounter.

¶ 108 Summary

Although raising revenues remains the primary reason behind our tax laws, social, economic, and political considerations play important roles in deciding how to allocate the tax burden. All governments, from the federal government to townships to local school districts, generate revenues by imposing taxes, and they have a variety of tax bases and tax rate structures from which to choose. Because taxes represent a transfer from the private sector to the government, minimizing taxes owed to the government results in increased private wealth. A solid understanding of how tax laws operate is crucial to achieving this goal.

The primary focus of this book is on the federal income tax laws that pertain to businesses. Regardless of the type of entity used to operate the business—sole proprietorship, partnership, S corporation, LLP, LLC, or C corporation—the rules in this textbook will allow the reader to gain a better understanding of how the federal income tax laws affect business decisions. This chapter introduced the federal taxable income formula and the concepts of income, deduction, and tax credit. These topics are covered more thoroughly in upcoming chapters. The final chapters of the book take a closer look at each type of entity choice and discuss the particular tax laws that pertain specifically to that type of entity.

GLOSSARY OF TERMS INTRODUCED IN THE CHAPTER

Ability-to-pay concept. Taxes are imposed on taxpayers that are in the best position to pay the taxes by having them pay a greater share of their tax bases toward the tax burden.

Administrative convenience. When a tax law is enacted because it reduces administrative costs or taxpayers' compliance costs.

Ad valorem tax. A tax that uses the value of property as the tax base.

Adjusted gross income (AGI). An intermediate step between gross income and taxable income that individuals calculate. Only deductions for AGI are subtracted from gross income in computing AGI.

All-inclusive approach. The method used to define income. Under this approach, all income is subject to income tax unless a provision in the tax laws allows it not to be taxed.

Average tax rate. The total tax liability divided by the tax base. Used in determining the portion of the tax base that is paid in taxes.

C corporation. An incorporated business entity other than an S corporation that is treated as a separate tax entity from its shareholders. The income of a C corporation is subject to two layers of taxation.

Capital recovery doctrine. When taxpayers dispose of property, in determining the amount of gain included in gross income (or loss deductible from gross income) they are allowed to recover their investment in the property.

Deduction. Expenditure made by a taxpayer that the government allows the taxpayer to use to reduce taxable income.

Direct tax. A tax levied on the party who ultimately bears the burden of the tax.

Employment tax. A tax imposed by the government on employee wages (FICA and FUTA) and on net earnings from a sole proprietorship (self-employment taxes).

Estate tax. A wealth transfer tax assessed on a decedent's taxable estate.

Excise tax. A tax on the production or consumption of specific goods or services, like tobacco products, alcohol, and gasoline.

Exclusion. An item of income that according to the tax laws is not subject to taxation.

Externality. The positive or negative effect of a transaction that occurs to persons or businesses that are not part of that transaction.

FICA (Federal Insurance Contributions Act). The combination of social security (OASDI) and Medicare taxes shared equally by the employee and the employer.

Fair market value (FMV). The amount that would induce a willing seller to sell and a willing buyer to buy certain property.

Flat tax. *See* Proportional tax.

Flow-through entity. A business entity that does not pay taxes, but files a tax return reporting the amounts of gross income, deductions, and credits generated by the business during the year, and passes information along to its owners regarding their respective shares of such items. Examples include partnerships, S corporations, limited liability corporations, and limited liability partnerships.

Franchise tax. An annual tax on the privilege of doing business in the state.

FUTA (Federal Unemployment Tax Act). A federal tax imposed on employers. The tax base is employee wages up to $7,000; the tax rate equals 6.2 percent.

GAAP (Generally Accepted Accounting Principles). The set of rules publicly-traded companies must adhere to when preparing financial statements.

Gift tax. A wealth transfer tax the government imposes upon the transferor for transfers to nonspouses in excess of a certain amount each year.

Gross income. All income from whatever source derived, except as specifically excluded by a provision in the Internal Revenue Code or other tax law. Represents the income the government has chosen to tax. Equals income minus exclusions.

Income. Broadly defined as increases in wealth that the taxpayer has realized.

Indirect tax. A tax levied on someone other than the one who ultimately bears the burden of the tax.

Inheritance tax. A tax levied on the beneficiary upon receipt of inherited property.

Intangible property. Personal property that has no physical characteristics. Examples include goodwill, patents, copyrights, mutual funds, stocks, and bonds.

Itemized deductions. A deduction from adjusted gross income that consists of various personal expenses that the federal government allows individuals to deduct in lieu of a standard deduction.

CCH® StudyMATE™
Your Personal Online Tax "Tutor"—24/7!

If you find taxes difficult, you're not alone! Now you have CCH® Study MATE™, a personal online "tutor." With Study MATE you can plug into online learning any time of day or night. Study MATE walks you through the most important concepts covered in your textbook using individual learning sessions designed to make learning as easy as possible.

Study MATE is easy to use, and since you've bought our book, you have free access to our Fundamental Tax Topics Library for a full year! Study MATE courses are designed with web learning in mind, so you can navigate your way through them independently. They are relatively short, but each course covers a substantial amount of material—including the top concepts covered in your textbook. These are student-centered courses with presentations that are different than those found in the text, so they give you another voice—another opportunity for concepts to sink in.

CCH® StudyMATE™
Mentor for Accounting and Tax Education

Home | Log In | Register

HOME >

Technical Support
866 798-5897 • support@learning.net

Welcome to Study MATE.
Study MATE provides a new and exciting way to expand your knowledge of taxes, auditing, and accounting. The courses provide examples, observations, and study questions to help you further develop your knowledge in these areas. Think of Study MATE as your own personal study partner.

Already enrolled?
Member Login

User Name:
Password:

Forget Password? | Login

New Users:

If you have an *access code* (provided with your CCH textbook)...
1. Whether you are a professor or student, register for an account by clicking on the appropriate sign up box.
2. Click on a library title or course name to enroll in a library and use your access code as payment.
3. Complete the courses in the library.

If you want to *purchase* a topic or entire library...
1. Whether you are a professor, student, or practitioner, register for an account by clicking on the appropriate sign up box.
2. Click on a library title to view the courses available, and then click on a library title or course name to enroll and pay by credit card.
3. Complete the courses you purchased.

» **Students** Sign up here if you are a student
» **Professors** Sign up here if you are a professor

» **Students** Sign up here if you are a student
» **Professors** Sign up here if you are a professor
» **Practitioners** Other members may sign up here.

How Many Courses Do I Take?

Your instructor may want you to access all the courses in the fundamental series, you may be asked to take selective courses on certain topics, or your instructor may leave it up to you to use Study MATE as you choose.

So, How Do I Get In?

Getting started is easy.

1 Go to www.cchstudymate.com and follow the instructions for New Users with an **access code** to sign up for a free account. Fill in the information on the registration page including a user ID and password of your choice.

2 Continue following the online instructions to enter your access code (provided below).

3 Click on MY COURSES to view the list of online courses, then click on the course title to begin.

ACCESS CODE:

CCHSM_10_TACL_1_984134

Technical Support: 866-798-5897 • support@learning.net

Over for course features ▶ ▶ ▶

Access CCH Study MATE at www.cchstudymate.com
For your records, print your User ID and Password below:

User ID: _____

Password: _____

Features of each course:

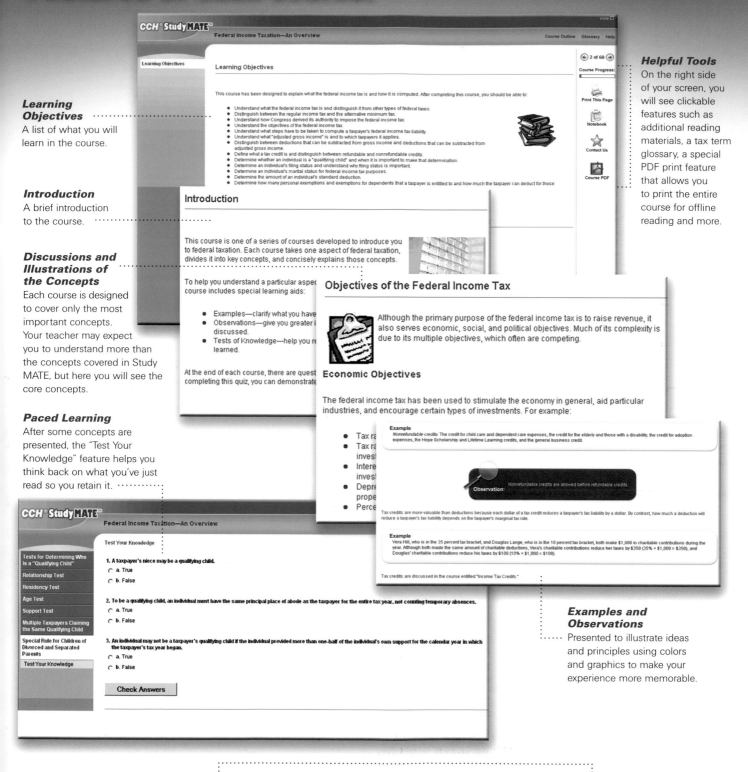

Learning Objectives
A list of what you will learn in the course.

Introduction
A brief introduction to the course.

Discussions and Illustrations of the Concepts
Each course is designed to cover only the most important concepts. Your teacher may expect you to understand more than the concepts covered in Study MATE, but here you will see the core concepts.

Paced Learning
After some concepts are presented, the "Test Your Knowledge" feature helps you think back on what you've just read so you retain it.

Helpful Tools
On the right side of your screen, you will see clickable features such as additional reading materials, a tax term glossary, a special PDF print feature that allows you to print the entire course for offline reading and more.

Examples and Observations
Presented to illustrate ideas and principles using colors and graphics to make your experience more memorable.

Testing—One, Two, Three
At the end of each course, a 15-question quiz is presented. The quiz questions are not easily answered—they really test whether you understand the concepts! You can take the quiz up to three times if you like and after successfully completing the quiz, you can print a certificate for your records and e-mail the certificate to your instructor to show you've successfully completed the course.

Get started! ▶ ▶ ▶

Limited liability. When an owner's liability with respect to the business is limited to the amount the owner has invested in the business.

Limited liability company (LLC). A business entity that can be treated as a partnership for tax purposes and whose owners enjoy limited liability.

Limited liability partnership (LLP). A business entity that can be treated as a partnership for tax purposes, but whose owners enjoy some aspects of limited liability.

Marginal tax rate. The rate of tax on the last dollar of taxable income or the amount of taxes saved on an additional dollar of deduction.

Nonrefundable tax credit. A tax credit that can only reduce a taxpayer's income tax liability.

Partnership. A flow-through entity that has at all times at least two owners, at least one of whom is responsible for the debts of the business.

Personal and dependency exemptions. A deduction from adjusted gross income the government allows to individual taxpayers. A deduction is allowed for the taxpayer, the taxpayer's spouse (if filing a joint return), and the taxpayer's dependents.

Personal property. Property that is not real estate. *See* Tangible personal property and Intangible property.

Progressive tax. A tax structure in which the average tax rate increases as the tax base increases.

Property tax. A tax assessed on property, including real property, tangible personal property, and intangible personal property.

Proportional tax. A tax structure in which the average tax rate does not change as the tax base changes (also referred to as flat tax).

Public good. A government-provided good or service for which enjoyment of the good cannot be limited.

Real property. Land and buildings (also referred to as real estate).

Realization principle. Gains and losses on property are not reported on the tax return until the year in which property is disposed of in a taxable transaction.

Refundable tax credit. A credit that can reduce a taxpayer's tax liability to zero and produce a refund for any amount of the credit in excess of the taxpayer's tax liability.

Regressive tax. A tax structure in which the average tax rate decreases as the tax base increases.

S corporation. A flow-through business entity that does not pay income taxes. An S corporation gets its name because it is a corporation that has elected to be taxed under Subchapter S of Chapter 1 of the Code. Only corporations that satisfy certain requirements can elect to be taxed as S corporations.

[handwritten margin note: Subchapter S of Chapter 1 of the Code.]

Sales tax. A broad-based tax on the comsumption of goods and services.

Self-employment tax. The employee and employer portions of FICA tax that are imposed on net earnings from self-employment.

Sole proprietor. The owner of an unincorporated business.

Standard deduction. A deduction from adjusted gross income that the federal government allows individual taxpayers to deduct in lieu of itemized deductions.

Tangible personal property. Property that has physical characteristics but is not real estate.

Tax avoidance. The art of reducing tax liability through legitimate means.

Tax base. Used in computing tax liability. It represents the amount subject to tax. The tax base is multiplied by the tax rate to determine the taxpayer's tax liability.

Tax credit. Amount that reduces a taxpayer's tax liability. Can be either refundable or nonrefundable.

Tax evasion. Understating taxes due to the government through unlawful means.

Taxable income. The difference between a taxpayer's gross income and the total deductions a taxpayer is allowed. The tax base used in the regular income tax system.

Use tax. A tax charged by states on the consumption, use, or storage of goods and services that are not subject to sales tax.

User fee. A tax charged to those that use a government-provided good or service.

Wealth transfer tax. The tax a government imposes on transfers of wealth between two individuals. *See also* Estate tax, Gift tax, and Inheritance tax.

Wherewithal-to-pay concept. The principle that taxes income at the point at which the taxpayer has the greatest ability to pay the tax on such income.

CHAPTER PROBLEMS

The following questions and problems relate to the discussion in Chapter 1, Introduction to Taxation, which begins at ¶ 100 in *Part I: Overview of Taxes and the Federal Income Tax System*.

Chapter 1 Discussion Questions

1. Government-provided goods and services can be categorized as public goods or nonpublic goods. Provide examples of each. For which goods and services is it appropriate to consider a user fee to raise revenues associated with the costs incurred in providing those goods and services? When the opportunity exists to cover the costs of those goods and services through user fees, why do governments often choose to raise taxes for those goods and services partly through other means?

2. What is the difference between a taxpayer's average tax rate and the taxpayer's marginal tax rate? Which of these rates is most useful in determining the benefits derived from additional deductions? Which of these rates is most useful in determining whether a tax rate structure is regressive, progressive, or proportional? Which of these rates is most useful in determining the benefits derived from a tax credit?

3. Tax rate structures can be regressive, proportional, or progressive. Provide an example of a tax that uses each of these tax structures.

4. All property owned can be categorized either as real property or as personal property. What is the distinction between these two types of property? Provide examples of each.

5. All personal property can be categorized either as tangible personal property or as intangible personal property. What is the distinction between these two types of property? Provide examples of each.

6. Are an individual's personal belongings always personal property? Explain.

7. FICA and FUTA are two types of unemployment taxes. Are FICA and FUTA regressive, proportional, or progressive taxes? Explain.

8. Some taxes are direct taxes, whereas others are indirect taxes. Among the taxes discussed in this chapter, which ones are direct taxes? Which ones are indirect taxes? Who bears the economic burden of these taxes? Explain.

9. What is the distinction between sales taxes and excise taxes?

10. Estate taxes and inheritance taxes are sometimes referred to as "death taxes" because the tax levied on the transfer of wealth is triggered by someone's death. On whom are these death taxes levied? Which levels of government levy these wealth transfer taxes? What tax base is used?

11. What is gross income and how is it computed?

12. Both exclusions and deductions reduce taxable income, so why do the income tax laws make a distinction between the two?

13. The income tax laws use an all-inclusive approach to defining income. What does this mean?

14. How does a tax credit differ from a tax deduction?

15. What is the difference between refundable and nonrefundable tax credits?

16. Tax avoidance and tax evasion are two ways a taxpayer can reduce the amount of taxes owed to the government. What is the important distinction between these two terms?

17. Fairness and efficiency are two goals of every tax system. Give an example that shows why it is difficult to achieve both at the same time.

18. In addition to using taxes for raising revenues, governments use them for a variety of other purposes. Name the other factors governments consider when deciding whom and what to tax. Provide examples of each.

19. Discuss the importance of taxes when making business decisions.

20. Explain why being able to accelerate the timing of a business deduction is valuable to a business.

Chapter 1 Problems

1. A major city recently entered into an agreement for a professional sports team to build its new stadium in the city. In exchange, the city will exempt the owners of the team from property taxes for the next 10 years. The mayor of the city is lauding the transaction because of all the positive externalities that building the stadium in the city will bring. Discuss some of the possible positive externalities from this transaction. Can you think of any negative externalities from this transaction?

2. If a taxpayer in the 25% marginal tax rate bracket is given the choice between a $1,000 deduction and a $300 tax credit, which would result in more tax savings?

3. Taxpayer A pays taxes of $3,000 on a $10,000 tax base. Taxpayer B pays taxes of $5,000 on a $15,000 tax base. Is this tax rate structure regressive, proportional, or progressive? Explain.

4. Taxpayer C pays taxes of $4,000 on a $10,000 tax base. Taxpayer D pays taxes of $4,800 on a $15,000 tax base. Is this tax rate structure regressive, proportional, or progressive? Explain.

5. Taxpayer E pays taxes of $3,500 on a $10,000 tax base. Taxpayer F pays taxes of $5,000 on a $15,000 tax base. Is this tax rate structure regressive, proportional, or progressive? Explain.

6. Taxpayer G pays taxes of $3,000 on a tax base of $10,000. If the tax rate structure is regressive, what is the maximum amount of taxes Taxpayer H would pay on a tax base of $15,000?

7. Taxpayer I pays taxes of $2,000 on a tax base of $10,000. If the tax rate structure is proportional, what is the amount of taxes Taxpayer J would pay on a tax base of $15,000?

8. Taxpayer K pays taxes of $2,500 on a tax base of $10,000. If the tax rate structure is progressive, what is the minimum amount of taxes Taxpayer L would pay on a tax base of $15,000?

9. Which entity choice(s) protect the owners from the general obligations of the business?

   a. Sole proprietorship

   b. C corporation

   c. S corporation

   d. Partnership

   e. LLC

   f. LLP

10. Which entity choice(s) only tax the profits of the business one time?

   a. Sole proprietorship

   b. C corporation

   c. S corporation

   d. Partnership

   e. LLC

   f. LLP

11. Which entity choice(s) are available for businesses with a single owner?

   a. Sole proprietorship

   b. C corporation

   c. S corporation

   d. Partnership

   e. LLC

   f. LLP

12. Which entity choice(s) are required to file an annual income tax return?

   a. Sole proprietorship

   b. C corporation

   c. S corporation

   d. Partnership

   e. LLC

   f. LLP

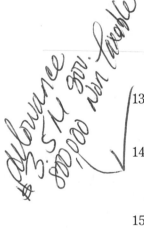

13. Julie and Ron Johansson are interested in making tax-free gifts to each of their six children and 14 grandchildren during 2009. What is the maximum amount that the Johanssons can transfer to their descendents tax free during 2009?

14. Eric Robertson died during 2009 leaving a taxable estate worth $3,000,000. During his lifetime, Eric made taxable gifts totaling $800,000, but since they did not exceed the $1,000,000 lifetime exemption amount, he never paid any gift tax. Will an estate tax be imposed on Eric's estate? Explain.

15. The federal government currently allows tax credits to consumers who purchase hybrid automobiles. What externalities do purchases of hybrid automobiles produce that are driving the federal government to provide this tax incentive?

16. In recent years, a debate has arisen over replacing the incredibly complex income tax system and the payroll tax with a simpler flat tax on all income. If the government were able to accomplish this, how might this affect the various equity, social, and economic issues that governments often consider when deciding how to raise revenues?

17. What is the primary tax or nontax advantage of operating a business as a C corporation over a sole proprietorship?

18. What is the primary tax or nontax disadvantage of operating a business as a C corporation over a sole proprietorship?

19. If a taxpayer in the 25% tax bracket is able to take a tax credit for 20 percent of the $10,000 of wages it pays a particular employee and deduct the rest as wage expense, how much more tax savings will the taxpayer generate over just being able to deduct the entire $10,000 as wage expense?

20. A single taxpayer has adjusted gross income of $35,000 and itemized deductions of $1,000 in 2009. What is the taxpayer's taxable income assuming no dependency exemptions?

21. A congressman is deciding between proposing a $1,000 increase in the child tax credit or a $5,000 increase in the deduction for the dependency exemption. Calculate the tax savings of the credit versus an increased deduction for a taxpayer in the 15% tax bracket with one who is in 28% tax bracket. Which person benefits most from the tax credit versus the increased deduction?

22. A congressman is trying to determine whether to propose a $1,000 increase in the child tax credit or a $5,000 increase in the dependency exemption. Calculate the tax savings of the credit versus exemption for a taxpayer in the 10% tax bracket with one who is in the 35% tax bracket. Which person benefits most from the tax credit versus the increased exemption?

23. A congressman is trying to determine whether to propose a $750 tax credit or a $4,000 tax deduction for the purchase of a hybrid car. Calculate the tax savings of the credit versus deduction for a taxpayer in the 10% tax bracket with one who is in the 35% tax bracket. Which person benefits most from the tax credit versus the deduction? In making your decision, does it matter that a wealthier individual is more likely to buy a $25,000 Prius than a less wealthy person?

24. A congressperson wants to encourage the establishment of renewable energy business in her state by providing tax incentives dealing with the start-up expenses of these businesses. Among the ideas she is considering are (1) allowing a write-off over 60 month of all start-up expenses; (2) allowing a deduction of $5,000 of start-up expenses with a 180 month write-off for any remaining start-up expenses; and (3) allowing a deduction of all start-up expenses up to $50,000 with no write-off allowed for expenses in excess of $50,000. What are the pros and cons of each option?

25. A congressman is trying to determine whether to propose a nonrefundable $500 tuition tax credit or a $2,500 tax deduction. Calculate the tax savings of the credit versus deduction for a taxpayer in the 10% tax bracket with one who is in the 35% tax bracket. Which person benefits most from the tax credit versus the deduction? If we assume that more students are in the 10% bracket and therefore prefer the tuition tax credit, will this proposed tax law provide them with a lot of assistance? Discuss whether the tuition tax credit should be refundable.

CHAPTER 2

Understanding the Federal Tax Laws

LEARNING OBJECTIVES

1. Explain the importance of understanding the various sources of tax law.
2. Distinguish between primary and secondary sources of tax law.
3. Understand which primary sources of tax law should be accorded the greatest authoritative weight.
4. Demonstrate how to locate primary sources of tax law.
5. Understand the ethical considerations involved when conducting tax research.
6. Explain how to effectively conduct tax research.

¶ 200 Introduction

Almost all business transactions have tax implications. When revenue is earned, questions are raised as to whether the revenue is taxable, how much is taxable, and when it is taxable. When an expenditure is incurred, businesses must determine whether an amount can be deducted, and if so, how much and when. They also must determine whether any credit is available with respect to the expenditure and, if so, the amount of the credit and when it may be taken. When businesses dispose of property, questions are raised as to the amount of gain or loss realized from the transaction, what amount must be recognized, and when that amount must be reported on the tax return. The answer to these and all other tax questions can be found in the tax laws of the U.S. income tax system.

The underlying foundation for the U.S. income tax laws is the Internal Revenue Code (the "Code"); however, the information in the Code alone may not be sufficient to adequately address the issue at hand. Consequently, taxpayers must consult with other sources of legislative, administrative, and judicial authority in order to determine the true tax consequences of a transaction.

The purpose of this chapter is to present the various sources of primary tax law, which include legislative, administrative, and judicial authority. In addition to introducing these various authorities, guidance will be provided to inform students how they can locate and use these sources to gain a better understanding of how the various U.S. federal income tax laws are derived. Guidance also will be provided to help students understand how decisions are to be made in situations involving ambiguous areas of the tax law. The chapter begins with a brief history of where the U.S. income tax laws originate, followed by a discussion of the various sources of tax authority. The chapter concludes with a discussion of the tax research process and ethical standards that are expected to be followed when researching tax issues.

¶ 201 History of the U.S. Federal Income Tax

Prior to the Civil War, the federal government relied primarily on tariffs and excise taxes to generate revenues. These taxes were imposed on imported goods (tariffs) and on the consumption of specific goods (excise taxes). The first federal individual income tax was enacted in 1861 to help pay for the costs associated with fighting the Civil War. A three-percent tax was imposed on a person's annual income in excess of $800, which is equivalent to almost $18,500 today. In 1862, a two-tiered rate structure was enacted with taxable incomes in excess of $10,000 being taxed at five percent. In 1872, Congress repealed the individual income tax and went back to relying primarily on excises taxes to generate revenues for the federal government.

The repeal of the income tax was short-lived. In 1894, Congress reinstated an individual income tax; however, this time it was challenged as unconstitutional on the grounds that the U.S. Constitution at the time allowed Congress to impose direct taxes only when they could be levied in proportion to each state's population. Since an individual income tax is levied on an individual's level of income and not collected based on the states' populations, the U.S. Supreme Court agreed with the petitioner and held that the individual income tax was unconstitutional.[1]

Congress recognized the problems of relying heavily on excises taxes, as it resulted in lower-income taxpayers spending disproportionately higher portions of their incomes in taxes. Consequently, in the years that followed the Supreme Court's decision, a great deal of debate ensued about how the government should raise its needed revenues. Industrialized states from the Northeast opposed high excise taxes because they drove up the price of goods and were paid disproportionately by less affluent Americans. Agricultural states feared that lost revenue from reducing excise taxes would be replaced by taxing property, which they owned in abundance.

The problem was resolved when Congress passed the Sixteenth Amendment to the Constitution, which made it possible for the federal government to impose an individual income tax. This amendment became effective on March 1, 1913. The first constitutional income tax rates ranged from one percent on the first $20,000 of "lawful" taxable income in excess of $3,000 for unmarried individuals ($4,000 for married individuals) to seven percent on "lawful" taxable income in excess of $500,000. The individual income tax return, Form 1040, was introduced as the standard tax reporting form, and though it has changed significantly over the years, it remains in use today. In 1913, fewer than one percent of individuals were required to pay any income tax.[2]

 Spotlight: An initial problem with the new income tax law was how to define "lawful" income. The problem was quickly addressed in 1915 by eliminating the word "lawful" from the definition of income and replacing it an all-inclusive approach to defining income. By taxing all income, even that which was earned by illegal means, many purported criminals who may have been able to escape justice for their crimes were incarcerated on tax evasion charges.

¶ 202 The Legislative Process

Income tax laws are enacted by a majority vote in both chambers of Congress along with the President's signature. Currently, 435 members of the House of Representatives and 100 members of the Senate comprise the two chambers of Congress. In accordance with the Constitution, changes to the income tax laws originate in the House of Representatives (House), where the responsibility rests with 41 members of the House who form the House Ways and Means Committee. Any changes to the tax laws initiated by the House Ways & Means Committee are drafted into a House Bill, which once it is passed with a majority vote by the committee is voted on by the House. If the

---

[1] *Pollock v. Farmers' Loan & Trust Co.*, SCt, 157 US 429, 15 SCt 673 (1895).

[2] U.S. Department of the Treasury Fact Sheets: History of the U.S. Tax System, available at *www.treas.gov/education/fact-sheets/taxes/ustax.shtml*.

bill passes the House with a majority vote, then the focus turns to the Senate, where changes to current tax laws are considered by the 23 senators that comprise the Senate Finance Committee (the Senate's equivalent to the House Ways & Means Committee). This committee is in charge of drafting a Senate Bill that will pass (with a majority vote) in both the Senate Finance Committee and the full Senate. Accordingly, since the Senate Finance Committee is not concerned with the Senate Bill passing in the House, the Senate Bill is almost always somewhat different from the House Bill.

Once the Senate Bill passes the full Senate with at least 51 votes, the legislative process shifts to reconciling the House and Senate bills in the Conference Committee. The Conference Committee, which is comprised of members of both the House Ways & Means Committee and the Senate Finance Committee, is responsible for generating a single tax bill (Conference Committee bill) that can be passed by a majority vote in both the House and the Senate. Once the Conference Committee Bill is passed with a majority vote by the Conference Committee and each chamber of Congress, it is sent to the President's desk for his signature or veto. A tax bill vetoed by the President can still be enacted into law with a two-thirds vote in both chambers of Congress. A summary of the five steps in the legislative process is illustrated in Figure 2-1.

Figure 2-1 The Legislative Process

Step	Event
1	Passage of a House Bill by the House Ways and Means Committee and then by the House of Representatives
2	Passage of a Senate Bill by the Senate Finance Committee and then by the Senate
3	Creation of a Bill which reconciles the House and Senate Bills, which is then passed by the Conference Committee
4	Passage of the Conference Committee Bill by both the House and Senate
5	Signing the bill into law by the President of the United States

---

(handwritten margin notes: "16th Am. of US Constitution gives power to Congress power to collect Taxes")

(handwritten margin note: "Primary Source of Authority")

(handwritten margin note: "Legislative administrative judicial")

.01 Internal Revenue Code — *the Code Title 26*

The ultimate source of federal tax law is the U.S. Constitution, which gives Congress the power "to lay and collect taxes, duties, imposts, and excises."[3] The tax laws enacted by Congress have been codified as the **Internal Revenue Code** (the "Code"), which is published as Title 26 of the U.S. Code. In its most basic form, the provisions in the Code are a collection of sections. Each section contains the tax law for a different topic, and each section is assigned a different number. For example, Section 163 contains the tax laws governing the deductibility of interest paid on loans and other debt obligations, whereas Section 164 describes the various types of taxes that can be deducted against taxable income.

.02 Amendment of the Code

Periodically, Code sections are amended, added, or deleted by a public law (abbreviated as "P.L.") enacted by Congress and signed into law by the President under the legislative process previously described in ¶ 202 and Figure 2-1. When a Code section is amended, added, or deleted, Congress specifies when the change will take place (the "effective date"). Congress also may specify a termination date for an amendment, addition, or deletion. For example, a provision in the Jobs and Growth Tax Relief Reconciliation Act of 2003 (P.L. 108-27) added paragraph (11) to Code Sec. 1(h), which specifies that qualified dividend income is taxed at the same rates as net capital gain (subject to a maximum tax rate of 15 percent for individuals). This change is effective for tax years beginning after December 31, 2002. Another provision in the Act states that this change will not apply to tax years beginning after December 31, 2008.[4] However, on May 11, 2006, Congress passed the Tax Increase Prevention and Reconciliation Act of 2005 (P.L. 109-222), which extended the lower tax rates on net capital gain and qualified dividend income an additional two years. The President signed the bill into law on May 17, 2006.[5] Thus, for tax years beginning after 2010, qualified dividend income once again will be taxed as ordinary income.

> **Planning Pointer:** Whenever taxpayers are using a published version of the Code, they should make certain that the version includes all changes that have been made, including the effective dates.

¶ 203 Primary vs. Secondary Sources of Tax Law

Although much of the U.S. federal tax law is covered in the provisions of the Code, when writing the tax laws, it is virtually impossible for Congress to anticipate every possible situation that taxpayers may encounter, and accordingly, many areas of the tax law are in need of interpretation and clarification. The provisions in the Code often must be studied in conjunction with other legislative authority, administrative interpretations (administrative authority), and court rulings (judicial authority). The various sources of legislative, administrative, and judicial authority comprise the U.S. tax laws and are called **primary sources of authority.**

Although primary sources of authority comprise a complete resource for understanding the U.S. tax laws, due to the vast amount of material they encompass, researchers often find it difficult to easily find the materials they need to answer their tax questions. Someone relying solely on primary sources would find it time consuming and highly ineffective to "wade through" all of the primary sources to find answers to a specific tax question. Although computerized tax research and key word searches help narrow down the amount of material that has to be perused, a good portion of irrelevant material may surface during the search for relevant authority.

---

[3] U.S. Const. art. I, § 8, cl. 1.

[4] Act Secs. 302 and 303 of the Jobs and Growth Tax Relief Reconciliation Act of 2003 (P.L. 108-27).

[5] Act Sec. 102 of the Tax Increase Prevention and Reconciliation Act of 2005 (P.L. 109-222).

Secondary sources of authority bring together pertinent primary sources on an area of the tax law and help explain the area in a relatively straightforward manner. Without secondary sources, a taxpayer would have to read all cases and rulings to determine which ones, if any, applied to the taxpayer's situation. Secondary sources of authority are various references that explain and comment on primary sources of authority. Popular examples of secondary sources include tax services and citators, as well as legal periodicals and other publications.

The discussion that follows introduces each of the three primary sources of tax law: legislative authority, administrative authority, and judicial authority. Once these primary sources of authority have been discussed, secondary sources are examined in conjunction with the tax research process.

LEGISLATIVE AUTHORITY

Legislative authority includes tax law that results from the legislative process, namely the involvement of the President of the United States and Congress during the enactment of tax legislation. In addition to the provisions in the Code, legislative authority includes committee reports, Blue Books, and treaties.

¶ 204 The Internal Revenue Code

The sections within Title 26 of the U.S. Code are organized by subtitle. There are 11 subtitles within the Code, which are designated sequentially with capital letters. All income tax laws are set forth in Subtitle A of the Code; the tax laws governing estate, gift, and generation-skipping transfer taxes are set forth in Subtitle B; employment tax laws are set forth in Subtitle C, etc. Within each subtitle are a series of chapters, each sequentially numbered. For example, in Subtitle A, Income Taxes, there are six chapters, beginning with Chapter 1, Normal Taxes and Surtaxes, followed by Chapter 2, Tax on Self-Employment Income, etc.

Each chapter can be further broken down into subchapters, which are various topics that fall within the chapter. For example, within Chapter 1, Normal Taxes and Surtaxes of Subtitle A, there are 25 subchapters as shown in Table 2-1.

Table 2-1 Subchapters within Chapter 1, Normal Taxes and Surtaxes

Subchapter	Description	Code Sections
A	Determination of Tax Liability	1-59A
B	Computation of Taxable Income	61-291
C	Corporate Distributions and Adjustments	301-385
D	Deferred Compensation, Etc.	401-436
E	Accounting Periods and Methods of Accounting	441-483
F	Exempt Organizations	501-530
G	Corporations Used to Avoid Income Tax on Shareholders	531-565
H	Banking Institutions	581-597
I	Natural Resources	611-638
J	Estates, Trusts, Beneficiaries, and Decedents	641-692
K	Partners and Partnerships	701-777
L	Insurance Companies	801-848
M	Regulated Investment Companies and Real Estate Investment Trusts	851-860G

Subchapter	Description	Code Sections
N	Tax Based on Income From Sources Within or Without the United States	861-999
O	Gain or Loss on Disposition of Property	1001-1092
P	Capital Gains and Losses	1201-1298
Q	Readjustment of Tax Between Years and Special Limitations	1301-1351
R	Election To Determine Corporate Tax on Certain International Shipping Activities Using Per Ton Rate	1352-1359
S	Tax Treatment of S Corporations and Their Shareholders	1361-1379
T	Cooperatives and Their Patrons	1381-1388
U	Designation and Treatment of Empowerment Zones, Enterprise Communities, and Rural Development Investment Areas	1391-1397F
V	Title 11 Cases	1398-1399
W	District of Columbia Enterprise Zone	1400-1400C
X	Renewal Communities	1400E-1400J
Y	Short-Term Regional Benefits	1400L-1400U-3

Many of the subchapters listed in Table 2-1 are topics that will be discussed in this textbook. Most of the tax laws behind the topics introduced in Chapters 3 through 7 are included in Subchapter A, Determination of Tax Liability, and Subchapter B, Computation of Taxable Income. Taxable corporations are often called C corporations since the tax laws specific to these business entities are located in Subchapter C, Corporate Distributions and Adjustments. Tax laws specific to corporate entities are discussed in Chapter 12. As mentioned in the previous chapter, businesses can operate as flow-through entities, which are taxed either as a partnership or S corporation. The partnership tax laws can be found in Subchapter K, whereas the tax laws that govern S corporations can be found in Subchapter S (hence the name S corporation).

Subchapters are further divided into parts and subparts. Parts are specific topics within a subchapter and are listed in numerical order using roman numerals. For example, Part I of Subchapter C describes the tax laws that govern distributions by a C corporation. These rules can be found in Code Secs. 301-318. Subparts A, B, and C within Part I contain subtopics on corporation distributions, including the tax consequences to the recipient (Subpart A), the tax consequences to the corporation (Subpart B), and definitions (Subpart C). A listing of the various parts within Subchapter C and subparts under Part I of that subchapter are provided in Tables 2-2 and 2-3.

Table 2-2 Parts within Subchapter C, Corporate Distributions and Adjustments

Part	Description	Code Sections
I	Distributions by Corporations	301-318
II	Corporate Liquidations	331-346
III	Corporate Organizations and Reorganizations	351-368
IV	[Repealed]	370-374
V	Carryovers	381-384
VI	Treatment of Certain Corporate Interest as Stock or Indebtedness	385

Table 2-3 Subparts within Part I, Distributions by Corporations

Subpart	Description	Code Sections
A	Effects on Recipients	301-307
B	Effects on Corporation	311-312
C	Definitions; Constructive Ownership of Stock	316-318

The actual tax laws are set forth in sections. For example, the two Code sections within Subpart B from Table 2-3 are Code Sec. 311, Taxability of Corporation on Distributions, and Code Sec. 312, Effect on Earnings and Profits. Each Code section describes very specific tax laws on a particular topic. For these particular Code sections, the tax consequences to both parties affected when a corporation distributes property to its shareholders are provided. Code sections are organized in outline form, as shown below with Code Sec. 311, which outlines the tax consequences to the corporation upon distributions of property to its shareholders.

Code Sec. 311 Taxability of Corporation on Distributions

(a) **GENERAL RULE.** — Except as provided in subsection (b), no gain or loss shall be recognized to a corporation on the distribution (not in complete liquidation) with respect to its stock of —

    (1) its stock (or rights to acquire its stock), or

    (2) property.

(b) **DISTRIBUTIONS OF APPRECIATED PROPERTY. —**

    (1) **IN GENERAL.** —If —

        (A) *a corporation distributes property (other than an obligation of such corporation) to a shareholder in a distribution to which subpart A applies, and*

        (B) the fair market value of such property exceeds its adjusted basis (in the hands of the distributing corporation),

        then gain shall be recognized to the distributing corporation as if such property were sold to the distributee at its fair market value.

    (2) **TREATMENT OF LIABILITIES.** —Rules similar to the rules of section 336(b) shall apply for purposes of this subsection.

    (3) **SPECIAL RULE FOR CERTAIN DISTRIBUTIONS OF PARTNERSHIP OR TRUST INTERESTS.** —If the property distributed consists of an interest in a partnership or trust, the Secretary may by regulations provide that the amount of the gain recognized under paragraph (1) shall be computed without regard to any loss attributable to property contributed to the partnership or trust for the principal purpose of recognizing such loss on the distribution.

To properly comprehend the tax laws described in a Code section, it is important to first understand the various components of a Code section. For example, the citation for the italic area of Code Sec. 311 from above is dissected below.

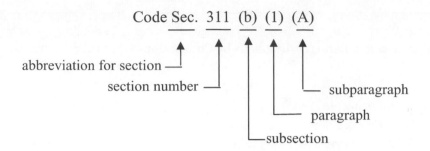

A section of the Code, such as Section 311, may be referred to as Code Sec. 311, Code §311, or as 26 U.S.C. §311. In the citation Code Sec. 311(b)(1)(A), the number after the words "Code Sec." designates the Code section, and the letter "b" refers to the second subsection in Code Sec. 311. The number "1" refers to the first paragraph under subsection (b), and the letter "A" refers to the first subparagraph under paragraph 1. After subsections, clauses are designated with small Roman numerals (i, ii, iii, etc.), followed by subclauses, which are designated with capital Roman numerals (I, II, III, etc.).

Subsection (a) of Code Sec. 311 provides a general rule regarding the tax consequences to corporations. Under this general rule, unless otherwise stated in subsection (b), the corporation does not recognize gain or loss when it distributes stock (or rights to acquire its stock) [paragraph (1)] or property [paragraph (2)]. Subsection (b) contains an exception to this general rule and provides that when a corporation distributes appreciated property (where the fair market value exceeds the corporation's adjusted basis in the property), the corporation is treated as having sold the property to the shareholder for its fair market value, and accordingly, the corporation will recognize gain.

Print versions of the Code are available from many commercial publishers. Also available from many commercial publishers are CD-ROMs that reproduce the Code and online subscriptions that include the Code. The Office of the Law Revision Counsel of the U.S. House of Representatives prepares and publishes the Code on its website at: *http://uscode.house.gov/search/criteria.shtml.*

¶ 205 Committee Reports

Although many tax questions can be answered in the provisions of the Code, there will be times when the language in the Code is ambiguous. In these situations, it is helpful to have access to the discussions that took place when the language in the Code was being written. As tax legislation proceeds through Congress, most bills are accompanied by a committee report. Although these reports are not as authoritative as the provisions in the Code itself, in situations where the language in the Code is ambiguous, these reports help explain what Congress intended when it enacted the new legislation. Among the three committee reports, reports that come from the committee bill that most closely matches the provisions eventually enacted into law are the ones that carry the greatest authoritative weight.

For example, assume that a Senate bill contains a provision that is eventually incorporated into the Conference Committee bill enacted into law. The House bill was silent on this matter. The appropriate committee reports to examine to determine Congressional intent would be the Senate Finance Committee report in conjunction with the Conference Committee report. It should be noted, however, that when Congress passes tax legislation, it votes on the provisions and words contained in the Conference Committee bill, not the words contained in any of the committee reports. For this reason, committee reports should never be relied upon when the language in the Code is clear.

For example, prior to the Tax Reform Act of 1986 (TRA 1986), individuals could deduct personal interest as an itemized deduction. Thus, if individual taxpayers were assessed interest on an underpayment of taxes resulting from an error made on their personal income tax returns, such interest would be deductible from adjusted gross income as an itemized deduction. In TRA 1986, Congress enacted Code Sec. 163(h), which no longer allows a deduction for personal interest. Personal interest is defined as all interest paid or incurred by a taxpayer that was not interest properly allocable to the taxpayer's business (subparagraph A), investment interest (subparagraph B), interest from a passive activity (subparagraph C), home mortgage and other residence-related interest (subparagraph D), certain interest paid in connection with estates (subparagraph E), and student loan interest (subparagraph F). Code Sec. 163(h) is reproduced below.

163(h)

(1) **IN GENERAL.** —In the case of a taxpayer other than a corporation, no deduction shall be allowed under this chapter for personal interest paid or accrued during the taxable year.

(2) **PERSONAL INTEREST.** —For purposes of this subsection, the term "personal interest" means any interest allowable as a deduction under this chapter other than —

(A) interest paid or accrued on indebtedness properly allocable to a trade or business (other than the trade or business of performing services as an employee),

(B) any investment interest (within the meaning of subsection (d)),

(C) any interest which is taken into account under section 469 in computing income or loss from a passive activity of the taxpayer,

(D) any qualified residence interest (within the meaning of paragraph (3)),

(E) any interest payable under section 6601 on any unpaid portion of the tax imposed by section 2001 for the period during which an extension of time for payment of such tax is in effect under section 6163, and

(F) any interest allowable as a deduction under section 221 (relating to interest on educational loans).

Although this Code section clearly states these six types of interest are not considered personal interest, it was unclear as to whether interest paid to the IRS on a tax deficiency resulting from a failure to report business income on the owner's individual income tax return constitutes business interest (which is not personal interest under Code Sec. 163(h)(2)(A)) or nondeductible personal interest (under the general rule in Code Sec. 163(h)(1)).

The IRS has taken the position that interest paid on an underpayment of individual federal, state, or local income taxes (or on indebtedness used to pay such taxes) is personal interest even though the source of the income generating the tax liability is business income.[6] This regulation has been upheld as a permissible and reasonable construction of the statute.[7]

The Library of Congress at its Thomas website (*http://thomas.loc.gov*) makes available committee reports published since 1995. Those committee reports and older committee reports can be found in *U.S. Code Congressional and Administrative News* and are available on CD-ROMs and online subscription services from commercial publishers.

¶ 206 Blue Books *[handwritten: is a General Explanation of Tax Legislation]*

The Joint Committee on Taxation assists Congress in all stages of the legislative process and works directly with Congress to help research and answer questions as a bill makes its way through the various stages in the legislative process. After legislation has been signed into law, the staff of the Joint Committee on Taxation prepares explanations of major tax acts called *General Explanation of Tax Legislation,* otherwise known as **blue books** because of the color of their cover.

Although written by the staff of the Joint Committee on Taxation, and not by actual members of Congress, the individuals who write blue books often can provide additional insight into understand-

---

[6] Temp. Reg. § 1.163-9T(b)(2)(i)(A).

[7] *D. Miller,* CA-8, 95-2 USTC ¶ 50,485, 65 F.3d 687; *J. L. Redlark,* CA-9, 98-1 USTC ¶ 50,322, 141 F.3d 936; *R.R. Allen, Sr.,* CA-4, 99-1 USTC ¶ 50,470, 173 F.3d 533; *M. McDonnell,* CA-6, 99-1 USTC ¶ 50,556, 180 F.3d 721; *N. Kikalos,* 99-2 USTC ¶ 50,823, 190 F.3d 791; *E. A.Robinson III,* 119 T.C. 44, CCH Dec. 54,863 (2002).

ing Congress's intent when enacting legislation. Both the IRS and the courts have been known to use information from the blue books in rendering their rulings and decisions.

Blue Books published in 1996 or a later year are available on The Joint Committee on Taxation's website (*www.house.gov/jct/*). Older Blue Books are available on CD-ROMs and online subscription services from commercial publishers.

¶ 207 Treaties

Tax treaties represent bilateral agreements between two countries to promote tax enforcement and prevent double taxation of income. In situations where income is taxed in more than one country, a treaty will specify in which country the income is taxed. Treaties between the United States and other countries are authorized by the U.S. Constitution. They are created by the President, with the advice and consent of the Senate. When the language in the Code and the provisions in a tax treaty conflict, the "later in time" rule applies, and the more recently enacted authority is the one that is to be followed.

> **Reason for the Rule:** When a treaty is enacted, it is done so with full knowledge of the existing statute, and accordingly, the language in the treaty was intended to override any existing Code provision. Likewise, when Congress enacts new tax legislation, it does so with full knowledge of the existing treaties that the United States has with other countries. Accordingly, if Congress uses language in the statute that specifically conflicts with a provision in a treaty, then it was Congress's intent to override the treaty provision.

ADMINISTRATIVE AUTHORITY

Administrative authority is tax law that comes from the Secretary of the Treasury and the Internal Revenue Service (IRS). Its role is to help taxpayers understand what the tax laws mean and how they are to be applied. Administrative authority includes Treasury regulations and various IRS pronouncements.

¶ 208 Treasury Regulations

Treasury regulations are the Secretary of the Treasury's official interpretation of the provisions in the Code and represent an important source of authority to consider when researching federal tax law. Regulations are especially valuable when the language in the Code is vague, as they interpret and give direction for complying with the Code. Regulations often define terms, clarify language used in the Code, and explain how the tax laws should be interpreted. They often contain examples of how the tax laws should be applied, which make them especially useful sources of authority.

For example, Code Sec. 41 allows businesses to take a tax credit equal to 20 percent of the excess of qualified research expenses over a base amount. Although "qualified research expenses" and "base amount" are defined in the Code, Reg. § 1.41-2 elaborates on the definition of qualified research expenses and provides numerous examples of these expenditures. In addition to defining what the base amount is, Reg. § 1.41-3 illustrates how the amount is calculated.

Like the Code, regulations are divided into parts. The citation for a final regulation might look like this:

Reg. § 1.301-1, Rules applicable with respect to distributions of money and other property.

The "§" in the citation is the symbol for section. The "301" indicates the regulation relates to Code Sec. 301. The number preceding the decimal point before "301" provides information as to the type of regulation. The "1" means that this is a regulation that discusses an income tax law. The other types of regulations that exist are listed in Table 2-4. The "1" following the hyphen indicates that this final regulation concerning Code Sec. 301 is numbered "1". Typically there is one or more regulation for each Code provision. Subsequent regulations within Reg. § 1.301 would be numbered -2, -3, etc.

Table 2-4 Regulation Types Used in Citations

Number	Area of Tax Law Discussed
1	Income tax
20	Estate tax
25	Gift tax and valuation issues
26	Generation-skipping transfer tax
31	Employment taxes
40-56	Excise taxes
156-157	Additional excise taxes
301	Procedure and administration
601	Procedural rules

[handwritten margin note: Regulations are guidance to interpreting provisions of the Code]

Regulations are published in the *Federal Register*. They are available online from GPO Access at *www.gopaccess.gov/cfr/index.html* and also through CD-ROMs and online subscription services offered by commercial publishers.

.01 Stages of Regulations

[handwritten note: Regulations are issued by Secretary of Treasury]

Regulations are issued by the Secretary of the Treasury under the authority of Congress. To ensure that regulations accurately interpret the provisions in the Code, regulations usually are first issued in proposed form (when guidance is needed quickly, temporary regulations may be issued at the same time as proposed regulations). The IRS publishes **proposed regulations** in the *Federal Register* as a Notice of Proposed Rulemaking and solicits comments from the public about the regulation. Although a proposed regulation is not binding on a taxpayer, often the provisions contained in a proposed regulation are those that appear in final regulations.

[handwritten margin note: Federal Register. - Proposed Regulation]

 Planning Pointer: The rules prescribed by a proposed regulation will not necessarily be the same rules included in a final regulation. Neither the IRS nor taxpayers are bound by proposed regulations. However, the IRS increasingly has been authorizing taxpayers to rely on proposed regulations so that they know how a transaction they engage in will be taxed.

Once the comments from the public have been taken into consideration, proposed regulations are revised and either reissued again as proposed regulations or issued as final regulations. **Final regulations** are published in the *Federal Register* as Treasury Decisions. The process of evaluating a proposed regulation, revising it, and issuing it as a final regulation can take several years to complete. For example, a proposed regulation pertaining to Code Sec. 280A was originally issued on August 7, 1980. The regulation was revised and released again as a proposed regulation on July 21,

[handwritten margin note: Final Regulations - are called Treasury Decisions and put also posted on Federal Register]

1983. This particular regulation has yet to be released in final form, which may suggest that problems inherent in the regulation continue to exist.[8]

Proposed regulations are distinguished from other types of regulations by including "Prop." at the front of the citation. For example, a citation for a proposed regulation referred to above is Prop. Reg. § 1.280A-1.

When Congress enacts major changes to the tax laws, it is often necessary that guidance be issued quickly so that taxpayers can correctly prepare their tax returns for the upcoming year. In situations where the changes are substantial, there may not be time to issue all of the needed regulations in proposed form and wait until the public has a chance to comment on them before issuing them in final form. In these situations, Congress allows the Secretary to issue **temporary regulations**, which have the same force and effect of final regulations, even though they have not been through the proposed stage.[9]

Temporary regulations, also published as Treasury Decisions in the *Federal Register,* provide interim guidance to tax practitioners and the public until final regulations can be issued. The rules contained in temporary regulations can be used as authority pending issuance of final regulations. Temporary regulations issued after November 20, 1988, expire three years after the date that they were issued. In addition, Congress requires that all temporary regulations be simultaneously issued as proposed regulations.[10] This allows the Secretary three years to make any necessary changes to the regulation before issuing it in final form.

Temporary regulations can be distinguished from other types of regulations because they include the word "Temp." and capital letter "T" in the citation. The citation for the ninth regulation for Code Sec. 163 is Temp. Reg. § 1.163-9T.

> **Reason for the Rule:** Prior to the Technical and Miscellaneous Revenue Act of 1988, temporary regulations did not expire. Since temporary regulations are accorded the same authoritative weight as final regulations, there was little incentive for the Secretary to make amendments to temporary regulations. Because temporary regulations are usually issued within a short period of time after major tax legislation is passed into law, Congress felt there needed to be a mechanism in place in the Code to ensure that these regulations eventually went through the proposed stage where potential problems with the regulation could be identified and corrected. Accordingly, Code Sec. 7805(e) was enacted into law and all temporary regulations issued after November 20, 1988, expire after three years.

.02 Types of Regulations

The nature of guidance provided by regulations can be classified as one of three types: interpretive, legislative, and procedural. Most regulations are **interpretive regulations,** which interpret the provisions in the Code under the general authority provided to the Secretary under Code Sec. 7805.[11] **Legislative regulations,** on the other hand, define a statutory term or prescribe a method for implementing a Code provision. These regulations are also written pursuant to authority granted by Congress, but through specific language in the Code section to which they relate. For example, in Code Sec. 1502, Congress wrote:

> The Secretary shall prescribe such regulations as he may deem necessary in order that the tax liability of any affiliated group of corporations making a consolidated return and of each corporation in the group, both during and after the period of affiliation, may be returned, determined, computed, assessed,

---

[8] Prop. Reg. § 1.280A-1; *The Brook, Inc.,* 51 TCM 133, Dec. 42,544(M), TC Memo. 1985-614.
[9] Code Sec. 7805.

[10] Code Sec. 7805(e).
[11] Code Sec. 7805(a).

collected, and adjusted, in such manner as clearly to reflect the income tax liability and the various factors necessary for the determination of such liability, and in order to prevent avoidance of such tax liability. In carrying out the preceding sentence, the Secretary may prescribe rules that are different from the provisions of chapter 1 that would apply if such corporations filed separate returns.

The above passage is the only provision in the Code that addresses how corporations in a consolidated group should file a consolidated income tax return. As this section directs, the tax law regarding this issue can be found in the regulations under section 1502. Accordingly, taxpayers interested in the tax laws governing consolidated income tax returns need to refer to Reg. §§ 1.1502-1 through 1.1502-100.

Code Sec. 611 provides that, "in the case of mines, oil and gas wells, other natural deposits, and timber, there shall be allowed as a deduction in computing taxable income a reasonable allowance for depletion and for depreciation of improvements, according to the peculiar conditions in each case; such reasonable allowance in all cases to be made under regulations prescribed by the Secretary." Thus, pursuant to the authority found in the language to Code Sec. 611, legislative regulations Reg. §§ 1.611-1 through 1.614-8 have been adopted.

 Reason for the Rule: Congress delegates to the Secretary of the Treasury responsibility for writing specified provisions of a tax law either because Congress cannot or prefers not to deal with the details of a tax provision.

A **procedural regulation** is a regulation that establishes procedure or practice requirements (such as prescribing how an election is made). For example, expenses whose useful life extends beyond the current tax year usually must be capitalized and expensed over a number of years. Code Sec. 190 allows businesses to elect to currently deduct up to $15,000 of expenditures incurred to make their trade or business more accessible to the elderly and disabled. Reg. § 1.190-3 explains how taxpayers can make this election.

There is no way to distinguish between the three types of regulations from looking at their citations. This distinction can only be found in the language of the Code. If the phrase "under regulations prescribed by the Secretary" or "The Secretary shall prescribe" appears in the Code section, this is indicative of a legislative regulation. If such language or similar language is absent, then the regulation is either an interpretative or procedural regulation. Due to the explicit directive given by Congress for the Secretary to write, rather than interpret, the tax laws, legislative regulations carry the same force and effect as the Code itself.

.03 Authoritative Weight Accorded to Regulations

The IRS is bound by regulations the Secretary issues. Regulations generally command the court's respect because Congress delegated to the Secretary the task of administering the tax laws.[12] Accordingly, taxpayers cannot ignore regulations. The amount of deference that the taxpayer or the courts are required to give a particular regulation depends on whether the regulation is an interpretive, legislative, or procedural regulation. A legislative regulation is given the force and effect of law unless it is arbitrary, capricious, or manifestly contrary to the statute.[13] Procedural regulations are considered to be directory rather than mandatory and do not have the force and effect of law.[14]

Although an interpretive regulation is accorded less deference than a legislative regulation, it cannot be ignored or set aside as long as it provides a reasonable interpretation of the Code.[15] An

---

[12] *Portland Cement Company of Utah*, SCt, 81-1 USTC ¶ 9219, 450 US 156, 101 SCt 1037.

[13] *Chevron U.S.A., Inc. v. Natural Resources Defense Council, Inc.*, 467 US 837, 104 SCt 2778 (1984).

[14] *H.G. Luhring, Jr.*, CA-4, 62-2 USTC ¶ 9547, 304 F2d 560.

[15] *Vogel Fertilizer Co.*, SCt, 82-1 USTC ¶ 9134, 455 US 16, 102 SCt 821.

interpretive regulation has particular force if it is a substantially contemporaneous construction of the statute by those presumed to have been aware of Congressional intent.[16]

In determining the authoritative weight that should be given an interpretative regulation, the Supreme Court has ruled that it is appropriate to first inquire as to whether the intent of Congress is clearly stated in the Code. If so, then the matter is resolved and the language in the Code controls. However, if the Code is silent or ambiguous with respect to the specific issue, then the question that remains is whether the Secretary's interpretation of the Code is based on a permissible construction of the statute. If the Secretary's interpretation fills in a gap or defined a term in such a way that it is reasonable in light of the Congress's revealed design, then taxpayers are to give the regulations "controlling weight."[17] It is important to note that there may be several ways to interpret a provision in the Code, and it is not necessary that the Secretary's interpretation be the best one. As long as it is a reasonable interpretation, the courts will uphold the regulation as valid.

Going back to the issue regarding the deductibility of deficiency interest discussed earlier in the chapter, the Secretary issued the following temporary regulation shortly after Congress passed TRA 1986 in regards to this matter.

> **Temp. Reg. § 1.163-9T.**, Personal interest (Temporary)
>
> (a) *In general.* —No deduction under any provision of Chapter 1 of the Internal Revenue Code shall be allowed for personal interest paid or accrued during the taxable year by a taxpayer other than a corporation.
>
> (b) *Personal interest*
>
> > (1) *Definition.* —For purposes of this section, personal interest is any interest expense other than —
> >
> > > (i) Interest paid or accrued on indebtedness properly allocable (within the meaning of § 1.163-8T) to the conduct of a trade or business (other than the trade or business of performing services as an employee),
> > >
> > > (ii) Any investment interest (within the meaning of section 163(d)(3)),
> > >
> > > (iii) Any interest that is taken into account under section 469 in computing income or loss from a passive activity of the taxpayer,
> > >
> > > (iv) Any qualified residence interest (within the meaning of section 163(h)(3) and § 1.163-10T), and
> > >
> > > (v) Any interest payable under section 6601 with respect to the unpaid portion of the tax imposed by section 2001 for the period during which an extension of time for payment of such tax is in effect under section 6163, 6166, or 6166A (as in effect before its repeal by the Economic Recovery Tax Act of 1981).
> >
> > (2) *Interest relating to taxes*
> >
> > > (i) *In general.* —Except as provided in paragraph (b)(2)(iii) of this section, personal interest includes interest —
> > >
> > > > (A) Paid on underpayments of individual Federal, State or local income taxes and on indebtedness used to pay such taxes (within the meaning of § 1.163-8T), regardless of the source of the income generating the tax liability;
> > > >
> > > > (B) Paid under section 453C(e)(4)(B) (interest on deferred tax resulting from certain installment sales) and section 1291(c) (interest on deferred tax attributable to passive foreign investment companies); or

---

[16] *National Muffler Dealers Association, Inc.*, SCt, 79-1 USTC ¶ 9264, 440 US 472, 99 SCt 1304.

[17] *Chevron U.S.A. Inc. v. Natural Resources Defense Council, Inc.*, 467 US 837, 842, 104 SCt 2778 (1984); *NationsBank v. Variable Annuity Life Ins. Co.*, 513 US 251, 115 SCt 810, 813-814 (1995).

(C) Paid by a trust, S corporation, or other pass-through entity on underpayments of State or local income taxes and on indebtedness used to pay such taxes.

(ii) *Example.* —A, an individual, owns stock of an S corporation. On its return for 1987, the corporation underreports its taxable income. Consequently, A underreports A's share of that income on A's tax return. In 1989, A pays the resulting deficiency plus interest to the Internal Revenue Service. The interest paid by A in 1989 on the tax deficiency is personal interest, notwithstanding the fact that the additional tax liability may have arisen out of income from a trade or business. The result would be the same if A's business had been operated as a sole proprietorship.

(iii) **Certain other taxes.** —Personal interest does not include interest —

(A) Paid with respect to sales, excise and similar taxes that are incurred in connection with a trade or business or an investment activity;

(B) Paid by an S corporation with respect to an underpayment of income tax from a year in which the S corporation was a C corporation or with respect to an underpayment of the taxes imposed by sections 1374 or 1375, or similar provision of State law; or

(C) Paid by a transferee under section 6901 (tax liability resulting from transferred assets), or a similar provision of State law, with respect to a C corporation's underpayment of income tax.

(3) **Cross references.** —See § 1.163-8T for rules for determining the allocation of interest expense to various activities. See § 1.163-10T for rules concerning qualified residence interest.

* * *

.01 Historical Comment: Adopted 12/21/87 by T.D. 8168 (corrected 3/18/2003).

In Temp. Reg. § 1.163-9T(b)(1), the Secretary merely restates the provisions in Code Sec. 163(h). In Temp. Reg. § 1.163-9T(b)(2)(i)(A), the Secretary interprets the provisions in Code Sec. 163(h) to mean that all interest paid by an individual taxpayer on a tax deficiency is personal interest, regardless of the source of the deficiency. This language is almost identical to that found in the Blue Book. The example in Temp. Reg. § 1.163-9T(b)(2)(ii) makes it absolutely clear from the Secretary's perspective that this rule applies to a sole proprietor. Since this temporary regulation was originally issued prior to November 20, 1988 (see historical comment), it does not expire and continues to have the same authority as a final regulation. Although several taxpayers have challenged the IRS's position on this matter, in the end, the courts ultimately concluded that the Secretary's interpretation is, in fact, a reasonable interpretation and therefore the temporary regulation is valid and must be followed.[18]

¶ 209 IRS Pronouncements

In addition to regulations, the IRS issues rulings and pronouncements that interpret and apply the tax laws to a specific set of facts. Some rulings are published to provide guidance for all taxpayers and typically cover areas of the tax law that affect many taxpayers. Other rulings are issued specifically for a particular taxpayer. IRS pronouncements disseminate information to taxpayers that is useful in helping them understand and comply with the tax laws.

---

[18] *J.E. Redlark,* CA-9, 98-1 USTC ¶ 50,322, 141 F3d 936, rev'g 106 TC 31, Dec. 51,104; *D. Miller,* CA-8, 95-2 USTC ¶ 50,485, 65 F3d 687; *R.R. Allen, Sr.,* CA-4, 99-1 USTC ¶ 50,470, rev'g DC N.C., 98-1 USTC ¶ 50,196; *D.V. Alfaro,* CA-5, 2003-2 USTC ¶ 50,715, 349 F3d 225; *E.A. Robinson III,* 119 TC 44, Dec. 54,863; *W.C. Fowler,* 84 TCM 281, Dec. 54,864(M), TC Memo. 2002-223.

.01 Revenue Rulings

A **revenue ruling** is an official interpretation of the tax laws by the IRS. It represents the IRS's conclusion as to the application of the tax laws to a specific set of facts. For example, expenses incurred to commute between the taxpayer's residence and the place of business or employment are nondeductible personal expenses. In contrast, expenses incurred in traveling from one business location to another are deductible business expenses. In Rev. Rul. 99-7, the IRS considered whether transportation expenses incurred between the taxpayer's residence and a temporary work location were deductible business expenses or nondeductible commuting expense. The IRS ruled that such costs were deductible business expenses, provided that the nature of the work was temporary. If the nature of the work was not temporary, then the travel to and from the work location would constitute a nondeductible commuting expense.[19]

Code Sec. 1031(a) provides that no gain or loss is recognized when property held for productive use in a trade or business or for investment is exchanged solely for like-kind property to be held either for productive use in a trade or business or for investment. Although the Code provides some general guidance as to what constitutes "like-kind property," it does not specifically address whether contracts of major league baseball players would be considered an exchange of like-kind property. In Rev. Rul. 67-380, the IRS concluded that when a major league baseball club trades one player contract for another player contract, the trade is treated as an exchange of like-kind property.[20]

Revenue rulings do not have the force and effect of Treasury regulations. Nonetheless, IRS personnel are required to follow the position contained in rulings, as it represents the IRS's position on that area of the tax law. Taxpayers may rely on a favorable revenue ruling, but they are not bound by unfavorable conclusions. However, any disputes between the taxpayer and the IRS may need to be eventually resolved by the courts, and accordingly, before taxpayers challenge the IRS's position in a revenue ruling, they should have a well-reasoned argument as to why the IRS's interpretation of the tax law is faulty or otherwise not appropriate to follow.

Revenue rulings are published weekly in the *Internal Revenue Bulletin* and then again in a semiannually bound publication called the *Cumulative Bulletin*. Weekly issues of the *Internal Revenue Bulletin* since July 7, 2003, are set forth on the IRS's website at *www.irs.gov/irb*. Revenue rulings are available from commercial publishers on CD-ROMs or through online subscription services.

The citation for Revenue Ruling 99-7 is:

Rev. Rul. 99-7, IRB 1999-5, 4 or

Rev. Rul. 99-7, 1999-1 CB 361.

From this citation, one can tell that this revenue ruling was the seventh revenue ruling issued in 1999. It begins on page 4 of the fifth issue of the *Internal Revenue Bulletin* published in 1999 and on page 361 of the first volume of the 1999 *Cumulative Bulletin*.

 Planning Pointer: When evaluating a revenue ruling, subsequent legislation, regulations, court decisions, revenue rulings, and revenue procedures must be considered. Revenue rulings may be modified, amplified, superseded, revoked, or made obsolete by subsequent changes in the law and court decisions. The current status of a revenue ruling can be determined by consulting the index to the most recent edition of the *Cumulative Bulletin* and the index to the most recent issue of the *Internal Revenue Bulletin*. Commercial publishers provide citators for determining the current status of a revenue ruling.

---

[19] Rev. Rul. 99-7, 1999-1 CB 361.   [20] Rev. Rul. 67-380, 1967-2 CB 291.

.02 Revenue Procedures

A **revenue procedure** is an official statement by the IRS of a procedure that affects the rights or duties of taxpayers under federal tax law. Whereas a revenue ruling states the IRS's position on a tax issue, a revenue procedure provides tax return filing and other instructions concerning an IRS position. For example, each year the IRS issues a revenue procedure explaining how taxpayers that use their automobile for business can use the standard mileage rate to compute their deduction. Revenue procedures, unlike revenue rulings, usually are not fact specific. For example, when an employer provides an employee with a company vehicle and permits the employee to use the vehicle for personal use, the value of that personal use is generally taxable and must be included in the employee's wages. In Rev. Proc. 2009-12,[21] the IRS explains how employers can value an employee's personal use in 2008. In Rev. Proc. 2006-45,[22] the IRS outlines specific procedures C corporations must follow in order to change their tax year. Corporations that comply with the requirements set forth in this revenue procedure automatically will be deemed to have received the IRS's consent to change their tax year.

Revenue procedures do not have the force and effect of Treasury regulations, but they may be relied on as authority. However, like a revenue ruling, they may be amplified, modified, superseded, revoked, or made obsolete by subsequent changes in the law or court decisions. When evaluating a revenue procedure, subsequent legislation, regulations, court decisions, revenue rulings, and revenue procedures must be considered.

 Planning Pointer: The current status of a revenue procedure can be determined by consulting the index to the most recent edition of the *Cumulative Bulletin* and the index to the most recent issue of the *Internal Revenue Bulletin*. Commercial publishers provide citators for determining the current status of a revenue procedure.

Revenue procedures are published weekly in the *Internal Revenue Bulletin* and in the semiannually published *Cumulative* Bulletin. Weekly issues of the *Internal Revenue Bulletin* since July 7, 2003, are set forth on the IRS's website at *www.irs.gov/irb*. Revenue rulings are available from commercial publishers on CD-ROMs or through online subscription services.

The citation for Revenue Procedure 2003-43 is:

Rev. Proc. 2003-43, IRB 2003-23, 998 or

Rev. Proc. 2003-43, 2003-1 CB 998.

This ruling is the forty-third revenue procedure issued in 2003. It begins on page 998 of the twenty-third issue of the *Internal Revenue Bulletin* for 2003 and on page 998 of the first volume of the 2003 *Cumulative Bulletin*.

.03 Written Determinations

The IRS issues three types of rulings in response to a taxpayer's specific fact situation. These rulings, known as **written determinations**, are binding only with respect to the taxpayer to whom they are issued. The rulings are made available to the public after all sensitive information has been eliminated, and represent a source of authority that that all taxpayers can use to determine how a particular item should be treated on their tax returns. The three types of written determinations the IRS issues include private letter rulings, technical advice memoranda, and determination letters.

Private letter rulings. A **private letter ruling** is a written statement that interprets and applies the tax laws to a specific set of facts presented to the IRS by the taxpayer. Letter rulings are issued by the National Office of the IRS and establish the federal tax consequences of a particular

---

[21] Rev. Proc. 2009-12, 2009-3 IRB 321.   [22] Rev. Proc. 2006-45, 2006-2 CB 851.

transaction. Letter rulings are written by the IRS's Associate Chief Counsel in response to a written request by the taxpayer. They can be issued for open fact situations (where the transaction has yet to be completed) or closed transactions (where the transaction has been completed). In either case, the letter ruling is requested prior to the taxpayer's filing of the tax return that involves the transaction. A user fee (up to $11,500 in 2009) is charged for a letter ruling.

Under Code Sec. 1031(a), no gain or loss is recognized when property held for productive use in a trade or business or for investment is exchanged solely for like-kind property to be held either for productive use in a trade or business or for investment. A taxpayer, however, may be uncertain as to whether an exchange of an interest in old-growth timberlands for reproduction timberlands constituted a like-kind exchange. In IRS Letter Ruling 200541037, the IRS held that such an exchange did, in fact, meet the qualifications of a like-kind exchange.

 Planning Pointer: Taxpayers can benefit by obtaining a letter ruling because it lets them know in advance the IRS's opinion regarding a proposed transaction. With that information, taxpayers can decide whether or not to proceed with the transaction. When a requested ruling involves an open-fact situation and the position in the letter ruling is not favorable to the taxpayer, the taxpayer has the opportunity to alter the facts in an effort to achieve a more favorable tax position before entering into the transaction. Alternatively, the taxpayer could decide not to pursue the transaction due to the potential unfavorable tax consequences.

A letter ruling is binding on the IRS with respect to a taxpayer's proposed treatment of an item unless there was a misstatement or omission of a material fact or the facts that subsequently develop are materially different from the facts on which the letter ruling was based. Although taxpayers may rely on a letter rulings issued to them personally as precedent, letter rulings issued to other taxpayers are not an established precedent for them. Instead they are a source of authority that they can use to determine the correct tax consequences of a transaction. **Precedent** refers to the principle in law of using the past decisions to assist in making current decisions. **Tax authority** is established tax law that can be used to help in reaching a conclusion about a tax issue.

Example 1: A company requested and paid for a letter ruling from the IRS regarding a planned transaction. The company received a favorable private letter ruling. The ruling is an established precedent for the company that requested it. If the company carries out the transaction as it is described in the ruling, it can follow the IRS's advice in the letter ruling and know with absolute certainty that it cannot be challenged by the IRS, even if at some later date the IRS changes its opinion with respect to the issue.

Example 2: Rushlow Supplies, who is not the taxpayer who requested the ruling in Example 1 above, is in the process of researching the tax consequences of a planned transaction. Through its research efforts, it comes across the letter ruling issued to the taxpayer in Example 1. The facts in the letter ruling describe a transaction that is identical to Rushlow's planned transaction. Although the transactions are identical, Rushlow cannot rely on a letter ruling issued to another taxpayer as an established precedent. The ruling can, however, be used as authority by Rushlow. Accordingly, if Rushlow goes through with the transaction and reports the tax consequences as described in the letter ruling, there is no guarantee that the IRS will accept Rushlow's position. To avoid uncertainty in this regard, Rushlow can request that the IRS issue a letter ruling to it based on its specific fact situation.

 Planning Pointer: Although a letter ruling can be used as precedent only by the taxpayer with respect to which it was issued, taxpayers and tax professionals benefit by reading letter rulings because they provide insight as to how the IRS may apply the tax

> law to taxpayers in similar situations. Taxpayers may rely on a letter ruling to avoid the penalty for a substantial understatement of income tax. (See ¶ 215.02.)

The contents of a letter ruling are made public after information that could identify the taxpayer to whom it was issued has been removed. Letter rulings that have been available to the public since 1997 are available in the IRS's Electronic Reading Room at *www.irs.gov/app/picklist/list/writtenDeterminations.html*. The full texts of letter rulings are available in print in *IRS Letter Rulings Reports* (published by CCH, a Wolters Kluwer business) and are available from commercial publishers through their online subscription services and CD-ROMs.

An example of a citation for a letter ruling is:

IRS Letter Ruling 200602045 (October 18, 2005).

The "2006" at the beginning of the citation refers to the year that the letter ruling was issued. The next two numbers "02" signify that the letter ruling was issued during the second week of 2006, and the next three digits "045" signify the letter ruling was the forty-fifth written determination issued that week. The date in parentheses is the date that the letter ruling was written. Prior to 1999, only two numerals were used to signify the year that a letter ruling was issued. For example, IRS Letter Ruling 9628006 was issued in 1996.

Technical advice memorandum. A **technical advice memorandum (TAM)** is issued by the National Office of the IRS and written by the IRS's Office of Associate Chief Counsel. Field offices request a TAM when an issue arises during an audit or review of a tax return and lack of uniformity exists within the IRS regarding the treatment of the issue. A TAM also may be requested when an issue is unusual or complex enough to warrant consideration. Accordingly, TAMs are issued only on closed transactions. No fee is charged to the taxpayer for a TAM.

For example, Code Sec. 1031(a) provides that no gain or loss is recognized when property held for productive use in a trade or business or for investment is exchanged solely for like-kind property to be held either for productive use in a trade or business or for investment. In Technical Advice Memorandum 200602034, the IRS rejected the taxpayer's argument that the exchange of any trademark or trade name for another trademark or trade name can qualify as an exchange of like-kind property.

The advice rendered in a TAM represents a final determination of the IRS's position, but only with respect to the specific issue in the specific case for which the advice is issued. The IRS is bound by its conclusion. However, a TAM that is adverse to a taxpayer does not preclude the taxpayer from litigating the issue.

> **Planning Pointer:** TAMs are useful because they permit taxpayers to settle disputes with the IRS during an audit. Although a TAM can be used as precedent only by the taxpayer with respect to which it was issued, taxpayers benefit from TAMs because they provide insight into how the IRS will apply the law to the particular facts presented and other factual circumstances. Taxpayers may rely on a TAM to avoid the penalty for a substantial understatement of income tax. (See ¶ 215.02.)

TAMs that have been made publicly available since 1997 can be found in the IRS's Electronic Reading Room at *www.irs.gov/app/picklist/list/writtenDeterminations.html*. The full texts of TAMs are available in print in *IRS Letter Rulings Reports* (published by CCH) and are available from commercial publishers through their online subscription services and CD-ROMs.

The citation for a TAM is similar to that of a letter ruling. An example of a citation for a TAM is:

Technical Advice Memorandum 200605011 (September 5, 2005).

This TAM was published in 2006, but it was actually written on September 5, 2005. It was issued during the fifth week of 2006 and was the eleventh written determination issued that week. Prior to 1999, only two numerals were used to signify the year that a TAM was issued. For example, Technical Advice Memorandum 9816007 was issued in 1998.

Determination letters. A written response issued by an IRS Director in response to a written request from a taxpayer is known as a **determination letter**. Determination letters differ from the two other types of written determinations because they are issued by an IRS Director rather than by the Office of Associate Chief Counsel. A determination letter applies the principles and precedents previously announced by the IRS to a specific set of facts. A determination letter will be issued only when the question presented is specifically answered by a statute, a tax treaty, the regulations, a conclusion stated in a revenue ruling, or an opinion or court decision that represents the IRS's position. A determination letter will not be issued if a question involves a novel issue. A determination letter will be issued only if it concerns a return that has been filed or is required to be filed. The fee for issuing a determination letter ($275 in 2009) is significantly less than the fee charged for a private letter ruling. A determination letter has the same effect as a letter ruling issued to a taxpayer. It is binding on the IRS and can be relied on only by the taxpayer to whom it is issued.

 Planning Pointer: Because a determination letter is issued only when the law applicable to a given set of facts is settled, it cannot be requested when a taxpayer needs guidance regarding an unsettled area of tax law. Under those circumstances, a taxpayer must request a letter ruling instead of a determination letter. A determination letter usually is requested with respect to the qualification of a retirement plan or tax-exempt organization.

.04 Other Pronouncements and Publications

In addition to rulings, the IRS provides other guidance to help people comply with the tax laws. These include notices, announcements, news releases, IRS publications, and actions on decision.

Notices. The IRS issues public **notices** to provide guidance involving substantive interpretations of the Code. They often are issued to provide taxpayers with guidance about recently enacted legislation or to alert taxpayers about pending regulations. For example, in Notice 2006-11, the IRS temporarily suspended certain requirements for low-income housing credit projects as a result of the destruction caused by Hurricane Rita.[23] In Notice 93-7, the IRS announced that effective January 1, 1993, the withholding rates on gambling winnings would increase from 20 percent to 28 percent for all winnings in excess of $5,000.[24]

The IRS normally gives notices the same status as revenue rulings and revenue procedures. Taxpayers can rely on them as authority unless the notice itself says otherwise. Notices are published in the *Internal Revenue Bulletin* and the *Cumulative Bulletin*. They also are available from commercial publishers through their online subscription services and CD-ROMs.

The citation for Notice 93-7 is:

Notice 93-7, 1993-5 IRB 13 or

Notice 93-7, 1993-1 CB 297.

This notice was the seventh notice issued in 1993. The full text of this notice can be found on page 13 of the fifth issue of the *Internal Revenue Bulletin* published in 1993, and on page 297 of the first volume of the *Cumulative Bulletin* for 1993.

---

[23] Notice 2006-11, 2006-1 CB 457.   [24] Notice 93-7, 1993-1 CB 297.

Announcements and news releases. Periodically, the IRS issues announcements and news releases. **Announcements** inform the public as to matters of general interest. They may provide guidance as to both substantive and procedural matters. **News releases** are issued to the media to announce items of general interest. They often are used to announce that an important new revenue ruling or revenue procedure is going to be released and set forth the text of that ruling or procedure. For example, in Announcement 2006-2, the IRS informed taxpayers claiming a low-income housing credit of new Form 8609-A, Annual Statement for Low-Income Housing Credit.[25] In News Release IR-2006-1, the IRS described the new look for its website and enhanced electronic services for taxpayers and tax return preparers, and in News Release IR-2006-31, the IRS announced that unclaimed refunds totaling more than $2 billion are awaiting persons who failed to file a federal income tax return for 2002.

Announcements are published in the *Internal Revenue Bulletin* and the *Cumulative Bulletin*. They also are available from commercial publishers through their online subscription services and CD-ROMs. News releases are available on the IRS's website at *www.irs.gov/newsroom/article/0,,id=108500,00.html*. They also are available from commercial publishers through their online subscription services and CD-ROMs.

The citation for IRS Announcement 2004-9 is:

Announcement 2004-9, 2004-6 IRB 441 or

Announcement 2004-9, 2004-1 CB 441.

This announcement was the ninth made in 2004. It can be found on page 441 of the sixth issue of the *Internal Revenue Bulletin* for 2004 and on page 441 of the first volume of the *Cumulative Bulletin* for 2004.

Acquiescence, nonacquiscence, and action on decision. When a court rules against the IRS on one or more issues, the IRS may announce whether it will follow the court's decision in similar situations in the future. When the IRS acquiesces it means that it will follow the court's decision and has accepted the court's conclusion, but not necessarily the reasons given by the court for its decision. When the IRS issues a nonacquiescence it means that it does not intend to follow the decision in disputes involving other taxpayers with similar situations. A nonacquiescence puts taxpayers on notice that the IRS will continue to challenge the position and force taxpayers in a similar situations to litigate the issue. The IRS is not bound by its announcement of acquiescence or nonacquiescence and may withdraw it at any time.

When the IRS issues an acquiescence or nonacquiescence to a decision, it announces it in an **Action on Decision (AOD)**. AODs issued since 1997 are available on the IRS's website at *www.irs.gov/foia/lists/0,,id=97630,00.html*. The IRS also announces its acquiescence or nonacquiescence to a court's decision at the beginning of *Internal Revenue Bulletins*. AODs also are available from commercial publishers on CD-ROMs and online subscription services.

An example of a citation for an AOD is:

AOD 2003-03 (October 20, 2003).

This citation tells the researcher that this AOD was the third one issued in 2003. It was issued on October 20, 2003.

IRS publications. The IRS publishes various publications for businesses and the general public. These publications are intended to provide guidance to taxpayers on specific tax topics. Examples of IRS publications include Circular E, *Employer's Tax Guide*; Publication 17, *Your Federal Income Tax*.; Publication 334, *Tax Guide for Small Business*; Publication 535, *Business Expenses*;

---

[25] Announcement 2006-2, 2002-1 CB 300.

Publication 538, *Accounting Periods and Methods*; Publication 541, *Partnerships*; and Publication 542, *Corporations*.

Publications contain explanations of the tax rules based on the Code, regulations, rulings, and important court decisions. Sometimes these publications contain information not found elsewhere. Publications can be obtained by telephoning the IRS or going to its website at *www.irs.gov/ formspubs/index.html*.

JUDICIAL AUTHORITY

When the IRS disputes an item or items reported on the taxpayer's tax return and the matter cannot be resolved through the appeals process within the IRS, the only recourse for the parties is to have the issue resolved by the courts. The federal court system consists of three trial courts and various appellate courts.

When a taxpayer and the IRS disagree with an interpretation of an area of tax law, the taxpayer may challenge the IRS's decision in the U.S. Tax Court, a U.S. district court, or the U.S. Court of Federal Claims. If either the taxpayer or the IRS is not satisfied with a trial court's decision, the litigant can appeal to the appropriate Court of Appeals. Litigants unhappy with a decision made by a Court of Appeal may request that the U.S. Supreme Court review their case. However, review usually is at the discretion of the U.S. Supreme Court, which accepts only a small percentage of the cases it is asked to review.

Judicial decisions represent a third primary source of federal tax law. The decisions made by federal courts provide additional guidance regarding the tax laws. The decisions can be relied upon not only by the taxpayer involved in the dispute but also by other taxpayers in similar situations. Therefore all court decisions are a source of authority for taxpayers, which can be used to determine the correct course of action to be taken on the tax return. However, only court decisions within the taxpayer's jurisdiction provide a precedent for the taxpayer in which it can rely on. Figure 2-2 shows the hierarchy of the various federal courts.

Figure 2-2 Federal Court System

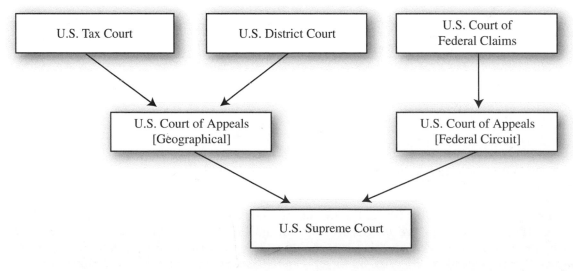

¶ 210 Trial Courts

Disputes between taxpayers and the IRS are first heard in one of three trial courts. Decisions rendered by a trial court can be appealed to the appellate court that has jurisdiction over the court. For example, appeals of decisions rendered by the Tax Court or a district court are heard by the geographical Court of Appeals located in the circuit in which the taxpayer works or resides (see Figure 2-3). The appeal of decisions rendered by the Federal Court of Claims is heard by the Federal Circuit Court of Appeals. Thus, a general understanding of each of these courts is required to understand which avenue taxpayers should pursue should they not be able to settle their dispute with the IRS. Also, decisions by courts within the taxpayer's jurisdiction carry considerably greater weight, as these decisions can establish precedent for the taxpayer should they choose to have their case heard by that particular court.

.01 Tax Court

The **U.S. Tax Court** is a special court established to provide a forum to dispute tax deficiencies determined by the IRS. Unlike other federal courts, the Tax Court hears only federal tax cases. Its 19 judges are nominated by the President and confirmed by the U.S. Senate to 15-year terms. The court is located in Washington, D.C., but the judges travel and conduct trials in various cities throughout the United States.

 Spotlight: The U.S. Tax Court was established so that taxpayers could dispute a deficiency assessed against them by the IRS without first having to pay the amount that the IRS claimed they owed. Prior to the establishment of the Tax Court, a taxpayer first had to pay the disputed amount and then file suit for a refund. Not having to pay the disputed amount before appealing the IRS's determination is a big advantage of litigating disputes in the Tax Court. Before litigating a dispute in either of the other two trial courts, a taxpayer first must pay the full amount of taxes, interest, and penalties that the IRS has determined that the taxpayer owes and then the taxpayer must sue the IRS for a refund.

Example 3: The IRS contends that Hand Shovels, Inc. owes $100,000 in additional income tax and interest because the company improperly characterized certain expenses as currently deductible business expenses rather than nondeductible capital expenditures. If the company appeals the IRS's determination to the Tax Court, it will not have to pay the $100,000 unless the Tax Court decides that the IRS's decision was correct. If the taxpayer loses in the Tax Court, interest on the $100,000 will be owed to the IRS in addition to the $100,000 currently in dispute. However, before Hand Shovels decides to litigate its dispute in the U.S. district court or U.S. Court of Federal Claims, it first must pay the $100,000. If the IRS loses the case in either the district court or Court of Federal Claims, interest on the $100,000 will be due to Hand Shovels in addition to the $100,000.

The Tax Court issues three types of opinions: regular, memorandum, and summary. Regular opinions are those that the Tax Court considers important or expressive of some new point not previously covered by one of its published opinions. In theory, a memorandum opinion applies well-established principles of law to facts found by the court. However, there are times when memorandum opinions also develop new law. If the taxpayer elects the small tax procedures (available for disputes involving $50,000 or less), a summary opinion is issued by the Tax Court.

Regular and memorandum decisions may be appealed to the Court of Appeals for the geographic area where the dispute was litigated. No appeal may be taken from a Summary opinion issued when a taxpayer has elected to have the case heard in small tax procedures court.[26]

---

[26] Code Sec. 7463(b).

Taxpayers may rely on regular and memorandum decisions as precedent but may not treat a summary opinion as a precedent.

Because the Tax Court is a national court, its decisions can be appealed to the Court of Appeals where the taxpayer works or resides (see Figure 2-3). Since decisions of each Court of Appeals are made independent of one another, it is possible that different decisions can be reached by different circuits on the same tax issue. The Tax Court is required to follow decisions made by the Court of Appeals to which its decision would be appealed (known as the ***Golsen* rule**).[27] As a result, the Tax Court may rule differently on identical factual patterns in two different cases if the taxpayers reside in different circuits and the Courts of Appeals for those circuits have made inconsistent decisions.

The IRS is not required to follow a decision by the Tax Court. The IRS signifies its agreement or disagreement by publishing its acquiescence or nonacquiescence to the decision in the *Internal Revenue Bulletin*. Tax Court regular decisions are published by the U.S. Government Printing Office in bound volumes under the title *United States Tax Court Reports* (cited as "TC"). Memorandum and summary opinions are not published by the U.S. Government Printing Office. Regular and memorandum opinions starting September 25, 1995, and summary opinions starting January 1, 2001, are available at the Tax Court's official website: *www.ustaxcourt.gov*. Regular, memorandum, and summary opinions are available in print from commercial publishers (such as CCH and Thomson Reuters/RIA) and as part of CD-ROMs and online subscription services. CCH publishes memorandum opinions under the title *Tax Court Memorandum Decisions* (cited as "TCM"); Thomson Reuters/RIA publishes memorandum opinions under the title *RIA Memorandum Decisions* (cited as "TC Memo").

Citing a Tax Court decision. The citation for the 2005 Tax Court decision involving *Van Der Aa Investments, Inc.* is:

Van Der Aa Investments, Inc., 125 TC 1, Dec. 56,086 (2005).

"Van Der Aa Investments, Inc." is the name of the taxpayer involved in the litigation. "125 TC" signifies that the opinion appears in volume 125 of the *United States Tax Court Reports*. The "1" indicates the page number in the volume where the decision starts. "Dec. 56,086" signifies that the decision is printed in paragraph 56,086 of CCH's *Tax Court Decisions*. The "2005" is the year that the opinion was filed. Because there is a delay in time between the date a decision is rendered and the date that it appears in the *United States Tax Court Reports*, a temporary citation form is used. An example of that temporary form is: 126 TC No. 6 (2006). This citation indicates that the opinion will be the sixth opinion in volume 126 of the *United States Tax Court Reports*.

The citation for a memorandum decision is slightly different, as regular and memorandum decisions are printed in different services. The citation for the 2005 memorandum decision for *S.J. Hauge is:*

S.J. Hauge, 90 TCM 538, Dec. 56,209(M), TC Memo. 2005-276.

The "90 TCM 538" signifies that the opinion begins on page 538 of volume 90 of CCH's *Tax Court Memorandum Decisions*. The "Dec. 56,209(M)" signifies that the opinion is in paragraph 56,209(M) of CCH's *Tax Court Decisions*. The "(M)" signifies that the decision is a Tax Court Memorandum decision. The "TC Memo. 2005-276" signifies that the opinion is printed in paragraph 2005-276 of Thomson Reuters/RIA's *Tax Court Reported and Memorandum Decisions*.

.02 District Court

Instead of litigating disputes with the IRS in the U.S. Tax Court, taxpayers may pay the amount of taxes, interest, and penalty the IRS says they owe and file a claim for a refund with the U.S. district court where they work or reside. Unlike the Tax Court, **district courts** hear a wide variety

---

[27] *J.E. Golsen*, 54 TC 742, Dec. 30,049, aff'd CA-10, 71-2 USTC ¶ 9497, 445 F2d 985.

of cases; they are not limited to disputes involving federal tax law. Each state has at least one district court.

 Planning Pointer: Taxpayers can request a jury trial when their dispute heard by a U.S. district court involves a question of fact (where the tax law is clear, but the taxpayer's facts are in dispute). Juries are not allowed to decide questions of law. The option of a jury trial for tax issues involving questions of fact is not available when taxpayers take their case to the U.S. Tax Court or U.S. Court of Federal Claims.

Example 4: On October 18, 2005, the IRS published proposed regulations reversing its previous position that an owner of a single-member limited liability company (LLC) is personally liable for the company's employment taxes. A taxpayer argued that this regulation should be applied retroactively to him and his single-member LLC. In *E. Kandi*,[28] the U.S. district court for the Western District of Washington decided that the IRS did not abuse its discretion by refusing to apply the proposed regulation retroactively.

Decisions by a U.S. district court may be appealed to the Court of Appeals having jurisdiction over the district court. The IRS is not required to follow a decision by a U.S. district court with respect to taxpayers other than those involved in the decision made by the U.S. district court. The IRS may signify its agreement or disagreement by publishing its acquiescence or nonacquiescence to the decision in the *Internal Revenue Bulletin*. When the IRS acquiesces or nonacquiesces a decision made by a court, it is published as an Action on Decision (see ¶ 209.04).

Many of the decisions made by U.S. district courts are reported in a series of books titled *Federal Supplement*. More recent cases are reported in the third series of the *Federal Supplement*. Tax decisions made by district courts are reported by CCH in its *United States Tax Cases* (cited as "USTC") and by Thomson Reuters/RIA in its *American Federal Tax Reports* (cited as "AFTR").

Citing a district court decision. An example of a citation for the 2000 U.S. district court case of *H.E. Butt Grocery Co.* is:

H.E. Butt Grocery Co., DC Tex., 2000-2 USTC ¶ 50,649, 108 FSupp2d 709, 86 AFTR2d 2000-5209.

"DC Tex." signifies that the court was a district court for Texas. "2000-2 USTC ¶ 50,649" signifies that the case is published in paragraph 50,649 of the second volume of the *United States Tax Cases* for the year 2000. The "108 FSupp2d 709" signifies that the first page of the case is located on page 709 of volume 108 of the *Federal Supplement, Second Series*. "86 AFTR2d 2000-5209" signifies that the case has been published at 2000-5209 in volume 86 of the *American Federal Tax Reports 2nd Series*.

.03 Court of Federal Claims

To have their cases heard by the U.S. Court of Federal Claims, taxpayers may pay the amount of taxes, interest, and penalties the IRS says they owe and file a claim for a refund. The court is located in Washington, D.C.; however, its judges periodically hear cases in major cities around the country.

The **U.S. Court of Federal Claims** was created by Congress solely to hear monetary claims against the United States based on the U.S. Constitution, federal statutes, executive regulations, and contracts with the United States. Approximately one-fourth of its cases involve tax refund suits; approximately one-third of its cases involve government contracts. The U.S. Court of Federal Claims consists of 16 judges nominated by the President and confirmed by the Senate for a term of 15 years.

---

[28] *E. Kandi*, DC Wash., 2006-1 USTC ¶ 50,231.

Decisions by the U.S. Court of Federal Claims may be appealed to the Federal Circuit Court of Appeals. That is the Court of Appeals whose decisions the U.S. Court of Federal Claims must follow, even when the U.S. Court of Federal Claims holds hearings in an area governed by a different (geographical) Court of Appeals.

The IRS is not required to follow a decision by the U.S. Court of Federal Claims with respect to taxpayers other than those involved in decisions made by the U.S. Court of Federal Claims. The IRS may signify its agreement or disagreement by publishing its acquiescence or nonacquiescence to the decision in the *Internal Revenue Bulletin*. When the IRS acquiesces or nonacquiesces a decision by a court, it is published as an Action on Decision (see ¶ 209.04).

Published decisions dating from July 3, 1997, are available on the court's website at *www.uscfc.uscourts.gov/opinions_decisions_general/Published*. Unpublished decisions dating from February 18, 2005, can be found at *www.uscfc.uscourts.gov/opinions_decisions_general/Unpublished*. Thomson Reuters/RIA publishes court decisions since 1992 in its *Federal Claims Reporter* (cited as "FedCl") and earlier decisions (when the court was named the "Claims Court") in its *U.S. Claims Court Reporter* (cited as "ClsCt").

Decisions by the court's predecessor, the Court of Claims, were published by the U.S. Government Printing Office in its *U.S. Court of Claims* Reports (cited as "CtCls"). West Publishing Co. published decisions of the Court of Claims from May 1960 through establishment of the Claims Court in its *Federal Reporter 2d* Series (cited as "F2d") and published earlier decisions in its *Federal Supplement* (cited as "FSupp"). Tax decisions made by the U.S. Court of Federal Claims and Court of Claims are reported by CCH in its *United States Tax Cases* (cited as "USTC") and by Thomson Reuters/RIA in its *American Federal Tax Reports* (cited as "AFTR").

Citing a Court of Federal Claims decision. The citation for the 2001 Court of Federal Claims of *Marsh & McLennan Companies, Inc.* is:

Marsh & McLennan Companies, Inc., FedCl, 2001-2 USTC ¶ 50,575, 50 FedCl 140, 88 AFTR2d 2001-5381.

The "FedCl" signifies that this is a Court of Federal Claims case. The "2001-2 USTC ¶ 50,575" signifies that the case is published in paragraph 50,575 of the second volume of the *United States Tax Cases* for the year 2001. The "50 FedCl 140" signifies that the first page of the case is on page 140 of volume 50 of the *Federal Claims Reporter*. The "88 AFTR2d 2001-5381" signifies that the case appears at 2001-5381 in volume 88 of the *American Federal Tax Reports, 2nd Series*.

¶ 211 Appellate Courts

There are two types of appellate courts to which trial court decisions can be appealed. The appellate court having jurisdiction over the trial court's decision is the court to which the case will be appealed. Decisions made by the U.S. Tax Court or a U.S. district court may be appealed to the **Court of Appeals** for the geographic area of the trial court. Appeals from the U.S. Court of Federal Claims are made to the Federal Circuit Court of Appeals. Review usually is limited to legal, not factual, issues.

.01 Geographical Courts of Appeals

There are 13 Courts of Appeals. Twelve cover specific geographic areas; the thirteenth (the Federal Circuit) hears particular types of cases. The geographical location of these courts, as well as the states that each court covers is depicted in Figure 2-3 that follows.

Figure 2-3 Geographical Courts of Appeals

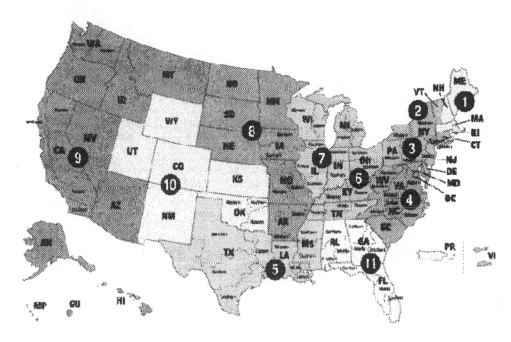

First Circuit:	Maine, Massachusetts, New Hampshire, Rhode Island, and Puerto Rico
Second Circuit:	Connecticut, New York, and Vermont
Third Circuit:	Delaware, New Jersey, Pennsylvania, and the Virgin Islands
Fourth Circuit:	Maryland, North Carolina, South Carolina, Virginia, and West Virginia
Fifth Circuit:	Louisiana, Mississippi, and Texas
Sixth Circuit:	Kentucky, Michigan, Ohio, and Tennessee
Seventh Circuit:	Illinois, Indiana, and Wisconsin
Eighth Circuit:	Arkansas, Iowa, Minnesota, Missouri, Nebraska, North Dakota, and South Dakota
Ninth Circuit:	Alaska, Arizona, California, Hawaii, Idaho, Montana, Nevada, Oregon, and Washington
Tenth Circuit:	Colorado, Kansas, New Mexico, Oklahoma, Utah, and Wyoming
Eleventh Circuit:	Alabama, Florida, and Georgia
D.C. Circuit:	District of Columbia

Source: *http://www.uscourts.gov/courtlinks/*

Decisions made by the geographical Court of Appeals for the area in which the taxpayer resides or does business establish precedent for the taxpayer. The IRS is required to follow a decision by a Court of Appeal, but only in the states within that court's jurisdiction. When the IRS acquiesces or nonacquiesces a decision of a court, it is published as an Action on Decision (see ¶ 200.04).

Example 5: Structural Clay, Inc. conducts its business in Illinois. During the year, Structural paid to have mold removed from one of its buildings. Structural is hoping that it can deduct these costs in the current year, rather than capitalize them. While researching this issue, it found a decision by the Ninth Circuit Court that disagreed with its planned tax treatment of its expenditures. However, a decision by the Seventh Circuit agreed that the costs could be expensed currently. Because Illinois is located the Seventh Circuit, the Seventh Circuit would have jurisdiction over Structural's case, and accordingly it can use that case as precedent and deduct the expenses in the current year.

Example 6: Assume the same facts as in Example 5, except that Structural Clay is located in Texas, which is located in the Fifth Circuit. Since neither of these cases establishes precedent to Structural, both cases can be used as authority in determining the course of action Structural should take with respect to these costs.

Example 7: Under the Code's all-inclusive approach to defining income, self-employment profits are subject to income tax. In addition, these profits are subject to self-employment taxes. Usually rental income from real estate is not considered self-employment income; however, an exception is made for farm rental income if the lessor materially participates in farm production. In *M. McNamara*,[29] the Eighth Circuit decided that the IRS must prove a nexus between the rents received by a taxpayer and the arrangement that requires the taxpayer's material participation. In AOD 2003-03, the IRS announced that it would not acquiesce to *McNamara*. Therefore, the IRS is bound by the Eighth Circuit's decision in the states making up the Eighth Circuit (Arkansas, Missouri, Iowa, Minnesota, Nebraska, South Dakota, and North Dakota), and accordingly, *McNamara* establishes precedent to taxpayers located in those states. For taxpayers living in states outside of the Eighth Circuit, the appellate court's decision in *McNamara* can be used as authority for avoiding substantial understatement penalties. (See ¶ 215.) However, the IRS has put these taxpayers on notice that it intends to exercise its right to challenge the issue and hopefully be able to litigate again in another circuit.

.02 Federal Circuit Court of Appeals

The Federal Circuit Court of Appeals hears appeals of tax and other cases from the U.S. Court of Federal Claims. It also hears appeals from a variety of other courts and government agencies. Decisions made by a Court of Appeals carry great weight because each Court of Appeals is independent from the others and can be overruled only by the U.S. Supreme Court, which agrees to hear very few tax cases each year. The Federal Circuit Court of Appeals is a national court. Consequently, all taxpayers that choose to have their tax case heard initially by the U.S. Court of Federal Claims can use decisions rendered by the Federal Circuit Court of Appeals as established precedent.

Decisions made by each U.S. Circuit Court of Appeals are reported on each court's website. Those sites are:

1st Circuit: *www.ca1.uscourts.gov*

2nd Circuit: *www.ca2.uscourts.gov*

3rd Circuit: *www.ca3.uscourts.gov*

4th Circuit: *www.ca4.uscourts.gov*

5th Circuit: *www.ca5.uscourts.gov*

6th Circuit: *www.ca6.uscourts.gov/internet/index.htm*

7th Circuit: *www.ca7.uscourts.gov*

8th Circuit: *www.ca8.uscourts.gov*

9th Circuit: *www.ca9.uscourts.gov*

10th Circuit: *www.ca10.uscourts.gov*

11th Circuit: *www.ca11.uscourts.gov*

D.C. Circuit: *www.cadc.uscourts.gov/internet/home.nsf*

Federal Circuit: *www.cafc.uscourts.gov*

---

[29] *M. McNamara*, CA-8, 2001-1 USTC ¶ 50,188, 236 F3d 410.

Decisions also are published in a series of volumes titled *Federal Reporter*. Tax decisions made by the U.S. Courts of Appeals are reported by CCH in its *United States Tax Cases* (cited as "USTC") and by Thomson Reuters/RIA in its *American Federal Tax Reports* (cited as "AFTR").

Citing an appellate court decision. The citation for the 2001 decision by the Eighth Circuit Court of Appeals in *M. McNamara* is:

M. McNamara, CA-8, 2001-1 USTC ¶ 50,188, 236 F3d 410, 87 AFTR2d 2001-310.

The "CA-8" signifies that the case was decided by the Eighth Circuit Court of Appeals. The "2001-1 USTC ¶ 50,188" signifies that the case is published in paragraph 50,188 of the first volume of the *United States Tax Cases* for the year 2001. The "236 F3d 410" signifies that the first page of the case is published on page 410 of volume 236 of the *Federal Reporter, Third Series*. The "87 AFTR2d 2001-310" signifies that the case has been published at 2001-310 in volume 87 of the *American Federal Tax Reports 2nd Series*.

 Planning Pointer: The appellate court having jurisdiction over the trial court's decision is the court to which the case will be appealed. Accordingly, when selecting a trial court to settle a dispute, taxpayers need to consider decisions made by the appellate court to which the decision will be appealed.

.03 The Supreme Court

The losing party of an appellate court decision may request that the **U.S. Supreme Court** hear an appeal of that decision. However, the U.S. Supreme Court grants very few of such requests. The U.S. Supreme Court usually will review a decision made by a U.S. Court of Appeals only if the decision conflicts with a decision made by another U.S. Court of Appeals, the U.S. Supreme Court itself, or the Supreme Court justices decide that the issue warrants their attention.

Example 8: Code Sec. 1221 defines a "capital asset" as property held by a taxpayer (whether or not connected with the taxpayer's trade or business) other than property that falls within one of the enumerated exceptions (e.g., for inventory). Arkansas Best Corporation, a diversified holding company, purchased shares of stock in the National Bank of Commerce to protect its reputation by giving the bank additional capital it needed to prevent its failure. It later sold the stock at a loss. Arkansas Best treated the loss as an ordinary loss rather than as a capital loss and deducted the loss in full on its tax return. (Capital losses would only have been deductible to the extent of Arkansas Best's capital gains.) The IRS disallowed the deduction.

The U.S. Tax Court agreed with the taxpayer that the company's loss on the sale of the stock was an ordinary loss and decided that stock acquired for a business purpose was not a capital asset. The Eighth Circuit reversed the Tax Court's decision on the grounds that the company's motivation for acquiring the stock was irrelevant to the determination whether the stock was a capital asset.[30] The U.S. Supreme Court agreed with the Eighth Circuit and ruled that the exceptions to the general rule regarding what constitutes a capital asset are exclusive, not just illustrative.[31] This standard now provides the final say in how capital assets are defined.

A decision by the U.S. Supreme Court is the final authority as to the interpretation of the language in the Code. Both taxpayers and the IRS must follow decisions rendered by the Supreme Court until such time that Congress enacts legislation that overrules the decision. For example, in *D.A. Gitlitz,* the U.S. Supreme Court held that discharge of indebtedness income excluded from an S

---

[30] *Arkansas Best Corp.*, CA-8, 86-2 USTC ¶ 9671, 800 F2d 215, rev'g., *Arkansas Best Corp.*, 83 TC 640, Dec. 41,581 (1984).

[31] *Arkansas Best Corp.*, SCt, 88-1 USTC ¶ 9210, 485 US 212, 108 SCt 971.

corporation's gross income nevertheless passes through to S corporation shareholders and increase their basis in their stock.[32] When it enacted the Job Creation and Worker Assistance Act of 2002 (P.L. 107-147), Congress amended Code Sec. 108, thereby making the Supreme Court's decision obsolete.

U.S. Supreme Court decisions are reported on the court's website at *http://www.supremecourtus.gov/*. They also are published in bound volumes. The official reporter of U.S. Supreme Court decisions is *U.S. Reports* (cited as "US"). Decisions are also reported in the *Supreme Court Reporter* (cited as "SCt") and *Lawyers' Edition* (cited as "LEd"). Supreme Court tax cases are also reported in the *United States Tax Cases* (CCH) (cited as "USTC") and the *American Federal Tax Reports* (RIA) (cited as "AFTR").

Citing a Supreme Court decision. An example of a citation for the Supreme Court case of *D.A. Gitlitz* is:

> *D.A. Gitlitz*, SCt, 2001-1 USTC ¶ 50,147, 531 US 206, 121 SCt 701, 148 LE2d 613, 87 AFTR2d 2001-417.

The "SCt" signifies that this is a Supreme Court decision. The "2001-1 USTC ¶ 50,147" signifies that this case is reported in the first volume of the *United States Tax Cases* for the year 2001 beginning at paragraph 50,147. The "531 US 206" signifies that this case is reported in Volume 531 of the *U.S. Reports* beginning on page 206. The "121 SCt 701" signifies that this case can be found in Volume 121 of the *Supreme Court Reporter* beginning on page 701. The "148 LEd2d 613" signifies that this case can be found beginning on page 613 in Volume 148 of the *Lawyers' Edition, Second Series*. The "87 AFTR2d 2001-417" is reported at 2001-417 in volume 87 of the *American Federal Tax Reports 2nd Series*.

RESEARCHING THE TAX LAW

Being able to structure a transaction to minimize the taxpayer's tax consequences is the goal of all tax planning. Eliminating taxes permanently is always a top priority, but sometimes being able to defer the tax to some point in the future provides taxpayers with temporary use of the tax dollars saved to spend or invest. Depending on the circumstances surrounding the taxpayer's situation, expenditures can either be currently deducted, deducted over a number of years, deducted at some later point in time, or never deductible. Thus, before taxpayers can determine whether to an item of income is subject to tax or whether an expenditure can be deducted in the current year, a general understanding of tax laws is a necessity.

¶ 212 Tax Planning vs. Compliance Research

Business decisions should be made only after thoroughly considering the tax consequences of the transaction. When tax research is conducted on a proposed transaction, it is known as tax planning. **Tax planning research** involves researching an "open fact" situation, where the transaction has yet to occur, and accordingly, taxpayers may have the opportunity to change the fact pattern to achieve optimal tax savings. **Tax compliance research**, on the other hand, involves researching a "closed fact" situation, where the transaction had already taken place and the goal at this point is to research the correct tax consequences of a completed transaction. Whenever possible, businesses should strive to conduct planning research, as it provides them with greater flexibility as the fact pattern is yet to be "set in stone." However, understanding how to conduct tax research, whether it is in a planning or compliance setting, is necessary in order to make the best decisions.

---

[32] *D.A. Gitlitz*, SCt, 2001-1 USTC ¶ 50,147, 531 US 206, 121 SCt 701.

¶ 213 Tax Evasion vs. Tax Avoidance

A legitimate goal of tax planning is **tax avoidance**, which is taking advantage of legal opportunities to reduce a taxpayer's tax liability. Sometimes these legal opportunities to reduce tax liability are referred to as "tax loopholes," although that term more often has a negative connotation of an unintentional omission or ambiguity in the tax law that permits a reduction in tax liability not intended by Congress. Tax avoidance should be distinguished from **tax evasion**, which involves illegally paying less federal income tax than one should.

Example 9: Water Colors, Inc. had its manufacturing plant destroyed by a hurricane. It receives $500,000 of insurance proceeds. The company knows that if it does nothing, it will have to report $400,000 of gain on the involuntary conversion in its taxable income. However, because the personnel in the tax department understand the tax laws governing these types of involuntary conversions, the company can legally avoid having to recognize any of that gain by reinvesting the $500,000 in another manufacturing plant in a timely manner.

Example 10: Howden Wired Music reduces its tax liability by taking deductions for expenditures it never made and by not reporting income that it received during the year. Howden is guilty of tax evasion and may be subject to civil and criminal penalties.

¶ 214 Tax Planning Strategies

A typical tax planning strategy is to defer receipt of income, accelerate deductions, and obtain credits. However, sometimes businesses can benefit by accelerating the receipt of income and deferring deductions.

Example 11: Ferucci Trailers, Inc. is in the 34-percent tax bracket. If it can defer $10,000 of income, it can save $3,400 ($10,000 × 34%) in federal income tax for the year. If it can take an additional $10,000 in deductions for the year, it also can save $3,400 in federal income taxes.

Example 12: Sopko Tube Fittings, Inc. expects to be in the 25-percent tax bracket for its current tax year but in the 39-percent tax bracket for its next tax year. If the company can accelerate $10,000 of income into the current year, it will pay $2,500 ($10,000 × 25%) of taxes on its income instead of $3,900 ($10,000 × 39%) if it waits to pay tax on the income until next year. The tax savings to Sopko would be $1,400 ($3,900 – $2,500).

Example 13: Assume the same facts as in Example 12, except that Sopko has a choice between spending $20,000 on business expenses during its current tax year or delaying its expenditures until its next tax year. If it makes those expenditures during its current tax year, it will save $5,000 ($20,000 × 25%) in federal income taxes. If it delays making those expenditures until its next tax year, it will save $7,800 ($20,000 × 39%). By delaying those expenditures, the company will save $2,800 ($7,800 – $5,000) in federal income taxes. However, it will have to wait an entire year to realize the $7,800 in tax savings.

Example 14: Geffers Venetian Blinds, Inc. had $10,000 in passive activity losses for its tax year. Pursuant to Code Sec. 469, such losses can be deducted only against income from passive activities. If the company can plan to recognize up to $10,000 in passive activity income (e.g., by selling its interest in a passive activity), the company can take advantage of the loss and not be taxed on any of the passive activity income that it recognizes.

¶ 215 Ethical and Professional Standards

Taxpayers and tax professionals must adhere to specific standards in situations involving ambiguous areas of the tax law. If these standards are not met, significant penalties can be imposed on the taxpayer, the tax professional, or both. In addition, professional organizations, such as the American Institute of Certified Public Accountants, impose their own set of professional standards that tax professionals must adhere to in addition to those imposed by the federal government.

.01 Professional Standards for Tax Research

The American Institute of Certified Public Accountants (AICPA) has adopted Statements on Standards for Tax Service that are enforceable against members of the AICPA. The AICPA's Statement on Standards for Tax Services No. 1, Tax Return Positions, sets forth standards to be followed when recommending tax return positions. Among those standards are:[33]

- As a general rule, a CPA should not recommend that a tax return position be taken unless the CPA has a good-faith belief that the position has a realistic possibility of being sustained administratively or judicially on its merits if challenged.

- A CPA may recommend a tax return position that does not satisfy the realistic possibility standard if the CPA concludes that the position is not frivolous and recommends appropriate disclosure of the position. A position is frivolous if it is knowingly advanced in bad faith and is patently improper.

To satisfy the *realistic possibility standard*, a CPA should in good faith believe that a tax return position is warranted by existing law or can be supported by a good-faith argument for an extension, modification, or reversal of existing law through the administrative or judicial process.[34] The likelihood of an audit or detection is not taken into consideration when determining whether the realistic possibility standard has been satisfied. The realistic possibility standard is less stringent than the "substantial authority standard" (¶ 215.02) and the "more likely than not standard" that apply to substantial understatements of liability taxpayers must adhere to, but is stricter than the "reasonable basis" standard.[35]

Example 15: Solar Energy, Inc. engaged in a transaction adversely affected by a new Code provision. Prior law was favorable to the company. The company and its adviser both believe that the new Code provision is unfair to taxpayers in the company's situation. However, the Code provision is unambiguous and constitutional. Because the Code provision is unambiguous and constitutional, a position contrary to the Code provision ordinarily would be considered frivolous.[36]

Example 16: Assume the same facts as in Example 15, except that the legislative history for the new Code provision addresses the company's situation and supports a position favorable to the company. Because the legislative history addresses the company's situation, taking a position based on that legislative history would satisfy the realistic possibility standard.[37]

Example 17: Assume the same facts as in Example 16, except that the legislative history does not specifically address the company's situation but can be interpreted as providing some authority for the company's position. Because the legislative history does not specifically address the company's situation, taking a position based on that legislative

---

[33] Statement on Standards for Tax Services No. 1, Tax Return Positions.

[34] Statement on Standards for Tax Services No. 1, Tax Return Positions, paragraph 7; Interpretation No. 1-1, "Realistic Possibility Standard" of Statement on Standards for Tax Services No. 1, Tax Return Positions, paragraph 2.

[35] Interpretation No. 1-1, "Realistic Possibility Standard" of Statement on Standards for Tax Services No. 1, Tax Return Positions, paragraphs 4 and 5.

[36] Interpretation No. 1-1, "Realistic Possibility Standard" of Statement on Standards for Tax Services No. 1, Tax Return Positions, paragraphs 12 and 13.

[37] Interpretation No. 1-1, "Realistic Possibility Standard" of Statement on Standards for Tax Services No. 1, Tax Return Positions, paragraphs 14 and 15.

history would not meet the realistic possibility standard. However, taking a position based on that legislative history would not be frivolous.[38]

Example 18: Assume the same facts as in Example 15 except that Solar Energy insists on taking the tax return position (even though the CPA concluded that it is frivolous) because the company did not believe that the position would be detected by the IRS on an audit. The likelihood of an audit or detection cannot be considered when determining whether the realistic possibility standard has been satisfied. A CPA cannot prepare or sign a return that contains a frivolous position even if that position is disclosed.[39]

Example 19: Brutger Machines, Inc. asked its adviser whether it could currently deduct an expenditure or whether it had to capitalize the expenditure and expense it over a number of years. The adviser found a revenue ruling requiring taxpayers to capitalize that type of expenditure. It also found a U.S. Tax Court decision permitting taxpayers to currently deduct that type of expenditure. The realistic possibility standard would be met by either tax return position.[40]

The AICPA does not impose any obligation on a tax researcher to inform a client about developments that affect prior advice unless the tax researcher is assisting the client in implementing plans or procedures associated with the advice given or the tax researcher has agreed to inform a client about developments that affect advice given by the tax researcher.[41]

.02 Federal Standards for Tax Research

Taxpayers who underpay their income tax will be subject to the accuracy-related penalty if they have a substantial understatement of income tax attributable to an undisclosed item and they do not have substantial authority for their tax treatment of the item.[42] If the substantial understatement is attributable to a disclosed item, taxpayers will be subject to the penalty if they do not have a reasonable basis for their tax treatment of the item.

> *Reasonable cause exception.* No penalty will be imposed if there was reasonable cause for the underpayment and the taxpayer acted in good faith.[43]

Substantial authority is an objective standard that is less stringent than the "more-likely-than-not" standard, but more rigorous than the "reasonable basis" standard.[44] Whether substantial authority exists for a position taken on a tax return is made based on all relevant sources of primary authority. The probability that the taxpayer's return will be audited is irrelevant for purposes of determining whether substantial authority exists.

As part of its standards of practice for tax professionals,[45] the IRS has provided standards applicable to those conducting tax research. Best practices require the following:[46]

- Establishing the facts, determining which facts are relevant, evaluating the reasonableness of any assumptions or representations, relating the applicable law (including potentially applicable judicial doctrines) to the relevant facts, and arriving at a conclusion supported by the law and the facts.

- Advising the client regarding the significance of the conclusions reached (including, for example, whether a taxpayer may avoid accuracy-related penalties under the Code if the taxpayer acts in reliance on the advice).

---

[38] Interpretation No. 1-1, "Realistic Possibility Standard" of Statement on Standards for Tax Services No. 1, Tax Return Positions, paragraphs 16 and 17.

[39] Interpretation No. 1-1, "Realistic Possibility Standard" of Statement on Standards for Tax Services No. 1, Tax Return Positions, paragraphs 28 and 29.

[40] Interpretation No. 1-1, "Realistic Possibility Standard" of Statement on Standards for Tax Services No. 1, Tax Return Positions, paragraphs 34 and 35.

[41] Statement on Standards for Tax Services No. 8, Form and Content of Advice to Taxpayers, paragraph 4.

[42] Code Sec. 6662.

[43] Code Sec. 6664(c)(1).

[44] Code Sec. 6662(d).

[45] Treasury Department Circular No. 230 (31 CFR pt. 10).

[46] Circular 230, 31 CFR § 10.33(a).

A tax return preparer can be penalized for preparing a return or claim of refund that understates tax liability if the understatement is due to an **unreasonable position** that the tax return preparer knew (or reasonably should have known) about.[47]

Reasonable cause exception. No penalty will be imposed if there was reasonable cause for the underpayment and the preparer acted in good faith.

What constitutes an "unreasonable position" Three different standards are used to determine whether a position is "unreasonable." Which standard applies varies depending on whether or not the position has been adequately disclosed and whether or not the position is with respect to a tax shelter or reportable transaction to which Code Sec. 6662A applies:

- If a position is adequately disclosed and is not with respect to a tax shelter or reportable transaction to which Code Sec. 6662A applies, it will be considered unreasonable unless the preparer had a reasonable basis for it (*reasonable basis standard*).

- If the position is with respect to a tax shelter or reportable transaction to which Code Sec. 6662A applies, it will be considered unreasonable unless it was reasonable for the preparer to believe that it would more likely than not be sustained on its merits (*more-likely-than-not standard*).

- If the position is not adequately disclosed and is not with respect to a tax shelter or reportable transaction to which Code Sec. 6662A applies, the position will be considered unreasonable unless there is or was substantial authority for it (*substantial authority standard*).

How to satisfy each of the standards used to determine whether a position is "unreasonable" The most difficult to satisfy of the three standards used to determine whether a position is "unreasonable" is the more-likely-than-not standard. The least difficult to satisfy is the reasonable basis standard.

- **Reasonable Basis Standard.** The reasonable basis standard is less stringent than the substantial authority standard or the more-likely-than-not standard but is significantly higher than not frivolous or not patently improper.[48] It is not satisfied by a position that is merely arguable or colorable. If a position is reasonably based on one or more of the authorities set forth in Reg. § 1.6662-4(d)(3)(iii), the position generally will satisfy the reasonable basis standard. A preparer can rely in good faith without verification on information furnished by the taxpayer and information and advice furnished by another tax professional.

- **Substantial Authority Standard.** The substantial authority standard is an objective standard involving an analysis of the law and application of the law to the relevant facts.[49] It is less stringent than the more-likely-than-not standard but more stringent that the reasonable basis standard. There is substantial authority for the tax treatment of an item only if the weight of authorities supporting the treatment is substantial in relation to the weight of authorities supporting contrary treatment. Conclusions reached in treatises, legal periodicals, or opinions rendered by tax professionals are not authority, but authorities used to form those conclusions may be. The possibility that a return will not be audited or, if audited, that an item will not be raised on audit, is not relevant in determining whether the substantial authority standard has been met.

- **More-Likely-Than-Not Standard.** The more-likely-than-not standard is satisfied if the tax return preparer analyzes the pertinent facts and authorities and reasonably concludes in good faith that a position has a greater than 50 percent likelihood of being sustained on its merits.[50] The authorities that can be considered are listed in Reg. § 1.6662-4(d)(3). The possibility that the position will not be challenged by the IRS (e.g., because the return may not be audited or because the issue may not be raised on audit) cannot be taken into account.

---

[47] Code Sec. 6694(a).
[48] Reg. § 1.6694-2(d)(2); Notice 2009-5, 2009-3 IRB 309.

[49] Notice 2009-5, 2009-3 IRB 309.
[50] Reg. § 1.6694-2(b)(1), (2).

Preparers may rely in good faith without verification on information furnished by the taxpayer and information and advice furnished by another tax professional.

Determining whether a position has been "adequately disclosed" Which standard is used to determine whether a position is "unreasonable" depends on whether or not the position has been adequately disclosed. Disclosure is adequate if:[51]

- The position is disclosed on a properly completed and filed IRS Form 8275, Disclosure Statement, or IRS Form 8275-R, Regulation Disclosure Statement, as appropriate, or on the tax return in accordance with the annual revenue procedure prescribing disclosure on a tax return.

- The tax return preparer provides the taxpayer with a prepared tax return that includes the disclosure.

- For returns or claims for refund subject to an accuracy-related penalty other than a penalty attributable to a substantial understatement of income tax, the preparer advises the taxpayer of the penalty standards applicable and contemporaneously documents the advice in the preparer's files.

¶ 216 Secondary Sources of Tax Authority

Given the professional and ethical standards taxpayers and tax professionals must abide by when preparing an income tax return, it is essential that they be able to thoroughly research a tax issue prior to taking a position on the tax return. However, the sheer volume and complexity of the federal tax law makes it difficult to efficiently research the tax implications of a proposed or completed transaction. Fortunately, secondary sources provide a needed guide through the complexity of federal tax law. There are various types of secondary sources that can be helpful to researchers. These include professional tax services, citators, and other publications such as legal periodicals and newsletters.

.01 Tax Services

A variety of tax services are available in print, online, or on a CD-ROM. A number of large publishing companies, including CCH, Thomson Reuters/RIA, and BNA, publish a variety of tax services. The distinguishing feature among tax services is how the information is arranged.

Some tax services are organized by Code section. For each Code section, the tax service provides the user with the full-text of the Code provision, committee reports and related regulations, as well as a brief summary of all cases and rulings relevant to the Code section and the publisher's commentary about the Code section. These brief summaries of cases and rulings are called annotations, which is why tax services organized by Code section are often referred to as **annotated tax services**. Annotated tax services typically provide the following information about each Code provision:

1. The full text of the Code provision;
2. Portions of the various committee reports where the Code provision was discussed;
3. The full text of any final, temporary, and proposed regulations issued for the Code section;
4. The publisher's explanation of the Code provision;
5. Annotations of IRS rulings and judicial decisions interpreting the Code provision and regulations; and
6. Any current developments pertaining to the tax law surrounding the Code section.

CCH's *Standard Federal Income Tax Reporter* and Thomson Reuters/RIA's *United States Tax Reporter: Income Taxes* are two annotated tax services that provide tax researchers with information relevant to federal income tax laws. CCH's *Federal Estate and Gift Tax Reporter* is an annotated tax

---

[51] Reg. § 1.6694-2(d)(3).

service that focuses on the tax laws surrounding federal gift, estate, and generation-skipping transfer taxes.

Topical tax services are arranged by topic. In these services, all tax law pertaining to a particular topic is located together within the tax service, regardless of which Code section the information lies with in the Code. For example, a discussion of the tax laws surrounding education deductions, exclusions, and credits are all located together, despite the fact that the tax implications of incurring education expenses are covered in Code Secs. 25A, 117, 127, 132, 262, among others. CCH's *Tax Research Consultant,* Thomson Reuters/West's *Mertens Law of Federal Income Taxation*, and Thomson Reuters/RIA's *Federal Tax Coordinator 2d* provide researchers with a discussion of the various areas of the tax law by topic.

.02 Citators

Before relying on relevant case law or rulings, it is necessary to establish that the tax law is still valid and remains authoritative. Citators are useful in this regard and can be used not only to determine whether a case or ruling has been modified or supplemented, but also whether other subsequent cases and rulings have mentioned the case. Some citators list secondary sources that have commented about a particular primary source. CCH and Thomson Reuters/RIA both publish citators as part of their professional tax services. Lexis-Nexis publishes *Shepard's Citators* and *Auto-Cite,* and Westlaw publishes *KeyCite.*

Example 20: In *Dow Chemical Company*,[52] the U.S. district court for the Eastern District of Michigan allowed Dow Chemical to deduct interest on loans obtained to purchase corporate-owned life insurance (COLI) policies on the lives of thousands of its upper management employees. It rejected the IRS's argument that the deductions should be disallowed because the COLI policies were economic shams with no practical economic purpose apart from generating tax deductions for interest payments. By consulting a case citator, a researcher would find that the district court's decision was reversed by the Sixth Circuit Court of Appeals because the Sixth Circuit decided that the COLI policies were, in fact, economic shams.[53]

Example 21: In Rev. Rul. 74-503,[54] a corporation transferred some of its own shares of stock to another corporation in exchange for stock in that other corporation. In that ruling, the IRS concluded that stock received had a zero basis. By consulting a citator, a researcher would find that the IRS revoked Rev. Rul. 74-503 in Rev. Rul. 2006-2.[55]

.03 Periodicals and Other Publications

Many law reviews and professional journals publish articles on tax law. Some cover a broad range of tax topics; others specialize in particular tax areas. Popular legal periodicals include CCH's *Taxes—The Tax Magazine*, Warren Gorman & Lamont's (WG&L) *Journal of Taxation*, the AICPA's *Tax Adviser*, and the American Bar Association's *Tax Lawyer*. CCH's *Federal Tax Articles* and WG&L's *Index to Federal Tax Articles* can be used to help locate pertinent articles in legal periodicals.

Many universities hold tax institutes during the year and then publish papers presented at their sessions. For example, the University of Chicago and New York University hold popular tax institutes and publish their annual proceedings. These papers are often used by tax professionals to help understand particularly difficult areas within the tax law.

Tax publishing companies send out newsletters to their subscribers to keep them abreast on current developments in tax law. These newsletters may be available online or may be delivered

---

[52] *Dow Chemical Company*, DC Mich., 2003-1 USTC ¶ 50,346.

[53] *Dow Chemical Company*, CA-6, 2006-1 USTC ¶ 50,126, 435 F3d 594.

[54] Rev. Rul. 74-503, 1974-2 CB 117.

[55] Rev. Rul. 2006-2, 2006-1 CB 261.

¶ 216.02

through the mail. CCH's *Federal Tax Day*, Tax Analysts' *Tax Notes Today*, BNA's *Daily Tax Report*, and Thomson Reuters/RIA's *Tax Alert* are examples of newsletters.

¶ 217 The Tax Research Process

Although there is no one "right way" to research tax law, below are some guidelines students can use to ensure that research is as complete as possible. The basic steps in researching a tax issue should include:

1. Gathering pertinent facts,
2. Identifying the tax issues,
3. Locating primary sources relevant to the tax issues,
4. Analyzing and evaluating authorities,
5. Applying the relevant authorities to the additional facts, and
6. Developing conclusions and recommendations.

At any stage in the research process, it may become necessary to gather additional facts. Sometimes while researching a tax issue other issues arise, making it necessary to repeat the steps in the research process. Once conclusions and recommendations have been developed (Step 6), they must be communicated to the taxpayer or a colleague.

.01 Gathering Facts

The first step in the tax research process is to gather the pertinent facts. Some preliminary facts that need to be established when conducting tax research for a business include:

- What type of legal entity is the business (i.e., a C corporation, S corporation, partnership, a limited liability company taxed as a partnership, or a limited liability company taxed as a corporation)?
- Is the business a U.S. or foreign business? Are the owners U.S. citizens and residents or foreign citizens and residents?
- What is the business's tax year and method of accounting?
- What is the transaction that the business has completed or is proposing to do?
- Is the business related to any of the parties involved in the transaction being researched?
- What is the business's marginal income tax rate expected to be for its current tax year and subsequent tax year?

Pertinent facts are not limited to the tax question being researched. They also include constraints on what tax strategies a tax researcher can recommend for a client. For example, although an exchange of property would produce the best tax consequences, a client may need the cash that a sale would realize.

.02 Identifying Issues

Once a tax researcher has gathered the pertinent facts, the adviser needs to identify which tax issues need to be researched. Being able to identify those issues is often the most difficult step in the legal research process. As a preliminary matter, tax researchers should determine whether they have been asked to determine whether income has to be recognized, whether a deduction or credit is available for an expenditure, or whether there has been a sale or exchange triggering the recognition of gain or loss.

If a tax researcher determines that there is a question about an item of income, the adviser must determine what type of income is involved, whether it is includible in gross income, and, if so, when it has to be recognized under the taxpayer's method of accounting. If a tax researcher determines that there is a question about an expenditure, the adviser must determine whether a deduction or credit is available for the expenditure and when it can be taken into account under the taxpayer's method of accounting.

Example 22: Genson Calculators, Inc. received interest on a bond and wants to know whether the interest has to be included in the company's gross income. The tax questions are whether the interest is the type of interest that can be excluded from gross income and, if so, when it has to be taken into account under the company's method of accounting.

Example 23: Milbrett Alabaster Products, Inc., a calendar year taxpayer, purchased some machinery in 2009 but did not pay for the machinery until 2010. The tax questions include whether the company is entitled to a deduction or credit for its purchase and, if so, for what year the expenditure is considered made.

If a tax researcher determines there is a question about a sale or exchange, the adviser must determine whether the sale or exchange is such that gain or loss may or must be deferred, when any gain or loss that must be recognized is taken into account, and how that gain or loss is characterized (i.e., as capital gain or ordinary income) for federal income tax purposes.

Example 24: Automatic Clocks, Inc. exchanged one piece of equipment for another. The tax questions are whether gain or loss must be recognized on the exchange and, if so, how much gain or loss must be recognized, and whether the gain or loss is capital or ordinary in nature.

.03 Locating Relevant Sources of Authority

After a tax researcher has gathered pertinent facts and identified which tax issues need to be researched, the adviser needs to locate the primary sources relevant to the tax issues being researched. Usually it is best to start by referring to a secondary source covering the tax issues being researched. Both annotated and topical secondary sources have a place in the research process. Topical secondary sources are a good place to start for those who do not know which Code provisions apply to the tax issue. Those who know which Code provisions apply to a tax issue may save time by using an annotated tax service to determine whether any particular Treasury regulation, IRS ruling, or judicial decision answers the research question.

Conclusions reached in commentaries (called treatises), legal periodicals, legal opinions, or opinions rendered by tax professionals cannot be used as authority for a tax return position. However, the authorities underlying such expressions of opinion can be treated as authority for a tax return position if they are applicable to the facts of the particular case.

Before relying on IRS rulings and judicial decisions identified as relevant, a citator should be used to determine whether the case or ruling is still current law. An authority cannot be relied on to the extent that it has been implicitly or explicitly overruled or modified. For example, a district court opinion is not an authority if overruled or reversed by the U.S. Court of Appeals for that district. However, a U.S. Tax Court opinion is not considered overruled or modified by a court of appeals to which the taxpayer does not have a right of appeal unless the Tax Court adopts the holding of that court of appeals.

.04 Analyzing and Evaluating Relevant Authorities

Once the primary sources relevant to a tax issue have been identified and reviewed, a researcher needs to assess what those authorities have to say about the tax questions that the researcher has identified. Sometimes the primary sources provide a clear answer. Other times there is no clear-cut answer. When there is no clear-cut answer, advisers need to assess the relative importance of those sources.

Primary sources are not given the same weight in answering a tax question. The U.S. Supreme Court is the final authority as to the meaning of a Code provision. All other things being equal, decisions by U.S. Courts of Appeals are given more weight than decisions by trial courts. Decisions by the U.S. Tax Court often are given greater weight than decisions by U.S. district courts and the U.S. Court of Federal Claims because Tax Court judges are considered to have special expertise in the tax law. Private letter rulings and TAMs have no precedential value except for the taxpayer to whom they were issued.

.05 Developing Conclusions and Recommendations

The final step in the research process is for a tax researcher to draw a conclusion and make recommendations. Often there is a clear conclusion. Other times it may be unclear how the tax law applies. Under such circumstances, researchers must use their professional judgment to determine how the tax law will be applied.

Before making a recommendation, a tax researcher must consider the preferences of their client and what it would cost their client to defend against a challenge by the IRS. The strategy that saves the most in taxes may not necessarily be acceptable to the client or save the taxpayer the most money over the long term.

Example 25: The IRS assessed a $500 deficiency against Schlaq Washing Machine Belts, Inc. Emmett Grassia, who Schlaq hires for professional tax advice, believes that the IRS's interpretation of the Code provision was incorrect, and some commentators agree with Emmett, but there were no judicial decisions either supporting or opposing the IRS's interpretation. Emmett estimates that it would cost the company $10,000 to challenge the IRS before the U.S. Tax Court and tens of thousands more if the case were appealed to a Court of Appeals. Although Emmett was confident that Schlaq would prevail, he could not recommend a strategy guaranteed to cost the company at least $10,000 but saving the company no more than $500.

While analyzing and evaluating primary sources of tax authority, a researcher may discover the need to obtain additional facts. If so, then those additional facts will have to be obtained, and the relevant authorities will have to be analyzed and evaluated in light of those additional facts.

Example 26: While researching whether Davino Pens, Inc. qualifies for the work opportunity credit, Melanie Skahan noticed that an increased credit now is available for hiring long-term family assistance recipients. Melanie went back to the taxpayer and made inquiries to determine whether any of the taxpayer's recent hires qualified as long-term family assistance recipients.

.06 Communicating Research Findings

Once a tax researcher has developed conclusions and recommendations regarding a tax issue, the researcher must be able to communicate those conclusions and recommendations to the adviser's client or to a colleague (typically the partner or supervisor who assigned the research project).

Properly communicating an answer to a tax question is as important as finding the correct answer to the question. If an answer is not properly communicated and it is misunderstood by the client or colleague, an item of income or expense may be improperly reported or a transaction may be improperly structured to achieve the best tax results. A typical memorandum communicating research results is divided into five parts:

1. *Facts.* This portion of a memorandum restates the pertinent facts.
2. *Issue.* This portion of a memorandum restates the assigned tax question and any ancillary questions that have arisen.
3. *Rule.* This portion of a memorandum mentions the tax laws that affect the issue.
4. *Analysis.* This portion of a memorandum applies the tax laws to the pertinent facts.

5. *Conclusion.* If the tax issue is a matter of compliance, this portion of a memorandum concludes how an item of income or expense or transaction should be reported. If the tax issue involves tax planning, this portion of a memorandum concludes how best to plan for income not yet received, expenses not yet incurred, and transactions that have not yet occurred to achieve the most favorable tax consequences. When the answer to a tax issue is not clear cut, the conclusions and recommendations will be a mixture of objective and subjective findings. Recommendations should include advice as to benefits, as well as risks.

Although a memorandum typically is structured as previously described, that is not the only form that a memorandum can take. If an issue is straightforward, the researcher may wish to start the memorandum by stating the conclusion and then explaining how that conclusion was derived.

¶ 218 Summary

Federal tax law includes not only the Code but also Treasury regulations, IRS rulings and other pronouncements, as well as judicial decisions. These are referred to as primary sources of tax law. Taxpayers need to know not only what primary sources of tax law are but where they can be found. Although secondary sources of tax law cannot be used as authority, they can provide essential guidance for locating and understanding primary sources of tax law.

The goal of a tax researcher is to locate and evaluate all relevant sources of tax law to determine whether a position favorable to a client is acceptable. If research involves an item of income that has been received, an expense that has been incurred, or a transaction that has been completed, tax research can help a business comply with tax reporting requirements. If the tax question involves income yet to be received, an expense yet to be incurred, or a transaction that has not yet occurred, tax researchers can help businesses time receipt of the income or the making of an expenditure or with the structuring of a transaction to achieve the most desirable tax consequences.

In addition, sometimes the tax law surrounding the taxpayer's tax issue is sufficiently vague such that no definitive answer as to the taxpayer's question exists. In these situations, professional assistance may be required to properly determine the tax consequences of the transaction.

GLOSSARY OF TERMS INTRODUCED IN THE CHAPTER

Action on decision. An IRS pronouncement that informs the public as to whether the IRS issued an acquiescence or nonacquiescence to a decision by a court other than the Tax Court.

Annotated tax service. A tax service that is organized by Code section rather than by topic. CCH's *Standard Federal Income Tax Reporter* is an example of an annotated tax service.

Announcements. IRS pronouncements that inform the public as to matters of general interest. They may provide guidance as to both substantive and procedural matters.

Blue book. An explanation of a tax act prepared by the staff of the Joint Committee on Taxation.

Court of appeals. The court to which decisions made by the U.S. Tax Court, a U.S. district court, or the U.S. Court of Federal Claims may be appealed. There are 13 Courts of Appeals: 12 geographical (11 numbers and one named) plus the Federal Court of Appeals.

Determination letter. A written determination issued by an IRS Director in response to a written request from a taxpayer or the taxpayer's authorized representative. A determination letter will be issued only when the question presented is specifically answered by a statute, a tax treaty, the regulations, a conclusion stated in a revenue ruling, or an opinion or court decision that represents the IRS's position.

District court. One of the trial courts to which taxpayers may appeal an IRS determination.

Final regulation. A proposed regulation that has been adopted as a regulation having the full force and effect of law.

***Golsen* rule.** This rule provides that the U.S. Tax Court will follow a Court of Appeals decision that is squarely on point when appeal of the Tax Court's decision lies to that Court of Appeals and that court alone.

Internal Revenue Code. The primary statutory source of federal tax law. It is set forth in Title 26 of the United States Code.

Interpretive regulation. A regulation that interprets the Code. It is promulgated pursuant to the Secretary of the Treasury's general authority to issue regulations.

Legislative regulation. A regulation that defines a statutory term or prescribes a method for implementing a Code provision. It is promulgated pursuant to a specific grant of authority by Congress.

News release. An IRS pronouncement issued to the media to announce items of general interest. They often are used to announce that an important new revenue ruling or revenue procedure is going to be released and set forth the text of that ruling or procedure.

Notices. IRS pronouncements issued to the public to provide guidance involving substantive interpretations of the Code. They often are issued to provide taxpayers with guidance about recently enacted legislation or to alert taxpayers about pending regulations.

Precedent. Refers to the principle in law of using past decisions to assist in making current decisions.

Primary sources of authority. Part of the tax law. Examples of primary sources include legislative authority (e.g., the Code, tax treaties, and Congressional reports), administrative authority (e.g., Treasury regulations and IRS rulings), and judicial decisions.

Private letter ruling. A written statement issued by the Associate Chief Counsel that interprets and applies the tax laws to a specific set of facts presented by a taxpayer. A letter ruling is issued at the request of a taxpayer and upon payment of a fee.

Procedural regulation. A regulation that establishes procedure or practice requirements (such as prescribing how an election is made).

Proposed regulation. A Treasury regulation that the Secretary of the Treasury proposes to issue.

Revenue ruling. An official interpretation by the IRS as to the application of the tax laws to a specific set of facts.

Revenue procedure. A ruling issued by the IRS that involves a procedural issue.

Secondary sources of authority. A reference that explains, comments on, or updates primary sources of tax authority. Examples include topical and annotated tax services, treatises, journals, papers from tax institutes, newsletters, and citators.

Substantial authority. An objective standard that is less stringent than the "more-likely-than-not" standard, but more rigorous than the "reasonable basis" standard.

Tax authority. Established tax law that can be used to help in reaching a conclusion about a tax issue.

Tax avoidance. The art of reducing tax liability through legitimate means.

Tax compliance research. The process of determining how an item of income already received, an expense already incurred, or a transaction already completed should be reported for tax purposes.

Tax evasion. Understating taxes due to the government through unlawful means.

Tax planning research. The process of determining how best to plan for income not yet received, expenses not yet incurred, and transactions that have not yet occurred to achieve the most favorable tax consequences.

Technical advice memorandum (TAM). Written advice from the IRS on the interpretation and proper application of the Code, tax treaties, regulations, revenue rulings, notices, or other precedents to a specific set of facts. A TAM is requested by IRS personnel, not taxpayers. No fee is charged a taxpayer for a TAM.

Temporary regulation. A Treasury regulation issued to provide interim guidance to tax practitioners and the public until final regulations are issued. The rules contained in temporary regulations can be used as authority pending issuance of final regulations.

Topical tax service. A tax service that is arranged by topic rather than by Code section. CCH's *Tax Research Consultant* is an example of a topical tax service.

Treasury regulations. The official interpretation of the Code by the Secretary of the Treasury.

U.S. Court of Federal Claims. One of the trial courts to which taxpayers may appeal an IRS determination.

U.S. Supreme Court. The last resort for those appealing a decision of a Court of Appeals and final authority as to what the Code means.

U.S. Tax Court. One of the trial courts to which taxpayers may appeal an IRS determination. Unlike the U.S. district court or U.S. Court of Federal Claims, there is no requirement that the taxpayer pay any alleged deficiency before the court will hear the taxpayer's appeal.

Unreasonable Position. A tax return preparer can be penalized for preparing a return or claim of refund that understates tax liability if the understatement is due to an unreasonable position. If a position (other than a position with respect to a tax shelter or reportable transaction to which Code Sec. 6662A applies) is adequately disclosed, it will be considered unreasonable unless the preparer had a reasonable basis for it (*reasonable basis standard*). If a position (other than a position with respect to a tax shelter or reportable transaction to which Code Sec. 6662A applies) is not adequately disclosed, it will be considered unreasonable unless there is or was substantial authority for it (*substantial authority standard*). If a position is with respect to a tax shelter or reportable transaction to which Code Sec. 6662A applies, it will be considered unreasonable unless it was reasonable for the preparer to believe that it would more likely than not be sustained on its merits (*more-likely-than-not standard*).

Written determinations. IRS rulings issued specifically to taxpayers. See private letter ruling, technical advice memorandum, and determination letter.

CHAPTER PROBLEMS

The following questions and problems relate to the discussion in Chapter 2, Understanding the Federal Tax Laws, which begins at ¶ 200 in *Part I: Overview of Taxes and the Federal Income Tax System*.

Chapter 2 Discussion Questions

1. What gives Congress the right to impose income taxes? *The ~~force the code~~* (16th admendment of the US Constitution)
2. What is a primary source of federal tax law?
3. What is a secondary source of federal tax law?
4. What is the Internal Revenue Code?
5. How can a committee report be helpful in the tax research process?
6. What is a temporary regulation, and what reliance can taxpayers place on it?
7. What is the difference between an interpretive and legislative regulation?
8. What is a revenue ruling?
9. What is the difference between a revenue ruling and a letter ruling?
10. What is the difference between a Technical Advice Memorandum (TAM) and a private letter ruling (PLR)?
11. What is an IRS notice of acquiescence or nonacquiescence?
12. If a taxpayer disagrees with the IRS's assessment of a deficiency, to which court can the taxpayer appeal?
13. What is the main advantage for a taxpayer in appealing an IRS's assessment of a deficiency to the U.S. Tax Court?
14. If a taxpayer doing business in Arkansas finds a decision of the Eighth Circuit Court of Appeals that supports the taxpayer's tax return position but a decision by the Fifth Circuit Court of Appeals that opposes the taxpayer's tax return position, which decision should the taxpayer follow?
15. If the U.S. Supreme Court interprets a Code provision differently than nine of the Circuit Courts of Appeal that have ruled on the same issue, which interpretation can a taxpayer follow?
16. What is the significance of the substantial authority standard in the tax research process?
17. Why is it not advisable for a researcher to rely solely on a secondary source to answer a research question?
18. What are the basic steps in researching a tax issue?
19. What are the similarities and differences between tax avoidance and tax evasion?
20. What obligation does the IRS impose on a tax researcher to question information furnished by a client?

Chapter 2 Problems

1. What types of tax provisions are included in Part VI of Subchapter B of Chapter 1 of Subtitle A of the Internal Revenue Code?
2. What types of expenses does Code Sec. 162(a) permit a business to deduct?
3. What does Reg. § 1.162-2 discuss?
4. What limit, if any, is imposed on the amount of charitable contributions that a corporation can deduct for a tax year? See Code Sec. 170.
5. Why did the Senate Finance Committee say that it proposed Code Sec. 199, the deduction for income attributable to U.S. production activities? See S. Rep. No. 108-192 (November 12, 2003).
6. If a taxpayer receives money for property that is compulsorily or involuntarily converted, how can the taxpayer avoid having to recognize gain on the conversion? See Code Sec. 1033(a)(2).
7. Is improved real estate similar or related in service or use to unimproved real estate? See Reg. § 1.1033(a)-2.

LLC

8. What is the issue in Rev. Rul. 2003-20, 2003-1 CB 465, and how was it resolved?

9. What is the status of Rev. Rul. 64-328, 1964-2 CB 11?

10. When is a work location temporary for purposes of determining the deductibility of transportation expenses? See Rev. Rul. 99-7, 1999-1 CB 361.

11. What is the maximum amount of depreciation that a business can deduct for a tax year beginning in 2008 with respect to a passenger automobile placed in service during calendar year 2008? See Rev. Proc. 2008-12, 2008-1 CB 658.

12. What did the IRS conclude in IRS Letter Ruling 200607003 (November 10, 2005)?

13. In TAM 200437030 (April 30, 2004), what was the issue and what did the IRS conclude?

14. In *W.J. Heitz*, 75 TCM 2522, Dec. 52,750(M), TC Memo. 1998-220, what factors did the court consider in determining whether the amount of compensation paid a shareholder-employee was reasonable?

15. What is the status of *W.J. Heitz*, 75 TCM 2522, Dec. 52,750(M), TC Memo. 1998-220?

16. What did the court decide in *S.B. Bufferd*, SCt, 93-1 USTC ¶ 50,038, 506 US 523, 113 SCt 927?

17. Zeches Box Partitions, Inc. owns a $1,000 bond that pays 4.4 percent interest. It sells the bond for a $100 loss. That same day, it purchases a $1,000 bond from the same issuer and with the same maturity date but a 5.5-percent interest rate. Can Zeches deduct its $100 loss? See Code Sec. 1091 and Rev. Rul. 60-195, 1960-1 CB 300.

18. Chambley Butter Cartons, Inc. read in the newspaper that the local government had decided to condemn its storage facility and thus it sells the facility to obtain what it believed would be a better price. The sales price was $200,000, and the company's adjusted basis in the facility was $50,000. A month later, the company reinvested all of the proceeds received in a new storage facility. Does it have to recognize any of the gain that it realized from its sale of the storage facility? See Code Sec. 1033 and Rev. Rul. 63-221, 1963-2 CB 332.

19. Huesman Farming, Inc. exchanged a farm for an apartment building. Does it have to recognize any gain or loss on the exchange? See Code Sec. 1031 and Reg. § 1.1031(a)-1.

20. Manzueta Magnetic Tapes, Inc. wants to know whether it is entitled to a work opportunity credit for any of its employees. What factual information do you need to obtain from the company? See Code Sec. 51.

21. What changes did the Tax Relief and Health Care Act of 2006 make to the research credit? See Joint Committee on Taxation, Technical Explanation of H.R. 6408, The "Tax Relief and Health Care Act of 2006," pp. 9, 10.

22. Which credits are included in the general business credit? See Code Sec. 38.

23. For purposes of the corporate alternative minimum tax, what is the exemption amount, and how much alternative minimum taxable income does a corporation have to have before the phaseout of the exemption amount is triggered? See Code Sec. 55.

24. Must legal action be taken to enforce payment before a debt can be considered worthless? See Reg. § 1.166-2.

25. Which businesses are eligible to take a credit for expenditures to provide access to individuals with a disability? See Code Sec. 44.

Chapter 2 Review Problems

1. Why did Congress increase the annual dollar limitation under Code Sec. 179 as part of the Jobs and Growth Tax Relief Reconciliation Act of 2003 (P.L. 108-27)? See House Ways and Means Committee Report No. 108-94 (May 8, 2003), p. 25.

2. Why did Congress repeal the Code Sec. 108 stock-for-debt exception to the general rule that income is recognized when debt is cancelled as part of the Revenue Reconciliation Act of 1993 (P.L. 103-66)? See Senate Finance Committee Report No. 103-36 (June 23, 1993), pp. 292-293.

Chapter 2 Research Question

Lempera Chutney, Inc. plans to sell real property but would prefer not to have to recognize any income from the sale until after the year of the sale. How could it structure its sale to achieve that goal? Refer to Code Sec. 453 when answering this question.

CHAPTER

3 Tax Accounting

1. Describe the differences between tax accounting and financial accounting and explain how the rules for each are determined.

2. List the requirements for selecting and changing a tax year.

3. Compare and contrast the rules governing the cash versus the accrual method of accounting.

4. Explain the accounting methods that apply to specific items such as long-term contracts and installment sales.

5. Explain the claim of right doctrine and the tax benefit rule.

¶ 300 Introduction

Income tax accounting, or **tax accounting**, is the official reporting of income and expenses so a taxpayer's taxable income for a particular period can be accurately determined. Congress enacts tax laws that, along with the administrative, judicial, and other legislative authorities introduced in Chapter 2, form the basis for the tax accounting rules. Tax accounting rules are the focus of this chapter; they apply to all forms of business. Tax accounting differs from financial accounting, which encompasses the rules corporations must abide by when preparing their financial statements.

Before businesses can report their taxable income to the Internal Revenue Service (IRS), they first must determine the period of time over which those taxable amounts are calculated and the rules for determining when income is taxed and when expenses can be deducted. The period over which a business's taxable income is reported is referred to as the "taxpayer's tax year." The rules for determining when a business must recognize income and when it may deduct expenses are referred to as the "taxpayer's method of accounting." This chapter focuses on how frequently businesses must report their taxable profits to the IRS and what methods must be used to report the appropriate amounts of taxable income on the taxpayer's federal income tax return.

¶ 301 Tax Accounting Distinguished from Financial Accounting

Businesses often keep two sets of books and records. They prepare a set of financial accounting records for financial statement purposes and keep a set of tax accounting records from which they prepare their income tax returns. Two sets of books and records are necessary because the financial accounting rules and the tax accounting rules are written by two different governing bodies that have differing, and sometimes contrary, objectives.

Financial accounting records are intended to provide useful information about a business so current and potential investors as well as creditors and other interested parties can make well-informed investment, credit, and other decisions. Corporations are required to prepare financial records in accordance with generally accepted accounting principles (GAAP), which use the accrual method of accounting to report the company's annual net income. Under the accrual method, events affecting the company are reported in the accounting periods in which they are earned (in the case of income) or incurred (in the case of expenses), rather than when the cash is received or paid. The objective of financial accounting is to ensure that the activities and profits of the business are accurately reflected in the company's financial statements, including the calculation of net income on the corporation's income statement.

Tax accounting records are kept to record the information necessary to analyze transactions and events to prepare the taxpayer's income tax return. Tax accounting focuses on those items of income and expense that are important for determining taxable income, which is the final amount of income the government taxes after allowed exclusions and deductions have been subtracted. The legislative, administrative, and judicial tax authorities discussed in Chapter 2 form the basis for the tax accounting rules that businesses must follow when preparing their federal income tax returns. As discussed in Chapter 1, Congress often enacts tax laws for any number of reasons, the most important being to raise revenue for the federal government in an equitable manner. However, many tax laws are enacted for various economic, social, and political reasons (see ¶ 106).

Not only are the rules governing the two sets of accounting records different, but a business's objectives when applying the two sets of rules are very different as well. For the most part, GAAP provides a series of rules that businesses must follow that are intended to fairly present a business's accounting income. GAAP, however, does provide some flexibility and sometimes allows businesses to choose among various acceptable accounting methods. For external (financial) reporting, management is interested in making sure the business is seen by investors and creditors as a successful and thriving business. When given a choice among acceptable accounting methods, management will often select the one that results in the greatest net income. This can involve accelerating accounting income into the current year or slowing down the rate at which expenses are taken on the income statement. For example, a business may choose to use the straight-line (SL) method of depreciation for financial reporting purposes in lieu of the various accelerated depreciation methods that GAAP allows.

In contrast, the goal in tax accounting is to pay the least amount of taxes as legally possible. Most often this involves using the tax laws to postpone income to future tax periods or to elect acceptable methods that will accelerate tax deductions into the current tax year. Thus, for tax purposes, businesses would elect to use the most accelerated depreciation method possible. However, when a business uses the straight-line method for financial accounting purposes and an accelerated depreciation method on its tax return, differences between net income and taxable income will arise.

Most students studying tax for the first time have previously been exposed to the financial accounting rules in an introductory or intermediate accounting course. As the federal income tax laws are presented in Chapters 4 through 9, any significant differences in how an item of income or expense is treated for tax accounting versus financial accounting purposes will be discussed in a shaded box entitled "GAAP vs. Code," as illustrated below.

 GAAP vs. Code: Large corporations are required to reconcile the differences between the amounts they report in net income on the income statement with the taxable income

> they report on the tax return. This reconciliation is done on the corporate income tax return. The reconciliation of net income to taxable income is discussed in Chapter 12.

ACCOUNTING PERIODS

A **tax year** is the period of time taxpayers use to calculate their taxable income. A business's tax year may or may not be the same as the annual accounting period used by the business for financial reporting purposes.[1] Businesses, as well as all other taxpayers, have become accustomed to computing their taxable income annually using the net results of all transactions within a 12-month period. However, that is not the only acceptable method for computing taxable income.

There is no Constitutional requirement that income be calculated on an annual basis. Businesses could be required to report their taxable income for shorter periods (such as monthly) or longer periods (such as every two years). Alternatively, they could wait to complete a transaction before having to determine their profits.

Example 1: Voice Communications signs a contract in December 2009 to install equipment. Voice incurs $16,000 of expenses but has no revenues during the 2009 calendar year. In 2010, it incurs an additional $4,000 of expenses and receives $20,000 for its work. If Voice were to report its taxable income using the calendar year, it would report a $16,000 tax loss in 2009. In 2010, it would report $16,000 of taxable income ($20,000 – $4,000). However, if Voice had been permitted to wait until it had completed its work on the contract, it would have reported no taxable income.

In 1931, the U.S. Supreme Court was asked to decide whether federal income tax could be assessed on the basis of fixed accounting periods or whether it must be assessed based on completed transactions. In upholding the government's right to assess federal income tax based on a fixed annual accounting period, the court ruled,

> It is the essence of any system of taxation that it should produce revenue ascertainable, and payable to the government, at regular intervals. Only by such a system is it practicable to produce a regular flow of income and apply methods of accounting, assessment, and collection capable of practical operation.[2]

It is possible that taxpayers may be aided or adversely affected by timing differences when income and deductions are reported on an annual basis. However, the Internal Revenue Code (the "Code") includes certain provisions to mitigate problems caused by assessing tax based on an annual accounting period.

Example 2: Referring back to Example 1, the $16,000 of expenses in 2009 did not reduce the amount of tax paid by Voice Communications that year because it was already operating at a loss for the year. However, in 2010 it reports $16,000 of taxable income, even though the entire transaction (when viewed over two years) produced no profits for the company. To mitigate this problem, the Code permits taxpayers to carry over net operating losses from one tax year to offset profits in other (profitable) tax years.[3] (See ¶ 1001.01.)

Example 3: In 2009, Hobbit Tool Bits received $200,000 from a defense contract. In 2009, Hobbit's marginal tax rate was 39 percent. In 2010, it is determined that Hobbit had been overpaid by $25,000. The company repays the $25,000 and deducts that amount when calculating its 2010 taxable income. In 2010, Hobbit's marginal tax rate is 25 percent, so when it deducts the $25,000, its tax liability decreases by $6,250 ($25,000 × 25%). However, in the year it reported the $25,000 overpayment in income, its tax liability

---

[1] Code Sec. 441.

[2] *Burnet v. Sanford & Brooks Company,* SCt, 2 USTC ¶ 636, 282 US 359, 51 SCt 150 (1931).

[3] Code Sec. 172.

increased by $9,750 ($25,000 × 39%). Absent any mitigating provision in the tax law, the company would pay an additional $3,500 ($9,750 – $6,250) in taxes because of the error. However, a provision in the Code protects the taxpayer in situations in which previously deducted amounts must be repaid (see the claim of right doctrine at ¶ 312).[4]

¶ 302 Permitted Tax Years

Most businesses use either a **calendar year,** which is a tax year that begins on January 1 and ends on December 31, or a **fiscal year,** which is a 12-month period that ends on the last day of any month other than December. Businesses that do not keep adequate books and records must report their taxable income using a calendar year.[5] Once a tax year has been selected, it generally must be used in all subsequent tax years unless permission is requested and granted from the IRS to change to a different year-end. In the first year of a business's existence or in a year in which a business changes its tax year, a tax return must be filed for a period of fewer than 12 months. This is referred to as a "short tax year" (see ¶ 304.02).

C corporations (defined as corporations other than S corporations) are generally allowed to use either a calendar or a fiscal year as long as they maintain their books and records using the annual accounting period they have selected. Other businesses, however, may be restricted in their tax year choices, and in some cases, they may be required to use a particular tax year. For example, partnerships and S corporations cannot select a tax year without following a strict set of rules that takes into consideration the year-end of their owners[6] (see ¶ 302.01).

Example 4: A business reports its income and expenses based on a year beginning January 1 and ending December 31. The business's tax year is a calendar year.

Example 5: A corporation uses as its tax year the 12-month period beginning on December 1 and ending on November 30. The corporation's tax year is a November 30 fiscal year.

Example 6: A business keeps its books based on a calendar year. Although the business might prefer to use a fiscal year, it cannot do so because it has not kept its books in accordance with a fiscal year.

Although a tax year generally may not include a period of more than 12 calendar months, taxpayers may elect to compute their taxable income on the basis of a fiscal year that varies from 52 to 53 weeks. Such a tax year must always end on the same day of the week and must always end on whatever date that day of the week occurs at the end of the calendar month.[7] For example, if a business uses as its tax year a year that always ends on the last Sunday of October, then its tax year is a fiscal year that varies from 52 to 53 weeks.

 Planning Pointer: Taxpayers may wish to use a fiscal year that varies from 52 to 53 weeks rather than a 52-week year if doing so would permit them to more reliably report their business activities. For example, a retailer that does most of its weekly business on the weekend might want to use a 52-to 53-week year ending on a Sunday to make sure that each year includes the same number of weekends.

.01 Required Tax Years

Although C corporations and individuals are allowed to select a fiscal tax year, certain types of businesses are required to use a particular tax year. For this discussion, a limited liability company

---

[4] Code Sec. 1341.
[5] Code Sec. 441(b).

[6] Reg. § 1.441-1(b)(2).
[7] Reg. § 1.441-2(a)(1).

treated as a partnership for tax purposes follows the same rules that pertain to partnerships. Businesses that have restrictive year-ends include:

- Partnerships,
- S corporations, and
- Personal service corporations.

Partnerships and S corporations are referred to as flow-through entities. The primary advantage of operating an activity as a flow-through entity is that the profits of the business are taxed directly (flow through) to its owners. Owners are considered to have recognized all profits or losses from a flow-through entity on the day of the flow-through entity's year-end. When the flow-through entity and its owners use the same year-end, all income earned by the entity during the year is taxed to its owners in the same tax year. However, when a flow-through entity uses a year-end that is different from the year-end of its owners, a deferral of income results.

For example, if a partnership uses a January 31 fiscal year-end, and its owners use a calendar year, partnership profits for the fiscal year that ends on January 31, 2010, would be reported on the calendar year partner's 2010 income tax return (the year that contains January 31, 2010). Thus, even though the entity's profits from February 1, 2009, through December 31, 2009, were actually earned during the 2009 calendar year, those profits are not taxed to the partner until the partner files its 2010 tax return. This delay (deferral) in the government receiving the taxes owed on this income has prompted Congress to enact rules regarding permitted year-ends for flow-through entities. Congress believed that without such rules, some owners would be able to improperly defer income received by their businesses.[8]

Required tax year for a partnership. A partnership's tax year must ordinarily be the same year the majority partners use. Thus, if a group of partners that collectively owns *more than* a 50-percent interest in the partnership's capital and profits has the same year-end, the partnership normally is required to use that same year-end ("majority partners rule").[9] If there is a not a majority of partners that have the same year-end, the partnership usually must use the same year-end of *all* of its principal partners ("principal partners rule"). "Principal partners" are partners who own at least five percent of the partnership's capital or profits.[10] If the year-end of *all* of the principal partners is not the same, the tax year that produces the least aggregate deferral is the partnership's required tax year.[11]

Example 7: Ryan Corporation owns a 45-percent profits and capital interest in a partnership. Ryan uses an October 31 fiscal year-end. Rachel Roth owns a 40-percent profits and capital interest in the partnership, and Alan Pascel owns the remaining 15 percent. Both Rachel and Alan use a calendar year-end. Since Rachel and Alan use the same year-end and together they own more than 50 percent of the partnership's profits and capital, the partnership's required tax year is the calendar year-end used by its majority partners.

Example 8: Birdland Partnership does not have a group of partners that owns a majority interest in capital and profits and has the same year-end. Thus, the majority partner rule does not apply, and Birdland must determine whether the principal partners rule is applicable. Ralph, Lane, and Dan are the only partners who own at least a five-percent capital or profits interest in Birdland. The three partners are the only principal partners, and if each of them uses the same year-end, then the partnership must use that same year-end. Thus, if Ralph, Lane, and Dan all use the calendar year, the partnership's required tax year is the calendar year.

---

[8] Joint Committee on Taxation, *General Explanation of the Tax Reform Act of 1986*, at 534.

[9] Code Sec. 706(b)(4).

[10] Code Sec. 706(b)(3).

[11] Code Sec. 706(b)(1)(B).

Example 9: Assume the same facts as in Example 8, except Creski Oil, which uses a fiscal year, purchases a five-percent interest in Birdland. Because all principal partners (which now includes Creski) no longer have the same tax year, Birdland's required tax year is the one that produces the least aggregate deferral of income.

The rules regarding the determination of a tax year that produces the least aggregate deferral of income are beyond the scope of this chapter. They are discussed in detail in Chapter 14 when the partnerships tax rules are discussed (see ¶ 1404.01). A partnership may use a tax year other than its required tax year if it (1) establishes to the IRS's satisfaction a business purpose for that requested tax year (see ¶ 304.01), (2) elects a particular tax year as allowed under Code Sec. 444 (see ¶ 302.02), or (3) elects to use a 52–53-week tax year that ends with reference to its required tax year or a tax year elected under Code Sec. 444.[12]

Required tax year for an S corporation. An S corporation's tax year must be one of the following:[13]

- A calendar tax year,
- A tax year elected under Code Sec. 444 (see ¶ 302.02),
- A 52- to 53-week tax year ending with reference to the calendar year or a tax year elected under Code Sec. 444, or
- Any other tax year for which the corporation establishes a business purpose to the IRS's satisfaction (see ¶ 304.01).

 Reason for the Rule: Due to the restrictive rules regarding the types of permitted shareholders of an S corporation, many S corporation shareholders are individuals (see ¶ 1503.01). Since most individuals use a calendar year-end, the rules regarding the permitted tax years of an S corporation require these corporations to use the calendar year as their tax year.

Required tax year for a personal service corporation. A personal service corporation must use the calendar year as its tax year unless it establishes to the IRS's satisfaction a business purpose for using a different period as its tax year.[14] A "personal service corporation" is a corporation engaged in performing services in the fields of health, law, engineering, architecture, accounting, actuarial science, performing arts, or consulting. A personal service corporation can use a tax year different from a calendar year if it makes a proper election under Code Sec. 444.

.02 Section 444 Election

Partnerships, S corporations, and personal service corporations may make an election under Code Sec. 444 to have a tax year other than the required tax year. However, the deferral period of the tax year they select cannot exceed three months. The "deferral period" is the length of time between the entity's year-end (when the owner is deemed to have earned its share of the entity's income) and its required year-end (the year-end that normally would control when the owner would be deemed to have earned the income).

Example 10: A newly formed partnership has a calendar year as its required tax year. Instead of using the calendar year, the partnership may elect a tax year ending September 30 because the number of months between the end of that year (September 30) and the close of the required tax year (December 31) does not exceed three months. It may also elect a tax year ending October 31 or November 30 because the deferral period of those tax years is fewer than three months (two months in the case of a tax year ending October 31; one month in the case of a tax year ending November 30).

---

[12] Reg. § 1.706-1(b)(2)(ii).
[13] Code Sec. 1378(a); Reg. § 1.1378-1(a).

[14] Code Sec. 441(i).

When a flow-through entity uses a tax year other than its required tax year, the government must wait to collect the tax owed on a portion of the income earned by the entity. In Example 10, the partnership would file a tax return reporting profits for the period from October 1, 2009, to September 30, 2010. The profits would not be taxed until reported by the owners in their tax years that contain September 30, 2010. For a calendar year partner, this would be the tax return for the 2010 calendar year. Consequently, income that the partnership earned for the period from October 1, 2009, to December 31, 2009, would not be taxed until the partner files its 2010 tax return. Thus, for the privilege of electing a tax year other than its required tax year, the entity must pay the IRS an amount representing the tax on the deferred income that its owners will not report until the next tax year.[15] The actual amount the entity must pay is calculated using Form 8752, *Required Payment or Refund Under Section 7519*.

Example 11: Continuing with Example 10, if the partnership elects to use a September 30 tax year, it must agree to prepay (keep on reserve with the IRS) any taxes associated with the profits generated during the first three months of its tax year. Thus, the partnership must pay the IRS the taxes its owners would owe on profits generated from October 1 to December 31. Each year the partnership must compute its estimated tax liability for the first three months of its tax year. If the estimate for the year is higher than the amount currently on reserve with the IRS, it must file Form 8752 and pay the additional taxes owed. If the estimate for the year is less than the taxes on reserve with the IRS, it can request a refund by filing Form 8752.

¶ 303 Adopting a Tax Year

New businesses may adopt any permitted tax year by filing their first income tax return using that tax year. Businesses *do not* adopt a tax year merely by filing an application for an employer identification number, by paying estimated taxes for a tax year, or by filing an application for an extension of time to file an income tax return.

Example 12: A corporation began operations on April 1. If the corporation files its first income tax return using December 31 as the last day of its tax year, it has adopted a calendar year as its tax year.

Example 13: A corporation files its first income tax return using September 30 as the end of its tax year. It has adopted a fiscal year beginning on October 1 and ending on September 30 as its tax year.

¶ 304 Changing a Tax Year

Once a business adopts a tax year, it must use that tax year to compute its taxable income and file its income tax returns unless it obtains the IRS's approval to change to a different tax year. The IRS ordinarily will approve a business's request to change to a different tax year if the taxpayer establishes a *business purpose* for the requested tax year and agrees to any terms, conditions, and adjustments required by the IRS to prevent any substantial distortion of income that otherwise would result from the change.

.01 Business Purpose Tax Year

If a partnership, S corporation, or personal service corporation can establish that it has an acceptable business purpose for using a tax year other than its required tax year, it may use a tax year that is different from its required tax year.[16] These entities can establish a business purpose to the IRS's satisfaction by showing that the requested tax year is their natural business year or by satisfying a facts and circumstances test.[17] Demonstrating that a tax year other than the taxpayer's required tax year is more of a natural business year for these particular entities generally requires

---

[15] Code Secs. 444(c)(1) and 7519.
[16] Code Secs. 706(b)(1)(C) and 1378(b)(2).

[17] Rev. Proc. 2002-39, 2002-1 CB 1046.

an entity to have been in business for several years to establish a track record that supports a natural business year.

Natural business year. A natural business year can be demonstrated by satisfying the "25-percent gross receipts test." This test requires a calculation of the percentage of gross receipts that comes from the last two months of the requested tax year. A partnership that meets the 25-percent gross receipts test will be granted automatic consent to change to its natural business year regardless of whether the use of the natural business year results in more deferral of income than the tax year the partnership is currently using.[18]

To satisfy the 25-percent gross receipts test, the business computes its gross receipts for the three previous 12-month periods ending on the last day of the requested year-end. For example, if a taxpayer that currently uses a calendar year wants to convince the IRS that a fiscal year ending May 31 is a more natural business year, it must calculate its gross receipts for the three previous 12-month periods ending on May 31. If at least 25 percent of the year's gross receipts comes from the last two months in each of those three years, then the 25-percent gross receipts test will have been satisfied. However, if using yet a different tax year passes the 25-percent gross receipts test for the previous three years, then the tax year that produces a higher percentage of gross sales during the last two months will be deemed the business's natural business year.

Example 14: JKL Partnership currently uses a calendar year as its tax year. JKL wants to change to a May 31 fiscal year. JKL would like the change to become effective after the short tax year of January 1 through May 31, 2010. The partnership's gross receipts for the period from June 1, 2008, through May 31, 2009, are $300,000, and its gross receipts for April 2009 and May 2009 total $90,000. Thus, gross receipts for the last two months are 30 percent of total gross receipts for the desired May 31 fiscal year ($90,000/$300,000). When JKL performs this same calculation for the 12-month periods ending May 31, 2008, and May 31, 2007, its percentages of gross receipts in the last two months are 26 and 28 percent, respectively. Since the percentages each exceed 25 percent, JKL has established a May 31 natural business year. However, JKL cannot adopt a May 31 year-end unless it can show that no other tax year would produce a greater percentage of gross receipts in the last two months.

A partnership, S corporation, or personal service corporation may also request a different year-end than its required year-end by showing a natural business year that ends soon after its annual peak period of business. Generally, one month is considered to be "soon after" the peak business period; however, a business that has been in existence less than three years typically has difficulty demonstrating its peak and nonpeak periods. A business whose income is steady from month to month will not be able to establish a natural business year using this special rule.[19]

A partnership, S corporation, or personal service corporation may also be able to establish a natural business year if it can show through its gross receipts for the previous three years that it is open only part of the year.[20] The natural business year of a taxpayer with a seasonal business ends at or within a month after the business operations end for the season. A seasonal business must have only insignificant receipts (less than 10 percent of the year's receipts) during the portion of the year it is not operational. Certain outdoor businesses that are seasonal due to weather conditions are likely to satisfy this requirement. These alternative ways for partnerships to show a natural business year are discussed in Chapter 14 (see ¶ 1401.01).

Facts and circumstances test. Partnerships, S corporations, and personal service corporations that have difficulty establishing a natural business year may establish a business purpose for a requested tax year that is different from their required tax year based on all the relevant facts and circumstances. The IRS, however, has stated that these entities will be granted permission to adopt,

---

[18] Rev. Proc. 2006-46, 2006-2 CB 859.

[19] Rev. Proc. 2002-39, 2002-1 CB 1046, § 503(1).

[20] Rev. Proc. 2002-39, 2002-1 CB 1046, § 5.03(2).

change, or retain a tax year under the "facts and circumstances test" only in rare and unusual circumstances. The following reasons *are not* sufficient to establish a business purpose for a requested tax year:[21]

- Deferral of income to owners;
- Use of a particular year for regulatory or financial accounting purposes;
- Hiring patterns of a particular business;
- Use of a particular year for administrative purposes;
- Partnership's business involves the use of price lists, model years, or other items that change on an annual basis;
- Use of a particular year by a related entity;
- Use of a particular year by competitors;
- Gaining an accountant's reduced rate;
- Record-keeping consistency; and
- Issuance of timely tax information forms to partners.

Businesses other than partnerships, S corporations, and personal service corporations that do not otherwise establish a business purpose for their requested tax years generally will be deemed to have established a business purpose if they provide a nontax reason for the requested tax year and agree to certain additional terms, conditions, and adjustments intended to neutralize the tax effects of any resulting substantial distortion of income.

 Planning Pointer: Selecting a tax year that coincides with a business's natural business year can be desirable for several reasons. First, income and expenses are matched. Second, because inventories usually are at their lowest level, it is easier to count and value them. Third, loans usually are at their lowest amounts, which means the business will have a more favorable balance sheet for credit purposes.

.02 Requesting a Change in Tax Year

Unless automatic consent to a change in tax years has been provided, businesses are required to file Form 1128, *Application To Adopt, Change, or Retain a Tax Year*, no earlier than the day after the end of the first year for which the change is to be effective and no later than the original due date (not including extensions) for filing a return for the first effective year. A change in tax years is automatically approved for certain businesses. For example, C corporations that comply with Rev. Proc. 2006-45[22] may change their tax years. Partnerships, S corporations, and personal service corporations that comply with Rev. Proc. 2006-46[23] may change their tax years. Unless the IRS has announced that it will automatically approve a change in tax year, the IRS charges a user fee for requests to change a tax year.

When a business changes from one tax year to another, it is required to file a tax return for the short tax year created by the change. A **short tax year** is a tax year of less than 12 months. If a short tax year return were not filed, the taxable income generated during the short period would never be taxed. When a short tax year return is filed, the taxpayer must compute its tax liability using an annualized taxable income. The taxpayer is only responsible for the tax liability for the portion of the year that represents the short tax year.

Example 15: A.G. Generators changes from a tax year ending October 31 to a tax year ending November 30. A.G. must file a tax return for the period beginning November 1 and ending November 30. In doing so, it annualizes taxable income on the short tax year

---

[21] Rev. Proc. 2002-39, 2002-1 CB 1046.
[22] 2006-2 CB 851.
[23] 2006-2 CB 859.

return by taking taxable income for the one-month period of November 1 to November 30 and then multiplying it by 12 to represent a full year of taxable income. A.G. then calculates the tax liability on its annualized taxable income. It then divides the tax liability by 12 to determine the amount of taxes it owes on one month of taxable income.

ACCOUNTING METHODS

As previously discussed, businesses must follow certain rules governing when they must recognize income and when they can deduct expenses. These rules are referred to as a business's **method of accounting**. The term includes not only the overall method of accounting used by a taxpayer but also the accounting treatment of any particular item.[24] For example, the cash method of accounting is a permissible accounting method. Under this method, cash is recognized as income in the year it is received, and expenses are deducted in the year they are paid. However, when a business enters into a long-term construction contract, it may be required to report its income in a tax year other than the year in which the cash is received. Although this method is inconsistent with the cash method of accounting, it nonetheless is the required method that must be used for this particular item of income.

Businesses must keep in mind that the method of accounting they use for financial accounting purposes is not necessarily the one they should use for tax accounting purposes. For financial accounting, businesses need to follow the rules provided under GAAP and to make choices that will maximize their net income and make the company look as profitable and successful as possible. For tax purposes, businesses want to select a method of accounting that will allow them to minimize their income tax liability. Because of the progressive nature of the U.S. income tax system, businesses often reduce their overall tax liabilities by keeping taxable income constant from year to year. They can also take advantage of the time value of money by selecting a method of accounting that allows them to defer income until a subsequent tax year or to accelerate expenses into the current tax year.

Example 16: S.W. Belts has a big order at the end of its tax year that will generate $25,000 in taxable income. The company anticipates its taxable income for the year will be $75,000 from other sources. It anticipates its taxable income for the following tax year will be $50,000. If its method of accounting permits it to delay recognizing the $25,000 in taxable income until its next tax year, it will report $75,000 of taxable income in each year and owe $13,750 in taxes each year (or a total of $27,500).

If its method of accounting does not allow S.W. Belts to delay recognition of the $25,000 in taxable income, its taxable income for the current tax year will be $100,000, and its taxable income for its next tax year will be $50,000. Due to the progressive nature of the corporate income tax rates, the company's total federal income tax for the two years will be $29,750 ($22,250 and $7,500, respectively). Although total taxable income for the two years is the same ($150,000 total), the timing of that income can cost S.W. Belts an additional $2,250 ($29,750 − $27,500) in federal income taxes.

Example 17: Mixon Signs purchases equipment for $50,000. Mixon is in the 34-percent tax bracket. For financial accounting purposes, Mixon uses a depreciation method that allows it to deduct $5,000 each year over the 10-year life of the equipment. If Mixon accounts for depreciation the same way for tax purposes, it will save $1,700 in federal income taxes each year ($5,000 × 34%). However, if for tax purposes it can elect to expense the entire $50,000 in the first year, it can reduce its tax liability by $17,000 ($50,000 × 34%) for the year the equipment is placed in service. Although Mixon will

---

[24] Reg. § 1.446-1(a)(1).

not be entitled to any tax depreciation deductions for the equipment in any subsequent years, it will generate an additional $15,300 in tax savings in the first year ($17,000 – $1,700) that it can immediately invest or otherwise use to its advantage.

¶ 305 Permissible Methods of Accounting

No uniform method of accounting for tax purposes is prescribed for all taxpayers.[25] A business usually can adopt any method of accounting, if the method clearly reflects its income and the business regularly uses the method in keeping its books. If the method of accounting used by a business does not clearly reflect its income, its taxable income must be computed under a method that in the IRS's opinion does clearly reflect its income.[26]

The two most common methods of accounting used by businesses are the cash receipts and disbursements method of accounting and the accrual method of accounting.[27] Under the **cash receipts and disbursements method**, a business includes in its gross income an item of income when it actually or constructively receives the cash or a cash equivalent, and it can deduct an expense when it is actually paid. Under the **accrual method**, an item of income must be included in gross income when all events have occurred that fix the right to receive the item and its amount can be determined with reasonable accuracy. An expense can be deducted when (1) all events have occurred that determine the liability, (2) the amount of the liability can be determined with reasonable accuracy, and (3) economic performance has occurred with respect to the liability. The accrual method should be familiar to students who have studied financial accounting, as publicly traded companies must use the accrual method to prepare their financial statements.

 GAAP vs. Code: GAAP requires taxpayers to use the accrual method of accounting instead of the cash method because reporting a company's financial transactions based on the cash method can give an incorrect view of the company's financial health and cause those relying on the company's financial reports to make bad decisions.

Businesses are also permitted to use a **hybrid method** of accounting, which combines elements of the cash and the accrual accounting methods. For example, the accrual method of accounting for purchases and sales of inventory may be combined with the cash method for other types of income and expenses. The cash method (see ¶ 306), accrual method (see ¶ 307), and hybrid method (see ¶ 308) are referred to as "overall methods of accounting" to distinguish them from methods of accounting required for particular items of income or expense (¶ 309).

A taxpayer that engages in more than one trade or business may use a different method of accounting for each trade or business.[28] A taxpayer can use one method of accounting for the taxpayer's business and a different method of accounting to compute income and deductions not connected with the business.

Example 18: Kim Striker is engaged in two businesses. Kim sells kaleidoscopes on eBay, and she sells antiques in her store. Kim uses the cash method for her eBay business and the accrual method for her antique store. She is permitted to use a different method of accounting for each of her businesses.

Example 19: Nina Zorman owns a card and party shop. She uses the accrual method for that business. Her use of an accrual method for her business does not prevent her from using the cash method for her personal income and expenses.

[25] Reg. § 1.446-1(a)(2).
[26] Code Sec. 446(a), (b).
[27] Code Sec. 446(c).
[28] Code Sec. 446(d).

.01 Limitations on the Use of the Cash Method

Although the cash method is simple to use and less costly to administer than the accrual method, it does have its shortcomings. Over the years, Congress has increasingly restricted its use. A major shortcoming of the cash method is that it is not in accordance with GAAP, and its use may result in the recognition of income and expense items without regard to the tax year in which the economic events giving rise to the items occurred and thus result in a mismatching of income with related expenses.[29] Use of the cash method can also produce a mismatching of income and deductions when one party to a transaction uses the cash method but another party uses the accrual method, as illustrated in Examples 20 and 21.

Example 20: Creative Designs uses the calendar year as its tax year and the cash method of accounting. During 2009, Creative Designs developed an advertising campaign for one of its clients. It finished the campaign in 2009 and billed the client $22,000 for its services; however, the client did not pay the bill until early in 2010. Under the cash method, the $22,000 is not taxed to Creative Designs until 2010. If the client uses the calendar year but uses the accrual method of accounting, the client would deduct the $22,000 in 2009—the year it incurred the advertising expense.

Example 21: Rob Guzi, who uses the calendar year as his tax year and the cash method of accounting, performs services in 2009 for Rossa, Inc., which uses an accrual method of accounting. Rob collects his $20,000 fee from Rossa in 2010 and properly reports it as taxable income on his 2010 tax return. However, since the services were performed in 2009, using the accrual method Rossa deducts the $20,000 in 2009 even though payment was not actually made until 2010.

Businesses required to maintain inventory. When a taxpayer is required to maintain inventory, it must use an accrual method of accounting with regard to its purchases and sales of such inventory.[30] A taxpayer is required to account for inventories when the production, purchase, or sale of merchandise is an income-producing factor in the taxpayer's business.[31] A business that must use the accrual method to account for purchases and sales of inventory can use the cash method for its other items of income and expense, provided the business is not required to use the accrual method of accounting as its overall accounting method (see the discussion that follows).

 Reason for the Rule: Since a business often purchases and pays for inventory prior to being able to sell it and collect the cash, allowing use of the cash method to account for inventory would result in a distortion of the business's true operating profits. A business that is required to maintain an inventory must use the accrual method to account for its purchases and sales because that method requires a business to match the proceeds from sales of goods with the costs associated with those goods.

The IRS exempts certain "qualifying small businesses" from the requirement to account for inventories using the accrual method of accounting. This exemption applies only to businesses whose *average annual gross receipts* over the previous three years do not exceed $10 million (and of course, only to businesses that are not otherwise required to use the accrual method). A qualifying small business may use the cash method for all of its trades or businesses if it satisfies one of the following three conditions:[32]

1. The taxpayer reasonably determines that its principal business activity is described in a North American Industry Classification System (NAICS) code other than an ineligible code (relating to manufacturing, retail trade, wholesale trade, information industries, and mining activities).

---

[29] Joint Committee on Taxation, *General Explanation of the Tax Reform Act of 1986*, at 474-475.

[30] Reg. § 1.446-1(c)(2)(i).

[31] Reg. § 1.471-1.

[32] Rev. Proc. 2002-28, 2002-1 CB 815.

2. The taxpayer's principal business activity is described in one of the ineligible NAICS codes, but the taxpayer reasonably determines that its principal business activity is the provision of services, including the provision of property incident to those services.

3. The taxpayer's principal business activity is described in one of the ineligible NAICS codes, but the taxpayer reasonably determines that its principal business activity is the fabrication or modification of tangible personal property upon demand in accordance with customer design or specifications.

 Reason for the Rule: The IRS adopted this rule to reduce administrative and tax compliance burdens on certain small businesses and to minimize disputes between the IRS and small businesses as to whether they are required to maintain inventories.[33]

C corporations and partnerships with a C corporation partner. Most C corporations and partnerships that have a C corporation as a partner cannot use the cash method of accounting if their average annual gross receipts for the three previous tax years exceed $5 million. Qualified personal service corporations are exempt from this rule,[34] and special rules apply to corporations and partnerships that engage in farming activities. This restriction on the use of the cash method applies regardless of whether inventory is material to the business.

 Reason for the Rule: In 1986 Congress limited the use of the cash method of accounting by C corporations and partnerships that have a C corporation as a partner because it concluded that the cash method of accounting frequently fails to reflect accurately the economic results of a taxpayer's trade or business over a tax year.[35] Congress continued to allow smaller businesses to use the cash method to avoid the higher compliance costs associated with changing to another method of accounting. It denied use of the cash method of accounting by a partnership that has a C corporation as a partner to prevent an entity that was prohibited from using the cash method from circumventing the rules by operating its business in partnership form.

Partnerships engaged in farming that have a C corporation as a partner must use the accrual method. Any C corporation engaged in farming must use an accrual method of accounting if its gross receipts for any tax year since 1975 exceeded $1 million. However, family corporations involved in farming must use the accrual method only if their gross receipts exceeded $25 million in any year after 1985. A "family corporation" is one in which at least 50 percent of the total combined voting power of all classes of stock to vote and at least 50 percent of all other classes of stock are owned by members of the same family.[36]

 Reason for the Rule: Congress enacted this provision as part of the Tax Reform Act of 1976. Congress denied large corporations entering into the farming business the benefit of the cash method of accounting because such corporations have ready access to skilled accounting assistance.[37] The primary justification for permitting farm operations to use the cash method of accounting is its relative simplicity, which, for example, eliminates the need to identify specific costs incurred in raising particular crops or animals.

---

[33] Rev. Proc. 2002-28, 2001- CB 815.

[34] Code Sec. 448(a), (b).

[35] Joint Committee on Taxation, *General Explanation of the Tax Reform Act of 1986*, at 474-476.

[36] Code Sec. 447.

[37] House Ways and Means Committee Report No. 94-658 (November 12, 1975), at 94.

A qualified personal service corporation is exempt from the rules restricting C corporations from using the cash method. A "qualified personal service corporation" is a C corporation in which 95 percent or more of its employees' time is devoted to the performance of services in the fields of health, law, engineering, architecture, accounting, actuarial science, performance arts, or consulting. In addition, 95 percent or more of the value of its stock must be held *directly or indirectly* by (1) employees performing services in a qualifying field, (2) retired employees who had performed such services for the corporation or the estate of any such employee or retired employee, or (3) any person who acquired stock by reason of the death of such an employee or retired employee (but only for the two-year period beginning on the date of the individual's death).[38]

.02 Special Methods of Accounting

Despite selecting an overall method of accounting in accordance with the rules previously discussed in this chapter, taxpayers may have to use special methods of accounting for certain items of income and expenses. For example, there are special methods of accounting for installment sales, long-term contracts, research and experimental expenditures, crops, and soil and water conservation expenditures. Regardless of which overall method (cash, accrual, or hybrid) the taxpayer uses on its tax return, special rules apply to these specific items. The details regarding these special rules follow the discussion of the overall accounting methods (see ¶ 309).

¶ 306 Cash Receipts and Disbursements Method

Most individuals and many small businesses use the cash receipts and disbursements method of accounting because it requires a minimum of recordkeeping and gives the taxpayer flexibility in reporting income and deducting expenses. Sole proprietors especially are inclined to use the cash method of accounting because they usually use it for the other items reported on their personal income tax returns.

 Planning Pointer: Subject to the constructive receipt of income doctrine (see ¶ 306.01), businesses that use the cash method of accounting can control the timing of when income (cash) is received. If towards the end of a tax year a business wishes to delay receipt of income until the next year, the business can delay sending invoices to customers. A business can accelerate or postpone deductions by accelerating or delaying purchases or payments for purchases.

.01 Accounting for Income

Under the cash method, taxpayers generally report income in the year during which they actually or constructively receive the cash or a cash equivalent.[39] Thus, amounts that cash method taxpayers receive as advance payments for goods or services must be included in gross income in the year they are received. If taxpayers receive property or services, they must include the fair market value (FMV) of the property or services in income. A credit sale is not included in income by a cash method taxpayer until the customer pays off the receivable, and a customer's promise to pay is not considered income by a cash method taxpayer.

Example 22: Mannox Confetti is a cash method taxpayer that uses the calendar year as its tax year. Mannox receives a promissory note in payment for some confetti it sold to a customer. The promissory note has no value and is not readily converted into cash. Receipt of the promissory note is not treated as income. As Mannox receives payments pursuant to the promissory note, it will include the payments in its calculation of gross income.

---

[38] Temp. Reg. § 1.448-1T(e).   [39] Code Sec. 446(b).

Example 23: Wax Aquariums is a cash method taxpayer that uses a calendar year as its tax year. In December 2009, Wax agrees to install and stock a custom aquarium in a dentist's office. Under the terms of the sale, $1,000 is payable up front on December 15 when the contract is signed. The remainder is due when the aquarium is installed. Wax finishes installing the aquarium on January 5, 2010. Wax includes the $1,000 advance in gross income in 2009.

Example 24: Morelli Shoes is a cash method taxpayer that uses a calendar year as its tax year. On November 30, 2009, Morelli sells $10,000 of shoes to a customer. Payment is due in 30 days, but payment is not actually received until January 2, 2010. Because the company uses the cash method, it does not include the $10,000 in its gross income until the year it receives the payment (2010).

Example 25: Pointe Carpet Cleaners accepts plumbing services from a customer in lieu of cash payment. The value of those plumbing services must be included in the company's gross income for the year.

Constructive receipt doctrine. Under the **constructive receipt doctrine**, a business constructively receives income in the tax year during which it is credited to the business's account, set apart for the business, or otherwise made available without any substantial limitation or restriction. A business may be treated as having constructively received income even though it does not have actual possession of the income until after the end of the year. If a business authorizes someone to receive income on its behalf as its agent, the business will be considered to have received income when its agent receives income on its behalf.[40]

A check is considered received when it is delivered into the hands of the payee, unless the check is later dishonored. However, if a check could have been delivered in one year but the payee requests that delivery be delayed, the payee will be considered to have constructively received the check in the year it could have been delivered.

Example 26: Pettway Check Printing is a cash method taxpayer that uses the calendar year. Pettway has a bank account that pays interest on the last day of the month. It must include the interest in its gross income when the interest is credited to its account, even if Pettway does not attempt to withdraw the interest from the bank account.

Example 27: Sealy Rentals authorizes Ming Sealy to act as its agent and to receive rental payments from tenants. The company is considered to have received rental payments when they are delivered to Ming.

Example 28: Sandy Fuller was out of town during the last two weeks of 2009 and did not return home until January 1, 2010. While she was away, Sandy received a check for $10,000 from a client for services previously rendered and billed. Sandy must report the $10,000 in income for 2009, even though she was unable to cash the check until the next year. The fact that the amount was made available to Sandy without substantial limitation or restriction during 2009 is sufficient for her to be required to pay tax on that amount during 2009.

Example 29: Assume the same facts as in Example 28, except the customer encloses a note along with the check and asks Sandy not to cash the check until after the first of the year because until then the bank account will not have sufficient funds to cover the check. Since there are substantial limitations placed on the check, Sandy does not take constructive receipt of the $10,000 until 2010.

Example 30: Matava Coffees received payment for an order of its products on December 31 but could not get to the bank to cash the check until January 2. The company is considered to have received the payment on December 31.

---

[40] Rev. Rul. 79-379, 1979-2 CB 204.

Example 31: Hendrix Extracts is a cash method taxpayer that uses a calendar year as its tax year. On December 10, 2009, Hendrix sells $2,000 of its products to Brian Hudnell. Payment is not due until January 9, 2010, but the invoice states that Brian can receive a one-percent discount if he pays by December 20. Brian tells Hendrix he will send a check by December 20; however, the company tells him it will honor the one-percent discount if he delays payment until January 1. Brian agrees to the new terms. Hendrix must include the $2,000 in its gross income for 2009 because it could have received the cash in 2009. Hendrix cannot avoid paying tax on the $2,000 that Brian had intended to pay to it in 2009 by refusing or altering the terms to accept the payment in another tax year.

 Reason for the Rule: The constructive receipt doctrine for income was developed to prevent taxpayers from refusing to accept income that was available to them. If taxpayers could refuse to accept income made available to them, they could indefinitely delay having to pay tax on that income or could time receipt to take advantage of lower marginal income tax rates. It is important to note that the constructive receipt doctrine does not prevent taxpayers from delaying billing for their goods or services.

Original issue discount. Because cash method taxpayers recognize income upon the receipt of cash, taxpayers using the cash method could avoid being taxed on interest income by structuring loans so that no payments for interest are received until the note matures. These types of loans are issued at a discount (below the amount due at maturity) and the difference between the loan proceeds and the amount due at maturity is interest that is called original issue discount (OID). If the borrower uses the accrual method, this type of loan arrangement could result in the accrual method borrower deducting interest expense over the life of the loan, while the cash method lender does not recognize income until the interest is paid at the end of the loan. To prevent such situations from occurring, the tax laws require that cash method taxpayers use the accrual method for recording interest income from loans involving OID.[41] The calculation of OID is discussed in Chapter 4 (see ¶ 410.06).

.02 Accounting for Expenses

Under the cash method of accounting, businesses ordinarily may not deduct (or capitalize) an expense until the year during which the expense actually is paid. Although it may seem feasible that there would be a tax law comparable to the constructive receipt doctrine for payments, no such rule exists. A taxpayer's mere promise to make a payment is not considered an actual payment, even though the promise is secured by collateral or a letter of credit. However, an expense may be deducted the year payment is made, even though payment is made with borrowed funds.

Amounts paid by check are considered paid when the check is mailed or delivered, provided that the bank honors the check. Amounts paid by credit card are considered paid when the amount is charged, regardless of when the taxpayer pays the credit card bill. If a taxpayer authorizes an agent to make a payment, payment is considered made by the taxpayer when made by the agent (e.g., when the agent mails a check).

 Reason for the Rule: Because of differences between the Code's treatment of income and deduction, the courts have rejected the notion of a constructive payment doctrine as a corollary to the constructive receipt of income doctrine.[42] "Gross income" is broadly construed because the Code is presumed to tax all income unless specifically excluded from gross income by the tax laws. In contrast, deductions are narrowly construed and

---

[41] Code Secs. 1272(a)(3) and 1273(a).

[42] *Vander Poel, Francis & Co., Inc.*, 8 TC 407, Dec. 15,628 (1947).

considered a matter of legislative grace. The constructive receipt of income doctrine helps prevent taxpayers from evading the intent of the Code to tax all income. A constructive payment doctrine would hinder Congress's intent to limit deductions to amounts actually paid.

Example 32: A cash method taxpayer uses the calendar year as its tax year. On December 10, 2009, the company purchases office supplies for $500 and pays for them on January 8, 2010. Because the company uses the cash method, it may not deduct its payment as a trade or business expense until 2010, the year it makes the payment.

Example 33: Harbor Motors is a cash method taxpayer that uses the calendar year as its tax year. On November 10, 2009, Harbor hires an advertising agency and agrees to pay $2 million for its services. The amount was billed and was due in 2009, but Harbor waited until 2010 to pay the bill. Because there is no rule comparable to the constructive receipt of income doctrine for payments, Harbor deducts the $2 million in 2010.

Example 34: Johnson Industrial Clothing is a cash method taxpayer that uses the calendar year as its tax year. On November 10, 2009, Johnson purchases exterminating services and gives the exterminator a $250 merchandise credit as payment for the services. Although the exterminator must include the $250 in its gross income for 2009, Johnson cannot deduct the $250 until the exterminator actually uses the credit to purchase merchandise from Johnson.

Example 35: Westly Moccasins is a cash method taxpayer that uses the calendar year as its tax year. On December 28, 2009, one of Westly's employees charges an airline ticket on the company's credit card. The company receives the credit card statement containing the airline ticket charge in January and pays the bill on February 2, 2010. Because amounts paid by credit card are considered paid when the amount is charged, regardless of when the bill is paid, the company deducts the travel expense in 2009.

Example 36: Ramone, Inc. is a cash method taxpayer that uses the calendar year as its tax year. On December 31, 2009, the company mails a check for $150 in payment for supplies that were delivered earlier in the month. Assuming there are sufficient funds in the bank, Ramone is considered to have paid for the supplies in 2009.

Example 37: Photographic Silk Screens is a cash method taxpayer that uses the calendar year as its tax year. On December 14, 2009, the company borrows $35,000 to purchase a minivan. On December 15, 2009, it uses the borrowed funds to purchase the minivan. It does not start repaying the loan until January 2010. The company will be treated as having paid for the minivan in 2009.

Example 38: Tes Realtors hires a real estate management firm to act as its agent in managing one of its apartment buildings. On June 14, 2009, the management firm pays $1,000 to a pesticide firm. The payment will be considered to be made by Tes Realtors on June 14, 2009.

Prepaid expenses. Prepaid expenses are treated the same way for cash method and accrual method taxpayers. As a general rule, prepaid expenses must be capitalized and amortized over the period to which the amounts paid apply.

Example 39: Goodwater Packaging is a cash method taxpayer that uses a calendar year as its tax year. On December 1, 2009, Goodwater pays $96,000 for a two-year lease of office space. Goodwater cannot deduct the $96,000 in 2009 but instead must amortize the $96,000 over the two-year term of the lease. For each month during the year that Goodwater occupies the office space, it may deduct $4,000 ($96,000/24). Thus, it deducts $4,000 in 2009, $48,000 in 2010 ($4,000 × 12), and $44,000 in 2011 ($4,000 × 11).

If the prepaid amount covers services that will be completed in accordance with the **12-month rule**, a cash method taxpayer can deduct the full amount paid in the current year. The 12-month rule applies if the amount paid creates (or facilitates the creation of) any right or benefit for the taxpayer that does not extend beyond the *earlier* of (1) 12 months after the first date on which the taxpayer realizes the right or benefit or (2) the end of the tax year following the tax year in which the payment is made.[43]

Example 40: Plastics Recycling is a cash method taxpayer that uses a calendar year as its tax year. On December 10, 2009, Plastics pays $5,000 for its annual premium on a property insurance policy effective from December 16, 2009, to December 15, 2010. Because the benefit (insurance coverage) attributable to the $5,000 payment does not extend more than a year beyond the *earlier* of December 16, 2010 (12 months from the date the first benefit was received) or the end of 2010 (the next tax year), Plastics Recycling may deduct the entire $5,000 in 2009 under the 12-month rule.

Example 41: Sacred Files is a cash method taxpayer that uses a calendar year as its tax year. On December 27, 2009, Sacred Files pays $1,825 for its annual premium for a property insurance policy effective January 2, 2010, to January 1, 2011. Because the benefit (insurance coverage) attributable to the $1,825 payment extends beyond the *earlier* of January 2, 2011 (12 months from the date the first benefit was received) or the end of 2010 (the end of the next tax year), it cannot deduct the payment in 2009 but instead must capitalize the payment. For each day of coverage during the year, it may deduct $5 ($1,825/365). Although it cannot deduct anything in 2009, it can deduct $1,820 ($5 × 364) in 2010, and $5 in 2011.

Interest. The special 12-month rule does not apply to interest expense. A cash method taxpayer can only deduct interest in the year it was paid. If interest is withheld from the proceeds of a loan or paid by means of an additional loan extended by the same lender, it cannot be deducted by the borrower for the year it was withheld or paid by means of an additional loan. Similarly, a cash method taxpayer can deduct prepaid interest only in the tax year to which the interest relates.[44]

Example 42: In 2009, Rick's Soft Pretzels borrows $1 million to help pay for a new office building. During 2010, the company falls behind on its payments, but the lender agrees to let the company pay the overdue amount (which includes $10,000 of interest) over a five-year period at a higher interest rate. Rick's cannot deduct the $10,000 of interest in 2010 because it was paid with the new loan.

Example 43: Assume the same facts as in Example 42, except Rick's borrows money from a different lender and uses the proceeds from that loan to pay the overdue amount. In this situation, Rick's may take a deduction in 2010 for the $10,000 of interest that it paid to the original lender.

Special rule for points. Individual taxpayers are allowed an itemized deduction for interest they pay in connection with loans associated with their personal residences (see ¶ 1304.03). Individual taxpayers who use the cash method of accounting may deduct as an itemized deduction the full amount of points paid for a mortgage loan in the year paid under certain conditions. **Points** represent prepaid interest a lender charges in exchange for a lower interest rate over the life of the loan. These amounts, sometimes called "loan origination fees," are expressed as a percentage of the loan amount and result in a lower interest rate to the borrower. When points are paid on the purchase or improvement of a principal residence, individuals can deduct the points as interest expense in the year paid. Points paid for any other reason, including the refinancing of a residence

---

[43] Reg. § 1.263(a)-4(f).   [44] Code Sec. 461(g)(1).

or the purchase of a residence other than the taxpayer's principal residence must be amortized over the life of the loan.[45] Businesses are required to amortize any points paid over the life of the loan.

Example 44: Janice Copper purchases a home for $500,000 in 2009 by paying $200,000 down and taking out a $300,000 mortgage. At the closing, Janice pays a two-percent loan origination fee. During 2009, Janice also pays $8,000 in interest on the loan. On her 2009 tax return, Janice can deduct the $8,000 as home mortgage interest plus the $6,000 ($300,000 × 2%) of points paid in connection with the loan used to purchase her principal residence.

Example 45: A business borrows $1 million to help pay for a new office building. In order to obtain a lower interest rate over the term of the loan, the business pays $10,000, which is equal to one percentage point ($1,000,000 × 1%). The business cannot take a deduction for the $10,000 for the year it borrowed the money, but it may deduct the $10,000 ratably over the term of the loan.

.03 Other Special Rules for Cash Method Taxpayers

Other provisions of the Code or regulations applicable to cash method taxpayers may change these general rules. For example, some expenses cash method taxpayers pay in the current year must be capitalized and deducted over several tax years.[46] Thus, the taxpayer will receive a deduction in years in which no cash is paid. Cash method taxpayers may also be required to capitalize certain costs associated with real or tangible personal property they produce or acquire for resale.[47] Finally, they may be required to use the percentage of completion method to account for certain long-term contracts. Each of these special rules is discussed at ¶ 309.

Example 46: Divine Stoves purchases a new office building in 2009 for $1,950,000. Divine cannot deduct the entire cost of the building in 2009, even though it paid cash for the building. Instead, the tax laws allow Divine to begin taking depreciation deductions for the building starting in 2009. Thus, in 2010 Divine will be entitled to a depreciation deduction against gross income, even though it will make no actual payment with respect to the building in 2010.

¶ 307 Accrual Method of Accounting

Under the accrual method of accounting, businesses generally report income in the tax year during which they earn the income, regardless of when they receive payment for it. They also deduct expenses in the tax year during which they incur the expenses, regardless of when the expenses are paid. Although the accrual method of accounting does not give businesses as much control over the year in which income and expenses must be taken into account, it still provides some limited flexibility. For example, a business using the accrual method of accounting can defer receipt of income to a subsequent tax year by delaying the shipment of goods to its customers.

.01 Accounting for Income

Under the accrual method, taxpayers include income on their tax returns for the tax year during which all events have occurred to fix their right to receive the income and the amount of the income becomes determinable with reasonable accuracy. This is referred to as the **all-events test.** Under the accrual method, it is not the actual or constructive receipt of income, but the right to receive income, that governs the timing of when income must be included in gross income. Taxpayers have a fixed right to receive income when *any* one of the following events occurs:

1. Required performance is completed,
2. Payment of the income becomes due, or
3. Payment is received.

---

[45] Code Sec. 461(g)(2)., Rev. Rul. 87-22, 1987-1 CB 146.
[46] Code Secs. 263 and 168.

[47] Code Sec. 263A.

Example 47: Capelli Architects uses the accrual method and a calendar year as its tax year. Capelli performs architectural services for a customer and bills the customer $3,000 on December 20, 2009. It receives payment from the customer on January 19, 2010. Although the company did not receive actual payment from the customer during 2009, it must include the $3,000 in its gross income for that year because all events occurred to fix the company's right to receive the income and the amount of the income became determinable with reasonable accuracy during 2009.

Example 48: Sluman Steel, Inc. is an accrual method taxpayer that uses a calendar year as its tax year. On December 23, 2009, Sluman sells steel to a customer for $100,000, but it does not bill the customer for the purchase until January 2, 2010. The customer pays the company's invoice on February 1, 2010. Sluman must include the $100,000 in its gross income for 2009, the year it sold the steel because that is when it had a fixed right to receive the income.

Although a taxpayer has a fixed right to receive income, the income need not be included in the taxpayer's gross income if there is a reasonable expectancy that the claim will not be paid.[48]

Advance receipt of payments for services. As a rule, advance payments received for services to be performed in a future tax year (or tax years) are included in the accrual method taxpayer's gross income in the year the payments are received. However, taxpayers may defer all or a portion of an advance payment for services beyond the current tax year if they include advance payments for services in whole or in part in their revenues for a subsequent tax year for financial statement purposes.[49]

Taxpayers who choose to use the deferral method must report advance payments for services in their gross income for the tax year that corresponds to the tax year in which they report the income on their financial statements.[50] Inclusion in gross income of any portion of an advance payment may not be postponed beyond the tax year following the year the advance payment is received, even though some services are performed after that tax year. This special rule does not apply to advance payments for interest because interest must be included in gross income in the year it is received, regardless of the taxpayer's method of accounting.

Example 49: DeSanto Musical Instruments is an accrual method taxpayer that uses a calendar year as its tax year. DeSanto offers lessons and has chosen to use the deferral method to report advance payments for its lessons. On November 1, 2009, the company received an advance payment of $1,200 for 48 music lessons. It provided eight lessons in 2009 and 40 lessons in 2010. In its applicable financial statement, it includes $200 ($1,200/48 × 8) of the advance payment in its revenues for 2009. It includes $1,000 ($1,200/48 × 40) of the advance payment in its revenues for 2010. For federal income tax purposes, it must include $200 of the advance payment in its gross income for 2009 and the remaining $1,000 of the advance payment in its gross income for 2010.

Example 50: Zedd Appliance Repairs is an accrual method taxpayer that uses a calendar year as its tax year. Zedd has chosen to use the deferral method to report advance payments for services. In 2009, Zedd receives $200 for a two-year contract under which it agrees to repair a customer's television set should any problems arise. In its applicable financial statement, it recognizes one-fourth of the payment in its revenues for 2009, one-half of the payment in its revenues for 2010, and the remaining one-fourth in its revenues for 2011. For federal income tax purposes, it must include $50 ($200 × ¼) in gross income for 2009 and the remaining $150 ($200 × ¾) in gross income for 2010. Although it actually will earn $50 ($200 × ¼) of the advance payment in 2011, it cannot delay paying taxes on the advanced payment beyond 2010 (the next tax year).

---

[48] *The Corn Exchange Bank*, CA-2, 2 USTC ¶ 455, 37 F2d 34; *M. Suffolk*, 40 BTA 1121, Dec. 10,925.

[49] Rev. Proc. 2004-34, 2004-1 CB 991.

[50] Rev. Proc. 2004-34, 2004-1 CB 991.

GAAP vs. Code: For financial reporting purposes, Zedd from Example 50 would recognize the $200 over three years as it earned the income. For tax purposes, the income is recognized over two years. This difference in the treatment of prepaid income for financial accounting and tax accounting purposes will result in a difference between Zedd's net income and taxable income in both 2010 and 2011.

Advance receipt of payments for sales of goods. As a rule, advance payments are included in gross income in the year they are received. However, an accrual method taxpayer can wait to recognize income from advance payments from the sale of goods as long as it accounts for the sale using the same method for financial and tax accounting purposes.[51] Under this alternative method of reporting, an advance payment is included in a taxpayer's gross receipts on the *earlier* of:

1. The tax year in which the payments are included in gross income under the accrual method of accounting, or

2. The tax year in which the taxpayer includes any portion of the advance payments in income for financial reporting purposes.

Example 51: Mahl Shoes, Inc. is a retailer that uses the accrual method of accounting and the calendar year as its tax year. On December 15, 2009, the company sells some shoes and receives an advance payment of $200. The shoes are shipped on January 2, 2010. Normally Mahl would include the $200 in gross income for 2009. However, if the company accounts for sales of goods when they are shipped for both tax and financial reporting purposes, under the alternative method, Mahl may include the $200 in gross receipts for 2010 (the year during which the goods were shipped).

 Planning Pointer: If it would benefit the business to delay receipt of income to the subsequent tax year, the business should consider taking advantage of the rules regarding when its right to income becomes fixed. For example, if income is accrued at the time goods are shipped, the business should consider delaying shipments to the next tax year. If income is accrued when title to goods changes, the business should consider shipping F.O.B. (free on board) destination.

Contested amounts. An accrual method business is not required to include in gross receipts amounts accrued but being contested. In such situations, the taxpayer recognizes gross income when the contested amounts are received.[52]

.02 Accounting for Expenses

Taxpayers using the accrual method of accounting may deduct or capitalize a business expense when the all-events test has been satisfied and economic performance has occurred with respect to the liability. The all-events test is satisfied when all events have occurred to establish the existence of the liability and the amount of the liability can be determined with reasonable accuracy.

Example 52: Berdin Tape, which uses as its tax year a fiscal year ending on September 30, purchases equipment on September 30 but does not pay for the equipment until December 1. Because the company uses the accrual method of accounting, it may capitalize the equipment and begin depreciating it in the tax year of the purchase. It need not wait until the year it pays for the equipment.

---

[51] Reg. § 1.451-5.

[52] *Burnet v. Sanford & Brooks Company*, SCt, 2 USTC ¶ 636, 282 US 359, 51 SCt 150 (1931).

Economic performance. The tax laws provide various principles to be used to determine when economic performance occurs.[53] In the case of interest, economic performance occurs as the interest economically accrues daily (as the borrower uses the borrowed funds), not as payments are made. When the taxpayer's liability arises from another party providing services or property to the taxpayer, economic performance occurs as the property or services are provided. If a taxpayer's liability arises out of the use of property by the taxpayer, economic performance occurs ratably over the period of time the taxpayer is entitled to the use of the property. When the taxpayer's liability requires the taxpayer to provide services or the use of property to another person, economic performance occurs as the taxpayer provides the services or the use of property.

Reason for the Rule: The requirement that economic performance must occur before all events establishing the existence of a liability will be considered to have occurred was added by the Tax Reform Act of 1984 to take into account the time value of money.[54] As Congress noted, permitting accrual method taxpayers to currently deduct expenses that are attributable to activities to be performed or amounts to be paid in the future overstates the true cost of the expense and causes revenue loss to the government (particularly in high inflationary times).

Recurring item exception. Under the "recurring item exception" to the economic performance requirement, a business can treat a liability as incurred for a tax year if the all-events test is met *and* the following requirements are satisfied:

1. Economic performance with respect to the liability occurs on or before the date the taxpayer files a timely (including extensions) return for that tax year or, if sooner, 8½ months after the close of the tax year.

2. The liability is recurring in nature and the taxpayer consistently treats similar liabilities as incurred in the tax year during which the all-events test is satisfied. A liability is recurring if it can generally be expected to be incurred from one tax year to the next. However, it need not actually be incurred by the taxpayer each year. A liability never previously incurred by a taxpayer may be treated as recurring if it is reasonable to expect that the liability will be incurred on a recurring basis in the future.

3. The amount of the liability is not material or accruing the liability for that tax year would result in a better matching of the liability with the income to which it relates than would result from accruing the liability for the tax year in which economic performance occurs.

To determine whether a liability is "material," the amount of the liability in absolute terms and in relation to the amount of other items of income and expense attributable to the same activity must be considered. A liability is material if it is material for financial statement purposes under GAAP. However, a liability that is immaterial for financial statement purposes under GAAP nevertheless may be material for tax purposes.[55]

Certain liabilities never qualify for the recurring item exception. Specifically, the regulations require that for the following situations, economic performance cannot be satisfied until the liability is paid:[56]

- Liabilities arising under a workers' compensation act or out of any tort, breach of contract, or violation of law;
- Rebates and refunds;
- Awards, prizes, and jackpots;
- Insurance, warranties, and service contracts; and

---

[53] Code Sec. 461(h).

[54] House Ways and Means Committee Report No. 98-432 (October 21, 1983, and March 5, 1984), at 917.

[55] Reg. § 1.461-5(b).

[56] Reg. §§ 1.461-4(g)(2)-(6) and 1.461-5(c).

- Taxes (except for real property taxes, if a taxpayer has elected to accrue the taxes ratably, and foreign income taxes).

Example 53: Digital Video Recorders is an accrual method taxpayer that uses the calendar year as its tax year. Digital offers customers a refund if they are not satisfied with their products. During 2009, 100 customers request a refund of the $500 purchase price. Digital refunds $30,000 on or before September 15, 2010, the extended due date for its 2009 tax return. It refunds the remaining $20,000 after September 15, 2010. If Digital adopts the recurring item exception with respect to these refunds, economic performance will be treated as having occurred in 2009 with respect to the $30,000 refunded on or before September 15, 2010. Economic performance will not be treated as having occurred with respect to the $20,000 refunded after September 15. That amount is not eligible for recurring item treatment because the refund occurred more than 8½ months after the end of the 2009 tax year.

Prepaid expenses. Unless the 12-month rule applies, prepaid expenses must be capitalized and amortized over the period covered by the payment. If the 12-month rule applies, a business deducts the amount of prepaid expenses in the year paid. The 12-month rule applies if the amount paid creates (or facilitates the creation of) any right or benefit for the taxpayer that does not extend beyond the *earlier* of (1) 12 months after the first date on which the taxpayer realizes the right or benefit or (2) the end of the tax year following the tax year in which the payment is made. This is the same 12-month rule that applies to taxpayers using the cash method of accounting (see ¶ 306.02).

Example 54: On November 1, 2009, Shatran Ticket Brokers, an accrual method taxpayer using the calendar year as its tax year, pays $72,000 for a two-year lease of office space. Shatran cannot deduct the entire $72,000 in 2009 but instead must amortize the $72,000 over the two-year lease term. For each month during the year that it occupies the office space, the company may deduct $3,000 ($72,000/24). Therefore, it can deduct $6,000 for 2009 ($3,000 × 2 months), $36,000 for 2010 ($3,000 × 12), and $30,000 for 2011 ($3,000 × 10).

Example 55: Babjeck Traders is an accrual method, calendar year taxpayer. On November 1, 2009, Babjeck pays the $2,000 annual premium for a property insurance policy effective November 15, 2009, to November 14, 2010. Because the benefit (the insurance coverage) attributable to the $2,000 does not extend beyond the *earlier* of November 15, 2010, or the end of 2010, Babjeck deducts the entire $2,000 in 2009.

Example 56: Danville Tubing is an accrual method, calendar year taxpayer. On December 27, 2009, Danville pays its $2,190 annual premium for a property insurance policy effective January 5, 2010, to January 4, 2011. Because the benefit (insurance coverage) attributable to the $2,190 payment extends beyond December 31, 2010 (the tax year following the tax year in which the payment was made), the company cannot deduct the payment in 2009 but instead must capitalize the payment. For each day of coverage during the year, it may deduct $6 ($2,190/365). Therefore, it deducts $0 for 2009, but it can deduct $2,166 in 2010 ($6 × 361) and $24 ($6 × 4) in 2011.

Expenses owed to a related party. When amounts are accrued to related parties, the tax laws require that the accrual method taxpayer postpone the timing of the deduction until the cash method recipient includes the amount in income.[57] This rule continues to apply even after a taxpayer's relationship with a person has ended. It ensures that the amount reported in income by the recipient and the deduction taken by the payer are accounted for at the same time.

Example 57: The employee of a corporation (who is also a shareholder) uses a calendar year as its tax year and the cash method of accounting. The corporation also uses a calendar year-end, but it uses the accrual method of accounting. If, in December 2009, the

---

[57] Code Sec. 267(a)(2).

corporation declares a $50,000 bonus to be paid to the employee in January 2010, the corporation normally would deduct the compensation incurred in December on its 2009 income tax return, and that would reduce the corporation's 2009 income tax liability. The cash method shareholder, however, will not include the $50,000 in income until 2010, and accordingly, the government will not receive the taxes due on that amount for an entire year. However, if the employee/shareholder and the corporation are related parties, then the corporation must wait until 2010 to take the deduction.

Whether the two parties are related is determined as of the close of the tax year for which the expense otherwise could be deducted. Figure 3-1 summarizes the relationships involving business entities that are considered related parties for purposes of this special rule. The rules regarding what relationships constitute a "related party" are discussed in Chapter 8 (see ¶ 804).

Figure 3-1 Related Parties

1. An individual and the individual's spouse, siblings, ancestors (parents, grandparents, etc.), or descendants (children, grandchildren, etc.);

2. An individual and a corporation in which the individual *directly or indirectly* owns more than 50 percent of the value of its outstanding stock;

3. An individual and a partnership in which the individual *directly or indirectly* owns more than 50 percent of the capital or profits interest;

4. Two corporations that are members of the same controlled group (in which one corporation owns at least 80 percent of both the voting shares and the value of the other corporation's stock);

5. A corporation and a partnership if the same person(s) own more than 50 percent of the outstanding value of the stock in the corporation and more than 50 percent of the capital or profits interests in the partnership;.

6. An S corporation and another S corporation if the same person(s) own more than 50 percent of the value in the outstanding stock of each corporation;

7. An S corporation and a C corporation if the same person(s) own more than 50 percent of the value in the outstanding stock of each corporation; and

8. Two partnerships in which the same persons *directly or indirectly* own more than 50 percent of the capital or profits interest.

Reason for the Rule: This rule prevents an accrual method business from claiming a deduction for an accrued expense that the related cash method taxpayer is not required to include in gross income until some subsequent time, if at all.[58] If in Example 57, the employee were also the sole shareholder of the corporation, the corporation and the shareholder would be related parties. The tax laws would delay the corporation's deduction of the bonus until 2008—the year the shareholder includes it in gross income. This will allow the government to receive the tax revenues from the employee's income in the same year that it provides a tax benefit to the corporation.

Contested liabilities. A business that transfers money or other property in satisfaction of a liability that it is contesting is allowed to take a deduction for the tax year in which the amount is

---

[58] House Ways and Means Committee Report 98-432 (October 21, 1983, and March 5, 1984), at 1578.

paid.[59] To take the deduction, the money or other property used to satisfy the asserted liability must be transferred beyond the taxpayer's control. It is not sufficient that the taxpayer transfer money or other property to an escrow agent or purchase a bond to guarantee payment.

If a business takes a deduction for a contested liability in the year that money or other property is transferred in satisfaction of the liability and a portion of the contested liability is recovered after the contest is settled, the business must include the recovered amount in gross income for the year of the settlement. See ¶ 313 for further discussion of the tax benefit rule.

Example 58: Medlock Vending is an accrual method taxpayer that uses the calendar year as its tax year. In 2009 Medlock pays a $10,000 real property tax bill that it receives but contests $500 of the amount owed. In 2011, the contest is settled and Medlock receives a $100 refund. Medlock deducts the $10,000 it paid in 2009 but must include the $100 refund in its gross income for 2011.

 Reason for the Rule: This provision was added to the Code by the Revenue Act of 1964 to reverse a 1961 U.S. Supreme Court decision holding that a contested amount could not be deducted until the contest terminated because all of the events that would determine whether the amount ultimately would have to be paid could not be determined until that time.[60] Congress believed that taxpayers should not be denied a deduction with respect to an item when payment actually has been made, even though the liability is still being contested.

¶ 308 Hybrid Method of Accounting

A business is not limited to either the cash or the accrual method of accounting. Instead, a business generally can use a combination of accounting methods if the combination clearly reflects its income and is consistently used.[61] For example, a taxpayer could use the accrual method to account for its purchases and sales of goods and the cash method to report all other items. This, of course, assumes that the tax law does not require the taxpayer to use the accrual method as its overall method of accounting (see ¶ 305.01). Furthermore, there are limitations on the combinations that a business may use.

For example, if a business is required to maintain an inventory to account for its income, it must use the accrual method to account for its purchases and sales. The business, however, may be allowed to use the cash method of accounting for all other items of income and expenses. A business that uses the cash method of accounting for reporting its income must use the cash method of accounting for reporting its expenses. Similarly, a business that uses the accrual method of accounting for reporting its expenses must use the accrual method for reporting its income. Finally, if a combination of accounting methods includes any special methods of accounting, the business must comply with the requirements relating to such special methods. (See ¶ 309.)

¶ 309 Special Accounting Methods

As previously mentioned in the chapter, special methods of accounting may apply to certain items of income and expense. These items include installment sales, long-term contracts, research and experimental expenditures, crops, and soil and water conservation expenditures. Each of these special methods is discussed in the sections that follow. When applicable, taxpayers must abide by these special rules, regardless of the overall method of accounting (cash, accrual, hybrid) they use.

---

[59] Code Sec. 461(t).

[60] Senate Finance Committee Report No. 88-830 (January 28, 1964), 1964 U.S. Code Congressional & Administrative News, at 1773.

[61] Reg. § 1.446-1(c)(1)(iv).

.01 Installment Method of Accounting

If a business disposes of property and at least one payment is received after the close of the tax year during which the disposal occurred, the business reports the gain from the sale using the **installment method** of accounting.[62] Under the installment method, gain is recognized as the payments are received rather than at the time the sale occurs. This is consistent with the "wherewithal-to-pay concept" introduced in Chapter 1 (see ¶ 104.07), which is based on the premise that the taxpayer's ability to pay taxes on income and gain is greatest at the time the cash becomes available.

The installment method more closely resembles the cash method of accounting because income is recognized as the cash is received. However, unless the taxpayer elects out of the installment method, this method must be used to recognize income from installment sales, regardless of the taxpayer's overall accounting method. When the taxpayer elects out of using the installment method, the entire gain is recognized in the year of the sale. This method more closely resembles the accrual method of accounting.

Under the installment method, the amount of gain recognized for a tax year is computed by multiplying the amount of payments received during the year by a fraction in which the numerator is the seller's gross profit from the sale and in which the denominator is the total contract price. Further details regarding the installment method are provided in Chapter 8 (see ¶ 810).

Example 59: Racket Accessories sells land on October 10, 2009. The terms of the sale require that equal payments are to be received over five years. The total contract price is $50,000, and the company's gross profit from the sale is $40,000. Thus, under the installment method, for every dollar of proceeds that Racket receives, 80 percent ($40,000/$50,000) represents gross profit from the sale. If Racket's payments during 2009 total $3,000, then under the installment method, Racket includes $2,400 of the gain in gross income in 2009 ($3,000 × 80%). If it receives $10,000 in 2010, it includes $8,000 in gross income in 2010 ($10,000 × 80%). If Racket elects out of using the installment method, it will report the entire $10,000 of gain on its 2009 tax return. Electing out of the installment method would be consistent with the accrual method of accounting, as the earnings process is completed in 2009 at the time of the sale.

 GAAP vs. Code: The installment method operates under the wherewithal-to-pay concept, in which the taxpayer's ability to pay tax on the gain is greatest when it receives the cash. Under the accrual method of accounting, the entire gain would be recorded in the year of the sale, as that is when the earnings process is complete. Accordingly, the installment method is not an acceptable method for financial accounting purposes. Businesses that do not elect out of the installment method will include different amounts of income from the sale in net income versus taxable income, not only in the year of the sale, but for all subsequent periods in which the cash is received.

.02 Long-Term Contracts

Businesses are required to use a special method of accounting to report income from long-term contracts, regardless of the overall method of accounting they have chosen.[63] Usually the method that businesses are required to use is the percentage of completion method. However, under limited circumstances a business may use the completed contract method. Under the completed contract method, income from the project is postponed until the tax year in which it is completed. For tax purposes, a contract is a "long-term contract" if it satisfies each of the following three requirements:

---

[62] Code Sec. 453.   [63] Code Sec. 460.

1. It is a contract for the manufacture, building, installation, or construction of property;
2. It will not be completed within the contracting year; and
3. If it is a contract for the manufacture of property, it must involve personal property that is a unique item not normally carried in the taxpayer's inventory or an item that normally requires more than 12 calendar months to complete.

Percentage of completion method. Under the **percentage of completion method (PCM),** taxpayers include in gross income each year the portion of the total contract price that corresponds to the percentage of the contract that they completed during the year. That amount is determined by multiplying the total contract price by the percentage of the total *estimated* contract costs that the taxpayer incurs during the tax year.

Example 60: Page Contracting is in the process of constructing an office building. The total contract price is $5 million, and Page estimates its total contract costs will be $3 million. During the first tax year, Page incurs $750,000 of contract costs. Since this amount represents 25 percent of the total estimated contract costs ($750,000/$3,000,000), it must include 25 percent of the contract price in its gross income. Thus, Page includes $1.25 million ($5,000,000 × 25%) in its gross income for the first year. From this amount, Page deducts the $750,000 of costs it incurs during the year. Thus, only $500,000 ($1,250,000 – $750,000) will increase Page's taxable income in the first year.

For tax purposes, businesses may elect not to include in their gross income any amount from a long-term contract until they have incurred at least 10 percent of the estimated total contract costs. An election is made on a business's original federal income tax return for the year of the election. An election applies to all long-term contracts entered into during and after the election year.[64]

Example 61: Steele Contracting is constructing a retail store. The total contract price is $3 million, and Steele estimates its total contract costs will be $1.5 million. During 20X0, its first year working on the contract, Steele incurs $125,000 of contract costs. Because the amount of costs incurred is less than 10 percent of the estimated total contract costs ($1,500,000 × 10% = $150,000), the company may elect not to include any amount from the contract in its gross income for 20X0. If Steele makes such an election and incurs an additional $375,000 of contract costs during 20X1, the amount it includes in its gross income for 20X1 must be based on the percentage of total contract costs incurred not only for the current year, but for 20X0 as well. Thus, in 20X1, Steele is considered to have incurred $500,000 of contract costs ($125,000 + $375,000). Since this amount represents one-third of the total contract costs ($500,000/$1,500,000), Steele must report one-third of the $3 million, or $1 million, of the contract price in gross income for 20X1. From this amount, Steele can deduct the $500,000 of contract costs incurred thus far on the contract.

 GAAP vs. Code: Unlike the Code, which permits businesses to use the completed contract method of accounting only in limited circumstances, GAAP permits businesses to use the PCM only if certain conditions are met. Consequently, there likely will be a difference between net income and taxable income when a corporation enters into a long-term contract. This difference will occur for all years during the contract period.

After a business completes a long-term contract using the PCM, it is required to go back to all prior tax years and reapply the PCM using its *actual total contract price* and its *actual contract costs.* This process is referred to as the "lookback method." The taxpayer must then pay interest on any amount of tax that was deferred because it underestimated the total contract price or overestimated total contract costs. It is entitled to receive interest on any extra tax that it paid because it

---

[64] Code Sec. 460(b)(5) and Reg. §1.460-4(b)(6).

overestimated the total contract price or underestimated total contract costs. The rate of interest for both underpayments and overpayments is the same interest rate the IRS pays taxpayers for overpayments of federal income tax. However, the lookback method does not correct for differences in tax liability resulting from tax rates changing during the term of the contract.[65]

Example 62: Destine Contractors is a cash method taxpayer that uses the calendar year as its tax year. In 2009, the company enters into a contract to construct an apartment building. The total contract price is $2 million. Destine estimates that its total contract costs will be $1 million. During 2009, it incurs $300,000 of contract costs. This represents 30 percent of its estimated contract costs; therefore, the amount that Destine includes in gross income for 2009 is $600,000 ($2,000,000 × 30%). Destine offsets its gross income by the $300,000 of contract costs incurred during the year.

During 2010, Destine incurs $450,000 of contract costs, which represents another 45 percent of its estimated total costs. Thus, in 2010, Destine will report $900,000 in gross income ($2,000,000 × 45%). It will offset its gross income by the $450,000 of contract costs incurred during 2010. During 2011, the company incurs $750,000 of contract costs to complete its construction of the apartment building. For 2011, it must include all amounts not previously included in gross income, or $500,000 ($2,000,000 − $600,000 − $900,000). It then must apply the lookback method to determine how much tax it over- or underpaid in 2009 and 2010.

Using its actual costs ($1.5 million), the company calculates that in 2009 it should have included 20 percent of the contract price in gross income ($300,000/$1,500,000). Thus, its 2009 gross income should have been $400,000 ($2,000,000 × 20%). In 2010, Destine would have included 30 percent ($450,000/$1,500,000) of the $2 million in gross income. Net income (gross income − contract costs) reported using the estimated contract price and costs, and net income reported using the actual price and costs are summarized below.

Year	Using Estimates	Using Actual Amounts	Overpayment
2009	$300,000	$100,000	$200,000
2010	450,000	150,000	300,000

Because of these overpayments, Destine overpaid taxes on $200,000 of income in 2009 and on $300,000 of income in 2010. If Destine's marginal tax rate is 34 percent in each of those years, it would have overpaid $170,000 in taxes ($500,000 × 34%). Destine is owed back interest on the overpayment of the taxes.

The lookback method is not required for any long-term contract completed within two years of the contract commencement date if the actual gross contract price does not exceed the *lesser* of $1 million or one percent of the taxpayer's average annual gross receipts for the three tax years preceding the tax year in which the contract was completed. In addition, taxpayers may elect not to apply the lookback method if their cumulative taxable income (or loss) under a contract as of the close of each prior contract year is within 10 percent of the cumulative lookback income (or loss) under the contract as of the close of that prior contract year.[66]

 Reason for the Rule: Congress requires that variances between the estimated and actual completion during each year of the contract be accounted for at the end of the contract through an interest charge or credit to the taxpayer. Congress does this because it recognizes that the use of the PCM may produce harsh results for taxpayers

---

[65] Reg. § 1.460-6.   [66] Code Sec. 460(b)(3)(B).

in some cases. For example, this can occur when the taxpayer has an overall loss on the contract or actual profits are significantly less than projected.[67]

Completed contract method. The PCM is not required for certain types of contracts. Instead, the income from these contrasts can be recognized either under the PCM or under the completed contract method. Under the **completed contract method**, no income or expenses related to the contract are recognized until the contract is completed. The types of contracts that are not required to use the PCM include exempt construction contracts and residential construction contracts.

A contract is an "exempt construction contract" if it is a home construction contract or another type of construction contract that the taxpayer estimates will be completed within two years, but only if the taxpayer's average annual gross receipts for the three tax years preceding the contracting year do not exceed $10 million. A long-term construction contract is a "home construction contract" if a taxpayer reasonably expects to attribute 80 percent or more of the estimated total allocable contract costs to (1) the construction of dwelling units in buildings containing four or fewer dwelling units and (2) improvements to real property directly related to, and located at the site of, the dwelling units. A "residential construction contract" is a home construction contract, except that the building or buildings constructed contain more than four dwelling units.[68] A "dwelling unit" is a home or apartment to provide living accomodations. It does not include a unit in a hotel, motel, or other establishment when more than half of the units are used on a transient basis.[69] "Allocable contract costs" include the cost of land, materials, and services as determined as of the close of the contracting year.

Example 63: On June 1, 20X1, Davidson Construction enters into a contract with Gina Kelsey to build a restaurant for $500,000. The estimated total costs for the contract are $400,000. On March 31, 20X2, the contract is completed, and Gina accepts the building. As of December 31, 20X1, Davidson incurred $370,000 of job costs tied to the contract. From January 1 to March 31, 20X2, another $30,000 of job costs were incurred. Using the completed contract method, Davidson must capitalize all the job costs related to the restaurant contract and wait to deduct them until the job is completed, which is the same time the income is reported in 20X2. As a result, Davidson's 20X2 taxable income will increase by $100,000 ($500,000 – $400,000 total contract costs).

 Reason for the Rule: Prior to the Tax Reform Act of 1986, taxpayers could elect to account for income from long-term contracts under either the PCM or the completed contract method. Congress decided to restrict use of the completed contract method of accounting for long-term contracts because it believed that use of that method of accounting permitted an unwarranted deferral of the income from long-term contracts.[70]

.03 Research and Experimental Expenditures

When taxpayers incur research and experimental expenditures, they have the option to (1) capitalize the expenditures (and do nothing else), (2) capitalize and amortize (expense) the expenditures over 60 months, or (3) deduct them entirely in the current year.[71] The second option (to capitalize and amortize) most closely reflects how the expenses are treated under the accrual method of accounting. The third option most closely resembles how expenses are treated under the cash method. However, any of the three options is available to all taxpayers, regardless of whether

---

[67] Joint Committee on Taxation, *General Explanation of the Tax Reform Act of 1986*, at 527

[68] Code Sec. 460(e)(1) and (6).

[69] Code Sec. 168(e)(2)(A)(ii).

[70] Joint Committee on Taxation, *General Explanation of the Tax Reform Act of 1986*, at 527.

[71] Code Sec. 174.

the taxpayer uses the cash, accrual, or hybrid method as its overall method of accounting. Thus, even when a corporation is required to use the accrual method of accounting, it has the option of expensing its research and experimental expenditures in the year in which the costs are incurred. The tax treatment of research and experimental expenditures is discussed in detail in Chapter 5 (see ¶ 507).

Example 64: Miller Presses incurs $60,000 of research and experimental expenditures during the year. The company has the option of capitalizing the expenditures (and not deducting them), capitalizing and then amortizing the expenditures ratably over 60 months, or expensing the entire $60,000 in the current tax year. It is irrelevant which method Miller uses as its overall accounting method.

.04 Crop Method of Accounting

Under the crop method of accounting, if crops are not harvested and sold in the same year during which they were planted, the cost of producing the crop cannot be deducted until the year in which the farmer realizes the gross income from the crop.[72] The use of the crop method is elective and requires the IRS's consent. The advantage of using the crop method is that it permits a farmer to deduct expenses attributable to the planting and growing of the crops in the year income is realized from the crops, thereby reducing taxable income for that year. If elected, the crop method applies to account for inventories of crops, regardless of which accounting method the taxpayer uses as its overall accounting method.

Example 65: Duett Farms incurs $30,000 in costs to plant wheat during 2009. It harvests the wheat in 2009 but delays selling the wheat until 2010. If Duett elects (with the IRS's consent) to use the crop method of accounting, it deducts its $30,000 in costs in 2010, the year it sells the wheat.

.05 Soil and Water Conservation Expenditures

Taxpayers engaged in the business of farming may treat as capital expenditures any expenses they pay or incur during the year related to soil or water conservation or to prevention of erosion of farmland, or they may elect to take a current deduction for such expenditures.[73] However, the amount currently deducted cannot exceed 25 percent of a farmer's gross income from farming.

Example 66: Shadow Farms pays $15,000 to construct a terrace to stop soil erosion. Shadow can treat the $15,000 as a capital expenditure, or it can elect to currently deduct the $15,000 as a soil and water conservation expenditure. These two options are the only options available to Shadow, regardless of which accounting method it uses as its overall accounting method.

¶ 310 Adopting an Accounting Method

Businesses may choose any permissible method of accounting when they file their first tax return. Business owners are not required to use the same method of accounting to determine how to report their personal income and expenses and their business income and expenses. Taxpayers with separate and distinct businesses may use a different method of accounting for each business, provided that they keep separate books and records for each business.

If the IRS decides that a taxpayer's method of accounting does not clearly reflect the taxpayer's income and expenses, the IRS may compute the taxpayer's taxable income under a method of accounting that the IRS believes does clearly reflect the taxpayer's income and expenses. The IRS's exercise of its discretion will be upheld unless its decision clearly was unlawful or an abuse of its discretion.[74] The IRS may not require a taxpayer to change from a method of accounting that clearly

---

[72] Reg. § 1.162-12(a).
[73] Code Sec. 175.

[74] *Thor Power Tool Co.*, SCt, 79-1 USTC ¶ 9139, 439 US 522, 99 SCt 773.

reflects the taxpayer's taxable income merely because a different method more clearly reflects the taxpayer's taxable income.[75]

¶ 311 Changing an Accounting Method

Once a business has selected a method of accounting, it may change that method of accounting only with the consent of the IRS.[76] Consent from the IRS must be obtained before a taxpayer can change from an impermissible to a permissible method of accounting. Taxpayers file Form 3115, *Application for Change in Accounting Method*, to request the IRS's consent to a change in method of accounting. Before the IRS will consent to a change, it will require the business to agree to terms and conditions intended to prevent any substantial distortion of income that otherwise would result from the change.

> **Planning Pointer:** Form 3115 must be filed during the year for which a change is desired and should be filed as early during the year as possible to give the IRS time to consider the request before the taxpayer's tax return for the year of the change is due. Unless the taxpayer is eligible to receive an automatic change (see ¶ 311.01 below), the IRS will charge the taxpayer a user fee.

.01 Automatic Changes

A business that complies with the applicable provisions of Rev. Proc. 2008-52[77] (as modified by certain subsequent revenue procedures) will be deemed to have obtained the IRS's consent to change its method of accounting, and accordingly, will not be required to pay a user fee for requesting a change. The Appendix to Rev. Proc. 2008-52 describes the accounting method changes that may be made using the automatic change request procedures and explains the terms and conditions that must be satisfied for each change. Form 3115 usually must be filed with a taxpayer's income tax return to request an automatic change. A list of the automatic changes for which Form 3115 must be filed is included in the instructions for that form. Approval of the change will be granted for the tax year for which a change is requested.

¶ 312 Claim of Right Doctrine

Under the **claim of right doctrine**, a business that receives money or other property under a "claim of right" (i.e., treats the property as its own) without restriction as to the disposition of the property must include the amount of money or the FMV of the property received in gross income for the year of receipt, regardless of the taxpayer's overall method of accounting. The amount of money or FMV of the property received must be included in gross income even though the business may not be entitled to keep the money or property and will be required to refund the money or property in a subsequent tax year. For the claim of right doctrine to apply, each of the following requirements must be satisfied:

1. The business must receive cash or other property,

2. The cash or other property must constitute income for the business under its method of accounting,

3. The business must have unrestricted control over the use and disposition of the cash or other property received, and

4. The business must possess the cash or other property under a claim of right.

Example 67: Scoundrels, Inc. creates a Web page that duplicates the Web page of a bank and encourages visitors to the site to provide the company with financial and personal

---

[75] *Wolf Bakery & Cafeteria Co.*, 5 TCM 389, Dec. 15,186(M); *H.L. Russell*, CA-1, 2 USTC ¶ 617, 45 F2d 100.

[76] Code Sec. 446(e).

[77] 2008-2 CB 587.

information. Scoundrels illegally obtains $500,000 from unsuspecting persons. Although the $500,000 was obtained through illegal actions, Scoundrels must include that amount in its gross income for the year under the claim of right doctrine.

> **Reason for the Rule:** The rule was adopted because the federal government did not want to wait to tax income until all disputes regarding the recipient's right to the income have been resolved.

A business that is required to refund an amount previously included in its gross income is entitled to a deduction for the amount refunded. However, because of the progressive nature of the federal income tax rates, the tax benefit of the deduction may not be as great as the tax cost of the income initially received. To mitigate this problem, taxpayers are entitled to reduce their tax liability for the year of repayment by the amount of the tax attributable to the inclusion of the item in gross income.[78] However, this mitigation rule applies only to deductions that exceed $3,000.

Example 68: Farmington Water Filtration is an accrual method taxpayer that uses the calendar year as its tax year. In 2009 Farmington's natural gas supplier gave Farmington a $5,000 refund. Because the claim of right doctrine applies, Farmington includes the refund in its gross income for 2009. However, in 2011 the natural gas supplier discovers that it made a mistake in making the refund and demands that the money be returned. Farmington deducts the $5,000 it returns to its natural gas supplier in 2011.

Example 69: Continuing with Example 68, in 2009 when Farmington includes the $5,000 in its gross income, its marginal income tax rate is 39 percent. This results in an additional payment of taxes of $1,950 ($5,000 × 39%) in that year. When it deducts the $5,000 in 2011, Farmington's marginal income tax rate is 25 percent, which results in a tax savings equal to $1,250 ($5,000 × 25%). The difference between the tax increase in 2009 and the taxes saved in 2011 is $700 ($1,950 − $1,250). However, because the amount of the deduction exceeds $3,000, Farmington can reduce its 2011 tax liability by the same $1,950 that it paid on the $5,000 in 2009. If its deduction did not exceed $3,000, the company would not have been able to recuperate the full amount of taxes the refund cost it in 2009.

¶ 313 Tax Benefit Rule

If a taxpayer deducts an expense for one tax year and later recovers all or a portion of the amount deducted, it must include the amount recovered in its gross income for the year the amount is recovered under the **tax benefit rule.** For this rule to apply, the taxpayer must have deducted an amount in a prior tax year that resulted in a tax benefit to the taxpayer.[79] Thus, none of the amount recovered is included in a taxpayer's gross income to the extent that the amount did not reduce the taxpayer's income tax liability in a prior tax year.[80]

Example 70: Kara Adhesives deducts $10,000 for real property tax that it paid in 2009. In 2011, the company receives a $500 refund of the real property tax that it paid in 2009. Under the tax benefit rule, the company includes that $500 in its gross income for 2011.

Example 71: Knipper Alarms deducts $1,000 as a bad debt expense in 2009. In 2010, it recovers $250 of the $1,000 it had been owed by the customer. Under the tax benefit rule, the company includes the $250 in its gross income for 2010.

Example 72: Assume the same facts as in Example 71, except in 2009 Knipper Alarms reported a net operating loss and therefore reported no income tax liability in that year. Because

---

[78] Code Sec. 1341.
[79] Code Sec. 111.

[80] Code Sec. 111.

Knipper did not benefit from the deduction in 2009, it does not include the $250 in its 2010 gross income. Instead it reduces its net operating loss carryover from 2009 by $250 (see ¶ 1001).

 Reason for the Rule: The purpose of the tax benefit rule is to approximate the results produced by a tax system based on transactional rather than annual accounting and to protect the government and the taxpayer from the adverse effects of reporting a transaction on the basis of assumptions that an event in a subsequent year proves to have been erroneous.[81]

¶ 314 Summary

Tax accounting rules should be distinguished from financial accounting rules. Both sets of rules are used to determine when income and expenses must be recognized; however, they differ in their derivation and objectives. The goal of financial accounting rules that govern financial reporting is to require corporations to provide useful information for a business's management, owners, creditors, potential investors, and other interested parties. By contrast, the goal of Congress when enacting federal income tax legislation is to raise revenues for the federal government in an equitable manner, along with a variety of other secondary reasons discussed in Chapter 1 (see ¶ 106).

For businesses to be able to determine their taxable income, they need to know their tax year and method of accounting. C corporations have the flexibility of using a calendar year or a fiscal year. Personal service corporations and flow-through entities, such as S corporations and partnerships, generally are required to have the same tax year as their owners to prevent undue deferral of tax. However, some flexibility exists in cases in which the entity is willing to pay the tax effects of the deferral in advance or in cases in which a valid business purpose exists for using a different tax year.

Small businesses generally use the cash method of accounting (or a combination of the cash and accrual methods) to determine when and how they should report their income and expenses. Large businesses usually use the accrual method of accounting. These methods of accounting are referred to as "overall methods of accounting." Other "special" methods of accounting are used to report particular types of income and expenses. Part I of this book introduced taxation, the federal tax laws, and the rules regarding tax year and accounting method. Part II takes a closer look at how business profits are taxed.

GLOSSARY OF TERMS INTRODUCED IN THIS CHAPTER

Accrual method. Income is included in gross income when all events have occurred that fix the right to receive the item and its amount can be determined with reasonable accuracy. Expenses are deducted when all events have occurred that determine the liability exists, the amount of the liability can be determined with reasonable accuracy, and economic performance has occurred with respect to the liability.

All-events test. A test used to determine when an accrual method taxpayer has to report income and can deduct or capitalize an expense.

Calendar year. A tax year that begins January 1 and ends December 31.

---

[81] *Hillsboro National Bank*, SCt, 83-1 USTC ¶ 9229, 460 US 370, 103 SCt 1134.

Cash receipts and disbursements method. A method of accounting under which a business is required to recognize income when it is received and may deduct expenses when they are disbursed.

Claim of right doctrine. A rule that requires taxpayers that receive money or other property under a claim of right without restriction to include the amount received in gross income for the year of receipt, regardless of the taxpayer's method of accounting.

Completed contract method. A special method of accounting for long-term contracts in which no income or expenses related to the contract are recognized until the contract is completed.

Constructive receipt doctrine. A rule that requires cash method taxpayers to report gross income in the tax year during which amounts are credited to the business's account, set apart for the business, or otherwise made available without any substantial limitation or restriction. A business may be treated as having constructively received income even though it does not have actual possession of the income until after the end of the year.

Financial accounting. Rules used to determine how information, including income and expenses, should be reported on a business's financial statements.

Fiscal year. A tax year that ends on the last day of any month other than December.

Hybrid method. A method of accounting that combines elements of the cash and accrual methods of accounting. *See also* Accrual method *and* Cash receipts and disbursements method.

Installment method. A special method of accounting in which a taxpayer recognizes gain as the payments are received rather than at the time the sale occurs.

Method of accounting. The rules that govern when a business must recognize income and when it may deduct expenses. It refers not only to the overall method of accounting that a taxpayer uses but also to a taxpayer's accounting treatment of any particular item.

Percentage of completion method (PCM). A special method of accounting that applies to long-term contracts for which the taxpayer reports in gross income each year a portion of the total contract price that corresponds to the portion of the total estimated contract costs actually incurred during the year.

Points. Term used to describe the prepaid interest a lender charges in exchange for a lower interest rate to the borrower over the term of the loan.

Short tax year. A tax year lasting fewer than 12 months.

Tax accounting. Rules used to determine when income and expenses are recognized for tax purposes.

Tax benefit rule. A tax rule under which an amount recovered must be included in gross income for the year of the recovery if all or a portion of the expense deducted in a prior tax year is recovered in a subsequent tax year and if the deduction resulted in a tax benefit for the taxpayer.

Tax year. The period of time over which taxable income is reported to the government.

12-month rule. A tax law that allows taxpayers to deduct as prepaid expense in full in the year it is paid provided that it creates (or facilitates the creation of) any right or benefit that does not extend beyond the earlier of (1) 12 months after the first date any right or benefit is realized or (2) the end of the tax year that follows the tax year in which the payment was made.

CHAPTER PROBLEMS

The following questions and problems relate to the discussion in Chapter 3, Tax Accounting, which begins at ¶ 300 in *Part II: Federal Taxation of Business Income and Deductions.*

Chapter 3 Discussion Questions

1. How does tax accounting differ from financial accounting? *[handwritten: internal Reports, we for investors]*
2. What is a fiscal year?
3. What is a tax year?
4. What is a required tax year, and to whom does it apply?
5. Can businesses that have a required tax year use any other tax year?
6. Can a business change its tax year? If so, how?
7. Which types of C corporations are prohibited from using the cash method of accounting?
8. What is the general rule for accounting for income under the cash method of accounting?
9. What is the general rule for accounting for expenses under the cash method of accounting?
10. What is the constructive receipt of income doctrine?
11. Is there a constructive payment of income doctrine?
12. How does a cash method taxpayer treat the advance payment of expenses?
13. When must a business using an accrual method of accounting include an item of income in its gross income?
14. When may a business using an accrual method of accounting take an expense into account?
15. If an accrual method business receives an advance payment for the sale of an item that it sells in the ordinary course of its business, how can it account for the payment?
16. What is a hybrid method of accounting and what restrictions are placed on its use?
17. What is the claim of right doctrine?
18. What is the tax benefit doctrine?
19. How are businesses supposed to account for income from most types of long-term contracts for tax accounting purposes?
20. How can a business change its method of accounting?

Chapter 3 Problems

1. Eader Jewelry is a partnership with six partners. Carey Sirin, which uses the calendar year as its tax year, owns a 10-percent interest in the profits and capital of the partnership. Delsie Ayudan, a calendar year taxpayer, owns a 20-percent interest in the profits and capital of the partnership. Ronin Pens, Inc., which has a fiscal year ending on January 31, owns a 30-percent interest in the profits and capital of the partnership. Goggles, Inc., which has a fiscal year ending February 28, owns a 25-percent interest in the profits and capital of the partnership. Three other partners, each using the calendar year as its tax year, own a five-percent interest each in the profits and capital of the partnership. What is the partnership's majority interest tax year?

2. Yero is a calendar year taxpayer that uses the cash method of accounting. On December 25, 20X1, it receives a check for $1,000; the company deposits the check in its bank account on December 28. On December 31, it receives a check for $1,500 too late in the day to be able to deposit the check in its bank account. It deposits the check on January 2, 20X2. Based on these facts, how much must Yero include in its gross income for 20X1?

3. A calendar year taxpayer uses the cash method of accounting. The company sold display boxes to two customers on December 20, 2009. It billed one customer $100 on December 21, received payment on December 31, and cashed the check on January 2. It waited until

January 2 to bill the second customer $3,000 because it wanted to include the $3,000 in its gross income for 2010. The company received a check for $3,000 on January 20 and cashed it on January 21. Based on these facts, how much does the company include in its gross income for 2009?

4. Stolberg Dyes is a calendar year taxpayer that uses the cash method of accounting. The company sells merchandise to Emily Kezar on November 1, 2009. Emily mails a check for $1,500 to Stolberg on November 30, and the company cashes it on December 4. Instead of mailing a check for the remaining amount due by January 1, Emily delivers a $1,000 check to her neighbor, Benita Stolberg, who is the daughter of the owner of Stolberg. Benita does not work for her mother's company. Benita gives the check to her mother on January 1, the next time they see each other. Based on these facts, how much does Stolberg include in its gross income for 2009?

5. Beaushaw Services is a cash method taxpayer that uses the calendar year as its tax year. Beaushaw pays $10,000 for an advertisement by mailing a check to the advertising firm on December 28, 2009. The firm receives the check on January 4 and cashes it on January 5. Beaushaw pays $2,000 for shipping supplies on December 31 by using its credit card. It pays its credit card charge on February 8 when its next statement is due. Based on these facts, what amount does the company deduct as expenses for 2009?

6. Blackhurst Cribs is a cash method taxpayer that uses the calendar year as its tax year. In 2009 the company receives a $200 advance for a crib to be delivered in 2010. It also receives a $1,000 promissory note for five cribs that it delivers in 2009. Based on these facts, how much income must the company include in its gross income for 2009?

7. Assume the same facts as in Problem 6, except Blackhurst receives payments totaling $800 with respect to the promissory note in 2010. Based on these facts, how much income must the company include in its gross income for 2010?

8. Trana Transmission is a cash method taxpayer that uses the calendar year as its tax year. During 2009 Trana borrows $10,000 to pay for an advertisement to be run in 2010. It also executes a $5,000 promissory note to pay for repairs to its manufacturing plant that were made in 2009. Based on these facts, how much of these expenses can the company take into account for 2009?

9. Assume the same facts as in Problem 8, except Trana makes $4,000 of payments with respect to the promissory note and repays $5,000 of the amount borrowed in 2010. Based on these facts, how much of these expenses can the company take into account for 2010?

10. Shimko Kitchens and Baths, Inc. is an accrual method taxpayer that uses the calendar year as its tax year. In 2009 it agrees to refurbish a homeowner's kitchen for $100,000. It receives $50,000 in 2009, $40,000 in 2010, and $10,000 in 2011. It has no applicable financial statement for any of those years, but its records show that it completed 25 percent of its work in 2009, another 50 percent of its work in 2010, and the remaining 25 percent of its work in 2011. How much does Shimko include in its gross income for 2010 if it uses the deferral method to account for advance payments for services?

11. A cash method taxpayer uses the calendar tax year. On December 28, 2009, the company makes a $24,000 advance payment for a lease commencing January 12, 2010, and ending January 11, 2011. How much of the advance payment may the company deduct as an expense in 2009?

12. An accrual method taxpayer uses the calendar year as its tax year. On September 1, 2009, the company prepays $2,400 for its premium for a property insurance policy covering the period beginning September 1, 2009, and ending August 31, 2010. How much of this expense may the company deduct in 2009?

13. An accrual method taxpayer uses the calendar year as its tax year. On July 1, 2009, the company borrows $4.8 million to construct a new manufacturing plant. To obtain the loan, which was repayable over 12 years, it paid one point, which amounted to $48,000 ($4,800,000 × 1%). How much of the $48,000 can the company deduct for 2009?

14. Assume the same facts as in Problem 13, except the company is a cash method taxpayer and uses a calendar year as its tax year. How much of the $48,000 can it deduct in 2009?

15. Marran Caskets is an accrual method taxpayer that uses the calendar tax year. On December 1, 2009, the company agrees to refund $2,000 of the price of a casket. It pays the refund on January 5, 2010. On December 15, 2009, it has its roof repaired but does not pay the $1,000 invoice until January 4, 2010. Based on these facts, how much can Marran deduct for 2009?

16. Hyrkas Checks, Inc. is an accrual method taxpayer that uses the calendar year as its tax year. On November 1, 2009, it became liable for a $20,000 workers' compensation award, but it did not pay the award until 2010. On August 1, 2009, it rented printing equipment for one year at an annual rental of $2,000 per month. How much of these expenses can it deduct in 2009?

17. Wunderlin Color Prints is an accrual method taxpayer that uses the calendar year as its tax year. On December 1, 2009, Wunderlin hires Raphael Bacot for one day to consult on a project. Raphael owns 60 percent of the common stock of Wunderlin and is a cash method taxpayer using the calendar year. Raphael bills Wunderlin $1,000 in December 2009 but is not paid until 2010. On November 25, 2009, Wunderlin hires a partnership owned by the same persons who own Wunderlin to repair its printing equipment. The partnership, which uses the accrual method and a calendar year-end, bills Wunderlin $2,000 for its services but does not receive payment until 2010. How much of its expenses may Wunderlin deduct in 2009?

18. Copper Castings is a cash method taxpayer that uses the calendar year as its tax year. On December 20, 2009, Copper was overpaid $100 by one of its customers for one of its invoices. Copper did not discover the error until 2010. On December 21, 2009, one of its employees discovered that a wallet containing $200 had been left on the company's premises and turned it over to a person in charge of "lost and found." Consequently, Copper never treated the money as its own. How much of these amounts does the company have to include in its gross income for 2009?

19. Jakobson Processing, Inc. is an accrual method taxpayer that uses the calendar year as its tax year. In 2009, it included $15,000 in its gross income under the claim of right doctrine. In 2010, it refunded the $15,000. In 2009, its marginal income tax rate was 25 percent. In 2010, its marginal income tax rate was 15 percent. How much does the $15,000 reduce its tax liability for 2010?

20. Diwan Remodeling, Inc., which is an accrual method taxpayer using the calendar year as its tax year, is remodeling a suite of offices. The total contract price is $2 million. It estimates that its total contract costs will be $1.2 million. During 2009, Diwan incurs $300,000 of contract costs. During 2010, Diwan incurs $600,000 of contract costs. During 2011, Diwan Remodeling completes the project and incurs $100,000 of contract costs. How much income from the contract must it include in its gross income for 2009, 2010, and 2011?

21. Malloy Partnership has 15 partners who each own four percent of the partnership's capital and profits, one partner who owns 25 percent of the partnership's capital and profits, and one partner who owns 15 percent of the partnership's capital and profits. Twelve of the 15 partners who each own four percent of the partnership's capital and profits use the calendar year as their tax year; the other three use as their tax year a fiscal year ending August 31. The other two partners each use a fiscal year ending January 31. What is the required tax year for Malloy Partnership?

22. Lair Laquers, Inc., an S corporation, wants to establish May 1 through April 30 as its tax year. It had $200,000 in gross receipts from sales for the 12 month period ending April 30, 2009. Its gross receipts from sales during March and April 2009 totaled $60,000. It had $180,000 in gross receipts from sales for the 12-month period ending April 30, 2008. Its gross receipts from sales during March and April 2008 totaled $45,000. It had $150,000 in gross receipts from sales during the 12-month period ending April 30, 2007. Its gross

receipts from sales during March and April 2007 totaled $42,000. Does an April 30 year-end qualify as Lair Laquers' natural business year?

23. Williamson Plumbing, Inc. is a cash method taxpayer that uses the calendar year as its tax year. On December 28, 2009, it accepted a $200 payment by credit card for plumbing services it had performed. The payment was credited to Williamson on January 5, 2010. On December 15, 2009, Williamson also received free accounting services (worth $1,000) in exchange for plumbing work it did for an accountant on November 20, 2009. How much of these amounts does it have to include in its gross income for 2009?

24. Same facts as Problem 23 except that Williamson Plumbing is an accrual method taxpayer that uses the calendar year as its tax year. How much does it have to include in its gross income for 2009?

25. Oday Ornamental Shrubs, Inc. is a cash method taxpayer that uses the calendar year as its tax year. On December 20, 2009, Oday charged to its credit card $2,000 for an advertisement in a local newspaper that ran the first week of January, 2010. Oday did not pay the credit card bill until January 16, 2010. On December 1, 2009, Oday obtained a 15-year mortgage loan for its new store and paid $3,600 in point for the loan. What amount of these expenses can Oday deduct from its gross income in 2009?

Chapter 3 Review Problem

How does the 12-month tax year fit in with notions of what makes for a good tax?

Chapter 3 Research Question

Does an amount paid or incurred to remediate environmental contamination that occurred in prior tax years qualify for special treatment under Code Sec. 1341 as an amount held under a claim of right that was restored? See Rev. Rul. 2004-17, 2004-1 CB. What argument did the taxpayer use, and how did the IRS respond?

PART II:
Federal Taxation of Business Income and Deductions

CHAPTER 4

Federal Income Taxes and Gross Income

LEARNING OBJECTIVES

1. Describe how and on whom the government taxes the profits from a business.
2. List the components of the taxable income formula and explain how taxpayers compute the taxes owed (or refund due) at the end of the accounting period.
3. Explain the tax rules regarding how taxpayers pay the taxes they owe for the year.
4. Describe how income is determined and list the types of income the government taxes and the types of income it excludes from the definition of gross income.

¶ 400 Introduction

One of the consequences of a successful business is the requirement that profits be shared with the federal government in the form of federal income taxes. Depending upon which form of business entity is used to operate the business, the income taxes on profits can be taxed to the business entity itself, to the owners of the business, or sometimes to both. The profits of a business operated as a sole proprietorship are included on the owner's personal income tax return, along with any nonbusiness gross income and deductions the owner generates during the year. The profits of a business operated as a C corporation are taxed to the corporation when the profits are earned and again when the after-tax profits are distributed to the shareholders in the form of dividends. Businesses that operate as a partnership, an S corporation, or a limited liability company are separate entities, but the entity itself does not pay income taxes. Instead, the business passes through to its owners its items of gross income, gain, deductions, losses, and credits. The owners are then responsible for reporting the items on their own income tax returns. Consequently, such entities are often referred to as "flow-through" or "pass-through" entities.

For the most part, the rules regarding what types of income are taxed and what expenses can be deducted are the same for all types of taxpayers. However, because the individual income tax return includes not only business activities but also the taxpayer's personal activities, a number of exclusions and deductions are available only to individual taxpayers. For example, individuals are entitled to deduct various personal expenses in computing their taxable income.

The purpose of the chapter is to set the stage for the upcoming chapters in the textbook. It begins with an overview of the basic taxable income formula, which is the focus of the next five chapters. It also introduces how taxes are calculated and how taxpayers can use tax credits to reduce the taxes they owe. The rules regarding the required prepayment of taxes are also presented in this chapter. The chapter concludes with a discussion of the types of income the federal government taxes, and more important, the types of income it does not tax.

CALCULATING TAXABLE INCOME

The true success of a business can only be measured over a long period, which starts with its inception and ends with the dissolution of the business. However, when a business generates profits during its existence, the government requires that those profits be taxed and that the taxes be periodically remitted to the government. As discussed in Chapter 3, the typical accounting period is one year in length. Part of the rationale for artificially breaking up the business cycle into accounting periods is the "wherewithal-to-pay principal," which posits that the taxpayer's ability to pay tax on business profits is highest when the profits are realized.

¶ 401 Taxable Income Formula

Before taxes owed can be calculated, it is first necessary to determine who is responsible for the taxes owed on business profits and what tax base is used to calculate those taxes. Only individuals and C corporations actually pay income taxes to the federal government. These taxpayers pay income taxes by applying a progressive income tax rate structure to a tax base known as **taxable income**. Gross income and deductions are the major components in the calculation of the taxable income, with taxable gains being part of gross income and deductible losses being part of deductions. The amount of a business's taxable income is the difference between its gross income and the sum of the deductions that the tax laws allow the business to deduct.[1] Simply put, a taxable income can be expressed by the following formula:

Income (broadly defined)	$ xx,xxx
Less: Exclusions	(xx,xxx)
Gross income	$ xx,xxx
Less: Deductions	(xx,xxx)
Taxable income	$ xx,xxx

Example 1: Ambrack, a C corporation, has a gross income of $300,000 for 2009 and deductions totaling $240,000. Its taxable income equals $60,000 ($300,000 – $240,000).

The federal government actually has two income tax systems that it uses to determine the taxpayer's fair share of taxes owed. The first income tax system is the "regular income tax system," which is the tax system introduced in Chapter 1 (see ¶ 104.07). The regular income tax system uses taxable income as its tax base, and it uses a progressive tax rate structure. The second income tax system is called the "alternative minimum tax system," which is introduced later in this chapter (see ¶ 406). Taxpayers are required to pay the tax associated with the *greater* of the amounts computed under the two income tax systems.

From income tax liability, taxpayers subtract tax credits, which can be refundable or nonrefundable. Nonrefundable tax credits can reduce a taxpayer's tax liability to zero, but they cannot create a refund. Refundable tax credits can reduce any remaining income tax liability, and any excess is refunded to the taxpayer. The formula for calculating taxes owed at the end of each accounting period is shown below:

Total income tax liability	$ xx,xxx
Less: Nonrefundable tax credits	(xx,xxx)

---

[1] Code Sec. 63(a).

Remaining tax liability (not less than $0)	$ xx,xxx
Less: Refundable tax credits, including prepayment of taxes	(xx,xxx)
Tax owed (refund due)	$ xx,xxx

Understanding how taxpayers compute their tax liability is important because proper tax planning involves understanding the tax benefits associated with a deduction or an exclusion, as well as with the costs associated with additional amounts of gross income. As introduced in Chapter 1, the taxpayer's "marginal tax rate" is the rate of tax the taxpayer pays on its last dollar of income. It also represents the tax savings that a taxpayer derives by reducing taxable income by $1.

The tax rates used in the regular income tax system are progressive. The regular income tax rates that apply to corporations range from 15 percent to 35 percent. However, surtaxes (additional taxes) apply to certain levels of corporate taxable income, which can make the actual federal marginal tax rate as high as 39 percent (see ¶ 405.01). Under the alternative minimum tax (AMT) system, the corporate tax rate is a flat 20 percent, but the tax base used to compute AMT (called alternative minimum taxable income (AMTI)) is much broader, due to its more restrictive exclusions and deductions. For individuals, the tax rates range from 10 percent to 35 percent. A two-tiered tax rate structure is used in the individual AMT system (26- and 28-percent). Again, the tax base used in the AMT system (AMTI) is much broader than that used in the regular income tax system.

If a taxpayer is subject to AMT, the marginal tax rate that should be used in determining the tax consequences of a proposed transaction should be the taxpayer's marginal tax rate under the AMT system. For example, if a corporation is subject to AMT and has the opportunity to generate an additional $10,000 of income for the year that will be included in the corporation's AMTI, then the tax associated with that income would be $2,000 ($10,000 × 20% corporate AMT rate). However, if the taxpayer is not subject to AMT, the marginal tax rate from the progressive income tax schedules should be used to determine the tax consequences of a transaction. Of course, all other relevant taxes, including state, local, and foreign income taxes as well as employment and other taxes, should be taken into consideration when computing the tax effects of any proposed transaction.

Example 2: Ambrack from Example 1 calculates its regular tax liability on its $60,000 taxable income using the progressive corporate income tax rates provided in Table 4-1 at ¶ 405.01. Taxable income of $60,000 falls between $50,000 and $75,000, which means that Ambrack's last dollar of income is taxed at 25 percent. Thus, assuming that Ambrack's AMT does not exceed its regular income tax liability, its marginal tax rate is 25 percent. If Ambrack were to earn an additional $10,000 of income during the year, the additional taxes owed would increase by $2,500 ($10,000 × 25%).

Flow-through entities do not pay income taxes, but instead keep track of their amounts of gross income (including gains), deductions (including losses), and tax credits using the same methods that other taxpayers use. At the end of each accounting period, the entity passes along the information to its owners, who are then responsible for reporting their respective shares of the amounts on their own income tax returns. Since ultimately the owners of all businesses are individuals, whether they are partners in a partnership, shareholders in a corporation, or owners of a sole proprietorship, it is important to understand not only how the profits of a C corporation are taxed, but also how the tax laws impact an individual taxpayer.

Example 3: Assume the same facts as in Example 1, except Ambrack is operated as an S corporation that has two equal shareholders. The shareholders would each include $30,000 ($60,000 × 50%) of the profits reported by Ambrack on their respective income tax returns.

GAAP vs. Code: Because of differences between the rules for determining income and expenses for financial accounting versus the rules for computing gross income and deduction on the tax return, a business's taxable income typically is different from the net income reported on the income statement. Larger corporations are required to reconcile these differences when they file their corporate income tax returns. Therefore, throughout this textbook, when differences between the financial accounting and tax accounting for an item arise, these differences will be pointed out and discussed in a separate box entitled, GAAP vs. Code. In Chapter 12, when the special tax rules that pertain to C corporations are discussed, the various differences between the financial accounting and tax accounting rules will be summarized.

¶ 402 Overview of Gross Income

Gross income is the starting point for determining the income tax liability for both corporate and individual taxpayers. Although flow-through entities do not pay tax on taxable income, they still must be able to compute their gross income for the year so they can pass the amounts on to their owners, who then report the gross income on their own income tax returns. **Gross income** is a tax term that represents the amount of income the government has decided to tax. It is similar to the concept of gross profit reported on the income statement; however, as discussed in Chapter 3, the accounting rules and tax rules often differ both in their objectives and in the application of their respective rules.

As discussed in Chapter 3, the tax laws take an all-inclusive approach to defining gross income. Specifically, if an event or transaction causes a taxpayer's wealth or net worth to increase, then income has been realized. Taking out a loan would not generate gross income because the increase in wealth from the cash received from the loan would be offset by the increase in the taxpayer's debt. However, if the taxpayer's debt is forgiven, "income" would be realized since the reduction in liabilities causes the taxpayer's wealth to increase. Thus, the amount of the forgiveness would be included in the taxpayer's income and would be included in gross income, unless a provision in the tax law allows the taxpayer to exclude the amount from gross income.

.01 Gains from Sales or Exchanges of Property

The tax accounting rules do not require mere appreciation in value of an asset to be included in income. Although such appreciation, if it did indeed exist, would cause the taxpayer's net worth to increase, it is difficult to ascertain what the true appreciation in the asset's value is prior to selling it to an unrelated party. Thus, the tax laws omit appreciation in value from income and instead operate under the "realization principle," in which income is realized only upon the disposal of the property. The realization principle follows the "wherewithal-to-pay concept," which recognizes that mere appreciation in value does not necessarily mean the owner has the resources (wherewithal) to pay the tax associated with the appreciation. The wherewithal-to-pay is assured when the property is disposed of and the proceeds can be used to pay the necessary taxes.

In addition to the realization principle, the "capital recovery doctrine" ensures that when taxpayers dispose of property, the portion of the proceeds that allows them to recover their investment in the property will not be taxed. Thus, only the excess of the proceeds over their investment is included in income. The tax term used to describe the taxpayer's investment in property is "adjusted basis," which is comparable to the term "net book value" used in financial accounting. The details regarding the calculation of adjusted basis are presented in Chapters 7 and 8. The capital recovery doctrine applies to all sales of property, including inventory. Therefore, only **gross profit** (computed as the excess of sales price over cost of goods sold) is included in the taxpayer's income.

Example 4: A corporation sells inventory for $10,000. Its adjusted basis in the inventory is $2,500. The corporation's income from the sale is $7,500 ($10,000 – $2,500). The $2,500 adjusted basis represents a return of its investment in the property sold.

In addition to selling inventory for profit, taxpayers can also sell other property, such as land held as an investment or long-lived assets like an office building, physical plant, machinery, or equipment. Code Sec. 1231 defines depreciable property and land used in a taxpayer's business (other than inventory or receivables) that has been held for more than one year as "Section 1231 property." If such property is held for one year or less, the property is classified as ordinary income property. Most property that is not inventory, accounts receivable, or other business property is classified as a "capital asset."

When a taxpayer sells a capital asset for more than its adjusted basis, a "capital gain" results. The proper classification of gain from the sale of a capital asset is particularly important because when capital assets are sold at a loss, the amount of loss allowed as a deduction against gross income depends largely on the amount of capital gains included in the taxpayer's gross income that year (see ¶ 901.01). If the taxpayer held the capital asset for more than a year prior to the sale or exchange, the capital gain is long-term capital gain. If held a year or less, the gain is short-term capital gain.

When Section 1231 property is sold, the gain or loss on the sale is Section 1231 gain or loss (subject to recapture rules described in ¶ 904.02). Section 1231 gains are included in gross income and Section 1231 losses are deducted from gross income (see the discussion at ¶ 403.02). There is no limit on the amount of Section 1231 losses that can be deducted against gross income. In some instances, however, the excess of Section 1231 gains over Section 1231 losses are treated as long-term capital gains. When a taxpayer sells depreciable property or land used in the taxpayer's business that was held for one year or less, the gain or loss is treated as ordinary gain or loss. Ordinary gains are included in gross income; ordinary losses are deductions from gross income.

Example 5: Waterman Enterprises sells land used in its business for a $10,000 gain. Waterman includes the $10,000 gain in its income for the year. Since the land was used in the taxpayer's business, the $10,000 gain will be classified as a Section 1231 gain if Waterman held the land for over one year. Otherwise, the $10,000 gain will be taxed as ordinary income.

Example 6: Assume the same facts as in Example 5, except the land was not used in Waterman's business but instead was land held as an investment. Since the land is not inventory or property used in the taxpayer's business, by default the land is classified as a capital asset, and accordingly, the $10,000 gain will be considered capital gain. If Waterman held the land for more than a year, the gain will be classified as a long-term capital gain. Otherwise, it will be classified as a short-term capital gain. The presence of capital gain will allow Waterman to deduct capital losses against the gain. (See ¶ 403.02.)

.02 Items of Gross Income Unique to Individual Taxpayers

The definition of gross income is the same for individual taxpayers as it is for all other taxpayers, including C corporations, partnerships, and S corporations. In addition, individual taxpayers must include in gross income any compensation they receive from an employer and certain types of income that business entities typically do not receive. While the discussion of these types of income items is beyond the scope of discussion for this chapter, gross income from these items increases the taxpayer's taxable income, and accordingly, may impact a sole proprietor's marginal tax rate. Hence, it is important to understand that the nonbusiness activities of a sole proprietor may have an effect on the amount of additional tax the business owner will pay on additional business profits as well as the tax savings derived from additional business deductions. Since married couples have the option of filing a joint return, the personal activities of the taxpayer's spouse will also impact the couple's taxable income and may affect the taxpayer's marginal tax rate. The following is a list of some of the types of nonbusiness income that may be included on an individual income tax return:

- Wages, bonuses, and other compensation;
- Pension and retirement income;
- Annuities;
- Unemployment compensation (up to $2,400 can be excluded from gross income for a tax year beginning in 2009);
- Alimony and separate maintenance payments;
- Prizes and awards;
- Gambling winnings (to the extent that they exceed gambling losses);
- Up to 85 percent of Social Security benefits;
- Income from an interest in an estate or trust; and
- Damage awards for back pay or replacing lost earnings.

.03 Exclusions

Despite the fact that the tax laws define income broadly, some income is exempt from federal income tax. Income the government does not tax is called an **exclusion**. For example, when a bondholder receives a semiannual interest payment from a corporation, the interest is included in income under the all-inclusive approach to defining gross income taken by the Internal Revenue Code (the "Code"). However, when the bond is issued from a state or local government, the interest received is excluded from gross income on the federal income tax return. This type of interest is known as "municipal interest" (or "muni interest" for short), since the bond was issued by a municipality rather than a private corporation. A more detailed discussion of the concepts of income and exclusions is included later in this chapter (see ¶ 411).

Example 7: During the year, a corporation receives $14,000 of interest from a bond issued by Alman, Inc., a private corporation. It also receives $41,000 of interest from State of Iowa municipal bonds it owns. The corporation computes its gross income from these bonds as follows:

Interest from the corporate bond	$14,000
Interest from the municipal bond	41,000
Total income	$55,000
Less: Exclusion for municipal interest	(41,000)
Gross income from interest	$14,000

¶ 403 Overview of Deductions

For the most part, deductions represent amounts by which the tax laws allow taxpayers to reduce taxable income. Typically, a deduction arises from an expenditure paid or incurred by the taxpayer. Because businesses are required to include in gross income the gross profits from sales of their products or services, it is only fair that they be allowed to deduct against gross income the costs they pay or incur in the normal course of generating the gross profits. Thus, only the excess of gross income over allowable deductions is subject to tax.

Unlike the all-inclusive approach to defining gross income, deductions are only allowed if a specific provision in the tax laws allows the expenditure to be deducted. Many business deductions are allowed under the general provision in Code Sec. 162(a), which allows a deduction for all "ordinary and necessary expenses incurred in the operation of a trade or business." Some of the more common types of deductible expenses include compensation paid to employees, rental expenses, repairs, maintenance, insurance, interest, and taxes. The year in which expenses can be deducted depends on the taxpayer's method of accounting in conjunction with the special accounting method rules discussed in Chapter 3. A detailed discussion of business deductions is the focus of Chapters 5 to 7. The discussion that follows provides an overview of the deductions businesses can subtract from gross income.

Example 8: A corporation spends $2,000 to repaint its office, $150 to repair a leaky faucet, and $500 to replace some shingles on the roof of its office building. The corporation deducts each of these expenses as ordinary and necessary business expenses.

The rules for determining what amounts can be deducted apply to all types of business entities. The only difference is that C corporations and sole proprietors use the deductions to reduce their taxable income and, thus, the amount of tax they must pay to the federal government. Flow-through entities offset ordinary deductions against ordinary gross income and pass through the net amount to their owners. Some deductions are passed through separately to the owners to be deducted on the owners' own income tax returns (see ¶ 1404.03 and ¶ 1506.01).

Example 9: Mineral Investments, Inc. receives $30,000 in royalties from the sale of minerals. The tax laws allow Mineral to take a $20,000 depletion deduction with respect to those royalties. Mineral must include the $30,000 in its gross income, but the company will be allowed to take a separate deduction for its depletion expense.

Example 10: Industrial Equipment receives $20,000 in royalties from a patent it owns. The tax laws allow Industrial to deduct (amortize) the cost of the patent over 15 years. Industrial must include the $20,000 in its gross income, but it may take a separate deduction for the amortization expense associated with the cost of the patent.

Example 11: A corporation has $100,000 in gross income from its business operations and $110,000 in business expenses. It also has interest income of $5,000. The corporation can offset its $110,000 of business expenses against both its income from business operations and its interest income.

.01 Capital Expenditures

Not all ordinary, necessary, and reasonable amounts paid or incurred by a business as part of its operations can be deducted as a business expense. If an expenditure creates an asset that can be expected to benefit the business for a period of time that extends beyond the current year, the expenditure is a **capital expenditure** that must be reported as a business asset. Some capital expenditures can be expensed over a specified period; however, others are never deductible.

Example 12: Home Remodelers purchases equipment for $50,000. The company expects to be able to use the equipment for 10 years. Because the $50,000 was expended for an asset with a useful life in excess of one year, Home Remodelers capitalizes the $50,000 to an asset account and uses the tax depreciation rules presented in Chapter 7 to determine how quickly it can expense (depreciate) the equipment.

Example 13: Ultrasonic Research pays $5,000 for a new roof. This expense is a capital expenditure because the benefits from the new roof will extend beyond the current tax year. Thus, Ultrasonic cannot deduct the $5,000 as a business expense; however, it may depreciate the roof using the depreciation rules discussed in Chapter 7.

 Reason for the Rule: If a business were allowed to reduce its taxable income for a year by the entire cost of an asset that has a useful life of more than one year, it would understate both its net income and taxable income for the year that the asset was purchased. In addition, the business would overstate its net income and taxable income

> for the remaining years that the asset was used. The depreciation deduction is intended to more closely match a business's income with its expenses.

.02 Losses from Disposing of Business or Investment Property

Gains on the sale of property are included in gross income (see ¶ 402.01). Losses on the sale of business and investment property are deducted from gross income, subject to certain limitations. When the property sold is a capital asset (see ¶ 402.01), the recognized loss is a capital loss. The tax laws limit the amount of capital losses that can be deducted in any one year. For corporate taxpayers, capital losses are deductible to the extent of the capital gains included in their gross income. Any excess capital losses over capital gains can be carried back three years to offset excess capital gains reported in gross income in those years, and the excess losses can then be carried forward five years to offset future capital gains[2] (see ¶ 901).

Example 14: Insulated Containers receives $6,000 on the sale of 100 shares of ABC stock. Insulated's adjusted basis in the stock is $4,000. Insulated also sells 100 shares of XYZ stock with an adjusted basis of $4,000 for $1,000. Since stock is not inventory, accounts receivable, or other business property, the gains and losses on the sale of these assets are capital gains and losses. Insulated recognizes a $2,000 gain on the sale of the ABC stock ($6,000 – $4,000) and a $3,000 loss on the sale of XYZ stock ($1,000 – $4,000). As a C corporation, Insulated can only deduct the loss on the sale of XYZ stock to the extent of the capital gains it includes in its gross income. Its loss is limited to $2,000 and it will carry back the $1,000 excess for up to three years, and it will carry forward any remaining loss for up to five years.[3]

Capital gain from the sale of ABC stock	$2,000
Less: Capital loss deduction	(2,000)
Amount included in taxable income	$ 0

The tax laws regarding the deduction for capital losses for individual taxpayers are different. When an individual taxpayer incurs capital losses, such losses are deductible to the extent of the capital gains included in gross income plus $3,000. Any excess capital losses are carried forward indefinitely to offset capital gains plus up to $3,000 of ordinary income in future tax years.[4]

Example 15: Pete Tallon operates a kitchen accessories business as a sole proprietor. During the year, Pete receives $4,000 when he sells 100 shares of ABC stock. His adjusted basis in those shares is $2,000. He also realizes $2,000 on the sale of 200 shares of XYZ stock that has an adjusted basis of $8,000. Pete's realized gain on the sale of the ABC stock is $2,000 ($4,000 – $2,000), and his realized loss on the sale of the XYZ stock is $6,000 ($2,000 – $8,000). Although Pete's capital losses exceed his capital gains by more than $3,000, he is allowed to deduct up to $5,000 of the capital loss against his gross income ($2,000 capital gain + $3,000). He carries forward the excess $1,000 loss indefinitely to future tax years.

Capital gain from the sale of ABC stock	$2,000
Less: Capital loss deduction	(5,000)
Amount that reduces Pete's AGI	($3,000)

As previously mentioned, when the taxpayer sells depreciable property and land used in business that has been held for more than a year (Section 1231 property), the gain or loss is a

---

[2] Code Sec. 1211(a).
[3] Code Sec. 1212(a).

[4] Code Sec. 1211(b).

Section 1231 gain or loss. Section 1231 gains are included in gross income and Section 1231 losses are deducted from gross income. These Section 1231 gains and losses are then summed up at the end of the year and if the taxpayer's Section 1231 gains exceed the amount of Section 1231 losses, the excess gain ("net Section 1231 gain") may be treated as a long-term capital gain. Although the gains are still taxed in gross income, by classifying the net Section 1231 gain as a long-term capital gain, the net gain can be used to increase capital gains, which will allow the taxpayer to deduct more capital losses incurred during the year.

Example 16: Amadia Golf Supplies, Inc. sells the following property during the year:

Gain on the sale of inventory	$50,000
Section 1231 gain	60,000
Section 1231 loss	(20,000)
Capital loss	(25,000)

Both the $50,000 gain on the sale of inventory and the $60,000 Section 1231 gain are included in the taxpayer's gross income. The $20,000 Section 1231 loss is deducted from Amadia's gross income. Normally the $25,000 capital loss would not be deductible because there are no capital gains in gross income for the capital loss to offset. However, the tax laws allow Amadia to treat the $40,000 net Section 1231 gain ($60,000 – $20,000) as long-term capital gain. Therefore, the entire $25,000 of capital loss can be deducted from gross income to offset the long-term capital gain.

Gain from the sale of inventory	$ 50,000
Section 1231 gain	60,000
Gross income	$110,000
Less: Section 1231 loss	(20,000)
Less: Capital loss deduction	(25,000)
Net increase in taxable income	$ 65,000

Example 17: Assume the same facts as in Example 16, except Amadia's Section 1231 loss is $40,000.

Gain on the sale of inventory	$50,000
Section 1231 gain	60,000
Section 1231 loss	(40,000)
Capital loss	(25,000)

Since Amadia's net Section 1231 gain is $20,000 ($60,000 – $40,000), the company can only use $20,000 of the capital loss to offset its $20,000 capital gain (from the net Section 1231 gain). The remaining $5,000 capital loss ($25,000 – $20,000) is carried over to another tax year.

Gain from the sale of inventory	$ 50,000
Section 1231 gain	60,000
Gross income	$110,000
Less: Section 1231 loss	(40,000)
Less: Capital loss deduction	(20,000)
Net increase in taxable income	$ 50,000

¶ 404 Expanded Taxable Income Formula for Individual Taxpayers

The steps in determining the taxable income of an individual are similar to those used to determine the taxable income of a corporation. Both must determine their total income, and both must exclude certain items of income from gross income. Both are entitled to deduct certain amounts from their gross income when calculating their taxable income. The major difference between the steps in determining the taxable income of a C corporation and the steps in determining the taxable income of an individual taxpayer is that individuals have two types of deductions. The first type of deduction is referred to as a deduction for **adjusted gross income** (AGI), sometimes called an "above the line" deduction. The second type of deduction is called a deduction from AGI. Such deductions are occasionally referred to as "below the line" deductions. The taxable income formula for individual taxpayers is expanded to include these two types of deductions and the intermediary calculation of AGI.

Income	$ xx,xxx
Less: Exclusions	(xx,xxx)
Gross income	$ xx,xxx
Less: Deductions for AGI	(xx,xxx)
Adjusted gross income (AGI)	$ xx,xxx
Less: Deductions from AGI	(xx,xxx)
Taxable income	$ xx,xxx

Deductions *for* AGI include many of the deductions corporations subtract from gross income. However, a few other deductions available only to individual taxpayers are allowed as deductions for AGI. The tax laws also allow individual taxpayers to deduct certain personal expenses when computing taxable income. These personal expenses consist of the deductions *from* AGI. Figure 4-1 lists the various deductions allowed on an individual taxpayer's income tax return. The items followed by an asterisk (*) are the business-related expenses that will be the focus of Chapters 5 to 9. Although most business expenses from a sole proprietorship are deducted for AGI on an individual's income tax return, some deductions are only available as itemized deductions to individual taxpayers.

Figure 4-1 Deductions Allowed in Computing Individual Taxable Income

Deductions for AGI
- Trade or business expenses*
- Losses from the sale or exchange of property*
- Health savings account deduction*
- Moving expenses*
- One-half of self-employment tax*
- Self-employed contributions to employer-sponsored qualified retirement plans*
- Self-employed health insurance deduction*
- Contributions to traditional IRAs
- Penalty on early withdrawals of savings
- Alimony paid
- Student loan interest
- Domestic production activities deduction*

Itemized Deductions

- Medical expenses
- State and local income taxes (or sales taxes)*
- Real estate taxes*
- Personal property taxes*
- Home mortgage interest
- Investment interest*
- Charitable contributions*
- Casualty and theft losses*
- Unreimbursed employee expenses
- Tax preparation fees*
- Investment fees and expenses*

---

* Designates business expenses that may be deducted on the individual tax return.

Example 18: Ray Alton operates a business as a sole proprietorship. The gross income, deductions, and tax credits generated by his business are reported on his individual income tax return. These amounts are added to his other items of gross income, deduction, and tax credit when computing his taxable income and taxes owed at the end of the year. Ray uses the taxable income formula for individuals to compute his taxable income.

Example 19: Assume the same facts as in Example 18, except the business is operated as a partnership, in which Ray owns a 75-percent interest. At the end of the partnership's accounting period, the partnership's gross income, deductions, and tax credits for the year are computed. Ray will include 75 percent of each item on his personal income tax return. He will add the amounts to his other items of gross income, deductions, and tax credit. Ray will then compute his taxable income using the taxable income formula for individual taxpayers.

CALCULATING TAXES OWED

Once taxable income has been calculated, corporate and individual taxpayers compute their regular income tax liability using their respective progressive income tax rates. In addition to income taxes based on taxable income, some taxpayers are also subject to the alternative minimum tax (AMT). The two taxes comprise a taxpayer's total income tax liability. Sole proprietors are subject to self-employment taxes on profits from the sole proprietorship. Although self-employment taxes are an employment tax rather than an income tax, they are included as part of an individual taxpayer's total tax liability.

Once a taxpayer's total tax liability is computed, the taxpayer reduces the tax liability by allowable tax credits. The taxpayer then offsets any remaining tax liability by amounts previously paid into the IRS for federal taxes owed, either through withholdings (as in the case of individual taxpayers), or prepayments (in the case of both individual and corporate taxpayers).

Example 20: Briss & Company determines that its regular tax for the year is $115,000 and that it owes an additional $10,000 under the AMT system. Briss's allowable tax credits for the year are $20,000, and it made estimated tax payments totaling $100,000 during the year. When it files its income tax return, Briss will owe an additional $5,000 in taxes.

Regular tax	$115,000
Plus: AMT	10,000
Total income tax liability	$125,000
Less: Tax credits	(20,000)
Less: Prepayments	(100,000)
Tax (refund) due	$ 5,000

Example 21: Rumill & Company determines that its regular tax for the year is $155,000 and that it is not subject to AMT. Rumill is entitled to $30,000 in tax credits, and it made a total of $135,000 in estimated tax payments during the year. When it files its income tax return, Rumill will request that a $10,000 overpayment be refunded.

Regular tax:	$155,000
Plus: AMT	0
Total income tax liability	$155,000
Less: Tax credits	(30,000)
Less: Prepayments	(135,000)
Tax (refund) due	($ 10,000)

¶ 405 Regular Income Tax Liability

The income tax system uses a progressive rate structure to promote equity among taxpayers by assessing a lower tax rate on taxpayers with lower amounts of taxable income. Although both an individual's taxable income and a corporation's taxable income are subject to progressive tax rates, different rates apply to each type of taxpayer.

.01 Tax Rates for Corporations

Corporations use the progressive tax rates from Table 4-1 to compute their regular income tax liability on their taxable income.[5] Unlike the tax brackets for individuals, the corporate tax brackets are not indexed for inflation. Thus, unless Congress enacts new legislation to change the corporate tax rates, the first $50,000 of corporate taxable income is taxed at 15 percent in each year.

Table 4-1 Corporate Income Tax Rates

If taxable income is over	But not over	The tax is:
$0	$50,000	15% of the amount over $0
$50,000	$75,000	$7,500 plus 25% of the amount over $50,000
$75,000	$100,000	$13,750 plus 34% of the amount over $75,000
$100,000	$335,000	$22,250 plus 39% of the amount over $100,000
$335,000	$10,000,000	$113,900 plus 34% of the amount over $335,000

[5] Code Sec. 11.

If taxable income is over	But not over	The tax is:
$10,000,000	$15,000,000	$3,400,000 plus 35% of the amount over $10,000,000
$15,000,000	$18,333,333	$5,150,000 plus 38% of the amount over $15,000,000
$18,333,333		35% of the amount over $0

Example 22: A corporation reports taxable income of $40,000. It calculates its $6,000 regular income tax liability for the year as follows:

Taxable income	$40,000
Times: Marginal tax rate	× 15%
Regular income tax liability	$ 6,000

Example 23: A corporation has $90,000 of taxable income. It calculates its regular income tax liability for the year to be $18,850, as shown below:

Taxable income	$90,000
Less: Threshold amount	(75,000)
Excess over $75,000	$15,000
Times: Marginal tax rate	× 34%
Tax on excess	$ 5,100
Plus: Additional tax	13,750
Regular income tax liability	$18,850

Example 24: A corporation has a taxable income of $140,000. It computes its regular income tax liability as follows:

Taxable income	$140,000
Less: Threshold amount	(100,000)
Excess over $100,000	$ 40,000
Times: Marginal tax rate	× 39%
Tax on excess	$ 15,600
Plus: Additional tax	22,250
Regular income tax liability	$ 37,850

Example 25: A corporation has a taxable income of $12 million. Its $4.1 million regular income tax liability for the year is calculated as follows:

Taxable income	$12,000,000
Less: Threshold amount	(10,000,000)
Excess over $10,000,000	$ 2,000,000
Times: Marginal tax rate	× 35%
Tax on excess	$ 700,000
Plus: Additional tax	3,400,000
Tax liability	$ 4,100,000

The highest corporate tax rate is actually 35 percent; however, at first glance at Table 4-1, there may appear to be both 38-percent and 39-percent tax brackets. The 39-percent rate for taxable income between $100,000 and $335,000 is actually the 34-percent marginal tax rate plus a five-percent surcharge intended to eliminate the tax benefits from the lower 15-and 25-percent tax rates for taxable income less than $75,000. Therefore, by the time taxable income reaches $335,000, corporations will have paid a flat tax rate of 34 percent on its taxable income, as shown below:

Tax on $335,000 of taxable income using Table 4-1:

Taxable income	$335,000
Less: Threshold amount	(100,000)
Excess taxed at marginal tax rate	$235,000
Times: Marginal tax rate	× 39%
Tax on excess	$ 91,650
Plus: Additional tax	22,250
Tax liability	$113,900

Tax on $335,000 using a flat 34-percent tax rate:

$335,000 × 34%	$113,900

The flat 34-percent tax rate continues for corporations with taxable income between $335,000 and $10 million. Once taxable income reaches $10 million, the rate increases to 35 percent until it reaches $15 million. At taxable income of $15 million, a three-percent surcharge is assessed until all taxable income that was taxed at 34 percent is taxed at 35 percent. This requires that the 38 percent tax rate (35% + 3% surcharge) remain in effect until taxable income reaches $18,333,333.

Tax on $18,333,333 taxable income using Table 4-1:

Taxable income	$18,333,333
Less: Threshold amount	(15,000,000)
Excess taxed at marginal tax rate	$ 3,333,333
Times: Marginal tax rate	× 38%
Tax on excess	$ 1,266,667
Plus: Additional tax	5,150,000
Tax liability	$ 6,416,667

Tax on $18,333,333 using a flat 35-percent tax rate:

$18,333,333 × 35%	$ 6,416,667

 Reason for the Rule: Congress believed that graduated income tax rates should be retained for smaller corporations to encourage their growth. However, it believed that larger corporations should not benefit from the lower rates and instead should pay a flat tax rate on their taxable income.[6]

---

[6] Joint Committee on Taxation, *General Explanation of the Tax Reform Act of* 1986, at 272.

¶ 405.01

Planning Pointer: Although the highest corporate tax rate is actually 35 percent, for tax planning purposes, the marginal tax rate that must be used when making decisions must include any surcharge in effect for the corporation's level of taxable income.

.02 Tax Rates for Individuals

The tax rates for individuals are graduated, ranging from 10 to 35 percent. However, unlike C corporations, individuals do not lose the benefit of the graduated rates as their taxable income increases. The amount of taxable income to which a particular tax rate applies varies, depending on an individual's filing status. There are five filing statuses: married filing jointly (MFJ), surviving spouse, head of household, married filing separately (MFS), and single. A different tax rate schedule applies to each filing status, with the exception of surviving spouse, which shares the MFJ tax rates. The 2009 tax rate schedules for individual taxpayers are reproduced in the Appendix at the back of this textbook.

Also unique to individual taxpayers are special rates that apply to net capital gains and qualified dividends. These special tax rates as well as the rules governing the taxation of sole proprietorships are discussed below and in Chapter 13 at ¶ 1306. Table 4-2 shows the 2009 tax rates for MFJ and surviving spouse.

Example 26: John Jacobs operates a sole proprietorship. John is married and files a joint return with his wife. During 2009, the couple's taxable income is $91,600. Using the tax rates from Table 4-2, the Jacobs' tax liability is $15,275 [$9,350 + ($91,600 – $67,900) × 25%].

Table 4-2 2009 Tax Rates for Married Filing Jointly and Surviving Spouse

If taxable income is:	The tax is:
Not more than $16,700	10% of taxable income
More than $16,700 but not more than $67,900	$1,670 plus 15% of the excess over $16,700
More than $67,900 but not more than $137,050	$9,350 plus 25% of the excess over $67,900
More than $137,050 but not more than $208,850	$26,637.50 plus 28% of the excess over $137,050
More than $208,850 but not more than $372,950	$46,741.50 plus 33% of the excess over $208,850
More than $372,950	$100,894.50 plus 35% of the excess over $372,950

Special tax rates on qualified dividends and net capital gains. Individual taxpayers have the advantage of paying lower tax rates on qualified dividends and net capital gains. Qualified dividends are taxed at a zero-percent tax rate (for tax years beginning in 2008, 2009, or 2010) for individual taxpayers in the 10- and 15-percent tax brackets and at a 15-percent rate for individual taxpayers in all higher tax brackets. **Qualified dividends** are dividends paid on stock of a U.S. corporation or a qualified foreign corporation that the individual held for 121 days surrounding the ex-dividend date.[7] Although most net capital gain is taxed at the same rates as qualified dividends, some can be taxed at a maximum 25 or 28 percent. Net capital gain arises from the sale of certain

---

[7] Code Sec. 1(h)(1) and (11).

property (including capital assets) held long-term. The rules that describe how net capital gain is calculated are discussed in Chapter 9.

Example 27: Gina Lopez's taxable income falls into the 28-percent tax bracket. Gina's taxable income includes $45,000 of net capital gain and qualified dividends. When Gina calculates her taxable income, she will back out $45,000 and calculate its tax at 15 percent. The remainder of her taxable income will be taxed using the progressive individual tax rates for her filing status. Gina's total tax liability will be the sum of the two amounts.

Example 28: Claude Van Dyke's taxable income falls in the 15-percent tax bracket. Included in his taxable income is $5,000 of qualified dividends. When Claude calculates his tax liability, his qualified dividends will be taxed at a zero-percent tax rate. The rest of his taxable income will be taxed using the progressive tax rates for his filing status. The sum of these two amounts will be Claude's total regular income tax liability.

.03 Tax Rate for Personal Service Corporations

"Qualified personal service corporations" are C corporations that are not entitled to use the graduated tax rates that apply to other C corporations. Instead they must pay a flat 35-percent tax on all taxable income.[8] A **qualified personal service corporation** (QPSC) is a corporation engaged almost exclusively in performing services in thc fields of health, law, engineering, architecture, accounting, actuarial science, performing arts, or consulting. In addition, at least 95 percent of the value of a QPSC's stock is held, directly or indirectly, by its employees, by retired employees who performed services for the corporation, or by an estate or other person owning stock because of the death of such employees or retired employees.[9]

Example 29: Cocco Engineering provides engineering consulting services. Its taxable income for the year is $100,000. Its employees devote 100 percent of their time providing consulting services, and all of Cocco's stock is owned by its employees. Cocco is a qualified personal service corporation, and therefore, its regular income tax liability equals $35,000 ($100,000 × 35%) In contrast, if Cocco were not a qualified personal service corporation, its regular income tax liability would be $22,250 (using Table 4-1).

Reason for the Rule: Qualified personal service corporations were denied the benefit of graduated income tax rates by the Revenue Act of 1987. Congress noted that the income from these corporations is taxed to employee-owners at the individual graduated income tax rates because it is paid out as salary. Congress believed that it was inappropriate to allow these amounts to be taxed at lower corporate graduated rates.[10]

¶ 406 Alternative Minimum Tax

Individual taxpayers and larger C corporations may be subject to the alternative minimum tax (AMT), which is a tax enacted to ensure that taxpayers pay their fair share of income taxes. The AMT is imposed in addition to the regular income tax. The corporate AMT system is described in Chapter 10; the individual AMT system is described in Chapter 13. Since the marginal tax rate for taxpayers subject to AMT will be affected, a brief overview of the tax is presented in this chapter.

Reason for the Rule: Congress imposes the AMT on corporations because it concluded that both the perception and the reality of fairness had been harmed by

---

[8] Code Sec. 11(b)(2).
[9] Temp. Reg. § 1.448-1T(e).

[10] House Ways and Means Committee Report No. 100-391 (October 26, 1987), at 1097.

instances in which corporations paid little or no tax in years when they reported substantial earnings and may even have paid substantial dividends to shareholders. The AMT is designed to attempt to ensure that companies with significant earnings pay at least some tax for the year.[11]

The AMT is a tax system that is parallel to the regular tax system. The AMT system has its own set of rules regarding exclusions and deductions (see ¶ 1008.05). Under the AMT system, a taxpayer's tentative minimum tax is computed. If this amount exceeds the taxpayer's regular income tax liability, the excess represents the taxpayer's AMT owed for the year.[12]

Example 30: A taxpayer's regular income tax liability is $30,000, and its tentative minimum tax is computed to be $35,000. The taxpayer's AMT equals $5,000 ($35,000 – $30,000).

Example 31: A taxpayer's regular tax liability for the year is $40,000 and its tentative minimum tax is $35,000. Because the amount of regular tax liability exceeds the tentative minimum tax, the taxpayer reports no AMT on its income tax return.

Although the AMT system is separate from the regular income tax system, many of the items of income and deduction that are used in computing taxable income are used in computing the alternative minimum taxable income (AMTI). Accordingly, the taxpayer starts the calculation of the tentative minimum tax by adjusting its taxable income to compute AMTI. The AMT system allows taxpayers to deduct an exemption from AMTI in arriving at the AMT tax base (the AMT equivalent to taxable income). The AMT tax rates are then applied to the AMT base to determine the minimum income tax the taxpayer will owe for the year. If the amount exceeds the amount of income tax computed under the regular income tax system, the excess represents the taxpayer's AMT liability for the year.

.01 Corporate AMT

Corporations calculate their tentative minimum tax using the following formula:[13]

Taxable income	$ xx,xxx
Plus or minus necessary adjustments	xx,xxx
AMTI	$ xx,xxx
Less: AMT exemption	(xx,xxx)
AMT base	$ xx,xxx
AMT tax rate	20%
Tentative minimum tax	$ xx,xxx

Example 32: Strole Industrial Paints has a regular tax liability for the year of $20,000. Its AMTI is calculated to be $150,000 and its AMT exemption amount is $40,000. Because Strole's $22,000 tentative minimum tax exceeds its $20,000 regular income tax liability, Strole is required to pay a minimum of $22,000 in income taxes for the year. Accordingly, Strole's AMT equals $2,000 ($22,000 – $20,000). When Strole files its tax return, it will report a regular income tax liability of $20,000 and an AMT of $2,000.

AMTI	$150,000
AMT exemption	(40,000)

---

[11] Joint Committee on Taxation, General Explanation of the Tax Reform Act of 1986, at 433-434.

[12] Code Sec. 55(a).

[13] Code Sec. 55(b).

AMT base	$110,000
AMT tax rate	× 20%
Tentative minimum tax	$ 22,000

.02 Individual AMT

Like corporations, individuals compute their AMT by starting with taxable income and making the necessary adjustments to compute AMTI. Because of the differences in how taxable income is calculated for individuals and corporations, the adjustments made to taxable income differ. Like corporations, individuals are allowed an exemption against AMTI, but the amount varies, depending on the individual's filing status. Unlike the corporate AMT rate, which is a flat 20 percent, a two-tier system of tax rates applies to individuals when computing tentative minimum tax. For individuals, the first $175,000 of AMT base is subject to a 26-percent tax rate; any excess is subject to a 28-percent tax. The threshold amount is halved for married taxpayers filing separate returns. In the AMT system, net capital gains and qualified dividends are subject to the same lower tax rates to which they are subject under the regular income tax system. The individual AMT is described in greater detail in Chapter 13.

Example 33: Shirley Augustine has a regular tax liability for 2009 of $15,000. Her AMTI is calculated to be $122,950, and her AMT exemption amount is $46,700. Thus, Shirley's AMT base is $76,250, and her tentative minimum tax is $19,825. Because Shirley's tentative minimum tax exceeds her $15,000 regular income tax liability, she is required to pay a minimum of $19,825 in income taxes for the year. Accordingly, her AMT equals $4,825 ($19,825 – $15,000). When Shirley files her tax return, she will report a regular income tax liability of $15,000 and AMT of $4,825.

AMTI	$122,950
AMT exemption	(46,700)
AMT base	$ 76,250
AMT tax rate	× 26%
Tentative minimum tax	$ 19,825

Example 34: Assume the same facts as in Example 33, except Shirley's regular income tax liability is $21,000. Because through the regular income tax system Shirley is paying at least the $19,825 minimum tax calculated under the AMT income tax system, she will not be subject to AMT in 2009.

¶ 407 Self-Employment Tax

In Chapter 1, the concept of employment taxes was introduced. Compensation is subject to Federal Insurance Contributions Act (FICA) taxes, which consist of social security and Medicare taxes. The responsibility for paying FICA taxes is shared equally by the employer and employee (see ¶ 104.06). The owner of a self-employed business acts both as an employee and as an employer of the business. Therefore, sole proprietors are required to contribute both the employer and employee portions of Social Security (OASDI) and Medicare taxes. When those taxes are paid on the profits of a sole proprietorship, they are called the "self-employment tax." For 2009, the self-employment tax rate is 15.3 percent on all *net earnings from self-employment* up to $106,800. After that, the self-employment tax rate drops to 2.9 percent. The details regarding the calculation of the self-employment tax are discussed in Chapter 13.

Sole proprietors add the amount of their self-employment taxes for the year to their income tax liabilities (regular income tax plus AMT). They are expected to make quarterly estimated tax payments during the year to cover any amounts of self-employment taxes that are not otherwise prepaid through other means (withholding). Failure to prepay these taxes during the year may result in substantial understatement penalties (see ¶ 409.02).

¶ 408 Tax Credits

The tax laws allow taxpayers to subtract from their total tax liability certain amounts known as "tax credits." In the case of flow-through entities, tax credits flow through to the owners of the business and are taken as tax credits on the owners' income tax returns. Tax credits are discussed in detail in Chapter 11, but a brief introduction is included in this chapter.

As introduced in Chapter 1, tax credits are different from deductions. A tax *credit* reduces a taxpayer's tax liability dollar for dollar. In contrast, a *deduction* reduces a taxpayer's tax liability by the amount of the taxpayer's marginal income tax rate. If the deduction is one that reduces a sole proprietor's self-employment taxes, the reduction in both income and self-employment taxes must be considered.

Example 35: Shetlar Hair Dyes, Inc. had $100,000 of taxable income for its tax year and owed $22,250 on its taxable income. Its tax credits for the year are $2,500. That credit reduces its tax liability dollar for dollar to $19,750 ($22,250 – $2,500).

Example 36: Assume the same facts as in Example 35, except Shetlar incurs $2,500 in deductible expenses for the year instead of a $2,500 tax credit. An additional $2,500 of expenses reduces the company's taxable income to $97,500 ($100,000 – $2,500). Without the deduction, the company's tax liability for the year on $100,000 of taxable income would have been $22,250 (see Example 35). When the deduction is taken, its tax liability on $97,500 of taxable income is $21,400 (using Table 4-1). The result is a reduction in taxes equal to $850 ($22,250 – $21,400). This amount is equivalent to the deduction multiplied by the taxpayer's marginal income tax rate ($2,500 × 34% = $850). In contrast, the $2,500 tax credit reduces the company's tax liability by $2,500.

Example 37: Mai Trammell operates a sole proprietorship. Mai is not subject to AMT, and her taxable income falls in the 28-percent tax bracket. If Mai incurs an additional $1,000 of business expenses that reduce both her sole proprietorship profits and her taxable income, her tax savings from this deduction equals approximately $433 ($1,000 × (28% income tax rate + a 15.3% self-employment tax rate)). Thus, the total cost of the expenditure to Mai is only $567 ($1,000 – $433).

Example 38: Assume the same facts as in Example 37, except the deduction is allowed to reduce Mai's taxable income, but it is not deductible in computing her business profits subject to self-employment taxes. Mai's tax savings from the deduction is $280 ($1,000 × 28%), and her out-of-pocket costs after considering the federal income tax savings is $720 ($1,000 – $280).

Three primary tax credits are available to businesses: the general business credit, foreign tax credit, and minimum tax credit. Businesses are also allowed a tax credit for any amounts they have prepaid toward the current year's tax liability. In addition to the various business tax credits, individual taxpayers also have a variety of personal tax credits that can be used to reduce their tax liabilities. These credits are introduced in Chapter 11.

.01 General Business Credit

The "general business credit" is a combination of a variety of business credits, each of which is computed under its own set of rules.[14] The various credits are combined into one general business credit to limit the amount of the combined credits that can offset a taxpayer's income tax liability and to prevent businesses from completely offsetting their income tax liability in any one tax year. Any

---

[14] Code Sec. 38.

unused general business credit can be carried back one year and then carried forward 20 years.[15] Both this limitation and the discussion of the credits that comprise the general business credit are discussed in Chapter 11. A partial list of credits that comprise the general business credit is shown in Figure 4-2.

Figure 4-2 Partial List of Tax Credits That Comprise the General Business Credit

Tax Credits Aimed at Encouraging Employers to Hire Certain Workers
- Work opportunity credit and
- Empowerment zone and renewal community employment credit.

Tax Credits Aimed at Encouraging Conservation of Energy
- Alternative motor vehicle (hybrid car) credit,
- Plug-in electric drive motor vehicle credit,
- Home builder's credit for new energy efficient homes,
- Manufacturer's credit for energy efficient appliances, and
- Carbon dioxide sequestration credit.

Tax Credits Aimed at Rewarding Research in Certain Areas
- Research credit and
- Orphan drug credit.

Tax Credits to Encourage Economic Development
- Empowerment zone and renewal community employment credit and
- New markets credit.

Tax Credits Used to Subsidize Businesses for Certain Expenditures Made during the Year
- Employer social security tax credit,
- Military differential wage payment credit,
- Rehabilitation credit,
- Low-income housing credit,
- Disabled access credit,
- Employer-provided child care credit, and
- Small employer pension plan start-up cost credit.

.02 Foreign Tax Credit

When U.S. businesses receive income from a foreign country, the foreign-source income may be subject to income tax by both the foreign country and by the U.S. government. To reduce the possibility of double taxation on the same income, U.S. citizens and residents as well as certain nonresident taxpayers are permitted to take an income tax credit for income taxes paid or accrued during the tax year to a foreign country or to a U.S. possession.[16] The details surrounding the availability and calculation of this credit are discussed in Chapter 11 (see ¶ 1117).

---

[15] Code Sec. 39.　　　　　　　　　　[16] Code Sec. 901(a).

.03 Minimum Tax Credit

The "minimum tax credit" is a tax credit allowed in certain situations when the taxpayer has previously been subject to AMT.[17] A discussion of the minimum tax credit can be found in Chapter 10 (see ¶ 1010).

.04 Prepayments of Federal Income Taxes

In addition to the various tax credits taxpayers are allowed to use to reduce their income tax liabilities, any amounts that the taxpayer has prepaid the government towards its tax liability are treated as a refundable credit when it files its income tax return. Thus, if the taxpayer has overpaid amounts into the government during the year, it can request a refund of the excess when it files its income tax return. Alternatively, the taxpayer can apply the overpayment to the next year's income tax liability and treat it as a refundable tax credit in the subsequent tax year.

Example 39: Ariel Industries determines that its regular tax for the year is $160,000 and that it is not subject to AMT. Ariel is entitled to $20,000 of tax credits, and it made a total of $155,000 in estimated tax payments during the year. When it files its income tax return, Ariel can request that its $15,000 overpayment be refunded, or alternatively, it can request that the overpayment be applied toward next year's taxes.

Regular tax	$160,000
Plus: AMT	0
Total tax liability	$160,000
Less: Tax credits	(20,000)
Less: Prepayments	(155,000)
Tax (refund) due	($ 15,000)

¶ 409 Estimated Tax Payments

Like a business, the federal government requires a steady source of revenues from which to pay its expenditures. Accordingly, the federal government requires taxpayers to periodically make payments toward their current year's tax liability. This includes amounts owed for regular income tax, AMT, and self-employment taxes plus any other taxes owed with the taxpayer's income tax return in excess of any allowable tax credits.

Employees (and retirees) can prepay their taxes by having taxes withheld from the checks they receive from their employers (or pension plans) to cover the taxes they will owe on those amounts. Taxpayers can also arrange to have amounts withheld from interest and dividend income they receive during the year. When taxes are prepaid through withholdings, the amounts are withheld by the payer and are remitted periodically to the government. For all other types of income, the government requires that taxpayers make **estimated tax payments** to cover their taxes owed for the year. The government imposes penalties if adequate amounts are not prepaid on a timely basis.

C corporations are required to make estimated tax payments during the year unless their total tax liability for the year, reduced by tax credits, is less than $500.[18] Individuals must make estimated tax payments on income not subject to withholding unless their total tax liability for the year, reduced by tax credits and amounts withheld from wages, etc., is less than $1,000.[19] A taxpayer that fails to make the appropriate amounts of estimated payments may be subject to an underpayment penalty when filing its tax return. The penalty is equivalent to the amount of interest that would have

---

[17] Code Sec. 53.
[18] Code Sec. 6655.

[19] Code Sec. 6654.

accrued on the tax underpayment during the period of the underpayment. In such situations, the "interest" charged is at the government's applicable federal rate.

 Reason for the Rule: Like most other businesses, the government needs a steady stream of revenues to operate efficiently. In addition, the taxpayers' wherewithal-to-pay tax is greatest when they realize income. Consequently, the government requires taxpayers to make payments periodically during the year. The requirement also helps the government avoid losing tax revenues because the taxpayer becomes insolvent or is otherwise is unable to pay the required taxes.

.01 Avoiding the Underpayment Penalty—Corporate Taxpayers

C corporations are required to pay the estimated tax in four installments during the year. These installments are due on the 15th day of the fourth, sixth, ninth, and twelfth months of the corporation's tax year. If the 15th of the month falls on a weekend or a federal holiday, the payment is due the next business day.

Example 40: Lyber Books uses the calendar year as its tax year. Lyber's estimated tax payments each year are due no later than April 15, June 15, September 15, and December 15. If any of these dates falls on a weekend or a federal holiday, the payment is due the next business day.

Example 41: Rhynard Stamps uses a January 31 fiscal year-end. Rhynard's estimated tax payments are due no later than May 15, July 15, October 15, and January 15. If any of these dates falls on a weekend or a federal holiday, the payment is due the next business day.

Large corporations are required to pay as estimated tax 100 percent of the tax shown on their returns for the current tax year. A "large corporation" is one whose taxable income is at least $1 million for any of the previous three tax years. The corporation's taxable income is computed without regard to any net operating loss (NOL) deduction (see ¶ 1002) or capital loss carryforward (see ¶ 901.01).

Example 42: Radiant Heating, which qualifies as a large corporation, owes $100,000 in taxes for 2009. For 2010, Radiant must make equal estimated tax payments that total at least 100 percent of its 2010 income tax liability. Its 2009 tax liability is irrelevant.

Example 43: Assume the same facts as in Example 42, except Radiant's tax liability in 2009 was $300,000. Since Radiant is a large corporation, its 2010 estimated tax payments are based on its 2010 tax liability.

To avoid an underpayment penalty, corporations that are not large corporations must make estimated payments equal to the *lesser* of (1) 100 percent of the tax shown on its return for the current tax year or (2) 100 percent of the tax shown on its return for the preceding tax year.

Example 44: Hawthorn is not a large corporation. Its federal tax liability for 2009 was $20,000. To avoid a penalty for underpayment of taxes, Hawthorn must make estimated payments totaling the *lesser* of $20,000 or its 2010 tax liability.

 Planning Pointer: If a corporation that is not considered a large corporation is uncertain as to its current year's tax liability, it should consider making estimated payments using 100 percent of the prior year's tax liability. This will ensure that the corporation is not subject to any underpayment penalty in case the actual tax liability for the year unexpectedly increases. For example, in Example 44, Hawthorn can make

> estimated payments based on the last year's actual tax liability of $20,000 and be guaranteed not to be subject to any underpayment penalty. The downside to using this "safe harbor" approach to paying estimated taxes is that if the taxpayer's actual tax liability in the current year is significantly less than in the prior year, the corporation will have allowed the federal government use of its overpayment for the entire year.

The amount of each required installment generally is one-fourth of the amount of estimated tax due for the year. Corporations that receive most of their taxable income toward the end of the year may benefit by annualizing their income and using the tax liability calculated based on that annualized income to determine the required amount of each installment.

 Planning Pointer: Businesses that receive most of their taxable income at the end of the year should consider using the annualized method to compute each required installment of estimated tax even though it results in a large payment at the end of the year. When businesses overpay their estimated tax during the year, they make an interest-free loan to the government. It is better for a business to retain that money for as long as possible and to let it earn money for the business.

.02 Avoiding the Underpayment Penalty—Individual Taxpayers

Sole proprietors and other individuals are required to make estimated tax payments when the amounts withheld from other sources are not sufficient to cover the amounts the government expects them to prepay during the year. Individual taxpayers (other than farmers and fishermen) must make total payments during the year equal to the *lesser* of (1) 90 percent of the tax shown on their tax return for the current tax year or (2) 100 percent of their tax liability for the preceding tax year. The percentage increases to 110 percent of the prior year's tax liability for taxpayers whose AGI exceeded $150,000 in the previous tax year ($75,000 if married filing separately). Farmers and fishermen are required to pay 66.67 percent of the *lesser* of (1) the tax reported on their current year's tax return for the year or (2) their tax liability for the preceding tax year.

Special rule for 2009. Qualified individuals can avoid a penalty for underpaying their estimated income tax for a tax year beginning in 2009 if they pay 90 percent of their tax liability for 2008. An individual is a "qualified individual" if the individual's adjusted gross income for 2008 was less than $500,000 ($250,000 if the individual was married but filing a separate return) and the individual certifies that more than 50 percent of that income was income from a small business (i.e., a trade or business whose average number of employees was fewer than 500 for the calendar year ending with or within the individual's 2008 tax year).

Example 45: George Cash is a sole proprietor who operates a pottery business. His AGI for 2009 was $100,000, and he paid $20,000 in federal income tax that year. George anticipates that his tax liability for 2010 (including his self-employment taxes) will be $22,000. If George's actual income tax liability for 2010 is $22,000, to avoid any underpayment penalty, George must have prepaid his taxes for 2010 of at least $19,800 (the *lesser* of (1) $20,000 or (2) $19,800 ($22,000 × 90%)). The $19,800 can be prepaid through withholdings (for example, from wages, interest, or dividend income) or through quarterly estimated payments to the federal government.

Example 46: Tommie Waldon is a sole proprietor whose 2009 AGI was $155,000. Tommie's tax liability for 2009 was $34,000, and she anticipates that her tax for 2010 will be $40,000. Assuming Tommie had no withholdings during the year and that her actual tax liability is $40,000, she will avoid any underpayment penalty if her required estimated tax payments for 2010 are at least $36,000 (the *lesser* of (1) $36,000 (90% of this year's $40,000 tax liability) or (2) $37,400 (110% of last year's $34,000 tax liability).

Individuals are required to pay their estimated taxes in four installments. Most individuals use a calendar year-end, and therefore their estimated payments are due on April 15, June 15, September 15, and January 15 of the following year. If the 15th of the month falls on a weekend or a holiday, the taxes are due the following business day. The amount of each required installment generally is one-fourth of the amount of the estimated tax due for the year. Individuals who receive most of their taxable income toward the end of the year may benefit by annualizing their income and using the tax liability calculated based on that annualized income to determine the required amount of each installment.

Example 47: Jay Keith is a sole proprietor who uses the calendar year as his tax year. His estimated tax payments for 2009 are due by April 15, 2009, June 15, 2009, September 15, 2009, and January 15, 2010.

 Planning Pointer: If an individual taxpayer is uncertain as to its current year's tax liability, the taxpayer should consider making estimated payments using 100 percent of the prior year's tax liability (110 percent if the prior year's AGI was more than $150,000). This will protect the taxpayer in situations where the actual tax liability for the year unexpectedly increases.

GROSS INCOME

Up to this point in the textbook, an overview of the entire federal income tax system has been presented. It is now time to begin taking a more in-depth look at some of the components of the taxable income formula. In this chapter, gross income is once again discussed and examined more closely. In Chapters 5 to 7, business deductions will be discussed, and in Chapters 8 and 9 the tax laws governing gains and losses on the disposal of business and investment property will be presented. The Code provides the following statutory definition of "gross income."[20]

> **General Definition**—Except as otherwise provided in this subtitle, gross income means all income from whatever source derived, including (but not limited to) the following items:
>
> 1. Compensation for services, including fees, commissions, fringe benefits, and similar items;
> 2. Gross income derived from business;
> 3. Gains derived from dealings in property;
> 4. Interest;
> 5. Rents;
> 6. Royalties;
> 7. Dividends;
> 8. Alimony and separate maintenance payments;
> 9. Annuities;
> 10. Income from life insurance and endowment contracts;
> 11. Pensions;
> 12. Income from discharge of indebtedness;
> 13. Distributive share of partnership gross income;
> 14. Income in respect of a decedent; and
> 15. Income from an interest in an estate or trust.

This definition is not intended to be comprehensive but instead provides a list of the more common types of gross income. As specifically provided in Code Sec. 61, all income is gross income, unless "otherwise provided." As a result, the presumption is that all receipts by a taxpayer are included, unless a specific statutory provision excluding them can be identified.

---

[20] Code Sec. 61.

Spotlight: Due to the all-inclusive approach to defining gross income, the IRS often uses a technique called the "bank deposits test" to search for unreported or underreported income. This test involves having the taxpayer bring in 12 months of bank statements. The IRS agent then totals all deposits into the taxpayer's bank accounts and compares that total to the gross income reported on the tax return. Any difference (if deposits exceed reported income) is presumed to be an underreporting, and the taxpayer must specifically provide evidence to counter this presumption.

¶ 410 Identifying Income

The Code takes an all-inclusive approach to determining what is included in gross income, which means that unless a provision in the tax law exists to not tax an item of income, the income is taxed.[21] This language has been interpreted as including all accessions to wealth, clearly realized, over which a taxpayer has complete dominion.[22] Accordingly, income only includes items that increase a taxpayer's wealth, and then only those that are realized during the tax year constitute income. Any items that reduce a taxpayer's wealth would be considered deductions, if anything at all. Wealth is considered realized when it is reduced to cash or property other than cash.

Example 48: Cratten Sealers borrows $1 million to purchase a new office building. The loan proceeds do not have to be included in the company's gross income because they do not increase the company's net wealth. Although the company receives an additional $1 million, its debt increased by $1 million, and consequently, no wealth has been created.

Example 49: Sidewalk Lighting has its manufacturing plant appraised and discovers it has increased in value by $50,000 since the beginning of the year. Although the company's wealth technically might have increased by $50,000, it does not have to include that amount in its gross income for the year because it did not realize any of the $50,000.

Reason for the Rule: The realization principle was adopted for several reasons. First, it would be costly to require taxpayers to have all of their property appraised each year to determine the change in net wealth during the year. Second, it would be costly and difficult for the government to determine whether taxpayers had properly appraised their property. Third, taxpayers might find it necessary to sell their property (perhaps in a forced sale at a loss) to pay tax owed on unrealized appreciation, and fourth, taxpayers might be able to save taxes by deducting a loss they might never actually incur.

Income is not limited to cash received; it also includes the fair market value (FMV) of property or services received.[23] This is true even though the business uses the cash method of accounting. Income usually is not realized when property is purchased, even though the property is purchased at a discount. However, gross income can be realized from the purchase of property at less than its FMV if the bargain element is a disguised dividend or a disguised compensation.

Example 50: Bigsby Management performs consulting services in exchange for a computer worth $2,000. Bigsby must include the $2,000 value of the computer in its income.

Example 51: McKenzie Chemical Engineers went shopping for a computer and found one with a retail price of $2,000 that was on sale for $1,750. The company does not have to include the difference between the computer's retail price and the sale price in its income.

---

[21] Code Sec. 61.
[22] *Glenshaw Glass Co.*, SCt, 55-1 USTC ¶ 9308, 348 US 426, 75 SCt 473.

[23] Reg. § 1.446-1(a)(3).

Example 52: Adu Boxes has its eye on some land with an estimated FMV of $300,000. When the owner of the land suffers a financial reversal and needs to sell the land in a hurry, the owner offers the land to Adu for $250,000. Although Adu purchases the property for $50,000 less than its estimated FMV, it does not recognize any income from the purchase.

Example 53: Taurus Industries performs consulting services for Wollmuth Flooring and charges Wollmuth $15,000 for the services, which was half its going rate. A week later, Wollmuth sells Taurus a vehicle worth $25,000 but charges Taurus only $10,000. If the IRS can establish that the $15,000 reduction in the vehicle's price was disguised compensation to Taurus, Taurus will be required to include the $15,000 in its income.

Income is not necessarily the same as **gross receipts**, which is the total FMV of property received in exchange for selling property or performing services. The concept of gross receipts is an even broader term than income and includes nontaxable returns of capital (such as the cost of goods sold) as well as income. The cost of goods sold must be subtracted from gross receipts when determining the amount to include in income. Income must also be distinguished from **gross sales**, which is the total amount of sales at invoice prices, not reduced by any discounts, returns, or allowances. The amount of any discounts, returns, and allowances is subtracted from gross sales to determine how much has to be included in income.

Example 54: Solt Telephones had gross sales of $100,000 during its tax year. Its cost of goods sold was $30,000. The value of returned goods was $5,000, and the amount of discounts and allowances was $8,000. The amount that Solt includes in income is $57,000.

Gross sales	$100,000
Less: Sales returns	(5,000)
Less: Sales discounts	(8,000)
Net sales	$ 87,000
Less: Cost of goods sold	(30,000)
Gross income from sales	$ 57,000

.01 Gross Profit

In accordance with the capital recovery doctrine, if a merchant purchases inventory costing $4,000 and later sells it for $10,000, the taxpayer's gross income from the transaction is $6,000 ($10,000 – $4,000). In this way, the tax concept of "gross income" is similar to the accounting term "gross profit."

Inventories. Gross profit from business operations is computed by deducting the cost of goods sold (COGS) from gross receipts. If inventories are material, then the accrual method must be used to compute gross profit from inventories (see ¶ 305.01). As is done in financial accounting, COGS is determined either (1) by aggregating the cost of each specific item sold or (2) by adding the cost of inventory from the beginning of the year to the cost of goods purchased or produced during the year and then subtracting out the cost of inventory remaining at the end of the year.

Example 55: Pink Co. is a small corporation that buys auto parts at wholesale and resells them to the general public. At the beginning of its tax year, the costs associated with its inventories were $60,000; at the end of the year they were $50,000. During the tax year Pink paid $30,000 for carburetors, $18,000 for mufflers, and $10,000 for air filters. Its gross receipts for the year were $110,000. Pink computes its gross profit as follows:

Gross receipts		$110,000
Less: Cost of goods sold		
Beginning inventory	$ 60,000	
Plus: Purchases	58,000	
Goods available for sale	$118,000	
Less: Ending inventory	(50,000)	(68,000)
Gross profit		$ 42,000

Uniform capitalization rules. Businesses that manufacture their own goods or acquire property for resale must abide by the uniform capitalization (UNICAP) rules and capitalize direct costs and an allocable portion of most indirect costs that are incurred because of production or resale activities.[24] Thus, certain expenses incurred during the year are included in the cost basis of property produced or in inventory costs, rather than being expensed immediately. These costs are recovered through COGS when the property is sold. This method is very similar to full absorption costing used to report inventories and COGS on the financial statements.

Under the UNICAP rules, direct material costs and direct labor costs incurred for production or resale of property must be capitalized. "Direct material costs" include the cost of those materials that become an integral part of the asset plus the cost of materials that are used in the ordinary course of the production of the asset. "Direct labor costs" include the cost of labor that can be identified or associated with a particular activity. This includes all types of compensation (basic, overtime, sick, vacation, etc.) plus payroll taxes and payments to a supplemental unemployment benefit plan. All costs other than direct material or direct labor are treated as "indirect costs." Certain types of costs may directly benefit a particular activity or be incurred because of a particular activity even though the same costs also benefit other activities. Therefore, costs that benefit more than one activity must be reasonably allocated to determine the portion that is attributable to each activity.

Inventory costing. Whether a business manufactures its own inventory or whether it purchases inventory from a supplier and resells it to customers, a method is needed for assigning a cost to the units sold during the year. Two common costing methods are the last-in, first-out (LIFO) and the first-in, first-out (FIFO) methods. Under LIFO, the last units produced/purchased are deemed to be the first units sold (and therefore the ones included in COGS). Under FIFO, the first units produced/purchased are the ones that are deemed to have been sold (and therefore the ones included in COGS). In inflationary times, the LIFO method produces the highest COGS (and thus, the lowest gross profit), whereas FIFO would produce lower COGS (and higher profits). Accordingly, many businesses would prefer to use the LIFO costing method for tax purposes and to use FIFO to calculate COGS on the income statement. Although this strategy is in the best interest of the business, the tax laws generally require that in order to use LIFO for tax purposes, the business must also use it for financial accounting purposes.[25]

Spotlight: In inflationary times the use of LIFO results in lower gross profit. Therefore, under such conditions, businesses that want to use LIFO for tax purposes will be selecting a method that results in higher cash flows (through paying less taxes) but lower profitability reported on the financial statements.

GAAP vs. Code: A corporation that wants to use LIFO for tax purposes must also use LIFO for financial reporting purposes. If a corporation does not want to use LIFO for

---

[24] Code Sec. 263A.   [25] Reg. § 1.472-2.

financial reporting purposes, it will use FIFO for both financial and tax purposes. Consequently, no differences between net income and taxable income should arise in the corporation's reports. However, any differences in the amounts required to be capitalized to cost of goods sold during the year would need to be accounted for when reconciling net income to taxable income on the corporation's income tax return.

Installment sales. As discussed in Chapter 3, regardless of the taxpayer's method of accounting, gross profit from installment sales is taxed when the cash flows are received, rather than when the income is realized. In this instance, the special accounting rules control the timing of the recognized gain on the tax return, unless the taxpayer elects to recognize the entire gain in the year of the sale. (See ¶ 309.01.)

 GAAP vs. Code: The installment sale method is not an acceptable method for reporting gross profit on the income statement. Therefore, corporations that use the installment method for tax purposes will report different amounts of gain on the tax return than on the income statement. For large corporations, this difference will need to be reconciled on the corporate income tax return. The details behind the calculation of gross profit reported each year from an installment sale are discussed in Chapters 8 and 9 (see ¶ 810 and ¶ 904.02).

.02 Gains from Sales of Property

When property is sold or exchanged, the amount included in income is the difference between the amount realized and the taxpayer's adjusted basis in the property.[26] A taxpayer's adjusted basis in property is the amount invested in the property reduced by certain amounts (such as deductions for depreciation, depletion, and amortization).[27] If the amount realized from a disposition of property exceeds the adjusted basis of the property, the difference is a loss, which is a deduction from gross income. (See ¶ 403.02.) The tax laws surrounding the calculation of the amount realized and the adjusted basis are the focus of Chapter 8. Also discussed in Chapter 8 are the situations in which gains realized from the sale or exchange of property are not recognized on the tax return and, therefore, are not included in the taxpayer's gross income. This occurs because a tax law either excludes the gain from gross income or postpones recognition of the gain to another tax year.

Example 56: Fire Gemstone invests $100,000 in a parcel of land, which it later sells for $250,000. Only $150,000 ($250,000 – $100,000) is included in gross income because that is the amount by which Fire Gemstone's net worth was increased. The remaining $100,000 represents a return of the company's investment in the land.

.03 Rental Income

The amounts owners of property receive from others for the rights to use their property are taxed as rental income. As discussed in Chapter 3, regardless of the taxpayer's method of accounting, receipt of rents in advance of providing the rental services generally must be included in gross income in the tax year in which the advance rent is received. Expenses for items such as repairs, interest, taxes, and depreciation that relate to the rental property are deductions and should not be treated as reductions in gross rental receipts.

Example 57: Syddel Realty receives $20,000 in rental income from an apartment building that it leases out to tenants. During the year, Syddel pays $1,000 for repairs made to the building. It also pays property taxes of $5,000 and interest on the mortgage loan it obtained to purchase the building of $4,000. Syddel also deducts a depreciation expense of $12,500. Although Syddel realized a $2,500 loss from its rental of the apartment building during the year ($20,000 – $1,000 – $5,000 – $4,000 – $12,500), it

---

[26] Code Sec. 1001(a).   [27] Code Sec. 1016.

must include $20,000 in its gross income. It can separately deduct the various rental expenses from its gross income.

Example 58: Redd Tooth, Inc. enters into a 10-year lease to rent a building that it owns. In addition to $7,000 for that year's rent, in the first year it receives $7,000 in advance as rent for the tenth and last year of the lease. Redd Tooth must include $14,000 in gross income in the first year.

 GAAP vs. Code: On the income statement, a corporate landlord "matches" rental income to the period to which the rental services are provided (when the revenue is earned). On the tax return, rents are included in gross income in the period in which they are received. This is particularly important in the case of advance lease payments, for which the advance payment is recorded on the books as unearned rent revenue but is included in gross income for tax purposes. This difference will be reversed in the year in which the rental services are finally provided. In Example 58, during the first year of the lease Redd Tooth includes $7,000 in net income and $14,000 in taxable income. Therefore, when reconciling net income to taxable income on that year's tax return, Redd Tooth will need to add $7,000 to its net income. In the tenth year of the lease, Redd Tooth will report $7,000 of rental income in net income, but nothing on the tax return. Thus, it will need to subtract out the $7,000 from net income when reconciling it with taxable income on that year's tax return.

Taxes and other expenses paid by a tenant. When a tenant pays a property owner's expenses, the amounts paid on the property owner's behalf are treated as additional rent,[28] and as such, are includible in the property owner's gross income. A common business lease type is a "triple net lease" in which the lessee pays taxes, insurance, and maintenance costs of the property. In this arrangement, the payments for taxes and insurance by the lessee are regarded as income to the lessor. These payments may be deductible rental expenses, although the timing of the expenses may differ from the recognition of income.

Example 59: Leonard Enterprises insures its factory building against fire. The premiums, payable every three years, are $3,500. As part of the terms of the lease, a new tenant agrees to pay the premiums on the policy by forwarding the money directly to the insurance company. The tenant's $3,500 payment is treated by the tenant as additional rent and the entire sum is to be included in Leonard's gross income. Leonard will be entitled to a deduction for the insurance expense, but it must apportion the $3,500 over the three-year period in accordance with its method of accounting.

.04 Dividend Income

When a corporation generates taxable income, it pays taxes on that income. When the board of directors of a C corporation decides to distribute the corporation's after-tax profits to the corporation's shareholders, the distribution is treated as a dividend to the extent of the corporation's current or accumulated earnings and profits.[29] Earnings and profits (E&P) is an account that keeps track of a corporation's ability to make distributions to shareholders from the corporation's current or accumulated profits. This account is increased by the after-tax amounts the corporation earns that enhance its ability to pay dividends and is decreased when it incurs expenses or makes distributions to shareholders. The calculation of a C corporation's E&P is described in detail in Chapter 12 (see ¶ 1207).

When a shareholder of a C corporation receives dividend income, the amount received causes the shareholder's wealth to increase, and accordingly, represents income to the shareholder. When the shareholder is another C corporation, some or all of the income may not be taxed (see

---

[28] Reg. § 1.61-8(c).

[29] Code Secs. 301 and 316(a).

discussion at ¶ 411.02 later in the chapter). When a shareholder of a C corporation is an individual and the individual receives dividend income, the full amount represents income to the shareholder. However, if the dividend is qualified dividend income, it may be taxed at a special, lower rate of tax. (See ¶ 405.02.)

Gross income from flow-through entities is taxed to its owners. Because the owners have already paid tax on the income, distributions from these entities are not dividends and are not part of gross income. The rules related to distributions received from various entities are summarized in Table 4-3. The tax consequences of gross income generated by flow-through entities are discussed in greater detail in Chapters 14 and 15, where the various flow-through entities are discussed.

Table 4-3 Summary of Distributions from Business Entities

Distributor	Recipient	Tax Consequences
Sole proprietorship	Proprietor	Tax-free distribution because the earnings have been taxed on the sole proprietor's individual income tax return.
Partnership	Partner	Tax-free distribution because the earnings have been taxed on the partner's income tax return.
S corporation	Shareholder	Tax-free distribution because the earnings have been taxed on the shareholder's income tax return.
C corporation	Individual	Taxed as dividend income.
	Partnership	Flows through to the partners as dividend income.
	S corporation	Flows through to the shareholders as dividend income.
	C corporation	Taxable after taking the dividends received deduction into consideration. (See ¶ 411.02.)

.05 Interest Income

Interest is the compensation allowed by law for the use, forbearance, or detention of money or its equivalent. This includes interest earned from certificates of deposit or money market accounts as well as interest earned from notes and bonds receivable. Although most interest is taxable, the tax laws exempt municipal interest from gross income. (See ¶ 411.01.)

Imputed interest on original issue discount bonds. When a corporation attempts to issue bonds that promise to pay a face rate of interest below the current market interest rate, the bonds cannot be sold at face value (the amount due at maturity). In other words, investors will not pay the corporation the same amount that they will redeem the bonds for at maturity because the periodic interest payments the corporation is agreeing to pay (based on the face rate) are less than the amounts they could earn elsewhere in the marketplace (market rate). Since the interest rate associated with the bonds is inadequate compared to the market rate investors can get elsewhere, the issuing corporation will find it necessary to issue the bonds at a discount (less than face value). The amount of the required discount (known as **original issue discount (OID)**) is a function of the difference between the face rate associated with the bond and the current market interest rate.

Some corporations issue bonds that make no periodic interest payments (that is, with a zero-percent face rate of interest). These bonds, which are issued at the deepest of discounts, are called "zero-coupon bonds." In all of these cases, the full face value of the bond is repaid when the bond matures, so in reality, the amount of the OID represents additional interest that the investor earns over the life of the bond.[30] As introduced in Chapter 3 (see ¶ 306.01), taxpayers must report OID interest in income in the year it is earned, regardless of the taxpayer's overall method of accounting. Accordingly, the tax laws require that the bondholders include in gross income the periodic cash payments they receive plus a portion of the OID. Thus, the total taxable interest income is the same amount the bondholder would have earned if the bonds had paid the market rate of interest when they were first issued.

The amount of each period's OID included in gross income is the carrying value of the bonds multiplied by the market rate of interest for the period (as determined at the time the bonds were issued). The carrying value of the bonds is then increased by the amount of the OID included in income. By increasing the carrying value of the bond by the taxable OID, the carrying value of the bonds will approach face value by the time the bonds mature. Therefore, when the bondholders receive full face value at maturity, no gain or loss will be realized by the bondholders.

Example 60: On July 1, 2009, a 10-year zero coupon bond with a face value of $10 million is issued by a corporation for $4,788,923. The bonds are issued to yield the equivalent of a 7.5-percent annual interest market interest rate, with interest compounded semiannually (therefore, a 3.75-percent semiannual interest rate). The OID associated with the bond is $5,211,077 ($10,000,000 − $4,788,923). Since the bonds pay a zero rate of interest, the owner of the bonds will receive nothing until maturity. However, over the next 10 years (20 semiannual periods), the bondholders will collectively earn income equal to $5,211,077. To determine the taxable OID for 2009 (the six months from July 1, 2009, to December 31, 2009), the carrying value of the bonds ($4,788,923) is multiplied by the semiannual market rate of interest at the time the bonds were issued (3.75%). Thus, the total taxable OID for the first six months is $179,585 ($4,788,923 × 3.75%). The carrying value of the bond is increased by this amount to $4,968,508 ($4,788,923 + $179,585).

To determine the taxable OID for each of the later periods, the periodic market rate is applied to the (adjusted) carrying value at the beginning of the accrual period. The carrying value of the bond is the sum of the original issue price plus all taxable OID over the prior accrual periods.

Example 61: The taxable original issue discount amount for the second accrual period of the bond (first half of 2010) in Example 60 is $186,319 ($4,968,508 × 3.75%). The amortization of OID for the first 2½ years of the bond's life is shown in the table below:

Payment	Taxable OID*	Carrying Value**
		$4,788,923
12/31/2009	$179,585	4,968,508
6/30/2010	186,319	5,154,827
12/31/2010	193,306	5,348,133
6/30/2011	200,555	5,548,688
12/31/2011	208,076	5,756,764

*Determined by multiplying the carrying value at the beginning of the period by the 3.75% market rate per period.

**Determined by adding the taxable OID to the carrying value of the bond.

 Spotlight: Amortizing OID accomplishes two results. First, the interest accrues to the owner as it is earned, not when it is received. Although this is consistent with the accrual method of accounting, both cash and accrual method taxpayers are required to report this imputed interest in income as it is earned. Second, the basis of the bond to

---

[30] Code Secs. 163(e) and 1272(a).

> the bondholder is increased on a regular basis, so when the bonds are sold or are redeemed at maturity, they are not taxed a second time on the OID. This also prevents the possibility of a bondholder reporting the difference between the amount of cash received at maturity and the cash paid for the bond as a capital gain, rather than as interest income.

De minimis **OID.** The tax laws treat OID as $0 if the total OID on a debt instrument is less than one-fourth of 1 percent (.0025) of the redemption price at maturity multiplied by the number of full years from the date of original issue to maturity.[31]

Example 62:   A corporation purchases a 10-year bond with a redemption price at maturity of $1,000. The bond is issued at $980 with OID of $20 ($1,000 – $980). One-fourth of 1 percent of $1,000 times 10 full years from the issue date to maturity is $25 ($1,000 × .0025 × 10). Under the *de minimis* rule, the taxpayer can disregard the OID since the $20 discount for the bond is less than $25.

Example 63:   Assume the same facts as in Example 62, except the bond was issued at $950. Because the $50 of OID is greater than the $25 *de minimis* threshold amount for the bond, the taxpayer must include part of the $50 OID in gross income each year. The amortized OID will be added to the carrying value of the bond so that at maturity its carrying value will equal the redemption price.

 Spotlight: The amount of interest required to be included in gross income by the recipient of the OID (bondholder) is the same as the amount of interest expense that is deducted by the payer (corporation issuing the bonds).

Imputed interest on below market loans. When a business loans money, it normally charges the borrower interest at the current market rate. Likewise, when a business borrows money, it expects to pay interest to the lender at the market rate. Thus, when a loan is made for which the interest charged is less than the market rate, it is usually because a special relationship exists between the lender and the borrower. For example, a corporation could loan money to an employee or to one of its shareholders. When the terms of a loan do not include an "adequate rate of interest," the IRS will consider that adequate interest was charged by the lender and paid by the borrower, even though it is not the same amount as the actual cash interest paid by the borrower. The term used to describe such loans is **below market loans**, and the amount of "deemed" interest paid by the borrower is called **imputed interest**.[32]

Adequate interest. The amount of interest deemed "adequate" depends on the type of loan arrangement the parties enter into. If the terms of the loan call for a scheduled date or dates at which the principal must be repaid, the loan is a "term loan." If the loan proceeds must be repaid immediately upon request of the lender, or if the terms of the loan do not specify a maturity date, the loan is a "demand loan." In the case of a term loan, adequate interest is based on the applicable federal rate (AFR) in effect as of the day on which the loan was made, compounded semiannually. The AFR is a statutory federal rate of interest that is adjusted monthly and is published by the IRS. The rates are based on the average market yield on outstanding marketable obligations of the United States during the one-month period ending on the 14th day of the preceding month.[33] There are three categories of AFRs, referenced by the term of the loan, as shown below. In the case of a demand loan, the loan amount is considered as a series of one-day term loans, and thus, adequate interest on such a loan would be interest that is computed on a daily basis using the federal short-term rate.

---

[31] Code Sec. 1273(a)(3).
[32] Code Sec. 7872.

[33] Code Sec. 1274(d).

Term of the Loan	Applicable Federal Rate
Not more than three years	The federal short-term rate
Over three years but not over nine years	The federal mid-term rate
Over nine years	The federal long-term rate

When a corporation makes a below market loan to a shareholder, the IRS treats the shareholder as having paid adequate interest to the corporation. To the extent the amount of adequate interest is less than the actual amount of interest paid according to the terms of the loan, the difference represents a "deemed" interest payment that the shareholder makes to the corporation. The corporation is then deemed to distribute back to the shareholder the same amount. Since the deemed payment by the shareholder to the corporation and the deemed distribution by the corporation to the shareholder are for the same amount, these amounts offset one another and no cash is actually ever exchanged. These deemed payments are depicted in Figure 4-3.

Figure 4-3 Corporation-Shareholder Below Market Loan

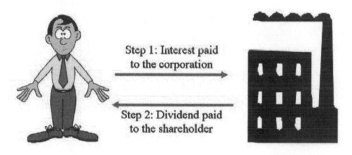

Step 1: Interest paid to the corporation

Step 2: Dividend paid to the shareholder

In a corporation-shareholder below market loan, the borrower (shareholder) is deemed to pay interest to the lender (corporation) in an amount equal to the amount of inadequate interest charged on the loan. The corporation includes the imputed interest in gross income, and the shareholder may or may not be able to deduct the interest (depending on the nature of the loan) (see ¶ 1304.03). The corporation is then deemed to pay a dividend to the shareholder for the amount of the inadequate interest. The distribution is treated as a dividend and is taxed as such to the shareholder. The corporation gets no deduction for the corresponding dividend distribution. Consequently, neither party has escaped taxation by using this arrangement.

Example 64: Greene & Company loans its sole shareholder, Margaret Greene, $200,000 for five years with no stated interest rate. At the time the loan was made, the current annual AFR mid-term rate (for loans between three and nine years) was nine percent, which when compounded semiannually yields 9.2025 percent. Since no interest is paid in cash on the note, each year Margaret is deemed to have paid $18,405 of interest to the corporation ($200,000 × 9.2025%), which it includes in gross income. Greene & Company is then deemed to pay a dividend to Margaret for $18,405. Margaret reports the dividend income of $18,405 in her gross income. She also has $18,405 of interest expense which she may or may not be able to deduct.

 Reason for the Rule: Since corporations cannot deduct dividends paid against gross income, corporations (particularly closely held corporations) have an incentive to attempt to characterize transfers of cash to their owners as something other than a dividend. One of these schemes is to call the payments a loan to the shareholder. In this case, the shareholder receives free use of cash from the corporation. As can be seen in Figure 4-3 and Example 64, the tax laws address this problem by treating the arrangement as dividend income to the shareholder and interest income to the corporation. Thus, both parties pay tax on income that was never actually exchanged.

The imputed interest rules also apply to any below market loan that involves a compensation-related loan between an employer and an employee or between an independent contractor and a person for whom the independent contractor provides services. The imputed interest rules also apply to any loan that has tax avoidance as one of its principal purposes. Figure 4-4 depicts the tax consequences of a compensation-related below market loan.

Figure 4-4 Employer-Employee Below Market Loan

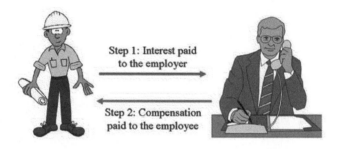

Step 1: Interest paid to the employer

Step 2: Compensation paid to the employee

In a compensation-related loan between an employer and its employee, the employee is deemed to pay interest to the employer for an amount equal to the amount of inadequate interest charged on the loan. The employer is then deemed to pay the employee compensation equal to the same amount. The employer reports the interest in gross income and the employee may or may not deduct the interest expense depending on the circumstances surrounding the loan (see ¶ 1304.03). The employer deducts the deemed amount paid as wage expense and the employee includes the amount in gross income as compensation.

Example 65: Assume the same facts as in Example 64, except Margaret is not a shareholder but, instead, is an officer and employee of the corporation. Each year, Margaret is deemed to pay $18,405 of interest to the corporation. The corporation is then deemed to turn around and pay $18,405 in compensation to Margaret. The corporation deducts the $18,405 as compensation paid, and Margaret includes the amount in gross income as compensation. The corporation includes the imputed interest in gross income and Margaret may or may not deduct the interest expense, depending on the use of the funds.

Example 66: Assume the same facts as in Example 65, except the terms of the loan require Margaret to pay interest equal to an annual rate of five percent (5.0625 percent when compounded semiannually). Each year, the deemed payment is reduced by the $10,125 of actual interest paid by Margaret ($200,000 × 5.0625%). Thus, the imputed interest deemed paid equals $8,280 ($18,405 – $10,125).

De minimis loans. A *de minimis* exception to the below market loan rules exists. In the case of any compensation-related or corporation-shareholder below market loan, no interest is imputed to either the borrower or the lender for any day on which the aggregate amount of all outstanding loans between the borrower and the lender does not exceed $10,000. This exception does not apply to loans for which tax avoidance is a principal purpose.[34]

.06 Distributive Shares from Flow-Through Entities

If the taxpayer is an owner in a flow-through entity, the taxpayer includes in its gross income its distributive share of the entity's items of gross income, regardless of whether the share is distributed to the taxpayer. The calculation of the taxpayer's distributive share of a flow-through entity's gross income is discussed in Chapters 14 and 15.

Example 67: Luffman Supplies is a partner in ABC Partnership. Luffman's share of the partnership's income for the year is $5,000; however, none of that amount was distributed to Luffman. Even though none of that $5,000 was distributed to Luffman, it includes the entire $5,000 in its gross income for the year. When the $5,000 is eventually distributed, Luffman will not pay tax on the $5,000 a second time.

Example 68: Donaldson Company is a partner in ABC Partnership. During the year ABC receives $10,000 of interest income from corporate bonds in which ABC invested. Donaldson's share of the interest is $3,000. The $3,000 represents taxable interest income to Donaldson.

.07 Other Items of Income

Some sources of income are less common, but they are subject to taxes nonetheless. Common forms of other income include damages and insurance, tax benefits, and income from the discharge of indebtedness.

Damages and insurance. Damage awards businesses receive for replacement of lost business profits or punitive damages must be included in income. Recoveries representing a replacement for lost income are taxed in the same manner as the lost income would have been taxed had it not been lost. Similarly, if the taxpayer is insured against a loss of net profits, the proceeds are taxable income. On the other hand, a recovery for property or property rights that were diminished in value is a nontaxable recovery of capital to the extent the recovery does not exceed the taxpayer's adjusted basis in the property or the property right. Any excess is taxed. If the amount of the recovery is less than the adjusted basis of the property or the property right, such adjusted basis is reduced by the amount of the recovery.

Example 69: Erne Compactors sues a competitor for antitrust violations and is awarded $150,000 in damages for its lost profits. Erne includes the $150,000 in its income.

Example 70: Lentine Gaskets successfully sues a company for illegally interfering with its suppliers and is awarded $50,000 in punitive damages. Lentine includes the damages in its income.

Tax benefit rule. If a taxpayer is able to deduct an item in one tax year that is refunded to the taxpayer in a subsequent tax year, the tax benefit rule (see ¶ 313) taxes the recovered amounts.

Example 71: In 2009, Bellomo (a calendar year corporation) deducts as a bad debt expense a $3,000 loan it made to an employee when the loan becomes uncollectible. In 2010, Bellomo receives $1,000 from the employee as partial repayment of the loan. The company includes the $1,000 in its gross income for 2010.

Income from discharge of indebtedness. The cancellation of a taxpayer's debt results in income to the taxpayer because the debt no longer must be repaid, thereby causing the taxpayer's net worth to increase. However, see ¶ 411.04 for situations in which discharge from indebtedness may be excluded from gross income. If a corporation satisfies its debt by transferring shares of its own corporate stock or the corporate stock of its parent company to the creditor, the corporation is

---

[34] Code Sec. 7872(c)(3).

treated as if it had paid the creditor with money equal to the FMV of the stock.[35] Thus, the corporation has income from the discharge of indebtedness to the extent that the principal of the debt exceeds the value of the stock (and any other property transferred).

Example 72: Finnigan Brass owes its creditors $10,000. The creditors reduce the debt owed to $8,000. The $2,000 reduction in indebtedness increases Finnigan's net worth and must be included in its gross income unless an exception applies (see ¶ 411.04).

Example 73: Olin Services owes $5,000 to one of its shareholders, James Olin. When James cancels the debt, it is likely to be viewed as a contribution to the capital of the corporation, and accordingly, none of the $5,000 represents income to Olin Services.

Example 74: Big Foot, Inc. owes a creditor $20,000. The creditor agrees to cancel the debt in exchange for $1,000 in cash and stock in Big Foot that has a FMV of $14,000. Big Foot recognizes income from the discharge of indebtedness in the amount of $5,000 ($20,000 − ($1,000 cash + $14,000 stock)).

¶ 411 Exclusions

Not all items of income are taxed by the federal government. The Code includes numerous provisions that specifically exclude certain items from gross income. These exclusions are considered matters of legislative grace that must be narrowly construed; taxpayers have the burden of proving that they qualify for an exclusion.[36] Exclusions should be distinguished from deductions. Deductions are amounts that are subtracted from gross income in order to arrive at a business's taxable income. By contrast, exclusions are items of income that are never taxed (and accordingly, never included in gross income).

.01 Municipal Interest

Interest income is specifically included in the list of broadly defined income in Code Sec. 61. However, Code Sec. 103 excludes from gross income interest received from state and local government bonds ("municipal bonds"). This exclusion does not extend to bonds issued by corporations or by the federal government. Furthermore, the exclusion only applies to the interest generated from the bonds. It does not extend to the gain realized on the sale of municipal bonds.

 Spotlight: In 1895, the Supreme Court set forth a doctrine of intergovernmental tax immunity whereby interest from state and local government bonds would not be subject to federal income tax.[37] In 1998, the Supreme Court set aside the doctrine and ruled that such interest was no longer immune from federal income taxes.[38] However, through enacting Code Sec. 103, Congress has chosen as a matter of public policy to confer these benefits on the holders of state and local government bonds (thus benefiting the issuing state and local governments by allowing them to offer lower interest rates than other taxable bonds).

.02 Dividends Received Deduction

Corporations are the only business entity for which the profits of the business are taxed twice—once for the corporation and a second time when the after-tax profits are distributed to shareholders. When the shareholder is a C corporation, the potential for triple taxation exists. To combat this, the tax laws allow corporations to reduce the amount of taxable dividends by granting them a **dividends received deduction (DRD)** of from 70 to 100 percent of the dividends received.

---

[35] Code Sec. 108.

[36] *See, e.g., A.J. Hackl Sr.*, CA-7, 2003-2 USTC ¶ 60,465, 335 F3d 664.

[37] *Pollock v. Farmers' Loan & Trust Co.*, SCt, 157 US 429, 15 SCt 673 (1895).

[38] *South Carolina v. Baker*, SCt, 88-1 USTC ¶ 9284, 485 US 505, 108 SCt 1355.

Although called a "deduction," the DRD does not result from an expenditure but instead is computed as a percentage of the dividends received during the year.

A C corporation may take a DRD for dividends received from either (1) a domestic (U.S.) corporation that is subject to income tax or (2) a foreign corporation that was once a domestic corporation if the distribution is made from the former domestic corporation's accumulated E&P. The DRD is 70 percent of dividends received if the corporation owns less than 20 percent of the stock of the distributing corporation. The deduction is increased to 80 percent if the corporation receiving the dividends owns at least 20 percent but less than 80 percent of the distributing corporation's stock. If the corporation receiving the dividends owns at least 80 percent of the distributing corporation's stock, the two companies are "affiliated companies." The tax laws allow a 100-percent DRD for dividends received from an affiliated company, thereby exempting the dividends entirely from federal income taxation.[39] For DRD purposes, stock ownership in another corporation is determined by the amount of voting stock as well as the value of the corporation's stock that the corporation receiving the dividend income owns in the distributing corporation. Shares of preferred stock owned in the distributing corporation are irrelevant to determining the ownership percentage for the DRD.

Example 75: During the year, Silk Finishers receives dividends from Folwell Publications. If Silk owns one percent of the outstanding common stock in Folwell, it is entitled to a 70-percent DRD.

Example 76: During the year, Isher Steel receives dividends from Razar Equipment. Isher owns 24 percent of the outstanding common stock of Razar. Isher's DRD is 80 percent.

Example 77: Assume the same facts as in Example 76, except Isher owns 80 percent of the outstanding common stock of Razar. Isher's DRD is 100 percent.

 Reason for the Rule: When a corporation earns income, that income is taxed, and when the corporation distributes that income to its shareholders the income is taxed a second time to the shareholders. Without the DRD deduction, a corporation's income could be taxed at least three times: once when earned by the corporation, a second time when distributed to corporate shareholders, and a third time when those corporate shareholders distribute the income to their shareholders.

Taxable income limitation. For corporations owning less than 20 percent of the stock in the distributing corporation, the DRD is limited to the *lesser* of (1) 70 percent of the dividends received or (2) 70 percent of the corporation's taxable income (with modifications). For corporations owning at least 20 percent but less than 80 percent of the stock in the distributing corporation, the DRD is limited to the *lesser* of (1) 80 percent of the dividends received or (2) 80 percent of the corporation's taxable income (with modifications). In neither instance does the taxable income limitation apply if after subtracting the full DRD, the taxpayer has a net operating loss for the year. The taxable income limitation also does not apply to dividends received from corporations that are part of an affiliated group.[40] For purposes of the taxable income limitation, taxable income is computed without deductions allowed for dividends received, net operating losses, income attributable to domestic production activities, any adjustment required when an extraordinary dividend is received, or any capital loss carryback to the year.

Example 78: Fulton Incorporated owns less than 20 percent of the stock in Dreamcasters, Inc. During 2009, Dreamcasters pays Fulton a $100,000 dividend. Fulton's taxable income is computed as follows:

---

[39] Code Sec. 243.   [40] Code Sec. 246(b).

Dividend income	$100,000
Sales revenue	40,000
Less: Business expenses	(80,000)
Taxable income before DRD	$ 60,000
Less: DRD ($100,000 × 70%)	(70,000)
Taxable loss	($ 10,000)

Because deducting 70 percent of dividends received produces a taxable loss, the taxable income limit does not apply, and Fulton's DRD equals $70,000 (70% × $100,000).

Example 79: Napier owns 20 percent of the stock in Rockpoint. During the year, Napier receives $100,000 of dividends from Rockpoint. Napier computes its taxable income as follows:

Dividends received	$100,000
Ordinary income	40,000
Less: Business expenses	(50,000)
Taxable income before DRD	$ 90,000
Less: DRD (limited to 80% of $90,000)	(72,000)
Taxable income	$ 18,000

Because Napier owns at least 20 percent but less than 80 percent of the stock in Rockpoint, its DRD cannot exceed 80 percent of the $100,000 of dividends it receives from Rockpoint during the year. However, if Napier were to deduct the full $80,000 ($100,000 × 80%) against its taxable income, the result does not create a tax loss, and therefore, the DRD is computed as the *lesser* of 80 percent of (1) the dividends received or (2) the taxable income before the DRD. Napier reduces its taxable income by $72,000 ($90,000 × 80%).

Example 80: Frampton, Inc. receives $150,000 of dividends from Ranmark Corporation, in which Frampton owns 80 percent of the stock. Since Frampton owns at least 80 percent of the stock in Ranmark, its DRD is 100 percent of the dividends received. The taxable income limitation does not apply to dividends between members of an affiliated group.

Example 81: Black, Inc. owns 75 percent of Yellow Co. The remaining 25 percent is held by unrelated parties. If Yellow declares and pays $4 million of dividends during the year, Black's dividend income would be $3 million ($4,000,000 × 75%). Assuming that the taxable income limitation does not apply, Black's DRD equals $2.4 million ($3,000,000 × 80%), which effectively reduces Black's taxable dividends to $600,000 ($3,000,000 – $2,400,000). If Black's marginal tax rate is 35 percent, its tax on the taxable portion of the dividend income is $210,000 ($600,000 × 35%). Thus, it effectively pays a seven-percent tax rate on the total dividends it receives during the year ($210,000 ÷ $3,000,000).

Example 82: White, Inc. receives $50,000 of dividends from short-term corporate investments in which it holds less than 10-percent ownership. Assuming the taxable income limitation does not apply, White recognizes $50,000 of dividend income, but will only pay tax on $15,000 after it reduces this amount by the $35,000 DRD ($50,000 × 70%). If White's taxable income is in the 35-percent tax bracket, then the tax associated with the taxable dividends equals $5,250 ($15,000 × 35%). Thus, White would effectively pay a 10.5-percent tax on the $50,000 of dividend income ($5,250 ÷ $50,000).

 GAAP vs. Code: The DRD is a tax concept. It has no equivalent in the financial accounting rules. Because the DRD may be subject to the taxable income limitation on the federal income tax, the DRD is one of the last items reported as a reduction in taxable income. When large corporations are required to reconcile their net (book) income to taxable income on the corporate tax return, they actually are required to reconcile net income with taxable income before the DRD or NOL deduction (see ¶ 1004). Consequently, there is no need to show the difference between these two methods in the reconciliation of net income and taxable income.

.03 Improvements Made by a Tenant

Ordinarily, a property owner reports no gross income in the year a tenant makes repairs or improvements on property that will revert to the property owner at the end of the lease term. However, if the parties intend the improvements to be, in whole or in part, a substitute for rental payments, then the property owner realizes rental income.[41] When such improvements do revert to the property owner at the end of the lease, the property owner takes a zero basis in the improvements. Thus, when the property owner eventually disposes of the property, any remaining value from the improvements will be recognized as taxable gain.

Example 83: Ponson Realty, Inc. leases land to Girard, Inc. for 20 years. Girard builds a manufacturing plant on the land. After 10 years, the tenant defaults on the lease, and Ponson repossesses the property. At that time, the manufacturing plant is worth $500,000. Ponson is not taxed on the $500,000. However, Ponson's adjusted basis in the plant is $0. Therefore, when it sells the plant the $500,000 previously untaxed income will be recognized.

.04 Cancellation of Indebtedness

Normally when a taxpayer's debt is forgiven, that constitutes income because the decrease in liabilities results in an increase in the taxpayer's wealth. However, when the forgiveness of debt results when a business is insolvent,[42] the taxpayer excludes from gross income the cancellation of debt to the extent of the insolvency.[43] A taxpayer is insolvent if its liabilities exceed the FMV of its assets. Thus, the extent of the insolvency is the amount by which the taxpayer's liabilities exceed the FMV of its assets. Accordingly, the taxable amount realized by an insolvent debtor from the cancellation of indebtedness is the *lesser* of (1) the amount of the indebtedness cancelled or (2) the excess of assets over liabilities after the cancellation of the debt. Cancellation of indebtedness while the taxpayer is going through bankruptcy proceedings is also excluded from gross income, regardless of the extent of the taxpayer's insolvency at the time the debt is forgiven.[44]

Example 84: Furber Fabrics' liabilities total $1 million and the FMV of its assets is $300,000. Because its liabilities exceed its assets, Furber is insolvent, and the extent of its insolvency is $700,000 ($1,000,000 – $300,000). In settlement of its debts to its creditors, Furber transfers all of its assets to its creditors. Because of that transfer, Furber is discharged of its $700,000 of liabilities. The $700,000 discharge of indebtedness constitutes income to Furber because it increases its wealth by that amount. However, because the amount discharged does not exceed the extent to which Furber is insolvent, the entire $700,000 is excluded from Furber's gross income.

---

[41] Code Sec. 109.
[42] Code Sec. 108(a)(1)(B).

[43] Code Sec. 108(a)(3).
[44] Code Sec.108(a)(1)(A).

Example 85: Helstrom Mailing's liabilities total $500,000, and the FMV of its assets total $450,000. Helstrom settles a $75,000 debt it owes one of its suppliers for $20,000. Accordingly, its income from discharge of indebtedness equals $55,000 ($75,000 – $20,000). Because the amount excluded under the insolvency exception cannot exceed $50,000 (the amount by which the company is insolvent ($500,000 – $450,000)), Helstrom can only exclude $50,000 from its gross income. Helstrom's gross income will increase by $5,000 ($55,000 – $50,000).

Example 86: Leander owes $10,000 to its supplier. Leander files for bankruptcy, and the debt is discharged. Because the debt was discharged in bankruptcy, Leander excludes the entire amount from gross income, regardless of the extent of its insolvency. None of the $10,000 will be included in Leander's gross income.

 Reason for the Rule: To the extent that a discharge of indebtedness does not make a taxpayer solvent, no additional income is considered made available to the taxpayer.

.05 Life Insurance Proceeds

The proceeds from a life insurance policy paid by reason of the death of the insured increase the beneficiary's wealth, and therefore represent income to the beneficiary. However, the tax law generally excludes these amounts from the beneficiary's gross income.[45] In the case of an employer-owned life insurance contract issued after August 17, 2006, the amount of death benefits received by the employer that the employer can exclude from gross income is limited to the amount of premiums and other amounts paid for the policy unless the insured was employed by the policy-holder during the 12-month period before the insured's death or was a director or highly compensated employee of the employer at the time that the policy was issued.[46] This exception to the general rule also does not apply to death benefits received by an employer that are paid to the insured's heirs. These are called "key-person life insurance" policies. To maintain equity, the premiums paid on these policies are not deductible by the company.[47]

¶ 412 Summary

C corporations and sole proprietorships pay federal income tax on their taxable income from business operations. Flow-through entities do not pay federal income taxes because they are not considered separate tax-paying entities. However, they still must compute the various components of the taxable income formula in order to properly pass along taxable amounts to their owners so they can report their respective shares on their income tax returns.

Taxable income is calculated by first determining gross income and then subtracting out allowable deductions. Taxable income is the tax base against which the regular income tax rates are applied to determine a business's regular income tax liability. Some individuals and larger corporations may be subject to AMT, which is an additional income tax that is added to the taxpayer's regular income tax liability. Sole proprietors also must pay self-employment taxes on their net earnings from self-employment.

Once a business calculates its total tax liability for the year, it determines the amount of tax it owes by subtracting out tax credits, which include any prepayments of income taxes that it made toward that year's tax liability. In order to avoid paying a penalty on amounts owed with the taxpayer's income tax return, individual and corporate taxpayers need to ensure that each year they properly prepay the minimum amounts required under the tax laws.

---

[45] Code Sec. 101(a).
[46] Code Sec. 101(j).

[47] Code Sec. 264(a).

The starting point of computing taxable income is gross income, which is all income the federal government taxes. Exclusions are one way taxable income is reduced. The other is through deductions, which are the focus of Chapters 5 to 7.

GLOSSARY OF TERMS INTRODUCED IN THIS CHAPTER

Adjusted gross income (AGI). An intermediate step between gross income and taxable income that individuals calculate. Only deductions for AGI are subtracted from gross income in computing AGI.

Applicable federal rate (AFR). A statutory federal rate of interest that is adjusted monthly and is published by the IRS. The rates are based on the average market yield on outstanding marketable obligations of the United States during the one-month period ending on the 14th day of the preceding month.

Below market loan. A loan arrangement in which the interest charged by the lender is less than adequate (below the market rate of interest).

Capital expenditure. An expenditure that creates an asset expected to benefit a business for more than one year.

Deduction. Expenditure made by a taxpayer that the government allows the taxpayer to use to reduce taxable income.

Dividends received deduction. The amount of dividend income received by a C corporation that is not subject to taxation. It can be 70, 80, or 100 percent of the dividend income.

Estimated tax payments. Amounts that C corporations and individuals with taxable income not subject to withholding must pay during the year in order to avoid an underpayment of tax penalty.

Exclusion. An item of income that according to the tax laws is not subject to taxation.

Gross income. All income from whatever source derived, except as specifically excluded by a provision in the Internal Revenue Code or other tax law. Represents the income the government has chosen to tax. Equals income minus exclusions.

Gross receipts. The total amount of money and the fair market value of any other property received for selling property or performing services.

Gross sales. The total amount of sales at invoice prices, unreduced by any discounts, returns, or allowances.

Imputed interest. The "deemed" interest payments a borrower makes to a lender on a below market loan, including a loan involving original issue discount. *See also* Below market loan *and* Original issue discount.

Municipal interest. Interest from state and local government bonds (municipal bonds, or "muni" bonds for short) that is not subject to federal income tax.

Original issue discount (OID). Additional interest income representing the difference between the issue price of indebtedness and the amount due at maturity (face value). It is a function of the difference between the face rate associated with the bond and the current market interest rate.

Qualified dividends. Dividends that are taxed to individual taxpayers at a rate lower than the taxpayers' marginal tax rates. They represent dividends paid on stock of a U.S. corporation or a qualified foreign corporation that the individual held for 121 days surrounding the ex-dividend date.

Qualified personal service corporation (QPSC). A corporation engaged almost exclusively in performing services in the fields of health, law, engineering, architecture, accounting, actuarial science, performing arts, or consulting. At least 95 percent of the value of its stock is held, directly or indirectly, by its employees, by retired employees who performed services for the corporation, or by an estate or other person owning stock because of the death of such employees or retired employees.

Taxable income. The difference between a taxpayer's gross income and the total deductions a taxpayer is allowed. The tax base used in the regular income tax system.

CHAPTER PROBLEMS

Chapter 4 Discussion Questions

1. What types of businesses pay federal income taxes? If a business does not have to pay federal income tax on its earnings, who, if anyone, does?

2. How is a taxpayer's taxable income computed?

3. What is adjusted gross income (AGI), and how is it different from gross income and taxable income?

4. How does the Code define "gross income"?

5. What is an exclusion, and how does it differ from a deduction?

6. What is a capital expenditure?

7. What steps are required to determine how much tax a corporation owes for the year? How does this differ from how a sole proprietor determines the amount of taxes it owes for the year?

8. Are C corporations taxed at progressive tax rates as individuals are?

9. What is a taxpayer's marginal tax rate?

10. How are personal service corporations taxed on their income?

11. What businesses may be subject to alternative minimum tax (AMT)?

12. What is the relationship between the alternative minimum tax and the regular income tax?

13. What steps are required to calculate a corporation's alternative minimum tax?

14. Under what circumstances does a C corporation have to make estimated tax payments?

15. When during a tax year must a calendar year C corporation make estimated tax payments? When must corporations using a fiscal tax year make estimated payments?

16. Are improvements made by a tenant taxable to the landlord?

17. A corporation loans an employee $100,000 for two years with no stated interest rate. At the time the loan is made, the current applicable federal rate (AFR) short-term, mid-term, and long-term rates are 4.5 percent, 5.6 percent rate, and 7.4 percent, respectively. Discuss how the tax laws treat this type of loan arrangement.

18. Assume the same facts as in Question 17, except the term of the loan is six years. Discuss how the tax laws treat this type of loan arrangement. Would your answer change if the terms of the loan required that the employee pay four-percent interest, compounded semiannually?

19. The X Corporation was engaged in the business of selling electrical appliances. Due to the discriminatory acts of certain distributors of electrical appliances, the corporation sustained damages and loss of profits. In a suit instituted under the Clayton Act, the court that tried the antitrust suit found that the corporation, but for the wrongful acts of the distributors, could have earned profits amounting to $150,000. The court awarded the X Corporation triple the amount of damages, as was required under the Clayton Act (i.e., treble damages).

Judgment in the amount of $450,000 was recovered. How much of the award is the taxpayer required to include in income?

20. How do the tax laws differ on the amount included in gross income from discharge of indebtedness when the taxpayer is insolvent versus going through bankruptcy procedures?

Chapter 4 Problems

1. Interior Decorators has a gross income of $200,000, deductions totaling $80,000, and tax credits totaling $25,000. What is its taxable income?

2. During its tax year, Kantz, Inc. receives a loan for $100,000 and sells for $70,000 equipment with an adjusted basis of $60,000. Based on these facts, what is the company's gross income for the year?

3. A corporation receives legal services with an FMV of $200 in exchange for a piece of luggage, and it receives a cabinet with an FMV of $50 in exchange for repairs on a piece of luggage. It also receives a 10-percent discount on a computer normally retailing for $2,000. Based on these facts, what amount must the company include in its gross income?

4. A corporation has gross receipts of $250,000 from sales of meat choppers during its tax year. The cost of the goods sold was $60,000, and the returns totaled $10,000. Based on these facts, what amount has to be included in the company's gross income for the year?

5. A corporation receives $20,000 in dividends from a U.S. company, $2,000 in interest from a Treasury bond, and $1,000 in interest from a state bond. The corporation owns five percent of the stock of the company paying the dividends. Based on these facts, how much of these amounts is taxable?

6. Real Property Development, Inc. receives $100,000 in rentals from one of its apartment buildings. During the same year, it pays $10,000 in real property taxes, $1,000 for repairs, and $20,000 in interest on a mortgage loan for the apartment building. Based on these facts, what amount must the company include in its gross income?

7. A corporation sells equipment with an adjusted basis of $30,000 for $50,000. It also sells stock with an adjusted basis of $25,000 for $15,000. Based on these facts, what amount must the company include in its gross income?

8. A corporation computes its regular tax to be $30,000 and its tentative minimum tax to be $40,000. The corporation's credits for the year totaled $20,000, and its estimated tax payments for the year totaled $35,000. Based on these facts, how much does the company owe in taxes at the end of the year?

9. A corporation has a taxable income of $400,000. What is the amount of its regular income tax?

10. A corporation has $400,000 of gross income, $200,000 of deductions, and $30,000 of credits. How much regular income tax does it owe?

11. A corporation (not qualifying as a large corporation) pays $30,000 in federal income tax for 2009 and anticipates that it will owe $35,000 in tax for 2010. The most taxable income the corporation has had in the last three years is $400,000. What is the amount of estimated tax payments that the company should make for 2010?

12. A corporation pays $170,000 in federal income tax for 2009. It anticipates that it will owe $300,000 in federal income tax for 2010. Its taxable income for 2007 was $1 million, but its taxable income for 2008 was $700,000, and its taxable income for 2009 was $500,000. What amount of estimated tax payments should it make for 2010?

13. Annett Kaizer, who is unmarried, works full time for a library but also publishes books. Her taxable income for 2009 was $90,000, and her tax was $18,920. She anticipates that her taxable income for 2010 will be $160,000 and her tax will be $38,520. Her full-time employer is withholding $9,165 from her wages. What amount of estimated tax payments must she make for 2010?

14. Stenson & Company loans its sole shareholder, Ralph Stenson, $100,000 for 10 years with no stated interest rate. At the time the loan is made, the current AFR short-term, mid-term, and long-term rates are 6.75 percent, 7.6 percent, and 8.4 percent, respectively.

   a. Compute the deemed payment if the terms of the loan require that Ralph pay a three-percent annual rate of interest, compounded semiannually.

   b. How does the deemed payment affect Stenson's taxable income?

   c. How does the deemed payment affect Ralph's taxable income?

15. Babson Enterprises owns 15 percent of the stock in a corporation. During the year, Babson receives dividends totaling $50,000 from the corporation. Babson's only other items of gross income and deduction are sales revenue of $80,000, cost of goods sold of $45,000, and business expenses of $20,000.

   a. What is its dividends received deduction and taxable income for the year?

   b. How would your answer differ if Babson's business expenses were $40,000?

16. Gonzolas, Inc. owns 35 percent of the stock in a corporation. During the year, Gonzolas receives dividends totaling $85,000 from the corporation. Its only other items of gross income and deductions are sales revenue of $120,000 and business expenses of $95,000.

   a. What are its dividends received deduction and its taxable income for the year?

   b. How would your answer differ if Gonzolas owned 80 percent of the corporation's stock?

17. A lessor rented property to a tenant for three years. The lessor buys an insurance policy to cover the property and the tenant agrees to pay the premiums of $3,000. What is the tax effect of this transaction on the lessor and the tenant?

18. A landlord receives the first year and last year lease payments of $10,000 each. In addition, the landlord receives a security deposit of $10,000. In addition, the landlord takes out a fire policy on the rental and the tenant agrees to pay the three-year premium of $3,000 in the first year. Also, in the first year of the lease the tenant spends $5,000 on improvements to the rental property for which no credit is given against rent. What is the effect of these transactions on the landlord's tax return in the first year of the lease?

19. A 30-year zero-coupon original issue discount bond was issued for $200,000. There is no provision for recalling the bond. The semiannual yield to maturity of the obligation is 6 percent. Compute the original issue discount for the first and second accrual periods.

20. A corporation receives $200,000 from a life insurance policy that it owned on a director's life. It also had a seller reduce the amount it owed on a purchase by $1,000. Based on these facts, what amount must the company include in its gross income?

21. For her 2009 tax year, Rita Picard, who was self-employed, had $50,000 of profits from her business, $10,000 in dividends, and $5,000 in taxable interest. She deducts $3,000 for self-employed health insurance and $3,532 for one-half of her self-employment taxes. She also deducts $8,000 for home mortgage interest, $2,000 for state income taxes, and $4,000 for real estate taxes. Rita is single with no dependents. Based on these facts, what is Rita's adjusted gross income?

22. Same facts as in Problem 21. Based on these facts, what is Rita's taxable income?

23. Mike Hyman had $40,000 net earnings from self-employment. How much does he owe in self-employment taxes?

24. Rhonda Dow had $120,000 net earnings from self-employment for 2009. How much does she owe in self-employment taxes?

25. Curtis Bergin, who is self-employed, had a regular tax of $5,000, a tentative minimum tax of $6,000, and an alternative minimum tax of $1,000. Based on these facts, how much does he owe in taxes?

Chapter 4 Review Problems

1. Downum Taffetas, Inc. is an accrual method taxpayer that uses the calendar year as its tax year. The company sold and delivered $1,000 of taffeta sheets to a customer on December 20, 2009, but was not paid for the sale until January 18, 2010. The cost of the goods sold was $250. The delivery of the sheets cost $50, but the company did not pay the delivery charge until January 12, 2010. Based on these facts, what is the company's taxable income for 2009?

2. Badasci Fishing Tours, Inc. is a cash method taxpayer using the calendar year as its tax year. On December 20, 2009, a customer chartered a fishing boat from Badasci for $2,000 but did not pay Badasci until January 3, 2010. Another customer chartered a boat on December 21, 2009. That customer gave the company a check for $1,500 on December 31, 2009, but Badasci could not deposit the check until January 2, 2010. The company hired someone to do repairs on the boats for $1,000 and paid for the repairs by credit card on December 30, 2009. It did not pay the credit card statement until 2010. Based on these facts, what is Badasci's taxable income for 2009?

Chapter 4 Research Question

Does the IRS have discretion to waive or disregard the statutory formula in Code Sec. 63 for determining taxable income? See the *CCH Standard Federal Income Tax Reporter.*

CHAPTER 5
Business Deductions: Ordinary and Necessary Business Expenses

¶ 500 Introduction

The focus of the previous chapter was the government's all-inclusive approach to defining income and the tax laws governing the various types of income and exclusions that businesses might encounter. In the next three chapters, the deductibility of the various expenditures businesses incur during the process of generating taxable income is discussed. As a rule, businesses are allowed to offset their business revenues by the expenses they incurred during the tax year that enable them to generate taxable revenues. If the tax laws did not permit these expenditures to be deducted against gross income, businesses would be taxed on their gross receipts from a trade or business and not on their net profit. However, special rules and limitations apply to certain expenditures.

This chapter provides an introduction to the general deductibility rules and provides a detailed discussion of some of the more common expenditures businesses must make in their pursuit of generating revenues. Chapter 6 continues with a discussion of the rules surrounding a business's employment-related expenses. In Chapter 7, the rules governing the depreciation, amortization, and depletion of long-term assets are introduced.

¶ 501 General Requirements for Deductibility

Unlike the government's all-inclusive approach to defining income, expenses are only deductible if the tax laws specifically state that they are. Many expenses are deductible under a general provision in the Internal Revenue Code (the "Code") that allows a deduction for all *ordinary and necessary* expenses paid or incurred in carrying on a trade or business. This provision allows businesses to reduce their gross income by various expenditures, including wages they pay to employees, as well as rent, insurance, interest, and taxes, to name a few. In addition to the ordinary and necessary test, expenditures must also be reasonable in amount and not items that are capital in nature. Finally, expenditures that tax law specifically identifies as nondeductible do not qualify as deductions, even if they have met all of the other general requirements for deductibility.

.01 Ordinary and Necessary

Under Code Sec. 162(a), taxpayers can deduct against gross income ordinary and necessary expenses paid or incurred in the conduct of a trade or business. Therefore, to deduct an expense currently under Code Sec. 162(a), the taxpayer must already be carrying on in a trade or business at the time the expenditure is paid or incurred. The Code does not define the terms ordinary and necessary, but when asked to interpret terms not specifically defined in the Code, the courts typically interpret them using their commonly accepted meanings. Accordingly, a **necessary expense** is one that is appropriate or helpful to the continuation of the taxpayer's business, and an **ordinary expense** refers to an expense that is customary and acceptable in the taxpayer's type of business.[1] An expense may be ordinary even though the particular taxpayer has only incurred the expense one time.[2]

To illustrate how the terms "ordinary" and "necessary" have been interpreted by the courts, the Tax Court ruled that the cost of gold coins purchased and melted down for use in dental castings was an ordinary and necessary business expense of a dental practice,[3] and payments by a cotton factory to a fund that was used to eradicate the boll weevil were considered ordinary and necessary business expenses.[4] However, the Tax Court also determined that amounts an attorney paid for a framed picture and a plant for an office furnished by her employer were not deemed necessary or helpful in the performance of her required services,[5] and amounts a sole proprietor paid to an ordained minister for spiritual advice provided to him and his employees were not "ordinary" in the taxpayer's industry.[6]

.02 Reasonable in Amount

The requirement that expenses be reasonable in amount is to prevent businesses from deducting lavish or extravagant expenditures. Although the Code specifically applies a reasonableness test only to compensation,[7] the courts have been known to apply this standard to all business expenses.[8]

The determination of whether an expense is reasonable depends upon the facts and circumstances of the particular situation. For example, the Tax Court held that the costs associated with providing a chauffeured luxury car to an employee who was a securities investment advisor were not extravagant given the "obnoxious traffic" the employee faced coupled with the fact that many of the employee's clients were wealthy Europeans. The costs were not only ordinary and necessary in the taxpayer's line of business, but also reasonable in amount.[9]

.03 Not Capital in Nature

The tax laws require that an expenditure be capitalized to an asset account if it creates an asset with a useful life extending substantially beyond the current tax year.[10] Since capital expenditures provide benefits to a business for a number of years, it is appropriate that their costs be spread out to offset gross income generated in those years. Often these expenditures are deducted over a

---

[1] *T.H. Welch,* SCt, 3 USTC ¶ 1164, 290 US 111, 54 SCt 8 (1933).

[2] *S.B. Heininger,* SCt, 44-1 USTC ¶ 9109, 320 US 467, 64 SCt 249.

[3] *M.L. Cochran,* 56 TCM 1433, Dec. 45,529(M), TC Memo. 1989-102.

[4] *Alexander Sprunt & Son, Inc.,* 24 BTA 599, Dec. 7250 (Acq.).

[5] *H.F. Henderson, Jr.,* 46 TCM 566, Dec. 40,233(M), TC Memo. 1983-372.

[6] *L.F. Trebilcock,* 64 TC 852, aff'd, CA-6, 77-2 USTC ¶ 9530, 557 F2d 1226.

[7] Code Sec. 162(a)(1).

[8] *Lincoln Electric Co.,* CA-6, 47-1 USTC ¶ 9282, 162 F2d 379.

[9] *R.J. Denison,* 36 TCM 1759, Dec. 34,799(M), TC Memo. 1977-430.

[10] Reg. § 1.263(a)-2.

period of years, but occasionally they remain as assets on the company's books and are never written off.

Prepaid expenses. When taxpayers pay expenses that relate to a future tax year, such amounts must be capitalized to an asset account and expensed in the period to which they relate. This rule applies to both cash and accrual method taxpayers. However, see ¶ 306.02 and ¶ 307.02 for a discussion of the *12-month rule* that applies to prepaid expenses that will be incurred within the next 12 months.

Example 1: During 2009, Triebina Corporation signs a lease for office space and pays $36,000 for three years' rent. The $36,000 represents a prepaid expense that must be capitalized and deducted over the next 36 months.

Depreciation, depletion, and amortization. The purchase of a machine used in a manufacturing business is another example of a capital expenditure. Since the machine will help generate revenues over several years, both cash and accrual basis taxpayers must write off its costs over a specified number of years. **Depreciation** is the annual deduction taken to recover the capitalized cost of business or income-producing property that is either tangible personal property or real property (other than land).

In Chapter 1, real property was defined as all real estate, which includes land and buildings. Apartment complexes, office buildings, warehouses, and parking lots are examples of real property. Personal property was defined as all property other than real property, and it could be tangible or intangible. Examples of tangible personal property that might be used in a trade or business include automobiles, machinery, and equipment. The furnishings in rental property are an example of tangible personal property that is also income-producing property. The rules that govern how quickly taxpayers can deduct the cost of depreciable property are a focus of Chapter 7.

Personal property that does not have physical characteristics is intangible property. The costs associated with the creation of an intangible asset that will benefit the business beyond the current tax year must be capitalized. Typically, the tax laws allow these costs to be expensed over a period of years; however, some intangible assets cannot be expensed and will remain as assets on the company's books. **Amortization** is the systematic recovery (expensing) of intangible assets. In financial accounting, goodwill, copyrights, patents, and trademarks are often given as examples of intangible assets. The rules for amortizing these types of intangible property are discussed in Chapter 7. In this chapter, the amortization of organizational costs and business start-up costs is discussed.

Costs incurred in the acquisition of natural resources, such as mines, oil and gas wells, and timber fields are another type of capital expenditure that taxpayers can deduct over the periods in which the asset provides usefulness to them.[11] The deduction for **depletion** is similar to depreciation, except that depletion allows owners to recover their investment in productive natural resources. As the natural resources are used up through the processes of mining (in the case of coal, metals and other minerals), quarrying (in the case of stone), drilling (in the case of oil and gas), and felling (in the case of timber), the taxpayer is allowed to expense (deplete) the costs associated with the extracted resources. Thus, depletion represents the reduction in the contents of the reserves from which the resource is taken.[12] The rules governing the two methods allowed for computing the depletion deduction are discussed in Chapter 7.

Operators of a domestic oil, gas, or geothermal wells may elect to currently deduct intangible drilling and development costs (IDC) rather than capitalize and recover them through depletion or depreciation. IDC generally includes all expenditures by the operator incident to and necessary for the drilling of wells and the preparation of wells for the production of oil, gas, or geothermal energy that are neither for the purchase of tangible property nor part of the acquisition price of an interest

---

[11] Code Sec. 611.

[12] *C.A. Ludey,* SCt, 1 USTC ¶ 234, 274 US 295, 47 SCt 608.

in the property. This includes the cost of labor, fuel and power, materials and supplies, tool rental, truck and auto hire, repairs to drilling equipment, and depreciation on drilling equipment.[13]

Uniform capitalization (UNICAP) rules. When real or tangible personal property is produced by a taxpayer, the **uniform capitalization (UNICAP) rules** require that certain costs be capitalized to the cost of the property. If the property produced is later placed in service in the taxpayer's business, the taxpayer can recover (expense) these capitalized costs over a number of years by taking annual depreciation deductions. If the property produced is subsequently sold, the taxpayer can use the capitalized costs to reduce the taxable amount realized from the sale.[14]

Under the UNICAP rules, the wages paid to employees engaged in the manufacture of a machine that will be used in the taxpayer's business must be capitalized to the cost of the machine and must later be recovered through depreciation expense. Since the machine is expected to help generate revenues for the taxpayer's business over many years, any expenses that are incurred in the production of the machine must be capitalized and depreciated. Thus, the UNICAP rules seek to match income and expenses, which is consistent with how prepaid expenses are treated under both the cash and accrual methods of accounting.

 Reason for the Rule: If given a choice between capitalizing and depreciating costs associated with an asset versus expensing the costs immediately, most taxpayers would choose immediate expensing since it normally would produce the greatest tax savings in the current year. When a taxpayer purchases depreciable property from the manufacturer, the costs the manufacturer incurred during production of the asset are included in the cost of the property. These costs are then recovered by the taxpayer over a number of years through annual depreciation deductions. When the taxpayer produces its own property, all of the same costs that a manufacturer incurs (materials, labor costs, etc.) are capitalized to the cost of the property under the UNICAP rules, and depreciated over several years. Without the UNICAP rules, taxpayers that produce their own property might be allowed to immediately expense certain costs that are part of the costs associated with long-lived assets. Thus, the UNICAP rules attempt to provide parity between taxpayers that purchase property directly from the manufacturer and those that manufacture their own property.

The UNICAP rules do not apply to property that is used for personal purposes or to any property that the taxpayer produces under a long-term contract (¶ 309.02 described how these costs are handled).[15] The rules also do not apply to certain types of expenses, including research and experimental costs, intangible drilling costs, mining exploration, and development costs,[16] or to the qualified creative costs of freelance artists, authors, and photographers.[17] Also, these rules only require that interest paid or incurred in the construction of certain types of property be capitalized to the asset. These special rules regarding the capitalization of interest are discussed later in the chapter (see ¶ 505.03).

 GAAP vs. Code: For financial reporting purposes, all costs incurred to prepare an asset for its intended use are capitalized, regardless of whether the asset is to be held for sale or used within the business. Depending on the business's materiality thresholds, certain amounts may not be capitalized for financial reporting purposes but would have to be capitalized for tax purposes. Any differences in amounts capitalized would result in a difference between the calculation of net income on the financial statements and taxable

---

[13] Code Sec. 263(c); Reg. § 1.612-4.
[14] Code Sec. 263A.
[15] Code Sec. 263A(c)(4).

[16] Code Secs. 59(e) and 263A(c)(6).
[17] Code Sec. 263A(h).

> income on the tax return. Such differences would need to be reflected when reconciling net income to taxable income on the corporate tax return.

Special rule for certain barrier removal costs. Despite the rule that denies a current deduction for expenditures that are capital in nature, the tax laws allow taxpayers to elect to currently deduct up to $15,000 of qualified architectural and transportational barrier removal expenses. To be expensed currently, the costs must be incurred to remove an existing barrier so that a business facility or public transportation vehicle owned or leased by the taxpayer for business use is made more accessible to and usable by handicapped or elderly persons.[18]

 Spotlight: Normally, capitalized costs such as these would be depreciated over the life of the asset to which they relate. For a building, this could be as long as 39 years. By allowing businesses to deduct up to $15,000 of these costs immediately, taxpayers can accelerate the timing of their tax savings. The amount of tax savings generated from the immediate expensing equals the amount expensed times the taxpayer's marginal tax rate. Therefore, a taxpayer in the 35-percent tax bracket who is allowed to write off $15,000 of these costs in the year in which they are paid will recuperate $5,250 ($15,000 × 35%) of the costs in the first year.

.04 Not Otherwise Disallowed

Sometimes an expenditure may appear to meet the general requirements for deductibility, but due to any number of policy considerations, tax law specifically states that it cannot be deducted. For example, the Code is clear that amounts paid to satisfy government-imposed fines and penalties cannot be deducted as business expenses.[19] The courts have denied a deduction for fines and penalties on the grounds that allowing them to be deducted would frustrate public policy by reducing the taxpayer's cost of the penalty by the amount of the tax benefit resulting from the deduction.[20] The Code also specifically disallows or limits the deductibility of lobbying costs and political contributions.

Violation of public policy. Under Code Sec. 162(a), ordinary and necessary business expenses are deductible against gross income. Thus, professional truck drivers might argue that traffic tickets are not only normal and customary in the trucking industry, but since drivers are often compensated by the haul and not by the hour, speeding tickets are also helpful in generating revenues. Although these arguments may seem valid given the environment of the trucking industry, the Supreme Court has ruled that any expenditure incurred while violating public policy is not a necessary expense[21] and, accordingly, is not deductible. Thus, fines and penalties paid to a government for the violation of any law are not deductible business expenses,[22] including settlement payments made to other persons or businesses. However, the tax laws do allow taxpayers to deduct legal fees and related expenses paid or incurred in the defense of an action that culminates in a fine or penalty, as well as any court costs imposed against the taxpayer.[23]

It is interesting to note that expenses that normally would constitute ordinary and necessary business expense are only disallowed on account of illegality if the expenditure itself constitutes an illegal payment under U.S. federal or state laws.[24] This rule allows taxpayers to deduct normal operating expenses incurred while carrying on an illegal business activity. For example, wages and rents paid in connection with operating an illegal gambling business would be deductible against the

---

[18] Code Sec. 190.

[19] Code Sec. 162(f).

[20] *B.T. Smith*, 34 TC 1100, Dec. 24,365 (1960), aff'd, *per curiam*, CA-5, 61-2 USTC ¶ 9686, 294 F2d 957; *W.L. Kolberg*, 24 TCM 913, Dec. 27,450(M), TC Memo. 1965-171.

[21] *Tank Truck Rentals, Inc.*, SCt, 58-1 USTC ¶ 9366, 356 US 30, 78 SCt 507.

[22] Code Sec. 162(f).

[23] Reg. § 1.162-21(b)(2).

[24] Code Sec. 162(c)(2); Reg. § 1.162-18(b).

gross income generated by the illegal activity.[25] Furthermore, an expenditure is deemed to be illegal under state law only when the state law is generally enforced.[26] Payments that violate an unenforced state law do not frustrate public policy and, accordingly, can be deducted against gross income.

Illegal bribes and kickbacks paid to public officials or government employees are never deductible because the kickbacks themselves are illegal under U.S federal laws. Similar rules apply to payments made to foreign officials that are unlawful under the Foreign Corrupt Practices Act of 1977.

Kickbacks include a payment in consideration of the referral of a client, patient or customer. Kickbacks paid to individuals who are not public officials may be legal or illegal, depending on local law. The Supreme Court has ruled that kickbacks that do not violate government laws are deductible as an ordinary and necessary business expense if they reflect an established and widespread practice in the taxpayer's industry.[27]

Example 2: A subcontractor at a mall construction site paid kickbacks to the supervisor of the site's primary contractor as a condition of continued employment and timely payment. There was a logical connection between the kickbacks, which were legal under local law (and deemed necessary), and the ability to continue work on the construction project. Thus, the kickbacks—a cost of doing business—were ordinary and were currently deductible by the subcontractor.[28]

However, the deduction for kickbacks was denied to a paving subcontractor who obtained contracts for the construction of a mall by paying for services and materials used in the construction of the personal residence of the person in charge of awarding subcontracts. The kickbacks were found to be unnecessary, since the subcontractor had obtained nearly all of its other contracts, including 20 from the same contractor, without paying kickbacks.[29]

Lobbying expenditures and political contributions. Amounts paid or incurred in connection with influencing legislation, including amounts paid to lobbyists and campaign contributions to a candidate for public office, are specifically not deductible.[30] Similarly, amounts paid to advertise in political convention programs and for tickets to political dinners, inaugural balls, and the like are not deductible.[31] This rule does not apply to professional lobbyists. It does, however, apply to amounts other businesses pay lobbyists.

Example 3: John Trippleton operates his consulting practice as a sole proprietorship. During 2009, John pays $475 in dues to the American Institute of Certified Public Accountants (AICPA). Included in the dues is $75 for a political action committee fee that enables the AICPA to lobby before Congress regarding legislation relevant to the accounting profession and its clients. In preparing his tax return for 2009, John is not permitted to deduct $75 of the dues paid to the AICPA. He can deduct the $400 of professional fees ($475 – $75) as an ordinary and necessary business expense.

 Reason for the Rule: Congress feared that allowing a deduction for lobbying expenditures and political contributions might enable taxpayers to exercise undue influence on the political process. Although taxpayers are entitled to make political contributions and hire professional lobbyists in an attempt to influence legislation that could affect the

---

[25] *N. Sullivan*, SCt, 58-1 USTC ¶ 9368, 356 US 27, 78 SCt 512.

[26] Code Sec. 162(c)(2); Reg. § 1.162-18(b)(3); *Greater Display & Wire Forming, Inc.*, 55 TCM 922, Dec. 44,802(M), TC Memo. 1988-231.

[27] *T.B. Lilly*, SCt, 52-1 USTC ¶ 9231, 343 US 90, 72 SCt 497.

[28] *Raymond Bertolini Trucking Co.*, CA-6, 84-2 USTC ¶ 9591, 736 F2d 1120, rev'g TC, 45 TCM 44, Dec. 39,474(M), TC Memo. 1982-643.

[29] *Car-Ron Asphalt Paving Co., Inc.*, CA-6, 85-1 USTC ¶ 9298, 758 F2d 1132, aff'g TC, 46 TCM 1314, Dec. 40,434(M), TC Memo. 1983-548.

[30] Code Sec. 162(e).

[31] Code Sec. 276.

taxpayer's business, the federal government will not subsidize the taxpayer's efforts, which would be the result if it allowed taxpayers to use political and lobbying expenditures to reduce their taxable income (and corresponding tax liability).

Taxpayers are allowed to deduct in-house expenditures paid or incurred during the tax year for lobbying activities, provided the expenditures do not exceed $2,000. In-house expenditures do not include amounts paid to lobbyists or amounts paid for dues to organizations to the extent that such dues are allocable to these types of activities.[32] Should the taxpayer exceed the $2,000 threshold, all in-house expenditures are nondeductible.[33]

Example 4: In 2009, Pradyolin Corporation approached members of Congress to gain their support for a pending bill. Pradyolin spent $1,200 to draft and print a position letter on the bill and $200 to distribute the letter to members of Congress. These were the only costs Pradyolin incurred for in-house lobbying activities in 2009. Pradyolin can deduct the entire amount of $1,400 incurred for in-house lobbying activities on its 2009 tax return.

Example 5: Assume the same facts as in Example 4, except that Pradyolin spent $3,200 to draft and print its position letter and $300 to distribute the letter to members of Congress. Since the amount spent exceeds the $2,000 *de minimis* threshold, none of the $3,500 can be deducted.

Taxpayers can deduct ordinary and necessary expenses directly attributable to appearances before local legislative councils in connection with existing or proposed legislation that will, or may reasonably be expected to, affect the taxpayer's trade or business. A deduction is also allowed for amounts spent to communicate information on legislative matters to business or trade organizations of which the taxpayer is a member, provided that the legislative matter is of direct interest to both the taxpayer and the organization.[34]

Example 6: John Smith, the President of Newbury Corporation, is invited to provide testimony at a county board hearing concerning a bill that will significantly affect Newbury's business. The expenses Newbury incurs for John's travel expenses are deductible.

 GAAP vs. Code: For financial reporting purposes, the payment of a governmental fine or penalty or payments for lobbying expenses and political campaign contributions are expensed in the period incurred. For tax purposes, these costs are generally not deductible. The difference in treatment creates a permanent difference between how net income and taxable income are calculated. For example, if a paint manufacturer is fined by the Environment Protection Agency for violating a federal toxic waste provision, the company will not be able to deduct the fine on its tax return. However, it will be required to expense this amount on the income statement in arriving at net income. Accordingly, when reconciling net income to taxable income on the corporate tax return, the corporation will need to add the amount paid for the fine back to its net income.

¶ 502 Timing of the Deduction

The year in which a tax deduction can be taken depends upon whether the taxpayer uses the accrual or cash method of accounting. As discussed in Chapter 3, under the accrual method, the taxpayer takes a deduction in the year in which an expense is incurred, regardless of when the expense is paid. Under the cash method, the taxpayer takes a deduction in the year in which the

---

[32] Code Sec. 162(c)(5)(B).

[33] Conference Committee Report to P.L. 103-66 (1993), H.R. Conf. Rep. No. 103-213.

[34] Code Sec. 162(e)(2).

expense is paid, regardless of when it was incurred. However, in the case of prepaid expenses, cash basis taxpayers must always wait until the year in which the expense is incurred before taking the deduction (however, see ¶ 306.02 and ¶ 307.02 for an exception under the *12-month rule*). Hence, cash and accrual basis taxpayers use the accrual method to handle prepaid expenses.

Example 7: Sand Co. (a calendar year, accrual basis corporation) pays its employees every Friday. During 20X1, December 31 ends on a Wednesday. On its 20X1 tax return, Sand will deduct the $26,240 of wages it accrued for work its employees performed from the previous Saturday through Wednesday, December 31.

Example 8: Assume the same facts as in Example 7, except that Sand uses the cash method. The deduction for the wages accrued in 20X1 will not be paid until Friday, January 2, 20X2. Accordingly, the $26,240 of wages cannot be deducted until 20X2, the year in which it is paid.

Example 9: On October 1, 2009, Triebina Corporation signs a lease for office space and pays $36,000 for three years' rent. The $36,000 represents a prepaid expense, which must be capitalized and deducted over the next 36 months, beginning on October 1, 2009. Thus, if Triebina uses a calendar year-end, it will be able to deduct $3,000 ($36,000/36 × 3 months) on its 2009 tax return, regardless of whether it uses the cash or accrual method of accounting. In 2010 and 2011, Triebina will deduct $12,000 for rent expense ($36,000/36 × 12 months), and in 2012 it will deduct $9,000 ($36,000/36 × 9 months).

¶ 503 Organizational Expenditures

Expenditures paid or incurred that are incidental to the formation of a corporation, including C corporations and S corporations, are known as **organizational costs**. Organizational costs include expenses for legal services to obtain the corporate charter, fees paid to the state of incorporation, and the expenses of temporary directors, such as costs of travel and office rent.[35] Only expenditures incurred before the end of the taxable year in which the corporation begins business qualify as organizational expenditures.[36]

Costs associated with the issuing and selling of stock, such as commissions, professional fees, and printing costs are not organizational costs.[37] Instead, these costs offset the proceeds from the stock issue and reduce the corporation's paid-in capital account.[38] The costs associated with reorganizing or merging activities are not organizational costs, but instead are costs that are capitalized and recovered upon liquidation of the corporation.

The Code allows corporations to elect to deduct up to $5,000 of organizational expenditures for the tax year in which the corporation begins its business operations. The $5,000 amount is reduced dollar for dollar when the total organizational costs exceed $50,000. Thus, no current deduction is allowed to corporations that incur over $55,000 in organizational costs. At the taxpayer's election, any costs not currently expensed may be amortized ratably over a 180-month period, starting in the month in which the business begins.[39] If the election is not made, these expenses are capitalized and recovered in the year the corporation is liquidated.

Example 10: Baker Industries incurred $52,000 of organizational costs prior to the end of 2009, the tax year in which it began operations. Since the organizational costs exceed $50,000, Baker can elect to expense only $3,000 ($5,000 – $2,000) in 2009; it can elect to amortize the remaining $49,000 ($52,000 – $3,000) over 180 months beginning with the month on which its business began.

---

[35] Reg. § 1.248-1(b)(2).
[36] Code Sec. 248(b); Reg. § 1.248-1(a)(2).
[37] Reg. § 1.248-1(b)(3).

[38] *Surety Finance Co. of Tacoma*, CA-9, 35-1 USTC ¶ 9354, 77 F2d 221.
[39] Code Sec. 248(a)(1), as amended by the American Jobs Creation Act of 2004 (P.L. 108-357).

Example 11: Shaw Company began its business operations on June 1, 2009. Shaw elected to use a calendar year to file its corporate tax return. Prior to December 31, 2009, Shaw incurred the following expenditures:

Date	Description of Expenditure	Amount
2/5/09	State incorporation fee	$ 150
4/7/09	Legal fees in the drafting of the Articles of Incorporation	5,000
5/15/09	Board of directors meeting	5,250
6/20/09	Other legal and accounting fees incident to organization	5,400
7/15/09	Stock printing costs	15,500
		$31,300

The stock printing costs are not organizational costs; therefore, Shaw's organizational expenditures total $15,800 ($150 + $5,000 + $5,250 + $5,400). Since the total organizational costs do not exceed $50,000, Shaw can elect to deduct $5,000 of these expenses in 2009, and it can elect to amortize the remaining $10,800 ($15,800 – $5,000) over a period of 180 months beginning in June 2009. If Shaw elects to amortize these remaining costs, it will deduct $420 against its 2009 gross income ($10,800/180 × 7 months) and $720 ($10,800/180 × 12 months) each year from 2010–2023. In 2024, Shaw will deduct the last $300 of organizational costs ($10,800/180 × 5 months).

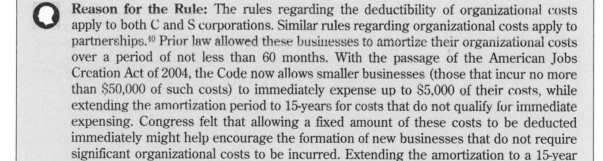

Reason for the Rule: The rules regarding the deductibility of organizational costs apply to both C and S corporations. Similar rules regarding organizational costs apply to partnerships.[40] Prior law allowed these businesses to amortize their organizational costs over a period of not less than 60 months. With the passage of the American Jobs Creation Act of 2004, the Code now allows smaller businesses (those that incur no more than $50,000 of such costs) to immediately expense up to $5,000 of their costs, while extending the amortization period to 15-years for costs that do not qualify for immediate expensing. Congress felt that allowing a fixed amount of these costs to be deducted immediately might help encourage the formation of new businesses that do not require significant organizational costs to be incurred. Extending the amortization to a 15-year period was consistent with the period over which most intangible assets are currently required to be amortized.[41]

.01 Beginning of Business Operations

The date on which a corporation begins business operations and is engaged in a "trade or business" for the purpose of taking current tax deductions is not the same date on which it enters into existence. A corporation comes into existence on the date of its incorporation, which is usually well before it is ready to begin operations. Thus, a mere organizational activity, such as obtaining a corporate charter, is not sufficient to establish the beginning of business operations. The actual date on which a corporation begins business operations can only be answered after taking into consideration all of the circumstances surrounding the activities of the corporation. For example, the acquisition of the operating assets necessary to the type of business being considered may indicate that business has begun.[42]

---

[40] Code Secs. 1363(b)(3) and 709.
[41] Senate Committee Report (S. Rep. No. 108-192).
[42] Reg. § 1.248-1(a)(3).

.02 Election to Amortize

An amortization deduction for organizational expenditures is claimed by filing Form 4562, *Depreciation and Amortization,* and attaching it to the corporate income tax return for the year in which its business begins. The costs that can be deducted currently can be reported on the "Other deductions" line of the applicable tax form. Prior to September 8, 2008, an election statement had to be attached to the tax return detailing the amount, description, and other information regarding the organizational expenditures. An election statement is no longer required for organizational expenditures paid or incurred after September 8, 2008. A corporation is deemed to have made an election by deducting the expense (up to the maximum allowed for the company) and amortizing any remaining portion of the expenditure on Form 4562.[43]

 GAAP vs. Code: For financial reporting purposes, organizational costs are expensed in the period in which they are incurred. For tax purposes, the expenses are capitalized or expensed (either immediately or amortized over 15 years). If no election is made to expense/amortize these amounts, then the amount expensed on the income statement must be added back to net income when reconciling net income to taxable income on the tax return. To the extent the election to immediately expense organizational costs is made, there will not be a difference between the amounts expensed on the income statement and on the tax return. However, to the extent the corporation amortizes any of the organizational costs, there will be a difference between net income and the amortization expense on the tax return for 16 tax years. In the first year, any excess amount deducted from net income would be added back in the reconciliation of net income and taxable income. In all subsequent years, the amortized costs deducted on the tax return would be subtracted from net income in reconciling net income to taxable income.

For example, Shaw Company from Example 11 would be required to expense the entire $15,800 against net income on its 2009 financial statements. However, for tax purposes, the best it can do is to deduct $5,420 on its 2009 tax return ($5,000 expensed immediately + $420 amortized in 2009). Consequently, in reconciling its net income and taxable income in 2009, Shaw would need to add back the $10,380 difference ($15,800 − $5,420) to net income to arrive at the amount reflected in taxable income. Each year from 2010–2024, Shaw would need to reduce its net income by the amortization expense taken on the tax return when it reconciled net income to taxable income on its tax returns for those years.

¶ 504 Start-Up Costs

Code Sec. 162 allows a deduction for ordinary and necessary costs paid or incurred in *carrying on a trade or business.* However, costs incurred prior to the start of business operations (see the discussion in ¶ 503) are not deductible under Code Sec. 162. Such expenditures may be start-up costs deductible in accordance with the rules of Code Sec. 195.

Start-up costs are costs that normally would be currently deductible if they were incurred in connection with the operation of an existing trade or business; they can include expenditures incurred to investigate entering into or acquiring a *new* active trade or business. The process of investigating the creation or acquisition of a *new* business might involve reviewing the prospective business prior to reaching a final decision on whether to acquire or enter into it. The costs associated with the analysis or survey of potential markets, products, labor supply, and transportation facilities generally qualify as start-up costs. Normally, any amounts paid or incurred in order to

---

[43] Temp. Reg. § 1.248-1T(c).

determine whether to enter a new business and which new business to enter are start-up expenditures, provided the costs themselves are not capital in nature (see ¶ 501.03).

The tax treatment of start-up costs is similar to that of organizational costs in that taxpayers may elect to deduct up to $5,000 of start-up expenditures, but the $5,000 is reduced by the amount by which the start-up expenditures exceed $50,000. The remainder may be ratably amortized over 180 months beginning with the month in which the active trade or business begins.[44] The rules that apply to start-up costs are available to all types of businesses, including sole proprietorships, C corporations, and the various flow-through entities.[45]

.01 Start-up Costs Distinguished from Other Types of Expenses

Organizational expenditures, acquisition costs, and expansion costs are sometimes mistaken for start-up costs, but their purposes and/or their tax treatments are different. Therefore, start-up costs must be distinguished from those other types of expenses.

Organizational expenditures. Although their tax treatment is similar, organizational expenditures and start-up costs are different types of expenses. Organizational expenditures are expenses incurred in forming a separate legal entity, while start-up costs are incurred in investigating the creation or acquisition of a new active trade or business.[46] Entities are allowed separate deductions for organizational and start-up expenditures. For example, when a corporation is formed and enters into a trade or business, it could conceivably expense up to $10,000 in costs associated with its formation and the start of its business: $5,000 of organizational expenses under Code Sec. 248 and $5,000 of start-up costs under Code Sec. 195.

Acquisition costs. Costs incurred in the attempt to acquire a specific business are not start-up expenditures but instead are acquisition costs that must be capitalized under Code Sec. 263. To distinguish between a start-up cost and an acquisition cost, the taxpayer must analyze the nature of the cost based on all the facts and circumstances of the transaction. The taxpayer must determine whether it is (1) an investigatory cost incurred to facilitate the taxpayer's decision regarding whether to enter into a new line of business or which new line of business to enter into or (2) a cost incurred to acquire or enter into a specific business. The former are start-up costs; the latter are acquisition costs. The label the taxpayer uses to describe the cost is not indicative of the true nature of the cost.[47]

Expansion costs. The expansion of an existing trade or business of a taxpayer is currently deductible as an ordinary and necessary business expense under Code Sec. 162. The distinction between the expansion of an existing business (for which the expenses are deductible under Code Sec. 162) and the creation or acquisition of a *new line of business* (for which the costs must be amortized over 180 months) is not always easily drawn.[48]

.02 Start-up and Acquisition Costs for Abortive Business Ventures

Acquisition costs a taxpayer incurs in the unsuccessful attempt to acquire a specific business, such as legal expenses incurred in drafting purchase documents, are deductible as losses under Code Sec. 165.[49] The rules applicable to start-up costs for businesses the taxpayer does not acquire or enter into are more complicated and less certain. The IRS and courts generally regard expenses incurred by an individual in the course of a preliminary investigation, that is, not connected with any specific line of business, to be nondeductible personal costs.[50] However, if an individual taxpayer's investigation advances beyond the preliminary stages, costs incurred may be deductible under Code Sec. 165 as losses incurred in a trade or business or for the production of income.[51] A corporation's

---

[44] Code Sec. 195(b).

[45] Code Sec. 195(b); Reg. § 1.195 1.

[46] Code Sec. 195(c)(1).

[47] Rev. Rul. 99-23, 1991-1 CB 998, as corrected by Announcement 99-89, 1999-2 CB 408.

[48] *Briarcliff Candy Corp.*, CA-2, 73-1 USTC ¶ 9288, 475 F2d 775.

[49] Rev. Rul. 77-254, 1977-2 CB 63.

[50] *Id.*; *R.C. Honodel*, CA-9, 84-1 USTC ¶ 9133, 722 F2d 1462.

[51] Code Sec. 165(c); *H.W. Seed*, 52 TC 880, Dec. 29,719 (1969) (Acq.).

losses are generally presumed not to be personal.[52] Accordingly, a corporation should be able to deduct start-up costs for businesses it does not acquire, including those incurred in the preliminary investigation of new trades or businesses, as losses under Code Sec. 165.

 Spotlight: As should be apparent from the above discussion, whether any particular expense is a start-up cost, an acquisition cost, an expansion cost, a loss, or a nondeductible personal expenditure is often a matter of interpretation. Taxpayers would generally prefer to deduct such expenditures as ordinary and necessary business expenses under Code Sec. 162 or losses under Code Sec. 165. However, the IRS can (and frequently does) challenge the treatment of such costs when they are deducted currently.

Example 12:   Maxis Corporation designs and manufactures clothing for teens. Maxis spent $25,000 to investigate expanding its existing line of teen clothing. Since the costs incurred are in the same line as Maxis's existing business, Maxis deducts the entire $25,000 in the current year.

Example 13:   Marvin Garden incurred $6,080 in qualified start-up expenses in connection with his landscaping business, which began operations on September 1, 2009. Marvin deducts $5,000 of the costs in 2009 and amortizes the rest over 180 months. His total deduction for 2009 equals $5,024 [$5,000 + (($6,080 – $5,000)/180 × 4 months)].

Example 14:   Gatewell Industries incurred $68,400 in qualified start-up costs in connection with investigating the acquisition of a new business. Gatewell acquired the business on November 2, 2009. Since the start-up costs exceed $55,000, Gatewell capitalizes and elects to amortize this amount over 180 months beginning in November 2009. Gatewell deducts $760 ($68,400/180 × 2 months) in 2009 and will deduct $4,560 ($68,400/180 × 12 months) each year from 2010–2023. In 2024, Gatewell will deduct the final $3,800 ($68,400/180 × 10 months) of amortization expense.

 GAAP vs. Code: For financial reporting purposes, start-up costs are expensed in the period in which they are incurred. For tax purposes, the expenses are capitalized and then expensed (either immediately or amortized over 15 years). To the extent that the election to immediately expense the costs is made, there will not be a difference between the amounts expensed on the income statement and on the tax return. However, if the taxpayer elects to amortize its start-up costs, there will be a difference between net income and the amortization expense on the tax return for 16 tax years. In the first year, any excess amount deducted from net income would be added back in the reconciliation of net income and taxable income. In all subsequent years, the amortized costs deducted on the tax return would be subtracted from net income in reconciling net income to taxable income.

For example, Gatewell Industries from Example 14 would be required to expense the entire $68,400 against net income on its 2009 income statement. However, for tax purposes, Gateway amortizes $760 of these costs on its 2009 tax return. Consequently, in reconciling its net income and taxable income in 2009, Gatewell will need to add back the $67,640 difference ($68,400 – $760) to net income to arrive at the amount reflected in taxable income. Each year from 2010–2024, Gatewell will reduce its net income by the amortization expense taken on the tax return when reconciling net income to taxable income on its tax returns for those years.

---

[52] *International Trading Co.*, CA-7, 73-2 USTC ¶ 9582, 484 F2d 707.

.03 Election to Amortize

A taxpayer elects to amortize eligible start-up costs by filing Form 4562, *Depreciation and Amortization*. The up to $5,000 expense deduction is generally claimed on the "Other deductions" line of the applicable tax form. Prior to September 8, 2008, an election statement had to be attached to the tax return detailing the amount, description, and other information regarding each start-up cost. Similar to organization costs, for start-up costs paid or incurred after September 8, 2008, an election statement is no longer required. A taxpayer is deemed to have made an election by deducting the expense (up to the maximum allowed for the company) and amortizing any remaining portion of the costs on Form 4562.[53]

¶ 505 Interest Expense

Because borrowing to finance business operations is normal and appropriate in any business, the Code allows a deduction for interest expense paid (in the case of a cash basis taxpayer) or incurred (in the case of an accrual basis taxpayer) during the year.[54] The rationale behind allowing the deduction for interest expense is that the proceeds from the indebtedness will be used to help generate taxable revenues for the business. In situations in which the taxpayer uses the proceeds to purchase assets that do not produce taxable income, the tax laws do not allow the related interest expense to be deducted. For example, if a taxpayer were to borrow $100,000 to purchase tax-exempt municipal bonds, the interest paid or incurred with respect to the loan would not be deductible.[55] Other examples in which the tax laws may limit the deductibility of interest paid or incurred during the year involve interest associated with the construction of certain long-lived assets and interest individual taxpayers pay on income tax deficiencies. Noncorporate taxpayers may also be limited on the amount of investment interest expense paid or incurred during the tax year.

.01 Deficiency Interest

When taxpayers fail to pay the proper amount of taxes on their income tax returns, the taxpayers must not only pay the taxes owed but also interest and penalties the government imposes on tax deficiencies. The interest charged on these tax deficiencies is called **deficiency interest**. Normally, if the deficiency interest paid or incurred during the year related to a deficiency in paying taxes owed on business profits, such interest would be deductible under the normal rules for deducting interest expense. However, the tax deficiency of an individual taxpayer is automatically considered to be personal in nature, and consequently, any interest on the deficiency constitutes nondeductible personal interest.[56] Thus, when individual taxpayers fail to pay the correct amount of taxes on income from their sole proprietorship activities (or on their distributive shares of partnership or S corporation income), any resulting interest is a nondeductible expense. This is one example in which operating a business as an entity other than a C corporation may result in greater taxes owed.

.02 Investment Interest Expense

Individual taxpayers can deduct investment interest only as an itemized deduction (deduction from adjusted gross income (AGI)) in computing their taxable income. Investment interest is interest paid or incurred on amounts borrowed to purchase taxable investments such as stock, corporate bonds, and mutual funds. This deduction is allowed because it relates to investments that generate taxable income. Accordingly, the tax laws limit the amount of investment interest expense individuals can deduct in any one tax year to the amount of taxable *net investment income* reported on their tax returns. As previously mentioned, interest on amounts borrowed to buy tax-exempt bonds is nondeductible. The rules governing the investment interest expense deduction are discussed further in Chapter 13.

---

[53] Temp. Reg. § 1.195-1T(b).
[54] Code Sec. 163(a).

[55] Code Sec. 265(a)(2).
[56] Code Sec. 163(h)(1); Temp. Reg. § 1.163-9T(b)(2)(i)(A).

Corporations are not subject to the investment interest expense limitation rules. Therefore, when corporations borrow money to purchase investments that produce taxable investment income, the interest associated with the loans is fully deductible. However, businesses that operate as flow-through entities often have individuals as their owners; consequently, any investment interest expense paid or incurred by flow-through entities must be tracked separately because the amounts flow through to the owners and are reported on the owners' tax returns. The separate reporting of these types of expenditures is discussed in greater detail in Chapters 14 and 15. As in the case of individuals, interest paid on amounts borrowed by corporations and flow-through entities to purchase investments that generate tax-exempt income is not deductible, regardless of the amount of the entity's taxable investment income.

.03 Required Capitalization of Interest

When interest is paid or incurred in conjunction with a loan associated with property produced by a taxpayer, special capitalization rules may apply. Specifically, interest on a debt must be capitalized if the debt is incurred or continues to exist in order to finance the construction, building, installation, manufacture, development, or improvement of real or tangible personal property produced by the taxpayer if any one of the following conditions is met:

1. The property being produced has a "long useful life,"

2. The estimated production period exceeds two years, or

3. The estimated production period exceeds one year and the property will cost more than $1 million to produce.[57]

Property with a long useful life is real property (such as land and buildings) or property with a class life of 20 years or more. For purposes of estimating the production period, the production period ends on the date the property is ready to be held for resale to customers or to be placed in service in the taxpayer's business.[58]

Example 15: In 2009, Py Co. begins building its own warehouse, which will replace its current storage facility. The cost of the building will be $2 million and it will take the company three years to complete. Py finances the cost of the building and incurs interest each year from 2009–2012 as it constructs the building. Since the building has a long useful life, Py must capitalize the interest costs to the cost of the building. Once the warehouse is placed in service, Py will depreciate the total cost of the building using the depreciation rules discussed in Chapter 7.

Example 16: Braylin Corporation, a furniture manufacturer, constructs its own machinery that it uses in the construction of sofa sleepers that it sells. It was estimated that the production period will last 18 months and the total costs to construct the machinery are $65,000. Braylin obtained financing for the project and paid interest on the loan balance in 2009 and in 2010. The machinery was placed in service in December 2010. Even though the production process took longer than a year, the costs did not exceed $1 million. Therefore, since the property is not realty (a "long-lived asset") and the machine took less than two years to complete, the interest on financing the project does not need to be capitalized and it can be deducted in the period in which it was paid or incurred.

Example 17: Assume the same facts as in Example 16, except that it cost Braylin $1,500,000 to produce the machine. Because the costs exceed $1 million and the estimated production period extends beyond one year, the interest incurred in financing the production of the machinery must be capitalized and added to the cost of the machinery. Once the machine is placed in service, Braylin will depreciate the total cost of the machine using the methods discussed in Chapter 7.

---

[57] Code Sec. 263A(f).   [58] Code Sec. 263A(f)(4)(B).

GAAP vs. Code: For tax purposes, the interest associated with the production of certain assets must be capitalized in accordance with the rules of Code Sec. 263A(f). For financial reporting purposes, interest must be capitalized only for the acquisition of "qualifying assets," since in some instances the benefits of capitalizing the interest may not justify the additional accounting and administrative costs involved in providing this information.[59] Due to the different standards used to determine whether interest must be capitalized or currently deducted, any differences between the two methods must be taken into consideration when reconciling net income to taxable income on the corporate tax return in the tax years when interest on construction of an asset is incurred.

¶ 506 Taxes

Businesses pay various taxes in the normal course of business. For example, property taxes are often levied annually on the owners of property. Businesses also regularly pay federal and state unemployment taxes on behalf of their employees[60] as well as the employer's share of social security and Medicare ("FICA") taxes. Sole proprietorships and partners pay self-employment taxes on their self-employment income.[61] Many of these taxes are currently deductible; however, some are nondeductible. Table 5-1 lists the various taxes the taxpayer may incur while engaging in a trade or business and the circumstances under which the taxes are currently deductible or must be capitalized.

Table 5-1 Tax Treatment of Taxes

Type of Tax	Deductible	Capitalized
Property[a]	Yes.	No.
Income (state and local)[b]	Yes, but always a deduction from AGI on an individual's income tax return.	No.
Sales (state and local)[c]	Yes, but always a deduction from AGI on an individual's income tax return.	Yes. May be added to cost basis of property.
Gasoline[d]	Yes.	No.
Foreign[e]	Yes. But only to the extent not claimed as a tax credit.	No.
Excise[c]	Yes.	No.
State Stamp[f]	Yes. Security dealers or investors in real property may deduct state stock transfer or real estate transfer taxes as a business expense.	No.
Unemployment[g]	Yes.	No.
Paid on shareholder's behalf[h]	Yes, if shareholders do not reimburse corporation for taxes paid on account of their ownership in the payor.	No.

---

[59] "Capitalization of Interest Cost," *Statement of Financial Accounting Standards No. 34* (Stamford, Conn: FASB 1979). "Determining Materiality for Capitalization of Interest Cost," *Statement of Financial Accounting Standards No. 42* (Norwalk, Conn: FASB 1980).

[60] Reg. § 1.162-10(a).

[61] Code Secs. 164(a) and (f).

Type of Tax	Deductible	Capitalized
Employment (FICA, FUTA)	Yes.	No.
Self-Employment[i]	Yes. Individuals may deduct one-half of the amount of their self-employment tax when computing AGI.	No.
Federal Income[j]	No.	No.
Estate and Gift[k]	No.	No.

[a] Code Secs. 164(a) and 63(c). Homeowners who claim the standard deduction can claim an additional standard deduction for state and local real property taxes, up to $500 ($1,000 for joint returns), for tax years 2008 and 2009.

[b] Code Sec. 164(a) and (b)(5); Reg. § 1.164-1(a). The sales tax deduction was extended through 2009. Individual taxpayers must choose between the deduction for state and local sales taxes and the deduction for state and local income taxes.

[c] *Id.* Code Sec. 164(a) and (b)(6). For tax year 2009, individual taxpayers are allowed a deduction from gross income for state sales and excise taxes imposed on the purchase of a qualified motor vehicle. The deduction is limited to the sales and excise tax on up to $49,500 of the price of a qualified motor vehicle. The deduction phases out for taxpayers with modified adjusted gross income between $125,000–$135,000 (joint return $250,000–$260,000). In addition, the deduction cannot be taken if the taxpayer elects to deduct state or local general sales taxes.

[d] Reg. § 1.164-5.

[e] Code Secs. 164(a) and 275(a)(4); Reg. § 1.164-2.

[f] Reg. § 1.164-1; Rev. Rul. 65-313, 1965-2 CB 47.

[g] *J.R. McGowan,* 67 TC 599, Dec. 34,200 (1976); *A. Trujillo,* 68 TC 670, Dec. 34,554 (1977); Rev. Rul. 75-156, 1975-1 CB 66; Rev. Rul. 75-444, 1975-2 CB 66.

[h] Code Sec. 164(e); Reg. § 1.164-7.

[i] Code Sec. 164(f).

[j] Code Sec. 275(a)(1).

[k] Code Sec. 275(a)(3).

Sales tax paid in connection with the purchase of property used in a business must be treated as part of the cost of the property.[62] If the property acquired is depreciable property, the capitalized sales tax will be depreciated along with the cost of the property. If the property acquired is currently deductible (for example, supplies), the sales tax is currently deductible as a business expense. Similar rules apply to use taxes and excise taxes paid or incurred during the year.[63]

State, local, and foreign income taxes businesses pay during the tax year are deductible,[64] but federal income taxes are not.[65] Foreign income taxes that taxpayers elect to take as a tax credit cannot be deducted. (See ¶ 1117.01 for a discussion of the option to claim a foreign tax credit in lieu of a deduction.) In addition, any state and local income taxes or, if elected, state and local general sales taxes, paid by an individual are automatically considered personal expenditures, and while still deductible, they are allowed only as itemized deductions and therefore cannot be used to reduce profits from a sole proprietorship.[66] As with the interest deduction for deficiency interest charged to a sole proprietor's business, the tax laws surrounding the deduction for state and local income, or general sales, taxes is another disadvantage to operating a business as a sole proprietorship.

---

[62] Code Sec. 164(a).

[63] Reg. § 1.164-2(f).

[64] Code Sec. 164(a).

[65] Code Sec. 275(a)(1); Reg. § 1.164-2(a).

[66] *D.H. Tanner,* CA-4, 66-2 USTC ¶ 9537, 363 F2d 36, aff'g, 45 TC 145.

GAAP vs. Code: Most taxes deducted on the income statement are also deductible on the tax return. However, a difference does exist in the treatment of federal income taxes. On the income statement, federal income taxes are reported as an expense deducted in arriving at net income. For tax purposes, no such deduction is allowed. This permanent difference in the treatment of this expenditure will result in less net income than taxable income for the year. Consequently, the amount of federal income taxes reported on the income statement must be added back to net income when the corporation reconciles its net income to taxable income. For example, if a corporation reports a deduction for federal income taxes of $640,000 on its income statement in arriving at net income, the amount must be added back when net income and taxable income are reconciled on the corporate tax return. Similar adjustments must be made for any taxes deducted in computing net income that are not deductible in the calculation of taxable income.

¶ 507 Research and Experimentation Expenditures

For businesses that regularly carry on research activities, research expenditures constitute ordinary and necessary business expenses. However, when a research project could provide benefits to a company for years to come, one might argue that the costs should be capitalized. However, once capitalized, it may be difficult to ascertain the project's useful life for purposes of amortizing the costs. To eliminate the need to make subjective determinations regarding such issues, the tax laws allow taxpayers to choose one of the following three methods for accounting for research and experimentation (R&E) costs paid or incurred in connection with a trade or business:[67]

1. Deduct the expenditures in the year in which they are paid or incurred,

2. Capitalize the expenditures and amortize them ratably over a period of at least 60 months beginning in the month that the benefits are first realized,[68] or

3. Capitalize the expenditures, but do not amortize them.

If the taxpayer chooses to currently deduct its R&E costs or to capitalize and amortize its costs, it must make an election. Generally the election must be made on the original tax return for the year in which the costs are paid or incurred. Once the election to use a method is made for a specific research project, it must be used in all subsequent tax years. If the taxpayer fails to make an election on the original tax return or would like to change to a different method, it must obtain the consent of the IRS.[69] If the taxpayer chooses to capitalize and not currently deduct or amortize its R&E costs, the capitalized amounts cannot be deducted until the research project is abandoned or deemed worthless.[70]

The choice of whether to deduct, defer and amortize, or capitalize R&E costs depends upon when it is best for the taxpayer to recover these costs. Generally, it will be preferable for the taxpayer to currently deduct its R&E expenditures. However, a business may elect to amortize its R&E costs if it believes it does not have sufficient income in the current year and has such significant net losses in prior years that it is worried that the losses generated by immediate expensing its R&E costs might not be fully utilized. In other instances in which the taxpayer anticipates a higher tax rate in future tax years, it may decide to amortize its R&E costs rather than take a current deduction.

Example 18: During 2009, Nycorm (a calendar year taxpayer), incurred $36,000 of R&E expenditures. Nycorm anticipates that it will have taxable income (before R&E) of $50,000 for both 2009 and 2010. Nycorm can select among the following three options for treating the R&E expenditures:

---

[67] Code Sec. 174(a).
[68] Code Sec. 174(b); Reg. § 1.174-4.

[69] Reg. § 1.174-3.
[70] Code Sec. 165.

1. Elect to deduct the full amount in 2009 and reduce its 2009 taxable income to $14,000 ($50,000 – $36,000). Its 2010 taxable income will be $50,000.

2. Elect to capitalize and amortize the R&E expenditures over a period of not less than 60 months. Assuming that Nycorm first realizes benefits on July 1, 2009, it could amortize $3,600 ($36,000/60 × 6 months) of R&E expenditures in 2009 and $7,200 ($36,000/60 × 12 months) in 2010. The amortization would reduce its 2009 taxable income to $46,400 ($50,000 – $3,600) and its 2010 taxable income to $42,800 ($50,000 – $7,200). Nycorm would amortize the rest of the R&E from 2011 to 2014.

3. Capitalize the $36,000 of R&E expenditures. Assuming that the research project is not abandoned or deemed worthless in 2009 or 2010, no deduction can be taken in either year. Thus, its taxable income will remain at $50,000 for both years.

.01 Activities That Constitute Research and Experimentation

To qualify as an R&E cost, the expenditure must be incurred in connection with the taxpayer's trade or business that represent research costs in the experimental or laboratory sense. It includes all such costs incident to the development or improvement of a product. This would include the development of any pilot model, process, formula, invention, technique or patent. Expenditures represent research costs in the experimental or laboratory sense if they are for activities intended to discover information that would eliminate uncertainty concerning the development or improvement of a product. Whether expenditures qualify as R&E expenditures depends on the nature of the activity to which the expenditures relate, not the nature of the product or improvement being developed.[71] R&E costs do not include expenditures for efficiency surveys, management studies, market research, advertising or promotions, normal product testing costs, the acquisition of another's patent, model, production or process, or research in connection with literary, historical or similar projects.[72] R&E expenditures are eligible for current deduction or deferral and amortization only to the extent the amount of the expense is reasonable under the circumstances.[73]

Example 19: On January 1, 2007, AXY Company began work on a special research project. During 2007, AXY purchased a building for $113,400 and used 50 percent of its facilities in connection with the special research project. AXY has not been profitable for the past several years, and it does not anticipate it will report taxable income until at least 2011. Thus, AXY elects to capitalize its R&E costs related to this project and amortize them over 60 months. In 2007, AXY incurred the following R&E expenditures:

Salaries	$40,000
Heat and light	1,200
Laboratory material	7,500
Attorney's fees	1,500
Depreciation on building attributable to the project (50% × $3,600 allowable depreciation)	1,800
Total R&E expenditures	$52,000

The $52,000 of expenditures resulted in a process that is marketable but not patentable and has no determinable useful life. If AXY first realizes benefits from the special research project in January 2009, on its 2009 tax return, AXY is entitled to deduct amortization of $10,400 ($52,000/60 × 12 months).

---

[71] Reg. § 1.174-2(a)(1).
[72] Reg. § 1.174-2(a)(3).

[73] Code Sec. 174(e); Reg. § 1.174-2(a)(6).

The options to deduct, amortize, or capitalize R&E expenditures do not extend to amounts spent for land or for depreciable property used in experimentation.[74] For example, a taxpayer cannot expense the cost of acquiring a site for a laboratory or the costs of constructing a laboratory. However, depreciation taken on property used in connection with a research project is considered an R&E expenditure. If the taxpayer elects to capitalize or amortize R&E expenditures that later result in the creation of depreciable property, any unamortized costs are added to the basis of the depreciable property and recovered through annual depreciation deductions.[75]

Example 20: In 2009, LED Corporation (a calendar year taxpayer) incurred R&E expenditures totaling $48,000 for a research project that did not relate to the creation of depreciable property. LED elected to capitalize and amortize the R&E costs over 60 months. The benefits were first realized on December 1, 2009. For 2009, LED can amortize $800 of its R&E expenditures ($48,000/60 × 1 month). For 2010, it can amortize $9,600 ($48,000/60 × 12 months).

On January 3, 2011, using the research from this project, machinery was produced that will be used in the company's manufacturing plant. In 2011, the $37,600 ($48,000 – $800 – $9,600) unamortized costs of R&E expenditures must be added to the basis of the machinery. Using the depreciation rules described in Chapter 7, LED will be able to recover these remaining costs through annual depreciation deductions.

.02 Research Credit in Lieu of a Deduction

The cost of certain research expenditures may be claimed as a tax credit, including a nonrefundable credit for the expenses paid or incurred for the clinical testing of a drug used for a rare disease or condition and amounts that represent an increase in the taxpayer's research activities. These credits are discussed in Chapter 11. If the taxpayer elects to take a tax credit for any R&E, it must reduce the amount of the tax deduction by the amount of the credit taken.

.03 Special Rule for Patents

A **patent** is an intangible asset that gives its owner the exclusive right to commercially profit from a specified product or process for a limited number of years. By filing for a patent, a business discloses its trade secrets regarding the product, but during the legal life of a patent (generally 20 years), others are specifically prohibited from profiting from the patented invention. The Code has established several alternatives regarding expensing the R&E costs associated with obtaining a patent.

First, R&E costs associated with the development of a patent can be deducted currently, regardless of whether the patent is eventually granted. These expenses may include the costs of obtaining a patent, such as the legal fees incurred in making and perfecting a patent application.[76] Second, the taxpayer can choose to capitalize the costs; however, if the patent is never obtained, the taxpayer must wait until the year the project is abandoned to deduct the costs.[77] Third, the taxpayer can elect to amortize the R&E costs over a period of no less than 60 months; however, if the patent is eventually issued, any unrecovered expenditures must be recovered through amortization deductions over the life of the patent (see ¶ 708).[78]

Example 21: Zyluss, Inc. reports its taxable income using a calendar year-end. In 2009, Zyluss elects to capitalize and amortize over a period of 60 months $60,000 of R&E expenditures made in connection with a particular project. During 2009, Zyluss developed a process that it seeks to patent. On July 1, 2009, Zyluss first realized

---

[74] Reg. § 1.174-2.
[75] Reg. § 1.174-4(a)(4).
[76] Rev. Rul. 68-471, 1968-2 CB 109.

[77] Code Sec. 165.
[78] Reg. § 1.174-4(a)(4).

benefits from the marketing of products resulting from the process. Therefore, the expenditures are deductible ratably over the 60-month period beginning July 1, 2009. On its 2009 tax return, Zyluss deducts $6,000 ($60,000/60 × 6 months), and on its 2010 tax return, Zyluss deducts $12,000 ($60,000/60 × 12 months). On October 1, 2011, a patent protecting the process is obtained. In its 2011 tax return, Zyluss is entitled to a deduction of $9,000, representing the amortizable portion of the R&E costs attributable to the period prior to October 1, 2011 ($60,000/60 × 9 months). The balance of the $33,000 of unamortized costs ($60,000 − $6,000 − $12,000 − $9,000) is recovered over the patent's useful life beginning October 1, 2011.

GAAP vs. Code: For financial reporting purposes, R&E expenditures are expensed in the period incurred unless the cost has an alternative future use (such as an intangible asset or property, plant, or equipment).[79] Depending on the tax treatment selected, there may or may not be a difference as to how these amounts are treated for financial reporting versus tax purposes. If the R&E costs are expensed immediately on the tax return, usually there will be no adjustment necessary between net income and taxable income. However, if the corporation chooses to amortize the R&E costs, then in the year the expenses are incurred, the corporation will need to add back to net income the difference between the amounts deducted in arriving at net income and the amortized expense deducted on the tax return. In all subsequent tax years, the amortization of the costs would need to be subtracted from net income in arriving at taxable income. Finally, if the R&E expenditures are capitalized and not amortized for tax purposes, then the amount expensed on the income statement in the first year would be added back to net income to arrive at taxable income.

For example, Zyluss, Inc. from Example 21 capitalizes the $60,000 of R&E expenditures for tax purposes and deducts (amortizes) $6,000 of the costs in 2009. On its financial statements, Zyluss expenses the entire $60,000 of R&E. Consequently, when reconciling net income to taxable income on its 2009 corporate tax return, Zyluss needs to add back the $54,000 ($60,000 − $6,000) difference between the amount deducted on the income statement and the deduction taken on the tax return. Adjustments will also need to be made in 2010 and 2011 when Zyluss continues to amortize the R&E costs on its tax return, with no such expense being deducted against net income.

Similarly, the amount a corporation is required to expense on the income statement for the costs associated with patents may not be the same as the amount a corporation is allowed to deduct on the tax return. An analysis similar to the one illustrated above with respect to R&E expenses would also apply to any amortization expense of a patent.

¶ 508 Dividends Received Deduction

Corporations are the one form of business entity for which the profits of the business are taxed twice—once by the corporation and a second time when the shareholders are paid a dividend from the corporation's earnings and profits. In the case of a corporate shareholder, the potential for triple taxation exists. Chapter 4 discussed the rules that allow corporations to reduce the amount of dividends they must report in their gross income to circumvent this potential problem. The percentage by which corporations can reduce their taxable dividends ranges from 70 percent to 100 percent, depending on the percentage of stock owned by the corporate shareholder. Although this amount is referred to as the "dividends received deduction," the deduction is not the result of an

---

[79] "Accounting for Research and Development Costs," *Statement of Financial Accounting Standards No. 2* (Stamford, Conn.: FASB, 1974), Para. 12.

expenditure; it is computed as a percentage of dividends received during the year. See ¶ 411.02 for more details on the calculation of this deduction.

¶ 509 Domestic Production Activities Deduction

Businesses that produce goods in the United States can claim a deduction, referred to as the manufacturers' deduction or domestic production activities (DPA) deduction.[80] The DPA deduction is available to all businesses engaged in domestic production activities, regardless of the type of entity under which the business is operated. Thus, sole proprietorships, partnerships, limited liability companies, limited liability partnerships, and corporations are all entitled to the DPA deduction if they meet the applicable requirements.

The DPA deduction is determined in accordance with the rules of Code Sec. 199, which contains a number of defined terms and is (perhaps needlessly) complex. However, the basic rule is simple enough: the DPA deduction is essentially a percentage of net income (gross receipts minus costs) derived from domestic production activities.

.01 Domestic Production Activities

Domestic production activities include not only traditional manufacturing but also such activities as construction, engineering, architectural services, and motion picture or video production. Taxpayers producing agricultural products can qualify for the deduction if they perform storage, handling, or other processing activities (other than transportation activities) within the United States.[81] Generally, the DPA deduction is for businesses that produce goods, not those that provide services (other than construction, engineering, or architectural services). The deduction is also unavailable for activities involving the sale of food and beverages prepared by the taxpayer at a retail establishment; the leasing, rental, licensing, sale, exchange or other disposition of land; or the leasing, licensing, or rental of property by the taxpayer for use by any related person.[82]

If a taxpayer is engaged both in producing goods and in providing services related to those goods, a distinction must be made between those activities related to producing the goods and those activities related to providing services. For example, producing electricity, natural gas, or potable water is considered a domestic production activity, but transmitting or distributing those products is not.[83] Therefore, in calculating its DPA deduction, a utility that both produces and transmits or distributes electricity, natural gas, or potable water must determine which of its activities relate to production and which relate to transmission or distribution.

.02 Calculating the Amount of the Deduction

Taxpayers are eligible for the DPA deduction if they derive income from domestic production activities. The DPA deduction rate is phased in through 2009. For tax years 2007, 2008, and 2009, the amount of the deduction is six percent of the *lesser of* a taxpayer's (1) qualified production activities income (QPAI) or (2) taxable income.[84] Beginning in 2010, the percentage increases to nine percent.[85] In no case can this deduction exceed 50 percent of employer's Form W-2 wages for the year that are used in computing QPAI.[86] For tax years beginning after May 17, 2006, wages taken into account in applying the 50 percent wage limitation only include wages that are allocable to domestic production gross receipts.[87]

---

[80] Code Sec. 199, as added by the American Jobs Creation Act of 2004 (P.L. 108-357), as amended by the Gulf Opportunity Zone Act of 2005 (P.L. 109-135), and the Tax Increase Prevention and Reconciliation Act of 2005 (P.L. 109-222).

[81] Code Sec. 199(c).

[82] Code Sec. 199(c)(4)(B).

[83] Code Sec. 199(c)(4).

[84] Code Sec. 199(a). The phased-in rates for tax years 2005 and 2006 are three percent.

[85] For tax years beginning after December 31, 2009, taxpayers having oil-related production activities income must reduce their DPA deduction by three percent of the least of (1) taxpayer's oil-related QPAI, (2) taxpayer's QPAI, or (3) taxpayer's taxable income (determined without regard to the DPA deduction). Code Sec. 199(d)(9), as added by the Emergency Economic Stabilization Act of 2008 (P.L. 110-343).

[86] Code Sec. 199(b).

[87] Code Sec. 199(b)(2) as amended by the Tax Increase Prevention and Reconciliation Act of 2005 (P.L. 109-222).

For the purposes of computing the DPA deduction, QPAI equals the taxpayer's receipts from domestic production activities (domestic production gross receipts) reduced by:

1. Cost of goods sold (COGS) that is allocable to domestic production gross receipts;

2. Other deductions, expenses, or losses directly allocable to domestic production gross receipts, such as selling and marketing expense; and

3. Proper share of other deductions, expenses, and losses not directly allocable to domestic production gross receipts or another class of income, such as general and administrative expense properly allocable to sales and marketing activities.[88]

For the purposes of reducing QPAI by COGS, an item or service brought into the United States is treated as acquired by purchase, and its cost cannot be less than its value immediately after it entered the United States.[89]

Example 22: Pentwater Manufacturing has domestic production gross receipts in the amount of $1 million derived from the sale of auto parts manufactured in the United States. The COGS for those auto parts is $500,000. Its sales and marketing expenses directly allocable to receipts from auto parts manufactured in the United States are $100,000, and it is proper to allocate $200,000 of indirect expenses to its receipts from the auto parts. Pentwater's QPAI is $200,000 ($1 million – ($500,000 + $100,000 + $200,000)).

Example 23: Burns Electric has as its sole business the production of electricity in its nuclear power plant. The electricity is transmitted to the town of Springfield by an unrelated company. For 2009, Burns has gross receipts of $1.5 million and expenses of $1 million, of which $500,000 is W-2 wages and $500,000 is other expenses. Because its sole activity (generating electricity) is a domestic production activity, all of its receipts and expenses are used in calculating its QPAI. Burns's QPAI equals $500,000 ($1.5 million – $1 million), and its DPA deduction equals $30,000 ($500,000 × 6%). Thus, for 2009 Burns's taxable income equals $470,000 ($500,000 – $30,000). If Burns's income and expenses stay the same over the next several years, its taxable income for 2010 will equal $455,000 ($500,000 – ($500,000 × 9%)), and in 2011 its taxable income will also equal $455,000 ($500,000 – ($500,000 × 9%)).

Example 24: Assume the same facts as in Example 23, except that the power plant is largely automated and Burns's W-2 wages are only $80,000. Its other expenses total $920,000. Burns's DPA deduction is limited to 50 percent of its W-2 wages, or $40,000. Because its DPA deduction for 2009 is less than that amount ($30,000), this limitation has no effect on its taxable income for the year. However, in 2010 and 2011, Burns's deduction will be limited to $40,000, and its taxable income will be $460,000 ($500,000 – $40,000) in those years.

Example 25: Moe's Taverns, Inc., a chain of bar-and-grill style restaurants, has gross receipts of $1.5 million and expenses of $1 million. Because Moe's does not engage in domestic production activities, it is not eligible for the DPA deduction. Therefore, its taxable income is $500,000 ($1.5 million – $1 million).

Domestic production gross receipts are the gross receipts the taxpayer derives from any lease, rental, license, sale, exchange, or other disposition of:

- Qualifying production property, a significant part of which was manufactured, produced, grown, or extracted by the taxpayer within the United States;

- Any qualified film produced by the taxpayer; or

- Electricity, natural gas, or potable water produced by the taxpayer in the United States.[90]

---

[88] Code Sec. 199(c); Prop. Reg. § 1.199-4(a). The "proper share" of indirect costs can be determined in several ways. The interested reader can consult Prop. Reg. § 1.199-4 or James M. Kehl, *Practical Guide to the Sec. 199 Deduction* (Chicago: CCH, 2007).

[89] Code Sec. 199(c)(3)(A).

[90] Code Sec. 199(c)(4)(A)(i).

"Qualified production property" includes all tangible personal property, computer software, and sound recordings (discs, tapes, etc.).[91] Gross receipts from the sale of real property are not eligible for the DPA deduction unless the taxpayer is in the construction business or provides architectural or engineering services in the construction of a building within the United States.[92] A "qualified film" is any motion picture film, video tape, or television program for which at least 50 percent of the total compensation relating to the film's production is compensation for services performed in the United States by actors, production personnel, directors, and producers. However, the term "qualified film" does not include pornography, and consequently, taxpayers cannot take a DPA deduction for income from pornographic films.[93]

Example 26: Mortiendi Corporation has the following gross receipts totalling $224.5 million and $102.5 million in direct costs for the current tax year for the following activities. Mortiendi also incurred $10 million of indirect costs during the year.

Item	Gross Receipts	Direct Costs (including COGS)
Electricity (produced in the United States)		
Consumed in the United States	$ 52,000,000	$ 25,000,000
Exported to Canada	1,500,000	1,000,000
Natural gas (produced in Canada)		
Consumed in Canada.	2,000,000	1,000,000
Exported to the United States	15,000,000	11,000,000
Corn syrup (produced in the United States)	5,000,000	4,000,000
Films		
Film 1 (shot overseas)	124,000,000	50,000,000
Film 2 (shot in the United States)	25,000,000	10,000,000
	$224,500,000	$102,000,000

Mortiendi's domestic production gross receipts include all receipts from electricity (because that is produced in the United States) but none of the receipts from natural gas (because that is produced in Canada). The gross receipts from corn syrup are included because the corn syrup is tangible personal property (and, thus, qualified production property) produced in the United States. The gross receipts from Film 1 are not included because the film was shot outside the United States. However, the gross receipts from Film 2 are included as domestic production gross receipts because the film was shot in the United States. Thus, Mortiendi's domestic production gross receipts equal $83.5 million ($52 million + $1.5 million + $5 million + $25 million).

Calculating domestic production gross receipts is the first step in determining a taxpayer's DPA deduction. Next, the taxpayer must deduct costs allocable to its domestic production gross receipts to determine its QPAI. The taxpayer's DPA deduction will be equal to a percentage of QPAI, but it cannot exceed 50 percent of its W-2 wages from its domestic manufacturing activities.

Example 27: Assume the same facts as in Example 26. To arrive at its QPAI, Mortiendi must reduce its domestic production gross receipts by costs directly allocable to domestic production gross receipts and an allocable portion of indirect costs. Directly allocable costs associated with the activities that are included in the calculation of domestic production gross receipts total $40 million ($25 million + $1 million + $4 million + $10 million). Indirect costs must be allocated between domestic production gross re-

---

[91] Code Sec. 199(c)(5).
[92] Code Sec. 199(c)(4)(A).

[93] Code Sec. 199(c)(6).

ceipts and Mortiendi's other receipts. One way to allocate these costs is on the basis of percentage of total gross revenues. Mortiendi's total gross revenues are $224.5 million. Its domestic production gross receipts total $83.5 million. Thus, its domestic production gross receipts are 37.2 percent of its total gross revenues ($83.5 ÷ $224.5). Accordingly, $3.72 million ($10 million × 37.2%) of its indirect costs are allocable to its domestic production gross receipts. Mortiendi's QPAI equals $39.78 million ($83.5 million − ($40 million + $3.72 million)). Mortiendi's DPA deduction will be a percentage of its QPAI.

Reason for the Rule: Congress chose to define broadly what constitutes qualified production activities so the deduction would be available to more businesses than just those that engage solely in traditional manufacturing activities. This is an example of Congress's use of the tax laws to encourage (and reward) certain activities (here, domestic production). However, it is important to note that in doing so, Congress introduces substantial additional complexity into the tax laws.

For the purposes of computing the DPA deduction, "W-2 wages" are defined as the taxable wages plus any elective deferral amounts reported on an employee's Form W-2. Taxable wages are those wages employees include in gross income when filing their personal income tax returns (typically the amount in box 1 on the employee's Form W-2). Elective deferrals are amounts an employee chooses to contribute to certain retirement plans and to exclude from the employee's current wages.[94] The most common example of an elective deferral is a contribution by an employee to a Code Sec. 401(k) plan (see discussion at ¶ 603.04).

Example 28: Bad Axe Manufacturing Corporation pays taxable wages allocable to domestic production activities reported in box 1 of its workers' Forms W-2 of $2 million. In addition, its employees make elective deferrals to their Code Sec. 401(k) accounts equal to $500,000. Bad Axe's W-2 wages are $2.5 million and its DPA deduction will be limited to $1.25 million ($2.5 million × 50%).

GAAP vs. Code: The DPA deduction is a tax incentive, not an expense, for financial reporting purposes. Accordingly, any amounts deducted on the tax return for the DPA deduction must be subtracted from net income when reconciling net income to taxable income on the corporate tax return. For example, assume that a corporation's taxable income for 2009 equals $523,000, but included in this amount is $34,000 for the DPA deduction. When preparing the reconciliation of net income to taxable income on the corporate tax return, net income must be reduced by $34,000.

¶ 510 Bad Debts

A bad debt occurs when money owed to a taxpayer becomes uncollectible. The tax laws allow a deduction for both business and nonbusiness bad debts, but the timing and character of the deductions differ. Business bad debts are deductible in full against business gross income. Nonbusiness bad debts are deductible as short-term capital losses. Taxpayers that incur a business bad debt can begin writing off the bad debt in the year it starts to become worthless. Nonbusiness bad debts must be fully worthless before they can be written off.[95]

All bad debts of a corporation are business bad debts. Individuals (including sole proprietors), partnerships, and S Corporations can have both business and nonbusiness bad debts. A **business bad debt** is one that is closely related to a taxpayer's trade or business.[96] There must have been a

---

[94] Code Sec. 199(b).
[95] Code Sec. 166.

[96] Code Sec. 166; Reg. § 1.166-5(b).

business reason for entering into the debt arrangement. Business bad debts are usually the result of credit sales of goods or services to customers and loans to suppliers, clients, employees, or distributors. A nonbusiness bad debt is any bad debt other than a business bad debt.

In order to claim a bad debt deduction, the taxpayer must have included the amount in gross income in the year the deduction is claimed or in a prior year. Thus, for businesses using the cash method of accounting, a bad debt deduction usually cannot be claimed from a receivable that is never paid because the defaulted payment would not have been included in gross income.

Furthermore, only a *bona fide* debt qualifies for a bad debt deduction. A *bona fide* debt arises from a debtor-creditor relationship based upon a valid and enforceable obligation to pay a fixed or determinable sum of money. A debt arising out of an accrual basis taxpayer's receivables is considered a legally enforceable obligation, deductible as a bad debt at the time of worthlessness, provided the amount of the debt is included in income of the current or a prior tax year. A gift or contribution to capital is not considered a debt for purposes of a bad debt deduction. Similarly, an advance by a taxpayer may not be written off if it is clear from the circumstances that repayment was not intended or expected.[97]

Example 29: Sol Winters owns all of the stock of a corporation. Sol advances $20,000 to the corporation so it could pay off its creditors. No payment of principal or interest was ever made by the corporation to Sol, and none was expected. The advance is a capital contribution or a gift, but it is not a loan. No bad debt deduction for the advance would be allowed.[98]

Example 30: Frank Wilson advanced $12,000 to his son-in-law to use in a new business venture. The son-in-law had no other income. Frank did not investigate the soundness or practicality of the venture. The $12,000 advance was not a loan, since the parties obviously did not intend a debtor creditor relationship. Therefore, if the business failed, no bad debt deduction would be allowed.[99]

Normally, losses from the sale or exchange of property between related persons (e.g., relatives or between a majority stockholder and the corporation) are disallowed under Code Sec. 267 (see ¶ 804). A bad debt loss, however, does not involve a sale or exchange, and therefore a bad debt between related parties may be deductible if the debt is legally enforceable and otherwise *bona fide*.

Example 31: Assume the same facts as in Example 30, except Frank has his son-in-law sign a note, and the terms of the note include terms for repayment of the loan, along with an interest rate comparable to the current market rate of interest. Under these conditions, if the son-in-law's business goes bankrupt, Frank will be able to deduct the amounts he cannot recover from the loan as a nonbusiness bad debt. Because the loan made to the son-in-law was personal in nature to Frank (the taxpayer), it does not qualify as a business loan.

An individual who operates a business as a sole proprietorship can have a business bad debt if the nature of the loan is related to the taxpayer's business. If the bad debt results from a loan to a relative, friend, or some other nonbusiness connection, the bad debt is a nonbusiness bad debt. Although a sole proprietor can deduct a nonbusiness bad debt as a short-term capital loss, such a loss is not deducted against the profits of the business but instead is used to reduce other capital gains the individual taxpayer generated during the year. The tax consequences of nonbusiness bad debts and ways to distinguish business bad debts from nonbusiness bad debts are discussed further in Chapter 13. The tax treatment of capital gains and losses is discussed in Chapter 9.

---

[97] *E.J. Cornish*, 22 BTA 474, Dec. 6750.
[98] *L. Rosenberg*, 5 TCM 138, Dec. 15,042(M).

[99] *J. Griffiths*, CA-7, 1934 CCH ¶ 9195, 70 F2d 946.

.01 Computing the Amount of the Deduction

If a debt becomes worthless, the amount allowed as a bad debt deduction is the adjusted basis of the debt.[100] The adjusted basis of the debt is the same as the amount that would be used to determine gain or loss from the sale of the debt.[101]

Example 32: A collection agency purchases a company's accounts receivable for $3,000. The face value of the receivables is $4,000. The accounts receivable became worthless in their entirety in the following year. For that year, the purchaser will report a bad debt of $3,000 because that amount would be used to compute the loss if the purchaser had sold the accounts receivable before they became totally worthless. If the agency had instead collected $3,500 from the receivables, it would recognize $500 of income ($3,500 – $3,000 adjusted basis).

The taxpayer's method of accounting must also be considered when computing the amount of the deduction. An accrual-basis taxpayer includes fees and rents in income when they are earned or become due and takes bad debt deductions when the debtor is unable to pay. A cash basis taxpayer can take a bad debt deduction only if the deducted amount was previously included in gross income. Since fees and rents are not included in income on the cash basis until they are received, they cannot be deducted as bad debts upon the default of the debtor. If notes are received by the cash basis taxpayer in payment of these debts and are included in income at their fair market value when received, that value can be deducted if the notes become worthless.

Example 33: An accountant using the cash method submitted a $400 bill to one of his clients. No part of the $400 was ever paid. The accountant will not include the unpaid bill in his gross income; therefore, he cannot take a bad debt deduction.

Example 34: Assume the same facts as in Example 33, except that the accountant uses the accrual method of accounting. The accountant reports the $400 in gross income at the time the services are performed. Assuming that the debt becomes worthless in a later year with the whole sum unpaid, the accountant can take a bad debt deduction for $400 in that year.

If a business debt becomes partially worthless, the part that has become worthless may be deducted on that year's tax return. In order to deduct a partially worthless business bad debt, the taxpayer must have evidence to support the probable amount that will be recovered at some point in the future.[102]

Example 35: A customer owes XYZ Company $12,000. In 2009, the customer files for bankruptcy, and an appraisal of the assets shows that only 25 percent of the amount due XYZ is recoverable. In 2009, XYZ can deduct $9,000 ($12,000 × 75%) as a partial bad debt.[103] If in 2010 the assets of the bankrupt company are disposed of and XYZ receives a final payment for $2,400, it can deduct the remaining $600 loss ($12,000 – $9,000 – $2,400) in 2010.

Example 36: Assume the same facts as in Example 35, except in 2010 XYZ receives $3,600 instead of $2,400. Since XYZ deducted $9,000 as a partial bad debt in 2009, the amount it deducted exceeds its actual loss of $8,400 ($12,000 – $3,600). Therefore, XYZ would report the $600 excess in gross income in 2010 under the tax benefit rule (see ¶ 313).

.02 Proof of Worthlessness

Except for a business bad debt that becomes partially uncollectible, a deduction is usually allowed only in the year a debt becomes worthless. A worthless debt is deductible in the year of worthlessness even when the debt is not due until a later year. The deduction is allowed in the year

---

[100] Code Sec. 166(b); Code Sec. 1011.
[101] Reg. § 1.166-1(d).

[102] Code Sec. 166(a)(2); Reg. § 1.166-3.
[103] *S.S. Denton Est.*, 11 TCM 802, Dec. 19,134(M).

the surrounding circumstances show that the debt is worthless and uncollectible, not when the taxpayer finally gives up attempting to collect the debt and decides to write it off.[104]

All the circumstances surrounding the situation are used to determine whether the debt is actually worthless. The running of the statute of limitations barring the creditor from bringing suit on the debt, the debtor's bankruptcy, or the death of the debtor leaving no assets are general indications, but not necessarily proof, of when a debt becomes worthless.

Example 37: Carl Dickenson loans Dan Hughes $180,000. In the following year, Dan is severely injured in an auto accident. It is unlikely that he will be able to work again and repay the loan. Carl can take a bad debt deduction for the year in which Dan was injured.[105]

Example 38: Jess Jones made a *bona fide* loan of $10,000 to Zeke Smith. Three years later, with the entire amount still unpaid, Zeke has left the state to places unknown, taking all of his property with him. On these facts, the $10,000 loan became worthless in the year of Zeke's departure. Therefore, Jess may deduct the bad debt in that year.[106]

 GAAP vs. Code: For financial reporting purposes, bad debt expense is an estimate taken in the year of sale in accordance with the matching principle. For tax purposes, the specific charge-off method is used. Therefore, the difference between the bad debt expense reported on the income statement and that which is deducted on the tax return would need to be taken into consideration when reconciling net income to taxable income on the corporate tax return.

¶ 511 Charitable Contributions

Contributions a taxpayer makes to a qualified charitable organization are usually deductible in computing taxable income. However, the amount of the deduction depends not only on the type of property contributed but also on the type of charitable organization to which the property was contributed. Different rules apply to contributions made to public versus private foundations as well as to contributions of ordinary income versus capital gain property. Finally, limitations on the amount that can be deducted in any one tax year differ depending on the type of taxpayer making the contribution.

.01 Qualified Charitable Organizations

Taxpayers can only deduct contributions they make to qualified charitable organizations. A **qualified charitable organization** is a tax-exempt, nonprofit organization formed and operated exclusively for the purposes specified in Code Sec. 501(c)(3).[107] Qualified charitable organizations can be classified as public charities or private foundations, depending upon whether they receive funding from the general public or from private sources. Churches, public universities, and many other organizations like the Red Cross, the United Way, and Goodwill receive their funding from the general public and are examples of **public charities**.

Private foundations, on the other hand, are entities formed with the express purpose of making grants to unrelated organizations or institutions or to individuals for scientific, educational, cultural, religious, or other charitable purposes. Private foundations typically receive most of their funding from one source, whether it be a family, a group of individuals, or a corporation.[108] **Private operating foundations** directly carry out their own activities; they are required to spend at least 85 percent of their earnings on carrying out these activities as well as to pass certain other tests. For example, a private operating foundation might conduct scientific research or operate a museum.[109] A

---

[104] Reg. § 1.166-2.

[105] *A.M. Smyth*, CA-10, 35-2 USTC ¶ 9405, 77 F2d 77.

[106] *E.K. Johnstone*, 17 BTA 366, Dec. 5417 (Acq.).

[107] Code Sec. 170(c).

[108] Code Sec. 509(a).

[109] Reg. § 53.4942(b)-1(b).

private nonoperating foundation is a privately funded, tax-exempt, nonprofit organization that does not meet the definition of a private operating foundation. Most private foundations make contributions to other qualifying charities in carrying out their role as qualified charitable organizations.

.02 Calculating the Amount of the Contributions

When taxpayers donate money to a qualified charitable organization, the deduction is the amount of money donated. When property is contributed, taxpayers usually are allowed to deduct the fair market value (FMV) of the contributed property, which is the price for which the property would sell on the open market on the date of contribution.[110] However, exceptions to this general rule exist, including exceptions for contributions of ordinary income and tangible personal property.

Contributions of ordinary income property. Ordinary income property is appreciated property that, if sold at its FMV on the date of contribution, would generate ordinary income or short-term capital gain. Appreciated property is property whose FMV exceeds its basis. Examples of ordinary income property include inventory, assets held for one year or less, and depreciable property used in a trade or business subject to depreciation recapture. When ordinary income property is contributed to a qualified charitable organization, the amount of the deduction is limited to the taxpayer's basis in the property.[111]

Example 39: BT Company donated to the United Way corporate stock it purchased six months earlier for $20,000. At the time of the donation to the United Way, the FMV of the stock was $28,000. Because BT donated stock it had held for less than one year (short-term property), its charitable contribution is limited to $20,000—its basis in the stock.

There are four exceptions to the ordinary income property rule that applies to corporations. Under the exceptions, the corporation is allowed to deduct its basis in the property plus half of the amount of the appreciation (FMV in excess of basis). However, the deduction is limited to twice the corporation's basis in the contributed property.[112]

One exception to the ordinary income property rule applies to corporations (other than S corporations) that contribute inventory and other ordinary income property to a qualified public charity or private operating foundation for use in the care of the ill, the needy, or infants. To qualify, the donee's use of the property must be related to its tax-exempt purpose or function; the organization cannot transfer the contributed property for money, property, or services; and the organization must provide the corporation with a written statement to this effect.[113]

Example 40: Mathis Corporation contributes men's overcoats with an FMV of $2,000 to a public charity. The charity will use the overcoats for the care of the ill and needy, which is consistent with its tax-exempt purpose. Mathis's basis in the overcoats is $600. Mathis initially computes its deduction as its $600 basis in the overcoats plus $700, which represents half of the appreciation (($2,000 – $600)/2). However, since this amount ($600 + $700 = $1,300) exceeds twice its basis in the overcoats of ($600 × 2 = $1,200), Mathis's charitable deduction is limited to $1,200.

A second exception to the ordinary income rules that applies to corporations (other than S corporations, personal holding companies, or service organizations) involves contributions of ordinary income property to colleges, universities, or scientific tax-exempt organizations for use in research. To qualify for this special rule:

1. The contributed property must be constructed or assembled by the donor and contributed within two years of its construction or assembly;
2. The original use of the property must be by the donee;

---

[110] Reg. § 1.170A-1(c)(2).
[111] Code Sec. 170(e)(1).

[112] Code Sec. 170(e)(3)(B), (e)(4)(A), and (e)(6)(A).
[113] Code Sec. 170(e)(3)(A).

3. The charitable organization must use the property at least 80 percent of the time for research or experimentation in the physical or biological sciences;

4. The charitable organization cannot exchange the property for money, other property, or services; and

5. The corporation must receive a written statement from the organization verifying that the previous two requirements have been met.[114]

Example 41: Gentran Corporation, a computer manufacturer, donates computers to Southern College; Gentran's basis in the computers is $100,000. The computers (FMV $140,000) will be used to assist in research projects conducted by Southern College's biology department. Gentran's charitable contribution deduction equals $120,000, which is the $100,000 basis in the computers plus $20,000 (50% of the $40,000 appreciation).

A third exception applies to corporations (other than S corporations, personal holding companies, or service organizations) that contribute computer technology or equipment. This exception applies to contributions made on or before December 31, 2009. An eligible donee for these purposes is:

1. An educational organization that normally maintains a regular faculty and curriculum and has a regularly enrolled body of pupils in attendance at the place where its educational activities are regularly conducted,

2. A Code Sec. 501(c)(3) entity that is organized primarily for purposes of supporting elementary and secondary education,

3. A private foundation that within 30 days after receipt of the contribution contributes the property to an eligible donee described in (1) and (2) above and notifies the donor of the contribution, or

4. A public library.

Computer technology and equipment is defined as computer software, computer or peripheral equipment, or fiber optic cable related to computer use. The contribution must be made within three years of the property's acquisition or substantial completion of its construction or assembly, and the original use of the property must be by the corporate donor or the donee. The donee may not transfer the donated property for money, services, or other property, except for shipping, transfer, and installation costs.[115]

Example 42: On January 3, 2009, BRE Inc., donated computer equipment to a public library in the U.S. that it had purchased new on March 1, 2006. At the time of the contribution, the equipment had an FMV of $80,000 and an adjusted basis of $50,000. BRE Inc.'s charitable contribution deduction is $65,000, which is the $50,000 basis in the computer equipment plus $15,000 (50% of the $30,000 appreciation).

The fourth exception to the ordinary income rules applies to any corporation (other than an S corporation) that makes a qualified book contribution to a public school on or after August 28, 2005, and before January 1, 2010. A qualified book contribution is a charitable contribution of books to a public school that provides elementary or secondary education (kindergarten through grade 12), which maintains a regular faculty and curriculum with a regularly enrolled student body. The donee educational institution must certify that (1) the books are suitable for use in the school's educational programs and (2) the school will actually use the books in its educational programs.[116]

---

[114] Code Sec. 170(e)(4)(B) as amended by the Tax Relief and Health Care Act of 2006 (P.L. 109-432).

[115] Code Sec. 170(e)(6), amended by The Tax Relief and Health Care Act of 2006 (P.L. 109-432), as amended by the Emergency Economic Stabilization Act of 2008 (P.L. 110-343).

[116] Code Sec. 170(e)(3)(D) as amended by the Emergency Economic Stabilization Act of 2008 (P.L. 110-343)

Contributions of capital gain property. Usually, taxpayers can deduct the FMV of property they contribute to a qualified charitable organization when they have held the property for more than a year (i.e., when it is long-term property). However, if capital gain property is donated to a private nonoperating foundation, then the amount of the deduction is limited to the taxpayer's adjusted basis in the property, except when the property is publicly traded stock, in which case FMV can still be deducted. Capital gain property is property that, if sold, would produce long-term capital gain or Section 1231 gain. This generally involves business property held long-term or property held long-term as an investment or as a personal belonging (in the case of an individual). Also, if tangible personal property is donated to a public charity where it is put to an unrelated use by the charitable organization, then the deduction again is limited to the taxpayer's adjusted basis in the property. Unrelated use is determined by reference to the purpose or function upon which the organization's tax-exempt status was based.[117] For charitable contributions made after September 1, 2006, unrelated use can also be determined by the sale, exchange, or disposal of property by the donee before the last day of the taxable year in which the contribution was made to which the donee has not made a certification as to the use, or intended use, of the donated property to the donee's exempt purpose.[118]

Example 43: TR Corporation donates a painting to a public university. The painting was purchased five years earlier for $10,000. At the time of the donation, the painting is worth $50,000. The university immediately sells the painting and uses the proceeds for educational purposes. TR's charitable contribution is limited to $10,000.

Example 44: Assume the same facts as in Example 43, except TR donates the painting to an art museum. TR's charitable contribution equals $50,000 because the tangible personal property donated to a charity is put to a use that is related to the organization's tax-exempt function.

Example 45: Angrella, Inc. donates land worth $100,000 to a public charitable organization. Angrella purchased the land for $20,000 several years earlier. Since land is not tangible personal property, no special limits apply and Angrella's charitable contribution equals $100,000.

Example 46: Deckright & Sons donates stock to a public charitable organization. Deckright paid $5,000 for the stock several years earlier, and it is currently worth $50,000. Although stock is considered personal property, it is intangible property, and therefore, the special limitations would not apply. Deckright's charitable contribution equals $50,000.

Recapture of charitable contribution deduction. For property donated after September 1, 2006, if a charitable organization receives appreciated tangible personal property as a charitable contribution in which the claimed value of the property exceeds $5,000 and later disposes of the property within three years of receiving it, the donor's charitable contribution deduction is limited to the amount of the property's basis. This recapture rule will not apply if the donee provides a certification that the property was intended to be used or was put to a use related to the donee's exempt purpose.[119]

 Planning Pointer: Taxpayers need to be aware of the rules for donating appreciated property to a charitable organization. In certain situations, the amount of the contribution may be limited to the taxpayer's basis in the property. In such situations, the taxpayer may be better off selling the property, paying any tax on the gain, and then making a cash donation to the charitable organization. For example, if tangible personal

---

[117] Code Sec. 170(e)(1)(B)(i).
[118] *Id.* As amended by The Pension Protection Act of 2006 (P.L. 109-280).

[119] Code Sec. 170(e)(7), as added by The Pension Protection Act of 2006 (P.L. 109-280).

property worth $20,000 is donated to a charitable organization that puts the property to a use that is unrelated to its charitable purpose, the taxpayer's charitable contribution will be limited to the taxpayer's basis in the property. If the taxpayer paid $5,000 for the property several years ago, it may be more advantageous to the taxpayer to sell the property for $20,000 and pay taxes on the $15,000 gain. The taxpayer can contribute some of the proceeds from the sale to the charitable organization. However, since this special rule only applies to appreciated tangible personal property, taxpayers can deduct the full FMV of donations of intangible assets (such as stock and bonds) or real property (land and buildings), provided the taxpayer has owned the property for more than one year.

.03 Timing of the Contributions

Contributions are typically deducted in the year in which they are paid, regardless of the taxpayer's method of accounting.[120] Payments made by credit card are deductible in the year in which the credit card is charged, regardless of when the taxpayer actually pays the credit card bill.[121] Since most corporations must use the accrual method, the tax laws allow accrual basis corporations to elect to accrue a contribution authorized by the board of directors by the end of the corporation's tax year, provided the contribution is paid within 2½ months after the close of the tax year. An election to treat such a contribution as having been paid during the tax year must be made at the time of filing the return for such year.[122]

Example 47: In December 2009, the board of directors of a corporation passes a resolution to contribute $500,000 to the local university. The corporation uses the accrual method of accounting and a calendar tax year. The check is mailed on February 10, 2010. At the time it files its 2009 tax return, the corporation may elect to deduct the contribution in 2009. If it fails to make the election, the deduction will be taken on the corporation's 2010 tax return.

.04 Limitations

The amount of the deduction that can be taken for charitable contributions in any given tax year is limited for both individuals and corporations. There is no overall limit imposed on businesses operated as flow-through entities, but the amounts of the contributions those entities make during the year are allocated separately to their respective owners, who then apply the limits on their own income tax returns. Although the details for the limitation imposed on individuals is discussed in detail in Chapter 13, it should be noted here that all contributions made by an individual are treated as itemized deductions, even if the contribution is paid from a business operated as a sole proprietorship or a flow-through entity. As mentioned in Chapter 1, only individuals whose total itemized deductions exceed their standard deduction benefit from itemized deductions; therefore, this rule is yet another disadvantage to operating an unincorporated business.

 Reason for the Rule: Charitable contributions made by a sole proprietor are always considered personal expenditures. A business operated as a sole proprietorship is not allowed to reduce taxable business profits by any charitable contributions made by the sole proprietor. To better understand why this rule exists, take as an example Sarah Conrad, who operates her greeting card business as a sole proprietorship. For 2009, Sarah's net profit from her business totals $50,000. Sarah is very active in her community and donates her time and money to a homeless shelter, which is a qualified

---

[120] Code Sec. 170(a)(1).

[121] Rev. Rul. 78-38, 1978-1 CB 67, distinguishing Rev. Rul. 68-174, 1968-1 CB 81.

[122] Code Sec. 170(a)(2); Reg. § 1.170A-11(b).

charitable organization. Several times during the year, Sarah writes checks from her business account as a donation to the homeless shelter. If Sarah were allowed to deduct her contributions of $4,000 to the homeless shelter as a business expense on Schedule C, *Profit or Loss From Business*, her federal income tax liability would be reduced due to the $4,000 reduction in her business profits. She would also pay less self-employment taxes as a result of having less profits subject to self-employment taxes. However, because Sarah is only able to deduct the $4,000 charitable contribution as an itemized deduction, it will only reduce her income taxes if her total itemized deductions exceed her standard deduction in 2009. The reason Congress only allows individual taxpayers to claim charitable contributions as itemized deductions is because anyone with a sole proprietorship would claim that his or her charitable contributions came from the business and were not made for personal reasons.

For corporate taxpayers, the allowable deduction for charitable contributions may not exceed 10 percent of the corporation's taxable income, computed before taking into consideration any of the following items:

- Charitable contribution deduction,
- Dividends received deduction (see ¶ 508),
- Deduction relating to the limitation of bond-premium deduction on repurchase,[123]
- Any capital loss carryback (see ¶ 901.01),
- Any net operating loss carryback (see ¶ 1004.02), and
- Domestic production activities deduction (see ¶ 509).

Any contributions in excess of the annual limit can be carried forward by the corporation to the next five tax years. At the end of five years, any excess contributions that could not be deducted are lost. The total deduction for the year to which an unused contributions deduction is carried over is also subject to the 10-percent limit. In years in which charitable contributions are being carried over, the current year's contributions are applied first against the limit, followed by the carryover contributions using a first-in, first-out method.[124]

Example 48: A corporation makes a $25,000 charitable contribution during the year. The corporation's taxable income before deducting the charitable contribution is $180,000; however, included in this calculation is a $12,000 deduction for domestic production activities and a $20,000 dividends received deduction. The corporation's charitable contribution deduction for the year is limited to $21,200. It carries over the remaining $3,800 ($25,000 – $21,200) of charitable contributions to the next five years. The corporation's taxable income for the year is $158,800 ($180,000 – $21,200).

Taxable income before the charitable contribution	$180,000
Plus: Dividends received deduction	20,000
Domestic production activities deduction	12,000
	$212,000
	× 10%
Charitable contribution limit	$ 21,200

Example 49: A calendar year corporation makes a charitable contribution of $30,000 in 2009. Its taxable income in 2009 determined without regard to the charitable deduction is $100,000. Therefore, the corporation's charitable contribution deduction for 2009 is

---

[123] Code Sec. 249.

[124] Code Sec. 170(d)(2)(A); Reg. § 1.170A-11(c).

limited to $10,000 ($100,000 × 10%). The $20,000 excess charitable contribution ($30,000 – $10,000) that could not be deducted in 2009 is carried forward to 2010. In 2010, the corporation has $125,000 of taxable income determined without regard to the charitable deduction. During 2010, it makes a $5,000 charitable contribution. For 2010, the corporation may deduct $12,500 as a charitable contribution ($125,000 × 10%). The corporation's $12,500 deduction consists of the $5,000 contribution made in 2010 and $7,500 carried over from 2009. The remaining $12,500 carryover from 2009 ($20,000 – $7,500) is carried forward to 2011.

.05 Sequencing of Deductions

In calculating taxable income, special consideration must be made for the order in which specific deductions, such as the charitable contribution deduction, dividends received deduction, capital loss carrybacks, NOL deduction and the domestic production activities deduction are taken. In calculating taxable income the sequence in taking the following five deductions must be followed:

1. Charitable contribution (CC) deduction,

2. Dividends received deduction (DRD),

3. Capital loss (CL) carryback,

4. NOL deduction, and

5. Domestic production activities (DPA) deduction.

The following example illustrates the sequencing of these deductions in calculating taxable income.

Example 50: The following is the 2009 tax information for Xtra, Inc.:

Sales revenue	$100,000
Dividend income from Rockpoint (Xtra, Inc. owns 15% of Rockpoint's stock)	50,000
Capital gains	15,000
Business expenses	25,000
Charitable contributions	20,000
Capital loss carryback	5,000
NOL carryback	40,000

For corporations, the charitable contribution (CC) deduction cannot exceed 10 percent of taxable income before taking any of the five deductions as listed. In determining the CC deduction, NOL carryforwards are reflected in computing taxable income for purposes of the 10-percent limitation.

Sales revenue	$100,000
Dividend income	50,000
Capital gain	15,000
Total income	$165,000
Less: Business expenses	(25,000)
Taxable income before CC, DRD, CL carryback, NOL and DPA	140,000
	× 10%
Charitable contribution (CC) deduction	$ 14,000

The amount of the CC deduction for 2009 is $14,000. The remaining amount of the charitable contributions of $6,000 ($20,000 – $14,000) will be carried over to 2010.

In determining the CC deduction, a capital loss **carryforward** (but not carryback—item #3) would be subtracted by the company to the extent it has capital gains. If Xtra, Inc. had a $5,000 capital loss carryforward, instead of a carryback, the CC deduction would have been limited to $13,500 ((($165,000 total income – $5,000 capital loss carryforward) – $25,000 business expenses) × 10%)).

After computing the CC deduction, the dividends received deduction (DRD) is calculated (see ¶ 411.02). When applying the taxable income limitation to the DRD, taxable income is computed before subtracting items 2–5 as listed. The CC deduction (item #1) is subtracted before computing the DRD.

Sales revenue		$100,000
Dividend income		50,000
Capital gain		15,000
Total income		$165,000
Less: Business expenses	$25,000	
Charitable contribution deduction	14,000	(39,000)
Taxable income before DRD, CL carryback, NOL and DPA		$126,000
Less: DRD ($50,000 × 70%)		(35,000)
Taxable income before CL carryback, NOL, and DPA		$ 91,000

The DRD is $35,000 calculated by taking the *lesser* of (1) 70 percent of the dividends received or (2) 70 percent of the corporation's taxable income before the DRD. If the corporation also received dividends subject to the 100 percent or 80 percent DRD, taxable income is first reduced by the 100 percent DRD then the aggregate amount of dividends subject to the 80 percent DRD before taking the 70 percent deduction.

After calculating the DRD, any capital loss carrybacks and/or NOL deduction are subtracted from taxable income.

Taxable income before CL carryback, NOL, and DPA		$ 91,000
Less: Capital loss carryback	$ 5,000	
NOL carryback	40,000	(45,000)
Taxable income before the DPA deduction		$ 46,000

The DPA deduction is calculated after all the items listed from 1–4 have been subtracted. In this example, Xtra, Inc. has determined its DPA deduction to be $1,380 after considering items 1–4. Xtra Inc.'s taxable income:

Taxable income before the DPA deduction	$ 46,000
Less: Domestic production activities deduction	(1,380)
Taxable income	$ 44,620

.06 Substantiation

Taxpayers making charitable contributions of cash, checks, or other monetary gifts must retain certain records of the gift, *regardless of the amount*. Taxpayers must maintain either: a bank record; *or* a receipt from the charity indicating the name of the charitable organization, the date the contribution was made, and the amount of the contribution. If these records are not kept for each donation made, no deduction is allowed for the charitable contribution.[125]

Taxpayers making noncash charitable contributions should file Form 8283, *Noncash Charitable Contributions,* to report information about the donated property. For noncash donations of property valued at more than $500, individuals, closely held corporations, personal service corporations, partnerships, and S corporations must file Form 8283 to report information about the donated property. When noncash donations exceed $500, the taxpayer must maintain a written record as to (1) the approximate date and manner of the acquisition of the property or the approximate date of completion if the taxpayer created the property and (2) the cost or other basis of the property held for a period of 12 months or less immediately preceding the date on which the contribution was made.[126] For contributions valued over $5,000, a qualified appraisal must be attached to the tax return when filed.

A deduction for the charitable contribution of a clothing or household item by a corporation, an individual, or partnership will only be permitted if the item is in good used condition or better.[127] The IRS will not deny a deduction for a charitable contribution of a clothing or household item if:

1. A deduction of more than $500 is claimed for the single clothing or household item, and

2. The taxpayer includes a qualified appraisal with respect to the item with the tax return on which the deduction is claimed.

"Household items" include furniture, furnishings, electronics, appliances, linens, and other similar items. The term does not include food, paintings, antiques, other objects of art, jewelry, gems, or collections.

Corporations, other than S corporations, personal service corporations, and closely held corporations, file Form 8283 only if the amount claimed as a deduction exceeds $5,000. For C corporations, the substantiation requirements for property exceeding the $5,000 level do not apply to donations of:

1. Cash,

2. Publicly traded securities,

3. Inventory, and

4. Any qualified vehicles sold by a donee organization without any significant intervening use or material improvement and for which an acknowledgement is provided.

 GAAP vs. Code: For financial reporting purposes, the amount of charitable contributions paid or accrued is expensed in the period incurred. For tax purposes, charitable contributions are subject to a 10 percent limitation. Thus, in any year in which a corporation's charitable contribution deduction is limited, the disallowed amount must be added back to net income when reconciling net income to taxable income. Likewise, in the years in which the carryover amounts are deducted on the corporation's tax return, such amounts must be subtracted from net income in arriving at taxable income.

For example, the corporation from Example 49 makes a $30,000 qualified charitable contribution during 2009. When computing its taxable income after applying the annual limit, only $10,000 of the contribution is allowed. When computing net income, the corporation deducts the $30,000 as a charitable contribution expense. When reconciling its net income to its taxable income in 2009, the corporation must add back the $20,000 difference to net income to compute taxable income. In 2010, the corporation deducts

---

[125] Code Sec. 170(f)(17), as added by the Pension Protection Act of 2006 (P.L. 109-280).

[126] Reg. § 1.170A-13(b)(3).

[127] Code Sec. 170(f)(16)(A), as added by the Pension Protection Act of 2006 (P.L. 109-280).

the $5,000 contribution it makes during the year in arriving at net income. However, due to the carryover, after applying the annual limit, the corporation deducts $12,500 on its 2010 tax return. The excess $7,500 of deductions taken on the tax return due to the charitable contribution carryover from 2009 must be subtracted from net income when reconciling net income to taxable income on the 2010 corporate tax return.

¶ 512 Business Gifts

Deductions for business gifts are limited to $25 per individual each year.[128] Items distributed by the taxpayer that do not cost more than $4 and on which the taxpayer's name is permanently imprinted (such as pens, key chains, etc.) are not subject to the $25 limit. Also, signs, display racks, or other promotional materials to be used by the recipient at the recipient's place of business are not subject to the $25 limit.

Achievement awards are not considered business gifts, but may be deductible by the employer as a business expense.[129] The employer's deduction depends on whether the award is a qualified plan award. The deduction to the employer for the cost of qualified plan awards made to any employee is limited to $1,600 per year, taking into account all other qualified and nonqualified awards made to that employee during a tax year. The employer's deduction for the cost of nonqualified plan awards made to any one employee during the tax year is limited to $400. A qualified plan award is one that is part of an established written plan or program set up by the employer that does not discriminate in favor of highly compensated employees as to eligibility for award benefits.[130]

 GAAP vs. Code: Because of the tax limitation on the amount paid for business gifts, there generally will be a difference between the amount expensed in arriving at net income versus that deducted on the tax return. For example, if a corporation sends out to 100 of its regular customers gifts costing $75 each, then the corporation will deduct $7,500 ($75 × 100) as gifts in arriving at its net income. On the tax return, the corporation will be able to deduct $2,500 ($100 × $25). The $5,000 difference would be added to net income when the corporation reconciles net income to taxable income on the corporate tax return.

¶ 513 Summary

Although most expenses taxpayers incur in the normal course of business meet the ordinary, necessary, and reasonable requirements, Congress has sought to deny or limit certain business expenses for a variety of reasons. Since every dollar taken as a deduction results in tax savings equal to the taxpayer's marginal tax rate, it is important that businesses understand all of their options with respect to the amount and timing of deductions available to them. This chapter focused on some of the more common expenses that businesses encounter during the normal course of business. This discussion continues in Chapter 6 with a discussion of employment-related expenses.

---

[128] Code Sec. 274(b)(1).
[129] Code Sec. 274(j)(2).

[130] Code Sec. 274(j)(3)(B).

GLOSSARY OF TERMS INTRODUCED IN THE CHAPTER

Amortization. The annual deduction taken to recover the cost of intangible assets over time.

Business bad debt. A *bona fide* debt that is closely related to a taxpayer's trade or business. There must have been a business reason for entering into the debt arrangement.

Deficiency interest. The interest charged on tax deficiencies when taxpayers fail to pay the proper amount of taxes on their income tax returns.

Depreciation. An annual deduction taken to recover the capitalized cost of business or income-producing property that is either tangible personal property or real property (other than land).

Depletion. The annual deduction taken to recover an investment in productive natural resources.

Domestic production gross receipts. The gross receipts the taxpayer derives from any lease, rental, license, sale, exchange, or other disposition of (1) qualifying production property, a significant part of which was manufactured, produced, grown, or extracted by the taxpayer within the United States; (2) any qualified film produced by the taxpayer; or (3) electricity, natural gas, or potable water produced by the taxpayer in the United States.

Necessary expense. An expense that is appropriate or helpful to the continuation of the taxpayer's business.

Nonbusiness bad debt. A *bona fide* debt that is not a business bad debt. *See also* Business bad debt.

Ordinary expense. An expense that is customary and acceptable in the taxpayer's type of business.

Organizational costs. Certain costs incurred in the process of incorporating a business.

Patent. An intangible asset that gives its owner the exclusive right to commercially profit from a specified product or process for a limited number of years.

Private nonoperating foundation. A privately funded, tax-exempt, nonprofit organization that does not meet the requirements of a private operating foundation.

Private operating foundation. A privately funded organization that directly carries out its own activities and is required to spend at least 85 percent of its earnings carrying out its activities and to pass certain other tests.

Public charities. Charitable organizations such as churches, public universities, the Red Cross, and the United Way that receive their funding from the general public.

Qualified charitable organization. A tax-exempt, nonprofit organization formed and operated exclusively for the purposes specified in Code Sec. 501(c)(3).

Start-up costs. Costs that normally would be currently deductible if they were incurred in connection with the operation of an existing trade or business and that are not organizational costs.

Uniform capitalization (UNICAP) rules. The rules that require a taxpayer to capitalize certain costs as part of the cost of real or tangible personal property the taxpayer produces.

CHAPTER PROBLEMS

The following questions and problems relate to the discussion in Chapter 5, Business Deductions: Ordinary and Necessary Business Expenses, which begins at ¶ 500 in *Part II: Federal Taxation of Business Income and Deductions.*

Chapter 5 Discussion Questions

1. Match the terms listed with the appropriate definition. A term can only be used once.

    (a) bad debt

    (b) domestic production activities deduction

    (c) charitable contribution deduction

    (d) illegal bribe paid to a public official

    (e) research and experimentation expenditure

    (f) ordinary, necessary, and reasonable

    (g) business creation and preopening costs

    (h) uniform capitalization rules

    (i) state incorporation fee

    1. Conditions for a business expense to be deducted.

    2. Organizational expenditure.

    3. Nondeductible business expense that violates public policy.

    4. Business taxpayers must capitalize and then depreciate costs that are incurred because of production or resale activities.

    5. Start-up expenditures.

    6. Business deduction that encourages businesses to engage in manufacturing activities within the United States.

    7. Money that is uncollectible that is owed to a taxpayer.

    8. Corporate deduction limited to 10 percent of the corporation's taxable income, computed with adjustments.

    9. Expenditure that includes all costs incident to developing or improving a plant process, product, formula, invention, or similar property.

2. Of the following, which are deductible as business expenses?

    a. Penalty for not filing an income tax return.

    b. Penalty for nonperformance of a contract.

    c. Fine for violation of a city housing code.

    d. Fine for truckers in violation of air quality laws.

    e. Fine for driving in excess of the speed limit.

    f. Kickbacks paid by tennis instructor to sporting goods dealer that violate state law (which is never enforced), but not federal law.

3. Smith & Wesson Investment Co. employed Wheeler Dealer, a securities broker with significant connections to the board rooms of several large, publicly traded corporations. During the course of a business lunch, Wheeler received some insider information that he promptly put to use in his trading activities, thereby turning a handsome profit for himself and Smith & Wesson. With almost equal promptness, Wheeler's activities were detected by the SEC and he was tried and found guilty on several criminal counts of securities law violations. Smith & Wesson incurs considerable legal expenses in Wheeler's defense. Nevertheless, Wheeler is found guilty on all counts. Are Wheeler's legal fees deductible by Smith & Wesson as an ordinary and necessary business expense?

4. A business pays a lobbyist to try to influence elected representatives concerning impending legislation. In addition, the business incurs expenses in communicating its concerns regarding the legislation to a trade organization in which the business is a member. Are these expenses deductible?

5. Which of the following are capital expenditures?

   a. Cost of partitions to convert a warehouse to an office building.

   b. Interest on a debt incurred to finance construction of a building.

   c. Cost of mending leaks in a roof.

   d. Cost of a building project to comply with the city building code.

6. At formation, WPJ Corporation incurred the following expenses: legal services to obtain charter—$500, state incorporation fees—$400, and stock issue costs—$300. How quickly will the corporation be allowed to deduct these costs?

7. Eleco and Ampco are public utilities that enter into an agreement to share the costs of constructing and operating a power plant. Eleco incurs costs in providing training to individuals on the operation of the plant prior to the start of its operation. Under the agreement Ampco reimburses Eleco for its share of the costs. May Ampco take a current deduction for the amounts?

8. Which of the following amounts must be capitalized and which may be deducted or capitalized at the election of the taxpayer?

   a. Interest paid by the taxpayer (contractor) in a special manufacturing contract in which there were no advance payments.

   b. Interest and taxes on unimproved real property.

   c. Interest paid by a contractor during the three-year construction period of an office building.

9. CYG Company purchases a number of computers. The total price of the computers purchased is $18,000, of which $1,200 is sales tax. Can CYG Company deduct the $1,200 on its current tax return?

10. A business pays property tax of $500, sales tax of $600 paid on the purchase of office equipment, gas tax of $200, and employment taxes of $500. Which taxes may be deducted in the current year?

11. In the current year, a taxpayer incurs $1,200 of research and experimentation costs. The taxpayer elects to amortize the research and experimentation cost, over 60 months, in the first year. Benefits from the cost of the project are realized in the first year only. At the end of the second year, the project is abandoned. What are the effects on the taxpayer's returns for both years?

12. What is the domestic production activities deduction, and what is the amount of the deduction for 2009?

13. What types of business entities can claim a domestic production activities deduction?

14. A taxpayer makes a personal loan to a friend, saying, "You need not pay it back unless you feel like it." Five years later the friend has not repaid the loan, and the taxpayer claims a bad debt deduction. Is this proper?

15. Determine the bad debt deduction that may be claimed for the current tax year by the taxpayers described below:

   a. A taxpayer charges off a $1,000 business debt in the current tax year. The debt became totally worthless during the preceding tax year.

   b. A $1,000 business debt becomes totally worthless during the current tax year. The debt is due in the following tax year.

16. The taxpayer, a merchandising corporation, ascertains in the current year that a debt owed to it is worthless. Had the corporation attempted to enforce the debt in the preceding year,

it would have found then that it could not be collected. However, there was no way in the ordinary course of business of determining the condition of the debt until this year, and therefore it charges the amount off this year. Can the debt be deducted as a bad debt for the current year?

17. For each situation described below, determine the allowable bad debt deduction.

   a. Star Painting Company, a cash basis taxpayer, agrees to paint Fred Blum's apartment building for $5,000. After completing the job, the company learns that Fred has sold the building and moved to Mexico. There is no reasonable prospect that Star will ever be paid.

   b. A collection agency purchases accounts receivable with a face value of $1,000 for $500. It collects $750 of the debt. The remainder becomes worthless.

18. A corporation wants to make a charitable contribution for the current tax year; however, the corporation wants to wait as long as possible to make the donation. If the corporation is a calendar-year corporation that uses the accrual method, how long can the corporation wait to make the contribution, and what process is necessary?

19. If a corporation contributes its inventory to a qualified charitable organization, what amount can it generally deduct?

20. What deduction is allowed to a corporation for a gift to a regular customer of a radio costing $50?

Chapter 5 Problems

1. PAZ Corporation incurred the following expenses during the year:

Federal (EPA) fine paid for violation of air quality laws	$ 50,000
Bribes paid to foreign officials to approve foreign construction project	200,000
Kickbacks paid to local police officers	25,000
Legal fees incurred in contesting EPA fine	250,000
Court costs incurred in contesting EPA fine	1,000

   What is the amount of expenses that PAZ Corporation can deduct for the year?

2. QT Corporation incurred the following politically related expenses:

Payments to state lobbyists to secure passage of favorable legislation	$550,000
Political contributions	250,000
Political dinner (table purchased)	10,000
Expenses incurred by QT President to appear before state congressional committee to discuss proposed legislation that will affect QT	2,000

   What is the amount of expenses that QT Corporation can deduct?

3. John Porter, sole shareholder of Canit Inc., incurred the following expenses for the year that were reimbursed by the company:

Parking tickets incurred while on business	$550
Traffic ticket for running a stop sign when going to a business meeting	150
Political contributions on behalf of the company	750

   What is the amount of expenses that Canit Inc. can deduct?

4. Kip Sims, a yacht broker, paid $15,000 to AB Marina and $35,000 to CU Marina as kickbacks for customer referrals. There is a state law against these payments, but the law is never enforced. There is no federal law against these payments. How much of the kickback payments can Kip Sims deduct, if any?

5. James Jacobs and Sons was a partnership operating a printing business. The partners decided to incorporate their business and consulted an attorney to file the Articles of

Incorporation. They also hired an accountant for audit work incidental to the incorporation. The following expenditures were made as a result of forming the corporation:

Attorney's fees relating to drawing up the corporate charter	$6,000
Accountant's fees incident to organization	3,000
State fee for incorporating	300
Expense of issuing stock	120
Transfer fees for transferring assets to the corporation	60

The corporation was formed on June 28, 2009, and began business in July of 2009. It elected to file its tax return using a calendar year. The officers of the corporation requested the bookkeeper to currently deduct expenses where possible and to amortize the remaining expenses over the shortest possible period for federal income tax purposes. What is the amount deductible on the corporation's tax return in 2009?

6. Zig Corporation incurs advertising and training costs of $52,500 before its business actually begins. Zig Corporation began business on May 1, 2009. Compute the maximum amount of Zig Corporation's deduction for start-up costs for 2009.

7. A trucking company had the following expenses for the tax year:

Stamps, stationery, and office supplies	$ 3,500
Office expense and salaries	150,000
Heat and light	10,000
Miscellaneous repairs to trucks	3,000
Tire replacements (consumed within one year)	4,000
Oil and gas for machines and trucks	30,000
Two new fax machines	980

The company also built an addition to its building to be used as a shipping room at a cost of $3,000. How are these items treated on the tax return for the year?

8. In 2009, Hat Co. purchased $160,000 of equipment to be used in its manufacturing plant. What is the correct tax treatment of this expenditure?

9. C&J Corporation incurred the following expenses at formation: legal services to obtain charter—$600, investigation costs leading to the decision to incorporate—$1,000, state incorporation fees—$500, and stock issue costs—$100. How quickly will the corporation be allowed to deduct these costs?

10. W&Z Corporation, a calendar year taxpayer, begins work on a project in 2007 and elects to amortize related research and experimental costs over a 60-month period. On September 1, 2009, W & Z Corporation begins to market products produced from a process resulting from the project. As of September 1, 2009, W & Z has deferred a total of $259,200 of research expenses. What is the amount of research and experimental costs that can be deducted by W & Z in 2009?

11. ABC Company incurs $15,200 in R&E costs in conjunction with developing a patent. How much can ABC Company deduct in the first year for the patent?

12. In 2009, a company hires a contractor to construct a building for its operations. The building cost $10 million. During construction, the company incurs interest costs of $100,000 in 2009 and $150,000 in 2010 related to construction financing. In 2011 during the first year following construction, the company uses the building and incurs an additional $75,000 of interest expense due to a mortgage on the building. How much interest should be capitalized?

13. The corporation's books, which are maintained on the accrual basis, show the following income and expense items for the 2009 tax year:

Net sales	$600,000
Cost of goods sold	250,000
Selling and marketing expenses	100,000
General and administrative expenses allocable to production	50,000
General and administrative expenses allocable to selling and marketing	25,000
W-2 wages for the year allocable to domestic production activities (not included in cost of goods sold)	120,000

If the corporation's QPAI for the year is $70,000, determine its 2009 taxable income.

14. Determine the allowable bad debt deduction for the current tax year in the situations described below:

   a. A business debt becomes partially worthless during the current tax year. The debt is for $1,000. However, only $600 of the debt is worthless.

   b. A $1,000 business debt becomes totally worthless during the current tax year.

   c. Tom makes a $1,000 *bona fide* loan to his friend. It is determined during the current tax year that the debt is worth only $500.

15. In 2007, the Jones Corporation sells merchandise to Doake for $5,000. In 2009, there was still a balance due of $3,000. Doake is adjudicated bankrupt. Although there are some substantial assets in the bankrupt estate, the Jones Corporation charges the entire balance off on December 31, 2009, while bankruptcy proceedings are still pending, and deducts the amount on its tax return for 2009. An examination of the bankruptcy file would have indicated a probable recovery of 20 percent. In 2010, the bankrupt's assets are liquidated, 16 percent of the debt is paid, and the bankruptcy debt is discharged.

   a. How much of the Jones Corporation's deduction on account of Doake's debt should be allowed for 2009?

   b. For 2010? Why?

   c. Can the Jones Corporation instead deduct the entire amount of $3,000 in 2010?

16. D Corporation, a computer manufacturer, donated some of its computers with a basis of $50,000 to LV University. The computers will be used in LV's biological sciences research lab. The fair market value of the computers is $160,000. Assume the requirements of Code Sec. 170(e)(4) are met. What is the amount of D Corporation's charitable contribution?

17. Comment on the deductibility of the following business expenses:

   a. Amounts paid to a lobbyist to secure the passage of favorable legislation.

   b. Fines paid by a trucker for inadvertently exceeding the state's maximum weight laws.

   c. Advertising by a public utility company to defeat public power legislation.

   d. Current research and development expenses incurred for the first time, assuming that the taxpayer desires to deduct the expenses.

18. M Company manufactures blankets. M Company donated its inventory of blankets with a fair market value of $15,000 to a public charity. The blankets will be used by the charity for the care of the ill and needy. M Company's basis in the blankets is $10,000. What is the amount of M Company's charitable contribution?

19. G Corporation uses the accrual method and reports on the calendar year. During the December meeting of the board of directors in 2009, the board authorized the corporation to make a $20,000 contribution to the Community Chest, and the check was mailed in January 2010. The corporation's taxable income for 2009 was $180,000, and for 2010 it was $250,000. What is the earliest year or years in which the contribution is deductible?

20. A C corporation has taxable income of $100,000 after all deductions except the charitable contribution deduction, but including a $7,000 dividends received deduction. The corpora-

tion made a $20,000 charitable contribution for the year. There are no charitable contribution carryforwards.

   a. Compute the charitable contribution deduction.

   b. Compute the charitable contribution carryforward (if any).

21. Outerwear, Inc., a clothing manufacturer, donated the following items to a local homeless shelter during the year. The shelter is a qualified public charity.

   a. Stock in ABC Corporation which was purchased nine months ago for $25,000, FMV $35,000;

   b. A painting which was purchased three years ago for $5,000, FMV $55,000;

   c. Stock in LMN Corporation which was purchased two years ago for $60,000, FMV $100,000;

   d. Coats, scarves, and sweaters from its inventory that cost $3,000 to manufacture, with an FMV of $10,000; and

   e. Unimproved land which was purchased five years ago for $5,000, FMV $20,000.

The shelter provided Outerwear with a certification that it will sell the stock, land, and painting immediately, and use the donated clothing in its care of the needy. Compute the value of Outerwear's charitable contribution deduction for the year (prior to taking into consideration the 10 percent taxable income limitation).

22. A corporation donated stock in another company, which it had held for five months, to a qualified public charity. The corporation had purchased the stock for $30,000 and at the time of its donation the stock was worth $45,000. The corporation's taxable income for the year, excluding its charitable contribution deduction, is $75,000. Included in taxable income is a $3,000 dividends received deduction and a $2,000 domestic production activities deduction. The corporation did not make any other charitable contributions for the year.

   a. What is the amount of the corporation's charitable contribution deduction for the year?

   b. What is the amount of the charitable contribution carryover?

23. Reflex, Inc., a calendar year company, prepaid three years' rent of $54,000 on August 1, 2009. If Reflex uses the cash method of accounting, how much rent can it deduct on its 2009 income tax return?

24. In 2009 Palmera Corporation, a cold cereal manufacturer, determined based on market conditions that it should expand its business. The corporation, which is on a calendar year, spent the following amounts in 2009 toward investigating the expansion of its business:

Marketing and cost analysis study in producing and selling frozen foods	$50,000
Legal and accounting fees incurred in locating a frozen foods manufacturing business	150,000
Feasibility study on producing a new organic cereal line	30,000
Marketing and cost analysis study in manufacturing specialty chocolates	45,000
Legal and accounting fees incurred in locating a chocolate manufacturing business	100,000

Palmera made an offer to purchase a frozen foods manufacturing plant, but at the last minute the deal fell through. The corporation decided not to start a new line of organic cereals because of the cost. On December 1, 2009, Palmera purchased a specialty chocolates manufacturing business. How should Palmera treat its business expansion costs incurred in 2009?

25. Bliss Inc.'s books, which use the accrual method, had the following income and expense items for the 2009 tax year:

Net sales	$450,000
Cost of goods sold	200,000

Operating expenses (100% allocable to production activities)	100,000
Charitable contributions	35,000
W-2 wages for the year	40,000

Determine Bliss Inc.'s taxable income for 2009.

Chapter 5 Review Problems

1. A corporation's books, which are maintained using the accrual method, show the following income and expense items for the 2009 tax year:

Gross sales and receipts	$800,000
Returns and allowances	2,000
Cost of goods sold	200,000
Taxable interest income	20,000
Office rent expense	50,000
Salaries and wages expense	300,000
Charitable contributions	25,000
Miscellaneous business expenses	75,000
School tuition paid for major shareholder's son's education	10,000
New truck purchased	25,000
Depreciation for new truck	5,000

   a. Determine the corporation's taxable income for the 2009 tax year. *(The company does not qualify to take the domestic production activities deduction.)*

   b. What is the amount of the corporation's charitable contribution carryover (if any)?

2. The corporation's books, which are maintained using the accrual method, show the following income and expense items for the 2009 tax year:

Gross sales	$950,000
Returns and allowances	5,000
Cost of goods sold	350,000
Taxable interest income	20,000
Office rent expense	60,000
Salaries and wages expense	150,000
Charitable contributions	55,000
Kickbacks paid to foreign government officials	65,000
Miscellaneous business expenses	75,000
New machines purchased	600,000
Depreciation on new machines	120,000
Research and experimentation expenses (corporation elected to currently deduct)	50,000

   a. Determine the corporation's taxable income for 2009. *(The company does not qualify to take the domestic production activities deduction.)*

   b. What is the amount of the corporation's charitable contribution carryover (if any)?

Chapter 5 Research Question

   ABC Corporation manufactures chemicals. The Environmental Protection Agency (EPA) brought a 10-count criminal indictment against ABC Corporation and two of its employees for misrepresenting to the EPA the amount of toxins discharged from ABC's manufacturing plant. The corporation was found guilty on all 10 counts and could have been fined $5 million and the two employees could have been sentenced to 10 years in prison.

ABC entered into a plea agreement with the government's attorney to pay the maximum fines and to pay $1 million to a trust fund designated by the government's attorney for the purpose of study and research in the field of toxic chemical cleanup. As part of the plea agreement, the government agreed to dismiss nine counts against ABC Corporation and to dismiss all counts against the two employees. The government also agreed not to institute further criminal or civil actions against ABC and the two employees. ABC paid the maximum fine and made a payment of $1 million to the trust fund.

You have been requested by the corporation to determine whether the $1 million payment made to the trust fund or a portion there of can be deducted as a business expense. Give your opinion. Show authorities, citing laws, regulations, interpretations, and decisions applicable, and cite the *CCH Standard Federal Tax Reporter* paragraphs where they may be found.

CHAPTER 6

Business Deductions: Employment-Related Expenses

1. Gain a better understanding for a business's total employment costs, including the difference in costs associated with hiring employees versus independent contractors.

2. Identify the costs involved when employers offer various employee benefit plans to their employees, including health care, flexible spending accounts, and educational assistance.

3. Explain the various retirement plans employers may offer their employees and the costs associated with each of these plans.

4. Explain the various ordinary and necessary business expenses that employers might reimburse their employees for and the tax consequences of the amounts businesses pay to reimburse their employers under an accountable versus a nonaccountable reimbursement plan.

5. Describe how the tax laws treat employment-related expenses incurred by sole proprietors, including amounts paid on behalf of their employees as well as amounts paid on behalf of themselves.

¶ 600 Introduction

Most businesses hire employees as part of the process of generating revenues and profits. Employment-related expenses are generally considered ordinary and necessary business expenses that are deductible against gross income. These expenses include not only the amounts that businesses pay to workers, but also business expenses they reimburse employees for travel, transportation, and relocation costs. It also includes amounts businesses pay for health insurance and educational assistance they provide to their employees, as well as contributions they make to their employees' retirement plans. This chapter introduces the tax laws regarding the deductibility of employment-related expenses.

For businesses operated as sole proprietorships, the owner generally performs the services for the business and, accordingly, incurs employment-related expenditures in conjunction with those services. Since the profits from the sole proprietorship are included on the owner's personal income tax return, different rules govern how employment-related costs are treated when incurred on behalf of the owner versus those paid by the business on behalf of an employee of the sole proprietor. The tax laws surrounding the deductibility of employment-related costs incurred by sole proprietors in connection with their own businesses are also discussed in the chapter.

¶ 601 Compensation Paid to Workers

When a business hires workers, it must compensate them for the services they perform for the company. Compensation paid to workers not only includes wages and bonuses paid to employees but also amounts paid to independent contractors. Although both amounts are deductible against business income,[1] the distinction between these two types of workers is significant, as the costs associated with hiring workers as employees is greater than those associated with hiring workers as independent contractors. The classification of a worker as either an employee or independent contractor is made based on the facts and circumstances surrounding the employment arrangement between the business entity and the worker.

.01 Employee vs. Independent Contractor

Independent contractors are self-employed individuals who perform services for another individual or business entity but are not employees of the persons or businesses that hire them. Although businesses can deduct the compensation they pay to workers, whether those workers are classified as employees or independent contractors will determine the employers' total out-of-pocket employment costs.

As a general rule, employers are responsible for withholding amounts from an employee's wages to cover any federal, state, and local income taxes the employee owes on the taxable wages. Employers also must withhold the employee's share of FICA taxes (social security and medicare). Although the amounts withheld are costs borne by the employees, the employer incurs administrative costs associated with making sure that the proper amounts are withheld and remitted to the appropriate government agencies. However, employers are required to make matching contributions for their employees' FICA taxes and are responsible for paying unemployment taxes on those wages. The costs for these taxes are borne by the employer.

In contrast, amounts paid to independent contractors are not subject to withholdings or unemployment taxes. Workers hired as independent contractors are self-employed individuals who operate their own businesses as sole proprietorships. Sole proprietors report the amounts they receive as an independent contractor as earnings from self-employment, and are allowed to offset these amounts by any businesses expenses paid or incurred in generating those earnings. Sole proprietors are subject to self-employment taxes on the net earnings from self-employment, which reflect their share of the employer and employee portions of FICA taxes. Furthermore, since no amounts are withheld from the compensation sole proprietors receive, sole proprietors are responsible for making quarterly estimated payments to cover both the income and self-employment taxes owed on any taxable amounts their businesses generate (see ¶ 409.02).

Table 6-1 summarizes some of the differences for the tax treatment of employees and independent contractors. It illustrates the difference in costs to the employer associated with hiring a worker as an employee versus hiring an independent contractor.

---

[1] Code Secs. 61(a)(1) and 162(a).

Table 6-1 Tax Implications of Classifying Workers as Employees vs. Independent Contractors

Issue	Workers Classified as Employees	Workers Classified as Independent Contractors
Party responsible for remitting income taxes on the compensation paid to the worker.	The employer withholds amounts from the employee's pay and remits these amounts to the appropriate government agencies. Therefore, the administrative costs are borne by the employer.	The worker is responsible for paying these amounts to the government by making quarterly estimated payments to cover the amounts owed.
Party responsible for the employee's share of FICA taxes.	The employer withholds amounts from the employee's pay and remits these amounts to the government.	The worker is responsible for paying these amounts to the government by making quarterly estimated payments to cover the amounts owed.
Party responsible for the employer's share of FICA taxes.	The employer matches the amounts it withholds from the employee's pay and remits the matching amount to the government.	The worker is responsible for paying these amounts to the government by making quarterly estimated payments to cover the amounts owed.
Party responsible for paying state and federal unemployment taxes.	The employer is required to contribute to these funds for each of its employees.	Sole proprietors are not required to pay unemployment taxes on self-employment income.
Eligibility for employer provided benefits, like health care and participation in employer-sponsored retirement programs.	Yes, but usually only for full-time employees. Amounts paid by the employer are generally excluded from employees' wages, but can be deducted as business expenses on the employer's tax return.	No. These items must be paid for and provided by sole proprietors themselves, who then deduct these costs from gross income on their personal income tax returns.

Most employers prefer to classify their workers as independent contractors since employers must pay unemployment taxes and the employer's share of FICA taxes on employees' wages. These additional taxes incurred plus the administrative costs associated with the withholding of employees' income and FICA taxes contribute to the higher costs associated with hiring workers as employees versus independent contractors. Employers are also finding that to stay competitive in the market-place and to continue to be able to attract the best workers, they often must offer a variety of benefit programs to their employees, the most common of which are participation in company's health care and retirement programs. Because employers that offer these programs are typically required to make them available to all full-time employees, not only does the employer incur the administrative costs associated with offering these programs, but usually a large portion of the funding for these programs comes from the employer. Since workers classified as independent contractors are not allowed to participate in these programs and they are responsible for all income and payroll taxes associated with their self-employment earnings, the employer's costs can be significantly reduced by hiring workers that can be classified as independent contractors.

Example 1: Becktel Company pays its employee, Susan Cross, an annual salary of $50,000. In addition to Susan's salary, Becktel pays $3,825 in FICA taxes, $378 in state unemployment taxes, and $56 in federal unemployment taxes. Becktel provides health insurance coverage for its full-time employees, and during the year, it paid health insurance premiums on behalf of Susan totaling $6,200. During the year, Becktel hires Bob Knight as an independent contractor and pays him a contractual fee of $50,000. As shown below, Becktel incurs significantly more employment-related costs by hiring Susan as an employee over Bob as an independent contractor. To accurately determine the company's true additional costs, the tax savings from being able to deduct these employment-related costs must be considered. For example, if Becktel's marginal tax rate is 35 percent, its total out-of-pocket costs of hiring Susan as an employee versus Bob as an independent contractor increase by $6,798 ($39,298 – $32,500).

	Susan Cross	Bob Knight
Compensation	$50,000	$50,000
Employee benefits	6,200	
Payroll Taxes:		
FICA	3,825	
State unemployment	378	
Federal unemployment	56	
Total employment-related costs	$60,459	$50,000
Less: Tax savings at 35%	(21,161)	(17,500)
Total out-of-pocket costs to Becktel	$39,298	$32,500

To prevent employers from inappropriately classifying workers as independent contractors to avoid these higher costs, the tax laws provide guidance on how to correctly classify workers. In some instances, the Code specifically categorizes workers as independent contractors. For example, real estate agents are self-employed workers for income tax purposes.[2] However, in most instances, the distinction hinges primarily on whether the worker is subject to the control and direction of the person who hires them, not only as to the results to be accomplished but also to the method of accomplishing them. If such control and direction exists, then the relationship is deemed to be one between an employer and employee. It is important to note that it is not necessary that the employer ever exercise control or direction over the worker; just having the right to do so is sufficient to classify a worker as an employee.[3] The IRS uses a 20-factor test to determine whether an employment relationship exists.[4]

Example 2: Abe Gable is the West Coast distributor for a movie company, Motion Pictures, Inc. The company is interested only in Abe's sales results, and accordingly, Abe is paid a commission for each movie he sells. Abe is required to furnish his own office and to find his own prospects. Motion Pictures properly classifies Abe as an independent contractor. Thus, the commissions it pays to Abe are deductible against business income and the company is not required to withhold amounts for income or FICA taxes. Likewise, Motion Pictures is not required to pay FICA or unemployment taxes on any commissions it pays to Abe, and Abe cannot participate in any benefit programs Motion Pictures offers its employees.

.02 Employee Compensation

Amounts paid to employees are included in the employee's gross income[5] and are deducted as wage expense by the employer.[6] Taxable wages include regular salary and wages, overtime pay,

---

[2] Code Sec. 3508.
[3] Reg. § 31.3401(c)-1(a) and (b).
[4] Rev. Rul. 87-41, 1987-1 CB 296.

[5] Code Sec. 61(a)(1).
[6] Code Sec. 162(a).

bonuses, vacation pay, back pay, severance pay, commissions and tips, as well as reimbursements for businesses expenses not covered under an accountable plan (see ¶ 601.03).

Reasonable compensation. The deduction for wages paid to employees is subject to the general deductibility requirements outlined in Chapter 5; therefore, only amounts paid to employees that are reasonable in amount can be deducted by the employer.[7] Because the profits of a corporation are subject to tax not only at the corporate level but also at the shareholder level when the profits are distributed to shareholders as dividends, the potential for abuse exists when a corporation has employees who are also shareholders in the corporation. Since wages are deductible, whereas dividends are not, the corporation pays less taxes by classifying a payment to an employee/shareholder as compensation rather than as a dividend distribution.

Although a corporation is liable for unemployment taxes and its share of FICA taxes (social security and medicare taxes) on employees' wages, federal unemployment (FUTA) taxes are only assessed on the first $7,000 of employee wages, and in 2009, employers are only required to pay the (matching) 6.2 percent social security taxes on the first $106,800 of employee wages and 1.45 percent medicare taxes on employee wages. Likewise, the employee is only responsible for paying social security taxes on the first $106,800 of wages received in 2009 and 1.45 percent medicare taxes on wages (see ¶ 604.01). Thus, when the tax consequences to both the employer and employee are considered together, there may be advantages to classifying a distribution to an employee-shareholder as wages rather than as a dividend.

The reasonableness test is more likely an issue with **closely-held corporations,** which are corporations whose stock is held by a small number of shareholders, possibly from the same family or a related group of individuals. Often employee-shareholders of closely-held corporations are officers of the corporation, and their total compensation already exceeds the maximum wages subject to social security taxes. Accordingly, when distributions to these officer-shareholders are treated as salaries, the corporation's tax liability is reduced significantly. The reasonableness requirement prevents the corporation from deducting as salaries what are actually distributions of corporate profits (dividends). The reasonableness requirement also might come up in situations where the salary is paid to a family member that is significantly higher than the value of the services the person is providing. In this case, the business may be attempting to shift the tax burden to a family member in a lower tax bracket, for example, a child.

Example 3: Heather Hill is the sole owner of HH Corporation. The marginal tax rate for both Heather and HH is 35 percent. During the year, HH pays Heather a salary totaling $120,000. In December, HH pays Heather a $50,000 bonus. Assuming the bonus is taxed as additional compensation to Heather, Heather's income tax liability will increase, and HH's income tax liability will decrease by the same $17,500 ($50,000 × 35%). Since Heather and HH have already paid in the maximum amounts for social security taxes for the year, both will be liable for an additional $725 in FICA taxes ($50,000 × 1.45%) on Heather's taxable wages. HH's tax savings on its $725 deduction of FICA taxes is $254 ($725 × 35%). In the end, Heather will net $31,775 after taxes from the $50,000 bonus ($50,000 − $17,500 additional income taxes − $725 additional payroll taxes), and the total costs of HH for paying the bonus will be $32,971 ($50,000 + $725 payroll taxes − $17,500 tax savings − $254 tax savings).

Example 4: Assume the same facts as in Example 3, except that the $50,000 is treated as a dividend distribution. Since corporations do not deduct amounts paid as dividends to their shareholders, HH does not derive any tax savings by making this distribution. Thus, the out-of-pocket costs to HH would be $50,000. The $50,000 of dividend income will be included in Heather's gross income. Her tax liability would increase by $7,500 ($50,000 × 15% tax rate on qualified dividends) (see ¶ 405.02). Although Heather would benefit from having the $50,000 payment treated as a dividend distribution (she

---

[7] Code Sec. 162(a)(1); Reg. § 1.162-7.

would net $50,000 – $7,500 = $42,500 vs. $31,775), HH's out-of-pocket costs would be significantly higher ($50,000 vs. $32,971).

A corporation will be unable to deduct compensation to the extent that it is determined to be unreasonable. The portion of the employee-shareholder's salary determined to be unreasonable is treated as a dividend distribution from the corporation to the employee-shareholder. The corporation can mitigate the loss of its compensation deduction by having entered into a repayment agreement with its employee-shareholders. A repayment agreement is an arrangement in which an employee agrees to repay the corporate employer an amount equal to the portion of compensation paid and deducted by the corporation but disallowed by the IRS. The employee is entitled to take a business deduction in the year of repayment.[8] However, the IRS has held in certain cases that the existence of a repayment agreement is evidence of excessive compensation. To thwart such an attack by the IRS, a corporation can include in its charter or by-laws a requirement that its employees must repay the corporation for disallowed deductions that relate to the employee.

The factors the courts use to determine whether salary and wages paid to employees are reasonable in amount include the following:

1. The employee's role in the company, responsibilities shouldered, and duties performed,
2. The ability and achievements of the employee,
3. How the employee's salary compares with similarly situated employees,
4. The character and condition of the company,
5. Whether the business is earning a satisfactory return on equity,
6. The cost of living in the locality, and
7. The internal consistency of salaries paid to all employees of the company.[9]

When no personal relationship exists between the employee and the employer or in situations where the employee has no real influence over the employer (for example, as a controlling shareholder), there is little need to question the amount deducted for salary and wages. However, when such influence or personal relationship exists, the IRS can reclassify the payment as a dividend distribution for any amounts it deems unreasonable in light of the facts and circumstances surrounding the business. The taxpayer may contest the IRS's decision to reclassify the payment, but the burden rests with the taxpayer to prove that the amount originally claimed is reasonable.[10]

Publicly-held corporations typically cannot deduct compensation paid to covered employees to the extent that the compensation exceeds $1 million per year.[11] **Publicly-held corporations** are corporations whose stock is traded on one of the U.S. stock exchanges, such as the American Stock Exchange, New York Stock Exchange, or NASDAQ. "Covered employees" are those who on the last day of the tax year are either the chief executive officer (CEO) of the corporation (or someone who acts in that capacity) or among the four highest paid officers of the corporation, other than the CEO.

There are a number of ways by which corporations can get around the $1 million limit. Exceptions to this limit include specified commissions, compensation based on performance goals, income payable under a written binding contract that was in effect on February 17, 1993, and compensation paid prior to the corporation becoming a publicly-held company.[12] Accordingly, businesses that pay their top executives more than $1 million annually will want to structure their employment arrangements to fall under one of these exceptions.

Example 5: Beta Corporation pays its CEO $1.35 million in 2009. Unfortunately, Beta cannot justify why the $1 million limit should not be imposed. Consequently, Beta can pay its CEO $1.35 million but only deduct $1 million on its 2009 tax return.

---

[8] Rev. Rul. 69-115, 1969-1 CB 50.

[9] *Elliots, Inc.* CA-9, 83-2 USTC ¶ 9610, 716 F2d 1241; *Mayson Manufacturing Co.*, CA-6, 49-2 USTC ¶ 9467, 178 F2d 115.

[10] *Long Island Drug Co.*, CA-2, 40-1 USTC ¶ 9446, 111 F2d 593, cert. denied, 311 US 680.

[11] Code Sec. 162(m). Financial institutions that are receiving government assistance which sell troubled assets to the Trea-sury Department through the Troubled Asset Relief Program (TARP) are restricted from deducting more than $500,000 of executive compensation to their (1) CEO and chief financial officer (CFO) (or someone acting in either capacity) and (2) the three highest compensated officers in the financial institution, other than the CEO or CFO.

[12] Code Sec. 162(m)(4)(C).

Example 6: In 2009, YUL Corporation, a calendar year, publicly-held corporation, establishes a bonus plan under which its CEO, Carl Smith, will receive a $500,000 cash bonus if year-end corporate sales increase by at least five percent. The bonus plan was established at the start of the year, and Carl's annual salary is $950,000 prior to any bonuses. YUL retains the right, if the performance goal is met, to reduce the bonus payment to Carl if, in its judgment, other subjective factors warrant a reduction.

At the end of the year, YUL's sales had increased by eight percent and the corporation agrees to pay Carl the $500,000 bonus. Because the bonus is based on acceptable performance goals, the bonus paid to Carl is not subject to the $1 million compensation limitation. For 2009, YUL will be able to deduct Carl's salary of $950,000 plus his year-end accrued bonus of $500,000.

 GAAP vs. Code: Since the $1 million limit on executive compensation is imposed by the Code, it does affect the amounts that corporations actually pay to their executives or the amount they expense on the income statement. Any amounts that are paid but cannot be deducted in arriving at taxable income must be added back to net income when the net income and taxable income are reconciled on the corporate tax return. In Example 5, Beta would need to add $350,000 to its net income as a result of the limitation imposed on the deduction for the compensation paid to its CEO.

Timing of the deduction. The timing of the deduction for compensation is largely governed by the employer's methods of accounting. If the employee uses the cash method (which most individual taxpayers use), then the amounts are taxed in the year in which they are received, regardless of when they are incurred by the accrual method employer. Consequently, when an accrual method business accrues compensation expense at the end of the tax year that is not paid until the next tax year, the tax benefits from taking the deduction are realized by the business one year in advance of when the income is taxed to the employee.

Example 7: On December 14, 2009, the Board of Directors of an accrual method calendar year corporation votes to pay each of its 10 managers a $10,000 year-end bonus and an additional $2,500 bonus in recognition of valuable services rendered in prior years. These amounts represent reasonable compensation. The corporation pays these amounts to the managers on January 5, 2010. These amounts are deducted by the corporation in 2009, the year in which they are incurred,[13] and would be taxed to the managers in 2010. The corporation would take a deduction for $125,000 ($12,500 × 10) on its 2009 tax return, and assuming the corporation's marginal tax rate is 35 percent, this deduction will reduce its taxes by $43,750 ($125,000 × 35%). Although the government will generate tax revenues by requiring that these amounts be included in the managers' gross income, these amounts will not be taxed until 2010, and consequently, the government loses out on the use of those revenues for an entire year.

In situations where the employee has significant influence over the company, the potential for abuse exists. For example, when a majority shareholder is also an employee of the corporation, the shareholder can influence when certain payments are accrued by the corporation and when such amounts are paid to employees. Although taxes on these amounts will eventually be paid, as illustrated in Example 7, the revenues the government generates from these amounts is delayed an entire year. Thus, when amounts are accrued to *related parties*, the tax laws require that the accrual method taxpayer postpone the timing of the deduction until the employee includes the amount in income.[14] For purposes of this rule, a corporation and an employee are related if the employee directly or indirectly owns more than 50 percent of the value of the outstanding stock in the

---

[13] *Lucas v. Ox Fibre Brush Co.*, SCt, 2 USTC ¶ 522, 281 US 115, 50 SCt 273.

[14] Code Sec. 267(a)(2).

corporation.[15] (See ¶ 804 for more on the related party rules.) This rule ensures that the amount reported in income by the employee and the deduction taken by the employer is accounted for at the same time.

Example 8: John Starks is an employee and sole shareholder of Markel Corporation. John uses the cash method; Markel uses the accrual method of accounting. Both use a calendar year end. In December 2009, John has Markel declare a $50,000 bonus to him to be paid in January 2010. Without the required "matching" rule for related parties, Markel could deduct this amount in 2009, and John would be able to defer the recognition of income in his tax return until 2010. However, the matching rule requires that Markel wait until 2010 to deduct the bonus it pays to John in that year.

Businesses can deduct wages and salaries for services rendered in prior years; however, payments for services to be provided in future tax years must be capitalized and deducted in the year in which the services are rendered.[16] Pursuant to the all-events tests introduced in Chapter 3, accrual method taxpayers may deduct an item if all the events have occurred that establish that a liability exists, the amount of the liability can be determined with reasonable accuracy, and economic performance has occurred with respect to the liability.[17] Accordingly, it is not required that the exact amount of compensation to be paid be known with absolute certainty by the end of the year in order for an accrual method taxpayer to deduct it in that year.[18] For example, when compensation is based on a percentage of sales, the amount of accrued sales revenue may not be known with certainty by the close of business on the last day of the tax year. As long as the percentage is known and the liability is fixed, accrual method taxpayers can accrue (deduct) these amounts as compensation in the year in which they are incurred.

 GAAP vs. Code: Generally the timing of the deduction for compensation will be the same for book and tax purposes. However, this is not the case where an employee/ shareholder has significant influence over when compensation is paid. In that instance, the corporation will accrue an expense on its books but will be unable to deduct the expense for tax purposes until the compensation is paid. In Example 8, Markel Corporation was unable to deduct the bonus to its employee and sole shareholder until 2010 when the amount was paid. On its 2009 financial statements, Markel reduces its net income by the $50,000 bonus. Accordingly, on its 2009 corporate tax return, Markel adds back the $50,000 bonus to its net income when reconciling net income to taxable income. Markel will then need to subtract the $50,000 bonus from its net income when reconciling net income to taxable income on its 2010 corporate tax return.

.03 Reimbursements from Nonaccountable Plans

When an employer reimburses employees for business expenses under an accountable plan, the reimbursements are excluded from the employee's gross income[19] and are deducted by the employer as the tax laws permit. Since these reimbursements are not taxable wages to the employee, they are not subject to income tax withholding, nor are they subject to FICA or unemployment taxes. An **accountable plan** requires that employees submit adequate documentation or receipts for any reimbursed expenses and requires that they return to their employers any advances they receive in excess of the substantiated expenses.[20]

Reimbursements paid through a system that does not meet the requirements for an accountable plan are considered reimbursements from a **nonaccountable plan**. Amounts paid to an employee under a nonaccountable plan are treated as taxable compensation to the employee and as

---

[15] Code Sec. 267(b)(2).

[16] Reg. § 1.162-7(b)(1).

[17] Code Sec. 461(h)(4); Reg. § 1.461-1(a)(2).

[18] Reg. § 1.162-7(b)(2); Rev. Rul. 61-127, 1961-2 CB 36, modifying Rev. Rul. 55-446, 1955 CB 531.

[19] Code Sec. 62(a)(2).

[20] Reg. § 31.3401(a)-4(a).

wage expense to the employer. Thus, the employee is subject to income and FICA tax withholdings on these amounts, and the employer is responsible for the employer's share of FICA plus unemployment taxes on the additional wages. Although the employee is allowed to deduct amounts reimbursed from a nonaccountable plan as employee business expenses, such expenses are miscellaneous itemized deductions and can only be deducted if the employee's total miscellaneous expenses exceed two percent of the employee's adjusted gross income (AGI) and the employee's itemized deductions exceed their standard deduction.[21]

Example 9: An employee of Macintye, Inc. is reimbursed $1,000 for expenses incurred while away on business. The amounts are reimbursed under a nonaccountable plan. Macintye is required to include the $1,000 in the employee's wages and accordingly, it deducts this amount as wage expense. Macintye also must pay its share of FICA and unemployment taxes on the $1,000, as well as withhold from the employee's pay income taxes and the employee's share of FICA taxes. The employee is allowed to deduct the $1,000 as an unreimbursed employee business expense, which is a miscellaneous itemized deduction subject to the two-percent AGI floor.

Example 10: Assume the same facts as in Example 9, except that the $1,000 was reimbursed from an accountable plan. Here, the $1,000 is excluded from the employee's gross income, and the full $1,000 is deducted as travel expense on Macintye's tax return.

Reason for the Rule: The different tax consequences of reimbursements made from accountable versus nonaccountable plans ensures that only valid business expenses are deducted on the tax return. Prior to these rules, employers could advance amounts to their employees to cover various out-of-pocket costs associated with their employment activities and deduct these amounts against business income without checking to make sure that the employees were spending these amounts on valid business expenses. One area where this was common involved monthly advances employers made to employees to cover the costs associated with business-use of their personal automobiles. Under the current tax laws, when these advances are made without any accountability, the employer is required to treat these amounts as additional wage expense (instead of transportation expense). The employee would be taxed on additional wages and only be allowed to deduct employee business expenses as miscellaneous itemized deductions subject to the two-percent AGI rule. Since the employer is responsible for unemployment taxes and its share of FICA taxes on amounts paid as wages to employees, Congress hoped that more businesses would make the effort to require substantiation before reimbursing employees for business-related expenditures. Amounts advanced to employees qualify as coming from an accountable plan as long as the plan requires that any excess amounts over substantiated business expenses be returned to the employer.

¶ 602 Employee Benefits

To attract and retain the best employees, employers often offer a variety of benefits to their employees, including health care coverage, educational assistance, and participation in employer-sponsored retirement programs. Since "income" generally includes all increases in net worth, from whatever source derived, fringe benefits provided to an employee in connection with the performance of services would be considered additional compensation and normally would be taxable to the employee.[22] However, certain provisions in the Code allow the costs associated with a variety of fringe benefits employers provide to their employees to be excluded from the employees' gross income but still be deducted by the employer.

---

[21] Code Sec. 67; Temp. Reg. § 1.67-1T(a).   [22] Code Sec. 61(a)(1).

.01 Contributions to Accident and Health Plans

Premiums employers pay to provide their employees (including coverage to the employee's spouse and dependents) with health or disability insurance are deductible by the employer and not taxed to the employee.[23] These rules apply regardless of the type of business entity the business is operated under. Thus, amounts corporations as well as amounts sole proprietors and partnerships pay for health and disability insurance for their employees are deducted from the gross income generated by their respective businesses. However, when sole proprietors pay the premiums for their own health insurance, these amounts are deducted in arriving at AGI on the proprietor's individual income tax return but not as a deduction against the profits of the sole proprietorship. Since a sole proprietor's self-employment tax is assessed on profits from the business, amounts paid for the proprietor's own health insurance reduce the amount of income taxes owed by the sole proprietor, but not their self-employment taxes. In contrast, amounts sole proprietors pay for their employees' health insurance reduce both their income and self-employment tax liabilities.

Example 11: Dr. Allen Bell operates a medical practice as a sole proprietorship. In 2009, Allen paid $4,000 for his employees' health insurance and $6,000 for his own health insurance. Allen's profits from his sole proprietorship are $84,000 before taking into consideration the health insurance paid during the year. On his 2009 tax return, Allen deducts the $4,000 of premiums paid for his employee's health insurance against the gross income from his business and reports $80,000 of business profits. This amount is included in Allen's AGI, along with his other personal items of AGI. Allen's AGI is reduced by the $6,000 paid for his own health insurance. If Allen's other items of AGI total $50,000, his AGI would equal $124,000 ($50,000 + $80,000 – $6,000). His regular income tax liability would be computed by applying the appropriate individual income tax rates to his taxable income ($124,000 AGI minus his deductions from AGI). Allen's self-employment tax will be computed based on his $80,000 net profit.

Example 12: Assume the same facts as in Example 11, except that Dr. Bell operates his medical practice as a personal service corporation, AB Medical. Allen Bell is an employee of the corporation and is included in the employees' group health insurance plan. In 2009, AB pays $10,000 for its employees' group health insurance. On its 2009 corporate income tax return, AB deducts the $10,000 paid for employees' health insurance. The FICA taxes owed on the salary paid to Allen will be shared by Allen and AB Medical.

 Spotlight: When employers deduct wage expense, it reduces their taxable income. The resulting tax savings to employers (and reduction in tax revenues by the government) from allowing deductions equals the amount of the deduction multiplied by the taxpayer's marginal tax rate. However, since these amounts are included in employees' gross income, the taxes generated from these wages equals the amount of taxable wages times the employee's marginal tax rate. Thus, while the government loses out on revenues when it allows a deduction for wage expense, it generates revenues by taxing the workers who ultimately use and control the amounts paid to them as compensation.

When employers pay health insurance premiums on behalf of their employees, the tax laws allow employers to deduct these costs against profits generated by the business and allow employees to exclude these benefits from gross income. The tax savings to businesses from the deduction represents the portion of the costs of providing health care to employees that is being subsidized by the government. To illustrate, take as an example a corporation with a 35-percent marginal tax rate that pays $10,000 in health insurance premiums for one of its employees during the year. The corporation's tax

---

[23] Code Sec. 106; Reg. § 1.106-1.

liability is reduced by $3,500 ($10,000 × 35%), and therefore, of the $10,000 of premiums paid, $6,500 of the costs are paid by the employer ($10,000 minus $3,500 reduction in tax liability) and $3,500 is paid by the federal government (via lost revenues). Because any medical expenses paid from this employer-provided health care plan are not taxable to the employee, the overall result is a net loss of revenues to the federal government.

The government's subsidizing of employee-provided benefits does not extend to all employee benefits. For example, the employer can deduct premiums it pays for disability insurance for its employees. Although the premiums paid by the employer are tax-free to the employee, any benefits the employee receives from the disability policy are taxable when the employer paid the premiums. Thus, if an employer pays the entire premiums on a disability insurance policy, each year the employer deducts the cost of the premiums from its gross income, and there are no tax consequences to the employees. However, if in a given year an employee is injured and receives $20,000 in disability benefits, the entire $20,000 is taxable to the employee since the entire premiums were paid for by the employer.[24]

.02 Flexible Spending Accounts (FSAs)

As a way of helping subsidize health care costs, the federal government allows employers to provide their employees with the opportunity to contribute to accounts from which unreimbursed health care costs (not including health insurance premiums) can be made. This type of account, called a **flexible spending account (FSA)**, can also be offered to employees to cover their dependent care costs. An FSA allows employees to elect to set aside each year pre-tax wages from which they can pay qualified health costs (in the case of medical FSAs) or up to $5,000 of their qualified child care costs (in the case of dependent care FSAs).[25] Amounts employees contribute to these accounts are done automatically through employer withholdings. FSAs benefit employees because amounts from their salaries that are contributed to FSAs do not show up as taxable wages on their W-2s, thus making them paid with pre-tax dollars. Accordingly, employees who contribute to FSAs pay less tax than they would if they did not participate.

Employees can contribute annually to each type of FSA their employer offers. Therefore, when an employer offers both types of FSAs and for medical FSAs allows its employees to contribute a maximum of $5,000, employees can elect to contribute up to $10,000 annually to their two FSA accounts. However, these two accounts are kept separate from one another, so only amounts spent on qualified health care can be reimbursed from the employee's medical FSA. Likewise, only amounts the employee spends on qualified dependent care can be reimbursed from the employee's dependent care FSA.

Example 13: Julie Adams' employer offers both medical and dependent care FSAs for its employees. Julie's employer allows its employees to contribute a maximum of $5,000 to their medical FSA. Julie has the option of participating in one, both, or neither FSA plan. Assuming that Julie elects to participate in both FSAs, she can contribute up to $5,000 annually to each account. If she contributes the maximum possible amount, Julie's taxable wages will be reduced by $10,000.

As employees pay for unreimbursed qualified medical costs, they submit their receipts for reimbursement from their medical FSA accounts. Likewise, as employees who contribute to dependent care FSAs pay qualified child care costs, they submit their receipts for reimbursement. Because these amounts are paid for with pre-tax dollars, each expenditure that is reimbursed through an FSA account reduces the employee's out-of-pocket costs for the expenditure.

---

[24] Code Secs. 104 and 105(a).

[25] Code Secs. 125(d)(2)(D) and 129; Prop. Reg. § 1.125-5.

Example 14: Todd Smalls works for a company that offers its employees a cafeteria plan that includes a medical FSA. Todd participates in the company's medical FSA by contributing $1,300 during the year. Todd does not participate in any other FSA or tax deferred compensation plan. In 2009, Todd earns $30,000, which includes his contributions to his health FSA. By participating in his employer's medical FSA, Todd's taxable wages are reduced by amounts he contributes to his FSA, and accordingly, his taxable wages for the year are $28,700 ($30,000 – $1,300). Had Todd not participated in the FSA, his taxable wages would have been $30,000. If Todd's marginal tax rate is 15 percent, he saves $195 ($1,300 × 15%) in federal income taxes by participating in the FSA.

Although his take-home pay is reduced by the $1,300 that the company withholds from his paychecks and contributes to the medical FSA plan, the first $1,300 of his out-of-pocket medical expenses are paid from the FSA plan. Accordingly, Todd's total out-of-pocket costs for the first $1,300 of unreimbursed medical expenses equal $1,105 ($1,300 – $195 taxes saved). In contrast, if Todd had not participated in the company's medical FSA plan, the $1,300 of unreimbursed medical costs would have cost him $1,300 and he likely would not receive any tax benefit for his medical expenses because only amounts in excess of 7.5 percent of AGI are deductible as itemized deductions. Thus, by participating in the medical FSA plan, Todd is able to pay for the first $1,300 of unreimbursed medical costs with pre-tax dollars.

The downside to FSAs is their "use it or lose it" feature. If the employee does not spend the amounts they contribute during the year on qualified expenses, then the amounts not used are forfeited back to the employer.[26] To be reimbursed for these amounts, employees must submit their documentation to their employer no later than March 31 of the subsequent year for calendar year plans. Amounts normally must be spent by the end of the plan year in which they were contributed in order to avoid being forfeited; however, the IRS allows employers to change their plans to allow employees a grace period of up to 2½ months after the end of the plan year (March 15 of the following year for calendar year plans) to spend amounts they contributed during the prior year.[27]

Example 15: In 2009, Julie Adams contributes $5,000 to her employer's medical and dependent care FSAs. Before the end of 2009, Julie's employer changes its FSA plans and allows employees until March 15, 2010, to spend amounts they contributed during 2009. During 2009, Julie submits receipts totaling $4,500 for her medical expenses and $4,000 for her dependent care expenses. This leaves Julie with unspent amounts in her medical and dependent care FSAs of $500 ($5,000 – $4,500) and $1,000 ($5,000 – $1,000), respectively. On March 15, 2010, Julie submits receipts for $500 in medical costs and $1,000 of dependent care costs paid between January 1, 2010, and March 15, 2010. Because Julie incurred these expenses during the grace period allowed under the plan, she will be reimbursed for these amounts and will not lose any of the $10,000 that she contributed to her FSA plans during 2009. As a result of contributing a total of $10,000 to her employer's FSA plans, Julie's taxable wages are reduced by $10,000. Assuming Julie's marginal tax rate is 25 percent, her tax liability will be reduced by $2,500 ($10,000 × 25%). Thus, Julie's total out-of-pocket costs for the $10,000 of receipts she submits for health and dependent care costs is actually $7,500 ($10,000 – $2,500).

Example 16: Assume the same facts as in Example 15, except that Julie's employer did not change its plans to allow reimbursement for expenses incurred after the end of the year. In this scenario, Julie would only have been reimbursed for expenses paid during 2009 that she submitted by the March 31, 2010, deadline. Consequently, she would have lost $500 of her medical FSA and $1,000 of her dependent care FSA. Julie's taxable wages for 2009 are still reduced by $10,000, and her 2009 tax liability is lower by

---

[26] Prop. Reg. § 1.125-5(c).   [27] Prop. Reg. § 1.125-1(e).

$2,500. However, the $1,500 withheld from her pay that she could not utilize from her FSAs is lost and effectively reduces her overall benefit to participating in the FSA plans to $1,000 ($2,500 taxes saved – $1,500 forfeited).

.03 Cafeteria Plans

A cafeteria plan is a written, employer-sponsored plan under which the participants have the opportunity to choose from a variety of benefits they want to receive and/or participate in. Only workers properly designated as employees can participate in a cafeteria plan.[28] A cafeteria plan gets its name because participants may choose among two or more benefits consisting of cash and qualified nontaxable benefits. If the participant chooses to receive cash from the plan, the amount received is included in the employee's gross income as compensation and is deductible as a wage expense by the employer. Because these amounts represent taxable wages, they are subject to withholding, as well as FICA and unemployment taxes. If the employee chooses to receive qualified benefits, these amounts are generally excluded from the employee's gross income. These types of benefits are often referred to as **perquisites,** as they represent a privilege employees are entitled to receive. Workers classified as independent contractors are not eligible for these benefits.

Qualified benefits include FSAs (previously discussed), up to $50,000 of group-term life insurance coverage, adoption assistance, disability benefits, and accident and health benefits. Although participation in a cafeteria plan is restricted to employees, employers can require a minimum of three years of employment before an employee is eligible to participate in the plan.[29] The three-year minimum employment requirement is optional, thus employers have the option of allowing employees with less than three years of employment to participate. However, whatever minimum employment requirement is chosen by the employer, it must apply equally to all eligible employees. Once the employment requirement is satisfied, the employee must be allowed to participate in the plan. Cafeteria plans are also subject to other discrimination rules that are beyond the scope of this discussion.[30] Employers deduct the costs they pay or incur in offering these benefits to their employees as employee benefits.

.04 Other Employee Fringe Benefits

Employers may provide their employees with several noncash fringe benefits that are not taxable to the employee but are deductible by the employer. These include reimbursing employees for qualified transportation and relocation costs, as well as providing qualified retirement planning services and educational assistance to employees.[31] These benefits are excluded from the employee's wages for purposes of income and FICA tax withholding. In addition, the employer is not responsible for FICA or unemployment taxes on these amounts.[32] A fringe benefit program may not discriminate in favor of officers, owners, and highly compensated employees. If the benefits are discriminatory, then only employees receiving benefits who are not members of the favored group can exclude the benefits from gross income. Those in the favored group who receive benefits must include the value of the benefits received in gross income as compensation.[33] Consequently, these taxable benefits would be subject to income and FICA tax withholdings, as well as FICA and unemployment taxes that must be paid by the employer.

Example 17: A department store offers a 15-percent discount as a noncash fringe benefit to its regular employees and a 25-percent discount to a favored group (officers, owners, and highly compensated employees). Because the fringe benefit program is discriminatory, the entire discount members of the favored group receive is includible in their gross income, while the nonfavored employees may continue to exclude the 15-percent discount they receive.

---

[28] Code Sec. 125(d); Prop. Reg. § 1.125 1.

[29] Code Sec. 125(g)(3); Prop. Reg. § 1.125-7(b)(2).

[30] For more on these restrictions, *see* Code Sec. 125(b)(2); Prop. Reg. §§ 1.125-7 and 416(i)(1)(A); and Notice 2007-87, IRB 2007-45, 966, November 5, 2007.

[31] Code Sec. 132 and Code Sec. 127.

[32] IRS Publication 15-B (For use in 2009).

[33] Reg. § 1.132-8.

Qualified transportation. In general, expenses employees pay in commuting to and from home and work are not deductible.[34] However, when an employer offers transportation fringe benefits to its employees, some of the employee's transportation and parking costs can be reduced by having them pay for these costs with pre-tax dollars. This is accomplished by having amounts withheld from the employees' pay (subject to monthly limits, see below) and then having the employee submit documentation to be reimbursed for qualified transportation and parking costs. In many ways, this is similar to how FSAs work.

Alternatively, an employer may provide their employees with parking benefits, transit passes, transportation to and from work in a commuter vehicle (such as a van), or may reimburse employees for the cost of such benefits on a tax-free basis, as long as the benefits are provided in addition to, and not in lieu of, other compensation. In the case of qualified parking, the excludable benefit in 2009 is limited to $230 per month. In the case of the aggregate value of transit passes and commuter highway vehicle transportation, the excludable benefit is $120 per month (for months January 2009 through February 16, 2009) and $230 per month (for any month beginning on or after February 17, 2009). For tax years beginning after December 31, 2008, qualified transportation fringes will also include qualified bicycle commuting reimbursements in which the employer provides benefit to employees who commute to work using a bike.[35] The excludable benefit is $20 per month in which (1) the employee uses a bike for a substantial portion of travel between the employee's home and the place of employment, and (2) the employee does not receive any other transportation fringe benefits. The limits for these benefits are adjusted annually for inflation (with the exception of the bicycle commuting fringe benefit).[36]

Example 18: In 2009, Warren Smith receives from his employer qualified parking valued at $240 per month. Because the value of the parking exceeds the amount allowed by $10 a month ($240 – $230), Warren's employer must include $120 ($10 × 12 months) in his 2009 taxable wages on his Form W-2. Warren's gross income increases by the $120 of additional wages; and the employer's wage expense increases by $120.

Relocation costs. Amounts employers pay or reimburse employees for qualified moving expenses are not taxable to employees, but are deducted by the employer.[37] Qualified moving expenses include costs incurred in relocating an employee and the employee's family so that the employer can begin work in a new location. These costs include the cost of hiring a moving company to pack and move the family's personal belongings as well as reimburse the employee to get to the new location (including $.24 per mile in 2009 if the employee's own automobile is used; however, no reimbursement is allowed for meals en route).[38]

Only reimbursement of qualified moving expenses for moves deemed necessary can be excluded from an employee's gross income (and therefore deductible as qualified moving expenses by the employer). A move is considered justified if it passes both the time and mileage tests. The *mileage test* is met if the employee's commute to the new job would increase by at least 50 miles. Thus, the distance between the employee's current residence and the location of the new job must be 50 miles further than the distance between the employee's current residence and the location of the old job. The *employment test* is met if the employee is employed full-time in the new location for at least 39 of the first 52 weeks after the move. It is not necessary that the 39 weeks be consecutive or with the same employer.[39]

Any amounts an employer reimburses its employees for moving expenses that do not qualify as deductible moving costs are taxable as additional wages to the employee and are deductible as wage

---

[34] Reg. § 1.162-2(e).

[35] Code Sec. 132(f)(1)(D), as added by the Emergency Economic Stabilization Act of 2008 (P.L. 110-343).

[36] Code Sec. 132(f), as amended by the Emergency Economic Stabilization Act of 2008 (P.L. 110-343); and the American Recov-ery and Reinvestment Tax Act of 2009 (P.L. 111-5); Rev. Proc. 2008-66, IRB 2008-45, 1107, October 16, 2008.

[37] Code Sec. 132(a).

[38] Rev. Proc. 2008-72, IRB 2008-50, 1286, November 24, 2008.

[39] Code Sec. 217(c)(2).

expense by the employer. Hence, these amounts would be subject to withholding from the employee's wages as well as FICA and unemployment taxes by the employer.[40]

Example 19: Luisa Landrey receives a promotion from her employer and must relocate to New York City where the company's corporate headquarters are located. Her employer pays her relocation costs, which include $3,000 to professional movers for packing and relocating her personal belongings and $220 for actual hotel and transportation costs en route to New York City. Her employer also reimbursed Luisa $600 that she had to pay to her landlord in Chicago to cancel her lease agreement.

Luisa's qualified moving expenses total $3,220 ($3,000 + $220). The lease cancellation costs are not qualified moving expenses. The $600 is added to Luisa's taxable wages and therefore is subject to income and FICA withholding. Her employer deducts the amounts it reimburses for qualified moving expenses against its taxable income. The nonqualified moving expenses are deductible as wage expense, as are the payroll taxes paid by her employer on the additional taxable wages.

Sole proprietors can deduct amounts they reimburse to their employees for relocation expenses provided that the amounts reimbursed are for qualified moving expenses. Sole proprietors can also deduct as moving expense amounts they pay to move themselves and their families to a new location, provided they pass the mileage test and a more stringent time test. In order for a sole proprietor to deduct moving expenses, the proprietor must also work full-time during 78 of the first 104 weeks after relocating to the new location. As with employees, these weeks need not be consecutive.[41] Although these qualified moving expenses are deducted in arriving at the proprietor's AGI, they cannot be used to reduce business profits.[42] Hence, these amounts reduce the proprietors' income tax liability but not their self-employment taxes. Self-employment taxes are discussed in greater detail in Chapter 13.

Educational assistance. Employers can provide their employees with and deduct amounts paid to further their employees' education. In return, employees can exclude up to $5,250 per year of employer-provided educational assistance. The exclusion is available for employer reimbursements for work-related undergraduate and graduate level course work.[43] If an employee works for more than one employer, then the $5,250 cap applies to the aggregate amount of educational assistance benefits received from all employers.[44] Any excess of benefits over $5,250 that cannot be excluded are included in the employee's wages, and therefore subject to income and employment taxes. The amounts included in the employees' gross income as wages would be deducted by the employer as wage expense.

Example 20: In 2009, the PG Law Firm, LLC establishes an educational assistance program for its employees that reimburses up to $5,250 per year for undergraduate and graduate level course work. Samuel Johnson, a paralegal who works for PG, is working on his law degree and incurs $5,000 of qualified educational expenses during the year. When PG reimburses Samuel $5,000 for his educational expenses, he is not required to include these amounts in his gross income. However, PG is allowed to deduct the $5,000 as an employee benefit on its tax return.

Adoption assistance. Employers can also provide their employees with financial assistance in the adoption of a child. Employees may exclude from gross income amounts paid or expenses incurred by an employer for the employee's qualified adoption expenses pursuant to a qualified adoption assistance program.[45] However, amounts excluded are subject to FICA tax. For 2009, the total amount excludable for the adoption of a child cannot exceed $12,150.[46] The exclusion is

---

[40] Code Sec. 82.
[41] Code Sec. 217(c)(2)(B); Reg. § 1.217-2(c)(4)(i)(b).
[42] Code Sec. 1402(a).
[43] Code Sec. 127; Notice 96-68, 1996-2 CB 236.
[44] Code Sec. 127(a)(2).
[45] Code Sec. 137.
[46] Rev. Proc. 2008-66, IRB 2008-45, 1107, October 16, 2008.

reduced starting when the employee's modified AGI exceeds $182,180 and is fully phased-out when modified AGI exceeds $222,180. The amount of the exclusion and the phase out range are adjusted annually for inflation.[47]

Qualified adoption expenses include reasonable and necessary adoption fees, court costs, attorney's fees, and other expenses that are directly related to, and the principal purpose of which is, the legal adoption of an eligible child. An eligible child is an individual who has not attained the age of 18 as of the time of adoption, or who is physically or mentally incapable of caring for him or herself.[48]

Example 21: In 2009, under its adoption assistance program, Universal Corporation pays $13,000 of qualified adoption expenses on behalf its employee, Sarah Knight, in connection with her efforts to adopt an eligible child. The $13,000 includes $4,000 of qualified adoption expenses to an agency for an unsuccessful attempt to adopt a child plus $9,000 of qualified adoption expenses to another agency for the successful final adoption of a different child. In 2009, Sarah's modified AGI is $80,000. Of the $13,000 that Sarah receives from Universal, $12,150 is excluded from her gross income. The remaining $850 ($13,000 – $12,150) is taxed to her as additional wages in 2009. Universal deducts the entire $13,000 on its tax return—$12,150 as a qualified employee benefit and $850 as wage expense.

¶ 603 Contributions Made to Employees' Retirement Plans

Contributions made by the employer to an employee's qualified retirement plan plus any subsequent amounts those contributions earn are not taxed to the employee until withdrawn. Some employer's plans allow employees to contribute to the retirement plans. In most cases the amounts are contributed with pre-tax dollars, meaning that the employee's taxable wages are reduced by any contributions they make during the year. Since the contributions both the employer and employee make plus any earnings that accumulate over the years are eventually taxed when withdrawn (presumably after retirement), these amounts are not tax-free, but instead grow tax deferred.[49] Income that is never taxed is known as an exclusion. When income or gain is postponed to some future point in time but is eventually taxed, the term used to describe this is **tax deferred**.

The annual contributions employers make to retirement plans for their employees are deductible and therefore reduce business profits. Self-employed individuals can establish a variety of retirement plans and make contributions to those plans for both themselves and their employees. Although amounts sole proprietors contribute to such plans are also deductible, only contributions made on behalf of the employees reduce business profits. Hence, contributions sole proprietors make to their own retirement plans reduce their income tax liability reported on their individual income tax returns, but they do not reduce net earnings from the business and, consequently, do not reduce a sole proprietor's self-employment taxes. The specific rules regarding retirement plans offered by self-employed businesses are discussed in Chapter 13. The following discussion focuses on the types of retirement plans businesses can offer their employees and the employer's costs associated with each type of plan. As you will see, some retirement plans are funded entirely by employer's contributions, whereas other plans are funded with contributions from employers and employees, or from employee contributions only.

.01 Qualified Retirement Plans

Only contributions to qualified retirement plans can receive tax deferred treatment. A qualified plan cannot be offered only to key employees, and consequently, most qualified retirement plans must be made available to all full-time employees after a specified length of service.[50] Although further discussion as to what constitutes a qualified retirement plan is beyond the scope of this

---

[47] Code Sec. 137(f).
[48] Code Sec. 23(d)(2).

[49] Code Sec. 401.
[50] Code Sec. 416.

textbook, employers only can deduct contributions they make to qualified plans.[51] Contributions to nonqualified plans are taxed to employees as additional compensation and accordingly would be deducted as wages expense (and be subject to income, employment, and unemployment taxes).

There are two basic types of qualified retirement plans: defined benefit plans and defined contribution plans. A **defined benefit plan** promises participants specified benefits during retirement years and continuing until the death of the participant, and often until the death of the spouse of the participant.[52] The amounts that can be expected upon retirement are often a function of the employee's length of service to the company as well as the level of compensation earned during those years. Typically the benefits are indexed annually to cover inflation.

Example 22: An employee's defined benefit plan specifies that for each year of service, the employee will receive benefits equal to two percent of the average pay during his last three years of service. Annual benefits are increased three percent annually for inflation, and payments to the participant's spouse are reduced by 50 percent upon the participant's death. Jake Winters retires after working for the company for 35 years. His salary averaged $80,000 during his last three years. Jake can expect to receive pension benefits of $56,000 during his first retirement year ($80,000 × 2% × 35 years) and $57,680 during the second year ($56,000 plus 3% of $56,000).

Under a defined benefit plan, benefits paid to employees are based on the employee's length of service and compensation earned over the years of employment. At the time contributions are made to these plans, these amounts are not known with any degree of certainty and therefore must be estimated. In addition, once benefits begin, they generally continue for the life of the participant (and of the spouse in many cases), and since this length of time is unknown, additional factors must be estimated adding to the uncertainty regarding the contributions necessary each year to adequately fund these types of retirement plans. The calculation of contributions to a defined benefit plan is extremely complex and generally must be performed by an actuary, who is a professional trained in this area. Amounts contributed to a defined benefit plan are contributed to one account and not designated to any of the plan participants.[53] Typically, the employer is responsible for a large portion of the contributions made to defined benefit plans. This reason, plus the costly administrative costs incurred in offering these plans, may explain why the number of employers offering defined benefit plans to their employees has declined significantly over the past couple of decades.

Under a **defined contribution plan**, the employer can make specific contributions on behalf of each employee covered under the plan. The amount of the contribution is usually a percentage of the employee's compensation. Unlike contributions to defined benefit plans, contributions to defined contributions plans must be allocated among individual accounts maintained for each participant. Thus, these accounts resemble individual retirement savings accounts. At retirement, employees are entitled to whatever the balance has accumulated in their own accounts.[54] A 401(k) plan is a popular defined contribution plan.

.02 Employer Contributions

Contributions to qualified plans are generally deductible by the employer in the year in which they are paid, regardless of whether the employer uses the cash or accrual method. However, in certain instances a payment will be considered as paid by the end of the preceding tax year.[55] Due to the attractiveness of the tax deferral feature of retirement accounts, the Code limits the amounts that can be contributed to retirement plans each year. Different limits apply depending on the type of retirement plan offered by the employer and the limits are indexed annually for inflation. The Code limits the maximum amount that employers can contribute on behalf of an employee to a defined contribution plan to the *lesser of* (1) 100 percent of a participant's compensation or (2) a

---

[51] Code Sec. 404.

[52] Code Sec. 414(j).

[53] Reg. § 1.401-1(b)(1)(i).

[54] Code Sec. 414(i).

[55] Code Sec. 404(a)(6); Rev. Rul. 76-28, 1976-1 CB 106, modified by Rev. Rul. 76-77, 1976-1 CB 107.

specified amount ($49,000 for 2009), which is adjusted annually for inflation.[56] The calculation of the amounts that need to be contributed to a defined benefit plan each year to provide adequate benefits to participants upon retirement is extremely complex and requires the assistance of an actuary.[57] However, the Code limits the amounts of an employee's compensation that may be taken into account in the calculation to the *lesser of* (1) a dollar amount ($245,000 for 2009), or (2) 100 percent of the participant's average compensation for the three highest consecutive years.[58]

To discourage taxpayers from using qualified retirement plans as tax deferred savings accounts for purposes other than retirement, Congress imposed a special 10-percent tax on early distributions.[59] The 10-percent tax on early distributions is assessed against the employee on their individual income tax return. The 10-percent tax will not apply if the distribution from the plan qualifies for one of the exceptions to the penalty (e.g., the employee is at least 59½).

 GAAP vs. Code: For tax purposes, accrual method taxpayers deduct contributions to qualified plans in the year in which they are paid. For financial statement purposes, corporations expense contributions in the year to which they are accrued, regardless of when they are paid. Thus, should a corporation accrue amounts that are not paid until the following tax year, this temporary difference will result in a difference between net income and taxable income in both the year accrued and in the year paid. The difference would require an adjustment to net income (that is, an increase to net income in the year accrued, followed by a decrease in the year paid) when reconciling net income to taxable income on the corporate tax return.

.03 Simplified Employee Pension (SEP) Plans

Simplified employee pension (SEP) plans are geared toward smaller employers who may be discouraged by the complexities of establishing a regular qualified plan.[60] Under a SEP, the employer agrees to make contributions to an individual retirement account (IRA) for each eligible employee. To establish a SEP plan, the following three conditions must be met.

1. The employer must execute a formal written agreement to provide benefits to all eligible employees,

2. The employer must provide certain information about the plan to each eligible employee, and

3. The employer must establish a SEP-IRA for each employee over the age of 20 whose compensation is at least $550 and who has performed services for the employer during at least three out of the preceding five calendar years.

For 2009, annual contributions by an employer to a SEP are excluded from the employee's gross income to the extent that the contributions do not exceed the *lesser of* (1) $49,000 or (2) 25 percent of the participant's compensation. If the employer exceeds the annual limit on contributions, the employee is generally taxed on the amount of the excess contributions as additional wages.[61]

The employer deposits its contributions in a SEP-IRA account set up for the individual employee. An employer is not required to make contributions every year, but in years the employer does make contributions, it must contribute amounts for each participant. Thus, if a sole proprietor establishes a SEP-IRA for himself and his employees, in order to contribute to his own retirement account, the sole proprietor must contribute to each eligible employee's respective accounts. The contributions that are made must be allocated among employees according to a written formula and must not discriminate in favor of highly compensated employees. A SEP can be established as late

---

[56] Code Sec. 415(c)(1)(A).

[57] See Code Secs. 412, 430, and 404(a)(1)(A)(ii) and (iii).

[58] Code Secs. 401(a)(17) and 404(l); IRS News Release 2008-118, October 16, 2008.

[59] Code Sec. 72(t)(1).

[60] Code Sec. 408(k).

[61] Code Sec. 402(h)(2) and 4973(a).

as the due date (including extensions) of the employer's tax return for the year.[62] Employers' SEP-IRA contributions for their employees are deductible as employee benefits and reduce business profits. Any contributions sole proprietors made to their own SEP-IRAs are deducted in computing AGI, but do not reduce business profits. Consequently, these contributions lower sole proprietors' income tax liabilities, but not their self-employment taxes.

Example 23: Paul Vargas is self-employed and has one employee, Cynthia Smith. Paul has adopted a SEP-IRA for his business and for 2009 decides to contribute the maximum 25 percent to the retirement plan. Cynthia's salary in 2009 is $30,000, and accordingly, Paul must contribute $7,500 ($30,000 × 25%) to her SEP-IRA. Paul will deduct the $7,500 contribution as a pension and profit-sharing expense against his business profits. The contribution he makes to his own SEP-IRA does not reduce business profits but is deducted in computing his AGI. Accordingly, the contribution Paul makes to his own retirement account reduces his income tax liability, but not his self-employment tax. The contribution he makes on behalf of his employee reduces both his income and self-employment taxes. Thus, Paul's out-of-pocket cost of contributing to his employee's retirement plan is less than his costs of contributing to his own retirement plan.

.04 401(k) and 403(b) Plans

401(k) plans are a very popular type of employer-sponsored defined contribution retirement plan. These plans, which are sometimes called cash or deferred arrangements (CODAs), allow employees to either elect to defer a portion of their salary or receive it in cash. Benefits paid in cash are taxable to the employee as wages and deducted as wage expense by the employer. Noncash benefits are not taxable to the employee, but are deducted by the employer as employee benefits. Most businesses can adopt 401(k) plans for their employees.[63] A 403(b) plan is very similar to a 401(k), except that a 403(b) plan is available to certain types of employees, including government workers. Unless otherwise stated in the discussion that follows, the rules that apply to 401(k) plans apply to 403(b) plans as well.

Limit on employee contributions. For 2009, the maximum amount of wages that employees can contribute to their 401(k) plans is $16,500. However, employees who will be at least 50 years old by the end of the year are able to make "catch up" contributions, which would allow them to contribute up to $5,500 more to their accounts.[64]

An employee's contributions to a 401(k) plan are not subject to income tax withholding to the extent that they do not exceed the maximum annual limit. However, these contributions are treated as taxable wages for purposes of FICA and unemployment taxes.[65] As a general rule, extra amounts contributed to an employee's 401(k) plan by the employer (matching contributions) are not subject to income tax withholding and are exempt from FICA and unemployment taxes. Furthermore, employers' contributions to employees' 401(k) plans do not count towards the maximum annual limit.[66]

Qualification requirements. To be a qualified 401(k) plan, the plan must satisfy the following requirements.[67]

1. The plan must give the participant the option of having the employer contribute amounts to the plan or receiving those amounts in cash.

2. The plan must prohibit distributions except in certain situations, such as the participant reaching age 59½, the participant being severed from employment, the participant being severed from employment due to death or disability, the participant enduring a financial hardship, or the employer terminating the plan without establishing a successor plan.

---

[62] Prop. Reg. § 1.408-7(b); Code Sec. 404(h).
[63] Code Sec. 401(k)(4)(B).
[64] Code Sec. 414(v).
[65] Code Secs. 3121(v)(1) and 3306(r)(1).
[66] Code Sec. 401(k)(3)(D).
[67] Code Sec. 401(k)(2) and (4).

3. The plan must provide that the amounts in the participant's account attributable to elective contributions are fully vested (nonforfeitable) at all times.

4. The plan can require as a condition of participation that an employee complete one year of service with the employer, but it cannot require any longer periods of employment to be completed.

5. The plan cannot place conditions on the benefits under the 401(k) plan or any other plan upon an employee's elective contributions. However, this rule does not prevent an employer from basing its contributions on the elective contributions of employees.

A hardship distribution is a distribution made because of the participant's immediate and heavy financial need, and is limited to the amount necessary to satisfy that financial need.[68] Amounts distributed to pay medical expenses; costs of post-secondary education for the participant, spouse, children or dependents; and expenditures to purchase, or to stave off eviction or foreclosure with respect to the participant's principal residence, all qualify as financial hardship distributions.[69] A hardship distribution is subject to the 10-percent tax on early distributions unless it qualifies for one of the exceptions to the tax penalty.[70]

In addition to the five special requirements listed above, a 401(k) plan must meet an annual nondiscrimination test. This test is used to determine if the contributions of highly-compensated employees exceed the contributions of rank and file employees by a specified ratio.[71] A safe harbor has been added for 401(k) plans, effective for plans beginning after December 31, 2006, that contain an automatic employee enrollment feature in which the employer makes elective contributions in an amount equal to a qualified percentage (not to exceed 10 percent) of the employee's compensation.[72] Plans that satisfy the safe harbor requirements will be treated as satisfying the nondiscrimination rules. If a plan adopts the safe harbor rules, an employee must affirmatively elect not to have elective contributions made or can elect to change the level of the elective contributions.

.05 Roth 401(k) Plans

Employers can offer Roth 401(k) plans to their employees. Employees' contributions to a Roth 401(k) are made with after-tax funds, meaning that the wages used to contribute to a Roth 401(k) are reported in their taxable wages on their Form W-2s. Only the participant can contribute to a Roth 401(k); employer contributions are not permitted.[73] Although contributions to Roth 401(k) plans are made with post-tax dollars, all amounts in a Roth 401(k) plan grow tax-free. Thus, when qualified distributions are eventually made from a Roth 401(k), both employee contributions and the accumulated earnings are exempt from tax. Roth 401(k) plans are subject to the same contribution limits that apply to 401(k) plans, including catch up provisions for participants age 50 or older.[74]

The amount of an individual's designated Roth contributions will be subject to the annual limit on elective deferrals, reduced by the amount of the participant's other elective deferrals under a 401(k) or 403(b) plan.[75] The applicable limit applies to the total of all of the employee's pre-tax elective deferrals (including contributions to a SEP and elective employer contributions to a SIMPLE plan) and after-tax Roth contributions.[76]

Example 24:   Earl Jones (age 46) participates in a 401(k) plan maintained by his employer. In 2009, he may designate up to $16,500 of his authorized elective deferrals as an after-tax Roth contribution if he makes no pre-tax contributions to his 401(k) plan. By contrast, if he makes pre-tax elective deferrals of $10,000 to his 401(k) plan, he may designate only $6,500 as a Roth contribution.

---

[68] Reg. § 1.401(k)-1(d)(3)(i).
[69] Reg. § 1.401(k)-1(d)(2)(iv)(A).
[70] Code Sec. 72(t)(2).
[71] Code Sec. 401(k)(3)(A).
[72] Code Sec. 401(k)(13), as added by the Pension Protection Act of 2006 (P.L.109-280); Prop. Reg. § 1.401(k)-3.

[73] Code Sec. 402A.
[74] Code Sec. 402A(c)(2); Code Sec. 402(g).
[75] Code Sec. 402A(c)(2); Code Sec. 402(g)(1).
[76] Code Sec. 402(g).

Unlike Roth IRAs, which are available only to taxpayers with an AGI below a certain level, qualified Roth contribution programs are available to any employee, regardless of income level, who is a participant in a 401(k) or 403(b) plan that allows Roth deferrals.

Qualified distributions from a Roth IRA are not included in the individual's gross income and are not subject to the 10-percent penalty for early withdrawals. To be treated as a *qualified distribution*, the Roth 401(k) must have been around for at least five years and distributions must be made for one of the following events:

1. The distribution is made on or after the date the participant reaches age 59½,
2. The distribution is made to a beneficiary (or the estate) after the participant's death,
3. The distribution is made because the participant is disabled, or
4. The distribution (up to $10,000) is used to pay for qualified first-time homebuyer expenses.[77]

.06 SIMPLE Plans

Employers with 100 or fewer employees that are paid at least $5,000 in compensation from the employer in the preceding year may adopt a retirement plan known as a Savings Incentive Match Plan for Employees (SIMPLE) plan.[78] Generally, the SIMPLE plan must be the employer's only qualified retirement plan. A SIMPLE plan allows employees to make elective contributions of up to $11,500 per year for 2009 and requires that employers make matching contributions.[79] Employees who are at least age 50 may make an additional catch-up contribution of $2,500 during 2009.

As with most other types of qualified plans, amounts contributed to the participant's account grow tax-deferred and are not taxed to the participant until withdrawn. Contributions employers make to their employee's SIMPLE accounts are deductible in the year the contributions are made. Unlike most qualified plans, SIMPLE plans are not subject to the nondiscrimination rules, top-heavy provisions, and other complex requirements that qualified plans must generally satisfy. Employers may set up a SIMPLE plan as a SIMPLE-IRA or as a SIMPLE-401(k).[80] Contributions employers make to their employees' SIMPLE-IRAs or SIMPLE-401(k)s are deducted as employee benefits and reduce business profits. However, contributions sole proprietors make to their own SIMPLE plans cannot reduce business profits, but are deducted in arriving at their AGI.

Table 6-2 Summary of Retirement Plans Employers May Offer Their Employees

Retirement Plan	*Requirements*	*Contribution Limits*
Defined Benefit Plans		
Pension Plan	Contributions are calculated by an actuary.	The amount that would be projected to yield a benefit not to exceed the *lesser of* (1) a dollar limit ($195,000 in 2009) or (2) 100% of the employee's compensation over the three highest consecutive years

---

[77] Code Sec. 402A(d)(2)(A).
[78] Code Sec. 408(p).

[79] Code Sec. 401(k)(11)(B)(i); IRS News Release 2008-118, Oct. 16, 2008.
[80] Code Secs. 408(p) and 401(k)(11); Prop. Reg. §1.401(k)-4.

Defined Contribution Plans

401(k) Plan	Employees contribute using either pre-tax or after-tax wages. Employer matching permitted, but not required.	$16,500 $5,500 catch-up contribution for employees age 50 and older
Roth 401(k)	Employees contribute with after-tax dollars. Employer matching is not allowed.	$16,500 $5,500 catch-up contribution for employees age 50 and older
SIMPLE Plan	Available to employers with 100 or fewer employees who received at least $5,000 of compensation in the previous year. Employer matching required.	$11,500 $2,500 catch-up contribution for employees age 50 and older
Simplified Employee Pension (SEP) Plan	Employers must contribute to a 401(k) or IRA for each eligible employee. Contributions made entirely by employers.	The *lesser* of (1) $49,000 or (2) 25% of the participant's compensation

---

 GAAP vs. Code: The amount of the employer's contribution accrued on the company's financial statements may be different from the actual amount contributed to the employees' retirement plan. For tax purposes, the employer is only able to deduct the actual amount contributed to the employees' retirement plan. Generally, the contribution must be paid before the due date of the tax return (including extensions), thereby allowing the employer some flexibility in determining the amount of the contribution in order to reduce the company's taxable income. Any difference between the amount deducted in arriving at net income and the deduction taken on the corporate tax return would be reported as an adjustment to net income when reconciling it with taxable income on the corporate tax return.

¶ 604 Employment Taxes

Employers are responsible for payroll taxes imposed on wages they pay to their employees. Employers must match the amounts of social security and medicare taxes that their employees pay and must also pay unemployment taxes on employees' wages. Businesses are not subject to payroll taxes on amounts they pay to independent contractors.

In 1935, Congress enacted the Federal Social Security Act, which established a federal unemployment insurance program and a program to provide old-age, survivors, and disability benefits to employees. Financing for the two programs is achieved through taxes imposed on both employers and employees under the **Federal Insurance Contributions Act (FICA)** and on employers under the **Federal Unemployment Tax Act (FUTA).** In 1950, the tax laws were amended to include FICA coverage for self-employed individuals. Financing for FICA for self-employed taxpayers is accomplished through the self-employment tax.

.01 Federal Insurance Contributions Act (FICA)

The old-age, survivors, and disability insurance (OASDI) portion of the FICA tax, commonly referred to as **social security taxes**, provides benefits to the elderly and their survivors as well as disabled individuals. In 1965, FICA was expanded to add a separate tax for hospital insurance (HI) for the elderly. This tax is commonly referred to as **Medicare taxes**. The FICA tax rate of 7.65 percent is comprised of 6.2 percent for social security taxes and 1.45 percent for Medicare taxes. The rate is imposed on both the employer and employee for a combined rate of 15.3 percent. For employees, the maximum amount of wages subject to the social security taxes in 2009 is $106,800; whereas all wages are subject to the Medicare tax.[81] The wage ceiling for social security taxes is adjusted annually for inflation.

The maximum amount of social security tax that an employee is required to pay in 2009 is $6,621.60 ($106,800 × 6.2%). Employers are required to withhold social security taxes on all wages up to the maximum limit. Therefore, employees who receive wages from more than one employer during 2009 may have more than $6,621.60 of social security tax withheld during the year. This excess is claimed as a tax credit on the employee's individual tax return.

FICA wages. For purposes of FICA, the term wages means all remuneration for employment, including both cash and noncash compensation.[82] FICA wages include, but are not limited to, employees' wages, tips, bonuses, commissions, most employer-provided prizes and awards, back pay awards, dismissal pay, employer-provided supplemental unemployment benefits, and reimbursements of employees' business expenses under a nonaccountable plan. FICA wages also include employee contributions to an employer-provided retirement plan. Excluded from FICA wages are certain nontaxable fringe benefits and reimbursements to employees under an accountable plan. Also excluded from FICA wages are wages paid to the taxpayer's children who are under age 18 and who work for their parents in a trade or business operated as a sole proprietorship or a partnership (provided that each partner is the child's parent).

Example 25: In 2009, Karen Hodges earns $150,000 working at Quentin Development Company. At the end of the year Quentin pays Karen a $20,000 bonus. Karen's FICA wages equal $170,000 ($150,000 + $20,000), and the amount of FICA withheld from Karen's earnings for the year include the maximum amount withheld for social security taxes of $6,621.60 ($106,800 × 6.2%) plus $2,465 for Medicare taxes ($170,000 × 1.45%). Quentin matches these amounts and pays FICA taxes totaling $9,086.60 ($6,621.60 + $2,465). Quentin remits to the federal government $18,173.20 ($9,086.60 withheld from Karen's earnings plus $9,086.60 it pays in payroll taxes).

Tips an employee receives in the course of employment are subject to both federal income tax and FICA tax. Every employee who receives cash tips of $20 or more per month with one employer must report to their employer the total amount of tips they received during the period.[83] These taxable tips are then included as taxable wages on the employee's Form W-2 and therefore are subject to FICA taxes as well as income tax withholding.[84]

Certain businesses are required to impute the amount of tips their employees earn and include those amounts in their employees' taxable wages. Consequently, these imputed tips are subject to income tax withholding and both the employer and employee's shares of FICA taxes. Normally, employers deduct their matching FICA contributions as an ordinary and necessary business expense. However, to encourage businesses to comply with the tax laws requiring them to impute tips on behalf of their employees, the federal government allows employers to take a tax credit equal to 100 percent of any matching amounts that result from amounts paid with respect to tips for food or beverages received by their employees, provided that the employee tips are not needed to allow the employee to earn a minimum wage.[85]

---

[81] Code Secs. 3101, 3111, and 3121.
[82] Code Sec. 3121(a).
[83] Code Sec. 6053.

[84] Code Sec. 3102.
[85] Code Sec. 45B(b).

Reason for the Rule: As you may recall from Chapter 1, all other things being equal, a tax credit is preferred over a tax deduction. By allowing employers to take a tax credit for 100 percent of the amounts they pay towards FICA on employees' tip income, the federal government is encouraging employers to report their employees' tips as taxable wages by rewarding them with tax incentives.

.02 Federal Unemployment Tax Act (FUTA) Taxes

FUTA was enacted by Congress to finance the federal unemployment program. Under FUTA, a tax is imposed on an employer at a specified rate on the first $7,000 in wages paid to each employee during a calendar year, regardless of the year used for accounting purposes. The FUTA tax rate for 2009 is 6.2 percent of the first $7,000 of wages paid to each employee in the calendar year.[86] For calendar years 2010 and thereafter, the FUTA tax rate is 6 percent.[87] The tax applies to the wages that are actually paid by the employer, regardless of the accounting method used.

FUTA wages. An employer is subject to FUTA taxes if the employer employs at least one person on one day in each of 20 weeks during the current or preceding calendar year or the employer pays at least $1,500 in wages during any calendar quarter in the current or prior years. Amounts paid for nontaxable fringe benefits, employer reimbursements under an accountable plan, and wages paid to children who are under age 21 who work for their parents (regardless of whether such work is in the taxpayer's trade or business) are not subject to FUTA tax. Also excluded from FUTA tax are wages paid to a spouse who works for the taxpayer's trade or business.

State unemployment taxes. Although the federal government provides funding for unemployment benefits, the responsibility for distributing those amounts to unemployed persons rests with the state governments. Accordingly, most states also impose unemployment taxes on employee wages. State tax rates range anywhere from zero percent to just over 10 percent, and the amount of wages subject to state unemployment taxes often exceeds the $7,000 maximum imposed by the federal government.

Employers are required to pay both the federal and state unemployment taxes. However, they are allowed to subtract from the amounts owed to the federal government contributions they make to the state, up to 5.4 percent of the first $7,000 of an employee's wages.[88] Thus, in a state that imposes a 5.4-percent tax rate or higher, the FUTA tax rate is reduced to .8 percent (6.2% minus 5.4%).

Example 26: The M&R Manufacturing Company has taxable FUTA wages of $300,000. M&R's federal unemployment tax liability equals $18,600 ($300,000 × 6.2%); its state unemployment tax liability is $25,000. The state's tax rate exceeds 5.4 percent. M&R pays $25,000 to the state and reduces its obligation to the federal government by $16,200 ($300,000 × 5.4%). Thus, M&R's payment to the federal government for unemployment taxes equals $2,400 ($18,600 – $16,200). M&R's total unemployment taxes for the year are $27,400 ($25,000 + $2,400). It deducts this amount from its gross income on its income tax return.

Table 6-3 summarizes the requirements for paying FICA and FUTA taxes on employee compensation. Any amounts subject to FICA tax are subject to both social security and medicare taxes (with social security taxes limited to the first $106,800 of compensation during 2009). FICA taxes are paid by both the employer and employee. Only employers are subject to FUTA taxes.

---

[86] Code Sec. 3301, as amended by the Emergency Economic Stabilization Act of 2008 (P.L. 110-343).

[87] Code Sec. 3301(2).

[88] Code Sec. 3302.

Table 6-3 Amounts Subject to FICA and FUTA Taxes

Type of Payment	*Subject to FICA Taxes?*	*Subject to FUTA Taxes?*
Compensation for services performed in the United States, including taxable tips	Yes	Yes
Cafeteria plan benefits under Code Sec. 125	Yes if the employee chooses cash; otherwise exempt from FICA taxes	Yes if the employee chooses cash; otherwise exempt from FUTA taxes
Amounts contributed to dependent care assistance programs	Only to the extent the annual limits are exceeded ($5,000 in 2009)	Only to the extent the annual limits are exceeded ($5,000 in 2009)
Reimbursements for qualified educational assistance	Only to the extent the annual limits are exceeded ($5,250 in 2009)	Only to the extent the annual limits are exceeded ($5,250 in 2009)
Reimbursements for parking, transportation, and bicycle commuting	Only to the extent the monthly limits are exceeded (Parking $230, Transportation $120 or $230, and Bicycle commuting $20 in 2009)[a]	Only to the extent the monthly limits are exceeded (Parking $230, Transportation $120 or $230, and Bicycle commuting $20 in 2009)[a]
Reimbursements from an accountable plan	No	No
Reimbursements from an nonaccountable plan	Yes	Yes
Payments to a child employed by a parent (or partnership where each partner is a child's parent)	Not until the child reaches the age of 18	Not until the child reaches the age of 21
Payments to a spouse employed in the taxpayer's business	Yes	No
Payments to parents employed in their child's business	Yes	No
Payments for accident and health insurance premiums and group life insurance premiums	No, except for costs associated with group term life insurance coverage in excess of $50,000	No

Type of Payment	Subject to FICA Taxes?	Subject to FUTA Taxes?
Employer contributions to a qualified retirement plan, including 401(k) or SEP-IRA plans	No	No
Employees' elective contributions to an employer's 401(k) or SIMPLE plan	Yes	Yes

a The excludable benefit for Transportation (transit passes and rides in a commuter highway vehicle) is $120 per month (for months January 2009 through February 16, 2009) and $230 per month (for months beginning on or after February 17, 2009).

¶ 605 Meals and Entertainment Expenses

Taxpayers generally can deduct meal and entertainment expenses provided that the expenses are directly related to or associated with the taxpayer's trade or business. The taxpayer must substantiate the amounts spent and the business nature of the expense. Even if the taxpayer meets these requirements, typically only 50 percent of the meals and entertainment can be used to reduce business profits.

.01 Meals

The costs associated with meals are not deductible if neither the taxpayer nor an employee of the taxpayer is present at the meal. Also, no deduction is allowed for food and beverages to the extent that they are lavish or extravagant under the circumstances.

Example 27: Lucia Jones spent $100 for a business-related meal. If $40 of that amount is considered lavish and extravagant, it is not deductible and the remaining $60 is subject to the 50-percent deduction limit. Therefore, Lucia may deduct only $30 ($60 × 50%) for the meal in arriving at business profits.

Transportation workers. A greater percentage of the cost of meals consumed by certain transportation workers is allowed.[89] Eighty percent of the cost of meals are allowed as a deduction. The increased meal deduction is available for food or beverages consumed while away from home by an individual during, or incident to, a period of duty subject to the Department of Transportation's hours of service limitations. Individuals subject to the hours of service limitations include:

- Certain air transportation employees, such as pilots, crew, dispatchers, mechanics, and control tower operators;
- Interstate truck operators and interstate bus drivers;
- Certain railroad employees, such as engineers, conductors, train crews; and
- Certain merchant mariners.

 Reason for the Rule: This increase in the amount allowed to be deducted by transportation workers is intended to restore meal deductions to certain workers who are forced to eat away from home and are unlikely to abuse the deduction.

---

[89] Code Sec. 274(n)(3).

GAAP vs. Code: For financial reporting purposes, all meals and entertainment expenses incurred are deducted in arriving at net income. For tax purposes, only a portion of deductible meals reduce taxable income. This differential treatment creates a permanent difference which must be added back to net income when reconciling net income to taxable income on the corporate tax return. For example, if a corporation incurs costs totaling $20,000 during the year for business meals, the entire $20,000 would be deducted in arriving at net income, but only $10,000 ($20,000 × 50%) would be deducted on the tax return. Therefore, when reconciling net income to taxable income, the $10,000 of disallowed expense would be added back to net income.

.02 Entertainment

No deduction is allowed for any expense of an activity considered to be entertainment, amusement, or recreation, except to the extent that it is established that the expense was *directly related to* the active conduct of a trade or business. However, entertainment expenses incurred directly before or after bona fide business discussions that are *associated with* the active conduct of the business are allowed even though they are not directly related to the business.[90] The Tax Court ruled that expenses incurred in entertaining 200 people at a cocktail party were not directly related to the active conduct of a taxpayer's dental practice, even though the expenditures were motivated by business considerations and generated referral patients for the taxpayer.[91] The Tax Court also held that an attorney could not deduct the costs of hosting a birthday party as promotion and public relations business expenses.[92] Entertainment costs that meet the directly related or associated with conditions are subject to the 50-percent limitation. Costs that do not qualify as entertainment expenses or any other deductible expense under the tax laws would be nondeductible expenditures.

Entertainment facilities. The deduction for tickets to any entertainment activity or facility is limited to the face value of the tickets.[93] This limitation does not apply to a ticket for a sports event that is organized for the primary purpose of benefiting a tax-exempt charitable organization, provided that all of the proceeds are contributed to the organization and the organization utilizes volunteers for substantially all of the work performed in carrying out the event. When a taxpayer leases a luxury skybox at a sports arena for more than one event, the deduction is limited to the cost of the highest-priced nonluxury box seat tickets generally held for sale to the public for the same event, multiplied by the number of seats in the skybox.[94]

Example 28: Playright Company paid $10,000 to rent a 10-seat skybox at Wrigley Field for three baseball games during the season. The cost of the highest-priced nonluxury box seat is $25. The deduction for the purchase of skybox seats is limited to 50 percent of the value of the highest priced nonluxury skybox seats. Thus, Playright's tax deduction of the skybox will be limited to $375 (($25 × 10) × 3 games × 50%).

Example 29: Tiana Smith, an employee of Warner Enterprises, purchased four concert tickets on behalf of her employer and gave them to a client. Tiana was reimbursed by her employer under an accountable plan. Tiana paid a ticket agency $300 for the four tickets, which had a face value of $240. Warner can deduct $120 as entertainment expense ($240 × 50%) on its corporate tax return.

 GAAP vs. Code: For financial accounting purposes, the entire amount of entertainment expenses incurred during the year is deducted in arriving at net income. When

---

[90] Code Sec. 274(a)(1)(A); Reg. § 1.274-2(a).

[91] *J.E. Gardner*, 45 TCM 1116, Dec. 40,000(M), TC Memo. 1983-171.

[92] *J.L. Flaig*, 47 TCM 1361, Dec. 41,091(M), TC Memo. 1984-150.

[93] Code Sec. 274(l)(1).

[94] Code Sec. 274(l)(2).

> calculating taxable income, only 50 percent of deductible entertainment expenses are allowed. The difference in these rules creates a permanent difference between net income and taxable income. When reconciling net income to taxable income on the corporate tax return, any disallowed amounts would need to be added back to net income. Thus, in Example 29, Warner Enterprises would add to net income the $180 ($300 - $120) disallowed entertainment expenses to arrive at the amount reflected in taxable income.

No deduction is allowed for amounts paid or incurred for dues and fees paid to social, athletic, sporting, or country clubs. Also, no deduction is allowed for any expense paid or incurred with respect to an entertainment, recreation, or amusement facility,[95] which includes any property that is owned, rented, or used by the taxpayer for entertainment. Entertainment facilities for which a taxpayer generally may not deduct any expenses include yachts, hunting lodges, fishing camps, swimming pools, tennis courts, bowling alleys, cars, airplanes, apartments, hotel suites, and homes located in a vacation resort. A taxpayer may, however, deduct out-of-pocket expenses for the business use of those facilities that are directly related to and associated with entertainment of customers at the facilities.

Example 30: Asten, Inc. owns a hunting lodge which is used by its executives for both business and personal purposes. During the year Asten incurs $10,200 of expenses to operate the lodge. The lodge was used by the company's executives 55 percent for business, which includes 35 percent for directly-related entertainment and 20 percent associated with entertainment. In addition, the corporation pays $2,000 for food and beverages in entertainment that was directly related to the active conduct of business and $1,200 for food and beverages in relation to entertainment that was associated with the active conduct of a trade or business. When preparing its tax return for the year, Asten will be allowed to deduct 50 percent of the $3,200 ($2,000 + $1,200) of meal and entertainment expenses directly related to or associated with the active conduct of its business. It will not be allowed to deduct the lodge's operating expenses of $10,200.

 GAAP vs. Code: For financial reporting purposes, all entertainment expenses reduce net income. However for tax purposes, the deduction for entertainment is limited or sometimes disallowed, depending on the circumstances. For example, in Example 30, the $10,200 of operating expenses for the lodge plus all $3,200 of meal and entertainment expenses would be deducted on the income statement in arriving at net income. However, it can only deduct $1,600 ($3,200 × 50%) on its tax return. Accordingly, when reconciling net income to taxable income, Asten will add back the $11,800 difference ($13,400 total costs – $1,600) to net income.

Example 31: Zander Company is a member of the Golf Duffs Country Club so that its executives can use the facilities to entertain clients. Zander pays annual dues of $1,200 to Golf Duffs. Meal and entertainment expenses incurred at the club meet the directly-related to or associated with tests and therefore, 50 percent are deductible. During the year, Zander incurs meal and entertainment expenses totaling $2,500. On its tax return, Zander is allowed to deduct $1,250 of the meals and entertainment costs ($2,500 × 50%). It cannot deduct the $1,200 of club dues.

---

[95] Code Sec. 274(a)(1)(B).

Planning Pointer: Detailed records showing dates, amounts, places, the business relationship to the persons involved, and the business purpose are the best proof to assure deductibility of entertainment expense. There is adequate substantiation if the taxpayer maintains a notebook or similar record in which the information as to each element of an expense is recorded in a contemporaneous and consistent manner throughout the tax year. In addition, documentary evidence (such as itemized receipts or paid bills) is required for each expenditure of $75 or more.

 Spotlight: Since only 50 percent of entertainment expenses can be deducted, businesses are better off classifying expenditures as something other than entertainment. For example, it would be to the taxpayer's advantage to classify an expenditure that could be viewed as either an entertainment or advertising expense as advertising. The furnishing of food and beverages, a hotel suite, a vacation cottage, or an automobile to a customer or member of his family is considered entertainment. Other activities generally considered to be entertainment include the entertaining of guests at nightclubs, football games, theaters, or prizefights, as well as the costs of hunting, fishing, vacation, and similar trips. However, the particular trade or business activity of the taxpayer claiming the deduction determines whether an activity is entertainment.[96] For example, a hunting trip is not entertainment to a professional big game hunter, but it would be considered entertainment to a clothing sales representative.

¶ 606 Travel Expenses

Travel and transportation are two types of expenses that employers may incur on behalf of their employees during the normal conduct of business. Accordingly, these amounts, whether paid directly by the employer or reimbursed to the employee under an accountable plan, are usually deductible under the general deductibility provisions of Code Sec. 162(a). Travel and transportation can also be deducted by a sole proprietor under this same Code provision. Travel expenses are those costs paid or incurred while traveling away from home overnight for business. Transportation expenses are costs paid or incurred while traveling around town on business.

Ordinary and necessary expenses incurred in the pursuit of business while away from home are deductible as business expenses.[97] Generally, business away from home expenses are travel costs incurred while temporarily away from home. Although the rules generally require an overnight stay, an individual does not have to be away from the tax home for an entire 24-hour day or from dusk to dawn, so long as the period of absence is substantially longer than a normal working day and, during the time away, it is reasonable for the traveler to need sleep or rest for the requirements of the job.[98]

The purpose of the travel may be to contact customers, to attend business and professional meetings, or to attend business and professional conventions and seminars. The types of expenses that may be incurred while traveling away from home include transportation costs (airplane, train or bus fares, and automobile expenses), meals and lodging to the extent that they are not lavish or extravagant and do not relate to purely personal activities, laundry and dry cleaning charges, taxicab fares, and tips.

.01 Away from Home

The location of a taxpayer's tax home for purposes of the "away from home" requirement is generally based on the facts surrounding the traveler's situation.[99] For years, the IRS insisted that for the purposes of deducting travel expenses, the tax home was the principal place of business or

---

[96] Reg. § 1.274-2(b)(1)(ii).

[97] Code Sec. 162(a)(2).

[98] Rev. Rul. 75-168, 1975-1 CB 58 and Rev. Rul. 75-170, 1975-1 CB 60.

[99] Rev. Rul. 75-432, 1975-2 CB 60.

employment, regardless of where a residence is maintained.[100] Although the courts generally agreed with this assessment, some support exists for the position that a taxpayer's home is where his residence is located.[101] However, even if it is accepted that the tax home is where the principal place of business is located, the taxpayer may have two places of business. Thus, to determine which one is the taxpayer's *principal place of business*, the IRS employs a three-prong test which examines (1) the length of time spent in each location performing duties, (2) the degree of business activity in each location, and (3) the relative amount of income derived from each location.[102]

Temporary vs. indefinite. Only costs incurred while temporarily traveling away from home overnight are deductible. If the assignment is temporary in nature, the individual is considered away from home, and a travel expense deduction is allowed. If the assignment is for an indefinite period of time, the location of the assignment becomes the individual's new tax home, and the taxpayer may not claim traveling expenses while there.

In determining whether an assignment is temporary or indefinite, the Code applies fixed time frames based on the expected and actual duration of the assignment or employment.[103] Employment in a single location away from home that is expected to and, in fact, does last one year or less will be considered temporary. Employment expected to last more than one year will be treated as indefinite, regardless of whether the employment exceeds one year. Employment initially expected to last one year or less which is later expected to last longer than a year will be treated as temporary until the date the expectation changes.[104]

Example 32: Leo Strauss lives in Atlanta, where he works as an employee at Sealproof, Inc. During the year, Sealproof sends Leo to the company's headquarters in Los Angeles for a temporary assignment of 10 months. After nine months in Los Angeles, the company asked Leo to stay an additional five months. The company reimburses Leo for his travel expenses. Since during the first nine months Sealproof believed that Leo's assignment would last for one year or less, the travel expenses are deductible against gross income from the business. However, once the assignment was extended by five months and it became clear that Leo's assignment no longer met the definition of "temporary," all costs incurred after that point are no longer deductible travel expenses. If Sealproof continues to pay Leo's living expenses, those amounts will be taxable as additional wages to Leo (as deductible wage expense to Sealproof).

 Reason for the Rule: Commuting expenses are not deductible. When a stay away from home is expected to last more than a year, then the trip between work and home begins to resemble a commute rather than travel while away from home.

.02 Combined Business and Personal Travel

Sometimes when business owners or their employees travel out of town for business, they stay a few extra days to sightsee or to visit with friends and family. Although the expenses incurred during these personal days are not deductible, it does not prevent the business owner from deducting the expenses that are properly allocable to business. Travel expenses of a spouse, dependent, or other person accompanying the traveler are disallowed unless the companion is also an employee of the person paying for or reimbursing the expenses, the travel serves a bona fide business purpose, and the expenses are otherwise deductible.[105]

---

[100] IRS Pub. 463, *Travel, Entertainment, Gift, and Car Expenses.*

[101] *W.R. Wallace,* CA-9, 44-2 USTC ¶ 9437, 144 F2d 407; *Burns v. Gray,* CA-6, 61-1 USTC ¶ 9294, 287 F2d 698; *R. Rosenspan,* CA-2, 71-1 USTC ¶ 9241, 438 F2d 905.

[102] *N.E. Soliman,* SCt, 93-1 USTC ¶ 50,014, 506 US 168, 113 SCt 701.

[103] Code Sec. 162(a).

[104] Rev. Rul. 93-86, 1993-2 CB 71.

[105] Code Sec. 274(m)(3).

Example 33: Susan Harris, a self-employed attorney, makes a trip to Washington, D.C. to attend a conference sponsored by the American Bar Association. The trip lasted seven days, but she spent three days sightseeing. Susan will be able to deduct the costs associated with the business portion of her trip against her business profits on her tax return.

Domestic travel. When business owners or their employees travel within the United States on business, the costs of traveling to and from the business destination are fully deductible, assuming that the purpose of the trip is primarily for business. Generally the number of days spent on business versus for personal travel is indicative of whether the trip is primarily for business or personal in nature. Days spent en route to the business destination are usually considered business days. Even if the nature of the trip is primarily for business, and thus all expenses of traveling to and from the destination are fully deductible, only the business portion of the other costs of the trip are deductible.[106]

Example 34: Continuing with Example 33, assume that Susan's costs for the trip were $415 for airfare, $150 a night for a hotel room, $95 per day for meals, and $300 for sightseeing tours. Because over half of the days Susan was gone were spent conducting business, her trip was primarily for business purposes, and therefore, she can deduct the entire costs of the airfare against business profits. She also can deduct the hotel costs for the four days that were spent conducting business as well as 50 percent of the meals for those four days. She cannot deduct the costs associated with the three days of meals and lodging or the costs of the sightseeing tours.

Example 35: Mary Bright is employed by a CPA firm located in Long Island, New York. The firm sends Mary to a five-day conference in Miami on estate planning. After the conference, Mary spends four days visiting with her sister, who lives in Miami. The cost of Mary's round trip airfare to Miami is $300. The cost of lodging is $750, and meals during the conference are $250. After the conference, while visiting her sister, Mary incurs meal and entertainment expenses of $300. Because over half of the days were spent conducting business, Mary's trip is primarily for business purposes. If the firm reimburses Mary for the business portion of her trip under an accountable plan, she will be reimbursed $1,300 ($300 total costs of domestic airfare + $750 + $250). This amount will be excluded from Mary's gross income because the company reimburses her from an accountable plan. However, the CPA firm can only deduct $1,175 since only 50 percent of the business meals and entertainment are deductible ($300 airfare + $750 lodging + ($250 × 50% for meals)).

Foreign travel. When business owners or their employees travel away from home outside of the United States for business, generally all costs, including the costs of traveling to and from the destination, must be allocated between business and personal. This rule applies to expenses of foreign travel away from home that lasts more than seven consecutive days or if the number of personal days during the trip represents at least 25 percent of the days away from home.[107] No allocation of the costs of traveling to and from the destination is required on a foreign trip if the individual had no substantial control over arranging the business trip or if the person's taking of a personal vacation was not a major consideration in making the trip.[108] However, only the business portion of all other costs (lodging, 50 percent of meals and entertainment, etc.) is deductible.

Example 36: The president and controlling stockholder of Appleview Corporation takes a 15-day European trip, spending two days flying, eight days on business, and five days sightseeing. Since the trip lasted longer than seven days and the five personal days exceeded 3.75 days (25% of the 15 days away from home), only the business portion of all expenses is deductible. Thus, under an accountable plan, Appleview can only reimburse the president for two thirds (10 business days ÷ 15 total days) of the cost

---

[106] Reg. § 1.162-2(b)(1).

[107] Code Sec. 274(c); Reg. § 1.274-4.

[108] Reg. § 1.274-4(f)(5).

of the trip. It can deduct the amounts reimbursed (minus 50 percent of meals and entertainment) on its tax return.

Example 37: Assume the same facts as in Example 36, except that later in the year the president takes a seven-day trip to Asia, spending two days flying, three days on business, and two days visiting relatives. Since the business trip outside the United States did not last longer than seven days, the entire cost of the airfare can be reimbursed (and deducted) by Appleview, along with 5/7ths of the other business-related travel costs.

.03 Attendance at Conventions

The deduction of convention expenses depends on whether attendance at the convention or other meeting benefits or advances the interests of the taxpayer's trade or business. If the convention is for political, social, or other purposes unrelated to the taxpayer's trade or business, the expenses are not deductible.[109] Furthermore, no deduction is allowed for travel or other costs incurred in connection with attending a convention, seminar, or other similar meeting relating to investments, financial planning, or other income-producing activities.[110]

Under certain circumstances, a limited business expense deduction is allowed for the cost of attending conventions, seminars, and similar meetings held on a U.S. cruise ship. However, no deduction is allowed for conventions held outside North America unless it is as reasonable for the convention to be held outside the North American area as within it.[111] A business deduction is allowed for attending conventions in certain Caribbean countries provided the country is a designated beneficiary country with which the United States maintains a bilateral or multilateral tax information exchange agreement.[112]

Example 38: Dr. Henry Stark is a self-employed doctor. Henry attends a five-day medical convention in San Juan, Puerto Rico. His wife, who is a nurse and a medical assistant for his medical practice, also attends the convention. Since the convention is held in Puerto Rico, it is considered as held in the "North American area," and accordingly, Henry's travel costs will be deductible. Because his wife works for him, her travel is for a bona fide business purpose and therefore also will be deductible.

 GAAP vs. Code: Because there are limitations on the amount that can be deducted for travel expenses, there usually is a difference between the amount reported as travel expenses for financial reporting purposes and the amount deducted on the tax return. For example, if a corporation reimbursed its employee $1,300 for deductible travel expenses but can only deduct $1,100 due to the 50-percent limitation on meals and entertainment, the $200 difference must be added to net income when reconciling it with taxable income.

.04 Substantiation

As with entertainment expenses, the taxpayer must obtain documentary evidence (like receipts or paid bills) for any lodging expense or any other expenditure of $75 or more.[113] In general, an employee who is required to account to the employer for reimbursed travel expenses connected with the employer's business is not required to furnish additional travel expense information.

Employers that have an accountable plan can use a per diem allowance for employees' away-from-home travel expenses. The **per diem** method covers three types of employer reimbursement arrangements: (1) an allowance for an employee's lodging, meals, and incidental expenses; (2) an

---

[109] Reg. § 1.162-2(d).
[110] Code Sec. 274(h)(7).
[111] Code Sec. 274(h).

[112] Code Sec. 274(h)(6); Act Sec. 212 of the Caribbean Basin Economic Recovery Act (P.L. 98-67).
[113] Code Sec. 274(d); Notice 95-50, 1995-2 CB 333.

allowance for an employee's meals and incidental expenses only (M&IE rate); or (3) an allowance for an employee's incidental expenses only. The per diem method can be used in lieu of actual receipts for employees' meals and lodging. Where the employee does not use the full per diem amount given by the employer, the excess does not have to be refunded to the employer. Any amount the employee generally spends over the per diem amount is not reimbursed by the employer, and any amount over the per diem rate that is advanced by the employer but is not accounted for by the employee or refunded to the employer must be included in the employee's wages. When travel costs are incurred by a sole proprietor in the pursuit of business, per diems for meals are allowed but the deduction for lodging must be based on the actual amount paid.

Example 39: Priscilla Thomas lives and works in San Diego, California. Her employer sends her to Little Rock, Arkansas on a three-day business trip in January 2009. Priscilla's employer reimburses her using the federal per diem rate for Little Rock, Arkansas of $142 per day ($88 lodging plus $54 M&IE).[114] Priscilla's actual expenses were $126 per day.

Because Priscilla did not spend more than the federal per diem rate, she does not have to refund the $48 excess to her employer (($142 – $126) × 3 days) and it is not included in her gross income. The employer is allowed to deduct $345 ($88 × 3 + 50% of the $54 × 3 for M&IE) as travel expenses on its tax return.

Example 40: In February 2009, Morris Dalcy, a self-employed architect, took a two-day business trip to Boston to meet with clients. The federal per diem rate for lodging is $203 and M&IE is $64. Morris's actual lodging cost was $115 per day. Morris uses the per diem rates. Because Morris is self-employed, he cannot use the per diem rate for his lodging costs. However, he can use the per diem rate for his meals and incidental expenses. Thus, Morris will be able to deduct against his business profit his actual lodging costs of $230 ($115 × 2 days) plus 50 percent of the per diem M&IE ($64 × 2 days × 50% = $64).

> **Reason for the Rule:** Each year, the IRS publishes per diem rates for various locations around the world as a way to help businesses reduce the administrative expenses associated with the substantiation requirements governing travel expenses. These rates can be found in IRS Publication 1542.

¶ 607 Transportation Expenses

Local transportation costs that are deductible as business expenses are the actual costs of transportation while the taxpayer or the taxpayer's employees are not away from the tax home. As such, these expenses include the costs of traveling from one work location or assignment to another during a day in the general geographical area where the taxpayer usually works. Costs of commuting between the individual's tax home and the place of employment are not deductible. When transportation costs are paid or incurred by sole proprietors, these costs can be used to offset their business profits, and therefore not only reduce their income taxes, but also their self-employment taxes.

Local transportation costs do not include meals and lodging. They do include transportation costs, whether the transportation is furnished by the employer, employee, or by others. Business transportation expenses include taxi fares, car rental, and other payments for transportation reimbursed to employees, as well as reimbursements to employees for expenses incurred in conjunction with the use of their cars for business purposes.

---

[114] IRS Publication 1542 (Rev. October 2008).

.01 Automobile Expenses

Expenses paid or incurred for automobiles used for business, such as gasoline, oil, tires, repairs, insurance, depreciation, parking fees and tolls, licenses, interest on a car loan, and garage rent are deductible against business profits. Expenses incurred by employees who are not reimbursed or who are reimbursed under a nonaccountable plan can be deducted only as itemized deductions, subject to the two-percent AGI floor. Furthermore, employees who are not reimbursed for their automobile expenses cannot deduct the business portion of any interest from their car loans.

Self-employed individuals and employees can compute their deductible expenses for operating an automobile for business purposes using one of two methods: by using the standard mileage rate or by using the actual expense method. When an employee is reimbursed for transportation expenses under an accountable plan (see ¶ 601.03), the employer deducts the amounts reimbursed as transportation expense.

Actual expense method. Taxpayers can deduct the business portion of actual expenses paid or incurred in operating an automobile. Actual expenses include such items as gas and oil, insurance, interest on car loans, repairs, licenses, tires, and depreciation. Generally, the deduction for actual expenses is based on a percentage that is computed by dividing the business miles driven in a tax year by the total miles driven in the tax year. The use of the actual expense method is required for automobiles owned by a corporation.

Example 41: Sharon Schmitt, a self-employed doctor, incurs the following automobile expenses during 2009.

Gas and oil changes	$2,755
Parking (100% for business)	100
Auto insurance	1,200
License renewal fees	80
Automobile repairs	750
Depreciation	3,000
Total costs	$7,885

Sharon drove her car a total of 21,150 miles during the year. Her business miles totaled 14,805. Since Sharon used her automobile 70 percent (14,805 ÷ 21,150) for business during the year, using the actual expense method, she can deduct $5,550 as automobile expenses against her business profits. The $100 of parking is entirely business-related and therefore not allocated with the other automobile expenses.

Gas and oil changes	$2,755
Auto insurance	1,200
License renewal fee	80
Automobile repairs	750
Depreciation	3,000
Total automobile expenses	$7,785
Business percentage	× 70%
	$5,450
Plus: Business parking	100
Deductible automobile expenses	$5,550

Standard mileage rate. Employers can deduct amounts they reimburse to employees for the business use of their vehicles up to the amount computed using the standard mileage rates. The standard mileage rate for business use of an automobile for 2009 is 55 cents a mile.[115] Sole proprietors can use the standard mileage rate to reimburse their employees. They also can deduct amounts as transportation expenses for the business use of their own automobiles.

Example 42: Mary Smith works for a consulting company and is reimbursed for her transportation costs based on business miles she accumulates meeting with clients and potential clients. Mary substantiates her business miles to her employer who reimburses her at the standard mileage rate. During 2009, Mary drove her automobile 20,000 business miles and is reimbursed $11,000 (20,000 × $.55) by her employer under an accountable plan. The $11,000 is not taxed to Mary and is deductible by her employer as transportation expense.

Example 43: Assume the same facts as in Example 42, except that the reimbursement is made from a nonaccountable plan. The $11,000 is included in Mary's taxable wages and deducted as a wage expense by her employer. Furthermore, this amount is subject to withholding and the employer is responsible for FICA and unemployment taxes on this amount. Mary will be able to deduct the $11,000 as a miscellaneous itemized deduction subject to the two-percent AGI floor.

The standard mileage rate replaces all actual operating and fixed expenses and depreciation in determining the deductible business costs of operating a passenger car, including vans and pickup trucks. However, parking and tolls and interest on loans attributable to business use of the vehicle are deductible in addition to the standard mileage deduction. Employees may not claim an interest deduction on car loans if they are not reimbursed for their transportation expense.[116]

The standard mileage rate deduction does away with the requirement that the taxpayer keep detailed records of expenditures associated with operating the automobile. This method may not be used to compute deductible costs of vehicles used for hire, such as taxicabs or limousines, nor can it be used if the taxpayer uses five or more automobiles simultaneously for business. However, the standard mileage method may be used by an employee irrespective of whether the employer reimburses the employee's business automobile expenses.[117]

Use of the standard mileage rate is restricted to individual taxpayers; therefore, corporations must use the actual expense method to compute their deductions for automobile expenses. However, if a corporation reimburses its employees for business use of their employees' own automobiles, the amounts reimbursed are deductible by the corporations, provided that they do not exceed the standard mileage rate in effect at the time. Some corporate employers opt to reimburse their employees for costs of operating their cars so that the standard mileage rate can be used.

 Reason for the Rule: Like per diems for travel expenses, the standard mileage method eliminates much of the paperwork and substantiation required under the actual method. The mileage rates vary and are published as a Revenue Procedure by the IRS in the Cumulative Bulletin.

¶ 608 Education

Employers can deduct amounts they pay for educating their employees, provided that the education maintains or improves the employee's skills required in the employer's trade or business or allows the employee to meet the employer's educational requirements or legal requirements which are imposed as a condition for retention of employment relationship, status, or rate of pay.

---

[115] Rev. Proc. 2008-72, IRB 2008-50, 1286, November 24, 2008.   [117] Rev. Proc. 98-63, 1998-2 CB 818.

[116] Code Sec. 163(h)(2)(A).

However, if the education allows the employee to meet the minimum education requirements for the position or allows the employee to enter into a new trade or business, the education costs are never deductible.[118]

Deductible educational expenses include tuition, books, supplies, lab fees, certain transportation and travel costs, and other educational expenses, such as costs of researching and typing a paper for a class. If the employer reimburses its employee for educational expense that qualifies for deduction, the tax treatment of the reimbursement depends upon whether the employer's reimbursement arrangement is an accountable plan or nonaccountable plan. Where the reimbursement is from an accountable plan, the educational reimbursement will not be included in the employee's income. Where the reimbursement is from a nonaccountable plan, the amount of the reimbursement is included in the employee's income and is subject to employment taxes.

Example 44: Lauren Smith has completed two years of a three-year course leading to a law degree. Lauren is hired by a law firm as a full-time paralegal. As a condition to continued employment, Lauren is required to obtain a law degree and pass the state bar examination. She completes her law school education by attending night school and takes a bar review course in order to prepare her for the state bar examination. The law courses and the bar review course constitute education that meet the minimum educational requirements in her intended business. Therefore, if these costs are reimbursed by her employer, these amounts will not be deductible as education expenses by her employer.

However, if these amounts were paid from the employer's established, written educational assistance program, Lauren would be able to exclude up to $5,250 of the benefits paid by her employer each year. The law firm would then deduct these amounts as an employee benefit. Otherwise the amounts paid would be taxable wages to Lauren and deducted as wage expense by the law firm (see ¶ 602.04).

¶ 609 Summary

In addition to the various ordinary and necessary business expenses that were discussed in Chapter 6, businesses can also deduct a number of employment-related expenditures they incur during the year. An understanding of the various tax laws surrounding the deductibility of employment-related expenses is essential in order to help businesses reduce the amount of income and payroll taxes they must pay each year.

GLOSSARY OF TERMS INTRODUCED IN THE CHAPTER

Accountable plan. Requires that employees submit adequate documentation or receipts for any reimbursed expenses and that any advances in excess of substantiated expenses be returned to the employer.

Closely-held corporations. Corporations whose stock is held by a small number of shareholders, typically from the same family or a related group of individuals.

Defined benefit plan. A type of retirement plan that promises participants specified benefits during retirement years and continuing until the death of the participant, and often until the death of the spouse of the participant.

Defined contribution plan. A type of retirement plan where the amounts are contributed to an employee's own account, and the amount available upon retirement depends on the performance of the investments in the account.

---

[118] Reg. § 1.162-5.

Federal Insurance Contributions Act (FICA). A program enacted under the Federal Social Security Act that established a federal unemployment insurance program (Medicare) and a program to provide old-age, survivors, and disability benefits to employees (social security). Contributions to this plan are shared by employers and employees through FICA withholding and self-employment taxes.

Federal Unemployment Tax Act (FUTA). FUTA was enacted by Congress to finance the federal unemployment program. Contributions to this plan are funded entirely by employers.

Flexible spending account (FSA). This type of account is offered to employees to cover their dependent care costs and/or medical costs. Employees can set aside each year pre-tax wages from which they can pay qualified health costs (in the case of Medical FSAs) or up to $5,000 qualified child care costs (in the case of Dependent Care FSAs).

Medicare taxes. The hospital insurance (HI) portion of the FICA tax.

Nonaccountable plan. Reimbursements paid through a system that does not meet the requirements for an accountable plan.

Per diem. Established amounts allowed by the IRS to be deducted in lieu of substantiation for an employee's lodging, meals, and incidental expenses or a sole proprietor's for meals and entertainment expenses.

Perquisites. Fringe benefits that represent privileges that businesses make available to their employees.

Publicly-held corporations. Corporations whose stock is traded on one of the U.S. stock exchanges, such as the American Stock Exchange, New York Stock Exchange, or NASDAQ.

Social security taxes. The old-age, survivors, and disability insurance (OASDI) portion of the FICA tax.

Tax deferred. When income or gain is postponed to some future point in time but is eventually taxed.

CHAPTER PROBLEMS

The following questions and problems relate to the discussion in Chapter 6, Business Deductions: Employment-Related Expenses, which begins at ¶ 600 in *Part II: Federal Taxation of Business Income and Deductions*.

Chapter 6 Discussion Questions

1. Edgar Berger is the VP of Marketing for Sandsun Corporation. Edgar is the fifth highest paid officer of Sandsun, other than its CEO. In 2009, Edgar's salary was $1.2 million dollars. How much can Sandsun Corporation deduct on its 2009 income tax return for Edgar's salary?

2. Cynthia Moss is an employee and sole shareholder of GO Corporation. Cynthia uses the cash method; GO Corporation uses the accrual method of accounting. Both Cynthia and GO use a calendar year end. In July 2009, Cynthia has the corporation declare a $30,000 bonus to her, which will be paid to her in February 2010. GO accrued the bonus on its books in 2009. In what tax year can GO deduct the bonus paid to Cynthia?

3. Herbert Cohn, who works for the RT Manufacturing Company, received a $1,200 reimbursement from RT for a business trip he took on behalf of the company. Herbert attached the receipts to his expense report to substantiate the expenses he incurred on his business trip. What is the tax treatment to RT and to Herbert if the company has an accountable

plan? What would be the tax treatment to RT and Herbert if the company has a nonaccountable plan?

4. What is the maximum amount that employees can elect to contribute to a flexible spending account (FSA)? What is the benefit to an employee in contributing to an FSA?

5. Under an employer-provided educational assistance plan, an employee receives reimbursement for tuition for an undergraduate course. The course is not related to the employee's job. Must the employee include the employer's tuition reimbursement in gross income? Can the employer deduct the amounts it reimburses its employees?

6. In 2009, the LB Advertising Company established a qualified adoption assistance program for its employees. What is the maximum amount an employee of the LB Advertising Company can exclude from his or her gross income for amounts paid or expenses incurred by LB for its employees' qualified adoption expenses? What costs are included as qualified adoption expenses? Are there any income limits the employee must meet to exclude the amount from his or her income? How does LB treat these amounts paid on its tax return?

7. What is the mileage test for purposes of being able to deduct moving expenses paid on behalf of an employee?

8. Ike entertains one of his employer's customers by taking him to a cocktail party at the yacht club and afterwards to the opera. No business discussions took place during the party or at the opera. However, earlier in the day, Ike and his customer had discussed business for several hours. Ike's employer fully reimbursed him under an accountable plan. Can Ike's employer deduct as an entertainment expense the cost of entertaining the customer?

9. DFG Company adopted a Roth 401(k) plan for its employees. The plan is not discriminatory. DFG's CEO, who is 55 years old, wants to participate in the Roth 401(k) plan. The CEO earns an annual salary of $350,000. What is the maximum contribution the CEO can make to the company's Roth 401(k) for 2009? How much can DFG make and deduct for contributions to its employees' Roth 401(k) plans?

10. A president and controlling shareholder of a corporation takes a seven-day trip to Europe. The corporation reimburses the president for his deductible travel expenses. The president spends half of the time during the trip on business and half for vacation. What amounts represent deductible travel expenses by the corporation?

11. Can independent contractors participate in an employer's cafeteria plan?

12. Paul Goddard is an accountant who works for a growing manufacturing company in Dallas, Texas, where he resides. Paul's company purchases another manufacturing plant in La Porte, Indiana, and the company sends Paul to the La Porte plant on a temporary nine-month assignment to update its accounting system. After seven months in La Porte, the company asks Paul to stay an additional four months. Paul works the additional four months and then returns home to Dallas. During his stay in LaPorte, the company reimburses Paul for his travel expenses for each of the 11 months. Can Paul's employer deduct the 11 months of travel expenses?

13. Sarah Croft, age 46, has been employed by Kybar Corporation for a number of years. Kybar has never offered any type of pension or retirement plan to its employees. Concerned with planning for her retirement, Sarah recently heard of a SIMPLE IRA that allows employees to contribute $11,500 to an IRA for 2009. She has asked your advice how she should go about opening a SIMPLE IRA. How would you advise Sarah?

14. Bruce Zen, age 55, is employed by Lee Corporation at a salary of $250,000. His employer allows him to contribute 10 percent of his salary to a 401(k) plan. For 2009, what is the maximum contribution that Bruce may make to his 401(k) plan?

15. Which of the following are characteristics of a SIMPLE plan?

    a. The maximum annual contribution that an employee may make is $4,000.

    b. The plan may be structured as an IRA or 401(k) arrangement.

c. The plan must follow strict nondiscrimination rules.

d. Self-employed individuals may participate.

16. The 10-percent penalty on early distributions from a Roth 401(k) will apply to which of the following distributions from a qualified retirement plan during 2009?

   a. A distribution to a former employee who is age 61.

   b. A distribution used to pay for qualified first time homebuyer expenses.

   c. A distribution to a disabled employee.

   d. A distribution made because of the death of the employee.

17. The FICA tax is made up of two component taxes. Discuss each tax.

18. Compare and contrast FICA and FUTA taxes as to their imposition and rate requirements.

19. What is the FUTA tax rate and its wage base limit for 2009?

20. Thomas Andrews, age 48, is employed as a designer by the Harlan and Wolff Corporation. The corporation permits its employees to contribute a maximum of 10 percent of their wages to a 401(k) plan. Depending on its profits for the year, the corporation has the option of making additional contributions to each employee's 401(k) plan account. During 2009, Andrews will earn a salary of $100,000, and he will contribute $10,000 to his 401(k) plan account. In December 2009, the corporation informs its employees that it will make an extra contribution to each employee's 401(k) plan account by the end of the year. Andrews is informed that the extra contribution to his 401(k) for 2009 will be $7,500. Late in 2009, while meeting with his accountant to discuss some year-end tax planning possibilities, the accountant mentions that because the maximum tax deferred contribution that can be made to a 401(k) plan for 2009, by an employee under age 50, is $16,500, Andrews will be required to include the excess contribution of $1,000 ($17,500 total amount contributed to his 401(k) minus $16,500 maximum contribution allowable) in his gross income for 2009. Is the accountant correct? How will the company treat its $7,500 contribution to Thomas's plan on its tax return?

Chapter 6 Problems

1. In 2009, Katy Jones received qualified parking valued at $260 per month from her employer for the year.

   a. Is any portion of the parking Katy received includable in her income for 2009?

   b. How does Katy's employer treat the amounts paid to Katy?

2. In 2009 under its adoption assistance program, RAY Corporation pays $15,000 of qualified adoption expenses on behalf of its employee Hugh Grand in connection with Hugh's effort to adopt an eligible child. The $15,000 included qualified adoption expenses from an adoption agency for a successful adoption of a baby. Hugh's modified AGI in 2009 is $100,000.

   a. What is the total amount that will be included in Hugh's income (if any) for qualified adoption expenses?

   b. How is the $15,000 treated by RAY?

3. Y Company paid $12,000 to rent a 15-seat skybox at Chicago's U.S Cellular Field for two baseball games. The cost of the highest-priced, nonluxury box seats is $20 a seat. How much can Y deduct for the cost of the luxury skybox?

4. To celebrate closing a profitable contract, Lester Briggs took his client and his client's wife out for dinner at an expensive French restaurant immediately after the contract had been signed. The bill for the meal was $550. Of the amount spent, $150 of the bill is considered lavish and extravagant. Lester's employer reimbursed him the amount he had spent under its accountable plan. How much can Lester's employer deduct for meals and entertainment expense?

5. In 2009, Sam Wilson took several graduate-level courses in business from a local university. The courses do not relate to the work Sam does. Sam's employer has an educational assistance program. The cost of the tuition, books, and fees, which were reimbursed by Sam's employer, totaled $8,000.

   a. How much is Sam's employer allowed to exclude from Sam's income?

   b. How much can the employer deduct?

6. A corporation, of which John Stevens is the sole owner, employs John's wife as secretary and treasurer at a salary of $28,000 per year. She performs certain work regularly, but efficient and bonded help for the same work can easily be obtained for $18,000 per year. How much may the corporation deduct regarding her salary, in arriving at its taxable income?

7. David Parks is president and the sole shareholder of the DP Retail Company. DP owns a yacht which David uses during the tax year for both personal and business purposes. The operating expenses of the yacht, including depreciation, totaled $16,200 during the tax year. David used the yacht 55 percent for business (35 percent for directly related entertainment and 20 percent for associated entertainment). In addition to these expenses, David incurred the following expenses in connection with entertaining customers on the yacht which were 100 percent reimbursed by DP:

   • $3,500 for food and beverages in entertainment that was directly related to the active conduct of DP's business.

   • $4,600 for food and beverages in entertainment that was associated with the active conduct of DP's business.

   • $2,000 for personal and family consumption of food and beverages.

   What is the amount of expenses that can be deducted by the DP Retail Company?

8. Peter Smalts is employed by Major Foods and works at the company's Los Angeles location. In 2009 Peter is transferred by his employer to Omaha, Nebraska. Major Foods pays $5,000 for Peter's moving, which includes $3,600 to professional movers; $1,000 to fly Peter and his family to Omaha; and $400 to cover temporary living expenses until their furnishings arrive. How is the $5,000 reimbursement under the company's accountable plan treated by Peter and Major Foods?

9. Humphrey Long, an employee of XYZ Company, uses his car for business. He drove his car a total of 30,000 miles in 2009, 25,000 of which were for business. Humphrey's employer has an accountable plan and reimburses its employees based upon the standard mileage rate. Humphrey submitted his business miles to his employer. How much was Humphrey reimbursed by his employer for 2009, and how is this amount handled on XYZ's tax return?

10. Jane Croft, an employee, uses her car 100 percent for business reasons. During 2009 she paid $2,000 in interest on her business car loan. May she deduct any of the interest expense? How would your answer change if Jane were self-employed?

11. Mr. Sands, an account executive at an advertising agency in San Francisco, incurs the following expenses in Los Angeles with respect to a client:

   • $200 for airfare to and from Los Angeles,

   • $250 for one overnight stay in a hotel in Los Angeles,

   • $600 for dinner for himself and five persons during which business was discussed, and

   • $600 for six tickets to a sports event directly following the dinner. The face value of the tickets is $270.

   Mr. Sands is reimbursed $1,650 by his company under a plan that requires an employee to substantiate the expenses and to return amounts in excess of the substantiated expenses. Will any portion of these expenditures be deductible on Mr. Sands's income tax return? Will any portion of these expenditures be deductible on the employer's tax return?

12. A.B. Call is employed as sales manager by the C-D Manufacturing Company. He incurs the following expenses for days away from home on business during 2010

  - $1,000 for meals,
  - $2,000 for lodging,
  - $1,000 for airfare, and
  - $3,000 for entertainment.

  A.B. was reimbursed by his company to cover his business expenses under an accountable plan. What amounts may be deducted by A.B. or C-D Manufacturing?

13. Alfredo, who operates a small manufacturing company, spent $1,500 for entertainment in a hospitality room at a business convention where he displayed and discussed his products. He also entertained his customers by taking them to a cocktail party at a country club and afterwards to the theater. No business discussions took place during the party or at the theater. However, they had spent several hours earlier discussing new product lines. The cost of entertaining the customers at the country club and theatre totaled $15,000. Alfredo's company has an accountable plan and reimbursed him for the amounts incurred. How much can the company deduct for entertainment expenses?

14. A corporation is on a calendar-year basis and uses the accrual method of accounting. The Board of Directors meets on December 4, 2010 and determines that the corporate officers, who are not related parties to the corporation, will be paid a bonus equal to one percent of profits. In February 2011, the profits are determined and the officers are paid. When can the corporation deduct the bonus?

15. Julie is employed as a waitress at two restaurants. In July, she received $18 in tips from one restaurant and $82 from the other. What amount of tips for the month of July must be reported and is subject to FICA withholding?

16. Michael's Mirror & Glass has three employees. The employees were paid $5,000, $6,000, and $10,000, respectively in 2009. What is the amount of wages subject to FUTA?

17. Bob made $120,000 while working at Williamston, Inc. during 2009. Compute the amount Williamston will pay (and deduct) for FICA taxes on Bob's wages.

18. For the calendar year 2009, a company paid its eight employees a total of $118,000. All of the employees earned over $7,000 a year. The company's wage base for state unemployment insurance purposes amounts to $64,000, which is subject to a six-percent state unemployment rate. Compute the FUTA tax that is payable.

19. In 2009, Joseph Sears earned $50,000 while working at JL Putz, Inc. Compute JL's FICA taxes on Joseph's wages.

20. Thomas Rigney has contributed six percent of his salary to his employer's 401(k) plan for a number of years. His total elective contributions in the plan now total $80,000. Rigney incurred $20,000 of medical expenses in the current year. Rigney wants to withdraw $20,000 from his 401(k) plan to pay his medical expenses. Based upon these facts, has Rigney satisfied the tests for a hardship withdrawal from the 401(k) plan?

21. Sam Stone is an employee and the sole shareholder of PPD Company. PPD paid Sam $950,000 as salary for its 2009 tax year. PPD did not pay any dividends for the year. A reasonable salary for Sam's job is $500,000. If the IRS selects PPD's tax return for audit, what may be their determination of Sam's salary of $950,000?

22. Tom Hughes, a corporate executive at MYH Co., went to China to investigate MYH's expansion into China. Tom's trip to China, which he scheduled, lasted 20 days. Two days were spent flying to and from China; ten days were spent attending meetings; and eight days were spent sightseeing. Tom's expenses were $1,500 airfare, $250 per day for lodging, $100 per day for meals. Tom also spent $300 on sightseeing tours. MYH reimbursed Tom for his expenses, except for the sightseeing tours, under its accountable plan. How much can MYH deduct for Tom's trip?

23. In 2009, Sam Jones, who is 16, worked part-time as an employee in his father's dry-cleaning business. Sam's gross salary was $8,000. In 2009, how much FICA and federal unemployment taxes should be paid regarding Sam's salary?

24. SQL Trucking Co. employs eight interstate truck drivers who are out on the road a continuous five days a week, 40 weeks per year. In 2009, SQL reimburses its trucker drivers $52 per day (federal per diem rate) for meals while away from home. How much can SQL deduct on its 2009 tax return of the truck driver's meals?

25. Payout Co. hired Sally Smith as an employee in its payroll department. Employees that work in the payroll department must have at least two semesters of college accounting to work in the department. When Sally was hired she did not have two semesters of college accounting. Sally spent a total of $1,200 for tuition and books for two accounting classes. This amount was reimbursed by Payout under its accountable plan. How much can Payout deduct of Sally's educational expenses? Would your answer be different if Payout had an educational assistance program?

Chapter 6 Review Problems

1. Tim Davis is president of a small manufacturing company. During the year, Tim incurred the following entertainment expenses that were reimbursed by the company:

   - $200 for dues to a social club. Tim took his customers to the social club for business conferences and did not use it in any other way.

   - $1,200 for the cost of the meals provided Tim's customers at the club in which business was discussed.

   - $200 for Tim's meals with customers.

   - $400 for gifts Tim gave to four customers costing $100 each.

   - $500 for watches (costing $100 each) given to five foremen in Tim's manufacturing plant as part of a plant safety achievement (non-qualified plan) award.

   What amount of the reimbursed expenses is deductible by the company?

2. On the draft of the tax return for XYZ Corporation, taxable income for the calendar year was $29,182. An examination developed the following questionable items:

   a. Salary paid to the sole shareholder was $800,000. A reasonable salary would be $250,000.

   b. 100-percent deduction taken on $25,500 of business meal expenses (which is subject to the 50-percent limitation).

   c. $2,500 deduction taken on country club dues.

   d. Mortgage interest of $12,500 paid on a hunting lodge used exclusively by the sole shareholder.

   What is the correct amount of taxable income that should be reported for XYZ Corporation?

Chapter 6 Research Question

Mr. Jones is the president of a corporation that is owned by him and members of his family. During a tax year under audit, Mr. Jones was paid a salary of $48,000 by the corporation. The corporation also contributed $12,000 to a pension plan on Mr. Jones's behalf in that year. A dispute has arisen over the compensation paid to Mr. Jones in that tax year. The IRS agent claims that both the salary paid to Mr. Jones and pension plan contribution made on his behalf must be taken into account in determining whether the total compensation is reasonable in amount. The agent is about to disallow a portion of the deduction for the compensation.

You have been requested by the corporation to determine whether the pension plan contributions must be taken into account in determining whether the compensation is reasonable. Give your opinion. In it show authorities, citing laws, regulations, interpretations and decisions applicable, and the *CCH Standard Federal Tax Reporter* paragraphs where they may be found.

CHAPTER 7

Depreciation, Depletion, and Amortization

LEARNING OBJECTIVES

1. Explain the cost recovery rules for depreciating real and tangible personal property and the differences between those rules and the financial accounting depreciation rules.

2. Describe how Code Sec. 179 immediate expensing can be used to write off the costs of tangible personal property and the rules regarding the Code Sec. 179 election.

3. Distinguish between the two methods for expensing the costs associated with the cost of acquiring a productive natural resource.

4. Illustrate how intangible assets are amortized for tax purposes and describe how the rules differ from those used in financial reporting.

¶ 700 Introduction

As discussed in Chapter 5, the costs of prepaid assets must be spread over the tax years in which they are utilized, regardless of whether the taxpayer uses the cash or accrual method of accounting. This rule extends to the cost of business or income-producing property that provides benefits beyond the current year. "Depreciation" is the annual deduction taken to recover the capitalized costs of tangible personal and real property (other than land). "Amortization" is the process used to recover the cost of intangible assets over time. "Depletion" is the method by which the cost of natural resources, so-called wasting assets, is recovered.

The concepts of depreciation, depletion, and amortization are similar to those used in financial accounting. However, the financial accounting and tax accounting rules are written by different governing bodies, each having its own agenda. In financial accounting, the cost recovery rules follow the matching concept, i.e., are intended to match the expensing of assets to the accounting periods in which the assets help generate revenues. Congress, on the other hand, is not as concerned with the proper matching of revenues and expenses, but instead often chooses to use the cost recovery rules to influence capital investment and economic growth.

The focus of this chapter is to introduce the methods taxpayers can use to depreciate business property and property used in the production of income. Unless otherwise indicated, the rules discussed in this chapter apply to all businesses, regardless of whether they are operated in corporation, partnership, or sole proprietorship form. This chapter also discusses the amortization rules that apply to the costs of acquiring intangible assets as well as the depletion rules that govern the expensing of the costs associated with the acquisition of productive natural resources.

In many instances, the tax laws provide some flexibility in selecting how quickly taxpayers can expense the costs associated with productive assets. Proper tax planning requires a general understanding of the various alternatives available because every dollar expensed on the tax return generates cash flows in the form of reduced tax liability. All other things being equal, the ability to accelerate the timing of these cash flows can benefit the company because the amounts can be invested or used to pay business expenses. However, before deciding whether to select a cost recovery method that accelerates deductions into earlier tax years, it is important to keep in mind that a taxpayer's marginal tax rate often varies from year to year.

DEPRECIATION

¶ 701 The Concept of Depreciation

Because capital expenditures benefit a business for a number of years, it is appropriate that their costs be spread out (deducted) to offset business income generated in the years of the asset's productivity. The same concept applies when a business acquires an asset with a useful life that extends beyond the current year. In financial accounting, depreciation involves matching the costs associated with the acquisition of a productive asset over the years in which the asset helps generate revenues for the business. If a business were to expense the entire cost in the year the asset was acquired, net income in the year the asset was purchased would be understated, and net income in all subsequent years the asset was used would be overstated. Thus, in order to accurately determine the net income of a business on a year-to-year basis, the cost needs to be allocated (depreciated) over the number of years that the asset is used in the business. Depreciation represents the periodic expensing of a productive tangible asset whose useful life extends over more than one year.

The tax laws regarding depreciation, on the other hand, are intended solely to write off the cost of tangible property in a systematic manner that is not necessarily intended to correspond to the expected usefulness of the asset in the taxpayer's business. As with all expenses deducted in arriving at taxable income, the amount a taxpayer deducts for depreciation expense produces tax savings equal to the amount of the deduction times the taxpayer's marginal tax rate. Since depreciation expense helps a taxpayer recuperate some of the initial costs associated with the acquisition of the asset, the quicker the asset is depreciated, the faster the taxpayer realizes the tax savings. Thus, the taxpayer can either invest the extra cash or use it to pay expenses. The depreciation rules have often been used by Congress as a mechanism to stimulate economic growth by temporarily accelerating the rate at which productive, long-lived assets can be expensed.

In 1981, Congress enacted the Accelerated Cost Recovery System (ACRS) as a means of recovering capital costs using accelerated methods over predetermined recovery periods that were much shorter than the properties' useful lives. Under ACRS, automobiles were depreciated over three tax years. Buildings were initially depreciated over 15 years (later extended to 18 and then 19 years). One of the principal reasons for enacting ACRS was to provide faster tax savings to businesses in an attempt to stimulate capital formation and the growth of the economy.[1] By allowing these assets to be written off over shorter periods, the tax savings from the depreciation deduction would be realized earlier, thereby accelerating cash flows into the earlier years of the assets' useful lives. In 1986, Congress enacted the Modified Accelerated Cost Recovery System (MACRS), which slowed down the pace at which assets were expensed, but still allowed cost recovery periods much shorter than the assets' actual useful lives. MACRS is the depreciation system in effect today.

---

[1] Staff of the Joint Committee on Taxation, 97th Cong., General Explanation of the Economic Recovery Tax Act of 1981, pages 75–76 (Comm. Print 1981).

.01 Financial Accounting Depreciation Rules

In financial accounting, the depreciable cost of the asset is written off over the accounting periods in which the company expects to use the asset in its operations (known as the asset's "estimated useful life"). The **depreciable cost** equals the costs associated with the acquisition of the asset minus the estimated salvage value. **Salvage value** of a depreciable asset is the amount the company estimates the asset's sales, trade-in, or scrap value will be at the end of its useful life. The difference between the amount the company pays for the asset and the amount it expects to receive when it sells it in the future is the company's out-of-pocket costs with respect to its investment in the asset. It is this amount that the financial depreciation rules attempt to allocate to expense over the asset's useful life.

Typically, the amount estimated for the salvage value of an asset is inversely related to the estimated useful life of that asset: The shorter the estimated useful life, the more the asset should be worth at the end of its useful life. For example, a new automobile costing $20,000 with an estimated useful life of three years may have a $12,000 salvage value, whereas that same automobile with a useful life of eight years may have a salvage value closer to $3,000. As depreciation expense is deducted each year in arriving at net income, the book value of the asset reported on the balance sheet decreases accordingly. **Book value** is the asset's cost plus any improvements made to the asset minus the accumulated depreciation taken on the asset over the years. Book value is deducted from the net sales price to determine the gain or loss reported on the income statement when the company eventually disposes of the asset.

The financial accounting rules allow for several acceptable methods of allocating the depreciable cost of a productive asset over its estimated useful life. Four common methods are the:

1. Straight-line method (the method that achieves the slowest write-off of costs);
2. Declining-balance method (an accelerated method that achieves a fast write-off of costs);
3. Sum-of-the-years' digits method (also an accelerated method); and
4. Units-of-production method (a method that relates depreciation to the usage of the asset). The calculation of depreciation expense for each method is discussed below.

Straight-line method. As the name suggests, the straight-line (SL) method allows for an even amount of depreciation expense each year. Under the straight-line method, annual depreciation equals the depreciable cost of an asset divided by the asset's estimated useful life.

Example 1: An asset costing $12,000 has an estimated useful life of five years and a salvage value of $2,000. The depreciable cost equals $10,000 ($12,000 – $2,000 salvage value), and under the SL method, this amount is expensed evenly over the asset's five-year useful life ($10,000 ÷ 5 = $2,000 annual depreciation). At the end of five years, a total of $10,000 of accumulated depreciation will have been taken on the asset, thereby reducing its book value to $2,000 ($12,000 – $10,000).

Year	Beginning Book Value	Depreciation Expense	Ending Book Value
1	$12,000	$ 2,000	$10,000
2	10,000	2,000	8,000
3	8,000	2,000	6,000
4	6,000	2,000	4,000
5	4,000	2,000	2,000
Accumulated Depreciation		$10,000	

Declining-balance method. The "declining-balance method" expenses a portion of the asset's book value each year. The amount expensed under this method is the asset's book value at the beginning of the year times a multiple of the straight-line rate. For example, under the "double declining balance (DDB) method," annual depreciation equals the asset's book value at the beginning of the year times twice (double) the straight-line rate. Under the "150-percent declining balance method," annual depreciation equals the book value at the beginning of the year times 150 percent of the straight-line rate. Since the beginning book value is used in computing the amount of annual depreciation expense, it is important that the amount of depreciation deducted for the year never cause the asset's book value to fall below its salvage value.

Example 2: Assume the same facts as in Example 1, except that the asset is depreciated using the DDB method. At the beginning of the first year, the book value of the asset equals $12,000 because there is no accumulated depreciation. Twice (double) the straight-line rate for an asset with a five-year life is 40 percent (1/5 × 2). Therefore, depreciation for the first year equals $4,800 ($12,000 × 40%). Book value of the asset at the beginning of year 2 equals $7,200 ($12,000 – $4,800).

Depreciation expense for the second year equals $2,880 ($7,200 × 40%), which further reduces the book value of the asset to $4,320 ($7,200 – $2,880). In the third year, depreciation expense equals $1,728 ($4,320 × 40%), and book value is reduced to $2,592 ($4,320 – $1,728). In the fourth year, the amount of depreciation expense is limited to $592 because depreciation equal to 40 percent of book value ($2,592 × 40% = $1,037) would cause the book value of the asset to fall below its estimated salvage value.

Year	Beginning Book Value	Depreciation Expense	Ending Book Value
1	$12,000	$ 4,800	$7,200
2	7,200	2,880	4,320
3	4,320	1,728	2,592
4	2,592	592	2,000
5	2,000	0	2,000
Accumulated Depreciation		$10,000	

As with the straight-line method, total depreciation expense over the asset's five-year assigned life using the DDB method equals $10,000. However, the amount deducted each year differs between these two methods. The declining-balance method is known as an "accelerated depreciation method" because depreciation expense is highest in the earliest years of the asset's useful life, while in the later years, depreciation expense decelerates. This can be seen by comparing the annual depreciation expenses in Examples 1 and 2.

Example 3: Assume the same facts as in Example 2, except the asset is depreciated using the 150-percent declining balance method. Since 150 percent of the straight-line rate for a five-year property life equals 30 percent (1/5 × 150%), first-year depreciation equals $3,600 ($12,000 × 30%) and book value is reduced to $8,400 ($12,000 – $3,600).

Depreciation for the second year would then equal $2,520 ($8,400 × 30%), which reduces the asset's book value. This process continues for years 3 to 5, while ensuring that the amount of depreciation expense does not cause book value to fall below the $2,000 salvage value.

Year	Beginning Book Value	Depreciation Expense	Ending Book Value
1	$12,000	$ 3,600	$8,400
2	8,400	2,520	5,880
3	5,880	1,764	4,116

Year	Beginning Book Value	Depreciation Expense	Ending Book Value
4	4,116	1,235	2,881
5	2,881	881	2,000
Accumulated Depreciation		$10,000	

Sum-of-the-years' digits method. Under the "sum-of-years' digits depreciation method," each year the depreciable cost is multiplied by a fraction. The numerator of the fraction is the number of years of the asset's useful life left at the beginning of the year; the denominator is the sum of the years in the asset's estimated useful life. For example, the denominator for an asset with a five-year estimated useful life would be 15 (5 + 4 + 3 + 2 + 1). For the first full year, the depreciable cost of the asset would be multiplied by 5/15 because there are 5 years of useful life remaining at the beginning of the first year.

Example 4: Assume the same facts as in Example 1, except that the asset is depreciated using the sum-of-the-years' digits method. In the first year, depreciation expense equals $3,333 ($10,000 × 5/15). In the second year, the depreciable cost would be multiplied by 4/15 to yield depreciation expense of $2,667 ($10,000 × 4/15). In the third year, the $10,000 would be multiplied by 3/15, etc.

Year	Beginning Book Value	Depreciation Expense	Ending Book Value
1	$12,000	$ 3,333	$8,667
2	8,667	2,667	6,000
3	6,000	2,000	4,000
4	4,000	1,333	2,667
5	2,667	667	2,000
Accumulated Depreciation		$10,000	

Units-of-production method. The "units-of-production depreciation method" attempts to expense the depreciable cost of an asset based on the usage of the asset. Each year the portion of the depreciable cost is multiplied by a fraction. The numerator of the fraction is the units produced during the year; the denominator is the total estimated units the asset is expected to produce during its useful life. Units can be measured in number of hours (in the case of a machine) or miles (in the case of an automobile). When this method is used, depreciation expense varies directly with production. Thus, among all of the depreciation methods that are acceptable methods for the purposes of financial accounting, this method does the best job at attempting to match the costs of the asset with the periods in which the asset is utilized.

Partial-year depreciation. Depreciable assets are rarely placed in service on the first day of the fiscal year or disposed of on the last day of the fiscal year. Consequently, for financial reporting purposes, each year's depreciation expense must be allocated between two fiscal years, which involves "partial-year depreciation." Although any reasonable, consistently applied method for selecting a day to begin and end depreciating an asset is allowed, the most common approach is starting and ending depreciation of an asset based on the nearest full month. Accordingly, assets placed in service during the first half of the month are assumed to have been placed in service on the first day of the month, and assets placed in service during the last half of the month are assumed to have been placed in service on the first day of the following month. The same rules apply to the disposition of assets. That is, assets disposed of in the first half of the month are deemed disposed of on the first day of that month, and those disposed of during the last half of the month are deemed disposed of on the first day of the following month.

To illustrate the "nearest month rules," assume that a calendar year corporation places an asset into service on May 12, 2008. Since the asset is deemed to have been placed in service on May 1, 2008, 8/12ths of the first year of depreciation is deducted in calculating 2008 net income. The remaining 4/12ths of the first-year depreciation plus 8/12ths of the second year depreciation would be deducted in 2009, and so forth. If the asset is later sold on October 25, the depreciation on that asset would be taken until November 1 of that year.

.02 Tax Depreciation Rules

Tax law generally allows property to be depreciated if it (1) is used in a trade or business or held for the production of income; (2) has a useful life that is longer than one year; and (3) wears out, decays, gets used up, becomes obsolete, or loses value from natural causes.[2] Consequently, land and artwork are not depreciable assets because they do not wear out, get used up, or become obsolete.[3] However, an asset does not necessarily need to decline in value to be a depreciable asset. For example, professional musicians were allowed to depreciate the cost of antique musical instruments that continue to appreciate in value because they established that these instruments used in their business were subject to wear and tear.[4] Similarly, individuals who were in the business of displaying exotic cars were entitled to depreciate the cars because they showed that the cars were subject to obsolescence.[5]

Since only property used in a trade or business or held for the production of income can be depreciated, no deduction for depreciation is allowed on "personal-use" assets.[6] It is important to distinguish between the terms "personal-use" and "personal property." Personal-use assets are thos such as a taxpayer's residence or an automobile that are used for personal purposes only. "Personal property" is property that is not realty (e.g., equipment and machinery). Many assets are "mixed-use assets," i.e., used partly for personal purposes and partly for business or investment purposes. Only the portion of the cost of the asset allocable to business or investment use of mixed-use assets is depreciable. Mixed-use assets are often found in businesses operated as sole proprietorships (see ¶ 1303.02).

Depreciation on property used by a business to construct a capital asset is generally not expensed; instead it is capitalized as part of the cost of the asset. The entire capitalized cost of the constructed asset may be depreciated once construction is completed and the asset is placed in service.[7]

Example 5: Pretty Good Construction, Inc. uses a payloader to construct a building in year 20X0. The payloader's sole use in 20X0 is to construct the building, and $20,000 of depreciation on the payloader is allowable to Pretty Good in that year. Pretty Good may not take a deduction for the $20,000 of depreciation on its 20X0 tax return. Instead, it must add the $20,000 to the basis of the building. Thus, Pretty Good will recover the depreciation expense on the payloader over the depreciation period of the building, not the payloader.

Although the concept of depreciation is similar to that used for financial reporting purposes, the tax laws surrounding the rules for deducting tax depreciation are somewhat different. Current tax depreciation rules allow taxpayers to recover the entire basis of depreciable assets over a specified recovery period (as if the salvage value were zero). The specified recovery periods for depreciable real property (such as apartment buildings and warehouses) are considerably longer than those assigned to personal property (like machinery and automobiles). However, the recovery periods used to determine depreciation are only indirectly related to, and are usually shorter than, the estimated useful lives of the properties depreciated. Assigning a specific recovery period to each type of property eliminates most controversies regarding the recovery periods that should be used

---

[2] Reg. § 1.167(a)-2.

[3] *See, e.g.,* Rev. Rul. 68-232, 1968-1 CB 79.

[4] *B.P. Liddle,* CA-3, 95-2 USTC ¶ 50,488, 65 F3d 329; *R.L. Simon,* CA-2, 95-2 USTC ¶ 50,552, 68 F3d 41.

[5] *B. Selig,* 70 TCM 1125, Dec. 50,975(M), TC Memo. 1995-519.

[6] Code Sec. 167(a).

[7] *B. Selig,* 70 TCM 1125, Dec. 50,975(M), TC Memo. 1995-519.

to depreciate assets. Furthermore, unlike for financial accounting, in which salvage value is considered when computing annual depreciation deductions, for tax purposes, the entire cost basis of depreciable property is expensed over the assigned recovery periods.

 Reason for the Rule: Prior to 1981, taxpayers could choose from a number of acceptable depreciation methods and write off the cost of assets over a variety of estimated useful lives. These depreciation rules were similar to those used in financial reporting, but they unfortunately required decisions to be made regarding the depreciation method to use, the asset's useful life, and its estimated salvage value. These rules resulted in a greater administrative burden on the IRS, whose job is to monitor whether the tax laws are properly observed. In 1981, Congress enacted the Accelerated Cost Recovery System (ACRS). A hallmark of ACRS was that it specified rates and methods for all classes of assets. This had the effect of lowering compliance and administrative costs by simplifying the methods that were acceptable for depreciating property and by assigning specific class lives to various categories of real and tangible personal property. The depreciation system in effect today is a modified version of ACRS, known as the Modified Accelerated Cost Recovery System (MACRS).

Adjusted basis is the tax equivalent to book value for financial statement purposes. Adjusted basis equals the initial basis of the asset (typically its cost in the case of an acquired asset) plus any capitalized improvements made to the property minus accumulated depreciation taken on the property. When property is disposed of, adjusted basis is used to determine the amount of gain or loss realized from the disposition. The tax laws require that the adjusted basis of property be reduced by the depreciation allowed or allowable, even if the taxpayer failed to deduct some or all of it. Where no depreciation deductions have been taken on an asset, "allowable depreciation" refers to depreciation that would have been allowed using the straight-line method.[8]

Example 6: Bradley Jones, a sole proprietor, purchased an item of machinery costing $12,000 for his business in 2006. He neglected to take depreciation on the machinery in 2006 through 2008 amounting to $3,500. Bradley sold the machine in 2008. The adjusted basis must be reduced by the $3,500 of depreciation deductions down to $8,500 so that the proper amount of gain or loss realized from the sale can be calculated.

Tax depreciation rules are currently governed under the **Modified Accelerated Cost Recovery System (MACRS).** MACRS allows taxpayers two options for depreciating real and tangible personal property: the general depreciation system (GDS) and the alternative depreciation system (ADS). The main distinction between the GDS (hereafter referred to as MACRS because MACRS incorporates the GDS) and ADS is how quickly the entire costs of depreciable property can be expensed. Unless the taxpayer elects to use ADS or the tax laws specially require that it be used, MACRS is used to compute tax depreciation. Under both MACRS and ADS, the cost of depreciable property (both new and used property) must be recovered using the applicable depreciation method, recovery period, and averaging convention.[9]

Depreciation methods and recovery periods. Under MACRS, most depreciable personal property has a recovery period of five or seven years. However, some personal property has a recovery period as short as three or as long as 10, 15, or 20 years. Under MACRS, taxpayers can depreciate personal property using the declining-balance or the straight-line methods. When the declining-balance method is used, the taxpayer switches to the straight-line method when the straight-line method starts producing higher depreciation. Because the tax savings are greater in the earlier years when the declining-balance method is used, businesses that use MACRS typically do

---

[8] Code Sec. 1016(a)(2); *B. Selig*, 70 TCM 1125, Dec. 50,975(M), TC Memo. 1995-519.

[9] Code Sec. 168.

not elect the straight-line method. Under ADS, the recovery periods for depreciating personal property are longer and only the straight-line method is allowed.

For purposes of depreciating real property under MACRS, only the straight-line method is available, and longer recovery periods apply to commercial realty (office buildings, warehouses, etc.) than to residential realty (apartment buildings). Under ADS, the straight-line method is used, and a 40-year recovery period is used to depreciate both commercial and residential real property.

 Planning Pointer: Even though the tax deductions are higher in the earlier years when the declining-balance method is used, taxpayers should look at the overall picture before automatically assuming that MACRS will yield the greatest overall tax savings. Lower depreciation deductions in the earlier years may be preferred when taxpayers are in a relatively low tax bracket and expect to be in a higher tax bracket in future years. In such situations, using ADS will allow the taxpayer to delay some of the depreciation to those tax years in which they can obtain greater tax savings. In making these decisions, taxpayers should consider the time value of money, i.e., whether the present value of the tax savings in future years exceeds the present value of the tax saved with the earlier deductions.

Averaging conventions (partial year depreciation). Under both MACRS and ADS, the day on which property is deemed to be placed in service (and when depreciation begins) is determined by reference to the applicable averaging convention.

Depreciable real property is governed by the **mid-month convention**, in which property is deemed to be placed in service in the middle of the month in which it is actually placed in service. Likewise, property is deemed to be disposed of in the middle of the month in which it is actually disposed of.[10] To illustrate the mid-month convention, assume that a calendar year corporation acquires and places in service a building on May 2, 20X0. For purposes of computing 20X0 depreciation, the property was deemed to be placed in service on May 15, 20X0. Accordingly, the corporation would deduct 7.5/12 of the first-year depreciation on its 20X0 tax return (the period from May 15, 20X0, to December 31, 20X0). In each subsequent year (until the final year), a full year of depreciation would be allowed, provided the property was not disposed of in that year. If the same corporation were to dispose of depreciable real property on November 29, 20X3, it would be able to deduct 10.5/12 of a full year of depreciation on the property on its 20X3 tax return for the period from January 1, 20X3, to November 15, 20X3, during which the property was deemed to be in service.

The mid-month convention applies only to depreciable real property. The date on which tangible personal property is deemed to be placed in service is governed by either the mid-quarter or the half-year convention. Under the **mid-quarter convention**, property is deemed to have been placed in service (or disposed of) in the middle of the quarter in which it is actually placed in service (or disposed of).[11] Therefore, when a calendar year taxpayer acquires and places in service property on July 5, 20X1, the property is placed in service during the third quarter. Accordingly, the taxpayer is deemed to have placed the property in service on August 15, 20X1 (the middle of the third quarter), and would be allowed to deduct 4.5/12 of the first year's depreciation in 20X1 (from August 15, 20X1, to December 31, 20X1). In each subsequent year (until the final year), a full year's depreciation would be allowed, assuming that the property was kept in service the entire year. If the same corporation were to sell the property on January 25, 20X5, under the mid-quarter convention it would be deemed to have disposed of the property on February 15, 20X5 (halfway through the first quarter). Consequently, the corporation would be entitled to 1.5/12 of a full year's depreciation in the final year (from January 1, 20X5, to February 15, 20X5).

---

[10] *B. Selig*, 70 TCM 1125, CCH Dec. 50,975(M), TC Memo.   [11] *Id.*
1995-519.

In contrast, the **half-year convention** deems that personal property is purchased and sold halfway through the taxpayer's tax year, regardless of the actual dates on which the events occur. Consequently, depreciation in the first and final years is always half of a full year's depreciation under the half-year convention.[12] The following examples illustrate the application of the various averaging conventions under MACRS and ADS.

Example 7: On November 5, 20X1, a calendar year business places in service an asset that costs $10,000. The asset is five-year property for the purposes of MACRS. Under the straight-line method, the entire $10,000 cost would be expensed evenly over the asset's five-year life. Assuming the half-year convention applies, only half of a full year's depreciation is allowed in the first year, and the depreciation expense for 20X1 equals $1,000 ($10,000/5 × ½). Assuming the asset is not sold, for each year from 20X2 to 20X5, depreciation of $2,000 ($10,000/5) is deducted against business income. In the sixth year (20X6), the remaining $1,000 of depreciation expense is deducted.

Year	Beginning Adjusted Basis	Depreciation Expense	Ending Adjusted Basis
20X1	$10,000	$ 1,000	$9,000
20X2	9,000	2,000	7,000
20X3	7,000	2,000	5,000
20X4	5,000	2,000	3,000
20X5	3,000	2,000	1,000
20X6	1,000	1,000	0
Accumulated Depreciation		$10,000	

The adjusted basis of the property is reduced by the amount of depreciation taken on the property each year. Because salvage value is ignored, the adjusted basis of the property will equal $0 when the property is fully depreciated, if the taxpayer does not dispose of the property during the recovery period.

Example 8: Assume the same facts as in Example 7, except the DDB method is used to depreciate the property. Depreciation expense is now calculated using twice the straight-line rate, or 40% (1/5 years × 2), and the first year's depreciation equals $2,000 ($10,000 × 40% × 1/2). This amount reduces the adjusted basis of the property at the end of 20X1 to $8,000 ($10,000 – $2,000), and is the starting point for calculating the depreciation expense for 20X2.

The depreciation expense for 20X2 equals $3,200 ($8,000 × 40%), and the property's adjusted basis is reduced to $4,800 at the end of 20X2 ($8,000 – $3,200). The depreciation expense for 20X3 equals $1,920 ($4,800 × 40%). At the end of 20X3, the adjusted basis of the property equals $2,880 ($4,800 – $1,920) and 2½ years of depreciation remain. If the adjusted basis of $2,880 were expensed using the straight-line method, annual depreciation would be $1,152 ($2,880/2.5). Under the DDB method, depreciation expense for 20X4 also equals $1,152 ($2,880 × 40%). Therefore, at the end of the third tax year, depreciation expense under the straight-line method has caught up with the depreciation expense under the DDB method. Accordingly, starting with 20X4, the switch is made to the straight-line method. The depreciation expense for 20X4 and 20X5 equals $1,152, and in 20X6 it equals $576 ($1,152 × ½).

---

[12] *Id.*

Year	Beginning Adjusted Basis	Depreciation Expense	Ending Adjusted Basis
20X1	$10,000	$ 2,000	$8,000
20X2	8,000	3,200	4,800
20X3	4,800	1,920	2,880
20X4	2,880	1,152	1,728
20X5	1,728	1,152	576
20X6	576	576	0
Accumulated Depreciation		$10,000	

Example 9: Assume the same facts as in Example 8, except the mid-quarter convention applies and the property is sold on April 10, 20X3. Since the property was placed in service during the fourth quarter of 20X1, for purposes of computing depreciation for 20X1, the property is deemed to have been placed in service on November 15, 20X1—halfway through the fourth quarter. Thus, the depreciation expense for the first year equals $500 ($10,000 × 40% × 1.5 months/12). This amount reduces the adjusted basis of the property to $9,500 ($10,000 – $500) at the end of 20X1.

For 20X2, a full year's depreciation is allowed ($9,500 × 40% = $3,800). This amount reduces the property's adjusted basis to $5,700 ($9,500 – $3,800) at the end of 20X2. In 20X3, the property was actually disposed of in the second quarter; therefore, it is deemed to have been disposed of on May 15, 20X3. Consequently, the property is depreciated from January 1, 20X3, through May 15, 20X3, and the depreciation expense for that year equals $855 ($5,700 × 40% × 4.5/12). The $4,845 adjusted basis of the property on the day it is sold is used in determining the gain or loss resulting from the sale (see ¶ 801).

Year	Beginning Adjusted Basis	Depreciation Expense	Ending Adjusted Basis
20X1	$10,000	$ 500	$9,500
20X2	9,500	3,800	5,700
20X3	5,700	855	4,845
Accumulated Depreciation		$5,155	

Spotlight: In financial accounting, depreciation expense for each year of the asset's useful life is computed and then allocated to the fiscal years to which it relates. When the declining-balance method is used to compute the depreciation expense on the income statement, the asset's book value on the anniversary of its deemed purchase date under the nearest month rule is multiplied by the declining-balance rate. For tax purposes, each tax year's depreciation is calculated independently. Therefore, under the declining-balance method, the adjusted basis at the beginning of the tax year is used to compute that year's depreciation expense. If the property is disposed of during that year, a portion of the full year's depreciation is deducted in accordance with the appropriate averaging convention.

GAAP vs. Code: Due to the different rules that govern the calculation of depreciation expenses for financial accounting versus tax reporting purposes, differences inevitably occur between the amount of depreciation deducted in arriving at net income and the amount deducted in computing taxable income. The difference must be taken into consideration when reconciling net income to taxable income on the corporate tax return. If the amount of depreciation taken on the tax return is greater, the excess must be subtracted from net income when reconciling net income with taxable income, and vice versa.

The differences due to the different methods used to depreciate property are merely timing differences that eventually will reverse themselves; however, this may not occur until the property is eventually sold in a taxable transaction. To illustrate, take an asset that costs $12,000 and has an estimated $2,000 salvage value. Because salvage value is used to compute depreciation for financial statement purposes, over several years a total of $10,000 will be deducted on the income statement with respect to this asset; however, on the tax return, a total of $12,000 (full cost basis) will be deducted. This $2,000 timing difference will be reflected in the adjustments made over the years when reconciling net income with taxable income on the corporate tax returns.

Once the asset is fully depreciated, its book value for financial statement purposes will be $2,000 ($12,000 – $10,000), but its adjusted basis for tax purposes will be $0. This last $2,000 difference in the treatment of depreciation expense will finally be reversed when the asset is disposed of in a taxable transaction. For example, if this fully depreciated asset is sold for $3,000, the $1,000 gain reported on the income statement ($3,000 – $2,000) will be less than the $3,000 gain reported on the tax return. Consequently, the extra $2,000 of depreciation deducted over the years on the tax return will be offset by the additional $2,000 gain recognized as taxable income in the year the property is sold. This $2,000 difference will result in an additional amount added to net income to reconcile it with taxable income on the corporate tax return in the year the corporation sells the asset.

¶ 702 Personal Property Depreciation Rules

The sections that follow present the rules for depreciating many common types of personal property. The topics included are general and alternative MACRS, additional first-year depreciation, Section 179 immediate expensing, and special rules for passenger automobiles.

.01 General and Alternative MACRS

The current tax laws categorize property into *property classes,* which establish the recovery periods under MACRS.[13] Rev. Proc. 87-56 lists the MACRS (general MACRS) and ADS (alternative MACRS) recovery periods for most assets.[14] The class life (MACRS recovery period) for many of the more common types of depreciable personal property is shown in Table 7-1.

---

[13] Code Sec. 168(e).

[14] 1987-2 CB 674, clarified and modified by Rev. Proc. 88-22, 1988-1 CB 785.

Table 7-1 MACRS Recovery Periods for Personal Property

Property Class (MACRS recovery period)	*Examples*
3-year property	Race horses that are over two years old, or any breeding or work horse over 12 years old at the time it is placed in service
	All race horses placed in service after 2008 and before 2014
	Qualified rent-to-own property (e.g., televisions and furniture) that a dealer leases to its customers
5-year property	Automobiles, taxis, limousines, buses, light general-purpose trucks, and noncommercial aircraft
	Computers and peripheral equipment (such as printers)
	Personal property used for research and experimentation
	Appliances, carpet, furniture, etc., used in residential rental property
	Office equipment, such as fax machines, phones, and copiers
	Certain farm equipment placed in service in the year 2009
7-year property	Office furniture
	Most machinery and equipment
	Commercial airplanes
10-year property	Water transportation assets (vessels, barges, tugs)
15-year property	Land improvements (sidewalks, roads, canals, drainage facilities, sewers)
	Wharves and docks, bridges, landscaping, and shrubbery
	Radio and transmitting towers
20-year property	Farming structures

MACRS allows personal property to be depreciated over the assigned recovery periods shown in Table 7-1 using either the declining-balance or straight-line methods. Most personal property is depreciated using the DDB method; however, the 150-percent declining balance method is used to depreciate 15- and 20-year property. In contrast, the applicable depreciation method under ADS is the straight-line method,[15] and the ADS recovery periods are generally longer than under MACRS. Although cars, light general-purpose trucks, and computer equipment have five-year ADS recovery periods, office furniture has a recovery period of 10 years under ADS.[16] Table 7-2 shows the differences in the recovery periods for several types of depreciable personal property. A full list can be found in Rev. Proc. 87-56.[17]

---

[15] Code Sec. 168(g)(2)(A).
[16] Code Sec. 168(g)(2) and (3).

[17] 1987-2 CB 674, clarified and modified by Rev. Proc. 88-22, 1988-1 CB 785.

Table 7-2 MACRS vs. ADS Recovery Periods for Personal Property

Examples	MACRS Recovery Period	ADS Recovery Period
Race horses that are over two years old, or any breeding or work horse over 12 years old at the time it is placed in service (but see exception in Table 7-1 for certain race horses placed in service after 2008 and before 2014)	3 years	12 years
Qualified rent-to-own property (e.g., televisions and furniture) that a dealer leases to its customers	3 years	12 years
Automobiles, taxis, limousines, buses, light general-purpose trucks, and noncommercial aircraft	5 years	5 years
Computers and peripheral equipment (such as printers)	5 years	5 years
Personal property used for research and experimentation	5 years	6 years
Office equipment, such as fax machines, phones, and copiers	5 years	6 years
Office furniture	7 years	10 years
Most machinery and equipment	7 years	12 years
Water transportation assets (vessels, barges, tugs)	10 years	18 years
Land improvements (sidewalks, roads, canals, drainage facilities, sewers, but *not* municipal sewers), wharves and docks, bridges, landscaping and shrubbery	15 years	20 years
Farming structures	20 years	25 years

ADS must be used to recover the cost of tangible personal property used predominantly outside the United States, tax-exempt personal use property, and personal property financed through the issuance of tax-exempt bonds. ADS must also be used to depreciate certain types of property (called "listed property) that are used 50 percent or less for business.[18] Listed property becomes an issue for businesses operated as sole proprietorships, which are discussed in Chapter 13. ADS is also sometimes required in the calculation of alternative minimum tax (AMT). This is discussed in Chapter 10.[19] In addition to the situations in which the use of ADS is required, taxpayers may irrevocably elect to use ADS to depreciate personal property placed in service during the year.[20] Such an election is made on a *class-by-class* basis. For example, if taxpayers want to elect ADS for a light, general-purpose truck placed in service during the year, they must also use ADS to depreciate all other five-year property placed in service during the year.[21] However, taxpayers may elect to use MACRS for all other classes of personal property placed in service during the year. They may also then use MACRS to depreciate five-year property placed in service in a subsequent year if they so choose.

Averaging conventions. Regardless of whether the taxpayer uses MACRS or elects to use ADS to depreciate personal property placed in service during the year, the appropriate averaging convention must be used. Averaging conventions determine the deemed placed in service date and the disposal date. Two averaging conventions apply to personal property: the half-year convention and the mid-quarter convention. Depreciation is allowed only for the portion of a tax year that property is treated as placed in service under the applicable convention.[22] The same averaging

---

[18] Code Sec. 280F(b)(2).
[19] Code Sec. 56(a)(1)(A).
[20] Code Sec. 168(g)(7).

[21] *Id.*
[22] Code Sec. 168(i)(4).

convention that applies to depreciable property in the year in which it is placed in service also must be used in the year the property is disposed of.

Example 8 illustrated the use of the DDB method under the half-year convention; Example 9 illustrated the use of the DDB method under the mid-quarter convention. These examples show how the depreciation calculations can be made manually; however, an easier way to calculate MACRS on personal property is to use depreciation tables provided by the IRS. These tables are reproduced in Tables 7-3 and 7-4 below for both five-and seven-year property. A full set of depreciation tables is presented in the Appendix to this chapter (see Tables 7A–7F at ¶ 725).

Table 7-3 MACRS 5-Year and 7-Year Recovery Rates (Half-Year Convention)

Recovery Year	5-Year Property	7-Year Property
1	20.00%	14.29%
2	32.00	24.49
3	19.20	17.49
4	11.52	12.49
5	11.52	8.93
6	5.76	8.92
7		8.93
8		4.46

Under the half-year convention, a full year's depreciation under the DDB method equals 40 percent of the straight-line rate for five-year property (1/5 × 2) and 28.57 percent for seven-year property (1/7 × 2). The first-year recovery rates from Table 7-3 are half of these rates (40% × ½ = 20%; 28.57% × ½ = 14.29%), which properly reflect the fact that the property was deemed to have been placed in service halfway through the year. Each subsequent year's recovery rate reflects a full year's depreciation.

For example, at the beginning of year 2, 80 percent of the asset's cost of five-year property has not been depreciated (100% – 20% expensed in year 1). In year 2, 40 percent of the remaining 80 percent adjusted basis equals 32 percent—the amount shown in Table 7-3. At the beginning of year 3, 52 percent of the asset has been depreciated (20% + 32%), leaving 48 percent yet to be depreciated. Forty percent of that amount equals 19.2 percent, which is the percentage shown for year 3 in the table. The asterisks in each column show when the switch to the straight-line method was made because at that point the straight-line method generated a greater depreciation expense. In the final year, the remaining half-year's depreciation (from taking only a half year in the first year) is allowed. If an asset subject to the half-year convention is sold in the last recovery year, no adjustment is made to the table percentage because the percentage already reflects six months' depreciation.

To calculate the amount of MACRS depreciation each year, the unadjusted cost of the property is multiplied by the applicable recovery rate from the table. However, if the property is disposed of prior to being fully depreciated (before the sixth year for five-year property; before the eighth year for seven-year property), the percentages from Table 7-3 must be reduced by half to reflect the deemed disposal of the property halfway through the year.

Example 10: Seven-year property costing $10,000 is placed in service during 20X6 and is sold during 20X9. The half-year convention applies to all seven-year property placed in service during 20X6.

Year	Cost Basis		Recovery Rate		Depreciation Expense
20X6	$10,000	×	14.29%	=	$1,429
20X7	10,000	×	24.49%	=	2,449
20X8	10,000	×	17.49%	=	1,749
20X9	10,000	×	12.49% × ½	=	625

Table 7-4 MACRS 5- and 7-Year Recovery Rates (Mid-Quarter Convention)

Placed in Service During:

Year	1st Quarter 5-year	1st Quarter 7-year	2nd Quarter 5-year	2nd Quarter 7-year	3rd Quarter 5-year	3rd Quarter 7-year	4th Quarter 5-year	4th Quarter 7-year
1	35.00%	25.00%	25.00%	17.85%	15.00%	10.71%	5.00%	3.57%
2	26.00	21.43	30.00	23.47	34.00	25.51	38.00	27.55
3	15.60	15.31	18.00	16.76	20.40	18.22	22.80	19.68
4	11.01	10.93	11.37	11.97	12.24	13.02	13.68	14.06
5	11.01	8.75	11.37	8.87	11.30	9.30	10.94	10.04
6	1.38	8.74	4.26	8.87	7.06	8.85	9.58	8.73
7		8.75		8.87		8.86		8.73
8		1.09		3.34		5.53		7.64

Under the mid-quarter year convention, the first full year's depreciation under the DDB method must be reduced to reflect the portion of the year that the property was deemed placed in service. For example, a calendar year taxpayer that places property in service during the third quarter would be deemed to have placed it in service on August 15. Consequently, depreciation is allowed from August 15 to December 31, or for 4½ months. Depreciation for the first year would equal 15 percent for five-year property (1/5 × 2 × 4.5/12) and 10.71 percent for seven-year property (1/7 × 2 × 4.5/12)—the percentages shown in the 3rd Quarter columns for year 1 in Table 7-4. Each subsequent year's recovery rate reflects a full year's depreciation. Therefore, if the property is disposed of prior to being fully depreciated, the percentages from Table 7-4 must be reduced to reflect only the portion of the year up until the middle of the quarter in which the property is disposed of.

Example 11: A calendar year corporation places in service seven-year property costing $10,000 on April 29, 20X1. The corporation sells the property on September 5, 20X5. The mid-quarter convention applies to all seven-year property placed in service during 20X1.

Year	Cost Basis		Recovery Rate		Depreciation Expense
20X1	$10,000	×	17.85%	=	$1,785
20X2	10,000	×	23.47%	=	2,347
20X3	10,000	×	16.76%	=	1,676
20X4	10,000	×	11.97%	=	1,197
20X5	10,000	×	8.87% × 7.5/12	=	554

Since the property was placed in service during the second quarter (April to June for calendar year taxpayers), the column that corresponds to the second quarter for seven-year property is used to depreciate the property each year. In 20X5 the property is sold in the third quarter (July to September), and accordingly, the property is deemed sold on August 15, 20X5—the middle of the third quarter. MACRS on the property during 20X5 is reduced to reflect the 7½ months during 20X5 that the property was deemed to have been in service.

Forty-percent test (when the mid-quarter convention applies). The mid-quarter convention applies to all depreciable personal property placed in service during a tax year if more than 40 percent of the aggregate cost of all depreciable personal property placed in service during such tax year is placed in service during the last three months of the tax year. In determining if the mid-quarter convention applies, only the basis of personal property placed in service during the year is used. Therefore, the depreciable basis of property not subject to MACRS is disregarded,[23] as is the cost of depreciable real property[24] or any portion of the property that is expensed under Code Sec. 179. All of these issues are discussed later in the chapter.[25] If the 40-percent test is not met, the half-year convention applies to all personal property placed in service during the year.

Example 12: During 20X0, John Frank purchases and places in service in his business a computer costing $3,000, a desk costing $700, and a copier costing $900. The computer is placed in service in January, the desk in August, and the copier in November. The aggregate basis of the personal property placed in service during the year equals $4,600. For the mid-quarter convention to apply to John's personal property placed in service during 20X0, more than $1,840 ($4,600 × 40%) must have been placed in service during the fourth quarter. Because the $900 copier is the only property placed in service during the fourth quarter, the mid-quarter convention does not apply and John uses the half-year convention (Table 7-3) to depreciate the personal property placed in service during 20X0.

The depreciation expense for the first two years for each of these assets is shown below. The rates used to compute the depreciation expense are from the applicable columns in Table 7-3.

Depreciation expense for 20X0

Item	Unadjusted Basis		Depreciation Rate		Depreciation Expense
Computer (5-year)	$3,000	×	20.00%	=	$ 600
Desk (7-year property)	700	×	14.29%	=	100
Copier (5-year property)	900	×	20.00%	=	180
Total depreciation expense					$ 880

Depreciation expense for 20X1

Item	Unadjusted Basis		Depreciation Rate		Depreciation Expense
Computer (5-year)	$3,000	×	32.00%	=	$ 960
Desk (7-year property)	700	×	24.49%	=	171
Copier (5-year property)	900	×	32.00%	=	288
Total depreciation expense					$1,419

Example 13: The facts are the same as in Example 12, except both the $900 copier and the $3,000 computer are placed in service in November. Since more than $1,860 of John's total personal property was placed in service during the fourth quarter, the mid-quarter

---

[23] Code Sec. 168(d)(3)(A).
[24] Code Sec. 168(d)(3)(B).

[25] Reg. § 1.168(d)-1(b)(4).

convention (Table 7-4) must be used to compute depreciation for each of the three assets placed in service during 20X0.

Depreciation expense for the first two years for each of these assets is shown below. The rates used to compute depreciation expense are from the applicable columns in Table 7-4 (third quarter for the desk and fourth quarter for the computer and copier).

Depreciation expense for 20X0

Item	Unadjusted Basis		Depreciation Rate		Depreciation Expense
Computer (5-year)	$3,000	×	5.00%	=	$ 150
Desk (7-year property)	700	×	10.71%	=	75
Copier (5-year property)	900	×	5.00%	=	45
Total depreciation expense					$ 270

Depreciation expense for 20X1

Item	Unadjusted Busis		Depreciation Rate		Depreciation Expense
Computer (5-year)	$3,000	×	38.00%	=	$1,140
Desk (7-year property)	700	×	25.51%	–	179
Copier (5-year property)	900	×	38.00%	=	342
Total depreciation expense					$1,661

Reason for the Rule: When ACRS was first enacted in 1981, Congress simplified the timing of when depreciation would begin and end by assuming that all personal property was placed in service halfway through the tax year. Although only a half-year's depreciation was allowed on property placed in service during the first half of the tax year, such loss of depreciation would be offset by allowing a half year of depreciation on property placed in service towards the end of the year. This simplified method was based on the assumption that property would be placed in service evenly throughout the tax year. Over the next several years, taxpayers began acquiring and placing in service personal property towards the end of the tax year to take advantage of the half-year convention. Taxpayers were able to deduct a half year of depreciation for property placed in service a few short days before the end of the year. In 1986, Congress attempted to curb any potential abuses by enacting the mid-quarter convention. If property is indeed placed in service evenly throughout the year, then only 25 percent of all personal property should be placed in service during the last quarter of the year. Accordingly, Congress decided that placing in service more than 40 percent of all personal property during the fourth quarter constituted abuse of the leniency of the half-year convention.

Under the mid-quarter convention, the percentages allowed in the first year for property placed in service during the first two quarters are greater than under the half-year convention. For example, 35 percent of five-year property placed in service during the first quarter is allowed in the first year under the mid-quarter convention (see Table 7-4), whereas only 20 percent is allowed under the half-year convention (see Table 7-3). However, with respect to five-year property placed in service in the fourth quarter, only five percent of the cost is depreciated in the first year. In order for the mid-quarter convention to apply, more than 40 percent of the cost of all personal property placed in service during the year is subject to the lower depreciation rates in the first year. Accordingly, overall depreciation expense is generally much lower in the first year when the mid-quarter convention applies, as evidenced by comparing the first years' total depreciation in Examples 12 and 13 ($880 versus $270).

MACRS optional tables. The IRS provides depreciation tables for each of the acceptable methods under MACRS, which include both 200-percent and 150-percent declining balance methods as well as the straight-line method. As with the tables reproduced in Tables 7-3 and 7-4, the percentages listed for the first year already reflect the portion of the first year that the property was deemed to be in service under the applicable averaging convention. All subsequent years (except the last one) reflect a full year's depreciation. These IRS tables are reproduced in the Appendix at the end of this chapter (see Tables 7A through 7F at ¶ 725). The following expenses show how depreciation is calculated using these optional tables.

Example 14: In August of 20X1, Glass On Demand, a wholesaler of automotive glass, pays $50,000 for new steel racks for transporting the glass to its customers. According to Rev. Proc. 87-56, the racks qualify as three-year property. Assuming Glass uses a calendar year and the half-year convention applies, its depreciation deduction for 20X1 equals $16,665 ($50,000 × 33.33%), and its deduction for 20X2 equals $22,225 ($50,000 × 44.45%). These percentages are from the 3-year recovery period column of Table 7A in the Appendix to this chapter (see ¶ 725).

Example 15: The facts are the same as in Example 14, except Glass elects to use straight-line depreciation for all three-year property placed in service in 20X1. The depreciation expense for the racks in 20X1 equals $8,335 ($50,000 × 16.67%), and depreciation for 20X2 equals $16,665 ($50,000 × 33.33%). These percentages are from the 3-year recovery period column of Table 7F in the Appendix to this chapter (see ¶ 725).

Example 16: The facts are the same as in Example 14, except the racks were placed in service in November and were the only property placed in service during the year. Since the 40-percent test has been met, the mid-quarter convention applies to all personal property placed in service during 20X1. Depreciation expense for 20X1 now equals $4,165 ($50,000 × 8.33%), and depreciation expense for 20X2 equals $30,555 ($50,000 × 61.11%). These percentages are taken from the 3-year recovery period column of the Table 7E in the Appendix to this chapter (see ¶ 725).

Example 17: In February of 20X1, John Smith purchases a machine for $20,000. The machine is used exclusively for business and the half-year convention applies. The machine is seven-year property for the purposes of MACRS, but its recovery period for the purposes of ADS is 10 years. If John elects ADS to depreciate all seven-year property placed in service in 20X1, his depreciation expense for 20X1 under the half-year convention equals $1,000 ($20,000 × 5%), and the depreciation in 20X2 and 20X3 equals $2,000 ($20,000 × 10%). These percentages are from the 10-year recovery period column of Table 7F in the Appendix to this chapter (see ¶ 725). If John sells the machine in 20X4, his depreciation expense that year will equal $1,000 ($20,000 × 10% × ½ year).

Example 18: In July of 20X2, J.W. Smith & Co., a calendar-year taxpayer, places in service a $700 desk in July and a $3,000 computer in November. The desk is seven-year property and the computer is five-year property. Assuming no other property is placed in service during the tax year, the mid-quarter convention applies since more than 40 percent of all personal property ($3,700 × 40% = $1,480) was placed in service in the last quarter. Depreciation for 20X1 and 20X2 for the desk equals $75 ($700 × 10.71%) and $179 ($700 × 25.51%), respectively. These percentages come from the column for 7-year property placed in service in the third quarter in Table 7-4 (and in Table 7D in the Appendix to this chapter (see ¶ 725)). Depreciation for 20X1 and 20X2 for the computer equals $150 ($3,000 × 5%) and $1,140 ($3,000 × 38%), respectively. These percentages also come from Table 7-4 (and Table 7E in the Appendix to this chapter (see ¶ 725)), except that they correspond to years 1 and 2 in the column for 5-year property placed in service in the fourth quarter.

Example 19: Continuing with Example 18, Smith sells the desk in January 20X3. Since the desk is deemed to have been sold on February 15, 20X3, depreciation on the desk for 2003 under the mid-quarter convention is $16 ($700 × 18.22% × 1.5/12). Depreciation for the computer in 20X3 equals $684 ($3,000 × 22.8%). Smith continues to depreciate the computer using the same column from the same depreciation table for as long as the property is used in its business.

.02 Additional First-Year Depreciation

During recent years, Congress amended the tax laws to allow taxpayers to claim additional depreciation on certain property in the first year they placed such property in service. These rules were first enacted in the wake of the events of September 11, 2001. Further changes were made in the aftermath of the destruction left by Hurricane Katrina in 2005, and in response to the economic slowdown in 2007. The developing economic crisis in 2008 motivated Congress to liberalize the additional first-year deprecation under the Economic Stimulus Act of 2008. The Emergency Economic Stabilization Act of 2008 provided even more liberal expensing rules for certain qualified disaster assistance property. The generous expensing rules provided for in the Economic Stimulus Act of 2008 were due to expire at the end of 2008. However, the American Recovery and Reinvestment Act of 2009 extends these allowances for the year 2009.

Hurricane Katrina. After hurricanes hit New Orleans and the surrounding areas in late summer 2005, Congress passed new legislation[26] allowing taxpayers in that region to claim additional first-year deprecation ("Katrina additional depreciation") on Qualified Gulf Opportunity Property. "Qualified Gulf Opportunity Property" is tangible property depreciable under MACRS with a recovery period of 20 years or less purchased after August 27, 2005 for original use in the Gulf Opportunity Zone and placed in service by December 31, 2007. It also includes residential and nonresidential real property placed in service by December 31, 2010. The deduction is equal to 50 percent of the adjusted basis of the property after reduction for any expensing allowance claimed under Code Sec. 179 (see ¶ 702.03). Taxpayers are allowed to claim the deduction only on certain depreciable property that is placed in service in the "Gulf Opportunity Zone" (the southern parts of Alabama, Louisiana, and Mississippi).

Example 20: Gulf Coast Enterprises is located in the Gulf Opportunity Zone. During 2007, Gulf Coast placed in service $50,000 of seven-year property that qualifies for Katrina additional depreciation. Gulf Coast deducted 50 percent of the cost ($25,000) in 2007 and depreciates the rest using MACRS from 2007 to 2014. MACRS depreciation on the property in 2008 equals $6,123 ($25,000 × 24.49%).

Economic Stimulus Package Act of 2008 and American Recovery and Reinvestment Act of 2009. In response to the housing and banking crisis and the overall economic slowdown that began in 2007, Congress enacted new tax law in hopes of staving off a recession. Two provisions in the tax law include enhanced Section 179 expensing (discussion at ¶ 702.03) and reinstatement of bonus depreciation for 2008 purchases. The 2008 and 2009 law changes allow taxpayers, in the first

---

[26] Code Sec. 1400N(d), as added by the Gulf Opportunity Zone Act of 2005 (P.L. 109-135).

year of ownership, to immediately depreciate (expense) 50 percent of the cost of qualifying property acquired during 2008 and 2009. Any remaining amounts could be depreciated under the MACRS rules discussed earlier in the chapter. Bonus depreciation for 2008 and 2009 is allowed on the acquisition of new MACRS property with a recovery period of 20 years or less, as well as on computer software that is depreciable over three years. The taxpayer reduces the adjusted basis of the property by the amount of bonus depreciation taken.

 Spotlight: Taxpayers that do not want to deduct the additional first year depreciation on 2008 and 2009 purchases may elect out of this provision. The taxpayer then depreciates the full basis of the property under the MACRS rules presented in ¶ 702.

 Reason for the Rule: Congress's motive in enacting bonus depreciation provisions was to encourage businesses to acquire new machinery, equipment, and other depreciable personal property, thereby providing a boost to the economy in the wake of certain events. Enacting the bonus depreciation rules provided businesses the opportunity to accelerate the timing of the cash flows. Congress hoped that would increase the demand for new tangible personal property, as well as residential and nonresidential real property. In turn, job growth would ensue because companies that manufacture (or construct) these assets would need to increase their workforce to meet the increased demand.

.03 Section 179 Immediate Expensing

Code Sec. 179 allows certain taxpayers to elect to immediately expense certain depreciable personal property (known as "Section 179 property"[27]) placed in service during the year rather than depreciate it over several tax years. When the taxpayer elects to expense a portion of the depreciable property under Code Sec. 179, the adjusted basis of the property is reduced for purposes of depreciating the remainder of the cost basis under MACRS or ADS, before determining the amount of bonus depreciation taken.[28]

Section 179 property is tangible personal property that is depreciable under MACRS and is acquired *by purchase* for use in the *active conduct of a trade or business*. Code Sec. 179 expensing is not allowed on property used outside the United States or on any real property.[29]

The "purchase" requirement is crucial to understanding key limitations on the Code Sec. 179 deduction. A property is not considered acquired by "purchase" if it is acquired from a related party or if it is acquired in a transaction on which recognition of gain or loss is deferred under the tax laws, such as a like-kind exchange or involuntary conversion (see ¶ 808 and ¶ 809, respectively). Accordingly, taxpayers may not take Code Sec. 179 deductions with respect to property they have acquired in such transactions.

Property acquired by trade-in. The cost of property for purposes of the expense election does not include the basis of other property held at any time by the person acquiring the property.[30] In other words, when used property is traded in for other property, only the boot paid is eligible for the expense election.

Example 21: Fred Farmer traded in his old combine which had an adjusted basis of $40,000 for a new combine. He paid cash boot of $60,000. Although the initial basis of his new

---

[27] Code Sec. 179(d)(1).
[28] Reg. § 1.179-1(f)(1).

[29] Code Sec. 179(d).
[30] Code Sec. 179(d)(3).

combine is $100,000 ($40,000 + $60,000), only the $60,000 boot paid is eligible for the expense election.

Dollar limitation. For tax years beginning before 2003, the maximum Code Sec. 179 expense deduction was $25,000. This amount is known as the "dollar limitation." To boost the economy after the September 11, 2001, terrorist attacks, Congress temporarily increased the dollar limitation. For tax years beginning in 2003, the maximum allowable Code Sec. 179 expense deduction increased to $100,000 and is adjusted annually for inflation from 2004 through 2009.[31] Congress again raised the dollar limitation as part of the Economic Stimulus Package Act of 2008 and the American Recovery and Reinvestment Act of 2009. The dollar limitation for 2008 and 2009 is $250,000.[32] The maximum deduction is currently scheduled to revert back to $25,000 in 2010. A taxpayer's dollar limitation amount may be reduced because of the investment limitation and taxable income limitation discussed below.

Example 22: Onandaga, Inc. purchases $288,000 of Section 179 property in 2009. It may elect to expense up to $250,000 of the property in 2009. It will have $38,000 ($288,000 – $250,000) of remaining basis that it may depreciate beginning in 2009.

Investment limitation. Code Sec. 179 expensing is intended to help small businesses, which are identified by the amount of Section 179 property they place in service during the year. To the extent that the taxpayer's total Section 179 property placed in service during the year exceeds a certain threshold, the dollar limitation is reduced dollar for dollar.[33]

Prior to 2002, the dollar limitation was $200,000. After September 11, 2001, Congress voted to raise the investment limitation to $400,000 for tax years beginning in 2003 through 2009 and to adjust it annually for inflation. As with the dollar limitation, in the Economic Stimulus Package of 2008, Congress increased the investment limitation for purchases made in 2008 and 2009. The investment limitation for 2008 and 2009 is $800,000.[34] For tax years beginning in 2010, the investment limitation is set to revert back to $200,000.

Thus, for tax years that begin in 2009, the investment limitation prevents taxpayers that place more than $1,050,000 ($800,000 + $250,000) of Section 179 property in service during the year from benefiting from Code Sec. 179. Amounts disallowed because of the investment limitation may not be carried forward to later tax years.

Example 23: During 2009, Amcast, Inc., a calendar year manufacturing company, places in service $1,017,000 of Section 179 property. Amcast can elect to immediately expense up to $33,000 of the property in 2008 ($250,000 – ($1,017,000 – $800,000)) and recover the remainder of the cost under the normal cost-recovery rules presented in this chapter, including bonus depreciation.

Reason for the Rule: In enacting Code Sec. 179, Congress wanted to give small businesses an incentive to purchase equipment and other depreciable personal property. For purposes of this rule, "small business" is defined by how much tangible personal property is placed in service during the year.

Planning Pointer: When deciding which property to expense under Code Sec. 179, taxpayers should consider expensing seven-year property in preference to five-year property placed in service in the same tax year. Since the cost of five-year property will be expensed over six years under MACRS (versus eight years for seven-year property), electing to first expense seven-year property will accelerate the deductions allowed to

---

[31] Code Sec. 179(b)(1), (5).

[32] Economic Stimulus Package Act of 2008, Sec. 102.

[33] Code Sec. 179(b)(2), (5).

[34] Economic Stimulus Package Act of 2008, Sec. 201.

> the taxpayer. All other things being equal, accelerating the timing of the tax savings will produce the greatest cash flows when the present value of the tax savings is considered.

Taxable income limitation. Taxpayers can elect to expense any amount allowed after the dollar and investment limitations have been considered. However, in order to deduct these amounts against taxable income, the taxpayer must have sufficient taxable income from business sources, as computed before consideration of any Code Sec. 179 expense. This is referred to as the **taxable income limitation**. The taxable income limitation disallows any deduction in the current year for amounts that exceed the aggregate of the taxpayer's taxable income derived from the active conduct of any trade or business. Taxable income attributable to services performed as an employee is considered taxable income from the active conduct of a trade or business. Taxable income from the active conduct of a trade or business is computed without regard to any Code Sec. 179 expense, but after all other business expenses, including MACRS.[35]

Any amounts disallowed because of the taxable income limitation are carried forward to the next tax year and are added to the amount allowable as a Code Sec. 179 deduction for that year, subject to the dollar and taxable income limitations for the year.[36] Generally, disallowed Code Sec. 179 deductions may be carried forward indefinitely. Furthermore, any amounts the taxpayer elects to expense under Code Sec. 179 (regardless of whether there is sufficient taxable income to deduct the full amount in the current year) reduces the basis of the property for purposes of depreciating it under MACRS or ADS.[37]

Example 24: Hagerton Company places in service $458,000 of Section 179 property during 2009. Hagerton elects to expense the full $250,000 that it is allowed under the dollar limit. It can then deduct the remaining $208,000 basis ($458,000 – $250,000) using bonus depreciation and MACRS. If Hagerton's taxable income derived from its trade or business is $70,000 in 2009, it may still elect to expense the full $250,000 in 2008. However, it will only be able to use $70,000 to reduce its taxable income in 2009. The remaining $180,000 ($250,000 – $70,000) will be carried over to 2010.

 Reason for the Rule: If the tax laws did not require taxpayers to reduce the property's basis by the full amount it elects to expense under Code Sec. 179, the potential exists for taxpayers to expense more than the total cost of the property. For example, if Hagerton from Example 25 is required to reduce its basis in the property by only $70,000, it will deduct $388,000 ($458,000 – $70,000) under MACRS over the next several years in addition to the $70,000 of Code Sec. 179 expense in 2009 and the $180,000 of Code Sec. 179 expense carried over to (and presumably utilized in) a future tax year.

Example 25: If, in Example 24, Hagerton is concerned that it may not be able to utilize the $180,000 of Code Sec. 179 expense carried over due to the taxable income limitation in the near future, it can elect to expense a smaller amount in 2009. For example, if Hagerton were to elect $70,000 of Code Sec. 179 expense in 2009, it would reduce its basis in the personal property to $388,000 ($458,000 – $70,000), and its bonus depreciation/MACRS deduction over the next several years would be higher than if it elected the full $250,000.

---

[35] Code Sec. 179(b)(3).
[36] Code Sec. 179(b)(3)(B).

[37] Reg. § 1.179-1(f)(1).

Planning Pointer: For the purposes of determining whether the half-year or mid-quarter convention applies to personal property placed in service during the year, any amount expensed under Code Sec. 179 is not considered when applying the 40-percent test. Therefore, when deciding which properties to elect to expense under Code Sec. 179, taxpayers should consider expensing property placed in service during the fourth quarter, if doing so will prevent the taxpayer from being subject to the mid-quarter convention.

Husband and wife. For the purposes of the Code Sec. 179 dollar limitation, a husband and wife who file a joint return are treated as one taxpayer, regardless of which spouse purchased the property or placed it in service. A husband and wife filing separate returns are treated as one taxpayer when applying the maximum dollar limit and the investment limit; however, the taxable income limit is applied separately on each spouse's separate return. Unless the spouses elect otherwise, 50 percent of the Code Sec. 179 expense is allocated to each spouse.[38]

Example 26: Marvin and Loretta English file separate returns in 2009. They place $815,000 and $144,000 of Section 179 property in service, respectively, for a combined total of $959,000. Marvin has $300,000 of taxable income from the active conduct of a trade or business; Loretta has $3,000. If they file a joint return, they could elect to expense up to $91,000 ($250,000 – ($959,000 – $800,000)), and they would be able to deduct the entire amount in 2008 because their combined taxable business income exceeds this amount. If Marvin and Loretta decide to file separate returns, absent a contrary election, each spouse is allocated 50 percent of the $91,000, or $45,500. Loretta's deduction would be limited to her $3,000, which is her taxable business income. She could carry the $42,500 excess over to future tax years. Amounts carried over would be subject to the applicable dollar and taxable income limitations each year.

Partnerships and S corporations. In the case of partnerships and S corporations, both the entity and each of its respective owners are subject to the annual dollar limitation and taxable income limitations. However, in determining whether more than $800,000 of Section 179 property has been placed in service during the tax year by the owner, the cost of Section 179 property placed in service by the *entity* is not taken into consideration by the owner.[39]

Example 27: In 2009, Christina Campbell and Colleen Collins form a partnership to operate a bakery. The partnership purchases an oven and a refrigerator for a total cost of $330,000. Both Christina and Colleen are active in the conduct of the business. In the same year, Colleen enters into a separate business venture, a flower shop operated as a sole proprietorship, for which she purchases $3,000 worth of equipment.

Assuming the partnership has sufficient taxable income, it can elect to expense up to $250,000 of the cost of the oven and refrigerator. Each partner's share of the expense deduction is $125,000. Colleen can elect to expense up to $128,000 ($125,000 + $3,000) if she has in aggregate at least $128,000 of taxable income from the partnership, flower shop, and/or other trade or business in which she actively participates. Christina may expense $125,000 if she satisfies the taxable income limitation.

Disposition of Section 179 property. A Code Sec. 179 expense deduction is treated as a depreciation deduction for purposes of computing the adjusted basis of the property. However, when a Section 179 expense is elected, but the deduction is disallowed due to the taxable income limitations, any amount of Section 179 expense carried over and not deducted before disposition of

---

[38] Code Sec. 179(b)(4).

[39] Code Sec. 179(d)(8); Reg. § 1.179-2.

the asset does not reduce the adjusted basis of the asset for the purpose of determining the gain or loss recognized on the disposition of the property.[40]

.04 Special Rules for Passenger Automobiles

The tax laws limit the amount of depreciation deductions that may be claimed each year on passenger automobiles. These rules are often referred to as the "luxury automobile limitations," even though they limit the amount of depreciation that may be claimed on all but the most inexpensive vehicles. A car is classified as a "passenger automobile" if its unloaded gross vehicle weight (curb weight) is 6,000 pounds or less. Trucks and vans, including sports utility vehicles (SUVs) built on a truck chassis, are classified as passenger automobiles if their gross vehicle weight rating (GVWR) is 6,000 pounds or less. GVWR is the curb weight of the vehicle plus its maximum allowable payload. Ambulances, hearses, taxis, and limousines are not considered passenger automobiles for the purposes of the limits imposed on such vehicles.[41]

Code Sec. 179 expense (¶ 702.03) and any bonus depreciation (¶ 702.02) are treated as depreciation deductions for purposes of the depreciation caps.[42] Consequently, the sum of any bonus depreciation, Code Sec. 179 expense, and MACRS or ADS depreciation in the first year may not exceed the applicable first-year depreciation cap. Note, however, that the depreciation cap is significantly increased for the years 2008 and 2009 because bonus depreciation is allowable for both years.

 Planning Pointer: Generally, there is no benefit in claiming a Code Sec. 179 expense allowance on a passenger automobile since the depreciation deductions without regard to Code Sec. 179 will almost always exceed the depreciation caps.

If a truck, SUV, or van has a GVWR in excess of 6,000 pounds, it is not subject to the annual depreciation limitations that apply to lighter vehicles. However, effective for SUVs weighing between 6,000 and 14,000 pounds that are placed in service after October 22, 2004, the maximum amount that may be expensed under Code Sec. 179 and not subject to the luxury automobile limits is $25,000.[43] The $25,000 limitation also applies to trucks with a GVWR in excess of 6,000 pounds if their interior cargo bed length is less than six feet. The limitation applies to passenger vans that seat fewer than 11 persons behind the driver's seat.

Example 28: A taxpayer places a passenger car with a GVWR of 2,500 pounds in service in the taxpayer's trade or business. The vehicle is subject to the lowest luxury automobile limitations described above, with no additional depreciation amount allowed for Code Sec. 179 expensing.

Example 29: A taxpayer places an SUV with a GVWR of 7,500 pounds in service in the taxpayer's trade or business after October 22, 2004. The vehicle is subject to the luxury automobile limitations, but the taxpayer may expense up to $25,000 of the vehicle's purchase price under Code Sec. 179.

 Reason for the Rule: When the luxury automobile rules were first enacted, most automobiles weighed less than 6,000 pounds. In recent years, taxpayers found that they could purchase a HUMMER or other SUV weighing more than 6,000 pounds and expense its entire cost in one year. Therefore, the new rules limit the deduction for

---

[40] Reg. § 1.179-3(f)(1).
[41] Code Sec. 280F.

[42] Code Sec. 280F(d)(1); Temp. Reg. § 1.280F-2T(b)(4); Temp. Reg. § 1.280F-3T(c), (d)(2).
[43] Code Sec. 179(b)(6).

these heavier vehicles to $25,000. Under the current tax laws, only vehicles weighing over 14,000 pounds are exempt from the limits imposed on expensing the costs of passenger automobiles under Code Sec. 179.

If the basis of a vehicle is not fully deducted during its recovery period because of the annual limitations on the depreciation deductions, any unrecovered basis attributable to the depreciation limits is recovered beginning with the first tax year after the regular depreciation recovery period. The deduction for each year in the post-recovery period, however, is limited to the maximum annual cap allowed as a deduction for the final year of the recovery period (or the remaining unrecovered basis, if less). This assumes, of course, that the vehicle is still being used for business purposes.

The maximum MACRS depreciation amounts for a passenger automobile for the first, second, third, and succeeding tax years in the depreciation period and in post-recovery period years are listed in Table 7G in the Appendix to this chapter (see ¶ 726).

Example 30: A new automobile used exclusively for business purposes is purchased in January 2009 for $40,000. The automobile is depreciated under MACRS. Assume the half-year convention applies and no Code Sec. 179 expense allowance or bonus depreciation is claimed. Also assume that the limits for 2009 are the same as for 2008. For each year of the recovery period, the taxpayer must compare the applicable depreciation limit with the depreciation computed under MACRS. The $2,960 first-year limit is compared to the sum of the regular first-year MACRS depreciation ($40,000 × 20% = $8,000) plus any Code Sec. 179 depreciation ($0). The allowable first-year deduction is $2,960 because that is less than $8,000. The taxpayer may deduct the lower of the limit or the depreciation allowed without regard to the limit as shown below.

Year	Limit	MACRS	Allowable Deduction
2009	$ 2,960	$ 8,000	$ 2,960
2010	4,800	12,800	4,800
2011	2,850	7,680	2,850
2012	1,775	4,608	1,775
2013	1,775	4,608	1,775
2014	1,775	2,304	1,775
Total depreciation taken after six years			$15,935

The unrecovered basis of $24,065 ($40,000 – $15,935) may be claimed at the rate of $1,775 per year beginning in 2015, assuming the vehicle continues to be used exclusively for business purposes.

Partial business use limitations. If a passenger automobile is used less than 100 percent in a trade or business or for the production of income (investment use), the depreciation deduction limits are determined by multiplying the limitation amount by the percentage of business and investment use. In addition, if the business use percentage for any year is less than 50 percent, depreciation must be computed using ADS and the appropriate averaging convention, as explained below.

Leased automobiles. In order to prevent lessees of automobiles from completely bypassing the depreciation limits to which they would be subject if they purchased the same automobile, instead of leasing, lessees may be required to reduce their allowable lease expense deduction by what is termed an "inclusion amount."[44]

The inclusion amount is a percentage of part of the fair market value (FMV) of the leased automobile multiplied by the percentage of business use of the vehicle for the tax year. The inclusion amount is prorated for the number of days of the lease term included in the tax year. Although the restrictions are not as severe as the luxury limits, these inclusion amounts tend to partially offset the benefits from leasing expensive autos to circumvent the luxury auto limits. In determining the proper inclusion amount, the taxpayer should use the tables that have been prepared by the IRS.[45] (See Table 7I in the Appendix at ¶ 727 for the inclusion amounts for leases that begin in 2008.)

Example 31:   Meisenheimer Corporation leases a passenger automobile with an FMV of $45,800 for use in its trade or business. Meisenheimer pays $700 per month for the automobile. The five-year lease term begins on February 1, 2008. Meisenheimer must reduce its deduction for each year of the lease by the appropriate amount from Table 7I in the Appendix at ¶ 727. The first-year inclusion for an automobile placed in service during 2008 with an FMV between $45,000 and $46,000 is $152. However, Meisenheimer's lease began on February 1, so this amount must be apportioned to reflect the 335 days the corporation leased the automobile during the year. Thus, for 2008, Meisenheimer must reduce its $7,700 lease expense ($700 × 11) by $139 ($152 × 335/366), so it only deducts $7,561 ($7,700 – $139).

In each subsequent year from 2009 to 2012, Meisenheimer pays $8,400 to lease the automobile ($700 × 12); however, it must reduce its deduction by the amounts from the lease inclusion table reproduced in Table 7I in the Appendix at ¶ 727 as shown below:

Year	Inclusion Amount	Allowable deduction
2008 (year 1)	$139	$7,561
2009 (year 2)	333	8,067
2010 (year 3)	495	7,905
2011 (year 4)	592	7,808
2012 (year 5)	682	7,718
2013 (year 6)	58	642

In 2013, Meisenheimer pays the final lease payment of $700 in January. It must reduce its deduction by the portion of the $682 inclusion amount to reflect the 31 days that it leased the automobile during the year ($682 × 31/365 = $58).

¶ 703 Real Property Depreciation Rules

The tax laws allow taxpayers to depreciate the costs associated with the acquisition of real property using the straight-line method. Because land does not wear out, decay, get used up, become obsolete, or lose its value from natural causes, it is nondepreciable real property.

As discussed below, the recovery period for depreciable realty is long—27.5 years or 39 years, depending on its use. Fortunately however, a not insignificant portion of the "cost" of a typical business or rental building is actually personal property, not realty. Once segregated for deprecia-

---

[44] Code Sec. 280F(c).
[45] Reg. § 1.280F-7. The IRS issues an annual Revenue Procedure containing such tables. For autos with lease terms begin-

ning in 2006, the percentages used to calculate the inclusion amount are found in Rev. Proc. 2006-18, IRB 2006-12, 645, March 20, 2006.

tion purposes (taxpayers often hire experts to do costs segregation), these separate personal property components may be depreciated over the prescribed period for personal property (usually five or seven years).

Generally, the cost of grading, clearing, planting, and landscaping are considered part of the cost of the land. However, land preparation costs may be depreciable if they are so closely associated with a depreciable asset that it is not possible to ascertain a life for the preparation costs that is separate from the life of the asset with which they are associated. Certain other land improvements that may be depreciated include sidewalks, roads, canals, drainage facilities, waterways, sewers, wharves, docks, bridges, and fences. These depreciable land improvements are treated as personal property and can be depreciated over a 15-year recovery period (see ¶ 702.01).

Example 32: Jones & Sons is in the process of constructing a new building for its business. Jones incurs costs for grading, clearing, seeding, and planting trees. Some of the bushes and trees are planted in the immediate vicinity of the building, while others are planted around the outer perimeter of the lot on which the new building is placed. If Jones were to replace the building, it would have to destroy the bushes and trees immediately adjacent to it. Therefore, Jones can depreciate the cost of landscaping right next to the building. It also can treat the cost of grading land directly under the building, including trenches for concrete footers, as part of the cost of the building. It cannot, however, depreciate the cost of the rest of the landscaping, which must be added to the basis of the land.

Under MACRS, the recovery period is 27.5 years for residential real property and 39 years for commercial real property. Prior to May 12, 1993, the cost recovery period for commercial realty was 31.5 years. Under ADS, all real property is depreciated over 40 years. The mid-month convention is used to determine the dates that real property is deemed to be placed in service and disposed of, regardless of whether MACRS or ADS is used.

Example 33: Depreciable real property is placed in service on February 3, 2008, by a calendar-year taxpayer. For 2008, depreciation may be claimed for 10.5 months (February 15, 2008, to December 31, 2008).

Example 34: Assume that the property in Example 33 was sold in March 2009. The property is considered in service in 2009 until March 15, 2009, and accordingly, 2½ months of depreciation may be deducted on the taxpayer's 2009 tax return with respect to the property.

Residential real property is rental property for which 80 percent or more of the gross rental income is derived from the rental of dwelling units. A **dwelling unit** is a house or apartment used to provide living accommodations. It does not include a unit in a hotel, motel, inn, or other establishment in which more than 50 percent of the units are used on a transient basis. Dwelling units include mobile homes and manufactured homes. Apartment buildings are an example of residential real property. Depreciable real property that does not meet the definition of residential realty is "commercial real property." Examples of commercial realty include warehouses, office buildings, and certain manufacturing facilities.

Example 35: On May 1, 2009, John Jones pays $240,000 for real property, of which $40,000 is allocable to land. The building consists of a single storefront and six similar upper-story apartments. Jones receives $400 per month for each of the six apartments and $700 per month for the store. Because the $2,400 gross rental income from the apartments ($400 × 6 units) is less than 80 percent of the gross rental income from the building ($2,400 + $700 = $3,100 × 80% = $2,480), the building is not residential rental property and must be depreciated over a 39-year recovery period under MACRS.

Example 36: The facts are the same as in Example 35, except that each apartment rents for $500 per month. Gross rental income from the building is then equal to $3,700 ($500 × 6 = $3,000 + $700). Because at least 80 percent of the gross rental income ($3,700 × 80% = $2,960) from the building comes from the gross rental income from the apartments ($500 × 6 = $3,000), the building is residential rental property and can be depreciated over 27.5 years under MACRS.

The IRS provides depreciation tables for real property that should be used; however because the straight-line method is used to depreciate real property, it is often easy to ensure that the correct amount has been used by calculating the depreciation manually.

Example 37: Continuing with Example 36, assume that the depreciable basis of the rental portion of the building is $172,973. The building is deemed placed in service on May 15, 2009; therefore, depreciation for 2009 equals $3,931 ($172,973/27.5 × 7.5/12). Depreciation for 2010 is $6,290 ($172,973/27.5).

Example 38: In December of 2009, Primex, Inc. (a calendar year taxpayer) purchases an office building for $450,000, of which $50,000 is allocable to the cost of the land. Depreciation expense for the building in 2009 equals $427 ($400,000/39 × .5/12).

Example 39: Continuing with Example 38, Primex sells the office building on November 10, 2013. Primex continues to depreciate the building until November 15, 2013. Therefore, from 2010 to 2012, Primex deducts $10,256 ($400,000/39), and on its 2012 tax return, it deducts $8,974 ($400,000/39 × 10.5/12). Primex's adjusted basis in the building at the time it is sold equals $359,831 ($400,000 – $427 – ($10,256 × 3) – $8,974).

Example 40: Assume the same facts as in Examples 38 and 39, except that Primex elects to depreciate the building using ADS. Under ADS, all real property is depreciated over 40 years. Therefore, 2009 depreciation equals $417 ($400,000/40 × .5/12), and depreciation from 2010 to 2012 is $10,000 ($400,000/40). In 2013, Primex's depreciation deduction is $8,750 ($400,000/40 × 10.5/12). Its adjusted basis in the building at the time of the sale equals $360,833 ($400,000 – $417 – ($10,000 × 3) – $8,750).

An irrevocable election may be made to use ADS for any class of property placed in service during a tax year. Unlike the election to use ADS for personal property which is done on a class-by-class basis, the ADS election for real property is made on a *property-by-property* basis.[46] Accordingly, taxpayers can elect to use ADS for one real property placed in service during the year, but still use MACRS to depreciate another piece of real property placed in service during the year.

¶ 704 Tax Depreciation of Improvements

Any depreciation deduction for any addition or improvement to property (including structural components that are added to a building after its construction) is computed in the same manner as the deduction for the underlying property would be computed if the property were placed in service at the same time as the addition or improvement.[47] For example, a roof replaced on a commercial building is separately depreciated as 39-year nonresidential real property beginning in the year the new roof is placed in service. The cost of an addition to or improvement of property, which must be depreciated, should be distinguished from a repair or maintenance expense, which can be deducted currently.

Example 41: In June 2009, the American Furniture Company purchases a new transmission for its 2005 model delivery truck (five-year property); the truck is four years old and has been driven 300,000 miles. The transmission costs $2,000. The depreciation period

---

[46] Code Sec. 168(g)(7).   [47] Code Sec. 168(i)(6).

for the transmission begins during 2009 following its installation in the truck. Assuming the half-year convention applies to personal property placed in service during 2009, the depreciation expense of $400 ($2,000 × 20%) would be calculated using the 5-year column in Table 7-3.

Additions or improvements made to real property that is leased are also treated as separate property items for depreciation purposes. MACRS depreciation on such additions or improvements is computed in the same way depreciation generally would be computed on the property added to or improved if such property had been placed in service at the same time as the addition or improvement.[48] Any unrecovered basis in property owned by the lessee and abandoned without compensation upon termination of the lease may be deducted as a loss. A lessor that disposes of or abandons a leasehold improvement owned by the lessor upon termination of the lease may also claim a loss.[49]

DEPLETION

The costs associated with the acquisition of natural resources (often called wasting assets) are recovered through an annual depletion expense. Examples of assets subject to depletion include, but are not limited to, coal, oil, gas, iron ore, sand, and timber. The tax laws allow two depletion methods: cost depletion and percentage depletion. For each year, taxpayers are required to use whichever method produces the highest deduction in that year;[50] however, in the case of timber, cost depletion is the only method allowed. The amount of depletion allowable reduces the adjusted basis of the property (but never below zero).

 Planning Pointer: A depletion deduction cannot be increased in a later year because no allowance, or an inadequate one, was taken in a prior year. The remedy for deducting less than the allowable depletion is to file an amended return for the year(s) involved.

¶705 Cost Depletion

The allowable **cost depletion** is equal to the adjusted basis of the depletable asset divided by the estimated recoverable reserves and then multiplied by the number of units sold during the tax year.[51] Recoverable reserves can be measured in tons (in the case of ore, gold, or other similar resources) or barrels (in the case of oil). The cost depletion method resembles the units-of-production depreciation method that is used for financial statement purposes.

Example 42: Smith & Sons bought a mine for $12,000; an engineer's estimate indicated that 60,000 tons of iron ore could be extracted from the mine. During 20X1, the first year, 6,500 tons were extracted and 6,000 sold. Cost depletion for 20X1 is computed as follows:

$12,000 (cost) ÷ 60,000 (tons available) = $.20 per ton (depletion rate)

6,000 (tons sold) × $.20 = $1,200 depletion expense for 20X1

$12,000 − $1,200 = $10,800 adjusted basis at the end of 20X1

Cost depletion can be deducted each year based on the estimated remaining recoverable units. If the estimate changes, the formula for computing cost depletion in future periods is adjusted to

---

[48] Code Sec. 168(i)(6) and (8).
[49] Code Sec. 168(i)(8)(B).

[50] Reg. § 1.611-1(a)(1).
[51] Reg. § 1.611-2(a).

reflect the new estimate. It is important to note that cost depletion is computed based on the number of units sold during the year, regardless of the number of units extracted.

Example 43: Assume the same facts as in Example 42, except that at the end of 20X1 it is estimated that another 90,000 recoverable tons remain. Another 6,000 tons are sold in 20X2. Cost depletion for 20X2 would then be calculated as follows:

$10,800 (adjusted basis) ÷ 90,000 (tons available) = $.12 per ton (depletion rate)

6,000 (tons sold) × $.12 cents (depletion rate) = $720 depletion expense for 20X2

$10,800 – $720 = $10,080 adjusted basis at the end of 20X2

The cost method must be used to calculate depletion on timber. Any costs associated with the land purchased in conjunction with the timber must be separated out and cannot be depleted.[52]

Example 44: A taxpayer bought a 500-acre timber tract for $20,000, of which $5,000 was for land and $15,000 was for timber. It was estimated that there were 150,000 board feet on the tract. During the first year, the taxpayer felled and sold 50,000 board feet. The depletion deduction is computed as follows:

$15,000 (adjusted basis) ÷ 150,000 = $.10 per board foot (depletion rate)

50,000 (board feet felled) × $.10 = $5,000 depletion expense

$15,000 – $5,000 = $10,000 adjusted basis at the end of the first year

¶ 706 Percentage Depletion

In general, **percentage depletion** is determined by multiplying the applicable percentage (as specified for the particular natural resource) by the gross income from the property. However, the deduction for percentage depletion is generally limited to 50 percent of the taxable income from the property before the depletion deduction. Exceptions to the general rule are provided for oil and gas properties. The limitation is 100 percent of taxable income for oil and gas properties (65 percent of taxable income for independent producers and royalty owners).[53] All expenses related to the property other than depletion are subtracted from gross income from the property when applying the limits.

The applicable percentage varies depending on the type of resource being extracted. Table 7-5 lists the applicable percentages for some of the more common types of natural resources.

Table 7-5 Percentage Depletion Rates

Natural Resource	Depletion Rate
Sulfur, lead, nickel, tin, and uranium	22%
Gold, silver, copper, and iron ore	15%
Coal and perlite	10%
Gravel, peat, and sand	5%

[52] Reg. § 1.611-3.   [53] Code Sec. 613(a).

Example 45: Refer back to Example 42, in which Smith & Sons purchased a mine for $12,000. If gross income from the mine is $15,000 and expenses connected with operating the mine are $12,000, the taxable income from the mine before depletion expense is $3,000 ($15,000 – $12,000). Applying the 15-percent depletion percentage to gross income yields preliminary depletion of $2,250 ($15,000 × 15%). However, allowable percentage depletion is limited to 50 percent of taxable income from the property, or $1,500 ($3,000 × 50%). Because the percentage depletion ($1,500) is greater than the $1,200 of cost depletion that would be allowed, the allowable depletion deduction is $1,500. The adjusted basis of the mine is reduced to $10,500 ($12,000 – $1,500). This adjusted basis is then used to compute cost depletion in 20X2.

 Spotlight: Percentage depletion is computed without regard to the adjusted basis of the property being depleted. Percentage depletion is a function of the applicable depletion rate and the gross income from the property. Therefore, the percentage depletion amount typically is greater than the depletion expense using cost depletion. However, because of the taxable income limit, in years in which the expenses (other than depletion) related to the property are very high, it is possible that the amount of percentage depletion will be limited.

.01 Percentage Depletion for Oil and Gas

Most large oil and gas producers are not allowed to use percentage depletion.[54] However, several exceptions exist to this general prohibition. A 22-percent allowance is allowed for production for certain domestic gas wells, and a 10-percent rate is allowed for certain natural gas from geo-pressured brine.[55] Independent producers and royalty owners are allowed a 15-percent rate for oil and gas, and certain marginal oil and gas wells are allowed a higher percentage depletion rate.[56] For oil and gas properties, the depletion deduction may not exceed the taxable income for the property, computed without regard to the depletion allowance.[57]

Example 46: Magic Gas Inc. purchases for $15,000 gas-producing wells that are eligible for the 22-percent depletion rate. In its first year of production, gross income from the property is $20,000 and its expenses are $5,000, generating $15,000 of taxable income from the property prior to depletion. Magic Gas computes percentage depletion, yielding a preliminary depletion deduction equal to $4,400 ($20,000 × 22%). Because this amount is less than its taxable income from the property, Magic Gas's percentage depletion deduction is $4,400. Assuming the cost depletion method yields a smaller deduction, the depletion deduction for the year would be $4,400, and Magic Gas would reduce its adjusted basis in the land to $145,600 ($150,000 – $4,400).

.02 Small Independent Producers and Royalty Owners

As mentioned above, percentage depletion for a small independent producer or a royalty owner for domestic production is calculated based on a 15-percent depletion rate.[58] The allowable percentage depletion is limited to the *lesser of* (1) 65 percent of the *taxpayer's taxable income* as computed without taking into account the depletion allowance, the domestic production activities deduction (¶ 509), NOL carrybacks (¶ 1001), or capital loss carrybacks (¶ 901.01) or (2) 100 percent of *taxable income from the property* before the depletion allowance.[59] The maximum depletable quantity is 1,000

[54] Code Sec. 613(d).
[55] Code Sec. 613A(b)(1) and (2).
[56] Code Sec. 613A(c)(1) and (6).
[57] Code Sec. 613(a).
[58] Code Sec. 613A(c) and (d).
[59] Code Sec. 613A(d)(1).

barrels of domestic crude a day or six million cubic feet of gas.[60] Any depletion deduction disallowed under the 65-percent limit may be carried over to subsequent tax years.

Example 47: Samuel Chavez, a taxpayer who owns royalty interests in various oil-producing properties, has taxable income (before depletion deductions) for the current year of $100,000. Samuel does not qualify for the domestic production activities deduction and does not have an NOL or capital loss carrybacks. He is allowed a depletion deduction of $70,000 with respect to his royalty interests. Because the amount exceeds 65 percent of his taxable income ($100,000 × 65% = $65,000), $5,000 of depletion allowances are disallowed for the current tax year and must be carried over and deducted in the next year.

Spotlight: Each year the taxpayer uses the depletion method that produces the greatest expense deduction. The amount reduces the adjusted basis of the property, which becomes the starting point for calculating the cost depletion for the subsequent tax year. Because percentage depletion is often much greater than cost depletion, it is possible that the adjusted basis of the property will be reduced to $0 before all of the resources have been extracted. The tax laws allow the taxpayer to continue to use the percentage depletion method for all subsequent tax years in which there is gross income from the property. The adjusted basis of the property cannot be reduced below $0, so it will remain at $0 during each of those years.

GAAP vs. Code: The cost method is the only acceptable method for financial statement purposes. The cost method used in financial reporting closely resembles the unit-of-production depreciation method, in that the depletable cost is allocated based on the estimated number of units the resource is expected to produce. Because the greater of cost depletion or percentage depletion is used for tax purposes, significant annual differences between the amount of depletion deducted on the income statement and that deducted on the tax return are likely to exist. Even when cost depletion is used for tax purposes, differences in amounts will likely occur. The income tax basis of the property may differ from the book value for financial purposes; thus, cost depletion beginning the first year may differ. In addition, tax depletion is based on the units sold, whereas depletion for financial purposes is based on units produced. Accordingly, the difference between the two depletion amounts needs to be considered when reconciling net income to taxable income on the corporate tax return.

¶707 Intangible Drilling and Development Costs

As discussed in Chapter 5, operators of a domestic oil, gas, or geothermal well may elect to currently deduct intangible drilling and development costs (IDC) rather than capitalize and recover the costs through depletion or depreciation. IDC generally includes all expenditures by the operator incident to and necessary for the drilling of wells and the preparation of wells for the production of oil, gas, or geothermal energy. However, IDC does not include the cost of tangible property nor part of the acquisition price of an interest in the property. IDC expenditures include the cost of labor, fuel and power, materials and supplies, tool rental, truck and auto hire, repairs to drilling equipment, and depreciation on drilling equipment.[61]

---

[60] Code Sec. 613A(c)(3) and (4).   [61] Code Sec. 263(c); Reg. §1.612-4.

Preliminary exploration costs are not considered IDC, but instead are considered capital expenditures in nature[62] and generally are recoverable through depletion. However, for taxable years beginning after August 8, 2005, certain of these costs (geological and geophysical (G&G) costs incurred with respect to oil and natural gas exploration) are amortizable over 24 months.[63] The exploration phase stops and the development stage begins at the point at which the preparation for exploratory drilling begins. The operator's decision to drill normally triggers the beginning of the development phase.[64]

The election to deduct these costs must be made in the first year in which the costs are paid or incurred and, once made, is binding for future years.[65] A failure to deduct the costs as expenses in the year they are incurred is deemed to be an election to capitalize them (i.e., add them to the basis of the property). The election, once made, is binding for all future years. If the operator has elected to capitalize IDCs, and the well proves to be nonproductive (a dry hole), the operator may elect to deduct the costs as an ordinary loss.

Example 48: End Run Oil company spends $50,000 investigating the oil producing capabilities of a piece of land: $25,000 in G&G costs and $25,000 in other exploratory costs. In the same year, the company buys the land for $250,000 and spends $100,000 sinking wells on the property. End Run may deduct the $100,000 as IDC and may amortize the $25,000 of G&G costs over 24 months. The remaining $25,000 in exploratory costs is added to the purchase price of the land, yielding an adjusted basis of $275,000. If End Run does not elect to deduct its IDC, they will be added to the adjusted basis of the land and recovered through depletion deductions.

AMORTIZATION

Depreciation and amortization are similar concepts, but they apply to two different types of assets: tangible assets are "depreciated;" intangible assets are "amortized." Intangible property is personal property that does not have physical characteristics, and includes, among others, copyrights, franchises, patents, trademarks, and trade names. The cost of intangibles used in a trade or business or for the production of income can often be recovered over time through amortization, much as the cost of depreciable business assets can often be recovered over time through depreciation. Amortizable intangible assets can be grouped into two broad categories: (1) intangibles that are amortized under Code Sec. 197 ("Section 197 intangibles") and (2) other amortizable intangibles.

¶708 Amortization of Section 197 Intangibles

Most intangible property falls under the category of Section 197 intangibles. A list of the intangible assets covered under Code Sec. 197 is shown in Figure 7-1. **Amortizable Section 197 intangibles** are intangibles listed in Code Sec. 197 that are *acquired by the taxpayer* and are held in connection with the conduct of a trade or business or for the production of income. Thus, intangibles that are not acquired by the taxpayer but are created by the taxpayer's own efforts are not Section 197 intangibles and are only amortizable if such treatment is allowed by some other provision in the tax law. Amortization under Code Sec. 197 is claimed ratably over 180 months (15 years) beginning on the first day of the month that the intangible is placed in service. Accordingly, a Section 197 intangible is amortized without respect to its actual or estimated useful life.

[62] Rev. Rul. 77-188, 1977-1 CB 76.

[63] Code Sec. 167(h), as added by §1310(a) of Energy Tax Incentives Act of 2005 (P.L. 109-58).

[64] *Gates Rubber Co.*, 74 TC 1456, Dec. 37,292, aff'd, CA-10, 82-2 USTC ¶9702, 694 F2d 648.

[65] Reg. §§1.612-4 and 1.612-5.

Figure 7-1 Section 197 Intangibles

- Goodwill and going concern value;

- Workforce in place, such as the portion of the purchase price of a business attributable to the existence of highly skilled employees;

- Business books and records, operating systems, or any other information base including customer lists, or other information with respect to current or future customers;

- Patents, copyrights, formulas, processes, designs, patterns, know-how, formats, or similar items;

- Customer-based intangibles, such as a business's market composition or market share;

- Supplier-based intangibles, such as a business's favorable relationships with distributors;

- Licenses, permits, or other rights granted by a governmental unit or agency, such as a liquor license, a taxi-cab medallion or license, or a television or radio broadcasting license (including issuance and renewal costs);

- Franchises, trademarks, or trade names; and

- Covenants not to compete if acquired in connection with the acquisition of a business.

Example 49: Kumquat Computer Corporation pays a departing executive, Stephanie Works, $10,000 not to compete with it for a period of three years. The covenant not to compete is not a Section 197 intangible because it was not entered into in connection with the acquisition of a trade or business.

Example 50: Specific Engines Corporation, as part of the acquisition of the business of Parrot Software on July 15, 2008, acquires substantially all of its assets. Of the purchase price, $18 million is allocated to goodwill. Since goodwill is a Section 197 intangible, the $18 million cost basis for the goodwill must be amortized using the straight-line method over 180 months beginning on July 1, 2008. If Specific Engines uses the calendar year, it can deduct $600,000 ($18,000,000/180 × 6 months) against gross income on its 2008 tax return. From 2009 until 2022, Specific Engines will deduct $1,200,000 ($18,000,000/180 × 12) of amortization each year. In 2022, Specific Engines can claim the final six months of amortization ($18,000,000/180 × 6 = $600,000).

When more than one amortizable Section 197 intangible is acquired in a single transaction, no loss may be claimed on any Section 197 intangible that is later separately disposed of. Instead, the amount of the loss is allocated proportionately among the remaining Section 197 intangibles acquired in the transaction as an increase in basis. As a result, the loss will be recovered through amortization deductions over the remainder of the 15-year amortization period.

Example 51: Assume the same facts as in Example 50, except that Parrot has three separate businesses, to which $6 million of goodwill is allocated. After taking $3 million of amortization ($1 million for the goodwill of each business), Specific Engines sells one of the businesses for a loss in an asset sale. It allocates $2 million of the loss to the business's goodwill. Specific Engines may not take an immediate loss deduction for this amount; instead it must add $1 million to the basis of the goodwill of each of the two remaining businesses and recover the loss through amortization deductions.

Reason for the Rule: The treatment of costs incurred to acquire intangible property has been a source of considerable controversy between taxpayers and the IRS. In an attempt to minimize the controversy surrounding the identification, valuation, and establishment of useful lives of intangible property, Congress added Section 197 to the Code in the Omnibus Budget Reconciliation Act of 1993 to provide a single method and recovery period for most acquired intangibles.[66]

¶ 709 Amorization of Non-Section 197 Intangibles

In Chapter 5, organizational costs, start-up costs, and research and experimental costs were discussed. These costs are all intangible costs that were capitalized and either expensed in the current period or amortized over 180 months (in the case of organizational costs and start-up costs) or 60 months (in the case of research and experimental costs) (see ¶ 503, ¶ 504, and ¶ 507). Certain other intangible property not specifically listed in Code Sec. 197 may be amortized, including leaseholds and computer software.

.01 Leaseholds

If a leasehold is acquired for business purposes, the taxpayer may amortize the cost of acquiring the lease over the term of the lease plus expected renewal options.[67] In addition, amounts paid to obtain a lease on property used in a business (such as commissions, bonuses, fees and other amounts) are amortized as part of the cost of the lease.

Example 52: On June 1, 2008, the American Pie Company (a calendar year corporation) purchases the leasehold interest of Don Donaldson in a one-story building from which American Pie operates a bakery. American Pie pays $25,000 for Donaldson's 15-year lease, on which 10 years (120 months) remain. American Pie deducts $1,458 ($25,000/120 × 7 months) as a business expense in 2008. It deducts $2,500 ($25,000/120 × 12) each year from 2009 to 2017, and it will deduct the final $1,042 ($25,000/120 × 5 months) in 2018.

.02 Computer Software

Computer software acquired in connection with a trade or business is amortizable over 15 years as a Section 197 intangible. Computer software that is not amortizable under Code Sec. 197 is depreciable over 36 months using the straight-line method beginning in the month of acquisition provided that it is readily available for purchase by the general public, is subject to a nonexclusive license, and has not been substantially modified.[68] Computer software whose cost is included in the total cost of a computer is not separately depreciated. It is considered part of the depreciable cost basis of the computer.

Example 53: St. Ignace Corporation purchases the business of Hancock Company in an asset acquisition. It allocates $100,000 of the purchase price to software owned by Hancock. In the same year, St. Ignace buys word processing software readily available for purchase by the public. St. Ignace may depreciate the cost of the word processing software over 36 months; however, it must recover the $100,000 of the purchase price allocated to the Hancock software over 15 years.

---

[66] House Committee Report, Omnibus Budget Reconciliation Act of 1993 (P.L. 103-66).

[67] Code Sec. 178.

[68] Code Sec. 167 (f) (1); Code Sec. 197 (e) (3).

GAAP vs. Code: For financial statement purposes, the costs associated with the acquisition of intangible assets having a finite life are amortized ratably over the asset's remaining useful life. Intangible assets with an infinite life are subject to an annual impairment test and are only written off when impaired. However, the economic downturn that began in late 2007 has resulted in the impairment, and resulting write-down, of a considerable amount of goodwill as well as other intangible assets. For tax purposes, most intangible assets are amortized ratably over 15 years, and accordingly, the amount of amortization expense reported on the income statement is rarely the same as amortization expense deducted on the tax return. This difference must be taken into consideration when reconciling net income to taxable income on the corporate tax return.

¶ 710 Summary

Generally, a taxpayer may not expense the purchase price of property that will provide benefits beyond the current tax year, but rather must depreciate (tangible personal property and depreciable real property), deplete (natural resource property) or amortize (intangible property) such assets. There are two main exceptions to the foregoing rule. First, land is not depreciable. Second, certain taxpayers can elect to expense a certain amount of the purchase price of certain depreciable assets under Code Sec. 179. Tax rules applicable to cost recovery deductions for depreciation, depletion, and amortization differ significantly from financial accounting rules for such deductions.

APPENDIX

¶ 725 MACRS and ADS Depreciation Tables

The following are some of the IRS depreciation tables used for 3-, 5-, 7-, 10-, 15-, and 20-year MACRS property. Table 7A is used if the half-year convention applies. Tables 7B through 7E reflect the mid-quarter convention. If the mid-quarter convention applies, use the table designated for the quarter that the asset was placed in service. Table 7F is used to compute depreciation under the general depreciation system (general MACRS) straight-line and MACRS alternative depreciation system (ADS) if the half-year convention applies. The straight-line and ADS mid-quarter convention tables are not reproduced. The 150-percent declining balance election half-year and mid-quarter convention tables are also not reproduced. These tables can be found in Appendix A in IRS Publication 946.

Table 7A

General Depreciation System (general MACRS)

Applicable Depreciation Method: 200 or 150 percent

Declining Balance Switching to Straight Line

Applicable Recovery Periods: 3, 5, 7, 10, 15, 20 Years

Applicable Convention: Half-Year

[All amounts in the table reflect percentages; only depreciation percentages for the first 10 recovery years are reproduced.]

If the Recovery Year Is:	and the Recovery Period Is:					
	3-year	5-year	7-year	10-year	15-year	20-year
			the Depreciation Rate Is:			
1	33.33	20.00	14.29	10.00	5.00	3.750
2	44.45	32.00	24.49	18.00	9.50	7.219
3	14.81	19.20	17.49	14.40	8.55	6.677
4	7.41	11.52	12.49	11.52	7.70	6.177
5		11.52	8.93	9.22	6.93	5.713
6		5.76	8.92	7.37	6.23	5.285
7			8.93	6.55	5.90	4.888
8			4.46	6.55	5.90	4.522
9				6.56	5.91	4.462
10				6.55	5.90	4.461
				. . .	. . .	. . .

Table 7B

General Depreciation System (general MACRS)

Applicable Depreciation Method: 200 or 150 percent

Declining Balance Switching to Straight Line

Applicable Recovery Periods: 3, 5, 7, 10, 15, 20 Years

Applicable Convention: Mid-quarter (property placed in service in first quarter)

[All amounts in the table reflect percentages; only depreciation percentages for the first 10 recovery years are reproduced.]

If the Recovery Year Is:	and the Recovery Period Is:					
	3-year	5-year	7-year	10-year	15-year	20-year
			the Depreciation Rate Is:			
1	58.33	35.00	25.00	17.50	8.75	6.563
2	27.78	26.00	21.43	16.50	9.13	7.000
3	12.35	15.60	15.31	13.20	8.21	6.482
4	1.54	11.01	10.93	10.56	7.39	5.996
5		11.01	8.75	8.45	6.65	5.546
6		1.38	8.74	6.76	5.99	5.130
7			8.75	6.55	5.90	4.746
8			1.09	6.55	5.91	4.459
9				6.56	5.90	4.459
10				6.55	5.91	4.459
				. . .	. . .	. . .

Table 7C

General Depreciation System (general MACRS)

Applicable Depreciation Method: 200 or 150 percent

Declining Balance Switching to Straight Line

Applicable Recovery Periods: 3, 5, 7, 10, 15, 20 Years

Applicable Convention: Mid-quarter (property placed in service in second quarter)

[All amounts in the table reflect percentages; only depreciation percentages for the first 10 recovery years are reproduced.]

If the Recovery Year Is:	and the Recovery Period Is:					
	3-year	5-year	7-year	10-year	15-year	20-year
	the Depreciation Rate Is:					
1	41.67	25.00	17.85	12.50	6.25	4.688
2	38.89	30.00	23.47	17.50	9.38	7.148
3	14.14	18.00	16.76	14.00	8.44	6.612
4	5.30	11.37	11.97	11.20	7.59	6.116
5		11.37	8.87	8.96	6.83	5.658
6		4.26	8.87	7.17	6.15	5.233
7			8.87	6.55	5.91	4.841
8			3.33	6.55	5.90	4.478
9				6.56	5.91	4.463
10				6.55	5.90	4.463
				. . .	. . .	. . .

Table 7D

General Depreciation System (general MACRS)

Applicable Depreciation Method: 200 or 150 percent

Declining Balance Switching to Straight Line

Applicable Recovery Periods: 3, 5, 7, 10, 15, 20 Years

Applicable Convention: Mid-quarter (property placed in service in third quarter)

[All amounts in the table reflect percentages; only depreciation percentages for the first 10 recovery years are reproduced.]

If the Recovery Year Is:	and the Recovery Period Is:					
	3-year	5-year	7-year	10-year	15-year	20-year
	the Depreciation Rate Is:					
1	25.00	15.00	10.71	7.50	3.75	2.813
2	50.00	34.00	25.51	18.50	9.63	7.289
3	16.67	20.40	18.22	14.80	8.66	6.742
4	8.33	12.24	13.02	11.84	7.80	6.237
5		11.30	9.30	9.47	7.02	5.769
6		7.06	8.85	7.58	6.31	5.336
7			8.86	6.55	5.90	4.936
8			5.53	6.55	5.90	4.566
9				6.56	5.91	4.460
10				6.55	5.90	4.460
				. . .	. . .	. . .

Table 7E

General Depreciation System (general MACRS)

Applicable Depreciation Method: 200 or 150 percent

Declining Balance Switching to Straight Line

Applicable Recovery Periods: 3, 5, 7, 10, 15, 20 Years

Applicable Convention: Mid-quarter (property placed in service in fourth quarter)

[All amounts in the table reflect percentages; only depreciation percentages for the first 10 recovery years are reproduced.]

If the Recovery Year Is:	and the Recovery Period Is:					
	3-year	5-year	7-year	10-year	15-year	20-year
	the Depreciation Rate Is:					
1........	8.33	5.00	3.57	2.50	1.25	0.938
2........	61.11	38.00	27.55	19.50	9.88	7.430
3........	20.37	22.80	19.68	15.60	8.89	6.872
4........	10.19	13.68	14.06	12.48	8.00	6.357
5........		10.94	10.04	9.98	7.20	5.880
6........		9.58	8.73	7.99	6.48	5.439
7........			8.73	6.55	5.90	5.031
8........			7.64	6.55	5.90	4.654
9........				6.56	5.90	4.458
10........				6.55	5.91	4.458
				. . .	. . .	. . .

Table 7F

General Depreciation System (MACRS SL) and Alternative Depreciation System (ADS)

Applicable Depreciation Method: Straight Line

Applicable Recovery Periods: 2.5—17 Years

Applicable Convention: Half-Year

[All amounts in the table reflect percentages; only depreciation percentages for the first 10 recovery years are reproduced.]

[IRS mid-quarter convention tables for depreciation under the general and alternative MACRS methods are not reproduced.]

If the Recovery Year Is:	and the Recovery Period Is:															
	2.5	3.0	3.5	4.0	4.5	5.0	5.5	6.0	6.5	7.0	7.5	8.0	8.5	9.0	9.5
	the Depreciation Rate Is:														
1 . . .	20.00	16.67	14.29	12.50	11.11	10.00	9.09	8.33	7.69	7.14	6.67	6.25	5.88	5.56	5.26
2 . . .	40.00	33.33	28.57	25.00	22.22	20.00	18.18	16.67	15.39	14.29	13.33	12.50	11.77	11.11	10.53
3 . . .	40.00	33.33	28.57	25.00	22.22	20.00	18.18	16.67	15.38	14.29	13.33	12.50	11.76	11.11	10.53
4 . . .		16.67	28.57	25.00	22.23	20.00	18.18	16.67	15.39	14.28	13.33	12.50	11.77	11.11	10.53
5 . . .				12.50	22.22	20.00	18.19	16.66	15.38	14.29	13.34	12.50	11.76	11.11	10.52
6 . . .						10.00	18.18	16.67	15.39	14.28	13.33	12.50	11.77	11.11	10.53
7 . . .							8.33	15.38	14.29	13.34	12.50	11.76	11.11	10.52
8 . . .								7.14	13.33	12.50	11.77	11.11	10.53
9 . . .									6.25	11.76	11.11	10.52
10 . . .										5.56	10.53

If the Recovery Year Is:	and the Recovery Period Is:														
	10.0	10.5	11.0	11.5	12.0	12.5	13.0	13.5	14.0	14.5	15.0	15.5	16.0	16.5	17.0
	the Depreciation Rate Is:														
1 . . .	5.00	4.76	4.55	4.35	4.17	4.00	3.85	3.70	3.57	3.45	3.33	3.23	3.13	3.03	2.94
2 . . .	10.00	9.52	9.09	8.70	8.33	8.00	7.69	7.41	7.14	6.90	6.67	6.45	6.25	6.06	5.88
3 . . .	10.00	9.52	9.09	8.70	8.33	8.00	7.69	7.41	7.14	6.90	6.67	6.45	6.25	6.06	5.88
4 . . .	10.00	9.53	9.09	8.69	8.33	8.00	7.69	7.41	7.14	6.90	6.67	6.45	6.25	6.06	5.88
5 . . .	10.00	9.52	9.09	8.70	8.33	8.00	7.69	7.41	7.14	6.90	6.67	6.45	6.25	6.06	5.88
6 . . .	10.00	9.53	9.09	8.69	8.33	8.00	7.69	7.41	7.14	6.89	6.67	6.45	6.25	6.06	5.88
7 . . .	10.00	9.52	9.09	8.70	8.34	8.00	7.69	7.41	7.14	6.90	6.67	6.45	6.25	6.06	5.88
8 . . .	10.00	9.53	9.09	8.69	8.33	8.00	7.69	7.41	7.15	6.89	6.66	6.45	6.25	6.06	5.88
9 . . .	10.00	9.52	9.09	8.70	8.34	8.00	7.69	7.41	7.14	6.90	6.67	6.45	6.25	6.06	5.88
10 . . .	10.00	9.53	9.09	8.69	8.33	8.00	7.70	7.40	7.15	6.89	6.66	6.45	6.25	6.06	5.88

* * *

¶726 Passenger Automobile Limits

The maximum MACRS depreciation amounts for a passenger automobile for the first, second, third, and succeeding tax years in the depreciation period and in post-recovery period years are listed in Table 7G. The limitation amounts in Table 7G do not apply to trucks (including SUVs built on a truck chassis) and vans placed in service after 2002 and which are subject to the depreciation caps because they have a gross vehicle weight rating of 6,000 pounds or less. The limits on these vehicles are listed in Table 7H. The official limits for 2009 were not available at the time this book went to the printer (instead, an unofficial estimate prepared by CCH staff is used).

Table 7G

For Cars Placed in Service After	Before	Depreciation Allowable in—			
		Year 1	Year 2	Year 3	Year 4, etc.
12/31/94	1/1/96	$ 3,060	$ 4,900	$ 2,950	$ 1,775
12/31/95	1/1/97	3,060	4,900	2,950	1,775
12/31/96	1/1/98	3,160	5,000	3,050	1,775
12/31/97	1/1/99	3,160	5,000	2,950	1,775
12/31/98	1/1/00	3,060	5,000	2,950	1,775
12/31/99	9/12/01	3,060	4,900	2,950	1,775
9/10/01	5/6/03	7,660*	4,900	2,950	1,775
5/5/03	1/1/04	10,710*	4,900	2,950	1,775
12/31/03	1/1/05	10,610	4,800	2,850	1,675
12/31/04	1/1/06	10,610*	4,800	2,850	1,675
12/31/05	1/1/07	2,960	4,800	2,850	1,775
12/31/06	1/1/08	3,060	4,900	2,850	1,775
12/31/07	1/1/09	10,960**	4,800	2,850	1,775
12/31/08***	1/1/10	10,960	4,800	2,850	1,775

*The first-year limit for an automobile placed in service after September 10, 2001, and before January 1, 2004, was reduced to $3,060 if bonus depreciation was not claimed on the vehicle. The limit was reduced to $2,960 for vehicles placed in service in 2004.

**The $8,000 of bonus depreciation allowed increased the 2008 limit from $2,960 to $10,960.

***Unofficial limits prepared by CCH staff.

Table 7H

For Trucks and Vans Placed in Service After	Before	Depreciation Allowable in—			
		Year 1	Year 2	Year 3	Year 4, etc.
12/31/02	5/6/03	$ 7,960*	$ 5,400	$ 3,250	$ 1,975
5/5/03	1/1/04	11,010*	5,400	3,250	1,975
12/31/03	1/1/05	10,910*	5,300	3,150	1,875
12/31/04	1/1/07	3,260*	5,200	3,150	1,875
12/31/06	5/6/08	3,260*	5,200	3,050	1,875
12/31/07	1/1/09	11,160**	5,100	3,050	1,875
12/31/08***	1/1/10	11,060	4,900	2,950	1,775

*The first-year limit is $3,360 in 2003 and $3,260 in 2004 if no bonus allowance is claimed.

**The $8,000 of bonus depreciation allowed increased the 2008 limit from $2,960 to $10,960.

***Unofficial limits prepared by CCH staff.

¶ 727 Inclusion Amounts for Leased Automobiles Placed in Service During 2008

Table 7I shows the inclusion amounts for leased automobiles placed in service during 2007 that have an FMV between $18,500 and $50,000. For inclusion amounts on leased automobiles placed in service prior to 2008, or on those placed in service during 2008 with an FMV in excess of $50,000, see Rev. Proc. 2008-22. (The 2009 inclusion amounts were not available at the time this book went to the printer).

Table 7I Dollar Amounts for Passenger Automobiles (That Are Not Trucks or Vans) with a Lease Term Beginning in Calendar Year 2007

Fair Market Value of Passenger Automobile		Tax Year During Lease				
Over	Not Over	Year 1	Year 2	Year 3	Year 4	Year 5 & later
$18,500	$19,000	$20	$42	$62	$73	$84
19,000	19,500	22	47	71	83	94
19,500	20,000	25	53	78	93	106
20,000	20,500	27	58	87	95	117
20,500	21,000	30	63	95	112	128
21,000	21,500	32	69	103	122	139
21,500	22,000	34	75	111	131	151
22,000	23,000	38	83	123	146	167
23,000	24,000	43	94	139	165	190
24,000	25,000	48	105	155	185	212
25,000	26,000	53	115	172	204	235
26,000	27,000	58	126	188	223	257
27,000	28,000	63	137	204	243	279
28,000	29,000	68	148	220	262	302
29,000	30,000	73	159	236	282	324
30,000	31,000	78	170	252	301	347
31,000	32,000	83	181	268	321	368
32,000	33,000	88	192	284	340	391
33,000	34,000	93	202	301	359	414
34,000	35,000	98	213	317	379	436
35,000	36,000	103	224	333	398	459
36,000	37,000	108	235	349	418	481
37,000	38,000	113	246	365	437	503
38,000	39,000	118	257	381	457	525
39,000	40,000	123	268	397	476	548
40,000	41,000	128	279	413	495	571
41,000	42,000	133	289	430	515	593
42,000	43,000	137	301	446	534	615
43,000	44,000	142	312	462	553	638
44,000	45,000	147	323	478	573	659
45,000	46,000	152	333	495	592	682
46,000	47,000	157	344	511	611	705
47,000	48,000	162	355	527	631	727
48,000	49,000	167	366	543	650	750
49,000	50,000	172	377	559	670	772

GLOSSARY OF TERMS INTRODUCED IN THE CHAPTER

Adjusted basis. The tax equivalent to book value. Adjusted basis equals the initial cost basis of the asset (typically its cost in the case of an acquired asset) plus any improvements made to the asset minus the accumulated depreciation taken on the asset over the years.

Alternative Depreciation System (ADS). An alternative to depreciating property under general MACRS in which the recovery periods tend to be longer and use of the straight-line method is required.

Amortizable Section 197 intangibles. Intangible assets for which amortization deductions may be taken under Code Sec. 197. Amortizable Section 197 intangibles are intangibles listed in Code Sec. 197 that are acquired by the taxpayer and held in connection with the conduct of a trade or business or for the production of income.

Book value. The financial accounting equivalent of adjusted basis, i.e., cost less accumulated depreciation.

Cost depletion. One of two acceptable tax methods for expensing the costs of a natural resource. This method is similar to the units-of-production method of depreciation and is the only acceptable method of depletion for financial reporting.

Depreciable cost. In financial accounting, it represents the portion of the cost of an asset that may be written off over the asset's useful life, i.e., the costs associated with the acquisition of the asset minus the estimated salvage value. *See also* Salvage value.

Dwelling unit. A house or apartment used to provide living accommodations; includes mobile homes and manufactured homes; does not include a unit in a hotel, motel, inn, or other establishment in which more than 50 percent of the units are used on a transient basis. *See also* Residential real property.

Half-year convention. Averaging convention used for tax depreciation in which any property put in service in a trade or business during a tax year is deemed to be placed in service in the middle of the year.

Mid-month convention. Averaging convention used for tax depreciation in which any property put in service in a trade or business during a month is deemed to be placed in service in the middle of the month.

Mid-quarter convention. Averaging convention in which any property put in service in a trade or business during a quarter of a tax year is deemed to be placed in service in the middle of the quarter.

Modified Accelerated Cost Recovery System (MACRS). A system of recovering the cost of capital expenditures through periodic depreciation deductions. MACRS applies to depreciable tangible property placed in service after 1986.

Percentage depletion. One of two acceptable tax methods for expensing the costs of a natural resource. Because the expense is calculated as a percentage of gross profits generated by the resource, over time, the costs expensed can exceed the income tax basis of the property.

Residential real property. Rental property for which 80 percent or more of the gross rental income is derived from the rental of dwelling units. *See also* Dwelling unit.

Salvage value. Term used in financial accounting. The amount for which the owner of an asset believes the asset could be sold at the end of its useful life.

Section 179 property. Property eligible for immediate expensing under Code Sec. 179. Section 179 property is tangible personal property that is depreciable under MACRS and is acquired by purchase for use in the active conduct of a trade or business.

Taxable income limitation. A limitation that disallows any Section 179 expense from being deducted in the current year for amounts that exceed the aggregate of the taxpayer's taxable income derived from the active conduct of any trade or business.

CHAPTER PROBLEMS

The following questions and problems relate to the discussion in Chapter 7, Business Deductions: Depreciation, Depletion, and Amortization, which begins at ¶ 700 in *Part II: Federal Taxation of Business Income and Deduction.*

Chapter 7 Discussion Questions

The following questions relate to the discussion in Chapter 7, Business Deductions: Depreciation, Depletion, and Amortization. Unless indicated otherwise in a particular question, assume:

- No amount is expensed under Code Sec. 179 and additional "bonus" depreciation is not claimed (with the taxpayer filing any necessary election).
- With respect to MACRS personal property, the half-year convention applies unless enough information is provided to determine whether more than 40 percent of assets were placed in service in the fourth quarter of the tax year.
- Depreciation deductions are computed using MACRS general depreciation system unless it can be determined from the facts that the alternative depreciation system (ADS) is required.
- No election is made to use the MACRS straight-line, MACRS 150-percent declining balance, or the ADS methods, unless otherwise stated.

1. Explain whether the following assets are eligible for depreciation or amortization:
   a. Car used only for personal reasons,
   b. Lubricating oil purchased for business machinery,
   c. Construction company truck,
   d. Truck used by utility company to construct towers for its power lines,
   e. Farmland used to grow corn,
   f. A new apartment building with construction completed but unoccupied,
   g. Boats held for sale by a marina,
   h. Broadcasting license acquired in connection with the purchase of a television station, and
   i. Leasehold improvements made by a tenant who has five years remaining on a lease.

2. What are the various cost recovery methods available to depreciate office furniture placed in service in 2009?

3. Fred Austin purchases a computer at a cost of $30,000 on January 1 and uses it in his business. Compute his maximum allowable MACRS deduction for the year of purchase. May Fred claim the Code Sec. 179 expense allowance?

4. Which of the following vehicles is subject to the luxury car depreciation limits if used for business purposes?

a. A farm tractor,

b. An SUV (sports utility vehicle) with a gross vehicle weight rating of 8,000 pounds that is built on a truck chassis,

c. A small truck with a gross vehicle weight rating of 5,000 pounds, and

d. A station wagon with an unloaded gross vehicle weight of 5,000 pounds.

5. Raymond George purchased a building in 20X1 for $100,000 and used it as nonresidential real property in a trade or business. In 20X9, he replaced the roof on the building at a cost of $20,000. How should he compute his depreciation deductions?

6. On January 1, 20X1, Sam Johnson agreed to lease 1,000 acres of pastureland for a period of five years. He uses the land to raise livestock. On March 1, 20X5, he erects a small fabricated storage building, which will be used primarily to store feed, for a total cost of $3,000. Assume that the building is 10-year MACRS property. Compute Sam's 20X5 MACRS depreciation deduction.

7. John Jacob operates a business as a sole proprietorship. In the current tax year, he will have a $5,000 loss before considering any Code Sec. 179 expense deduction. John's wife, Denise, operates a word processing business as a sole proprietorship; it generates $50,000 in net profits. The couple has no other items of gross income and reports the tax items from their businesses on Schedule C of their joint Form 1040 tax return. If John were to purchase $15,000 in computer equipment and office furniture and fixtures, would he be able to expense them as a Code Sec. 179 deduction on his Schedule C?

8. In Question 7, assume that instead of having her own business, Denise is employed by Veriti Corporation and earns W-2 income of $50,000. How would your answer change regarding John's ability to take the Code Sec. 179 election for the $15,000 in new acquisitions he made for his business?

9. Sherry is a 50-percent partner in three separate partnerships, A, B, and C, in which she actively participates. For one tax year, she received three Form 1065 K-1s, each indicating a $7,000 Code Sec. 179 expense allocation from the partnerships. Assume that each of the partnerships met all the requirements for electing Code Sec. 179 (i.e., the dollar limit, the investment limit, and the aggregate taxable income limit). Sherry is engaged in other business activities that generate losses and her aggregate taxable income from her businesses for the year, including her partnership income allocations, is $9,000. How much may Sherry expense on her Form 1040?

10. A taxpayer depreciates the entire $10,000 cost of an item of MACRS property placed in service in a trade or business. If the taxpayer sells the property in a later year for $1,000, what is the gain from the sale?

11. Onondaga Corporation, a calendar year taxpayer, begins business operations on March 15, 20X1. During 20X1, Onondaga placed in service $10,000 of five-year MACRS property. On what date does the recovery period for the property begin, and on what date does it end under the half-year convention?

12. Chris's Cutlery, Inc. is opening a new retail outlet. The building it purchased has three unfinished walls, an unfinished ceiling, basic plumbing and electrical connections, a concrete slab floor, and no front wall. Chris's plans to have the following improvements made to make the site suitable for its use:

a. Electrical connections,

b. Plumbing connections,

c. Permanent interior walls,

d. Front wall and window,

e. Side and rear walls,

f. Drop ceiling,

g. Lighting fixtures, and

h. Heating and cooling system.

In addition, Chris's purchases the following assets for use at the site:

   i. Computers and

   j. Office furniture.

Assume that items (a) through (h) are structural components. What are the MACRS depreciation periods of the items?

13. What method of cost recovery can be used in Question 12 if Chris's goal is to deduct as much depreciation as possible in the first year?

14. What is the ADS depreciation period of the items in Question 12?

15. How is computer software amortized for tax purposes?

16. A taxpayer owned a building that was used in the taxpayer's business. The building cost $100,000 and the depreciation taken was $20,000. The building was idle for two years and the taxpayer took no depreciation. The depreciation that could have been taken during the idle period was $10,000. The taxpayer sold the building for $110,000 without using the building again. Ignoring any recapture considerations, what is the taxpayer's adjusted basis in the building?

17. Which of the following elections is *not* available under MACRS:

   a. 200-percent declining balance election,

   b. 150-percent declining balance election,

   c. Straight-line election, or

   d. Alternative depreciation system (ADS) election.

18. The cost of seven-year MACRS property placed in service by a calendar year taxpayer is depreciated over:

   a. Six tax years,

   b. Seven tax years,

   c. Eight tax years, or

   d. Nine tax years.

19. A taxpayer places property in service that costs $10,000 and expenses it under Code Sec. 179. Three years later, the property is sold for $4,000. How is the adjusted basis of the property determined for purposes of computing the gain or loss on the sale?

20. To which of the following do the luxury automobile limitations apply?

   a. Leased passenger automobile,

   b. 5500-pound four-wheel truck,

   c. 7500-pound SUV, or

   d. Hearse.

Chapter 7 Problems

The following problems relate to the discussion in Chapter 7, Business Deductions: Depreciation, Depletion, and Amortization. Unless indicated otherwise in a particular problem, assume:

- No amount is expensed under Code Sec. 179, and additional "bonus" depreciation is not claimed (with the taxpayer filing any necessary election).

- With respect to MACRS personal property, the half-year convention applies unless the midquarter convention applies because more than 40 percent of assets were placed in service in the fourth quarter of the tax year.

- Depreciation deductions are computed using MACRS unless it can be determined from the facts that the alternative depreciation system (ADS) is required.

- No election is made to use the MACRS straight-line, MACRS 150-percent declining balance method, or the ADS, unless otherwise stated.

1. As part of the purchase price of a business, on January 1, Sam Farrow pays $100,000 for the patent to an industrial gear. In addition, as part of the same purchase, Sam pays $10,000 for the business's goodwill and another $10,000 for the seller's covenant not to compete for the next five years. Compute Sam's amortization deduction for the year of purchase.

2. Seymour Scagnetti bought an apartment building for $180,000 and rented all of the units out to tenants. Land accounted for $30,000 of the purchase price. What is Seymour's depreciable basis for the property?

3. A corporation places in service two properties during the year. The first property is five-year property costing $55,000 that was placed in service on June 6. The second is seven-year property costing $39,000 that was placed in service on December 6. Compute MACRS depreciation on these properties for the current year.

4. A calendar year corporation places in service machinery costing $810,000 on April 8, 2009. This is the only property placed in service during the year. Assuming the corporation elects to expense as much of the machine as possible under Code Sec. 179, and takes the "bonus depreciation" allowed in 2009, what is the adjusted basis in the machinery on December 31, 2009, if the corporation's taxable income of the corporation (before Section 179 expense) is $1,000,000.

5. On January 31, 1997, a corporation with a calendar tax year purchased and placed in service land and a commercial building for $125,000, of which $25,000 is properly allocable to the land. The building qualifies as depreciable property under MACRS. It has an expected useful life of 30 years. Compute the corporation's MACRS depreciation deduction for 2009.

6. Assume the same facts as in Problem 5, except compute the corporation's depreciation deduction assuming it uses ADS to depreciate the property.

7. Jackson Corporation purchases a computer on December 31, 2009, for use in its trade or business. The computer cost $20,000. Determine its 2009 MACRS and ADS deductions. Assume this was the only depreciable personal property Jackson purchased in 2009.

8. Assume, in Problem 7, that Jackson also purchases a computer at a cost of $20,000 on November 1, 2009. What are the MACRS and ADS deductions for the computers in 2009 and 2010?

9. Popcorn Inc. purchases a sports sedan on June 1, 2008, for $30,000. The vehicle is used 100 percent for business reasons by the company president, Colonel Popper. Taking the luxury car depreciation limits into consideration, and assuming that the maximum bonus depreciation is taken, compute the company's MACRS depreciation deduction for the years 2008–2012.

10. Kedzie Company places nonresidential real property that cost $200,000 (exclusive of land cost) in service on December 31, 2009. Compute the MACRS deductions on the property for 2009 and 2010.

11. Hargarten Corporation, a calendar year taxpayer, purchases a depreciable two-story building for $120,000 on March 1, 2009. Of the total purchase price, $20,000 was for the land. The corporation rents the upper story to a family for $500 per month. The downstairs is rented to a retailer for $1,000 per month. Compute the MACRS depreciation allowance for 2009 and 2010.

12. James Johnson, a real estate developer, purchased an abandoned warehouse as an investment in 2005 for $70,000, of which $50,000 was attributable to depreciable real property. He converted the warehouse into apartments at a cost of $1 million; he placed the apartments in service in a trade or business on October 1, 2009. The fair market value of the building on October 1, 2009, was $1,150,000. Compute his 2009 MACRS depreciation deduction.

13. Coldwater Properties, Inc. purchases and places an apartment building in service on May 16, 1993. The building cost $80,000. On March 1, 2009, Coldwater replaced the roof at a cost of $3,000. Compute the 2009 depreciation deduction on the roof.

14. Shreve Corporation, a calendar year taxpayer, is planning its 2009 asset acquisitions. All the acquisitions will be five-year property, and Shreve will use MACRS. The company would

like to know the difference in the total first- and second-year depreciation deductions resulting from the two cost acquisition patterns outlined below:

Property Acquisition Dates:	Plan A	Plan B
1/28/2009	$200,000	$200,000
5/2/2009	150,000	50,000
11/16/2009	100,000	200,000
Total:	$450,000	$450,000

15. Olga Corporation, a calendar year taxpayer, purchased an item of three-year property costing $10,000 on February 1, 2007. It sells the property on October 21, 2009.

    a. Compute Olga's depreciation expense for 2007–2009 assuming the half-year convention applies to all three-year property placed in service during 2007.

    b. Compute Olga's depreciation expense for 2007–2009 assuming the mid-quarter convention applies to all three-year property placed in service during 2007.

16. A calendar year taxpayer placed in service on June 10, 2009, listed property (computer and peripheral equipment) that cost $100,000. The property was used 10 percent of the time in the taxpayer's trade or business. Compute the 2009 depreciation allowed on the property.

17. A computer costing $5,000 is placed in service on February 3 in a calendar year business and is used 80 percent for business. Compute the first-year depreciation.

18. A taxpayer bought a mine in 20X1 for $80,000 and estimated there were 100,000 tons of ore to be extracted. In 20X1, he mined 7,500 tons and sold 7,000. In 20X2, he mined 6,000 tons and sold the 500 tons remaining from 20X1 and 5,500 tons of the ore mined in 20X2. However, at the end of 20X2, he estimated that 180,000 tons of ore remained, including the ore extracted but unsold. Compute the taxpayer's allowable cost depletion for 20X1 and 20X2.

19. A corporation bought 100 acres of timber for $40,000, of which $30,000 was allocable to the timber and $10,000 was allocable to the land. It was estimated that there were 1.5 million board feet of timber on the land. The first year, the corporation felled 500,000 board feet and sold 300,000 board feet for $18,000. The corporation's deductible expenses from these operations amounted to $8,000. Compute the depletion allowable for the first year.

20. A taxpayer buys a mine for $100,000. The mine is estimated to hold 50,000 tons of ore at the beginning of the tax year. During the first year, 4,000 tons are sold from the 5,000 tons extracted. No change in the original estimate is made for the first year. In the second year, 6,000 tons of ore are extracted and 5,000 tons are sold. The mine is estimated to have 60,000 tons at the end of the second year. Compute the cost depletion for both years.

21. A corporation places in service on May 1, 2009, property that qualifies as seven-year property under MACRS that cost $730,000. The corporation has taxable income of $2,000,000 in 2009. There is no other Section 179 property acquired in 2009. What are the allowable Section 179 and other depreciation deductions if additional "bonus depreciation" is taken? How much tax savings will this produce if the corporation is in the 35-percent tax bracket?

22. During 2009, Pitterle, Inc, a calendar year manufacturing company, places in service $880,000 of Section 179 property. How much can Pitterle, Inc. elect to immediately expense?

23. A corporation places in service $900,000 of seven-year property in 2009. Before deducting the Section 179 expense election, the corporation has taxable income of $120,000. If the corporation elects the maximum Section 179 expense allowed by law, compute its total depreciation deduction for 2009, including bonus depreciation.

24. Schoeberle, Inc. acquired substantially all the assets of Luke, Inc. on June 15, 2009. Luke had four separate businesses. $16 million of the purchase price was allocated to goodwill. After taking $2 million of amortization ($500,000 per business), Schoeberle, Inc. sells one of the businesses in a loss in an asset sale. It allocates $3.5 million of the loss to the business's

goodwill. What is the amount of the immediate loss deduction that can be taken for the business' goodwill?

25. On August 1, 2009, Meitner, Inc. (a calendar year corporation) purchases the leasehold interest of Cats R Us in a one-story business from which Meitner, Inc. operates a pet shop. Meitner pays $75,000 for Cats R Us' 10- year lease on which 5 years (60) months remain. How much does Meitner, Inc. deduct as a business expense in 2009 and 2010?

Chapter 7 Review Problems

1. In January 2009, Alder Corporation purchased a coal mine for $800,000. The mine had been producing minerals for several years, but it had an estimated 120,000 tons remaining at the time of purchase. During 2009, 16,800 tons were mined and sold for $386,400. Costs of operating the mine were as follows:

Labor for operating and servicing mining equipment	$120,000
Repairs to equipment	21,000
Real estate taxes on mine	46,000
Costs of gasoline to operate equipment	5,200

   a. Compute Alder's taxable profit from the mine after taking into consideration all expenses incurred in operating the mine.

   b. What is Alder's basis in the mine at the end of 2009?

2. Menominee Corporation, whose books were kept on the accrual method, showed the following cash receipts and disbursements for 2009:

Receipts:

Cash sales	$245,862
Collection of receivables	833,317
Interest on notes receivable	654

Disbursements:

Purchases	$639,034
Bank loan ($794 interest and $12,048 principal)	12,842
Fire and casualty insurance premium	3,870
Other operating expenses	374,377
Payments for returned merchandise	5,629

Receivables collected in 2009 included 2008 receivables totaling $32,561. Interest collected on notes receivable included $78 accrued in 2008. Disbursements included payment for 2008 purchases of $21,725 and other 2008 operating expenses of $7,541. The bank loan payments were on amounts that accrued in 2009.

The following amounts were accrued as of December 31, 2009:

Accounts and notes receivable	$41,578
Interest on notes receivable	27
Accounts payable	27,652
Other operating expenses	6,687

Merchandise inventories were valued at $123,428 on January 1, 2009, and at $135,223 on December 31, 2009.

The fire and casualty insurance premium paid in 2009 was for a two-year period beginning May 1, 2009. The three-year policy that expired on April 30, 2009, had cost $1,785.

Menominee is entitled to depreciation on the following assets:

Description of Property	Date Acq.	Cost
Office building	1/1/1992	$68,000
Copy machine	1/1/2007	8,000
Printer	6/1/2007	4,000
Computer	4/10/2005	700
Furniture	8/1/2008	6,781

Assume that this is the only depreciable property that Menominee has placed in service in a trade or business for the relevant time frame. Of the $68,000 cost of the office building, $5,000 is allocable to land. The corporation did not take the Code Sec. 179 deduction for any of these properties. Assume also that Menominee did not claim any first-year additional "bonus depreciation," making any necessary elections.

Compute Menominee's taxable income in 2009.

Comprehensive Review Question

Webster, Inc. has the following items of income and expense for 2009, its first year of operations. Webster began operations on April 1 and uses a calendar year end.

Gross receipts from sales	$912,649
Charitable contributions	15,000
Employment taxes	10,250
Interest expense	30,000
Organizational costs	52,600
Office rent expense	31,000
Real estate taxes	15,600
Utilities expense	11,300
Wage expense	93,540

In addition to these items, Webster purchased machinery and equipment costing $930,000 and furniture costing $112,000 on April 9, 2009, and a warehouse costing $190,000 on May 2, 2009.

Webster wants to minimize its 2009 income tax liability, which means electing Section 179 expense for the maximum the tax law allows, as well as taking additional "bonus depreciation" in 2009. Compute Webster's 2009 taxable income and income tax liability.

Chapter 7 Research Question

Are there any conditions under which a depletion deduction may be taken on water? Use the complete CCH Federal Tax Library in your school or local library to find your answer and provide the following:

1. Give your opinion. In it, show authorities, citing law, regulations, decisions applicable, and the *CCH Standard Federal Tax Reporter* paragraph references where they may be found.

2. Explain carefully every step you take in reaching your result.

PART III:

Transactions Involving Business Property

CHAPTER 8

Property Transactions: Realized and Recognized Gains and Losses

LEARNING OBJECTIVES

1. Calculate the realized gain or loss on the sale or exchange of property and determine which gains and losses are recognized on the tax return.
2. Define the loss disallowance provisions for wash sales and related party transactions and explain what happens to the disallowed loss.
3. List the rules behind the nonrecognition of gain or loss on like-kind exchanges and explain how the gains and losses are eventually recognized on the tax return.
4. Describe what constitutes an involuntary conversion and the circumstances under which realized gains can be postponed.
5. Explain when gains from the sale of certain securities can be excluded or postponed.
6. Describe how the tax laws and financial reporting rules differ with respect to disposing of property.

¶ 800 Introduction

The accountant's definition of income rests on the revenue principle, also known as the realization concept. For income to be realized, generally there must be an exchange with an outsider. The realization concept is based on the accountant's desire to have an objective basis for measuring income. Therefore, unrealized gains and losses and imputed income are generally rejected as being too subjective to allow recognition. Income tax law generally follows the realization concept. Therefore, increases and decreases in value of assets that are held (often called paper gains and losses) generally do not constitute gross income.

Furthermore, mere appreciation in value is not indicative of the owner's wherewithal to pay taxes on the income generated. Instead, the wherewithal is realized when the owner sells the property and can use the proceeds from the sale to pay the corresponding taxes. Under the realization principle, gross income from changes in the value of property is reported only when taxpayers realize gain or loss from disposing of property.

Good tax planning requires an understanding of the tax laws regarding gains and losses on the disposition of property so that businesses can take advantage of opportunities to exclude or postpone gains. Likewise, businesses need to understand how the tax laws operate so they can avoid situations in which a realized loss is postponed or lost. This chapter introduces the tax laws that govern the sale or exchange of property and discusses the exceptions to the general rule regarding the taxation of gains and the deductibility of losses on the disposal of business and investment property.

¶ 801 Realized vs. Recognized Gains and Losses

Realized gain or loss is the term used to describe taxpayers' gain or loss when they dispose of property. As a rule, the tax laws require taxpayers to include realized gains in gross income but allow taxpayers to deduct only losses that result from the sale or exchange of business or investment property. Realized gains and losses result when taxpayers dispose of property in a sale or exchange, or abandonment of property. Gains and losses resulting from mere appreciation or decline in value are **unrealized gains and losses**. Although most realized gains and losses from the sale or exchange of business or investment property are recognized (i.e., taken into gross income), unrealized gains and losses generally are not included in the calculation of taxable income.

Realized gain is the portion of "the amount realized" that exceeds the taxpayer's adjusted basis in the property.[1] "The amount realized" is equal to the sales price minus the expenses of sale, i.e., the net sales price. When the adjusted basis exceeds the amount realized, the taxpayer has a loss. "Adjusted basis" represents the taxpayer's unrecovered investment in the property. (Adjusted basis is discussed later in the chapter.) Although most realized gains and losses are reported on the tax return, exceptions do exist. These exceptions are the focus of much of this chapter.

Recognized gain or loss is the term used to describe the amount of realized gain or loss that taxpayers report on their tax returns. Only recognized gains and losses affect the taxpayer's tax liability. As a general rule, all realized gains and losses from the sale or exchange of business and investment property are recognized.[2] In situations in which all of a realized gain or loss is not recognized, often, recognition of the gain or loss is merely postponed. However, in a few instances, the gain or loss is never recognized.

When a transaction results in gain that is excluded from gross income, the gain is never taxed, and the benefits to the taxpayer are obvious. When gain is postponed, the associated taxes are deferred until some point in the future. Until the gain is recognized, the taxpayer has full use of the temporary tax savings either to invest or to spend. When a transaction results in losses that are postponed, the tax savings that would have been generated from deducting the loss are postponed as well. If the transaction results in the permanent disallowance of the loss, the tax savings are forever lost.

 GAAP vs. Code: The objective of financial reporting is to provide users of financial statements the most relevant and reliable information about a company's financial activities. Because the market value of publicly traded stocks and bonds (collectedly called "marketable securities") is a readily available and highly reliable measure of their true value, generally accepted accounting principles (GAAP) require that unrealized gains and losses from trading securities be reported on the income statement. "Trading securities" are stocks and bonds a corporation buys primarily for the purpose of selling them in the near future.[3]

The tax laws, on the other hand, operate under the realization principle, and unrealized gains and losses on securities are generally not reported on the tax return. Thus, to the extent unrealized gains and losses are reflected in the calculation of net income, such amounts must be backed out of net income when reconciling net income to taxable income on the corporate tax return. "Backing out" the amounts involves adding back to net income any unrealized losses and subtracting out any unrealized gains. The

---

[1] Code Sec. 1001(a).
[2] Code Sec. 1001(c).

[3] "Accounting for Certain Investments in Debt and Equity Securities," *Statement of Financial Accounting Standards No. 115* (Norwalk, Conn.: FASB, 1993).

difference in how unrealized gains and losses are treated for financial purposes versus tax purposes is merely a timing difference that will reverse when the securities are eventually sold. In the year trading securities are sold, the difference between the gain or loss reported on the income statement and the amount reported in the calculation of taxable income must be considered in the reconciliation of net income to taxable income.

¶ 802 Realized Gains and Losses

As previously mentioned, realized gains and losses represent the gains or losses that result from the sale, exchange, or abandonment of property. Realized gains and losses can also result from condemnations and casualties. An **exchange** involves two parties trading property other than cash. Sometimes the properties exchanged are similar; sometimes they are not similar. Exchanges of similar property, known as "like-kind exchanges," are discussed later in the chapter (see ¶ 808). All other transactions between a buyer and a seller that are not exchanges are sales. In a typical sale, the seller receives cash in exchange for the property, but other forms of consideration may be included (see ¶ 802.01).

Under the capital recovery doctrine, taxpayers that dispose of property are allowed a tax-free recovery of their investment in the property. Thus, only the excess of the amount realized over a taxpayer's adjusted basis in the investment is taxed. Adjusted basis is the tax term used to describe the taxpayer's investment in property at disposition (see ¶ 802.02). Thus, realized gains and losses are computed as follows:

Amount realized	$ xx,xxx
Less: Adjusted basis	(xx,xxx)
Realized gain (or loss)	$ xx,xxx

Example 1: Swanson Company sold a machine it used in its business for $45,000. The adjusted basis in the machine is $36,000. Swanson's realized gain equals $9,000 ($45,000 – $36,000).

Example 2: Sanders Company sells land it used in its business for $27,000. If Sanders's adjusted basis in the land is $32,000, the realized loss equals $5,000 ($27,000 – $32,000).

 Spotlight: When a company purchases land for $100,000, its cash decreases by $100,000. If the company later does a cash sale of the land for $150,000, its cash will increase by $150,000. When these two transactions are viewed together, the company's assets increase by $50,000 ($150,000 – $100,000). This amount is the company's realized gain from owning the land. Now consider a company that purchases stock for $60,000 and later sells it for $35,000. The company spends $60,000 to purchase the stock but only receives $35,000 from the sale. When viewed together, the company's cost of the transaction is $25,000, which represents its realized loss from owning the stock. Accordingly, realized gains and losses represent the taxpayer's true economic gains and losses from the sale or exchange of property.

.01 Amount Realized

The starting point in the calculation of realized gain or loss is determining the **amount realized**, which is the amount the seller receives from the buyer minus any expenses related to the sale (selling expenses). The amount realized includes cash received and the fair market value

(FMV) of property as well as any services received in the sale or exchange.[4] As previously discussed, FMV is the amount that a willing buyer would pay to a willing seller if neither party were compelled to complete the transaction and if both parties had reasonable access to the same information. The seller often receives cash, but sometimes the seller provides financing to the buyer. Accordingly, the value (generally the face amount) of any notes received from the buyer is included in the seller's amount realized.

Example 3: Stephens Company sold land to Bragg Company. Bragg paid Stephens $90,000 in cash and gave Stephens industrial diamonds worth $50,000. Stephens's amount realized from the sale is $140,000.

Cash received	$ 90,000
FMV of diamonds received	50,000
Amount realized	$140,000

Example 4: Southard Company sold land to Bradshaw Company. Bradshaw paid $50,000 cash and signed a $200,000 interest-bearing note. The note is secured by a mortgage on the land and bears annual interest of 10 percent. Southard's amount realized from the sale is $250,000. Only the face value (principal) of the note is included in the amount realized. Southard will include the interest income it receives on the note as it is accrued or received, depending on Southard's accounting method.

Cash received	$ 50,000
Face value of the note received	200,000
Amount realized	$250,000

 Reason for the Rule: When property is disposed of, taxpayers must include the FMV of all property they receive from the transaction. Otherwise, if the amount realized only included the cash received from the transaction, taxpayers could avoid paying taxes by structuring the transaction to involve only the receipt of noncash property.

In addition to cash and notes, the amount realized sometimes includes noncash property received. The sections that follow discuss some common examples: (1) release from liability; (2) payment of real estate taxes; (3) selling expenses; (4) casualties, thefts, and condemnations; and (5) worthless securities.

Release from liability. The amount realized includes any debt of which the seller is relieved as a part of the sale or exchange.[5] The seller of a property can be released from recourse or nonrecourse liabilities. A **recourse liability** is a liability for which the seller is personally liable. A **nonrecourse liability** is a liability for which the seller is not personally liable, but for which the creditor can only look to property specified in the loan agreement for satisfaction of the debt. Nonrecourse liabilities are discussed further in ¶ 802.02.

Example 5: Tom Gonzalez takes out a nonrecourse loan from Franklin Savings and Loan to buy a house. The loan agreement specifies that Franklin can repossess the house if Tom fails to make required payments on the loan. Tom defaults on the loan. Franklin can repossess the house, but it cannot look to Tom's other assets to satisfy the debt.

Example 6: Assume the same facts as in Example 5, except the loan is for an office building and is a recourse loan. Franklin can repossess Tom's office building and, if the proceeds from

---

[4] Code Sec. 1001(b).   [5] Reg. § 1.1001-2(a)(1).

¶ 802.01

the sale of the office building do not fully satisfy the amount of the loan, it can pursue Tom individually for the balance.

Release from recourse liability occurs when the buyer assumes the seller's debt, takes property subject to the seller's debt, or when the buyer pays off the seller's debt. In these instances, the seller's liabilities decrease, thereby creating wealth to the seller. Consequently, liability release constitutes the equivalent of cash and must be included in the amount realized.

Example 7: Milwood, Inc. sells a building to Jefferson Company for $700,000. Milwood's amount realized from the sale equals the $700,000 cash received. At the time of the sale, Milwood still owes $200,000 on the mortgage it took out when it purchased the property. Milwood can use $200,000 of the cash it receives from Jefferson to pay off the remaining balance of the mortgage. The lender will likely require Milwood to pay off the $200,000 mortgage because many mortgages include a due-on-sale clause.

Example 8: Assume the same facts as in Example 7, except the terms of the sale stipulate that Jefferson will pay Milwood $500,000 cash and issue a five-year interest-bearing note for $200,000. Milwood's amount realized equals $700,000 ($500,000 + $200,000). Milwood can then use some of the cash it receives from Jefferson to pay off the remaining balance of the mortgage.

Example 9: Assume the same facts as in Example 7, except the terms of the sale stipulate that Jefferson will pay Milwood $500,000 cash and assume the remainder of Milwood's mortgage with the consent of the lender. The lender thereby discharges Milwood from any liability on the $200,000 balance on the mortgage. Milwood's amount realized on the sale equals $700,000 ($500,000 cash + $200,000 release from debt).

In each of the three examples, the seller (Milwood) received consideration from the buyer (Jefferson) equal to the FMV of the building ($700,000), which was the total FMV the seller received in each of the examples. The difference in the examples is how the transaction was structured. In all three, the seller is no longer responsible for the debt. In Examples 7 and 8, Milwood uses some of the cash it receives from the sale to pay off its remaining mortgage. In Example 9, Jefferson takes over the mortgage and thus no further action is required by Milwood. In each example, Milwood had cash of $500,000 left after the debt was satisfied/assumed.

Example 10: JP Richards & Co. exchanges land for a building owned by Kettlemore, Inc. At the time of the exchange, the land is worth $150,000 and the FMV of the building is $200,000. Kettlemore still owes $50,000 on the building, and as part of the exchange, Richards agrees to take over the mortgage payments with the consent of the lender. As depicted in the diagram below, each party receives property worth $200,000 on the exchange. Richards receives a building worth $200,000, and Kettlemore receives land valued at $150,000 plus release from $50,000 of debt.

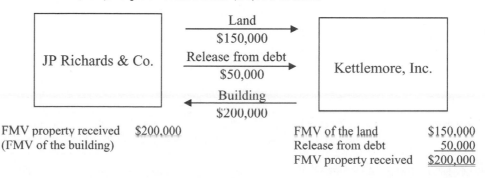

FMV property received $200,000	FMV of the land $150,000
(FMV of the building)	Release from debt 50,000
	FMV property received $200,000

> **Spotlight:** When property is sold, the amount that the buyer is willing to pay and the seller is willing to receive determines the FMV of the property. When property is sold for cash, the amount of cash represents the FMV of the property sold. When property is sold for something other than cash, the FMV of the property received by the seller is likely to be approximately equal to the FMV of the property being sold, otherwise the parties might not agree to the exchange. Therefore, on exchanges of property, the FMV of the property (or properties) given up is considered for income tax purposes to be equal to the FMV of the property (or properties) received. This was illustrated in Example 10 because each party receives $200,000 in the exchange.

Real estate taxes. Local governments levy real estate taxes on the owners of real property. When real property is sold during the year, for federal income tax purposes, the seller is presumed to be responsible for any real estate taxes accrued for the year up until the day of the sale, and the buyer is presumed to be responsible for any real estate taxes accrued on and after the day of the sale.[6] However, since real estate taxes are generally paid once a year, the owner at the time the taxes are levied is responsible under local law for paying the taxes due for the entire year. Thus, as part of the sales agreement, the buyer should require the seller to pay at the closing the seller's share of the real estate taxes for the year. If this is done, each party will pay and deduct its respective share of the real estate taxes for the year.

Example 11: Dean Enterprises (a calendar year taxpayer) sold land on May 11, 20X6, for $600,000. Real estate taxes on the land for 20X6 are estimated to be $10,000. At the closing, Dean remits to the buyer $3,561.64 ($10,000 × 130/365), which represents its share of the real estate taxes for the 130 days it owned the land during 20X6. Dean deducts this amount on its 20X6 tax return. At the end of the year, the local government will send the $10,000 property tax bill to the (new) owner of the property. However, the buyer's out-of-pocket costs will be $6,438.36: the $10,000 taxes owed minus the $3,561.64 that it received from Dean at the closing. Therefore, the buyer may deduct $6,438.36 on its income tax return for real estate taxes.

The apportionment of real estate taxes at the closing is standard in most real estate contracts. If the real estate taxes for the year of the sale are not apportioned between the seller and the buyer at the closing, then the costs for the entire amount of real estate taxes owed will be borne by the new owner. However, taxpayers may deduct only the portion of the taxes associated with the period of time they owned the property. When the buyer bears the entire burden of taxes for the year, the seller receives a benefit equal to the amount of taxes that were the seller's responsibility but were paid by the buyer. Accordingly, this amount is included in the seller's amount realized at the time of the sale. The buyer is then allowed to add this amount to the basis of the property being purchased.[7]

Example 12: Assume the same facts as in Example 11, except that no amounts are allocated or paid to the buyer at the closing for real estate taxes owed by Dean for the period during 20X6 in which it owned the property. In this case, Dean's amount realized from the sale increases to $63,561.64 ($60,000 + $3,561.64). The purchaser's basis in the property equals $63,561.64 ($60,000 + $3,561.64).

Selling expenses. Once the FMV of the property received has been determined, any costs paid in conjunction with the sale or exchange are subtracted from the cash and FMV of the property received to determine the amount realized from the sale or exchange. Common examples of selling expenses include commissions paid to stockbrokers and real estate agents and advertising expenses.

Example 13: Gibson Properties, LLC sells land for $500,000 and in the process pays a $30,000 commission. Gibson's amount realized equals $470,000 ($500,000 − $30,000).

---

[6] Code Secs. 164(d) and 1001(b)(2).   [7] Code Sec. 1001(b)(2).

Example 14: Smith Company sold land to Bennett Company. Bennett paid Smith $20,000 in cash, assumed Smith's mortgage of $80,000 on the land, and issued Smith an interest-bearing note for $10,000. Smith incurred $7,000 in selling expenses. Smith's $103,000 amount realized is calculated as follows:

Cash received	$ 20,000
Plus: Release from liability	80,000
Plus: Face value of the note received	10,000
Total FMV of the property received	$110,000
Less: Selling expenses	(7,000)
Amount realized	$103,000

Casualties, thefts, and condemnations. Although not a sale in the traditional sense, taxpayers realize a gain or loss on the condemnation of real property. A **condemnation** occurs when the government compensates the owner of real property upon taking possession of the property, usually through the process of eminent domain. Typically, the owner is compensated with money, but sometimes the compensation can be in the form of other property. For the purpose of computing the realized gain or loss from the condemnation, the amount realized equals the amount of money or FMV of the other property the owner receives.

Like condemnations, realized gains and losses from casualties and thefts do not result from sales or exchanges. Casualties are sudden and unexpected events that result in damage to the taxpayer's property. Examples include natural disasters, such as tornadoes, hurricanes, and earthquakes, as well as damage caused by storms and accidents. When the property is insured and the amount of insurance proceeds exceeds the taxpayer's adjusted basis in the property, a casualty gain results. (See ¶ 802.02.)

Worthless securities. Tax law treats worthless securities (stocks and bonds) as being sold for $0 on the last day of the tax year in which they become worthless, regardless of the actual date on which the securities lose all of their value.[8] Because no amount is realized from a worthless security, the realized loss is equal to the taxpayer's adjusted basis in the securities.

Example 15: Wineland, Inc. purchased 100 shares of Wentbroke Corporation for $2,500 on October 6, 20X1. On May 8, 20X3, Wineland was notified that Wentbroke filed for bankruptcy and that its stock was worthless. Wineland is deemed to have sold the 100 shares for $0 on December 31, 20X3. Its realized loss from the deemed sale equals $2,500.

Planning Pointer: If the taxpayer is having difficulty proving that a security is worthless, the taxpayer could sell it to an unrelated party in an arm's length transaction for a small amount (for example, $1). The taxpayer would then realize a loss on the sale. However, the taxpayer must be careful not to sell the security to a related party because the related-party rules would prohibit the seller from recognizing the loss. (See ¶ 804.)

Call options and put options are not considered securities for purposes of this rule. A call (put) option involves the payment for a right to purchase (sell) stock for a certain price in the future. If the holder of a call option or a put option allows the option to expire, the expiration of the option is treated as a sale or exchange of the option on the expiration date.[9]

Example 16: On January 24, 20X7, Holt Company bought 100 call options on Andrews Company as an investment for $2.20 per option, including commissions and fees. Therefore, Holt

---

[8] Code Sec. 165(g).

[9] Rev. Rul. 78-182, 1978-1 CB 265.

paid $2,200 for the 100 call options ($2.20 × 100). The price of Andrews's stock began to go down rapidly after Holt bought the call options. On May 18, 20X7, the call options expired, worthless. Holt is treated as if it sold the call options for $0 on May 18, 20X7, the date of expiration.

.02 Adjusted Basis

After the amount realized is computed, the next step in determining the realized gain or loss involves calculating the taxpayer's adjusted basis in the property at the time of the sale or exchange. Adjusted basis is the tax term that is similar to book value in financial accounting. **Adjusted basis** is the initial basis plus any capital improvements minus any cost recovery amounts deducted on the property (such as accumulated depreciation, amortization, or depletion).

As in financial reporting, the "initial cost" of an asset includes all of the costs necessary to get the property in place and ready for use. Thus, the initial cost of equipment would include the purchase price, sales taxes, delivery costs, and insurance while in transit as well as amounts paid for installation and testing. The "initial basis" in real property includes many of the closing costs incurred in acquiring the property. Closing costs included in the initial basis of property include recording fees, taxes on the deed or mortgage, fees charged to obtain credit reports, appraisals, and title insurance plus any legal fees or surveying costs.

Example 17: Weaver Company ordered a specialized machine to use in its business. The invoice price of the equipment was $35,000. Weaver also paid $2,100 in sales taxes, $250 in delivery charges, $50 for insurance while in transit, $150 for installation, and $80 for testing. Each of these amounts is included in Weaver's $37,630 initial cost for the equipment. As the equipment is depreciated under MACRS or expensed under Code Sec. 179, Weaver reduces its adjusted basis in the equipment. (See ¶ 702).

To determine the adjusted basis, the taxpayer adds any capital improvements it has made to the initial basis. The taxpayer then subtracts the accumulated cost recovery amounts. The sections that follow present some examples: (1) liabilities; (2) basket purchases; (3) abandonments; and (4) properties involved in casualties or theft.

 Reason for the Rule: Adjusted basis represents taxpayers' unrecovered costs in property they own. The unrecovered cost is equivalent to the amounts invested in the property (initial cost plus any improvements) minus any amounts recovered over the years (for example, from depreciation or casualty loss deductions). Under the capital recovery doctrine, a taxpayer's unrecovered costs are subtracted from the amount realized in determining the taxpayer's true economic gain or loss from owning the property.

Liabilities. As a rule, the initial basis also includes the amount of any nonrecourse liabilities secured by the property and any recourse liabilities assumed by the purchaser of the property.

Example 18: Petosky Corporation purchases a tract of land from Escanaba, Ltd. Petosky pays $1 million cash and agrees to assume Escanaba's $500,000 recourse liability. In addition, the land is subject to a $100,000 nonrecourse liability. Petosky's basis in the property is $1.6 million ($1,000,000 + $500,000 + $100,000).

The tax rules with respect to nonrecourse liabilities were discussed by the Supreme Court in *B.B. Crane*.[10] The court held that because a taxpayer that purchases property subject to nonrecourse liabilities includes the amount of such liabilities in the basis, the taxpayer must also include the amount of such nonrecourse liabilities in the amount realized when the property is sold.

---

[10] SCt, 47-1 USTC ¶ 9217, 331 US 1, 67 SCt 1047.

Example 19: Alpena Company sells a property for $1.5 million cash. The property is subject to a nonrecourse liability of $250,000. Alpena's amount realized on the sale is $1.75 million ($1,500,000 + $250,000).

Basket purchases. When a taxpayer acquires more than one property in a single transaction, called a "basket purchase," the purchase price is generally allocated to the various items acquired based on each property's relative FMV.[11] "Relative FMV" is the FMV of the individual property divided by the total FMV of all properties acquired in the purchase. A common example of a basket purchase is the purchase of real property with one or more items of personal property. Another example involves the purchase of land (nondepreciable realty) and a building (depreciable realty) for a single, lump sum amount.

Example 20: Brenda Davis operates a sole proprietorship. Brenda pays $480,000 for land, an office building, a refrigerator, and a conference table. The FMV of the land and the office building were $100,000 and $498,000, respectively. The FMV of the refrigerator and conference table were $700 and $1,300, respectively. Brenda must allocate the $480,000 purchase price to the various properties based on their relative FMVs as shown below.

	FMV	Relative FMV		Cost		Basis
Land	$100,000	$100,000/$600,000	×	$480,000	=	$ 80,000
Office building	498,000	$498,000/$600,000	×	$480,000	=	398,400
Refrigerator	700	$700/$600,000	×	$480,000	=	560
Conference table	1,300	$1,300/$600,000	×	$480,000	=	1,040
Totals	$600,000					$480,000

Reason for the Rule: Land is not depreciable and different depreciation rules apply to different types of depreciable property. In addition, the various properties acquired may be sold at different times. Therefore, an initial basis must be assigned to each property acquired. If left to their own discretion, taxpayers typically would assign as much of the cost as possible to depreciable property with the shortest recovery period, as it would produce the greatest tax savings in the quickest period of time. Thus, an objective method for allocating the purchase price among the various assets acquired is needed. The relative FMV approach to allocating the initial cost is an objective method, and it is also used to allocate costs in these types of situations for financial reporting purposes.

Abandonments. An **abandonment** occurs when the owner walks away from property and receives no consideration. Because no amount is realized upon the disposition, the taxpayer's realized loss equals its adjusted basis in the property.[12]

Example 21: Mark Grooms operates a sole proprietorship. During the year, a truck that Mark used exclusively in his business broke down while he was traveling in a remote location. Mark's adjusted basis in the truck is $950. At the time the truck broke down, it was worth $600. When Mark learned that the cost to repair the truck would be $800, he abandoned it rather than have it repaired. Mark's realized loss on the abandonment equals $950 ($0 amount realized – $950 adjusted basis).

Property involved in a casualty or theft. When the insurance proceeds exceed the taxpayer's adjusted basis in business property damaged in a casualty, the excess results in a realized casualty gain. For the purpose of computing a realized loss from a casualty, the amount used to offset the

---

[11] Note that this rule does not apply when the basket of assets purchased constitutes a trade or business. In that case, the residual allocation method of Code Sec. 1060 must be used.

[12] *L&C Springs Associates*, CA-7, 99-2 USTC ¶ 50,777, 188 F3d 866, aff'g, 74 TCM 928, TC Memo. 1997-469.

insurance proceeds depends on whether the property was partially or completely destroyed in the casualty. When business property is *completely destroyed*, the adjusted basis of the property is offset by the insurance proceeds and the excess is the taxpayer's realized loss from the casualty. When business property is only *partially destroyed* in the casualty, the realized casualty loss is equal to the *lesser of* the decline in FMV of the property or its adjusted basis, offset by the insurance proceeds.[13]

Example 22:   Dunlap Company's delivery van was damaged in an accident. The FMV of the van before the accident was $4,000; its FMV after the accident was $3,000. Dunlap Company chose not to repair the van because the damage was only cosmetic. The adjusted basis of the van at the time of the accident was $2,500. Since the van was only partially destroyed, the amount of Dunlap's loss is measured as the *lesser of* the $1,000 decline in FMV ($4,000 – $3,000) of the van or its $2,500 adjusted basis. Thus, Dunlap's realized casualty loss equals $1,000 because there are no insurance proceeds to further reduce the loss.

When business property is stolen, the business incurs a loss equal to the adjusted basis of the property. If the property is covered by insurance, the amount of the theft loss is reduced accordingly. The term "theft" includes, but is not necessarily limited to, larceny, embezzlement, and robbery.[14] When the insurance proceeds exceed the adjusted basis of the stolen property, the taxpayer realizes a theft gain. Taxpayers recognize a theft loss in the year in which they discover the property has been stolen.[15]

Example 23:   On December 30, 20X8 the offices of Midwestern Supply, Inc. were broken into and $800 in petty cash was stolen. The theft was discovered on January 2, 20X9 when the company reopened after the holidays. The theft loss is deductible in the year 20X9.

¶ 803 Recognized Gains and Losses

As previously mentioned, recognized gains and losses are realized gains and losses that the taxpayer must include in gross income. They are the gains and losses that taxpayers report on their tax returns. Figure 8-1 lists the situations in which realized gains and losses are not recognized on the tax return. Sometimes the gains and losses are never taxed; often, however, the gain or loss is merely postponed. The remainder of this chapter focuses on the tax laws that govern these special transactions.

Figure 8-1 Summary of Realized Gains and Losses Postponed or Never Taxed

- Losses from the sale, exchange, or abandonment of personal-use property;
- Losses on the sale of property to a related party;
- Losses on the sale of securities that are involved in a wash sale;
- Gains and losses from exchanges of like-kind property;
- Gains from involuntary conversions of business or investment property;
- Gains from the sale of Section 1244 stock; and
- Gains from the sale of SSBIC stock.

 GAAP vs. Code: When corporations dispose of depreciable property, the gain or loss reported on the income statement often is different from that reported on the tax return

---

[13] Reg. § 1.165-7(b)(1).
[14] Reg. § 1.165-8(d).
[15] Reg. § 1.165-8(a)(2).

due to the different methods used to depreciate property. The amount of depreciation expense deducted on the tax return is reflected in the adjusted basis of property and therefore impacts the amount of gain or loss reported on the tax return. Similarly, the amount of depreciation expense deducted on the income statement is reflected in the book value of the asset and impacts the gain or loss reported in the calculation of net income in the year the asset is sold. Thus, just as the differences in depreciation expense taken each year are taken into consideration when reconciling net income and taxable income, in the year the corporation disposes of property, the cumulative differences are reversed when the amount of gain or loss included in net income is reconciled with the amount reported in taxable income.

¶ 804 Losses between Related Parties

Taxpayers can generally deduct losses on the sale or exchange of business or investment property. However, when the buyer and seller are related, no loss deduction is allowed.[16] The tax laws disallow the loss even when the property is sold at its FMV and would appear to be an arms-length transaction. Related parties include certain family members; however, other relationships among parties, including those involving business entities, cause them to be considered "related" for this purpose. Figure 8-2 describes several types of relationships between parties that will result in a disallowed loss on a sale or an exchange of property.[17]

Figure 8-2 Related Parties

1. An individual and the individual's spouse, siblings, ancestors, or descendants;

2. An individual and a corporation in which the individual *directly or indirectly* owns more than 50 percent of the value of the outstanding stock;

3. An individual and a partnership in which the individual *directly or indirectly* owns more than a 50-percent capital or profits interest;

4. Two corporations that are members of the same controlled group;

5. A corporation and a partnership if the same person or persons own more than 50 percent of the outstanding value of the stock in the corporation and more than a 50-percent capital or profits interests in the partnership;

6. An S corporation and another S corporation if the same person or persons own more than 50 percent of the value in the outstanding stock of each corporation;

7. An S corporation and a C corporation if the same person or persons own more than 50 percent of the value in the outstanding stock of each corporation; and

8. Two partnerships in which the same person or persons *directly or indirectly* own more than a 50-percent capital or profits interest.

For the related party rules, "siblings" include an individual's brothers and sisters, as well as half brothers and half sisters. "Descendents" of the individual include the individual's children and grandchildren; "ancestors" include parents and grandparents. In determining whether a taxpayer directly or indirectly owns more than 50 percent of a corporation's stock, the IRS considers stock the taxpayer actually owns as well as stock the taxpayer constructively owns. Similar rules apply to constructive ownership of partnership interests (see ¶ 804.01).

---

[16] Code Sec. 267(a)(1).   [17] Code Secs. 267(b) and 707(b).

The term "controlled group" covers two distinct types of ownership arrangements: "brother-sister controlled groups," and "parent-subsidiary controlled groups." Two corporations can be related through a brother-sister controlled group where five or fewer persons own more than 50 percent of either the voting shares or value of the stock in both corporations. Parent-subsidiary controlled groups for purposes of the loss disallowance rules consist of one or more chains of corporations connected through stock ownership with a common parent corporation if two conditions are met:

1. one or more of the corporations own either a minimum of 50 percent of the total *combined voting power* of all stock eligible to vote, or a minimum of 50 percent of the total value of shares of all classes of stock, and

2. the common parent corporation owns directly stock (options are counted as stock for this purpose) with at least 50 percent of either the total *combined voting power* of all stock eligible to vote, or at least 50 percent of the total *value* of shares of all classes of stock.[18]

Example 24: Delightful Foods owns 70 percent of the outstanding stock of Baker Supply and 40 percent of Pantry Supply. Baker Supply also owns 60 percent of Pantry Supply. The relationship among these corporations is illustrated below.

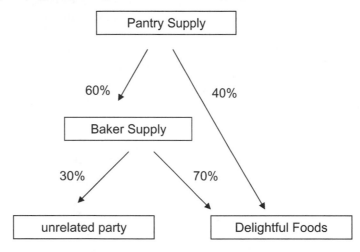

More than 50 percent of Pantry Supply is owned by Baker Supply (60 percent) and Delightful Foods (40 percent). In addition, more than 50 percent of Baker Supply is owned by Delightful Foods (70 percent) and Pantry Supply (zero percent). Thus, for purposes of the loss disallowance rules, Delightful Foods, Baker Supply, and Pantry Supply are members of a parent-subsidiary controlled group with Delightful Foods as the common parent.

Example 25: Sara sold land to her brother Bill for $60,000. Sara purchased the land for $100,000 several years earlier. Sara's realized loss equals $40,000 ($60,000 – $100,000), but she cannot recognize the loss because she sold the land to a related party.

Example 26: Bea sold land to her nephew Andy for its FMV of $16,000. Bea purchased the land for $18,000 two years earlier. Bea's realized loss is $2,000 ($16,000 – $18,000), and even though she and her nephew are relatives, they are not considered related parties for tax purposes, and accordingly, Bea recognizes the $2,000 loss on her tax return.

> **Reason for the Rule:** The tax laws allow taxpayers to deduct losses on the disposal of business and investment property based on the assumption that the seller has suffered a true economic loss. When related parties are involved in a sale or an exchange, the

---

[18] Code Secs. 267(f)(1) and 1563(a)(1).

seller may be able to formally dispose of the property without truly relinquishing control over it because of the special relationship that exists between the buyer and the seller. Therefore, the taxpayer may be able to influence the (related) buyer to sell the property back to the (related) seller at its lower FMV. This practice would allow taxpayers to turn unrealized losses into recognized losses.

The tax laws do not attempt to determine whether the seller's motive for selling the property is something other than a valid business or investment reason. Instead, an objective test is used to determine whether such a motivation might exist. The tax laws normally assume that certain transactions, such as those between family members or those between a corporation and a controlling shareholder, are made to generate recognized losses without actually relinquishing control of the property. For the purpose of defining family members, the government applies an objective test and automatically assumes that taxpayers can control the decisions and actions of certain close family members. Accordingly, a taxpayer is allowed to recognize a loss on the sale of property to an aunt, but not to a sister, even when a closer bond exists between the taxpayer and the aunt. A taxpayer may not avoid the application of the rules by showing that the sale was a *bona fide* sale for the FMV of the property,[19] nor can the tax consequences of the related party rules be avoided by demonstrating that the taxpayer and a related party do not have an amicable relationship.[20]

.01 Constructive Ownership

Under the **constructive ownership** rules, a taxpayer may be treated as owning stock that is actually owned by another person or entity in which the taxpayer has an ownership interest. For example, stock owned by a business entity (corporation or partnership) is treated as owned proportionately by the entities' owners.[21] Thus, if a partnership with two equal partners owns 10 percent of the stock in a corporation, each partner is treated as owning five percent of the stock in that corporation, even though neither partner actually owns any stock in the corporation. Similarly, if ABC Corporation owns 40 percent of the stock in DEF Corporation, a shareholder who owns 30 percent of the stock in ABC is treated as owning 12 percent (30% × 40%) of the stock in DEF.

The constructive ownership rules extend to stock owned by some of an individual's family members. For these rules, stock owned by the taxpayer's spouse, descendants, ancestors, or siblings is treated as owned by the taxpayer.[22] Furthermore, the tax laws treat relationships established by legal adoption the same as those established by blood when applying the constructive ownership rules.[23] For example, if a taxpayer and the taxpayer's spouse each own 35 percent of the stock in a corporation, they are treated as owning each other's stock. Therefore, each is treated as owning 70 percent of the corporation, and any transactions between the corporation and either spouse would fall under the related party rules.

The constructive ownership rules also involve a series of complex rules regarding individuals and any business entities they own. For example, under the constructive ownership rules, a partner who owns stock in a corporation is treated as owning any stock his or her partner actually owns in that corporation.[24] However, if the partner does not personally own stock in a corporation, he is not considered to constructively own stock that his partner owns. For example, if Anne and Bob (unrelated to one another) are 50-50 partners in Anne & Bob's, and each owns 30 percent of the stock in XYZ Corporation, each is treated as owning 60 percent of the stock in XYZ. However, if Bob

---

[19] *R.C. Camp*, 31 TCM 297, Dec. 31, 316(M), TC Memo. 1972-74.

[20] *D.L. Miller*, 75 TC 182, Dec. 37,376 (1980).

[21] Code Sec. 267(c)(1).

[22] Code Sec. 267(c)(2) and (c)(4).

[23] Reg. § 1.267(c)-1(a)(4).

[24] Code Sec. 267(c)(3).

does not actually own any stock in XYZ, then he is not treated as owning the 30 percent that his partner (Anne) owns.[25]

Example 27: Edward Blake and Ralph Davis are 50-50 partners in BD partnership. Edward and Ralph each own stock in General Distributors Corporation, which is owned by the following individuals:

	Actual Ownership
Edward Blake	35%
Patsy Blake (Edward's wife)	35%
Susan Rogers (the Blakes's daughter)	15%
Ralph Davis (Edward's partner)	15%
	100%

Because Edward owns stock in General Distributors, in addition to the 35 percent that he personally owns, he is deemed to own the 15 percent that his partner, Ralph Davis, owns. He is also treated as owning the 35 percent owned by his spouse and the 15 percent owned by his daughter. Therefore, Edward's total ownership (actual + constructive) is 100 percent of General Distributors.

Patsy actually owns 35 percent of the stock in General Distributors; however, through the constructive ownership rules, she is deemed to also own stock owned by her husband (Edward) and her child (Susan). Thus, Patsy's total ownership (actual + constructive) is 85 percent (35% + 35% + 15%). The stock Edward is deemed to own through his partner, Ralph, is not "reattributed" to any of his family members. Similarly, Susan's total ownership is 85 percent because she is deemed to own the stock that her parents own (15% + 35% + 35%).

Ralph is deemed to own the stock actually owned by Edward, so his total ownership in General Distributors is 50 percent (15% + 35%). Edward's constructive ownership of the stock owned by his family members is not reattributed to Ralph.

	Actual Ownership	*Constructive Ownership*	*Total Ownership*
Edward Blake	35%	65%	100%
Patsy Blake (Edward's wife)	35%	50%	85%
Susan Rogers (the Blakes's daughter)	15%	70%	85%
Ralph Davis (Edward's partner)	15%	35%	50%

Because Edward, Patsy, and Susan each own (directly or indirectly) own more than 50 percent of General Distributors, any realized loss from the sale of property between any of them and General Distributors would be disallowed under the related party rules. However, any realized loss from a sale between Ralph and General Distributors would be recognized because Ralph's ownership does not exceed 50 percent.

 Reason for the Rule: The related party rules exist because Congress believes that taxpayers may be able to influence the decisions and actions of certain persons or entities. The constructive ownership rules go one step further and assume that stock owned by certain (related) parties is stock they can control as well. Without the

---

[25] Code Sec. 267(c)(5).

constructive ownership rules, taxpayers could have family members and certain related entities purchase the property from them, thereby turning an unrealized loss into a realized and deductible recognized loss without truly relinquishing control over the property.

.02 Subsequent Use of Disallowed Loss by Purchaser

When property is sold to a related party, the seller's realized loss is permanently disallowed with respect to the seller. The related party purchaser, however, may use the disallowed loss to reduce or eliminate any gain realized on the subsequent sale or exchange of the property. However, the disallowed loss cannot cause or increase a loss.[26] The related party purchaser may be unable to use some or all of the disallowed loss if the property acquired does not appreciate enough to produce sufficient realized gain to absorb the disallowed loss. Consequently, before selling or exchanging property that will generate a realized loss, it is important that taxpayers, and especially business entities, understand the related party rules and be cognizant of the tax consequences associated with related party transactions.

Example 28: Fletcher Corporation sells land to Kevin Barnes for $14,000. Fletcher's adjusted basis in the land is $25,000. Kevin owns 60 percent of the outstanding stock of Fletcher, and accordingly, Fletcher cannot recognize any of its $11,000 realized loss ($14,000 – $25,000) on the sale. Kevin's basis in the land is what he paid for it ($14,000). If Kevin later sells the land for $31,000, his realized gain equals $17,000 ($31,000 – $14,000). He can use the $11,000 disallowed loss realized by Fletcher to reduce his recognized gain to $6,000 ($17,000 – $11,000).

Example 29: Assume the same facts as in Example 28, except Kevin sells the land for $22,000. Kevin's realized gain equals $8,000 ($22,000 – $14,000). He can use $8,000 of the $11,000 disallowed loss to reduce his recognized gain to $0. He cannot use the remaining $3,000 of the disallowed loss to create a loss from the sale. The $3,000 of disallowed loss is lost, and neither Fletcher Corporation nor Kevin Fletcher will benefit from it on their respective tax returns.

Example 30: Assume the same facts as in Example 28, except Kevin sells the land for $12,000. Kevin realizes and recognizes a $2,000 loss ($12,000 – $14,000). Neither he nor Fletcher will benefit from the $11,000 disallowed loss, as it is gone forever.

 GAAP vs. Code: When computing net income on the income statement, all losses are deducted from net income, regardless of who buys the property. Thus, when a corporation sells property to a related party, the disallowed loss must be added back to the corporation's net income when reconciling net income to taxable income on the corporation's income tax return. When a corporation purchases property from a related party and is later able to use some or all of the seller's disallowed loss to reduce its recognized gain, the corporation must subtract from net income the difference between the gain reported on the income statement and the (reduced) gain recognized on the tax return when reconciling net income to taxable income on the tax return.

¶ 805 Wash Sales

A **wash sale** occurs when a taxpayer realizes a loss on the sale of securities (stocks and bonds) and purchases the same or substantially identical securities within 30 days before or after the date of the sale. The tax laws do not allow taxpayers to recognize losses that result from wash sales. For

---

[26] Code Sec. 267(d) and Reg. § 1.267(d)-1.

purposes of the wash sale rules, call options and put options on stock are treated as securities unless the regulations state otherwise.[27]

Example 31:   Rickers Company purchased 1,000 shares of common stock in Appleton, Inc. several years ago for $50,000. As of December 31, 20X1, the stock was selling for $10,000. Because the decline in value represents an unrealized loss, Rickers cannot deduct the loss in computing taxable income on its 20X1 tax return.

Example 32:   Assume the same facts as in Example 31, except on December 31, 20X1, Rickers sells the 1,000 shares in Appleton. Rickers's realized loss on the sale equals $40,000 ($10,000 – $50,000). Under the general rules, Rickers would recognize the $40,000 loss when computing its 20X1 taxable income.

Example 33:   Assume the same facts as in Example 32, except on January 2, 20X2, Rickers repurchases 1,000 shares of Appleton common stock for $10,000. Since Rickers repurchased the same stock in the same company within 30 days after the sale that resulted in a realized loss (the December 31 sale), Rickers's realized loss is disallowed on its 20X1 tax return.

Example 34:   Deborah Williams bought 1,000 shares of High Hope Corporation on September 21, 20X1, for $30,500. She bought another 1,000 shares of High Hope on April 2, 20X3, for $29,000. On April 23, 20X3, she sold the 1,000 shares that she had bought on September 21, 20X1, for $28,100 and realized a loss of $2,400 ($28,100 – $30,500). Deborah may not recognize the loss because she bought the same or substantially identical stock within 30 days before she sold the shares at a loss.

Reason for the Rule: The wash sale rules were enacted in 1921 to prevent taxpayers from reducing their tax liability by taking losses on the sale of securities and then reacquiring the same securities within a short time, thereby essentially leaving them in the same economic position.[28] In Example 33, Rickers originally owned 1,000 shares of common stock in Appleton and, except for a few short days, it continues to own 1,000 shares of Appleton common stock. Without the wash sale rules, Rickers would have been able to turn what was otherwise a nondeductible unrealized loss into a deductible loss. The language applying the wash sale rules to repurchases 30 days before or after the sale was included to make it clear that a window period was intended. The statutory language enacted in 1921 is essentially the same as the language that exists today.

.01 Substantially Identical

The wash sale rules apply if the taxpayer repurchases the *same or substantially identical* securities within 30 days before or 30 days after selling securities at a loss. In determining whether securities are substantially identical, all the facts and circumstances must be considered. With respect to shares of stock sold at a loss, substantially identical securities would be shares of stock in the same company. Normally, common stock of one corporation is not substantially identical to common stock of another corporation, and nonconvertible preferred stock of a corporation is not substantially identical to common stock of the same corporation.[29] Bonds or preferred stock of a corporation are not ordinarily considered substantially identical to the common stock of the same corporation. However, when the bonds or preferred stock are convertible into common stock of the same corporation, the relative values, price changes, and other circumstances may make the bonds or preferred stock and the common stock of the corporation substantially identical.[30]

---

[27] Code Sec. 1091(a).
[28] H.R. Rep. No. 350-67, at 11 (1921).

[29] Reg. § 1.1233-1(d)(1); Rev. Rul. 77-201, 1977-1 CB 250; GCM 37004 (Feb. 15, 1977).
[30] Rev. Rul. 1977-1 CB 250.

Bonds are not substantially identical if they are significantly different with respect to any material feature or when differences in several features are significant when considered together. Maturity date, face rate of interest, call, and convertible features are all features associated with bonds. To determine whether a difference in maturity dates is material, it is necessary to compare the differences in maturity dates in conjunction with the length of time until the bonds mature. Thus, two bonds issued by the same company that have similar features except for maturity dates that are three months apart would be substantially identical if their maturity dates were 14 years away. Differences in interest payment dates would not be considered substantial when the bonds have the same number of annual interest payments. For example, the difference in bonds that pay interest every February 1 and August 1 and bonds that pay interest every October 1 and April 1 would not be considered a substantial difference since both bonds pay interest semiannually.[31]

 Spotlight: The wash sale rules only apply to losses realized on the sale of securities. Taxpayers who sell securities for a gain and purchase the same or substantially identical securities within 30 days on either side of the sale date recognize the gain under the normal recognition rules. Therefore, the basis of the newly acquired securities would be their cost.[32]

.02 Eventual Recognition of the Loss from the Wash Sale

Unlike the related party rules, which permanently deny recognition of the loss to the seller, the wash sale rules merely postpone the loss until the taxpayer sells the securities in a nonwash sale transaction.[33] This is accomplished by either selling the repurchased securities at a gain or by selling the securities for a loss without repurchasing the same or substantially identical securities within the 61-day window surrounding the sales date.

To ensure that taxpayers eventually benefit from the disallowed loss, the disallowed loss is added to the basis of the newly acquired shares that caused the loss to be disallowed. If within the 61-day window the taxpayer purchases the same number of shares that were sold, none of the realized loss is recognized and the entire unrecognized loss is added to the basis of the new shares purchased. The holding period of the shares purchased includes the holding period of the shares sold that resulted in a wash sale.[34]

Example 35: In Example 33, Rickers Company's $40,000 disallowed loss would be added to the basis of the shares purchased on January 2, 20X2. Therefore, the basis in the new shares will be $50,000 ($10,000 + $40,000 disallowed loss). If Rickers immediately sells the newly acquired shares for their $10,000 FMV, the realized loss would equal $40,000 ($10,000 – $50,000). If Rickers can avoid repurchasing these shares for the 61 days surrounding the date of the sale, it will recognize the $40,000 loss that was originally disallowed under the wash sale rules.

If the taxpayer purchases fewer shares than those sold, only a portion of the loss is disallowed and the taxpayer is allowed to recognize the loss on the shares of stock that were sold and not repurchased within the 61-day window. The disallowed loss is added ratably to the basis of the shares repurchased within the 61-day window.[35]

Example 36: On August 11, 20X2, Leah Starnes sold 600 shares of stock in Skate Rinks Corporation for $6,000. Leah's purchases of stock in Skate Rinks were as follows:

---

[31] Rev. Rul. 58-210, 1958-1 CB 523.
[32] Code Sec. 1012.
[33] Code Sec. 1091(d).

[34] Code Sec. 1091.
[35] Reg. § 1.1091-1.

Date	Number of Shares	Price Per Share	Total Paid
June 14, 20X1	600	$25	$15,000
August 28, 20X2	400	14	5,600
September 13, 20X3	200	13	2,600

Leah's realized loss on the sale of the 600 shares sold on August 11, 20X2, equals $9,000 ($6,000 – $15,000). Since she repurchased 400 shares of the stock within 30 days before or after that date, $6,000 of the loss is disallowed ($9,000 × 400/600) and must be added to the basis in the shares involved in the wash sale (the 400 shares purchased on August 28, 20X2). Thus, Leah will recognize $3,000 of the loss ($9,000 – $6,000), and her basis in the shares acquired on August 28, 20X2, equals $11,600 ($5,600 + $6,000). Leah's holding period for those shares dates back to June 14, 20X1—the date on which the shares involved in the wash sale were originally purchased.

 GAAP vs. Code: For financial reporting purposes, all gains and losses on the sale of securities are reported in the calculation of net income. For tax purposes, the wash sale rules affect the timing of the recognition of loss on the sale of securities involved in a wash sale. Since the disallowed loss from a wash sale is eventually recognized, the difference between net income and taxable income in the year the securities are sold at a loss will later be reversed when the repurchased shares are sold at either a gain or in a nonwash sale transaction. Thus, in the year of the wash sale, the disallowed loss must be added back to net income when reconciling net income to taxable income. In the year in which the disallowed loss is finally recognized on the tax return, the loss must be subtracted from net income when reconciling net income to taxable income on that year's corporate tax return.

¶ 806 Qualified Small Business Stock

When a noncorporate taxpayer sells or exchanges qualified small business stock (sometimes referred to as "Section 1202 stock") that the taxpayer held for more than five years, 50 percent of the realized gain is excluded from the taxpayer's gross income.[36] The American Recovery and Reinvestment Act of 2009 (ARRA09) temporarily increases the exclusion percentage to 75 percent. The 75 percent exclusion applies to qualified small business stock acquired after February 17, 2009, and before January 1, 2011.[37] The excluded gain from selling stock in any one corporation cannot exceed the *greater of* (1) $10 million ($5 million for married taxpayers who file separate returns from their spouses) minus all amounts excluded from previous tax years with respect to stock in that particular corporation or (2) 10 times the aggregate bases of qualified small business stock issued by the corporation and sold or exchanged by the taxpayer during the year.[38] Thus, each year in which noncorporate taxpayers sell qualified small business stock, they must ensure that the amount of the exclusion does not exceed either limit.

A "qualified small business" is a domestic C corporation with assets that do not exceed $50 million. The corporation must be actively engaged in business, which is assumed when at least 80 percent of the value of its assets is used in an active trade or business. However, tax law specifically excludes from qualified small business status any business that provides services, such as health, law, engineering, architecture, accounting, consulting, or financial services, among others. It also excludes businesses involving leasing, farming, or operating establishments such as hotels, motels, restaurants, or similar businesses.[39]

---

[36] Code Sec. 1202(a)(1).
[37] Code Sec. 1202(a)(3), after amendment by AARA09.
[38] Code Sec. 1202(b).
[39] Code Sec. 1202.

Example 37: Beth Yarbrough purchased common stock in a qualified small business in 20X0 for $36,000. She sold the stock in 20X7 for $86,000. Her realized gain is $50,000 ($86,000 − $36,000). Beth may exclude $25,000 ($50,000 × 50%) of the gain from her gross income because she held the qualified stock for more than five years.

Reason for the Rule: Code Sec. 1202 was enacted as part of the Omnibus Budget Reconciliation Act of 1993 to encourage investment in new ventures, small businesses, and specialized small business investment companies (SSBICs). Due to the higher risk involved in such investments, Congress hoped that offering special tax incentives to noncorporate investors who invested in these businesses would encourage them to take a chance on these investments. For example, although Beth's realized gain from Example 37 is $50,000, she is only taxed on $25,000 of the gain. If her tax rate on the gain is 15 percent, then Beth will pay a total of $3,750 of tax on the $50,000 gain ($25,000 × 15%), which makes her tax rate on the realized gain 7.5 percent ($3,750 ÷ $50,000).

¶ 807 Rollover of Gain on the Sale of Publicly Traded Stock

Generally, gain realized on the sale of stock must be recognized. A special provision in the tax law allows individuals and C corporations to postpone the realized gain on the sale of publicly traded stock by investing the entire proceeds from the sale in the common stock of or in a partnership interest of an SSBIC.[40] Publicly traded securities include stocks and bonds traded on an established securities market[41] such as the New York Stock Exchange, the American Stock Exchange, or the NASDAQ. If the stock in the SSBIC is small business stock under Code Sec. 1202, then an individual investor may also be able to exclude 50 percent of the gain on the sale of the stock after five years. However, the 50-percent exclusion is only available on the appreciation in the stock after it is purchased by the individual investor (see ¶ 807.02).[42]

Reason for the Rule: SSBICs are licensed by the Small Business Administration. They are financial institutions that invest in and provide financing to the small business community. Currently over 100 SSBICs operating in the United States provide financing to small businesses. These small businesses are primarily owned by socially or economically disadvantaged persons. Since such companies are often riskier investments, Congress enacted Code Sec. 1044 as part of the Revenue Reconciliation Act of 1993 to provide tax incentives to individuals and corporations that invest in SSBICs. Individuals who hold stock in an SSBIC for more than five years may also qualify to exclude 50 percent of the gain on the sale of the SSBIC stock under Code Sec. 1202.

.01 Calculating the Postponed Gain

When a taxpayer realizes a gain on the sale of publicly traded securities and within 60 days reinvests the entire sales proceeds in the stock of or in a partnership interest of an SSBIC, the taxpayer may elect to postpone recognition of the gain. If the taxpayer reinvests only part of the proceeds of the sale of the publicly traded securities in the stock or a partnership interest of an SSBIC, the taxpayer must recognize the *lesser of* (1) the gain realized or (2) the excess of the sales proceeds over the amount reinvested in an SSBIC.[43] The postponed gain may not exceed either the annual or lifetime limits discussed below.

Example 38: During the year, Bucknell, Inc. sold publicly traded stock for $600,000. Its adjusted basis in the stock was $125,000. The sale produced a $475,000 realized gain

---

[40] Code Sec. 1044(c)(3).
[41] Committee Reports on P.L. 103-66 (Omnibus Budget Reconciliation Act of 1993).

[42] Code Sec. 1044(d).
[43] Code Sec. 1044(a).

($600,000 – $125,000). Within 60 days of the sale, Bucknell invests $460,000 of the $600,000 proceeds in an SSBIC and files an election on its tax return to postpone the gain to the extent allowed under the tax law. Even if the election to postpone gain is made, Bucknell must recognize *at least* $140,000 that it failed to reinvest in an SSBIC ($600,000 – $460,000). However, annual and lifetime limits apply to determine whether any of the $335,000 of remaining gain ($475,000 – $140,000) must be recognized.

Annual and lifetime limits. An individual taxpayer may elect to annually postpone up to $50,000 of gain, subject to a lifetime maximum of $500,000. These limits are halved for married taxpayers who file separate returns. C corporations can elect to annually postpone up to $250,000 of gain, subject to an aggregate $1 million limit. The tax laws treat all C corporations that are members of a controlled group of corporations as one corporation.[44] (See ¶ 804 for the definition of a controlled group.)

Example 39:   Continuing with Example 38, since Bucknell's $335,000 remaining gain exceeds the $250,000 annual limit allowed to corporations, Bucknell will be allowed to exclude $250,000 of the realized gain but will be required to recognize an additional $85,000 of gain ($335,000 realized gain – $250,000 annual limit). Thus, Bucknell's total recognized gain will be $225,000 ($140,000 + $85,000). Another way to compute the recognized gain is to subtract the postponed gain from the realized gain ($475,000 – $250,000 = $225,000). Bucknell's $1 million aggregate limit is reduced by the $250,000 it excludes in the current year. If Bucknell has never before postponed gain by investing in an SSBIC, its remaining aggregate limit to use in subsequent tax years equals $750,000 ($1,000,000 – $250,000).

 Planning Pointer: The special provision under Code Sec. 1044 is available only to individuals and C corporations. Accordingly, all other taxpayers, including partnerships and S corporations, must recognize the realized gain on the sale of publicly traded stock, even if the proceeds are reinvested in an SSBIC.[45]

.02 Reduction of Basis

To ensure that the postponed gain is eventually recognized (and not permanently excluded), the basis in the stock or partnership interest of the SSBIC is reduced by the postponed gain. However, for purposes of calculating the 50 percent exclusion of gain available to individuals on the sale of Section 1202 stock (which includes SSBIC stock held for more than five years) (see ¶ 806), the adjusted basis of the SSBIC stock is not reduced by the postponed gain.[46] If the basis reduction were allowed for Section 1202 purposes, some of the postponed gain under Code Sec. 1044 would possibly be excluded under Code Sec. 1202. This provision prevents the deferred gain from qualifying for the exclusion. However, the exclusion under Code Sec. 1202 is available for all appreciation that occurs *after* the taxpayer buys the stock in the SSBIC.

Example 40:   Fagan Corporation, a C corporation, purchased publicly traded bonds in 20X1 for $2 million. In prior years, Fagan postponed under Code Sec. 1244 a total of $450,000 of gain on the sale of publicly traded securities by investing in the stock of an SSBIC. In 20X3, Fagan sells the bonds for $2.4 million and realizes a $400,000 gain ($2,400,000 – $2,000,000). Within 60 days after selling the bonds, Fagan invests $3 million in the stock of an SSBIC. Because the $400,000 realized gain exceeds the annual maximum gain deferral of $250,000 for C corporations, Fagan must recognize at least $150,000 of the gain ($400,000 – $250,000). However, Fagan can elect to postpone $250,000 of the $400,000 realized gain because it invested more than the proceeds from the sale

---

[44] Code Sec. 1044(b).
[45] Code Sec. 1044(c)(4).

[46] Code Sec. 1044(d).

in an SSBIC within 60 days of the sale. Because the aggregate postponed gain of $700,000 ($450,000 in prior years + $250,000 in the current year) does not exceed the aggregate limit of $1 million, Fagan can postpone recognition of the remaining $250,000 gain. The postponed gain reduces the basis in the stock of the SSBIC to $2.75 million ($3,000,000 – $250,000).

Example 41: Dawn Foster operates a business as a sole proprietorship. In 20X1, Dawn purchased stock in a publicly traded corporation for $460,000. In 20X3, she sells the stock for $550,000 and realizes a $90,000 gain ($550,000 – $460,000). Within 60 days of the sale, Dawn pays $550,000 for stock in an SSBIC. She elects to defer the $50,000 of the gain (the annual limit for individual taxpayers) and reduces her basis in the stock in the SSBIC. Dawn's basis in the stock in the SSBIC is only $500,000 ($550,000 – $50,000). However, Dawn's basis in the stock for the purpose of calculating the gain eligible for the 50-percent exclusion under Code Sec. 1202 is the $550,000 that she paid for the stock. In order to meet the provisions of Code Sec. 1202, Dawn will have to hold the stock for at least five years.

Example 42: Continuing with Example 41, Dawn sells the stock in the SSBIC in 20X5 for $1 million. Because she did not hold the stock in the SSBIC for more than five years, her realized and recognized gain equals $500,000 ($1,000,000 – $500,000).

Example 43: Assume the same facts as in Example 42, except Dawn sells the stock in the SSBIC in 20X9 for $1 million. Because Dawn held the stock in the SSBIC for more than five years, her realized gain from the sale equals $500,000 ($1,000,000 – $500,000). However, for purposes of the exclusion under Code Sec. 1202, she may exclude only $225,000, which is 50 percent of the amount realized ($1 million) minus the $550,000 that she paid for the stock. Thus, her recognized gain equals $275,000 ($500,000 – $225,000).

 GAAP vs. Code: On the company's financial statements, all realized gains from the sale of stock are included in net income. Corporations that elect to postpone the gain on the sale of publicly traded securities by reinvesting the proceeds in SSBICs, must subtract out the postponed gain from net income when reconciling net income to taxable income in the year the stock is sold. Because the amount of postponed gain reduces the corporation's basis in the SSBIC, in the year the SSBIC stock is sold, the amount of gain reported on the tax return will exceed the amount included in the calculation of net income. Accordingly, the difference in the amount of the gain must be added to net income when reconciling net income to taxable income in the year in which the corporation sells the SSBIC stock.

.03 Making the Election

Taxpayers make the election to rollover (postpone) gain on the sale of publicly traded stock by attaching a statement to the tax return and filing the return on or before its due date (including extensions). The statement must show (1) how the postponed gain was calculated, (2) the SSBIC in which the investment was made, (3) the date on which the investment was made, and (4) the basis of the stock or the partnership interest in the SSBIC.[47]

¶ 808 Like-Kind Exchanges

When the consideration received on the sale of property is other property, the amount realized equals the FMV of the property received in the exchange, minus any selling expenses. The excess of the amount realized over the adjusted basis in the property sold is the realized gain or loss on the

---

[47] Reg. § 1.1044(a)-1(b).

exchange. Under the general rules, any realized gain or loss would have to be recognized if the property sold is business or investment property. When taxpayers exchange similar property, they, in essence, leave themselves in the same economic position as before the exchange, since both parties enter the transaction with property worth a certain amount and after the exchange they each own similar property presumably worth that same amount. However, one party could receive property of more value than the property received by the other party. In the absence of a relationship between the parties, the IRS makes no attempt to determine if like-kind exchanges benefit both parties equally. In addition, parties that exchange similar assets do not necessarily have the funds needed to pay the tax on the gain. The Internal Revenue Code (the "Code") allows taxpayers to postpone the gain realized on the exchange of like-kind properties, but because the government must wait to receive the tax revenues generated from the realized gain, the tax law also requires that realized losses on the exchange of like-kind property be postponed.[48] Accordingly, taxpayers who realize a loss on a like-kind exchange must wait to receive the tax benefits associated with deducting the loss.

.01 Like-Kind Exchange Requirements

A like-kind exchange occurs when a taxpayer transfers property and receives in exchange property of "like-kind." Property of "like-kind" refers to the nature or character of the property and not to its grade or quality.[49] The various types of property that are never considered to be like-kind are listed in Figure 8-3.

Figure 8-3 Property Never Considered Like-Kind

- Property used by the taxpayer for personal purposes;
- Real property located outside the United States;
- Personal property used predominately outside the United States;
- Partnership interests;
- Stocks (however, for exchanges after May 22,2008, certain mutual ditch, reservation or irrigation stock is not considered stock for this purpose and therefore may be exchanged for other real property as a like-kind exchange.[50]), bonds, and notes receivable; and
- Inventory.

Because an individual's personal belongings do not qualify as like-kind property, a like-kind exchange must involve the exchange of business or investment property for other property to be used for business or investment purposes.[51] With respect to exchanges of real property (other than real property located outside the United States), any other business or investment real property qualifies as like-kind property.[52] Thus, the exchange of land for an office building qualifies as like-kind property, as would the exchange of a vacant lot for a warehouse or an apartment building.

With respect to tangible personal property, like-kind property must be of like class. Personal property that has the same use qualifies as property of like class.[53] For example, a like-kind exchange would occur when a business trades in a truck as a part of the consideration in the purchase of a new truck. For property to be of a "like class," it must be within the same *general asset class* or within the same *product class*.[54] Property cannot be classified within more than one general

---

[48] Code Sec. 1031(a)(1).

[49] Reg. § 1.1031(a)-1(b).

[50] Code Sec. 1031(i), after amendment by the Heartland, Habitat, Harvest, and Horticulture Act of 2008.

[51] Code Sec. 1031(a)(1).

[52] Reg. § 1.1031(a)-1(b).

[53] Reg. § 1.1031(a)-1(c).

[54] Reg. § 1.1031(a)-2(b)(1).

asset class or within more than one product class. Furthermore, property that is classified within a general asset class cannot qualify as like-class property using the product class designations. Table 8-1 lists the various general asset classes as designated in the regulations.[55]

Table 8-1 General Asset Classes

Asset Class	Includes
00.11	Office furniture, fixtures, and equipment
00.12	Computers and peripheral equipment
00.13	Data handling equipment other than computers
00.21	Helicopters and airplanes (except those used in commercial or contract carrying of passengers or freight)
00.22	Automobiles and taxis
00.23	Buses
00.241	Light general purpose trucks
00.242	Heavy general purpose trucks
00.25	Railroad cars and locomotives (except those owned by railroad transportation companies)
00.26	Tractor units for use over the road
00.27	Trailers and trailer-mounted containers
00.28	Vessels, barges, tugs, and similar water-transportation equipment (except those used in marine construction)
00.4	Industrial steam and electric generation and/or distribution systems

---

Example 44: Hall Company exchanges a computer for Ruiz Company's color laser printer. The exchange qualifies as a like-kind exchange because both the computer and the color laser printer are in the same general asset class of 00.12.[56]

Example 45: Gregory Company exchanges a heavy general purpose truck for Fisher Company's automobile. The exchange does not qualify as a like-kind exchange under the general asset class criterion because the heavy general purpose truck is in the 00.242 general asset class, and the automobile is in the 00.22 general asset class. Because the properties are included in a general asset class, the taxpayer cannot classify the properties as like class using product class designations. Therefore, the exchange does not qualify as a like-kind exchange.

Properties are like-kind properties if they are in the same product class, but *only* if the property is not listed in a general asset class.[57] A "product class" consists of depreciable tangible personal property described in a six-digit product class within Sectors 31, 32, and 33, of the North American Classification System (NAICS) Manual, prepared under the auspices of the Office of Management and Budget. This manual is available online at *http://www.census.gov/naics.* If the last digit of an NAICS code for a product class is "9" (a miscellaneous category), the product class is not considered a product class for the like-kind exchange rules.[58]

Example 46: Rhodes Company exchanges a grader for Flowers Company's scraper. Neither property is listed in a general asset class (see Table 8-1), but both properties are in

---

[55] Reg. § 1.1031(a)-2(b)(2); Rev. Proc. 87-56, 1987-2 CB 674.
[56] Reg. § 1.1031(a)-2(b)(7), Ex. 1.

[57] Reg. § 1.1031(a)-2(b)(1).
[58] Reg. § 1.1031(a)-2(b)(3).

the same product class (NAICS Code 333120). Therefore, the properties are of like class, and the exchange qualifies as a like-kind exchange.[59]

Example 47: Michaels Company exchanges a stamping machine for Hammer Company's drill press. Neither property is listed in a general asset class (see Table 8-1). The stamping machine is classified in product class code 333513, and the drill press is classified in product class code 333512. Since the properties are not of like class, the exchange is not considered a like-kind exchange.

.02 Time Frame for Taking Possession of Like-Kind Property

Although direct exchanges of like-kind property fall under the nonrecognition rules for like-kind exchanges, the exchange of the like-kind properties does not have to be simultaneous. Often taxpayers wishing to engage in like-kind exchanges do not have specific properties in mind for which to make a trade. Fortunately, in most areas of the country there are specialized intermediaries who act as escrow agents and hold the property until finding another party interested in completing the exchange. To qualify for a like-kind exchange, the property the taxpayer receives in the exchange must be identified within 45 days of the date the taxpayer transfers property to the other party. In addition, the taxpayer must receive the like-kind property by the *earlier of* (1) 180 days after the transfer of the like-kind property to the other party or (2) the due date of the taxpayer's income tax return, including extensions.[60] If the exchange does not meet both conditions, the exchange will not qualify as a like-kind exchange, and any realized gain or loss would be recognized.

Example 48: On June 20, 20X1, Harris Corporation transfers land held for investment to a qualified intermediary in anticipation of exchanging the land for another parcel of land that it will hold for investment. Harris uses the calendar year as its tax year, and accordingly, the due date of its 20X1 tax return is March 15, 20X2. Harris must take possession of the new land from the other party through the qualified intermediary no later than the *earlier of* (1) December 17, 20X1, which is 180 days after Harris transferred its land to the intermediary, or (2) the due date of Harris's 20X1 tax return. Since December 17, 20X1 occurs before the due date of for filing its tax return, Harris must receive the like-kind property no later than that date.

Example 49: O'Connor Corporation transfers an office building on December 16, 20X1, to a qualified intermediary. O'Connor uses the calendar year as its tax year. The 180-day period after the initial transfer ends on June 14, 20X2. If O'Connor does not extend the deadline for filing its income tax return, the like-kind property must be received no later than March 15, 20X2 (the *earlier of* June 14, 20X2, or March 15, 20X2).

Example 50: Assume the same facts as in Example 49, except O'Connor Corporation is granted a six-month extension to file its 20X1 income tax return. O'Connor must receive the like-kind property no later than June 14, 20X2 (the *earlier of* June 14, 20X2, or the September 15, 20X2 extended due date), in order for the exchange to qualify as a like-kind exchange. By obtaining the extension to file its income tax return, O'Connor has three additional months (June 14 versus March 15) to receive the like-kind property for the exchange to qualify as a like-kind exchange.

 Planning Pointer: If an exchange meets the conditions for a like-kind exchange, the like-kind exchange rules are mandatory. Most taxpayers prefer to recognize losses immediately because of the tax savings associated with reducing taxable income. Likewise, taxpayers typically prefer to defer the recognition of gains because of the time value of money. However, if the taxpayer is in a low tax bracket and expects to be in a

---

[59] Reg. § 1.1031(a)-2)b)(7), Ex. 3.   [60] Code Sec. 1031(a)(3).

much higher tax bracket in the future, the taxpayer may want to recognize the gain on the exchange. Also, if the taxpayer has expiring loss carryovers (for example, capital losses (¶ 901.01) or net operating losses (¶ 1001.01)), the taxpayer may want to recognize the gain in the year of the exchange to utilize the expiring carryovers.

To recognize a gain or loss on an exchange, a taxpayer can structure the transaction as a sale followed by a purchase of the new property. The taxpayer could also negotiate to modify the terms of an exchange of tangible depreciable personal property so the property received is not of the same general asset class or the same product class as the asset given in the exchange. If the exchange is not a direct exchange, the taxpayer could recognize the gain or loss by ensuring that the property to be received was not identified within 45 days after the initial transfer or that it was not received within the time frame allowed under the tax laws. A taxpayer also could negotiate to receive enough nonlike-kind property in the exchange so all realized gain will be recognized (see ¶ 808.03).

.03 Tax Consequences of a Like-Kind Exchange

The realized gain or loss on the exchange of like-kind property is not recognized. Instead, any gain or loss is postponed until the taxpayer disposes of the newly acquired like-kind property in a nonlike-kind transaction.[61] To make sure the postponed gain or loss is not forgotten, the tax laws require the taxpayer to take a substituted basis in the newly-acquired like-kind property. This is accomplished by decreasing the FMV of the like-kind property by any postponed gain and increasing the FMV of the like-kind property by any postponed loss.[62] The holding period of the like-kind property includes the holding period of the like-kind property given up in the exchange.[63]

Example 51: Rodgers & Moore, LLC exchanges a building worth $50,000 for land worth $50,000 owned by Gartner & Associates, LLP. Rodgers & Moore's adjusted basis in the building is $30,000; Gartner's basis in the land is $60,000. Each party uses the property in its business and neither property is located outside of the United States. Thus, the exchange qualifies as a like-kind exchange for both parties.

In determining the tax consequences of the exchange, each party first determines its realized gain or loss. As depicted in the diagram below, the FMV of the property received is the same for each party. Assume neither party incurred any selling expenses resulting from the exchange. Therefore, their realized gain equals the $50,000 amount realized, minus their respective adjusted basis in the property given up in the exchange. The result is a $20,000 realized gain for Rodgers & Moore and a $10,000 realized loss for Gartner.

---

[61] Code Sec. 1031(a)(1).
[62] Code Sec. 1031(d).

[63] Code Sec. 1223(1).

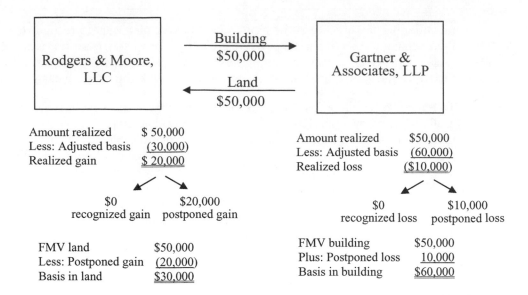

In this example, the like-kind exchange rules require that all realized gains and losses be postponed and reflected in the basis of the newly acquired like-kind property. Therefore, none of Rodgers & Moore's $20,000 realized gain is recognized, and its basis in the land is reduced to $30,000 ($50,000 – $20,000). Similarly, none of Gartner's $10,000 realized loss is recognized, and its basis in the building increases to $60,000 ($50,000 + $10,000). Furthermore, the holding period of the land acquired by Rodgers & Moore includes the holding period of the building. Thus, if Rodgers & Moore purchased the building in 1998, the land will be deemed to have been acquired in 1998. Similarly, Gartner's holding period in the building will begin on the date it acquired the land. Gartner's depreciable basis in the newly acquired building is its $60,000 basis after the exchange.

 Reason for the Rule: Under the wherewithal-to-pay principle, taxpayers are in the best position to pay tax when the property is sold or otherwise disposed of and the proceeds can be used to pay the corresponding tax. When a like-kind exchange occurs, the proceeds consist of the FMV of the like-kind property. If gain were required to be recognized, taxpayers might be forced to sell the property in order to pay the taxes owed on any recognized gain. Thus, under the like-kind rules, the gain is postponed until the taxpayer has the wherewithal to pay the taxes on the gain.

Receipt of boot. If in the exchange, the taxpayer receives property (including cash) that is not of like-kind, the nonlike-kind property is referred to as **boot**. When taxpayers receive boot in addition to like-kind property, any realized gain is recognized to the extent of the boot received. Thus, taxpayers recognize gain equal to the *lesser of* (1) the FMV of the boot received or (2) the amount of gain realized.[64] Receipt of boot in a like-kind exchange does not trigger a recognized loss on the exchange.[65]

Example 52: Assume the same facts as in Example 51, except Gartner's land was only worth $42,000, so to even up the exchange Gartner pays Rodgers & Moore $8,000 cash. Accordingly, each party still receives property totaling $50,000. Under this scenario, the tax consequences to the two parties are as follows:

---

[64] Code Sec. 1031(b).　　　　[65] Code Sec. 1031(c).

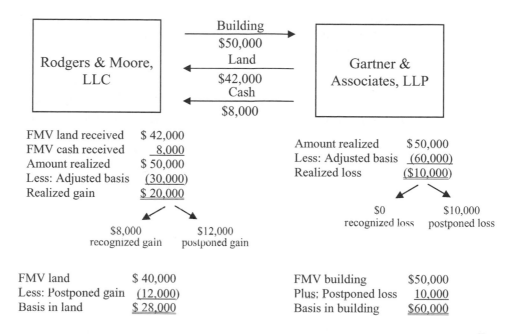

FMV land received	$ 42,000
FMV cash received	8,000
Amount realized	$ 50,000
Less: Adjusted basis	(30,000)
Realized gain	$ 20,000

$8,000 recognized gain $12,000 postponed gain

Amount realized	$ 50,000
Less: Adjusted basis	(60,000)
Realized loss	($10,000)

$0 recognized loss $10,000 postponed loss

FMV land	$ 40,000
Less: Postponed gain	(12,000)
Basis in land	$ 28,000

FMV building	$50,000
Plus: Postponed loss	10,000
Basis in building	$60,000

Because Rodgers & Moore received boot on the exchange, the *lesser of* the FMV of the boot received ($8,000) or the realized gain ($20,000) is taxed, and the remainder of the realized gain is deferred and reflected in the basis of the like-kind property acquired in the exchange. The payment of cash boot by Gartner does not trigger recognition of any realized gain or loss that it might realize on the exchange of like-kind property.[66] However, see ¶ 803.03 for a discussion of instances when boot given results in gain recognition.

 Reason for the Rule: The premise behind the like-kind exchange rules is the wherewithal-to-pay principle. When taxpayers receive boot in an exchange, the government considers that they have the ability to pay taxes associated with the realized gain. Therefore, taxpayers recognize gain to the extent of the boot received.

The tax laws treat a party's release from liability as though the taxpayer received cash, which was then used to pay off the debt. Thus, the amount of liability from which the taxpayer is relieved in a like-kind exchange is treated as boot received and represents the taxpayer's wherewithal to pay tax on the recognized gain.[67] The party that assumes debt is treated as having given boot. When the two parties assume one another's debts as part of the exchange, the party that is relieved of more debt than it assumes is treated as having received boot for the difference in the amount of debt. Likewise, the party that assumes more debt than it is relieved of is treated as having paid boot for the net difference of the debt. However, the debt incurred by the taxpayer does not reduce boot from money or nonlike-kind property the taxpayer receives. Therefore, it is possible for both parties to receive boot in a like-kind exchange if one party receives cash and the other party is treated as having received boot by having been released from more debt than it assumed on the exchange.[68]

Example 53: Brock Company purchased land for investment purposes in 20X1 for $190,000 by making a down payment and signing a note secured by a mortgage. Smyth Company purchased land in 20X0 for $245,000 by making a down payment and signing a note secured by a mortgage. On August 27, 20X4, Brock and Smyth agree to exchange properties and to assume one another's outstanding mortgage with the consent of

---

[66] Code Sec. 1031(c).
[67] Reg. § 1.1031(b)-1(c).

[68] Reg. § 1.1031(b)-1(c); Reg. § 1.1031(d)-2, Ex. 2.

the lenders. On the date of the exchange, the FMV of Brock's land is $400,000 and the outstanding mortgage is $200,000; the FMV of Smyth's land is $360,000 and its outstanding mortgage is $160,000.

Since Brock and Smyth swap debt, it is first necessary to calculate the net amount of debt and determine which party is deemed to have paid boot and which party is deemed to have received boot. The net amount of debt exchanged is $40,000 ($200,000 – $160,000). Since Brock is relieved of $200,000 of debt and only assumes $160,000 of debt, Brock is treated as having received $40,000 boot. This amount is included in Brock's amount realized. On the other side of the transaction, Smyth has taken on $200,000 of debt in exchange for being relieved of $160,000 of debt, and therefore Smyth is treated as having paid $40,000 boot. Like the adjusted basis of the property given up in the exchange, any boot given is subtracted from Smyth's amount realized in determining its realized gain or loss from the exchange. The tax consequences of the exchange are illustrated below.

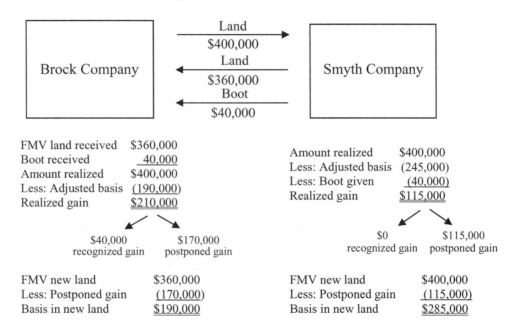

FMV land received	$360,000
Boot received	40,000
Amount realized	$400,000
Less: Adjusted basis	(190,000)
Realized gain	$210,000

$40,000 recognized gain $170,000 postponed gain

FMV new land	$360,000
Less: Postponed gain	(170,000)
Basis in new land	$190,000

Amount realized	$400,000
Less: Adjusted basis	(245,000)
Less: Boot given	(40,000)
Realized gain	$115,000

$0 recognized gain $115,000 postponed gain

FMV new land	$400,000
Less: Postponed gain	(115,000)
Basis in new land	$285,000

Both parties realize gain on the exchange; however, only Brock recognizes gain. Brock is treated as having the wherewithal to pay the tax on gain due to the boot (net release of debt) it received on the exchange. The remainder of Brock's gain is postponed and reduces the basis in the new land that it received from Smyth. Because Smyth did not receive any boot on the exchange, the entire $115,000 of realized gain is postponed, and the FMV of the land received from Brock is reduced by $115,000 when Smyth computes its basis in the land.

Example 54: In 20X1, Beck Company purchased land held for investment for $245,000 by making a down payment and signing a note for the remainder. In 20X0, Snyder Company paid $257,000 for land held for investment by making a down payment and signing a note for the remainder. On April 2, 20X4, Beck and Snyder exchange properties, each assuming the other's outstanding debt with the consent of the lenders. In addition, on the date of the exchange, Beck's property is worth $345,000 and its outstanding loan amount is $195,000. Snyder's property is worth $260,000 and its outstanding mortgage is $200,000. Snyder pays Beck $90,000 in cash to even up the exchange.

Because the two parties swap debt, only the net debt is considered boot. Since Snyder is relieved of $5,000 more debt than it assumes from the exchange, Snyder is treated as having received $5,000 boot on the exchange. Beck also receives $90,000 boot from the cash it receives from Snyder. The tax law does not allow these two types of boot to be netted against one another.[69]

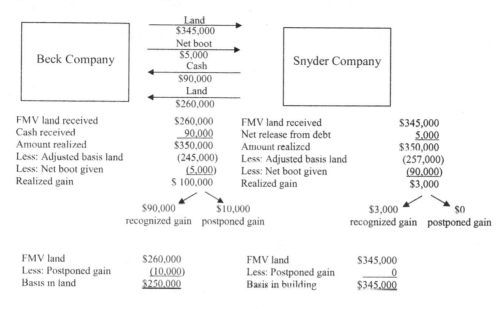

	Land $345,000		
Beck Company	Net boot $5,000	Snyder Company	
	Cash $90,000		
	Land $260,000		

FMV land received	$260,000	FMV land received	$345,000
Cash received	90,000	Net release from debt	5,000
Amount realized	$350,000	Amount realized	$350,000
Less: Adjusted basis land	(245,000)	Less: Adjusted basis land	(257,000)
Less: Net boot given	(5,000)	Less: Net boot given	(90,000)
Realized gain	$ 100,000	Realized gain	$3,000

$90,000 recognized gain $10,000 postponed gain $3,000 recognized gain $0 postponed gain

FMV land	$260,000	FMV land	$345,000
Less: Postponed gain	(10,000)	Less: Postponed gain	0
Basis in land	$250,000	Basis in building	$345,000

Each party's amount realized on the exchange is $350,000, and both parties realized a gain on the exchange. Since Beck received $90,000 cash from Snyder, Beck must recognize $90,000 of its $100,000 realized gain. Accordingly, Beck's basis in the land it receives in the exchange is reduced by the $10,000 of postponed gain. On the other side of the transaction, Snyder benefits from having been relieved of $5,000 more of debt than it assumes on the exchange, and therefore, it recognizes the entire $3,000 of realized gain. Since none of the gain is postponed, Snyder's basis in the new land is its $345,000 FMV at the time of the exchange.

Reason for the Rule: Normally, the receipt of boot triggers the recognition of realized gain on a like-kind exchange. Thus, under the normal rules, when each party assumes the other's debt, both parties would be treated as having received boot. Since the like-kind exchange rules operate under the wherewithal-to-pay principle, it is difficult to tax the gain to the party that assumes more debt because that party has less liquidity (from the standpoint of having taken on more debt) than before the exchange. The special rule allowing the parties to offset each other's debt prevents the party assuming net debt from having to recognize gain on a like-kind exchange when the only boot is debt relief.

Gain or loss on transfer of boot. Although boot typically is cash or involves the assumption of debt, boot can also consist of other types of nonlike-kind property. When the FMV of the boot given is different from the transferor's adjusted basis in the boot, the transferor is treated as having sold the boot for its FMV. Consequently, any realized gain or loss on the sale of boot (any difference between its FMV and adjusted basis) is recognized by the transferor under the normal rules that govern gains and losses on the sale of property.[70]

[69] Reg. § 1.1031(d)-2, Ex. 2.   [70] Code Sec. 1001(c).

GAAP vs. Code: The revenue recognition principle governs the financial accounting rules regarding exchanges of similar assets. Under GAAP, gains from the exchange of similar assets must be postponed and subtracted from the basis of the similar property received on the exchange. Losses, on the other hand, are reported on the income statement. If the corporation receives a monetary (cash) consideration as part of the exchange, the earnings process is considered to have been partially completed, and part of the realized gain is recognized on the income statement. These rules are similar to the tax laws requiring recognition of gain upon the receipt of boot. However, the amount of gain reported on the income statement is the proportion the amount of cash bears to the total FMV of the properties received in the exchange.[71] Thus, if the corporation receives a total consideration of $100,000 on the exchange, of which $20,000 is cash, 20 percent of the realized gain would be reported on the income statement. These rules are different from the tax laws governing the recognition of gains on like-kind exchanges. If the above situation were a like-kind exchange, the *lesser of* the amount of realized gain or $20,000 would be recognized on the tax return.

.04 Special Rules for Like-Kind Exchanges between Related Parties

When related parties exchange like-kind property that results in the deferral of gain or loss, the postponed gain or loss is recognized if within two years of the transfer either party disposes of the like-kind property. Such gain or loss is recognized in the tax year in which the like-kind property is subsequently sold. Thus, if related parties enter into a like-kind exchange transaction, they must each hold onto the like-kind property they receive for at least two years to take full advantage of the nonrecognition of gain or loss under Code Sec. 1031. The rules defining related parties presented earlier in the chapter also apply to like-kind exchanges (see ¶ 804 and Figure 8-2.) Exceptions do exist for dispositions due to a death or to a subsequent involuntary conversion of the like-kind property. The taxpayer may also avoid gain recognition by proving to the IRS that avoidance of federal income tax was not one of the principal purposes of the like-kind exchange or the disposition.[72] If a sale or taxable exchange does occur within the two-year period, a basis adjustment is required. Any recognized gain would then be added, and any recognized loss would be subtracted from the basis of the like-kind property from the exchange.

Example 55: In 2008, Eagle Eye Corporation exchanges land used in its business for land held for investment by its sole shareholder Amanda Eagle. Eagle Eye realizes a $10,000 gain on the exchange of its land. Amanda realizes a gain of $12,000, but neither recognizes any gain because no boot was exchanged. In 2009, Amanda sells her land to an unrelated party and recognizes a $14,000 gain. The sale of Amanda's land triggers recognition of the $10,000 gain by Eagle Eye in 2009.

Example 56: Anzelt Corporation owns as an investment an apartment building (Building A) worth $1 million and with an adjusted basis of $100,000. Bakkert owns an apartment building (Building B) worth $1 million, but it has an adjusted basis of $900,000. Anzelt and Bakkert are members of the same controlled group. Therefore, they are related parties. The controlling shareholders of the two companies have decided they would like Anzelt to dispose of Building A because they are concerned about it holding its value in the long term. However, they would also like for Bakkert to sell its investment in the apartment building and invest the $1 million in its operations.

If Anzelt were to sell Building A, it could use the proceeds to purchase Building B (which is a much more promising investment in the long run) from Bakkert;

---

[71] "Accounting for Nonmonetary Transactions," *Opinions of the Accounting Principles Board No. 29* (Stamford, Conn.: FASB, 1973).

[72] Code Sec. 1031(f).

however, it would recognize gain of $900,000 ($1 million – $100,000). Bakkert would recognize gain of $100,000 on the sale of Building B to Anzelt ($1,000,000 – $900,000 adjusted basis). Anzelt's basis in Building B would be its cost of $1 million.

Since the two corporations are related, they could arrange for the two companies to exchange their respective properties. Each company would postpone recognition of its realized gain and reduce its basis in the new property accordingly. Anzelt would take a basis of $100,000 in Building B; and Bakkert would take a basis of $900,000 in Building A as shown below.

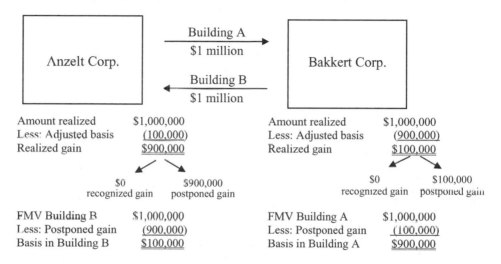

Amount realized	$1,000,000
Less: Adjusted basis	(100,000)
Realized gain	$900,000

$0 recognized gain $900,000 postponed gain

FMV Building B	$1,000,000
Less: Postponed gain	(900,000)
Basis in Building B	$100,000

Amount realized	$1,000,000
Less: Adjusted basis	(900,000)
Realized gain	$100,000

$0 recognized gain $100,000 postponed gain

FMV Building A	$1,000,000
Less: Postponed gain	(100,000)
Basis in Building A	$900,000

Immediately after the exchange, Bakkert could turn around and sell Building A for $1 million and pay tax on the resulting $100,000 gain ($1,000,000 – $900,000). Thus, Bakkert would achieve its goal of getting out of its investment in the apartment building in exchange for proceeds of $1 million. By structuring the sale as an exchange, Anzelt is able to get out of its investment in Building A but continue its investment in a (more desirable) apartment building (Building B) while postponing payment of tax on the appreciation of Building A until Building B is sold.

Under the related party rules for like-kind exchanges, because Bakkert sells its apartment building within two years of the exchange, Anzelt must recognize the postponed gain in the year Bakkert sells Building A. Anzelt's basis in Building B would equal $1 million ($100,000 + $900,000 recognized gain). Therefore, the result to each party is the same as if the two parties had initially sold their respective buildings.

 Reason for the Rule: When like-kind property is exchanged, each party takes a substituted basis for the property it receives. Congress feared that related parties might engage in like-kind exchanges of property so property with a higher adjusted basis (like Building B in Example 55) could be substituted for property with a lower adjusted basis (like Building A) so the owner of the lower basis property (Anzelt) could avoid recognizing gain on the sale. Congress believed that if a related party exchange were followed shortly thereafter by a disposition of the property, the related parties would, in effect, have "cashed out" of the investment, and the original exchange should be taxed as such [73]

---

[73] Senate Committee Print and Conference Committee Report to P.L. 101-239.

¶ 809 Involuntary Conversions

An involuntary conversion occurs when property that taxpayers own is taken from them against their wishes. Examples of **involuntary conversions** include the various casualties described earlier plus instances in which the government seizes the taxpayer's property in a condemnation. The gross amount realized from an involuntary conversion is equal to the insurance proceeds (in the case of property destroyed in a casualty) or the compensation received from the government (in the case of a condemnation). Any expenses incurred in connection with receiving the proceeds from the involuntary conversion are deducted from the gross amount realized to arrive at the amount realized.

When a taxpayer realizes a loss from the involuntary conversion of business or investment property, the tax laws allow the loss to be deducted.[74] If the taxpayer acquires replacement property, the basis of the property (for depreciation and subsequent sale) is equal to its cost, and the holding period of the property begins on the day the taxpayer purchases it.[75]

When a taxpayer realizes a gain from an involuntary conversion, the tax laws allow the taxpayer to postpone the gain if the entire proceeds are reinvested in qualified replacement property.[76] The taxpayer must reduce the basis in the newly acquired replacement property by any postponed gain just as the taxpayer must in a like-kind exchange. This basis reduction ensures that the gain is eventually recognized when the taxpayer sells the replacement property. As with the like-kind exchange rules, the holding period of the new property usually includes the holding period of the converted property.[77] If the government threatens to condemn a property and the taxpayer sells the property prior to the government taking possession of it, any realized gain from the sale can be postponed under the involuntary conversion rules if the proceeds from the sale are reinvested in qualified replacement property within a specified time frame.[78]

Taxpayers also have the option of electing to recognize the entire realized gain and to not postpone any of the realized gain. If this election is made and replacement property is purchased, the taxpayer's basis in the replacement property is equal to its cost, and the holding period begins on the date the property is purchased.[79]

 Planning Pointer: Most people might assume that postponing gain is always in the taxpayer's best interest. However, it is important to look closely at the overall picture if the taxpayer has a choice between postponing and recognizing gain. If the taxpayer has carryovers that are about to expire (for example, charitable contributions (¶ 511), capital losses (¶ 901.01), net operating losses (¶ 1004.02) or tax credits (¶ 1103.02 and ¶ 1117.04)), recognizing the gain immediately may allow the taxpayer to avoid losing the tax benefits associated with the carryover amounts. This is especially important to consider if the taxpayer plans to sell the replacement property in the near future and would recognize gain anyway. It may also be advantageous to recognize the gain if the taxpayer is currently in a low tax bracket and is expected to be in a higher tax bracket in future tax years. In that event, the taxpayer may want to pay tax today at the lower tax rates rather than pay more tax in the future. Because the amount of postponed gain reduces the taxpayer's basis in the replacement property, more depreciation will be taken in upcoming (higher tax rate) years if the gain is recognized and the depreciable basis is the (unreduced) cost of the replacement property.

---

[74] Code Sec. 1001(c).
[75] Code Sec. 1012.
[76] Code Sec. 1033(a)(2)(A).

[77] Code Sec. 1223(1).
[78] Rev. Rul. 81-180, 1981-2 CB 161.
[79] Code Sec. 1012.

.01 Postponing the Realized Gain

The taxpayer can postpone part or all of the realized gain on an involuntary conversion by acquiring qualified replacement property within the allowable time. To the extent that the proceeds are not reinvested in qualified replacement property, the taxpayer recognizes gain equal to the *lesser of* the realized gain or the amount not reinvested.[80] If the cost of the qualified replacement property is greater than or equal to the amount realized on the involuntary conversion, all of the gain can be postponed.

 Reason for the Rule: To the extent the taxpayer reinvests the entire proceeds in qualified replacement property, the taxpayer is not considered to have the wherewithal to pay the tax on the gain realized.

The postponed gain equals the realized gain minus the recognized gain. The basis of the qualified replacement property is its cost minus the postponed gain.[81] The holding period of the qualified replacement property typically includes the holding period of the property involuntarily converted.[82]

 Planning Pointer: The taxpayer does not have to spend all of the cash received in an involuntary conversion on the qualified replacement property. The taxpayer's reinvestment also includes debt incurred in the process of acquiring qualified replacement property.

.02 Qualified Replacement Property

For property used in the taxpayer's business, "qualified replacement property" is property that is similar to or related in service or use to the property involuntarily converted.[83] Typically, the replacement property must have the same *functional use* as the property that was involuntarily converted. For example, if the property involuntarily converted was a warehouse, qualified replacement property would be another building with the same functional use (a storage facility for inventory). For property held as an investment, qualified replacement property would be property that will be used in similar investment endeavors.[84] For example, if the taxpayer's investment in an apartment building is involved in an involuntary conversion, the owner can replace it with any other rental property, not just another apartment building. This special rule allows investors more flexibility in defining qualified replacement property. A more flexible rule also applies if business or investment property is located in a disaster area and is involuntarily or compulsorily converted as a result of a federally declared disaster. In that event, tangible property of a type held for productive use in a trade or business is considered as qualified replacement property.[85]

When the government condemns business or investment real estate, the definition of qualified replacement property is expanded to include any like-kind property.[86] Thus, the proceeds from a condemnation can be used to purchase any business or investment realty.

Example 57: Steele Corporation's machine is destroyed in an accident. Steele receives insurance proceeds in excess of its basis in the machine and realizes an $8,000 gain. To defer the gain, Steele must invest the entire insurance proceeds in another similarly-functioning machine within the time allowed. In an involuntary conversion of per-

---

[80] Code Sec. 1033(a)(2)(A).
[81] Code Sec. 1033(b)(1).
[82] Code Sec. 1223.
[83] Reg. § 1.1033(a)-1(a).

[84] Rev. Rul. 79-261, 1979-2 CB 295.
[85] Code Sec. 1033(g)(2).
[86] Code Sec. 1033(g)(1).

sonal property, the replacement asset must have the same function as the asset involuntarily converted.

Example 58: The office building of Drew Corporation is destroyed in a fire. Drew receives insurance proceeds that result in a $100,000 realized gain. To postpone the gain, Drew must reinvest the entire insurance proceeds in another office building within the time allowed. In an involuntary conversion of real estate used in a business, the replacement property must have the same function as the property involved in the involuntary conversion.

Example 59: Dan Breaux, LLC owns an investment in an apartment building that is completely destroyed by a tornado. The insurance company pays Breaux $500,000, which results in a realized gain of $240,000. To defer the gain, Breaux must reinvest the entire $500,000 proceeds in any type of investment real estate in which Breaux acts as the landlord and receives rental income from the property. The proceeds need not be used to purchase another apartment building. Because the property was held by Breaux as an investment rather than used in a business, the tax law allows Breaux more flexibility in replacing the converted property.

Example 60: Wood Company's warehouse is condemned by the state under the power of eminent domain to use as a part of the right-of-way for a new highway. The state pays Wood the FMV of the property, and Wood realizes a gain on the condemnation. Wood can defer the gain by investing the entire amount received from the state in any other business or investment real property within the time allowed. Qualified replacement property for condemned business or investment real estate is any business or investment realty.

.03 Time Frame for Making the Purchase

To defer part or all of the gain realized on an involuntary conversion, the taxpayer must obtain qualified replacement property within a certain period of time. This period begins on the date of the involuntary conversion (or on the date the government threatened condemnation) and generally ends two years after the end of the tax year in which the taxpayer realized the gain from the involuntary conversion.[87] That is, the year in which the taxpayer received the insurance proceeds (in the case of a casualty) or the condemnation award (in the case of a condemnation). However, if business or investment realty is condemned by the government, the period is extended an additional year (to three years).[88]

Example 61: Zuckerman Industries paid $50,000 for land on September 16, 20X2. On October 6, 20X5, the state condemns the land under the power of eminent domain to build a new highway. The state pays Zuckerman $90,000 for the land on January 4, 20X6. Zuckerman's realized gain in 20X6 equals $40,000 ($90,000 – $50,000), and the company has until December 31, 20X9 (three years from December 31, 20X6), to purchase any business or investment realty. If Zuckerman reinvests at least $90,000 during this period, it can postpone the entire $40,000 of realized gain.

Example 62: Continuing with Example 61, assume that during 20X6, Zuckerman pays $75,000 for new land and does not plan to reinvest the remaining $15,000 in qualified replacement property prior to December 31, 20X9. Zuckerman recognizes a gain of $15,000 in 20X6 (the *lesser of* the $40,000 realized gain or $15,000) and defers $25,000 of the gain ($40,000 – $15,000). Its basis in the new land is $50,000 ($75,000 cost of replacement property – $25,000 postponed gain). The holding period includes the holding period of the land purchased on September 16, 20X2.

---

[87] Code Sec. 1033(a)(2)(B).

[88] Code Sec. 1033(g)(4).

Example 63: Donna Underwood's business machine is destroyed by fire. An insurance company reimburses her $45,000 for the loss on September 5, 20X6. The machine originally cost $62,000, but Donna had deducted Section 179 and Modified Accelerated Cost Recovery System (MACRS) totaling $34,000 up until the time of the casualty. Thus, her adjusted basis in the machine was $28,000 ($62,000 − $34,000). Donna's realized gain equals $17,000 ($45,000 − $28,000) on the involuntary conversion. Donna has until December 31, 20X8 (two years after December 31, 20X6, the year in which she realized the gain), to purchase another similarly functioning machine for her business. As long as the new machine costs at least $45,000, all $17,000 of the realized gain can be postponed.

Example 64: Continuing with Example 63, assume that during 20X7 Donna purchases a similarly functioning machine for $50,000. Donna recognizes no gain on the involuntary conversion because the cost of the new machine exceeds the proceeds she received from the insurance company. Therefore, all of her realized gain of $17,000 is deferred, and her basis in the new machine is $33,000 ($50,000 − $17,000). Donna depreciates the machine's $33,000 basis using the rules discussed in Chapter 7.

Example 65: Assume instead that Donna Underwood from Example 63 reinvests $40,000 in a new machine during the allowed period. Since Donna does not reinvest the entire proceeds, she will recognize $5,000 of the $17,000 realized gain ($45,000 − $40,000). The remaining $12,000 of realized gain ($17,000 − $5,000) will be postponed, and the basis of her new machine will be $28,000 ($40,000 − $12,000).

 GAAP vs. Code: For financial accounting purposes, realized gains and losses resulting from involuntary conversions are reported on the income statement.[89] Thus, when taxpayers postpone gain for tax purposes, the postponed gain must be subtracted from net income when reconciling net income to taxable income on the corporate tax return.

¶ 810 Installment Sales

An **installment sale** involves the sale of business or investment property from which the seller receives at least one payment in a subsequent tax year. When taxpayers sell property in an installment sale that produces a loss, they generally recognize the loss in the year of the sale or the exchange.[90] When taxpayers sell property in an installment sale and realize gain, they generally recognize the gain over the tax years in which they collect the proceeds from the sale.[91]

Under the installment method, gain recognized each year equals the amount the taxpayer actually or constructively receives during the year multiplied by the gross profit percentage.[92] There are some limitations on the use of the installment sales method. Generally, for installment sales that exceed $150,000, taxpayers who borrow money using the installment notes as collateral must treat the borrowed funds as installment payments received. In addition, to the extent that deferred principal payments exceed $5 million, taxpayers must inpute and pay interest to the federal government on the tax that is deferred from the installment sale.[93] Exceptions to this requirement exist for sales of personal use property, certain farm property, and certain time shares and residential lots.[94] The impact is to largely remove the tax deferral benefits for those installment sales that are subject to these rules. Taxpayers that regularly sell property for which the proceeds are collected over more than one tax year generally must recognize the entire gain in the year of the sale. Thus, for example, inventory is not eligible for the installment method of reporting.[95]

---

[89] FASB Interpretation No. 30, *Accounting for Involuntary Conversions of Nonmonetary Assets to Monetary Assets.*

[90] Code Secs. 165 and 1001(c).

[91] Code Sec. 453.

[92] Code Sec. 453(c).

[93] Code Sec. 453A(b)(1) and (2).

[94] Code Sec. 453A(b)(3).

[95] Code Secs. 453(b)(2)(A) and 453(l)(1)(B).

Reason for the Rule: Under the installment method, taxpayers recognize the gain as they receive cash or its equivalent under the terms of the sale. That is when they are considered to have the wherewithal to pay the tax on the gain.

.01 Operating Rules

When taxpayers use the installment method, the payments received during the year are multiplied by the gross profit percentage to determine the amount of gain to include in gross income for the year. The "gross profit percentage" equals the gross profit from the sale divided by the "total contract price." The "total contract price" is equal to the sales price minus any debts on the property that the buyer assumed or to which the property was subject. "Gross profit" is equal to the gross sales price minus the adjusted basis of the property. If the seller pays commissions on the sale of real property, the selling expenses (commissions) are added to the taxpayer's adjusted basis in the property sold; they do not reduce the gross sales price.[96]

Example 66: Johnson Manufacturing sells land to Able Manufacturing for $150,000. The terms of the sale require Able to pay cash of $20,000 and issue an installment note that calls for five annual payments of $20,000 on principal plus interest at the market rate. In addition, Able assumes Johnson's $30,000 mortgage on the land with the consent of the lender. Johnson incurs $8,000 in selling expenses on the sale. Johnson purchased the land two years earlier for $82,000. Since Johnson will receive payments over more than one tax year, it will report the $60,000 gross profit from the sale over the next six years.

Gross sales price	$150,000
Less: Adjusted basis*	(90,000)
Gross profit from the sale	$ 60,000

Gross sales price	$150,000
Less: Debt assumed by buyer	(30,000)
Total contract price	$120,000

$60,000 gross profit ÷ $120,000 total contract price = 50% gross profit percentage

---

* Includes $8,000 of commissions paid on the sale of the land

In the year of the sale, Johnson's recognized gain equals $10,000 ($20,000 cash payment × 50%). Johnson will recognize $10,000 gain for each of the next five years as it collects each payment on the installment note ($20,000 × 50%). In addition, Johnson will include the interest it receives from the note in gross income. At the end of five years, Johnson will have recognized the entire $60,000 of gross profit from the sale ($10,000 in the year of the sale + $10,000 annually for five years).

If the amount of debt the buyer assumes exceeds the taxpayer's adjusted basis of the property, the seller adds the excess to the total contract price. In these cases, the gross profit percentage will always be 100 percent. When the amount of the assumed debt exceeds the seller's adjusted basis in

---

[96] Temp. Reg. § 15A.453-1(b)(2).

the property, the seller is deemed to have been paid cash equal to such excess amount in the year of the sale.

Example 67: Assume the same facts as in Example 66, except Johnson's remaining mortgage on the land is $100,000, and the terms of the sales agreement call for Able to assume the debt and pay Johnson $10,000 at the time of the sale and the rest of the purchase price in five installment payments of $8,000 each.

Gross sales price	$150,000
Less: Adjusted basis	(90,000)
Gross profit from the sale	$ 60,000

Gross sales price	$150,000
Less: Debt assumed by buyer	(100,000)
Plus: Excess of $100,000 debt assumed over $90,000 adjusted basis	10,000
Total contract price	$ 60,000

$60,000 gross profit ÷ $60,000 total contract price = 100% gross profit percentage

Because Johnson is relieved of $10,000 more of debt than its adjusted basis in the land, Johnson is deemed to have received a total of $20,000 cash from the buyer in the year of the sale ($10,000 down payment + $10,000 from excess release from debt). Johnson will recognize the entire $20,000 in the year of sale ($20,000 × 100%), and then recognize 100 percent of each $8,000 payment it receives over the next five years. At the end of five years, Johnson will have recognized the entire $60,000 of gross profit from the sale ($20,000 plus $8,000 annually for five years).

.02 Sale of an Installment Note

The face value of an installment note consists of two elements:

1. the unrecovered cost of the asset sold, and

2. the postponed gain.

The adjusted basis of the installment note is its unrecovered cost. Therefore, if a taxpayer sells an installment note before collecting all the payments on the note, the taxpayer recognizes a gain or loss on the sale of the note equal to the difference between the amount realized and the adjusted basis of the note. The "adjusted basis" of the note is its uncollected principal minus the deferred gain.[97]

Example 68: On December 4, 20X1, Lofton Enterprises sold land used in its business for $150,000. Its basis in the land was $60,000. Lofton received $50,000 cash and an installment note for $100,000 that calls for annual payments of $20,000 over the next five years beginning December 4, 20X2. The note also provides for Lofton to receive interest at the market rate on any outstanding balance of the note. Lofton's realized gain from the sale equals $90,000 ($150,000 amount realized less $60,000 adjusted basis), and its gross profit percentage is 60 percent ($90,000 ÷ $150,000). Accordingly, in 20X1, Lofton's recognized gain is $30,000 ($50,000 cash received × 60%). In each subsequent year, Lofton's recognized gain from the installment sale will equal $12,000 ($20,000 × 60%).

---

[97] Code Sec. 453B.

On January 9, 20X5, after having collected three of the five installment payments, Lofton sells the note for $29,000. At the time of the sale, the balance due on the principal of the note equals $40,000 ($100,000 minus three installments of $20,000 each), and the amount of deferred gain is $24,000 [$90,000 – $30,000 – ($12,000 × 3)]. Accordingly, the adjusted basis in the installment note equals $16,000 ($40,000 uncollected principal minus $24,000 of deferred gain). In 20X5, Lofton recognizes $13,000 of gain from the sale of the note ($29,000 amount realized minus $16,000 adjusted basis in the note).

> **Reason for the Rule:** When the taxpayer sells an installment note, the taxpayer has the wherewithal to pay the tax on the resulting gain.

.03 Installment Sales between Related Parties

The tax law allows related parties to sell property at a gain in an installment sale. However, when two family members enter into a transaction that involves an installment sale, special rules apply if the (related party) purchaser disposes of the property within two years of the sale. When the property is disposed of within two years of the sale, the original seller is required to recognize all remaining gain in the year the original purchaser sells the property.[98] For this rule, the term "family members" has the same meaning it has for sales between related parties, discussed earlier in the chapter (see ¶ 804).

.04 Electing Out of the Installment Method

If an installment sale is made, the default method of reporting the recognized gain is the installment method. However, taxpayers have the option of electing out of the installment method and instead recognizing the entire gain in the year of the sale. Such election normally must be made by the due date of the tax return, including extensions. Once an election is made, it cannot be revoked without permission from the IRS.[99]

> **GAAP vs. Code:** For financial accounting purposes, any gain or loss realized on the sale of property is recognized immediately—with rare exceptions. The financial accounting rules require sellers of real estate to recognize all the profit in the year of sale provided the collection of the sales proceeds is reasonably assured or the seller can reasonably estimate the uncollectible amount. In addition, the terms of the sale must not require the seller to perform significant services after the sale.[100] Consequently, when taxpayers report a gain from an installment sale, the amount of net income must be adjusted each year for the difference between the gain reported on the income statement and the gain reported on the tax return.

¶ 811 Summary

Under the realization principle, taxpayers generally do not recognize gains and losses from the sale of business or investment property until the property is disposed of in a taxable transaction. Realized gains and losses from the disposal of business and investment property are generally recognized; however, exceptions do exist. Proper tax planning requires that taxpayers understand the circumstances under which realized gains can be excluded or postponed as well as the circumstances under which realized losses can be disallowed, either permanently or temporarily.

---

[98] Code Sec. 453(e)(2).
[99] Code Sec. 453(d).

[100] "Accounting for Sales of Real Estate," *Statement of Financial Accounting Standards No. 66* (Stamford, Conn.: FASB, 1973).

Deferring gains is not always in the taxpayer's best interest. However, a good understanding of the tax laws will allow taxpayers to structure transactions to best serve their interests.

GLOSSARY OF TERMS INTRODUCED IN THE CHAPTER

Abandonment. The situation in which the owner of property permanently and intentionally relinquishes any claim to the property without receiving any consideration in return.

Adjusted basis. The initial basis of property adjusted upward for capital improvements and any deferred losses and downward for capital recoveries and deferred gains. Used in determining the realized gain or loss from the sale of property.

Amount realized. The sum of the cash, other non-like-kind boot, FMV of property, and release of mortgage received in a sale or an exchange of property minus any selling expenses. Used in determining the realized gain or loss from the sale of property. *See also* Realized gain or loss.

Boot. A term tax practitioners use to describe nonlike-kind property involved in a like-kind exchange. *See also* like-kind.

Condemnation. A legal action in which the government takes possession of property under the power of eminent domain.

Constructive ownership. A rule under which a taxpayer may be treated as owning stock that is actually owned by another person or entity in which the taxpayer has an ownership interest.

Exchange. A transaction in which two parties exchange property. Various types of boot (see definition above) may also constitute part of the proceeds.

Installment sale. A sale or exchange of property in which the seller receives payments in more than one tax year.

Involuntary conversion. An event caused by casualty, theft, or condemnation in which the taxpayer's property is damaged or destroyed.

Nonrecourse liability. A liability for which the seller is not personally liable, but for which the creditor can only look to property specified in the loan agreement for satisfaction of the debt.

Realized gain or loss. Measure of the taxpayer's true economic gain or loss resulting from the disposal of property in a sale, an exchange, or an abandonment.

Recognized gain or loss. The amount of the realized gain or loss that is reported on the tax return.

Recourse liability. Liability for which the seller is personally liable.

Unrealized gains and losses. The difference between the FMV of property and its adjusted basis at a time other than when the property has been disposed of. Sometimes referred to as paper gains and losses because they represent the appreciation or decline in value of property that has yet to be sold.

Wash sale. A sale of securities (stocks and bonds) in which a taxpayer realizes a loss on the sale and then purchases the same or substantially identical securities within 30 days before or 30 days after the date of the sale; tax laws do not allow taxpayers to recognize losses that result from wash sales.

CHAPTER PROBLEMS

The following questions and problems relate to the discussion in Chapter 8, Property Transactions: Realized and Recognized Gains and Losses, which begins at ¶ 800 in *Part III: Transactions Involving Business Property.*

Chapter 8 Discussion Questions

1. When computing realized gain or loss from the sale of property, why does the amount realized include the fair market value of property received?

2. When computing realized gain or loss, why does the amount realized include debt relief?

3. A business owns land used in its business. The land increased $100,000 in value this year. Why does the tax law not require the business to pay taxes on the increase in the value of the land? Explain.

4. Discuss what is meant by an exchange. How does it differ from a sale? How does the tax law treat the gains and losses on exchanges? Are the rules the same for financial accounting?

5. What is the income tax treatment of a holder of a call option or put option on common stock who allows the option to expire worthless? How does this treatment compare to stocks or bonds that become worthless?

6. Distinguish between unrealized, realized, and recognized gains and losses and explain their importance in computing taxable income.

7. What is a wash sale? How do the tax laws treat realized losses from a wash sale?

8. Discuss the annual and lifetime limits that individuals may exclude on the gain from the sale of publicly traded securities when they invest the proceeds in a specialized small business investment company (SSBIC). How do these limits differ from the annual and lifetime limits for a C corporation?

9. How do the tax laws treat losses on a sale between related parties? What happens to any disallowed loss? What is the significance of the disallowed loss with respect to sales or exchanges between related parties?

10. What does "like class" mean in a like-kind exchange?

11. When a like-kind exchange is not simultaneous, what is the allowable time after the initial transfer to identify the property to be received in the exchange? Within what period must the taxpayer receive the like-kind property in a like-kind exchange?

12. May a taxpayer elect out of the like-kind exchange rules? If so, how? If not, can a taxpayer structure the transaction in a different manner so as to make the exchange taxable?

13. What is "boot" in a like-kind exchange? How is a release from debt treated when it is part of a like-kind exchange?

14. Do the tax laws allow like-kind exchanges between related parties? Explain.

15. What constitutes an "involuntary conversion," and how do the tax laws treat realized gains and losses resulting from an involuntary conversion of business property?

16. What constitutes "qualified replacement property" in an involuntary conversion?

17. In an involuntary conversion, what period does a taxpayer have in which to purchase qualified replacement property to avoid recognition of gain?

18. Sam Kinder sold land he used in his business in 20X1. The buyer gave him 10 percent down and a note for the remaining 90 percent due in 20X2. Sam realized a gain on the sale of the land. Does the sale qualify as an installment sale?

19. What is the meaning of "total contract price" in an installment sale?

20. May a taxpayer elect out of the installment method of recognizing gain from an installment sale? If so, how?

Chapter 8 Problems

1. Tennison Company sells a machine used in its business. Tennison receives $18,000 in cash and a promissory note for $75,000 that bears interest at the market rate. Tennison incurs $500 in selling expenses. Compute Tennison's amount realized.

2. Roberts Company exchanged a truck used in its business for a new truck. The new truck was worth $58,000. Roberts Company paid $5,000 in cash for the new truck and signed a note for $36,000 that is secured by the new truck. The dealer agreed to pay $11,000 that Roberts still owed on the old truck. What is the amount realized by Roberts on the exchange of the old truck?

3. Jenkins Corporation sold equipment used in its business for cash. The amount realized was $80,000. The equipment originally cost $140,000, but it had an adjusted basis of $60,000 at the time of the sale. What is the gain or loss realized by Jenkins Corporation?

4. Lockwood Corporation purchased land. The contract sales price was $122,000 and Lockwood Corporation had to pay all of the closing costs, including the unpaid real estate taxes from the first of the year. The estimated real estate taxes for the year are $1,200. The date of sale was June 1. The closing costs other than the real estate taxes and prepaid items were $3,100. What is Lockwood Corporation's adjusted basis in the land?

5. Martin Company bought land with an FMV of $20,000, a building with an FMV of $70,000, and equipment with an FMV of $10,000 at an estate auction for a lump sum payment of $60,000. What is the basis of each asset?

6. Sanchez Company sold land for $100,000 to Belita Sanchez, who owns 60 percent of the outstanding stock of Sanchez. The company's adjusted basis in the land is $120,000.

    a. Compute the company's realized and recognized gain or loss on the sale of the land.

    b. What is Belita's adjusted basis in the land?

    c. If Belita sold the land for $90,000 two years after she purchased it, compute her realized and recognized gain or loss.

    d. If Belita sold the land for $105,000 two years after she purchased it, compute her realized and recognized gain or loss.

    e. If Belita sold the land for $145,000 two years after she purchased it, compute her realized and recognized gain or loss.

7. Warren Davis owns 20 percent of the outstanding stock of Davis Corporation. Warren's sister, Sara Smith, owns 30 percent of the stock; his cousin, Reggie Anderson, owns 20 percent of the stock; and his father, Ben Davis, owns 30 percent of the stock. Determine Warren's actual and constructive ownership in Davis Corporation under the related party rules.

8. Biggs Company bought 1,000 shares of RXA Corporation for $50,000 on May 10, 20X0. Biggs Company sold the 1,000 shares for $40,000 on July 14, 20X1. On July 28, 20X1, Biggs Company purchased 600 shares of RXA Corporation for $26,400.

    a. Calculate Biggs's realized and recognized gain or loss from the sale of the 1,000 shares sold.

    b. Compute Biggs's basis in the new shares purchased on July 28, 20X1.

9. Julie Waters sold qualified small business stock (Section 1202 stock) that she had owned for more than five years. She realized a gain of $400,000. Compute Julie's recognized gain.

10. Giese Corporation, a C corporation, sold publicly traded bonds for $897,000. Giese's adjusted basis in the bonds was $600,000. Two days after receiving the proceeds from the sale, Giese invested $750,000 in an SSBIC.

    a. How much gain must Giese recognize on the sale of the bonds?

    b. What is Giese's adjusted basis in the stock in the SSBIC?

11. Jeannie Lynne sold stock in a publicly traded corporation for $480,000 and realized a gain of $160,000. Within 60 days of selling the stock, she purchased stock in an SSBIC that cost $500,000.

    a. Calculate Jeannie's recognized gain if she elects to postpone as much gain as possible from the sale of the stock.

    b. Calculate her adjusted basis in the SSBIC stock.

    c. Calculate her adjusted basis in the SSBIC stock for purposes of determining the 50-percent exclusion that could result under Code Sec. 1202 if she holds the stock for at least five years.

12. Lopez Company transfers a computer used in its business that has an adjusted basis of $300 and an FMV of $1,000 to Greene Company and receives in exchange a laser printer with an FMV of $600 that it will use in its business and cash of $400.

    a. Calculate Lopez's realized and recognized gain or loss.

    b. What is Lopez's basis in the laser printer?

13. Wheeler Corporation transferred land to a qualified intermediary on March 1, 20X1, as a part of a like-kind exchange. The tax year for Wheeler Corporation is the calendar year.

    a. By what date must the land be identified that Wheeler Corporation will receive in exchange?

    b. By what date must Wheeler Corporation actually receive the land?

14. Garrison Corporation transfers unimproved land to Rucker Corporation and receives in exchange improved land with an FMV of $600,000 and $250,000 of cash. Rucker's adjusted basis in the improved land is $750,000. Garrison's adjusted basis in the unimproved land is $400,000 and the FMV of the land is $900,000. At the time of the exchange Garrison's unimproved land is subject to a $200,000 mortgage that Rucker assumes. Rucker's improved land is subject to a mortgage of $150,000 that Garrison assumes.

    a. Compute Garrison's realized and recognized gain or loss on the exchange of the unimproved land and its basis in the newly acquired improved land.

    b. Compute Rucker's realized and recognized gain or loss on the exchange of the improved land and its basis in the newly acquired unimproved land.

15. Harris Corporation transfers unimproved land to Newman Corporation and receives in exchange improved land worth $850,000 and $100,000 of cash. Newman's improved land is subject to a $120,000 mortgage, which Harris assumes. Harris's unimproved land has an FMV of $830,000 and an adjusted basis to Harris of $700,000. The unimproved land is not subject to any mortgage at the time of the exchange. Newman's basis in the improved land is $770,000.

    a. Compute Harris's realized and recognized gain or loss on the exchange and its adjusted basis in the newly acquired improved land.

    b. Compute Newman's realized and recognized gain or loss on the exchange and its adjusted basis in the newly acquired unimproved land.

16. The business equipment of Connor Corporation was destroyed in a fire. The insurance company reimburses Connor $221,000. At the time of the fire, the adjusted basis in the equipment was $171,000. Two months after receiving the insurance proceeds, Connor Corporation purchases similarly functioning equipment that costs $215,000.

    a. Compute Connor's realized and recognized gain or loss from the casualty.

    b. What is Connor's basis in the new equipment?

17. Murray Corporation's office building is destroyed in a tornado. Murray receives $2 million in insurance proceeds. Murray's adjusted basis in the office building at the time of the tornado was $2,150,000. Within three months of receiving the insurance proceeds, Murray purchases a new office building at a cost of $1,950,000.

    a. Compute Murray's realized and recognized gain or loss from the casualty.

    b. What is Murray's basis in the new office building?

18. Tanger Company's warehouse is destroyed in a fire on October 4, 20X4. Tanger's adjusted basis in the warehouse at the time of the fire is $140,000. The insurance company reimburses Tanger $200,000 for the loss on January 14, 20X5. Tanger has a calendar year-end.

    a. How much must Tanger reinvest in qualified replacement property to avoid recognizing any gain on the involuntary conversion?

    b. How long does Tanger have to reinvest in qualified replacement property?

    c. What constitutes qualified replacement property?

    d. How would your answers to a., b., and c. change if the warehouse were condemned by the government?

19. Walker Corporation sold land on the installment basis in 20X1. Walker Corporation received $70,000 in cash at the time of the sale and an installment note for $630,000 that called for seven annual payments of $90,000 of principal plus interest at 10 percent per year. In addition, the purchaser assumed a mortgage on the land in the amount of $100,000. Walker Corporation had an adjusted basis in the land of $450,000. Walker Corporation paid selling expenses of $70,000 in 20X1.

    a. Compute Walker's gross profit percentage on the sale.

    b. How much of the realized gain must Walker recognize in 20X1?

    c. How much of the realized gain must Walker recognize each year from 20X2 through 20X8?

20. Cahill Corporation sells land on the installment basis. Cahill receives $50,000 in cash at the time of sale. The purchaser assumes a mortgage on the land in the amount of $400,000. Cahill also receives an installment note that calls for five annual payments of $50,000 of principal plus interest at the market rate. Cahill's adjusted basis in the land is $300,000. Cahill pays $20,000 in commissions on the sale.

    a. Compute Cahill's gross profit percentage on the sale.

    b. How much of the realized gain must Cahill recognize in the year of the sale?

    c. How much of the realized gain must Cahill recognize each year for the next five years?

21. Sedita Company sold land on the installment basis to Benson Company. Sedita received $50,000 in cash and an installment note for $350,000 that calls for annual payments of $70,000 plus interest at the market rate for five years. Sedita had a basis in the land of $160,000. Calculate the gain realized by Sedita. Calculate the gain that Sedita would recognize in the year of sale and in each of the next five years.

22. Carper Company sold land it held for investment for $100,000. Carper received in exchange $10,000 in cash and an installment note for $90,000 that calls for annual payments of $10,000 plus interest at the market rate for nine years. Carper had a basis in the land of $60,000. After collecting two installment payments, Carper sold the note for $62,000. Calculate the gain or loss that Carper realized on the sale of the installment note.

23. Orosz Company bought land for $10,000 cash and by signing a nonrecourse note for $90,000. Five years later, when the balance on the nonrecourse note was $50,000, Orosz sold the land to Reyes Company for $130,000 in cash and Reyes took the land subject to the nonrecourse liability with the consent of the lender. Calculate Orosz's gain or loss on the sale of the land.

24. Albright Company bought 800 shares of LoTech Company for $32,000 ($40 per share) on November 16, 20X6. On March 9, 20X7, Albright sold the 800 shares of LoTech for $22,400 ($28 per share). Soon thereafter, the shares of LoTech began to increase in value. On April 2, 20X7, Albright bought 1,000 shares of LoTech for $36,000 ($36 per share).

   a. Calculate the gain or loss that Albright realized on the sale of the 800 shares of LoTech on April 2, 20X7.

   b. How much of the realized gain or loss is recognized?

   c. What is Albright's basis in the 1,000 shares of LoTech?

25. Grossman Company received land with a fair market value of $90,000 and $10,000 in cash from Francona Company. In exchange, Grossman transferred land to Francona that had an FMV of $100,000 and an adjusted basis of $130,000.

   a. Calculate the gain or loss that Grossman realized on the exchange.

   b. How much of Grossman's realized gain or loss is recognized?

   c. What is Grossman's adjusted basis in the land it received from Francona?

Chapter 8 Review Problems

1. Benson Corporation purchased office furniture for $300,000 in 2007 at a bargain price at a bankruptcy auction. Benson did not claim Code Sec. 179 deduction on the office furniture. In 2009, Benson Corporation exchanged the office furniture for new office furniture. The old office furniture was subject to a debt of $50,000, which the other party assumed. The fair market value of the new office furniture was $340,000, and it was subject to a debt of $40,000, which Benson assumed. Benson Corporation also received $60,000 cash in the exchange.

For Benson Corporation, calculate the following:

   a. Depreciation allowed on the old office furniture under MACRS for 2007–2009 (assume the half-year convention applies).

   b. Benson's adjusted basis in the old furniture.

   c. The realized gain or loss on the exchange of the old office furniture.

   d. The recognized gain or loss on the exchange of the old office furniture.

   e. Benson's basis in the new office furniture.

2. In January 2007, Karen Sparks purchased land with a building situated on it for $320,000. It was determined that the building accounts for 62.5 percent of the FMV of the property and the land for the other 37.5 percent. Karen immediately began using the land and building in her business, which she operates as a sole proprietorship. On September 1, 2009, the building was completely destroyed in a fire. She received insurance proceeds of $500,000 on September 21, 2009. She built a new building on the land and used it for the same purpose. The new building cost $480,000. She began using it on December 22, 2009. She wants to defer as much gain as possible.

Based on this information, determine the following:

   a. The initial basis in the land and in the original building.

   b. The depreciation on the building for years 2007–2009.

   c. The adjusted basis in the building at the time of the fire.

   d. Realized gain or loss on the involuntary conversion of the building.

   e. Recognized gain or loss on the involuntary conversion of the building.

   f. The adjusted basis in the new building.

Chapter 8 Research Question

Melton Company bought land for $100,000 that it held for a possible future plant site. Melton Company bought the property for a $20,000 cash payment and by signing a note secured by a mortgage on the land in the amount of $80,000.

Property values in the area increased significantly. When the land was worth, $300,000, Melton Company took out a new mortgage loan of $250,000 and paid off the $100,000 existing mortgage loan.

Property values in the area then decreased a great deal, and Melton Company could no longer make the payments on the mortgage. When Melton Company's land had a fair market value of $175,000, the lender foreclosed on the mortgage. The balance of the mortgage loan at the time of the foreclosure was $240,000. The mortgage loan was a recourse loan. Although the lender could have held Melton Company liable for any deficiency resulting from the foreclosure, the lender forgave the entire debt because of Melton Company's deteriorating financial condition. However, Melton Company was not bankrupt or insolvent.

How much gain or loss did Melton Company realize on the foreclosure? How much, if any, gain or loss must it recognize? How much gross income does Melton Company recognize as income from the discharge of indebtedness?

CHAPTER 9
Property Transactions: Character of Gain or Loss

1. Explain the importance of distinguishing between a capital gain or loss and an ordinary gain or loss.

2. Describe the capital losses limitations that apply to corporate versus noncorporate taxpayers.

3. Calculate the tax associated with an individual taxpayer's net capital gain.

4. Explain how the gains and losses on the sale or other disposal of business property are treated on the tax return.

5. Describe the special capital gains tax rates that apply to individual taxpayers.

¶ 900 Introduction

In the previous chapter, the tax laws that govern realized and recognized gains and losses were presented. Any gain that the taxpayer realizes represents income, but only recognized gains are included in gross income under federal income tax law. Thus, recognized gains are the only gains reported on the taxpayer's income tax return. Realized losses are only reported on the income tax return if the tax laws allow them to be recognized. Although recognized losses are reported on the tax return, the tax laws may limit the amount of losses the taxpayer may deduct against gross income in a particular tax year. Any loss disallowed would be carried over to another tax year to be utilized in that year. Therefore, while recognized losses are deductible, they may not be deducted from gross income in the tax year in which they are realized. This chapter discusses the loss limitation rules that affect both corporate and individual taxpayers.

Ultimately, all recognized gains and losses from the sale, exchange, or other disposal of property are treated either as ordinary gains and losses or as capital gains and losses. The distinction is important because preferential treatment is given to both capital gains and ordinary losses. Initially, recognized gains and losses may be characterized as any one of the following: ordinary gains and losses, short-term capital gains and losses, long-term capital gains and losses, Section 1231 gains and losses, or business casualty and theft gains and losses. The proper classification of recognized gains and losses is critical not only for determining the amount of losses taxpayers can deduct in a particular tax year, but also for calculating an individual taxpayer's federal income tax liability. The rules regarding the characterization of gains and losses are the focus of this chapter.

¶ 901 The Significance of Capital Gains and Losses

Although recognized gains and losses can initially be characterized in several ways, all recognized gains are ultimately treated either as capital gains or as ordinary income. Likewise, all recognized losses are treated either as capital losses or as ordinary losses. The distinction between capital and ordinary gains and losses is important for two reasons. First, the tax laws limit the amount of capital losses that can be deducted in a particular tax year. No such limits apply to ordinary losses. Second, lower tax rates may apply to capital gains recognized by individual taxpayers. Ordinary income, however, is taxed at the taxpayer's marginal tax rate.

The lower tax rates for capital gains of individual taxpayers are limited to special instances in which an individual recognizes a "net capital gain." This occurs when the taxpayer's net long-term capital gains exceed net short-term capital losses (see ¶ 901.02). Typically, capital gains and losses result from the sale or exchange of a capital asset; however, capital gain treatment can be generated from the sale of certain other assets. The definition of what constitutes a capital asset and the various other ways in which capital gain treatment can be generated are discussed in this chapter (see ¶ 903 and ¶ 904). A long-term capital gain or loss generally results from the sale or exchange of a capital asset that the taxpayer held for more than one year.[1] For most property, the taxpayer's "holding period" begins on the day after the taxpayer acquires property and ends on the day the taxpayer disposes of the property.[2] However, special holding period rules may apply (see ¶ 901.03).

.01 Limitations on Capital Losses

The tax laws limit the amount of capital losses that can be deducted in a particular tax year. Different limitations apply to corporate and individual taxpayers. Flow-through entities are not subject to capital loss limitations because those entities are merely conduits through which capital gains and losses recognized by the business during the year are summarized and passed along to their owners. The owners of the flow-through entity are then responsible for combining the capital gains and losses that are allocated to them from the flow-through entity with the other capital gains and losses that they recognize during the year.

Corporate taxpayers. When corporations recognize capital losses, the capital loss deduction in any one tax year is limited to the amount of capital gains included in gross income that year.[3] Any excess capital loss can be carried back three years and carried forward five years to offset capital gains in those tax years.[4] When a capital loss is carried back, it must be applied first to offset capital gains in the third preceding tax year. To the extent there are not sufficient capital gains to offset the loss in that year, the excess loss is carried to the second preceding year to offset capital gains in that year. Any remaining unutilized capital loss from the second preceding year would carry over to the immediately preceding tax year and then carry forward for up to five tax years. A capital loss carryback, however, cannot create or increase a corporation's net operating loss (see ¶ 1001).[5]

When capital gains and losses are reported on the corporation's tax return, short-term capital gains and losses are reported separately from long-term capital gains and losses. Although both short-term and long-term capital gains are taxed at the same rates for corporate taxpayers, the tax laws require that short-term capital losses first offset short-term capital gains and long-term capital losses first offset long-term capital gains.[6] This process is commonly referred to as the "netting process" of capital gains and losses. If netting the short-term and long-term classifications of gains and losses produces both a net gain and a net loss, then the net losses are used to offset the net gains. The netting process of capital gains and losses is illustrated in the examples that follow.

Example 1: Amblyn, a C corporation, recognizes the following capital gains and losses during 20X4:

---

[1] Code Sec. 1222.
[2] Rev. Rul. 66-7, 1966-1 CB 188.
[3] Code Sec. 1211(a).

[4] Code Sec. 1212(a)(1).
[5] Code Sec. 1212(a)(1).
[6] Code Sec. 1222.

Short-term capital gain	$10,000
Short-term capital loss	(4,000)
Long-term capital gain	12,000
Long-term capital loss	(16,000)

The first step in the netting process is to offset short-term capital losses against short-term capital gains. Then, long-term capital losses are offset against long-term capital gains.

Short-Term	*Long-Term*
$10,000	$12,000
(4,000)	(16,000)
$ 6,000	($ 4,000)

Because there is a net gain and a net loss remaining, the corporation uses the net loss to offset the net gain as follows.

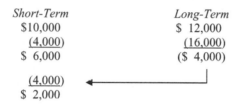

Amblyn has an overall gain; therefore, the entire $22,000 of capital gain ($10,000 + $12,000) is included in its gross income and the entire $20,000 of capital losses ($4,000 + $16,000) can be deducted from gross income in 20X4. Amblyn's taxable income therefore increases by the $2,000 overall net short-term gain.

When a corporation's capital losses exceed its capital gains, the excess is carried back three years and forward five years to offset the *capital gains* that were recognized in those years. Even when the taxpayer's excess capital loss stems partly or entirely from a long-term capital loss, the amount carried over to another tax year is treated as a short-term capital loss in the carryover year.[7] Therefore, the capital loss carried back or forward from another tax year first offsets any short-term capital gains.

Example 2: Assume the same facts as in Example 1, except Amblyn suffers a $26,000 long-term capital loss instead of a $16,000 long-term capital loss during 20X4. Once again, the netting process begins by offsetting short-term capital losses against short-term capital gains, followed by offsetting long-term capital losses against long-term capital gains.

Short-Term	*Long-Term*
$10,000	$12,000
(4,000)	(26,000)
$ 6,000	($14,000)

Because the initial netting of short-term and long-term capital gains and losses produces a net gain and a net loss, Amblyn uses $6,000 of the net long-term capital loss to offset its net short-term capital gain.

---

[7] Code Sec. 1212(a)(1)(C).

Short-Term	Long-Term
$10,000	$ 12,000
(4,000)	(26,000)
$ 6,000	($ 14,000)
(6,000)	
$ 0	

Amblyn's $30,000 ($4,000 + $26,000) in capital losses exceed its $22,000 ($10,000 + $12,000) of capital gains. Therefore, it can only deduct $22,000 of its capital losses in 20X4, and it must carry back $8,000 of its capital losses ($30,000 − $22,000) to the third preceding tax year as a short-term capital loss.

Example 3: Continuing with Example 2, assume that on its 20X1 tax return (the third preceding tax year), Amblyn originally had reported the following capital gains and losses:

Short-Term	Long-Term
$15,000	$6,000
(2,000)	(5,000)
$13,000	$1,000

On Amblyn's 20X1 tax return, the entire $21,000 of capital gains ($15,000 + $6,000) were included in gross income and the $7,000 of capital losses ($2,000 + $5,000) were deducted from gross income. Thus, Amblyn's 20X1 taxable income increased by $14,000 as a result of its capital gains and losses. When the $8,000 excess capital loss from 20X4 is carried back to 20X1 as a short-term capital loss, the netting process from 20X1 changes, as shown below:

	Short-Term	Long-Term
Carryback from 20X4	($ 8,000)	
	15,000	$6,000
	(2,000)	(5,000)
	$ 5,000	$1,000

When Amblyn adds the $8,000 short-term capital loss to the netting process, its taxable income is reduced by $8,000 ($14,000 overall net gain reported originally versus $6,000 overall net gain as recomputed). Amblyn files for a refund of the taxes paid on the $8,000 of capital gain by filing Form 1139, *Corporation Application for Tentative Refund.* If Amblyn's marginal tax rate in 20X1 was 35 percent, the IRS will refund Amblyn $2,800 ($8,000 × 35%), which represents the overpaid taxes for that year.

Example 4: Blyth Enterprises recognizes the following capital gains and losses during 20X4:

Short-term capital gain	$20,000
Short-term capital loss	(45,000)
Long-term capital gain	15,000
Long-term capital loss	(62,000)

Blyth begins the netting process by offsetting its short-term capital gains and losses, and then by offsetting its long-term capital gains and losses. This initial netting produces a $25,000 net short-term capital loss and a $47,000 net long-term capital loss.

Short-Term	Long-Term
$20,000	$15,000
(45,000)	(62,000)
($25,000)	($47,000)

Because there are no net gains to offset, Blyth's capital losses for 20X4 will be limited to its $35,000 ($20,000 + $15,000) of capital gains included in gross income. Blyth carries back the excess $72,000 loss ($62,000 + $45,000 – $35,000 utilized in 20X4) to 20X1. When it performs the netting process for 20X1, Blyth includes the $72,000 as a short-term capital loss carryback.

Example 5: Continuing with Example 4, assume that on its 20X1 tax return Blyth's netting of its capital gains and losses was as follows:

Short-Term	Long-Term
$ 25,000	$ 9,000
(28,000)	(2,000)
($ 3,000)	$ 7,000
	(3,000)
	$ 4,000

When Blyth reconstructs the netting process after including its $72,000 capital loss carryback from 20X4, only $4,000 of the loss carryback can be utilized to offset the excess capital gains recognized in that year. As shown below, $68,000 of the loss carryback was not utilized and must be carried over to 20X2 ($75,000 net short-term loss – $7,000 utilized to offset net long-term capital gains). Blyth will request a refund of taxes paid on the $4,000 of capital gains originally reported on its 20X1 tax return that were offset by the 20X4 capital loss carryback.

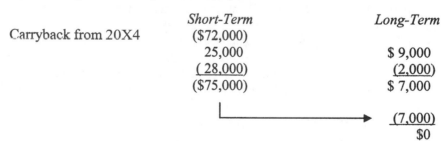

	Short-Term	Long-Term
Carryback from 20X4	($72,000)	
	25,000	$ 9,000
	(28,000)	(2,000)
	($75,000)	$ 7,000
		(7,000)
		$0

Example 6: Continuing with Example 5, assume that on its 20X2 tax return, Blyth reported an $8,000 short-term capital loss, a $26,000 long-term capital gain, and a $6,000 long-term capital loss. (The netting process follows). On its 20X2 tax return, Blyth included the $26,000 capital gain in gross income and deducted the entire $14,000 from its gross income ($6,000 + $8,000). Thus, Blyth's 20X2 taxable income increased by $12,000 ($26,000 – $14,000) as a result of the capital gains and losses recognized in that year.

Short-Term	Long-Term
($ 8,000)	$26,000
	(6,000)
	$20,000
	(8,000)
	$12,000

When Blyth includes its $68,000 capital loss carryover and reconstructs the netting process for 20X2, only $12,000 of the loss carryover can be utilized to offset the excess capital gains recognized in that year. As shown below, $56,000 ($76,000 – $20,000) of the loss carryover was not utilized and must be carried over to 20X3.

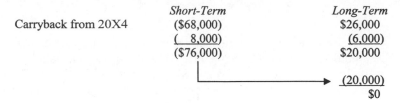

	Short-Term	Long-Term
Carryback from 20X4	($68,000)	$26,000
	(8,000)	(6,000)
	($76,000)	$20,000
		(20,000)
		$0

Blyth will include the $56,000 capital loss carryback as a short-term capital loss when it redoes the netting process from its 20X3 tax return. To the extent that the entire $56,000 capital loss carryback cannot be utilized on its 20X3 tax return, it will carry over any remaining loss to its 20X5 tax return. Blyth has a total of five years after 20X4 to fully utilize its capital loss recognized in 20X4. Thus, if in 20X9 Blyth still has any remaining capital loss carryover from 20X4, it should plan to sell property during the year to produce sufficient capital gain to absorb all of its capital losses (including any capital loss carryovers).

 GAAP vs. Code: On a corporation's income statement, a capital loss is deducted in the year the loss is realized. Therefore, in a year in which a corporation's capital losses exceed its capital gains, the excess loss will create a difference between net income and taxable income. This difference must be added back to net income when reconciling net income to taxable income. Likewise, when the capital loss carryover is utilized in a subsequent tax year, the amount used must be subtracted from net income during the reconciliation process in the carryover year.

Individual taxpayers. For individuals, the deduction for capital losses is limited to the capital gains included in gross income plus $3,000. (The limit is $1,500 for individuals who are married but file separate tax returns).[8] Any unused capital losses are carried forward indefinitely, but may not be carried back. Unlike corporate taxpayers, whose capital loss carryovers are carried over as short-term capital losses, an individual taxpayer's capital loss carryovers retain their long-term and short-term nature. When an individual's capital losses exceed capital gains, the $3,000 deduction is taken first from net short-term capital losses; any remaining amount needed to reach the $3,000 limit is taken from the long-term capital losses. Thus, as required of all taxpayers, individuals must properly classify each capital gain or loss as a short-term or a long-term capital gain or loss.

Example 7: In 20X6, Nan Jones has a net short-term capital gain of $10,000 and a net long-term capital loss of $24,000. Nan uses $10,000 of her long-term capital loss to offset her short-term capital gain (see below). This leaves Nan with an overall capital loss of $14,000 ($10,000 – $24,000). Nan uses $3,000 of the net capital loss to reduce her ordinary income. She carries over to 20X7 a long-term capital loss of $11,000 ($14,000 – $3,000). She adds this amount to her other long-term capital gains and losses in 20X7.

Short-Term	Long-Term
$10,000	($24,000)
(10,000)	
$0	

---

[8] Code Sec. 1211(b).

As mentioned previously, the tax laws do not limit the number of years individual taxpayers can carry over a capital loss. However, if an unmarried taxpayer dies with an unused capital loss carryover, the capital loss carryover expires, and it cannot be used by any other taxpayer.[9] If a married taxpayer dies with a capital loss carryover from a joint return, the decedent's spouse can continue to use the capital loss carryover during his or her lifetime.

Example 8: Brenda Puckett was unmarried when she died in 20X6. At the time of her death, Brenda had a $23,000 capital loss carryover from 20X5. During 20X6, but prior to her death, Brenda did not recognize any capital gains or losses. On her final individual income tax return for 20X6, $3,000 of the capital loss carryover may be used to reduce ordinary income. The remaining $20,000 ($23,000 – $3,000) expires, and it cannot be deducted on Brenda's estate tax return or on any other income tax return.

Example 9: In 20X4, Don and Alma Smith, joint filers, incur a $46,000 net capital loss. They utilize $13,000 of the loss in 20X5, and carry over the rest to 20X6. Don dies during 20X6. Alma can utilize the $33,000 ($46,000 – $13,000) capital loss carryover in 20X6 first to offset any capital gains and then to reduce $3,000 of ordinary income. She can then carry over any remaining capital loss to 20X7 and future tax years.

 Spotlight: The carryover rules for capital losses are different for corporate and individual taxpayers in two ways. Excess losses for individual taxpayers are defined as capital losses in excess of capital gains plus $3,000. However, for corporate taxpayers, excess losses are defined as simply the excess of capital losses over capital gains. A second difference has to do with capital loss carrybacks and carryforwards. Corporations can carry back excess losses three years; individual taxpayers can only carry forward excess losses. The carryforward period for individuals is indefinite; for corporate taxpayers it is five years.

Other business entities. Flow-through entities, i.e., partnerships, S corporations, limited liability companies, and certain trusts, are not subject to capital loss limitations. Instead, these entities keep track of all short-term and long-term capital gains and losses during the year. At the end of the year the entity calculates its "net short-term capital gain or loss" and its "net long-term capital gain or loss" and reports these amounts, along with each owner's share of these net gains and losses, on the entity's tax return. The owners then report their respective amounts of net short-term and net long-term capital gain or loss in the netting process on their own income tax returns. Thus, any net long-term or net short-term capital loss that flows through from a flow-through entity to its owner is included in the owner's netting process along with other short-term and long-term capital gains and losses the owner recognizes during the year. Because the owners of these entities can be individuals, corporations, or other flow-through entities, when flow-through entities recognize capital gains and losses, they must also report which of the capital gains and losses are long-term and which are short-term.

.02 Special Tax Rates on Net Capital Gains

Although a progressive tax rate structure applies to an individual's taxable income, net capital gain recognized by an individual taxpayer is taxed at a lower tax rate than other types of (ordinary) income. **Net capital gain** is defined as the excess of the taxpayer's net long-term capital gains over its net short-term capital losses.[10] If the individual does not have a net long-term capital gain, then net capital gain equals zero. If the individual does not have a net short-term capital loss, then net capital gain equals the amount of its net long-term capital gain (if any).

---

[9] Rev. Rul. 74-175, 1974-1 CB 52.   [10] Code Sec. 1(i)(2).

The tax rate on ordinary income currently ranges from 10 to 35 percent for individual taxpayers.[11] The tax rate on most net capital gains for taxpayers in the 10- and 15-percent tax brackets is zero percent for the years 2009–2010. For taxpayers in all other tax brackets, the tax rate on most net capital gains is 15 percent through 2010.[12] While most net capital gain is subject to these special tax rates, special rules apply to certain gains. Unrecaptured Section 1250 gain is taxed at a maximum 25-percent tax rate and net capital gain on the sale of collectibles is taxed at a maximum 28-percent tax rate. (See ¶ 907 and ¶ 1306.01.) Generally, corporations do not receive any preferential tax rate treatment for net capital gains. Capital gains are taxed to corporations like any other taxable income. However, the Heartland, Habitat, Harvest, and Horticulture Act of 2008 (HHHHA08) provides a one-year window of opportunity for C corporations to get a tax break on their timber holdings. The corporations may elect under Code Sec. 631 to treat the cutting of timber as a Section 1231 gain. The corporations will then be taxed on the FMV at the time the timber is cut at a maximum rate of 15 percent. The special rate applies only to a taxable year ending after May 22, 2008, and beginning on or before May 22, 2009.[13]

Example 10: Janice Jacks is a single taxpayer in the 35-percent tax bracket. In the current tax year, Janice sold the following capital assets:

Description	Gain (Loss)
Stock held 6 months	$6,000
Stock held 3 years	(3,000)
Land held 5 years	1,000
Land held 8 months	(1,000)

Janice begins the netting process by offsetting short-term capital losses against short-term capital gains. This yields a net short-term capital gain of $5,000. Long-term capital gains and losses are then netted to yield a $2,000 net long-term capital loss. The netting process is complete after the net long-term capital loss is used to offset the short-term gain.

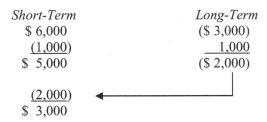

Short-Term	Long-Term
$ 6,000	($ 3,000)
(1,000)	1,000
$ 5,000	($ 2,000)
(2,000)	
$ 3,000	

Because Janice does not have a net long-term capital gain, her net capital gain is $0 and the lower tax rates do not apply. Her $3,000 overall short-term capital gain increases her adjusted gross income (AGI) by that amount. From her AGI, Janice subtracts out her deductions from AGI (see ¶ 1304) to compute her taxable income. Her income tax liability is calculated by applying the progressive income tax rates for single taxpayers to her taxable income (see the Appendix at the back of this book).

Example 11: Liam Watson is a single taxpayer. In 2009, he sold the following capital assets. Before considering these items, Liam's AGI is $75,000 and he has $9,350 of deductions from AGI.

Description	Gain (Loss)
Stock held 5 months	$5,000
Stock held 12 years	2,000

---

[11] Code Sec. 1(i)(2).
[12] Code Sec. 1(h)(1)(C).

[13] Code Sec. 1201(b), as amended by HHHA08.

Description	Gain (Loss)
Land held 13 years	(1,000)
Land held 3 months	(2,000)

Liam's netting process begins by netting his short-term capital gains and losses to yield a $3,000 net short-term capital gain. He then nets his long-term capital gains and losses to yield a $1,000 net long-term capital gain.

Short-Term	Long-Term
$5,000	$2,000
(2,000)	(1,000)
$3,000	$1,000

Because Liam does not have a net short-term capital loss, his net capital gain is equal to his $1,000 net long-term capital gain. The capital gains and losses increase his AGI to $79,000 ($75,000 + $4,000 overall capital gains). From this amount, Liam subtracts out his deductions from AGI to compute his taxable income of $69,650 ($79,000 – $9,350). When he calculates the income tax on his taxable income, Liam backs out the $1,000 net capital gain and taxes it at 15 percent because his taxable income falls in the 25 percent tax bracket (see the tax rates for Single Individuals in the Appendix at the back of this book). He computes his 2009 tax liability as follows:

Tax liability on $68,650 ($69,650 – $1,000)	$13,350
Plus: Tax on net capital gain ($1,000 × 15%)	150
Total 2009 tax liability	$13,500

Example 12: Assume the same facts as in Example 11, except Liam's AGI after considering his capital gains and losses is $35,000, which puts his $25,650 taxable income ($35,000 – $9,350) in the 15 percent tax bracket (see the Appendix at the back of this book).

Tax liability on $24,650 ($25,650 – $1,000)	$3,280
Plus: Tax on net capital gain ($1,000 × 0%)	0
Total 2009 tax liability	$3,280

Example 13: Misty Jenkins is a single taxpayer. In 2009, she sold the following capital assets. Before considering these items, her AGI is $105,000 and she has $9,350 of deductions from AGI.

Description	Gain (Loss)
Stock held 5 months	($ 1,000)
Stock held 9 months	2,000
Land held 13 months	11,000
Land held 3 months	(6,000)

Misty's netting process begins by netting her short-term capital gains and losses to yield a $5,000 net short-term capital loss. She then uses the net short-term capital loss to offset the $11,000 net long-term capital gain. Misty's net capital gain is $6,000 ($11,000 net long-term capital gain in excess of $5,000 net short-term capital loss).

Short-Term	Long-Term
($1,000)	$11,000
2,000	
(6,000)	
($ 5,000) ⟶	(5,000)
	$ 6,000

The $6,000 net capital gain increases Misty's AGI to $111,000 ($105,000 + $6,000). From this amount, she subtracts out her deductions from AGI to arrive at her taxable income of $101,650 ($111,000 – $9,350). When she calculates income tax on the taxable income, Misty backs out the $6,000 net capital gain and taxes it at 15 percent because her taxable income falls in the 28 percent tax bracket (see the Appendix at the back of this book). She then computes her 2009 tax liability as follows:

Tax liability on $95,650 ($101,650 – $6,000)	$20,502
Plus: Tax on net capital gain ($6,000 × 15%)	900
Total 2009 tax liability	$21,402

Gains and losses from the sale or exchange of property are not included in the calculation of business profits, from which self-employment taxes are calculated. Consequently, a net gain from the sale of business property increases the taxpayer's AGI (and the taxpayer's income tax liability), but it does not increase the amount of self-employment tax a sole proprietor or partner owes during the year. Likewise, losses from the sale of business property reduce the taxpayer's AGI but do not reduce the self-employment taxes owed by a sole proprietor or partner.

Example 14: Owen Jacobs operates a research and marketing business as a sole proprietorship. During the year, Owen sells all rights to a patent he held for designing a new computer chip and recognizes a $25,000 long-term capital gain. Although the patent was obtained as a result of Owen's business, it is classified as a capital asset. Any gain or loss realized from the sale of a capital asset produces capital gain or loss. Owen therefore includes the $25,000 in gross income and reports it as long-term capital gain in his netting process for the year. If Owen recognizes any capital losses during the year, he can use up to $25,000 of the loss to offset his capital gain from the sale of the patent, and he can use another $3,000 to offset ordinary income. The $25,000 gain is not reflected in Owen's sole proprietorship profits, and consequently, he will not be subject to self-employment taxes on the gain. Furthermore, if the netting process results in a net capital gain, then Owen will pay a maximum tax rate of 15 percent on this net capital gain.

.03 Holding Periods

Reduced tax rates apply to certain long-term gains reported in an individual taxpayer's taxable income. Although the focus of this textbook is not individual income taxation, an understanding of the rules that govern individual taxpayers is necessary because when a business is operated as a flow-through entity, an individual owner's allocated share of gains and losses from the flow-through entity are reported on the individual's income tax return. Thus, in addition to computing a taxpayer's recognized gain or loss (see Chapter 8), it is important to be able to determine the short-term or long-term nature of that gain or loss.

If at the time the property was sold, the taxpayer's holding period in the property was more than one year, the resulting gain or loss is usually long-term gain or loss. The taxpayer's **holding period** in property generally begins the day after the taxpayer acquires property and ends on the day the taxpayer disposes of the property.[14] When property is disposed of in a sale or exchange, the "disposal date" is the date of the sale or exchange. For stocks and bonds traded on an established exchange (like the New York Stock Exchange or the American Stock Exchange), the "trade date" with respect to a security is considered the date that the taxpayer acquires or disposes of a security. The actual delivery of the security is irrelevant for determining the taxpayer's holding period.[15]

If property is partially or completely destroyed in a casualty, the disposal date is the date of the casualty. If property is stolen, the disposal date is the date on which the taxpayer becomes aware of the theft. In the case of stocks or bonds that are considered worthless, the tax laws treat a worthless security as having been sold for $0 on the last day of the tax year in which it becomes worthless (see ¶ 802.01). This rule regarding the date of the deemed sale can affect whether the worthless security produces a short-term or a long-term loss.

Example 15: On March 5, 20X4, a taxpayer sells property for $30,000 that was purchased for $45,000 on January 22, 20X1. The taxpayer's capital loss of $15,000 ($30,000 – $45,000) is long-term because the asset was held for more than one year.

Example 16: A taxpayer purchases property for $31,600 on September 1, 20X1. The taxpayer's holding period begins on September 2, 20X1. The taxpayer sells the property for $40,000 on September 2, 20X2, and recognizes an $8,400 short-term gain ($40,000 – $31,600). Had the taxpayer held the asset for one more day, the gain would have been a long-term gain. To qualify as long-term gain, the taxpayer must have held the property for *more than* one year.

Example 17: Mike Faulkner purchases 500 shares of stock in NuHome Décor. The trade date is May 14, 20X1, but the shares are not credited to his brokerage account until May 17, 20X1. Mike's purchase date for the stock is May 14, 20X1, and his holding period begins on May 15, 20X1. If Mike sells the stock any time on or after May 16, 20X2, he will have held the shares for investment for more than one year, and his gain or loss will be classified as long-term capital gain or loss.

Example 18: Ivan Miller bought 200 shares of DotCom common stock for $8,000 on July 8, 20X1. The shares became worthless on April 6, 20X2, when the company declared bankruptcy. Ivan is deemed to have sold the 200 shares for $0 on December 31, 20X2. Therefore, his $8,000 loss is a long-term capital loss.

Properties having a transferred basis. When the basis of the taxpayer's property is determined in whole or in part by reference to another asset (often termed a substituted basis), the holding period of the taxpayer's property includes the holding period of the other asset. This generally occurs when gain is postponed due to an involuntary conversion (see ¶ 809) or when gain or loss is postponed as a result of a like-kind exchange (see ¶ 808). The taxpayer's holding period will also "tack on" when a realized gain from the sale of publicly traded stock is postponed when the taxpayer purchases stock in a specialized small business investment company (SSBIC) (see ¶ 806).[16]

Example 19: A corporation acquires land worth $100,000 in a like-kind exchange by giving up land also worth $100,000. The corporation's basis in the land it exchanged was $80,000, and accordingly, the corporation realizes a $20,000 gain on the exchange ($100,000 – $80,000). Since no boot was received on the exchange, the corporation's gain is postponed, and its basis in the new land is reduced to $80,000 ($100,000 FMV of the new land – $20,000 postponed gain). The corporation's holding period for the land it acquired in the like-kind exchange begins on the day of the holding period for the old land it exchanged.

Example 20: On May 2, 20X3, Bucknell, Inc. sells publicly traded stock in Bannister, Ltd. that it bought on January 21, 20X1. Bucknell's amount realized from the sale is $600,000; its

---

[14] Rev. Rul. 66-7, 1966-1 CB 188.

[15] Rev. Rul. 93-84, 1993-2 CB 225.

[16] Code Sec. 1223.

adjusted basis in the stock was $125,000. Bucknell's realized gain is $475,000 ($600,000 – $125,000). Within 60 days of the sale, Bucknell invests $460,000 of the $600,000 proceeds in Alpena Corporation, an SSBIC, and files an election on its tax return to postpone $335,000 of the gain. Bucknell's holding period in the Alpena stock includes its holding period in the Bannister stock, which began on January 22, 20X1.

The transferred basis rules also apply in most instances in which the taxpayer receives property as a gift. If an individual receives property from a spouse, the spouse's basis in the property carries over and becomes the individual's basis in the property. In instances where the donor's basis in the property carries over to the donee, the donor's holding period includes the donee's holding period.[17] However, if the FMV at the time of the gift is less than the donor's basis, such FMV becomes the basis to the donee, and a new holding period begins the day after the gift.

Example 21: On October 24, 20X1, Henry Waters gave to his daughter, Debra, 100 shares of HiFly Company stock, worth $5,000 at the time of the gift. Henry had purchased the 100 shares for $4,000 on May 2, 20X1, and as a result of the gift, Debra takes her father's $4,000 basis in the shares. Debra's holding period begins on May 3, 20X1 (the day after Henry purchased the stock). Debra sells the shares on May 4, 20X2. Her gain or loss will be classified as a long-term capital gain or loss.

Example 22: Assume the same facts as in Example 21 except that the stock was worth only $3,500 at the time of the gift. Debra's holding period began on October 25, 20X1.

Inherited property. The disposition of inherited property results in a long-term capital gain or loss, regardless of the actual time the taxpayer holds the property or the decedent had held the property.[18] Furthermore, the beneficiary's basis in inherited property is generally the FMV of the inherited property on the decedent's date of death. This basis rule is known as the "step-up" in basis, because if the property is appreciated in value, the basis to the heir is stepped-up from the decedent's basis to FMV. However, the executor of the estate may elect to value the estate six months later (as allowed) on the alternative valuation date. In that event the FMV on such date generally becomes the heir's basis. If the alternate valuation date is used and the property is sold after death, but before the alternate valuation date, the basis becomes FMV at the date of sale.

Example 23: Vance Enterprises inherits a parcel of land from one of its shareholders. The shareholder purchased the land on October 6, 20X0, for $16,250. The shareholder dies on November 23, 20X4, when the land is worth $28,100. The executor of the shareholder's estate does not use the alternative valuation date. If Vance Enterprises sells the land for $30,400 on October 24, 20X5, it will recognize a $2,300 long-term capital gain ($30,400 – $28,100), even though the corporation did not actually own the land for more than one year.

 Spotlight: The special basis and holding period rules that govern gifted and inherited property are less likely to affect businesses. Instead, these rules are more likely to affect individual taxpayers. If an individual is an owner in a flow-through entity or operates a business as a sole proprietorship, all of the owner's tax items for the year (not just those of the business) are reported on the individual's income tax return. This would include any gains from the sale of gifted or inherited property plus losses on the sale of such property assuming that the property is held as an investment. Accordingly, it is important to be aware of the special basis and holding period rules that apply to such property so all tax aspects of the individual owner's tax return can be taken into consideration when tax planning for businesses and their owners.

---

[17] Reg. § 1.1223-1(b).   [18] Code Sec. 1223(9).

¶ 902 Generating Capital Gains and Losses

Recognized gain or loss from the sale or exchange of a capital asset usually produces capital gain or loss. If the taxpayer's holding period for the capital asset exceeds one year, the recognized gain or loss is a **long-term capital gain or loss.** If the holding period is one year or less, a **short-term capital gain or loss** results (see ¶ 901.03). In addition to selling a capital asset, there are other ways to generate capital gains and losses. For example, when a taxpayer recognizes a nonbusiness bad debt, the loss is recognized as a short-term capital loss, regardless of how long the debt that went bad was outstanding. (See ¶ 510.) Nonbusiness bad debts pertain primarily to individual taxpayers, as the debts of all other business entities typically involve business bad debts, which are deductible as ordinary losses.

Example 24: Larry Mahan owns and operates a sole proprietorship. In 20X0, Larry loaned his friend Bill Eastin $5,000 so Bill could start up his own business. The nature of Larry's loan is not related to his business. Bill defaults on the loan and declares bankruptcy in 20X3. Larry is entitled to take a short-term capital loss for the difference between the $5,000 loan amount and the amount he receives as a distribution from the bankruptcy court.

The tax laws also allow taxpayers to generate long-term capital gains through the sale of depreciable business property and land used in the taxpayer's trade or business, but only when the property is held long-term (more than one year). When long-term business property ("Section 1231 property") is sold, the resulting gain or loss is classified as a Section 1231 gain or loss. When a taxpayer's Section 1231 gains exceed its Section 1231 losses for the year, the excess gain (net Section 1231 gain) may be eligible to be treated as a long-term capital gain (see ¶ 903) for purposes of the netting process of capital gains and losses. However, there are instances in which Section 1231 gain does not receive long-term capital gain treatment (see ¶ 904.03 for a discussion of nonrecaptured Section 1231 losses). If long-term capital gain treatment is allowed, net gains from the sale of long-term business property can help taxpayers deduct more capital losses for the year. They also can help individual taxpayers pay less tax because net capital gain is taxed at a lower rate (see ¶ 901.02).

Example 25: Perry Corporation has the following gains and losses during the year:

Long-term capital loss	($15,000)
Section 1231 gain	30,000
Section 1231 loss	(10,000)

Perry's net Section 1231 gain equals $20,000 ($30,000 – $10,000). Assuming that the tax laws allow the net Section 1231 gain to be treated as a long-term capital gain, Perry may deduct the entire $15,000 long-term capital loss. If the tax laws do not allow the net Section 1231 gain to be treated as a long-term capital gain in the netting process, Perry will have no capital gains included in gross income, and accordingly, its capital loss deduction for the year will be zero.

¶ 903 Sale or Exchange of Capital Assets

The most straightforward way to generate capital gains and losses is to dispose of a capital asset in a taxable transaction. Although the term capital asset may conjure up images of buildings, equipment, machinery, and the like, for tax purposes, capital assets are specifically defined in the Internal Revenue Code (the "Code"). Although the general rule for classifying gains and losses from the sale of capital assets as long-term (held for more than one year) and short-term (held for one year or less) applies to most capital assets, special rules apply to the sale of certain assets. The tax treatment of these assets is discussed later in the chapter.

.01 Capital Assets Defined

Code Sec. 1221 defines **capital assets** by exclusion, meaning that its definition of capital assets includes assets other than the nine types of assets listed below. In other words, capital assets are *all assets except*:

1. Inventory or other property held primarily for resale in the ordinary course of business.

2. Accounts or notes receivable received for the sale of services or inventory.

3. Supplies used in the ordinary course of business.

4. Depreciable property and land used in a trade or business.

5. Copyrights, works of art, letters, or similar property held by the taxpayer who created the works. (However, certain taxpayers can elect to treat self-created musical works or copyrights of such works as capital assets.[19])

6. Letters, memoranda, or similar property held by the taxpayer for whom the letters or memoranda were prepared or produced.

7. Publications of the U.S. government except those acquired by purchase at their FMV or those acquired by other means where the taxpayer's basis is the same FMV of the publication that the original purchaser used as its basis.

8. A commodities derivative financial instrument held by a commodities derivatives dealer, unless the instrument has no relationship to the dealer's activities as a dealer and the instrument is shown in the records of the dealer on the date of acquisition as not being held by the dealer as part of the dealer's ordinary business activities.

9. Any hedging transaction that the taxpayer identifies as such on the date the taxpayer enters into the transaction.

Any asset not included on the above list is a capital asset. The first three types of business assets listed above involve assets that when sold produce ordinary income or loss. The fourth item listed involves depreciable property as well as land used in the taxpayer's trade or business. The remaining items on the list are specialized items that are not the focus of this discussion.

The most common types of capital assets are properties held for investment or personal use (in the case of an individual taxpayer). Personal use assets should not be confused with tangible personal property (see ¶ 104.01). The former includes all assets that individuals possess and use in their personal lives. The latter consists of all tangible property other than real estate. Personal use assets include assets such as a taxpayer's home, automobile, furniture, and other personal belongings. A gain on the sale of a personal use asset is recognized as a capital gain, unless a tax law specifically excludes the gain from gross income. A loss on the sale or exchange of a personal use asset is not deductible unless it stems from a casualty or theft loss (see ¶ 1304.03).[20]

Example 26: Chris Riley owns and operates a business as a sole proprietorship. Chris owns the properties listed below:

> Vacation home
>
> 100 shares of stock in Omega Company
>
> Automobile used entirely for personal use
>
> Inventory from his sole proprietorship
>
> Computer used in his sole proprietorship

Among the property Chris owns, only the inventory and the computer are on the list of property that is specifically not a capital asset (items 1. and 4., respectively). Thus, the remaining items are capital assets. If any of these items is sold at a gain, the gain is reported in Chris's gross income. However, if Chris sells either his

---

[19] Act Sec. 204(a), amending Code Sec. 1221(b), Tax Increase Prevention and Reconciliation Act of 2005 (P.L. 109-222).   [20] Code Sec. 165(c).

residence or his automobile at a loss, neither loss would be deductible because the items are Chris's personal belongings. When Chris sells the inventory, the gain or loss from the sale will be reported as ordinary income or loss. The tax law governing the tax treatment of a gain or loss on the sale of the computer is discussed at ¶ 904.

 Spotlight: Stocks and bonds are common types of capital assets. Thus, when bonds are sold at a gain, a capital gain results, even if the bonds sold are state or local government bonds ("municipal bonds"). Although the interest on municipal bonds is excluded from gross income (see ¶ 411.01), taxpayers recognize capital gain or loss on the sale or exchange of municipal bonds.

.02 Capital Assets Sold to a Related Party

Generally when a taxpayer realizes a gain on the sale or exchange of a capital asset, the gain is treated as a capital gain. If acquired in a purchase or taxable exchange, the purchaser's basis in the acquired property is its cost. If the property acquired is depreciable property in the hands of the purchaser, the depreciable basis in the property is its purchase price. Since capital gains and ordinary deductions receive preferential tax treatment, the tax laws require that the gain on the sale of a capital asset to a *related person* be taxed as ordinary income.[21] In accordance with this rule, the appreciation in value included in the purchaser's (depreciable) basis will be taxed as ordinary income to offset the ordinary deductions the purchaser will take as the property is depreciated.

Example 27: Arden Wright sells to a related person artwork that he currently holds as an investment (a capital asset). The artwork is sold for its $25,000 FMV; Arden purchased the artwork for $5,000. The (related) purchaser plans to use the artwork as a business property and plans to depreciate the $25,000 depreciable basis over its useful life in accordance with the tax laws described in Chapter 7. Thus, over the years, the purchaser will be taking ordinary deductions against gross income totaling $25,000. Because Arden sold the artwork to a related person, his $20,000 gain ($25,000 – $5,000) must be recognized as ordinary income on his tax return in the year of the sale.

 Reason for the Rule: Code Sec. 1239 was enacted to prevent "related persons" from selling capital assets to one another at a capital gain and having the purchaser receive a stepped-up depreciable basis. Rather than deny the stepped-up basis to the purchaser (who does, in fact, pay the FMV for the property), the tax law instead requires the seller to report the gain as ordinary income. By taxing the gain as ordinary income, the seller loses out on the ability to use the gain to offset capital losses, and in the case of an individual, the ability to tax the gain at a lower tax rate. Furthermore, the government's taxing of the gain on the stepped-up basis at the ordinary income rates will more closely offset the tax benefits the related purchaser will realize as the property is depreciated.

For purposes of this rule regarding the sale of capital assets, "related persons" are defined as the following:

- A person and a corporation if the person owns, *directly or indirectly*, more than 50 percent of the value of the outstanding stock of the corporation;

- A person and a partnership in which the person owns, *directly or indirectly*, more than 50 percent of the capital or profits interest;

---

[21] Code Sec. 1239.

- Two corporations that are members of the same controlled group (applying the rules from ¶ 804, except that more than 50-percent ownership is required instead of at least 80-percent ownership);

- A corporation and a partnership, if the same persons own both more than 50 percent of the value of the outstanding stock of the corporation and more than 50 percent of the value of the capital or profits interest in the partnership;

- Two S corporations, if the same persons own more than 50 percent of the value of the outstanding stock of each entity; and

- An S corporation and a C corporation, if the same persons own more than 50 percent of the value of the outstanding stock of both entities.

.03 Patents

A "patent" is an intangible asset that gives its owner the exclusive right to profit commercially from a specified product or process for a limited number of years. By filing for a patent, the inventor discloses trade secrets regarding the product, but during the legal life of a patent, others are specifically prohibited from profiting from the patented invention. A patent is included in the list of Section 197 intangibles from Chapter 7 (see Table 7-6 at ¶ 708), and accordingly, the costs associated with a patent are amortized over 15 years. Since patents are neither depreciable business property nor any of the other eight items of property that are specifically excluded from the definition of a capital asset (see ¶ 904.01), patents are a capital asset. Thus, the sale of a patent normally produces capital gain or loss (unless the taxpayer is in the business of buying and selling patents or is holding the patent as inventory to sell to customers in the ordinary course of business).

If certain requirements are met, the tax laws treat gain or loss from the sale of patents as long-term capital gain or loss, regardless of how long the taxpayer has held the patent and regardless of whether the patent is a capital asset to the taxpayer. The long-term capital gain treatment also applies to transfers of patent rights, even when the patent itself or the patent application for the invention does not yet exist.[22] One appellate court has held that secret formulas and trade names are similar enough to patents to warrant the special treatment accorded to patents.[23]

 Spotlight: A patent that meets the requirements of Code Sec. 1235 does not have to be held for more than a year to qualify for long-term capital gain treatment because the transfer by a holder of a patent is considered a sale or exchange of a capital asset held long-term. Thus, from the moment property capable of being patented is created, it is considered long-term capital gain property. The seller recognizes long-term capital gain on the sale, even if the seller is in the business of buying and selling patents or is holding the patented property as inventory to sell to its customers.[24]

To qualify for long-term capital gain treatment, the "holder" must sell *all substantial rights* in the patent or an undivided interest in all substantial rights in the patent. The holder of the patent is the individual whose efforts resulted in the patent (the "inventor"). The holder can also be any other party that bought the patent from the inventor before the invention was tested successfully under operating conditions or before any commercial exploitation of the invention occurs.[25] However, neither the employer of the inventor nor certain parties related to the inventor can qualify as the holder of the patent for this special rule.[26] The main issue involving the sale of a patent is whether the sale is for *all substantial rights* in the patent. If a taxpayer sells less than all substantial rights in the patent, the taxpayer has sold a license to use the patent, and the sale of a right to use a patent results in ordinary income in the form of royalties.

---

[22] Reg. § 1.1235-2(a).

[23] *J.H. Pickren*, CA-5, 67-2 USTC ¶ 9477, 378 F2d 595.

[24] Reg. § 1.1235-2(d).

[25] Reg. § 1.1235-2(e).

[26] Code Sec. 1235.

Example 28: Ray Kelly works for a corporation. During the year, Ray invents a secret formula to which his employer holds the rights. The corporation sells the formula for a $100,000 gain. Since the employer of the inventor does not qualify as a holder of the patent, the employer recognizes $100,000 of ordinary income.

Transfer of all substantial rights. In determining whether a taxpayer has transferred *all substantial rights* to a patent, all of the facts and circumstances surrounding the transfer are examined, rather than the language used in the sales contract. The sale of rights to a patent for a limited geographical area or for a limited time that is less than the remaining life of the patent does not qualify as the transfer of all substantial rights; it is instead treated as a license. The receipt of payments for granting a license is taxed as ordinary income. If, however, the holder retains legal title or a lien on the patent to secure payment from the buyer, this alone will not cause the holder to recognize ordinary income instead of capital gain.[27] A holder may obtain capital gain treatment on the sale of a patent even though another person holds nonexclusive rights to use the patent.[28]

 Planning Pointer: When considering the sale of all substantial rights to a patent versus granting a license to use the patent, the holder of the patent should consider the preferential tax treatment accorded long-term capital gains over ordinary income.

Example 29: Nancy Allegan patents a new design for a motorboat. She sells the right to both manufacture and sell the motorboat in Kazakhstan to Allegan Corporation. Nancy has not sold her patent but has rather granted a license to Allegan Corporation. Accordingly, the Code Sec. 1235 rules do not apply to payments received from Allegan, and the payments give rise to ordinary income and not to long-term capital gain.

Related persons. The special rules that apply to patents do not apply to sales between the holder and certain related parties. "Related" parties for purposes of the special rule for patents are very similar to those described in Table 8-2 (see ¶ 804) that pertain to the tax law that disallows losses between certain related parties. However, the ownership percentages for purposes of the special rule for patents is *25 percent or more* (instead of more than 50 percent), and siblings are not considered related to the holder of a patent. The list of "related persons" for purposes of Code Sec. 1235 is as follows:

1. An individual and the individual's spouse, ancestors, or descendants;

2. An individual and a corporation in which the individual *directly or indirectly* owns 25 percent or more of the value of the outstanding stock;

3. Corporations that are members of the same controlled group;

4. A corporation and a partnership if the same person(s) own 25 percent or more of the outstanding value of the stock in the corporation and 25 percent or more of the capital or profits interests in the partnership;

5. An S corporation and another S corporation if the same person(s) own 25 percent or more of the value in the outstanding stock of each corporation;

6. An S corporation and a C corporation if the same person(s) own 25 percent or more of the value in the outstanding stock of each corporation;

7. An individual and a partnership in which the individual *directly or indirectly* owns more than 25 percent of the capital or profits interest; and

8. Two partnerships in which the same persons own, *directly or indirectly*, more than 25 percent of the capital or profits interest.

---

[27] Reg. § 1.1235-2(b)(2).

[28] *D.C. MacDonald,* 55 TC 840, Dec. 30,665 (1971).

Planning Pointer: If capital gain treatment is denied for the sale of a patent by an inventor because the transfer was made to a related person, the tax consequences of the transfer are determined under the general rules for determining gain or loss on the sale of property. Thus, if the property is a capital asset in the hands of the inventor, the gain can still be treated as long-term capital gain if the inventor holds the property for more than one year prior to selling it.

.04 Subdivided Realty

Taxpayers who purchase a large tract of real estate often find it easier to resell the land if they subdivide it into smaller parcels (lots). In addition, they may find that the sale of the land is usually quicker and more lucrative if they engage in efforts that involve advertising and/or promoting the property. Unfortunately, when real estate owners undertake such efforts, they may no longer be considered merely investors but instead may be considered dealers in real estate. The distinction between property held as an investment and property held in the normal course of business is important because the sale of the former generates capital gain or loss, while the latter involves the sale of inventory, which generates ordinary income or loss.

Investor versus dealer in real estate. Normally, the determination as to whether an owner is an investor or dealer in real estate must be made based on the facts and circumstances of the case. To avoid having the IRS repeatedly challenge these types of issues, Congress enacted Code Sec. 1237, which provides that individuals, partnerships, and S corporations *will not* be treated as real estate dealers merely because real estate acquired as an investment or for use in a trade or business is later subdivided and sold in lots. Although the sale of the lots may resemble sales of inventory, the gain on the sale of subdivided realty *will not* automatically be considered ordinary income. However, in order for Code Sec. 1237 to apply, the tax law requires that there be no substantial evidence to suggest that the taxpayer is holding the land primarily for sale to customers in the ordinary course of a trade or business and that the following three conditions be met:

1. The taxpayer did not hold either the lot sold or the tract from which the lot came as inventory in any tax year, nor did the taxpayer hold any other real property primarily for sale in the ordinary course of a trade or business during the year the lot was sold. (This rule automatically excludes real estate dealers from being eligible for this special provision.)

2. The taxpayer has not made any substantial improvements to the tract of land.

3. The lot or parcel is held by the taxpayer for a period of at least five years (an exception exists for property acquired by inheritance).[29]

Substantial evidence to suggest that the taxpayer is holding the real estate primarily for sale to customers in the ordinary course of a trade or business might include a prior history by the taxpayer of being engaged in subdividing or selling activities with respect to the subdivided tract. Evidence might also include the taxpayer's intention in prior years (or at the time of acquiring the property currently being subdivided) to hold the tract primarily for sale in a trade or business or the construction of a permanent real estate office the taxpayer could use in selling other real property. If the only evidence of the taxpayer's purpose in holding real property is one of the following factors, then such evidence alone would not be considered substantial evidence for purposes of assuming the taxpayer's intention to be that of a real estate dealer. However, if more than one of these factors exists, the circumstances may or may not constitute substantial evidence, depending upon the particular facts in each case.[30]

- Holding a real estate dealer's license,
- Selling other real property that was clearly investment property,

---

[29] Code Sec. 1237(a).

[30] Reg. § 1.1237-1(b)(3).

- Acting as a salesperson for a real estate dealer but without any financial interest in the business, or

- Merely owning other vacant real property without engaging in any selling activity whatsoever with respect to it.

Code Sec. 1237 does not apply if the taxpayer *substantially improves* the property. Examples of substantial improvements include building a shopping center or other commercial or residential buildings as well as installing hard surface roads or utilities such as sewers, water, gas, or electric lines. However, surveying, filling, draining, leveling, and clearing operations as well as the construction of minimum all-weather access roads (including gravel roads when required by the climate) will not be considered substantial improvements. Erecting a temporary structure used as a field office will not be considered a substantial improvement. In addition, an improvement will not be considered substantial if *all four* of the following conditions are met:

1. The taxpayer has held the property for 10 years. (The full 10-year period must elapse, whether the taxpayer inherited the property or not. Although the taxpayer must hold the property 10 years, the property need not be held for 10 years after it is subdivided.)

2. The improvement consists of the building or installation of water, sewer, drainage facilities (either surface, subsurface, or both), or roads, including hard surface roads, curbs, and gutters.

3. The IRS is satisfied that without the improvement the lot or parcel would not have been marketable at the prevailing local price for similar building sites.

4. The taxpayer elects not to capitalize the cost of the improvement to the basis of the lot sold or to the basis of any other property held by the taxpayer, and also agrees not to expense any such costs.[31]

Planning Pointer: As long as the taxpayer has owned the land for at least five years, subdividing the property will not affect the taxpayer's ability to be considered an investor in real estate. However, if the taxpayer improves the property to enhance its marketability or price and then sells it before the full 10-year holding period has elapsed, the taxpayer risks being deemed a dealer in real estate and accordingly, all gain on the sale of the lots would then be recognized as ordinary income.

Character of the gain. Assuming Code Sec. 1237 applies, the tax law allows the taxpayer to treat the gain on the sale of all lots as long-term capital gain until *the tax year* in which the sixth lot is sold. In that year and for all subsequent tax years, the gain from all sales of all lots or parcels is treated as ordinary income to the extent of five percent of the *selling price*; the remainder is long-term capital gain.[32] Any selling expenses (commissions, advertising) incurred in the sale are first used to offset the portion of the gain that is taxed as ordinary income. Any excess is offset against the selling price to determine the amount of long-term capital gain.[33]

Example 30: In 20X0, Dwane Carter purchased a large tract of real estate for $50,000. In 20X6, he subdivided the tract into 20 lots of equal size and engaged in advertising, promotional, and selling activities in connection with the lots. Dwane sold two lots (lots numbers 1 and 2) during 20X7 for $8,000 each. He incurred $1,000 in total selling expenses in connection with the sale of the lots. Dwane's amount realized from the sale is $15,000 ($16,000 selling price minus $1,000 in selling expenses). His basis in each lot is $2,500 ($50,000/20), and accordingly, his adjusted basis in the lots sold is $5,000 ($2,500 × 2). Since Dwane did not sell the sixth lot during 20X7, he will recognize $10,000 long-term capital gain from the sale ($15,000 – $5,000).

---

[31] Reg. § 1.1237-1(c)(5)(i)(d).
[32] Code Sec. 1237(b)(1); Reg. § 1.1237-1.
[33] Code Sec. 1237(b)(2).

Example 31: Continuing with Example 30, in 20X8, Dwane sells another three lots (lots 3, 4, and 5) for a total of $35,000. He incurs $1,500 in selling expenses on the sale. Because Dwane did not sell the sixth lot in 20X8, he recognizes a $26,000 long-term capital gain ($35,000 – $1,500 – $7,500).

Example 32: Assume the same facts as in Example 31, except Dwane sells four lots (lots 3, 4, 5, and 6) in 20X8 for a total of $44,000 and incurs $2,000 in selling expenses on the sale. His amount realized on the sale is $42,000 ($44,000 – $2,000). Dwane's gain from the sale is $32,000 ($42,000 – $10,000). Since he sold the sixth lot during the year, five percent of the *sales price* ($44,000 × 5% = $2,200) must be recognized as ordinary income. However, the selling expenses are used first to reduce the amount taxed as ordinary income and then to reduce the amount taxed as long-term capital gain. Thus, of the $32,000 gain, $200 ($2,200 – $2,000) is taxed as ordinary income and $31,800 ($32,000 – $200) is taxed as long-term capital gain.

Example 33: Continuing with Example 32, in 20X9 Dwane sells another five lots (lots 7–11) for a total of $50,000. He incurs $2,800 in selling expenses on the sale. Dwane's realized and recognized gain is $34,700 ($50,000 – $2,800 – $12,500). He does not recognize any ordinary income because the $2,800 of selling expenses exceeds five percent of the $50,000 selling price ($50,000 × 5% = $2,500). Thus, the entire $34,700 gain is taxed as long-term capital gain.

 Spotlight: Code Sec. 1237 does not apply to C corporations. Thus, no assumptions are made regarding the actions of a C corporation that subdivides realty and sells the lots individually. The determination of whether the C corporation acted as a dealer or as an investor must be made based on the facts and circumstances on a case-by-case basis.

.05 Section 1244 Stock

Because stock is a capital asset for most taxpayers, gains and losses on the sale of stock normally produce capital gains and losses. Due to the limitations that apply to capital loss deductions, certain more risky corporations could find it difficult to find investors to purchase their stock. In an effort to help smaller corporations in this regard, Code Sec. 1244 allows individual taxpayers to recognize annually ordinary losses of up to $50,000 on the sale of "Section 1244 stock." Married couples who file a joint return are allowed to recognize up to $100,000 in ordinary losses on the sale of Section 1244 stock each year.[34] Any recognized loss on the sale of Section 1244 stock that exceeds these amounts is treated as a capital loss. Only individuals are entitled to this ordinary loss treatment on the sale of Section 1244 stock.

 Spotlight: Section 1244 applies only to individuals who own stock directly and to individuals who are partners in partnerships that own stock. An individual who is a partner in a partnership at the time the partnership acquired the Section 1244 stock may deduct an ordinary loss under Section 1244 if the partner's distributive share of partnership items reflects the loss sustained by the partnership.

The ordinary loss deduction is limited to the *lesser* of the partner's distributive share at the time of the issuance of the stock or the partner's distributive share at the time the partnership realized the loss. In order to claim a deduction under Section 1244 the individual, or the partnership, sustaining the loss must have held the stock from the date of issuance (be the original owner of the stock).[35]

---

[34] Code Sec. 1244(a) and (b).

[35] Reg. § 1.1244-1(b)(2).

> A corporation, trust, or estate may not deduct an ordinary loss under Section 1244.[36] Individuals who are shareholders of an S corporation may not deduct an ordinary loss under Section 1244 on the sale of small business stock owned by the S corporation.[37]

Section 1244 stock is stock purchased directly from a domestic corporation after July 18, 1984.[38] To qualify as Section 1244 stock, the corporation must qualify as a "small business." A "small business" is a corporation whose contributed capital does not exceed $1 million at the time the stock is issued.[39] In addition, during the previous five tax years before the taxpayer realized the loss, more than 50 percent of the corporation's gross receipts must have come from sources other than royalties, rents, dividends, interest, annuities, and gains on the sale of stock and securities.[40] If the corporation has not been in existence for five years when the taxpayer realizes the loss, the corporation must not have violated the 50-percent rule for any year since its formation.[41] When property is contributed in exchange for stock in the corporation, the amount counted as contributed capital for purposes of the $1 million limitation is the adjusted basis of the property, reduced by any liabilities assumed by the corporation.[42]

Example 34: On November 14, 20X1, Dan and Sue Jones contributed $300,000 to a corporation in exchange for 1,000 shares of the corporation's common stock. The corporation qualifies as a small business under Code Sec. 1244. The Joneses sell all 1,000 shares in the corporation on December 12, 20X6, for $140,000. Their recognized loss from the sale is $160,000 ($140,000 – $300,000). Assuming this is the only capital asset sold during the year, the Joneses may deduct $100,000 of this loss as an ordinary loss under Code Sec. 1244. The remaining $60,000 loss is a long-term capital loss. Because they did not sell or exchange any other capital assets during the year, they will be able to deduct $3,000 of the long-term capital loss against their ordinary income. They will carry over the remaining $57,000 loss as a long-term capital loss to the next tax year.

Example 35: In exchange for 100 percent of the stock, Edgar Jones contributed equipment, building, and land to a corporation in a Code Sec. 351 transaction. The corporation assumed a $300,000 mortgage on the building. The FMV and adjusted basis of the property contributed was as follows:

	FMV	Adjusted Basis
Equipment	$200,000	$250,000
Building	1,100,000	800,000
Land	150,000	90,000
Total	$1,450,000	$1,140,000

For purposes of the $1 million limitation, the contributed capital is only $840,000 ($1,140,000 – $300,000). Therefore, the corporation does qualify under Code Sec. 1244.

 Reason for the Rule: Congress wanted to encourage individuals to invest in small corporations to stimulate the economy and create jobs. Investments in small corporations are risky, especially newer ones. While the lower tax rates on net capital gains and

---

[36] Reg. § 1.1244-1(b)(2).

[37] V.D. Rath, 101 TC 196, Dec. 49,266.

[38] Committee Report on P.L. 98-369, Deficit Reduction Act of 1984.

[39] Code Sec. 1244(c)(1)(A) and (c)(3)(A).

[40] Code Sec. 1244(c)(1)(C) and (c)(2)(B).

[41] Code Sec. 1244(c)(2)(A).

[42] Code Sec. 1244(c)(3)(B).

dividends are an incentive to buy stock, the favorable tax treatment in the event of a loss provides investors with an additional incentive to invest directly in small corporations.

 Planning Pointer: The limit on deducting a loss on the sale or exchange of Code Sec. 1244 stock as an ordinary loss is an annual limit. Therefore, a taxpayer who would realize a loss on the sale of Code Sec. 1244 stock that exceeds the limit should consider selling the stock over two or more years. For example, in Example 33, the Joneses could have waited to sell some of their shares until the next tax year. That would have allowed them to deduct the entire $140,000 as an ordinary loss over two tax years. Furthermore, the $50,000/$100,000 annual limit is an aggregate limit applied to each tax return. It is not a limit that is applied on a per corporation basis. Thus, losses on sales of all Section 1244 stock make during the years are included in applying this annual limit.

¶ 904 Section 1231 Gains and Losses

Code Sec. 1221 specifically excludes depreciable property and land used in the taxpayer's trade or business from the definition of a capital asset. If these business properties are held for one year or less at the time they are disposed of, the recognized gain or loss is taxed as ordinary gain or loss. However, if these business properties are held for more than one year (exceptions exist for certain livestock), they fall under the definition of "Section 1231 property." When taxpayers sell Section 1231 property, it usually results in a Section 1231 gain or loss.

.01 Significance of Net Section 1231 Gains

A Section 1231 gain or loss is generally recognized when the taxpayer disposes of Section 1231 property. **Section 1231 property** consists of business property held long-term (more than one year). However, inventory, receivables, and supplies do not qualify as Section 1231 property. Section 1231 gains and losses typically result from sales or exchanges of Section 1231 property. However, they can also result from gains and losses on condemnations of business or investment property that the taxpayer holds for more than one year (see ¶ 809).[43] When accelerated depreciation methods are used to depreciate certain business assets, some of the Section 1231 gain may be recharacterized as ordinary income (see ¶ 904.02). However, since land is nondepreciable property, all recognized gains and losses from the sale or exchange of land that qualifies as Section 1231 property are always treated as Section 1231 gains and losses. Loss recognized on the sale of Section 1231 property is always **Section 1231 loss**, regardless of whether the Section 1231 property was depreciable or nondepreciable property.

When a taxpayer combines all Section 1231 gains and losses for the year and the result is a net Section 1231 loss, all Section 1231 gains and losses are treated as ordinary gains and losses.[44] If a net Section 1231 gain results, the net gain has the potential to be treated as a long-term capital gain.[45] However, the amount equal to any nonrecaptured Section 1231 losses from the previous five years must first be characterized as ordinary income (see ¶ 904.03). Any excess gain is then treated as long-term capital gain.

Example 36: During the year, Hale Co., Inc. sells the following five properties:

Property	Section 1231 Gain (Loss)
Equipment	($ 2,500)
Land	44,000
Machinery	(1,000)

---

[43] Code Sec. 1231(a)(3).

[44] Code Sec. 1231(a)(2).

[45] Code Sec. 1231(a)(1).

Property	Section 1231 Gain (Loss)
Building	35,000
Truck	(6,400)
Net Section 1231 gain	$69,100

Because Hale has a net Section 1231 gain for the year, its taxable income will increase by $69,100 because of the gains and losses from these five transactions. The $69,100 net Section 1231 gain is added to Hale's long-term capital gain in the netting process of capital gains and losses (assuming that Hale does not have any nonrecaptured Section 1231 losses that recharacterize the gain as ordinary income). By allowing the net Section 1231 gain to be included as long-term capital gain in the netting process, the tax law potentially allows Hale to deduct more capital losses.

Example 37: Assume the same facts as in Example 36, except the land is sold for a $44,000 loss (instead of a $44,000 gain).

Property	Section 1231 Gain (Loss)
Equipment	($ 2,500)
Land	(44,000)
Machinery	(1,000)
Building	35,000
Truck	(6,400)
Net Section 1231 loss	($18,900)

Because Hale has a net Section 1231 loss for the year, all of the Section 1231 gains and losses are treated as ordinary gains and losses. Thus, Hale's taxable income is reduced by the $18,900 net loss. A net Section 1231 loss does not affect the amount of the taxpayer's capital gains and losses involved in the netting process.

 Spotlight: As illustrated in Examples 34 and 35, Code Sec. 1231 provides taxpayers with the "best of both worlds"—the possibility of including net Section 1231 gains as long-term capital gains in the netting process and the potential for deducting net Section 1231 losses as ordinary losses. By allowing taxpayers to increase the amount of long-term capital gains in the netting process, the tax law allows individual taxpayers to often pay a lower tax rate on net Section 1231 gain. Although corporate taxpayers pay the same rate of tax on ordinary income and capital gains, the ability to count net Section 1231 gains as long-term capital gains helps corporations (as well as individuals) avoid being limited on the amount of capital losses they can deduct. Since corporations are allowed to carry back excess capital losses three years, any long-term capital gain recognized in the current year may benefit the corporation for the next three tax years to the extent the corporation incurs capital losses.

.02 Depreciation Recapture

If a taxpayer sells depreciable personal property held for one year or less and realizes a gain, the entire gain is taxed as ordinary income. Code Sec. 1231, which allows for the possibility of long-term capital gain treatment on net Section 1231 gains, only applies to business property held long-term. If the taxpayer sells depreciable personal property held for more than one year and recognizes a gain, some or all of the gain may be treated as ordinary gain rather than as Section 1231 gain. Due to the accelerated methods available to depreciate tangible personal property (Modified Accelerated Cost Recovery System (MACRS), Section 179, and additional first-year "bonus" depreciation), it is likely that much if not all of the gain on the sale of depreciable property may be due to reducing the adjusted basis by depreciation deductions, rather than from an actual increase in the value of the property sold.

Section 1245 depreciation recapture. Although the tax laws allow taxpayers to use MACRS and Code Sec. 179 to depreciate tangible personal property, to even out the effects illustrated in Example 36, the tax laws require that any gain from the sale of tangible personal property that is attributable to depreciation (and not to an increase in the property's value) be taxed as ordinary income under Code Sec. 1245. For depreciable property placed in service after 1986, depreciation recapture under Code Sec. 1245 only applies to tangible personal property. Real property placed in service after 1986 is not subject to Code Sec. 1245 depreciation recapture.

The amount of **Section 1245 gain** is equal to the *lesser* of (1) the accumulated depreciation taken on the property or (2) the recognized gain. Accumulated depreciation includes all depreciation taken, including MACRS depreciation, bonus depreciation, and any Section 179 expense. Use of the alternative depreciation system (ADS), does not avoid the Code Sec. 1245 recapture provisions, i.e., the entire amount of straight-line depreciation taken is subject to recapture. Generally, the entire gain on Section 1245 property sales will be taxed as ordinary income. However, if the sales price of the property exceeds the basis before depreciation is deducted (usually the original basis if no adjustments other than depreciation have been made), then *some* of the gain will be Code Sec. 1231 gain.

Example 38: Cross Company sells a machine used in its business for $38,000. The company purchased the machine two years earlier for $40,000 and has claimed depreciation deductions (including Section 179) totaling $22,000. Thus, Cross's adjusted basis in the machine equals $18,000 ($40,000 – $22,000) and the recognized gain on the sale is $20,000 ($38,000 – $18,000). Cross must recognize all $20,000 of the gain as ordinary income under Code Sec. 1245 gain (the *lesser* of (1) $22,000 of depreciation taken or (2) $20,000 of recognized gain). Cross's Section 1231 gain is zero ($20,000 – $20,000).

Example 39: Assume the same facts as in Example 38, except Cross sold the machine for $45,000. The recognized gain on the sale is $27,000 ($45,000 – $18,000). Cross must recognize $22,000 of the gain as ordinary income under Code Sec. 1245 gain (the *lesser* of (1) $22,000 of depreciation taken or (2) $27,000 of recognized gain). Cross's Section 1231 gain is $5,000 ($27,000 – $22,000). Notice that the $5,000 Section 1231 gain is equal to the excess of the sales price over the original basis.

Planning Pointer: Self-employed taxpayers can benefit from claiming depreciation deductions and Section 179 expense in more ways than just the obvious time value of money considerations. Depreciation and Section 179 expense reduce net earnings from self-employment, and accordingly, the amount of self-employment tax the owner pays. When these amounts are later recaptured on a sale or exchange of the property and taxed as ordinary income, they are not included in the taxpayer's self-employment income. Likewise, Section 1231 losses are not deductible in computing an owner's self-employment tax. Consequently, claiming the maximum depreciation deduction and Section 179 expense allowed often produces additional tax benefits for self-employed taxpayers.

Section 1250 depreciation recapture. If a taxpayer sells depreciable real estate (buildings) and realizes a gain, the gain is referred to as **Section 1250 gain** to the extent that the accumulated depreciation taken on the property exceeds what the accumulated depreciation would have been had the straight-line method been used. Because straight-line depreciation is the only method available under MACRS, Section 1250 recapture does not apply to the sale of real property placed in service after 1986. Furthermore, because pre-ACRS property (acquired before 1987) is by now fully depreciated, there is no excess depreciation to recapture on its sale. However, Code Sec. 1250 is relevant for two purposes:

- It applies to Section 291 gain (discussed next); and
- It affects the tax rate that is applied to individuals on the sale of buildings. This is termed "unrecaptured Section 1250 gain" and is discussed at ¶ 907.

Section 291 gain. Even though Section 1250 recapture no longer applies to depreciable realty placed in service after 1986, Code Sec. 291 requires C corporations to treat as ordinary income 20 percent of the gain that would result if the property were Section 1245 property over the amount of ordinary income recognized under Section 1250. Since Section 1250 gain is always zero for property placed in service after 1986, a corporation's **Section 291 gain** (ordinary income from the sale of real property) equals the *lesser* of (1) 20 percent of the accumulated depreciation taken on the property or (2) the recognized gain. Any gain not taxed as ordinary income is treated as Section 1231 gain.

Example 40: DuRite Corporation sells its office building for $500,000 in 20X0. DuRite purchased the building for $400,000, and the corporation has taken $80,000 of straight-line depreciation on the building over the years. Thus, its adjusted basis in the building at the time of the sale is $320,000 ($400,000 – $80,000). DuRite's recognized gain is $180,000 ($500,000 – $320,000). If the building were subject to Section 1245 recapture, its Section 1245 gain would be $80,000 (the *lesser* of the $80,000 accumulated depreciation taken or the $180,000 gain). Under Code Sec. 291, DuRite must recognize $16,000 ($80,000 × 20%) of the gain as ordinary income. The remaining gain of $164,000 ($180,000 – $16,000) is Section 1231 gain.

Example 41: Continuing with Example 40, in addition to selling the building, DuRite also realized the following gain and loss during 20X0:

Gain on the sale of business land held for 12 years	$88,000
Loss on the sale of a warehouse held for 3 years	(40,000)

DuRite computes its net Section 1231 gain or loss as follows:

	Section 1231 Gain (Loss)	Ordinary Gain (Loss)
Office building	$164,000	$16,000
Land	88,000	- 0 -
Warehouse	(40,000)	- 0 -
Total	$212,000	$16,000

DuRite's net Section 1231 gain will be treated as a long-term capital gain for determining the amount of capital losses DuRite can deduct from gross income in 20X0 (assuming the nonrecaptured Section 1231 gain rules do not apply, see ¶ 904.03.)

Example 42: Assume the same facts as in Example 41, except the land was sold for a loss of $188,000 (instead of an $88,000 gain). Under this scenario, DuRite has a $64,000 net Section 1231 loss for the year, as shown below:

	Section 1231 Gain (Loss)	Ordinary Gain (Loss)
Office building	$164,000	$16,000
Land	(188,000)	- 0 -
Warehouse	(40,000)	- 0 -

	Section 1231 Gain (Loss)	Ordinary Gain (Loss)
Total	($ 64,000)	$16,000

Code Sec. 1231 does not limit the losses that DuRite can deduct. DuRite treats all Section 1231 gains and losses as ordinary gains and losses. Therefore, all of DuRite's $180,000 of gains for the year ($164,000 + $16,000) are included in gross income, and the entire $228,000 ($188,000 + $40,000) of losses for the year are deducted from gross income. None of DuRite's Section 1231 transactions affects the amounts included in DuRite's netting process of short-term and long-term capital gains and losses.

Depreciation recapture and nontaxable transactions. The general rule relating to the recognition of ordinary income upon the disposition of Section 1245 property does not apply if the property is disposed of in a like-kind exchange (see ¶ 808) or in an involuntary conversion (see ¶ 809). If any gain is recognized in a like-kind exchange or in an involuntary conversion of Section 1245 property, Section 1245 gain must be recognized to the same extent.

Example 43: Alan Starker, who operates a printing shop, trades a used printing press that has a market value of $50,000 for a newer, smaller press that has a market value of $25,000. In the exchange he also receives cash of $10,000 and undeveloped land having a market value of $15,000. Alan originally purchased the printing press for $60,000 and had taken $40,000 in depreciation over the years. Thus, Alan's basis in the old press is $20,000 ($60,000 – $40,000). Alan's realized gain on the exchange is $30,000 ($50,000 – $20,000); however, his recognized gain is limited to the $25,000 of boot received ($10,000 cash + $15,000 FMV of the nonlike-kind property). If Alan had sold the printing press for $50,000 cash, he would have recognized the entire $30,000 as ordinary income under Section 1245; however, since Alan's recognized gain under Code Sec. 1031 is limited to $25,000 ($10,000 cash plus the $15,000 FMV of the nonlike-kind property), he will recognize $25,000 of Section 1245 gain.

Depreciation recapture from an installment sale. In an installment sale, the taxpayer recognizes gain each year equal to the amount the taxpayer actually or constructively receives during the year multiplied by the gross profit percentage (see ¶ 810.01).[46] However, if the property sold is subject to depreciation recapture, the tax law requires that the *entire amount* of depreciation recapture be recognized as ordinary income in the year of sale, regardless of the amount of cash the taxpayer receives during the year. The amount of the depreciation recapture is then added to the adjusted basis of the property to calculate the gross profit from the sale. The Section 1231 gain the taxpayer will recognize each year is equal to the gross profit percentage multiplied by the cash or its equivalent received as a down payment or as a payment on the principal of the installment note.[47]

Example 44: In 20X1, Anthony Samari paid $45,000 for equipment that he uses in his business. Over the years, Anthony claimed depreciation (including Section 179 expense) totaling $28,000. In 20X3 he sells the equipment for $60,000. The terms of sale require the buyer to make a $20,000 cash payment at the time of sale and to pay $20,000 on the principal of the installment note one year after the sale date and another $20,000 on the principal of the installment note two years after the sale date. The buyer also agreed to pay the accrued interest on each payment date. The payments to be made were evidenced by a $40,000 installment note that bears interest at the market rate. The tax consequences of the installment sale are as follows:

Cash paid at the time of sale	$20,000
Installment note	40,000

---

[46] Code Sec. 453(c).

[47] Reg. § 1.1245-6(d).

Amount realized	$60,000
Less: Adjusted basis ($45,000 – $28,000)	(17,000)
Realized gain	$43,000

Anthony recognizes $28,000 as ordinary income in the year of sale. The amount taxed as Section 1245 gain is the *lesser* of (1) the $28,000 of accumulated depreciation or (2) the $43,000 gain from the sale. He adds the $28,000 to the adjusted basis of the asset to calculate his gross profit on the installment sale. Anthony computes his gross profit and gross profit percentage from the installment sale as follows:

Selling price	$60,000
Less: Adjusted basis ($17,000 + $28,000)	(45,000)
Gross profit from the sale	$15,000

Gross profit percentage = $15,000 ÷ $60,000 = 25%

In the year of the sale (20X3), Anthony recognizes a Section 1231 gain of $5,000 ($20,000 × 25%) from the cash received at the time of the sale. He also recognizes the $28,000 of Section 1245 gain (ordinary income). The $5,000 of Section 1231 gain will be offset against other Section 1231 gains and losses for the year. In 20X4, Anthony will recognize a Section 1231 gain of $5,000 ($20,000 × 25%), and in 20X5, he will recognize the remaining $5,000 of Section 1231 gain ($20,000 × 25%). Anthony will also recognize the interest from the note that the buyer pays. Over the three years, Anthony will recognize $43,000 of total gain as follows:

Character of the gain:

Section 1245 gain	$28,000
Section 1231 gain ($5,000 + $5,000 + $5,000)	15,000
Total gain recognized	$43,000

.03 Nonrecaptured Section 1231 Losses

If the taxpayer incurs a net Section 1231 loss for the year, the loss is treated as an ordinary loss. However, when the taxpayer has a net Section 1231 gain in a subsequent tax year, the net gain is normally treated as long-term capital gain. Like the depreciation recapture rules which attempt to counteract the tax benefits associated with ordinary deductions in one year followed by preferential long-term capital gains in another, the tax laws require that net Section 1231 gain be recaptured as ordinary income to the extent that the taxpayer has "nonrecaptured Section 1231 losses" from the previous five tax years.

Example 45: In the current year, a corporation has $55,000 of net Section 1231 gains. Over the past five tax years, the corporation has deducted net Section 1231 losses as ordinary deductions, and the amount of nonrecaptured net Section 1231 losses at the beginning of the year is $35,000. Although the entire $55,000 of net Section 1231 increases the taxpayer's taxable income, the corporation is taxed on the first $35,000 of the gain as ordinary income. It can then treat the remaining $20,000 of net Section 1231 gain ($55,000 – $35,000) as long-term capital gain in the netting process. Therefore, $20,000 of the gain can be used to offset capital losses in the current year. If the corporation's capital losses in the current year are less than its capital gains, the excess capital gain can be used to offset excess capital losses recognized over the next three years when such excess losses are carried back three tax years.

Reason for the Rule: Before the Deficit Reduction Act of 1984, when a taxpayer had a net Section 1231 gain, it was treated as a long-term capital gain. Good tax planners advised their clients to claim their Section 1231 losses in one tax year and their Section 1231 gains in another tax year. Taxpayers who did this could recognize all of their Section 1231 losses as ordinary losses and all their Section 1231 gains as long-term capital gains. Congress decided to minimize the benefits of this tax planning strategy by requiring taxpayers to treat net Section 1231 gains as ordinary income to the extent of their net Section 1231 losses recognized in the previous five years.

The Section 1231 look back provision requires that net Section 1231 gain in the current year be recognized as ordinary income to the extent of the taxpayer's nonrecaptured net Section 1231 losses from the previous five years. Any remaining net Section 1231 gain can be treated as a long-term capital gain in the netting process. The look back provision requires that in any year in which a taxpayer reports a net Section 1231 gain, it must determine how much of the net Section 1231 losses in the previous five years have not yet been "paid back" through the recharacterization of net Section 1231 gain as ordinary income. These net Section 1231 losses from the last five tax years that have not been "paid back" are called **nonrecaptured net Section 1231 losses**. The calculation of nonrecaptured net Section 1231 losses is illustrated in the McMillan example below.

Example 46: McMillan, Inc. has recognized the following net Section 1231 gains and losses over the past five years. McMillan's first year of operations was 20X1.

Year	Net Section 1231 Gain (Loss)
20X1	$12,000
20X2	(14,200)
20X3	3,700
20X4	(18,900)
20X5	5,200

In 20X1, McMillan reports a net Section 1231 gain of $12,000. Because 20X1 is McMillan's first year of operations, there are zero nonrecaptured Section 1231 losses, and therefore the entire $12,000 is treated as long-term capital gain. As of the end of 20X1, McMillan has no nonrecaptured Section 1231 losses.

In 20X2, the company has a net Section 1231 loss of $14,200. This amount is deducted as an ordinary loss from McMillan's gross income in 20X2. Because McMillan benefits from being able to deduct this amount against income that is taxed at the ordinary income tax rates, the $14,200 becomes McMillan's nonrecaptured Section 1231 loss at the end of 20X2.

In 20X3, McMillan reports a $3,700 net Section 1231 gain. This gain is taxed as ordinary income to counteract the ordinary deduction it received in the prior tax year. Since McMillan "pays back" $3,700 of its prior net Section 1231 losses, its nonrecaptured Section 1231 loss at the end of 20X3 is reduced to $10,500 ($14,200 – $3,700).

In 20X4, McMillan reports an $18,900 net Section 1231 loss and deducts this amount as ordinary loss. McMillan's nonrecaptured Section 1231 losses for the past five years increase to $29,400 ($10,500 + $18,900).

In 20X5, the company reports a $5,200 net Section 1231 gain, the entire gain is taxed as ordinary income under the look back provision, and McMillan's nonrecaptured Section 1231 losses are reduced to $24,200 ($29,400 – $5,200).

McMillan's nonrecaptured Section 1231 losses are summarized as follows:

Year	Amount of Net Section 1231 Gain (Loss)	Amount of Nonrecaptured Section 1231 Losses
20X1	$12,000	$ 0
20X2	(14,200)	14,200
20X3	3,700	10,500
20X4	(18,900)	29,400
20X5	5,200	24,200

If in 20X6 McMillan has a net Section 1231 gain of $29,800, only the first $24,200 of this gain is treated as ordinary income. The remaining $5,600 ($29,800 – $24,200) is treated as a long-term capital gain and is included as such in the netting process for 20X6. The company's nonrecaptured Section 1231 losses would be reduced to zero at the end of 20X6.

Planning Pointer: If a taxpayer recognizes Section 1231 gains and has no nonrecaptured net Section 1231 losses in the previous five years, the taxpayer may treat the net Section 1231 gain as a long-term capital gain. Net section 1231 losses incurred in subsequent years will be deductible as ordinary losses. Therefore, a good tax-planning strategy for taxpayers who have no nonrecaptured net Section 1231 losses is to first sell Section 1231 assets that create gains. Then in the following tax year, sell any Section 1231 assets that will produce losses. This point is illustrated in Example 46.

Example 47: Frank Adams operates a farming business as a sole proprietor. His long-term capital gains are taxed at 15 percent; his ordinary income is taxed at 25 percent. Frank is considering selling a tractor and a parcel of land used in his farming business. Based on good estimates of their FMVs, Frank concludes that the sale of his tractor would result in an $8,000 Section 1231 loss and the sale of his farmland would result in a $12,000 Section 1231 gain. These are the only assets Frank will be selling during the year.

If Frank sells both assets in the current year, he will have a net Section 1231 gain of $4,000 ($12,000 – $8,000), which will be taxed as a long-term capital gain. His tax associated with the net gain would be $600 ($4,000 × 15%). However, if Frank waits to sell the tractor until the next tax year, he will report a $12,000 net Section 1231 gain in the current year, which will be taxed as a long-term capital gain. His tax associated with that gain would be $1,800 ($12,000 × 15%). In the next year Frank would report an $8,000 net Section 1231 loss that he can fully deduct as an ordinary loss. His tax savings from the loss would be $2,000 ($8,000 × 25%). When the tax consequences for the two years are combined, Frank would save $200 in taxes ($2,000 reduction in taxes in the second year – $1,800 taxes owed in the first year).

When the two alternatives are compared, Frank would pay $600 in taxes under the first scenario, but save $200 in taxes under the second scenario. This $800 difference in tax liability is due to the tax benefits of deducting losses as ordinary losses and taxing gains as long-term capital gains.

Planning Pointer: In Example 47, Frank was able to engage in effective tax planning by selling Section 1231 property at a gain the year before he sold Section 1231 property at a loss. If the situation were reversed and Frank had sold the loss property first, the

> Section 1231 look back provision would have taxed the subsequent Section 1231 gain as ordinary income.

¶ 905 Business Casualty and Theft Gains and Losses

When business property is involved in a casualty or theft, the amount of the loss depends on whether the business property is partially or completely destroyed. For completely destroyed business property, the amount of the loss is the taxpayer's adjusted basis in the property minus any insurance reimbursement. If the insurance proceeds exceed the taxpayer's adjusted basis in the property, a casualty gain results. For partially destroyed business property, the amount of the loss is measured as the *lesser* of (1) the taxpayer's adjusted basis in the property or (2) its decline in FMV. Any insurance reimbursement the taxpayer receives is then subtracted from the lesser of the two amounts. (see ¶ 802.02). Once again, if the insurance proceeds exceed the taxpayer's adjusted basis in the partially destroyed business property, a casualty gain results.

Gains and losses from business property held one year or less (short-term) that is involved in a casualty or theft are treated as ordinary gains and losses. A loss recognized on a casualty or theft of business property held for more than one year (long-term) is treated as a "business casualty or theft loss." A gain recognized on a casualty or theft of business property held for more than one year is subject to the same depreciation recapture rules as discussed previously in the chapter (see ¶ 904.02). After the appropriate amount of the gain from business property involved in a casualty or theft has been taxed as ordinary income, any remaining gain is treated as a "business casualty or theft gain."

Example 48: Anniston's corporate warehouse is completely destroyed by a fire. Anniston purchased the warehouse for $300,000; it had taken depreciation deductions over the years of $100,000. The insurance company reimburses Anniston $250,000 for its loss. Since the amount of the reimbursement ($250,000) exceeds the taxpayer's $200,000 ($300,000 – $100,000) adjusted basis in the warehouse, Anniston recognizes a $50,000 business casualty gain ($250,000 – $200,000). Although Code Sec. 1250 depreciation recapture does not apply to realty placed in service after 1986, C corporations are required to recognize as ordinary income under Code Sec. 291 the *lesser* of (1) 20 percent of the $100,000 depreciation taken on the property or (2) the $50,000 gain. Thus, of the $50,000 gain, Anniston must recognize $10,000 as ordinary income ($50,000 × 20%) and $40,000 ($50,000 – $10,000) as business casualty and theft gain.

Example 49: A taxpayer has three casualty and theft events during the year that involve business property held for more than a year. The first involves an automobile; the second involves the taxpayer's office building; and the third involves computer equipment. The taxpayer's adjusted basis in the property, along with the FMV before and after the casualty or theft and any insurance proceeds is as follows.

Property	Adjusted Basis	FMV Before	FMV After	Proceeds
Automobile	$ 2,000	$ 7,000	$ 0	$ 6,500
Office building	180,000	220,000	190,000	28,000
Computer	1,500	1,000	0	0

The automobile is completely destroyed in the casualty (evidenced by the $0 FMV after the event), and therefore the amount of the casualty loss is measured as the adjusted basis ($2,000) minus the amount of the insurance reimbursement ($6,500). When the insurance proceeds are subtracted from the adjusted basis, a casualty loss does not result. Thus, the taxpayer recognizes a gain to the extent that the insurance proceeds exceed its adjusted basis in the property, or $4,500 ($6,500 – $2,000). However, to the extent that this gain is attributable to depreciation (and not a decline in the value of the automobile), the gain will be taxed as ordinary income under Code Sec. 1245.

The office building is partially destroyed in the casualty, and therefore the amount of the casualty loss is measured as the excess of the *lesser* of the adjusted basis of the property ($180,000) or its decline in value ($220,0000 – $190,000 = $30,000) over the $28,000 of insurance proceeds. Therefore, the taxpayer's business casualty loss equals $2,000 ($30,000 – $28,000). The computer equipment was stolen and therefore it is completed destroyed. Accordingly, the amount of the theft loss is measured as its adjusted basis ($1,500) minus the amount of the insurance reimbursement ($0).

All business casualty and theft gains and losses are netted against one another at the end of the year. If a net business casualty and theft loss results, the business casualty and theft gains and losses are treated as ordinary gains and losses.[48] If, however, the taxpayer has a net business casualty and theft gain, the gains and losses are treated as Section 1231 gains and losses, and accordingly, the net gain is added to the taxpayer's other Section 1231 gains and losses.[49]

Example 50: Continuing with Example 49, assuming that the taxpayer's entire $4,500 gain on the automobile is taxed as ordinary income under Code Sec. 1245, the taxpayer's business casualty and theft loss for the year equals $3,500 ($2,000 + $1,500). This net business casualty and theft loss is deducted as an ordinary loss from the taxpayer's gross income.

¶ 906 Review of the Netting Process

As stated previously in the chapter, all gains and losses are ultimately taxed either as ordinary gains and losses or as capital gains and losses. The netting process of gains and losses from the disposal of long-term business property and capital assets is used to determine the taxpayer's ordinary versus capital gains or losses. When completing the taxpayer's income tax return, this netting process starts with computing the taxpayer's recognized gain or loss for each property disposed of during the year (see Chapter 8). Once the taxpayer's recognized gain or loss is determined, it is important to apply the rules from this chapter to determine the character of the recognized gain or loss. Initially gain or loss can be classified into one of the following five categories:

1. Casualty or theft gains and losses from long-term business property (Note that condemnations of business property and property held for the production of income are automatically Code Sec. 1231 items, and are *not* included with casualty gains and losses);

2. Section 1231 gain or loss (after Code Secs. 1245, 1250, and 291 have been considered and the ordinary income component of any gain has been removed);

3. Short-term capital gain or loss;

4. Long-term capital gain or loss; and

5. Ordinary income (includes all depreciation recapture, Section 1231 gains recharacterized as ordinary income due to nonrecaptured Section 1231 losses as well as gains and losses from short-term property that is not a capital asset).

Using the above listed items in the order presented, the netting process is illustrated in Figure 9-1. In order to make sure that all capital gains and losses are properly recorded and the rules of the netting process are followed, the netting process must begin with the netting of business casualty and theft gains and losses, followed by the netting of Section 1231 gains and losses, and then followed by the netting of capital gains and losses.

---

[48] Code Sec. 1231(a)(4).

[49] Code Secs. 1231(a)(3)(A)(ii) and 1231(a)(3)(B).

Figure 9-1 Summary of the Netting Process

*In addition to ordinary income derived from business profits, interest, or dividend income, etc., amounts in this column include any depreciation recapture under Code Secs. 1245, 1250, or 291 resulting from the sale, exchange, or destruction of Section 1231 property. The column also includes any gain from the sale or exchange of business property held short-term (one year or less) or from casualty gains involving short-term business property.

**In addition to ordinary losses resulting from business activities, this amount includes losses from the sale of business property held short-term as well as casualty and theft losses involving business property held short-term.

[1] The amounts reported in this far left column only reflect the gains and losses from long-term business property damaged or destroyed in a casualty or theft. Business gains reported in this column are shown after any depreciation recapture associated with the casualty or theft gain has been removed and placed in the far right column as ordinary income (designated by an asterisk "*"). If a net business casualty and theft gain results, the net gain is included in the column along with other Section 1231 gains and losses. If a net business casualty and theft loss results, the net loss reduces ordinary income.

[2] The amounts reported in the Section 1231 gains (losses) column are those amounts that represent Section 1231 gains and losses from the sale or exchange of Section 1231 property (business property held long-term) as well as gains and losses resulting from the condemnation of business property held long-term. Any amounts representing depreciation recapture of Section 1231 property are not included in this column but instead are reported in the far right column as ordinary income (designated by an asterisk "*"). If a net Section 1231 gain results, the gain is either ordinary income (to the extent of nonrecaptured Section 1231 losses) or long-term capital gain. A net Section 1231 loss reduces ordinary income, and it is therefore shown as a negative amount in the ordinary income (loss) column.

Example 51: After taking into consideration the depreciation recapture rules, Basken, a C corporation, has the following casualty and theft gains and losses resulting from business property held for more than one year:

Business casualty gain	$54,000
Business casualty loss	(36,000)
Theft loss	(6,000)

Basken's net business casualty and theft gain equals $12,000 ($54,000 – $36,000 – $6,000). It treats the $12,000 as Section 1231 gain and adds this amount to its other Section 1231 gains and losses for the year.

Example 52: Continuing with Example 51, during the year Basken has a Section 1231 gain of $15,000 and a Section 1231 loss of $4,000. Basken's net Section 1231 gain of $23,000 is computed as follows:

Section 1231 gain	$15,000
Section 1231 loss	(4,000)
Business casualty gain treated as Section 1231 gain	12,000
Net Section 1231 gain	$23,000

If Basken has $5,000 of nonrecaptured Section 1231 losses from the last five years, it taxes $5,000 of its net Section 1231 gain as ordinary income and treats the remaining $18,000 ($23,000 – $5,000) as long-term capital gain in the netting process of capital gains and losses. Thus, to the extent that Basken incurs capital losses during the year, the $18,000 can be used to offset those losses.

Example 53: Continuing with Example 52, during the year Basken has a long-term capital loss of $6,000 and a short-term capital loss of $3,000. Basken's netting of capital gains and losses is as follows:

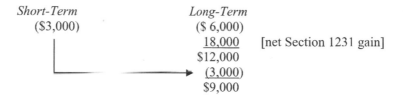

Short-Term
($3,000)

Long-Term
($ 6,000)
18,000   [net Section 1231 gain]
$12,000
(3,000)
$9,000

Basken is able to use the $18,000 net Section 1231 gain that is treated as long-term capital gain to reduce its $9,000 total capital losses for the year. The $9,000 excess of capital gains increases Basken's taxable income by $9,000 for the year.

Example 54: George Restin has the following gains and losses during the year (after taking into consideration the depreciation recapture rules):

Section 1231 gain	$25,000
Section 1231 loss	(9,000)
Business casualty gain treated as Section 1231 gain	12,000
Net Section 1231 gain	$28,000

In addition to those gains and losses, George also has $30,000 of long-term capital losses during the year. If George has no nonrecaptured Section 1231 losses from the last five years, the entire $28,000 is treated as long-term capital gain in the netting process of capital gains and losses. Because George is an individual taxpayer, he is allowed to deduct up to $3,000 of capital losses in excess of capital gains. Therefore, his capital losses are limited to the $28,000 of long-term capital gain (from net Section 1231 gains) plus $3,000, or $31,000. Therefore, George will be allowed to deduct the entire $30,000 capital loss on his individual income tax return. When George includes the $28,000 of long-term capital gain in his gross income and deducts the $30,000 capital loss from gross income, his AGI will decrease by $2,000 ($28,000 – $30,000).

Example 55: Assume the same facts as in Example 54, except George does not have any other capital gains or losses during the year except those that result from his net Section 1231 gain. George's AGI will increase by the $28,000 gain; however, when George computes the tax liability on his taxable income, the maximum tax rate on his $28,000 net capital gain ($28,000 net long-term capital gain in excess of $0 short-term capital losses) will be 15 percent (see ¶ 405.02).

.01 Netting Process for Flow-Through Entities

The full netting process presented in this chapter applies only to individual and corporate taxpayers. Because flow-through entities do not pay income taxes, the tax consequences of the gains and losses recognized by those entities are determined on the owners' income tax returns. Because different rules apply to individual and corporate taxpayers and because the limitations that apply to capital losses must be applied independently for each taxpayer, flow-through entities are responsible for summarizing the various categories of gains and losses they recognize during the year. This includes not only the net short-term capital gain (loss) and net long-term capital gain (loss) but also the amount of net Section 1231 gain (loss) and net business casualty and theft gain (loss).

When a flow-through entity sells property at a gain and the property is subject to depreciation recapture, the amount recaptured is determined by the entity and separated out from the remaining gain. Gains and losses from business casualties and thefts, Section 1231 property, and capital assets must be kept separate from ordinary income because the owners include their respective shares of the gains and losses in their own netting process on their income tax returns. Since all taxpayers pay tax on ordinary income at the regular tax rates, amounts set aside for depreciation recapture are combined with the other items of ordinary income or loss recognized by the entity.

¶ 907 Long-Term Capital Gains for Individual Taxpayers

As mentioned previously in the chapter, individual taxpayers have the advantage of paying lower tax rates on net capital gains. Individuals and corporations use a similar netting process to determine the tax consequences of gains and losses on the sale of business and investment property. Both allow capital losses to be netted against capital gains and both separate long-term gains and losses from short-term gains and losses during the netting process. However, corporate taxpayers pay the same rate of tax on all types of income, including gains from the sale of property, whereas the tax rates on long-term capital gains for individual taxpayers can be 0, 15, 25, or 28 percent. The expanded netting process for individual taxpayers is discussed in Chapter 13, along with other special rules that apply to the individual income tax return. However, in this chapter, a brief introduction to the various long-term capital gain rates is presented.

Gains from the sale of Section 1202 small business stock that qualify for the 50-percent exclusion (see ¶ 806) plus gains and losses on the sale of collectibles held for more than a year are taxed at a maximum 28-percent tax rate (instead of the lower 0- or 15-percent tax rate). **Collectibles** include antiques, stamp and coin collections, rugs, artwork, gems, and metals.[50]

As discussed previously in the chapter, after Section 1231 gains and losses are netted against one another, any net Section 1231 gain is taxed as ordinary income to the extent of nonrecaptured Section 1231 losses for the past five years. Any excess gain is treated as long-term capital gain. Consequently, when individual taxpayers sell depreciable real business property at a gain, the Section 1231 gain may end up being taxed at the lower capital gain tax rate. Often, the reason depreciable property is sold at a gain is because its adjusted basis had been significantly reduced by depreciation expense. When depreciation is taken on the tax return, the taxpayer's income tax liability is reduced by the amount of the deduction times the taxpayer's marginal tax rate. Since an individual taxpayer's marginal (ordinary) tax rates are generally higher than the 15-percent maximum net capital gains tax rate, the tax laws require that to the extent the gain on the sale of depreciable real property is due to depreciation (and not appreciation in value), such gain is subject to a maximum 25-percent tax rate (instead of the lower 0- or 15-percent tax rate). The gain taxed due to depreciation of real property is known as **unrecaptured Section 1250 gain.** The amount of this gain equals the *lesser* of (1) the amount of the recognized gain or (2) the amount of accumulated depreciation taken on the property.[51]

---

[50] Code Sec. 1(h)(5)(A).   [51] Code Sec. 1(h)(1).

Example 56: Joe Ackers sells an apartment building for $440,000. Joe purchased the building years ago for $300,000, and over the years, he deducted MACRS totaling $100,000. Joe's adjusted basis in the building is $200,000 ($300,000 – $100,000) and his gain on the sale equals $240,000 ($440,000 – $200,000). Because Joe took depreciation deductions totaling $100,000 with respect to this property, $100,000 of the gain is unrecaptured Section 1250 gain, which is taxed at a maximum 25-percent tax rate. The remaining $140,000 of gain ($240,000 – $100,000) is taxed at a maximum 15-percent rate. The amount taxed at the 15-percent maximum rate represents the gain due to appreciation during Joe's ownership of the building ($440,000 – $300,000 cost basis).

 Spotlight: The 25-percent maximum tax rate applies only to *gains* from the sale of depreciable realty. When depreciable realty is sold at a loss, the loss is treated as a Section 1231 loss. When Section 1231 losses exceed Section 1231 gains, the net Section 1231 loss is deducted against ordinary income and is not part of the netting process involving capital gains and losses.

¶ 908 Summary

The process of computing the correct amount of recognized gain or loss (Chapter 8) along with the process of determining the character of that gain or loss (Chapter 9) are critical to correctly calculating a taxpayer's taxable income and income tax liability. Both corporate and individual taxpayers are limited on the amount of capital losses they can deduct in any given tax year. The best way to ensure that capital losses are not limited is to generate sufficient capital gains during the tax year.

Although capital gains are generated through the sale of capital assets, as seen in this chapter, there are several other ways in which capital gains and losses can be generated. The most common is through the sale of Section 1231 (long-term business) property. The tax laws governing Section 1231 property are, for the most part, taxpayer-friendly. However, the depreciation recapture and Section 1231 look back rules work to counteract the tax benefits associated with taking ordinary deductions, thereby making it more difficult for taxpayers to generate capital gains from the sale of business property.

GLOSSARY OF TERMS INTRODUCED IN THE CHAPTER

Capital asset. An asset other than the property listed in Code Sec. 1221. In general, a capital asset is either an asset held for investment or is a personal-use asset.

Collectibles. Works of art, antiques, rugs, metals, gems, stamps, coins, and other similar items of tangible personal property. If held more than a year, collectibles are subject to a maximum 28-percent tax rate when sold.

Holding period. Time period that generally begins the day after a taxpayer acquires property and ends on the day the taxpayer disposes of the property. Used in determining the short-term versus long-term nature of a recognized gain or loss.

Long-term capital gain or loss. A capital gain or loss on a capital asset held for more than one year.

Net capital gain. The excess of a net long-term capital gain over any net short-term capital loss. Relevant to individual taxpayers, as it represents the amount of capital gain subject to reduced tax rates.

Net long-term capital gain. The excess of long-term capital gains over long-term capital losses.

Net long-term capital loss. The excess of long-term capital losses over long-term capital gains.

Net short-term capital gain. The excess of short-term capital gains over short-term capital losses.

Net short-term capital loss. The excess of short-term capital losses over short-term capital gains.

Nonrecaptured net Section 1231 losses. The net Section 1231 losses recognized in the previous five tax years that have not previously caused a net Section 1231 gain to be treated as ordinary income.

Section 291 gain. Ordinary income recognized on the sale of depreciable real property that is sold by a C corporation.

Section 1231 gain. The gain on the sale, exchange, or condemnation of Section 1231 property other than ordinary gain due to depreciation recapture.

Section 1231 loss. A loss on the sale, exchange, or condemnation of Section 1231 property.

Section 1231 property. Land or depreciable property used in a business and held for more than one year.

Section 1244 stock. Stock issued by a domestic corporation in exchange for money or property at a time the corporation does not have more than $1 million in paid-in capital. The corporation must also meet an active business requirement unless it is a new corporation.

Section 1245 gain. The (ordinary income) gain that results from depreciation recapture on depreciable personal property held for more than one year. The amount of gain is equal to the *lesser* of the amount of the gain or the accumulated depreciation taken on the property.

Section 1250 gain. The (ordinary income) gain on the sale of depreciable real property that is recaptured as ordinary income. The amount recaptured is the *lesser* of the amount of the gain or the excess of the depreciation taken over the amount that would have been allowed under the straight-line method.

Short-term capital gain or loss. A capital gain or loss on a capital asset held for one year or less.

Unrecaptured Section 1250 gain. A term applicable only to individual taxpayers. The portion of the gain on the sale of depreciable realty that is taxed at a maximum 25-percent tax rate.

CHAPTER PROBLEMS

The following questions and problems relate to the discussion in Chapter 9, Property Transactions: Character of Gain or Loss, which begins at ¶ 900 in *Part III: Transactions Involving Business Property.*

Chapter 9 Discussion Questions

1. How is net capital gain calculated? What tax rates apply to net capital gains recognized by individual taxpayers?
2. Discuss the significance of a capital gain or loss.

3. a. What are the tax consequences to an individual who has an overall capital loss of $8,000?

    b. What are the tax consequences to a corporate taxpayer that has an overall net capital loss of $8,000?

4. a. What tax treatment applies to a capital loss carryover when an unmarried individual dies?

    b. What tax treatment applies to a capital loss carryover when a married individual dies and the couple files a joint return?

5. What is the tax treatment of a nonbusiness bad debt?

6. What rules apply to the recognition of a loss on a worthless security?

7. Why is equipment used in the taxpayer's business not considered a capital asset?

8. Under what circumstances would the gain on the sale of land be an ordinary gain, a capital gain, or a Section 1231 gain?

9. a. How long must a taxpayer hold a capital asset for the gain on its sale or exchange to be a long-term capital gain?

    b. How is the holding period determined if the taxpayer received the asset by inheritance?

    c. How is the holding period determined if the taxpayer received the asset in a like-kind exchange?

10. How do the tax laws treat the gain on the sale of a capital asset to a related person?

11. What special rule applies to the sale of a patent? What is the difference between a sale of a patent and a licensing of the right to use the patent?

12. Sharon Moss bought a tract of land in 20X1 as an investment. In 20X3, she subdivided the land into 20 lots but made no further improvements on them. In 20X7, she sold nine lots for a total of $315,000. The adjusted basis of each lot is $5,000. The total selling expense for the nine lots was $3,510. How are the gains on the lots and their selling expense treated for income tax purposes?

13. How much of a loss on the sale of Section 1244 stock may an unmarried individual recognize as an ordinary loss? How much of a loss on the sale of Section 1244 stock may a married couple recognize as an ordinary loss on a joint return? What is the tax treatment of any loss recognized on the sale of Section 1244 stock that exceeds the amount the taxpayer may recognize as an ordinary loss?

14. Discuss how taxpayers receive "the best of both worlds" with respect to Code Sec. 1231.

15. The gain on the sale of an asset used in a business can be comprised of both a Section 1245 gain and a Section 1231 gain. Can a loss on the sale of business property be comprised of both a Section 1245 loss and a Section 1231 loss?

16. Does an individual who operates a business as a sole proprietorship include capital gains and losses recognized on the sale or exchange of business property in calculating the net profit or loss from the business?

17. Does a taxpayer recognize ordinary income on the sale of depreciable personal property if the straight-line method (under ADS) is used?

18. Is depreciation recapture on the sale of depreciable realty placed in service after 1986 relevant to C corporations?

19. Explain the rationale of Congress when it enacted the depreciation recapture rules of Code Sec. 1245?

20. If a taxpayer sells a depreciable asset on the installment basis, what effect does Section 1245 recapture have on the amount of gain that must be recognized in the year of sale?

Chapter 9 Problems

1. Higgins Corporation realized the following capital gains and losses during 20X6:

Short-term capital gain from the sale of land held for investment	$10,000
Short-term capital loss from the sale of common stock	(18,000)
Long-term capital gain from the sale of corporate bonds	6,000
Long-term capital loss from the sale of common stock	(4,000)

Determine the effects of these transactions. Assume that Higgins Corporation had a net long-term capital gain of $1,000 in 20X3, a net long-term capital gain of $1,500 in 20X4, and a net short-term capital gain of $2,500 in 20X5.

2. Skagway Co., Inc. recognizes the following capital gains and losses during 20X4:

Short-term capital gain	$ 10,000
Short-term capital loss	(33,000)
Long-term capital gain	15,000
Long-term capital loss	(44,000)

On its 20X1 tax return, Skagway's netting of its capital gains and losses produced a net capital gain of $7,000.

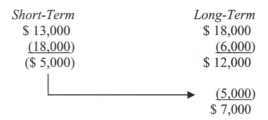

Short-Term	Long-Term
$ 13,000	$ 18,000
(18,000)	(6,000)
($ 5,000)	$ 12,000
	(5,000)
	$ 7,000

Compute Skagway's capital loss carryback to 20X1 and determine its capital loss carryover to 20X2.

3. Answer the same questions posed in Problem 2, except assume that the taxpayer is Damon Skadden, an individual taxpayer.

4. Roger Dales has $10,000 of ordinary income. In addition, Roger has a $5,000 long-term capital loss and a $500 short-term capital gain. How much of the capital loss can be used against ordinary income? What happens to the remaining loss?

5. Tony Rogers recognizes the following capital gains and losses during 2009:

Short-term capital gain from the sale of stock held for investment	$20,000
Short-term capital loss from the sale of land held as an investment	(22,000)
Long-term capital gain from the sale of corporate bonds	20,000
Long-term capital loss from the sale of common stock	(14,000)

Compute Tony's net capital gain. If Tony's taxable income (before considering the above items of gain or loss) is $55,000, what would be his 2009 tax liability? Tony's filing status is single.

6. Mark and Sara Hopkins are married and file a joint return. In 20X1, they invested $600,000 in NuTech Company. The stock qualifies as Section 1244 stock. On December 17, 20X6, they sold all of their NuTech Company stock for $100,000. They did not realize any other capital gains or losses during 20X6. What are the tax effects of the sale of the stock? If they called you just before they sold all of their NuTech Company stock, what advice would you give them that would provide them with a more favorable tax result?

7. Hank Jarbee bought 1,000 shares of WentLo Company for $20,000 on November 6, 20X5. The company declared bankruptcy on February 5, 20X6. The bankruptcy case was closed on October 12, 20X6, and at that time, the court informed the shareholders that their shares were worthless. What is the tax effect of Hank's loss?

8. A taxpayer purchases land held as an investment for $280,000 on January 5, 20X1. The taxpayer sells the land for $300,000 on January 5, 20X2. Compute the amount and character of the taxpayer's gain or loss.

9. Assume the same facts as in Problem 8, except the land was used in the taxpayer's trade or business. Compute the amount and character of the taxpayer's gain or loss.

10. A C corporation purchased an office building on January 1, 20X1, for $225,000 (exclusive of the land on which it was located). On January 1, 20X7, the corporation sells the building for $375,000. Depreciation of $93,750 was taken on the building using MACRS. Compute the amount and character of the recognized gain or loss from the sale.

11. Carla Anderson loaned her friend Debbie Jarvis $1,000 for personal purposes on May 8, 2007. On November 16, 2008, Debbie declared bankruptcy. Carla has learned that her loan is worthless. What is the tax effect to Carla?

12. Three years ago, Roswell Copying purchased a color copier for $80,000 and expensed it under Code Sec. 179 in the year it was placed in service. In the current year, Roswell traded in the old copier for a newer, smaller model worth $15,000. In exchange for the new copier, the manufacturer took Roswell's old copier and gave Roswell $5,000 cash. Compute the amount and nature of Roswell's gain or loss from the exchange.

13. Terrance Vincent sold a capital asset to a corporation in which he owned 60 percent of the value of the outstanding shares of stock. Terrance paid $50,000 for the asset three earlier, and the sales price to the corporation is $120,000.

    a. What are the tax consequences if the property is a capital asset in the hands of the corporation?

    b. What are the tax consequences if the property is depreciable Section 1231 property in the hands of the corporation?

    c. How would your answer to parts a. and b. change if Terrance owned 50 percent of the value of the outstanding shares in the C corporation?

14. John Adner, a farmer, subdivided an unimproved tract of land that he acquired approximately 20 years ago. In 20X1, he sold four lots for $10,000 each. The basis of each lot is $2,000, and the selling expenses are $400 per lot.

    a. What is the gain or loss on these transactions, and how will these transactions be taxed?

    b. If John sells five lots in 20X2 at the same price with selling expenses of $400 per lot, what will be the gain or loss, and how will these transactions be taxed?

15. Joan Miller purchased equipment for $50,000 and placed it in service in her business. Two years later, she sold the equipment after having claimed $33,000 in depreciation and Section 179 expense. Calculate the amount and character of Joan's recognized gain or loss assuming that the amount realized from the sale is:

    a. $12,000.

    b. $45,000.

    c. $60,000.

16. Finley Enterprises sold an apartment building in 2009 for $1 million. Finley purchased the building years ago for $780,000. Over the years, it claimed straight-line depreciation of $200,000 on the building. Finley has no other Section 1231 gains or losses or capital gains or losses during 2009. Finley does not have any nonrecaptured net Section 1231 losses from prior years. What are the tax consequences from the sale of the apartment building?

17. Cavanaugh Inc. sold a machine in 20X5. The terms of the sale stipulate that Cavanaugh is to receive a cash payment of $10,000 at the time of the sale and an installment note that calls for four annual payments of $20,000 on principal plus interest at 10 percent beginning one year after the date of sale. Cavanaugh purchased the machine in 20X1 for $59,000 and at the time of sale had claimed $40,000 in depreciation and the Section 179 expense. The machine

was subject to a mortgage of $14,000, which the buyer assumed. Based on this information, calculate:

   a. Cavanaugh's realized gain or loss;

   b. Cavanaugh's gross profit from the sale, total contract price, and gross profit percentage;

   c. The amount and character of the gain recognized in 20X5; and

   d. The amount and character of the gain to be recognized in each year from 20X6 though 20X9.

18. Max Wyatt has a $2,000 short-term capital gain on the sale of common stock, a $6,000 short-term capital loss on the sale of land held for investment, a $5,000 long-term capital loss on the sale of land held for investment, a $4,000 Section 1245 gain from the sale of depreciable equipment, and a $10,000 long-term capital gain on the sale of common stock.

   a. What is Max's net short-term capital gain or loss?

   b. What is Max's net long-term capital gain or loss?

   c. What is Max's net capital gain?

19. For 20X6, Brandon Manufacturing has a net Section 1231 gain of $28,000. Brandon reported the net Section 1231 gains or (losses) for the previous five years shown below. None of the losses ever caused a net Section 1231 gain in any year before 20X1 to be treated as an ordinary gain.

20X1	($14,000)
20X2	(7,000)
20X3	9,000
20X4	6,000
20X5	(2,000)

How much of the $28,000 Section 1231 gain realized in 20X6 is treated as ordinary income? How much is treated as a long-term capital gain?

20. After taking into consideration the depreciation recapture rules, Danik, Inc., a C corporation, has the following gains and losses resulting from business property held for more than one year:

Business casualty gain	$53,000
Business casualty loss	(22,000)
Theft loss	(6,000)
Section 1231 gain	5,000
Section 1231 loss	(14,000)

As of the beginning of the year, Danik's nonrecaptured Section 1231 losses are $12,000. Discuss the tax consequences of these gains and losses on Danik's corporate tax return.

21. Fuente Company sold its warehouse for $1,000,000. The company paid $1,400,000 for the building several years ago and over the years had properly claimed $216,000 of depreciation using the straight-line method. What is the amount and character of Fuente's gain or loss?

22. Two years ago, Drew Corporation (a C corporation) purchased 3,000 shares of stock in Nuco Corporation directly from Nuco for $300,000 in cash. The total capital of Nuco at that time was $900,000. Drew holds the shares in Nuco as an investment. Calculate the amount and character of the loss assuming that Drew sold all 3,000 shares for $180,000. What if the stock had been held by Frank Drew, a single individual, rather than by Drew Corporation?

23. Sara Lantz began to invest some of her excess cash from the income generated from her sole proprietorship in stamps to hold as an investment. She sold one of her stamp collections during the year for $20,000. She had purchased the collection in three years ago for $12,000. She is in the 35-percent marginal tax bracket for ordinary income. Sara did not

sell or exchange any other capital assets during the current year. How much will her income tax liability increase because of the sale of this stamp collection?

24. Nathan Pace realized a net Section 1231 gain of $8,000 on the sale of land used in his business. He had no nonrecaptured Section 1231 losses from previous tax years. He realized a $20,000 short-term capital gain on the sale of bonds he held for investment. Nathan realized a $5,000 long-term capital loss on the sale of stock held for investment. He did not sell or exchange any other capital assets during the year. What is his net capital gain? If he is in the 35-percent marginal tax bracket for ordinary income, how much additional tax will he pay due to these gains and loss?

25. Brenda Sizemore bought land in her own name for $6,000 on March 1, 20X7. She died in an accident on November 29, 20X7. At the date of her death, the land was worth $7,000. Her living trust specified that Sizemore Corporation was to receive the land in the event of her death. Her executor did not elect the alternate valuation date. Sizemore Corporation received the land from the trustee on December 15, 20X7, when it had a fair market value of $7,100. The corporation sold the land on February 11, 20X8, for $7,500. What is the amount and character of Sizemore Corporation's gain on the sale of the land?

Chapter 9 Review Problems

1. Years ago, Robert Reese purchased land for an investment at a cost of $50,000. In the current year, when his land was worth $150,000, he exchanged his land for other land that he would hold for investment. The new land had an FMV of $120,000. He also received $30,000 in cash.

   a. What is Robert's amount of realized gain or loss?

   b. What is the amount and character of Robert's recognized gain or loss?

   c. What is Robert's basis in the newly acquired land?

2. Howard Corporation had equipment destroyed in a fire. The equipment had an original cost of $400,000, and it had accumulated depreciation recorded to the date it was destroyed of $140,000. Howard Corporation collected $325,000 in insurance proceeds and 10 days later bought equipment with the same functional use for $300,000.

   a. What is Howard's adjusted basis in the old equipment?

   b. What is Howard's realized gain or loss?

   c. What is the amount and character of Howard's recognized gain or loss?

   d. What is Howard's basis in the new equipment?

Chapter 9 Comprehensive Review Question

Kyle Brown bought computer equipment (five-year property) for his business on May 1, 2007, at an auction for a bargain price of $200,000. He immediately placed the equipment in service in his business. He claimed $20,000 of Section 179 expense on the computer equipment and began depreciating the remaining $180,000 using MACRS and the half-year convention.

On June 16, 2009, he sold the property on an installment basis. He received $40,000 cash on the date of sale. The buyer assumed Kyle's $50,000 debt on the property and gave Kyle a $210,000 installment note that called for $30,000 payments each year on principal plus interest for seven years beginning on June 16, 2010. The note carried interest at the market rate. Kyle's nonrecaptured net Section 1231 losses are $2,000 at the beginning of 2009.

a. Compute Kyle's adjusted basis in the five-year property at the time of the sale.

b. Compute the gross profit, total contract price, and gross profit percentage.

c. What is the amount and character of the gain recognized in 2009?

d. What is the amount and character of the gain recognized in 2010?

Chapter 9 Research Question

Bruce Wilson won $2 million in the state lottery. The lottery pays out the prize money in 20 annual installments of $100,000 each. After receiving three $100,000 installments, Bruce sold the remaining $1.7 million of payments for $1 million, reported the $1 million as a long-term capital gain on his tax return, and paid tax on that amount at the 15-percent tax rate. Bruce's tax return has been selected for audit by the IRS. Is he likely to prevail on his treatment of the $1 million sale of his future lottery payments as a long-term capital gain?

PART IV:
Calculating Tax Liability and Taxes Owed

CHAPTER 10

NOLs, AMT, and Other Business Taxes

LEARNING OBJECTIVES

1. Explain the concept of a net operating loss (NOL), demonstrate how it is calculated, and illustrate how it can be used to offset taxable income in other tax years.

2. Explain the concept of the alternative minimum tax (AMT) and the reason it exists in the income tax system.

3. Demonstrate how the AMT is calculated for both corporate and individual taxpayers.

4. List the reasons for the accumulated earnings tax and the personal holding company (PHC) tax.

5. Determine which corporations are subject to the accumulated earnings tax and the PHC tax and compute the taxes.

¶ 1000 Introduction

After corporate or individual taxpayers compute their taxable income, they calculate their regular income tax liability using the applicable progressive income tax rates. Taxpayers reporting negative taxable income do not have any regular income tax liability and may be allowed to carry over the amounts to other tax years and to deduct them against gross income generated in those years. The amount taxpayers are allowed to carry over to other tax years is known as a net operating loss (NOL), which may be a different amount from the amount of negative taxable income reported on the taxpayer's income tax return. The calculation of the NOL and a discussion of how it can be used to offset gross income in other tax years are presented in this chapter.

Besides regular income taxes, C corporations may be subject to several additional taxes enacted to address issues that arose over time when Congress felt it was necessary to take corrective action to ensure a more accurate determination of the proper taxes owed. These taxes include the alternative minimum tax (AMT), the accumulated earnings tax, and the personal holding company (PHC) tax. Although the accumulated earnings tax and the PHC tax apply only to C corporations, individuals may be subject to the AMT.

The AMT system is an alternative method of calculating income tax; it has its own definitions of exclusions from or deductions against gross income. The AMT is an add-on income tax that represents the excess of a taxpayer's tentative minimum tax (computed under the AMT system) over the taxpayer's regular income tax (computed using the rules discussed in Chapters 1–9). The AMT system was enacted to prevent taxpayers from taking advantage of exclusions and deductions available under the regular tax system to such an extent that their income tax obligation was eliminated or reduced to very low levels. For the most part, the exclusions and deductions allowed under the AMT system are less generous than those allowed in the regular income tax system. Consequently, taxpayers who take advantage of the exclusions and deductions incorporated into the regular income tax system may find themselves subject to AMT. The AMT applies to both corporate and individual taxpayers.

The accumulated earnings tax is a penalty tax developed to keep corporations from avoiding the second layer of taxation by retaining previously taxed earnings in the corporation beyond the reasonable needs of the business in lieu of distributing these earnings as dividends. The PHC tax is another penalty tax designed to prevent individual taxpayers from gaining a tax advantage by shifting their investment portfolios into corporate form. Each of these topics will be taken up sequentially in this chapter.

NET OPERATING LOSSES

In broad terms, the Internal Revenue Code (the "Code") taxes income from all sources except those specifically identified as exclusions from gross income. As discussed in Chapters 5 through 9, businesses can deduct from gross income various expenditures associated with generating income. However, because the life of the business is arbitrarily divided into tax years for reporting gross income and expenses, the taxable income or loss reported on the tax return for any particular year may not accurately reflect the overall, long-term performance of the business. Consequently, if the government did not allow taxpayers to offset losses from one tax year against profits in another, businesses could owe taxes on net profits from years of good performance without deriving any tax benefits from net losses generated in years of weaker performance. That situation might deter taxpayers from starting new businesses because losses in the earlier years are common.

The NOL rules were enacted to ease the unduly drastic consequences of taxing income strictly on an annual basis.[1] They were designed to permit a taxpayer to offset gross income from profitable years with losses from unprofitable years. The current tax law generally allows taxpayers to carry back a NOL to the previous two tax years and then to carry forward any unutilized NOL another 20 years.

 Reason for the Rule: Since a carryback requires amending a tax return that has already been filed with the IRS, the carryback period typically is limited to tax years for which the statute of limitations for amendment by the taxpayer has not yet expired. Since the carryforward goes into years for which the taxpayer has not yet filed returns, the carryforward period tends to be longer.

¶ 1001 Tax Treatment of NOLs

The tax laws allow NOLs generated from carrying on a trade or business to offset gross income generated in other tax years. A NOL may arise from losses generated either by a corporation or by an individual engaged in a trade or business. Flow-through entities, like partnerships and S corporations, do not pay income taxes, and consequently, do not generate NOLs that need to be carried over to other tax years. Instead, any operating losses from such entities are passed on to their owners and may result in a NOL on the owner's income tax return. NOLs reported on an individual's income tax return are introduced in this chapter and then are discussed in greater detail in Chapter 13.

---

[1] Code Sec. 172.

.01 Carryover Provisions

The current tax law generally allows taxpayers to carry back a NOL to the two previous tax years. Any amounts not utilized in those years can be carried forward to the following 20 years.[2] When a NOL is carried back, the NOL must first be offset against gross income from the second preceding tax year before it can be carried over to the first preceding year. Any unutilized losses during the carryback period are carried over sequentially for 20 years, or until fully utilized.

Special carryback and carryover rules for certain types of losses. There are special carryback and carryover rules for certain types of net operating losses (e.g., a casualty loss, farming loss, specified liability loss, excess interest loss, bad debt loss of a commercial bank, or loss sustained by a real estate investment trust).

Special carryback period for 2008 losses. An eligible small businesses may elect to carry back a net operating loss for a tax year beginning or ending in 2008 for three, four, or five years. A business is an eligible small business if its average annual gross receipts did not exceed $15 million for the three-tax-year period ending with the prior tax year.

Taxpayers have the option of electing to forego the entire carryback period and to carry the NOL forward for 20 years instead.[3] The election must be made by the due date (including extensions) of the return for the year of the loss; it can be made by attaching a statement to the taxpayer's tax return. The election, once made, is irrevocable.

Example 1: A taxpayer generates a NOL in 2009. The taxpayer carries back the NOL to 2007. To the extent the NOL is not fully utilized in 2007, the taxpayer carries over the NOL to 2008. Any NOL not utilized in 2008 is carried over to offset gross income on the taxpayer's 2010 through 2029 tax returns until fully utilized. Alternatively, the taxpayer can elect to forego the carryback period and carry forward the entire NOL to 2010. Any NOL not utilized in 2010 would be carried forward to 2011 through 2029.

¶ 1002 Calculating a Corporation's NOL

Simply put, a NOL is the excess of allowed deductions over gross income. When a corporation reports negative taxable income, it generally indicates that the corporation may have incurred a NOL. All expenses deducted on the corporate tax return are business related, but one adjustment that must be made to negative taxable income is to add back any NOL deduction from a previous year. Without this adjustment, the taxpayer would be taking a double deduction for the same NOL. Also, the tax law does not allow the domestic production activities deduction to create or increase a taxpayer's NOL.

Example 2: In 2009, Centrol Corporation reports a negative taxable income of $50,000. Included in this calculation is a NOL deduction of $30,000 carried over from 2008. In calculating Centrol's 2009 NOL deduction, the NOL carried over from 2008 is disregarded. Centrol's NOL from 2008 remains $30,000, and its NOL for 2009 is $20,000 (assuming no adjustment for the domestic production activities deduction must be made).

.01 The DRD and the NOL

The DRD is not a typical deduction because it is computed as a percentage of dividends, and it is not the result of an expenditure made by the taxpayer. Nonetheless, the tax law does not require that corporations add back to negative taxable income any of the DRD when computing its NOL for the year. Consequently, the DRD can produce or contribute to a corporation's NOL.

Chapter 4 indicated that the DRD is equal to 70, 80, or 100 percent of dividend income, depending on the corporation's percentage ownership of stock in the corporation paying the dividends (see ¶ 411.02). Only corporations that are part of an affiliated group (in which the

---

[2] Code Sec. 172(b)(1). [3] Code Sec. 172(b)(3).

corporation's ownership is at least 80 percent) are allowed to deduct 100 percent of the dividends included in income. For corporations that are not part of an affiliated group, the DRD is limited to 70 percent or 80 percent of taxable income.

If a corporation computes its DRD using the applicable 70 or 80 percent of dividends received and if deducting the full DRD causes the corporation to sustain a NOL for a tax year, the taxable income limit on the DRD does not apply in computing the corporation's NOL. Accordingly, the full DRD can contribute to the taxpayer's NOL for the year.

Example 3: Abbet, Inc. owns less than 20 percent of the stock in Bahara. During 2009, Bahara pays Abbet a $100,000 dividend. Abbet's taxable income is computed as follows:

Dividend income	$100,000
Ordinary income	40,000
Less: Business expenses	(80,000)
Taxable income before DRD	$ 60,000
Less: DRD ($100,000 × 70%))	(70,000)
Taxable loss	($ 10,000)

Deducting 70 percent of the dividends received produces a taxable loss; therefore, the taxable income limit on DRDs does not apply, and Abbet's DRD equals $70,000 (70 percent of the dividends received). Since Abbet's negative taxable income is not due to a NOL carryover from another tax year, its NOL for the year equals $10,000.

Example 4: Mavelton owns less than 20 percent of the stock in Reiter, Inc. During 2009, Mavelton receives $100,000 of dividends from Reiter. In addition, Mavelton reports $40,000 of income and $50,000 of deductions from business operations. Mavelton computes its 2009 taxable income as follows:

Dividends received	$100,000
Business income	40,000
Less: Business expenses	(50,000)
Taxable income before DRD	$ 90,000
Less: DRD (limited to 70% of $90,000)	(63,000)
Taxable income	$ 27,000

Because Mavelton owns less than 20 percent of the stock in Reiter, its DRD cannot exceed 70 percent of the $100,000 of dividends it receives during the year. However, if Mavelton were to deduct the full $70,000 ($100,000 × 70%) against its taxable income, it would not create a tax loss, and therefore, the DRD is computed as the *lesser* of 70 percent of (1) the dividends received or (2) the taxable income before the DRD. Mavelton reduces its taxable income by $63,000 ($90,000 × 70%).

 Planning Pointer: When a corporation's DRD is limited by the taxable income limitation, the amount by which the DRD is reduced is lost and will never create a tax benefit to the corporation. For example, in Example 4, Mavelton's DRD normally would be $70,000 ($100,000 × 70%). Thus, the taxable income limitation effectively increases Mavelton's taxable income by $7,000 ($70,000 − $63,000), and Mavelton ends up paying more income taxes as a result of the limitation.

A corporation can avoid losing the benefit of the DRD by (1) accelerating income to the year and/or postponing deductions to a subsequent year, or (2) accelerating sufficient deductions and/or postponing sufficient income to create a NOL and avoid the taxable income limitation on the DRD.

For example, if Mavelton were to be able to accelerate $20,001 of deductions into the current year, its taxable income before the DRD would be $69,999 ($90,000 – $20,001). If Mavelton subtracted the full $70,000 DRD from that amount, a NOL would result. Thus, Mavelton's taxable loss for the year would equal $1 ($69,999 – $70,000 DRD). Mavelton reduces its 2009 taxable income by an additional $27,001, and its tax liability in 2009 is reduced to zero. Assuming a 15-percent tax rate, the tax savings from these deductions equals $4,050 ($27,001 × 15%). Normally a taxpayer with a 15-percent marginal tax rate would expect $3,000 in tax savings from a $20,001 deduction ($20,001 × 15%); therefore, accelerating expenses into the current year results in an additional $1,050 ($4,050 – $3,000) in tax savings.

Example 5: Continuing with Example 4, in 2011 Mavelton incurs a $30,000 NOL that it carries back to 2009.

Taxable income before DRD and NOL deduction	$90,000
Less: DRD (no change, still limited to 70% of $90,000)	(63,000)
Taxable income before NOL carryback	$27,000
Less: NOL deduction (limited to taxable income)	(27,000)
Taxable income	$ 0

Since the taxable income is less than the NOL carryback, the NOL deduction is limited to the taxable income, and the $3,000 difference between the $30,000 NOL carryback and the $27,000 taxable income may be carried over to a subsequent year.

¶ 1003 Calculating an Individual Taxpayer's NOL

As discussed in Chapters 1 and 4, the calculation of an individual taxpayer's taxable income includes both business and nonbusiness deductions. In particular, incorporated into the tax laws are deductions from adjusted gross income (AGI) for various personal expenses (itemized deductions) as well as "free" deductions like the standard deduction and personal exemptions. Since the tax laws governing NOLs are intended to allow businesses to deduct operating losses against gross income generated in other tax years, when an individual taxpayer reports negative taxable income, it is important to determine the extent to which the taxpayer's negative amount is attributable to business losses versus that which is due to personal deductions taken on the tax return.

The actual calculation of an individual's NOL is presented in Chapter 13 where the rules regarding the calculation of an individual's taxable income are described in greater detail than presented thus far in this textbook. However, with few exceptions, an individual's deductions from AGI (which include the taxpayer's personal and dependency exemptions plus the *greater* of the taxpayer's standard deduction or itemized deductions) are not permitted to generate an individual taxpayer's NOL that can be used to offset gross income in other tax years. Furthermore, any reductions to taxable income that result from the domestic production activities deduction (see ¶ 509) or NOL carryovers are added back to an individual's taxable income in computing the NOL generated during the year. Capital losses in excess of capital gains that are deducted in computing taxable income are limited when computing the individual's NOL. (See ¶ 1305.)

¶ 1004 Utilizing a NOL

Like any other business deduction, a NOL carryover is a deduction from gross income. The NOL deduction is applied against income in general and is not restricted to offsetting only business income. A taxpayer's **NOL deduction** is the total of the NOL carryforwards and carrybacks to the tax year. Each carryback and carryforward is separately computed under the rules described at ¶ 1002 and ¶ 1003 and then is combined with the others into one total NOL deduction.[4]

Example 6: For 2009, a corporation has income totaling $110,000 and deductions of $50,000. The corporation has an unused NOL from 2008 of $40,000 that originated in 2007. This amount is carried over to 2009 and becomes the corporation's NOL deduction for 2009. The NOL deduction reduces the corporation's taxable income to $20,000 ($110,000 – $50,000 – $40,000).

A NOL generally can be carried back two years, and if taxable income for the carryback years is not sufficient to absorb the entire loss, any remaining NOL can be carried forward for 20 years following the year it is generated. Alternatively, the taxpayer can elect to forego the carryback period and just carry forward the NOL for the next 20 years. If the NOL carried over to another tax year exceeds the taxable income in that year, the corporation must modify its taxable income to determine how much of the NOL is utilized in the carryover year. The excess of the NOL carryover over the corporation's modified taxable income is the amount of NOL that can be carried over to the next subsequent tax year.

Example 7: A corporation reports negative taxable income of $25,000 in 2009. The corporation carries back the NOL to 2007, when it reported taxable income of $14,000. Since the amount of the NOL exceeds the taxable income from 2007, the corporation carries over the $11,000 excess to 2008 ($25,000 – $14,000).

Example 8: Lax Corporation incurs a NOL of $100,000 for calendar year 2009. After carrying the NOL back to its two previous tax years, Lax carries forward a $30,000 NOL to 2010. In 2010, Lax reports $500,000 of gross income and business expenses of $540,000. Lax's taxable income for 2010 is computed as follows:

Gross income	$500,000
Less: Business expense	(540,000)
Taxable income before NOL deduction	($ 40,000)

Since Lax's taxable income before any NOL deduction is negative, it is unable to utilize any of the NOL carryover from 2009. Lax carries forward to 2011 the $30,000 NOL from 2009 and the $40,000 NOL from 2010. The combined $70,000 NOL will be deducted against Lax's gross income in 2011. To the extent that Lax can utilize any of the $70,000, it will be deemed to utilize the NOL carryover from 2009, followed by the NOL carryover from 2010.

.01 Modified Taxable Income

A NOL carried back to a previous tax year is used to offset gross income in that year. Accordingly, taxable income is reduced as well. The amounts for several exclusions and deductions taken on the tax return are based on a percentage of taxable income. For example, both individual and corporate taxpayers are limited on the amounts they can deduct for charitable contributions. Therefore, the question may be raised as to whether these items must be recomputed when determining the extent to which a NOL carryover has been utilized.

---

[4] Code Sec. 172(a); Reg. § 1.172-1.

Modified taxable income for corporate taxpayers. A corporation's taxable income is used both in determining the amount of the charitable contribution deduction (see ¶ 511) and the dividends received deduction (DRD) (see ¶ 411.02). However, in the process of recomputing the taxable income in a carryback year, the tax laws specifically state that the taxpayer does not recompute these deductions. Instead, the NOL is deducted after both the DRD and the charitable contribution deduction have been taken into consideration. The NOL is utilized in the carryback year to the extent that it does not reduce taxable income below $0. Any excess NOL represents the taxpayer's NOL carryover to the next subsequent tax year.[5]

Corporations can claim a refund of taxes attributable to a NOL carryback on Form 1139, *Corporation Application for Tentative Refund,* or on an amended Form 1120, *U.S. Corporation Income Tax Return;* however, filing Form 1139 produces the quickest refund. The difference between the taxes originally paid in the carryback year and the tax on the taxable income recomputed with the NOL deduction may be claimed as a refund.

If the recomputed taxable income is zero or negative, the entire tax originally paid is refunded. For example, Mavelton from Example 5 would be entitled to a refund for the entire amount of taxes paid in 2009. When taxable income is reduced to less than zero after the entire NOL carryover is taken into consideration, a portion of the NOL may remain for carryover to the next subsequent year. For example, in Example 5, Mavelton has a $3,000 NOL carryover to a subsequent year.

Example 9: Assume the same facts as in Example 5, except that in 2011, Mavelton incurs a $20,000 NOL that it carries back to 2009.

Taxable income before DRD and NOL deduction	$90,000
DRD (no change, still limited to 70% of $90,000)	(63,000)
Taxable income before NOL carryback	$27,000
NOL deduction	(20,000)
Taxable income	$ 7,000

Here, Mavelton is able to fully absorb the NOL carryback in 2009. When filing its claim for a refund for 2009, Mavelton will request a refund of the difference between the taxes it paid on $27,000 of taxable income and the taxes it would have paid on $7,000 of taxable income.

Example 10: In 2009, Cablenet, Inc. reports taxable income of $100,000 before taking into consideration a $25,000 charitable contribution. Cablenet's charitable contribution for 2009 is limited to $10,000 ($100,000 × 10%). After deducting its charitable contribution, Cablenet reports taxable income of $90,000, which results in an $18,850 tax liability. Cablenet carries forward the unutilized $15,000 charitable contribution to 2010 ($25,000 – $10,000). In 2010, Cablenet reports sufficient taxable income to fully utilize the carryover.

In 2011, Cablenet reports a $210,000 net operating loss, which it carries back to 2009—the first available carryback year. When determining how much of the NOL is utilized in the carryback year, Cablenet does not recompute the DRD or the charitable contribution deduction. Therefore, the starting point in the calculation is taxable income before the NOL deduction.

Taxable income before NOL deduction	$90,000
NOL deduction (limited to taxable income)	(90,000)
Taxable income	$ 0

---

[5] Code Sec. 172(b)(2); Reg. § 1.172-5(a)(2)(iii).

Cablenet uses $90,000 of the NOL from 2011 to offset its 2009 taxable income to zero. Since there is no tax liability on $0 taxable income, Cablenet files an amended return for 2009 or Form 1139 to claim a refund for the $18,850 of taxes it paid that year. Cablenet carries forward the remaining $120,000 NOL ($210,000 – $90,000) to 2010 and recomputes its taxable income (without recomputing its DRD or charitable contribution deduction) and its tax liability in that year.

 Spotlight: The tax law specifically requires that modified taxable income be computed without recalculation of the DRD or charitable contribution deductions. This rule prevents taxpayers from losing out on the tax benefits of any charitable contribution carryovers. In Example 10, Cablenet was able to fully utilize the $15,000 charitable contribution carryover from 2009 in 2010. Thus, between 2009 and 2010, Cablenet generated tax savings from making a $25,000 charitable contribution in 2009.

If Cablenet had been required to recompute its charitable contribution limit in 2009 after the NOL deduction, none of the $25,000 contribution would have been deductible since recomputed taxable income would have been $0. Cablenet would have been able to utilize $100,000 of the NOL (to reduce original taxable income of $100,000 to $0) and carry forward $110,000 ($210,000 – $100,000) to 2010. It also would have carried forward the full $25,000 charitable contribution to 2010 since none of it would have been deducted in 2009. Because the charitable contributions can be carried forward only five years (see ¶ 511.04), Cablenet may have some difficulty utilizing the full $25,000 carryover. If the tax laws required that Cablenet recompute the taxable income limitation for 2010 after deducting the NOL carryover from 2009, it is likely that its charitable contribution deduction would be limited. Since we know that Cablenet generated a NOL in 2011, only 2012, 2013, and 2014 would remain to absorb the charitable contribution carryover.

Modified taxable income for individual taxpayers. Because both personal and business expenses are deducted on an individual's income tax return, the computation of modified taxable income is more complicated for individual taxpayers. For several items that are deductible on the individual tax return, the amount of the deduction depends on the taxpayer's AGI for the year. For example, medical expenses, personal casualty and theft losses, and miscellaneous itemized deductions are all deductible as itemized deductions; however, only amounts that exceed a certain percentage of the AGI can be deducted. When carrying back a NOL from another tax year, the taxpayer's deductions for such items must be recomputed. The NOL rules for individuals are discussed in Chapter 13 (see ¶ 1305).

.02 Carryback and Carryover Periods

When applying a NOL to the allowed carryover years, the taxpayer must start by carrying the NOL to the second preceding tax year. To the extent that the NOL is not fully utilized in that year, it is carried over to the immediately preceding tax year. Any NOL that cannot be utilized in the carryback period is carried forward to the year immediately following the loss year, then to the second year following the loss year, until the loss is used up or the carryover period expires, whichever occurs first.[6] If the taxpayer elects to forego the carryback period, the NOL must first be applied to the first tax year following the year the NOL is generated before it can be deducted in the second subsequent year.

---

[6] Code Sec. 172(b).

Example 11: A corporation generates a $52,000 NOL in 2009. The corporation's modified taxable income is computed as follows:

2007	$ 9,000
2008	4,000
2010	13,000
2011	12,000
2012	80,000

The $52,000 loss is first carried back to 2007. After offsetting the $9,000 of modified taxable income in that year, the corporation carries the remaining $43,000 ($52,000 – $9,000) over to 2008 and uses it to offset the $4,000 of modified taxable income in that year. The $39,000 ($43,000 – $4,000) of remaining NOL is then carried forward to 2010, 2011, and 2012 until it is entirely used up.

Carryovers from multiple periods. If a taxpayer has NOLs for more than one year and each is carried to the same tax year, the NOLs are applied in the order in which they occurred. This method ensures that the oldest carryovers (those that would expire first) are utilized first.

.03 Deriving Tax Benefits from a NOL

Because a NOL deduction reduces the taxpayer's gross income, tax savings are derived when a NOL is carried over to a previous or to a subsequent tax year. Like all deductions, the tax savings produced depend on the taxpayer's marginal tax rate. For example, in Example 11, the $52,000 NOL is carried over to multiple tax years, and although the taxpayer must wait until filing the tax returns for the carryforward years to derive the tax savings from the NOL deductions, assuming that the taxpayer generates sufficient taxable income in the carryover period, the taxpayer eventually will realize the tax benefits of the NOL.

Example 12: Continuing with Example 11, by utilizing the $52,000 NOL generated in 2009 by carrying back the NOL to 2007 and 2008, the taxpayer can file a claim for a refund of taxes paid in those years of $1,350 and $600, respectively. When the corporation carries forward the remaining NOL to 2010 through 2012, it will generate additional tax savings in those years.

Year	Tax Savings
2007	$1,350 ($9,000 × 15%)
2008	600 ($4,000 × 15%)
2010	1,950 ($13,000 × 15%)
2011	1,800 ($12,000 × 15%)
2012	3,950 [($9,000 × 25%) + ($5,000 × 34%)]
Total tax savings	$9,650

Alternatively, the taxpayer could elect to forego the carryback period and could carry over the NOL to 2010 through 2012. This would produce total tax savings of $10,950.

Year	Tax Savings
2010	$ 1,950 ($13,000 × 15%)
2011	1,800 ($12,000 × 15%)
2012	7,200 [($22,000 × 25%) + ($5,000 × 34%)]
Total tax savings	$10,950

Planning Pointer: The decision whether to waive the carryback of a NOL depends on the taxpayer's particular situation. For example, if the taxpayer expects substantially more gross income in future years, the waiver would be useful because the marginal tax rate would be higher. The additional tax savings in those later years would need to be weighed against the (perhaps lower) immediate tax benefits derived from filing a claim for a refund of taxes from the two carryback years.

For example, the taxpayer in Example 12 would generate greater tax savings ($10,950 versus $9,650) by electing to forego the carryback period because its marginal tax rate in 2012 is higher than the 15-percent tax rate in 2007 to 2008. However, the additional tax savings will not be realized for three years. Because the marginal tax rate in the third carryforward year is not known with certainty at the time the election must be made, the taxpayer must weigh the possibility of generating additional tax savings against the certain refund amount generated in the carryback period.

ALTERNATIVE MINIMUM TAX

Many provisions in the Code allow taxpayers to reduce their total income by investing or participating in activities that produce income that is excluded from gross income or in activities that produce expenses that reduce taxable income. By properly investing in these types of activities, taxpayers are able to reduce their tax liability to relatively low amounts when compared to their total economic income. The **alternative minimum tax (AMT)** was first enacted to enhance equity in the income tax system by ensuring that all taxpayers pay at least some minimum income taxes each year.

Statistics indicated that many individual and corporate taxpayers were taking such effective advantage of deductions and credits afforded to them under the regular federal income tax system that they were often able to reduce or eliminate their federal income tax obligations. Before the Tax Reform Act of 1969, many high-income taxpayers who could take advantage of tax preferences paid a significantly lower effective tax rate on their economic income than did other taxpayers. In some instances, millionaires paid little or no tax. In an attempt to curb this practice, Congress enacted a minimum tax system that created a different, more restrictive, set of rules for calculating what deductions and exclusions would be allowed under the alternative system. Taxpayers calculate their tax liability under both the regular tax system and the alternative tax system and pay the higher of the two taxes.

¶ 1005 Taxpayers Subject to AMT

Both C corporations and individuals may be subject to AMT. The calculation of AMT is similar for both types of taxpayers; however, because personal deductions are permitted on the individual tax return, differences also exist in the calculation of corporate and individual AMT. Only certain larger corporations are subject to the corporate AMT, and only those whose tax liability under the AMT system exceeds their regular tax liability actually pay AMT. All individuals are subject to AMT when their regular income tax liabilities are less than the amount of tax computed using the AMT system.

.01 Corporate Taxpayers Subject to AMT

Large corporations are subject to AMT; small corporations are not. A corporation is not subject to AMT in its first year of existence.[7] After the first year, a corporation qualifies as a small corporation and is not subject to AMT if:

1. Its *average* annual gross receipts for its first three years after 1993 but before the current year did not exceed $5 million and

---

[7] Code Sec. 55(e)(1)(C).

2. Its *average* annual gross receipts for all subsequent three-year periods before its current tax year did not exceed $7.5 million.[8]

For the average annual gross receipts test, gross receipts in the first year must be annualized if the corporation is in existence for less than 12 months during its first year.[9]

Example 13: A calendar year corporation is incorporated on October 5, 2009. The corporation will qualify as a small corporation in 2009 regardless of its gross receipts for the year. To qualify as a small corporation in 2010, its *average* annual gross receipts for 2009 and 2010 must not exceed $5 million. The corporation's gross receipts for 2009 must be computed on an annualized basis in accordance with Code Sec. 448(c)(3)(B).

Once a corporation qualifies as a small corporation, it will continue to be exempt from AMT for as long as its *average* gross receipts for the prior three-year period do not exceed $7.5 million. Once a corporation fails to qualify as a small corporation, it cannot qualify in any subsequent tax year.

Example 14: Brownett Corporation, a calendar year taxpayer, has been in existence since January 1, 2001. To qualify as a small corporation in 2009, Brownett's *average* gross receipts for the three tax years from 2001–2003 must have been $5 million or less, and its *average* gross receipts for the periods 2004–2006, 2005–2007, and 2006–2008 must have been $7.5 million or less. If Brownett qualifies as a small business in 2009, it will continue to qualify as a small business for 2010 as long as its *average* gross receipts for the period 2007–2009 are $7.5 million or less. If it fails to qualify as a small business in 2009, it cannot qualify as a small corporation in 2010 or in any subsequent tax year.

.02 Individual Taxpayers Subject to AMT

Technically, all individuals are required to compute their income tax liability under both the regular and the AMT systems and to pay the higher of the two tax amounts. In reality, most taxpayers pay sufficient tax under the regular tax system and therefore are not subject to AMT. However, recent reductions in regular tax rates, the continuing addition of deductions and credits under the regular income tax system, and a lack of inflation adjustments in the AMT structure have resulted in more individual taxpayers being subject to AMT than ever before. In 1969 when the AMT was first introduced, 155 individual taxpayers were subject to AMT. If Congress had not increased the exemption amounts for 2008, 26.8 million individuals were expected to have to pay the AMT (up from 4.1 million individual taxpayers for 2007).

¶ 1006 The Corporate AMT Formula

The AMT is an add-on tax that taxpayers owe in addition to regular income taxes, if the income tax computed under the AMT system exceeds the income taxes they owe under the regular tax system. The AMT system is like any other tax system in which a tax rate is applied to a tax base. The tax base used in the AMT system is called the **AMT base**. This amount is analogous to taxable income in the regular income tax system. The AMT rate for corporations is 20 percent of the AMT base.

Example 15: A corporation subject to AMT has an AMT base of $60,000. The minimum amount of income tax it will owe for the year is $12,000 ($60,000 × 20%). If its regular income tax exceeds that amount, the corporation will not owe any AMT.

The AMT base is computed by subtracting out an exemption amount from the **alternative minimum taxable income (AMTI).** The corporate AMT exemption is $40,000 for corporations with AMTI that does not exceed $150,000. For corporations with AMTI in excess of $150,000, the AMT exemption is reduced by 25 percent of the excess.[10] The AMT exemption is zero for corporations with AMTI of $310,000 or more.

---

[8] Code Sec. 55(e).

[9] Code Secs. 55(e)(1)(D) and 448(c)(3)(B).

[10] Code Sec. 55(d)(3).

Example 16: A corporation subject to AMT has $120,000 of AMTI. Since this amount does not exceed $150,000, its AMT exemption equals $40,000. Thus, the corporation's AMT base is $80,000 ($120,000 – $40,000). The minimum amount of income tax it will owe for the year is $16,000 ($80,000 × 20%). If the corporation's regular income tax exceeds this amount, it will not owe any AMT.

Example 17: A corporation subject to AMT has $220,000 of AMTI. Since this amount exceeds $150,000, the corporation's initial AMT exemption is reduced to $22,500.

Initial exemption		$40,000
AMTI	$220,000	
	(150,000)	
	$ 70,000	
	× 25%	(17,500)
AMT exemption		$22,500

The corporation's AMT base equals $197,500 ($220,000 – $22,500), and the minimum amount of income tax the corporation will owe for the year is $39,500 ($197,500 × 20%). If the corporation's regular income tax is $23,000, its AMT will be $16,500 ($39,500 – $23,000). Through the regular income tax system the taxpayer pays $23,000. When the $16,500 of AMT is added to this amount, the taxpayer pays a total of $39,500, which is equal to the minimum amount of income tax owed as computed under the AMT system.

Example 18: A corporation subject to AMT has $320,000 of AMTI. Since this amount exceeds $310,000, its AMT exemption is $0. The corporation's AMT base equals $320,000, and the minimum amount of income tax it will owe for the year is $64,000 ($320,000 × 20%). If the corporation's regular income tax is less than this amount, it will owe the difference as AMT.

Many of the tax rules governing the calculation of AMTI are the same as those used in computing taxable income. Therefore, the calculation of AMTI involves adjusting the taxpayer's taxable income for various adjustments and preferences.[11] The calculation of the corporate AMT is shown in Figure 10-1.

---

[11] Code Sec. 55.

Figure 10-1 Calculation of Corporate AMT

	Corporate taxable income
+	Tax preferences
±	AMT adjustments
±	ACE adjustment*
=	AMTI
–	AMT exemption
=	AMT base
×	20% (corporate AMT rate)
=	Tentative minimum tax
–	Regular income tax
=	AMT (only if a positive amount)

*Note: The adjusted current earnings (ACE) adjustment is discussed at ¶ 1009.

Example 19: A corporation reports taxable income of $200,000 and owes regular income tax on this amount of $61,250. Included in taxable income are tax preference items totaling $100,000, negative AMT adjustments totaling $20,000, and a $40,000 positive ACE adjustment. The corporation computes its AMT as follows:

Corporate taxable income	$200,000
Plus: Tax preferences	100,000
Less: Negative AMT adjustments	(20,000)
Plus: Positive ACE adjustment	40,000
AMTI	$320,000
Less: AMT exemption	(0)
AMT base	$320,000
20% (corporate AMT rate)	× 20%
Tentative minimum tax	$ 64,000
Regular income tax	(61,250)
AMT (only if a positive amount)	$ 2,750

Example 20: A corporation reports taxable income of $300,000 and owes regular income tax on this amount of $100,250. Included in taxable income are tax preference items totaling $40,000, positive AMT adjustments totaling $20,000, and a $30,000 negative ACE adjustment. The corporation computes its AMT as follows:

Corporate taxable income	$300,000
Plus: Tax preferences	40,000
Plus: Positive AMT adjustments	20,000
Less: Negative ACE adjustment	(30,000)

AMTI	$330,000
Less: AMT exemption	(0)
AMT base	$330,000
20% (corporate AMT rate)	× 20%
Tentative minimum tax	$ 66,000
Regular income tax	(100,250)
AMT (only if a positive amount)	$ 0

¶ 1007 Tax Preferences

Tax preferences are deductions or exclusions allowed in the calculation of taxable income that the government has specifically singled out as excessive and therefore not allowed in the calculation of AMTI. Since these deductions and exclusions are taken away in the AMT system, tax preferences are always added back to taxable income in arriving at a taxpayer's AMTI. Figure 10-2 provides a list of tax preferences that must be added to taxable income when computing AMTI.[12]

Figure 10-2 AMT Tax Preferences

1. Percentage depletion in excess of the adjusted basis in the property,

2. Excess intangible drilling costs, and

3. Tax-exempt interest on specified private activity bonds.

In an effort to encourage domestic oil and gas production, Congress enacted tax incentives that allow domestic oil and gas companies to immediately expense intangible drilling costs that would normally be capitalized expenditures and to take "percentage depletion"—a deduction that has no connection to actual expenses. To the extent that these two deductions result in "excessive" deductions, the amounts deducted represent tax preference items that must be added back to taxable income when computing AMTI.

.01 Percentage Depletion

If the percentage depletion deduction taken in computing taxable income exceeds the taxpayer's adjusted basis in the property at the end of the tax year (computed before reduction of the basis by the depletion deduction), the difference is a tax preference added back to taxable income when computing AMTI. The preference item is computed separately for each piece of depletable property. Excess percentage depletion is not considered a tax preference item with respect to independent oil and gas producers and royalty owners; accordingly, this amount does not have to be added back when computing the AMTI of these taxpayers.[13]

Example 21: An oil and gas company (not an independent producer) deducts $70,000 for percentage depletion on its tax return. Its adjusted basis in the property (before the depletion deduction) was $50,000. To compute AMTI, the taxpayer adds back $20,000 to taxable income.

.02 Intangible Drilling Costs

Operators of domestic oil, gas, or geothermal wells may elect to currently deduct intangible drilling and development costs (IDCs) rather than capitalize and recover them through depletion or

---

[12] Code Sec. 57.   [13] Code Sec. 57(a)(1).

depreciation.[14] (See ¶ 501.03 and ¶ 707.) Excess IDCs are treated as a tax preference item to the extent that the excess exceeds 65 percent of the net income from oil, gas, and geothermal properties. "Excess IDCs" equal the amount of the IDCs the taxpayer deducted in computing taxable income over the amount that would have been deducted if such amount had been capitalized and amortized ratably over a 120-month period. Alternatively, the taxpayer can elect to compute the deduction for IDCs under the AMT system using the amounts that would have been allowed through cost depletion (in lieu of amortization over 120 months).

Example 22: Marquette Oil Company incurs $120,000 of IDCs with respect to oil wells that are placed in service in July 20X0. Marquette elects to deduct the entire amount of the IDCs when computing its regular taxable income. If Marquette had amortized its IDCs over 120 months, it would have been allowed a $6,000 deduction in 20X0 ($120,000/120 months × 6 months). Therefore, it has excess IDCs of $114,000 ($120,000 immediately expensed minus the $6,000 amortized amount). If Marquette has net income from oil, gas, and geothermal properties of $150,000 in 20X0, 65 percent of its net income equals $97,500 ($150,000 × 65%). Thus, its excess IDC that exceeds 65 percent of the net income from the property is $16,500 ($114,000 − $97,500). Therefore, Marquette Oil must add back to taxable income a tax preference of $16,500 when computing its AMTI for 20X0.

.03 Tax-Exempt Interest from Private Activity Bonds

Chapter 4 explained that the tax laws allow as an exclusion the interest earned from state and local government bonds, more commonly referred to as "municipal bonds." (See ¶ 411.01.) Tax-exempt interest from these bonds ("municipal interest") is a preference item when the interest is paid on a *specified private activity bond*. Under the AMT system, a specified private activity bond is a type of private activity bond issued after August 7, 1986, that pays interest that can be excluded from gross income for regular tax purposes. Although interest paid with respect to a private activity bond usually has to be included in gross income for regular tax purposes, an exception is made for interest payable with respect to a private activity bond that is a *qualified bond*. A bond is a **private activity bond** if more than 10 percent of its proceeds are used for a private business use (a five percent test is used for private business not related, or disproportionate, to government use financed by the issue).[15] A private activity bond is a qualified bond if the proceeds are used for certain specified purposes (e.g., to build an airport, sewage facility, finance owner-occupied residences, or student loans).[16]

Certain types of bonds are excluded from the definition of specified private activity bond:

- Qualified 501(c)(3) bond (a bond whose proceeds are used to benefit a charitable Code Sec. 501(c)(3) organization or governmental unit).

- Certain housing bonds (i.e., an exempt facility bond whose proceeds are used to provide qualified residential rental projects, qualified mortgage bond, or qualified veterans' mortgage bond).

- Any bond issued in 2009 or 2010.

In the AMT system, interest from specified private activity bonds does not qualify for the exclusion allowed for qualified private activity bonds. Thus, any interest from specified private activity bonds received during the year is added back to taxable income when computing AMTI. Interest incurred in connection with the investment in tax-exempt bonds is not deductible in the regular income tax system (see ¶ 505). In the AMT system, interest expense associated with private activity bond investments can be used to offset the interest income. Thus, only the difference represents a tax preference item.[17]

---

[14] Code Sec. 263(c); Reg. § 1.612-4.
[15] Code Sec. 141(a).

[16] Code Sec. 141(e).
[17] Code Sec. 57(a)(5).

Example 23: A corporation receives $10,000 of interest from a *specified private activity bond*. The corporation paid $500 in interest on a temporary loan to purchase the bonds. For computing taxable income, the $10,000 is not included in gross income, and the $500 is not deductible from gross income. For computing AMTI, the $10,000 is taxable and the $500 is deductible. Accordingly, the taxpayer's tax preference amount is $9,500 ($10,000 – $500).

 Spotlight: Private activity bonds are issued by or on behalf of municipalities to provide financing for projects of private business users. Investors typically purchase the bonds from the municipality, and then the municipality loans the proceeds to private users for completion of their projects, such as airports, certain residential rental projects, and the like.

¶ 1008 AMT Adjustments

AMTI is computed by making certain adjustments to the taxpayer's taxable income in addition to tax preferences. Like tax preference items, "AMT adjustments" are intended to eliminate the tax advantages of items that, in the aggregate, reduce the taxpayer's taxable income to such an extent that the taxpayer is paying too little in income taxes relative to the taxpayer's economic income. However, unlike preference items for which the amount that reduces taxable income is always greater than the amount permitted to reduce AMTI, AMT adjustments can be positive or negative.

Figure 10-3 lists some of the more common AMT adjustments required when calculating corporate AMTI.[18] Although these adjustments also apply to individuals, the list of AMT adjustments for individual taxpayers is more extensive due to the number of personal expenses they are allowed to deduct from AGI.

Figure 10-3 AMT Adjustments

- Adjusted current earnings,
- Depreciation on realty and personal property,
- Gain or loss from property with an AMT adjusted basis,
- Amortization of certified pollution control facilities,
- Amortization of mining exploration and development costs,
- Amortization of circulation expenditures,
- Long-term contracts, and
- NOL recomputed using AMT income and deductions.

AMT adjustments typically involve items for which the method used to compute the deduction on the tax return is different than the method allowed in the AMT system. If the deduction is accelerated on the tax return (as it typically is with such items), in later years the deduction allowed for computing AMTI will be greater. These types of differences are known as **timing differences.** The distinguishing feature of timing differences is that they reverse themselves over time.

With respect to income items, if the recognition of income occurs earlier for AMT than under the regular income tax system, a positive adjustment will be necessary in the year the income is

---

[18] Code Sec. 56.

recognized under the AMT system. In the year the item is included in taxable income, it must be subtracted from taxable income to compute AMTI.

.01 AMT Adjustment for Depreciation

One area in which timing differences cause AMT adjustments is depreciation. AMT rules may require recovery periods that are similar to or different from those the regular tax system requires. In addition, the same or different depreciation methods may apply under the AMT system.

For example, if the tax laws governing the calculation of taxable income allow for more accelerated methods of depreciation than those allowed under the AMT system, then in the earlier years of an asset's recovery period, depreciation expense deducted in computing taxable income will be greater than that allowed in computing AMTI. Thus, in the earlier years, the difference between these two depreciation amounts must be added back to taxable income to arrive at AMTI. In the latter years of the asset's recovery period, the opposite will occur, and the necessary adjustment will be a subtraction from taxable income.

Example 24: Assume that the following rules apply to the depreciation of an asset. For purposes of computing taxable income, the tax laws allow property to be depreciated over five years using the double declining balance (DDB) method, switching to the straight-line (SL) method when that method produces greater deductions. Under the AMT system, depreciation is allowed over the same five years, but the straight-line method must be used. Both methods require taxpayers to use the half-year convention to depreciate five-year property. (See ¶ 702.01.)

Under each tax system, depreciation during the six tax years for property costing $50,000 would be as follows:

Year	Regular Tax System*	AMT System**	Required Adjustment
1	$10,000	$ 5,000	$5,000
2	16,000	10,000	6,000
3	9,600	10,000	(400)
4	5,760	10,000	(4,240)
5	5,760	10,000	(4,240)
6	2,880	5,000	(2,120)
	$50,000	$50,000	$ 0

* These amounts were computed using the column for 5-year property from Table 7A in the Appendix to Chapter 7.

** These amounts were computed using the column for 5-year property from Table 7F in the Appendix to Chapter 7.

As you can see from this example, during the earlier years of the recovery period, a positive adjustment would be required. The $11,000 of positive adjustments required during the first two years of the recovery period is reversed by the negative adjustments in the last four years.

Now assume that the tax laws governing the depreciation of an asset under the regular income tax and under the AMT systems allow for the same depreciation methods, but the recovery periods are longer under the AMT system. Up to the last year in which the property is depreciated under the regular income tax system, the amount deducted against taxable income will exceed the amount deducted in computing AMTI. Accordingly, a positive adjustment will be necessary in those years.

However, once the property has been fully depreciated for regular income tax purposes, the amount allowed in the AMT system must be subtracted from taxable income to properly calculate AMTI.

Example 25: Assume that the following rules apply to the depreciation of an asset. For computing taxable income, the tax laws allow property to be depreciated over three years using the straight-line method. For computing AMTI, the property must be depreciated over five years using the straight-line method. Both methods require taxpayers to use the half-year convention to depreciate property.

Depreciation during the respective recovery periods for property costing $30,000 would be as follows:

Year	Regular Tax System*	AMT System**	Required Adjustment
1	$ 5,000	$ 3,000	$2,000
2	10,000	6,000	4,000
3	10,000	6,000	4,000
4	5,000	6,000	(1,000)
5	0	6,000	(6,000)
6	0	3,000	(3,000)
	$30,000	$30,000	$0

* These amounts were computed using the column for 3-year property from Table 7F in the Appendix to Chapter 7.

** These amounts were computed using the column for 5-year property from Table 7F in the Appendix to Chapter 7.

As you can see from this example, until the year in which the property is fully depreciated under the regular tax system, positive adjustments are needed. In the year the property is fully depreciated and in all subsequent tax years, negative adjustments to taxable income will be required.

Under the Modified Accelerated Cost Recovery System (MACRS), taxpayers have the option of using regular (accelerated) MACRS, straight-line MACRS, or the alternative depreciation system (ADS) to depreciate personal property. (See ¶ 702.) Taxpayers that qualify can also elect to expense some or all of their personal property under Code Sec. 179. (See ¶ 702.03.) The AMT system also allows Code Sec. 179 immediate expensing, but it prohibits taxpayers from using the 200-percent (double) declining balance method and instead requires that taxpayers depreciate personal property using the 150-percent declining balance or the straight-line methods using the same recovery periods as allowed under regular MACRS. Thus, an AMT adjustment is required when 3-, 5-, 7-, or 10-year property is depreciated using the double declining balance method.

Because MACRS uses only the SL method to depreciate real property, fewer adjustments are required to real property depreciation for AMT purposes. In the regular income tax system, real property placed in service after 1986 is depreciated using regular MACRS over 27½, 31½, or 39 recovery periods, depending on whether the property is residential or commercial realty, and if the latter, when the property is placed in service. (See ¶ 703.) Under the AMT system, real property placed in service after 1986, but before 1999, is depreciated using the SL method over a 40-year recovery period. This is the same depreciation that is allowed under the ADS. Consequently, unless ADS was used to depreciate real property placed in service after 1986 and before 1999, an adjustment is required each year when computing AMTI. The tax laws were changed so that real property placed in service after 1998 is now depreciated using the same method under both the regular income tax system and the AMT system. Thus, no AMT adjustment is required for real property placed in service after 1998.

Table 10-1 outlines the differences in depreciation methods under the regular income tax system and the AMT system and discusses the types of adjustments that are needed each year.

Table 10-1 Comparison of Allowable Depreciation Methods

Description	Regular Tax System	AMT System	Required Adjustment
Real property placed in service after 1986, but before 1999	Under regular MACRS, taxpayers use the straight-line (SL) method over 27½, 31½, or 39 years, depending on the type of property. Under ADS, taxpayers depreciate real property over 40 years using the SL method.	Taxpayers must depreciate real property over 40 years using the SL method.	If regular MACRS is used, positive adjustments are required to taxable income until the end of the regular MACRS recovery period. Negative adjustments will be required for all subsequent years. If ADS is used under the regular tax system, no adjustments will be needed.
Real property placed in service after 1998	Same as for real property placed in service after 1986, but before 1999.	Same as the regular depreciation system.	No adjustments required.
Personal property	Taxpayers can use regular (DDB) MACRS, SL MACRS, or ADS. (See ¶ 702.)	Taxpayers must use 150% declining balance using the same recovery periods as allowed under MACRS.	If the double declining balance method under MACRS is used, positive adjustments will be required during the earlier recovery periods, and negative adjustments will be required during the later periods.

Example 26: DuMont Enterprises placed an office building in service on June 5, 1998. The building cost $500,000; under MACRS, it is depreciated using the SL method over 39 years. To compute AMTI, the building must be depreciated over 40 years. From 1998 through 2009, depreciation under each of these methods is as follows:

Year	Regular Tax System*	AMT System**	Required Adjustment
1998	$ 6,945	$ 6,771	$174
1999–2009	$12,821 a year	$12,500 a year	$321

*For 1999–2009, this amount equals $500,000/39. For 1998, the depreciation is allowed for the last 6½ months of the year, so depreciation equals $12,821/12 × 6.5.

**For 1999–2009, this amount equals $500,000/40. For 1998, the depreciation is allowed for the last 6½ months of the year, so depreciation equals $12,500/12 × 6.5.

¶ 1008.01

.02 Adjusted Gain or Loss

When gain is realized from the disposition of depreciable property that was subject to AMT adjustments, the adjusted basis must be determined for purposes of AMT using the amount of depreciation taken into account for computing AMTI. Thus, the amount of gain will differ for regular and for AMT purposes. This difference will result in an adjustment to taxable income when computing AMTI.

If the amount of gain included in taxable income is greater than the gain computed under the AMT system, the amount of gain is a negative adjustment to taxable income. Likewise if the loss included in taxable income is less than the loss computed under the AMT system, the amount of loss is a negative adjustment to taxable income. Positive adjustments are required if the gain is greater or the loss is smaller under the AMT system.

Example 27: Continuing with Example 26, assume that on February 19, 2009, DuMont sells the office building for $700,000. The depreciation deduction for regular tax purposes for 2009 would equal $1,603 ($500,000/39 × 1.5/12). For computing AMTI, depreciation expense would be $1,563 ($500,000/40 × 1.5/12). Thus, the $40 difference ($1,603 – $1,563) would be reported as a positive adjustment to taxable income in 2009. During the years 1998 to 2009, DuMont will have reported positive AMT adjustments totaling $3,424 ($174 + ($321 × 10) + $40).

DuMont's adjusted basis in the office building as well as its realized and recognized gain under both the regular income tax and the AMT systems are computed as follows:

	Regular Tax System		AMT System	
Amount realized		$700,000		$700,000
Less:				
Cost	$500,000		$500,000	
Accumulated depreciation	(136,758)*	(363,242)	(133,334)**	(366,666)
Recognized gain		$336,758		$333,334

*$6,945 + ($12,821 × 10 years) + $1,603
**$6,771 + (12,500 × 10 years) + $1,563

The $3,424 difference ($336,758 – $333,334) in the gain reported in taxable income and the gain allowed under the AMT system must be reported as a negative adjustment to taxable income. This amount is equal to the cumulative positive adjustments made over the years when depreciation was taken on the building. Thus, the timing differences resulting from depreciation reverse themselves at the time the asset is sold or fully depreciated, whichever occurs first.

Although the above example illustrates the adjustments required on the sale of depreciable property, similar rules apply to all sales of property. To the extent that the adjusted basis of the property under the regular tax system and the adjusted basis under the AMT system differ, so too will the amount of gain or loss reported under each system.

.03 Amortization of Circulation Expenditures, Certified Pollution Control Facilities, and Mining Exploration and Development Costs

For purposes of computing taxable income, the tax laws allow taxpayers to immediately expense circulation costs.[19] Alternatively, corporations may elect to amortize (expense) their circulation costs over three years. **Circulation costs** are amounts paid or incurred to establish, maintain, or increase the circulation of a newspaper, magazine, or other periodical. When a corporation immediately expenses its circulation costs for regular income tax purposes, the AMT rules do not allow the corporation to expense its circulation costs. Consequently, the fully expensed circulation costs would be a positive adjustment to taxable income when computing AMTI. However, if the corporation elects to amortize its circulation costs for regular tax purposes, the AMT rules allow the same deduction for computing AMTI.[20] Hence, no adjustment would be needed.

The costs associated with certified pollution control facilities and mining exploration and development would normally be capitalized as the taxpayer benefits from such expenditures beyond the current year. However, when computing taxable income, these costs may be deducted immediately. When computing AMTI, these costs must be capitalized and amortized ratably over a 10-year period (in the case of mining exploration and development costs) or depreciated using ADS (in the case of certified pollution control facilities). Under ADS, the costs of the certified pollution control facility would be depreciated using the SL method over the facility's class life. (See ¶ 702.01.)

.04 Long-Term Contracts

In very limited situations involving real estate construction contracts, taxpayers may be allowed to compute taxable income using the completed contract method. (See ¶ 309.02.) For purposes of computing AMTI, the percentage of completion method must be used for all long-term contracts, with the exception of certain home construction contracts.[21] The completed contract method is allowed for home construction contracts for computing both regular tax and AMT. All other differences between the amount of income from a long-term contract recognized during the year for regular tax purposes and that recognized under the percentage of completion method for AMT purposes result in an adjustment to taxable income. When the amount included in AMTI exceeds the amount included in taxable income, a positive adjustment to taxable income is required.

Example 28: In 2007, a corporation enters into a long-term contract to construct a building that it reasonably expects to complete within two years. The corporation is eligible to use the completed contract method under the regular income tax system. The taxpayer recognizes the entire $50,000 in 2009, the year in which the construction is completed. Under the percentage of completion method, the corporation would have recognized $20,000 in 2007, $20,000 in 2008, and $10,000 in 2009. For computing the AMTI, the following adjustments must be made to taxable income:

Year	Regular Income Tax	AMT	AMT Adjustment
2007	$ 0	$20,000	$20,000
2008	0	20,000	20,000
2009	50,000	10,000	(40,000)

.05 Recomputed Deductions Using the AMT System

The deduction for domestic production activities (see ¶ 509) uses amounts and limits based on the regular income tax system. Taxpayers who take a deduction for domestic production activities must recompute their deduction using the AMT system rules.[22] If the deduction allowed in calculating regular taxable income is larger than the deduction allowed in calculating the AMTI, the excess must be added to taxable income as a positive adjustment when computing the AMTI. On the

---

[19] Code Sec. 173.
[20] Code Sec. 56(b)(2).

[21] Code Sec. 56(a)(3).
[22] Code Sec. 199(d)(6).

other hand, if the deduction taken in the calculation of taxable income is less than the deduction under the AMT system, a negative adjustment to taxable income would need to be made.

Taxpayers that have a NOL for a tax year must recompute the NOL using the AMT system. The NOL calculated under the AMT system can be carried back and forward in the same manner as regular NOLs. This rule ensures that to the extent the NOL is attributable to accelerated depreciation, depletion, or other favorable provision under the regular income tax system, such amounts cannot be used in reducing the taxpayer's AMTI.

¶ 1009 ACE Adjustment

Preference items and AMT adjustments apply both to corporations and to individuals. Corporations are also subject to a third calculation, called **adjusted current earnings** (ACE). The calculation of ACE closely resembles the calculation of **current earnings and profits** (current E&P), which is the amount (together with accumulated E&P) from which corporations pay dividends to their shareholders (see ¶ 1204). E&P attempts to measure a corporation's ability to pay dividends from its current year earnings, and accordingly, many of the tax incentives incorporated into the regular and AMT systems are not included in the calculation of E&P.

Generally, a corporation's ACE exceeds its AMTI because the ACE rules are more restrictive with respect to allowable exclusions and deductions. The AMT rules require a C corporation to increase its AMTI by 75 percent of the amount by which its ACE exceeds its unadjusted AMTI (AMTI computed without regard to the ACE adjustment and the AMT NOL deduction). This adjustment is known as the ACE adjustment.

If a corporation's unadjusted AMTI exceeds the ACE, AMTI is reduced by 75 percent of the difference. However, the AMTI is reduced only to the extent that the aggregate amount of the negative ACE adjustments used against positive ACE adjustments from prior years does not exceed the aggregate positive ACE adjustments from prior years.[23]

Example 29: Handell, Inc., a calendar year corporation, has an unadjusted AMTI equal to $330,000 each year from 2007 to 2009. Handell's ACE and ACE adjustment during those years is as follows:

Year	ACE	AMTI	Difference	ACE Adjustment
2007	$400,000	$330,000	$ 70,000	$52,500
2008	330,000	330,000	0	0
2009	140,000	330,000	(190,000)	(52,500)

In 2007, ACE exceeds its unadjusted AMTI by $70,000 ($400,000 – $330,000). Therefore, 75 percent of this amount ($52,500) must be included as an ACE adjustment when computing its AMTI in 2007. In 2008, there is no increase (or decrease) to AMTI because the difference between ACE and the unadjusted AMTI is zero. In 2009, its unadjusted AMTI exceeds its ACE by $190,000 ($330,000 – $140,000), creating a potential negative adjustment to the AMTI equal to $142,500 ($190,000 × 75%). The aggregate increases to the AMTI for prior years equal $52,500 (from 2007), and accordingly, only $52,500 of the potential $142,500 negative adjustment can reduce its AMTI in 2009.

Example 30: Assume the same facts as in Example 29, except that in 2009 Handell's unadjusted AMTI once again is $330,000, but its ACE for 2008 equals $360,000. Because Handell's ACE exceeds its unadjusted AMTI by $30,000 ($360,000 – $330,000), 75 percent of the $30,000 ($22,500) must be included as a positive ACE adjustment when computing the AMTI in 2009. If in 2010, Handell's unadjusted AMTI exceeds

---

[23] Code Sec. 56(g).

its ACE, 75 percent of the difference, up to $22,500, can be used as a negative adjustment to AMTI.

.01 Concept of E&P

Earnings and profits (E&P) will be discussed in more detail in Chapter 12; however, the basic concepts, which are important to understanding ACE, are discussed here. As a corporation earns income and pays expenses, current E&P attempts to capture the corporation's capacity to distribute amounts to shareholders without returning any portion of their investment in the corporation. Such distributions are classified as dividends. Unlike the regular income tax system or the AMT system, in which exclusions and deductions are included for various social, economic, and political reasons, the calculation of current E&P focuses on how much an item of income or expense affects the corporation's ability to pay dividends to its shareholders.

For example, interest from state and local municipal bonds ("municipal interest") generally is excluded from gross income. However, interest paid on specified private activity bonds is included in the calculation of the AMTI. Despite the fact that most other types of municipal interest are exempt from both regular income tax and AMT, the reality is that when the corporation receives the interest, the amount received from that interest can be distributed to the shareholders. Thus, both taxable and tax-exempt interest are included in the calculation of E&P.

Example 31: A corporate taxpayer receives $150,000 of municipal interest, which includes $40,000 of interest from specified private activity bonds. Taxable income under the regular income tax system is $400,000. Under the AMT system, only the municipal interest on specified private activity bonds is taxable, and accordingly, the corporation's AMTI equals $440,000 ($400,000 + $40,000). However, all municipal interest is included in current E&P. Thus, the taxpayer's current year E&P equals $550,000 ($400,000 + $150,000).

As discussed in previous chapters, some expenditures are not deducted from gross income. These include federal income taxes paid during the year; bribes, fines and penalties that violate public policy; and 50 percent of meals and entertainment expenses (M&E). Although there are valid reasons as to why the government does not allow these amounts to be deducted in the calculation of regular income tax and AMT, these expenditures nonetheless affect the corporation's ability to pay dividends. Accordingly, these amounts are deducted in computing a corporation's E&P.

Example 32: In its first year of operations, a corporation reports business income of $100,000 and incurs $60,000 of ordinary and necessary business expenses. The corporation also incurs $2,000 in M&E and $5,000 in penalties for activities that violate public policy. The corporation computes its $39,000 taxable income and $33,000 of current year E&P as follows:

Business income		$100,000
Less: Operating expenses	$60,000	
50% of M&E	1,000	(61,000)
Taxable income		$ 39,000

Taxable income		$ 39,000
Less: Nondeductible portion of M&E	$ 1,000	
Nondeductible penalties	5,000	(6,000)
Current year E&P		$ 33,000

Although the corporation reports $39,000 of taxable income, if it distributes more than $33,000 to its shareholders, the excess will represent a return to shareholders of some of their investment in the corporation. The tax consequences of dividend and return capital distributions is discussed in Chapter 12 (see ¶ 1204).

.02 Calculating ACE

Although the concepts behind the ACE are similar to the concepts involved in the calculation of current E&P, differences exist between the two calculations. For example, current E&P attempts to measure the corporation's capacity to pay dividends from current period earnings; the ACE calculation is intended to measure pretax income before any distributions. Thus, while federal and foreign income taxes are not deducted in computing taxable income or AMTI, these amounts reduce the corporation's dividend-paying capacity and therefore reduce E&P. However, neither of these items nor any dividends paid during the year is considered when computing the corporation's ACE. (E&P is discussed in greater detail in Chapter 12, which introduces corporate distributions.)

The starting point for the calculation of ACE is AMTI. Differences between the amounts of income and deduction items taken into account in the calculation of AMTI and the amounts taken into account in the calculation of ACE are handled as positive and negative adjustments to AMTI. Thus, if an item of income is excluded from AMTI but is included in ACE, the amount is a positive adjustment to AMTI. Likewise, if a deduction is allowed in computing AMTI, but not in computing ACE, the deductible amount would be added back to AMTI for purposes of computing the corporation's ACE. On the other hand, an expense that is not deductible for computing AMTI but is deductible for computing ACE would be a negative adjustment to AMTI.

Some ACE adjustments reflect timing differences that eventually reverse themselves. For example, if AMT tax law allows a greater deduction for an item than is allowed under the provision governing the ACE calculation, the excess amount would be a positive adjustment to AMTI. However, in the year that the deduction for computing ACE exceeds the deduction allowed for computing AMTI, the difference would result in a negative adjustment.

Positive adjustments for exclusion items. Items that are excluded from gross income for computing AMTI but that are included in determining ACE must be reported as positive adjustments and are added to AMTI when computing a corporation's ACE. Deductions related to the exclusion that normally would not be deducted in computing AMTI offset the positive ACE adjustment. For example, AMTI would be increased by interest on tax-exempt bonds and would be reduced by any interest expense associated with financing the bonds. However, this rule would not apply to interest on specified private activity bonds, since such amounts have already been reflected in AMTI.[24] ACE does not include interest from certain housing bonds (i.e., an exempt facility bond whose proceeds are used to provide qualified residential rental projects, qualified mortgage bond, or qualified veterans' mortgage bond) or from any bond issued in 2009 or 2010.

Example 33: A corporate taxpayer receives $130,000 of municipal interest, which includes $60,000 of interest from specified private activity bonds. Taxable income under the regular income tax system is $600,000. The taxpayer incurs $10,000 of interest expense on municipal bonds other than specified private activity bonds. Because this expense relates to property that produces tax-exempt income, the $10,000 is not deductible under the regular income tax system.

Under the AMT system, the interest on specified private activity bonds is taxable. Accordingly, the corporation's AMTI equals $660,000 ($600,000 + $60,000). The $10,000 of interest expense is not deductible because the income from the bonds to which the interest pertains is exempt from AMT. However, $720,000 ($600,000 + $130,000 − $10,000) represents the corporation's capacity to pay dividends from current year's earnings. Accordingly, this amount is included in the corporation's

---

[24] Code Sec. 56(g)(4)(B).

ACE. When computing the corporation's ACE, $60,000 ($720,000 – $660,000) would be shown as a positive adjustment to AMTI.

Positive adjustments for deduction items. As a general rule, no deduction from ACE is allowed for an item that is not deductible for purposes of computing a corporation's E&P. The deduction for domestic production activities is not based on expenditures but instead is computed as a percentage of domestic production activity income. However, a special rule makes it deductible when computing a corporation's ACE.[25]

Like the domestic production activities deduction, the dividends received deduction (DRD) does not reduce the corporation's ability to pay dividends. Although it would make sense that this deduction would not be allowed in computing the ACE, corporations that own at least 20% of another corporation's stock and thus qualify for the 80- or 100-percent DRD for dividends received from that corporation subtract the DRD when computing their ACE. However, corporations that are "portfolio investors" with respect to another corporation because they own less than 20 percent of the stock in that corporation must add back the amount of their (70-percent) DRD to AMTI when computing their ACE.[26] The DRD was discussed in Chapter 4 (see ¶ 411.02).

Other expenses allowed in the calculation of AMTI that are not recognized as deductions in computing a corporation's ACE include deductions for circulation costs (amortized over three years for AMTI) and organizational expenses (either expensed (up to $5,000) or amortized over 180 months for AMTI). Any amounts deducted from AMTI for these items are positive adjustments to AMTI when computing a corporation's ACE for the year.

Example 34: Amica Corporation began its business operations on March 1, 2009. Amica Corporation incurred $80,000 of organizational costs, but since this amount exceeds $55,000, it cannot immediately expense any of the costs (see ¶ 503), but instead elects to amortize the costs over 180 months. Amica files its first tax return using a calendar year-end. On its 2009 tax return, Amica deducts $4,444 ($80,000/180 × 10 months) as amortization of its organizational costs. Although this amount is also allowed for purposes of computing AMTI, it is not deductible in computing Amica's ACE. Thus, the $4,444 must be added back to Amica's AMTI in 2009 when computing its ACE.

Adjustments for timing differences. Some differences between the calculation of ACE and AMTI stem from timing differences, which eventually reverse themselves. Required adjustments due to timing differences are listed in Table 10-2.

Table 10-2 ACE Adjustments Due to Timing Differences

Item	AMTI System	ACE Calculation
Depreciation of personal property	Taxpayers must use 150% DB using the same recovery periods as allowed under MACRS. (See ¶ 1008.01.).	Personal property must be depreciated using ADS. (See ¶ 702.01.)[a] The difference between the AMTI amount and the ACE amount is a timing difference. In years when the AMTI deduction is greater, a positive ACE adjustment results. In years when ADS expense is greater, a negative ACE adjustment results.

---

[25] Code Sec. 56(g)(4)(C)(v).

[26] Code Sec. 56(g)(4)(C)(ii).

Item	AMTI System	ACE Calculation
Depletion	Percentage depletion in excess of the adjusted basis of the property is added back to AMTI. (See ¶ 1007.01.)	With the exception of independent oil and gas producers, taxpayers must use cost depletion.[b] Therefore, the excess of the amount deducted against taxable income minus any depletion preference item used in computing AMTI over the ACE amount is a positive ACE adjustment, and accordingly, it is added to AMTI when computing ACE.
Installment sale method	Allowed for computing AMTI.	Income from installment sales is reported in the year of the sale.[c] Therefore, in the first year, a positive ACE adjustment will occur, followed by negative ACE adjustments in years in which installment method gain is reported in AMTI.
Intangible drilling and development costs (IDCs)	IDCs are usually expensed immediately in computing taxable income, but in computing AMTI, they are amortized over 120 months and result in a preference item only if the excess of the amount expensed over the amortized amount exceeds 65 percent of the net income from the property. (See ¶ 1007.02.)	IDCs are amortized over 60 months.[d] The ACE adjustment equals the difference between the amount deducted in determining AMTI and the amortized amount allowed for the ACE calculation. When the deduction allowed in computing AMTI exceeds the deduction allowed in computing ACE, the adjustment is positive; when the ACE deduction exceeds the AMTI deduction, the adjustment is negative.
LIFO	Last-in, first-out (LIFO) or first-in, first-out (FIFO) can be used to compute inventory costs.	LIFO must be used.[e] Therefore, the excess of the inventory amount reported on the balance sheet using FIFO over the inventory amount using the LIFO method is a positive ACE adjustment if the taxpayer uses the FIFO method to calculate regular taxable income.

[a] Code Sec. 56(g)(4)(A).

[b] Code Sec. 56(g)(4)(F)

[c] Code Sec. 56(g)(4)(D)(iv).

[d] Code Sec. 56(g)(4)(D)(i).

[e] Code Sec. 56(g)(4)(D)(iii).

Example 35: An oil and gas company (not an independent producer) deducts $70,000 for percentage depletion on its 2009 tax return. Its adjusted basis in the property (before the depletion deduction) was $60,000. If the cost method had been used, the taxpayer's depletion deduction would have been $35,000.

For AMT purposes, the taxpayer's depletion deduction would be limited to the taxpayer's basis in the property. Consequently, the taxpayer adds back to taxable income the $10,000 excess of percentage depletion over the taxpayer's basis in the property ($70,000 – $60,000) to arrive at AMTI. For computing the corporation's ACE, the $25,000 difference between the deduction used in computing AMTI

($60,000) and the deduction using the cost depletion method ($35,000) is included as a positive ACE adjustment for the year. This amount is added to AMTI in the calculation of the corporation's ACE.

Example 36: A corporation sells land for $500,000, resulting in a $150,000 profit. The terms of the sale require that the buyer pay $200,000 at the time of the sale and $100,000 annually for each of the next three years. The corporation reports the gain on the installment method. On its tax return for the year of the sale, the corporation recognizes a $60,000 gain ($200,000/$500,000 × $150,000). In each of the next three years, $30,000 of gain is recognized ($100,000/$500,000 × $150,000). Under the ACE calculation, the entire $150,000 of gain is recognized in the year of the sale. The AMT adjustment required each year is as follows:

Year	AMTI	ACE	Adjustment to AMTI
1	$60,000	$150,000	$90,000
2	30,000	0	(30,000)
3	30,000	0	(30,000)
4	30,000	0	(30,000)

The $90,000 positive ACE adjustment in the first year is reversed in years 2 to 4 with negative adjustments of $30,000 in each of the three years.

¶ 1010 Minimum Tax Credit

Certain tax credits can be used to offset the AMT and certain tax credits cannot. Tax credits are discussed in detail in Chapter 11. However, we discuss one tax credit here: the **minimum tax credit**. Code Sec. 53 provides that the amount of AMT paid by a corporation in one year can be used to offset the corporation's regular tax liability for a subsequent year. The amount of AMT paid by an individual can offset the individual's regular tax liability for a subsequent year only to the extent that the AMT is attributable to timing differences (as opposed to exclusions). The minimum tax credit, however, in combination with other tax credits (see Chapter 11) cannot be used by corporations to reduce the regular tax below the tentative minimum tax in that subsequent tax year. Further, the minimum tax credit may not be used to offset any future AMT tax liability. An individual with a long-term unused minimum tax credit (i.e., a minimum tax credit attributable to tax years more than three years before the current tax year) for a tax year beginning before 2013 is entitled (subject to a modified adjusted gross income limitation) to a refund of all or a portion of the credit. Minimum tax credits paid in one year may be carried forward (but not back) indefinitely as an offset against regular tax liability.

Example 37: In 2009, Reyas Inc. reports $16,000 of AMT stemming from specified private activity bond interest that was exempt from regular income tax. The $16,000 can be used to reduce the taxpayer's regular income tax liability to the extent that it exceeds the taxpayer's AMT liability for a subsequent tax year.

Example 38: In 2009, Dreyfus Tools, Inc. pays $16,000 in AMT. In 2010, the taxpayer's regular income tax liability is $149,000, and its tentative minimum tax is $135,000. Dreyfus can use $14,000 of its minimum tax credit to reduce its total 2010 taxes to $135,000 ($149,000 − $14,000). Dreyfus can carry over the remaining $2,000 ($16,000 − $14,000) of minimum tax credit to 2011 and subsequent tax years.

¶ 1011 Individual AMT

Individuals are subject to an alternative minimum tax (AMT) when the amount of tentative minimum tax exceeds the amount of regular income taxes owed.[27] The formula for computing the AMT is similar to that which corporations use to calculate AMT. Individual taxpayers are subject to the same tax preferences as corporations. Figure 10-4 shows the calculation of individual AMT.

Figure 10-4 Calculation of Individual AMT

	Taxable income
±	Tax preferences and adjustments
=	AMTI
–	AMT Exemption
=	AMT tax base
×	AMT rates
=	Tentative Minimum Tax
–	Regular income tax
=	AMT (if positive amount)

.01 AMT Preferences and Adjustments for Individual Taxpayers

Individuals do not have an ACE adjustment. However, individuals have a number of additional adjustments that must be taken into consideration when computing AMTI due to the many personal expenses deductible on the individual tax return. Table 10-3 summarizes the adjustments that an individual taxpayer must make to taxable income.

Many of these adjustments have been discussed in Chapter 10; however, a few adjustments that are unique to individual taxpayers are listed in Table 10-3. For example, individuals are allowed to reduce taxable income by a standard deduction or itemized deductions, plus personal exemptions (see ¶ 104.07). Some itemized deductions are not allowed in computing AMTI. Likewise, neither the standard deduction nor personal exemptions is allowed in the calculation of AMTI. Instead, a larger AMT exemption is allowed.[28] The standard deduction (except to the extent attributable to a disaster loss deduction or motor vehicle sales tax deduction) and personal exemptions are added back to regular taxable income as positive adjustments in computing AMTI.

Table 10-3 Summary of AMT Preferences and Adjustments

Item	Adjustment Necessary to Taxable Income
Standard deduction*	Added back to taxable income.
Personal exemptions	Added back to taxable income.
State and local income taxes	Added back to taxable income.
State and local real property taxes	Added back to taxable income.

[27] Code Sec. 55.   [28] Code Sec. 56(b)(1)(E).

Item	Adjustment Necessary to Taxable Income
State and local personal property taxes	Added back to taxable income.
Miscellaneous itemized deductions	Added back to taxable income
MACRS depreciation	Same rules as for a corporation. (See ¶ 1008.01.)
Circulation costs	Same rules as for corporations. (See ¶ 1008.03.)
Research and experimental expenditures	Individuals must amortize these costs over 10 years. (See discussion that follows.)
Mining exploration and development costs	Same rules as for corporations. (See ¶ 1008.03.)
Long-term contracts	Same rules as for corporations. (See ¶ 1008.04.)
Pollution control facilities	Same rules as for corporations. (See ¶ 1008.03.)
Gain excluded on the sale of Section 1202 stock	Add back seven percent of the exclusion to taxable income. (See discussion that follows.)
Incentive stock options	Excess of FMV over the option price at date of exercise is added back to taxable income.
Passive activity losses	Net losses from passive activities, including tax shelter farm activities, are not allowed.
Intangible drilling costs	Same rules as for corporations. (See ¶ 1007.02.)
Alternative tax net operating loss	Recompute NOL using AMT rules and make any necessary adjustments to taxable income.

* Except to the extent attributable to a disaster loss deduction or motor vehicle sales tax deduction

---

Deductions from AGI. No deduction for personal and dependency exemptions is allowed in computing AMTI.[29] Thus, these amounts are added back to regular taxable income as positive adjustments to taxable income when computing AMTI. Many itemized deductions are not allowed or are further limited in the AMT system. (See ¶ 1307.01.)

Research and experimental expenditures. As discussed in Chapter 5, when computing taxable income, businesses have the following three options for handling research and experimental expenses. (See ¶ 507.01.)

1. Deduct the costs in full in the year incurred,

2. Capitalize and amortize the costs over a period of 60 months, or

3. Capitalize the costs, but do not amortize them.

For the AMT system, individual taxpayers must amortize these expenditures over ten years.[30] Therefore, the differences in the amount deducted under the regular income tax system and the AMT system result in an adjustment to taxable income when computing an individual's AMTI.

Gain on the sale of small business stock. Individual taxpayers can exclude up to 50 percent of the gain on the sale of Section 1202 stock held for at least five years (75 percent in the case of Section 1202 stock acquired after February 17, 2009, and before January 1, 2011, see ¶ 806). Consequently, only half of the gain is subject to regular income tax. For computing AMTI, seven percent of the 50-percent exclusion for gain on small business stock is treated as a tax preference item in computing AMTI. As a result, 3.5 percent (50% × 7%) of the investor's total realized gain from the sale or exchange of small business stock will be added back in the computation of AMTI.[31]

---

[29] Code Sec. 56(b)(1)(E).
[30] Code Sec. 56(b)(2).

[31] Code Sec. 57(a)(7).

.02 AMT Exemption for Individual Taxpayers

The AMT exemption for individual taxpayers varies depending on the taxpayer's filing status. The five filing statuses are: married filing jointly (MFJ), married filing separately (MFS), surviving spouse, head of household, and single. The initial AMT exemption for individuals is as follows:

MFS $22,500 ($35,475 for a tax year
beginning in 2009)

Single and head of household $33,750 ($46,700 for a tax year
beginning in 2009)

MFJ and surviving spouses $45,000 ($70,950 for a tax year
beginning in 2009)

For individuals whose AMTI exceeds a specified amount ($150,000 for MFJ and surviving spouses; $75,000 for MFS; and $112,500 for all others), the exemption amount is reduced by $.25 for every dollar of excess.[32]

Example 39: A couple that files MFJ has AMTI equal to $200,000 in 2010. Because this amount exceeds the $150,000 threshold by $50,000, the couple is required to reduce the $45,000 initial exemption by $12,500 ($50,000 × $.25). Thus, the couple's AMT exemption is reduced to $32,500 ($45,000 – $12,500).

Spotlight: To prevent tens of millions of individuals from having to pay the AMT, Congress has been periodically enacting legislation to temporarily increase the exemption amounts above the 2000 amounts ($45,000 for married individuals filing joint returns and surviving spouses; $33,750 for unmarried individuals and heads of household; and $22,50 for married individuals filing separate returns). The American Recovery and Reinvestment Act of 2009 (P.L. 111-5) increased the exemption amounts for 2009.

.03 AMT Tax Rates for Individual Taxpayers

The tax structure of the individual AMT is a two-tier progressive tax. The first $175,000 of AMT base is taxed at a 26-percent rate. Any excess over that amount is taxed at 28 percent. As is the case when computing the regular tax, net capital gains and qualified dividends under the AMT system are taxed at a maximum 15-percent rate (five percent for individuals in the 10-percent or 15-percent tax brackets). (See ¶ 405.02.) Gain from the sale of certain types of capital assets is subject to a higher maximum capital gains rate. For example, a portion of the gain from the sale or exchange of depreciable real property may be taxed at the maximum rate of 25 percent. Since the gain on the sale of collectibles (such as coins or stamps) and net gain from small business stock are subject to a maximum tax rate of 28 percent, any such gain is taxed at the taxpayer's normal AMT rates. (See ¶ 1307 for additional discussion of the Individual AMT.)

¶ 1012 Tax Planning for AMT

Although the AMT system is more restrictive than the regular tax system, it remains possible that by choosing the right strategies and investments taxpayers can eliminate their tax liabilities under both the regular tax system and the alternative minimum tax system. For example, although tax-exempt interest from specified private activity bonds is subject to AMT, all other types of state and local government bonds remain exempt both from regular tax and from AMT for individual taxpayers. For corporations, municipal interest (other than from specified private activity bonds) is an AMT adjustment if the corporation's AMTI exceeds its ACE.

---

[32] Code Sec. 55(d)(3).

For taxpayers subject to AMT, the impact of the AMT on the taxpayer's marginal tax rate must be considered in determining the tax savings of a deduction or costs associated with additional income. For example, if a corporation is in the 15 -percent tax bracket for regular tax purposes but is subject to AMT due to the extensive preferences and adjustments taken in computing taxable income, the corporation's federal MTR for tax planning is 20 percent. State and local income taxes (both regular tax and AMT) must be considered as well.

ACCUMULATED EARNINGS TAX

Because a corporation's after-tax profits are taxed a second time when distributed to shareholders in the form of a dividend, the board of directors may be hesitant to distribute profits. Accumulation of profits often results in higher stock prices because the cash retained by the corporation adds value to the company. Instead of receiving periodic dividend payments, taxpayers could sell their shares of stock for a higher price, thereby generating capital gains. In addition to the lower capital gain rates that apply to individual taxpayers, capital gains generated by both individual and corporate taxpayers can be used to offset capital losses.

Historically, dividend income has been taxed at an individual taxpayer's ordinary income rates, thereby making capital gains more attractive than dividend income. The reduced tax rates that apply to qualified dividends in recent years has taken some of the "sting" out of receiving dividend distributions; however, the fact that capital gains can be used to offset capital losses remains an attractive feature of generating capital gain over dividend income. In addition, capital gains are only taxed when the stock is sold, whereas dividend income is taxed in the year it is received. Accordingly, being able to defer the tax consequences of the second level of taxation is another reason for not distributing corporate profits. Although the accumulated earnings tax has almost always been applied to closely held corporations, its application is not limited to only those corporations.[33]

¶ 1013 Corporations Subject to the Accumulated Earnings Tax

The **accumulated earnings tax** applies only if the corporation is formed or continues to exist for the purpose of preventing individual shareholders from paying tax on the profits of the corporation by allowing E&P to accumulate instead of distributing corporate earnings.[34] The accumulated earnings tax, however, does not apply to personal holding companies, as these companies are subject to their own penalty tax (see ¶ 1015).

A presumption of tax-avoidance intent arises when a corporation accumulates E&P in excess of the reasonable needs of its business. However, this presumption can be overcome by a preponderance of evidence that the accumulation was not motivated by a desire to avoid the income tax on the part of the shareholders of the corporation.[35] A presumption of tax-avoidance intent also arises when a corporation is found to be a mere holding or investment company.[36] Thus, the original burden of disproving the allegation that it has accumulated earnings beyond its reasonable needs rests upon the corporation.[37] The circumstances that tend to negate the presumption of tax-avoidance intent include:

- The fact that little or no tax savings was achieved as a result of the corporation's accumulation of earnings and profits,

- The fact that the corporation's accumulation of earnings was for the reasonable needs of the business,

[33] Code Sec. 532(c) and *Technalysis Corp.*, 101 TC 397, Dec. 49,378 (1993).

[34] Code Sec. 532(a); Reg. § 1.532-1.

[35] Code Secs. 532 and 533; Reg. § § 1.532-1 and 1.533-1.

[36] Code Sec. 533(b).

[37] *Iowa School of Men's Hairstyling, Inc.*, 64 TCM 1114, Dec. 48,591(M), TC Memo. 1992-619; *MYCO Industries, Inc.*, 63 TCM 2355, Dec. 48,068(M), TC Memo. 1992-147; *Yates Petroleum Corporation*, 63 TCM 2347, Dec. 48,067(M), TC Memo. 1992-146.

- The absence of loans to shareholders or the payment of their personal expenses by the corporation,
- The absence of investments that have no reasonable connection with the business, and
- A good dividend-paying record.

¶ 1014 Calculating the Accumulated Earnings Tax

Assuming the IRS can prove the corporation was formed or continues to exist for the purpose of preventing individual taxpayers from paying tax on the corporation's profits, the accumulated earnings tax equals 15 percent of the corporation's accumulated taxable income. The calculation of the "accumulated taxable income" starts with the corporation's taxable income, which is adjusted to reflect the corporation's current year earnings, or an amount called the "adjusted taxable income." The adjusted taxable income is then reduced by the dividends paid deduction and the accumulated earnings credit.

The "dividends paid deduction" generally is the amount of dividends the corporation paid during the tax year. The corporation can elect to treat dividends paid during the first 2½ months of the following year as dividends paid in the current year. However, those dividends are then not eligible for the dividends paid deduction in the following year.[38] The **accumulated earnings credit** is the amount of current year earnings considered to be for the reasonable needs of the business. The formula for computing the accumulated earnings tax is shown in Table 10-4.

Table 10-4 Calculation of Accumulated Earnings Tax

Taxable income	$xxx,xxx
Plus/minus: Adjustments	xx,xxx
Adjusted taxable income	$xxx,xxx
Less: Dividends paid deduction	(xx,xxx)
Less: Accumulated earnings credit	(xx,xxx)
Accumulated taxable income	$xxx,xxx
Accumulated earnings tax rate	× 15%
Accumulated earnings tax	$ xx,xxx

Example 40: Dodge and Company reports taxable income of $550,000 during 2009 and has $200,000 of positive adjustments to taxable income to reflect current earnings. Dodge uses the calendar year. On October 5, 2009, Dodge distributes $45,000 of dividends to its shareholders, and on February 18, 2010, it distributes $90,000. Its accumulated earnings credit is $250,000. Assuming that Dodge elects to treat the dividends paid on February 18, 2010, as paid in 2009, its accumulated earnings tax is computed as follows:

Taxable income	$550,000
Plus: Adjustments	200,000
Adjusted taxable income	$750,000

---

[38] Code Secs. 561 and 563(a) and (d); Reg. §§ 1.561-1, 1.563-1, and 1.563-3.

Less: Dividends paid deduction	$135,000	
Accumulated earnings credit	250,000	(385,000)
Accumulated taxable income		$365,000
Accumulated earnings tax rate		× 15%
Accumulated earnings tax		$ 54,750

.01 Adjustments to Taxable Income

Several adjustments to taxable income are made in determining the accumulated taxable income. These adjustments attempt to provide a more accurate measure of the corporation's earnings for the year that could be distributed to shareholders. The required adjustments to taxable income include:[39]

1. A negative adjustment for amounts paid for federal income taxes and certain foreign income taxes accrued during the year because these amounts are not deducted in the calculation of taxable income, but they reduce the corporation's capacity to pay dividends.

2. A negative adjustment for any charitable contributions made during the year that were disallowed in the calculation of taxable income due to the 10-percent taxable income limitation. Although the charitable contribution deduction is limited for computing taxable income, the full amounts contributed reduce the corporation's ability to pay dividends.

3. A negative adjustment for any capital losses in excess of capital gains, as these losses incurred during the year affect the corporation's dividend-paying capacity.

4. A positive adjustment for any DRD and NOL deduction taken in the calculation of taxable income. The NOL deduction related to a previous tax year does not impact the corporation's ability to pay dividends from current year earnings. The DRD reduces the amount of dividends taxed under the regular tax system, but the deduction does not reduce the corporation's ability to distribute the full amount of dividends received during the year to its shareholders.

5. A deduction is allowed for the net capital gain (excess of net long-term capital gain over net short-term capital loss) for the tax year, reduced by the taxes attributable to the net gain.

6. A negative adjustment for any charitable contribution carryover from a previous tax year deducted in arriving at taxable income. The contribution to which this deduction relates reduced the corporation's ability to pay dividends out of the prior year's earnings and was taken into consideration in the year in which the contribution was made. (See the explanation in item number 2. above.)

7. A positive adjustment for any capital loss carryover from a previous tax year that offsets capital gains in the current year. The capital loss from another tax year affected the corporation's ability to pay dividends out of earnings in the year in which the loss was incurred. (See the explanation in item number 3. above.)[40]

Many of the adjustments involve deductions that either are limited for the purpose of calculating taxable income or are nondeductible, but because these amounts were paid by the corporation, they reduce the amounts available to be distributed to shareholders. Examples include the deduction for federal income taxes and the limitations that are applied to charitable contributions and capital losses. Other adjustments, like the requirement that the NOL deduction and the DRD be added back to taxable income, are necessary because they reduce taxable income but are not associated with a cash outflow that would reduce the corporation's ability to pay dividends to its shareholders.

---

[39] Code Sec. 535; Reg. §§ 1.535-1 and 1.535-2.   [40] Code Sec. 111(d).

Example 41: Dawning Corporation reports business profits of $100,000 during 2009. Dawning made charitable contributions during the year totaling $50,000. It received dividends from another domestic corporation of $100,000; Dawning owns five percent of the stock in the corporation. Dawning Corporation's dividends paid deduction is $10,000, and its accumulated earnings credit is $35,000.

Business profits		$100,000
Dividend income		100,000
		$200,000
Less: Charitable contribution deduction		
(limited to $200,000 × 10%)		(20,000)
DRD ($100,000 × 70%)		(70,000)
Taxable income		$110,000
Regular tax on $110,000 taxable income		$ 26,150

Taxable income		$110,000
Less: Excess charitable contributions	$30,000	
Federal income tax	26,150	(56,150)
Adjusted taxable income		$ 53,850
Less: Dividends paid deduction	$10,000	
Accumulated earnings credit	35,000	(45,000)
Accumulated taxable income		$ 8,850
Accumulated earnings tax rate		× 15%
Accumulated earnings tax		$ 1,328

.02 Accumulated Earnings Credit

Accumulated earnings and profits (accumulated E&P) represent the corporation's dividend-paying ability from previous years' E&P. It represents the amount of E&P the corporation has generated over the years that has not been distributed. A corporation is not subject to the accumulated earnings tax if its accumulated E&P does not exceed an amount that the corporation needs to retain to cover the reasonable needs of the business. At a minimum, the tax laws allow corporations to retain $250,000 of accumulated E&P ($150,000 for personal service corporations (PSCs), which are corporations engaged in performing services in the fields of health, law, engineering, architecture, accounting, actuarial science, performing arts, or consulting).

The accumulated earnings credit is intended to measure the amount of current year E&P the corporation needs to hold onto in addition to its accumulated E&P to meet the reasonable needs of the business. The accumulated earnings credit is the amount by which the *greater* of (1) the corporation's foreseeable reasonable financial needs or (2) $250,000 ($150,000 for PSCs) exceeds the corporation's accumulated E&P at the beginning of the year.[41] Only the greater of the two amounts over the amounts already retained from previous years (beginning balance in accumulated E&P) is allowed as a credit against adjusted taxable income when computing the current year's accumulated earnings tax. If the corporation can show that its reasonable needs exceed $250,000, it will be able to retain a total of that amount in accumulated E&P.

Example 42: A corporation has accumulated E&P of $50,000 at the beginning of 2009. Its adjusted taxable income for 2009 is $330,000. The corporation paid $20,000 of dividends

---

[41] Code Secs. 531-537.

during 2009. Assuming that the corporation cannot establish the need for more than $250,000 of accumulated earnings, its accumulated earnings credit for the year equals $200,000 ($250,000 – $50,000). The corporation's accumulated taxable income for 2009 is computed as follows:

Adjusted taxable income	$330,000
Less: Dividends paid deduction	(20,000)
Accumulated earnings credit	(200,000)
Accumulated taxable income for 2009	$110,000

Assuming that the IRS can show that the corporation was formed or continues to exist to avoid taxation of profits to individual shareholders, its accumulated earnings tax for 2009 equals $16,500 ($110,000 × 15%). This tax is paid in addition to the regular income tax and the AMT the corporation owes during the year.

Planning Pointer: A corporation with individual shareholders that has accumulated E&P in excess of $250,000 should be prepared to justify its reasons for needing to hold onto those accumulated earnings. If no reason exists, the corporation should consider distributing its excess earnings before 2½ months after the close of the tax year to avoid any possibility of being assessed the accumulated earnings tax. With tax rates on qualified dividends equal to a maximum of 15 percent through 2010, even corporations that may be able to justify retaining excess accumulations of earnings may want to consider making dividend distributions to avoid this tax in future tax years.

Reasonable accumulations. Accumulations that are considered reasonably necessary to meet the needs of the business include accumulations for business expansion or plant replacement, debt retirement, acquisition of a business through purchase of stock or assets, working capital, investments or loans to suppliers or customers necessary to the maintenance of the corporation's business, and some stock redemptions.[42]

Unacceptable grounds for having excess accumulations include loans to shareholders and expenditures for their personal benefit, loans to relatives or friends of shareholders or to others that have no reasonable connection with the business, loans to a sister corporation, investments that are not related to the business, and accumulations to provide against unrealistic hazards.[43]

Example 43: A corporation has taxable income in year 2009 of $200,000, but its adjusted taxable income is $233,850. The corporation paid $86,000 in dividends during 2009. Accumulated E&P at the beginning of 2009 equals $250,000 and the corporation cannot show a need for accumulations in excess of the $250,000 allowed without justifying its reasonable needs. The corporation's $22,178 accumulated earnings tax for 2009 is computed as shown below. The corporation owes this amount in addition to the regular income tax and any AMT it owes during the year.

Adjusted taxable income		$233,850
Less: Dividends paid deduction	$86,000	
Accumulated earnings credit	0	(86,000)
Accumulated taxable income		$147,850
		× 15%
Accumulated earnings tax		$ 22,178

---

[42] Reg. § 1.537-2(b).   [43] Reg. § 1.537-2(c).

Example 44: Assume the same facts as in Example 43, except the corporation can demonstrate that its reasonable needs for accumulations of E&P are $400,000. Under this scenario, the corporation would not be subject to any accumulated earnings tax.

Adjusted taxable income		$233,850
Less: Dividends paid deduction	$ 86,000	
Accumulated earnings credit ($400,000 – $250,000)	150,000	(236,000)
Accumulated taxable income		$ 0

Spotlight: Unlike the regular income tax or the AMT, enforcement of the accumulated earnings tax often requires the IRS to reach a decision about the reasonable needs of the corporation. Thus, unsophisticated management may not be aware of a potential accumulated earnings tax liability until an IRS agent in the course of an audit brings the liability to management's attention.

PERSONAL HOLDING COMPANY TAX

In addition to the regular corporate income tax and the AMT, a special tax is imposed on any corporation that is classified as a personal holding company (PHC). This tax exists to prevent individuals from holding investments (the income from which they would not use) in corporations in which the income could be taxed at a lower rate. The PHC tax is 15 percent of the corporation's undistributed PHC income.[44]

Reason for the Rule: When the PHC tax was originally enacted in 1934, the maximum corporate tax rate was 13.5 percent and the top individual tax rate was 63 percent. The difference in these two rates created huge incentives for individuals to form closely held corporations where the income from their personal investments could be taxed at much lower tax rates. When the individual needed access to the investments in the corporation, the corporation could be liquidated on a tax-free basis under the tax laws in effect at the time. Today, the top tax rate for both individuals and corporations is 35 percent, and a PHC can no longer be liquidated free of tax. Thus, even though the PHC rules continue to exist in the tax law, the advantages of forming a PHC have diminished significantly over time.

¶ 1015 Personal Holding Company Defined

A **personal holding company (PHC)** is any corporation for which (1) at any time during the last half of the tax year, more than 50 percent of the corporation's stock is owned, *directly or indirectly*, by five or fewer individuals and (2) at least 60 percent of the corporation's adjusted ordinary gross income for the tax year is PHC income.[45]

A corporation is specifically exempt from this definition if it is a bank, life insurance company, surety company, foreign corporation, small business investment company, or a corporation that is

---

[44] Code Sec. 541.

[45] Code Sec. 542(a).

subject to court jurisdiction in a federal or state bankruptcy, receivership, foreclosure, or similar proceeding; in some circumstances a lending or finance company may also be exempt.[46]

.01 Stock Ownership Requirement

A corporation meets the stock ownership requirement of being a PHC if at any time during the last half of its tax year more than 50 percent in value of its outstanding stock was owned, *directly or indirectly,* by or for five or fewer individuals. Corporations with a considerably greater number of shareholders may also meet the test when the constructive ownership rules are applied.[47] These rules were first introduced in Chapter 8 with the discussion of the related party rules (see ¶ 804.01). Two of the more common constructive ownership rules are:

1. Stock owned by a corporation or partnership is considered owned proportionately by its shareholders or partners.

2. An individual is considered to own the stock owned by family members (only siblings, spouse, ancestors, or lineal descendants) or by a partner.

.02 Income Requirement

A corporation meets the income requirement of being a PHC if at least 60 percent of its adjusted ordinary gross income for the tax year is PHC income.[48] The purpose of this requirement is to determine whether the income of the corporation is weighted with certain types of passive or investment income so as to indicate that the corporation has no substantial purpose other than to hold income-producing properties for its shareholders.

The ordinary gross income of a PHC is gross income reduced by capital gains and gains from sales or disposition of property used in a trade or business.[49] "Adjusted ordinary gross income" is ordinary gross income minus certain deductions associated with rents, mineral royalties, working interests in oil and gas wells, and certain interest income.[50] **PHC income** includes eight specific types of ordinary income: (1) dividends, interest, and royalties; (2) rents; (3) mineral, oil, and gas royalties; (4) copyright royalties; (5) produced film rents; (6) amounts received by a corporation for the use of its property; (7) compensation under personal services contracts; and (8) estate or trust income.[51]

Example 45: Gamma Corporation, which meets the stock ownership requirement of a PHC, owns a department store, some rental property, and some securities. Its adjusted ordinary gross income for the tax year is $110,000, consisting of gross income from the mercantile business of $40,000, adjusted rental income of $25,000, dividend income of $35,000, and interest income of $10,000. Gamma is a PHC because its $70,000 of PHC income (rents of $25,000 + dividends of $35,000 + interest of $10,000) represents at least 60 percent of its adjusted ordinary gross income of $110,000 ($70,000/$110,000 = 63.6%).

¶ 1016 Undistributed Personal Holding Company Income

The amount subject to the PHC tax is a corporation's **undistributed personal holding company income**. This amount is determined by applying certain adjustments to the taxable income of the corporation to arrive at the adjusted taxable income.[52] A 15-percent tax rate is assessed on undistributed PHC income.[53] The adjustments to taxable income include many of the adjustments necessary for the accumulated earnings tax. (See ¶ 1014.01.)

As in the calculation of the accumulated taxable income, dividends paid during the year are deducted in computing a corporation's undistributed PHC income. This includes dividends paid

---

[46] Code Sec. 542(c).

[47] Code Sec. 544; Reg. §§ 1.544-1-1.544-7.

[48] Code Sec. 542(a)(1).

[49] Code Sec. 543(b)(1).

[50] Code Sec. 543(b)(2).

[51] Code Sec. 543(a).

[52] Code Sec. 545.

[53] Code Sec. 541.

during the first 2½ months of the following year that the taxpayer elects to treat as paid in the current year. This deduction makes it possible for a corporation that has not been able to avoid PHC status to avoid payment of the penalty tax on its undistributed PHC income.[54]

Example 46: A PHC's taxable income for 2009 is $200,000, computed without taking into account the deductions for charitable contributions or for dividends received deduction (DRD). The PHC made contributions of $45,000 to a charitable organization during the year. It also received $100,000 of dividends from other domestic corporations in which it owned five percent of the stock. The PHC paid $70,000 of dividends to its shareholders in 2009, and it paid an additional $14,000 of dividends prior to March 15, 2010. The PHC elects to treat the dividends paid before March 15, 2010, as paid during 2009.

Taxable income		$200,000
Less: Charitable contribution deduction		
($200,000 × 10%)	$20,000	
DRD ($100,000 × 70%)	70,000	(90,000)
Taxable income		$110,000
Regular tax on $110,000 taxable income		$ 26,150
Taxable income		$110,000
Add: DRD		70,000
Deduct: Excess charitable contribution deduction	$25,000	
Federal income taxes paid	26,150	
Dividends paid during year	70,000	
Dividends paid before March 15, 2010	14,000	(135,150)
Undistributed PHC income		$ 44,850
		× 15%
Personal holding company tax		$ 6,728

¶ 1017 Summary

If after using the tax laws presented in Chapters 1 to 9, an individual or corporate taxpayer has negative taxable income, the taxpayer may have a NOL that can be used to offset gross income in other tax years. If taxable income results, regular income taxes must be paid by individual and corporate taxpayers, and for some taxpayers, AMT taxes might be due. In addition to income taxes, the accumulated earnings tax and the PHC tax are penalty taxes corporations will want to avoid because they are imposed in addition to the income taxes corporations pay during the year.

GLOSSARY OF TERMS INTRODUCED IN THE CHAPTER

Accumulated earnings and profits. The amount of E&P a C corporation has generated over the years that has not been distributed as of the beginning of its current tax year.

Accumulated earnings credit. Used in the calculation of the accumulated earnings tax. A credit allowed a corporation in computing accumulated taxable income that represents the amount by which the *greater of* (1) the corporation's foreseeable reasonable financial needs or (2) $250,000

---

[54] Code Sec. 561.

($150,000 for personal service corporations) exceeds the corporation's accumulated E&P at the beginning of the year.

Accumulated earnings tax. A penalty tax imposed on C corporations formed or that continue to exist for the purpose of preventing individual shareholders from paying tax on the profits of the corporation by allowing E&P to accumulate.

Adjusted current earnings (ACE). An alternative minimum tax concept similar to current earnings and profits. ACE differs from current E&P in that current E&P attempts to measure the corporation's capacity to pay dividends from current period earnings, while the ACE calculation is intended to measure pretax income before any distributions.

Alternative minimum tax (AMT). Rules in the federal tax system enacted to enhance equity in the income tax system by ensuring that all taxpayers pay at least some minimum income taxes each year.

Alternative minimum taxable income (AMTI). Term used in the alternative minimum tax system. AMTI is determined by making certain adjustments to regular taxable income. *See also* Alternative minimum tax.

AMT base. The tax base used in the AMT system; determined by subtracting the exemption amount from the alternative minimum taxable income. This amount is analogous to taxable income in the regular income tax system. *See also* Alternative minimum tax *and* Alternative minimum taxable income.

Circulation costs. Amounts paid or incurred to establish, maintain, or increase the circulation of a newspaper, magazine, or other periodical.

Current earnings and profits. A C corporation's earnings and profits for its current tax year. A corporate tax concept that attempts to capture a corporation's capacity to pay dividends from its current year's earnings.

Minimum tax credit. A tax credit equal to the amount of alternative minimum tax paid in one year that is attributable to adjustments due to timing differences. The minimum tax credit can be carried forward and used to offset the regular tax liability of a subsequent year. *See also* Alternative minimum tax *and* Timing differences.

Net operating loss deduction. The total of a taxpayer's net operating loss carryforwards and carrybacks to a tax year.

Personal holding company (PHC). Any corporation for which (1) at any time during the last half of the tax year, more than 50 percent of the corporation's stock is owned, *directly or indirectly*, by five or fewer individuals and (2) at least 60 percent of the corporation's adjusted ordinary income for the year is PHC income.

Personal holding company income. Eight specific types of ordinary income, including: (1) dividends, interest, and royalties; (2) rents; (3) mineral, oil, and gas royalties; (4) copyright royalties; (5) produced film rents; (6) amounts received by a corporation for the use of its property; (7) compensation under personal services contracts; and (8) estate or trust income.

Personal service corporation (PSC). A corporation engaged almost exclusively in performing services in the fields of health, law, engineering, architecture, accounting, actuarial science, performing arts, or consulting. At least 95 percent of the value of its stock is held, directly or indirectly, by its employees, by retired employees who performed services for the corporation, or by an estate or other person owning stock because of the death of such employees or retired employees.

Private activity bond. A bond issued by a state or other municipality from which more than 10 percent of the proceeds are used to finance private business activities. Interest paid on these bonds is exempt from regular income tax if the issuer has complied with certain limitations concerning the volume of the bonds issued and the use of the bond proceeds.

Tax preference. A deduction or exclusion allowed in the calculation of regular taxable income that the Internal Revenue Code specifically singles out as excessive and, therefore, not allowed in the calculation of alternative minimum taxable income.

Timing difference. In the alternative minimum tax system, a difference in the treatment of an item for determining regular taxable income and alternative minimum taxable income that reverses itself over time.

Undistributed personal holding company income. The amount subject to the personal holding company tax, determined by applying certain adjustments to the taxable income of the corporation.

CHAPTER PROBLEMS

The following questions and problems relate to the discussion in Chapter 10, NOLs, AMT, and Other Business Taxes, which begins at ¶ 1000 in *Part IV: Calculating Tax Liability and Taxes Owed.*

Chapter 10 Discussion Questions

1. A taxpayer has a net operating loss. In looking over the past several tax returns and the anticipated future growth of his business, the taxpayer believes it would be advantageous from a tax perspective to utilize its NOL in future tax years. Can this be done, and if so what steps must the taxpayer take?

2. Sig and Tom are equal partners in a partnership that reports an ordinary loss of $17,000. Is this loss a NOL? Who is entitled to the loss?

3. Under what circumstances can the dividends received deduction create or increase a corporation's NOL?

4. Are all taxpayers subject to AMT? Discuss.

5. If a corporation fails to qualify as a small corporation in 2009 for purposes of the alternative minimum tax (AMT), what must it do in 2010 to avoid being subject to AMT?

6. What role does "tentative minimum tax" play in the calculation of AMT?

7. The maximum corporate AMT exemption amount is $40,000. At what point does a corporation subject to AMT have a $0 exemption?

8. What two AMT tax preferences relate to owners and/or produces of oil and gas property?

9. AMT preferences items are always positive adjustments to taxable income for purposes of computing AMTI. Explain.

10. AMT adjustments resulting from timing adjustments may be positive or negative. Explain.

11. Do taxpayers that experience a net operating loss (NOL) for the tax year need to recompute the NOL for AMT purposes?

12. While corporate earnings and profits (E&P) attempt to measure a corporation's capacity to pay dividends from current period earnings, what is the adjusted current earnings (ACE) calculation intended to measure?

13. When can AMT paid in one year be carried forward as a credit against regular tax in a subsequent year?

14. Is the AMT tax rate the same for corporate and individual taxpayers?

15. Which taxpayers are subject to the accumulated earnings tax and under what circumstances does it apply?

16. Which party (the corporation or the IRS) has the burden of proving that earnings and profits are not being accumulated for a tax avoidance purpose?

17. How is the accumulated earnings credit computed?

18. What might constitute "reasonable needs of the business" for purposes of computing the accumulated earnings credit?

19. What is a personal holding company (PHC)?

20. What tax law changes have contributed to the decline in the attractiveness of personal holding companies?

Chapter 10 Problems

1. In 2009, Acme Corporation reports negative taxable income of $350,000, including a net operating loss (NOL) carryforward from 2008 of $70,000. What is Acme's NOL for 2009?

2. An individual taxpayer reports a $19,000 NOL in 2009. To which tax years can this NOL be applied? How would your answer change if the taxpayer were a C corporation, rather than an individual?

3. Failing Corporation incurred a NOL of $90,000 for the calendar year 2009. Failing carried this loss back to 2007. In 2007, Failing had $400,000 of gross income and business expenses of $325,000. Included in the business expenses was a deduction for a charitable contribution of $3,000. In addition, a NOL of $40,000 from 2008 had been carried back to 2007. What is the Failing's NOL to be carried forward from 2007?

4. The Simplex Machine Corporation presents you with the following profit and loss statement of its operations for 2009 and requests that you prepare its tax return.

Sales	$570,000
Less: Cost of goods sold	(480,000)
Gross profit	$ 90,000
Less: Operating expenses	(110,000)
	($ 20,000)
Section 1231 gain from sale of building	4,000
Taxable income (loss)	($ 16,000)

Simplex Machine's taxable income for 2007 and 2008 was $9,000 and $33,000, respectively.

a. Compute the NOL deduction, if any, for the Simplex Machine Corporation for 2009.

b. What else should you do for your client once you apply the loss to the prior years' income?

5. A corporation generates a $72,000 NOL in 20X6. The corporation's modified taxable income for the following years is as follows.

20X1	$ 19,000
20X2	25,000
20X3	3,000
20X4	10,000
20X5	12,000
20X7	22,000
20X8	21,000

a. Compute the corporation's NOL carryover to 20X9 assuming that the corporation does not elect to forego the NOL carryback.

b. Compute the corporation's NOL carryover to 20X9 assuming the corporation elects to forego the NOL carryback.

6. Assume that the marginal tax rate of the corporation in Problem 5 is 15 percent from 20X1–20X5 and 34 percent from 20X7–20X9. Compute the total tax savings generated from the NOL assuming (a) that the corporation does not forego the carry back period, and (b) the corporation elects to forego the carry back period. For purposes of this calculation, assume that any remaining NOL carryover is utilized in 20X9.

7. For the prior tax year, XYZ Corp. had an asset with a basis of $20,000, for both regular tax and AMT purposes, with respect to which a $700 depreciation deduction was calculated for regular tax purposes but a $500 depreciation deduction was calculated for AMT purposes.

What will be the basis for determining gain in the current year under both the regular tax system and the AMT system?

8. ACME Corporation sells a piece of equipment with an adjusted tax basis of $300,000 for $400,000. The terms of the sale have ACME receiving $100,000 at the time of the sale and $100,000 annually over the next three years. ACME does not elect out of the installment method. Compute the positive or negative adjustments that must be made to AMTI in each of the four years for purposes of computing ACME's adjusted current earnings.

9. A corporation's taxable income and AMTI are $130,000 and $280,000, respectively. Assuming the corporation is subject to AMT, compute the corporation's total income tax liability for the year.

10. A calendar-year corporation's first tax year is 20X1. Its unadjusted AMTI is $150,000 each year from 20X1–20X3. The corporation's ACE during those years is $200,000, $120,000, and $100,000, respectively. Compute the ACE adjustment in each of these three years 20X1–20X3.

11. A corporate taxpayer receives $50,000 of municipal interest, which includes $10,000 of interest from specified private activity bonds. What amount of the $50,000 interest is included in the corporation's taxable income, alternative minimum taxable income, and current year earnings and profits (E&P)?

12. A corporation in the retail industry with calendar-year end has $300,000 in taxable income in 2009. This figure includes $1,000 for an installment sale made in 2006; the total gain from the sale was $5,000. The taxable income reflected $30,000 in depreciation, $20,000 of which represented the excess of accelerated depreciation over straight-line. The corporation received $10,000 of tax-exempt interest from a specified private activity bond. No nondeductible expenses were related to this income. The corporation's ACE equaled $800,000. Determine the corporation's alternative minimum tax for 2009.

13. Widget Corporation has taxable income of $500,000 for the current year. There are net positive adjustments to taxable income for purposes of the accumulated earnings tax of $50,000. Widget paid dividends during the year of $45,000, and its accumulated earnings credit is $200,000. Calculate Widget's accumulated earnings tax for the year.

14. A retail hardware store was organized on January 1, 2009. Its taxable income in the first year is $300,000. It makes no distributions to its shareholders during that year or during the first 2½ months of the second year. The only adjustments to taxable income for purposes of the accumulated earnings tax is for federal income taxes paid on its taxable income.

   a. Will the corporation be subject to the accumulated earnings tax for the first tax year?

   b. Assuming that the corporation has the same taxable income the second year and that it makes no distributions during the second year or the first 2½ months of the third year, will it be subject to the accumulated earnings tax for the second year?

   c. If the corporation had distributed $115,000 to shareholders in its first year of existence and nothing in the second year, would it be subject to the accumulated earnings tax for the second year?

15. West Corporation had taxable income of $200,000 in 2009 and $250,000 for 2010. How much, if any, of the 2009 income must the West Corporation distribute in order to be sure to avoid the accumulated earnings tax for 2010 if it cannot justify taking more than the minimum credit? Assume that the only adjustment to taxable income for purposes of the accumulated earnings credit is for its federal tax paid.

16. The Axel Construction receives 90 percent of its gross income during the tax year from interest on industrial bonds and dividends on railways stocks. Dan Majors owns 20 percent of Axel, Dan's son owns 10 percent, and the son's wife owns five percent. The rest of the shares are owned by 13 unrelated employees each of whom own five percent. Is Axel Construction a personal holding company? Explain.

17. A corporation that meets the stock ownership requirement of a personal holding company (PHC), owns a hardware store, residential rental property, and some corporate stocks and bonds. Its adjusted ordinary gross income for the tax year is $180,000, consisting of gross

income from the mercantile business of $50,000, adjusted rental income of $35,000, dividend income of $55,000, and interest income of $40,000. Is the corporation a PHC?

18. Assume the same facts as in Problem 17, except that the corporation's dividend income is $5,000. Assume all other income items and amounts remain the same. Is the corporation a PHC?

19. A personal holding company's taxable income for 2009 is $200,000, which includes a $90,000 dividends received deduction. The PHC has a $13,000 charitable contribution carryover due to its current year contributions being subject to the taxable income limitation. It paid $45,000 of dividends to its shareholders in 2009 and an additional $26,000 of dividends on March 19, 2010. The PHC elects to treat dividends paid within the first 2½ months of 2010 as paid during 2009. Compute the company's PHC tax for 2009.

20. Assume the same facts as in Problem 19, except that the PHC makes a dividend distribution on March 15, 2010. Compute the company's PHC tax for 2009. Comment on the difference between the answers to Problems 19 and 20.

21. Godsey Corporation has a net operating loss of $60,000 for its 2009 tax year. For its 2007 tax year, its taxable income was $55,000 and its modified taxable income was $45,000. For its 2008 tax year, its taxable income was $35,000 and its modified taxable income was $30,000. For its 2010 tax year, it expects its taxable income to be $30,000 and its modified taxable income to be $25,000. For its 2011 tax year, it expects its taxable income to be $120,000 and its modified taxable income to be $100,000. Based on this information, how should the corporation treat its NOL for 2009, and how much will it save if it follows your recommendation?

22. Jernigan Corporation, which uses the calendar year as its tax year, started business on December 1, 2007. Its gross receipts for 2007 totaled $500,000. Its gross receipts for 2008–2010 were $4,500,000, $4,900,000, and $6,000,000, respectively. Will the corporation be subject to AMT in 2010? Explain your answer.

23. Hoffman, Inc. had to pay $50,000 in AMT for its 2009 tax year. If its taxable income for 2010 is $170,000 and it is not subject to the AMT that year, how much tax will it owe?

24. For her 2009 tax year, Rosie Longo, who is unmarried, received $75,000 in wages (her only source of AGI for the year). During the year she exercised an incentive stock option and purchased 100 shares of her company's stock (with a fair market value of $40 per share) for $10 per share. She took the standard deduction and personal exemption. What is her tentative minimum tax for the year? Does she owe any AMT?

25. Hyman, Inc. has four shareholders. John Hyman owns 20% of the corporation's stock. Mae Ritter, who is not related to John, owns 15% of the corporation's stock. The Bracket Partnership owns the remaining 65% of the corporation's stock. That partnership consists of John and four unrelated partners, who each owns the same interest in the partnership. Does John satisfy the stock ownership requirement for a personal holding company?

Chapter 10 Review Problems

1. After an investigation by the IRS, the following facts were discovered from the books and records of the Shady Tree Nursery, which began business on January 1, 2007.

	2007	2008	2009	2010
Gross profit on sales	$100,000	$210,000	$160,000	$70,000
Net capital gains			5,000	
Net capital losses		(5,000)		(3,000)
Gross income	$100,000	$205,000	$165,000	$67,000
Business expenses	(130,000)	(155,000)	(145,000)	(87,000)
Net income per books	($ 30,000)	$ 50,000	$ 20,000	($20,000)

a. In computing taxable income for 2008 and 2010, are the net capital losses deductible?

    b. Compute the taxable income for 2008 after taking into account any net operating loss carrybacks and carryforwards from 2007 and 2010.

2. A personal holding company's taxable income for 2009 is $250,000, computed before taking into account the charitable contributions deduction and the dividends received deduction. Included in the $250,000 is $120,000 of dividends it received from other domestic corporations in which it owns 25 percent of the stock. The PHC makes contributions of $55,000 to a charitable organization during the year. It paid $75,000 of dividends to its shareholders in 2009 and an additional $40,000 of dividends on March 8, 2010. What amount of PHC tax does it owe for 2009?

3. A calendar year corporation has $100,000 in taxable income for 2009. In calculating its alternative minimum tax (AMT), it has positive adjustments and tax preferences of $140,000 and $60,000, respectively. Its adjusted current earnings for the year are $500,000.

    a. Compute the corporation's 2009 AMT.

    b. What would have been the corporation's AMT given its average gross receipts for all three-tax-year periods ending before its current tax year was below $5 million?

Chapter 10 Comprehensive Review Question

For its tax year ended December 31, 2009, Beneficial Corporation had the following income and expenses:

Income:

Sales	$4,000,000
Interest income ($100,000 of tax-exempt interest other than from specified private activity bonds)	200,000
Short-term capital gain	50,000

Expenses:

Cost of goods sold	$2,000,000
Wages	400,000
Interest expense	50,000
Depreciation*	150,000
Charitable contributions	100,000
Miscellaneous	500,000

* Under GAAP, depreciation expense is $100,000; for purposes of AMT depreciation is $125,000.

Beneficial's QPAI for purposes of the domestic production activities deduction is $600,000. Compute Beneficial's 2009 regular income tax liability and its AMT.

Chapter 10 Research Question

You are approached by a corporation with a long-standing dispute with the IRS. The corporation incurred alternative minimum tax net operating losses in the years subsequent to the enactment of the corporate alternative minimum tax in 1986. The corporation seeks to carryforward these AMT net operating losses so that it can obtain tax refunds for subsequent tax years. The IRS contends that these AMT net operating losses must first be carried back and applied against regular tax in the years prior to the enactment of the corporate AMT. Determine whether you can find any authority on this issue that would support the taxpayer's or the IRS's position.

CHAPTER 11

Tax Credits

LEARNING OBJECTIVES

1. Review the concept of a tax credit and distinguish it from a tax deduction.

2. Review the distinction between a refundable tax credit and a nonrefundable tax credit.

3. Explain the government's motives behind offering tax credits.

4. Describe how tax credits reduce a business's transaction costs.

5. List the various tax credits available to businesses and explain the calculation of the more common business credits.

6. Describe the limitations that apply to business tax credits and explain the rules that allow tax credits that cannot be utilized in one tax year to be carried over to other tax years.

¶ 1100 Introduction

As discussed in Chapter 1, the federal government often uses tax laws to provide incentives aimed at encouraging certain types of behavior. One tool used to accomplish this is the **tax credit**, which is an amount by which the government allows a taxpayer to reduce its tax liability. This chapter reintroduces the concept of a tax credit and reviews the advantages of tax credits over tax deductions. This chapter also introduces the various tax credits that are available to businesses and discusses some of the more commonly used business tax credits, including the requirements and limitations that apply to each business credit. Most credits available to businesses are computed individually and then grouped together as part of the general business credit. A separate limitation applies to the general business credit each year. The limitations on and treatment of any unutilized credits are discussed.

Since tax credits reduce a taxpayer's tax liability, anyone involved in making decisions on behalf of a business needs to understand how tax credits can be used to reduce transaction costs. What otherwise might be considered an unattractive endeavor might become attractive when available credits are taken into consideration.

 GAAP vs. Code: Financial reporting has no equivalent to a tax credit. A tax credit is a tax concept only.

¶ 1101 Tax Savings Generated from a Tax Credit vs. a Tax Deduction

A tax credit is an amount that is subtracted from a taxpayer's tax liability. Thus, the tax savings derived from a $1 tax credit equals $1.

Example 1: Berglund Thermometers, Inc. had a gross income of $200,000, deductions of $106,000, and a business tax credit of $10,000. Burglund's taxable income equals $94,000 ($200,000 – $106,000), and its tax liability using the corporate income tax rates is $20,210. The $10,000 tax credit is subtracted from Berglund's tax liability, thereby reducing its taxes owed by $10,000.

In contrast, a tax deduction reduces a taxpayer's taxable income. The tax savings derived from a $1 tax deduction equals $1 multiplied by the taxpayer's marginal tax rate, which is the rate of tax paid on the last dollar included in taxable income. Therefore, all other things being equal, the tax benefits of a tax credit always outweigh the tax savings produced by a tax deduction.

Example 2: Assume the same facts as in Example 1, except instead of a $10,000 tax credit, Berglund has additional tax deductions of $10,000. The additional deductions reduce Berglund's taxable income to $84,000. Since Berglund's taxable income falls into the 34-percent tax bracket, its tax liability will be reduced by $3,400 ($10,000 × 34%). Hence, the $10,000 tax savings from the $10,000 tax credit illustrated in Example 1 outweigh the $3,400 tax savings produced by the $10,000 tax deduction illustrated here.

Because the tax savings derived from a deduction vary with the taxpayer's marginal tax rate, taxpayers in higher tax brackets benefit more from tax deductions than those in lower tax brackets. Under a progressive rate structure, higher tax rates are imposed on taxpayers with higher taxable incomes. Consequently, tax deductions favor higher-income taxpayers. Tax credits, on the other hand, benefit all taxpayers equally, and consequently, tax credits often are seen as a fairer way to offer tax incentives to taxpayers.

Example 3: Godsey Handles, Inc. and Arbuckle Co. are each entitled to a $50,000 depreciation deduction and a $10,000 business tax credit. Godsey's taxable income falls in the 25-percent tax bracket; Arbuckle's falls in the 34-percent tax bracket. The $10,000 tax credit reduces each company's respective tax liability by $10,000. The $50,000 depreciation deduction reduces Godsey's tax liability by $12,500 ($50,000 × 25%), which is less than the $17,000 ($50,000 × 34%) that Arbuckle's tax liability is lowered. The $4,500 difference is due to the nine-percent difference in the companies' marginal tax rates ($50,000 × 9% = $4,500 additional tax savings to Arbuckle).

Recall that the government takes an all-inclusive approach to defining gross income but allows deductions for expenses only by legislative grace. Thus, when the government allows businesses to deduct expenses from gross income, less tax revenues are generated and the government in essence subsidizes a portion of the company's expenditures. Alternatively, if the entire cost of the expenditures were offered as a tax credit, the actual cost of the item would be borne entirely by the government. Therefore, most tax credits are computed as a percentage of the actual expenditure. In some instances when the government allows a portion of the cost to be taken as a tax credit, it then allows the remainder to be deducted from gross income.

Example 4: As discussed in Chapter 6, the tax laws allow businesses to deduct wages they pay their employees as an ordinary and necessary business expense against their gross income. In the current year, Roland Enterprises (whose taxable income falls in the 35-percent tax bracket) pays an employee wages totaling $20,000. Roland's tax savings from those wages equals $7,000 ($20,000 × 35%). Accordingly, Roland's actual out-of-pocket costs for the wages paid to the employee were only $13,000 ($20,000 – $7,000).

Example 5: Assume the same facts as in Example 4, except the tax laws allow businesses to take a tax credit equal to 40 percent of the first $10,000 of first-year wages paid to a long-term family assistance recipient. Any wages not taken as a credit can be deducted from the taxpayer's gross income. Accordingly, if Roland hires a long-term family assistance recipient and pays him $20,000 in the first year, Roland's tax credit will equal $4,000 ($10,000 × 40%). Roland will then be able to deduct the remaining $16,000 ($20,000 – $4,000) from its gross income, thereby generating an additional tax savings of $5,600 ($16,000 × 35%). Roland's total tax savings from hiring this employee would be $9,600 ($4,000 + $5,600), and its actual out-of-pocket costs with respect to the wages would be $10,400 ($20,000 – $9,600).

Examples 4 and 5 illustrate how a company's understanding of the tax laws can generate additional cash flows by reducing the amounts the company pays in federal income taxes. Comparing the cash savings in the two scenarios, Roland can reduce its out-of-pocket costs for this worker by $2,600 ($13,000 – $10,400) by hiring a long-term family assistance recipient over a worker who is not a long-term family assistance recipient. Another way to compute the $2,600 of cash savings is to compare the tax savings of hiring a long-term family assistance recipient ($9,600) to that of hiring someone who is not a long-term family assistance recipient ($7,000).

¶ 1102 Types of Tax Credits

Tax credits can be business or personal. They can also be refundable or nonrefundable. A **refundable tax credit** can reduce a taxpayer's tax liability to zero and produce a refund for any amount of the credit in excess of the taxpayer's tax liability. A **nonrefundable tax credit** can only reduce a taxpayer's tax liability to zero. Most tax credits are nonrefundable; however, a few refundable credits exist. For example, amounts taxpayers prepay toward their current year's tax liability, whether through withholdings or by making estimated tax payments, are a refundable tax credit used first to reduce the amount of taxes owed when filing their annual income tax returns but refunded if not needed to cover the taxpayer's current year's tax liability (see ¶ 409). Most other refundable tax credits are personal credits available only to individual taxpayers.

.01 Business vs. Personal Tax Credits

Tax incentives, whether they are offered as exclusions, deductions, or credits, are a mechanism governments often use to encourage and reward taxpayers for making certain types of decisions. **Business tax credits** are a way governments reward businesses by subsidizing a portion of the expenditures they incur when participating in certain types of activities. An example of a business tax credit is the work opportunity credit, which was illustrated in Example 5. This credit rewards businesses that hire members of a targeted group by reducing the company's tax liabilities. Business tax credits are available to all types of business entities, including corporations, sole proprietorships, and the various flow-through entities.

Personal tax credits are available only to individual taxpayers. Like business tax credits, many personal tax credits represent a portion of an expenditure that the government allows individual taxpayers to use to offset their tax liabilities. However, a few personal credits are available without any corresponding cash expenditures. For example, the federal government allows an earned income credit to taxpayers who report relatively low amounts of earned income on their individual income tax returns. It also allows a $1,000 tax credit for each dependent child under the age of 17 for low- and moderate-income taxpayers. Most personal tax credits are nonrefundable; however, a few are refundable. Since the focus of this book is how taxes impact business decisions, the details regarding the various personal credits are beyond the scope of this chapter. However, a list of the more common personal tax credits available to individual taxpayers is provided in Figure 11-1.

Figure 11-1 Personal Tax Credits

Nonrefundable Personal Credits

- Lifetime Learning, Hope Scholarship, and American Opportunity education credits,
- Child and dependent care credit,
- Adoption expenses credit,
- Credit for the elderly and the disabled,
- Elective deferrals and IRA contributions credit,
- Mortgage interest credit,
- Nonbusiness energy property credit,
- Residential energy efficient property credit,
- Hybrid automobile credit,
- Qualified plug-in electric drive motor vehicle credit, and
- Child tax credit (for certain taxpayers).

Refundable Personal Credits

- Credit for prepayment of taxes,
- Credit for overpayment of social security taxes,
- Earned income credit,
- Child tax credit (for certain taxpayers),
- First-time homebuyer credit,
- Health insurance costs credit, and
- Making Work Pay credit.

 Reason for the Rule: As mentioned in Chapter 1, individuals are allowed a standard deduction and exemption amounts that are intended to reduce taxable income to zero or near zero for many lower-income individuals. Since nonrefundable tax credits are of little or no value to taxpayers with little or no taxable income, some personal tax credits, like the earned income credit and the child tax credit, were enacted to provide financial assistance to lower-income individuals. These tax credits were enacted as refundable tax credits so they could produce a refund to taxpayers the federal government has identified as needing additional financial assistance. Because the earned income credit is available only to taxpayers who report taxable earned income to the federal government on their income tax returns, the earned income credit serves the dual purposes of reallocating wealth to lower-income taxpayers and of increasing tax compliance for lower-income taxpayers by requiring them to file an annual tax return in order to claim the credit.

.02 The Motivation Behind Offering Tax Credits

Offering tax credits to individuals and businesses serves many purposes. Some tax credits exist to prevent taxpayers from overpaying taxes that they owe, like the refundable tax credit for prepaid income taxes. Other examples include the foreign tax credit and the credit for overpayment of social security taxes.

When income included in taxable income is taxed by both the United States and a foreign country, the federal government allows a tax credit for the taxes paid to the foreign country to ensure that the taxpayer is taxed only once on the income. The foreign tax credit is available to all types of taxpayers, including individuals and all business entities. It is discussed later in this chapter.

The tax credit for overpayment of social security taxes is necessary because the tax laws require employers to withhold a 6.2-percent social security tax on the first $106,800 of wages earned in 2009. Thus, employees who have more than one employer during the year will have more than $6,621.60 ($106,800 × 6.2%) withheld from their wages during the year if their total wages exceed $106,800. The refundable credit for overpayment of social security taxes ensures that any excess social security tax withheld during the calendar year is refunded to workers when they file their income tax returns.

Although a few tax credits exist to ensure that taxpayers are refunded any taxes they overpay during the year, most tax credits exist to encourage businesses to make certain types of decisions. For example, the federal government offers tax incentives for businesses to hire certain groups of economically disadvantaged workers. It also helps subsidize the costs businesses incur in rehabilitating a historical structure or providing access to physically disabled persons. Such credits are the focus of this chapter.

¶ 1103 General Business Credit

Numerous tax credits are available to businesses. With the exception of the foreign tax credit (which will be discussed later in the chapter), tax credits aimed at businesses are part of what is known as the **general business credit**. As with deductions, each business credit is subject to its own set of eligibility requirements and limitations. Each credit that is part of the general business credit is computed separately, and then the various credits are aggregated to compute the general business credit for that tax year. In addition to the limits imposed with each separate credit, Congress also limits the amount that taxpayers can claim as a general business credit in any one tax year. Although the general business credit is a nonrefundable credit, any amount of general business credit that cannot be taken in any one tax year can be carried over to other tax years. Unused general business credits can be carried back one year and forward for up to 20 years.[1]

 Reason for the Rule: Due to the ability of tax credits to offset a taxpayer's tax liability dollar for dollar, the various business credits that comprise the general business credit are subject to an overall limitation. The limitation prevents taxpayers from being able to entirely offset their income tax liabilities in any given tax year. However, the generous carryover provisions help ensure that taxpayers will eventually utilize the tax credits in tax years when they have sufficient amounts of tax liabilities.

.01 Calculating the General Business Credit

Businesses are allowed a nonrefundable general business credit equal to the sum of the following amounts:

1. The current year general business credits;

2. The general business credit carried forward from prior tax years to the current tax year; and

3. The general business credit carried back to the current tax year from a subsequent tax year.[2]

Example 6: Taggert Company claimed a $20,000 general business credit on its 2009 corporate tax return. During 2010, Taggert Company generates a $50,000 general business credit; however, due to the limitations imposed on the amount of general business credit allowed in any one year, only $35,000 of the credit was allowed. Taggert carries back the $15,000 of disallowed general business credit to 2009 and recomputes its taxes

---

[1] Code Sec. 39(a).   [2] Code Sec. 38(a).

owed in that year using a $35,000 recomputed general business credit ($20,000 current year [2009] credit + $15,000 credit carried back from 2010).

Example 7: Assume the same facts as in Example 6, except when Taggert reapplies the general business credit limitations in 2009, $3,000 of the general business credit is disallowed. Taggert carries forward the $3,000 to 2011 and adds it to any general business credit generated in that year.

Like many credits, the credits that comprise the general business credit were enacted to elicit and reward certain types of behavior. The various types of activities and behaviors that the government was hoping to encourage include (1) hiring certain types of workers; (2) conserving and exploring new sources of energy; (3) conducting research in specified areas; and (4) assisting in economic development. Other business tax credits were enacted to subsidize businesses for certain socially or economically desirable expenditures made during the year. Figure 11-2 summarizes the various tax credits that comprise the general business credit. The more common general business credits plus the foreign tax credit (which is not part of the general business credit) are the focus of the discussion for the remainder of this chapter.

Figure 11-2 Tax Credits That Comprise the General Business Credit

Tax Credits Aimed at Encouraging Employers to Hire Certain Workers
- Work opportunity credit,
- Empowerment zone and renewal community employment credit, and
- Indian employment credit.

Tax Credits Aimed at Encouraging Conservation of Energy and Reduction of Greenhouse Gases
- Alternative motor vehicle credit,
- Plug-in electric drive motor vehicle credit
- Alternative fuel vehicle refueling property credit,
- Home builder's credit for new energy efficient homes,
- Manufacturer's credit for energy efficient appliances,
- Energy credit,
- Credit for producing fuel from a nonconventional source,
- Alcohol used as fuel credit,
- Biodiesel and renewable diesel used as fuel credit,
- Low sulfur diesel fuel production credit,
- Renewable electricity and refined coal production credit,
- Carbon dioxide sequestration credit,
- Qualifying advanced coal project credit,
- Qualifying gasification project credit,
- Advanced energy project credit,
- Enhanced oil recovery credit, and
- Marginal oil and gas well production credit.

Tax Credits Aimed at Rewarding Research in Certain Areas
- Research credit and
- Orphan drug credit.

Tax Credits to Encourage Economic Development

- Empowerment zone and renewal community employment credit and
- New markets credit.

Tax Credits Used to Subsidize Businesses for Certain Expenditures during the Year

- Employer social security tax credit,
- Differential wage payment credit,
- Rehabilitation credit,
- Low-income housing credit,
- Disabled access credit,
- Employer-provided child care credit,
- Small employer pension plan start-up cost credit,
- Distilled spirits credit,
- Railroad track maintenance credit,
- Mine rescue team training credit,
- Agricultural chemicals security credit, and
- Advanced nuclear power facility credit.

.02 Overall Limitations on the Amount of General Business Credit

The amount of a taxpayer's general business credit for any tax year is limited to the amount by which the taxpayer's net income tax exceeds the *greater* of (1) the taxpayer's tentative minimum tax for the tax year or (2) 25 percent of the amount by which the taxpayer's net regular tax liability exceeds $25,000.[3] Any amount of general business credit that is not allowed in the current year can be carried back one year and then carried forward 20 years.[4]

Tentative minimum tax was introduced in Chapter 10. When tentative minimum tax exceeds the taxpayer's regular tax liability, the excess represents the taxpayer's alternative minimum tax (AMT) for the year. "Regular tax liability" is the tax liability computed on taxable income using the applicable progressive income tax rates. **Net regular tax liability** is the taxpayer's regular tax liability minus certain tax credits like the foreign tax credit and personal tax credits (in the case of an individual, including a sole proprietor).[5] **Net income tax** equals the sum of the net regular tax liability and any AMT minus the same tax credits used in computing net regular tax liability. Thus, the difference between net regular tax liability and net income tax is usually the taxpayer's AMT for the year.

Example 8: For 2009, Norris Machine Shop calculates $170,000 of regular tax liability on its taxable income and takes a $10,000 foreign tax credit. Norris's tentative minimum tax equals $120,000, and since this amount does not exceed its regular tax liability, Norris is not subject to AMT in 2009.

For the purposes of computing the limitation in its general business credit, net regular tax liability equals $160,000 ($170,000 regular tax liability − $10,000 foreign tax credit). Since Norris is not subject to AMT in 2009, net income tax also equals $160,000 ($170,000 regular tax liability + $0 AMT − $10,000 foreign tax credit). If in 2009 Norris generates a total general business credit of $50,000, it will be allowed to reduce its 2009 tax liability by $40,000 as calculated below. The $10,000 ($50,000 − $40,000) that Norris is not allowed to use in 2009 can be carried back to 2008. If not

---

[3] Code Sec. 38(c).

[4] Code Sec. 39(a)(1).

[5] Code Sec. 38(c)(1).

fully utilized in 2008, the remaining credit can be carried forward from 2010 through 2029, and it can be applied against the company's income tax liability in those years.

Net income tax	$160,000
Less: The *greater of* (1) $120,000 or	
(2) $33,750 [25% × ($160,000 – $25,000)]	(120,000)
General business credit allowed in 2009	$ 40,000

Example 9: For 2009, McMurray, Inc. had a regular tax liability and a tentative minimum tax of $175,000 and $210,000, respectively. Since the amount of tentative minimum tax exceeds the taxpayer's regular tax liability, McMurray reports the $35,000 excess as AMT on its 2009 tax return. McMurray has no foreign tax credit in 2009. McMurray's net income tax is $210,000 ($175,000 regular tax + $35,000 AMT). In 2009, McMurray generated a total general business credit of $20,000, but as shown below, the company cannot utilize any of the credit in 2009. The $20,000 can be carried back to 2008, and if not utilized in that year, any unused credit can be applied against its income tax liability from 2010 through 2029.

Net income tax	$210,000
Less: The *greater of* (1) $210,000 or	
(2) $37,500 [25% × ($175,000 – $25,000)]	(210,000)
General business credit allowed in 2009	$ 0

Planning Pointer: Taxpayers entitled to a tax refund after carrying any unused general business credit back to the previous tax year can obtain a quick refund by filing Form 1139, *Corporation Application for Tentative Refund,* or Form 1045, *Application for Tentative Refund* (for individuals, estates, and trusts). These forms are filed in lieu of filing an amended income tax return.

The entire amount of an unused credit is first carried to the prior tax year. To the extent that an unused credit cannot be used in the prior tax year, it is carried to each of the other 20 tax years in the carryforward period.[6]

Example 10: After applying the annual limitation to the general business credit on its 2009 tax return, Warden Dormers, Inc. had an excess general business credit of $25,000 that it carried back to 2008. In 2008, Warden's regular income tax liability and its net income tax were $200,000; its tentative minimum tax was $180,000. Warden's 2008 general business credit (before considering the $25,000 carryback) was $17,500. The amount of general business credit that Warden is entitled to take for 2008 is recomputed to $20,000.

Net income tax	$200,000
Less: The *greater of* (1) $180,000 or	
(2) $43,750 [25% × ($200,000 – $25,000)]	(180,000)
Recomputed general business credit for 2008	$ 20,000

For 2008, Warden is allowed a general business credit of $20,000; however, since it has already claimed a $17,500 credit on its originally filed corporate tax return,

---

[6] Code Sec. 39(a)(1).

Warden can only utilize $2,500 ($20,000 – $17,500) of the general business credit carried back to 2008. The remaining $22,500 ($25,000 – $2,500) of the excess general business credit from 2009 will be carried forward and utilized in 2010 through 2029.

The first-in, first-out method (FIFO) is used to determine the order in which credits are carried back and forward. The oldest credits are used first in determining the amount of a taxpayer's general business credit for a tax year.[7] Allowing taxpayers to use the FIFO rule to utilize carryovers reduces the risk that a taxpayer will lose the benefit of a general business credit because the carryover period has expired.

Example 11: Kendell-Jenkins, Inc. generates a $20,000 general business credit for 2009. Kendell-Jenkins has general business credit carryforwards from prior tax years as follows:

Year	Amount
2004	$11,000
2005	7,500
2006	16,000
2007	2,000
2008	5,000
	$41,500

Kendell-Jenkins's total general business credit for 2009 equals $61,500 ($20,000 current year business credit + $41,500 carryforward from prior tax years). After computing the limitation imposed on the general business credit, Kendell-Jenkins determines that its allowable general business credit for 2009 is $36,000. Using the FIFO method, the $36,000 credit for 2009 consists of the $11,000 carried over from 2004; the $7,500 carried over from 2005; $16,000 carried over from 2006; and $1,500 from 2007. The amount of general business credit unused at the end of 2009 totals $25,500 ($61,500 – $36,000 utilized in 2009). This carryforward amount is attributable to the following years:

Year	Amount
2007	$ 500
2008	5,000
2009	20,000
	$25,500

.03 Claiming the General Business Credit

Taxpayers must file Form 3800, *General Business Credit,* if they claim more than one of the credits included in the general business credit or if one of the credits (not including the low-income housing credit) is from a passive activity. Taxpayers carrying over credits from other tax years must also file Form 3800 in order to compute the correct amount of general business credit for the year. In the sections that follow, some of the more common tax credits that are included as part of the general business credit are discussed in greater detail.

---

[7] Code Sec. 39(a).

BUSINESS TAX CREDITS AIMED AT ENCOURAGING EMPLOYERS TO HIRE CERTAIN WORKERS

The federal government provides tax incentives to businesses that hire certain workers. In many instances, these are typically individuals for whom finding work is difficult and for whom the federal government is providing (or will soon be providing) assistance because they are unable to support themselves. By offering tax credits to businesses that hire these workers, the amount of taxes the federal government collects is lowered, but the savings the government derives from no longer having to provide assistance to these individuals exceeds the loss in revenues. Two tax credits the federal government uses to encourage employers to hire certain workers are discussed in the sections that follow.

¶ 1104 Empowerment Zone and Renewal Community Employment Credit

Empowerment zones and renewal communities are specific geographic areas within the United States that the federal government has identified as being in need of revitalization. To date, 41 empowerment zones (including the District of Columbia Enterprise Zone, which is treated as an empowerment zone) and 40 renewal communities have been designated by the federal government. Employers that hire individuals who both live and work in either an empowerment zone or a renewal community are entitled to tax credits for a portion of the wages paid to those workers. Employers can determine whether their business or an employee's residence is located in an empowerment zone or renewal community by using the RC/EZ/EC address locator at *http://egis.hud.gov/egis/cpd/rcezec/welcome.htm*.

.01 Calculating the Amount of the Credit

Only wages paid to workers who both live *and* work in an empowerment zone or in a renewal community qualify for the **empowerment zone and renewal community employment credit**. Each calendar year, up to $15,000 of qualified zone wages paid to (in the case of a cash basis taxpayer) or incurred for (in the case of an accrual basis taxpayer) each qualified empowerment zone employee plus up to $10,000 of qualified zone wages paid to or incurred for each qualified renewal community employee are eligible for the credit.[8] The employer's credit equals the sum of the following:

1. Twenty percent of qualified wages paid to or incurred for qualified empowerment zone employees during a calendar year (up to $15,000 per qualified employee) and

2. Fifteen percent of the qualified wages paid to or incurred for qualified renewal community employees during the calendar year (up to $10,000 per qualified employee).[9]

Only qualified wages paid or incurred in the calendar year that ends with or within the employer's tax year can be used in computing the employer's empowerment zone and renewal community employment credit. If the employer uses a calendar year-end, then all qualified wages paid during the employer's tax year (up to the $15,000/$10,000 limits) are used in computing the credit. However, employers that use a fiscal year-end can only use qualified wages paid during the prior calendar year to compute their current year credit.

Example 12: Deschamp Window Blinds, Inc. uses a fiscal year that ends on March 31. For the tax year that began on April 1, 2008, and ended on March 31, 2009, only qualified zone wages paid or incurred during the 2008 calendar year can be used in computing Deschamp's credit during that fiscal year. Any qualified zone wages paid or incurred during the 2009 calendar year will be included in the calculation of Deschamp's tax credit for the fiscal year ending March 31, 2010.

---

[8] Code Secs. 1396(a), (b), and 1400H(b)(1).   [9] Code Secs. 1396(c)(2) and 1400H(b)(2).

The $15,000 and $10,000 limits are reduced by the amount of wages paid or incurred during the year that are used to compute the work opportunity credit (discussed later in the chapter).[10] Furthermore, an employer's wage expense deduction must be reduced by the amount of any credit taken during the year.

Example 13: During 2008, Deschamp Window Blinds, Inc. (from Example 12) paid $20,000 of qualified zone wages to Jorge Calahan and $11,000 of qualified zone wages to Rosa Gonzalez. Jorge's services were provided in an empowerment zone where he also resides; Rosa's were provided in a renewal community where she resides. Deschamp's empowerment zone and renewal community employment credit for the fiscal year ended March 31, 2009, equals $4,500 ($15,000 × 20% = $3,000 for Jorge's wages; $10,000 × 15% = $1,500 for Rosa's wages). Deschamp reduces its wage deduction by $4,500 on its tax return for the fiscal year ended March 31, 2009.

 Reason for the Rule: The empowerment zone and renewal community employment credit was enacted because Congress believed federal tax incentives could play a role in revitalizing economically distressed urban and rural areas.[11] Congress hoped the credit would lead to revitalization in distressed areas by expanding business and employment opportunities and would help alleviate both economic and social problems, including those caused by crime and narcotics.

.02 Qualified Zone Wages

Qualified zone wages include wages paid or incurred by an employer for services performed by an employee while working as a qualified zone employee.[12] A **qualified zone employee** is an employee who performs substantially all of his or her services for an employer within an empowerment zone or renewal community and whose principal residence while performing such services is located within an empowerment zone or a renewal community. Usually employees must work for the employer for at least 90 days to have their wages qualify for the credit; however, the wages of employees who are unable to complete 90 days of employment due to becoming disabled or to being fired for cause constitute qualified zone wages. Wages paid to or incurred for employees who are related to the employer are never considered qualified zone wages.[13]

.03 Claiming the Credit

Employers claim the empowerment zone and renewal community employment credit by completing and filing Form 8844, *Empowerment Zone and Renewal Community Employment Credit*. Although the credit is part of the general business credit, a special (slightly higher) tax liability limit applies, and accordingly, the allowed credit is calculated on Form 8844, not on Form 3800 with the other general business credits generated during the year.[14]

¶ 1105 Work Opportunity Credit

Employers that hire workers from a targeted group of individuals may receive a **work opportunity credit** for a portion of the wages they pay those workers during their first year of employment (and second-year wages in the case of long-term family assistance recipients).[15] This credit is scheduled to expire with respect to workers who begin work for an employer after August 31, 2011.[16]

---

[10] Code Secs. 1396(c)(3) and 1400H(b)(2).

[11] House Ways and Means Committee Report No. 103-11, H.R. 2141 (May 19, 1993), at 353.

[12] Code Sec. 1396(c)(1).

[13] Code Secs. 1396(d) and 1400H(a).

[14] Code Sec. 38(c)(2)(A).

[15] Code Sec. 51(a).

[16] Code Sec. 51(c)(4)(B).

> **Reason for the Rule:** The work opportunity credit was enacted to give employers an incentive to provide jobs and training for economically disadvantaged individuals, many of whom are underskilled and/or undereducated.[17]

.01 Qualifying for the Credit

Employers are entitled to a work opportunity credit for a portion of the qualified first-year wages (and second-year wages in the case of long-term family assistance recipients) they pay to eligible workers during the year. Eligible workers are individuals from one of the targeted groups that have been identified as having a particularly high unemployment rate or other special employment needs.[18] In order to qualify for the credit, the worker must have performed services for the employer for no less than 120 hours during the year, cannot be related to the employer, and cannot have previously worked for the employer.[19]

The Internal Revenue Code (the "Code") specifies the following targeted groups from which eligible workers can be hired for the purpose of obtaining the work opportunity credit:[20]

1. *Qualified IV-A recipient.* Any individual who has been a member of a family receiving Temporary Assistance for Needy Families (TANF) for any nine months during the 18-month period leading up to the individual's hiring date.

2. *Qualified veteran.* Any veteran who (1) has been member of a family receiving assistance under a supplemental nutrition assistance program under the Food and Nutrition Act of 2008 for at least a three-month period ending during the 12-month period ending on the hiring date; or (2) is entitled to compensation for a service-connected disability and either is hired no more than one year after being discharged or released from active duty in the U.S. Armed Forces, or has been unemployed during the one-year period ending on the hiring date for periods aggregating at least six months.

3. *Qualified ex-felon.* Any individual who has been convicted of a felony and who, as of the hiring date, is not more than one year past the date of release from prison or the date of the conviction.

4. *Designated community resident.* An individual who is at least age 18 but under age 40 on the hiring date and who has his or her principal place of abode within an empowerment zone, enterprise community, renewal community, or rural renewal county.

5. *Vocational rehabilitation referral.* Any individual who has a physical or mental disability that results in a substantial handicap to employment and who has been referred to the employer upon completion of (or while receiving) rehabilitative services pursuant to an individualized written plan for employment under a state plan for vocational rehabilitation services, a vocational rehabilitation program, or an individual work plan developed and implemented by an employment network pursuant to the Social Security Act.

6. *Qualified summer youth employee.* Any person age 16 or 17 on the date hired who performs services for the employer between May 1 and September 15. A qualified summer youth employee cannot have worked for the employer during any period prior to the 90-day period prior to being hired. In addition, the youth must reside within an empowerment zone, enterprise community, or renewal community, as designated by the federal government.

7. *Qualified Supplemental Nutrition Assistance Program Benefits Recipient.* Any individual at least 18 but younger than 40 on the hiring date who is a member of a family that either (1) received assistance under a supplemental nutrition assistance program under the Food and Nutrition Act of 2008 (P.L. 110-246) for the six-month period ending on the hiring date or,

---

[17] Senate Finance Committee Report on the Small Business Job Protection Act of 1996 (June 19, 1996), at 32.

[18] Code Sec. 51(b).

[19] Code Sec. 51(i).

[20] Code Sec. 51(d).

(2) in the case of a member of a family who ceased to be eligible for such assistance under Section 6(o) of the Food and Nutrition Act of 2008, received such assistance for at least three months of the five-month period ending on the hiring date.

8. *Qualified Supplemental Security Income (SSI) recipient.* Any individual who has been receiving SSI benefits for any month ending within the 60-day period leading up to the hiring date.

9. *Long-term family assistance recipient.* Any individual who (1) is a member of a family that has received Temporary Assistance for Needy Families (TANF) for a period ending on the hiring date that has lasted at least 18 months, (2) is a member of a family that has received TANF for at least 18 months and was hired within two years after the end of the earliest such 18-month period, or (3) is a member of a family that ceased to be eligible for TANF because of a limitation on the maximum period such assistance is payable and was hired within two years after the family's eligibility ceased.

10. *Unemployed veteran hired in 2009 or 2010.* A veteran who (1) was discharged or released from active duty in the Armed forces at any time during the five-year period ending on the hiring date and (2) received unemployment compensation for no fewer than four weeks during the one-year period ending on the hiring date.

11. *Disconnected youth hired in 2009 or 2010.* An individual who (1) has attained age 16 but not age 25 on the hiring date, (2) did not regularly attend any secondary, technical, or post-secondary school during the six-month period preceding the hiring date, (3) was not regularly employed during the six-month period preceding the hiring date, and (4) is not readily employable by reason of lacking a sufficient number of basic skills

.02 Calculating the Amount of the Credit

The amount of the work opportunity credit equals 40 percent of up to $6,000 ($10,000 in the case of long-term family assistance recipients and $12,000 in the case of qualified veterans) of an employee's qualified first-year wages for workers who provide at least 400 hours of service during their first year.[21] The percentage drops to 25 percent for workers who perform between 120 and 400 hours of service during the first year.[22] No credit is available for an individual who has worked fewer than 120 hours.[23] For summer youth employees, only the first $3,000 of qualified first-year wages are used in computing the credit, and the credit is equal to 25 percent of those wages.[24] Qualified first-year wages include all eligible wages paid (in the case of a cash basis employer) or incurred (in the case of an accrual basis employer) during the first year that begins on the date the individual is hired (the "hiring date").[25] An additional credit equal to 50 percent of up to $10,000 of an employee's qualified second-year wages is provided for hiring a long-term family assistance recipient.[26] Qualified second-year wages include all eligible wages paid or incurred with respect to a long-term family assistance recipient during the second year following the individual's hiring date.

Example 14: Tiles, Inc. paid $8,000 in wages to Ana Hoffman during her first year of employment. Ana is a qualified IV-A recipient. Thus, $6,000 of Ana's first-year wages are used in computing Tiles's work opportunity credit. If Ana works at least 400 hours during her first year, Tiles will be able to take credit equal to $2,400 ($6,000 × 40%) as part of the general business credit.

Example 15: In the summer of 2009, Tiles, Inc. paid $3,500 in wages to Norman Godsey, a qualified summer youth employee. Only $3,000 of Norman's wages are eligible for the work opportunity credit. Assuming Norman worked at least 120 hours for Tiles during the summer, Tiles would be able to claim a $750 ($3,000 × 25%) work opportunity credit for the wages it paid Norman during the summer months.

---

[21] Code Sec. 51(a).

[22] Code Sec. 51(i)(3)(A).

[23] Code Sec. 51(i)(3)(B).

[24] Code Sec. 51(d)(7)(B)(ii).

[25] Code Sec. 51(b)(2).

[26] Code Sec. 51(e)(1).

Example 16: Lairs Pest Control paid $9,000 in qualified first-year wages and $11,500 in qualified second year wages to a qualified long-term family assistance recipient. Since the qualified worker is a long-term family assistance recipient, up to $10,000 of qualified wages paid during the worker's first two years qualify for the work opportunity credit. For the worker's first year, Lairs's work opportunity credit equals $3,600 ($9,000 × 40%). For the worker's second year, the credit equals $5,000 ($10,000 × 50%).

Example 17: Oday Flowers, Inc. paid $4,000 in wages to Lorraine Arnette, who worked 390 hours during her first year of employment. Lorraine is a qualified SSI recipient. Oday's work opportunity credit with respect to Lorraine's first-year wages equals $1,000 ($4,000 × 25%). If Lorraine had worked another 10 hours during her first year, Oday's work opportunity credit would have increased to $1,600 ($4,000 × 40%).

When the employee's first year of employment spans two of the employer's tax years, the employer can take the credit over those two tax years. (Likewise, in the case of long-term family assistance workers, if the employee's first and second year wages span over three of the employer's tax years, the employer can take the credit over those three tax years.) However, only the wages earned in each of those years are allowed in computing that year's work opportunity credit. Furthermore, an employer's wage expense deduction must be reduced by the amount of the work opportunity credit.[27]

Example 18: On November 14, 2009, Eloise Meyers was hired by Jakelin Enterprises, a calendar year taxpayer. Eloise is a qualified food stamp recipient. Eloise's first-year wages were $11,200, of which $1,100 was received during 2009. Jakelin is entitled to a work opportunity credit equal to $440 ($1,100 × 40%) in 2009 and a credit equal to $1,960 ($6,000 − $1,100 = $4,900 × 40%) in 2010. During 2009, Jakelin paid $1,100 in qualified first year wages, which resulted in a $440 tax credit. Jakelin can deduct the remaining $660 ($1,100 − $440) of wages paid to Eloise in computing its 2009 taxable income.

Example 19: Lairs Pest Control (from Example 16) paid $9,000 of qualified first year wages to a long-term family assistance recipient. Of this amount, $2,000 was paid during 2009 and the rest ($7,000) in 2010. Lairs also paid $11,500 in qualified second years wages, of which $2,700 were paid in 2010 and the rest ($8,800) in 2011. Lairs is entitled to take an $800 work opportunity tax credit in 2009 ($2,000 × 40%). In 2010, Lairs's work opportunity credit equals $4,150 (($7,000 first year wages paid in 2010 × 40% first year rate) + ($2,700 second year wages paid in 2010 × 50% second year rate)). Its work opportunity credit for 2011 will equal $3,650 (($10,000 maximum − $2,700 paid in 2010) × 50%).

Of the $2,000 of qualified wages paid in 2009, Lairs can deduct $1,200 ($2,000 − $800) as wage expense in computing its taxable income. Likewise, of the $9,700 of qualified wages paid in 2010, Lairs can deduct $5,550 in computing its 2010 taxable income ($9,700 − $4,150). Finally, of the $8,800 of qualified wages paid in 2011, Lairs will be able to deduct $5,150 as wage expense ($8,800 − $3,650).

.03 Coordination with the Empowerment Zone and Renewal Community Employment Credit

When a worker's wages qualify for the work opportunity credit and for the empowerment zone and renewal community employment credit, the tax laws do not permit the same wages to be used in computing both credits. Thus, any of an eligible worker's wages used in computing the work opportunity credit must reduce both the worker's qualified zone wages as well as the

---

[27] Code Sec. 280C(a).

$15,000/$10,000 limitation used in computing the employer's empowerment zone and renewal community employment credit.[28]

The empowerment zone and renewal community employment credit is based on wages paid to qualified workers during a given calendar year, and the credit is available each year as long as qualified zone wages continue to be paid to the qualified zone employee.

Planning Pointer: The wages eligible for the empowerment zone and renewal community employment credit ($15,000 and $10,000, respectively) exceed the $6,000 limit ($10,000 limit in the case of long-term family assistance recipients and $12,000 limit in the case of qualified veterans) for first-year wages that are eligible for the work opportunity credit. However, the percentage of wages that qualify for the work opportunity credit (40 percent) exceeds that allowed for the empowerment zone and renewal community employment credit (20 and 15 percent, respectively). Accordingly, when a worker's wages qualify for *both* credits, employers may benefit by using the first $6,000 ($10,000 in the case of long-term family assistance recipients and $12,000 in the case of qualified veterans) of the employee's qualified wages in the calculation of the work opportunity credit and then reducing the amount of wages eligible for the empowerment zone employment credit by the wages used in computing the work opportunity credit. This decision affects only the tax years in which the work opportunity credit is available to the employer.

Example 20: On October 5, 2009, Raskin Enterprises hired John Sanchez, a qualified IV-A recipient whose wages qualify both for the empowerment zone and renewal community employment credit and for the work opportunity credit. John lives and works in an empowerment zone. During John's first year of employment (October 5, 2009–October 4, 2010), Raskin paid him $13,500 in total wages, of which $3,200 were paid in 2009. During 2010, John's wages were $16,000. Raskin files its corporate tax return using the calendar year.

Because the $3,200 of wages paid during the 2009 calendar year qualify for both credits, Raskin would be better off using those wages to claim a $1,280 work opportunity credit ($3,200 × 40%), rather than a $640 ($3,200 × 20%) empowerment zone and renewal communities credit. In computing its 2009 taxable income, Raskin must reduce its wage expense deduction by the $1,280 credit taken in that year.

In 2010, the first $2,800 ($6,000 − $3,200) of wages paid to John qualify for both credits. Thus, on its 2010 tax return, Raskin should claim a $1,120 work opportunity credit ($2,800 × 40%) and reduce the wages eligible for the empowerment zone and renewal community employment credit by the $2,800 of wages used in computing the work opportunity credit. Raskin's empowerment zone and renewal community employment credit for 2010 would equal $2,440 ($15,000 maximum qualified wages − $2,800 = $12,200 × 20%). Raskin would then reduce its 2010 wage deduction by the total $3,560 ($1,120 + $2,440) tax credits taken in that year.

In Example 20, had Raskin chosen to use the entire wages paid to John Sanchez in computing its empowerment zone and renewal community employment credit, the tax credit for 2009 would have been $640, and the 2010 tax credit would have been $3,000 ($15,000 × 20%). Accordingly, the tax credits over the two years would have totaled $3,640 ($640 + $3,000). Under this scenario presented in Example 20, Raskin took the work opportunity credit on the first $6,000 of the worker's first-year wages and then reduced the amount of wages eligible for the empowerment zone and renewal community employment credit. Raskin's tax credits over the same two tax years totaled

---

[28] Code Sec. 1396(c)(3).

$4,840 ($1,280 + $3,560). Thus, by using its understanding of the tax laws, Raskin can claim an additional $1,200 ($4,840 − $3,640) in tax credits. However, because the amounts taken as a tax credit reduce the amounts that can be deducted as wage expense, the true tax savings can only be measured after taking the difference in taxes Raskin will pay on taxable income due to the differing amounts of wage expense deducted under each scenario.

Assuming Raskin's taxable income for each of the two years falls in the 35-percent tax bracket, the $1,200 additional wage expense that Raskin would take if all wages were used in computing the empowerment zone and renewal community employment credit would produce an additional $420 in tax savings ($1,200 × 35%) over the approach used in Example 20. Thus, Raskin's actual tax savings would be $780 ($1,200 additional tax credit − $420 additional tax liability due to less wage expense deduction). Hence, Raskin is still better off using the planning technique illustrated in Example 20 to reduce its taxes owed to the federal government over the two tax years.

.04 Claiming the Credit

Employers file Form 5884, *Work Opportunity Credit*, with their federal income tax returns to claim the work opportunity credit. The amount of the credit is included as part of the general business credit on Form 3800, *General Business Credit*. To claim the credit for an employee's wages, an employer must request and be issued a certification for the employee from the state employment security agency. If an employer does not receive the certification by the day that an employee begins work, the employer must complete Form 8850, *Pre-Screening Notice and Certification Request for the Work Opportunity and Welfare-to-Work Credits*, on or before the individual is offered a job. The employer must submit this form to the state employment security agency no later than 28 days after the employee begins to work for the employer.[29]

TAX CREDITS AIMED AT ENCOURAGING CONSERVATION OF ENERGY

¶ 1106 Energy Credits

Several tax credits aimed at encouraging taxpayers to help conserve energy and reduce greenhouse gases are available to individuals and businesses. Although the details of these credits are beyond the scope of this textbook, the types of credits the tax laws provide include:

- Credit for the use or production of qualified biodeisel and renewable diesel,
- Alcohol fuels credit,
- Enhanced oil recovery credit,
- Renewable electricity production credit,
- Credit for small business refiners of low-sulfur diesel fuels,
- Credit for producing oil and natural gas from qualified marginal wells,
- Alternative motor vehicle credit,
- Qualified plug-in electric drive motor vehicle credit,
- Home builder's credit for new energy efficient homes,
- Manufacturer's credit for energy efficient appliances,
- Energy credit,
- Carbon dioxide sequestration credit,
- Qualifying advanced coal project credit,
- Qualifying gasification project credit, and
- Advanced energy project credit.

---

[29] Code Sec. 51(d)(13).

TAX CREDITS AIMED AT REWARDING RESEARCH IN CERTAIN AREAS

¶ 1107 Tax Credit For Increasing Research Activities

Employers who conduct research and experimentation may qualify for a nonrefundable **research activities credit**, which is part of the general business credit.[30] This credit is not scheduled to apply to any amount paid or incurred after December 31, 2009.[31] However, Congress has been renewing it from year to year.

 Reason for the Rule: The research activities credit was enacted in 1981 based on concerns that the United States' lead in research and development had diminished and on a belief that from research and development come technological advances that are essential to increased productivity and competitiveness.[32] Congress hoped that the tax incentives of offering a research credit would encourage businesses to increase the amounts they spend towards qualified research activities.

The research activities credit is different from the deduction allowed for research and experimental expenditures that was discussed in Chapter 5. The research activities credit is intended to reward businesses that conduct research in specific areas and those that increase the amounts they spend each year on specified research and development activities. Some research expenditures qualify for both the research activities tax credit and the deduction for research and experimental expenditures. In these situations, the taxpayer has the option of taking the full amount as a deduction and then reducing the allowable credit to 65 percent of the amount otherwise allowed to be taken. Alternatively, the taxpayer may take a credit for these expenditures and then reduce the amount of its deduction (or amortizable amount) by the amount of the credit taken.[33]

Example 21: Biotechnologies, Inc. incurred $200,000 in expenditures during the year that qualify for both the research activities credit and the deduction for research and experimental expenditures. Biotechnologies' marginal tax rate is 35 percent. The computed amount of the tax credit available for these expenditures is $40,000. Biotechnologies has the option of deducting the entire $200,000 in computing its 2008 taxable income and reducing the amount of its credit to $26,000 ($40,000 × 65%). This would generate tax savings equal to $96,000 ($200,000 × 35% plus $26,000). Alternatively, Biotechnologies can choose to take the full $40,000 tax credit and reduce its research and experimental expenditures deduction to $160,000 ($200,000 – $40,000). This latter option would generate the same $96,000 in total tax savings ($160,000 × 35% plus $40,000).

 Planning Pointer: As illustrated in Example 21, taxpayers with a marginal tax rate of 35-percent generate the same tax savings under both options. Only taxpayers with a marginal tax rate of less than 35 percent will generate greater tax savings from electing to take the full tax credit and reduce the amount eligible for the deduction. It is not a coincidence that the 35-percent "indifference" rate corresponds to the highest corporate tax rate (not including the three- and four-percent surtaxes that are imposed in addition to the top 35-percent tax rate in order to eliminate the tax benefits of the lower tax rates) (see ¶ 405.01).

---

[30] Code Sec. 41.
[31] Code Sec. 41(h)(1).

[32] Senate Finance Committee Report No. 97-144 (July 6, 1981), at 120.
[33] Code Sec. 280C(c).

.01 Calculating the Amount of the Credit

The research activities credit is the sum of the (1) incremental credit, (2) university basic research credit, and (3) qualified energy research credit. The amount included in the research activities credit is 20 percent of each of the amounts.[34]

Incremental credit. The "incremental credit" is intended to reward businesses that increase the amounts spent toward research activities. The amount of the credit equals 20 percent of the amount by which a business's qualified research expenses for the tax year exceeds its base amount. (The base amount is discussed later in this chapter at ¶ 1107.04.) Alternatively, businesses can elect to compute an alternative simplified credit amount.[35]

Example 22: Tann Communications, Inc. incurred $80,000 of qualified research expenses during its most recent tax year. If Tann's base amount is $50,000, its incremental credit for the year equals $6,000 ($80,000 – $50,000 = $30,000 × 20%).

Example 23: Martin Enterprises incurred $100,000 of qualified research expenses during its most recent tax year. If Martin's base amount is $90,000, its incremental credit for the year equals $2,000 ($100,000 – $90,000 = $10,000 × 20%).

Instead of computing the incremental credit using 20 percent of the excess of qualified research expenses over the base amount, taxpayers have the option of electing an alternative simplified credit:[36]

Alternative simplified credit. The alternative simplified credit is equal to 14 percent of its qualified research expenses in excess of 50 percent of the average of its qualified research expenses for the three preceding tax years for which the credit is being determined. If a taxpayer had no qualified research expenses for any of the three preceding tax years, the credit is six percent of the taxpayer's qualified research expenses for the tax year. An election applies to the tax year for which it is made and all subsequent tax years unless revoked with the IRS' consent.[37]

Example 24: Pickard Telecommunications, Inc. incurred $500,000 in qualified research expenses during 2010. The average of its qualified research expenses for 2007, 2008, and 2009 was $300,000. Its alternative simplified research credit is $42,000, computed as follows:

$$14\% \times [\$500,000 - (50\% \times \$300,000)] = \$49,000$$

Example 25: Helget Industries, Inc. had $60,000 of qualified research expenses during the year. It had no qualified research expenses for one of the three preceding years. Its alternative simplified credit is 6% × $60,000 = $3,600.

University basic research credit. The "university basic research credit" equals 20 percent of the difference between the basic research payments and the qualified organization base period amount. Like the incremental credit, this component of the research activities credit is available to businesses that increase their research expenditures during the year. Basic research includes any original investigation for the advancement of scientific knowledge that does not have a specific commercial objective. Expenditures paid or incurred for research conducted outside the United States or research conducted in the social sciences, the arts, or humanities do not qualify for the university basic research credit, regardless of the amount spent on the research.[38]

Qualified energy research credit. The "qualified energy research credit" equals 20 percent of amounts paid or incurred by the taxpayer (including contributions) in carrying on any trade or business during the tax year with an energy research consortium. Unlike the other two components

---

[34] Code Sec. 41(a).
[35] Code Sec. 41(a)(1).
[36] Code Sec. 41(c)(5).

[37] Code Sec. 41(c)(5)(C).
[38] Code Sec. 41(e)(7).

of the research activities credit, the amount of the qualified energy research credit is not dependent on the company increasing its research expenditures over prior tax years.

An "energy research consortium" is an organization that satisfies each of the following requirements.[39]

- It is either a tax-exempt public charity (as defined in Code Sec. 501(c)(3)) organized and operated primarily to conduct energy research or an organization operated primarily to conduct energy research in the public interest;
- It is not a private foundation;
- During the calendar year in which the organization's tax year begins, at least five unrelated persons provide amounts to the organization for energy research; and
- No single person provides 50 percent or more of the total amounts provided to the organization for energy research during the calendar year.

.02 Qualified Research

"Qualified research" for purposes of the research activities credit includes (1) research with respect to which expenditures qualify for the research and experimentation deduction discussed in Chapter 5 (see ¶ 507.01) and (2) research undertaken for the purpose of discovering information that is technological in nature and the application of which is intended to be useful in the development of a new or improved business component of the taxpayer.[40] Substantially all (defined as 80 percent or more) of the research activities must constitute elements of a process of experimentation relating to a new or improved function, performance, reliability, or quality. Research will *not* be treated as conducted for a qualified purpose if it relates to style, taste, cosmetic, or seasonal design factors.[41] Other disbursements that do not constitute qualified research expenditures include any efficiency survey; activity relating to management function or technique; marketing research, testing, or development (including advertising or promotions); routine data collection; or routine or ordinary testing or inspection for quality control.

Research is "undertaken for the purpose of discovering information" if it is intended to eliminate uncertainty concerning the development or improvement of a business component. "Uncertainty" exists if the information available to the taxpayer does not establish the capability or method for developing or improving the business component or the appropriate design for the business component.[42] Information is "technological in nature" if the process of experimentation used to discover the information fundamentally relies on the principles of the physical or biological sciences, engineering, or computer science. A taxpayer may employ existing technologies and may rely on existing principles of the physical or biological sciences, engineering, or computer science to satisfy this requirement.[43]

Example 26: Odom Shelving, Inc. decides it wants to manufacture shelving in a different color. Odom researches the available colors and surveys its customers to determine which color they prefer. The research does not constitute qualified research because it relates to style, taste, cosmetic, or seasonal design factors.

Example 27: After selecting a color for its shelving, Odom Shelving from Example 26 determines that it cannot use its existing painting-spraying machine because the new color has characteristics that differ from those of the paints it previously used. Odom consults with the manufacturer of its paint-spraying machine and learns that a new nozzle is needed. Odom purchases the nozzle and performs tests to ensure the nozzle will satisfy the company's needs. Odom's research does not constitute qualified research because the company did not conduct a process of evaluating alternatives to eliminate uncertainty regarding the modifications required for painting the shelving.

---

[39] Code Sec. 41(f)(6).
[40] Code Sec. 41(d).
[41] Reg. § 1.41-4(a)(6).

[42] Reg. § 1.41-4(a)(3).
[43] Reg. § 1.41-4(a)(4).

Instead, the manufacturer eliminated any uncertainty by informing Odom of the nozzle that was needed. Odom's testing of the new nozzle falls into the category of routine or ordinary testing or inspection for quality control.

Example 28: Perrault Food Grinders, Inc. decided to manufacture a smaller version of its grinder. Because a smaller version of the blade the company used for its current model was not commercially available, it developed a blade that it could manufacture using its current production line. Perrault engages in a systematic trial-and-error process of analyzing blade designs and materials to determine what design and material would be best. The research constitutes qualified research because the appropriate design and material were uncertain when Perrault began its research activities. Perrault went through the process of identifying and evaluating alternatives, and the process of evaluating alternatives was technological in nature.

Research conducted after commercial production of the business component begins does not constitute qualified research, nor does research related to the adaptation of an existing business component to a particular customer's requirement or need. Expenses incurred in connection with computer software developed primarily for internal use do not qualify for the research activities credit. Expenditures do not qualify if they are related to research that reproduces an existing business component (in whole or in part) from a physical examination of the business component itself or from plans, blueprints, detailed specifications, or publicly available information with respect to the business component. Research usually must be conducted within the United States, Puerto Rico, or any U.S. possession to be eligible for the research activities credit. However, expenditures paid or incurred for research in the social sciences, the arts, or humanities do not qualify for the credit.

.03 Qualified Research Expenses

"Qualified research expenses" are the sum of (1) in-house research expenses and (2) contract research expenses paid or incurred by the taxpayer during the tax year in carrying on a trade or business of the taxpayer.[44] *In-house research expenses* include wages paid to or incurred for the services of an employee who is engaged in qualified research or in the direct supervision or direct support of research activities that constitute qualified research. In-house research expenses also include amounts paid or incurred for supplies and amounts paid to another person or incurred for the right to use computers to conduct qualified research.[45] *Contract research expenses* are 65 percent of any amount a taxpayer pays to any person (other than a taxpayer's employee) or incurs for qualified research. However, if the amounts are paid to or incurred for an eligible small business, an institution of higher education, or a federal laboratory, 100 percent of such amounts are considered in computing the research activities credit.[46]

For any calendar year, a small business is one whose average number of employees did not exceed 500 during either of the two preceding calendar years. A small business is an *eligible small business* if the taxpayer does not directly or indirectly own 50 percent or more of the outstanding value or voting shares of its stock (if the business is a corporation) or 50 percent or more of the business's capital and profits interests (if the business is not a corporation).[47]

.04 Base Amount

For the purposes of the research activities credit, the "base amount" equals a fixed-base percentage multiplied by the average annual gross receipts of the taxpayer for the previous four tax years. In no event may the base amount be less than 50 percent of the taxpayer's qualified research expenses for the credit year.[48]

---

[44] Code Sec. 41(b)(1).
[45] Code Sec. 41(b)(2).
[46] Code Sec. 41(b)(3)(D).

[47] Code Sec. 41(b)(3)(D)(ii).
[48] Code Sec. 41(c).

Example 29: In the current year, Sidhu Cloths, Inc. incurred $30,000 in qualified research expenditures. Sidhu's fixed-base percentage is two percent and its average annual gross receipts for the four prior tax years was $1 million. Two percent of Sidhu's average annual gross receipts equals $20,000 ($1,000,000 × 2%). Since this amount is not less than $15,000 (50% of the $30,000 qualified research expenditures), Sidhu's base amount for the year is $20,000.

Example 30: Assume the same facts as in Example 29, except that Sidhu's qualified research expenditures for the current year are $45,000 (instead of $30,000). Since 2 percent of Sidhu's average annual gross receipts ($20,000) is less than 50 percent of its current year's expenditures ($45,000 × 50% = $22,500), Sidhu's base amount for the year is $22,500.

Fixed-base percentage. The calculation of the fixed-base percentage depends on how long the taxpayer has been in business. The maximum fixed-base percentage is 16 percent.[49] The actual computation of the fixed-base percentage can be quite involved, and it is beyond the scope of this discussion. However, as a rule, the fixed-base percentage is calculated by dividing the taxpayer's aggregate qualified research expenses for tax years beginning after December 31, 1983, and before January 1, 1989, by the taxpayer's aggregate gross receipts for those tax years.

Example 31: Eccles Imaging, Inc. had $270,000 in qualified research expenses for tax years beginning after 1983 and before 1989. During that same period, its aggregate gross receipts were $3 million. Eccles' fixed-base percentage is nine percent ($270,000 ÷ $3,000,000).

Code Sec. 41(c)(3) provides a series of complex rules for determining a company's fixed base percentage if the company was not in existence for at least three years from 1984–1988.

.05 Claiming the Credit

Taxpayers can claim the credit by filing Form 6765, *Credit for Increasing Research Activities*. Since this credit is part of the general business credit, amounts reported on Form 6765 flow through to Form 3800, *General Business Credit*, and they are used in determining the taxpayer's general business credit for the current year.

¶ 1108 Orphan Drug Credit

The tax laws allow a larger tax credit for research conducted in the clinical testing of drugs for rare diseases and conditions. This credit, often called the "orphan drug credit," is similar to the research activities credit in that both in-house and contract research expenses are allowed in computing the credit. However, for the purposes of computing the orphan drug credit, 100 percent of contract research expenses are allowed (up from 65 percent for the research activities credit). The calculation of the credit is similar to the research activities credit, except the credit is equal to 50 percent of the qualified clinical testing expense (up from 20 percent for the incremental credit).[50]

Since expenses that qualify for the orphan drug credit also qualify for the research activities credit, any expenses used in computing the orphan drug credit cannot be used in computing the taxpayer's research activities credit. However, such amounts are included in the company's base amount when computing its incremental research activities credit.[51]

Example 32: In 2009, Biogene Company incurred $200,000 in the clinical testing of a drug for a rare disease. Biogene also incurred $50,000 in other qualified research expenses. Biogene's orphan drug credit for 2009 equals $100,000 ($200,000 × 50%). Since the entire $200,000 is used in computing its orphan drug credit, it cannot use any of this amount in computing its research activities credit. Accordingly, Biogene will com-

---

[49] Code Sec. 41(c)(3).
[50] Code Sec. 45C(a).

[51] Code Sec. 45C(c).

pute its research activities credit based on the $50,000 of other qualified research expenses it incurred during 2009.

The orphan drug credit is computed on Form 8820, *Orphan Drug Credit,* and the amount of the credit is transferred to Form 3800, *General Business Credit*, where it is used to compute the taxpayer's general business credit for the current year.

TAX CREDITS AIMED AT ENCOURAGING ECONOMIC DEVELOPMENT

Although discussed earlier in this chapter as a credit aimed at encouraging employers to hire certain workers, the empowerment zone and renewal community employment credit also exists to provide tax incentives for businesses that relocate to distressed urban and rural areas that the federal government believes to be in dire need of revitalization.[52] As previously mentioned, Congress hoped that by enacting this credit, businesses would expand to those areas, bringing with them employment opportunities that would help alleviate both economic and social problems. The new markets credit is another tax credit aimed at encouraging economic development in low-income communities.

¶ 1109 New Markets Credit

Taxpayers that invest in a qualified community development entity may be entitled to a new markets credit.[53] The **new markets credit** is a nonrefundable credit that is part of the general business credit. It is scheduled to end after 2009, but Congress has been renewing it from year to year.

A **qualified community development entity**(qualified CDE) is a domestic corporation or partnership whose primary mission is serving, or providing investment capital for, low-income communities or low-income persons. During its first six years, a qualified CDE must use at least 85 percent of the cash it raises to make qualified low-income community investments. After the sixth year, a qualified CDE need only use 75 percent of its cash towards low-income community investments.[54] In addition, a qualified CDE must maintain accountability to the residents of low-income communities through their representation on any governing board of the entity or on any advisory board to the entity. Finally, a qualified CDE must be certified as such by the Community Development Financial Institutions (CDFI) Fund of the Department of the Treasury.[55]

An equity investment in a qualified CDE is an investment in the stock of a qualified CDE (in the case of a corporation) or an investment in a capital interest of a qualified CDE (in the case of a partnership). The taxpayer must pay cash to purchase its investment in a qualified CDE, although the taxpayer may borrow the funds to generate the cash necessary to purchase the investment.[56]

.01 Calculating the Amount of the Credit

The amount of the credit equals the applicable percentage multiplied by the amount invested in a qualified CDE. The applicable percentage is five percent for the first three credit allowance dates and six percent for the next four credit allowance dates. The "credit allowance date" is the date on which the investment initially was made and each of the next six anniversaries of that date.[57]

Example 33: On July 1, 2009, Creekmore Illustrators, Inc. paid $100,000 for a qualified equity investment in a CDE. Creekmore (a calendar year corporation) is entitled to a new markets credit equal to $5,000 (5% × $100,000) for 2009 and will be entitled to

---

[52] House Ways and Means Committee Report No. 103-11, H.R. 2141 (May 19, 1993), at 353.

[53] Code Sec. 45D(a).

[54] Temp. Reg. § 1.45D-1T(c)(5).

[55] Code Sec. 45D(c).

[56] Code Sec. 45D(b)(6).

[57] Code Sec. 45D(a); Reg. § 1.45D-1(b).

another $5,000 credit on its 2010 and 2011 tax returns. The company will be entitled to a $6,000 (6% × $100,000) credit on its 2012–2015 tax returns.

.02 Claiming the Credit

Taxpayers can claim the credit by filing Form 8874, *New Markets Credit*. The new markets credit is part of the general business credit. Accordingly, any credit generated on Form 8874 is transferred to Form 3800, *General Business Credit*, and used to compute the taxpayer's general business credit for the year. Furthermore, the taxpayer's basis in its investment in the CDE is reduced by the new markets credit taken with respect to that investment.[58]

Example 34: Continuing with Creekmore Illustrators from Example 33, over the seven years, Creekmore will receive tax credits equal to $39,000 ($5,000 for each of the first three years + $6,000 for each of the next four years). If these amounts were considered as reducing Creekmore's cost in its investment in the CDE, its out-of-pocket costs would effectively be reduced to $61,000 ($100,000 – $39,000). However, because Creekmore must reduce its basis in the CDE by the $39,000 of tax credits taken, the $39,000 will eventually be taxed when Creekmore disposes of the investment. Until then, Creekmore will have the use of the amounts it receives from the tax savings generated by the tax credits.

.03 Recapture of the Credit

If at any time during the seven-year period beginning on the date of the taxpayer's investment in the qualified CDE, (1) the investment ceases to be a qualified CDE, (2) the taxpayer's investment is redeemed by the qualified CDE, or (3) the proceeds from the investment are not substantially used by the qualified CDE to make qualified low-income community investments, the taxpayer's tax liability must be increased by an amount equal to the amount by which the taxpayer's general business credit would have been reduced if there had been no new markets credit, plus interest at the federal government's underpayment rate.[59]

Reason for the Rule: The new markets credit was enacted as part of the Community Renewal Tax Relief Act of 2000 to encourage taxpayers to invest in CDEs, whose primary mission is to serve or provide investment capital for low-income communities and low-income individuals.[60]

TAX CREDITS USED TO SUBSIDIZE BUSINESSES FOR CERTAIN EXPENDITURES MADE DURING THE YEAR

¶ 1110 Employer Social Security Credit

Tips constitute income and therefore are taxable to the recipient. However, since most tips are paid in cash, they are difficult for the government to trace (and therefore to tax), and consequently, compliance with this tax law is extremely low. To combat this, the government has enacted tax laws requiring certain businesses to impute the amount of tips their employees earn and include those amounts as employee wages on their employees' Form W-2s.

As discussed in Chapter 6, employers must withhold federal, state, and FICA taxes from their employees' wages. In addition, employers are required to match any amounts withheld for FICA taxes. Normally, employers deduct their matching FICA contributions as ordinary and necessary business expenses. However, to encourage businesses to comply with the tax laws requiring them

---

[58] Code Sec. 45D(h).
[59] Code Sec. 45D(g).

[60] Joint Committee on Taxation, *General Explanation of Tax Legislation Enacted in the 106th Congress* (J.C.T. Rep. No. JCS-2-01), at 122 and 123.

to impute tips on behalf of their employees, the federal government allows employers to take a tax credit cqual to 100 percent of any matching amounts that result from amounts paid with respect to tips for food or beverages received by their employees, provided the tips are not needed to allow the employee to earn a minimum wage.[61]

 Reason for the Rule: By allowing employers to take a tax credit for 100 percent of the amounts they pay towards FICA on employees' tip income, the federal government encourages employers to report their employees' tips as taxable wages. Although by allowing the tax credit (versus deduction), the government is subsidizing a much larger portion of the employer's cost for FICA matching, in return, the tips the employer reports are subject to the employee's portion of FICA as well as state, local, and federal income taxes. Hence, the government is willing to pay businesses for their efforts to increase employees' compliance by allowing the businesses a tax credit instead of a tax deduction for their share of the FICA on tip income.

¶ 1111 Rehabilitation Credit

Businesses are entitled to a **rehabilitation credit** for costs associated with the substantial rehabilitation of a certified historic structure or other depreciable building that was originally placed in service prior to 1936.[62]

.01 Calculating the Amount of the Credit

The rehabilitation credit is the sum of (1) 20 percent of the qualified rehabilitation expenditures with respect to any certified historic structure and (2) 10 percent of the qualified rehabilitation expenditures with respect to any qualified rehabilitated building that is not a certified historic structure.[63]

Example 35:   Bourn Leasing, Inc. purchased an apartment building that is a qualified rehabilitated building that is not a certified historic structure. During the year, Bourn made $100,000 in qualified rehabilitation expenditures with respect to five of the apartments and made the apartments available to renters by the end of the year. Bourn is entitled to a rehabilitation credit of $10,000 ($100,000 × 10%).

.02 Expenditures Qualifying for the Rehabilitation Credit

An expenditure qualifies for the rehabilitation credit if it is a qualified rehabilitation expense with respect to a qualified rehabilitated building.[64] Qualified rehabilitation expenditures are capital in nature and relate to depreciable residential or nonresidential realty. In addition, the expenditure must be incurred in connection with the rehabilitation of a qualified rehabilitation building.[65]

Qualified rehabilitated building. A certified historic structure is a **qualified rehabilitated building** if sometime after purchasing the building, the taxpayer pays or incurs substantial expenditures to rehabilitate it. A building is a certified historic structure if it is listed in the National Register or if it is located in a registered historic district and is certified by the Secretary of the Interior as being of historic significance to the district.[66]

A building that is not a certified historic structure is considered a qualified rehabilitated building only if it was originally placed in service before 1936 and if sometime after purchasing the building, the taxpayer pays or incurs substantial rehabilitation expenditures. Once the rehabilitation is completed, at least 50 percent of the building's original external walls must still be external walls;

---

[61] Code Sec. 45B(b).
[62] Code Sec. 47.
[63] Code Sec. 47(a).

[64] Code Sec. 47(a).
[65] Code Sec. 47(c)(2).
[66] Code Sec. 47(c)(3).

at least 75 percent of its original external walls must have been retained as either internal or external walls; and at least 75 percent of its internal structural framework must have been retained.[67]

Example 36: Samuel Industries paid $200,000 for a building that is not a certified historic structure. The building was originally placed in service in 1940. Since the building is not a certified historical structure, and it was not first placed in service before 1936, any expenditure the company makes to rehabilitate the building will not qualify for the rehabilitation credit.

Substantially rehabilitated. A building must be substantially rehabilitated after the taxpayer purchases it in order for the rehabilitation expenditures to qualify for the credit. A building has been "substantially rehabilitated" if during any 24-month period ending within the taxable year in which the property is placed in service, the qualified rehabilitation expenditures exceed the *greater* of (1) $5,000 or (2) the adjusted basis of the building and its structural components. The adjusted basis of the building is determined as of the beginning of the 24-month period or the beginning of the holding period for the building, whichever is later.[68]

Example 37: Tarrik Inc. pays $100,000 for a building that is a certified historic structure. During the next 24-months, Tarrik incurs $50,000 in costs associated with rehabilitating the building. Since the $50,000 costs do not exceed $100,000 (the *greater* of Tarrik's adjusted basis or $5,000), the building is not considered to have been substantially rehabilitated.

Example 38: On May 5, 2007, Rycline Industries pays $200,000 for a building that is not a certified historic structure. Rycline is a calendar year taxpayer. The building was originally placed in service in 1922. Rycline places the property in service on October 9, 2009. Between August 10, 2007, and August 9, 2009, Rycline incurs $250,000 to rehabilitate the building. Since the $250,000 exceeds $200,000 (the *greater* of Rycline's adjusted basis or $5,000), the building is considered to have been substantially rehabilitated.

 Reason for the Rule: The rehabilitation credit is intended to encourage businesses to rehabilitate and modernize older structures rather than build new structures or relocate their businesses to new structures. The credit is also intended to encourage the preservation of historic structures. Congress believed that a tax incentive was needed because businesses otherwise would be deterred from rehabilitating older or historic buildings because of the extra costs of undertaking such rehabilitation and because the social and aesthetic values of rehabilitating and preserving older structures are not necessarily taken into consideration when businesses decide whether to rehabilitate an older structure or to move a new structure.[69]

.03 When Expenditures May Be Taken into Account

As a rule, qualified rehabilitation expenditures with respect to any qualified rehabilitated building are taken into account for the tax year in which the qualified rehabilitated building is placed in service.[70] This tax year must also contain the end of the 24-month period used to determine whether the building placed in service was substantially rehabilitated.

Example 39: Rycline Industries from Example 38 will claim a $25,000 rehabilitation credit ($250,000 × 10% for buildings that are not certified historic structures) as part of its general business credit on its 2009 tax return.

---

[67] Code Sec. 47(c)(1).
[68] Code Sec. 47(c)(1)(C)(i).

[69] Joint Committee on Taxation, *General Explanation of the Tax Reform Act of 1986* (J.C.T. Rep. No. JCS-10-87), at 149.
[70] Code Sec. 47(b)(1).

Example 40: On May 5, 2007, Northeastern Company (a calendar year taxpayer) pays $50,000 for a building that qualifies as a certified historic structure. From May 6, 2007, until August 28, 2009, Northeastern incurs $75,000 to rehabilitate the building. The building is placed in service on August 31, 2009. Because the rehabilitation expenditures exceed $50,000 (the *greater* of $5,000 or its $50,000 adjusted basis), Northeastern can take a $15,000 rehabilitation credit ($75,000 × 20% credit for certified historic structures) as part of its general business credit on its 2009 tax return.

.04 Claiming the Credit

Businesses claim the rehabilitation credit on Form 3468, *Investment Credit*. The rehabilitation credit is one of the components of the nonrefundable investment credit.[71] Other credits that make up the investment credit are the energy credit, the qualifying advanced coal project credit, the qualifying gasification project credit, and qualifying advanced energy project credit. The aggregate of these investment credits are reported as part of the general business credit on Form 3800, *General Business Credit*. Taxpayers claiming the rehabilitation credit must reduce their basis in the property by the amount of the credit.[72]

.05 Recapture of the Credit

If a taxpayer disposes of rehabilitated property, or if such property otherwise ceases to be investment credit property to the taxpayer within five years after it was placed in service, the taxpayer's tax liability is increased by an amount equal to the recapture percentage times the original credit taken. The recapture percentages, summarized in Table 11-1, reflect the equivalent of the amount by which the taxpayer's general business credit would have been reduced if no credit for rehabilitation expenditures had been allowed.[73] Taxpayers file Form 4255, *Recapture of Investment Credit*, when property ceases to qualify as investment credit property within five years after it was placed in service. Amounts recaptured are added back to the adjusted basis of the building.[74]

Table 11-1 Recapture Percentages for the Rehabilitation Credit

Period of Time After Property Was Placed in Service That It Ceases To Be Investment Credit Property	*Recapture Percentage*
Within 1 full year	100%
More than 1 but within 2 years	80%
More than 2 but within 3 years	60%
More than 3 but within 4 years	40%
More than 4 but within 5 years	20%
More than 5 years	0%

Example 41: On its 2007 tax return, Oday Tambourines took a $10,000 rehabilitation credit for a building with a total cost basis of $180,000. Oday Tambourines placed the building in service on April 1, 2007. Oday reduces its basis in the building to $170,000 ($180,000 – $10,000) and begins depreciating the building using this depreciable basis and the cost recovery rules from Chapter 7. On February 2, 2009, Oday sells the building for $300,000. Because Oday disposed of the property within two years after it was placed in service, the amount of additional income tax that Oday must pay in 2009 is $8,000 (80% × $10,000). Oday increases its adjusted basis in the building by $8,000.

---

[71] Code Sec. 46.
[72] Code Sec. 50(c)(1).

[73] Code Sec. 50(a).
[74] Code Sec. 50(c)(2).

Reason for the Rule: The recapture provisions prevent taxpayers from taking undue advantage of the investment credit. However, since in the year the credit is taken the taxpayer's adjusted basis in the building was reduced by the full amount of the credit, it is only fair that any amounts recaptured be added back to the building's basis, thereby reducing the amount of realized gain (or increasing the amount of loss) upon its disposition.

¶1112 Low-Income Housing Credit

Taxpayers who purchase or substantially rehabilitate residential rental property used for low-income housing may take a **low-income housing credit**.[75] The nonrefundable credit is part of the general business credit.

.01 Calculating the Amount of the Credit

The amount of the low-income housing credit is the applicable percentage of the qualified basis of each qualified low-income building.[76] The amount of the low-income housing credit may be taken each year for a total of 10 years, beginning with the tax year during which the building is placed in service or, at the building owner's election, the following tax year. If the taxpayer elects to start the 10-year period in the year subsequent to the year in which the building is placed in service, such election is irrevocable.[77]

Example 42: In 2009, McIlwain Real Estate Investors, LLC purchased a residential building and began renting it to low-income persons. At the time the building was placed in service, the applicable percentage was eight percent and the qualified basis was $1 million. McIlwain will include an $80,000 ($1,000,000 × 8%) low-income housing credit as part of its 2009 general business credit. Since McIlwain is a flow-through entity, its owners will report their respective shares of the general business credit on their respective income tax returns. LLCs are discussed in Chapter 14.

Example 43: McIlwain Real Estate Investors, LLC from Example 42 is able to take an $80,000 low-income housing credit each year from 2009 to 2018. Alternatively, McIlwain can irrevocably elect to forego taking any credit in 2009 and instead take an $80,000 credit each year from 2010 to 2019.

Qualified low-income building. A "qualified low-income building" is a residential rental building that is part of a qualified low-income housing project during the 15-year compliance period. A "qualified low-income housing project" is a residential rental property project that satisfies either of the following tests:[78]

1. *20-50 test.* This test is satisfied if 20 percent or more of the residential units in the project are rent-restricted and are occupied by individuals whose income is 50 percent or less of the area median gross income.

2. *40-60 test.* This test is satisfied if 40 percent or more of the residential units in the project are rent-restricted and are occupied by individuals whose income is 60 percent or less of the area median gross income.

Applicable percentage. The "applicable percentage," which the IRS redetermines each month, is the percentage that will yield a credit over the 10-year credit period with a present value equal to 70 percent of the qualified basis of new buildings that are not federally subsidized and 30 percent of the qualified basis of existing buildings and new buildings that are federally subsidized. In the case of a new building placed in service after July 30, 2008, and before December 31, 2013, that is not federally subsidized, the applicable percentage must be a minimum of nine percent. A new

---

[75] Code Sec. 42.
[76] Code Sec. 42(a).

[77] Code Sec. 42(f).
[78] Code Sec. 42(c)(2), (g), and (i)(1).

building will be treated as federally subsidized if, at any time during the tax year or any prior tax year, there is or was outstanding any state or local obligation paying tax-exempt interest whose proceeds are or were used (directly or indirectly) with respect to the building or its operation.[79]

 Planning Pointer: Owners of federally subsidized buildings can take advantage of the higher credit percentage by electing to reduce their eligible basis by the balance of the loan or by the proceeds of the obligation.

Qualified basis. The "qualified basis" of any qualified low-income building is an amount equal to the applicable fraction times the eligible basis of the building. The "applicable fraction" is the *smaller* of the unit fraction or the floor space fraction. The *unit fraction* is the fraction whose numerator is the number of low-income units in the building and whose denominator is the number of residential rental units (whether or not occupied) in the building. Alternatively, the *floor space fraction* is the fraction whose numerator is the total floor space of the low-income units in the building and whose denominator is the total floor space of the residential rental units (whether or not occupied) in the building.[80]

The "eligible basis" of a building varies depending on whether it is a new or existing building. For new buildings, the eligible basis is its adjusted basis as of the close of the first tax year in the credit period. For existing buildings, the eligible basis is its adjusted basis as of the close of the first tax year in the credit period provided (1) the taxpayer purchased the building; (2) at least 10 years have elapsed since the building was last placed in service by the previous owner; (3) the building was not previously placed in service by a party related to the taxpayer; and (4) a low-income housing credit is allowed with respect to the building. If any of these conditions is not met, the eligible basis of the existing building will be zero.[81]

 Reason for the Rule: Congress enacted the low-income housing credit as part of the Tax Reform Act of 1986 because it believed that tax incentives (for example, accelerated depreciation) in existence at the time were not effective in providing affordable housing for low-income individuals. Congress realized the shortcomings of other tax subsidies offered at the time. In particular, these subsidies were not linked to the number of units serving low-income persons; they were not targeted to persons of truly low income; and they did not limit the amount of rent that low-income individuals could be charged.[82] Through the provisions enacted in the low-income housing credit, Congress addressed these issues and provided tax incentives that it hoped would make providing affordable housing to low-income persons and families an attractive investment for businesses.

.02 Claiming the Credit

The credit is claimed by filing Form 8586, *Low-Income Housing Credit*. The low-income housing credit is part of the general business credit, so the credit computed on Form 8586 is transferred to Form 3800, *General Business Credit*, when computing the business's general business credit for the year.

.03 Recapture of the Credit

If a building is not owned and operated as low-income housing for 15 years, a portion of the credit usually must be recaptured. However, no recapture will be required when a building is disposed of before the end of the compliance period if it is reasonably expected that the building will

---

[79] Code Sec. 42(b)(2) and (i)(2).
[80] Code Sec. 42(c)(1)(D).

[81] Code Sec. 42(d).
[82] Joint Committee on Taxation, *General Explanation of the Tax Reform Act of 1986* (J.C.T. Rep. No. JCS-10-87), at 152.

continue to be operated as a qualified low-income building for the remaining compliance period. The amount of the credit that must be recaptured is the sum of the difference between the amount of the credit taken and the amount that would have been allowed if the credit had been spread over 15 years instead of 10 years plus the interest from the dates the recaptured credits were claimed. The interest rate used is the rate paid on overpayment of taxes.[83]

Example 44: Garoutte Investors, LLC placed a qualified low-income building in service and started taking a $1.5 million credit in annual installments of $150,000. After claiming the credit for six years, the company ceased operating the building as a low-income building. If the credit had been taken over 15 years, the company would have been able to take a $100,000 credit each year. Therefore, $50,000 for each year the credit was claimed, or $300,000 ($50,000 × 6 years), must be recaptured. Interest (using the federal government's overpayment rate) will be charged from the date each recaptured $50,000 credit was claimed until the date the credit was recaptured.

¶ 1113 Disabled Access Credit

Eligible small businesses may take a disabled access credit for amounts paid or incurred to enable them to comply with applicable requirements under the Americans with Disabilities Act of 1990.[84] The nonrefundable credit is part of the general business credit.

> **Reason for the Rule:** Congress enacted this credit as part of the Revenue Reconciliation Act of 1990 because it was concerned that complying with the requirements included in the Americans with Disabilities Act of 1990 would impose a severe financial burden on certain small businesses.[85]

.01 Eligible Small Business Defined

A business qualifies as an "eligible small business" if during the preceding tax year it met either of the following conditions: (1) its gross receipts did not exceed $1 million or (2) it employed no more than 30 full-time employees. A "full-time employee" is an employee who works at least 30 hours per week for 20 or more calendar weeks during the tax year.[86]

Example 45: During the previous tax year, Riggers, Inc. reported gross receipts totaling $1,150,000 and employed 31 individuals full-time. Riggers does not qualify as an eligible small business because in its previous tax year its gross receipts exceeded $1 million and it employed more than 30 full-time individuals.

Example 46: During the previous tax year, Collins, Inc. had gross receipts of $1,200,000 and employed 29 full-time individuals. Even through Collins's gross receipts in the previous tax year exceeded $1 million, in that year it did not have more than 30 full-time employees. Accordingly, Collins qualifies as an eligible small business in the current year.

.02 Computing the Amount of the Credit

The amount of the disabled access credit equals 50 percent of the amount by which the eligible access expenditures during the tax year of an eligible small business exceed $250 but do not exceed $10,250.[87] Thus, when eligible expenditures exceed $10,250, the maximum credit allowed is $5,000 ($10,250 – $250 = $10,000 × 50%). The adjusted basis of the building is increased by the amount by which the expenditures exceed the taxpayer's disabled access credit.[88]

---

[83] Code Sec. 42(j)

[84] Code Sec. 44(a).

[85] Senate Finance Committee Report, S. 3209 (October 13, 1990), at 71.

[86] Code Sec. 44(b).

[87] Code Sec. 44(a).

[88] Code Sec. 44(d)(7).

Example 47: Christiansen Lighting is an eligible small business that made $10,000 of eligible access expenditures during the tax year. Christiansen may take a disabled access credit equal to $4,875 ($10,000 – $250 = $9,750 × 50%). Christiansen increases the basis in its building by $5,125, the amount by which its eligible capital expenditures exceed the disabled access credit ($10,000 – $4,875) and will depreciate this amount using the MACRS rules discussed in Chapter 7.

Example 48: Davidson & Sons is an eligible small business. During the year, Davidson made $15,000 of eligible access expenditures. Davidson's disabled access credit equals the maximum $5,000 since its eligible access expenditures exceed $10,250. Davidson increases its basis in the building by $10,000 ($15,000 – $5,000) and can depreciate this amount under MACRS.

.03 Eligible Access Expenditures

"Eligible access expenditures" are amounts paid or incurred by an eligible small business to enable it to comply with applicable requirements under the Americans with Disabilities Act of 1990. They include ordinary and necessary expenditures paid or incurred for any of the following purposes:[89]

- Removal of architectural, communication, physical, or transportation barriers that prevent a business from being accessible to, or usable by, individuals with disabilities, but not if the amounts are paid or incurred in connection with a facility first placed in service after November 5, 1990;

- Provision of qualified interpreters or other effective methods of making aurally delivered materials available to individuals with hearing impairments;

- Provision of qualified readers, taped texts, and other effective methods of making visually delivered materials available to individuals with visual impairments;

- Acquisition of or modification of equipment or devices for individuals with disabilities; or

- Provision of similar services, modifications, materials, or equipment.

.04 Claiming the Credit

Taxpayers claim the credit by filing Form 8826, *Disabled Access Credit*. Since the disabled access credit is part of the general business credit, amounts reported on Form 8826 are transferred to Form 3800, *General Business Credit*.

As mentioned in Chapter 5, businesses normally can elect to currently deduct up to $15,000 each year of such expenses as qualified architectural and transportation barrier removal expenses.[90] If a disabled access credit is taken, the amount of any deduction must be reduced by the amount of the credit taken. Since taxpayers are almost always better off taking a tax credit rather than a tax deduction, the tax savings (and therefore cash flow) will be greater when the disabled access credit is taken and the deduction is reduced.

Example 49: Cable Corporation incurs $22,000 in costs to install wheelchair ramps at the entrances to its office building. Cable has the option of expensing $15,000 of its costs in the current year. Alternatively, Cable can take a $5,000 disabled access credit and deduct $10,000 of the remaining costs in the current year. In both scenarios, the excess $7,000 ($22,000 – $15,000) would be added to the basis in the building and depreciated under MACRS. Assuming that Cable's marginal tax rate is 35 percent, if it were to choose to deduct $15,000 in the current year, its tax savings would equal $5,250 ($15,000 × 35%). If Cable were to take the $5,000 disabled access credit, the tax savings from the $10,000 deduction ($15,000 maximum – $5,000 credit taken) would be $3,500 ($10,000 × 35%) and its total tax savings would equal $8,500 ($3,500

---

[89] Code Sec. 44(c).   [90] Code Sec. 190.

+ $5,000). The additional tax savings from taking the credit equals $3,250 ($8,500 – $5,250). Because the $7,000 in excess of the $15,000 eligible for immediate expensing will be depreciated under MACRS in either scenario, the tax savings from the depreciation deductions is the same under both scenarios and consequently is not relevant for purposes of considering the tax advantages of taking the credit over the $15,000 deduction.

¶ 1114 Employer-Provided Child Care Credit

Employers are allowed a nonrefundable **employer-provided child care credit** when they provide employee child care and child care resource and referral services.[91] The credit is part of the general business credit.

.01 Calculating the Amount of the Credit

The amount of the credit is the sum of 25 percent of the qualified child care expenditures and 10 percent of the qualified child care resource and referral expenditures.[92] The amount of the credit cannot exceed $150,000.[93]

Example 50: P. Mackey, Inc. made $30,000 of qualified child care expenditures and $10,000 of qualified child care resource and referral expenditures during its tax year. Its employer-provided child care credit equals $8,500 [($30,000 × 25%) + ($10,000 × 10%)].

Qualified child care expenditures. Twenty-five percent of the taxpayer's qualified child care expenditures are used in computing the employer-provided child care credit. "Qualified child care expenditures" are amounts paid or incurred for any of the following purposes:[94]

- Acquisition, construction, rehabilitation, or expansion of property to be used as part of a qualified child care facility of the taxpayer if the property is depreciable (or amortizable) and if the property is not part of the principal residence of the taxpayer or any employee of the taxpayer;

- Payment for operating costs of a qualified child care facility of the taxpayer, including expenses for training employees, scholarship programs, and the provision of increased compensation to employees with higher levels of child care training;

- Provision of child care services to the taxpayer's employees under a contract with a qualified child care facility.

A qualified child care facility has as its principal purpose providing child care assistance. The facility must meet the requirements of all applicable laws and regulations of the state or local government in which it is located, including the licensing of the facility as a child care facility, and it cannot be the principal residence of the person who operates the facility. Enrollment in the facility must be open to the taxpayer's employees during the tax year, and at least 30 percent of the enrollees must be dependents of the taxpayer's employees. Finally, a qualified child care facility cannot discriminate in favor of the taxpayer's highly compensated employees.[95]

Example 51: Kehoe Tack Boards, Inc. sets aside part of its facility for child care. The child care facility is open to the children of all employees, and only employees and their dependents can use the facility. However, special teachers were brought in for the children of the owners and top executives (all of whom are highly compensated). Because the facility discriminates in favor of highly compensated employees, it is not a qualified child care facility. Therefore, the costs incurred in operating the facility do not qualify for the employer-provided child-care credit.

[91] Code Sec. 45F.
[92] Code Sec. 45F(a).
[93] Code Sec. 45F(b).
[94] Code Sec. 45F(c)(1).
[95] Code Sec. 45F(c)(2).

Qualified child care resource and referral expenditures. Ten percent of the taxpayer's qualified child care resource and referral expenditures are used in computing the employer-provided child care credit. "Qualified child care resource and referral expenditures" are amounts paid or incurred under a contract to provide child care resource and referral services to a taxpayer's employee.[96] Such services will not be qualified if the contract discriminates in favor of highly compensated employees.

 Reason for the Rule: The credit was enacted as part of the Economic Growth and Tax Relief Act of 2001 to encourage employers to provide child care for their employees.

.02 Claiming the Credit

Taxpayers can claim the credit by filing Form 8882, *Credit for Employer-Provided Childcare Facilities and Services*. This credit is part of the general business credit; accordingly, the amount computed on Form 8882 is transferred over to Form 3800, *General Business Credit*.

Since qualified child care expenditures include amounts paid or incurred to acquire, construct, rehabilitate, or expand property, any credit allowed for qualified child care expenditures with respect to such property must reduce the taxpayer's basis in the property. Furthermore, if an expenditure used to qualify an employer for the credit is otherwise a deductible expenditure (for example, wages paid to workers to operate the facility), the amount of the employer's deduction for that expenditure must be reduced by the amount of the credit taken.[97]

Example 52: In 2009, Kambell Company pays wages totaling $40,000 to workers who operate its child care facility. Since the costs are qualified child care expenditures, Kambell is eligible for a $10,000 tax credit ($40,000 × 25%) on its 2009 tax return. In computing its taxable income, Kambell must reduce its wage expense deduction by $10,000. Thus, on its 2009 tax return, Kambell can only deduct $30,000 of the wages it paid to the workers of its child care facility.

.03 Recapture of the Credit

If a recapture event occurs with respect to any qualified child care facility during any of the 10 tax years after the facility was placed in service, the employer's tax liability is increased by an amount equal to the applicable recapture percentage, as shown in Table 11-2, times the amount by which the general business credit for all prior tax years would have decreased if the taxpayer's qualified child care expenditures had been zero.[98] The recapture provision is similar to the provisions that apply to the low-income housing and rehabilitation tax credits.

Cessation of the operation of the facility as a qualified child care facility constitutes a recapture event, unless the cessation is due to a casualty loss and the loss is restored by reconstruction or replacement within a reasonable period. Disposition of the taxpayer's interest in the qualified child care facility is also a recapture event, unless the person acquiring the taxpayer's interest agrees in writing to assume the taxpayer's recapture liability. The applicable recapture percentage depends on when the recapture event occurs, as shown in Table 11-2.

---

[96] Code Sec. 45F(c)(3).
[97] Code Sec. 45F(f).
[98] Code Sec. 45F(d).

Table 11-2 Applicable Recapture Percentages for the Employer-Provided Child Care Credit

Recapture Event Occurs in	Applicable Recapture Percentage
Years 1-3	100%
Year 4	85%
Year 5	70%
Year 6	55%
Year 7	40%
Year 8	25%
Year 9 or 10	10%
Year 11 or thereafter	0%

Example 53: Lockridge Shoes, Inc. took a $50,000 employer-provided child care credit in 2006 for a qualified child care facility that it constructed and operated. In 2007, Lockridge took a $20,000 credit for operating expenses; in 2008, it took a $30,000 credit for operating expenses. In 2009, the company closed the facility because it had become too costly to operate. If its credit for the previous years had been zero, its general business credit would have been reduced by $100,000 ($50,000 + $20,000 + $30,000). Because the recapture event took place in year 4, the applicable recapture percentage is 85 percent. Thus, the recapture amount equals $85,000 ($100,000 × 85%).

¶ 1115 Foreign Tax Credit

When U.S. businesses receive income from a foreign country, the foreign-source income may be subject to income tax both by the foreign country and by the United States. To reduce the possibility of double taxation on the same income, U.S. citizens and residents and certain nonresident taxpayers are permitted to take a **foreign tax credit (FTC)** for income, war profits, and excess profits taxes (collectively referred to as income taxes) that they paid or accrued to a foreign country or to a U.S. possession during the tax year.[99]

 Reason for the Rule: U.S. citizens and residents are taxed on their worldwide income, meaning that they are taxed on all income they receive from both U.S. and foreign sources. U.S. businesses and residents are permitted to take a tax credit or a deduction for foreign income taxes they paid so they will not be taxed on the same income twice (once by the foreign country and a second time by the United States).

.01 Election To Take a Deduction Instead of a Credit for Foreign Income Taxes Paid

In lieu of claiming a tax credit for foreign taxes paid, taxpayers can instead take a deduction for the foreign taxes paid or accrued.[100] For businesses, this deduction would offset business profits and, therefore, reduce the taxpayer's tax liability by the amount of the deduction times the taxpayer's marginal tax rate. However, any foreign taxes paid by an individual taxpayer are considered personal taxes and, therefore, must be taken as itemized deductions (deductions from AGI). Thus, foreign taxes that result from profits earned by sole proprietors do not reduce their sole proprietorships' profits or their adjusted gross income. Payment of such taxes can only reduce a sole

---

[99] Code Sec. 901(a).

[100] Code Sec. 164(a)(3).

proprietorship's taxable income if the taxpayer's total itemized deductions exceed the standard deduction amount.

As a rule, taxpayers benefit more by taking a credit for foreign income taxes paid because each dollar of the credit reduces the taxpayer's tax liability by one dollar. However, the amount of foreign tax credit taxpayers can claim is limited to the ratio of their income from foreign sources to total income; therefore, under certain circumstances taxpayers may be better off taking a deduction for foreign taxes paid instead of a credit. For example, if the rate of tax on the foreign income was high and the taxpayer's foreign income was a small proportion of the taxpayer's U.S. income, the tax benefits to taking a deduction may outweigh the amount of the tax credit.

Example 54: Elkin Teak Floors, Inc. paid $1,000 in foreign taxes during the year. Because of limitations on the foreign tax credit, the company's credit for the year is only $10. Elkin's taxable income falls in the 34-percent tax bracket. If Elkin elects to deduct the $1,000 in foreign taxes paid rather than to take the credit, it will save $340 (34% × $1,000) in income taxes for the year. This amount exceeds the $10 foreign tax credit it could take by $330.

 Planning Pointer: Taxpayers may take a credit for all qualified foreign taxes they paid or accrued during the year or they may take a deduction for all qualified foreign taxes they paid or accrued during the tax year. They may *not* take a credit for some foreign taxes and a deduction for other foreign taxes. However, taxpayers who claim a foreign tax credit one year may claim a foreign tax deduction the next year, and vice versa.

.02 Taxpayers Eligible for the Credit

U.S. citizens and residents and domestic corporations are eligible to take a credit for the amount of foreign income tax paid or accrued during the tax year to any foreign country or to a U.S. possession. Partners, S corporation shareholders, and beneficiaries of a trust or estate are allowed a credit for their proportionate share of foreign income tax paid by their partnership, corporation, estate, or trust to a foreign country or to a U.S. possession.[101] Nonresident alien individuals and foreign corporations engaged in a trade or business within the United States are allowed a credit for foreign income tax paid or accrued (or deemed paid or accrued) to any foreign country or U.S. possession with respect to income effectively connected with the conduct of their trade or business within the United States.[102]

Example 55: Bracken Inc., a U.S. corporation, paid $20,000 in foreign income taxes during the year. Because the company is a U.S. corporation, Bracken is eligible for the foreign tax credit.

Example 56: Elkins Company is incorporated under the laws of a foreign country. During the year, the company engaged in business within the United States and had $100,000 of income effectively connected with that business. Half of that income was considered foreign-source income and was taxed by a foreign country. Elkins can take a foreign tax credit for the foreign income taxes it paid.

.03 Taxes Eligible for the Foreign Tax Credit

Not every amount a business pays to a foreign government qualifies for the foreign tax credit. A business is allowed a credit for income taxes paid or accrued to a foreign country or to a U.S. possession.[103] To be eligible for the foreign tax credit or deduction, a foreign tax must be a levy whose predominant character is that of an income tax in the U.S. sense. A penalty, fine, interest, or

---

[101] Code Sec. 164(a)(3).
[102] Code Sec. 906(a).

[103] Code Sec. 901(b).

customs duty is not considered a tax. A foreign levy is not considered a tax to the extent that a person subject to the levy receives (or will receive), directly or indirectly, a specific economic benefit from the foreign country in exchange for payment pursuant to the levy.[104] In some instances, foreign income taxes paid by an entity in which the taxpayer owns an interest are "deemed" to have been paid by the taxpayer. Foreign taxes "deemed" to have been paid are also eligible for the credit.[105]

Deemed taxes paid. If a domestic (U.S.) corporation, other than an S corporation, owns at least 10 percent of the voting stock of a foreign corporation from which it receives dividends, the domestic corporation will be "deemed" to have paid a portion of the foreign corporation's foreign income taxes paid. However, the amount of deemed taxes cannot be attributable to dividends distributed by the foreign corporation in prior tax years.[106] The calculation of a deemed payment can be expressed as follows:

$$
\begin{array}{l}
\text{Foreign taxes} \\
\text{"deemed"} \\
\text{paid by the} \\
\text{domestic} \\
\text{shareholder} \\
\text{(corporation)}
\end{array}
=
\begin{array}{l}
\text{Foreign income} \\
\text{taxes} \\
\text{actually paid by the} \\
\text{foreign corporation}
\end{array}
\times
\frac{\text{Dividends paid to the domestic (corporation) shareholder}}{\text{Foreign corporation's post-1986 undistributed earnings}}
$$

Example 57: Pulido Inc., a U.S. corporation, owns 30 percent of the voting stock of Outright, Inc., a foreign corporation. When Pulido receives a dividend from Outright, it will be deemed to have paid a portion of Outright's foreign income taxes.

When a U.S. taxpayer claims a foreign tax credit or deduction for deemed taxes paid under this special rule, the corporation must add the amount of the foreign taxes to the dividend income it received from the foreign corporation. Thus, while the deemed taxes may result in a higher foreign tax credit, additional income taxes will be owed on the additional dividend income reported by the taxpayer.

Example 58: Domestics, Inc., a U.S. corporation, owns 40 percent of the voting stock of First-Tier, a foreign corporation. During 2009, First-Tier pays a $20,000 dividend to Domestics. As of the end of 2009, First-Tier has $100,000 of post-1986 undistributed earnings and has paid $40,000 in foreign income taxes. The $20,000 of dividends paid to Domestics during the year represents 20 percent ($20,000/$100,000) of First-Tier's post-1986 accumulated earnings; thus, Domestics is deemed to have paid 20 percent of First-Tier's $40,000 of foreign income taxes, or $8,000 ($40,000 × 20%). If Domestics includes this amount as foreign taxes paid during the year in computing its tax credit, it will report $28,000 of dividend income from First-Tier on its 2009 tax return ($20,000 + $8,000).

.04 Limitations on the Amount of the Credit

A taxpayer's foreign tax credit is limited to the portion of its U.S. income tax liability that is attributable to foreign income being taxed by both the United States and a foreign government.[107] The overall limitation can be expressed as follows:

$$
\begin{array}{l}
\text{U.S. Income tax} \\
\text{(before any FTC)}
\end{array}
\times
\frac{\text{Taxable income from foreign sources}}{\text{Worldwide taxable income}}
$$

The taxpayer's credit is the *lesser* of the foreign taxes paid or the calculated amount of the overall limitation.

---

[104] Reg. § 1.901-2(a)(2)(ii).
[105] Code Sec. 903.

[106] Code Sec. 902; Reg. § 1.902-1(a).
[107] Code Sec. 904(a).

Example 59: Seale Clothes, Inc. had a total taxable income of $1 million and a pre-credit U.S. income tax of $340,000. Its taxable income from foreign sources was $400,000, and it paid $175,000 in foreign income tax during the year. The maximum amount of foreign income tax credit Seale can take is $136,000.

$$\$340,000 \times \frac{\$400,000}{\$1,000,000} = \$136,000$$

Since only 40 percent ($400,000/$1,000,000) of Seale's worldwide income came from foreign sources, only 40 percent of its U.S. income tax liability is attributable to foreign income. Consequently, the maximum amount of foreign tax credit that Seale Clothes can take is $136,000 (the *lesser* of the $175,000 foreign taxes paid or the $136,000 overall limitation).

 Reason for the Rule: The overall limitation prevents taxpayers from using foreign tax payments to reduce their U.S. tax liability on income from U.S. sources. Permitting taxpayers to use the foreign tax credit to reduce the U.S. income tax on their U.S. income would give foreign countries the right to tax income earned in the United States.[108]

Example 60: Murdell Distributors, Inc. paid $500,000 in foreign income taxes on $1 million in foreign-source income and owed $680,000 in U.S. income tax on its $2 million of taxable income from both U.S. and foreign sources. If Murdell had only the $1 million in taxable income from U.S. sources, its U.S. income tax liability would have been $340,000 (using the tax rates from Table 4-1 at ¶ 405.01). If Murdell were permitted to take a credit and reduce its U.S. tax liability by the full $500,000 paid in foreign income taxes from its U.S. tax liability, its U.S. income taxes would be reduced to $180,000 ($680,000 – $500,000). Accordingly, if no limitation were imposed on the amount of foreign tax credit, Murdell would pay $160,000 ($340,000 – $180,000) less in taxes to the U.S. government than it would have paid without its foreign activities.

A second limitation based on the aggregate of separate limitations also applies. The calculation of these separate limitations is quite involved and beyond the scope of this discussion. However, when taxpayers report different types of foreign-source income, the taxes attributable to each category of income will be limited to the amount of taxable income from that activity.[109]

.05 Foreign Tax Credit Carryback and Carryover

The amount of foreign income taxes not allowed as a credit because of the overall and separate limitations can be carried back one year and carried forward 10 years.[110] Foreign income tax payments in excess of the limitations are deemed paid in the prior (or subsequent) tax year.

Example 61: Because of the overall and separate limitations, Benton Document could not take a credit for $50,000 in foreign income taxes that it paid. Benton adds the $50,000 to its foreign income taxes paid for the prior tax year. After applying the overall and separate limitations to the recomputed amount of foreign income taxes, Benton is able to increase its foreign tax credit for its prior tax year by $5,000. Benton can carry forward the $45,000 ($50,000 – $5,000) that it could not use for its prior tax year for up to 10 subsequent tax years.

---

[108] Joint Committee on Taxation, *General Explanation of the Tax Reform Act of 1986* (J.C.T. Rep. No. JCS-10-87), at 854.

[109] Code Secs. 901(b) and 904.
[110] Code Sec. 904(c).

Foreign income tax payments carried back to the prior tax year or carried forward to a subsequent tax year cannot be deducted for that year. The deduction for foreign taxes is only allowed in the year in which the foreign taxes are paid or incurred.

.06 Claiming the Credit

Corporations claim the foreign tax credit by completing Form 1118, *Foreign Tax Credit—Corporations*, and attaching it to their income tax returns. A separate form must be completed for each separate category of income against which a separate limitation is applied. The foreign tax credit is not part of the general business credit; therefore, the credit from Form 1118 is reported directly on Form 1120, *U.S. Corporation Income Tax Return*. Corporations that elect to take the deduction report the amount of foreign taxes paid during the year on Form 1120.

Individuals usually must complete Form 1116, *Foreign Tax Credit* (Individual, Estate, or Trust), and attach it to the income tax return to claim the credit. A separate form must be completed for each separate category of income against which a separate limitation is applied. Individuals who choose to take a deduction for foreign taxes paid report the deduction on Schedule A, *Itemized Deductions*.

Flow-through entities report both the amount of foreign-source income as well as the amount of taxes accrued or paid during the year on the entities' tax returns. The owners then use their respective shares of these amounts to compute the amount of the foreign tax credit they are allowed to claim on their own tax returns.

¶ 1116 Summary

Whenever a business calculates the financial cost of a proposed transaction, it should consider whether a tax credit is available to offset some or all of its costs. Tax credits are available to reimburse a business for the additional costs that may be required to train an individual who has had trouble finding employment. Tax credits also are available to encourage businesses to reduce their use of oil and natural gas, conduct research, invest in economically disadvantaged areas, and rehabilitate older structures.

Each of the tax credits discussed in this chapter illustrates the many ways businesses can reduce the overall costs of certain expenditures by having the federal government, in essence, subsidize a greater portion of the costs associated with particular expenditures. Accordingly, knowledge about which expenditures qualify for a tax credit and how to comply with the requirements for each of the credits is an essential element of good tax planning.

GLOSSARY OF TERMS INTRODUCED IN THE CHAPTER

Business tax credit. Tax credit used by governments to reward businesses for participating in certain types of activities by subsidizing a portion of the expenditures that they incur by participating in those activities.

Disabled access tax credit. A nonrefundable credit that eligible small businesses may take for amounts paid or incurred to enable them to comply with applicable requirements under the Americans with Disabilities Act of 1990.

Employer-provided child care credit. A nonrefundable income tax credit for employers who provide employees with child care and child care resource and referral services.

Empowerment zones and renewal communities. Specific geographic regions within the United States that the federal government has identified as being in need of revitalization.

Empowerment zone and renewal community employment credit. A nonrefundable tax credit for employers who hire individuals who both live *and* work in an empowerment zone or renewal community.

Foreign tax credit (FTC). A nonrefundable income tax credit for income, war profits, and excess profits taxes paid or accrued to a foreign country or to a U.S. possession during the tax year.

General business credit. A combination of business credits, each of which is computed under its own set of rules.

Low-income housing credit. A nonrefundable income tax credit for taxpayers who purchase or substantially rehabilitate residential rental property used for low-income housing.

Net income tax. Term used in the alternative minimum tax system. The sum of the net regular tax liability and any alternative minimum tax minus the same tax credits used in computing net regular tax liability.

Net regular tax liability. Term used in the alternative minimum tax system. A taxpayer's regular tax liability minus certain tax credits, such as the foreign tax credit and personal tax credits.

New markets credit. A nonrefundable income tax credit for taxpayers who make a qualified equity investment in a qualified community development entity. See also *Qualified community development entity.*

Nonrefundable tax credit. A tax credit that can only reduce a taxpayer's income tax liability.

Personal tax credit. A tax credit available only to individuals.

Qualified community development entity (qualified CDE). A domestic corporation or partnership whose primary mission is serving, or providing investment capital for, low-income communities or low-income persons.

Qualified rehabilitated building. A building that is a certified historic structure or a building that originally was placed in service before 1936 and with respect to which the taxpayer paid or incurred substantial rehabilitation expenditures.

Qualified zone employee. An employee who performs substantially all of his or her services for an employer within an empowerment zone or renewal community and whose principal residence while performing such services is located within an empowerment zone or renewal community.

Qualified zone wages. Wages paid or incurred by an employer for services performed by an employee while working as a qualified zone employee.

Recapture of a tax credit. If a taxpayer ceases to use property for the purposes that qualified the property for a tax credit, all or a portion of the credit may have to be added to the taxpayer's tax liability for the year that the property ceased to be used for the qualified purpose.

Refundable tax credit. A credit that can reduce a taxpayer's tax liability to zero and produce a refund for any amount of the credit in excess of the taxpayer's tax liability.

Rehabilitation credit. A nonrefundable credit available for substantially rehabilitating a depreciable building that was placed in service before 1936 or that qualifies as a certified historic structure. *See also* Substantially rehabilitated *and* Qualified rehabilitated building.

Research activities credit. A nonrefundable income tax credit for conducting qualified research.

Tax credit. Amount that reduces a taxpayer's tax liability. Can be either refundable or nonrefundable.

Work opportunity credit. A nonrefundable income tax credit for employing individuals from certain targeted groups.

CHAPTER PROBLEMS

Chapter 11 Discussion Questions

1. What is a tax credit?

2. How does a tax credit differ from a tax deduction in terms of affecting a taxpayer's tax liability?

3. Why are the various tax credits combined into a general business credit?

4. How many years can a general business credit in excess of the annual limitation be carried back and carried forward?

5. Whom can an employer hire if the employer wants to qualify for the empowerment zone and renewal community employment credit?

6. When will a member of a targeted group be ineligible for the work opportunity credit?

7. What is the work opportunity credit for hiring a long-term family assistance recipient?

8. What role does the state employment security agency have in determining whether an employer qualifies for the work opportunity credit?

9. When does research constitute "qualified research," thereby entitling a business to a research activities credit?

10. How is the base amount calculated for purposes of determining the research activities credit, and what is the minimum base amount?

11. What types of expenditures qualify for the new markets credit?

12. Expenditures to rehabilitate what types of buildings can qualify for the rehabilitation credit?

13. A taxpayer pays $250,000 for a certified historical structure originally placed in service in 1948. Over the next 20 months, the taxpayer spends $180,000 rehabilitating the building. Does the taxpayer qualify for the rehabilitation credit?

14. What does "recapture a credit" mean?

15. For how many years may a taxpayer take a low-income housing credit, and for how many years must the property be owned and operated as low-income housing?

16. What businesses may be eligible to take a disabled access credit?

17. What types of expenditures are eligible for the disabled access credit?

18. What types of expenditures qualify for the employer-provided child care credit?

19. What limitations are placed on the amount of a taxpayer's foreign tax credit?

20. What happens to foreign tax payments for which no foreign tax credit is allowed?

Chapter 11 Problems

1. Hoang Skis, Inc. has a tentative general business credit of $60,000. Its net income tax is $250,000, its tentative minimum tax is $200,000, and its net regular tax liability is $250,000. How much of its tentative general business credit can it take for the tax year?

2. For the tax year, Carlson, Inc., had regular tax of $100 million, tentative minimum tax of $80 million, and current year general business credit components of $50 million. What is Carlson's general business credit for the tax year?

3. During the tax year, Reimer Office Designers, Inc. made $200,000 of qualified rehabilitation expenditures with respect to two qualified rehabilitated buildings, one of which qualified as a certified historic structure. Of the qualified rehabilitation expenditures, $120,000 was

made with respect to the certified historic structure. What is the company's rehabilitation credit for the tax year?

4. Pizzo Nursing Homes, Inc. took a $100,000 rehabilitation credit for a building and sold the building 18 months after it was placed in service. How much of the credit has to be recaptured?

5. During 2009, Allgood Tubing, Inc. hired Pedro Urrutia and Shane Earhart as full-time employees. At the time, Pedro was 19 and lived in an empowerment zone, and Shane was a veteran who had been receiving food stamp assistance for the four months prior to his hiring date. Allgood paid Pedro $15,000 and Shane $16,000 during their respective first years of employment. What amount of work opportunity credit may Allgood take for these two employees?

6. After having success with its hiring of Pedro and Shane, Allgood Tubing, Inc. from Problem 5 hired Rachelle Bleich and Herman Weinstock. Rachelle, age 16, was hired to work full time from May 30 to September 1. Rachelle lives in a renewal community. Herman has a mental disability that was a substantial handicap to his employment, but he was referred to Allgood after he successfully completed rehabilitative services under a state vocational rehabilitation program. During the employees' first year of employment, Allgood paid Rachelle $3,500 and Herman $10,000. What amount of work opportunity credit may Allgood take with respect to these employees?

7. Lemelle Mufflers, Inc. qualified for the work opportunity credit by employing Candy Macedo, a long-term family assistance recipient. She was hired on June 1, 2009. From June 1, 2009, through December 31, 2009, Lemelle paid Candy $9,000 and took a work opportunity credit based on that amount. From January 1, 2010, through May 31, 2010, Lemelle paid Candy $10,000 in wages. For the remainder of 2010, the company paid Candy $15,000 in wages. What is the amount of its work opportunity credit for 2010?

8. Chew Plastic Balls, Inc. paid Roberto Haycraft $20,000 of qualified zone wages during the calendar year for his services in a renewal community. What is the amount of empowerment zone and renewal community employment credit the company may take with respect to Roberto's wages?

9. Izzi Sheet Metal, Inc. had $60,000 of qualified research expenses for the year, and its base amount was $30,000. What is Izzi's research activities credit for the year?

10. Assume the same facts as in Problem 9, except that Izzi decided to calculate its alternative simplified credit. Its average qualified research expenses for the three preceding tax years was $40,000. What is its alternative simplified credit?

11. Sayer Music Systems, Inc. had a fixed-base percentage of three percent and average annual gross receipts for its previous four tax years of $3 million. What is its base amount for the current tax year for purposes of determining its research activities credit?

12. Sudduth Precision Imagers, Inc. made a $200,000 qualified equity investment in a qualified community development entity on October 1, 2009. What amount of new markets credit will it be entitled to in 2012?

13. A taxpayer has research expenditures in the current year of $800,000 that qualify for the increased research expenditure credit. The taxpayer does not elect the alternative simplified credit. The applicable aggregate qualified research expenses are $400,000 and the applicable aggregate gross receipts are $2,000,000. The average annual gross receipts for the four preceding tax years are $3,000,000. There are no university basic research payments. Compute the credit for increased research expenditures.

14. Clifton Investors, LLC was eligible for a low-income housing credit of $900,000. After 10 years, the company ceased using the property as low-income housing. What amount, if any, of the credit has to be recaptured?

15. Norwood Compactors, Inc., an eligible small business, made $8,000 of eligible disabled access expenditures for the tax year. What is the amount of disabled access credit that it may take?

16. Jahn Heating, Inc. pays $50,000 of qualified child care expenditures and $20,000 of qualified child care resource and referral expenditures during its tax year. What is the amount of its employer-provided child care credit?

17. Dutcher Garden Tillers, Inc. took a $50,000 employer-provided child care credit in 2009 for a qualified child care facility that it constructed that year. If the company were to sell the facility in 2014, how much of that credit taken in 2009 would have to be recaptured? Could the company do anything to avoid having to recapture the credit?

18. Fenton Millers, Inc., a U.S. C corporation, owns 15 percent of the voting stock of Beane Millers, Inc., a foreign corporation. Beane distributed a $30,000 dividend to Fenton. The amount of post-1986 foreign income taxes paid by Beane was $100,000, and the amount of the company's post-1986 undistributed earnings at the end of the year during which the dividend was paid was $200,000. What amount, if any, of the foreign income taxes paid by Beane can be taken as a foreign tax credit by Fenton?

19. Lenz Jewelers, Inc. is a U.S. corporation. Its total taxable income for the year is $750,000, its taxable income from foreign sources is $150,000, and its pre-foreign tax credit income tax is $255,000. Applying the overall limitation, what is the maximum amount of the company's foreign tax credit for the year? What happens to any excess?

20. A taxpayer has worldwide income of $200,000 and a tentative U.S. tax liability of $65,000. The taxpayer earned $40,000 in a foreign country. Compute the maximum allowable foreign tax credit.

21. Bracken Batteries, Inc. is thinking about opening a manufacturing plant in an empowerment zone and asks you what its after-tax cost will be if it hires individuals who live in the empowerment zone. It plans to pay each of these individuals $20,000 a year. Its marginal tax bracket is 34 percent.

22. Torrey Trucks, Inc. hired a long-term family assistance recipient on January 1, 2008, and a qualified veteran on January 1, 2009. Both employees qualify Torrey Trucks for a work opportunity credit. If it pays each one qualified wages of $25,000 in 2009, what is its work opportunity credit for that year?

23. Pulido Power Tools, Inc. had $300,000 in qualified research expenses during 2009. The average of its qualified research expenses for the prior three years was $200,000. What is its alternative simplified credit?

24. Seale Coffee Roasters, Inc. invested $100,000 in a qualified community development entity. What is the total amount of new markets credit to which it will be entitled?

25. Benton Linens, Inc. spent $75,000 during its tax year to operate a qualified child care facility for its employees. The company also paid $5,000 to a business to provide child care referral services to the company's employees. How much is its employer-provided child care credit for the year?

Chapter 11 Review Problems

1. Salter Technological Solutions, Inc. incurred $50,000 in qualified research expenses during its tax year. Its base amount is $30,000. How much of its expenses can the company deduct, and how much can it take as a credit?

2. A corporation that uses the calendar year hires a new employee on March 1, 2009. The employee works for the corporation full-time and is paid the following amounts during the first two years of employment. The corporation's marginal tax rate is 35 percent.

Time Period	Amount Paid
3/1/09 – 12/31/09	$ 7,500
1/1/10 – 2/28/10	2,450
3/1/10 – 12/31/10	8,000
1/1/11 – 2/28/11	2,500
Total wages paid	$20,450

Compute the tax savings that the corporation would generate for 2009–2011 if the employee qualifies for the work opportunity credit (other than as a long-term family assistance recipient). Determine the amount of the company's out-of-pocket costs for the $20,450 wages that it pays this employee during the first two years of employment. What percentage of the $20,450 gross wages paid is the actual cash paid by the company (net of tax savings)?

Chapter 11 Comprehensive Review Question

Stella Clay, Inc. purchased a manufacturing plant for $1 million and made $500,000 in improvements. A few years later it constructed a child care facility in the plant for $200,000 and took an employer-provided child care credit with respect to those expenditures. Over the next five years, it spent $300,000 on operating expenses and took an employer-provided child care credit for those expenditures. In the sixth year after opening the child care facility, Stella sold the manufacturing plant (including the child care facility), and the buyer refused to assume liability for any recapture tax. As of the date of the sale, Stella had taken $250,000 in depreciation deductions. If the amount realized from the sale is $1,750,000, compute the amount and character of the corporation's gain or loss on the sale.

Chapter 11 Research Question

Stephen Aguilera, who owns a business, wants to save fuel costs by purchasing more fuel-efficient automobiles and light trucks for himself and his employees. He remembers reading about a tax credit for hybrid vehicles and asks you how much the credit is. Using the CCH *Standard Federal Income Tax Reporter*, determine the credit.

PART V:
Business Entity Issues

CHAPTER 12

Corporate Formation, Distributions, and Other Corporation-Related Tax Issues

LEARNING OBJECTIVES

1. Explain how a transfer of property to a corporation in exchange for stock is taxed.
2. Describe how distributions from a corporation are treated by both the corporation and the shareholders.
3. Discuss the importance of E&P in determining how a distribution is treated as a dividend.
4. Explain the concept of a constructive dividend and specify its impact on the corporation and the affected shareholders.
5. Explain how distributions of a corporation's own stock to its shareholders are taxed.
6. Distinguish between the way net income is calculated on the income statement and the way taxable income is computed on the tax return, and explain how to reconcile the two amounts.

¶ 1200 Introduction

When a corporation is formed, property often is transferred to the corporation in exchange for stock. Such a transaction usually is tax-free if the transferor, or two or more transferors as a group, control the corporation following the transfer. However, under certain situations gain has to be recognized. Those situations and what constitutes "control" are discussed in this chapter.

Many C corporations regularly distribute cash or other property to their shareholders. They usually make these distributions because shareholders expect to share in the profits of the corporation. However, corporations are sometimes forced to make distributions to avoid triggering additional taxes, such as accumulated earnings or personal holding company taxes. (See ¶ 1013 and 1014.)

A distribution of money or property has tax consequences for the corporation as well as for its shareholders. Distributions of property from a corporation to its shareholders can be treated as dividends or as a return of capital. When a shareholder receives a distribution that is a return of capital, it can be a tax-free distribution, a capital gain, or some of each, depending on the shareholder's basis in the stock at the time of the distribution. This chapter explains how to determine which type of distribution shareholders receive and what the tax consequences of the distribution to the shareholder are. This chapter also discusses the tax consequences of distributions of stock dividends and the concept of constructive dividends. Finally, the differences between the financial reporting rules and the tax laws and the reconciliation between net income and taxable income are reviewed.

FORMATION OF A CORPORATION

¶ 1201 Transfer of Property to a Controlled Corporation

Although property may be transferred to a corporation in exchange for the corporation's stock at any time, such a transaction occurs most frequently when a corporation is being formed. As a general rule, the transferor will not have to recognize any gain realized when property is transferred in exchange for stock provided that the transferor, or the transferor and one or more other persons transferring property to the corporation, control the corporation following the transfer.[1] However, there are situations when the transferor will have to recognize gain:

- The transferor receives "boot" in addition to stock.

- The corporation assumes "excess liabilities."

 Spotlight: A loss realized on the transfer of property to a controlled corporation is never recognized.

The exchange of securities other than stock issued by a controlled corporation is not tax-free.

.01 "Control" Defined

A transferor has **control** of a corporation if the transferor or the transferor and one or more other transferors as a group own stock possessing at least 80 percent of the total combined voting power of all classes of stock entitled to vote and at least 80 percent of the total number of shares of all other classes of stock of the corporation.[2] Control must exist immediately after the exchange.[3] "Immediately after the exchange" does not necessarily require simultaneous exchanges by two or more persons, but comprehends a situation where the rights of the parties have been previously defined and the execution of the agreement proceeds with an expedition consistent with orderly procedure.[4] If control exists, it is immaterial whether the stock received by two or more transferors is in the same proportions as the transferors' interests in the properties before the exchange or whether the transferor, if a corporation, distributes the stock received.[5]

Example 1: Kelvin Labate transferred land to a newly formed corporation for $260,000 of common stock and $140,000 of nonvoting preferred stock. The land had a fair market value of $400,000 and an adjusted basis of $200,000. Robin Harsch transferred machinery with a fair market value of $100,000 and an adjusted basis of $150,000 for $60,000 of common stock and $40,000 of nonvoting preferred stock. After the transfers, Kelvin and Robin possessed more than 80 percent of the combined voting power of all classes of stock entitled to vote and more than 80 percent of the total number of the shares of all other classes of stock. As a result, Kelvin does not recognize any gain (even though he received stock worth $200,000 more than the adjusted basis of the property transferred), and Robin cannot recognize any of the $50,000 loss that she realized on the transfer.

---

[1] Code Sec. 351(a).
[2] Code Sec. 368(c).
[3] Code Sec. 351(a).

[4] Reg. § 1.351-1(a)(1).
[5] Reg. § 1.351-1(a)(1), (b)(1).

.02 Excepted Transactions

Under certain circumstances, stock will not be treated as having been issued in return for property (and thus not eligible for tax-free treatment).

Stock for property of relatively small value. Stock or securities issued for property that has a value less than 10 percent of the value of the stock and securities already owned (or to be received for services) by the transferor will not be treated as having been issued in return for property if the primary purpose of the transfer is to enable other transferors to qualify for tax-free treatment under Code Sec. 351.[6]

Stock for services rendered. Stock issued for services rendered is never considered issued for property.[7]

 Reason for the Rule: One reason for this rule is that stock issued for services is nothing more than compensation. Another reason for this rule is to prohibit stock issued for services from being considered when determining whether transferors have control of a corporation following one or more transfers of stock.

.03 "Boot"

If a transferor receives money or property other than the controlled corporation's stock (such property is referred to as **boot**) in addition to stock, the transferor will have to recognize gain to the extent of the amount of money and the fair market value of the other property received.[8] If the property transferred to the corporation is depreciable by the corporation, any gain recognized will be treated as ordinary income.[9] No loss can be recognized by the transferor.

Example 2: Roxanna Niland transferred property with a fair market value of $50,000 and an adjusted basis of $40,000 to a controlled corporation for stock worth $45,000 and $5,000 in cash. Roxanna has to recognize $5,000 of her gain.

Multiple assets transferred If more than one asset is transferred to a controlled corporation, the amount of cash and fair market value of property received from the corporation has to be allocated to each transferred asset in proportion to its fair market value.[10]

Property subject to a liability. When property transferred to a corporation is subject to a liability, the amount of liability is not treated as "boot" unless the amount of debt exceeds the transferor's adjusted basis in the property.[11]

Example 3: Gary Shirtzinger transferred property to a controlled corporation. The property had a fair market value of $500,000 and an adjusted basis of $225,000. It was subject to a $150,000 mortgage. In return, he received stock worth $350,000. Because the debt is not considered boot, Gary does not have to recognize any of the $125,000 gain that he realized.

Liabilities in excess of basis. A liability will be treated as boot to the extent that the amount of liabilities assumed and the amount of liabilities on property taken subject to a liability exceed the adjusted basis of the property transferred to the corporation.[12]

Example 4: Assume the same facts as in the previous example except that the property transferred was subject to a $300,000 mortgage. Gary has to recognize $75,000 of his $125,000 gain.

---

[6] Reg. § 1.351-1(a)(1); Rev. Proc. 77-37, 1977-2 CB 568.

[7] Code Sec. 351(d); Reg. § 1.351-1(a)(1).

[8] Code Sec. 351(b).

[9] Code Sec. 1239.

[10] Rev. Rul. 68-55, 1968-1 CB 140.

[11] Code Sec. 357(a), (c).

[12] Code Sec. 357(c), (d).

.04 Basis in Property Received

Following an exchange of stock for property, both the corporation and the transferor have to determine their basis in the property that they receive.

Corporation's basis. As a general rule, a corporation's basis in property acquired in a nontaxable exchange for stock is the transferor's adjusted basis in the property plus any gain recognized by the transferor on the exchange.[13] However, the corporation's basis cannot be increased above the fair market value of the property by reason of any gain recognized to the transferor as a result of the assumption of a liability.[14]

Transferor's basis. A transferor's basis in stock acquired in a nontaxable exchange is the same as the transferor's adjusted basis in the property transferred, with the following adjustments:[15]

Decreases

- The amount of any money received by the transferor.
- The fair market value of any property other than stock received by the transferor.
- The amount of any liability assumed by the corporation from the transferor.
- Any loss recognized on the exchange.

Increases

- The amount of any gain realized.
- Any amount treated as a dividend.

 Spotlight: Although a liability to which transferred property is subject (such as a mortgage) is not treated as boot, it is treated as money received by the transferor for purposes of determining the transferor's basis in property received in the exchange.[16]

Example 5: Lori Forquer transferred property with a fair market value of $50,000 and an adjusted basis of $20,000 to a controlled corporation in exchange for stock worth $50,000. Lori's basis in the stock is $20,000.

Example 6: Assume the same facts as in the previous example except that Lori received stock worth $45,000 plus $5,000 in cash. Her basis in the stock is $25,000 ($20,000 plus the $5,000 of gain that she has to recognize).

Example 7: Dominic Kjos transferred land to a controlled corporation in exchange for stock. The land had a fair market value of $500,000. Its adjusted basis was $200,000, and it was subject to a $150,000 mortgage. Dominic's basis in the stock received is $50,000 (his adjusted basis of $200,000 minus the $150,000 mortgage).

The basis of any property other than stock received by the transferor is its fair market value.[17]

CORPORATE DISTRIBUTIONS

When a corporation distributes money or other property to its shareholders, the corporation classifies the distribution either as a dividend or as a return of capital. From the shareholders' perspective, a distribution from a corporation in which they own stock produces dividend income, a tax-free return of their investment in the stock, or a capital gain. A **dividend** is a distribution of current or accumulated **earnings and profits (E&P)** by a C corporation to its shareholders.[18] E&P

---

[13] Code Sec. 362(a).
[14] Code Sec. 362(d).
[15] Code Sec. 358(a)(1).

[16] Code Sec. 358(d)(1).
[17] Code Sec. 358(a)(2).
[18] Code Sec. 316(a).

was introduced in Chapter 10 (see ¶ 1009.01). It represents a corporation's ability to make distributions to shareholders from the corporation's current or accumulated profits. (See ¶ 1207.)

Dividends usually are paid in cash, but they may involve a distribution of other property, such as land or equipment. Distributions of noncash property are known as **property distributions**. Distributions of stock in the corporation making the distribution are not considered property dividends, but instead are stock dividends. (See ¶ 1206.) Thus, in this chapter, the term "property distribution" or a wording that suggests a distribution of property refers to a distribution from the corporation of property that is not cash and is not the corporation's own stock.

¶ 1202 Calculating the Amount of a Distribution

When a corporation distributes cash or other property to its shareholders, the amount of the distribution equals the sum of (1) the money distributed and (2) the fair market value (FMV) of any property distributed (determined as of the date of the distribution).[19] When a corporation makes a distribution to its shareholders, to the extent the corporation has current or accumulated E&P, the distribution is considered to have come from E&P. A *proportional* distribution from current or accumulated E&P is treated as a dividend distribution.

When a property distribution is treated as a dividend, the shareholder recognizes ordinary income equal to the FMV of the property. The shareholder's basis in the property received is also equal to the FMV. When a corporation distributes appreciated property to its shareholders, it must recognize gain equal to the amount it would have recognized had it sold the property for its FMV immediately prior to the distribution.[20] A corporation does not recognize a loss when it distributes property that has declined in value.

Example 8: Pacer Trucking has $50,000 in current and accumulated E&P at the time it distributes $10,000 to its owners. The distribution is treated as a dividend because it was distributed from Pacer's current and accumulated E&P.

Example 9: Image Consultants distributes to its sole shareholder, Al Jones, 100 shares of stock that it owns in Prince Enterprises. Image's current and accumulated E&P equals $100,000. The FMV of the 100 shares on the date distributed is $40,000. Since the property distributed is not shares of Image's own stock and is made from Image's current and accumulated E&P, the distribution is treated as a $40,000 property distribution.[21] Al reports the $40,000 as dividend income on his income tax return, and his basis in the Prince Enterprises stock will be $40,000.

Example 10: Faulk Furnishings distributes a $15,000 dividend to each of its two shareholders. It distributes $15,000 cash to shareholder A and property worth $15,000 to shareholder B. Faulk is treated as having made a $30,000 proportional distribution to its shareholders. Each shareholder reports $15,000 of dividend income in its gross income.

Example 11: Continuing with Example 10, Faulk's basis in the property distributed is $12,000. Since the appreciated property is distributed, Faulk recognizes $3,000 gain ($15,000 – $12,000) on the distribution. Shareholder B's basis in the property it receives from the distribution is $15,000.

Example 12: Assume the same facts as in Example 11, except Faulk's basis in the property distributed is $26,000. Because property that had declined in value is distributed, Faulk does not recognize a loss on the distribution. Shareholder B's basis in the property received is $15,000.

---

[19] Code Sec. 301(b)(1).
[20] Code Sec. 311(b)(1).

[21] Code Sec. 301(d).

Planning Pointer: Corporations should not distribute property that has declined in value. Those that do so miss the opportunity to deduct the loss. If Faulk from Example 12 had sold the property for its $15,000 FMV, it would have recognized an $11,000 loss ($15,000 – $26,000). Assuming it could deduct the loss, its tax liability would have decreased by its marginal tax rate times $11,000. If Faulk's marginal tax rate is 35 percent, its tax savings from the loss would equal $3,850 ($11,000 × 35%). Faulk could have then distributed the $15,000 proceeds from the sale as a cash dividend. In both scenarios, the shareholder receives property worth $15,000. However, the $11,000 decline in value (and the associated tax savings) is lost if the property is distributed instead of the cash.

.01 Reduction for Liabilities

If the property distributed is subject to a liability, the amount of a distribution must be reduced (but not below zero) by the amount of any liability (1) to which the property is subject or (2) that the shareholder assumes in connection with the distribution.[22]

Example 13: Electronic Supplies distributes equipment with an FMV of $10,000 to its sole shareholder. The equipment is subject to a $6,000 liability. The amount of the distribution equals $4,000 ($10,000 minus the $6,000 liability to which the equipment is subject).

¶ 1203 Tax Consequences of Dividend Distributions to Shareholders

The tax consequences of dividend income to the shareholder depend on whether the shareholder is a corporate or a noncorporate shareholder. When a partnership, S corporation, or other flow-through entity is a shareholder in a C corporation, any dividends it receives from the corporation are passed through to its owners and are taxed accordingly on the owners' income tax returns.

.01 Corporate Shareholders

When a corporation owns stock in another corporation, only a portion of the dividends it receives is taxable. The dividends received deduction allows corporate shareholders to reduce the amount of the dividend subject to tax to between 0 percent and 30 percent. Table 12-1 summarizes the amount of the dividends received deduction for corporate shareholders depending on their ownership percentage in the other corporation.[23] (See ¶ 411.02.)

Table 12-1 Summary of Dividends Received Deduction Rates

Ownership At Least	Percentage No More Than	Dividends Received Deduction	Percentage Taxed in Gross Income
0%	20%	70%	30%
20%	80%	80%	20%
80%	100%	100%	0%

Example 14: Liscana Enterprises receives $5,000 in dividends from Windows Framing, Inc. Liscana currently owns 10 percent of the outstanding shares in Windows. Because Liscana does not own at least 20 percent of the stock, it receives a 70-percent

---

[22] Code Sec. 301(b)(2).　　　[23] Code Sec. 243.

dividends received deduction; therefore, it is taxed on only 30 percent of the dividends it receives from Windows. $1,500 of the dividends it receives ($5,000 – $3,500 dividends received deduction) is taxed like any other income the corporation earns during the year.

Example 15: Duke Steel receives $50,000 in dividends from Ketchun Equipment. Duke's ownership in Ketchun represents 25 percent of Ketchun's shares. Because Duke owns at least 20 percent but not more than 80 percent of the stock of Ketchun, it is only taxed on 20 percent of the dividends it receives from Ketchun. Of the taxable dividends Duke receives, $10,000 ($50,000 – $40,000 dividends received deduction) is taxed like any other income at Duke's marginal tax rate.

Reason for the Rule: The dividends received deduction is designed to prevent triple taxation of a corporation's income. When a corporation earns income, the income is taxed for the first time. When the corporation distributes income to its shareholders, the income is taxed a second time when reported as dividend income on the shareholder's tax return. Without this deduction, a corporation's income could be taxed at least three times: once when earned by the corporation, a second time when distributed to corporate shareholders, and a third time when the corporate shareholders distribute the income to their shareholders. If any of the shareholders were themselves corporations, in the absence of the dividends received deduction, the income would then be taxed a fourth time. The stacking of layers of taxation in this manner could potentially be unlimited without the dividends received deduction.

.02 Individual Shareholders

How dividends received by individual taxpayers are taxed depends on whether the dividend is qualified dividend income. **Qualified dividends** are dividends received from U.S. corporations and qualified foreign corporations.[24] A foreign corporation is a "qualified foreign corporation" if the corporation is incorporated in a U.S. possession, the corporation is eligible for the benefits of a comprehensive income tax treaty with the United States, or the stock of the corporation with respect to which the dividend is paid is readily tradable on an established securities market in the United States. (See ¶ 405.02 and ¶ 1306.)

A dividend that is not qualified dividend income is taxed like all other ordinary income using the progressive tax rates that apply to individuals; the rates range from 10 percent to 35 percent (see the Appendix at the back of this book). Qualified dividend income is taxed at the same rates as net capital gains to individual taxpayers.[25] For taxpayers in the 10- or 15-percent tax bracket, qualified dividends are taxed at a zero-percent rate for a tax year beginning in 2009 or 2010. For a taxpayer in a higher tax bracket, qualified dividends are taxed at 15 percent. For a tax year beginning after 2010, qualified dividends are taxed at the same rates as other ordinary income.

Example 16: In 2009, Elijah Coppersmith received $1,000 in dividends from a U.S. corporation. Because Elijah is taxed at the 15-percent rate, he will pay $0 on the dividends. If Elijah had received $1,000 of nonqualified dividends, his tax on the dividends would have been $150 ($1,000 × 15%).

Example 17: In 2009, Boyd Willet receives $1,000 in dividends from a U.S. corporation. Because Boyd was in the 35 percent tax bracket, the tax he owes on the dividend income is $150 ($1,000 × 15%). If Boyd had $1,000 in nonqualified dividends, his tax owed on the dividend income would have been $350 ($1,000 × 35%).

---

[24] Code Sec. 1(h)(11)(B).   [25] Code Sec. 1(h)(11)(A).

Reason for the Rule: Prior to the Jobs and Growth Tax Relief Reconciliation Act of 2003 (P.L. 108-27), dividends received by noncorporate shareholders were taxed as ordinary income at rates that ranged up to 38.6 percent. Congress reduced the tax on dividends received by noncorporate taxpayers for three reasons. First, it believed the reduction of the tax on dividends (and thus the cost of capital needed by corporations to finance new investments) would lead to increased national investment, increased output, productivity, employment, and higher real wages. Second, it believed the tax rate reduction would reduce the incentive of corporations to finance their operations with debt (and its tax-deductible interest) rather than equity and would thus reduce the risk of corporate bankruptcies during economic downturns. Third, Congress believed taxing dividend income at a higher rate than income from capital gains encouraged corporations to retain earnings rather than to distribute them as dividends, even though shareholders might have an alternative use for the funds that could offer a higher rate of return than that earned on retained earnings.[26]

¶ 1204 Distributions Treated as Dividends vs. Return of Capital

The corporation is responsible for letting the shareholders know the extent to which the distribution constitutes a dividend versus return of capital. Distributions of cash or property to shareholders are treated as dividends to the extent that the distribution can be made out of current or accumulated earnings and profits (E&P). **Current E&P** refers to E&P that the corporation generates in the current year. **Accumulated E&P** refers to E&P generated in prior tax years that the corporation had not distributed to shareholders. Therefore, as long as the corporation has current and/or accumulated E&P at the time of the distribution, the distribution is treated as a dividend.

Any portion of the distribution that is not considered a dividend is treated as a return of capital. When shareholders receive a **return of capital distribution**, it is a tax-free return of their investment in the stock and thus reduces their adjusted basis in the stock (but not below zero).[27] To the extent shareholders receive a return of capital distribution in excess of their adjusted basis in stock, they are treated as having recognized gain from the sale or exchange of their stock. The gain is "capital gain" if the stock is a capital asset to the shareholder (which it will be unless the shareholder is a dealer in stock). The capital gain is "long-term capital gain" if the shareholder held the stock for more than one year as of the date of the distribution; it is "short-term capital gain" if the shareholder held the stock for one year or less on the date of the distribution.

Example 18: Demere Air Cylinders distributes $100 per share to each of its shareholders. Of this amount, $60 per share is from current or accumulated E&P. One of its shareholders, Santos Martell, owns 100 shares of stock in Demere. His adjusted basis in those shares is $50 per share, or $5,000. Santos includes $6,000 ($60 per share × 100 shares) of the distribution as ordinary dividend income on his current year income tax return. The remaining $40 per share reduces his adjusted basis in each share of stock to $10 ($50 – $40). Santos's basis in his 100 shares will be $1,000 ($10 × 100) after the distribution.

Example 19: Continuing with Example 18, Boyd Milden also owns 100 shares of stock in Demere as an investment. Boyd's adjusted basis in each share is $30. Boyd includes $6,000 ($60 × 100 shares) in gross income as a dividend. The remaining $40 per share is treated as a return of capital distribution. The first $30 per share reduces Boyd's basis in each share to $0. The excess $10 per share that he receives ($40 – $30) is treated as gain from the sale or exchange of the stock. Because the stock is a capital

---

[26] House Ways and Means Committee Report No. 108-94 (May 8, 2003), pp. 30, 31.

[27] Code Sec. 301(c).

asset for investors, Boyd's $1,000 gain ($10 × 100 shares) is capital gain. If Boyd held the stock for more than one year on the date of the distribution, his capital gain would be long-term capital gain. If he held the stock for one year or less, his capital gain would be short-term capital gain.

Example 20: Continuing with Example 19, assume that Boyd sells his 100 shares of Demere for $4,500. Since Boyd's basis in the stock is $0, he will recognize a $4,500 capital gain ($4,500 – $0). Whether the gain will be treated as short-term or long-term capital gain depends on how long Boyd held the stock prior to selling it. (See ¶ 901.03.)

How a shareholder's original basis is determined depends on how the stock was acquired. If the shares are purchased, then the original basis of the stock is its purchase price, including any purchase costs (such as commissions and transfer fees). The purchase price includes amounts paid in cash and the fair market value (FMV) of any other property transferred. If the shares are acquired in return for services rendered, then the original basis of the stock is the FMV of the stock received. This amount corresponds to the amount taxed to the shareholder upon receipt of the stock. The basis of property transferred to a corporation for stock in a nontaxable exchange under Code Sec. 351 is discussed in ¶ 1201.04.

Example 21: Deedra Stasiuk purchased 100 shares of stock for $5,000 (including commissions and transfer fees). Deedra's original basis in those shares is $5,000. Her basis in each share is $50 ($5,000 ÷ 100).

Example 22: Fidel Brech performed accounting services for a corporation in return for two shares of stock with an FMV of $100. His original basis in those two shares of stock is $100. His original basis in each share is $50 ($100 ÷ 2).

Example 23: Rod Zinkievich is one of three individuals who contributed cash and other property to a newly formed corporation in exchange for 100 percent of the stock in the corporation. Rod contributed $10,000 plus land with an FMV of $500,000 and an adjusted basis of $200,000 in return for 10,000 shares in the corporation. Rod's original basis in the 10,000 shares is $210,000 ($10,000 + $200,000). His basis in each share is $21 ($210,000 ÷ 10,000).

Special rules apply to stock acquired by gift, inheritance or in a divorce. If stock is received from a spouse or from a former spouse as part of divorce, then the taxpayer's original basis is the same as the transferor spouse's basis in the stock. If the shares are inherited, then the taxpayer's original basis in the stock usually is its FMV at the time of the decedent's death.

When the taxpayer is gifted stock, the donor's basis in the stock generally becomes the donee's (taxpayer's) basis. If the FMV of the gifted property at the time of the gift exceeds the donor's adjusted basis in the stock, then a portion of any gift tax paid on the transfer by the donor is added to the donee's basis. However, when the FMV of the gifted property at the time of the gift is less than the donor's adjusted basis in the stock, the donee's basis cannot be determined until the donee sells the stock. If the donee subsequently sells the stock for more than the donor's basis, then the donee's basis is the donor's basis. If the donee subsequently sells the stock for less than the FMV of the stock at the time of the gift, then the donee's basis is the FMV of the stock at the time of the gift. In situations where the donee sells the stock for an amount greater than the FMV at the time of the gift but less than the donor's basis, then the donee's basis in the stock is equal to the amount realized from the sale.

Example 24: When Ileen Oflaherty divorced her husband Bernie, he gave her 100 shares of stock. The shares had an FMV of $5,000. Bernie's adjusted basis in the shares was $3,000. Ileen's original basis in the shares is $3,000. Her original basis in each share is $30 ($3,000 ÷ 100).

Example 25: Alvaro Amacker inherited 100 shares of stock from his uncle Miguel. The shares had an FMV of $6,000 at the time of Miguel's death. Miguel's adjusted basis in the shares was $1,000. Alvaro's original basis in the share is $6,000. His original basis in each share is $60 ($6,000 ÷ 100).

Example 26: Laveta Berver's mother Janice gifted her with 100 shares of stock. At the time of the gift, the 100 shares had an FMV of $4,000. Janice's adjusted basis in the shares was $2,000. Laveta's original basis in the shares is $2,000. Her original basis in each share is $20 ($2,000 ÷ 100).

Basis of stock is adjusted for certain events that occur after its acquisition. For example, basis is adjusted when there is a nondividend distribution (described later in this section), a stock split, or additional contributions are made to a corporation's capital.

Example 27: Lavenia Cockrel acquired 100 shares of stock for $3,000. Her original basis in each share is $30 ($3,000 ÷ 100). Three years after her purchase, the company declared a stock split, and Lavenia received 100 additional shares. Lavenia's original basis does not change, but her basis in each share becomes $15 ($3,000 ÷ 200 total shares).

Example 28: Same facts as in Example 27 except that Lavenia received a $1,000 return of capital distribution. This distribution reduced her basis in the 200 shares to $2,000 ($3,000 – $1,000 tax-free return of capital), and her basis in each share becomes $10 ($2,000 ÷ 200).

Example 29: Same facts as in Example 27 except that Lavenia contributed an additional $1,500 to the corporation to help finance a new business operation. She received no additional shares for the contribution. Her contribution increases her basis in the 200 shares to $3,500 ($2,000 + $1,500), and her basis in each share becomes $17.50 ($3,500 ÷ 200).

.01 Distributions That Do Not Exceed Current Year E&P

Corporate distributions are considered to be made from the most recently accumulated E&P. Thus, a distribution is considered to come first from the current year's E&P; once all current E&P has been exhausted, any remaining distribution is considered to be paid from accumulated E&P.[28] If a corporation generates sufficient current E&P to cover the total distribution made during the year, the entire distribution is considered to have come from current E&P, and current E&P is reduced accordingly. Any remaining current year E&P would then be added to the corporation's accumulated E&P to determine its accumulated E&P for the next tax year. As long as the corporation has current E&P, a distribution may be treated as having come from current E&P, even if the corporation has a deficit balance in its accumulated E&P.

Example 30: Shune Automobile Parts has $20,000 in current year E&P and $10,000 in accumulated E&P. Shune distributes $12,000 during the year. Because its total distribution did not exceed its current E&P, the entire amount of the distribution is treated as a dividend distribution out of current E&P. Shune reduces its current E&P by $12,000, and the remaining $8,000 ($20,000 – $12,000) of current year E&P is added to its accumulated E&P. For the following year, Shune's accumulated E&P will equal $18,000 ($8,000 + $10,000).

Example 31: McClour Wall Plaques has a $15,000 deficit in its accumulated E&P at the beginning of its tax year. During the year the company generates $10,000 of E&P and distributes $10,000 to its shareholders. The $10,000 distribution will be treated as a dividend (out of current year E&P), even though the corporation still has negative accumulated E&P for the prior years it has been in existence.

---

[28] Reg. § 1.316-2(a).

Reason for the Rule: In Example 31, McClour's $10,000 distribution is considered to come from its current year E&P, even though its combined current and accumulated E&P are a negative amount. The distribution is taxed to the shareholders as a dividend because the Internal Revenue Code (the "Code") defines dividends as distributions out of either the accumulated earnings *or* the current year earnings.[29]

.02 Distributions When Current Year E&P Has a Negative Balance

If a corporation has a deficit in E&P for the tax year in which a distribution is made, but has a positive balance in accumulated E&P, the current year deficit is prorated as of the day the distribution is made, and it is subtracted from the corporation's accumulated E&P before determining the source of the distribution.[30]

Example 32: Klement Building Blocks, a calendar year corporation, has $15,000 in accumulated E&P at the beginning of its tax year. During the year, its current E&P is negative $21,900. On January 5, Klement distributes $14,500 to its sole shareholder, whose adjusted basis in the Klement stock is $16,000. Of the corporation's $21,900 negative current E&P, only $300 ($21,900/365 days × 5 days) is attributable to the portion of the year from January 1 to January 5. This allocation of current E&P deficit reduces Klement's combined current and accumulated E&P to $14,700 ($15,000 – $300). Therefore, the entire $14,500 distribution will be treated as a taxable dividend to the shareholder since the distribution does not exceed Klement's current and accumulated E&P at the time of the distribution.

Example 33: Assume the same facts as in Example 32, except the distribution was made on November 30 instead of January 5. As of November 30, $20,040 ($21,900/365 × 334 days) of the corporation's current year negative E&P must be taken into consideration when determining Klement's current and accumulated E&P. Since combined E&P on November 30 is negative ($15,000 – $20,040), none of the distribution is treated as a dividend, but instead it is treated as a return of capital. Because the shareholder's adjusted basis in its stock is greater than the amount of the distribution, the shareholder recognizes no income or gain on the return of capital. The shareholder's adjusted basis in the stock immediately following the distribution will be reduced to $1,500 ($16,000 – $14,500 tax-free return of capital).

.03 Distributions in Excess of Current Year E&P

If current year E&P is not sufficient to cover the amounts distributed during the year, the distribution is considered to come first from current year E&P and then from accumulated E&P. Even when the corporation has a deficit balance in accumulated E&P, distributions are considered to have been made first from current year E&P. Any distribution in excess of current E&P would then be treated as a return of capital and would be tax free to the shareholder to the extent of the shareholder's basis in the stock. Any excess would be taxed as capital gain.[31]

Example 34: Olman Corporation has $20,000 in current year E&P and a $15,000 deficit balance in accumulated E&P. The company distributes $25,000 during the year. The first $20,000 of the distribution is treated as coming from current E&P. This amount is taxed as dividend income on the shareholder's income tax returns. Because total distributions exceed Olman's current E&P and because Olman has a deficit in accumulated E&P, the remaining distribution is treated as a return of capital to the shareholders and is tax free to them to the extent of their respective bases in the stock. Any return of capital distribution in excess of a shareholder's basis is taxed as

[29] Code Sec. 316(a)(2).
[30] Rev. Rul. 74-164, 1974-1 CB 74.

[31] Code Sec. 301(c).

a capital gain. Olman's accumulated E&P at the beginning of the next year remains a $15,000 deficit.

If the amount of a corporation's distributions with respect to its stock for a year exceeds the corporation's current and accumulated E&P, it is necessary to determine first what part of each distribution is made from current E&P at the time of the distribution. Any part of the distribution that does not come from current E&P is considered a distribution from accumulated E&P to the extent thereof. Any distribution that is not from either current or accumulated E&P is not a dividend but is instead considered a return of capital, which will be tax free to the shareholders to the extent of their respective adjusted bases in the stock. Return of capital distributions in excess of adjusted basis are taxed as capital gains.

To determine what portion of the distribution was made from current E&P that existed at the time of the distribution, it is necessary to first determine the percentage of the distributions for the year that came from current E&P. This is computed by dividing current E&P by the total distributions for the year. This percentage is then multiplied by each distribution made during the year.[32]

Example 35: Bassinet, Inc. has current year E&P of $10,000 and accumulated E&P of $16,000. During the year, Bassinet distributes $20,000 to each of its shareholders, Fred and Alice. Fred and Alice each own 50 percent of the stock in Bassinet. Fred's basis in his shares of stock is $10,000; Alice's basis in her shares of stock is $5,000.

Date	Total Distribution
April 1	$ 5,000
September 1	15,000
December 1	20,000
	$40,000

Since Bassinet's total distributions ($40,000) exceed its total current and accumulated E&P ($26,000), it must determine how much of each distribution comes from current E&P. Of the total amounts distributed during the year, $10,000 is deemed to have come from current E&P. Thus, 25 percent ($10,000/$40,000) of each distribution is considered to come from current E&P.

Date	Amount		Current E&P
April 1	$ 5,000	× 25% =	$ 1,250
September 1	15,000	× 25% =	3,750
December 1	20,000	× 25% =	5,000
	$40,000		$10,000

Of the $5,000 distributed on April 1, $1,250 is considered to come from current E&P and the rest ($3,750) from accumulated E&P. This reduces Bassinet's accumulated E&P to $12,250 ($16,000 – $3,750). With respect to the September 1 distribution of $15,000, $3,750 is considered to come from current E&P and $11,250 from accumulated E&P ($15,000 – $3,750). After the September 1 distribution, Bassinet's accumulated E&P have been reduced to $1,000 ($12,250 – $11,250). Thus, of the $20,000 distribution on December 1, $5,000 is considered to come from current E&P and $1,000 from accumulated E&P. Bassinet will have a zero balance in its accumulated E&P. The remaining $14,000 ($20,000 – $5,000 – $1,000) of the December 1

---

[32] Reg. 1.316-2(b).

distribution is treated as a return of capital to the shareholders. A summary of the allocation of each distribution between dividend and return of capital is shown below.

Date	Dividend	Return of Capital
April 1	$ 5,000	$ 0
September 1	15,000	0
December 1	6,000	14,000
	$26,000	$14,000

Of the $20,000 distribution that each shareholder receives during the year, a total of $13,000 is considered to come from current and accumulated E&P ($26,000 × 50%). The shareholders report this amount as dividend income on their respective income tax returns. The remaining $7,000 distribution ($14,000 × 50%) is treated as a return of capital. Since Fred's basis in his stock is $10,000, the entire $7,000 is treated as a tax-free return of his investment in Bassinet and his basis in the stock is reduced to $3,000 ($10,000 – $7,000). Since Alice's basis in her stock is $5,000, only $5,000 of her $7,000 return of capital is treated as a tax-free return of her investment in Bassinet; thus her basis in the stock is reduced to $0. The $2,000 excess is taxed as a capital gain.

In the above example, a total of $10,000 ($1,250 + $3,750 + $5,000) of the total $40,000 distribution is considered to come from current E&P and a total of $16,000 from accumulated E&P ($3,750 + $11,250 + $1,000). This same result would have occurred without allocating each distribution between current and accumulated E&P and just treating each distribution as coming first from current E&P until exhausted and then from accumulated E&P. However, when stock is sold during the year, it is important to allocate each distribution between current and accumulated E&P to determine what portion of each distribution represents a taxable dividend versus what portion is a return of capital to each shareholder receiving a distribution during the year.

Example 36: Assume the same facts as in Example 35, except on August 16 of the current year, Alice sells her shares of stock in Bassinet to Julia for $9,000. Because Fred's ownership in Bassinet remains the same throughout the year, he still reports $13,000 as dividend income on his tax return and treats the remaining $7,000 of the distribution as a tax-free return of capital. However, Alice is entitled only to her share of the April 1 distributions ($5,000 × 50%) and not to later distributions. Accordingly, the entire $2,500 distribution Alice receives during the year is a taxable dividend because the April 1 distributions to Fred and Alice do not exceed Bassinet's current and accumulated E&P as of that date. Alice reports a $4,000 capital gain from the sale of her stock to Julia ($9,000 amount realized – $5,000 basis in the stock).

As the owner of 50 percent of the stock as of August 16, Julia receives her share of the September 1 and December 1 distributions from Bassinet. All $15,000 of the September 1 distribution was paid from current and accumulated E&P. Julia's share of this amount is $7,500. Of the $20,000 distribution on December 1, only $6,000 is considered a dividend distribution. Julia's share of this amount is $3,000. Therefore, Julia will report a total of $10,500 ($7,500 + $3,000) as dividend income for the year. Her share of the $14,000 return of capital is $7,000; that accordingly reduces her basis in the Bassinet stock to $2,000 ($9,000 – $7,000). The allocation of each distribution between dividend and return of capital (RofC) is summarized below.

	Fred		Alice		Julia	
Date	Dividend	RofC	Dividend	RofC	Dividend	RofC
April 1	$ 2,500	$ 0	$2,500	$0		
Sept. 1	7,500	0			$ 7,500	$ 0
Dec. 1	3,000	7,000			3,000	7,000
	$13,000	$7,000	$2,500	$0	$10,500	$7,000

¶ 1205 Constructive Dividends

Before making a dividend payment, a C corporation's board of directors usually declares that it will be paying a dividend to shareholders of record as of a specific date. However, a **constructive dividend** may occur when a corporation confers an economic benefit on a person in that person's capacity as a shareholder.

.01 The Need for the Constructive Dividend Rules

A constructive distribution is treated like all other distributions, in that it is considered a dividend distribution to the extent that it comes from the corporation's current and/or accumulated E&P. The constructive dividends rules were enacted to prevent corporations and their shareholders from avoiding tax on a corporation's earnings at the corporate or the shareholder level (or both) by disguising dividends as another form of payment. Examples 37 to 39 illustrate the possible abuse that might occur and the need for the constructive dividends rules.

Example 37: Pecelli Distributors has E&P of $300,000 for the year and pays a federal income tax of $100,250 to the IRS on its taxable income. It distributes $100,000 to its sole shareholder, Renee Pecelli, and she pays $15,000 tax on the dividend income ($100,000 × 15%). When the corporation's $39,000 federal income tax liability on the $100,000 distributed ($100,000 × 39%, Pecelli's marginal tax rate) is added to Renee's $15,000 tax on that same $100,000, a total of $54,000 in federal income tax is paid on the $100,000 earned by the corporation.

Example 38: Assume the same facts as in Example 37, except Renee is also an employee of Pecelli and instead of paying her a dividend, the company increases the compensation it pays Renee for the year by $100,000. Renee must pay tax on the additional compensation at a higher rate of tax than that imposed on dividends because compensation is taxed at a higher rate than qualified dividends. In this case, Renee's tax on that additional $100,000 of compensation is $35,000 ($100,000 × 35%, Renee's marginal tax rate). However, because compensation paid to employees is deductible by a corporation, the $100,000 in additional compensation paid to Renee reduces the corporation's taxable income for the year by $100,000. Thus, the $100,000 escapes tax at the corporate level, and only a total of $35,000 in federal income tax is paid on the $100,000 Pecelli paid to Renee. Overall, $19,000 in federal income tax is saved ($54,000 – $35,000).

Example 39: Assume the same facts as in Example 38, except instead of increasing Renee's compensation, Pecelli increases the amount of nontaxable fringe benefits (see ¶ 602) provided to her by $20,000. Because the fringe benefits are nontaxable to Renee, she receives $20,000 in benefits without having to pay any tax on the benefits. At the same time, the $20,000 in benefits paid by the company reduces the company's taxable income by $20,000. As a result, no tax is paid at either the corporate or shareholder levels on the $20,000.

.02 Identifying a Constructive Dividend

Whether a constructive dividend has been paid depends on the particular facts and circumstances of a transaction. Sometimes a transaction inadvertently results in a constructive dividend. Other times it is found that a transaction was intentionally designed to disguise a dividend as a different type of payment so tax at the corporate and/or shareholder levels could be avoided. Whether intentional or unintentional, when the economic substance of a transaction indicates that it is the payment of a dividend, the transaction will be recharacterized as a constructive dividend. Examples of transactions that may be recharacterized as constructive dividends include:

1. *Unreasonable compensation.* A constructive dividend may occur when a C corporation pays an unreasonable amount of compensation to a shareholder-employee.

2. *Payment of a shareholder's personal expenses.* A constructive dividend may result when a corporation pays a shareholder's personal expenses.

3. *Use of a corporation's property by a shareholder or person related to a shareholder.* A constructive dividend may result when a corporation allows a shareholder or a shareholder's relative to use corporate property for personal purposes without having to pay the fair rental value for the use of the property.

4. *Payment of an amount owed by a shareholder.* A constructive dividend may result when a corporation pays an amount owed by a shareholder.

5. *Loan to the corporation by a shareholder.* A constructive dividend may result when a shareholder makes a loan to a corporation if the loan can be characterized as a contribution to the corporation's capital.

6. *Loan by a corporation to a shareholder.* A constructive dividend may result when a corporation makes a loan to a shareholder on terms that would not be expected following arm's-length negotiations.

7. *Bargain sale of property to a shareholder.* A constructive dividend may result when a corporation sells property to a shareholder at a bargain price.

8. *Overpaying for a shareholder's property.* A constructive dividend may result when a corporation purchases property from a shareholder for more than its FMV.

Example 40: Samuelson Corporation has $100,000 in earnings for the year. Rather than pay tax on those earnings and have its sole shareholder and CEO, Samantha (Sam) Davis, pay a second tax on those earnings when they are distributed to her as a dividend, the corporation increases Sam's compensation by $100,000 for the year. If Sam's total compensation is unreasonably high, the corporation will be treated as having made a constructive dividend to Sam equal to the amount by which her compensation exceeds what would be deemed reasonable.

Example 41: Assume the same facts as in Example 40, except Samuelson pays $50,000 to remodel the family room in Sam's home. The $50,000 will be treated as a constructive dividend to Sam except to the extent that the corporation and Sam can show a business purpose for the remodeling and business use of the family room.

Example 42: Assume the same facts as in Example 40, except Samuelson purchases a ship for $100,000 and leaves it in Sam's exclusive possession. The $100,000 will be treated as a constructive dividend to Sam except to the extent that the corporation and Sam can show a business purpose for the purchase and a business use for the ship.

Example 43: Assume the same facts as in Example 40, except Samuelson pays $50,000 for the college tuition and living expenses of Sam's daughter. The $50,000 payment will be treated as a constructive dividend to Sam.

Example 44: Assume the same facts as in Example 40, except Sam makes a $100,000 loan to Samuelson. Interest at the rate of eight percent per year is payable on the loan. The corporation was not required to make any repayments at any specified intervals, and it was not required to provide any security for repayment. Given these facts, it is likely that the loan will be treated as a contribution of capital to the corporation, and interest payments to Sam will be treated as constructive dividends.

Example 45: Assume the same facts as in Example 40, except Samuelson makes an interest-free demand loan of $100,000 to Sam. Sam will be treated as making interest payments to the corporation, and the corporation will be treated as transferring those amounts back to Sam as constructive dividends.[33] If, as is likely, the interest payments are treated as nondeductible personal interest, the net tax effect to Sam will be that she will be required to include the entire amount of the deemed interest in her taxable income as a dividend without any offsetting deduction for the interest payment.

Example 46: Assume the same facts as in Example 40, except Samuelson purchases a motor vehicle for $30,000 and then sells it to Sam for $5,000. The company will likely be treated as having made a $25,000 constructive dividend to Sam ($30,000 – $5,000).

Example 47: Assume the same facts as in Example 40, except Samuelson pays $600,000 for a parcel of land that Sam owned and that had been appraised as having an FMV of $500,000. The corporation will be treated as having made a constructive dividend of $100,000 to Sam.

 Planning Pointer: The above examples should not cause tax planners to discourage corporations and their shareholders from entering into the types of transactions characterized in the examples. Changes in some of the facts can avoid characterization of a transaction as a constructive dividend. For example, if a shareholder loans money to a corporation on terms that would be expected in any arm's-length negotiation between unrelated parties (such as adequate interest and security for repayment), then the interest payments will not be recharacterized as constructive dividends and the corporation will be able to deduct them when calculating its taxable income. The parties can achieve their original goal—avoiding the corporate level of tax on some of the corporation's income—without conflicting with the constructive dividend rules.

¶ 1206 Stock Dividends

The term used to describe the distribution by a C corporation of its own stock to its shareholders is a **stock dividend**. As a rule, receipt of a stock dividend is not taxable to the shareholders, provided the stock dividend does not alter their interests in the corporation. Thus, if after receiving a stock dividend, the shareholders' ownership percentages in the corporation have not changed, then the stock dividend is excluded from shareholders' gross incomes.[34] When a stock dividend is not taxable to the shareholders, it does not affect the corporation's E&P.

Example 48: Rugg Equipment distributes one share of its own stock to the holder of each of its outstanding shares of stock. Following the distribution, each shareholder owns twice as many shares of Rugg as each owned prior to the distribution. No amount of the distribution is included in a shareholder's gross income. Ruggs's E&P is not reduced by the nontaxable stock dividend.

 Reason for the Rule: A stock dividend commonly is thought of as a mere bookkeeping change, not as income.[35] For example, if a corporation with only common stock outstanding issues more common stock as a dividend, each shareholder's ownership in the corporation is the same as it was before the distribution. Since no corporate assets are paid out, the distribution merely gives each stockholder more pieces of paper to represent the same interest in the corporation.

---

[33] Code Sec. 7872.
[34] Code Sec. 305(a).

[35] Senate Finance Committee Report No. 91-552 (November 21, 1969), 1969 United States Code Congressional and Administrative News, p. 2182.

Not treating stock dividends as taxable events stems from the premise that the shareholders have not received anything of real value in the distribution because no assets were transferred to the shareholders and no change in ownership interests resulted. When stock dividends alter the shareholders' interests in a corporation, the FMV of the stock distributed is taxable to the shareholders to the extent that the distribution is made out of current or accumulated E&P of the corporation. Taxable stock dividends also occur when a disproportionate distribution (see below) is made to shareholders.[36]

.01 Distributions in Lieu of Money or Other Property

If a corporation allows its shareholders the option of electing to receive cash or other property in lieu of stock, all shareholders receiving a distribution will be treated as having received a taxable dividend to the extent the distribution is made from the corporation's accumulated or current E&P. Any distribution not treated as a dividend is treated as a return of capital distribution.[37]

Example 49: A corporation offers its shareholders one share of its stock for each share they currently own, or $10 for each share of stock. Because shareholders have the option of receiving cash in lieu of stock, the stock dividend will be treated as a distribution of property and will be taxed as a dividend to the extent of the corporation's current and/or accumulated E&P.

Reason for the Rule: If a corporation with only common stock outstanding declares a dividend payable at the election of each shareholder either in additional common stock or in cash, the shareholder who receives a stock dividend is in the same position as if the shareholder had received a cash dividend and purchased additional stock with the proceeds.[38]

.02 Disproportionate Distributions

If a corporation's distribution of its stock results in some shareholders receiving money or other property and other shareholders increasing their proportionate interests in the assets or E&P of the corporation, the distribution will be treated as a dividend to the extent it is made from the corporation's current or accumulated E&P.[39]

Example 50: Variety Merchandise has two classes of stock, Class A common stock and Class B preferred stock. The company declares a stock dividend payable to the Class A shareholders and a cash dividend to Class B preferred stock shareholders. Because the distribution does not increase the proportionate interests of the Class A shareholders in the E&P of the company, it is not considered a disproportionate distribution.

Example 51: Pulos Trailers, Inc. pays a cash dividend to the owners of its Class A common stock and one share of its stock to the owners of each share of its Class B common stock. Because the result of the distribution is that some shareholders (Class A) receive cash and other shareholders (Class B) increase their proportionate interests in the E&P of the corporation, the distribution is treated as a dividend to the extent that the distribution comes from the corporation's current or accumulated E&P.

---

[36] Code Sec. 305(b).

[37] Code Sec. 305(b)(1).

[38] Senate Finance Committee Report No. 91-552 (November 21, 1969), 1969 United States Code Congressional and Administrative News, p. 2182.

[39] Code Sec. 305(b)(2).

Planning Pointer: A distribution of common stock to some shareholders and preferred stock to other shareholders will not be treated as a taxable distribution if the transaction effects a reshuffling of a corporation's capital structure—as long as the recapitalization has a *bona fide* business purpose and is an isolated transaction and not part of a plan periodically to increase the proportionate interest of any shareholder in the assets or earnings and profits of a corporation.[40]

.03 Shareholders' Basis Adjustments and Holding Period

If a corporation distributes a taxable stock dividend, the shareholder's basis in the stock is the FMV of the stock on the date of the distribution. This is the same amount the shareholder reports as dividend income from the stock dividend. When the shareholder receives a taxable stock dividend, the holding period begins on the date the dividend is distributed to the shareholders.

Shareholders that receive a nontaxable stock dividend must allocate their basis in their stock prior to the distribution (their "old stock") between their old stock and their new stock in proportion to the FMVs of each on the date the stock is distributed.[41] If the stock distributed is the same class as the stock with respect to which the distribution was made (e.g., common stock was distributed to common stock shareholders), the new basis of each share is determined by dividing the aggregate basis of the old shares by the total number of old and new shares.

Example 52: Kathlyn Ross owns 100 shares of the single class of stock of Mins Glass. Kathlyn's basis in the stock is $6,000. On August 1, Mins issues a stock dividend of one share for each two shares that a shareowner already owned. Because the shares distributed are identical to the shares Kathlyn already owned, she allocates her $6,000 basis to the total number of shares after the distribution. Prior to the distribution, Kathlyn's basis per share was $60 ($6,000/100); after the distribution, her basis per share is $40 ($6,000/150).

If the stock dividend is made in a different class of stock (for example, a common stock dividend on preferred stock, or a preferred stock dividend on common stock), the shareholder's new basis calculation becomes more complicated. In such situations, the basis of the stock with respect to which the dividend was paid must be allocated to the old stock and new stock based on the *respective FMV* of each class of stock on the date of distribution.

Example 53: Chemists Supplies distributes one share of preferred stock for each five shares of common stock its shareholders own. Dom Lanzarin, who owns 100 shares of common stock, receives 20 shares of preferred stock (100 ÷ 5). Dom's basis in his 100 shares of common stock was $4,000 ($40 per share). The FMV of the common stock on the date of distribution was $60 per share; the FMV of the preferred stock was $15 per share.

	FMV	Relative FMV	New Basis
Common	$6,000	$6,000/$6,300 = 95.24%	$3,810
Preferred	300	$300/$6,300 = 4.76%	190
Total FMV	$6,300		$4,000

The FMVs of the 100 shares of common stock and of the 20 shares of preferred stock are computed. The FMV of the common shares is $6,000 (100 shares × $60); the FMV of the preferred shares is $300 (20 shares × $15). By comparing the FMV of each type of stock to the FMV of all types of stock Dom owns, the relative FMV percentage of each type of stock can be determined. Since the FMV of the common shares represents 95.24 percent of the total FMV of the total shares, that percentage

---

[40] Rev. Rul. 86-25, 1986-1 CB 202.   [41] Code Sec. 307(a).

of Dom's $4,000 basis is allocated to his common shares ($4,000 × 95.24% = $3,810). When he does the same calculations for the preferred shares, he allocates a total of $190 of the $4,000 original basis to those shares.

If nontaxable stock dividends are received, the shareholder's holding period for the stock received includes its holding period for the stock with respect to which the distribution was made.

Example 54: Shelly Larran acquires 100 shares of stock on July 1, 2007. On August 8, 2009, Shelly receives a stock dividend with respect to her 100 shares. Her holding period in the shares she receives on August 8 runs from July 2, 2007.

¶ 1207 Keeping Track of E&P

Because only distributions from current or accumulated E&P are treated as dividend distributions, each time a corporation makes a distribution to its shareholders it must know its balance in both current and accumulated E&P. Therefore, it is important to understand the rules for computing E&P and to be able to keep track of a corporation's current and accumulated E&P balances.

In many ways, E&P resembles the retained earnings of a company. However, the calculation of retained earnings is determined under the rules that govern generally accepted accounting principles (GAAP), whereas E&P is computed under the tax laws enacted by Congress. E&P is used as a gauge of a corporation's ability to pay dividends without refunding the shareholder's investment in the corporation's stock. Therefore, the calculation of E&P differs in many ways from the calculation of taxable income. However, since many items included in the calculation of taxable income are also included in the calculation of E&P, the starting point for computing E&P is taxable income. From taxable income, various adjustments are made for those items for which the treatment of the item for computing taxable income is different from the treatment of the item for computing E&P. In making these adjustments, corporations must use the same basic method of accounting for calculating their E&P that they use for calculating their taxable income.[42]

Example 55: A corporation uses the accrual method of accounting to report its income and expenses. It must use the accrual method of accounting to report its income and expenses for purposes of determining its E&P.

The required adjustments to taxable income may be positive or negative. Positive adjustments include income not reported on the tax return that increases the corporation's ability to pay dividends as well as deductions taken on the tax return that do not reduce the corporation's ability to pay dividends. Negative adjustments to taxable income include income reported on the tax return that does not increase the corporation's ability to pay dividends as well as expenses that cannot be deducted on the tax return that reduce the amount of dividends a corporation can pay.

.01 Adjustments Due to Permanent Differences

Differences between amounts reported in taxable income and those reported in E&P result from the different rules that govern how the two amounts are computed. If one method includes an item of income, whereas the other method never recognizes it, a permanent difference results. Likewise, permanent differences occur when one method allows an expense to be deducted, while the other method never allows a deduction for it. Permanent differences between the two methods can result in positive or negative adjustments to taxable income, depending on whether the item disallowed results in lower or higher taxable income in relation to the corporation's E&P.

Negative adjustments resulting from permanent differences. Many expenses that are not deductible against gross income reduce the corporation's capacity to pay dividends. Such amounts must be subtracted from taxable income to arrive at a corporation's E&P for the year. For example, federal income taxes are not allowed as a deduction in the calculation of taxable income, but when a

---

[42] Reg. § 1.312-6.

corporation pays $50,000 in federal income taxes, the payment reduces the amount that can be distributed to shareholders. Likewise, penalties, fines, and other expenditures that violate public policy are not deductible in computing taxable income, but they reduce the amount of profits available to be distributed to shareholders.

Example 56: Wedge Photo pays $40,000 in federal income tax for the year. Although Wedge Photo cannot reduce its taxable income by this amount, the payment reduces the amount of money available to the corporation for making distributions to shareholders without refunding their investment in the corporation's stock. Therefore, the company must reduce its E&P by the $40,000 of federal income tax paid. It subtracts the $40,000 negative adjustment from its taxable income to properly reflect the reduction in E&P.

Losses disallowed for tax purposes affect a corporation's ability to pay dividends. For example, a corporation cannot deduct a loss resulting from a sale to a related party. However, when a corporation realizes a loss on the sale or exchange of an asset, that indicates the amount realized from the transaction was less than the corporation's adjusted basis in the property. Thus, the loss reduces the corporation's ability to pay dividends. Accordingly, losses from related party transactions are deducted in computing E&P. These disallowed losses are negative adjustments to taxable income. Figure 12-1 provides a list of negative adjustments to taxable income.

Figure 12-1 Negative Adjustments Due to Permanent Differences

- Federal income taxes paid;
- Disallowed losses from related party transactions;
- Life insurance premiums paid for a policy benefiting the corporation;
- Interest and expenses relating to tax-exempt income;
- Nondeductible, unreasonable amount of compensation paid to officers;
- Disallowed portion of meals and entertainment;
- Disallowed deduction for gifts in excess of $25; and
- Nondeductible fines and other penalties that violate public policy.

Example 57: Kalan Enterprises makes gifts worth $55 each to 100 of its top customers. On its tax return, the deduction is limited to $2,500 ($25 × 100); however, its dividend-paying capacity is reduced by $5,500 ($55 × 100). Thus, the $3,000 difference is a negative adjustment to taxable income when computing the corporation's E&P.

Example 58: Macro Services, Inc. incurs $20,000 in meal and entertainment expenses for the year, but it can deduct only half of such expenses on its tax return. However, the entire $20,000 paid reduces Macro's ability to pay dividends to its shareholders. Therefore, it must subtract the disallowed portion of the expenses ($10,000) from taxable income when computing its current year E&P.

Positive adjustments due to permanent differences. The tax laws specifically allow certain types of income to be excluded from federal income tax. These amounts, known as "exclusions," are not included in the calculation of taxable income, but they increase a corporation's capacity to pay dividends. For example, interest on state and local government bonds is specifically excluded from federal income tax. However, when a corporation receives $15,000 of interest from such a bond, its capacity to distribute earnings to its shareholders increases by $15,000. Accordingly, this amount would be a positive adjustment to taxable income when computing E&P. Other examples of positive adjustments of this nature include tax-exempt life insurance proceeds and federal income tax refunds. When computing E&P, a corporation's organizational expenditures are never deductible.

For tax purposes, such costs are immediately expensed or amortized over 180 months. (See ¶ 503.) These and other permanent differences are listed in Figure 12-2.

Figure 12-2 Positive Adjustments Due to Permanent Differences

- Municipal bond interest,
- Federal income tax refunds,
- Amortization of organizational expenses,
- Any deduction related to construction period carrying charges, and
- Circulation expenditures deducted from gross income.

Example 59: Culkin Tractors has $1,000 in interest on a state bond that was not included in its taxable income but was included in its E&P because it increased the corporation's economic capacity to make distributions. Although the income was not taxable to the corporation, when it is distributed to a shareholder it will be taxed as a dividend.

Example 60: A corporation receives $15,000 of tax-exempt interest on a municipal bond and a $5,000 federal income tax refund. Although neither amount is included in the corporation's gross income, each amount increases the amount of funds available to the corporation to make distributions and therefore increases its E&P.

Not all amounts excluded from gross income that increase the amount of assets available to make distributions increase a corporation's E&P. Items excluded from gross income that increase a corporation's capital, but not its income, do not increase a corporation's E&P. Such items include contributions to capital.

Example 61: Fuqua Decorators was organized as a corporation on April 1. At that time, five individuals transferred a total of $100,000 to the corporation in return for stock in the corporation. Although the capital contributed to the corporation increased the amount available for it to make distributions, any of that $100,000 distributed to the corporation's shareholders would be a return of the capital they contributed to the corporation, not a distribution of any income the corporation had earned. Therefore, the $100,000 is not included in the calculation of the company's E&P.

 Reason for the Rule: E&P is a measure used to determine what portion of a distribution consists of income earned by a corporation that should be taxed when received by a shareholder. Amounts that increase a corporation's capital but do not constitute income are not included in E&P.

.02 Adjustments Due to Timing Differences

Up to this point, the discussion concerning adjustments to taxable income has been about permanent differences in the way the regular income tax system and the E&P rules handle a particular item. Some expenses are allowed under both sets of rules; however, the two rules differ as to how quickly the item is expensed. For example, both the federal income tax laws and the rules governing the calculation of E&P allow certain assets to be depreciated. The income tax laws allow personal property to be depreciated under the Modified Accelerated Cost Recovery System (MACRS) (see ¶ 702.01), which uses the double-declining balance method. Furthermore, some corporations are eligible to expense some or all of the cost of personal property under Code Sec. 179. These accelerated methods of depreciation were incorporated into the income tax laws especially to allow taxpayers to enjoy the tax benefits associated with depreciation expense quicker in hopes of making investments in such assets more attractive to businesses.

For computing E&P, the cost of depreciable property is recovered using the alternative depreciation system (ADS) over specified periods (see Table 7-2 at ¶ 702.01 and ¶ 703), and the cost of property expensed under Code Sec. 179 is instead expensed ratably over five years. Thus, in years in which tax depreciation is higher than allowed under the E&P rules (typically the early years), a positive adjustment to taxable income will be required. In the latter years of the asset's life, when depreciation allowed for E&P is greater than tax depreciation, a negative adjustment will be required.

Because different methods are used to depreciate property for determining corporate taxable income than for determining E&P, the adjusted basis in depreciable property will also differ. Thus, when depreciable property is sold, the gain or loss reported on the tax return must be compared to the gain or loss recognized for computing E&P. The difference between these two amounts will result in either a positive or a negative adjustment to taxable income.

Other examples of timing differences involve intangible drilling costs as well as mining exploration and development costs. For tax purposes, these costs are generally expensed in the year they are incurred. For E&P purposes, intangible drilling costs are deducted ratably over 60 months, and mineral exploration and development costs are deducted ratably over 120 months. Table 12-2 summarizes the more common timing differences that require adjustments to taxable income.

Table 12-2 Adjustments Due to Timing Differences

Description of the Item	*Discussion*
Installment sales	For tax purposes, gain from an installment sale is recognized as the cash is received. For E&P purposes, the gain is earned in the year of the sale. Thus, in the year of the sale, a positive adjustment to taxable income will be required. In subsequent tax years when the cash is received, a negative adjustment will be required.
Depreciation of personal property	Differences between the depreciation taken under the two methods result in a timing difference. The difference will reverse itself either at the end of the depreciation periods or when the property is sold.
Capital losses in excess of capital gains	In the year the loss is disallowed, a negative adjustment to taxable income must be made. In a subsequent year when the carryover loss is allowed, a positive adjustment must be made.
Charitable contributions in excess of the 10-percent limit	In the year the charitable deduction is limited, a negative adjustment to taxable income is necessary. In the year in which the charitable contribution carryover is utilized, a positive adjustment to taxable income must be made.
Intangible drilling costs	In the first year, a positive adjustment must be made, but for the next five years, negative adjustments will be required.
Mining exploration and development costs	In the first year, a positive adjustment must be made, but for the next 10 years, negative adjustments will be required.

Example 62: Kovar Shipping sells stock, resulting in a $60,000 capital loss. Because corporations can only deduct capital losses to the extent of capital gains, Kovar cannot deduct the $60,000 loss on its tax return and instead must carry the loss over to the next year. However, the loss reduced the corporation's capacity to pay dividends and therefore must be subtracted from taxable income to accurately reflect the corporation's E&P.

Example 63: Bartek Moving purchases a delivery truck on September 1, 2009, for $45,000 and depreciates it under general MACRS. The truck weighs more than 6,000 pounds and is not subject to the luxury automobile depreciation limits. Bartek's depreciation deduction for federal income tax purposes is computed using the five-year column from Table 7A in the Appendix to Chapter 7. Depreciation for computing E&P is calculated using ADS, which depreciates trucks over five years using the straight-line (SL) depreciation method (see Table 7F in the Appendix to Chapter 7).

Year	MACRS Depreciation	E&P Depreciation
2009	$ 9,000 ($45,000 × 20%)	$4,500 ($45,000 × 10%)
2010	14,400 ($45,000 × 32%)	9,000 ($45,000 × 20%)
2011	8,640 ($45,000 × 19.2%)	9,000 ($45,000 × 20%)

Because Bartek's depreciation deduction for 2009 using MACRS exceeds the depreciation deduction under ADS (for purposes of computing E&P) by $4,500 ($9,000 – $4,500), the difference must be added back to taxable income. In 2010, the $5,400 difference ($14,400 – $9,000) must also be added back to taxable income when computing the company's E&P for the year.

In 2011, Bartek uses $9,000 of depreciation to compute E&P compared to $8,640 of depreciation deducted in computing taxable income. Because its depreciation using ADS exceeds its depreciation deduction on the tax return, the corporation must subtract an additional $360 ($9,000 – $8,640) from its taxable income when computing its E&P for 2011.

Effect of sale of property on E&P. When a corporation sells an asset, the gain or loss realized will increase or decrease the corporation's E&P. The amount of gain or loss realized for the purpose of determining the adjustment to a corporation's E&P may differ from the amount of gain or loss realized in computing a corporation's taxable income because property may have a different adjusted basis for determining E&P than it does for determining taxable income. When computing gain for E&P, adjusted basis using E&P depreciation deductions must be used.

Example 64: On January 1, 2008, Katch Oils, a calendar year taxpayer, purchases a delivery truck for $45,000 and expenses the entire cost. As a result, the truck's adjusted basis for tax purposes is $0. On January 1, 2010, Katch sells the delivery truck for $30,000 and reports a $30,000 gain on its tax return.

To compute E&P each year, Katch expenses the Section 179 property over five years. Accordingly, it deducts $9,000 each year, so when the truck is sold, Katch's total depreciation deductions are $18,000 ($9,000 × 2 years). Katch's adjusted basis in the truck for E&P equals $27,000 ($45,000 – $18,000), and its E&P gain equals $3,000 ($30,000 – $27,000).

In 2008, Katch makes a $36,000 positive adjustment to taxable income. This amount is the difference between the depreciation expense reported on the tax return ($45,000) and the expense allowed for E&P ($9,000). In 2009, the entire $9,000 deducted against E&P requires a $9,000 negative adjustment to taxable income. In 2010, Katch makes a negative adjustment to taxable income equal to the difference between the $30,000 gain reported on the tax return and the $3,000 gain included in E&P.

Year	Positive Adjustment	Negative Adjustment
2008	$36,000	
2009		$ 9,000
2010		27,000
	$36,000	$36,000

As this example illustrates, the initial $36,000 difference between these two depreciation methods reverses itself as the property is depreciated or at the time the property is subsequently sold.

Although realized gains and losses generally do not affect a corporation's E&P until they are recognized, an exception is made for installment sales. A corporation's E&P is computed as if the corporation did not use the installment method to report gain from the sale.

Example 65: Scheve Foods sold vacant land with an adjusted basis of $100,000. The proceeds from the sale were $250,000, payable in five equal annual installments. The entire $150,000 gain ($250,000 – $100,000) is included in E&P in the year of the sale, even though for tax purposes the gain is recognized over the next five years.

.03 Items Requiring No Adjustment to E&P

Certain items of income whose recognition is deferred to a subsequent tax year do not increase a corporation's E&P in the year the gain is realized, but only in the year in which the gain is finally recognized. That is because an increase in E&P in the year of realization could result in the income being taxed twice to the shareholders as dividend income if E&P were also increased in the year income was recognized. Items that do not increase E&P include gains from like-kind exchanges and the involuntary conversion of property. Income from the discharge of indebtedness that is excluded from gross income does not increase E&P to the extent that the amount discharged is applied to reduce the corporation's basis in assets.

Example 66: Gramm, Inc. exchanges an office building with an FMV of $500,000 and an adjusted basis of $200,000 for an office building with an FMV of $600,000. As part of the exchange, Gramm transfers $100,000 to the other party. No amount of Gramm's $300,000 realized gain ($500,000 – $200,000) is recognized because the transaction qualifies as a like-kind exchange. However, recognition of that gain is only deferred, and Gramm's basis in its new office building is reduced by the postponed gain ($600,000 – $300,000 = $300,000). If Gram subsequently sells the office building for $600,000, it will have to recognize the $300,000 of postponed gain ($600,000 – $300,000). If the company were required to include that $300,000 in E&P at the time the gain was realized (but unrecognized) and a second time when the new office building was sold and the gain was recognized, E&P would include the $600,000 instead of the proper $300,000, which reflects the corporation's ability to pay a dividend from previously taxed profits.

Example 67: Stalling, Inc. does not recognize any income when $50,000 of its debt is discharged in bankruptcy. The tax laws require Stalling to apply the $50,000 to reduce the basis of the assets it retained following its bankruptcy. Thus, when Stalling sells those assets, it will realize $50,000 more in gain than it would have realized absent the discharge of indebtedness. If both the $50,000 discharge of indebtedness income and $50,000 gain realized from the sale of assets were included in the corporation's E&P, the shareholders could be taxed on an additional $50,000 of income that the corporation never actually earned, since distributions from current and accumulated E&P are taxed as dividends to the shareholders.

> **Reason for the Rule:** Examples 66 and 67 demonstrate that income from transactions that result in deferred gain cannot be included in E&P in the year in which the realized gain is deferred because it creates the potential for shareholders to be taxed twice on income the corporation only earns once. When a corporation's current and accumulated E&P are exhausted, any distributions are treated as a return of capital, which is tax free to shareholders to the extent of their basis in the corporate stock. Thus, in Example 66, if the corporation's E&P incorrectly increase by $600,000 (rather than $300,000), an additional $300,000 of distributions from the corporation has the potential of being treated as a dividend distribution to shareholders. In Example 67, if the corporation's E&P increase by $100,000, an additional $50,000 of distributions will be treated as a dividend rather than as a return of capital.

.04 Effects of Distributions on E&P

As a general rule, when C corporations distribute money or property with respect to their stock, they must decrease their E&P (but not below zero) by the sum of the following amounts:[43]

1. The amount of money distributed,

2. The principal amount of any obligations of the corporation that are distributed,[44]

3. The adjusted basis of property (other than appreciated property) distributed, and

4. The FMV of appreciated property distributed.

For purposes of reducing E&P for property distributions, the adjusted basis of property (in the case of distributions other than of appreciated property) is its adjusted basis for purposes of computing E&P.[45] When a C corporation distributes appreciated property, its E&P is increased by the gain it recognizes on such distribution. After E&P is increased by the gain, it is reduced by the FMV of the property distributed.

Example 68: Hahl Engines distributes equipment with an FMV of $10,000 and an adjusted basis of $2,000 to its sole shareholder. Hahl increases its E&P by the $8,000 gain it recognizes for the difference between the FMV of the equipment and its adjusted basis. Hahl then reduces its E&P by the $10,000 FMV of the equipment. Because of the distribution, the company's E&P is reduced by $2,000, which is the amount of the adjusted basis of the property distributed.

When a corporation makes a nontaxable distribution of its own stock, the corporation does not reduce its E&P. However, if a corporation makes a distribution that results in a taxable dividend that is included in shareholders' gross income, the corporation's E&P must be reduced by the taxable amount of the distribution.[46]

Example 69: Machine Coolants declares a stock dividend and distributes two shares of stock for each share of stock held by a shareholder. Because the distribution is nontaxable, the company does not reduce its E&P.

Example 70: Medical Alarms has two classes of common stock outstanding: Common Stock A and Common Stock B. The company distributes $10 per share to the owners of Common Stock A outstanding and distributes one share of its own stock to the owner of each share of Common Stock B. Because this is a disproportionate distribution, the FMV of the stock distributed to the Common Stock B shareholders must be included in

---

[43] Code Sec. 312(a).
[44] Code Sec. 312(c).

[45] Code Sec. 312(b).
[46] Reg. § 1.312-1(d).

their gross income. As a result, the company must reduce its E&P by both the amount of cash and the FMV of the stock distributed.

RECONCILIATION OF NET INCOME AND TAXABLE INCOME

Larger C corporations are required to maintain two sets of accounting records: one for financial reporting purposes and a second for tax reporting purposes. Different records are required because financial statements and tax returns are prepared with different objectives and in compliance with different rules. For financial accounting purposes, corporations need to comply with Generally Accepted Accounting Principles (GAAP). For tax reporting purposes, corporations need to comply with the *tax laws*, which Chapters 1–11 have shown to be different from the financial reporting rules. Most differences between the two methods of computing net earnings stem from the different objectives of the two governing bodies in charge of the rules.

The rules that govern GAAP are written with the objective of providing users of financial statements with the most relevant and reliable information about the activities and financial position of the business. When writing the tax laws, Congress is concerned first with raising revenues for the federal government and second with maintaining certain economic, social, or political agendas. (See ¶ 106.)

Corporations with total receipts of at least $250,000 *and/or* at least $250,000 in total assets are required to reconcile the disparities between their **net income per books** and their **taxable income per return** on their income tax returns (before any net operating loss (NOL) or dividends received deduction (DRD)).

¶ 1208 Differences between Book Income and Taxable Income

The different rules for reporting income for financial accounting purposes and for tax purposes result in differences in a corporation's net income and taxable income. These differences can be characterized as permanent differences or timing differences.

.01 Permanent Differences

Permanent differences result when certain items of income or expenses reported for financial accounting purposes are *never* reported for tax purposes. They can also occur when deductions taken on the tax return are *never* reported in net income. When the item results in more net income than taxable income, the item must be subtracted from net income in order to reconcile net income with the taxable income reported on the company's tax return. For example, interest from state and local government bonds is exempt from federal income tax; however, the interest is included in the calculation of net income. Thus, the amount of municipal interest must be subtracted from net income in order to reconcile net income (per books) and taxable income (per return). When the item results in less net income than taxable income, the item must be added to net income in order to reconcile it with taxable income reported on the corporation's tax return.

Example 71: Bolles Forklifts receives $2,000 of tax-exempt interest during the year. The tax-exempt interest increases its net income by $2,000 but is excluded from its taxable income. In order to reconcile the amounts reported in net income to those reported on the tax return, the $2,000 must be subtracted from net income.

The permanent differences between the calculation of taxable income and net income that have been the focus of discussion in this textbook are shown in Table 12-3.

Table 12-3 Permanent Differences Between Taxable Income and Net Income

Item	Tax Return	Financial Reporting
Municipal interest (see ¶ 411.01.)	Not taxable*	Included
Life insurance proceeds	Not taxable**	Included
Expenses related to tax-exempt investments (see ¶ 505.)	Not deductible	Deductible
Federal income taxes paid	Not deductible	Deductible
Premiums paid for life insurance in which the corporation is named as a beneficiary	Not deductible	Deductible
Fines and penalties (see ¶ 501.04.)	Not deductible	Deductible
Meals and entertainment (see ¶ 605.)	50% limitation	Entirely deductible
Unreasonable compensation (see ¶ 601.02.)	Not deductible	Deductible
Loss on the sale of property to a related party (see ¶ 804.)	Not deductible	Deductible
Depletion expense (see ¶ 705 and ¶ 706.)	The greater of percentage or cost depletion	Cost depletion
Organizational and start-up costs (see ¶ 503.)	Deduct up to $5,000 immediately or amortize over 180 months	No deduction
Intangible assets with an infinite life (see ¶ 708 and ¶ 709.)	Amortize over 15 years	No deduction
Business gifts (see ¶ 512.)	Limited to $25	Entirely deductible
Domestic production activities deduction (see ¶ 509.)	Deductible	No deduction
Dividends received deduction (see ¶ 411.02 and ¶ 508.)	Deductible	No deduction
Net operating loss deduction (see ¶ 1002.)	Deductible	No deduction

* Interest may be taxable if it is paid with respect to a private activity bond that is not a qualified bond, an arbitrage bond, or a bond not in registered form.

** Life insurance proceeds may be taxable if the transfer for value rule applies or the policy is on the life of an employee.

Example 72: Howell Industries incurs $10,000 of meals and entertainment expenses during the year. Howell reduces its net income by the $10,000, but can only reduce its taxable income by $5,000. When reconciling net income to taxable income, Howell must add back the disallowed meals and entertainment.

For tax purposes, corporations can deduct the *greater* of percentage depletion (subject to the taxable income limitations) or cost depletion. For financial accounting purposes, only the cost depletion method can be used. Although differences in these two methods are usually timing differences that will reverse themselves over time, if the amount deducted for percentage depletion exceeds the corporation's adjusted basis in the property, a permanent difference results. Any excess deducted on the tax return would require a negative adjustment to net income to reconcile net income to taxable income on the corporate tax return.

Example 73: A corporation owns oil and gas property, which as of the beginning of the year had been fully depleted. During the year, gross income from the property was $250,000, and percentage depletion equals $37,500 ($250,000 × 15%). (See ¶ 706.) Because the property is fully depleted, cost depletion is zero, and accordingly, no amount is subtracted in computing net income on the income statement. On its tax return, the corporation deducts $37,500 as depletion expense (the *greater* of $0 or $37,500). The $37,500 difference is a permanent difference.

.02 Timing Differences

Timing differences result when income and expenses are reported for tax purposes in a different tax year than they are reported for financial accounting purposes. Timing differences originate in one tax year but reverse themselves in a subsequent tax year. For this reason, in the year in which the difference is created, it is often called an **originating difference**. In the subsequent year(s) when the difference is reversed, it is called a **reversing difference**.

Example 74: Scribb Equipment purchases equipment costing $10,000 on July 1, 2009. Scribb deducts depreciation expense over the years in accordance with the tax laws (on its tax return) and GAAP (on its financial statements) as shown below.

Year	Tax Depreciation	Book Depreciation	Difference
2009	$ 2,000	$ 1,000	$1,000
2010	3,200	2,000	1,200
2011	1,920	2,000	(80)
2012	1,152	2,000	(848)
2013	1,152	2,000	(848)
2014	576	1,000	(424)
	$10,000	$10,000	$ 0

During 2009 and 2010, depreciation deductions on the tax return exceed depreciation taken against net income. However, the differences reverse from 2011 through 2014 when book depreciation exceeds the tax depreciation. Nonetheless, the total amount of depreciation deductions that Scribb takes from 2009 to 2014 is the same. Therefore, the differences merely involve timing.

Four basic types of timing differences create differences between a corporation's net income and its taxable income:

1. Income is included in net income but not in taxable income during the same year.

2. Income is included in taxable income but not in net income during the same year.

3. Amounts are deducted when calculating net income but are not deducted when calculating taxable income for the same year.

4. Amounts are deducted when calculating taxable income but are not deducted when calculating net income for the same year.

Throughout Chapters 1 to 9, as the tax laws governing the tax treatment of income and expense were discussed, significant differences between how the tax laws and GAAP require that the item be handled were presented in the *GAAP vs. Code* sections. Therefore, most of the differences should look familiar. The differences are summarized in Tables 12-4 and 12-5.

Table 12-4 Differences between Net Income and Taxable Income Due to the Timing of Gains and Other Income

Item	Originating Difference	Reversing Difference
Installment sales (see ¶ 309.01 and ¶ 810.)	In the year of the sale, the entire gain is included in net income, whereas only a portion of the gain is reported on the tax return. This difference will require a negative adjustment to net income.	In each subsequent tax year as payments are received, gain is recognized on the tax return. This will require a positive adjustment to net income.
Gains from involuntary conversions (see ¶ 809.)	Gain from an involuntary conversion is not taxable if the proceeds are reinvested in qualified replacement property. This will require a negative adjustment to net income in the originating year.	Because the adjusted basis of the replacement property for tax purposes is reduced by the postponed gain, the originating difference is reversed through differences in depreciation taken on the replacement property or when the property is eventually sold.
Gains from like-kind exchanges (see ¶ 808.)	Gain is recognized on the income statement to the extent that the earnings process has been completed. Gain is recognized on the tax return to the extent of boot received. Any difference between the two amounts will need to be shown as an adjustment to net income in the year of the exchange.	Because the basis of the like-kind property received is reduced by any postponed gain, any originating difference will be reversed either through differences in depreciation expense taken on the like-kind property or when the property is subsequently sold.
Income received in advance (see ¶ 307.01.)	Can be taxed in the year received or over no more than two tax years. Income is included in net income in the year it is earned.	When income is eventually taxed in the second tax year, a positive adjustment to net income will be needed.
Long-term contracts (see ¶ 309.02.)	If the completed contract method is used for financial accounting purposes, each year until the final year, the gain reported on the tax return (under the percentage-of-completion method) will result in an originating difference due to higher taxable income being reported.	In the year the project is completed, the entire gain is reported in net income. Thus, in the final year, net income will be greater than taxable income and a positive adjustment to net income will be required.
Rollover of gain from the sale of publicly traded securities (see ¶ 807.)	Gain from the sale of publicly traded securities can be postponed for tax purposes if the proceeds are invested in a specialized small business investment company (SSBIC). This would require a negative adjustment to net income in the year of the sale of publicly traded stock.	Since the tax basis in the SSBIC stock is adjusted for any postponed gain, this difference will reverse itself when the corporation sells the SSBIC stock.

Item	Originating Difference	Reversing Difference
Unrealized gain on marketable securities (see ¶ 801.)	GAAP requires that unrealized gains and losses on marketable trading securities be reported on the income statement in the year in which the unrealized gain or loss occurs. This will cause a difference between the calculation of net income and taxable income.	Any remaining unrealized gain or loss previously reported on the income statement will be reversed in the year in which the securities are sold.

Example 75: On December 20, 2009, Kraft Dyes sells a parcel of land for $150,000. The adjusted basis of the land is $50,000. The terms of the contract call for five annual payments of $30,000 beginning on January 20, 2010. Kraft uses the calendar year as its tax year.

For 2009, the company must include its entire $100,000 gain ($150,000 – $50,000) in its net income. However, since none of the proceeds is received in 2009, none of the gain is included in the calculation of taxable income. Kraft will report a $100,000 negative adjustment to net income when it reconciles its net income to taxable income on its corporate tax return. From 2010 to 2014, Kraft will report $20,000 of the gain in taxable income each year ($100,000/5 years). The amounts will be reported as positive adjustments to net income in those years.

Example 76: On November 1, 2009, Rennell, Inc. receives a $36,000 payment for rent covering the three-year period beginning on November 1, 2009, and ending on October 31, 2012. Rennell uses the calendar year as its tax year. In 2009, Rennell includes $2,000 ($36,000/36 × 2 months) in income on both its tax return and on its financial statements. In 2010, it reports $12,000 in net income ($36,000/36 × 12 months). It must include the remaining rents ($34,000) in gross income on its tax return because taxpayers cannot defer prepaid amounts beyond the subsequent tax year (see ¶ 307.01).

In 2010, Rennell must add the $22,000 difference to net income when it reconciles net income to taxable income on its corporate income tax return. In 2011 and 2012, Rennell will report the amount reported on the income statement ($12,000 and $10,000, respectively) as a negative adjustment to net income.

Table 12-5 Differences between Net Income and Taxable Income Due to the Timing of Losses and Deductions

Item	Originating Difference	Reversing Difference
Depreciation (see ¶ 702.)	When accelerated methods of depreciation are used to depreciate property for tax purposes, the amounts deducted in the earlier years of an asset's life will result in originating differences that will need to be subtracted from net income.	In the latter years of an asset's life, depreciation expense on the income statement will exceed depreciation deducted on the tax return.

Item	Originating Difference	Reversing Difference
Depletion (see ¶ 705 and ¶ 706.)	For tax purposes, corporations deduct the *greater* of percentage depletion or cost depletion. On the income statement, depletion expense must be computed using the cost method. When the amount of percentage depletion taken on the tax return exceeds the amount deducted on the income statement, the corporation will be required to make a negative adjustment to net income. However, any difference due to depletion expense on the tax return exceeding the adjusted basis of the property is a permanent, not a timing, difference (see Table 12-4 and Example 66).	In years in which the depletion taken on the income statement exceeds that which is deducted on the tax return, the difference will be a positive adjustment to net income.
Intangible assets with finite lives (see ¶ 708 and ¶ 709.)	Any differences between the amortization of such assets over their useful lives for financial accounting purposes and over 15 years for tax purposes will result in timing differences.	Any difference between the amortization methods is a timing difference that will eventually be reversed.
Research and experimentation costs (see ¶ 507.)	If the corporation elects to amortize these costs over 60 months (rather than to expense them immediately), the expense reported on the income statement in the year the costs are incurred will exceed the amount deducted on the tax return. This difference will require a positive adjustment to net income.	In each subsequent year as the costs are amortized on the tax return, a negative adjustment will be required to net income when reconciling it to taxable income on the corporate tax return.
Wash sale transactions (see ¶ 805.)	In the year in which a wash sale occurs, the loss disallowed for tax purposes will require a positive adjustment to net income	Because the adjusted basis of the stock for tax purposes is increased by the postponed loss, when the stock is subsequently sold, a negative adjustment to net income will be required.
Losses from like-kind changes (see ¶ 808.)	Losses from like-kind exchanges must be recognized on the income statement but must be postponed for tax purposes. Thus, the postponed loss will be a positive adjustment to net income in the year of the exchange.	Because for tax purposes the adjusted basis of the like-kind property received is increased by any postponed loss, the originating difference will be reversed through differences in depreciation expense taken on the like-kind property or when such property is subsequently sold.

Item	Originating Difference	Reversing Difference
Bad debts (see ¶ 510.)	Because the direct write-off method, which is the only acceptable method for tax purposes, is not allowed for financial accounting purposes, differences in timing for writing off bad debt expenses will require an adjustment to net income.	As amounts estimated to be bad debts on the financial statement become actual bad debts, the originating differences will reverse and require an adjustment to net income.
Charitable contribution and capital losses (see ¶ 511 and ¶ 901.01.)	When these deductions are limited on the tax return, an originating difference will require a positive adjustment to be made to net income.	As these carryover amounts are utilized, the originating differences will be reversed and a negative adjustment to net income will be required.

Example 77: W.R. Leasing uses the calendar year as its tax year. During 2009, it sells for $10,000 stock that has an adjusted basis of $15,000. W.R. has no capital gains for 2009. On its 2009 income statement, W.R. reduces its net income by the $5,000 loss ($10,000 – $15,000), but cannot utilize the loss on its 2009 tax return. This $5,000 originating difference will be reversed in the tax year in which the $5,000 capital loss carryover is utilized.

Example 78: Damkor Fixtures uses the calendar year as its tax year. During 2009, Damkor exchanges equipment with an adjusted basis of $10,000 for like-kind equipment worth $8,000. Damkor must reduce its 2009 net income by the $2,000 loss ($8,000 - $10,000), but it must postpone the loss for tax purposes. Damkor increases its tax basis in the new equipment by the $2,000 postponed loss. This will cause Damkor's tax depreciation on the new equipment to be greater than its book depreciation over the asset's depreciable life. Any part of the originating difference not reversed through depreciation deductions will be reversed when the property is eventually sold and different bases for the property are used for book versus tax purposes.

¶ 1209 Schedules M-1 and M-3

C corporations whose total receipts are at least $250,000 *and/or* whose total assets are at least $250,000 are required to reconcile the net income reported on their income statement with the taxable income reported on their income tax returns (before any NOL deduction or DRD). This reconciliation is reported either on Schedule M-1 or on Schedule M-3, both of which are part of the U.S. corporate income tax return.

A corporation's *total receipts* are the sum of the corporation's gross receipts or sales (not reduced by returns and allowances or by the cost of goods sold), dividends (not reduced by the dividends received deduction), interest, gross rents, gross royalties, capital gain net income, net gain or loss from sales of business property, and other income reported on the corporation's income tax return.

.01 Schedule M-1

C corporations whose total receipts are at least $250,000 *and/or* whose total assets are at least $250,000 but are less than $10 million are required to complete Schedule M-1, *Reconciliation of Income (Loss) Per Books With Income Per Return*. Schedule M-1 is part of Form 1120, *U.S. Corporation Income Tax Return*. Corporations complete Schedule M-1 to reconcile their financial accounting net income or loss for the year with their taxable income or loss (before any NOL deduction or DRD) reported on their federal income tax returns.

Example 79: Coffee Roasting, Inc. has gross receipts of $235,000, returns and allowances of $5,000, and cost of the goods sold of $50,000. It has also earned $5,000 of interest income and $10,000 of dividend income (all of which is eligible for the 70-percent DRD). Its total gross receipts equal $250,000 ($235,000 + $5,000 + $10,000). Assuming that its total assets are not at least $10 million, Coffee Roasting will be required to complete Schedule M-1 of its corporate income tax return.

Reason for the Rule: Schedule M-1 is designed to help the IRS identify matters that require extended examination. Small corporations have been exempted so they can use record keeping based on their checkbook or cash receipts and disbursements journal instead of additional accounting methods solely for tax reporting.[47]

Schedule M-1 starts by adding to net income or loss as reported on the income statement all items that result in positive adjustments to net income (lines 2–5). These are items for which the amount of income recognized on the tax return exceeds that reported in net income or for which the expenses deducted on the income statement exceed those reported on the tax return. Positive adjustments from both permanent and timing differences are reported in the first part of Schedule M-1.

The second half of Schedule M-1 takes into account the negative adjustments to net income (lines 7–9). These include items of income that are included in net income but are not recognized for tax purposes or expenses that are allowed on the tax return that are not deducted in computing net income. Negative adjustments stemming from both permanent and timing differences are reported on the latter half of Schedule M-1. Any NOL deduction or DRD is not included as an adjustment, as net income is reconciled to taxable income or loss on the tax return before either of these items is deducted. After all positive and negative adjustments to net income have been made, the result must equal the corporation's taxable income before any NOL deduction or DRD.

Schedule M-1 Reconciliation of Income (Loss) per Books With Income per Return

1. Net income (loss) per books $_____
2. Federal income tax per books   _____
3. Excess of capital losses over capital gains   _____
4. Income subject to tax not recorded on books this year (itemize)   _____
5. Expenses recorded on books this year not deducted on this return (itemize):

    a.   Depreciation $_____

    b.   Charitable contributions   _____

    c.   Travel and entertainment   _____

    d.   _____   _____   _____

6. Add lines 1 through 5 $_____
7. Income recorded on books this year not included on this return (itemize):

    Tax-exempt interest $_____

    _____   _____

    _____   _____ $_____

8. Deductions on this return not charged against book income this year (itemize):

    a.   Depreciation $_____

---

[47] IRS News Release IR-2002-48 (April 10, 2002).

b.	Charitable contributions	_____	
	_____	_____	
	_____	_____	

9.   Add lines 7 and 8 $_____

10.   Line 6 minus line 9. The result should be the same as taxable income
      before any NOL or dividends received deductions $ _____

Example 80: In 2009, Lotan Containers reports net income per books of $365,600 and taxable income of $410,000. Lotan does not show any deduction for an NOL or dividends received deduction on its tax return. Lotan's federal income tax for 2008 was $139,400. The taxable income reflected $3,000 more than the amount reflected in net income due to differences in adjusted basis used to compute the gains for book and tax purposes. The difference in adjusted basis stems from accelerated depreciation taken to depreciate the property for tax purposes (versus straight-line for financial statement purposes). Taxable income also included an additional $40,000 in depreciation expense over the amount used in determining its net income. Items that were reflected in the net income but not on the tax return included $12,000 of charitable contributions in excess of the 10-percent taxable income limit, $10,000 of interest expense incurred on amounts borrowed to purchase tax-exempt bonds, $30,000 of tax-exempt interest, and $50,000 of nontaxable insurance proceeds. Lotan's completed Schedule M-1 is shown below.

Schedule M-1 Reconciliation of Income (Loss) per Books with Income per Return

1.	Net income (loss) per books			$365,600
2.	Federal income tax per books			139,400
3.	Excess of capital losses over capital gains			_____
4.	Income subject to tax not recorded on books this year (itemize):			
	Additional gain due to accelerated depreciation			3,000
5.	Expenses recorded on books this year not deducted on this return (itemize):			
	a. Depreciation	$_____		
	b. Charitable contributions	12,000		
	c. Travel and entertainment	_____		
	d. Interest to carry tax-exempt bonds	10,000	22,000	
6.	Add lines 1 through 5			$530,000
7.	Income recorded on books this year not included on this return (itemize):			
	a. Tax-exempt interest	$30,000		
	b. Insurance proceeds	50,000		
	c. _____	_____	80,000	
8.	Deductions on this return not charged against book income this year (itemize):			
	a. Depreciation	$40,000		
	b. Charitable contributions	_____		
	c. _____	_____		
	d. _____	_____	40,000	

9.   Add lines 7 and 8 $120,000

10. Line 6 minus line 9. The result should be the same as taxable income before
     any NOL or dividends received deductions $410,000

.02 Schedule M-3

Schedule M-3, *Net Income (Loss) Reconciliation for Corporations With Total Assets of $10 Million or More,* is required for all corporations with $10 million or more in assets. Schedule M-3 is an expanded version of Schedule M-1. Corporations with at least $10 million in total assets must complete Schedule M-3 in lieu of Schedule M-1. Other C corporations may voluntarily file Schedule M-3 in lieu of Schedule M-1.

Reason for the Rule: Schedule M-3 was developed to increase the transparency of corporate tax returns by making the differences between financial accounting net income and taxable income more transparent and to help the IRS determine whether a return should be audited and, if so, what portions of the return should be audited.[48] Schedule M-3 is also intended to address two problems with Schedule M-1: (1) no uniform reporting requirement regarding the definition of book income and (2) no uniform disclosure requirements for reporting differences between financial accounting net income and taxable income.[49]

Schedule M-3 requires more detail regarding the source of the differences between net income and taxable income; it is divided into three parts. Unlike Schedule M-1, which has 10 numbered lines, Schedule M-3 has more than 90 numbered lines.

Part I: The corporation identifies the source of its financial statement information among the following: an SEC Form 10-K income statement; a certified audited income statement; an income statement prepared by the corporation; or the corporation's books and records.

Part II: The corporation reconciles net income (or loss) reported on its income statement with the taxable income (or loss) reported on its U.S. income tax return.

Part III: The corporation reconciles expenses and other deductions reported on its income statement with expenses and other deductions reported on its U.S. income tax return.

Spotlight: The information provided on Schedule M-1 and on Schedule M-3 helps the federal government identify areas in which corporations use different methods to compute net income and taxable income. While some of these differences result from differences in the requirements in the two sets of rules used to report the information, some differences result from actions of the corporation to (legally) avoid paying income taxes.

The SEC and the IRS Commissioner have discussed whether corporations should be required to provide investors with a side-by-side presentation of tax reporting and financial reporting and whether corporate income tax returns should be made public. During a March 14, 2006, speech at the National Press Club, the IRS Commissioner was quoted as saying, "If we are not willing to operate the two systems by the same set of rules, it makes sense to discuss whether corporate tax returns should be (made) public." In response to these discussions, a spokesperson for the National Taxpayers Union commented that allowing such disclosure "would be one of the most radical

---

[48] IRS News Release 2004-14 (January 28, 2004).   [49] 2004 ARD 019-5 (January 29, 2004).

> departures in tax history" as tax return information "is often regarded as the most private in American society."[50]

¶ 1210 Schedule M-2

C corporations that are required to complete Schedule M-1 or Schedule M-3 also are required to complete Schedule M-2, *Analysis of Unappropriated Retained Earnings Per Books*. Schedule M-2 requires that corporations explain changes in their unappropriated retained earnings per books during the year.

 Reason for the Rule: Schedule M-2 is another tool the IRS uses to ensure compliance with the tax laws.

Schedule M-2 Analysis of Unappropriated Retained Earnings per Books

1.	Balance at beginning of year	$_____
2.	Net income (loss) per books	_____
3.	Other increases (itemize):	
	_____	_____
	_____	_____
4.	Add lines 1, 2, and 3	$_____
5.	Distributions:	
	a. Cash	_____
	b. Stock	_____
	c. Property	_____
6.	Other decreases (itemize):	
	_____	_____
	_____	_____
7.	Add lines 5 and 6	$_____
8.	Balance at end of year (line 4 less line 7)	$_____

The analysis begins with the balance of the unappropriated retained earnings per books at the beginning of the year. This amount is then adjusted for the items that affect retained earnings during the year. The amount resulting from these calculation is the corporation's unappropriated retained earnings per books at the end of the current year. This amount should agree with the retained earnings reported on the corporation's balance sheet.

Example 81: On January 1, 2009, the unappropriated retained earnings per books for Kenniston Frozen Custards were $1.2 million. At the end of the year, the unappropriated retained earnings were $915,000. The corporation's net income per books for 2008 was $365,000. During the year, Kenniston paid a cash dividend of $150,000 and transferred $500,000 to its appropriated retained earnings account to cover the projected liability of a products liability claim made against the company for which there was no insurance coverage. Schedule M-2 would be completed as follows.

---

[50] "SEC, IRS May Seek Tax Data Disclosure," *L.A. Times*, May 2, 2006.

Schedule M-2 Analysis of Unappropriated Retained Earnings per Books

1.	Balance at beginning of year	$1,200,000
2.	Net income (loss) per books	365,000
3.	Other increases (itemize):	
4.	Add lines 1, 2, and 3	$1,565,000
5.	Distributions:	
	a. Cash	150,000
	b. Stock	
	c. Property	
6.	Other decreases (itemize):	
	Appropriated retained earnings	500,000
7.	Add lines 5 and 6	$ 650,000
8.	Balance at end of year (line 4 less line 7)	$ 915,000

¶ 1211 Summary

As a general rule, a person who transfers property to a corporation in exchange for stock will not have to recognize any gain realized if that person, or that person and one or more other persons transferring property to the corporation, control the corporation following the transfer. However, gain has to be recognized if the transferor receives "boot" in addition to stock or the corporation assumes excess liabilities.

When a C corporation distributes cash or other property to its shareholders, the distribution is treated as a dividend to the extent of the corporation's accumulated and current E&P. Sometimes a corporation will be deemed to have made a constructive distribution with respect to its stock. That may occur, for example, if a corporation pays a shareholder-employee an unreasonable amount of compensation or lets a shareholder use corporate property for personal purposes.

As a rule, when a C corporation distributes any of its own stock, no amount of the distribution has to be included in a shareholder's gross income unless the distribution is in lieu of money or other property or is a disproportionate distribution. In such instances, the distribution is taxable to the shareholders as a dividend to the extent it is paid out of the corporation's current or accumulated E&P.

When large corporations file their U.S. income tax, they are required to reconcile the net income or loss reported on the financial statements with the taxable income or loss reported on the tax return. Differences result because of timing and permanent differences between the methods used to report net income on the books and those used to report taxable income on the tax return.

GLOSSARY OF TERMS INTRODUCED IN THE CHAPTER

Accumulated earnings and profits. The amount of E&P a C corporation has generated over the years that has not been distributed as of the beginning of its current tax year.

Boot. Cash and other property added to an exchange to equalize the value of exchanged items. When made part of an otherwise nontaxable exchange, the portion of realized gain equal to the value of the boot will have to be recognized.

Constructive dividend. A payment to or for the benefit of a shareholder that is treated as a dividend even though it may not be denoted as such by the corporation.

Control. Persons control a corporation if they own stock possessing at least 80 percent of the total combined voting power of all classes of stock entitled to vote and at least 80 percent of the total number of shares of all other classes of stock of the corporation. Code Sec. 368(c).

Current earnings and profits. A C corporation's earnings and profits for its current tax year. A corporate tax concept that attempts to capture a corporation's capacity to pay dividends from its current year's earnings.

Dividend. A distribution of current and/or accumulated earnings and profits by a C corporation to its shareholders.

Earnings and profits (E&P). A tax term used to reflect a C corporation's economic capacity to make a distribution from corporate earnings that is not a return of a shareholder's capital. It is computed by making adjustments to the corporation's taxable income.

Net income per books. The net income a corporation reports for financial accounting purposes.

Originating difference. The initial difference that occurs in the year in which a timing difference is created. *See also* Reversing difference *and* Timing difference.

Permanent difference. The condition that exists when items of income or expense are reported for financial accounting purposes but *never* for tax purposes, or vice versa.

Qualified dividends. Dividends that are taxed to individual taxpayers at a rate lower than the taxpayers' marginal tax rates. They represent dividends paid on stock of a U.S. corporation or a qualified foreign corporation that the individual held for 121 days surrounding the ex-dividend date.

Return of capital distribution. A distribution of cash or other property from a corporation that is not made from current or accumulated earnings and profits.

Reversing difference. Timing difference that occurs in years subsequent to the year in which the originating difference occurs. *See also* Originating difference *and* Timing difference.

Schedule M-1. Part of Form 1120, *U.S. Corporation Income Tax Return*; it requires corporations to reconcile their net income for financial accounting purposes with their taxable income. Must be filed by corporations with total receipts and/or total assets of at least $250,000 (but total assets less than $10 million).

Schedule M-2. Part of Form 1120, *U.S. Corporation Income Tax Return*; it requires corporations to explain changes during the year in their unappropriated retained earnings. Must be filed by corporations that file Schedule M-1 or Schedule M-3.

Schedule M-3. An expanded version of Schedule M-1. Must be filed by corporations with total assets of at least $10 million.

Stock dividend. A dividend payable in shares of the distributing corporation's own stock.

Taxable income per return. A corporation's taxable income, as reported on the U.S. federal income tax return.

Timing difference. Difference that results when income and expenses are reported in one year for financial accounting purposes and in a different year for tax purposes. *See also* Originating difference *and* Reversing difference.

CHAPTER PROBLEMS

The following questions and problems relate to the discussion in Chapter 12, Corporate Distributions and Other Corporation-Related Tax Issues, which begins at ¶ 1200 in *Part V: Business Entity Issues.*

Chapter 12 Discussion Questions

1. What is a dividend?
2. How are dividends received by a C corporation taxed?
3. How are dividends received by an individual taxed?
4. If a corporation distributes property other than money or stock in the distributing corporation to a shareholder, what is the shareholder's basis in that property?
5. If the amount of a C corporation's distribution exceeds the amount of its current and accumulated E&P, how is the distribution taxed?
6. How is the amount of a distribution to a shareholder calculated?
7. Zeff Polishing distributes shares of its own stock to its shareholder, Kim Zeff, as a nontaxable stock dividend. Kim originally acquired her shares of Zeff stock on February 1, 2009, and Zeff Publishing distributed the stock to Kim on September 1, 2009. When does her holding period in the new stock begin?
8. Why do corporations have to calculate their E&P for tax purposes?
9. What is the starting point for determining a corporation's E&P for tax purposes?
10. When may a corporation be treated as having paid a constructive dividend?
11. Why was the concept of a constructive dividend developed?
12. Pegboard Hooks distributes one share of its common stock to the holder of each of its outstanding shares of common stock. How is the distribution taxed?
13. Industry Leaders has two classes of common stock, Class A and Class B. On January 1, 2009, Industry Leaders distributes one share of Class A common stock to the owner of each outstanding share of Class A stock. On October 15, 2011, the company distributes a cash dividend of $1 per share to the owner of each share of Class B stock. How is each distribution taxed?
14. How does payment of a dividend affect a corporation's taxable income?
15. How does a payment of a dividend affect a corporation's E&P for tax purposes?
16. Why can a corporation's net income for financial accounting purposes differ from its taxable income?
17. What is meant by a "timing difference" in the reporting of income and expenses for financial accounting and tax accounting?
18. What is meant by a "permanent difference" in the reporting of income and expenses for financial accounting and tax accounting?
19. What is Schedule M-1, and who must complete it?
20. What is Schedule M-2, and who must complete it?

Chapter 12 Problems

1. Lamonte Absorbents has two shareholders, each of whom owns an equal share in the corporation. Lamonte has $50,000 in accumulated and current E&P. During the year it

distributes $5,000 in cash to one shareholder and property with an adjusted basis of $2,000 and a FMV of $5,000 to its other shareholder. What amount of its distribution constitutes a dividend?

2. A U.S. corporation distributes $80 in cash to the owner of each of its shares. Of that $80, $60 is distributed from the corporation's current or accumulated E&P. If Sheila Pano owns 100 shares, each with an adjusted basis of $80, how is she taxed on the distribution?

3. Assume the same facts as in Problem 2, except Tommie Mu owns 150 shares of stock, each with an adjusted basis of $15. How is he taxed on the distribution?

4. A calendar year corporation has a $10,000 deficit (negative) E&P at the beginning of the year. During the year, the company's E&P is $8,000. On November 30, it distributes $5,000 to its shareholders. How much of the distribution is treated as a dividend? How much is treated as a return of capital?

5. A calendar year corporation has current year E&P of $15,000 and accumulated E&P of $10,000. It distributes $30,000 to its shareholders during the year. The $30,000 was distributed as follows: $10,000 on April 1 and $20,000 on December 1. How much of each distribution is treated as a dividend, and how much is treated as a return of capital?

6. At the beginning of its calendar tax year a corporation has $10,000 in accumulated E&P. During the year, it reports negative E&P of $18,250. On April 30, the company distributes $10,000. How much of the distribution is treated as a dividend, and how much is treated as a return of capital?

7. Assume the same facts as in Problem 6, except the corporation made an additional distribution of $2,000 on May 10. How much of the distribution is treated as a dividend, and how much is treated as a return of capital?

8. A calendar year corporation has $4,000 of accumulated E&P at the beginning of the year. Its current year E&P is $10,000. On June 30, the corporation distributes $15,000 to the owners of its common stock. How is the distribution taxed?

9. Broc Exercise Equipment distributes $500 in cash and an elliptical exerciser with an FMV of $600 to one of its shareholders. Broc's adjusted basis in the exerciser is $100. What is the amount of the distribution?

10. Riven Printing distributes $5,000 cash and 100 shares of its stock (with an FMV of $4,000) to its sole shareholder, Roman Riven, who agreed as part of the distribution to assume a $5,000 loan obtained by the corporation. What is the amount of the distribution?

11. A corporation has taxable income of $50,000. The company received $1,000 of tax-exempt interest and made $2,000 of charitable contributions in excess of the deduction limit. It also paid federal income taxes of $7,500. Based on these facts, what is the corporation's E&P for tax purposes for the year?

12. A corporation has taxable income of $100,000. During the year it makes an installment sale of equipment and includes $5,000 of its $20,000 gain in its taxable income. During the year it paid $10,000 in meal and entertainment expenses that it could not deduct from its taxable income and incurred federal income taxes of $22,250. At the end of the year, the company paid a $20,000 dividend to its shareholders. Based on these facts, what is the corporation's current year E&P?

13. Abel Blackhurst owns 100 shares of common stock in his mother's company, Blackhurst Machines. His adjusted basis in the shares is $4,500. The company distributes to each of its shareholders one share of common stock for every two the shareholder owns. Abel is issued another 50 shares of common stock. The common stock had an FMV of $60 per share at the time of the distribution. What is Abel's basis in the 50 shares distributed to him and in the 100 shares he already owned?

14. Elijah Soro owns 100 shares of common stock, each with an adjusted basis of $40, in Dowe Magazine Racks. Dowe distributes one share of common stock for every 10 shares of

common stock a shareholder owns. On the date of the distribution, each share of the common stock had an FMV of $50. What is Elijah's adjusted basis in his stock?

15. Kady Switches distributes one share of preferred stock to the owner of each share of its Class A common stock and one share of common stock to the owner of each share of its Class B common stock. Each share of preferred stock had an FMV of $40 on the date of the distribution, and each share of common stock had an FMV of $30 on the date of the distribution. Aubrey Kady receives 100 shares of common stock. The FMV of the common and preferred stock distributed did not exceed the corporation's accumulated and current E&P. How is Aubrey taxed on the distribution?

16. Sage Paper sells land with an adjusted basis of $150,000 for $300,000. Payment of the purchase price is to be made over five years, with the first payment due the year after the sale. How much income does the company have to include in its net income, and how much income does the company have to include in its taxable income for the year of the sale?

17. One of a corporation's motor vehicles is destroyed in a casualty, and the corporation reinvests the insurance proceeds in another motor vehicle during the same year as the casualty. Its basis in the destroyed motor vehicle was $0 for income tax purposes and $18,000 for financial accounting purposes; the insurance proceeds were $20,000. How does this event affect the corporation's net income and taxable income?

18. A corporation incurs $15,000 in federal income tax for the year. It incurs $1,000 in expenses with respect to tax-exempt income and pays $3,000 in premiums on a life insurance policy that names the corporation as the beneficiary. How do these expenditures affect its net income for financial accounting purposes and taxable income?

19. On January 1, 2009, Hansbrough Corporation has unappropriated retained earnings per its books of $980,000. During the year, it reports net income of $411,300 and taxable income on its tax return of $380,000. On the tax return, it shows a dividends received deduction of $120,000. Federal income taxes for the year were $129,200. Because Hansbrough took accelerated depreciation deductions on its machinery, its taxable income included $5,000 more in gain from the sale of the machinery than its net income included. The corporation's tax depreciation exceeds its book depreciation by $32,000.

During the year, the corporation received $25,000 in tax-exempt interest and paid $9,500 in interest on a loan obtained to purchase the tax-exempt bonds. The corporation also received $10,000 from a life insurance policy naming the corporation as the beneficiary. These three items are reflected in net income but not in taxable income. The corporation made charitable contributions that exceeded the 10-percent limitation by $12,000.

During 2009, Hansbrough paid a cash dividend of $120,000 and transferred $300,000 from its unappropriated retained earnings per books to its appropriated retained earnings per books to cover an unsettled tort claim. Using this information, complete Schedule M-1 for the corporation.

20. Assume the same facts as in Problem 19. Complete Schedule M-2 for the corporation. What are the corporation's unappropriated retained earnings per books as of December 31, 2009?

21. At the beginning of its 2010 tax year, Harness Hostels, Inc. had $10,000 in accumulated earnings and profits. Its earnings and profits for the year were a negative $32,850. On January 31, 2010, the company distributed $10,000 to its two shareholders, Billy Harness and his sister Tawny Harness, who each owned 50 percent of the corporation. Billy's adjusted basis in his shares was $6,000. How is he taxed on the distribution?

22. The facts are the same as in Problem 21 except that the distribution was made on April 30. How is Billy taxed on the distribution?

23. Warden Communications, Inc. permitted its sole shareholder, Mabel Warden, to use one of its hospitality suites free of charge. The hospitality suite had a fair rental value of $150 a day, and Mabel used it for 50 days during the year. The company had $15,000 in earnings and profits for its current year and $50,000 in accumulated earnings and profits. Mabel received a cash distribution of $10,000 during the year. If her adjusted basis in her stock is

$15,000, how will she be taxed on amounts she received during the year from the corporation?

24. Bourn Office Furniture, Inc. offered its shareholders the option of receiving one share of its stock for each share that they currently owned or the fair market value of such shares ($25 per share). Dean Bourn chose to receive 100 shares. What amount of taxable distribution, if any, did he receive?

25. Allgood Textiles, Inc. started the year with $200,000 in accumulated earnings and profits. During the year, it earned $75,000 from its business operations, received a $2,000 federal income tax refund, received a $10,000 contribution to capital from its shareholders, paid $13,750 in federal income taxes, and could not deduct $1,000 of its meal expenses. What is the amount of its accumulated earnings and profits at the end of the year?

Chapter 12 Review Problems

1. Bauk Printing uses the calendar year. Bauk purchases a digital printer for $140,000 and places it in service on April 1, 2009. The company estimates that the digital printer will have a useful life of 10 years and no salvage value. If it uses MACRS and the half-year convention to compute its depreciation deduction, how will the purchase affect its net income and its taxable income in 2009? In 2013?

2. Desmond Photocopying and Supplies, Inc. exchanges an old photocopying machine (with an adjusted basis of $0 and an FMV of $5,000) plus $3,000 in cash for a new photocopying machine. Desmond's book value in the machine is $4,000. The FMV of the new machine is $8,000. How does this exchange affect the company's taxable income and its net income for financial accounting purposes for the tax year of the exchange? What is its adjusted basis in the new photocopying machine?

Chapter 12 Comprehensive Review Question

Wahlgren Reed Furniture, Inc. is an accrual method taxpayer that uses the calendar year as its tax year. Its gross sales for 2009 were $500,000, and its cost of goods sold was $150,000. In addition to its gross sales, at the end of the year it received $50,000 in advance payments for furniture to be constructed in January 2011. It received $6,000 in interest on a municipal bond, and it paid $5,000 in interest on a loan obtained to purchase the municipal bond.

In 2008, it purchased machinery with an estimated useful life of 10 years for $5,000. Wahlgren uses MACRS and the half-year conversion to depreciate the machinery. The machine has no salvage value.

Wahlgren had $6,000 of capital losses and $2,000 of capital gains for the year. Wahlgren paid $15,000 in research and experimental expenditures on October 1, 2009, and elected to amortize the expenditures over 60 months. It paid $3,000 in premiums for life insurance insuring a key employee and naming the corporation as the beneficiary. It paid $10,000 for meals and entertainment during the year. It received $20,000 in dividends from a U.S. corporation; it owned five percent of the stock of that corporation. Its qualified production activities income was $250,000. (Assume that Wahlgren has sufficient W-2 wages to take the full amount of the deduction based on the applicable percentage for 2009.) Based on these facts, what are its net income and taxable income for the year?

Chapter 12 Research Question

Tashia Dux is the sole shareholder of Dux Digital Cameras. Her daughter Elena is the sole shareholder of Dux Photographic Lenses. Dux Digital Cameras loans Dux Photographic Lenses $100,000 to help Dux Photographic Lenses develop a new lens that Dux Digital Cameras could use for its cameras. No interest was payable on the loan, no security was provided, and no repayments were scheduled. Has Dux Digital Cameras paid a constructive dividend? See *R. Fenn, Jr.*, 40 TCM 559, Dec. 37,040(M), TC Memo. 1980-229.

CHAPTER 13

The Sole Proprietorship and Individual Tax Return

LEARNING OBJECTIVES

1. Learn more about the expanded taxable income formula for individual taxpayers.
2. Learn more about the differences in how incorporated and unincorporated businesses are taxed.
3. Understand which business deductions reduce only a sole proprietor's income taxes versus those that reduce both the owner's income and self-employment taxes.
4. Learn more about an individual's deductions from adjusted gross income.
5. Understand how net capital gains and qualified dividends are taxed on an individual's tax return.
6. Understand the limitations placed upon the deduction of losses from hobby activities and passive activity losses.

¶ 1300 Introduction

Sole proprietorships are a popular form of doing business. In 2006, slightly more than 22 million of the 138 million individual tax returns filed reported self-employment income from nonfarm businesses.[1] The popularity of forming a business as a sole proprietorship stems, in large part, to the lack of the formality that other types of business entities require. However, unlike shareholders of a corporation that enjoy limited liability from the activities of the corporation, owners of a sole proprietorship are generally liable for both the contractual debts incurred by the business plus any liabilities caused by the actions of the owners or their employees when representing the business.

Unlike a corporation, which is a separate business entity for tax purposes, the activities of a sole proprietorship are reported on the owner's individual income tax return. Consequently, the income, deductions, gains, and losses from the sole proprietorship are included among the owner's personal items of income, deduction, gain, and loss in calculating the owner's taxable income. Furthermore, individual tax rates are used to compute the sole proprietor's tax liability. Although the tax rates for individuals are also progressive, they vary depending on the taxpayer's filing status.

Like corporations, individuals may be subject to alternative minimum tax (AMT); however, because taxable income is calculated differently for individuals and corporations, so too is AMT.

---

[1] Statistics of Income (SOI) Bulletin, Fall 2008, Individual Income Tax Returns, 2006, Dent, J., Curry, J., and Bryan, J. (2008).

Like corporations, a variety of tax credits are available to individuals to reduce their regular and AMT income tax liabilities. However, in addition to the business credits and the foreign tax credit described in Chapter 11, many personal tax credits are available to individual taxpayers. Most personal credits are nonrefundable, but some can create a refund when the amount of the credit exceeds the individual's tax liability.

The most important distinguishing feature of a business operated as a sole proprietorship is the owner's responsibility for both the employer and employee portions of FICA taxes on any profits generated by the business. These amounts, known as self-employment taxes when paid by sole proprietors, are reported directly on the owners' individual tax returns and are added to their regular income tax liabilities. The calculation of self-employment tax begins with computing net profit or loss from the business. Although most of the business income, deductions, gains, and losses discussed in Chapters 4 through 9 are reflected on the sole proprietor's income tax return, some of these amounts are not part of the calculation of net profit from the business but are reported elsewhere on the individual's income tax return.

The focus of this chapter is how activities from businesses operated as a sole proprietorship are reported on the individual tax return. To fully understand the differences in the tax consequences of operating an unincorporated business (sole proprietorship) versus an incorporated business (corporation), more must be understood about the tax laws regarding the taxation of individuals. Thus, this chapter begins with an overview of how the individual taxable income formula differs from the taxable income formula used by corporations.

¶ 1301 Taxable Income Formula for Individual Taxpayers

When an individual enters into a business venture without the formality of incorporation, the business is known as a sole proprietorship. The net profit or net loss from a sole proprietorship is included with the owner's other items of income and deduction on Form 1040, *Individual Income Tax Return*. Because an individual's personal items of income and deductions are each reported on the tax return, the taxable income formula is expanded to include two types of deductions: deductions for adjusted gross income (AGI) and deductions from AGI.

Deductions from AGI are deductions for expenditures that are personal in nature, as well as "free" (i.e., no cost) deductions that the federal government gives individual taxpayers to reduce their taxable income. Deductions for AGI include not only business expenses and losses but also expenses individual taxpayers paid during the year that the tax laws give preferential treatment to. AGI is an important calculation, as many formulas used in computing the amounts allowed as deductions or the amounts included in gross income involve the taxpayer's AGI.[2] The expanded taxable income formula for individuals is shown below in Figure 13-1.

Figure 13-1 Taxable Income Formula for Individuals

Income	$ xx,xxx
Less: Exclusions	(xx,xxx)
Gross income	$ xx,xxx
Less: Deductions for AGI	(xx,xxx)
AGI	$ xx,xxx
Less: Deductions from AGI	(xx,xxx)
Taxable income	$ xx,xxx

---

[2] Code Sec. 62; Reg. § 1.62-1; Temp. Reg. § 1.62-1T.

.01 Deductions for vs. from AGI

The distinction between deducting an expense for versus from AGI is important because only deductions for AGI are guaranteed to reduce an individual's taxable income. Deductions from AGI consist of the taxpayer's personal and dependency exemptions plus the *greater of* the taxpayer's itemized deductions or standard deduction amount. Thus, only when an individual's itemized deductions exceed the standard deduction amount will taxable income be reduced by an expense that is deductible as an itemized deduction.

Most business expenses paid or incurred by sole proprietors are deducted for AGI; however, a few business-related expenses deducted in arriving at a corporation's taxable income are not deductible by individual taxpayers, and a few can only be deducted as itemized deductions. For example, charitable contributions made by an individual can only be deducted as an itemized deduction.

When a business is operated as a corporation, all deductible business expenses are subtracted from gross income in computing the corporation's taxable income. This includes deductible losses from the sale of business property, as well as amounts the corporation pays or incurs on behalf of its employees. Thus, when a corporation pays health insurance premiums for its employees or makes contributions to their retirement plans, these amounts are deducted by the corporation even when the employee is also an owner (shareholder) of the corporation. When a corporation reimburses an employee for deductible business expenses, like travel, transportation, or moving costs, it deducts the reimbursed amounts from gross income of the business, regardless of whether the employee is also a shareholder of the corporation. Finally, corporations are responsible for unemployment taxes and the employer's share of FICA taxes on wages paid to its employees, including those who are shareholder/employees.

When a business is operated as a sole proprietorship, most of the same business expenses that corporations deduct from gross income are deductible on the individual's income tax return as deductions for AGI. However, not all of these expenses are used in calculation of net profit or loss from the business, which is the starting point for computing the owner's self-employment taxes owed on profits generated during the year. The following five expenses are deducted for AGI but not included in the calculation of net profit from the business when paid by owners on their own behalf:

1. Qualified moving expenses,

2. Amounts paid for premiums on their own health insurance coverage,

3. One-half of self-employment taxes,

4. Contributions to their own retirement plans, and

5. Domestic production activities deduction (see ¶ 509).

In addition to these expenses, both gains and losses from the disposal of business property are not reflected in the calculation of net profits from the business. Thus, when sole proprietors dispose of business property, the gains and losses are netted against one another, in a manner similar to that described in Chapter 9; however, these amounts are not included in the net profit or loss from the business and, therefore, only impact the owners' income tax liability and not the amount of their self-employment tax. Similarly, when sole proprietors pay for their own health insurance coverage, contribute to their own retirement plans, or pay qualified moving expenses for themselves, they deduct these amounts for AGI but cannot use them to reduce their profits from their business. And even though one-half of their self-employment taxes represents the employer's share of FICA taxes and is deducted for AGI by individual taxpayers, it does not reduce their profits from the business.

Finally, while sole proprietors are responsible for paying unemployment taxes on their employees' wages, unemployment taxes are not assessed on the profits from their businesses.

Self-employment taxes can be as high as 15.3 percent of net earnings from self-employment; however, in 2009, the 12.4-percent social security component of FICA only applies to the first $106,800 of earnings. Once a sole proprietor's earnings exceed this amount, the self-employment tax rate drops to 2.9 percent. To the extent that business expenses are deductible in determining AGI and can be used in computing net profit or loss from the business, these expenses reduce both owners' regular income tax liability and self-employment taxes. However, business expenses that can be deducted in determining AGI but are not considered when computing profits from the business only reduce the owner's income tax liability. Accordingly, the tax savings from an expense can be significantly greater when it not only reduces AGI but also reduces net profits from the business. The calculation of self-employment taxes is discussed later in the chapter (see ¶ 1303.03).

Example 1: Jack Abrams reports $100,000 of business income and $30,000 of business expenses from his sole proprietorship. Thus, Jack's net profits from his business equal $70,000 ($100,000 - $30,000), and his AGI increases by this amount. If Jack makes a $10,000 contribution to his own retirement plan, his AGI is reduced by $10,000, but his net profits from the business remain at $70,000. The amount of Jack's income tax liability is based on his taxable income, which includes the $60,000 from business-related income and expenses. However, his self-employment tax will be assessed on the $70,000 of profits from his sole proprietorship.

.02 Method of Accounting

As with corporations, the owners of sole proprietorships must select a method of accounting for the business. Sole proprietors can use either the cash or accrual methods and have the option of selecting different accounting methods if they have multiple businesses.[3] Generally, the cash method requires that income be reported in the tax year it is actually or constructively received and deductions be taken in the tax year in which they are paid (see ¶ 306). The accrual method generally requires that income be taxed in the period in which the business has the right to receive it, and deductions be taken in the year in which they are incurred (see ¶ 307).

For businesses where inventory is a material income producing item, the tax laws require that sole proprietors use the accrual method of accounting for sales and the cost of goods sold of the business, but allows them to use the cash method for other items of income and deduction for the business.[4] The combined use of these two methods is referred to as the hybrid method of accounting (see ¶ 309).

Example 2: Mark Jamison is an architect and reports his income using the cash method of accounting. For 2009, Mark has the following business activities.

Business Income	
Services performed and billed in 2009	$80,000
Fees collected in 2009 from billings sent out in 2008	25,000
Fees collected in 2009 from billings sent out in 2009	65,000

Business Expenses	
Accrued expenses in 2009 (unpaid at year end)	$10,000
Expenses incurred and paid in 2009	15,000
Expenses accrued in 2008 but paid in 2009	8,000

---

[3] Code Sec. 446.   [4] Reg. § 1.446-1(c)(2).

Under the cash method of accounting, Mark's 2009 income would include the $90,000 of cash collected in 2009 ($25,000 + $65,000), and he would deduct the $23,000 of expenses paid during the year ($15,000 + $8,000). Thus, under the cash method, Mark's net profits would equal $67,000 ($90,000 - $23,000). Under the accrual method, Mark's net profits would equal $55,000, which he computes by subtracting the $25,000 of expenses he incurred during the year ($10,000 + $15,000) from the $80,000 billed for services performed. Although all amounts of income expense will be eventually reported to the government, the timing of when the government receives its revenues both from Mark's income taxes and his self-employment taxes is different depending upon which method he chooses to use to compute his business profits.

Example 3: Assume that Mark's business from Example 2 involves inventory that is a material income producing item and that his cost of goods sold using the accrual method was $30,000. Although Mark would be required to report gross profit of $50,000 ($80,000 of income less $30,000 of cost of goods sold) using the accrual method, he would be allowed to deduct his expenses using the cash method. The hybrid method would produce a net income of $27,000 ($50,000 gross profit – $23,000 cash basis expenses).

Planning Pointer: Many sole proprietors utilize the cash method of accounting, which permits them to report items of income and deduction in the tax year in which income is received or expenses are paid. The cash method gives sole proprietors limited ability to control the amount of net income from self-employment by timing the recognition of income and/or expenses. Thus, through judicious year-end tax planning, sole proprietors may shift income or expense to the next tax year. This opportunity can reduce both the income tax assessed on the business income and the self-employment tax assessed on the self-employment income.

Once an accounting method is selected, it must be consistently used each year unless permission to change to another method is requested and granted from the IRS.[5] When taxpayers do not maintain proper books and records, they must report their income using the cash method.[6] Individuals often prepare their first tax returns by using the wages reported on their W-2s or the interest and dividends reported to them on Form 1099s, and they (perhaps unknowingly) have chosen to report their taxable income using the cash method. Although individuals are required to continue using the cash method for their nonbusiness income and deductions, they can still choose to use the accrual or hybrid methods for reporting business profits, provided that they properly maintain their books and records.

¶ 1302 Gross Income

The Code's all inclusive approach to defining income along with the specific exclusions the Code allows in computing gross income apply to all taxpayers, including individual taxpayers. However, in addition to the items of gross income discussed in Chapter 4, individuals also may receive other (personal) gross income that they are required to report on their income tax returns. For example, a divorced individual may receive alimony payments from a former spouse, an elderly taxpayer may receive taxable pensions and social security benefits, or a student may receive a taxable scholarship. Although a detailed discussion of these topics is beyond the scope of this chapter, it is important to note that when these amounts are included in an individual's gross income, they increase taxable income but are not included in the computation of net profits for purposes of computing self-employment taxes. Because the individual income tax rates are progressive, higher taxable income may result in a higher marginal tax rate. Since proper tax planning requires knowing how to compute the tax savings derived from an exclusion or a deduction,

---

[5] Code Sec. 446(e); Reg. §1.446-1(e).

[6] *J.W. England, Jr.,* 34 TC 617, Dec. 24,257 (1960); *S. Greengard,* CA-7, 1929 CCH D-9002, 29 F2d 502.

understanding how these personal items impact an individual's marginal tax rate is essential to proper tax planning. Some items of gross income that are not usually reported by business entities are:

- Compensation for services (as an employee), including commissions, tips, and bonuses;
- Alimony and separate maintenance payments;
- Unemployment compensation;
- Social security benefits received;
- Annuity and pension distributions; and
- Miscellaneous income, such as lottery winnings, prizes, and awards.

.01 Investment Income

When taxpayers invest in corporate bonds, the semiannual interest bondholders receive is included in gross income. Likewise, dividends shareholders receive from corporations in which they own stock are included in gross income. Most taxpayers that purchase corporate stocks and bonds do so as an investment, and consequently, the interest and dividends generated from these investments produce investment income. This type of income is also called **portfolio income**. For corporations, investment income is treated the same as all other types of income, and accordingly, corporations do not distinguish between investment income and other types of income. However, when individuals earn interest, dividends, gains, and losses from their investments, these items are treated differently from business income, and consequently, investment income is not included in the calculation of a sole proprietor's net profit or loss from the business.

Corporations pay income tax on the profits they generate, and their shareholders pay tax on those profits a second time when the profits are distributed to them as dividends. Thus, when a corporation owns stock in another corporation, the possibility of triple taxation exists. To remedy this problem, corporations are entitled to a dividends received deduction, which reduces the amount of dividends subject to corporate income tax (see ¶ 411.02). When individuals own corporate stock, there is no risk of triple taxation, and accordingly, individuals are not entitled to a dividends received deduction. However, the tax laws allow any qualified dividends received by an individual taxpayer to be taxed at a lower tax rate. Nonqualified dividends are also included in gross income and are taxed at the normal (ordinary) tax rates.

Qualified dividends paid to individual taxpayers are subject to a maximum tax rate of 15 percent (zero percent for taxpayers in the 10- and 15-percent tax brackets) through December 31, 2010, after which the tax rates will revert to the taxpayer's tax rate on ordinary income. These same lower tax rates also apply to an individual's net capital gains. (A zero percent tax rate replaced a five percent rate on qualified dividends and net capital gains for tax years after December 31, 2007 through December 31, 2010). **Qualified dividends** are dividends paid on the stock of a U.S. corporation or a qualified foreign corporation that the individual held for 121 days surrounding the ex-dividend date.[7] The ex-dividend date is generally two business days prior to the date dividends are paid to shareholders of record and represents the day after the last date the stock of the corporation can be purchased in order to be the shareholder to whom the dividend will be paid.

Example 4: Janet Wilson's taxable income falls in the 25-percent tax bracket. If Janet were to receive $1,000 in nonqualified dividends, her tax liability would increase $250 ($1,000 × 25%). However, if the dividends she receives are qualified dividends, her tax liability would increase only by $150 ($1,000 × 15%).

 Reason for the Rule: Since dividend income represents the second time that corporate earnings are subject to income tax, Congress believed that reducing the individual tax

---

[7] Code Sec. 1(h)(1) and (11).

on dividends lowers the cost of capital and will lead to economic growth and the creation of jobs. By reducing the total tax burden on investments made by individuals, corporations would lower the cost of capital needed to finance new investments, which would lead to increased aggregate national investment and employment in the private sector. Congress believed that through such investment, the U.S. economy would increase output, employment, and productivity, which, in turn, would result in workers earning higher real wages and all Americans benefiting from a higher standard of living.[8]

.02 Gains on the Sale of Business and Investment Property

Chapter 9 introduced the concepts of capital assets and Section 1231 property and discussed how the netting process works to offset gains and losses produced by these assets. Although more on this topic is discussed later in the chapter, it is important to point out that when an individual taxpayer reports net capital gain on the tax return (the excess of net long-term capital gain over net short-term capital loss), such gain is taxed at the same maximum 15-percent (or zero-percent) tax rates accorded to qualified dividends.[9] Furthermore, although these gains are included in an individual's gross income, they are not considered business income for purposes of computing a sole proprietor's net profits from the business.

Example 5: Paul Santom sells several investments during the year which produce the following capital gains and losses.

Short-term capital loss	($ 3,500)
Short-term capital gain	18,000
Long-term capital gain	11,000

Paul offsets his short-term capital loss against his short-term capital gain. The result is a net short-term capital gain of $14,500 ($18,000 - $3,500). Both this net short-term capital gain and the $11,000 long-term capital gain are included in his AGI. When Paul goes to calculate his tax liability, the $11,000 net capital gain ($11,000 net long-term capital gain minus $0 net short-term capital loss) will be taxed at a maximum 15-percent tax rate.

¶ 1303 Deductions for AGI

Certain expenses are deducted from gross income in arriving at an individual's AGI.[10] Deductions allowed for AGI are given preferential treatment, as all deductions for AGI reduce a taxpayer's taxable income. Itemized deductions (deductions from AGI) only reduce taxable income if the taxpayer's itemized deductions exceed the standard deduction amount. The calculation of AGI is important, as many deductions on the individual tax return are limited to a percentage of AGI. Some of the more common deductions for AGI are:

1. Expenses paid or incurred in carrying on a trade or business,

2. Losses from the sale or exchange of business or investment property,

3. Contributions made to a self-employed taxpayer's own retirement plan,

4. Premiums self-employed persons pay for their own health insurance,

5. One-half (the employer's share) of self-employment taxes,

6. Qualified moving expenses,

7. Expenses paid or incurred in the production of rental income,

---

[8] H.R. Rep. No. 108-94.

[9] Code Sec. 1(h)(1).

[10] Code Sec. 62; Reg. § 1.62-1; Temp. Reg. § 1.62-1T.

8. Certain contributions individuals make to a traditional IRA,

9. Alimony and separate maintenance payments, and

10. Interest on student loans.

.01 Certain Business-Related Expenses Not Deductible for AGI

Every business, whether operated as a corporation, partnership, or sole proprietorship, incurs expenses in the normal process of generating profits. For the most part, the deductions discussed in Chapters 5 through 9 are available to all business entities, including sole proprietorships. When a business is operated as a corporation, there is usually little doubt that all expenses relate to business activities. However, when a business is operated as a sole proprietorship, it becomes important that proprietors keep their business activities separate and distinct from their personal activities to avoid any confusion as to what is a valid business expense versus a nondeductible personal expense.

Certain items reported by individual taxpayers on the individual tax return are automatically considered personal expenses. For example, charitable contributions are always considered a personal expense, as are state, local, and foreign income taxes an individual pays during the year. Fortunately, the tax laws allow these expenses to be deducted as itemized deductions, so the tax benefits are not necessarily lost. However, because these amounts cannot be used in the computation of net profit or loss from the business, they do not reduce the owner's self-employment taxes. Furthermore, since itemized deductions are only deductible if the total of all itemized deductions exceeds the standard deduction amount, the possibility exists that some, if not all, of the tax benefits associated with these expenses could be lost.

Example 6: Bev Thomas operates a sole proprietorship. During 2009, Bev generates $100,000 of business income and $30,000 of deductible business expenses. Also during 2009, Bev donates $10,000 to a local charity from her business checking account. Because Bev's business is operated as a sole proprietorship, the $10,000 charitable contribution is deducted as an itemized deduction. Assuming Bev's other itemized deductions exceeded the standard deduction amount, the full $10,000 will reduce Bev's taxable income; however, her self-employment taxes will be based on the $70,000 ($100,000 – $30,000) of net profit from her business that is included in AGI. If the charitable contribution was Bev's only itemized deduction and she was a single taxpayer, the additional tax deduction resulting from her charitable contribution would be $4,300, which is the amount by which the $10,000 charitable contribution exceeds her $5,700 standard deduction amount for 2009. The standard deduction is discussed further in ¶ 1304.02.

Deficiency interest. When errors are subsequently discovered in the calculation of taxes owed to the government, the IRS charges interest on the back taxes owed. This interest, referred to as "deficiency interest," is normally deductible if assessed as a result of an income tax deficiency arising from business activities (see ¶ 505.01). Thus, when a corporation pays deficiency interest, it is deducted against its business profits. However, when deficiency interest is imposed on an individual taxpayer, the interest is always considered nondeductible personal interest, even when the deficiency stems from errors made in computing net profits from a sole proprietor's business.[11] Unfortunately, this is one area of the tax law where operating a business as a sole proprietorship has its disadvantages.

Example 7: A business makes an error in computing its 2006 taxable income. The error is discovered early in 2009 and results in an additional $50,000 of taxes owed. The IRS charges $14,000 of interest on the back taxes, which the business pays in 2009. If the business is operated as a corporation, the $14,000 would be deducted as interest expense on the 2009 corporate tax return. Assuming the corporation is in the 34-percent tax bracket, the corporation reduces its taxes that year by $4,760 ($14,000 × 34%),

---

[11] Temp. Reg. § 1.163-9T.

and the true cost to the corporation for the interest charged is $9,240 ($14,000 − $4,760). If the business is operated as a sole proprietorship, the $14,000 is nondeductible personal interest, and, therefore, the true cost to the business for the interest charged is the full $14,000.

Hobby activities. In order to deduct expenses paid or incurred in carrying on a trade or business, it goes without saying that the taxpayer must already be carrying on a trade or business. Unless the facts and circumstances indicate that a taxpayer entered into or continued the activity with the objective of making a profit, it is considered an activity not engaged in for profit, or what is commonly referred to as a hobby.

The tax consequences of having an activity treated as a hobby can be quite severe. First, any income that the activity generates is included in the individual's gross income under the Code's all-inclusive approach to defining income. Second, expenses related to the activity are limited to the amount of gross income from the hobby activity, and any excess expenses cannot be carried over to any other tax year. Third, the deductible expenses are treated as miscellaneous itemized deductions subject to the two-percent AGI floor.[12]

Example 8: John Baron is a professional musician who also raises Black Angus cattle. John's AGI from sources other than the activity is $50,000. During the year, John paid $1,500 for feed for the cattle and raised $1,000 from the sale of cattle. If the activity is deemed a business, the entire $1,500 would be deductible against the $1,000, and John's AGI would decrease to $49,500 ($50,000 + $1,000 - $1,500). However, if the activity is considered a hobby, John's expenses would be limited to $1,000 and would be deductible as miscellaneous itemized deductions that are subject to the two-percent AGI floor. However, the $1,000 from the sale of the cattle would be included in John's gross income, causing his AGI to increase to $51,000.

The tax laws presume that if an activity generates a profit in any three of five consecutive years, it is one that has a profit motive and as such, the IRS has the burden of proving that the activity is instead a hobby.[13] Activities that fail to generate a profit during any three of five consecutive years will automatically be considered a hobby and the burden of proving that the activity is actually a business rests with the taxpayer. (The time frame for generating a profit is two of seven years for activities related to horse racing and breeding.) Although the party with the burden of proof often has the more difficult task, it does not mean that it cannot be done. The Tax Court held in one case that despite 12 consecutive years of losses, the taxpayers established a profit motive in connection with the operation of their ski lodge.[14] A list of nine factors the courts use in making its determination of whether an activity should be treated as a business or as a hobby are listed below.[15]

1. The manner in which the taxpayer carried on the activity,
2. The expertise of the taxpayer or the taxpayer's advisors,
3. The time and effort expended by the taxpayer in carrying on the activity,
4. The expectation that assets used in the activity may appreciate in value,
5. The success of the taxpayer in carrying on other similar or dissimilar activities,
6. The taxpayer's history of income or loss with respect to the activity,
7. The amount of occasional profit, if any, which is earned,
8. The financial status of the taxpayer, and
9. Whether elements of personal pleasure or recreation are involved.

---

[12] Code Sec. 183.
[13] Code Sec. 183(d).

[14] *T. Allen*, 72 TC 28, Dec. 35,977 (1979).
[15] Reg. § 1.183-2(b); *L.D. Boyer*, 69 TC 521, Dec. 34,900 (1977).

Reason for the Rule: In almost all income tax matters, the burden of proof rests with the taxpayer claiming the exclusion, deduction, or tax credit, so normally the burden of proving that an activity was entered into for a profit motive would rest with the taxpayer. However, Congress realized that many businesses struggle to earn a profit during the first few years, and it wanted to give businesses a few years to "get on their feet" before judging whether the activity was entered into for a profit motive. Although any activity can generate profits, only those considered to be business endeavors can use business expenses to offset the income generated from the activity. Nonetheless, when an activity generates profits in any three of five consecutive years, the tax laws shift the burden of proof over to the IRS to prove that the activity is not a business endeavor.

 Spotlight: Because many hobbies generate some income and may occasionally turn a profit, it is not always easy to distinguish a business from a hobby. Some activities, such as raising cattle or horse breeding, can be either. Therefore, the determination must be made on a case-by-case basis. Two Tax Court decisions involving similar fact situations resulted in different outcomes. In one case, the Tax Court held that one horse breeding venture was operated for profit,[16] and, in the other, it held that no profit motive existed.[17]

.02 Expenses Paid or Incurred in Carrying on a Trade or Business

Assuming an activity is considered a trade or business, business expenses (other than those previously mentioned as either nondeductible or deductible only as itemized deductions) are deducted for AGI by sole proprietors. However, as previously discussed, losses on the sale of business property and certain expenses sole proprietors pay or incur on their own behalf are not part of the calculation of net profit or loss from the business. The tax laws regarding these items are discussed later on in the chapter. The remainder of this section focuses on some special rules that pertain to the expenses that sole proprietors deduct for AGI in the calculation of net profit of loss from their businesses.

Schedule C. Net profits from a sole proprietorship are computed on Schedule C, *Profit or Loss from Business.* This profit or loss is transferred to page 1 of the owner's Form 1040 and included in the calculation of the owner's AGI. Any net profit from Schedule C is also transferred to Schedule SE, *Self-Employment Tax,* and becomes the starting point for calculating the sole proprietor's self-employment taxes for the year. A list of business expenses that sole proprietors deduct against business profits on Schedule C is shown in Figure 13-2.

Figure 13-2 List of Business Expenses Deducted on Schedule C

- Advertising,
- Car and truck expenses,
- Commissions and fees,
- Contract labor costs,
- Contributions to employees' benefit plans,
- Depletion,
- Depreciation, amortization, and Section 179 expense deduction,
- Employee benefit programs,

---

[16] *T. Engdahl,* 72 TC 659, Dec. 36,167 (1979).   [17] *S. Golanty,* 72 TC 411, Dec. 36,111 (1979).

- Insurance (other than health),
- Interest,
- Legal and professional services,
- Meals and entertainment (subject to a 50-percent limitation),
- Office expense,
- Rent,
- Repairs and maintenance,
- Supplies,
- Travel,
- Utilities,
- Wages (less employment tax credits), and
- Other expenses (education, dues, etc.).

As the list in Figure 13-2 shows, many of the expenses discussed in Chapters 5 through 7 are reported on Schedule C. For example, advertising, interest, taxes, rent, and wage expense are each listed as deductions against gross income from the business, along with many other business expenses. Amounts sole proprietors pay for employee benefit programs (such as health care coverage) and contributions to pension and profit-sharing plans are reported on Schedule C. Note, however, that only amounts they pay on behalf of their employees can be deducted against business income. Contributions owners make to their own retirement plans, and premiums they pay for their own health care coverage are deducted for AGI on Form 1040.

Example 9: Jay Reynolds operates his business as a sole proprietorship. The business earns gross income of $100,000 during the year before considering the following expenses.

Advertising	$ 5,000
Rent	6,700
Contributions to employees' retirement plans	1,760
Contributions to Jay's retirement plan	2,640
Employee benefits (health insurance for employees)	8,500
Jay's health insurance premiums	6,000
Charitable contributions	1,000
Wages paid to employees	30,000
Payroll taxes	3,600
Total business expenses	$65,200

Because Jay operates his business as a sole proprietorship, he deducts the charitable contributions as an itemized deduction. He deducts the contributions made to his own retirement plan and amounts paid for his own health insurance premiums for AGI, but cannot use these amounts to calculate the profits from his business. Jay's net profit from his business will be computed on Schedule C as follows.

Gross income from the business		$100,000
Business expenses:		
Advertising	$ 5,000	
Rent	6,700	
Employees' retirement plan contributions	1,760	
Employee benefits	8,500	

Wages paid to employees	30,000	
Payroll taxes	3,600	(55,560)
Net profit from the business		$ 44,440

Jay will include the $44,440 net profit from his business in his AGI. He will then deduct for AGI the $2,640 contributions he made to his own retirement plan and the $6,000 of premiums he paid for his own health insurance. Jay also will be able to deduct the employer's share (one-half) of the self-employment taxes for AGI. Jay calculates his self-employment tax using the $44,440 of profits from his business.

In contrast, if Jay operated the business as a corporation, the entire $65,200 of business expenses would have been deducted against business profits. In addition, any wages paid to Jay as an employee (plus the employment taxes assessed on those wages) would be deducted by the corporation. The corporation would also withhold social security and Medicare taxes on wages paid to Jay.

Although the tax laws that apply to most deductions are the same for all business entities, because the activities of businesses operated as sole proprietorships are reported on the owner's individual tax return, some additional rules may apply. These rules are the focus of the discussion that follows.

Bad debts. An individual can have a business bad debt if the nature of the loan is related to the sole proprietor's business.[18] As with all other business entities, business bad debts of a sole proprietorship are deductible against the gross income from the business. Business bad debts generally result from credit sales of goods or services to customers, as well as loans to suppliers, clients, employees, or distributors. Sole proprietors that use the cash method for their business activities cannot deduct a bad debt for uncollectible accounts receivable since those amounts were never included in gross income.

Example 10: Arthur Nelson is an attorney who reports his business activities using the cash method. During 2009, Arthur bills a client for $10,000 who subsequently files for bankruptcy and has the entire debt discharged in 2010. As a cash basis taxpayer, Arthur does not report any income during 2009 when the invoice is sent and will not be entitled to a bad debt deduction when the debt is discharged by the bankruptcy court in 2010.

Example 11: Referring to Example 10, if Arthur reports his income using the accrual method of accounting, he would report the $10,000 as income for 2009 when the income was earned and then be entitled to a bad debt deduction during 2010 when the debt is discharged.

A business bad debt is one that is closely related to a taxpayer's trade or business. A nonbusiness bad debt is a debt which comes about from a debt incurred or acquired in some manner other than through a trade or business (see ¶ 510). When a sole proprietor loans money to friends or relatives for use in their respective businesses, the loan still constitutes a nonbusiness loan to the sole proprietor. When a nonbusiness bad debt becomes worthless, the loss will be recognized as a short-term capital loss. Individual taxpayers can deduct capital losses to the extent of any capital gains included in gross income plus $3,000[19] (see ¶ 901.01).

Example 12: Jan Russell makes a *bona fide* loan to a friend for $10,000 so that her friend can start her own business. The friend later files for bankruptcy. In the year that the loan becomes worthless, Jan would be entitled to a nonbusiness bad debt deduction. Assuming Jan has no other capital gains or losses in that year, her loss deduction

---

[18] Code Sec. 165; Reg. § 1.166-5(b).   [19] Code Sec. 1211.

would be limited to $3,000 and the remaining $7,000 would carry forward to the next tax year.

Transportation expense. Sole proprietors that use their personal automobile for business can deduct the business portion of their automobile expenses against business income on Schedule C. As discussed in Chapter 6, the owner's transportation expense deduction can be computed using either the actual expense method or the standard mileage rate ($.55 per mile in 2009).[20] Any business-related parking and tolls also can be deducted. Sole proprietors have the option of using the standard mileage rate to reimburse their employees as well as to deduct amounts for the business use of their own personal automobiles. However, the actual method must be used by sole proprietors who use five or more automobiles simultaneously for business[21] (see ¶ 607.01).

Example 13: John Harris is a self-employed attorney who used his personal automobile for travel between his office and the courthouse. For 2009, John properly documents the 10,000 business-related miles his automobile was driven during the year. The total miles during the year were 15,000 miles. John's actual operating expenses include $7,600 for gas, oil, insurance, repairs, maintenance, and depreciation, plus $500 for business-related parking and tolls. Because John used his automobile 66.67 percent of the time for business (10,000/15,000), he is allowed to deduct $5,567 (($7,600 × 66.67%) + $500) against his business income on Schedule C. Had John elected to use the standard mileage rate, his deduction would have been $6,000 ((10,000 × $.55) + $500).

Spotlight: The Internal Revenue Service (IRS) released Rev. Proc. 2008-72 establishing the optional standard mileage rates effective January 1, 2009, at 55 cents per mile for business miles driven. The IRS stated that the higher rates for 2009 reflected the generally higher transportation costs related to business automobile usage compared to the prior year. The optional standard mileage rate for the first half of 2008 was 50.5 cents per mile for business miles driven and increased to 58.5 cents per mile for the second half of the year. These rates are established based upon a study of the fixed and variable costs of operating an automobile. Thus, while the price of gasoline is a significant factor in the mileage rate, other operating costs are included in the calculation which can be a moderating factor when considering volatile gasoline prices.[22]

Depreciation and Section 179 expense. The rules for calculating depreciation from Chapter 7 apply to all business entities, including sole proprietorships. Individuals starting out a business may find it financially beneficial to take their own personal assets and convert them into business property. When personal-use property, such as part of the owner's home or the owner's personal automobile or furniture, is converted to business use, the amount that can be depreciated is the *lesser* of the property's fair market value (FMV) on the date of the conversion or its adjusted basis.[23]

Example 14: Alan Landon operates a sole proprietorship. On June 15, 2009, Alan decides to convert his SUV from personal use to business use. The SUV cost Alan $32,000 when he acquired it in 2008. On June 15, 2009, the SUV had a FMV of $26,000. Alan can depreciate the SUV using a $26,000 depreciable basis.

Another issue unique to businesses operated as sole proprietorships is the owner's use of listed property. **Listed property** is property that is easily used for both business and personal use, and includes cellular phones, automobiles, computers, and peripheral equipment. When listed property is not used more than 50 percent of the time for business, the tax laws prohibit the taxpayer from taking Section 179 or accelerated depreciation on the business use of the property.[24] Thus, listed

---

[20] Rev. Proc. 2008-72, IRB 2008-38.

[21] Rev. Proc. 2003-76, IRB 2003-43, 924.

[22] IR-2008-131, Nov. 24, 2008.

[23] Reg. §1.167(g)-1 and Reg. §1.168(i)-4(b).

[24] Code Secs. 280F and 179, Temp. Reg. §§1.280F-1T - 1.280F-6T.

property that is not used primarily for business must be depreciated using the alternative depreciation system (ADS). Recall from Chapter 7 that ADS uses the straight-line method of depreciation over slightly longer recovery periods. See Table 7-3 at ¶ 702.

Also recall from Chapter 7 that depreciation expense taken on an automobile is subject to annual limits. The amounts provided in Table 7G (see ¶ 726) represent the limits for automobiles used 100 percent for business. For purposes of depreciating automobiles used less than 100 percent for business, the luxury automobile limits from the table must be reduced to reflect the portion of business use during the year.

Example 15: Joanne Smith operates her business as a sole proprietorship. During 2008, Joanne acquires a new automobile for $14,000 and uses it 40 percent of the time for business. The half-year convention applies. Since the business use percentage for the automobile does not exceed 50 percent, Joanne uses Table 7F from Chapter 7 to depreciate her automobile using ADS over a five-year recovery period. The maximum depreciation allowed in 2008 for an automobile used 40 percent for business is $1,184 ($2,960 × 40%). Since Joanne's ADS depreciation deduction of $560 ($14,000 x 40% business use × 10% ADS first year recovery rate) does not exceed $1,184, she can deduct $540 on her Schedule C.

Example 16: Assume the same facts as in Example 15, except that the business use percentage of the automobile is 80 percent. Joanne would be entitled to use regular (accelerated) MACRS to depreciate the automobile. She uses the recovery percentages from the column for 5-year property in Table 7-3 at ¶ 702 to compute the MACRS depreciation deduction on the automobile of $2,240 ($14,000 × 80% × 20%). Since this amount does not exceed 80 percent of the first year limit for luxury automobiles placed in service during 2008 ($2,960 × 80% = $2,368), Joanne would deduct $2,240 for depreciation expense on her Schedule C in 2008.

In determining whether listed property is used primarily for business, for transportation vehicles, usage should be based on mileage driven during the year. For other types of listed property, hours used during the year is appropriate. If listed property originally used primarily for business is later used 50 percent or less of the time for business, then any depreciation taken over the years in excess of what would have been allowed under ADS must be included in gross income in the year the property is no longer used primarily for business.

Example 17: Continuing with Example 16, if Joanne's business use drops to 40 percent in 2009, she would be required to begin depreciating the 40 percent business use using ADS starting in 2009. In addition, she would be required to go back and recalculate what her depreciation deduction would have been had she elected to use ADS on the 80-percent business use in 2008 and recapture the excess of the amount she deducted ($2,240) and the amount that would have been allowed under ADS. She adds this excess to her income reported on Schedule C in 2009.

 Planning Pointer: *The American Recovery and Reinvestment Tax Act of 2009* (P.L. 111-5) extended the limitation on first-year depreciation of "luxury" automobiles for a qualifying vehicle purchase during 2009. The maximum first-year depreciation allowance would be the amount otherwise allowable plus an additional $8,000 of bonus depreciation permitted by the new tax Act. Taxpayers contemplating the purchase of a qualifying vehicle after the 2009 tax year should consider this opportunity for accelerating the acquisition and receiving this enhanced deduction in 2009. Further discussion of bonus depreciation and Section 179 expensing elections can be found at ¶ ¶ 702.02 and 703.03.

Interest and taxes. Most of the rules discussed in Chapter 5 with respect to the deduction for interest and taxes also apply to sole proprietorships and are deducted on Schedule C. However, any interest an individual taxpayer pays on a tax deficiency, even one that stems from mistakes made on Schedule C, represents nondeductible personal interest (see ¶ 1303.01). Also, any state, local, or foreign income taxes paid by an individual are considered personal taxes; however, these taxes can be deducted as itemized deductions on the individual's tax return. Federal income taxes are not deductible by any taxpayer or business entity, including sole proprietors and individuals. Individuals, like all taxpayers, can chose to take a foreign tax credit in lieu of a deduction for any foreign income taxes paid during the year. The rules discussed in Chapter 11 regarding the limits that apply to the foreign tax credit apply to individual taxpayers as well as corporate taxpayers.

Example 18: A business generates profits totaling $30,000 during the year. The state in which the business operates taxes profits at a rate of six percent. Accordingly, $1,800 ($30,000 × 6%) is paid to the state government for state income taxes. If the business is operated as a corporation, then the $1,800 is deducted in computing corporate taxable income in the year the taxes are paid. If the corporation is in the 25-percent tax bracket, the corporation's tax liability is reduced by $450 ($1,800 × 25%) as a result of the deduction. Alternatively, if the business is operated as a sole proprietorship, then the owner deducts the $1,800 of taxes as an itemized deduction in the year the taxes are paid. If the taxpayer's itemized deductions do not exceed the standard deduction amount, then no tax benefit will be derived from this deduction. Furthermore, the $1,800 cannot reduce business profits on Schedule C and, therefore, will not reduce the owner's self-employment taxes owed on business profits.

Office in the home deduction. Sole proprietors that rent office space can deduct amounts they pay to their landlords as rent expense on Schedule C. As another option, sole proprietors can convert a part of their personal residences into an office and use it regularly and exclusively for business. They can then deduct the costs associated with that part of their home on Schedule C against the gross income from the business,[25] including a portion of any home mortgage interest, real estate taxes, and utilities paid during the year. They also can deduct depreciation on the portion of the taxpayer's home that represents an office. Although residences are considered residential realty, the portion of the home that is being depreciated is an office, and, as such, the home office is nonresidential realty that must be depreciated over 39 years under MACRS.[26] Furthermore, since the office is personal property being converted to business use, the depreciable basis for the office is the *lesser* of the FMV of the home or its adjusted basis at the time it is converted to an office, multiplied by the percentage of the square footage of the home that represents the home office.

Example 19: Tony Johnson operates a business as a sole proprietorship. On March 2, 2009, Tony converts one of his bedrooms into a home office. The size of the bedroom is 196 square feet; his entire home is 2,000 square feet. Tony purchased the home in 1995 for $130,000, and at the time he converted the space to an office, it was worth $200,000. Of these amounts, $20,000 is associated with the costs of the land. On his 2009 tax return, Tony will deduct 9.8 percent (196/2,000) of the expenses related to his home, including his mortgage interest, real estate taxes, utilities, and insurance. Tony also will be able to depreciate 9.8 percent of the $110,000 basis in his home (the *lesser* of (1) $130,000 minus $20,000 for the land, or (2) $200,000 minus $20,000) over 39 years starting on March 15, 2009, under the mid-month convention.

Individual taxpayers deduct home mortgage interest and real estate taxes as itemized deductions. Thus, the portion of these amounts they deduct for AGI as home office expenses cannot also be deducted as itemized deductions. Also, the tax law does not allow home office expenses, other than for mortgage interest, real estate taxes, and casualty losses, to generate a loss from the business. Any amounts not deductible in the current tax year due to this limitation can be carried

---

[25] Code Sec. 280A(c)(1).

[26] Code Secs. 168(b)(3)(A), 168(c), and 168(d)(2).

over to subsequent tax years and deducted as home office expenses when the sole proprietor generates enough profits to cover these amounts.[27]

Example 20: Continuing with Example 19, assume that in 2009, Tony's home mortgage interest and real estate taxes are $8,400 and $2,200, respectively. Tony will be able to deduct $823 ($8,400 × 9.8%) and $216 ($2,200 × 9.8%), respectively, on Schedule C to offset his business profits. He can then deduct the remaining $7,577 ($8,400 – $823) and $1,984 ($2,200 – $216) as itemized deductions.

Example 21: Continuing with Examples 19 and 20, assume the Tony generates business income of $13,000 and has $6,000 of business expenses in 2009. After subtracting out the business portion of his mortgage interest and real estate taxes, Tony's net profits equal $5,961 ($13,000 – $6,000 – $823 – $216). Therefore, Tony's other deductible home office expenses (for utilities, insurance, depreciation, etc.) cannot exceed this amount.

.03 Other Business Expenses Deductible for AGI

Once net profits from the business are calculated, sole proprietors calculate the amount of self-employment taxes owed on those profits. They also can then determine the amount they are allowed to contribute and deduct to their own retirement plans.

Deduction for one-half of self-employment taxes. Self-employment taxes represent both the 7.65 percent employer and 7.65 percent employee contributions to FICA.[28] In 2009, the maximum net earnings subject to the social security portion is $106,800, whereas all net earnings from self-employment are subject to the Medicare tax.[29] Because one-half of these amounts present the employer's responsibility, self-employed taxpayers can deduct one-half of their self-employment taxes for AGI. If the one-half of self-employment taxes were allowed to be deducted as a business expense on Schedule C, they would reduce the amount of net profits subject to self-employment tax; however, this would create additional problems in how the tax is calculated. Therefore, the tax laws require that the one-half of self-employment taxes be deducted for AGI on page 1 of Form 1040. However, when computing the amount of self-employment taxes owed for the year, only 92.35 percent (100 percent minus the 7.65 percent employer share of FICA taxes) of net profits from the business are subject to self-employment tax.[30] This 92.35 percent of net profits from the business is referred to as **net earnings from self-employment**. Self-employed taxpayers with at least $400 of net earnings from self-employment are subject to self-employment taxes on their earnings.[31]

Example 22: Grace Williams, a sole proprietor, reports a net profit from her business of $40,000. Grace's self-employment tax is calculated below.

Net profit from the business	$40,000
	× 92.35%
Net earnings from self-employment	$36,940
Self-employment tax rate	× 15.3%
Self-employment tax	$ 5,652

When Grace files her tax return, she will add the $5,652 of self-employment taxes to her regular income taxes. In computing her taxable income and regular income tax liability, Grace will deduct one-half of the self-employment taxes ($2,826) for AGI on page 1 of her Form 1040.

---

[27] Code Sec. 280A(c)(5).
[28] Code Sec. 1401.
[29] Code Secs. 3101, 3111, and 3121.

[30] Code Secs. 164(f) and 1402(a)(12).
[31] Code Secs. 1402(b)(2) and 6017.

> **Reason for the Rule:** Since one-half of self-employment taxes that sole proprietors pay represent the employer's share of FICA taxes, it is appropriate that one-half of these taxes be deducted for AGI. However, since the calculation of self-employment taxes starts with net profits of the business, the calculation of the self-employment taxes becomes more complicated if the deduction for one-half of these taxes were required in determining net profits from the business. Using only 92.35 percent of these profits in the calculation of self-employment taxes attempts to solve this issue by subtracting from 100 percent of business profits the 7.65 percent of the employer's share of FICA taxes.

Since only the first $106,800 of earnings during 2009 is subject to social security taxes (otherwise known as OASDI), sole proprietors who also earn wages as an employee during the year will have already contributed towards the social security portion of FICA. Consequently, the amounts they and their employers have already contributed to FICA need to be considered in the calculation of the 12.4 percent component of self-employment tax. Accordingly, when computing the OASDI component of the self-employment tax, the 12.4 percent is applied to the *lesser* of (1) 92.35 percent of net profit from the business or (2) the excess of the maximum earnings subject to OASDI ($106,800 in 2009) over the taxpayer's social security wages.

Example 23: Glen Smith is an employee of a construction corporation and has taxable wages subject to FICA of $64,200 in 2009. Glen also operates a sole proprietorship that generates profits totaling $50,000 during the year. Glen's self-employment tax is $6,621.

Net profit from the business	$50,000
	× 92.35%
Net earnings from self-employment	$46,175
Maximum earnings subject to OASDI	$106,800
Less: Social security wages	(64,200)
Remaining earnings subject to OASDI	$42,600
Lesser of: net earnings from self-employment or the remaining earnings subject to OASDI	$42,600
OASDI rate	× 12.4%
OASDI component of self-employment tax	$ 5,282
Net earnings from self-employment	$46,175
Medicare rate	× 2.9%
Medicare component of self-employment taxes	$ 1,339
Total self-employment tax ($5,282 + $1,339)	$ 6,621
Deduction for one-half of self-employment tax	$ 3,310

Sole proprietor's health insurance premiums. Self-employed individuals can deduct against their business profits on Schedule C health insurance premiums they pay for their employees' health coverage.[32] However, amounts they pay for their own health insurance premiums are deductible for AGI on page 1 of Form 1040 but do not reduce their net profits from the business.[33] Any amounts paid during months when sole proprietors are eligible to participate in any employer-sponsored health plan (including their spouses' plans) are not deductible for AGI.[34]

Example 24: John Martin operates a sole proprietorship. During the year, John pays insurance premiums on the policy that covers himself and his two employees. The amount of the premiums for each covered individual is $10,000. John can deduct the $20,000 of premiums paid for his two employees as a trade or business expense on Schedule C. He can also deduct the $10,000 of premiums paid for his own policy as a deduction for AGI on page 1 of Form 1040 as self-employed health insurance. John will pay less self-employment tax due to the $20,000 deduction taken on Schedule C for health insurance premiums paid on behalf of his employees. He will pay less income taxes as a result of reducing his taxable income by $30,000 ($20,000 + $10,000).

Contributions to the sole proprietor's own retirement plan. Self-employed persons can deduct contributions they make to their own qualified retirement plans, provided that those plans are also made available to all eligible employees.[35] Many self-employed individuals establish defined contribution or Simplified Employee Pension (SEP) plans because of the larger amounts they can contribute (and deduct). However, for sole proprietors who have employees, these plans generally require the owners to make contributions on behalf of their employees as well, so many sole proprietors may offer 401(k) plans and Savings Incentive Match Plans for Employees (SIMPLE). The rules regarding the amounts that employers and employees can contribute annually to each of these plans are essentially the same as those discussed in Chapter 6 (see ¶ 603).

A sole proprietor also must follow the rules regarding participation of the employees of the business. Contributions to a plan must be separated between those contributions on behalf of the employee and sole proprietor. The contributions on behalf of the employee are deductible in arriving at the net profits from the business and, therefore, reduce the taxpayer's self-employment taxes. Sole proprietors' contributions to their own retirement plans are deductible as a deduction for AGI but do not reduce the net income from the business for purposes of the self-employment tax.

Example 25: Justin Church is self-employed and has one employee. Justin contributes $8,000 to the company's retirement plans during the year: $5,000 for himself and $3,000 for his employee. Net profit from the business before considering these contributions equals $55,000. Justin's AGI from sources other than his sole proprietorship total $10,000. After deducting the retirement contributions, net profit from the business equals $52,000 ($55,000 - $3,000). This amount will be included in Justin's AGI, which increases it to $62,000 ($52,000 + $10,000). The $5,000 Justin contributes to his own retirement plan reduces his AGI to $47,000 ($52,000 - $5,000) but does not affect the amount of net profit from his sole proprietorship. Thus, the $8,000 Justin contributes to the company's retirement plans reduce his taxable income and his income tax liability, but only the $3,000 that he contributes to his employee's plan reduces his self-employment tax.

Qualified moving expenses. Amounts employers pay or reimburse their employees for qualified moving expenses are not taxable to employees and are deducted by the employer. Qualified moving expenses were discussed in Chapter 6 and include costs incurred in relocating employees and their families to the new location. It also includes the costs of lodging en route as well as $.24 per mile for moves that take place during 2009 (see ¶ 602.04).[36]

---

[32] Reg. § 1.132-1(a).

[33] Code Sec. 162(l)(4).

[34] Code Sec. 162(l)(2)(B) and *C. Reynolds*, 79 TCM 1376, Dec. 53,721(M), TC Memo. 2000-20.

[35] Code Secs. 401-404.

[36] Code Secs. 162 and 217(b)(1) and Rev. Proc. 2008-72, IRB 2008-38, September 28, 2008.

Qualified moving expenses are for moves that pass both the time and mileage tests. The *mileage test* is met if the employee's commute to the new job would be increased by at least 50 miles. Thus, the distance between the employee's current residence and the location of the new job must be 50 miles further than the distance between the employee's current residence and the location of the old job. The *employment test* is met if the employee is employed full-time in the new location for at least 39 of the first 52 weeks after the move. It is not necessary that the 39 weeks be consecutive or with the same employer.[37]

Any amounts an employer reimburses its employees for moving expenses that do not qualify as deductible moving costs are taxable as additional wages to the employee and are deductible as such by the employer. Hence, these additional wages would be subject to income and FICA tax withholding and the employer would be responsible for its share of FICA tax and any unemployment taxes on those wages.

Sole proprietors can also deduct qualified moving expenses they pay for their own moves. However, the sole proprietor must pass the distance test and a more stringent time test. In addition to being employed full-time in the new location at least 39 of the first 52 weeks following the move, sole proprietors must also be employed full-time for 78 of the first 104 weeks following the move.[38]

Example 26: Norman Stockington is self-employed. In May 2009, Norman moves to a new town 1,000 miles away. Norman paid $3,500 to a moving company to move his household goods and personal effects. He drove himself and his family to the new location traveling 1,000 miles and incurring $150 for lodging and $110 for meals during the trip.

On his 2009 tax return, Norman deducts $3,890 for AGI ($3,500 + $150 + $240 for mileage at $.24 a mile). This amount reduces his AGI but does not affect his net profits reported on Schedule C. Furthermore, as a self-employed individual, Norman will be required to be employed full-time at the new location 39 of the first 52 weeks and 78 out of the first 104 weeks after the move.

Losses from the sale of property. In Chapter 9, the calculation of gain or loss on the disposal of business property was discussed. These same rules apply to sole proprietors. Although the netting of Section 1231 gains and losses and capital gains and losses is similar to that discussed in Chapter 9 (see ¶ 904), these amounts are not reflected on Schedule C, but are included in the calculation of AGI. Individual taxpayers are allowed to deduct up to $3,000 of net capital losses against ordinary income, and any excess retains its short-term or long-term character and can be carried forward indefinitely. (Recall that corporations can only offset capital losses against capital gains, and any excess loss is carried back three years and forward five years as a short-term capital loss.) (See ¶ 901.01.)

Example 27: Gwen Wolfe operates a small retail shop as a sole proprietorship. During the 2009 tax year, Gwen realizes gains and losses from the disposition of business assets and investments as follows.

Loss from sale of business equipment (held 4 months)	($ 5,000)
Gain from sale of business land (held 3 years)	8,000
Loss from sale of stock (held 6 months)	(40,000)
Gain from sale of stock (held 2 years)	25,000

The business property held short-term is deducted for AGI against Gwen's ordinary income. The business land held long-term is the only Section 1231 property sold during the year. Assuming no nonrecaptured Section 1231 losses from the last five years, the $8,000 of Section 1231 gain is treated as long-term capital gain, thus

---

[37] Code Sec. 217(c) and Reg. § 1.217-2.   [38] Code Sec. 217(f).

making Gwen's total long-term capital gain $33,000 ($25,000 + $8,000). When Gwen nets the $40,000 of net short-term capital loss against the $33,000 of net long-term capital gain, she ends up with a $7,000 net short-term capital loss. Gwen is allowed to deduct $3,000 of this loss against her other income in computing her AGI. The remaining $4,000 ($7,000 – $3,000) is carried over to 2010 and netted against short-term capital gains and losses generated that year.

.04 Passive Activity Losses

A provision enacted in the Tax Reform Act of 1986 limits the deductibility of losses resulting from certain trades or businesses, as well as and rental activities. Deductions from a passive activity, including expenses such as interest attributable to acquiring or carrying on an interest in a passive activity, generally may not be deducted from other income for the tax year to the extent that the deductions exceed income from all of the taxpayer's passive activities. The effect of this rule is to prohibit the offsetting of passive losses against income that can be termed "nonpassive," such as compensation for services, portfolio income (interest, dividends, royalties, and gain from the sale of property held for investment), and income from a trade or business in which the taxpayer materially participates. Likewise, credits from passive activities generally are limited to the tax allocable to such activities.[39]

Example 28: Katie Harris has three business activities that are classified as passive activities for the 2009 tax year. In addition, she has income in the form of compensation for services of $50,000, business income of $20,000 from a business activity considered "nonpassive" and interest income of $3,000. The taxable income or (loss) from each passive activity is as follows:

A	$15,000
B	(9,000)
C	(8,000)

For 2009, the net passive activity loss of $2,000 (the $15,000 of passive income from Activity A minus the $17,000 of passive losses from Activities B and C) cannot be used to reduce Katie's other income of $73,000 stemming from compensation for services, "nonpassive" business income, and interest income.

Reason for the Rule: Prior to the enactment of the Tax Reform Act of 1986, taxpayers could fully deduct losses from rental activities and from trades or businesses, regardless of the level of participation of the taxpayer in the activity. This gave rise to a significant number of tax shelters, which allowed taxpayers to deduct losses from activities in which they had little or no participation against wages and investment income. The Tax Reform Act of 1986 added Code Sec. 469, which limits taxpayers' ability to deduct losses from most rental activities and from trades or businesses in which they do not materially participate.

The passive activity loss rules are applied at the individual taxpayer level and extend to virtually every business or rental activity whether reported on Schedule C, Profit or Loss from Business (Sole Proprietorships); Schedule F, Profit or Loss from Farming; or Schedule E, Supplemental Income or Loss (Rental Activities), as well as to flow through income and losses from partnerships, S corporations, and trusts. The passive loss limitations also apply to personal service corporations. They also apply to closely held C corporations, but have a limited application.

Deductions from passive activities for the tax year that exceed passive income may not be deducted in that year, but instead, the excess (passive activity loss) is "suspended" and carried

---

[39] Code Sec. 469.

forward to offset passive activity income generated in future years. Similarly, credits from passive activities that exceed the tax liability allocable to passive activities for the tax year must be suspended and utilized to offset tax liability associated with passive activities in future years.

Example 29: Continuing with Example 28, Katie would be able to carry forward the nondeductible portion of the passive activity losses to 2010. If in 2010 the three passive activities produced a net passive activity income of $5,000, the $2,000 suspended loss would be allowed as a deduction reducing her taxable income from these activities in 2010 to $3,000 ($5,000 less $2,000).

To fully deduct losses from a trade or business, the taxpayer must participate in the activity on a regular, continuous, and substantial basis. This is known as the **material participation**. Both losses and income from businesses in which the taxpayer materially participates are treated as "nonpassive" and generally all losses are fully deductible. For activities other than rental realty, the tax law provides seven tests to measure whether a taxpayer's participation in a trade or business is material. The four most common tests are quantitative in nature and are based upon a taxpayer's hours of participation during the tax year. These four tests are listed in Table 13-1.

Table 13-1 Tests for Material Participation by the Taxpayer

1. Participation in the activity for more than 500 hours during the tax year.

2. Participation constitutes substantially all of the participation in the activity of all individuals (including the taxpayer and nonowners) for the tax year.

3. Participation in the activity for more than 100 hours during the tax year, and the taxpayer's participation is not less than the participation of any other person.

4. The activity is a significant participation activity for the tax year, and the taxpayer's aggregate participation in all significant participation activities during the year exceeds 500 hours. A *significant participation activity* is one in which the taxpayer has more than 100 hours of participation during the tax year but fails to satisfy any other tests for material participation. A rental activity may not be included in the significant participation activity test. If the sum of all the time spent in the significant participation activities exceeds 500 hours, then all such activities of the taxpayer are considered "nonpassive."

Example 30: Jason Johnson has six separate businesses in which he participates. The numbers of hours he participated and the hours his other employee, Sandy Smith, participated in the activities during the current tax year are as follows. Sandy is Jason's only employee.

Business	Jason's Hours	Sandy's Hours
A	615	1,100
B	82	0
C	135	50
D	385	435
E	215	375

All of the business activities would constitute material participation and would be considered "nonpassive" activities, thereby allowing any loss resulting from them to be deductible against income from "nonpassive" sources. Business A is "nonpassive" because Jason participated for more than 500 hours and passes the Test 1 from Table

13-1. His participation in Business B is "nonpassive" because his participation constitutes substantially all the participation of all employees for the tax year (Test 2) and would not meet the requirement for any of the other tests because his participation is less than 100 hours (the threshold hours for Tests 3 and 4). Jason's participation in Business C is deemed material because his participation was more than 100 hours and Sandy did not participate for more hours than him (Test 3). Jason's participation in Businesses D and E do not meet the requirements of Test 3 because of the number of hours Sandy participated in the businesses; however, they do meet the criteria for significant participation activities with a cumulative participation in excess of 500 hours.

A rental activity is generally considered to be a passive activity, regardless of the extent of the taxpayer's participation in the activity. Thus, classification of an activity expected to produce losses as a rental activity is generally disadvantageous to those persons who would otherwise have materially participated had the activity been a trade or business. To compensate for this possible inequity, a more stringent, two-prong, material participation test applies to rental activities. First, the taxpayer must participate in the rental activity for at least 750 hours during the year. Second, the taxpayer's hours of participation in all rental activities during the year must be more than the taxpayer's participation in all other activities during the year.[40]

Taxpayers not meeting the material participation test for rental activities generally cannot deduct losses from such activities in excess of income from passive activities. However, up to $25,000 of rental losses may be deducted by anyone whose modified adjusted gross income (MAGI) does not exceed $100,000. MAGI is AGI calculated without including certain items of income and deduction, such as other passive activity losses and the deduction for IRA contributions.[41] To qualify for this special deduction, the taxpayer must meet the **active participation** test with respect to the rental activity, own at least a 10 percent interest in the activity, and not be a limited partner. The $25,000 exception is phased out at the rate of $.50 for every dollar of MAGI over $100,000. Thus, when a taxpayer's MAGI exceeds $150,000, the no loss deduction is allowed.

Planning Pointer: Taxpayers wanting to take advantage of the $25,000 real estate loss deduction need to satisfy both the active participation and MAGI components of the test. While active participation is not as stringent as material participation, the taxpayer is required to participate in making management decisions, such as selecting tenants, or arranging for services for the property in a significant and bona fide sense, such as arranging for repairs. To meet the active participation test, the taxpayer must fulfill the requirements both in the year the loss arose and in the year the loss is deducted. The MAGI component requires taxpayers to project their income and deductions from other sources and plan to keep their MAGI under $100,000, when possible.

Example 31: Daryl Williams has an AGI of $118,000 prior to claiming any deduction for a $20,000 rental real estate loss, but after deducting $2,000 for an IRA contribution. The rental activity is one in which Daryl actively participates and he does not have any other passive activity losses. Under the general rules for the passive activity loss deduction the $20,000 would not be deductible, however, since Daryl's $120,000 of MAGI ($118,000 + $2,000) is less than $150,000, the special rule for allowance of losses from rental real estate applies. The $20,000 of excess MAGI ($120,000 – $100,000) reduces the amount of the possible loss deduction by $10,000 ($20,000 × $.50). Daryl's loss deduction will be $15,000, which is the *lesser* of the $20,000 of rental real estate loss or $15,000 ($25,000 – $10,000 phase-out for excess MAGI).

---

[40] Code Sec. 469(c)(7).   [41] Code Sec. 469(i)(3)(E).

Any unused suspended loss deductions are allowed in full when the taxpayer disposes of the entire interest in the activity in a fully taxable transaction. Suspended credits are not allowed on disposition of a taxpayer's interest in an activity. A taxpayer may be involved in several activities, and, to compute the passive activity loss (if any) for a tax year, the income and deductions from all passive activities must be aggregated. Nevertheless, for some purposes it is necessary to account for the net income or loss of each activity separately. One major reason for separating an activities and allocating losses and income among activities is to be able to determine the tax treatment upon disposition of an interest in an activity.

Example 32: On January 1, 2009, John Olsen pays $500,000 for an investment in a restaurant and hires a full-time manager and staff. As an owner he does not participate in the restaurant and his interest in the restaurant is passive. John has no other passive activities. Assume that for 2009, John's loss from the restaurant is $100,000. The loss is not deductible in 2009, and must be suspended until 2010. In 2010, John realizes $60,000 of taxable income from the restaurant, which continues to retain its status as a passive activity to John. Accordingly, John would report no net income or loss from the restaurant for 2010 and would have a suspended loss carry forward to 2011 of $40,000 ($100,000 loss from 2009 less a $60,000 profit in 2010). On January 1, 2011, John disposes of his entire interest in the restaurant at a passive activity gain of $25,000. The $25,000 gain would be applied against the $40,000 loss carry forward to 2011 leaving $15,000 to be deductible in 2011 against "nonpassive" trade or business income and portfolio income.

 Planning Pointer: When a taxpayer is faced with continuing passive activity losses from a trade or business, there can be devastating results from the inability to deduct the losses on the taxpayer's tax return. There are a few potential courses of action that can be taken to have the passive losses become deductible. First, the taxpayer can acquire an investment that generates passive income. Since passive losses can be deducted against passive income, this will allow the taxpayer to absorb the passive losses that would otherwise not be currently deductible. Second, the taxpayer can become a material participant in the activity. If a taxpayer has substantial losses from a passive activity, it could be worthwhile to increase the level of the taxpayer's involvement to that of a material participant. Finally, the taxpayer can dispose of the entire interest in the passive activity since any suspended losses can be deducted in the year of complete disposition in a taxable transaction.

¶ 1304 Deductions from AGI

As previously mentioned, some expenses that normally would be deductible business expenses if paid or incurred by a corporation must be deducted as itemized deductions by an individual who operates a sole proprietorship. Since itemized deductions only reduce taxable income if the taxpayer's total itemized deductions exceed the standard deduction amount, it is important to understand a little more about the various expenses that are allowed as itemized deductions, as well as how the standard deduction amount is determined. Furthermore, since deductions from AGI reduce an individual's taxable income, an individual taxpayer's marginal tax rate may be affected by deductions from AGI.

.01 Personal and Dependency Exemptions

In determining taxable income, taxpayers may claim two types of exemptions as deductions from their AGI: personal and dependency exemptions.[42] In 2009, each personal and dependency

---

[42] Code Sec. 151(b).

exemption reduces taxable income by $3,650;[43] however, the total personal and dependency exemptions of higher-income taxpayers are reduced.[44]

 Spotlight: The deduction for personal and dependency exemptions may be reduced or eliminated for higher-income taxpayers. The total exemption amount for a taxpayer whose AGI exceeds the set threshold amount is reduced by 2 percent for each $2,500 ($1,250 for a married person filing separately) or fraction thereof by which AGI exceeds the threshold amount. The 2009 threshold amounts are: $240,200 for surviving spouse or married couples filing a joint return, $208,500 for a head of household, $166,800 for single taxpayers and $125,100 for married persons filing separately. The amount of the exemption phaseout reduction is reduced by two-thirds for tax years beginning in 2008 and 2009. For tax years beginning after 2009, the exemption phase-out is repealed.[45]

Example 33: For 2009, Rita Williams lived alone as a single taxpayer, did not support any other persons, and no other taxpayer provided over 50 percent of Rita's support. On her 2009 tax return, Rita will deduct $3,650 from AGI in arriving at her taxable income as a result of having one personal exemption.

Personal exemption. A personal exemption may be claimed for the person filing a return. A married couple filing a joint return may claim two personal exemptions on their return. A married individual filing a separate return may claim a personal exemption for his or her spouse only if the spouse has no gross income, and if the spouse is not a dependent of another taxpayer.[46] Taxpayers who can be claimed as dependents on another person's tax return may not claim a personal exemption on their own personal returns. For example, a student who works part-time during the year or during the summer may not claim a personal exemption on his return if his parents (or another taxpayer) are entitled to claim him as a dependent on their return.[47]

Example 34: The Robertsons file a joint return in 2009 and claim three dependency exemptions. On their 2009 tax return, the Robertsons will deduct $18,250 ($3,650 × 5) from AGI in arriving at their taxable income related to their two personal and three dependency exemptions.

Dependency exemption. In 2009, individual taxpayers are allowed to deduct $3,650 from AGI for each person whom they can claim as a dependent. Although the rules regarding who qualifies as a dependent are beyond the scope of this chapter, in order for someone to qualify as a dependent, the taxpayer must generally provide over half of the person's support during the year. In addition, the person must be related to the taxpayer or live with the taxpayer during the entire year and be a U.S. citizen or resident. Furthermore, persons who qualify as a dependent generally cannot have gross income that exceeds the exemption amount ($3,650 in 2009). However, a "qualifying child" that is either under the age of 19 or between the ages of 19 and 23 and a full-time student will qualify as a dependent even when the qualifying child's gross income exceeds the exemption amount. An additional requirement of the age component of the test is the child must be younger than the taxpayer claiming the dependency exemption.[48] For purposes of the dependency exemption, the Code considers a sibling and a descendent of the taxpayer (child or grandchild) as a "qualifying child."

.02 Standard Deduction

The federal government allows taxpayers to deduct from AGI the *larger of* a standard deduction[49] or the taxpayer's itemized deductions. The standard deduction consists of two components: a basic standard deduction plus any additional standard deductions.

---

[43] Rev. Proc. 2008-66, IRB 2008-31, August 4, 2008.

[44] Code Sec. 151(d)(3)(E).

[45] Code Sec. 151(d).

[46] Code Sec. 151(b).

[47] Code Sec. 151(d)(2).

[48] Code Sec. 152(c)(3)(A).

[49] Code Sec. 63(c).

The basic standard deduction. The basic standard deduction is determined by reference to the taxpayer's filing status. There are five filing statuses available to taxpayers.

1. Married filing jointly,
2. Surviving spouse,
3. Married filing separately,
4. Head of household, and
5. Single.

Couples who are married as of the last day of the tax year have the option of filing a joint return with their spouse. When a joint tax return is filed, the couple combines their gross income and deductions and computes taxable income and tax liability on the same tax return. This filing status is called married filing jointly (MFJ). MFJ filing status is also available to widows and widowers in the year that their spouse dies, provided that they have not remarried by the last day of the tax year. Married couples that do not want to file a joint tax return must file separate tax returns, with the spouses reporting their respective gross income and deductions for the year. This filing status is referred to as married filing separately (MFS).

Taxpayers who are not married on the last day of the tax year but were widowed during one of the two preceding tax years can file as a **surviving spouse** if they have a dependent son or daughter living with them the entire year. Taxpayers who file as surviving spouses have many of the benefits that MFJ couples are provided, including a higher basic standard deduction and use of the more favorable MFJ tax rates.

Example 35: Jean Soranston's husband passed away in 2008, leaving her to raise their nine-year-old daughter for whom Jean is entitled to claim a dependency exemption. Jean files a joint return with her husband in 2008 and qualifies to file as a surviving spouse in 2009 and 2010.

Unmarried individuals who do not qualify as surviving spouses must file their tax returns as either head of household or single filing status. **Head of household** filing status is available to taxpayers who are not married and do not qualify as a surviving spouse, but maintain a household for more than one-half of the tax year where a qualifying child of the taxpayer or any other person who is a dependent of the taxpayer lives. Abandoned spouses are considered unmarried taxpayers and, therefore, may qualify for head of household filing status. An **abandoned spouse** is a married individual who lives with a dependent child but has not lived with his or her spouse for the last six months of the year. An unmarried taxpayer who does not qualify as a surviving spouse or for head of household filing status must file as a single taxpayer.

Example 36: Continuing with Example 35, beginning in 2011, Jean will file as head of household since surviving spouse filing status is only available for the two years that follow the year in which the taxpayer's spouse dies.

The additional standard deduction. Additional standard deduction amounts are allowed for taxpayers who are blind or over age 64. Like the basic standard deduction, the amount of the additional standard deduction is also determined in accordance with the taxpayer's filing status. If the taxpayer is both blind and over age 64, two additional standard deduction amounts are added to the basic standard deduction to arrive at the taxpayer's total standard deduction. Table 13-2 shows the standard deduction amounts allowed in 2009.

Table 13-2 2009 Standard Deduction Amounts

Filing Status	Basic standard deduction	Additional deduction for over age 64	Additional deduction for blindness
Single	$ 5,700	$1,400	$1,400
Head of households	$ 8,350	$1,400	$1,400
Married filing jointly	$11,400	$1,100	$1,100
Surviving spouse	$11,400	$1,100	$1,100
Married filing separately	$ 5,700	$1,100	$1,100

Taxpayers are presumed to reach age 65 on the day that precedes their 65th birthday. Thus, a person whose birthday is on January 1 is considered to be age 65 on December 31.[50] Taxpayers whose eyesight is not correctable (with contact lenses or glasses) to vision of at least 20/400 are entitled to the additional deduction for blindness. When a married couple files a tax return, each spouse is allowed an additional standard deduction for each incident (age or blindness) that applies to them.

Example 37: Mary Alexander's filing status for 2009 is single. Mary is 70 years old and her eyesight is bad, but she is able to see 20/20 with the help of glasses. Mary's 2009 standard deduction equals $7,100 ($5,700 basic + $1,400 additional for age).

Example 38: Mark and Margaret Matthews are married and file a joint return for 2009. On December 31, 2009, Mark is 64 years old; Margaret is 69. Margaret lost her eyesight entirely in 1972. The Matthews's 2009 standard deduction equals $13,600 ($11,400 basic + $1,100 additional for Margaret's age + $1,100 for Margaret's blindness).

Spotlight: Reacting to a slump in the housing market, rising unemployment and to the general weakness in the credit markets, *The Housing Assistance Act of 2008* (P.L. 110-289) added a new additional standard deduction amount for taxpayers who are homeowners and claim the standard deduction. Qualifying taxpayers may add to the basic standard deduction amount the lesser of (1) the amount allocable as a deduction for state and local property taxes if the taxpayer had claimed itemized deductions, or (2) $500 ($1,000 in the case of joint filers). This additional standard deduction amount applies to any tax year commencing in 2008 and *The Emergency Economic Stabilization Act of 2008* (EESA) (P.L. 110-343) extended the eligibility to include tax years beginning in 2009. The EESA further added an additional standard deduction amount equal to the net disaster loss incurred in a federally declared disaster area which will apply for tax years beginning after December 31, 2007, and before January 1, 2010.

Continuing with Example 37, if Mary was a homeowner and paid $3,500 in real estate taxes on her primary residence, she would be permitted to increase her standard deduction $500 under this provision increasing her standard deduction to $7,600 ($5,700 basic + $1,400 additional for age + $500 additional for real estate taxes).

Reacting to the economic crisis in the automobile industry and the continuing weakness in the general economy, *The American Recovery and Reinvestment Tax Act of 2009* (P.L. 111-5) added a provision permitting taxpayers a deduction from gross income with respect to "qualified motor vehicle taxes." The deduction may be claimed in calculating both the taxpayer's regular income tax and alternative minimum tax liability. The

[50] Reg. § 1.151-1(c)(2).

amount of the deduction is limited to the portion of the state sales or excise tax imposed on the first $49,500 of the purchase price of a qualified motor vehicle. If a taxpayer elects to deduct state or local general sales taxes in lieu of deducting state and local income taxes, then she may not "double dip" and also claim the deduction for qualified motor vehicle taxes. Original use of the vehicle (the vehicle must be of a new, not a used, vehicle) must commence with the taxpayer and the taxpayer must purchase the vehicle on or after February 17, 2009, and before January 1, 2010. The amount of the deduction is subject to a phase out for high-income taxpayers. The phase out begins to apply when a taxpayer's modified adjusted gross income (MAGI) exceeds $125,000 ($250,000 for joint filers).

Continuing with Example 38, if Mark had purchased a qualifying motor vehicle on July 10, 2009, for $40,000 and paid $2,400 in sales tax to his state Mark and Margaret would be entitled to an additional deduction from gross income of $2,400. The Matthews's 2009 standard deduction would equal $16,000 ($11,400 basic + $1,100 additional for Margaret's age + $1,100 for Margaret's blindness + $2,400 for sales tax).

.03 Itemized Deductions

Expenses that are not deductible for AGI may be allowable from AGI as itemized deductions and reported on Schedule A, *Itemized Deductions*. As previously discussed, expenses related to the sole proprietorship for charitable contributions as well as state and local income taxes are considered itemized deductions rather than trade or business expenses of the sole proprietorship. While this classification as an itemized deduction creates parity amongst individual taxpayers who are employees as well as sole proprietors, it creates a differential treatment between a sole proprietorship and a corporation, since the latter are allowed to deduct these amounts directly against gross income.

Figure 13-3 Categories of Allowable Itemized Deductions

- Medical and dental expenses,
- Taxes,·
- Interest,
- Charitable contributions,
- Nonbusiness casualty and theft losses, and
- Job expenses and certain miscellaneous itemized deductions.

While the Code permits the deduction of certain personal expenses which meet one of the categories listed in Figure 13-3, several of these deductions must exceed a certain level of AGI to be deducted as itemized deductions. These limits are often referred to as "AGI floors." For example, only medical expenses that exceed 7.5 percent of AGI are deductible. Other itemized deductions subject to AGI floors are certain miscellaneous itemized deductions, which are subject to a two-percent AGI floor, and personal casualty and theft losses, which are subject to a 10-percent AGI floor. In addition, only total itemized deductions that exceed the taxpayer's total standard deduction amount are deductible in computing the taxpayer's taxable income.

 Reason for the Rule: The use of AGI floors promotes administrative convenience. Taxpayers who take the standard deduction do not need to keep receipts documenting their itemized deductions, and the IRS does not need to verify that these expenditures exist. Likewise, these rules prevent most taxpayers from having to bother with keeping receipts for unreimbursed medical expenses and casualty losses, as well as many miscellaneous expenses.

Unreimbursed medical and dental. Individual taxpayers are allowed to deduct unreimbursed medical and dental expenses paid during the year for themselves, their spouse, and dependents. Only unreimbursed amounts that exceed 7.5 percent of AGI are deductible as an itemized deduction. Common medical expenses include amounts the taxpayer pays for doctor's visits, hospital stays, dental exams and procedures, prescription medicines, and health insurance premiums. Capital expenditures, like crutches, eyeglasses, hearing aids, and contact lenses, are also deductible. Transportation (at $.24 per mile)[51] and lodging ($50 maximum per night) are also allowed. However, over-the-counter medicines and cosmetic procedures are not deductible.

Interest expense. Interest that an individual pays in connection with business debts are deducted for AGI against the income generated by the business. Similarly, interest paid on loans associated with rental property is deducted for AGI against rental income. The federal government also allows individuals to deduct for AGI interest paid on student loans.[52] All other interest individuals pay is considered personal interest, and for the most part, personal interest is a nondeductible expenditure. The federal government does, however, allow individuals to deduct certain types of interest from AGI. Because these types of interest are only deductible from AGI as itemized deductions, only taxpayers whose total itemized deductions exceed their standard deductions can reduce their taxable income (and thus, their tax liability) by paying the interest.

Home mortgage interest. Individuals can deduct interest on debt incurred in acquiring, constructing, or substantially improving a qualified residence that is secured by that residence. This debt is referred to as "acquisition indebtedness" and can be deducted only on the taxpayer's principal residence plus one other residence. The second residence can be any other residence the individual owns that is rented for less than 15 days during the year. If the second residence is rented for more than 14 days, then to qualify as a second residence, the taxpayer must personally use it at least 14 days and 10 percent of the number of days it is rented during the year.[53] Each year, a taxpayer who has more than two residences may select the second residence that will be used to determine the amount of interest expense.

Example 39: John and Karen Raymond own a primary residence. They also own a second residence that they occasionally rent out. The vacation home was rented a total of 10 days during 2009. For 2009, the Raymonds paid interest on the primary residence of $12,000 and the interest on the second home of $18,000. The vacation home qualifies as a residence since it was rented for less than 14 days during 2009. Therefore, the interest paid on both mortgages can be deducted as home mortgage interest.

The tax laws allow only interest associated with the first $1 million of acquisition indebtedness to be deducted as an itemized deduction.[54] In addition, the tax laws allow a deduction for interest on up to $100,000 of home equity indebtedness, which is debt other than acquisition indebtedness that is secured by a qualified residence.[55] Interest on the home equity indebtedness is deductible even if the proceeds are used for personal expenditures.[56] These limits are halved for married taxpayers who file separate tax returns. Any interest paid on loan amounts that exceed these limits is nondeductible personal interest.

Example 40: Paul Cooper borrows $1,300,000 at a six-percent interest rate to acquire a new principal residence. During 2009, interest paid on the debt was $77,000. However, since the amount of the indebtedness exceeds $1 million, only $60,000 of the interest is deductible as acquisition indebtedness ($1,000,000 × 6%). Of the remaining inter-

---

[51] Rev. Proc. 2008-72, IRB 2008-38, September 28, 2008.
[52] Code Sec. 221(d)(1).
[53] Code Sec. 280A(g).

[54] Code Sec. 163(h)(3)(B)(ii).
[55] Code Sec. 163(h)(3)(C)(ii).
[56] Code Sec. 163(h)(3)(C).

est, $6,000 can be deducted as home equity indebtedness ($100,000 × 6%). The rest of the interest is nondeductible personal interest.

Example 41: Nancy Thompson owns a house worth $175,000 that is fully paid for. During 2009, Nancy takes out a home equity loan for $25,000 to purchase an automobile and pays $1,200 of interest on the loan. The interest is home equity indebtedness, which Nancy deducts as an itemized deduction.

"Points" represent prepaid interest a lender charges in exchange for a lower interest rate over the life of the loan. These amounts, often called loan origination fees, are considered points when they are expressed as a percentage of the loan amount and result in a lower interest rate to the borrower. When points are paid on the purchase of a principal residence, individuals are allowed to deduct the points as interest expense in the year paid. Points paid on the refinancing of a residence or in connection with the purchase of a residence other than the taxpayer's principle residence must be amortized over the life of the loan[57] (see ¶ 306.02 for a further discussion of points).

Example 42: Janice Copper purchases a home for $500,000 in 2009 by paying $200,000 down and taking out a $300,000 mortgage. At the closing, Janice pays a two-percent loan origination fee. During 2009, Janice also pays $8,000 in interest on the loan. On her 2009 tax return, Janice can deduct the $8,000 as home mortgage interest plus $6,000 ($300,000 × 2%) points paid in connection with the loan used to purchase her principal residence.

Investment interest. Investment interest is interest that individuals pay to allow them to purchase or continue to own investment property, like stocks and bonds. Investment interest may be deducted only to the extent of "net investment income," which generally includes gross income from investment property such as interest, dividends, and capital gains minus deductible investment expenses. Interest that cannot be deducted because of this limitation is carried over to the next tax year and treated as having been paid in that year. Consequently, investment interest expense will be subject to the net investment income limitations in the carryover year.

Example 43: During 2009, Joyce Rivers pays $13,000 of investment interest expense and has net investment income of $10,000. Joyce's investment interest expense deduction for 2009 is limited to $10,000 (the amount of her net investment income), and the excess $3,000 is carried over to 2010. During 2010, Joyce pays $9,500 of investment interest and has $12,000 of net investment income. Joyce is treated as having incurred $12,500 of investment interest expense ($9,500 paid in 2010 plus $3,000 carried over from 2009). She will be allowed to deduct $12,000 of this amount in 2010 (up to the amount of her net investment income) and will carryover $500 to 2011.

As previously discussed in this chapter, qualified dividends that individuals receive are taxed the same as net capital gain and are eligible for either a zero- or 15-percent tax rate (see ¶ 1302.01 for a further discussion of capital gain tax rates and changes). Individuals may elect to forgo the use of the reduced tax rate and allow the qualified dividends to be taxed as nonqualified dividends at the regular ordinary tax rate applicable to the taxpayer. In return for allowing the income to be taxed at the higher rate, the dividend income may be included in the calculation of net investment income. If the taxpayer opts to have the qualified dividends taxed at the lower tax rate, they cannot be included in net investment income for the purpose of computing the deductible investment interest amount.[58]

Personal taxes. Taxes paid or accrued in connection with the acquisition of property are added to the basis of the property, and taxes paid or accrued in connection with the disposal of property are subtracted from the amount realized. Some taxes that an individual pays are deductible in computing AGI. For example, taxes that a landlord pays on rental property are deducted for AGI against rental income. Likewise, taxes that a sole proprietor pays on business property are deducted for AGI against business profits. Employment taxes paid by a sole proprietor are also deductible for

---

[57] Rev. Rul. 87-22, 1987-1 CB 146.

[58] Code Sec. 163(d)(4)(B).

AGI. These include social security, Medicare, and federal and state unemployment taxes employers pay on behalf of their employees, as well as one-half of the self-employment taxes paid on net earnings from self-employment.

All other taxes that individuals pay are personal taxes. The three types of personal taxes that individuals can deduct as itemized deductions include:

1. State, local, and foreign real property taxes;

2. State and local personal property taxes; and

3. State, local, and foreign income taxes or state and local general sales tax.[59]

State, local, and foreign real property taxes are generally deductible as itemized deductions by the person upon whom the taxes are imposed in the year in which they are paid or accrued.[60] Real estate taxes are imposed upon the value of real property levied; however, no deduction is allowed when the taxes are imposed for local benefit such as special assessments for property improvements, like the paving of sidewalks and curbs.[61] When real estate is bought or sold during the year, the real property tax is apportioned between the buyer and seller on the basis of the number of days each one held the property during the real property tax year. (See ¶ 802.01.)

To qualify as a deductible personal property tax, the tax base must use the value of the personal property being taxed. In addition, the tax must be imposed on an annual basis, even if collected more frequently. *Ad valorem* (value-based) taxes imposed on both tangible personal property and intangible property are deductible as itemized deductions.[62]

State and local income taxes a taxpayer pays during the year are deductible as an itemized deduction. This includes amounts withheld from an employee's pay for state and local income taxes. As a cash method taxpayer, amounts paid to state and local governments are deductible in the year paid, regardless of the year to which they were applied. Thus, taxpayers deduct as itemized deductions all amounts paid during the year as estimated payments to state and local governments, as well as any amounts paid during the year to satisfy the amount owed when filing a prior year's state or local income tax return. Even if a portion of the estimated taxes paid or amounts owed when filing one's tax return are attributable to profits reported from a sole proprietorship, state and local income taxes are considered a personal expense of the individual taxpayers and, as such, are only deductible as an itemized deduction.

Example 44: Karen and John Bolton file a joint tax return. In 2009, Karen began her own business and made timely quarterly estimated payments to the state government of $500 on April, June, and September of 2009, and January of 2010. During 2009, John had $3,500 of state income tax withheld from his wages by his employer, and on April 10, 2009, the Boltons paid $800 to the state government when they filed their 2008 state income tax return. On April 15, 2010, the Boltons paid $950 to the state government when they filed their 2009 state income tax return. The Boltons will deduct from AGI a total of $5,800 in 2009 for state and local income taxes.

April 15, 2009 (1st quarter estimate payment)	$ 500
June 15, 2009 (2nd quarter estimate payment)	500
September 15, 2009 (3rd quarter estimate payment)	500
State and local income taxes withheld during 2009	3,500
Amount paid when filing 2008 state income tax return	800
Total deduction for state and local income taxes in 2009	$5,800

---

[59] Code Sec. 164(a).
[60] Code Sec. 164(a)(1) and Reg. § 1.164-1(a).

[61] Reg. § 1.164-3(b).
[62] Reg. § 1.164-3(c).

The $500 paid to the state for the fourth quarter estimated tax payment for 2009 was not paid until 2010, and under the cash method, the Boltons cannot deduct this amount until 2010. Similarly, the $950 paid on April 15, 2010, is deductible as an itemized deduction in 2010.

Planning Pointer: The *Emergency Economic Stabilization At of 2008* (P.L. 110-343) extended through December 31, 2009, the election to deduct state and local general sales taxes in lieu of state and local income taxes. Individual taxpayers may elect to deduct either state and local income taxes or state and local general sales taxes as an itemized deduction on their federal income tax returns.[63] The deduction is the greater of either: (1) the total of actual general sales taxes paid as substantiated by accumulated receipts; or (2) an amount from the IRS generated sales tax tables plus, if any, the amount of general sales taxes paid in the purchase of a motor vehicle, boat, or other items as prescribed by the IRS. The sales tax paid upon the purchase of qualified motor vehicles may also be permitted to increase the standard deduction as a result of the enactment of *The American Recovery and Reinvestment Tax Act of 2009* (P.L. 111-5) (see ¶ 1304.02).

Income tax paid to foreign governments can be deducted as an itemized deduction. Chapter 11 mentioned that taxpayers may qualify to take a tax credit for income taxes paid. Similar rules apply to individual taxpayers. As you may recall, a foreign tax credit is allowed only in situations where the taxpayer has enough foreign-source income to justify claiming a tax credit (see ¶ 1117.04). Since the tax benefits to claiming a tax credit always outweigh a tax deduction, when amounts paid for foreign income taxes qualify for a tax credit, taxpayers are better off opting to claim the credit over an itemized deduction. Taxpayers have the option of deducting foreign income taxes as an itemized deduction or taking them as a tax credit, but not both.

Charitable contributions. Individuals can deduct as itemized deductions contributions they make to qualified charitable organizations. As discussed in Chapter 5, qualified charitable organizations can be classified as public charities or private foundations, depending upon whether the charitable organization receives its funding from the general public or private sources. Churches, public universities, and many other organizations like the Red Cross, United Way, and Goodwill receive their funding from the general public and are examples of public charities.

Private foundations, on the other hand, are entities formed with the express purpose of making grants to unrelated organizations or institutions or to individuals for scientific, educational, cultural, religious, or other charitable purposes. Private foundations typically receive most of their funding from one source, whether it be a family, a groups of individuals, or a corporation.[64] Private operating foundations directly carry out their own activities and are required to spend at least 85 percent of their earnings on carrying out these activities, as well as pass certain other tests. A private nonoperating foundation is a privately-funded tax-exempt non-profit organization that does not meet the requirements of a private operating foundation. Most private foundations make contributions to other qualifying charities in carrying out their role as a qualified charitable organization.

Planning Pointer: To determine whether or not a contribution is made to a qualifying organization, taxpayers can check IRS Publication 78, which lists most qualifying organizations. Taxpayers can also contact the IRS Exempt/Government Entities Division to find out when an organization is a qualified charitable organization.

[63] Code Sec. 164(b)(5).

[64] Code Sec. 170(b)(1)(E).

As with corporate taxpayers, both cash and property contributions can be deducted. In most instances, the FMV of the property contributed is used in computing the charitable contribution deduction; however, special rules apply to contributions of ordinary income and capital gain property.[65] Taxpayers cannot deduct the full FMV for contributing ordinary income property (like inventory and property held short-term) to a charity. Instead the deduction is limited to the taxpayer's (lower) adjusted basis in the property. Likewise, a taxpayer's charitable contribution deduction is limited to the property's adjusted basis when capital gain property that is not publicly traded stock is contributed to a private nonoperating foundation. However, the contribution of capital gain property to a public charity is not subject to this same limitation unless the property is tangible personal property and the public charity uses the property in a way that is unrelated to the charity's purpose. In those situations, the taxpayer's deduction would once again be limited to the property's adjusted basis. (See ¶ 511.02.)

The value of an individual's personal services rendered to a charitable organization is not deductible, and payments for admission to or for participation in a charity event (for example, a ball, banquet, or athletic event) are treated as charitable contributions only to the extent that the payment exceeds the FMV of the admission price or other privileges associated with the event.[66] Taxpayers who use their own personal automobile for charitable purposes can deduct a standard mileage rate of $.14 per mile in 2009. Parking fees and tolls may be deducted in addition to this amount. Expenses related to travel for charitable purposes can be deducted, but only 50 percent of meals are allowed.[67]

 Reason for the Rule: All charitable contributions made by an individual, including those made from income generated by a sole proprietorship, are deductible as itemized deductions. This prevents the sole proprietor from being able to classify all of their charitable contribution as a trade or business expenses and using them to reduce both AGI as well as their profits from the business. To do so would allow sole proprietors an unfair advantage over individual taxpayers who do not operate a sole proprietorship. This rule is also administratively convenient, as it prevents individual taxpayers and the IRS from spending time and money determining the "true" nature of the contribution.

Example 45: During the year, Daryl Chesterfield makes a $100 donation to a family who lost all their possessions in a fire that destroyed their home. From his business checking account Daryl contributes $500 to his college alma mater, $250 to the Girl Scouts, and $100 to the local public broadcasting station receiving in return a DVD valued at $20. Of these amounts, Daryl can deduct $830 ($500 + $250 + $80) as an itemized deduction for his contributions. The donation to the fire victims is not deductible because it was not made to a qualified charitable organization, and the $100 donation to the public broadcasting station must be reduced by the $20 FMV of the DVD Daryl received.

Deductions for contributions are generally limited to 50 percent of an individual taxpayer's AGI, but in some cases a 20- or 30-percent limit applies. An overall 50-percent limit generally applies to all contributions made to qualified public charities and private operating foundations; however, when appreciated property is contributed and its FMV is deducted, these contributions are subject to a 30-percent limit. The overall 30-percent AGI limit applies to all cash contributions made to nonoperating private foundations, with a 20-percent limit imposed on contributions of appreciated capital gain property when its FMV is deducted.

---

[65] Code Sec. 170.

[66] Rev. Rul. 67-246, 1967-2 CB 104, amplified by Rev. Proc. 90-12, 1990-1 CB 471; Rev. Proc. 92-102, 1992-2 CB 579; Rev. Proc. 93-49, 1993-2 CB 581.

[67] Reg. § 1.170A-1(g); Rev. Proc. 2008-72, IRB 2008-38, September 28, 2008.

¶ 1304.03

Spotlight: The Pension Protection Act of 2006 not only made changes to pensions, but also to the ability to deduct charitable contributions by all types of taxpayers, including individuals and corporations. Donors of charitable contributions of cash, checks or other monetary gifts must now retain certain records of the gift, regardless of the amount. Specifically, the donor must maintain either: (1) a bank record; or (2) a receipt, letter, or other written communication from the donee indicating the name of the donee organization, the date the contribution was made, and the amount of the contribution. If these records are not kept for each donation made, then no deduction is allowed for the charitable contribution.[68]

A deduction under Code Sec. 170 for the charitable contribution of a clothing or household item by an individual, partnership or corporation will only be permitted if the item is in good used condition or better. By regulation, the IRS can deny a deduction for the contribution of a clothing or household item that has minimal monetary value. However, these restrictions do not apply if: (1) a deduction of more than $500 is claimed for the single clothing or household item, and (2) the taxpayer includes a qualified appraisal with respect to the item with the tax return on which the deduction is claimed.

A special rule applies to individuals for contributions of appreciated capital gain property where (a higher) FMV is deducted. This would include contributions of certain long-term property including real or intangible property (stocks and bonds), or tangible personal property that the charity puts to related use (for example, artwork to an art museum). Because the (higher) FMV of these items is deductible, normally the taxpayers must apply a lower AGI ceiling (30 percent). However, individual taxpayers have the option of electing to reduce the amount of the deduction by the amount of appreciation (and, therefore, only deduct the adjusted basis of the property) and use the higher 50 percent AGI ceiling.

Example 46: Robert Pringle's AGI is $50,000 for 2009. During the year Robert donates capital gain property with a FMV of $18,000 to a qualified public charity. Robert's basis in the property is $16,000. He also contributes $5,000 cash to a private operating foundation. If Robert deducts the $18,000 FMV for the appreciated property, it will be subject to an overall 30-percent AGI limit ($50,000 × 30% = $15,000). Since the $18,000 FMV of the property exceeds 30 percent of his AGI, Robert's deduction for the capital gain property is limited to $15,000. When applying the 50-percent limit to the $5,000 cash contribution, Robert's total contributions of $20,000 ($15,000 for the property + $5,000 cash) do not exceed 50 percent of his AGI ($50,000 × 50% = $25,000). Thus, Robert's total charitable contribution for 2009 is limited to $20,000, and the $3,000 excess contribution for the contribution of capital gain property ($18,000 − $15,000) is carried over to 2010.

Example 47: Assume the same facts as in Example 46, except that Robert elects to reduce his contribution in the capital gain property and deduct his $16,000 basis instead of FMV. Both contributions are now subject to an overall 50-percent limit. Robert's total contribution of $21,000 ($16,000 for the capital gain property + $5,000 cash) does not exceed his $25,000 limit ($50,000 × 50%), and consequently, the entire $21,000 can be deducted as itemized deductions on his 2009 tax return.

As illustrated in Examples 46 and 47, two options can produce very different results, both in the year the property is contributed and in future tax years to which the disallowed amounts are carried over. Under the first option, Robert can deduct the full FMV and apply the 30-percent limit. This will produce a $20,000 deduction for 2009 and a $3,000 carryover that can be utilized in 2010–2014. Thus,

---

[68] Code Sec. 170(f)(17).

if Robert believes that he will be able to utilize the $3,000 in the next five years, his total contribution deduction will equal $23,000 ($20,000 in 2009 + $3,000 in subsequent carryover years).

Under the second option, Robert reduces the amount of his deduction by the $2,000 appreciation associated with that property ($18,000 - $16,000) and applies the higher 50-percent AGI limit. However, the amount by which the contribution is reduced ($2,000 in Robert's case) cannot be carried over to any other tax year. If Robert elects this second option, his total charitable contribution deduction would be the $21,000 deducted in 2009. The $2,000 difference between the two options represents the reduced deduction Robert would give up in exchange for the higher AGI limit and the opportunity to deduct more in 2009.

 Planning Pointer: Individual taxpayers concerned that any carryovers may never be fully utilized may find it advantageous to elect to deduct the (lower) adjusted basis and use a higher AGI limit. This decision becomes easier to make the smaller the amount of appreciation on the contributed property. For example, it would be easier to permanently reduce the amount available to be deducted if the difference between FMV and adjusted basis were $500 versus if the difference were $50,000. When the full FMV is deducted, amounts carried over to subsequent tax years will be subject to the same 30 percent (20 percent) reduced ceilings. Since the carryover period expires after five years, the amount of the carryover generated by deducting the higher FMV needs to be taken into consideration.

The rules regarding the contribution limits are summarized in Table 13-3.

Table 13-3 Charitable Contribution Limits for Individual Taxpayers

	Amount Deducted	50% limit applies	30% limit applies	20% limit applies
Public Charities and Private Operating Foundations:				
Cash contributions	FMV	X		
Ordinary income property	Adjusted basis	X		
Capital gain property	FMV		X	
Capital gain property	Adjusted basis	X		
Private Nonoperating Foundations:				
Cash contributions	FMV		X	
Ordinary income property	Adjusted basis		X	
Capital gain property	FMV			X
Capital gain property	Adjusted basis		X	

Personal casualty and theft losses. Individual taxpayers can deduct as itemized deductions losses arising from fire, storm, shipwreck, or other casualty, or from theft of nonbusiness property.[69] A casualty loss is generally deductible in the year in which the casualty occurred, even if the taxpayer does not repair or replace the property until a later tax year. If the casualty loss occurs

---

[69] Code Sec. 165(c)(3).

from a disaster in a Presidentially-declared disaster area, the deduction for the loss can be made on the tax return or amended tax return for the year in which the casualty occurred or the year immediately prior to the year the disaster occurred.[70]

The amount of the deductible loss for nonbusiness casualties is calculated differently than for business casualty losses which were discussed in Chapter 8 (see ¶ 802.01). Like the rules for business casualties, only uninsured losses are deductible; however, the amount of the loss for nonbusiness property is always the *lesser* of its decline in FMV or its adjusted basis.[71] In addition, a nonbusiness casualty loss is reduced by $100 and only nonbusiness casualty losses that in aggregate exceed 10 percent of the individual taxpayer's AGI are deductible as itemized deductions.[72]

Example 48: Jim Thomas acquired a new home in 2004 for $260,000. During 2009, a fire destroyed the home. This was Jim's only casualty loss during the tax year. An appraiser had assessed the value of the home prior to the casualty to be $300,000; after the fire, the home was appraised at $100,000. During 2009, the insurance company paid Jim $180,000 in full settlement for the loss. If Jim's AGI in 2009 was $75,000, his deductible casualty loss equals $12,400.

Lesser of adjusted basis before the casualty ($260,000) or decline in FMV ($300,000 – $100,000 = $200,000)	$200,000
Less: Insurance reimbursement	(180,000)
Less: $100 per casualty	(100)
Less: 10% of AGI	(7,500)
Casualty loss deduction	$ 12,400

Spotlight: The *Emergency Economic Stabilization Act of 2008* (P.L. 110-343) permits personal casualty losses attributable to a federally declared disaster occurring in 2008 and 2009 to be deductible without regard to whether the losses exceed 10 percent of a taxpayer's adjusted gross income (AGI). The deduction for any casualty attributable to a federally declared disaster occurring in 2009 is limited to the amount of the loss that exceeds $500. As an example, if the disaster referred to in Example 48 had been the result of a federally declared disaster, the calculation of the casualty loss would have been as follows:

Lesser of adjusted basis before the casualty ($260,000) or decline in FMV ($300,000 – $100,000 = $200,000)	$200,000
Less: Insurance reimbursement	($180,000)
Less: $500 per casualty	($500)
Casualty loss deduction	$12,400

Additionally, for tax years beginning after December 31, 2007, the basic standard deduction amount may be increased due to the federally declared disaster loss if the taxpayer does not itemize on the tax return. As a further example from above, the taxpayer would be able to add the net disaster loss from the declared disaster area of $12,400 to the basic standard deduction amount as determined by the taxpayers filing status.

Miscellaneous itemized deductions. Miscellaneous itemized deductions are deductible only to the extent that in aggregate they exceed two percent of AGI.[73] Deductions subject to the two-percent limit include unreimbursed employee expenses, tax preparation fees, investment expenses

---

[70] Code Sec. 165(i).
[71] Reg. § 1.165-7(b).
[72] Code Sec. 165(h).
[73] Code Sec. 67.

(other than investment interest), and expenses related to hobby activities. Unreimbursed employee expenses include valid business expenses that individuals pay in as an employee. They also include expenses that were reimbursed by their employers under a nonaccountable plan (and hence the reimbursement is included in their taxable wages). Examples of deductible employee expenses which are subject to the two-percent limit are listed below.

- Business bad debts of an employee;
- Education that is work-related;
- Licenses and regulatory fees;
- Malpractice insurance fees;
- Subscriptions to professional journals and trade magazines related to work;
- Travel, transportation, entertainment, and gifts related to work;
- Home office expenses;
- Job search expenses;
- Union dues and expenses;
- Work clothes and uniforms not adaptable to "street wear;" and
- Tools used in work as an employee.

Some miscellaneous deductions are not subject to the two-percent AGI floor. Examples of these miscellaneous itemized deductions are listed below.

- Amortizable premium on taxable bonds,
- Casualty and theft losses from income-producing property,
- Federal estate tax on income in respect of a decedent,
- Gambling losses up to the amount of gambling winnings,
- Impairment related work expenses for persons with disabilities,
- Repayments of more than $3,000 under a claim of right, and
- Unrecovered investment in an annuity.

Example 49: Mary and Larry Smith file a joint return and report AGI of $70,000. The Smiths pay the following expenses during the year that otherwise qualify as itemized deductions.

Home mortgage interest	$5,800
Real property taxes	1,700
Subscriptions to professional journals	500
Charitable contributions	900
Tax return preparation	100
Job hunting costs	200

The Smiths's total itemized deductions equal $8,400 ($5,800 + $1,700 + $900). Although the subscriptions to professional journals, tax preparation fees, and job hunting costs all qualify as miscellaneous itemized deductions, the aggregate for these expenses ($500 + $100 + $200 = $800) does not exceed two percent of AGI ($70,000 × 2% = $1,400).

 Spotlight: When AGI exceeds certain threshold amounts, itemized deductions are reduced. The threshold for 2009 is AGI in excess of $166,800 ($83,400 for MFS), and for most taxpayers the amount of their total itemized deductions is reduced by three percent of the excess amount.[74] Although the details regarding the phase out of

---

[74] Code Sec. 68.

> itemized deductions for higher-income individual taxpayers is beyond the scope of this discussion, it is important to note that any amounts that are included in gross income increase the taxpayer's AGI and, accordingly, may further reduce their itemized deductions.

¶ 1305 Net Operating Loss

Negative taxable income on an individual income tax return is not indicative of a net operating loss (NOL) since many personal expenses are allowed in the calculation of taxable income. However, individuals who operate their businesses as sole proprietorships may, in fact, have an NOL. As with corporate taxpayers, NOLs can be carried back two tax years and carried forward 20 years. An NOL carried over to another tax year is treated as an ordinary loss when computing (or recomputing in the case of an NOL carry back) AGI for that carryover year.

.01 Calculating the Amount of NOL

In determining the extent to which an individual's negative taxable income is attributable to a net operating loss, the following adjustments must be made.

1. Any NOL carryovers from other tax years that are included in the calculation of taxable income must be added back.

2. All personal and dependency exemption amounts deducted from AGI must be added back to taxable income.

3. Itemized deductions (other than deductible casualty and theft losses) in excess of nonbusiness income must be added back to taxable income. If the taxpayer does not itemize, then the standard deduction in excess of nonbusiness income is added back.

4. Nonbusiness capital losses in excess of nonbusiness capital gains must be added back.

5. Business capital losses in excess of the *sum of* (1) business capital gains and (2) any nonbusiness capital gains in excess of nonbusiness capital losses and other nonbusiness deductions must be added back.[75]

6. Any 50-percent exclusion on the gain from qualified small business stock must be added to taxable income.[76]

7. The domestic production activities (DPA) deduction is added back (see ¶ 509).

Nonbusiness income includes income from investments, such as interest, dividends, annuities, etc. It also includes capital gains on the sale of investment. Salary is considered business income, and losses from rental property are considered business losses. Deductible contributions to a self-employed individual's own retirement plan are considered nonbusiness deductions.[77]

Example 50: Jim and Kim Yates have two dependent children and file a joint tax return for 2009. The Yates compute their taxable income and NOL for 2009 as follows.

Calculation of Taxable Income

Gross Income:

Salaries	$ 52,000
Interest income	4,000
Loss from sole proprietorship	(100,000)
Nonbusiness long-term capital loss	(3,000)
Adjusted Gross Income	($ 47,000)

---

[75] Reg. § 1.172-3(a)(2).
[76] Code Sec. 172(d)(2)(B).

[77] Code Sec. 172(d)(4) and Reg. § 1.172-3(a)(3)(iv).

Less: Itemized deductions		
Mortgage interest	$8,000	
Real estate taxes	2,100	
State income taxes	900	
Charitable contributions	5,000	(16,000)
Less: Personal exemptions (4 × $3,650)		(14,600)
Taxable Income (Loss)		($ 77,600)

Calculation of NOL

Taxable Income (Loss)	($ 77,600)
Add back: Personal exemptions	14,600
Add back: Nonbusiness losses ($3,000) over nonbusiness gains ($0)	3,000
Add back: Itemized deductions, other than casualty losses ($16,000) over nonbusiness income ($4,000)	12,000
NOL generated in 2009	($ 48,000)

.02 Carryover Provisions

NOLs can be carried back to the two years preceding the loss year and then forward to the 20 years following the loss year. Taxpayers may elect to forgo the entire carryback period and just carry forward the NOL 20 years. Once this election is made, it is irrevocable. The election must be made by the return due date (including extensions) for the tax year of the NOL. The election may also be made on an amended return filed within six months of the due date of an original timely-filed return (excluding extensions).[78]

In a year in which an NOL is carried back, any income, deductions, or credits that are based on or limited to a percentage of AGI must be recomputed based on the recomputed AGI after applying the NOL deduction in the carryback year. However, tax law allows the limit on charitable contributions in a carryback year to continue to be applied using the original amount of AGI. After taxable income is recomputed with the NOL carryback, regular income tax, alternative minimum tax, and tax credits are recomputed. The difference between taxes owed or refunded on the original tax return and the newly recomputed return are refunded to the taxpayer. If the recomputed taxable income is negative, the seven adjustments to convert negative taxable income into NOL for the year are repeated.[79]

¶ 1306 Calculation of Taxes Owed or Refund Due

Individual taxpayers compute their regular tax liability by applying progressive tax rates to their taxable income. In addition, individual taxpayers who do not pay sufficient amounts of tax through the regular income tax system may be subject to AMT. Taxpayers who operate a business as a sole proprietorship add the self-employment taxes from their net earnings from the business to their total income taxes to determine their total tax liabilities.

Like corporate taxpayers, individual taxpayers have a variety of tax credits that can be used to offset tax liability. In addition to the nonrefundable business tax credits and the foreign tax credit introduced in Chapter 11, several personal tax credits are available to individual taxpayers. These tax credits are listed in Figure 13-4.

---

[78] Code Sec. 172(b); Reg. § 1.172-4.   [79] Reg. § 1.172-5.

Figure 13-4 Personal Tax Credits

Nonrefundable Personal Credits

- Lifetime learning education credit
- American Opportunity Tax Credit (for certain taxpayers)
- Child and dependent care credit
- Adoption credit
- Credit for the elderly and the disabled
- Mortgage interest credit
- Nonbusiness energy property credit
- Residential energy efficient property credit
- Hybrid automobile credit
- Child tax credit (for certain taxpayers)

Refundable Personal Credits

- Credit for prepayment of taxes
- Credit for overpayment of social security taxes
- Earned income credit
- Child tax credit (for certain taxpayers)
- Making work pay credit
- First-time home buyer credit
- American Opportunity Tax Credit (for certain taxpayers)

Reason for the Rule: Reacting to the nationwide slump in housing sales, rising unemployment, and the weakness in the credit markets, *The Housing and Economic Recovery Act of 2008* (P.L. 110-289) created a tax credit for first-time homebuyers who purchased a principal residence in the United States after April 8, 2008, and before July 1, 2009. To qualify, the taxpayer could not have an ownership interest in a principal residence in the prior three years. The refundable income tax credit was equal to 10 percent of the purchase price of the home, up to a maximum credit of $7,500 ($3,750 for a married taxpayer filing a separate return) and was subject to a phase out for higher-income taxpayers.

For homes purchased after 2008 and before December 1, 2009, *The American Recovery and Reinvestment Tax Act of 2009* (P.L. 111-5) increased the first-time homebuyer credit to $8,000 ($4,000 for a married taxpayer filing a separate return) and it does not have to be repaid unless within 36 months of the date of purchase the taxpayer sells the home or the taxpayer (and spouse if married) cease to use the home as their primary residence.

Eligible taxpayers who purchased a home after April 8, 2008, and before January 1, 2009, and claimed the credit in 2008 must begin repaying the credit over a 15-year period, beginning in 2010. The changes made by *The American Recovery and Reinvestment Tax Act of 2009* (P.L. 111-5) do not modify the requirement for the repayment of the 2008 credit amount. In addition, if the taxpayer claiming the 2008 credit sells the home or stops using it as his or her principal residence, he or she must repay the entire

> remaining unpaid balance of the credit in the year in which the sale or change of use occurs. This provision contained in *The Housing and Economic Recovery Act of 2008* (P. L. 110-289) can be a burden for taxpayers who cease to use a home as a principal residence but do not sell it.

The nonrefundable personal tax credits, along with any general business credit or foreign tax credit, can be used to offset an individual's income tax liability (both regular and AMT). Since these credits are nonrefundable, they can only reduce the taxpayer's income tax liability to zero. The refundable credits, which include any amounts withheld during the year and amounts paid as estimated tax payments, can then be used to offset any remaining income tax liability and self-employment taxes. Any excess, of course, would be refunded to the taxpayer or can be applied against next year's taxes owed. Figure 13-5 summarizes the process of determining the amount of taxes owed by or to be refunded to an individual taxpayer.

Figure 13-5 Calculation of an Individual Taxpayer's Taxes Owed (or to be Refunded)

Regular income tax liability (based on taxable income)	$xx,xxx
Plus: Alternative minimum tax (if any)	xx,xxx
Less: Nonrefundable tax credits	(xx,xxx)
Remaining tax liability (cannot be less than zero)	$xx,xxx
Plus: Self-employment taxes	xx,xxx
Less: Refundable tax credits	(xx,xxx)
Taxes owed (to be refunded)	$xx,xxx

The remainder of this chapter discusses in further detail some of the distinguishing features of the individual regular income tax calculation and the computation of AMT.

.01 Regular Income Tax Liability

Progressive tax rates are applied to an individual's taxable income depending on the taxpayer's filing status. The four tax rates can be found in the Appendix at the back of this textbook (MFJ and surviving spouse share the same tax rates). Currently, there are six tax brackets for individuals: 10, 15, 25, 28, 33, and 35 percent. The level of taxable income needed to move into each of these brackets is different for each filing status. As a general rule, the most favorable filing status is MFJ; the least favorable is MFS.

Example 51: Karen and John Snyder file a joint tax return for 2009. They have taxable income of $150,000. Using Schedule Y-1, *Married Filing Jointly or Qualifying Widow(er),* found in the Appendix of this textbook and reproduced below, the Snyders' taxable income falls in the 28-percent tax bracket. Therefore they multiply the $12,950 excess of $150,000 over $137,050 by 28 percent and add this amount to $26,637.50. The Snyders's tax liability is $30,263.50 (($12,950 × 28%) + $26,637.50).

Schedule Y-1 — Married Filing Jointly or Qualifying Widow(er) - 2009

If taxable income is over—	But not over—	The tax is:
$0	$16,700	10% of the amount over $0
$16,700	$67,900	$1,670.00 plus 15% of the amount over $16,700
$67,900	$137,050	$9,350.00 plus 25% of the amount over $67,900
$137,050	$208,850	$26,637.50 plus 28% of the amount over $137,050
$208,850	$372,950	$46,741.50 plus 33% of the amount over $208,850
$372,950	no limit	$100,894.50 plus 35% of the amount over $372,950

Special tax rates on qualified dividends and net capital gains. Individual taxpayers have the advantage of paying lower tax rates on qualified dividends and net capital gains. Individuals and corporations use a similar netting process to determine the tax consequences of gains and losses on the sale of business and investment property. Both allow capital losses to be netted against capital gains and both separate long-term gains and losses from short-term gains and losses during the netting process (see ¶ 901). However, corporate taxpayers pay the same rate of tax on all types of income, including gains from the sale of property, whereas the tax rates on long-term capital gains for individual taxpayers can be zero, 15, 25, or 28 percent. To understand which tax rate applies, it is first necessary to understand the types of property that are subject to the maximum 25-percent and 28-percent tax rates. Long-term capital gains that are not taxed at a maximum 25-percent or 28-percent rate are taxed at the 15-percent rate (zero percent for taxpayers in the 10- and 15-percent tax brackets). For the tax years 2008 through 2010, the capital gains tax rate for taxpayers in the 10 and 15 percent tax brackets is reduced to zero on property that had previously been taxed at five percent in 2007.

Planning Pointer: In 2009, taxpayers holding capital gain property with a five-year holding period are taxed the same (zero- or 15-percent) upon disposition of such property as they are for any long-term capital gain property. After 2010, however, the maximum tax rate for capital gains will revert to 20 percent and the tax rate for property held for more than five years will become 18 percent. Taxpayers who would qualify for a 10 percent capital gain tax rate (taxpayers in the 10 percent or 15 percent tax brackets) would pay only 8 percent on five-year capital gain property. The earliest holding period for the acquisition of property to qualify for these five-year holding period tax rates was January 1, 2006. Taxpayers need to plan dispositions of capital assets with the five-year holding period in mind during the period of time leading up to 2011. Retaining assets which would meet the five-year holding period after 2010 would reduce the income tax upon the disposition of such assets in 2011 and thereafter.[80]

Capital gains taxed at a maximum 28-percent tax rate. Gains from the sale of Section 1202 small business stock that qualify for the 50-percent exclusion (see ¶ 806) plus gains and losses on the sale of collectibles held for more than a year are netted against one another separately from other long-term capital gains and losses. The net gains from the sale of collectibles and Section 1202 stock is taxed at a maximum 28-percent tax rate. Collectibles include antiques, stamp and coin collections, rugs, artwork, gems, and metals.[81]

Spotlight: When Section 1202 stock is sold for a gain, 50 percent of the gain is excluded (see ¶ 806). Therefore, when the tax laws require that this gain be taxed at a 28-percent

---

[80] Tax Increase Prevention and Reconciliation Act of 2005 (P. L. 109-222) Act Sec. 102.   [81] Code Sec. 1(h)(5)(A).

maximum rate, the effective tax rate is actually only 14 percent of the realized gain. For example, when an individual taxpayer realizes $100,000 gain on the sale of Section 1202 stock, only 50 percent of the gain is taxed. If the maximum tax rates applies to the recognized gain, then the taxes owed on the gain equal $14,000 ($50,000 × 28%). Hence, the true tax rate on the realized gain is 14 percent ($14,000 ÷ $100,000). This 14-percent tax rate is close to the 15-percent maximum tax rate that applies to most long-term capital gains.

Capital gains taxed at a maximum 25-percent tax rate. In Chapter 9, you learned that after Section 1231 gains and losses are netted against one another, any net Section 1231 gain is treated as long-term capital gain (after any nonrecaptured Section 1231 losses for the past five years have been considered). Consequently, when individual taxpayers sell depreciable real business property at a gain, it is possible that the Section 1231 gain may end up taxed at the lower capital gain tax rate. Often, the reason depreciable property is sold at a gain is because its adjusted basis has been significantly reduced by accumulated depreciation. When depreciation is taken on the tax return, the taxpayer's income tax liability is reduced by the amount of the deduction times the taxpayer's marginal tax rate. Since taxpayers' (ordinary) marginal tax rates are generally higher than the 5- or 15-percent maximum net capital gains tax rate, the tax laws require that to the extent that the gain on the sale of depreciable real property is due to depreciation (and not appreciation) such gain is subject to a maximum 25-percent tax rate. The gain taxed attributable to depreciation of real property is known as **unrecaptured Section 1250 gain.** The amount of this gain equals the *lesser* of (1) the amount of recognized gain or (2) the amount of accumulated depreciation taken on the property.[82]

Example 52: Tammy Bryant sold an office building for $400,000. Tammy purchased the office building six years ago for $300,000 and, over the years, she has deducted MACRS totaling $120,000. Tammy's adjusted basis in the building is $180,000 ($300,000 – $120,000) and her gain on the sale equals $220,000 ($400,000 – $180,000). Because Tammy took depreciation deductions totaling $120,000 with respect to this property, $120,000 of the gain is unrecaptured Section 1250 gain, which is taxed at a maximum 25-percent tax rate. The remaining $100,000 of gain ($220,000 – $120,000) is taxed at a maximum 15-percent rate. The amount taxed at the 15-percent maximum rate represents the gain due to appreciation during Tammy's ownership of the building ($400,000 – $300,000 cost basis).

 Spotlight: The 25-percent maximum tax rate applies only to *gains* from the sale of depreciable realty. When depreciable realty is sold at a loss, the loss is treated as a Section 1231 loss. When Section 1231 losses exceed Section 1231 gains, the net Section 1231 loss is deducted against ordinary income and is not part of the netting process involving capital gains and losses (see ¶ 904).

The netting process. All capital gains and losses are netted against one another within their own "groups." Thus, short-term capital losses (including short-term loss carryovers from a prior year) are netted against short-term capital gains, gains and losses from property taxed at a maximum 28-percent rate are netted against one another, and finally long-term capital gains and losses taxed at 15 percent are netted against one another. After the gains and losses are netted within their own columns, the focus of the netting process is utilizing net losses to offset net gains. Using the diagram in Figure 13-6, the various columns represent the different types of capital gains and losses. They are listed in order in which gains are taxed. Short-term capital gains are taxed at the taxpayer's marginal tax rate, and, therefore, are shown first (Column A), followed by long-term

---

[82] Code Sec. 1(h)(1).

capital gains taxed at a maximum 28-percent rate (Column B), and then long-term capital gains taxed as a maximum 25-percent rate (Column C). The last column of gains to be offset is those that are taxed at the lowest (zero- or 15-percent maximum) rate (Column D). Figure 13-6 explains the steps involved in the continuation of the netting process for individual taxpayers.

The first two steps involve utilizing as much of the long-term capital loss as possible. Only after all net long-term losses have been offset by net long-term capital gains can any net long-term loss offset net short-term capital gains. The goal in the netting process is to continue offsetting gains and losses until every column reports a gain or every column reports a loss.

Figure 13-6 Netting Process for Capital Gains and Losses by Individual Taxpayers

A Short-term	B Long-term (28% maximum)	C Long-term (25% maximum)	D Long-term (0% / 15% maximum)
$xx,xxx	$xx,xxx	$xx,xxx	$xx,xxx
(xx,xxx)	(xx,xxx)	(xx,xxx)	(xx,xxx)
Net ST gain (loss)	*Net 28% gain (loss)*	*25% gain*	*Net 15% gain (loss)*

Step 1: If there is a net loss in Column D, the loss is first used to offset any long-term capital gain in Column B and then any gain in Column C. This process of offsetting long-term gains and losses ensures once again that the gains taxed at the highest 28-percent rate are offset first. Any remaining loss can then be used to offset short-term capital gains (Column A). If there is no net loss in Column D, or if the entire net loss from Column D is utilized during this netting process, continue with Step 2.

Step 2: If there is a net loss in Column B, the loss is first used to offset any long-term capital gain in Column C and then any gain in Column D. Any remaining loss can then be used to offset net short-term capital gain in Column A.

Step 3: Offset the loss in Column A against any net long-term capital gain in Column B, and then Column C, and finally Column D. This order ensures that the long-term gains taxed at the highest rates are offset first.[83] At this point, all gains and losses should be netted.

Example 53: Jim Henderson had AGI of $70,000 before considering the following capital gains and losses that he incurred during the year. Jim also has a $10,000 short-term capital loss carryover from the previous tax year.

Gain on the sale of a property held 11 months (Column A)	4,000
Loss on the sale of a collectible (Column B)	4,000
Unrecaptured Section 1250 gain (Column C)	25,000
Gain on the sale of long-term property (Column D)	11,000
Loss on the sale of long-term property (Column D)	8,000

Jim starts the netting process by putting each gain and loss in its respective group (column) and netting gains and losses within groups, as shown below.

---

[83] Code Sec. 1(h)(5).

A	B	C	D
Short-term	Long-term (28% maximum)	Long-term (25% maximum)	Long-term (0% / 15% maximum)
($10,000)	($4,000)	$25,000	$11,000
4,000			(8,000)
($ 6,000)			$ 3,000

Jim then continues the netting process, starting with Step 2 (he skips Step 1 after having reported a net gain in Column D). He offsets his net long-term capital losses against long-term capital gains, starting with the gains subject to the highest tax rate. Jim's net loss from Column B is used to offset the gain from Column C. Once the entire loss net long-term capital losses has been utilized, Jim's focus shifts to Step 3, where he offsets his short-term losses against long-term gains, again starting with the highest taxed gain. Jim utilizes the net loss from Column A to offset the remaining net gain from Column C. Once the entire loss from Column A is utilized, the netting process is complete as there are no more losses to offset against the remaining gains.

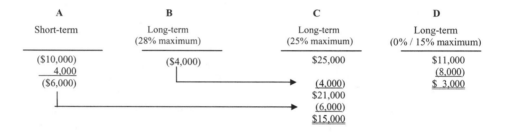

Jim includes the net $18,000 of net capital gain ($15,000 + $3,000) in AGI. When Jim goes to calculate his regular tax liability on his taxable income, he will be sure to tax the $15,000 at no more than a 25-percent tax rate, and the $3,000 at a maximum of 15 percent (along with any qualified dividends Jim includes in AGI).

For example, if Jim's taxable income for 2009 is $79,700, which includes $5,000 of qualified dividends and $18,000 of net capital gain from above, as a single taxpayer, he computes his tax liability as follows.

Tax on $56,700 ($79,700 – $18,000 – $5,000) using Schedule X from the Appendix	$10,363
Tax on $15,000 at 25%	3,750
Tax on $8,000 at 15%	1,200
Total regular income tax liability	$15,313

¶ 1307 Alternative Minimum Tax

Individuals are subject to alternative minimum tax (AMT) to the extent that it exceeds their regular income tax liability.[84] The individual AMT was designed to prevent high-income taxpayers from avoiding significant tax liability through the use of certain exclusions and deductions, referred to as tax preference or adjustment items.

---

[84] Code Sec. 55.

Like the calculation of corporate AMT discussed in Chapter 10, the calculation of an individual's AMT begins by adjusting taxable income for certain adjustments and preferences to arrive at Alternative Minimum Taxable Income (AMTI). Although many of the adjustments and preferences introduced in Chapter 10 also apply in the calculation of individual AMTI, due to the differences in how corporation taxable income and individual taxable income are calculated, differences also exist in how these two taxpayers calculate AMTI.

For example, the adjusted current earnings (ACE) adjustment that applies to corporations does not apply to individuals. Also, many of the personal deductions on the individual income tax return result in additional adjustments and preferences in the calculation of an individual's AMTI. Figure 13-7 summarizes the calculation of AMT for individuals. Table 13-4 summarizes the more common preferences and adjustments that individuals make in computing AMTI.

Figure 13-7 Calculation of Individual AMTI

	Taxable income
±	Tax preferences and adjustments
=	AMTI
-	AMT exemption
=	AMT tax base
×	AMT rates
=	Tentative minimum tax
-	Regular income tax
=	AMT (if positive amount)

Many of these adjustments you may recognize from Chapter 10; however, a few unique to individual taxpayers are listed in Table 13-4. For example, individuals are allowed to reduce taxable income by a standard deduction, itemized deductions, and exemption amounts. Some itemized deductions are not allowed for purposes of computing AMTI. Likewise, neither the standard deduction nor personal exemptions are allowed in the calculation of AMTI. Instead, a larger AMT exemption is allowed.[85] Thus, these amounts are added back to regular taxable income as positive adjustments in computing AMTI.

Table 13-4 Summary of AMT Preferences and Adjustments

Item	Adjustment Necessary to Taxable Income
Standard deduction	Added back to taxable income
Personal exemptions	Added back to taxable income
Itemized deductions	See discussion that follows (¶ 1307.01)
Gain excluded on the sale of Section 1202 stock	Add back seven percent of the exclusion to taxable income (¶ 806)
MACRS depreciation	Same as discussed in Chapter 10 (¶ 1008.01)

---

[85] Code Sec. 56(b)(1)(E).

Item	Adjustment Necessary to Taxable Income
Circulation expenditures	Same as discussed in Chapter 10 (¶ 1008.03)
Research and experimental expenditures	Same as discussed in Chapter 10 (¶ 1011.01)
Mining exploration and development costs	Same as discussed in Chapter 10 (¶ 1008.03)
Long-term contracts	Same as discussed in Chapter 10 (¶ 1008.04)
Pollution control facilities	Same as discussed in Chapter 10 (¶ 1008.03)
Certain incentive stock options	Excess of FMV over the option price at date of exercise is added back to taxable income
Passive activity losses	Net losses from passive activities, including tax shelter farm activities, not allowed
Certain tax-exempt interest	Same as discussed in Chapter 10 (¶ 1007.03)
Depletion	Same as discussed in Chapter 10 (¶ 1007.01)
Intangible drilling costs	Same as discussed in Chapter 10 (¶ 1007.02)
Alternative tax net operating loss	Recompute NOL using AMT rules and make any necessary adjustments to taxable income.

The 2009 AMT exemption amount for married individuals filing joint returns and surviving spouses is $70,950 ($35,475 for MFS) and $46,700 for unmarried individuals. For individuals whose AMTI exceeds a specified amount ($150,000 for MFJ and surviving spouses, $75,000 for MFS, and $112,500 for all others), the exemption amount is reduced by $.25 for every dollar of excess.[86] Unlike the standard deduction, personal exemptions, and other amounts used in calculating taxable income, the AMT exemption amounts are not indexed for inflation. The AMT for individuals is computed with a 26 percent tax rate applied to the first $175,000 ($87,500 for married individuals filing separately) of AMT tax base and 28 percent applied to the excess.

Example 54: A couple that files MFJ has AMTI equal to $250,000. Because this amount exceeds the $150,000 threshold by $100,000, they are required to reduce their $70,950 initial exemption by $25,000 ($100,000 × $.25). Thus, the couple's AMT exemption is reduced to $45,950 ($70,950 – $25,000).

 Spotlight: AMT was originally enacted on the premise that higher-income taxpayers tended to have greater opportunities than lower- and average-income taxpayers to take advantage of the many tax savings available through the exclusions and deductions offered in the Code. As a result, many high-income taxpayers were able to reduce their tax liability to such an extent that they paid very little (and sometimes no) tax given their true level of income generated for the year. By creating a parallel, alternative tax system, the government hoped to promote tax equity between wealthy and lower-income taxpayers.

AMT is only assessed when the tentative minimum tax from the AMT calculation exceeds the taxpayer's regular income tax liability. Unlike the regular tax rates, which are indexed annually for inflation, the AMT exemption and rates are not indexed. Accordingly, over the years a greater number of taxpayers have been subject to AMT. When first enacted in 1969, 155 individual taxpayers were subject to AMT. In 2006, this number rose to 4 million. In an effort to reduce the number of moderate-income taxpayers subject to AMT, on a number of occasions Congress has temporarily increased the AMT exemption amount. The latest effort designed to insulate an estimated 25 million middle income taxpayers from the effects of AMT occurred on February 17,

---

[86] Code Sec. 55(d)(3).

2009, when President Obama signed into law *The American Recovery and Reinvestment Act of 2009* (P.L. 111-5). This Act provided another temporary increase in the AMT exemption amounts for 2009. Although Congress continues to work on a permanent correction for the AMT, as of the date of publication of this book, no solution has been achieved and the exemption amounts for 2010 have been returned to the amounts in force before the temporary patch. Thus, the exemption amounts for tax years beginning after 2009 are scheduled to be: (1) $45,000 for married individuals filing a joint return and surviving spouses; (2) $33,750 for unmarried individuals; and (3) $22,500 for married individuals filing separate returns.

.01 AMT Itemized Deductions

Most itemized deductions allowed for purposes of calculating taxable income are deductible in computing AMTI. However, a few differences exist. For example, for purposes of computing AMTI, medical expenses are allowed only if they exceed 10 percent of AGI (versus 7.5 percent). Also, no taxes or miscellaneous deductions subject to the two-percent floor are allowed in computing AMTI. Therefore, all deductions for income and property taxes and miscellaneous deductions in excess of two percent of AGI must be added back to taxable income when computing AMTI.[87]

 Planning Pointer: When a taxpayer is regularly subject to the AMT, one strategy available is to spread out AMT preference items over two or more years rather than bunching them into one year. The sole proprietor must look at both the business AMT adjustments, such as MACRS, and the personal AMT adjustments, such as the standard deduction and personal exemptions. If the sole proprietor is subject to the AMT year after year, they may wish to look at the depreciation practices they have in place and adjust them to extend the depreciation expense over a longer period of time, and thus reducing the AMT adjustment. A sole proprietor who is borderline for AMT each year does not want to accelerate or defer revenue of the business and may want to avoid the use of bunching strategies for itemized deductions. Bunching strategies utilize the concept of accelerating deductions into one year so the taxpayer can itemize their deductions, followed by a year with very low itemized deductions in which the taxpayer then uses the standard deduction.

Example 55: Larry and Helen Bolles file a joint return. For 2009, they have four dependents and taxable income of $60,696 as shown below.

Schedule C profits	$206,000
Interest income	5,000
One-half of self-employment tax	(8,804)
Health insurance premiums	(12,500)
Contribution to self-employed retirement plans	(40,000)
AGI	$149,696
Less: Itemized deductions:	
Home mortgage interest	(25,000)
Charitable contributions	(15,000)
Real estate taxes	(28,000)
Less: Exemptions ($3,650 × 6)	(21,900)

[87] Code Sec. 56(b).

Taxable income	$ 59,796
Regular income tax (using Schedule Y-1 from the Appendix)	$ 8,134
Calculation of AMT:	
Taxable income	$ 59,796
Plus: Real estate taxes	28,000
Exemptions	21,900
AMTI	$109,696
Less: AMT exemption	(70,950)
AMT base	$ 38,746
AMT rate	× 26%
Tentative minimum tax	$ 10,074
Less: Regular income tax liability	(8,134)
AMT	$ 1,940

The Bolles will pay regular income taxes of $8,134 and AMT of $1,940. They will subtract from this amount any nonrefundable tax credits (but not reduce their total tax liability below zero), and then add to any remaining amount the self-employment taxes owed on the net earnings from self-employment.

Spotlight: The AMT does not tax qualified dividends or net capital gains taxed at a maximum 15-percent rate at the higher 26-percent/28-percent AMT rates. Instead, the special (lower) tax rates continue to apply in computing a taxpayer's AMT liability. For example, if a taxpayer's AMT base of $110,000 includes $20,000 of qualified dividend income and net capital gain, the taxpayer's tentative minimum tax would equal $26,400 (($90,000 × 26%) + ($20,000 × 15%)).

¶ 1308 Summary

While forming a sole proprietorship comes without the complexity involved in the formation of other business entities, the tax consequences of operating a business as a sole proprietorship must be considered. Although businesses that operate as sole proprietorships escape the double taxation that C corporations face, sole proprietors must remember that self-employment taxes are reported on their personal income tax returns, along with their regular income tax and AMT. The costs associated with each of these taxes needs to be considered when computing the marginal tax rate that applies to the individual taxpayers. In addition, they must be able to understand the tax laws that govern the taxation of individuals to ensure that they pay the proper amount of estimated taxes to cover each of type of tax in order to avoid penalties for underpayment of taxes.

GLOSSARY OF TERMS INTRODUCED IN THE CHAPTER

Abandoned spouse. A married individual who lives with a dependent child but had not lived with his or her spouse for the last six months of the year.

Active participation. A requirement for a taxpayer to be able to take advantage of the exception permitting a $25,000 real estate loss deduction under the passive activity loss rules. A taxpayer must own at least a 10-percent interest in the rental activity, not be a limited partner, and participate in making management decisions.

Head of household. A filing status available to taxpayers who are not married and do not qualify as a surviving spouse but maintain a household for more than half of the tax year in which a qualifying child of the taxpayer or any other person who is a dependent of the taxpayer lives.

Listed property. Certain personal property susceptible to both business and personal use. Examples include passenger automobiles, computers, and cellular telephones.

Material participation. A taxpayer who participates in a trade or business on a regular, continuous, and substantial basis is considered to materially participate in the trade or business. The tax law provides seven tests to measure whether a taxpayer's participation in a trade or business is material.

Net earnings from self-employment. The amount from which self-employment taxes of a sole proprietor are based. It equals 92.35 percent of net profits reported on Schedule C.

Passive activity loss. A loss from a rental property or a trade or business activity in which the owner does not materially participate.

Portfolio income. Income derived from investments, such as stocks, bonds, and mutual funds.

Qualified dividends. Dividends that are taxed to individual taxpayers at a rate lower than the taxpayers' marginal tax rates. They represent dividends paid on stock of a U.S. corporation or a qualified foreign corporation that the individual held for 121 days surrounding the ex-dividend date.

Surviving spouse. A filing status available to taxpayers widowed during one of the two preceding tax years who have a dependent son or daughter living with them the entire year.

Unrecaptured Section 1250 gain. A term applicable only to individual taxpayers. The portion of the gain on the sale of depreciable realty that is taxed at a maximum 25-percent tax rate.

CHAPTER PROBLEMS

The following questions and problems relate to the discussion in Chapter 13, Sole Proprietorships, which begins at ¶ 1300 in *Part V: Special Business Entity Issues*.

Chapter 13 Discussion Questions

1. What are the steps individuals use to compute taxable income and the amount of taxes owed (refunded)?

2. Given that both deductions for AGI and deductions from AGI reduce taxable income, why are deductions for AGI preferred to itemized deductions?

3. a. What are the three accounting methods that are available to a sole proprietor and how do they differ?

   b. How many accounting methods may an individual use on his or her income tax return for the same tax year?

4. What are the standard deduction amounts for 2009 and under what circumstances are they increased?

5. Individuals are required to include dividends received from C corporations in their gross income.

    a. What tax benefits are available to an individual to reduce the amount of tax paid on the dividends received?

    b. How does any tax benefit received by an individual differ from that granted to a C corporation?

6. What type of interest is deductible as an itemized deduction?

7. a. What amount is a taxpayer allowed to deduct regarding a qualified residence mortgage?

    b. What amount is a taxpayer allowed to deduct regarding points paid on a loan to acquire a principal residence?

8. What is the tax base used to compute the self-employment tax, and what is the self-employment tax rate?

9. A sole proprietor may deduct certain expenses resulting from the operations of the business either for or from AGI. Which of these expenses are deductible in computing only AGI, and which reduce both AGI and are deductible for purposes of computing net profits from the business?

10. The rules for deducting a casualty and theft loss differ depending upon whether the property involved is business property or a personal belonging. Discuss how these rules differ.

11. Some personal income taxes paid by a sole proprietor may be deductible.

    a. What types of taxes are deductible and what type of deduction are they, for or from AGI?

    b. In what accounting period are each of the taxes discussed in part (a.) deductible, the period incurred or the period in which paid?

12. In order for an individual to deduct a contribution to a charitable organization, it must first be a qualified organization.

    a. What organizations are considered "qualified" organizations?

    b. What are the limitations placed upon these organizations?

13. A sole proprietor is generally permitted to deduct losses from their trade or business in the tax year in which they occur. If the trade or business is determined to be a passive activity, how does this impact the year in which the loss is deductible? Under what circumstances may the sole proprietor be able to classify the trade or business as a nonpassive activity?

14. Does reporting negative taxable income on an individual income tax return mean that the taxpayer experienced a net operating loss for the year? Explain.

15. What is the difference between the alternative minimum tax adjustments and preferences?

16. How are the revenue and expenses of a hobby activity reported on an individual's tax return?

17. How are capital gains taxed differently than ordinary income?

18. How are gains and losses on the disposition of business assets treated by the sole proprietor different than by a C corporation?

19. Distinguish between a business and nonbusiness bad debt and the difference in the tax treatment between them?

20. What expenses may an individual deduct as a miscellaneous itemized deduction subject to the two-percent AGI limitation?

Chapter 13 Problems

1. Randy Sutton is in the process of preparing Tim James's income tax return. Tim is single, employed, and owns investment rental property. Which of the following items of expense or loss incurred by Tim may be claimed as a deduction against his gross income in arriving at adjusted gross income (*for AGI*) and which may be claimed as a deduction from his adjusted gross income (*from AGI*)?

a. Alimony payment to former spouse.

b. Loss from sale of rental property.

c. Real estate taxes on personal residence.

d. Loss from sale of investments.

e. Contribution to individual retirement account (IRA).

f. Contribution to American Cancer Society.

g. Tax preparation fees.

h. Repairs to rental property.

i. Safety deposit box fee.

j. Depreciation on rental property.

k. Employee moving expense.

l. Unreimbursed tuition for course required by employer.

m. Premiums for health insurance paid by an employee.

2. Fred and Carol Dickson have a gross income for 2009 of $25,000. Compute their AGI if they have the following allowable deductions in 2009.

- Itemized deductions—$4,750.

- One dependency exemption.

- Two personal exemptions.

- Alimony paid—$3,000.

- Contribution to IRA—$1,500.

3. Determine the standard deduction amount (including any additional standard deduction for age or blindness) that should be claimed on the returns filed by the following taxpayers in 2009.

a. Husband and wife filing jointly, both under age 65.

b. Unmarried taxpayer age 69.

c. Unmarried taxpayer born on January 1, 1945, filing as unmarried.

d. Husband and wife filing jointly, both age 55. Wife is permanently disabled and legally blind.

e. Husband filing a separate return. Wife will not file a return because her gross income is insufficient to require filing. She will not be claimed as a dependent on any person's return.

f. Married individual filing a joint return. Wife died in May of the tax year. Both husband and wife are under the age of 65 and are not considered legally blind.

4. A taxpayer has a taxable income of $150,000 for the year 2009. Calculate the regular income tax for each of the following filing statuses. There is no net capital gain or qualified dividends included in the $150,000 of taxable income.

a. Single.

b. Married filing jointly.

c. Married filing separately.

d. Head of household.

5. The following facts relate to the tax return for 2009 of a married couple who file a joint return.

Qualified-residence interest on home mortgage	$10,000
Net business income	25,000
Business interest	40,000

Net investment income	12,000
Investment interest expense	30,000

   a. Compute the amount of investment interest expense deductible on the joint return.

   b. What happens to any portion of the investment interest expense that is not deductible on the joint return?

6. In January 2009, Sydney Griffin had a mortgage on her summer beach house and a separate one for her primary residence; each loan funded the initial acquisition cost of the property. The following information pertains to the mortgages.

	Beach House	*Principal Residence*
Date of loan	January 1, 2006	January 1, 2009
Term	10 years	20 years
Mortgage origination fee (1%) paid in year loan taken out	$1,500	$2,000
Deed registration fees	200	400
Legal fees	75	115
Qualified-residence interest for tax year	4,000	9,000

What is Sydney's interest deduction for the tax year?

7. Larry's personal taxes for 2009 were as follows:

   a. County real property taxes on personal residence—$800.

   b. Special assessment paid to city for new road—$750.

   c. County real estate taxes paid on summer vacation home—$200.

   d. Federal income taxes:

      Paid in March of 2009 with 2008 tax return—$200.

      Withheld during 2009—$3,200.

      Taxes refunded when 2009 tax return was filed in April 2010—$200.

   e. State income taxes:

      Paid in March of 2009 with 2008 tax return—$30.

      Withheld during 2009—$420.

      Paid in April of 2010 when 2009 tax return was filed—$20.

   f. State sales tax—$200.

   g. State and local gasoline taxes on car driven for personal purposes—$60.

   h. State inheritance taxes—$150.

   i. Driver's license fee (for three years)—$20.

Larry uses the cash method and uses a calendar year-end. What amount of taxes can Larry claim on his 2009 federal income tax return?

8. What is the amount of the charitable contribution deduction for each of the following situations?

   a. The community's Boy Scout leader lost all his possessions when a fire destroyed his home. James gave him $2,500 to help him purchase new clothing. How much can James deduct as a charitable contribution if his adjusted gross income is $25,000?

   b. Ariel contributed $200 to each of the following organizations for the tax year: First Community Church, the American Red Cross, Private Country Club, the United Way, and the Girl Scouts of America. What amount may Ariel deduct as charitable contributions?

9. Leona Henderson, a part-time employee of the City School System, also operates a business as a swimming instructor. In 2009, Leona's salary is $10,000. She also gives private lessons from which her income is $20,000. Compute:

   a. The maximum amount of net self-employment earnings that she can earn in 2009 that will be subject to the social security component of the self-employment tax.

   b. Leona's self-employment tax for 2009.

   c. The amount Leona will deduct for AGI for the employer's share of her self-employment tax.

10. A single taxpayer has taxable income of $52,000. In addition, the taxpayer has adjustment and preference items for purposes of computing alternative minimum taxable income (AMTI) of $13,300 and $40,000, respectively. Compute the taxpayer's total income tax liability for 2009.

11. During the current tax year, a taxpayer raises dogs as a hobby. The taxpayer has the following hobby-related items:

    Hobby income—$1,150

    Taxes on real property—$350

    Dog food—$1,600

    The taxpayer's AGI (not including the hobby activity) is $52,350, and the taxpayer has $500 other miscellaneous itemized deductions not related to the hobby.

    a. Compute the amount of the deductible hobby-related expenses

    b. If the taxpayer has the following income or losses from prior years, how would this affect the determination as to whether the taxpayer's activity is a business or a hobby? What arguments can the taxpayer use to justify this as a trade or business?

       2008—$5,000 profit

       2007—$1,000 profit

       2006—$(1,000) loss

       2005—$(15,000) loss

       2004—$500 profit

       2003—$ 1,000 profit

12. Kevin Harris has AGI of $40,000 for 2009. For the tax year 2009, how much in charitable contribution deductions may Kevin be permitted under each of the following independent circumstances?

    a. Cash contributions to the Bishop's Appeal for the local Catholic Diocese in the amount of $20,000, $5,000 cash contributions to the capital campaign for Eastern University, and a $2,000 contribution to miscellaneous public charities.

    b. Cash contributions of $20,000 to a private nonoperating foundation.

    c. Cash contributions of $5,000 and a contribution of appreciated capital gain property with a FMV of $30,000 and a tax basis of $25,000. Both contributions made to a public charity.

    d. What factors should Kevin take into consideration before deciding whether to deduct the full FMV of the capital gain property or deduct the adjusted basis and use the higher 50-percent limitation?

13. George Hampton is a self-employed computer programmer with no employees. George has the following income and expenses related to the operating of his business:

Gross billings to customers during 2009	$150,000
Collections on billings during 2009	160,000
Bad debts on 2009 billings	10,000

Advertising expense	5,000
Commissions and fees paid	25,000
Insurance	8,000
Office expense	9,000
Taxes and licenses	10,000
Repairs and maintenance	20,000
Contribution to self-employed retirement plan	15,000
Payment of health insurance for George	12,000
Mileage driven using personal automobile for business	15,000 miles

a. Calculate the net profit or loss from the trade or business assuming that George uses the cash method of accounting. Assume all expenses listed above were expenses both paid and incurred during 2009.

b. Calculate George's 2009 self-employment tax.

c. What other amounts are deductible for AGI that are not allowable in calculating the net profit or loss of the business?

14. Carol Jones is an employee with wages in 2009 of $70,000. This is her only item of income for the year. Carol has the following personal expenses for 2009.

Fee paid for preparation of personal income tax return	$ 300
Subscriptions to professional journals	2,000
Home office expenses related to her employment	2,500
Unreimbursed professional license	500
Unreimbursed malpractice insurance expense	6,250
Cash contributions to public charities	2,000
State and local income taxes	2,800
Real estate taxes on primary residence	5,500
Unreimbursed medical expenses	3,800

a. What amount is Carol permitted to deduct as itemized deductions for 2009?

b. Assume that Carol is self-employed, married filing a joint tax return, and the $70,000 was her net profit before considering any of the deductions listed in part (a.) and the unreimbursed employee expenses were related to her business. How would the calculation of her deductions from AGI change?

15. Paul and Mary Thomas do not itemize and they have no dependents. Their taxable income for 2009 is $270,000 including a net long-term capital gain of $30,000 and qualified dividends of $10,000.

a. Calculate the Thomases' regular tax liability for 2009.

b. Will the Thomases' be subject to alternative minimum tax in 2009 if their only adjustments and preferences are their $11,400 standard deduction and $7,300 of personal exemptions?

16. Linda Sullivan converted her personal automobile to business use on July 1, 2008. At the time of purchase of the automobile (April 1, 2007) the purchase price was $22,800, and at the date of conversion to business use, the fair market value was $12,000.

a. What is the amount that would be used to calculate depreciation for business purposes for the automobile?

b. If the property is used 65 percent for business, what would be the maximum amount of depreciation that Linda could claim as a deduction for 2009?

c. If the property is used 35 percent for business, what would be the maximum amount of depreciation that Linda could claim as a deduction for 2009?

d. If Linda used the automobile for 6,000 properly documented business mileage and incurred $300 in parking fees and tolls, what would be the transportation deduction if she elects to use the standard mileage rate method?

17. John Church has a business operated out of his home. The business portion of the home consists of a room (400 square feet), which is used regularly and exclusively to see clients and the only location at which he operates his business. His home has a total of 2,000 square feet. For 2009, John incurs the following expenses related to his home.

Real estate taxes	$5,500
Qualified mortgage interest	7,500
Utilities	4,800
Depreciation	6,000
Insurance	500

a. If the net income from John's business is $45,000 prior to the deduction of home office expenses, what amount will he be able to deduct against the net profits from his business?

b. How do the expenses related to business use of the home affect the computation of the self-employment tax?

c. How much is John entitled to as a deduction from AGI related to these home office expenses?

d. If John were an employee and the home office was related to his employment, how would the deduction be taken on his 2009 tax return?

18. For each of the following expenditures indicate if they are deductions for AGI, from AGI, or not deductible. For deductions for AGI, be sure to mention whether they reduce net profits from the business as well as AGI, or only reduce AGI.

a. Qualified moving expenses.

b. Personal grooming items.

c. Self-employment taxes.

d. Medical expenses.

e. State income tax on business profits.

f. Contributions to retirement plan for employees.

g. Contributions to self-employed retirement plan for owner.

h. Personal mileage on automobile used for both business and personal uses.

i. Health insurance coverage paid by self-employed individual with no other coverage.

j. Loss on sale of business property.

k. Loss on sale of capital asset.

l. Deficiency interest resulting from IRS audit of business.

m. Credit card interest.

n. Hobby expenses.

o. Non-business bad debt.

19. Beth Adams had a series of transactions from the sale of investments. The sales resulted in the following transactions:

Crescent Corporation stock	$5,000	Long-term capital gain
Smith Machine Corporation stock	9,000	Long-term capital gain
Thomas Corporation stock	(6,000)	Long-term capital loss
Professional Services stock	(2,000)	Short-term capital loss
Columbia Corporation stock	4,000	Short-term capital gain

| Business land | 6,000 | Section 1231 gain |
| Business furnishings | (3,000) | Section 1231 loss |

How are the above transactions taxed on Beth's income tax returns if these are the only capital gain and loss transactions, and she is in the 25-percent marginal tax bracket? Beth has no nonrecaptured Section 1231 losses.

20. Samantha Dolan operates a small consulting business as a sole proprietor. During 2009, she has the following transactions related to the business.

Customer sales on account	$75,000
Collections from 2009 credit sales	55,000
Collections from 2008 credit sales	18,000
Business bad debts	8,000
Operating expenses incurred during 2009	44,000
Operating expenses from 2009 paid in 2009	33,000
Operating expenses from 2008 paid in 2009	10,000

 a. Calculate the net income or loss from Samantha's business using the accrual method of accounting.

 b. Calculate the net income or loss from Samantha's business using the cash method of accounting.

 c. What accounts for the difference in the two net incomes and how does this benefit or cause a problem for a trade or business?

21. Donald Maxwell is a Certified Public Accountant (CPA) who is a partner in a national CPA firm and has several other business ventures. The businesses and the hours of participation are as follows:

Description of Business	Hours worked by Donald	Hours worked by other employees	Income or (loss) from the business for 2009
Commercial real estate rental property	50	500	($25,000)
Italian ice retail store	250	2,845	15,000
Collectable train mail order sales business	185	-0-	(6,000)

With regards to the rental property, Donald is actively involved in the selection of tenants and handling of maintenance issues. Donald has an AGI of $500,000 before considering any of the above businesses.

 a. Which of the above businesses are considered to be passive activities?

 b. What will Donald's AGI be after considering the income and losses from these three other activities?

 c. What happens to any losses not deductible in 2009?

 d. How would your answer to part b. differ if Donald's AGI were $90,000 before considering any of the three activities?

 e. How would your answer to part b. differ if Donald's AGI were $140,000 before considering any of the three activities?

22. At the beginning of the year, Arthur Miller lived in Philadelphia, PA where he operated a residential real estate sales business from his personal residence as a sole proprietorship. Arthur decides to move with his family to Florida where he will reopen his sole proprietorship. On July 1, 2009, Arthur and his family drove the 1,200 miles to Florida, incurring $400

in lodging, $250 in food costs, and $15 in tolls along the way. The Millers paid $5,500 to a moving company that packed and transported their household belongings.

a. What amount may Arthur deduct on his 2009 tax return as a result of the move?

b. As a sole proprietor Arthur would like to take any moving deduction as a deduction from his business income and thus reduce his self-employment income. How will the amount be deducted?

c. How long must Arthur be employed at his new business location in order to meet the time test for purposes of deducting his moving expenses?

23. Glen Williams, a single taxpayer, had the following items of income and loss related to the preparation of his 2009 income tax return:

Gross Income

Compensation from employment (W-2)	$25,000	
Dividend income	1,000	
Loss from operation of business (nonpassive activity)	(75,000)	
Long term loss on sale of capital asset	(3,000)	
Adjusted Gross Income		($52,000)

Deductions from AGI:

Personal exemption	$3,650	
Mortgage interest	5,500	
Real estate taxes	2,500	
State income taxes	1,100	($12,750)
Taxable Income (loss)		($64,750)

Calculate the amount of Glen's 2009 NOL.

24. Flo Wolfe has seven separate businesses in which she participates, none of which involve rental property. The numbers of hours she participated and the hours of participation of her three employees in the activities during the current tax year are as follows:

Business	Flo's Hours	Employee A	Employee B	Employee C
A	115	0	0	330
B	55	0	0	25
C	525	0	0	850
D	270	200	600	200
E	215	1,900	1,600	750
F	77	0	0	0

Indicate which of the business activities would be considered to be passive activities for the current tax year.

25. Marc and Mary Lathrop, married taxpayers with two dependent children, file a 2009 joint federal income tax return containing the following information:

Gross Income:

Compensation from employment (W-2)	$ 45,000
Interest income	3,500
Income from operation of business (nonpassive activity)	100,000

Deductions from AGI:

Mortgage interest	$ 5,500
State and local income taxes	12,500
Real estate taxes	8,500
Charitable contributions	10,100

AMT Adjustment—MACRS depreciation	$ 15,000

a. Compute the Lathrops' 2009 regular income tax liability.

b. Compute the Lathrops' 2009 AMT.

Chapter 13 Review Problems

1. Joe and Cheryl Peterson are filing a joint tax return for 2009 and have two children whom they will also claim on the tax return as dependents. They are both 48 years of age in good health. Joe and Cheryl are both teachers with the local school district and in these positions have health care available for themselves and their children paid for by the school district. Cheryl has been operating a small gift shop as a supplemental source of income since 2007 in space rented from a local shopping mall operator. Information regarding their income and deductions is as follows:

Joe's gross wages and social security wages	$50,000
Cheryl's gross wages and social security wages	60,000
Interest earned—Third Community Bank	2,500
Qualified dividends—Public Utility Corporation	1,000
Alimony paid to a former spouse	12,000
State and local sales taxes paid	1,800
State and local income taxes paid	3,000
Real estate taxes paid on personal residence	6,000
Cash contributions to a private nonoperating foundation	5,000
Interest on $100,000 home equity loan—proceeds used to acquire investments	8,000

Business income and expenditures

Sales revenue	$200,000
Cost of goods sold	150,000
Health insurance Cheryl paid in addition to coverage provided by her employer	4,800
Contribution to employees' retirement plans	2,000
Home office expenses (excludes real estate taxes and mortgage interest listed above)—the office is 200 of the 2,000 total square feet of the residence	7,500
Cost of automobile used for business (acquired 1-1-08)	12,000
Operating expenses of automobile (insurance, gas, oil, and repairs)	8,600
Business tolls and parking fees	340
Business miles—8,000; total miles—20,000	
Salary and wages paid to employees	30,000
Taxes and licenses	5,000
Rent expense for equipment	16,000

Calculate the Petersons's regular income tax liability and Cheryl's self-employment taxes for 2009.

2. Philip and Pat Richardson are engaged in a business that removes and disposes of various toxins from buildings prior to demolition. The business has been very successful in past

years and the Richardsons plan on donating stock worth $100,000 to their church. The Richardsons will file a joint tax return for 2009. They have no dependents and will report in their AGI $100,000 profit from Pat's sole proprietorship and $20,000 of taxable interest. Itemized deductions (before considering the charitable contribution) include state and local income taxes of $3,000, real estate taxes of $4,000, and home mortgage interest of $6,500. They have presented you with the following options. For each option they would like you to calculate and explain the impact on their regular income taxes and Pat's self-employment tax, plus any charitable contribution carryovers that may result.

Option 1: The Richardsons elect to deduct the full FMV of the stock.

Option 2: The Richardsons elect to reduce the amount of the deduction and instead deduct the adjusted basis of the stock. Philip purchased the stock years ago for $73,000.

Chapter 13 Research Question

Jennifer Woods is 32 years old and for the last six years has been employed as a manager by Ski USA, a distributor of ski equipment and boots. In the past two years as a professional bicycle racer she has participated in approximately 50 races annually. Although she has won some of the races in which she was entered, Jennifer has incurred annual expenses that far exceed her annual income from racing. Jennifer trains extensively on a daily basis; she has sponsors who have provided her with the bicycles, clothing, and, occasionally, entry fees required for participation in these races. Otherwise she pays her own expenses which include the costs of bicycle repairs, transportation, lodging, and most entry fees. During racing season, she works a lighter schedule at Ski USA and also utilizes her vacation time. The National Bike Racing Association ranked Jennifer in two events—the dual slalom and downhill races—for which she wears a full-face helmet, chest protector, knee protection, elbow pads, goggles, and heavy-duty clothing. Jennifer wants to know if she was correct in deducting her expenses as a deduction for AGI against the winnings from the races in which she has won prize money and the sponsorship income she has received.

CHAPTER 14

Flow-Through Entities: Partnerships, LLPs, and LLCs

LEARNING OBJECTIVES

1. List the tax and nontax aspects of flow-through entities.

2. Describe how a partnership is formed and the tax implications to both the partnership and its partners when property is contributed to the partnership.

3. Illustrate the tax consequences of partnership operations and the allocation of income and deductions to the partners.

4. Distinguish between a partner's capital account and the partner's tax basis in the partnership interest and demonstrate how each is calculated.

5. Describe limited liability companies and explain how those entities are treated for tax purposes.

¶ 1400 Introduction

Sole proprietorships were the focus of the last chapter. Sole proprietorships involve businesses with a single owner and are a popular business entity choice, especially among owners just starting a new business. However, as the business grows and becomes successful, there may come a point when additional funding is needed beyond what can be raised either though borrowing or from the owner's own personal assets. In these situations, the business owner may find it necessary to raise additional capital by taking on new owners. If these new owners are merely investors in the business who are interested in sharing in the profits of the business but have no interest in being involved in its day-to-day operations, then incorporating the business may make sense. By holding a majority interest in the corporation's stock, the business owner can still manage and control the direction of the business, while at the same time protecting himself or herself and the other shareholders from the liabilities of the business. Unfortunately, incorporation comes at a steep price, as the profits of an incorporated business that operates as a C corporation are subject to double taxation.

Business owners that wish to avoid being taxed twice on the business's profits may consider operating the business either as a partnership or as an S corporation. These business entities are called flow-through entities because the business entity does not pay tax on the profits it generates, but instead its profits "flow through" to the owners. Although a flow-through entity does not pay tax, it is required to file an annual income tax return that summarizes the business's gross income, deductions, gains, losses, and credits for the year and provides both the IRS and the owners with information regarding the items and amounts to be reported on the owners' respective income tax returns. S corporations are the focus of Chapter 15. This chapter focuses on the tax laws that govern the income taxation of partnerships.

A partnership is a business entity with at least two owners (partners). Tax laws unique to partnerships include (1) the tax consequences of forming the partnership; (2) the reporting of business operations, including the allocation of partnership profits and losses to the partners; and (3) making sure that the partnership items of income, gain, deduction, and loss are taxed one time. These areas are the focus of discussion for this chapter. The rules discussed in this chapter also pertain to limited liability partnerships (LLPs) and limited liability companies (LLCs) that choose to be taxed as partnerships. LLCs and LLPs are governed under the state laws of the states in which they are formed. Although the Internal Revenue Code (the "Code") does not specifically recognize these two business entities, the federal government now allows LLPs and LLCs to be taxed as partnerships using the partnership rules discussed in this chapter. This chapter begins with an overview of the taxation of partnerships and their partners. In the overview, the tax concerns of forming and operating a partnership are introduced. The chapter continues with a discussion of these issues and concludes with a discussion of LLCs and LLPs.

¶ 1401 Tax and Nontax Aspects of Partnerships

Flow-through entities are a popular form for operating a business, primarily because of the single layer of taxation on profits. Unlike the profits of a C corporation, which are taxed a first time at the entity level and again when distributed to shareholders as dividends, flow-through entities are not treated as separate taxable entities, and accordingly, their profits are taxed a single time to the owners. Although both partnerships and S corporations are flow-through entities, the income taxation of partnership profits is the primary focus of this chapter and the income taxation of S Corporation profits is the focus of Chapter 15.

.01 Responsibility for Partnership Liabilities

The shareholders of a C corporation are not responsible for the liabilities of the corporation. The shareholder's liability is limited to the shareholder's basis in the shares of stock it owns in the corporation plus any indebtedness owed to the shareholder by the corporation. Although an S corporation is a flow-through entity and is taxed differently than a C corporation, the owners of an S corporation are shareholders, and they are accorded the same protection from the corporation's liabilities as are shareholders of a C corporation.

The owners of a partnership are partners, and the rules regarding the liability of partners depend upon the classification of the partnership as a general partnership or a limited partnership. A **general partnership** arises from an agreement among two or more partners to operate a business for profit. In a general partnership all the partners are classified as "general partners," each of whom has unlimited liability for the debts of the partnership. The liabilities can be those that come about from the operations of the business or from the negligence of the other partners as it relates to the operations of the business. The formation of a general partnership is fairly easy and only requires that the partners come to an agreement regarding the terms and conditions that surround the operation of the partnership. It is recommended that this agreement be made in writing and signed by the partners; however, verbal partnership agreements can exist and can be respected (see ¶ 1403.01).

Example 1: Paul Stone and Mary Brice are general partners operating a retail store as a general partnership. The partnership has outstanding invoices to its vendors for $10,000. Both Paul and Mary are liable for the entire $10,000 that the partnership owes its vendors.

Example 2: Brent Meyers and Trina Williams are physicians who operate a medical practice as a general partnership. One of Mary's patients is suing the partnership for negligence. If the patient prevails, as general partners both Brent and Trina will be liable for any amounts for which the partnership is liable but cannot satisfy.

When a partnership operates as a **limited partnership**, some partners have limited liability with respect to the debts of the partnership. The partners with limited liability are called "limited partners." When a limited partnership is formed, the federal tax laws require that there be at least one general partner responsible for the actions of the partnership. The general partner or partners are subject to unlimited liability and manage the day-to-day operations of the partnership. Limited partners do not participate in the management of the partnership, and their liability for partnership debts is limited to the amount they have invested in the partnership plus any guarantees the limited partners may have extended to the partnership. Amending a partnership agreement to give original limited partners a voice in the management of the partnership has been held to convert the limited partners to general partners.[1]

A limited partnership does not come into existence with the same ease or lack of formality with which a general partnership may be formed. Forming a limited partnership requires a certificate of limited partnership to be filed with the appropriate state government office. The filing of the certificate of limited partnership along with the requirement that the name of the partnership include a term such as "LP" or "Limited Partnership" gives notice to potential creditors of the partnership that not all partners are unlimitedly liable for the business's debt.

Example 3: A retail store operates as a limited partnership in which P.G. Giles, Incorporated is the general partner and Mary Wright is a limited partner. The partnership currently has $10,000 in outstanding invoices to its vendors. Mary's capital account balance is $2,000, which represents the amount she has invested in the limited partnership. P.G. Giles's capital account balance is $5,000, which represents its investment in the limited partnership. As the general partner, P.G. Giles is liable for the entire $10,000 in liabilities despite the fact that it only has $5,000 in its capital account. As a limited partner, Mary is liable to the extent of the $2,000 in her capital account.

Reason for the Rule: After all partners' capital accounts have been used to satisfy a partnership's liabilities, creditors' only remaining recourse is to go after the general partners to satisfy any outstanding loan amounts. When the general partner is a corporation, the possibility exists that all of the owners could be protected from the partnership's debts because the shareholders of a C corporation enjoy limited liability from the debts of the corporation. Thus, the general partner is really only liable for the partnership's debts to the extent of the corporation's net assets. By requiring a limited partnership to be formally registered as an "LP" or "Limited Partnership," potential creditors are forewarned that they may have limited avenues for satisfying amounts loaned to the partnership.

.02 Single Level of Taxation

The most appealing feature of a flow-through entity is the single layer of taxation. All flow-through entities are required to file an annual income tax return reporting their activities during the year regarding gross income, deductions, gains, losses, and tax credits. The entity is then required to allocate those items among its owners so the owners can include those amounts on their respective income tax returns. These allocated amounts are deemed to be taxed to the owners on the last day of the entity's tax year, regardless of the amounts that have been distributed to the owners.

Example 4: Alan Kraig owns a one-fifth interest in Tillman partnership. Both Alan and Tillman use a calendar year-end. During 2009, Tillman reports profits of $35,000, of which Alan's share is $7,000. Also during 2009, Tillman distributes $7,000 to Alan. Alan includes the $7,000 on his 2009 individual income tax return, which causes his adjusted gross

---

[1] *Financial Dynamics, Ltd.*, (DC Fla.) 80-2 USTC ¶ 9585.

income (AGI), taxable income, and tax liability to increase. The $7,000 distribution is not taxed to Alan because it represents a tax-free return of the profits in Tillman on which Alan has already paid tax.

Example 5: Assume the same facts as in Example 4, except Tillman distributes $3,000 to Alan during 2009 (instead of $7,000). Alan still reports his $7,000 distributive share of partnership profits on his 2009 income tax return. The $3,000 represents a tax-free return of Alan's investment in Tillman, which now includes his initial contribution to the partnership plus his $7,000 distributive share of previously taxed profits.

.03 Responsibility for Making Accounting Elections

As discussed throughout this textbook, the amount and timing of gross income and deductions can vary depending upon the accounting method and other elections made by the taxpayer. For example, the time when gross income is reported and when expenses are deductible against gross income depends largely on the method of accounting the taxpayer uses, such as the cash or accrual methods of accounting discussed in Chapter 3. If the taxpayer sells property and receives the proceeds over more than one tax year, the gain from the sale is normally recognized over more than one year. However, at the election of the taxpayer, the entire gain from the installment sale can be taxed in the year of the sale (see ¶ 309.01). If the taxpayer realizes a gain from an involuntary conversion of business or investment property, at the taxpayer's election, the gain can be postponed by investing the entire proceeds in qualified replacement property within a specified period of time (see ¶ 809.01). When tangible personal property is purchased and placed in service in a trade or business, at the taxpayer's election, the property may be immediately expensed under Code Sec. 179 to the extent that the tax laws provide (see ¶ 702.03). With a C corporation, the entity reporting the activities is also the one that is responsible for paying the tax on the profits. Therefore, having the corporate entity make these and other elections does not raise any issues. However, with respect to flow-through entities, the issue arises as to which party should make such elections—the entity reporting the activities or the owners, who are ultimately affected by the elections made.

 Planning Pointer: The election to expense qualified Code Sec. 179 property, up to the limit of $250,000 for 2009, is made at the partnership level. The amount of the deduction and the reduction in such, as discussed further in ¶ 702.03 and ¶ 1404.03, are applied at both the partnership and partner levels.[2] Once the partnership calculation is made, the partner's allocable share is added to the partner's tax return to calculate the amount each partner is entitled to deduct. In the case of a partner who has Code Sec. 179 elections in place in other pass through entities or from a sole proprietorship, that partner may not be able to take advantage of the entire amount of expense allocated to them.

For example, if Marc owns a 50 percent interest in three partnerships, all of which elect to expense the maximum $250,000 under Code Sec. 179, his total Code Sec. 179 expense would be $375,000 ($250,000 × 50% × 3). Marc would not be able to take advantage of the excess deduction of $125,000 ($375,000 – $250,000) due to the limitations applied at the partner level. Because the excess is not due to the taxable income limitation, the $125,000 excess cannot be carried over to a future tax year, but is instead permanently lost. Thus, it is critical that there be coordination between the elections made at the partnership and partner levels for electing to expense property under Code Sec. 179 in order to maximize potential tax savings.

The American Recovery and Reinvestment Act of 2009 extended the 50-percent first-year bonus depreciation deduction on qualified new property acquired and placed in service through December 31, 2009. The bonus depreciation is taken on top of the regular

---

[2] Code Sec. 179(d)(8).

> depreciation reported for the year the property is placed into service. Unlike the Code Sec. 179 expensing allowance referred to above, there is no taxable income limitation or investment limitation on the bonus allowance at either the partnership or partner level as illustrated in the previous example.

The tax laws require that most elections affecting the calculation of gross income and the timing of expenses be made by the partnership.[3] Thus, the partnership makes the elections regarding which accounting period and which overall accounting method to use to report partnership items. Other elections made by the partnership include the depreciation method used to expense real and tangible personal property and the election not to use the installment sale method. The partnership also makes the election to immediately expense intangible drilling and development costs or research and development expenditures or to postpone gain from an involuntary conversion when qualified replacement property is purchased within the specified time period.[4] These elections, once made, are binding on the partners of the partnership, and the methods used by the partnership apply to all of its partners.[5] All other elections are made individually by each partner. For example, each partner decides whether to deduct or take a tax credit for foreign taxes paid during the year. A list of the elections made by the partnership is shown in Figure 14-1.

Figure 14-1 List of Elections Made at the Partnership Level

- The accounting period used to report partnership activities (see ¶ 302.01), including the election to use a tax year other than a required tax year under Code Sec. 444 (see ¶ 302.02)
- The accounting method used to compute partnership income (see ¶ ¶ 306–308)
- The depreciation method used to expense depreciable property, including any election to expense tangible personal property under Code Sec. 179 (see ¶ 702.03)
- The election to opt out of using the installment method (see ¶ 309.01 and ¶ 810.04)
- The option to expense intangible drilling and developments costs (see ¶ 501.03)
- The election to deduct research and experimentation expenditures (see ¶ 507)
- The election to deduct up to $5,000 of a partnership's organizational and start-up costs and then amortize the rest over 180 months[6]
- The election to postpone gain from an involuntary conversion (see ¶ 809.01)

¶ 1402 Why Study Partnership Taxation?

The single layer of taxation on profits makes any flow-through entity a popular business entity choice. The tax laws governing the taxation of partnerships are one of the most complex areas of tax law. However, the flexibility in the types and number of owners that partnerships can have and the ability of the partners to decide how to allocate partnership profits and losses give partnerships an edge over S corporations. Unfortunately, the one disadvantage of operating a business as a partnership has been the requirement that every partnership have at least one general partner with unlimited liability. In the last three decades, all 50 states have come to recognize limited liability companies (LLCs) as an alternative to partnerships. In an LLC, all owners (called members) have limited liability for the general debts of the business entity, and there is no requirement that any owner be ultimately responsible for the entity's debts. More recently, the federal government has

---

[3] Code Sec. 703(b).

[4] *Demirjian*, 72-1 USTC ¶ 9281, 457 F2d 1.

[5] Code Sec. 703(b); Reg. § 1.703-1(b).

[6] Code Sec. 709(b), as amended by the American Jobs Creation Act of 2004, P.L. 108-357; Reg. § 1.709-1(b)(1) and § 1.709-2(c).

come to accept limited liability partnerships (LLPs) as a business entity that can be taxed as a partnership. Like LLCs, all partners in an LLP have limited liability from the partnership's debts. Since the owners of LLCs and LLPs have limited liability similar to that offered by corporations (but unlike with corporations, the profits are taxed only one time), these entities have become the latest trend of business entity choice.

As the information presented in Table 14-1 shows, in 2006 the number of partnership tax returns filed had increased 101 percent over the number filed in 1993. However, a closer look at the table shows that traditional general partnerships displayed a continuing pattern of decline over this same period of time. The increase in entities filing tax returns with the Internal Revenue Service that are classified as a partnership results from an increase in the number of LLCs, LLPs and Limited Partnerships. These three entities constituted 2,172,000 tax returns filed for the 2006 tax year and made up 74 percent of all entities filing tax returns as partnerships.

Table 14-1 Partnership Tax Returns Filed by Type of Entity[7]

Year	Total Number of Returns (000's)	Domestic General Partnerships (000's)	Domestic Limited Partnerships (000's)	Domestic Limited Liability Companies (000's)	Domestic Limited Liability Partnerships (000's)	Other (000's)
1993	1,468	1,176	275	17	——	——
1994	1,494	1,163	283	48	——	——
1995	1,581	1,167	295	119	——	——
1996	1,654	1,116	311	221	——	5
1997	1,759	1,069	329	349	——	13
1998	1,855	945	343	470	26	71
1999	1,937	898	354	589	42	52
2000	2,058	872	349	718	53	64
2001	2,132	815	369	809	69	70
2002	2,242	780	377	946	78	61
2003	2,375	757	379	1,092	88	58
2004	2,547	725	402	1,270	89	61
2005	2,764	729	414	1,465	100	56
2006	2,947	718	433	1,630	109	50

¶ 1403 Forming a Partnership

Since a partnership involves two or more owners, forming a partnership requires a little more formality than forming a sole proprietorship. The first step in forming a partnership is for the partners to enter into a **partnership agreement**, which provides, among other things, how the partners will share in the partnership's profits and losses. Although there is no requirement that the partnership agreement be in writing, as with any contract, it is highly recommended that the partners enter into a written partnership agreement to avoid any disputes in the future over any of the partnership arrangements.

[7] Wheeler, Tim and Shumofsky, Nina, "Partnership Returns, 2006," *Statistics of Income Bulletin*, Fall, 2008.

After a partnership agreement has been established, the partners must contribute capital (assets) to the partnership so the partnership can begin operations. Often the partners will contribute cash to the partnership in exchange for a partnership interest; however, sometimes property other than cash or services is contributed.

.01 Partnership Agreement

The partnership agreement is a contract between the parties that usually establishes how the partnership's income, gains, losses, deductions, and credits will be allocated among the partners. These allocated amounts are known as the partner's **distributive shares** of partnership items. If the partnership agreement does not specify each partner's distributive share of such items, the partners' shares are determined according to each partner's interest in the partnership, taking all the facts and circumstances into consideration. Although the partnership agreement normally controls the allocation of partnership items, the allocations provided in the agreement are disregarded if they lack substantial economic effect. (See ¶ 1404.04.) Partnership agreements are interpreted under the law of the state in which the entity is formed.

 Spotlight: A partnership agreement may be an oral or written understanding between the partners and need not even be referred to as a partnership agreement for it to be a binding agreement. Since the partnership agreement is considered to be the governing instrument for tax allocation purposes as well as the contract to be relied upon by the partners for the effective management of the partnership, its importance cannot be overstated.[8] Provisions that are commonly included in a partnership agreement that have tax implications include: (1) initial capital contributions by the partners (¶ 1403.01 and .02); (2) method of accounting (¶ 1404.02); (3) fiscal year of the partnership (¶ 1404.01); (4) determination of the partnerships profit or loss for the tax year (¶ 1404.03); (5) division of profits and losses amongst the partners (¶ 1404.04); and, (6) maintenance of partners capital accounts (¶ 1404.04). This chapter addresses each of these provisions, as well as other topics that should be considered in drafting a partnership agreement.

The partnership agreement also contains many nontax-related provisions that govern the operations of the partnership. For example, the partnership agreement will specify who will manage the partnership operations, including how disputes among the various partners will be resolved. The agreement may restrict the partners' abilities to transfer their partnership interests, or it may provide a formula to determine the amount at which one partner will buy out another partner should a partner retire or otherwise decide to leave the partnership. The partnership agreement also states how partners will distribute the partnership assets upon dissolution of the partnership.

.02 Contributions of Property

Before any business can begin operations, it must first generate capital. Typically, the partners contribute property (including cash) to the partnership in exchange for a capital interest in the partnership. A partner's interest in the partnership is similar to a shareholder's shares of stock in a corporation. It represents the partner's ownership rights in the partnership. A capital interest in a partnership is an asset that a partner can sell for cash or for another consideration, provided the terms of the sale do not violate any limitations specified in the partnership agreement. As with the disposal of any asset, the partner recognizes gain or loss on the sale equal to the difference between the amount realized and the partner's adjusted basis in the partnership interest.

When a partner contributes money or property to a partnership solely in exchange for an interest in the partnership, no gain or loss is recognized by either the partner or the partnership.[9]

---

[8] Code Sec. 704(a).   [9] Code Sec. 721.

Instead, the realized gain or loss is deferred (postponed) and will be recognized at a later point in time. Nonrecognition of gain, however, does not extend to the contribution of services. If the partner performs services for the partnership in exchange for an interest in the partnership, the partner includes the fair market value (FMV) of the partnership interest received as gross income.[10] When the FMV of a partnership interest a partner receives exceeds the FMV of the property the partner contributes to the partnership, the difference represents the value of the services rendered by the partner in exchange for a capital interest in the partnership. Thus, the difference between the FMV of the partnership interest received and the value of the property contributed to the partnership is the amount of taxable services the partner reports in gross income.

Example 6: Joan Andrews and David Busbee agree to form an equal partnership. Each contributes $5,000 of property in exchange for his or her respective partnership interests. Joan contributes $5,000 cash; David contributes $5,000 worth of property with an adjusted basis of $3,000. Although David realizes a $2,000 gain ($5,000 – $3,000) on the transfer, neither the partnership nor the partners recognize any gain or loss on the exchange.

Example 7: Jessica Adams owns and operates a business as a sole proprietorship. Three years earlier she hired Eric DuPree and promised to make him a 50-percent partner in her business if he was still employed at the end of three years. At the end of three years, Eric is still working for Jessica, and in accordance with their agreement, a partnership is formed with net assets (total assets minus total liabilities) of $150,000. David's share of those net assets equals $75,000 ($150,000 × 50%). Upon formation of the partnership, David receives $75,000 in exchange for no consideration other than his prior services, and accordingly, the $75,000 is taxable to him as ordinary income.

Example 8: Erica Harris and Jeff Jenkins form an equal partnership. In exchange for her interest, Erica contributes $50,000 cash. In exchange for his 50-percent interest, Jeff performs services for the partnership and contributes $20,000 cash. Since Jeff receives a 50-percent capital interest in the partnership, the FMV of the amounts he contributed must be the same as the $50,000 Erica contributes in exchange for her 50-percent interest. Therefore, in order to receive a 50-percent interest in the partnership, Jeff must have contributed services worth $30,000. Thus, Jeff will report the $30,000 of services rendered in gross income and will pay tax on that amount at the ordinary income (marginal) tax rates.

Profits-only interest in the partnership In the previous three examples, each partner received a share of the partnership's capital in exchange for contributing property, services, or both. When a partner has an interest in the future profits the partnership generates as well as an interest in the partnership's assets upon his liquidation from or dissolution of the partnership, the partner has a **capital and profits interest**. If the partner is entitled to a share of future partnership profits but does not have an ownership interest in the partnership capital, the partner receives a **profits-only interest**. A partner with a profits interest does not receive anything upon the dissolution of the partnership beyond any previously taxed profits that have yet to be distributed to the partner.

The receipt of a profits interest in exchange for the contribution of services is taxable upon receipt only if the FMV of the profits interest is determinable. Thus, if an individual contributes past services in exchange for a profits interest, and the profits interest has only speculative value, the individual recognizes income only as the profits are received.[11] According to the IRS, a partner's receipt of a profits interest is not taxable unless *any* of the following circumstances exists:

1. The interest relates to a substantially certain and predictable stream of income from partnership assets, such as from a high-grade lease of real property,

2. Within two years of receipt, the partner disposes of the profits interest, or

3. The interest is a limited partnership interest in a publicly traded partnership.[12]

---

[10] Reg. § 1.721(1)(b)(1).
[11] *W.G. Campbell*, CA-8, 91-2 USTC ¶ 50,420.

[12] Rev. Proc. 93-27, 1993-2 CB 343, clarified by Rev. Proc. 2001-43, 2001-2 CB 191.

Example 9: Edwina Stewart is admitted as a partner in the ABC partnership. Edwina does not contribute anything to the partnership in exchange for her interest, but she nonetheless receives 15 percent of partnership profits in exchange for remaining with the partnership. During the year the partnership's profits are $200,000, and in accordance with the partnership agreement Edwina is allocated $30,000 of the partnership income. Edwina will be taxed during the current year on the $30,000 distributive share of the partnership profits. However, neither she nor the partnership will be taxed on the value of her interest in the partnership (i.e., her right to future profits).

Example 10: Sally Jensen is given a 20-percent interest in the future profits from the operation of an apartment building that has guaranteed leases that have produced a $150,000 profit for the past 10 years. The building will produce the same profit for the next 10 years, which will complete the terms of the guaranteed leases. Sally is taxed on the value of the partnership interest based upon the predictable nature of the income.

 Spotlight: Receipt of a profits-only interest differs from a capital and profits interest in that the owner of the latter is entitled to a portion of the partnership assets upon dissolution of the partnership. For example, Eric DuPree from Example 7 was taxed on $75,000 because that amount represented the FMV of the 50-percent capital and profits interest he received in the partnership due to past services he rendered to Jessica's business. Thus, if Eric were to sell his 50-percent capital and profits interest immediately upon becoming a partner, his interest should be worth $75,000 because the purchaser would be buying a claim to half of the $150,000 FMV of partnership assets. Contrast this to Examples 9 and 10, in which Edwina and Sally have no claim to partnership assets. Should either Edwina or Sally decide to sell her profits-only partnership interest, the buyer would be purchasing only an interest in the future profits of the partnership. In Example 9, a high degree of uncertainty exists regarding the value of Edwina's future profits, and accordingly, she is not taxed until her distributive share of partnership profits is realized.

.03 Partnership's Basis and Holding Period in Contributed Property

The contributing partner's realized gain or loss from the contribution of property in exchange for a partnership interest is not recognized but is merely deferred and eventually must be taxed. One way this is accomplished is by requiring that the partnership use as its basis in the contributed property the contributing partner's basis in the property.[13] Thus, when the partnership sells the property, the unrealized gain or loss will be recognized by the partnership and taxed to the partners.

Example 11: Jay Morrill contributes land that is worth $50,000 to a partnership. Jay's adjusted basis in the land is $33,000. In return for the land, Jay receives a one-third interest in the partnership. Jay realizes $17,000 gain ($50,000 – $33,000); however, he does not recognize any gain on the exchange. The partnership takes Jay's $33,000 basis in the land. If the partnership later sells the land for $50,000, it will both realize and recognize a $17,000 gain ($50,000 – $33,000). Thus, Jay's $17,000 gain is merely postponed. (See ¶ 1404.04 for special rules regarding the allocation of the recognized gain or loss.)

Example 12: Daria Monroe and Monica Edwards form an equal general partnership. Each partner contributes $100,000. Daria contributes $100,000 cash; Monica contributes land worth $100,000. Monica's adjusted basis in the land is $140,000. The partnership's basis in the cash is $100,000; its basis in the land is $140,000. Monica does not recognize the $40,000 loss ($100,000 FMV less $140,000 basis) upon transfer of the land to the general partnership.

---

[13] Code Sec. 723.

If the partner contributes nonbusiness property to the partnership (such as a personal automobile or other personal belonging), the basis of the property to the partnership is the *lesser* of (1) the FMV of the property at the time of contribution or (2) its adjusted basis to the contributing partner.[14]

Example 13: Jake Matthews contributes his personal automobile to a partnership in exchange for a 10-percent capital and profits interest in the partnership. The automobile is worth $15,000 at the time he contributes it to the partnership. Jake paid $35,000 for the automobile, and since it is a personal asset, this amount represents his adjusted basis in the property. Although the general rule stipulates that the partnership take Jake's $35,000 basis in the automobile, the special rule governing the contribution of a partner's personal belongings limits the partnership's basis to $15,000 (the *lesser* of $15,000 FMV or $35,000 adjusted basis). This amount also represents Jake's basis in his partnership interest.

 Reason for the Rule: Almost all personal belongings individuals own decline in value over time. Since personal belongings cannot be depreciated, their adjusted basis usually is their cost. Thus, when these personal belongings are sold, the realized loss cannot be recognized on the tax return (see ¶ 803). If the partnership tax laws allowed individuals to contribute their personal belongings to a partnership and to follow the general rule and allow the partnership's basis in those assets to be the (higher) adjusted basis, then the partnership would benefit from the partner's realized loss on the property contributed. For example, if in Example 13, the partnership were to immediately sell Jake's automobile for its $15,000 FMV, no gain or loss would be recognized by the partnership. However, if the tax laws had permitted the partnership to use Jake's $35,000 adjusted basis in the automobile, it would recognize a $20,000 loss ($15,000 – $35,000). This, in effect, would allow the partnership (and the partners) to benefit from the $20,000 realized loss on the exchange of a personal belonging for a partnership interest which would not have been deductible if sold by Jake outside the partnership.

The holding period of property contributed to the partnership includes the period during which the contributing partner held the property.[15] This holding period determines whether any gain upon a sale will be treated as long-term or short-term gain.

.04 Partner's Tax Basis and Holding Period in the Partnership Interest

A partnership interest represents an investment in a partnership, and like any other investment, it is important to keep track of its tax basis. When an interest in a partnership is sold, the partner recognizes gain or loss for the difference between the amount realized from the sale and the adjusted basis of the partnership interest. The partner's tax basis in the partnership interest is also used to ensure that the profits of the partnership are taxed only one time.

The contributions a partner makes to a partnership represent the partner's investment in the partnership. Therefore, contributions the partner makes to the partnership are included in the calculation of the partner's basis in the partnership interest. As partnership income and gain is allocated (and taxed) to the partner, the partner's basis in the partnership is increased by these amounts. Likewise, the partner's allocable share of partnership deductions and losses reduces the partner's tax basis in the partnership interest. When the partnership makes distributions to its partners, the partners reduce their basis in the partnership interest as they receive a tax-free return of capital to the extent of their basis in the partnership interest. The only time a partner is taxed on a distribution from the partnership is when the amount of cash distributed exceeds the partner's basis in the partnership interest.[16]

---

[14] *L.Y.S. Au*, CA-9, 64-1 USTC ¶ 9447, 330 F2d 1008.

[15] Code Sec. 1223(2); Reg. § 1.723-1.

[16] Code Sec. 731.

When a partner sells its partnership interest, the partner only recognizes gain to the extent that the amount realized from the sale exceeds its adjusted basis in the partnership interest. Thus, to the extent that a partner's share of allocated partnership profits has not been distributed at the time the partner sells the interest in the partnership, a higher adjusted basis will cause the partner to recognize less gain or a greater loss from the sale. The discussion of how a partner's basis in the partnership interest is computed is discussed at ¶ 1405.

Example 14: Kelly Moore and Julie Costas are equal partners in JK general partnership. To form the partnership, each partner contributed $10,000. Kelly and Julie's initial basis in their respective partnership interests is $10,000. During the first year of operations, JK reports taxable profits of $4,000, which it allocates 50 percent to each partner. Each partner's basis in the partnership interest increases by $2,000, to $12,000 ($10,000 + $2,000). If Kelly sells his interest in JK for $12,000, he will not recognize any gain, thus ensuring that the $2,000 of partnership profits is not taxed a second time and that he receives a tax-free return of his original $10,000 investment.

Example 15: Continuing with Example 14, if JK distributes $8,000 to Julie at the beginning of the second year, this amount reduces the basis in her partnership interest to $4,000 ($12,000 – $8,000), but she does not recognize gain on the distribution. The $8,000 distribution she receives represents a tax-free return of the previously taxed partnership profits ($2,000) and part of the amount she contributed to JK ($6,000).

The partner's tax basis is calculated differently from the partner's capital account. The **partner's capital account** keeps track of what the partner is entitled to receive upon dissolution of the partnership. Initially, the partner's capital account includes the *value* of the property the partner contributes to the partnership because this amount represents the partner's contribution of assets to the partnership relative to the other partners. The partner's capital account is increased by the partner's allocable shares of partnership income and gain, as determined in accordance with the partnership agreement. Likewise, the partner's capital account is decreased by the partner's allocable shares of partnership deduction and loss, as well as the *value* of property distributed to the partner, as determined in accordance with the partnership agreement. The partner's capital account is often referred to as the partner's "book" basis.

Example 16: Isabel Anderson and Miranda Bates form a 50-50 general partnership. Isabel contributes property that has an adjusted basis of $20,000 and a value of $50,000. Miranda contributes $50,000 cash. For book purposes, each partner contributes property worth $50,000, and therefore this amount represents each partner's capital account balance. If the partnership were to dissolve, each partner would be entitled to 50 percent of the partnership net assets, as determined by their respective capital account balances.

Initial basis. When a partner contributes property (including cash) to a partnership in exchange for an interest in the partnership, the partner's initial (tax) basis in a partnership interest is the amount of money contributed plus the partner's adjusted basis of any property contributed.[17] When a partner contributes services to the partnership in exchange for a partnership interest, the taxable amount of those services increases the partner's basis in the partnership interest. The partner's capital account (book basis) is computed using the FMV of the contributed property and the taxable services rendered. Because a property's *value* often is different from the taxpayer's adjusted (tax) basis in the property, the partner's basis in the partnership interest is often different from the balance in the partner's capital account.

Example 17: Continuing with Example 16, for tax purposes, Isabel's basis in her partnership interest is $20,000 (the adjusted basis in the property she contributes), while Miranda's basis in her partnership interest is $50,000. The tax and book balances of each account are shown below. In both cases, the partnership's assets are equal to its

---

[17] Code Sec. 722, Reg. § 1.722-1.

liabilities and the partners' capital. However, the rules for computing the account balances are different.

Assets	Tax Basis	Book Basis	Partner's Capital	Tax Basis	Book Basis
Cash	$50,000	$ 50,000	Isabel	$20,000	$ 50,000
Property	20,000	50,000	Miranda	50,000	50,000
	$70,000	$100,000		$70,000	$100,000

Example 18: Jim Chan, Mary Dunn, and Charles Edger form an equal three-member general partnership. In exchange for their respective one-third interests, Jim contributes $150,000 in cash; Mary contributes $75,000 in cash plus stock worth $75,000; and Charles contributes land worth $150,000. Mary's adjusted basis in the stock is $45,000; Charles's adjusted basis in the land is $160,000. Each partner contributes property worth $150,000 in exchange for his or her one-third interest in the partnership, and therefore, each partner's capital account balance is credited for $150,000. Although each partner contributed property worth equivalent amounts, the tax bases of their interests differ.

Jim's basis in his partnership interest is $150,000, the amount of cash he contributes. Mary's basis is $120,000 ($75,000 cash plus $45,000 adjusted basis of the stock). Charles's basis is $160,000 (adjusted basis of the land). Thus, if the three partners were to sell their interests to three other individuals for $150,000 each, Jim would not report any gain or loss ($150,000 – $150,000); Mary's gain would be $30,000 ($150,000 – $120,000); and Charles's loss would equal $10,000 ($150,000 – $160,000).

Assets	Tax Basis	Book Basis	Partner's Capital	Tax Basis	Book Basis
Cash	$225,000	$225,000	Jim	$150,000	$150,000
Stock	45,000	75,000	Mary	120,000	150,000
Land	160,000	150,000	Charles	160,000	150,000
	$430,000	$450,000		$430,000	$450,000

Example 19: Ed Rentara and Jessica Sampson form an equal general partnership. In exchange for his 50-percent interest, Ed contributes $20,000 cash and stock worth $30,000. Ed's adjusted basis in the stock is $25,000. In exchange for her 50-percent interest, Jessica performs services for the partnership and contributes land worth $40,000. Jessica's adjusted basis in the land is $45,000. Ed contributes $50,000 in exchange for his 50-percent interest ($20,000 cash + $30,000 FMV of property). Therefore, in order for Jessica to receive the same 50-percent interest in partnership capital, she must have contributed $50,000 as well. Since the property Jessica contributes is worth $40,000, the services she contributes must be worth $10,000. Thus, Jessica reports the $10,000 of services rendered in gross income and will pay tax on that amount at her ordinary income (marginal) tax rates.

Neither Ed nor Jessica recognizes any gain or loss on the contribution of property to the partnership solely in exchange for his or her partnership interest. Ed's (tax) basis in his partnership interest is $45,000 ($20,000 cash + $25,000 adjusted basis in the stock). Jessica's (tax) basis in her partnership interest is $55,000 ($45,000 adjusted basis in the land + $10,000 recognized as ordinary income for her services rendered).

Spotlight: The tax laws governing the partner's basis in a partnership interest are similar to the tax laws that govern the taxpayer's basis in property received in a like-kind exchange. In a like-kind exchange, any realized gain or loss is postponed and reflected in the taxpayer's basis in the newly acquired property (see ¶ 808.03). Thus, when the taxpayer later sells the like-kind property, the postponed gain or loss is recognized. The tax laws operate similarly to "hide" the partner's realized (but unrecognized) gain or loss on the contribution of property to a partnership in exchange for a partnership interest. As illustrated in Example 19, Jessica receives a partnership interest worth $50,000 in exchange for property and services of which her basis is $55,000 (property with an adjusted basis of $45,000 + $10,000 of taxable services) Thus, Jessica's realized loss on the exchange is $5,000 ($50,000 − $55,000). The tax laws do not allow her to recognize this loss but instead postpone it until later by allowing her to take the $55,000 as her basis in the partnership. Thus, if Jessica were to immediately turn around and sell her partnership interest she would recognize a $5,000 loss.

Liabilities associated with contributed property. Since the partners are ultimately responsible for the debt of the partnership, when contributed property is transferred subject to indebtedness or when a partner's indebtedness is assumed by the partnership, the contributing partner's basis in the partnership interest is reduced by the amount of the indebtedness assumed by the other partners. Likewise, the noncontributing partners' bases in their partnership interests increase by their respective amounts of partnership debt for which they are now responsible.[18]

A partner's basis in a partnership interest cannot be reduced below zero. Therefore, if the debt assumed by the other (noncontributing) partners exceeds the contributing partner's adjusted basis in the property, the basis of that partner's interest is reduced to zero, and the excess of the debt assumed by the other partners over the contributing partner's basis for the property is taxable to the contributing partner. Generally, the excess is taxed as capital gain.[19] However, the amount of the taxable excess does not increase the contributing partner's basis.

Figure 14-2 Initial Basis of Contributing Partners

The initial basis of a contributing partner is calculated as follows:

Money Contributed by Partner

Plus:	Partner's adjusted basis in contributed property
Plus:	Taxable amount of partner's services contributed to the partnership
Plus:	Amount of existing partnership indebtedness assumed by the contributing partner
Minus:	Amount of indebtedness assumed by noncontributing partners of indebtedness transferred to the partnership by the contributing partner
Equals:	Initial Basis of Contributing Partner

Example 20: Fred Ackers contributes land worth $105,000 to a general partnership in exchange for a one-third interest in the partnership. The other partner, Jeff Rowley, contributes $120,000 cash in exchange for a two-thirds interest in the partnership. Fred's basis in the land is $55,000, and the land is subject to a $45,000 mortgage that the partnership assumes. Prior to contributing the property, Fred was entirely responsible for the $45,000 mortgage associated with the land. After the contribution, all liabilities of the

---

[18] Code Sec. 752; Reg. § 1.752-1.   [19] Code Sec. 731(a).

partnership are borne by the partnership (and ultimately, its partners), and Fred's share of the mortgage held by the partnership is $15,000. Jeff's responsibility is $30,000. By contributing the land to the partnership, Fred's responsibility for the mortgage decreases by $30,000 ($45,000 – $15,000). Each partner's basis in his partnership interest is shown below:

Fred

Adjusted basis in the land contributed	$ 55,000
Less: Liabilities assumed by other partners	(30,000)
Fred's initial basis in his partnership interest	$ 25,000

Jeff

Cash contributed	$120,000
Plus: Share of partnership liabilities	30,000
Jeff's initial basis in his partnership interest	$150,000

Example 21: Assume the same facts as in Example 20, except Fred's basis in the land is $20,000. Fred reduces his basis in the partnership interest by the $30,000 decrease in his responsibility for the mortgage; however, the tax laws do not allow his basis to fall below zero. Fred is taxed on the $10,000 excess ($30,000 – $20,000). Each partner's basis in his partnership interest is shown below:

Fred

Adjusted basis in the land contributed	$ 20,000
Less: Liabilities assumed by the other partners	(30,000)
Fred's initial basis in his partnership interest	$ 0

Jeff

Cash contributed	$120,000
Plus: Share of partnership liabilities	30,000
Jeff's initial basis in his partnership interest	$150,000

Allocating the debt among the various partners depends on whether the debt assumed by the partnership is a recourse or nonrecourse debt. If the debt assumed is a recourse debt, each partner's share of the assumed liability is that portion of the liability for which he or a related person[20] bears the economic risk of loss.[21] A nonrecourse debt is usually shared in the same ratio as the partnership profits.[22]

A **nonrecourse debt** gets its name because the lender has no recourse (no ability to collect the debt) directly from the borrower in the event the borrower defaults on the loan. Instead, the lender has recourse against property, called **collateral**, that can be used to satisfy the debt in the event the borrower defaults on the loan. If a lender makes a nonrecourse loan and the borrower defaults on the loan, the lender can use the collateral to satisfy the remaining balance on the loan. If the collateral is not sufficient to satisfy the entire loan amount, the lender has no further recourse (hence the term, nonrecourse debt) and is out of pocket for any remainder of the debt.

Example 22: A partnership acquires land costing $200,000 by making a down payment of $20,000 and taking out a nonrecourse loan for $180,000. The land is used as collateral for the loan. After making several payments on the loan, the partnership defaults on the loan

---

[20] Reg. § 1.752-4(b).
[21] Reg. § 1.752-2.
[22] Reg. § 1.752-3.

when the loan balance is $160,000. The lender takes possession of the land and sells it for $150,000. The lender uses the entire $150,000 of proceeds to satisfy $150,000 of the $160,000 outstanding balance. Because the loan was nonrecourse debt, the lender cannot go back to the partnership for the remaining $10,000 owed on the debt. The lender will incur a $10,000 loss on the amount of debt that it cannot collect.

With a **recourse debt**, the lender can proceed directly against the debtor for any debt on which the debtor has defaulted. Typically, if property is pledged as collateral for a recourse debt, the lender will first look to the collateral to satisfy the debt and will then try to attach the debtor's other assets. In the case of a partnership, if the collateral is insufficient to satisfy a recourse debt or if no property is pledged as collateral on the debt, the lender can go after the partnership assets (and accordingly, the partners) to satisfy the debt. In the case of a limited partnership, the limited partners would be liable to satisfy their portions of the debt for the amount equal to their capital account balances in the partnership plus any loans they have made to the partnership. The general partners of a partnership have unlimited liability with respect to the debts of the partnership, and thus, should the partnership assets be insufficient to satisfy the recourse debt, the general partners' assets other than their interests in the partnership are at risk for satisfying any remaining portion of the partnership's debt.

Example 23: Assume the same facts as in Example 22, except the $180,000 loan is structured as a recourse debt. The partnership defaults and $150,000 of the outstanding loan amount is satisfied with the proceeds from the sale of the property. Because the debt was structured as a recourse debt, the lender is able to require that the remaining $10,000 be satisfied using other partnership assets. If the partnership is unable to satisfy the remainder of the debt, the lender will have recourse to go after the general partner's personal assets.

If the debt assumed is a recourse debt, each partner's share of the assumed liability is that portion of the liability for which the partner bears the economic risk of loss. To determine each partner's economic risk of loss for recourse debt, a "constructive sale and liquidation" is deemed to take place, and the resulting loss is allocated among the partners in accordance with the loss allocation provisions in the partnership agreement. The losses are then applied against the partner's capital account balances. The negative balances in the partner's capital accounts represent the partner's risk of economic loss. Thus, the steps taken to determine a partner's risk of economic loss are as follows:

1. The partnership is deemed to sell all of its assets (including cash) for $0 and the resulting loss (based on the book value of the assets) is then allocated to each of the partners in accordance with each of their loss allocation ratios.

2. The allocated loss reduces each partner's respective capital account balances.

3. The resulting negative balances in the partners' capital accounts represent each partner's share of economic loss with respect to the recourse debt.[23]

Example 24: Tim Roberts and Chip Frasier form a general partnership. The partnership agreement provides that Tim and Chip will share profits equally, but they will share partnership losses 60/40. Tim contributes $100,000 in cash; Chip contributes land worth $140,000 that is subject to a recourse mortgage of $40,000. Chip's adjusted basis in the land is $70,000. Chip's lender agrees to release Chip from liability for the mortgage and to substitute the partnership as the obligor. Both partners contribute property worth $100,000. Although the property Chip contributes is worth $140,000, it is contributed along with a $40,000 liability, which reduces the total value of his contribution to $100,000 ($140,000 – $40,000). Thus, each partner's "initial capital account balance" (the amount each partner would be entitled to upon the dissolution of the partnership) is $100,000.

---

[23] Reg. § 1.752-2.

By contributing the encumbered property to the partnership, Chip is discharged from personal responsibility for the $40,000 liability; however, through his 50-percent ownership interest in the partnership, he will be responsible for a portion of the $40,000 recourse mortgage. To determine Tim and Chip's respective shares of the $40,000 recourse debt, each partner is allocated his share of the economic risk of loss from the $40,000. This amount can be determined by going through the calculations of a hypothetical sale of all of the partnership's assets for $0 and then allocating the loss (calculated based on the book value of the assets) among the partners. The resulting negative balances in each partner's capital account represent each partner's economic risk of loss from the property. If the partnership were to sell all of its assets, including cash, for $0, the partnership would realize a $240,000 loss (based on book value) which would be allocated 60 percent to Tim and 40 percent to Chip.

Asset	Sales Price	Book Value	Loss
Cash	$0	$100,000	($100,000)
Land	0	140,000	(140,000)
			($240,000)

Tim's initial capital account balance	$100,000
Tim's distributive share of $240,000 loss	(144,000)
Tim's economic risk of loss	($ 44,000)

FMV of property Chip contributes	$140,000
Less: Personal release of liability	(40,000)
Chip's initial capital account balance	$100,000
Chip's distributive share of $240,000 loss	(96,000)
Chip's economic risk of loss	$ 4,000

The hypothetical liquidation shows that if all of the partnership assets were sold for $0, the entire $40,000 recourse debt would be borne by Tim. Therefore, Tim's adjusted (tax) basis in his partnership interest is $140,000 ($100,000 cash contributed plus his $40,000 share of the recourse liability). Chip's adjusted (tax) basis in his partnership interest is $30,000 ($70,000 adjusted basis in the property contributed minus $40,000 of the liability assumed by the partnership plus his $0 share of the recourse liability). The allocation of the mortgage among the partners is the proportion of the liability, if any, for which each partner or related person bears the economic risk of loss. The ratio at which the partners agree to share partnership income is irrelevant when allocating recourse debt between the two partners.

Example 25: Assume the same facts as in Example 24, except the debt is a nonrecourse liability. Nonrecourse debt is allocated in accordance with the partner's profit-sharing ratio. Thus, Tim and Chip would each add $20,000 ($40,000 × 50%) of the nonrecourse debt to his basis in his interest in the partnership.

Partnership interest acquired from another partner. If a partner acquires an interest in the partnership by purchasing it from a partner, rather than from the partnership itself, a different rule applies to determine the partner's initial basis in the partnership interest.[24] The purchasing partner receives an initial basis in the interest equal to its cost to the partner, including the selling partner's share of partnership liabilities assumed by the purchasing partner.

---

[24] Code Sec. 742 and Code Sec. 1011.

Holding periods. The holding period of a partner's interest determines the nature of the gain (or loss) as long-term or short-term. Gain or loss from the sale or other disposition of a partnership interest held by a partner for over one year generally qualifies as long-term capital gain or loss. Partnership interests held one year or less generally give rise to short-term capital gain or loss.[25] If a partner pays cash to a partnership in exchange for a partnership interest, the partner's holding period for the interest begins as of the time the partner acquires the interest. In the case of a contribution of property, if the contributed property was a capital asset or a Code Sec. 1231 asset in the hands of the contributing partner, the holding period of the contributed property carries over to the acquired partnership interest.[26] Thus, an interest acquired from a partnership in exchange for contributing property that is a capital asset or a Code Sec. 1231 asset not only takes the adjusted basis of the contributing property but also takes its holding period.

¶ 1404 Reporting Partnership Operations

Once the partners have entered into a partnership agreement and assets have been contributed to the partnership, the partnership is ready to begin operations. Like any other business, a partnership must select a tax year and an overall accounting method. A partnership is not a tax-paying entity, but nonetheless it is required to keep track of its gross income, gains, deductions, and losses using the accounting method it has selected. It then files an income tax return reporting these items in accordance with its tax year. It also allocates the items among its partners in accordance with the terms of the partnership agreement.

.01 Required Tax Year

As first discussed in Chapter 3, a partnership's required tax year is the one that best conforms to the tax year of its partners, as determined using a series of rules prescribed in the Code. The first rule requires that a partnership adopt the year-end of its majority partners. If a partnership does not have a majority of partners with the same year-end, the tax laws require that the partnership adopt the year-end of *all* its principal partners. For partnerships that do not have either a majority of partners or all principal partners with the same year-end, then the tax laws require that the partnership use as its year-end the tax year that produces the least aggregate deferral of income. Although a partnership's required tax year is determined by sequentially following these three sets of rules, the tax laws allow a partnership to have a tax year other than its required tax year if it (1) establishes to the IRS's satisfaction a business purpose for that requested tax year, (2) elects a particular tax year as allowed under Code Sec. 444 (see ¶ 302.02), or (3) elects to use a 52- to 53-week tax year that ends with reference to its required tax year or a tax year elected under Code Sec. 444.[27] (See ¶ 302.02.)

 Reason for the Rule: When a partnership computes taxable income, each of the partners includes their allocated share of partnership income, gain, loss, deduction, or credit from the partnership tax year ending within or with the partner's tax year. Without the rules outlined in ¶ 1404, when a partnership's tax year ended on January 31, 2009, a calendar-year partner's income from the partnership would be reported by the partner in his tax year ending on December 31, 2009, thereby resulting in an 11-month deferral of income recognition and payment of tax. To prevent this deferral of income and payment of tax, a provision of the Tax Reform Act of 1986 added the "least aggregate deferral of income" rule to the Code. When combined with the majority partner's and principal partners' year-end tests, the ability to defer the payment of tax through the selection of a tax year end has been substantially curtailed.

---

[25] Code Sec. 1222.
[26] Code Sec. 1223(1).
[27] Reg. § 1.706-1(b)(2)(ii).

Majority partners' year-end. This rule provides that the partnership's tax year must conform to the year-end used by its partners that own a majority interest in the partnership. The **majority partners rule** only applies if a partner, or group of partners, owns more than a 50-percent interest in partnership capital *and* profits. This test is applied annually on the first day of the partnership's tax year.[28] If a partnership's required tax year is determined under the majority partners rule, the partnership must use the year-end of that used by those partners, unless the partnership makes an election under Code Sec. 444 to use a different year-end or the partnership can prove a natural business year.

Example 26: ABC partnership is formed on April 6, 2009, when Klatten Industries and Joanna McNeal contribute property in exchange for an 80-percent and a 20-percent interest in capital and profits, respectively. Klatten uses a June 30 year-end; Joanna uses the calendar year-end. Since Klatten is a majority partner in ABC, the partnership's required tax year is a June 30 fiscal year.

Example 27: Assume the same facts as in Example 26, except that on June 30, 2012, Klatten Industries sells half of its interest in ABC (equal to 40 percent of its interest in the capital and profits of ABC) to Jeremy Odam, a calendar year taxpayer. As of July 1, 2012, Klatten no longer owns a majority interest in ABC. Instead, Joanna and Jeremy now collectively own 60 percent (20% + 40%) of ABC. Thus, effective July 1, 2012, ABC's required year-end changes to a calendar year. ABC is required to file a short year income tax return for the period July 1, 2012, to December 31, 2012.

Example 28: Assume the same facts as in Example 27, except Klatten Industries sells its one-half interest in ABC to a corporation that uses a March 31 fiscal year. As of July 1, 2012, ABC no longer has a majority partner because its three partners, each with a different year-end, now own 20 percent, 40 percent, and 40 percent, respectively. The majority interest rule does not apply to ABC, and it must decide if its required tax year is determined under the principal partners rule.

Principal partners' year-end. The second of the conformity rules is the principal partner rule, which applies only when partners having the same year-end do not own a majority interest in partnership capital and profits. The **principal partner rule** requires that the partnership adopt a tax year used by *all* of its principal partners. A **principal partner** is a partner that has at least a five-percent interest in the profits *or* capital of the partnership. The principal partner rule does not apply unless ALL partners who own at least a five-percent interest in capital *or* profits have the same year-end. If neither the majority interest nor the principal partners rules applies, the partnership's required tax year is the tax year that results in the least aggregate deferral of income.[29]

Example 29: Hensley, Inc. and Ingram Enterprises both use a fiscal year that ends on September 30. Each corporation owns a 20-percent interest in the DEF partnership. Each of the remaining partners in DEF owns less than a five-percent interest in DEF. Hensley and Ingram are the only two principal partners of DEF, and since they have the same year-end, DEF's required tax year is the fiscal year that ends on September 30.

Example 30: Assume the same facts as in Example 29, except Angela Lenox is admitted to the partnership as a partner owning a five-percent profits-only interest in DEF. Angela uses a calendar year-end. Since Angela owns at least a five-percent interest in capital *or* profits, DEF's principal partners no longer all have the same year-end. Accordingly, DEF's required tax year is no longer the year-end of its principal partners. Instead, it must now determine which year-end results in the least aggregate deferral of partnership income.

Least aggregate deferral of income. When the partnership and its partners do not use the same tax year, the tax laws require that each partner's allocable share of partnership items be

---

[28] Code Sec. 706(b)(1)(B)(i), (4).   [29] Code Sec. 706(b)(1)(B)(ii)(3).

reported in that partner's tax year that includes the year-end of the partnership. If the tax year of a partner is different from that of the partnership, the partner's share of the partnership taxable income is to be reported as if the entire amount were received by the partner on the closing date of the partnership tax year.

Example 31: Tom Reynolds (a calendar year taxpayer) is a partner in JKL partnership. JKL uses an approved January 31 year-end. Tom reports his share of JKL's income for the year ended January 31, 2009, on his 2009 calendar year individual income tax return. Thus, even though $^{11}/_{12}$ths of JKL's income was earned during 2008 (February 1, 2008–December 31, 2008), all of JKL's income for the 2008–2009 fiscal year is reported on Tom's 2009 calendar year tax return that includes JKL's January 31, 2009 year-end.

When a partnership cannot determine its required tax year using either the majority interest or the principal partners rule, that fact indicates that its partners use a variety of year-ends. The government's goal in this situation is to have the partnership use as its year-end the one that produces the shortest time for the government to wait to tax the income earned by the partnership. This method, called the **least aggregate deferral of income rule,**[30] involves performing a test using each of the year-ends of its partners and determining which of those year-ends, on average, will allow the government to collect taxes on the partnership income the most quickly. Using each of its partners' tax years as possible tax years, the number of months of deferral is measured and then weighted in accordance with the percentage of ownership of the partners using that particular year-end. The sum of the weighted deferrals for each tax year is compared. The tax year with the shortest (least) aggregate deferral is the partnership's required tax year.

Example 32: RST partnership has three equal partners. Robbins, Inc. uses a March 31 year-end; Schutsler, Inc. uses a July 31 year-end; and Terry Teranto uses a calendar year-end. Since no one partner or group of partners owns more than 50 percent of the capital and profits of RST, and since the three principal partners have a different year-end, RST's required year-end is determined using the year-end that produces the least aggregate deferral of income. In determining which of these three possible year-ends meets this requirement, the deferral period for each partner using each of the year-ends is determined. The deferral period is the number of months from the selected year-end until the partner's year-end. These deferral periods are then weighted by the partner's percentage of ownership in RST (one-third for each partner in this example). The sum of the deferrals for each of the partners for a particular year-end equals the aggregate deferral for that possible year-end.

If March 31 were used as RST's year-end

Partner	Months of Deferral			Weighted Deferral Period
Robbins	0	×	1/3	0
Schutsler	4 (April–July)	×	1/3	1.33
Terry	9 (April–December)	×	1/3	3.00
Aggregate deferral using a March 31 year-end				4.33

---

[30] Code Sec. 706(b)(1)(B)(iii) and Reg. § 1.706-1T.

If July 31 were used as RST's year-end

Partner	Months of Deferral			Weighted Deferral Period
Robbins	8 (August–March)	×	1/3	2.67
Schutsler	0	×	1/3	0
Terry	5 (August–December)	×	1/3	1.67
Aggregate deferral using a July 31 year-end				4.34

If December 31 were used as RST's year-end

Partner	Months' Deferral			Weighted Deferral Period
Robbins	3 (January–March)	×	1/3	1.00
Schutsler	7 (January–July)	×	1/3	2.33
Terry	0	×	1/3	0
Aggregate deferral using a December 31 year-end				3.33

The least of the three weighted aggregate deferrals is 3.33, which corresponds to using a December 31 year-end. Thus, RST's required tax year is a calendar year.

Example 33: Assume the same facts as in Example 32, except Robbins's ownership in RST is 40 percent; Schutsler's ownership is 40 percent; and Terry's ownership is 20 percent. To determine RST's required tax year, the aggregate deferral periods are computed as follows:

If March 31 were used as RST's year-end

Partner	Months of Deferral			Weighted Deferral Period
Robbins	0	×	40%	0
Schutsler	4 (April–July)	×	40%	1.6
Terry	9 (April–December)	×	20%	1.8
Aggregate deferral				3.4

If July 31 were used as RST's year-end

Partner	Months of Deferral			Weighted Deferral Period
Robbins	8 (August–March)	×	40%	3.2
Schutsler	0	×	40%	0
Terry	5 (August–December)	×	20%	1.0
Aggregate deferral				4.2

If December 31 were used as RST's year-end

Partner	Months of Deferral			Weighted Deferral Period
Robbins	3 (January–March)	×	40%	1.2
Schutsler	7 (January–July)	×	40%	2.8
Terry	0	×	20%	0
Aggregate deferral				4.0

The least of the three aggregate deferrals is 3.4, which corresponds to a March 31 fiscal end. Thus, RST's required year-end is the fiscal year that begins on April 1 and ends on March 31, unless it shows that it has a business purpose for using another year-end or elects a different year-end under Code Sec. 444.

Natural business year. Although the Code prescribes various rules that must be followed to determine a partnership's required tax year, a partnership is allowed to select a different tax year if it can establish to the IRS's satisfaction that a business purpose exists for using the requested tax year. A business purpose exists if the partnership's tax year coincides with its natural business year, which is a tax year in which the partnership receives at least 25 percent of its gross receipts in the last two months.[31] However, to demonstrate a natural business year, the 25-percent gross receipts test must be met for the preceding three consecutive 12-month periods ending with the desired year-end.[32] If more than one tax year exists in which the 25-percent gross receipts test can be met for the previous three years, the tax year that produces a higher percentage of gross sales during the last two months is the business's natural business year. (See ¶ 304.01.)

Example 34: M&N partnership currently uses a June 30 year-end. M&N wants to change to a March 31 fiscal year. M&N would like the change to become effective after the short tax year July 1, 2009, through March 31, 2010. During the last 12-month period ending on the desired year-end (April 1, 2008, to March 31, 2009), the partnership's gross receipts were $300,000, and its gross receipts for February 2009 and March 2009 total $90,000. Thus, gross receipts for the last two months are 30 percent of the total gross receipts for the desired March 31 fiscal year ($90,000/$300,000). When M&N performs this same calculation for the 12-month periods ending March 31, 2008, and March 31, 2007, its percentage of gross receipts in the last two months is 31 and 27 percent, respectively. Since the percentages are at least 25 percent, M&N passes the gross receipts test. However, M&N cannot adopt a March 31 year-end unless it can show that no other tax year would produce a greater percentage of gross receipts in the last two months. Thus, M&N would need to perform this test for each of the 11 other possible tax years before it can determine whether it can adopt March 31 as its tax year.

Section 444 election. A partnership may elect a different tax year under Code Sec. 444, provided that the selected year-end does not result in a deferral of income more than three months over the partnership's required tax year. In Example 33, RST is required to use a March 31 fiscal year-end; however, RST can elect to use either a December 31, January 31, or February 28 year-end because none of these year-ends would cause a deferral of partnership income of more than three months. (The deferral period from December 31 to March 31 is exactly three months).

For the privilege of electing a tax year other than its required tax year, the partnership must prepay to the government an amount that represents the tax on the deferred income that the owners will not report until a later year.[33] The exact amount that must be prepaid is calculated using Form 8752, *Required Payment or Refund Under Section 7519.*

---

[31] Code Sec. 706(b)(1)(C).
[32] Rev. Proc. 2002-38, 2002-1 CB 1037.

[33] Code Secs. 444(c)(1), 7519.

Example 35:   Refer back to Example 33, in which RST's required year-end is March 31. Under Code Sec. 444, RST can elect to use a calendar year, provided it agrees to prepay (keep on reserve with the IRS) any taxes associated with the profits generated from January 1 to March 31 of its tax year. Each year the partnership computes its estimated tax liability for those three months of the year. If the estimate for the year is higher than the amount currently on reserve with the IRS, it must file Form 8752 and pay the additional taxes owed. If the estimate for the year is less than the taxes on reserve with the IRS, RST can request a refund by filing Form 8752.

.02 Permissible Accounting Methods

As a rule, a partnership may elect to use any method of tax accounting that clearly reflects its income and that is regularly used in keeping its books and records. The permissible methods of accounting introduced in Chapter 3 include the cash receipts and disbursements method, the accrual method, and the hybrid method (see ¶¶ 306–308). However, a partnership usually cannot use the cash method of accounting if one of the following applies:

1. The partnership has at least one corporate partner, average annual gross receipts of more than $5 million, and it is not a farming business or

2. The partnership is a tax shelter as defined in Code Sec. 448(d)(3).

In addition to selecting an overall accounting method, partnerships are also required to abide by the special methods of accounting for certain items, such as installment sales, long-term contracts, and research and development expenditures, as discussed in Chapter 3 (see ¶ 309).

.03 Calculating Partnership Income

At the end of each tax year, a partnership (including an LLP or an LLC that elects to be taxed as a partnership) is required to file Form 1065, *U.S. Partnership Income Tax Return*. On Form 1065, the partnership provides a summary of all income, gains, deductions, losses, and credits generated during the tax year using the appropriate methods of accounting. The various partnership items are then allocated among the partners in accordance with the partnership agreement, and each partner is issued a Schedule K-1, *Partner's Share of Income, Deductions, Credits, etc.*, which reports each partner's distributive shares of the various partnership items.

The partners include the amounts reported on their respective Schedule K-1s on their income tax returns for the year that includes the last day of the partnership's tax year, regardless of whether any or all of the income was distributed to them during the year.[34] Even if restrictions exist that prevent a partner from withdrawing its share of partnership income, the partner must include the amounts reported on Schedule K-1 in the tax year that contains the day of the partnership's year-end.[35] If the partnership has more than one closing date within a partner's tax year, the partner's distributive shares from more than one partnership period are included in the partner's return.[36]

Example 36:   AB partnership has two equal partners, A and B. During its tax year ending August 31, 2009, AB generates profits of $200,000. Of this amount, $50,000 was distributed to each partner during the year, and the remaining $100,000 was retained in the partnership. Although A and B receive only $50,000 each from the partnership during the year, each must report its entire $100,000 distributive share of the partnership income on its own respective income tax return for the tax year that includes August 31, 2009.

Example 37:   CDE partnership currently uses a fiscal year ending June 30. Carla Tucker is a calendar year taxpayer who is a partner in CDE. On July 1, 2009, CDE performs the required tests for its year-end and determines that it must change to an October 31 year-end effective November 1, 2009. Thus, CDE will file its normal 12-month income tax return for the period from July 1, 2008, to June 30, 2009, and it will then file a

---

[34] Code Sec. 706(a).

[35] Reg. §1.702-1; *J.A. Basqe*, SCt, 73-1 USTC ¶ 9250, 410 U.S. 441.

[36] Code Sec. 706.

short period return for the period from July 1, 2009, to October 31, 2009. CDE's next income tax return will be for the period from November 1, 2009, to October 31, 2010. As a calendar year taxpayer, Carla will report on her 2009 individual income tax return her distributive share of partnership items for CDE's tax returns that end during Carla's 2009 tax year (June 30, 2009, and October 31, 2009). On her 2010 income tax return, Carla will report her distributive share of partnership items reported on CDE's tax return for the year ending October 31, 2010.

Guaranteed payments. If any partner is paid amounts from the partnership that are determined *without regard* to the profits generated by the partnership during the year, such amounts are referred to as **guaranteed payments.** Although partners are not considered employees of the partnership, guaranteed payments is the closest thing to salary or wage payments that a partnership can make to any of its partners. However, guaranteed payments can be made for services provided other than personal services.

Guaranteed payments are ordinary income to the partner and can be deducted by the partnership if made for services that are not capital in nature. Thus, if a partner rents out a building that it owns to the partnership for $10,000 a month, the landlord partner is guaranteed to be paid $120,000 ($10,000 × 12 months) over the course of the partnership's tax year, regardless of how well or poorly the partnership performs during the year. The tax laws require that the partner report and pay tax on the rental income it receives from the partnership and that the partnership deduct the rental expense paid to the partner from its gross income for the year. Consequently, the amount of partnership profits that are allocated to the partners is reduced by $120,000.

Example 38: GHI partnership is owned equally by three partners. In addition to being a one-third partner in GHI, Hugh Dunkin performs accounting and tax services for GHI. GIII agrees to pay Hugh $20,000 a year for his services, regardless of the partnership's performance during the year. During the year, the GHI's profits (not including the amounts paid to Hugh for his accounting and tax services) are $140,000. When reporting its activities on Form 1065, GHI deducts the $20,000 of guaranteed payments made to Hugh during the year and reports an overall profit of $120,000 ($140,000 – $20,000). Each partner's distributive share of these profits is $40,000 ($120,000/3), which is reported on each partner's respective Schedule K-1. In addition, GHI reports the $20,000 guaranteed payment on Hugh's Schedule K-1. When Hugh completes his individual income tax return for the year that includes GHI's year-end, he will include both the $20,000 of guaranteed payments and the $40,000 of partnership profits in his AGI and pay taxes on those amounts.

 Spotlight: Since partners are not considered employees of the partnership, the partnership does not withhold amounts paid to partners for personal services rendered to the partnership. When a general or limited partner performs personal services for the partnership and receives a guaranteed payment from the partnership, the partner is required to pay self-employment taxes on such income. In addition, ordinary income that is allocated to an individual who is a general partner is also considered earnings subject to self-employment tax. (The calculation of ordinary income is discussed in the next part of this section). These earnings from self-employment are added to an individual partner's other sources of self-employment income and self-employment taxes are then calculated on these amounts using the rules from Chapter 13. Individual taxpayer can deduct one-half of their self-employment tax for AGI. (See ¶ 1303.03).

Ordinary income versus separately stated items. At the end of the tax year, the partnership totals up its various items of income, loss, deduction, gain, and credit. It then separates out those items that are treated differently by different taxpayers.[37] For example, when a partnership makes a charitable contribution, it determines the amount that is deductible under the tax laws described in Chapter 5 (see ¶ 511.02). However, since the tax laws apply different charitable contribution limits

---

[37] Code Sec. 702 and Reg. § 1.702-1(a).

to corporate and individual taxpayers, it would be inappropriate to deduct charitable contributions against partnership gross income.

Example 39: Albert Shaffer is a partner in ABC partnership. During the year, ABC contributes to various qualified public charities. Albert's share of those contributions is $1,000. During that same year, Albert personally contributes $5,000 to a qualified public charity. When preparing his individual income tax return, Albert's total charitable contributions for the year are $6,000 ($5,000 + $1,000). Since these amounts were contributed to qualified public charities, he applies the 50-percent AGI limit to determine how much of the $6,000 he can deduct as an itemized deduction on his income tax return. (See ¶ 511.04 and ¶ 1304.03.)

Example 40: Continuing with Example 39, Byron Industries is also a partner in ABC. Byron's share of ABC's charitable contributions is $2,500. Bryon adds this amount to any contributions it makes to qualified charitable organizations for the year and applies the 10-percent taxable income limitation to determine how much it can deduct from its gross income on its corporate tax return. (See ¶ 511.04).

In addition to separately stating items for which the tax laws are different for corporate and individual taxpayers, any item for which the tax treatment *could* differ among two partners must be separately stated on the partnership tax return. For example, both corporate and individual taxpayers are limited in 2009 to a total of $133,000 of Section 179 expense, subject to the taxpayer having sufficient taxable income (see ¶ 702.03). Since the amount of taxable income from the business differs among the partners, any Section 179 expense elected by the partnership during the tax year must be separated from the other partnership items, and each partner's respective share of Section 179 expense must be separately reported on the partner's Schedule K-1.

Example 41: Morton, Inc. owns a 75-percent interest in MNO partnership. Because Morton is a majority partner, MNO's required tax year is the same as Morton's calendar year-end. During the year, MNO purchases Section 179 property and elects to expense the maximum $250,000 that is allowed in 2009. As a 75-percent partner in MNO, Morton's share of MNO's Section 179 expense is $187,500 ($250,000 × 75%). This amount flows through separately from ordinary income on Morton's Schedule K-1. When preparing its 2009 tax return, Morton adds the $187,500 to any Section 179 property it elects to expense during 2009, keeping in mind that it can only elect a total of $250,000 of Section 179 expense for 2009. In addition, any amounts that Morton elects to expense in 2009 (including the $187,500 from MNO) can only be deducted if Morton's taxable income from the business is sufficient to absorb these amounts in 2009. Any amounts not deducted in 2009 are carried forward to Morton's 2010 tax year as Section 179 expense deduction in that year. (See ¶ 702.03.)

Figure 14-3 lists items that a partnership must state separately from the partnerships ordinary income or loss when preparing its tax return.

Figure 14-3 Separately Stated Items

- Guaranteed payments made to partners (see ¶ 1404.03).
- Gains and losses from sales or exchanges of capital assets held for one year or less (see ¶ 901).
- Gains and losses from sales or exchanges of capital assets held for more than one year (see ¶ 901), including a breakdown of those that may be subject to a maximum 28-percent tax rate (from the sale of collectibles and Section 1202 stock) and any unrecaptured Section 1250 gain subject to a maximum 25-percent tax rate (see ¶ 1306.01).
- Gains and losses from sales or exchanges of Section 1231 property (see ¶ 904).

- All other items included in the calculation of investment income and investment expense that are necessary to compute an individual's investment interest expense limitation (see ¶ 1304.03). This includes interest income, dividend income (keeping separate any amounts of qualified dividends that are eligible for the reduced tax rates applicable to individual taxpayers (see ¶ 907 and ¶ 1306.01)), and (investment) expenses for the production of income that are not business deductions (see ¶ 1304.03).

- Rental income and royalties that may be used as passive income in computing an individual's passive loss limitation.

- Section 179 deduction (see ¶ 702.03).

- Charitable contributions (see ¶ 511).

- Any special allocations of income, gain, loss, or deduction under the partnership agreement (see ¶ 1404.04).[38]

- Foreign income taxes paid or accrued plus the partner's share of foreign source income that the partner can use to compute its foreign tax credit (see ¶ 1117).

- Any tax credits generated by the partnership during the year (see Chapter 11).

- The partner's net earnings from self-employment. For general partners, this amount includes the partner's distributive share of ordinary income during the year plus any guaranteed payments the partner received for personal services rendered to the partnership.[39] A limited partner's distributive share of partnership income is not earnings from self-employment.[40]

- The partner's share of any alternative minimum tax (AMT) (see ¶ 1005), tax preference items (see ¶ 1007), and AMT adjustment items (see ¶ 1008) that are attributable to partnership operations during the year.

- Dividends for which there is a dividends received deduction available (see ¶ 1203.01).

The partnership need only separately track those items of income, deduction, gain, or loss that could be treated differently on the partners' own respective income tax returns. Items that are treated identically for all types of taxpayers can be lumped together and reported as one lump sum amount called "ordinary income (loss)." Therefore, amounts recognized as gross receipts or sales (net of any cost of goods sold) are included in the partnership's ordinary income (loss). Also included would be any gains or losses taxed as ordinary income from the disposal of property, which includes gains and losses from business property held short-term and any depreciation recapture on the sale or exchange of depreciable property. Likewise, salaries, wages, and amounts paid for employee benefit programs would be ordinary deductions included in the calculation of the partnership's ordinary income (loss). Also included in the calculation would be guaranteed payments made to partners (assuming the costs are not capital in nature), repairs, bad debts, interest, taxes, rent, depreciation expense (Modified Accelerated Cost Recovery System (MACRS) or alternative depreciation system (ADS)), depletion expense, and other similar ordinary deductions.

Example 42: Susie Reeser owns a 25-percent interest in QRST partnership. Both Susie and QRST use a calendar year-end. For the year ended December 31, 2009, QRST reports the following items of partnership income, gain, loss, deduction, and credit.

Gross sales	$400,000
Cost of goods sold	120,000
Wage expense	80,000
Depreciation recapture	5,000
Net Section 1231 gain	24,000
Equipment rental	18,000

---

[38] Reg. § 1.702-1.
[39] Code Sec. 1402(a).

[40] Code Sec. 1402(a)(13).

Mortgage interest	10,000
Real estate taxes	5,000
MACRS depreciation	11,000
Contribution to employee retirement plans	3,000
Charitable contributions	10,000

On its partnership tax return, QRST lumps together all items that are taxed as ordinary income or loss without limitation to any partner as follows:

Gross profit (net of cost of goods sold)			$280,000
Depreciation recapture			5,000
Less:	Wage expense	(80,000)	
	Rent expense	(18,000)	
	Interest	(10,000)	
	Taxes	(5,000)	
	MACRS depreciation	(11,000)	
	Retirement plan contributions	(3,000)	(127,000)
Ordinary income of the partnership			$158,000

QRST then allocates the $158,000 of ordinary income to its partners on their respective Schedule K-1s. On her personal income tax return, Susie includes $39,500 of ordinary income in her gross income ($158,000 x 25%).

In addition to allocating a 25-percent share of the ordinary income to Susie, QRST allocates 25-percent of its net Section 1231 gain and charitable contributions to her. Susie adds her $6,000 share ($24,000 × 25%) of the Section 1231 gain to the netting process on her income tax return to determine whether any of the gain can be considered long-term capital gain subject to a maximum 15-percent tax rate. Both the $39,500 ($158,000 × 25%) and $6,000 increase Susie's AGI. Susie then adds her $2,500 ($10,000 × 25%) share of QRST's charitable contributions to her own contributions and then applies the AGI limits to determine the amount she can deduct as an itemized deduction (see ¶ 1304.03).

 Planning Pointer: Since amounts allocated to partners are not subject to withholding, partners will need to make sure that the proper amount of taxes are prepaid to the federal and state governments during the year. If an individual partner (or partner's spouse if filing a joint return) is also an employee, the partner (or partner's spouse) can arrange to have additional amounts withheld from wages to cover the additional taxes owed on partnership income. In all other cases, the partner will need to make quarterly estimated payments to avoid any underpayment penalties. (See ¶ ¶ 409.01 and 409.02.) In addition to income taxes, individual partners must also consider any self-employment taxes that will be assessed on income allocated from the partnership that is considered self-employment income. This includes any guaranteed payments for personal services, as well as a general partner's distributive share of ordinary income.

Character of gain or loss from the sale of contributed property. Normally, the character of the gain or loss recognized by the partnership depends on the type of property sold and the partnership's holding period of the property. For example, if a partnership purchases a capital asset and sells it for a gain after holding it for nine months, the partnership will report a short-term capital gain on its tax return and will allocate the short-term capital gain among its partners on their respective Schedule K-1s. However, special rules apply to the character of the gain or loss recognized on the sale or other disposition of contributed property. "Contributed property" is property the partnership acquires as a contribution from a partner in exchange for a capital and profits interest in the partnership. When a partnership sells contributed property, the nature and character of the gain or loss is sometimes determined by the character and holding period of the property in the hands of the contributing partner.[41] These special rules apply to the sale of unrealized receivables, inventory, and capital loss property.

An **unrealized receivable** includes any right to income for services or goods that are not capital assets that have not been previously recorded in gross income under the contributing partner's method of accounting.[42] Thus, if a cash method partner contributes to a partnership amounts due from customers, the receivables are unrealized receivables because those amounts have yet to be reported in income. The amounts will be recognized as ordinary income as they are collected by the partnership, regardless of the partnership's method of accounting.[43]

Example 43: In exchange for a capital and profits interest in ABC partnership, Anthony Ryan contributes $50,000 of accounts receivable he had obtained in the course of operating his sole proprietorship. Anthony used the cash method of accounting in his sole proprietorship, and therefore, had not reported these accounts receivable in his gross income prior to contributing them to ABC. Thus, Anthony's basis in the accounts receivable is $0, which becomes ABC's basis in the receivables. When ABC collects the $50,000 from Anthony's former clients, it will include the $50,000 in its gross income as part of partnership profits for the year.

If the contributed property is inventory in the hands of the contributing partner, then for five years after the date the partner contributes the property to the partnership, any gain or loss recognized from the sale of the property will be taxed as ordinary income or loss to the partnership. This rule applies regardless of whether the property is inventory in the hands of the partnership. After five years, the character of the gain is determined based on how the property is used by the partnership.[44]

Example 44: On April 29, 2009, Frank Simmons contributes inventory from his sole proprietorship in exchange for a 30-percent capital and profits interest in EFG partnership. At the time of the contribution, the FMV of the inventory is $50,000. Frank's basis in the inventory is $22,000. EFG's basis in the inventory also is $22,000. If EFG sells the inventory within five years of April 29, 2009, the gain will be taxed as ordinary income or loss to EFG.

Example 45: Continuing with Example 44, Frank is a real estate developer, and the property he contributes to EFG is land that was inventory in his business. If EFG is in the real estate business, the land will be inventory to the partnership and any gain or loss upon its sale will always produce ordinary income or loss.

Example 46: Assume the same facts as in Example 45, except EFG is a law firm and it uses the land as an employee parking lot. If EFG sells the land in 2011 for $60,000, it will recognize $38,000 of ordinary income ($60,000 – $22,000). If, however, EFG sells the land for $60,000 after five years have passed, it will recognize $38,000 of Section 1231 gain.

Example 47: Assume the same facts as in Example 45, except that EFG holds the land as an investment. The $38,000 gain on the sale of the land will be characterized as long-term capital gain if EFG waits more than five years to sell the land.

---

[41] Code Sec. 724.
[42] Code Sec. 751(c) and Reg. § 1.751-1(c).

[43] Code Sec. 724(a).
[44] Code Sec. 724(b).

> **Reason for the Rule:** The tax laws limit the amount of capital losses that can be deducted on both an individual and a corporate taxpayer's income tax returns. When taxpayers generate more capital gains, they are allowed to deduct more capital losses. In addition, individual taxpayers may be taxed at lower tax rates on long-term capital gains. When writing the partnership rules, Congress was concerned that taxpayers might attempt to use partnerships as a vehicle for converting ordinary income into capital gain by contributing appreciated ordinary income property to a partnership, having the partnership use the property as a capital asset, and then having the partnership recognize a capital gain on the subsequent sale of the property. To prevent such abuses, Congress enacted the tax laws that require unrealized receivables (which the partner would eventually recognize as ordinary income) to be taxed as ordinary income when recognized by the partnership. The tax laws also require that gain or loss on the subsequent sale of any inventory in the hands of the contributing partner be recognized as ordinary income or loss if sold within five years after it is contributed.

For property that was a capital asset in the hands of the contributing partner, any loss on the disposal of the property by the partnership within five years is a capital loss to the extent that the adjusted basis of the property to the contributing partner exceeded the property's FMV immediately before the contribution.[45] This special rule applies only if property that had declined in value is contributed to the partnership and within five years is sold by the partnership at a loss.

Example 48: On March 8, 2009, Dottie Britten contributes land worth $50,000 in exchange for a capital and profits interest in XYZ partnership. Prior to contributing the land, Dottie held it as an investment. Her basis in the land is $130,000, which becomes XYZ's basis in the land and Dottie's adjusted basis in XYZ. The land is Section 1231 property in the hands of XYZ. If XYZ sells the land for less than its $130,000 basis within five years of March 8, 2009, it will recognize the first $80,000 of loss as a capital loss. Any additional loss would be characterized as a Section 1231 loss.

Example 49: Continuing with the Example 48, assume that XYZ sells the land for $100,000 on January 15, 2011. XYZ recognizes a $30,000 capital loss ($100,000 – $130,000).

Example 50: Assume the same facts as in Example 49, except XYZ sells the land for $30,000. XYZ recognizes a $100,000 loss ($30,000 – $130,000), of which the first $80,000 is a long-term capital loss. The remaining $20,000 ($100,000 – $80,000) loss is recognized as a Section 1231 loss.

Example 51: Assume the same facts as in Example 49, except XYZ sells the land for $160,000. XYZ recognizes a $30,000 gain ($160,000 – $130,000), which XYZ recognizes as a Section 1231 gain.

> **Reason for the Rule:** Because of the tax laws that limit the amount of capital losses that can be deducted on both an individual and a corporate taxpayer's income tax return, Congress was concerned that taxpayers might attempt to use partnerships as a vehicle for converting capital losses into ordinary losses. To prevent abuses in this area, Congress requires that the partnership recognize a capital loss on the sale of contributed property that was a capital asset in the hands of the contributing partner. However, the amount of the loss that must be characterized as a capital loss is limited to the amount by which the adjusted basis of the property to the contributing partner exceeds the property's FMV at the time it is contributed to the partnership.

---

[45] Code Sec. 724(c).

.04 Allocating Partnership Items

The partners are liable for the tax on the partnership income, regardless of whether the income is actually distributed to them.[46] For the most part, the allocation of any item of income, gain, loss, deduction, or credit among the partners is controlled by the partnership agreement. If the partnership agreement does not provide for the allocation of any item, the partner's distributive share of each item will be determined by reference to the partner's interest in the partnership, after taking into account all facts and circumstances. The partner's distributive share of each item will be determined by the partner's interest in the partnership if the partnership agreement lacks substantial economic effect.[47]

Example 52:   Eric Brown owns 25 percent of ABCD partnership. The partnership agreement calls for all depreciation expense and dividend income to be allocated to Eric. As a 25-percent partner in ABCD, Eric normally would be allocated 25 percent of these items. However, if the allocation of 100 percent of these items has substantial economic effect, then the allocation will be respected, and ABCD will be allowed to allocate these items in accordance with the terms in the partnership agreement.

Special allocations. To determine whether an allocation specified in the partnership agreement has **substantial economic effect**, it is first necessary to determine whether the allocation has economic effect and then determine whether that effect is substantial.[48] An allocation in the partnership agreement has *economic effect* if (1) the partnership maintains separate capital accounts in accordance with prescribed regulatory rules for each partner; (2) upon liquidation of the partnership or any partner's interest in the partnership, liquidating distributions are required to be made in accordance with positive capital account balances of the partners; and (3) each partner with a deficit balance in his or her capital account following the liquidation must restore the deficit (negative) balance.[49] Normally, an economic effect will be deemed *substantial* if (1) a reasonable possibility exists that the allocation will substantially affect the dollar amount of the partners' shares of the partnership's tax items independently of tax consequences and (2) the partner to whom an allocation is made actually receives the economic benefit or bears the economic burden corresponding to the allocation.[50]

The rules governing what constitutes substantial economic effect are very complex and beyond the scope of this chapter; however, it is important to note that if certain conditions are met, partnership items can be specially allocated among the partners. For example, assuming the requirements of substantial economic effect are met, a partner that owns a 40-percent interest in capital and profits may be allocated none of one item—the partnership's tax-exempt income, for example—and instead be allocated 100 percent of another partnership item, such as dividend income. Any specially allocated items must be separately stated on the partners' Schedule K-1s and are not included as part of the partnership's ordinary income or loss.

Reason for the Rule: Much of the complexity of the tax rules surrounding partnerships stems from Congress's concern that partners may use the partnership to manipulate the reporting of income or loss, thus distorting their tax liabilities. For example, there is a requirement that each partnership allocation of a tax item must have substantial economic effect. This is designed to prevent the allocation of income to partners with tax losses that the income would offset or the allocation of deductions to partners with high incomes for whom the loss allocations would have more value due to their higher income tax brackets. In these situations, the total tax liabilities of all the partners could be less if the partnership were to allocate income among partners for the

---

[46] Code Sec. 701; Reg. § 1.701-1.
[47] Code Secs. 704(a) and (b), 706(d), Reg. § 1.706-1(c)(2).
[48] Reg. § 1.704-1(b)(2).

[49] Reg. § 1.704-1(b)(2)(ii)(b).
[50] Reg. § 1.704-1(b)(2).

> sole purpose of reducing taxes without any business purpose or consequence to any of the partners.

Required allocations. The tax laws require that certain partnership items be allocated to the partners in a particular manner, despite the allocations that may be specified in the partnership agreement. Like special allocations, these required allocations are separately stated on the partner's Schedule K-1. Although the tax laws surrounding these required allocations are extremely complex and beyond the scope of this introductory chapter on partnership taxation, a brief discussion of a couple of the required allocations provides an idea of how the rules work.

When a partner contributes appreciated property to the partnership, the amount of the appreciation represents realized gain that neither the partner nor the partnership immediately recognizes. Instead, the contributing partner's adjusted basis in the contributed property becomes the partnership's basis in the property and is added to the partner's basis in the partnership interest. By having both parties take a "substituted basis" (and by the special allocation rules discussed in the paragraphs that follow), the tax laws ensure that the contributing partner eventually recognizes (and pays tax on) the gain. This occurs either when the partnership sells the property or when the partner sells the partnership interest.

When a partnership sells property, the recognized gain or loss is normally allocated among the partners in accordance with the terms in the partnership agreement (assuming the allocation has substantial economic effect). However, when contributed property is sold, the realized gain or loss must be allocated to the contributing partner to the extent of any deferred gain or loss to the contributing partner.[51] Any remaining gain or loss is allocated in accordance with the partnership agreement.

Example 53: David Cotton contributes land worth $100,000 in exchange for a one-third capital and profits interest in ABC partnership. ABC plans to use the land as a parking lot for its employees, thus making the land Section 1231 property in the hands of the partnership. David purchased the land several years earlier as an investment for $30,000. Thus, when David contributes the land to ABC, he realizes a $70,000 gain ($100,000 – $30,000); however, recognition of the gain is postponed, and both David's basis in his ABC partnership interest and ABC's basis in the land are $30,000. Furthermore, David's long-term holding period for the land carries over and becomes the holding period for both David's interest in ABC and ABC's holding period in the land. If David immediately sells his partnership interest for $100,000, he will recognize a $70,000 ($100,000 – $30,000) long-term capital gain.

Example 54: Assume the same facts as in Example 53, except David does not sell his interest in ABC. Instead, ABC sells the land for $100,000, and the partnership recognizes a $70,000 Section 1231 gain ($100,000 – $30,000). The tax laws require that ABC allocate the entire gain to David, which will cause his basis in ABC partnership to increase to $100,000 ($30,000 + $70,000). (See ¶ 1404.04.) If David then sells his partnership interest, the increase to his partnership basis will ensure that the $70,000 gain from the sale of the land is not taxed a second time.

Example 55: Assume the same facts as in Example 54, except ABC sells the land for $120,000. The partnership recognizes $90,000 of Section 1231 gain ($120,000 – $30,000). The tax laws generally require that ABC allocate the first $70,000 of gain to David. The remaining $20,000 gain ($90,000 – $70,000) is then allocated among the partners in accordance with the partnership agreement.

---

[51] Code Sec. 704(c)(1)(C).

Reason for the Rule: Code Sec. 704(c) is designed to prevent taxpayers from allocating built-in gains on an asset transferred to a partnership away from the contributing partner to another partner. While Code Sec. 721 generally permits the tax-free transfer of appreciated assets to a partnership, the subsequent sale of these assets will result in the deferred built-in gain upon contribution being allocated to the contributing partner, overriding any provisions that may be included in the partnership agreement. This rule furthers the desire of Congress to prevent the use of partnerships as a means of manipulating the reporting of income and deductions where the result would be the understatement of tax liability.

When a partnership purchases a depreciable asset, the cost of the asset is depreciated over a number of years, and the depreciation expense is allocated among the partners. When a partner contributes depreciable property in exchange for an interest in the partnership, the partner's adjusted basis in the property becomes the partnership's tax basis, and accordingly, becomes the depreciable basis in the property. If the adjusted basis is less than the FMV of the contributed property, the partnership's total depreciation deductions will be less than they would have been had the partnership purchased the property for its FMV. This, in turn, means the partners will be allocated less depreciation than normally would have been allocated to them if the partnership had acquired the property for its FMV. Since the contributing partner is responsible for this difference, the tax laws require that the depreciation expense be specially allocated to the noncontributing partners to make up for any difference in total depreciation expense.[52]

Example 56: Amber Trane contributes depreciable property worth $50,000 in exchange for a 50-percent interest in AB partnership. Amber's basis in the property is $40,000. AB's basis in the depreciable property is $40,000, and therefore over the years AB will deduct depreciation expense totaling $40,000. The tax laws require that depreciation expense be allocated to the other partners to compensate for the $10,000 ($50,000 − $40,000) of depreciation that AB will never deduct because it uses Amber's substituted basis. In accordance with this rule, over the years the noncontributing partners would be entitled to 50 percent of the depreciation ($25,000) based upon the FMV at the date of contribution ($50,000). Amber would be entitled to $15,000 in depreciation expense, the actual depreciation allowed ($40,000) less the amount allocated to the noncontributing partners ($25,000).

Character of allocated items. The character of the gain or loss recognized by the partnership retains it character when it flows through to the partners. Thus, if property that is Section 1231 property to the partnership is sold at a gain, then each partner's share of Section 1231 gain is allocated to each partner, regardless of the character the property sold would have had in the hands of the partner. Similarly, when the partnership sells contributed property and is required to recognize ordinary income or loss (in the case of unrealized receivables or inventory) or capital loss (in the case of a capital asset), the character of the income or loss recognized by the partnership flows through to the partners in accordance with the allocation rules described in this chapter.

Example 57: ABC partnership owns 100 shares of common stock that is a capital asset in the hands of ABC. The partnership has owned the stock for several years. ABC sells the stock at a gain of $10,000, which is treated as long-term capital gain. If this gain were not reported separately from ABC's other income and deductions, it would be treated as ordinary income and could not be used to offset capital losses generated on its partners' own tax returns. Thus, it is important that ABC separately state this long-term capital gain on the partnership tax return and on the partners' Schedule K-1s.

---

[52] Code Sec. 704(c)(1)(A).

Example 58: In 2007, Bob Everett (a real estate developer) contributed land worth $50,000 in exchange for a 50-percent interest in BD partnership. Bob's adjusted basis in the land was $30,000. In 2009, BD sells the land for $75,000. BD realizes a $45,000 gain ($75,000 – $30,000) on the sale of the land. Since the land was inventory to the contributing partner and was sold within five years after it was contributed to BD, the $45,000 gain is ordinary income to BD. The tax laws require that the first $20,000 of the deferred gain upon contribution ($50,000 – $30,000) be allocated entirely to Bob. The remaining $25,000 ($45,000 – $20,000) is allocated to the partners in accordance with the terms in the partnership agreement. Bob's total share of the gain would be $32,500 ($20,000 + ($25,000 × 50%)).

Example 59: Assume the same facts as in Example 58, except the land is sold for $40,000. BD recognizes $10,000 of ordinary income ($40,000 – $30,000), which must be entirely allocated to Bob since it represents deferred gain from the contribution of the asset to the partnership.

Example 60: On January 5, 2005, Clint Wix contributes land held as an investment in exchange for a one-third interest in WXY partnership. The land is worth $100,000. Clint's basis in the land is $120,000, which becomes WXY's basis in the land. The land is Section 1231 property in the hands of WXY. In 2009, WXY sells the land for $90,000 and recognizes a $30,000 loss ($90,000 – $120,000). Because the property was sold within five years after it was contributed, the first $20,000 of the loss ($120,000 – $100,000) must be allocated to Clint and will be characterized as a capital loss. The remaining $10,000 of the loss is allocated to the partners in accordance with the terms of the partnership agreement and will be characterized as a Section 1231 loss. (The partnership is only required to recognize a capital loss to the extent that the contributing partner's adjusted basis in the property exceeded the FMV of the property at the time it was contributed to the partnership.)

¶ 1405 Keeping Track of a Partner's Interest in the Partnership

The adjusted basis in property is the mechanism used to make ensure that the amount that represents a return of the taxpayer's investment is tax-free to the taxpayer when the property is sold (see ¶ 802.02). This same principle applies to the partner's basis in a partnership interest. The partner's basis in the partnership interest is also used to ensure that the profits of the partnership are not taxed a second time when distributed to the partners. The amount of the partner's basis in the partnership interest also determines the maximum amount of any allocated loss from the partnership that the partners can deduct on their respective income tax returns.[53]

The initial basis of the partner's interest in the partnership was discussed at ¶ 1403.04. The tax law normally increases the partner's basis in the partnership interest by the adjusted basis of the property and taxable services that the partner contributes to the partnership in exchange for an interest in partnership capital and profits (minus the partner's net release of any debt associated with the contributed property). These same rules also apply to any subsequent contributions a partner makes to the partnership. The tax law then requires that the partner's basis in the partnership interest be increased by the partner's allocable share of partnership income and gain items to ensure that the taxable profits and gains of the partnership are taxed only one time or, in the case of tax-exempt income, never taxed at all. Likewise, the tax law requires that the partner's basis in the partnership interest be decreased by the partner's allocable share of partnership deduction and loss items to ensure that the partners only benefit once from those items (or that in the case of nondeductible expenses, the partner never benefits at all).

---

[53] Reg. § 1.704-1(d).

.01 Increases to Basis

After the partner's initial partnership tax basis has been determined, the basis of the partner's interest is increased by the partner's distributive share of partnership items of income and gain. The partner's basis is not only increased by the partner's share of taxable partnership income and gain but also by the partner's share of tax-exempt income. The partner's basis in the partnership interest is also increased by any additional contributions the partner makes during the year using the rules described in ¶ 1403.04.

Example 61: Mark Witherspoon contributes $10,000 in exchange for a 10-percent interest in MNO partnership. During its first year of operations, MNO allocates $5,000 of ordinary income and $1,000 of tax-exempt income to Mark. Mark's basis in his partnership interest increases by the $6,000 of taxable and tax-exempt income he is allocated during the year. Assuming MNO does not make any distributions to Mark during the year, Mark's basis in MNO at the end of the first year is $16,000 ($10,000 + $6,000).

Reason for the Rule: Through the use of a partner's tax basis in a partnership interest, the tax laws ensure that a partner only pays tax one time on partnership income. It also ensures that the partner will never pay tax on tax-exempt income. When a partnership earns tax-exempt income, its assets increase by the amount of income the partnership receives. In turn, the partners' value in their partnership interest also increases. Thus, if a partner's tax basis does not increase by the partner's share of tax-exempt income, the partner will eventually be taxed on the income when it sells the partnership interest. In Example 61, if Mark's basis were only increased by his allocable shares of taxable items of income and gain, his basis in MNO would be $15,000 ($10,000 + $5,000). If Mark were to sell his partnership interest for $16,000 (its FMV), he would be taxed on a $1,000 gain ($16,000 – $15,000), which means that the tax-exempt income was merely tax deferred, not tax exempt. To prevent this from happening, the tax laws allow Mark's basis in MNO to increase to $16,000 so that he will never be taxed on his share of MNO's tax-exempt income.

Increase in partner's share of partnership liabilities. One distinctive feature of operating a business as a partnership is that a partnership's owners are ultimately responsible for the debts of the partnership. Thus, the tax laws allow partners to include as part of the tax basis in their partnership interests their respective shares of partnership liabilities. This is done by treating the partner's share of partnership liabilities the same as if the partner had made a cash contribution to the partnership.[54] Thus, when the partnership takes on additional liabilities, each partner's tax basis in the partnership interest increases accordingly.

A partner's share of partnership recourse liabilities generally is determined by the ratio for apportioning partnership losses. If, however, none of the partners has personal liability (a nonrecourse debt), the liability generally is shared by all partners, including any limited partners, in the same proportion as they share profits.[55] (See ¶ 1403.04 for a more detailed discussion of how recourse and nonrecourse liabilities are allocated among the partners). However, if a partner personally guarantees a nonrecourse liability, the liability is allocated to the guarantor partner to the extent of the guarantee. For example, if the general partner of a limited partnership personally guarantees a nonrecourse loan assumed by the partnership, the general partner's tax basis is increased by the amount of the loan. The tax basis of the other (nonguaranteeing) partners is not affected by this particular loan.

---

[54] Code Sec. 752(a).

[55] Reg. § 1.752-3(a).

Example 62: Art Myers and Ken Norman form AK equal partnership. AK takes out a loan from the bank for $100,000. Art and Ken's bases in their respective partnership interests are increased by $50,000 ($100,000 × 50%).

Example 63: Brian Michaels and Jeannie Richards are equal partners in BJ partnership. During the year, BJ's liabilities increase from $200,000 to $260,000. Accordingly, each partner is treated as having contributed $30,000 cash at the end of the tax year, which represents each partner's one-half share of the $60,000 increase in partnership debt ($260,000 – $200,000). Brian and Jeannie increase their respective bases in their partnership interests by $30,000 at the end of the partnership's tax year.

 Spotlight: Since a partner's basis cannot be reduced below zero, allowing the tax basis in the partnership to be increased by the partner's share of partnership debts makes it less likely that the partner will be taxed on cash distributions or limited on the amount of partnership losses that it can deduct. A partner faced with not being able to deduct a loss as a result of lack of basis can have the partnership increase its debt at year end which increases basis at the partner level and thus permits a tax deductible loss from what would have been a nondeductible loss. The ability to utilize debt to increase basis also can create a problem when the partnership debts are reduced. Partnerships must evaluate any change in debt, including accounts payable, notes payable, and other accrued liabilities, before the end of the year to make certain they have not inadvertently created a circumstance where partnership losses become nondeductible due to a lack of basis.

.02 Decreases to Basis

When the partnership makes a distribution to a partner, the distribution generally represents the partner's share of previously taxed partnership profits or amounts representing contributions the partner made to the partnership. Therefore, the basis of a partner's interest in the partnership is decreased (but not below zero) when the partner receives a distribution from the partnership. The partner's basis in the partnership is also reduced (again, not below zero) by the partner's distributive share of partnership losses, deductions, and nondeductible expenses that are not capital in nature.[56]

Example 64: Donna Chapel contributes $100,000 to the ABCD equal partnership. During the first year, Donna's share of the partnership taxable income is $25,000, but only $10,000 is actually distributed to her. At the end of the year, Donna includes her $25,000 distributive share of partnership income on her individual income tax return. Her basis in ABCD at the end of the first year is $115,000. This amount represents Donna's initial investment in ABCD ($100,000) plus $15,000 ($25,000 – $10,000) of previously taxed partnership income that has not yet been distributed to her.

Contributions to the partnership	$100,000
Plus: Allocable share of partnership income	25,000
Less: Distributions made during the year	(10,000)
Tax basis at the end of the year	$115,000

Example 65: At the beginning of the year, Antwon Nasim's basis in his partnership interest is $100,000. Antwon's share of the partnership's ordinary loss for the year is $40,000, and his share of tax-exempt municipal bond interest is $3,000. The partnership distributes $33,000 to Antwon during the tax year. Antwon's basis at the end of the year is computed as follows:

[56] Code Sec. 733.

Tax basis at the beginning of the year	$100,000
Plus: Allocable share of tax-exempt income	3,000
Less: Distributions made during the year	(33,000)
Less: Allocable share of partnership loss	(40,000)
Tax basis at the end of the year	$ 30,000

Example 66: Continuing with Example 65, during the subsequent tax year, Antwon contributes an additional $20,000 to the partnership in exchange for an interest in partnership capital and profits. His share of the partnership ordinary income for the year is $25,000, and his share of separately stated Section 1231 losses is $6,000. Also during the year the partnership paid and incurred a nondeductible fine. Antwon's allocable share of the fine was $2,000. The partnership distributes $40,000 to Antwon during the tax year. Antwon's basis at the end of the year is computed as follows:

Tax basis at the beginning of the year	$30,000
Plus: Additional contribution	20,000
Plus: Allocable share of partnership income (loss)	25,000
Less: Distributions	(40,000)
Less: Allocable share of Section 1231 loss	(6,000)
Less: Allocable share of nondeductible expenditures	(2,000)
Tax basis at the end of the year	$27,000

 Reason for the Rule: When a partnership pays an expense that is not deductible, its assets decrease by the amount of the expense. This, in turn, reduces the value in the partnership assets. If a partner's tax basis does not decrease by the partner's share of the nondeductible expense, the partner will eventually benefit from the nondeductible expense (either by recognizing less gain or more loss on the sale of the partnership interest or by being able to have additional basis from which to receive tax-free distributions).

Decrease in partner's share of partnership liabilities. As previously discussed, if the partnership's liabilities increase during the year, the tax law treats the increase as though the partners made additional cash contributions to the partnership. The reverse happens when the partnership's liabilities decrease during the year. A decrease in partnership liabilities is treated as though the partnership made a cash distribution to the partners for their respective shares in the decrease in partnership liabilities.[57]

Example 67: Daryl Tristin and Glen Ackers are equal partners in DG partnership. During the year, DG's liabilities decrease from $300,000 to $160,000. Because of the $140,000 decrease ($300,000 – $160,000) in partnership liabilities, each partner is deemed to have received a $70,000 cash distribution from the partnership. The cash distribution reduces the partner's basis in the partnership interest. If the cash distribution exceeds the partner's basis in the partnership interest, the partner recognizes gain for the amount of the excess.

---

[57] Code Sec. 752(b).

Spotlight: Allocating partnership liabilities, both recourse and nonrecourse liabilities, requires the partnership to recognize differences in the allocation due to the two types of liabilities. The partnership is also required to report to partners their shares of the allocated liabilities on their Schedule K-1s, including the breakdown between recourse and nonrecourse, to help in facilitating the calculation of each partner's basis in capital and to allow the IRS to know the amounts of the different categories of liabilities. In the case of a general partnership, each partner's share of the partnership's recourse liabilities is that partner's share of the economic risk of loss relating to that liability computed as if the partnership were liquidated and all the assets were of no value.[58] (See ¶ 1403.04.) Special rules apply in cases in which partners guarantee all or part of the debt. Generally, a guarantee creates an economic risk of loss, and a partner's basis is increased to the extent of that risk.[59] In the case of a limited partnership, the limited partners are, by definition, liable generally only to the extent of their original contributions to the partnership. Therefore, a limited partner generally cannot increase his or her basis in a partnership interest because of recourse debt, unless he or she guarantees all or part of the debt.

.03 Ordering Rules

The tax law never allows a partner's tax basis to go below zero. A partner never recognizes gain or loss from the allocation of losses and deductions in excess of the partner's basis in the partnership interest. The only time a partner recognizes gain from a distribution from the partnership is when the amount of the cash distribution exceeds the partner's basis in the partnership interest.[60] Since both distributions and the partner's share of partnership losses and deductions reduce the partner's basis in the partnership interest, it is necessary to establish an order in which items of income, gain, deduction, and loss are taken into account in determining a partner's basis.

The tax law requires that, at the end of the year, all items that increase a partner's basis be taken into account first. Such items include the partner's distributive share of partnership taxable income, tax-exempt income, and gain. Also taken into account are any contributions the partner made to the partnership during the year, including any cash contributions the partner was deemed to have made due to an increase in partnership liabilities. Any taxable services the partner provided in exchange for a capital interest in the partnership are also taken into account.

After the partner's basis in the partnership interest is as high as it can be made, the tax law next requires that the partner's basis be reduced by any distributions by the partnership, including deemed cash distributions due to a decrease in partnership liabilities during the year.[61] If the amount of the cash distributions during the year exceeds the partner's basis in the partnership interest, the excess is a taxable gain to the partner.[62]

After the distributions have been subtracted from the partner's basis, the last items taken into consideration are the partner's allocable share of partnership losses, deductions, and nondeductible (but not capitalized) expenditures.[63] To the extent that these items exceed the partner's remaining basis in the partnership interest, they are carried over to the next tax year.[64]

Example 68: Richard purchases a partnership interest for $5,000. During the current tax year, Richard receives a $3,000 cash distribution from the partnership. At the end of the tax year, Richard's distributive share of partnership losses is $6,000. The distribution reduces Richard's basis in the partnership interest to $2,000 ($5,000 – $3,000). Thus, only $2,000 of Richard's share of partnership losses is deductible on Richard's income tax return in the current year. His basis in the partnership is reduced to zero.

---

[58] Reg. § 1.752-2(a), Reg. § 1.752-2(b).
[59] Reg. § 1.752-2(e).
[60] Code Sec. 731(a).
[61] Rev. Rul. 66-94, 1966-1 CB 166.

[62] Code Sec. 731(a)(1).
[63] Rev. Rul. 66-94, 1966-1 CB 166.
[64] Code Sec. 704(d).

The $4,000 disallowed loss is carried forward to the next tax year. Richard will be allowed to deduct the suspended loss when he generates sufficient basis in his partnership interest to absorb the loss.

Amount paid for partnership interest	$5,000
Less: Distributions	(3,000)
	$2,000
Less: Allocable share of partnership losses	(6,000)
Tax basis at the end of the year	$ 0

Example 69: Florena Santiago, a partner of FGH partnership, has an $80,000 basis in her partnership interest at the beginning of the year. During the year, Florena's share of partnership losses is $40,000 and the partnership distributes $50,000 to her. Florena's basis in her partnership interest at the end of the year is $0, and $10,000 of her partnership loss ($40,000 – $30,000) will be suspended until her basis in the partnership interest increases.

Basis at beginning of year	$80,000
Less: Cash distributions	(50,000)
	$30,000
Less: Distributive share of losses (cannot reduce basis below zero)	(40,000)
Adjusted tax basis at the end of the year	$ 0

Example 70: On May 5, 2009, Jade Avery contributes $10,000 in exchange for a 50-percent partnership interest in JK partnership. During 2009, JK has $3,000 of ordinary income, of which Jade's allocable share is $1,500. JK also distributes $2,000 to Jade. Her share of partnership liabilities is $1,000. Jade increases her basis in JK by the $1,500 of partnership income and the $1,000 representing her share of partnership liabilities. She then reduces her tax basis in JK by the $2,000 distribution. Jade's basis in JK at the end of 2009 is $10,500.

Initial basis	$10,000
Plus: Allocable share of partnership income	1,500
Plus: Share of partnership liabilities	1,000
Less: Distributions during 2009	(2,000)
Tax basis at the end of 2009	$10,500

Example 71: Continuing with Example 70, in 2010 JK generates a $5,000 loss, of which Jade's distributive share is $2,500. Also during 2010 JK distributes $3,000 to Jade, and at the end of the year, Jade's share of partnership liabilities is $200 (down from $1,000 at the beginning of the year). Jade's $4,200 basis at the end of 2010 is computed as follows:

Tax basis at the beginning of 2010	$10,500
Less: Decrease in share of partnership liabilities	(800)
Less: Distributions during 2010	(3,000)
Tax basis for purposes of loss limitations	$ 6,700
Less: Allocable share of partnership loss	(2,500)
Tax basis at the end of 2010	$ 4,200

Example 72: Continuing with Example 71, in 2011 JK generates a $15,000 loss, of which Jade's distributive share is $7,500. JK distributes $500 to Jade during 2011, and her share of partnership liabilities at the end of 2011 is $2,000 (up from $200 at the beginning of the year). Jade's zero basis at the end of 2011 is computed as follows:

Tax basis at the beginning of 2011	$4,200
Plus: Increase in share of partnership liabilities	1,800
Less: Distributions during 2011	(500)
Tax basis for purposes of loss limitations	$5,500
Less: Allocable share of partnership loss	(7,500)
Tax basis at the end of 2011	$ 0

Jade's losses for 2011 are limited to her $5,500 tax basis in JK after taking into consideration all increases and her distributions during the year. Jade's tax basis in JK at the end of 2011 is $0. She carries over to 2012 the $2,000 ($7,500 − $5,500) disallowed loss from 2011. The suspended loss will be deductible once Jade's tax basis in JK increases.

Example 73: Continuing with Example 72, in 2012 JK generates $10,000 of ordinary income, of which Jade's distributive share is $5,000. JK distributes $2,000 to Jade during 2012, and Jade's share of partnership liabilities at the end of 2012 is $1,200 (down from $2,000 at the beginning of the year). On her income tax return, Jade includes her $5,000 distributive share of partnership income and the $2,000 suspended loss from 2011. Jade's basis at the end of 2012 is computed as follows:

Tax basis at the beginning of 2012	$ 0
Plus: Allocable share of partnership income	5,000
Less: Distributions during 2011	(2,000)
Less: Decrease in share of partnership liabilities	(800)
Tax basis for purposes of loss limitations	$2,200
Less: Release of suspended losses from 2011	(2,000)
Tax basis at the end of 2012	$ 200

Figure 14-4 summarizes items for which a partner's basis in its partnership interest is adjusted upward or downward.

Figure 14-4 Summary of Adjustments Made to a Partner's Basis

A partner's basis is adjusted upward for the following items:

• The partner's distributive share of partnership ordinary income plus all separately stated items of income and gain,

• The partner's distributive share of tax-exempt partnership income, and

• Contributions the partner makes to the partnership, including the partner's share of increases to partnership liabilities (treated as cash contributions).

A partner's basis is adjusted downward (but never below zero) by the following items:

- Distributions made to the partner from the partnership, including the partner's share of any decrease in partnership liabilities (treated as a cash distribution),
- The partner's distributive share of partnership losses and deductions, and
- The partner's distributive share of nondeductible partnership expenditures.

¶ 1406 Impact of Distributions to Partners

A "distribution" is a payment, either in money or other property, made by a partnership to a partner. Partnership distributions fall into two categories: (1) those made in complete liquidation of a partner's interest in the partnership and (2) all other partnership distributions.[65] The latter type of distribution is also known as a "current distribution."[66] Liquidating distributions, disproportional distributions, and distributions involving noncash property can involve very complex tax laws, and accordingly, are beyond the scope of this introductory chapter on partnership taxation. All distributions described in this chapter are assumed to be current distributions in the form of cash that the partnership makes proportionally to each of its partners.

Current distributions do not completely liquidate a partner's interest in a partnership. They include distributions of the current profits of the partnership, pro rata distributions of the partners' capital interests, and disproportionate distributions that reduce the distributees' proportionate interests in the partnership. An advance or drawing of money or property against a partner's distributive share of income is treated as a current distribution made to the partner on the last day of the partnership tax year. No prorating of profits to the withdrawal dates is necessary.[67] A partner who receives a current cash distribution recognizes a taxable gain only to the extent that the amount of cash received exceeds the basis of the partner's partnership interest.[68] The ordering rules described in ¶ 1405.03 are used to determine how the cash distribution is taken into consideration in determining a partner's tax basis in the partnership interest. If there is a gain, it is considered a gain from the sale or exchange of the partner's interest and is usually taxed as a capital gain. Losses are never recognized on a current distribution since the partner still retains an interest in the partnership and there is no closed transaction (no sale of distributed property) from which a loss can arise.[69]

¶ 1407 Limited Liability Companies (LLCs) and Limited Liability Partnerships (LLPs)

The tax laws generally do not allow businesses that provide professional services (for example, law firms, medical practices, and CPA firms) to shield themselves from the liabilities of the business by incorporating their businesses and hiding behind corporate partners. Thus, many of these businesses operate as general partnerships in which each and every partner is personally responsible for the actions of the partnership and of each of its individual partners acting on behalf of the partnership.

In 1977, Wyoming became the first state to authorize the limited liability company (LLC) as a business entity. In an LLC, the owners (called "members") are protected from most debts of the entity, much as limited partners are protected in a limited partnership. However, unlike the limited partnership rules that require that at least one general partner be responsible for the partnership's liabilities beyond those covered by the limited partners, in an LLC all members have limited liability. The tax laws generally prohibit professional services firms (for example, law firms or CPA firms) from operating as limited partnerships, and accordingly, most states' LLC laws prohibit these firms from operating as LLCs. In 1991, Texas became the first state to authorize the limited liability

---

[65] Code Sec. 731.

[66] Reg. § 1.761-1(d).

[67] Reg. § 1.731-1(a)(1)(ii).

[68] Code Sec. 731(a)(1); Reg. § 1.731-1(a)(1).

[69] Reg. § 1.731-1(a)(2).

partnership (LLP) as a business entity. Today, most states recognize LLCs and LLPs as legal business entities.

 Planning Pointer: The Code and the IRS have made converting from a general partnership to an LLC taxed as a partnership a tax-friendly option. The conversion is considered a tax-free conversion from one partnership to another with the contribution of assets to the new partnership considered a tax-free transaction governed by Code Sec. 721 (see ¶ 1403.02). In addition, the treatment is the same whether the resulting LLC is formed in the same state or in a different state from the converting partnership. After the conversion, the tax year of the converting partnership does not close with respect to any or all of the partners, and the resulting LLC operates under the same taxpayer identification number as the general partnership had previously.[70]

The Code does not specifically address the taxation of LLCs and LLPs, except to acknowledge that at the entity's election, they can be treated for income tax purposes either as a corporation or as a partnership. Much like a corporation or limited partnership, the LLC is formed and operates in conformity with the law of the state in which it is organized. To form an LLC, articles of organization, much like articles of incorporation, must be filed with the appropriate state office. The owners of an LLC are referred to as members. The members are similar to partners, and when the LLC is taxed as a partnership, they are treated as a partner would be in a partnership. The determination of the interests and responsibilities of the members can be found in the "operating agreement" of the LLC, an agreement similar to the partnership agreement (See ¶ 1403). While an LLC operates under state law to limit claims of liability by third parties against the members to the amount of the members investment in the LLC plus any guarantees of LLC debt by the member, along with that benefit come responsibilities to comply with the statute. For example, most statutes require the name of the LLC to be distinctive, including at the end of the name such terms as "LLC" or "Limited Liability Company." While the operating agreement cannot waive such conditions as the name requirement, other default provisions within the statutes can be overridden by the agreement of the partners. Figure 14-5 lists the advantages and disadvantages of limited liability companies.

Figure 14-5 LLC Advantages and Disadvantages

LLC advantages:

- The primary advantage of a two-or-more member LLC is that the entity is not subject to federal income tax as a corporation if it elects to be treated as a partnership; it thus avoids the double taxation of the C Corporation.

- A member of an LLC has no personal liability for the entity's debts, while at the same time it receives tax advantages similar to those of a limited partner.

- LLCs can have a single owner, but the tax consequences of a single member LLC are similar to those of a sole proprietorship.

- Members of an LLC have the freedom to allocate entity tax items in the same manner that partners do in partnerships. As will be discussed in Chapter 15, shareholders in an S corporation must allocate income, deductions, and other items on a *pro rata* basis.

- LLC members have the right to participate in the management of the LLC, while limited partners who participate in management risk losing their limited liability status.

- As will be discussed in Chapter 15, S corporations have restrictions on the number and type of shareholders they can have. These limits and restrictions do not apply to LLCs, and therefore, LLCs provide more flexibility in this regard.

---

[70] Rev. Rul. 84-52.

- Members of an LLC can make tax-free contributions of property for interests in the LLC at any time (similar to partnerships). As mentioned previously in Chapter 12, shareholders of a C corporation can make tax-free contributions of property to a C corporation in exchange for stock and securities only if they own at least 80 percent of the stock in the corporation after the exchange.

LLC disadvantages:

- The Code does not specifically address LLC issues as such. The only real authority in this area is the acceptance that LLCs with two or more members can elect to be taxed as partnerships, even if they offer limited liability to all of their members.

- A single member LLC is disregarded for tax purposes. Although a single member LLC is treated as a sole proprietorship, the member continues to be protected from lawsuits in state court.

- State LLC statutes are not uniform, thereby raising jurisdictional issues. For example, if an LLC is organized in California but does business in another state, which state's statutes will control? Jurisdictional issues always have been a part of U.S. law, but with LLCs being relatively new entities, there is substantial uncharted territory to be explored.

.01 Entity Classification

An LLC files Form 8832, *Entity Classification Election*, to elect a business entity classification.[71] If the LLC does not file the Form 8832, an entity with two or more members will automatically be classified as a partnership. However, an LLC is more like a corporation than a partnership in that members of the LLC have limited liability with respect to the LLC's debts and to any claims against the LLC. In addition, all members of an LLC are eligible to participate in the management of the LLC, unlike a limited partner in a partnership. A single member LLC will be disregarded for federal tax purposes and will be treated as a sole proprietorship for federal income tax purposes.

 Spotlight: While the complexities of the tax rules governing partnerships require a careful study of the tax laws, the number of businesses filing partnership tax returns continues to increase. From 1993 to 2005, the number of partnership returns filed increased by 1,296,000, which was an 88-percent increase over the number of returns filed in 1993. However, this increase was not the result of an increase in traditional general or limited partnerships but instead was the result of the increasing number of LLPs and LLCs that chose to be taxed as partnerships. In fact, the number of general partnerships decreased from the 1,176,000 partnership returns filed in 1993 to 729,000 filed in 2005 with the increase in filings from 2004 to 2005 of 4,000 general partnership returns being the first annual increase since the increase from 1994 to 1995. The increase in filing of partnership tax returns has come from LLCs and LLPs which increased from 17,000 in 1993 to 1,565,000 in 2005.

¶ 1408 Summary

The taxation of pass-through entities allows taxpayers the opportunity to enter into business ventures with options ranging from ease of formation (general partnerships) to limited liability either for a select group of partners (limited partners) or for all the members of the firm (LLCs). To understand the differences and make an informed selection requires a review of the tax and nontax considerations for the formation of a general partnership, limited partnership, LLC, or LLP. With the

---

[71] Reg. § 301.7701-1, -2, -3.

option to be taxed as a partnership for any of these four business entities, the selection process can generally proceed without concern over any significant tax differences among the entities.

GLOSSARY OF TERMS INTRODUCED IN THE CHAPTER

Capital and profits interest. The term used to describe a partner's interest in a partnership when the partner has an interest in the future profits the partnership generates as well as an interest in the partnership's assets upon liquidation of the partner's interest or dissolution of the partnership.

Collateral. Property offered by the borrower that the lender can use to satisfy the debt in the event the borrower defaults on the loan.

Current distributions. Distributions from a partnership to a partner that do not completely liquidate the partner's interest in the partnership.

Distributive share. A partner's allocated share of partnership income, gains, losses, deductions, and credits as specified in either the partnership agreement or in accordance with each partner's interest in the partnership.

General partnership. A business entity that arises from an agreement among two or more persons, all of whom have unlimited liability for the debts of the partnership, to operate a business for profit.

Guaranteed payments. Amounts paid from the partnership to a partner that are determined *without regard* to the profits generated by the partnership during the year.

Least aggregate deferral of income rule. The last of three tests used to determine a partnership's required tax year. It involves performing a test using each of the year-ends of its partners and determining which of those year-ends, on average, will allow the government to collect taxes on the partnership income the most quickly. *See also* Majority partners rule *and* Principal partner rule.

Limited partnership. A business entity that arises from an agreement among two or more partners to operate a business for profit in which one or more of the partners has limited liability with respect to the debts of the partnership and at least one partner is responsible for the debts of the partnership.

Majority partners rule. The first of three tests used to determine a partnership's required tax year. It requires that a partnership adopt the year-end of the partner, or group of partners, that owns more than a 50-percent interest in partnership capital *and* profits. *See also* Least aggregate deferral of income rule *and* Principal partner rule.

Nonrecourse debt. The type of debt arrangement in which the lender has no recourse (no ability to collect the debt) directly from the borrower in the event the borrower defaults on the loan.

Partner's capital account. An account on the partnership books that keeps track of what a partner is entitled to receive upon the liquidation of the partner's interest or upon dissolution of the partnership.

Partnership agreement. A written or oral agreement among the partners in a partnership that provides, among other things, how the partners will share in the partnership's profits and losses and how the assets of the partnership will be divided upon dissolution of the partnership.

Principal partner. A partner that has at least a five-percent interest in the profits *or* capital of the partnership.

Principal partner rule. The second of three tests used to determine a partnership's required tax year. If the majority interest rule does not apply, this rule requires that a partnership adopt the tax year of *all* of its principal partners. *See also* Least aggregate deferral of income rule *and* Majority partners rule.

Profits-only interest. The term used to describe a partner's interest in a partnership when the partner is entitled to a share of future partnership profits but does not have an ownership interest in the capital of the partnership.

Recourse debt. The type of debt arrangement in which the lender can proceed directly against the borrower for any debt on which the borrower defaults.

Substantial economic effect. The standard that must be met before allocations of partnership items can be made to the partners as specified in the partnership agreement.

Unrealized receivable. Any right to income for services or goods that are not capital assets that have not been previously recorded in gross income under the taxpayer's method of accounting.

CHAPTER PROBLEMS

The following questions and problems relate to the discussion in Chapter 14, Flow-Through Entities: Partnerships, LLPs, and LLCs, which begins at ¶ 1400 in *Part V: Business Entity Issues.*

Chapter 14 Discussion Questions

1. Explain the increase in the number of partnership tax returns filed with the Internal Revenue Service over the past decade.

2. Discuss the nontax differences between a general partnership, limited partnership, and limited liability company.

3. Are the following elections made at the partner or partnership level?

   a. Election to expense property under Code Sec. 179.

   b. Replacement of property under involuntary conversion rules.

   c. Use of foreign taxes as a deduction or credit.

4. What methods of accounting are available to the partnership and how is the method used by the partnership selected?

5. A partnership has 10 partners, each of whom owns a 10-percent interest in partnership capital and profits. Four of the partners use the calendar year, and the other partners all have different fiscal years. How is the required tax year of the partnership determined?

6. How does the partnership agreement affect the operations of a partnership?

7. How does a contribution of a personal asset to the partnership by a partner differ from the contribution of a business asset by the partner?

8. Under what circumstances does the contribution of services to a partnership in exchange for a partnership capital interest constitute taxable income to the contributing partner?

9. How is the partner's initial basis in a partnership interest determined if the property contributed is subject to a recourse liability that the partnership assumes?

10. How is the partner's initial basis in a partnership interest determined if the property contributed is subject to a nonrecourse liability that the partnership assumes?

11. Which of the following is a separately stated item for partnership reporting, and why?

    a. Business bad debts

    b. Charitable contributions

    c. Gains and losses from sales or exchanges of capital assets held for one year or less

    d. Real estate taxes

12. What are guaranteed payments to partners and how are they treated by the partnership and the partner?

13. What constitutes an unrealized receivable in the hands of the partnership? What rules are associated with it?

14. How does a change in liabilities owed by the partnership at the end of a tax year affect the basis of a partner's interest in the partnership?

15. If a partnership distributes only cash to its partners in a current distribution, do the partners recognize gain or loss on the distribution?

16. How is the character of the gain or loss from the sale of property contributed to the partnership by one of its partners determined?

17. How is the concept of double taxation as discussed in reference to C corporations eliminated or mitigated through the use of a partnership?

18. In what order are increases and decreases to a partner's basis in the partnership determined at the end of the year?

19. When a partnership does not distribute the entire net income of the partnership for the tax year, does a partner have the option to exclude the income from his or her tax return and report it when it is received?

20. Does a limited liability company have an agreement similar to the partnership agreement? What is it and what are the similarities and differences?

Chapter 14 Problems

1. Adam, Brian, and Cynthia are equal partners in ABC partnership. In exchange for their one-third interests, Adam contributes $90,000; Brian contributes business property worth $90,000 with an adjusted basis of $60,000; and Cynthia contributes a capital asset with a fair market value and adjusted basis of $90,000.

   a. How much gain is recognized by each of these partners on the contribution of property to ABC partnership?

   b. What is each partner's basis in his or her respective partnership interests?

   c. What is the partnership's basis in each of these assets?

2. Nicole O'Conner and Jonathan Rix form NJ Partnership. In exchange for equal interests in NJ, each contributes the following property. Jonathan also performs services for NJ.

   Nicole:

	Adjusted Basis	FMV
Cash	$600,000	$600,000
Inventory (held 3 months)	70,000	150,000

   Jonathan:

	Adjusted Basis	FMV
Office equipment (held 18 months)	$400,000	$600,000

   a. How much gain or loss is recognized by the partners and the partnership at formation because of the contributions?

   b. What is each partner's basis in his or her partnership interest at formation?

   c. What is NJ Partnership's basis and holding period at formation for each asset contributed to it?

3. The ABC partnership agreement provides for guaranteed payments for services rendered of $70,000, $64,000, and $60,000 for Adam, Brian, and Cynthia, respectively. After the guaranteed payments are deducted, the partnership agreement calls for sharing of profits

and losses as follows: Adam, 40 percent; Brian, 35 percent; and Cynthia, 25 percent. Each partner is a general partner. If net profits before the guaranteed payments are $176,000, what amount of income from the partnership should each partner report on his or her individual income tax return?

4. Katie and Grace operate their business as a calendar-year partnership. They share profits and losses equally. During 2008, the partnership had a $16,000 loss and in 2009 it reported a $20,000 profit. At the beginning of 2008, Katie's adjusted basis in her partnership interest was $5,000. The partnership made no distributions during 2008 or 2009, and Katie made no additional contributions.

   a. What is the adjusted basis of Katie's partnership interest at the end of 2008?

   b. What is Katie's basis in her partnership interest in 2009?

5. Timothy Nesbith owns a 40-percent interest in capital and profits of TNT partnership. Timothy and TNT both have calendar year-ends. Timothy's basis in his TNT interest at the beginning of 2009 is $140,000. For 2009, TNT has $600,000 of ordinary income and $100,000 of dividend income from stocks it holds in various corporations. TNT also makes $150,000 of contributions to qualified charitable organizations. During 2009, TNT distributes $280,000 to Timothy. In 2010, TNT reports $250,000 of ordinary loss, and distributes $100,000 to Timothy.

   a. What is Timothy's basis in his TNT at the end of 2009?

   b. How much of the TNT loss may Timothy deduct on his 2010 individual income tax return?

   c. What is Timothy's basis in TNT at the end of 2010?

6. Samuel Todd became a member of the STX partnership when it was organized in 2003. At that time he contributed $45,000 in cash and land worth $20,000. He had purchased the land for $15,000. His share of the partnership earnings (loss) and the amounts withdrawn for the years 2003 to 2009 are as follows:

Year	Share of Profit (Loss)	Amounts Withdrawn
2003	$18,000	$12,000
2004	12,000	15,000
2005	(6,000)	0
2006	25,000	15,000
2007	35,000	30,000
2008	15,000	10,000
2009	(15,000)	5,000

What is Samuel's basis in STX's partnership interest at the end of 2009?

7. Nancy Carter contributes property with a fair market value of $150,000 to a new partnership in exchange for a 50-percent interest in the partnership. The property has an adjusted basis of $45,000 and is subject to an $80,000 (nonrecourse) mortgage that is assumed by the partnership. What is Nancy's basis in her partnership interest?

8. ABCD Partnership begins business on January 19, 2009. ABCD consists of four partners, Albert, Brandon, Carol, and Daryl. Consider the following independent situations:

   a. Albert, who uses a fiscal year ending on September 30, owns a 60-percent interest in ABCD. Brandon, Carol, and Daryl have fiscal years ending June 30. Brandon owns a 20-percent interest, and Carol and Daryl own a 10-percent interest each. What is ABCD's required tax year?

   b. Albert uses a fiscal year ending June 30, and he owns a 47-percent interest in ABCD. Brandon uses a fiscal year ending June 30 and owns 47 percent of the partnership.

Partners Carol and Daryl use fiscal years ending May 31, and each owns a 3-percent partnership interest. What is ABCD's required tax year?

c. May ABCD adopt a tax year other than the one required in a. or b. without declaring a business purpose for the selection of the year? If so, how may it do so, and what tax year(s) can it use?

9. A partnership has three equal partners. One partner uses a March 31 year-end. The second partner uses a June 30 year-end, and the third partner uses an October 31 year-end. Discuss the possible tax years the partnership can select.

10. A sole proprietor offers an employee the chance to become a partner. If the employee works an additional two years, the sole proprietor has agreed to transfer half the business to the employee. The employee meets the requirement and receives half ownership in the capital and profits of the partnership. What is the tax effect on the employee at the time the promise is made? At the time the transfer occurs?

11. Danielle Jefferson and Waylon Evans form an equal partnership. In exchange for her interest, Danielle contributes $30,000 of cash and property worth $70,000. Danielle's adjusted basis in the property is $50,000. In exchange for his 50-percent interest, Waylon performs services for the partnership and contributes $40,000 cash.

a. What amount of gain or loss does each partner recognize on the exchange of his or her contributions for a 50-percent share in the partnership?

b. What is each partner's basis in his or her respective partnership interest?

c. What is the partnership's interest in the property Danielle contributes to the partnership?

12. Justin contributes land worth $100,000 to a general partnership in exchange for a 50-percent interest in JM partnership. Mike contributes $50,000 cash in exchange for a 50-percent interest in JM. Justin's basis in the land is $60,000, and the land is subject to a $50,000 mortgage, which the partnership assumes. The partnership agreement allocates profits equally between the partners and allocates losses 45 percent to Justin and 55 percent to Mike. These allocations have substantial economic effect.

a. Compute the tax consequences to each partner on the receipt of his respective partnership interest, including each partner's basis in the respective partnership interests assuming that the $50,000 mortgage is nonrecourse debt.

b. Compute the tax consequences to each partner on the receipt of his respective partnership interest, including each partner's basis in the respective partnership interests assuming that the $50,000 mortgage is recourse debt.

13. Ahmeek partnership is owned equally by four partners. John Barley, a partner in Ahmeek, receives a guaranteed payment of $30,000 a year in exchange for services. During the year, Ahmeek's profits (not including the amounts paid to John for his accounting and tax services) are $150,000. How much income does each partner recognize for the year?

14. Angela Peterson owns a 25-percent interest in Ishpeming Partnership. Both Angela and Ishpeming use a calendar year-end. For the year ended December 31, 2009, Ishpeming reports the following items of partnership income, gain, loss, deduction, and credit.

Gross sales	$380,000
Cost of goods sold	110,000
Wage expense	90,000
Depreciation recapture	8,000
Net Section 1231 gain	60,000
Casualty loss	7,000
Interest	12,000
Real estate taxes	8,000

MACRS depreciation	14,000
Business bad debt	8,000
Charitable contributions	20,000

Calculate Angela's distributive share of partnership ordinary income and separately stated items. How does she report these items on her individual income tax?

15. What is the amount and character of gain/loss recognized by the partnership in the following situations?

   a. A partner contributes inventory from his sole proprietorship to a partnership in exchange for an interest in the partnership. At the time of the contribution, the FMV of the inventory is $60,000. The partner's basis in the inventory is $22,000. The property is a capital asset in the hands of the partnership, which sells it for $60,000 within five years of the contribution.

   b. In 2000, a real estate developer contributes land (with a basis of $36,000 and a fair market value of $40,000) to a manufacturing LLC in which he is a member. The land was inventory to the real estate developer. The LLC uses the land as an employee parking lot. The LLC sells the land in 2009 for $50,000.

   c. A partner contributes property with a basis of $4,000 and a fair market value of $6,000 to a partnership. The property is inventory in the hands of both the partner and the partnership. The partnership sells the property after five years for $8,000.

16. How is the gain and loss from the sales in Problem 15 allocated among the partners?

17. How much gain or loss is recognized by the partnership in the following transactions?

   a. Jeri Holden contributes land worth $80,000 in exchange for a capital and profits interest in a partnership. Prior to contributing the land, Jeri held it as an investment. Jeri's basis in the land is $160,000. The partnership uses the land in its trade or business and then sells it within five years for $100,000.

   b. How does the answer in a. change if the partnership sells the land for $70,000?

   c. How does the answer in a. change if the partnership sells the land for $170,000?

18. Andrew Springer has a partnership interest with a basis of $20,000. The partner receives a $24,000 current cash distribution that is proportional. What are the tax consequences of the distribution to Andrew?

19. A partner contributes $15,000 in exchange for a 50-percent partnership interest in a partnership. During the tax year, the partnership has $8,000 of ordinary income, of which the partner's allocable share is $4,000. The partnership also distributes $3,000 to the partner. Her share of partnership liabilities is $2,000. What is her tax basis in her partnership interest at the end of the year?

20. A partner purchases a partnership interest for $6,000. During the current tax year, the partner receives a $2,000 cash distribution from the partnership. At the end of the tax year, the partner's distributive share of partnership losses is $8,000. What portion of the partner's share of losses is deductible in the current year? What happens to any portion that is not deductible? What is the partner's tax basis in the partnership at the end of the year?

21. Phyllis and Sally are equal partners in the income and losses of the PS Partnership. The partnership's balance sheet at the end of the current year is as follows:

Cash	$100,000
Inventory	160,000
Land (Collateral for Third Mortgage Corp Mortgage Payable)	150,000
Total Assets	$410,000
Note Payable—First Bank (recourse note)	$100,000

Mortgage Payable—Third Mortgage Corp. (nonrecourse mortgage)	150,000
Capital—Phyllis	110,000
Capital—Sally	50,000
Total Liabilities and Capital	$410,000

a. If both Phyllis and Sally are general partners, what is the maximum amount of the partnership's liabilities each would be liable to repay in the event of a default by the partnership?

b. If Phyllis is a general partner and Sally is a limited partner, what is the maximum amount of the partnership liabilities each would be liable to repay in the event of a default by the partnership?

c. If Phyllis and Sally had registered the partnership as a limited liability company (LLC), what is the maximum amount of the liabilities each would be liable to repay in the event of a default by the partnership?

d. Phyllis and Sally ask you to calculate their respective share of the year end liabilities from the partnership Balance Sheet to be included in the basis of their respective partnership interests. Assume that the liabilities shown in the problem represent the entire amount of liabilities of the partnership and land with a book value of $150,000 is used as collateral for the nonrecourse liability to Third Mortgage Corporation. Further assume that the partnership capital accounts represent the year end adjusted basis in their capital after allocating the current year's profit and before any allocation of partnership liabilities.

22. Bob Sanford and Michelle Thomas form an equal general partnership. Bob contributes $65,000 in cash and land with a FMV of $35,000 and an adjusted basis of $50,000 in exchange for his 50 percent interest. Michelle contributes services of $20,000 and equipment with a FMV of $80,000 and adjusted basis of $40,000 in exchange for her 50 percent interest.

a. What amount of gain or loss must Bob recognize as a result of his contributions to the partnership?

b. What amount of gain or loss must Michelle recognize as a result of his contributions to the partnership?

c. What is Bob's initial basis in his partnership interest?

d. What is Michelle's initial basis in his partnership interest?

23. Referring to the facts in Problem 22, the partnership depreciates the equipment contributed by Michelle utilizing MACRS depreciation over a seven-year life. Over the life of the equipment, how much of the depreciation expense will be allocable to Bob and Michelle?

24. Sarah Austin is a 25 percent general partner in the SBS partnership with a basis in her capital account of $50,000 as of the first day of the 2009 tax year. During 2009, SBS sustained a $60,000 tax loss and Sarah withdrew $20,000 from the partnership. During 2009, the amount of partnership liabilities remains unchanged.

a. Compute Sarah's tax basis in her capital account at December 31, 2009.

b. What amount may Sarah deduct as a loss on her 2009 tax return?

c. During 2010, the SBS partnership sustains a loss of $80,000 and reduces its liabilities (all recourse) by $40,000 over the prior year. Compute Sarah's tax basis in her capital account at December 31, 2010.

d. What amount may Sarah deduct as a loss on her 2009 tax return?

25. Janet Miller and Terry Wood form a general partnership. As part of the general partnership agreement, Janet and Terry will share profits equally and losses 75 percent and 25 percent, respectively. Terry has an initial contribution to the capital of the partnership of $20,000 cash and land with a FMV of $80,000 (adjusted tax basis $50,000) and the partnership

assumes a mortgage against the land of $50,000 which the lender releases Terry from liability and adds the partnership as mortgagee. After the reduction in FMV of the land by the amount of the mortgage assumed and the cash contribution, Terry's contribution has a net FMV of $50,000 for her 50 percent interest ($20,000 + $80,000 − $50,000 mortgage). Janet contributes $50,000 in cash for her 75 percent interest in the partnership.

   a. How much of the $50,000 is allocated to Janet in the determination of her tax basis if the debt is nonrecourse debt to the partners?

   b. How much of the $50,000 is allocated to Janet in the determination of her tax basis if the debt is recourse debt to the partners?

Chapter 14 Review Problems

1. Schedule K-1, Form 1065, filed by the ABC Partnership discloses the following amounts attributable to a partner for the year:

Ordinary income	$33,000
Guaranteed payments to partners—salaries and interest	20,500
Charitable contributions	200
Net long-term capital gain	1,500

Indicate the total amount of ordinary income from the partnership that the partner should report on his individual income tax return.

2. Clark Huber, a calendar-year taxpayer, is a member of a partnership with a tax year ending on October 31. During the partnership year ended October 31, 2009, Clark is paid a guaranteed payment for services rendered of $12,500 a month for each of the 12 months, and his distributive share of partnership ordinary income was $50,000. How much must Clark report on his 2009 return as ordinary income from the partnership? How much of this amount is subject to self-employment tax if Clark is a general partner?

Chapter 14 Comprehensive Review Question

A has a one-fourth and B a three-fourths interest in a partnership that operates a toy manufacturing company. The partnership files its partnership return on the calendar-year basis. The partnership books disclose the following information for the current calendar year:

Sales	$235,000
Returns and allowances	10,000
Opening inventory	50,000
Purchases	50,000
Cost of labor and supplies	105,000
Closing inventory	61,000
Royalties received for use of a patent	1,100
Salaries	26,000
Guaranteed payments to partners ($8,400 to each)	16,800
Rent paid	17,000
Interest expense on business debt (other than payments to partners)	550
Taxes	8,500
Bad debt written off	1,000
Repairs	3,000
Depreciation	2,470
Light, postage, stationery, etc.	1,680

Net long-term capital gain	600
Dividends	200

Compute the partnership income and the partners' distributive shares of items that are required to be separately stated.

Chapter 14 Research Questions

1. Taylor Tamblyn is a partner in three partnerships. Earlier in the year, Taylor received her Schedule K-1s from her partnerships and discovered that she had been allocated amounts under Code Sec. 179 of $100,000, $104,000, and $72,000, respectively. Taylor is familiar with Code Sec. 179 and knows that she will not be able to deduct more than $250,000 on her 2009 tax return. What alternatives are available for the excess section 179 expense Taylor was allocated in 2009? By what amount is her basis in each partnership reduced by the allocation of section 179 expense? See Rev. Rul. 89-7, 1989-1 CB 178.

2. Florena Santiago is a general partner in Santiago and Johnston Partnership (SJ) with a 50-percent interest in profits and losses. SJ files partnership tax returns on a calendar year basis and uses the cash receipts and disbursements method of accounting. At the close of the current taxable year at issue, SJ had liabilities for accrued expenses of $100,000 and accounts payable of $250,000. At the end of the prior tax year, SJ had liabilities for accrued expenses of $160,000 and accounts payable of $285,000. Florena had a basis in her partnership interest at the end of the prior tax year of $50,000 excluding any allocation of partnership liabilities. What are the tax ramifications of the Santiago and Johnston Partnership having a $210,000 loss for the current tax year on Florena's basis and deductibility of losses? See Code Sec. 752 and Revenue Ruling 88-77, 1988-2 CB 128.

CHAPTER 15

Flow-Through Entities: S Corporations

LEARNING OBJECTIVES

1. Understand the advantages and disadvantages of operating a business as an S corporation and be able to compare S corporations to other types of business entities.

2. Learn about the requirements for qualifying to elect S corporation status.

3. Understand how an S corporation can terminate its S status and the tax consequences of doing so.

4. Understand how an S corporation's taxable income is calculated and how S corporation shareholders are taxed on their share of the corporation's profits.

5. Understand how distributions by an S corporation to its shareholders are taxed.

6. Learn about the special taxes that apply to S corporations that were C corporations prior to electing S status.

¶ 1500 Introduction

For federal income tax purposes, a corporation generally is treated as an entity separate from its shareholders. Taxable income of the corporation is taxed when earned by the corporation and again when distributed to its shareholders. Shareholders of a corporation enjoy limited liability from the debts and other activities of the corporation, thereby making corporations a widely-used business entity choice. As discussed in Chapter 14, partnerships are also considered separate entities distinct from their owners; however, taxable income earned by a partnership is taxed directly to the owners, regardless of whether any amounts are distributed to them during the year. Although limited partners in a limited partnership enjoy limited liability similar to that of corporate shareholders, the limited partnership rules require that at least one partner (general partner) be responsible for the debts of the partnership.

In an ideal world, business owners would like to operate a business that enjoys the corporate aspects of limited liability but pay only a single level of taxation. In addition, they would like any corporate losses to be passed through to them so that they can deduct the losses on their own income tax returns. In 1958, Congress enacted Subchapter S of Chapter 1 of the Code, providing for certain corporations to be taxed as flow-through entities. S corporations provide business owners the "best of both worlds," by combining the limited liability aspects of a corporate entity with the single layer of taxation associated with a partnership. For many years S corporations were the only entity choice that shared these two features. Today, business owners can achieve similar results by organizing their businesses as limited liability companies (LLCs) or limited liability partnerships

(LLPs) and electing to have them be treated as partnerships for tax purposes (as discussed in Chapter 14).

Nonetheless, S corporations continue to be a popular corporate entity choice. During the IRS's 2007 fiscal year, 4,099,000 S corporation returns were filed (accounting for 62 percent of all corporate returns filed).[1] The number of S corporation returns filed was 7.2 percent more than the number filed the previous year. Many of the tax laws presented in this textbook also pertain to S corporations.[2]

This chapter focuses on the areas where an S corporation and its owners are treated differently from other types of business entities. It begins with an overview of the history of the S corporation. The chapter then presents the rules for how corporations can elect S status, and continues by discussing how S corporations calculate taxable income and allocate it to their shareholders. The tax consequences of distributions from an S corporation are discussed, as are other features that distinguish an S corporation from other types of business entities.

¶ 1501 The History Behind the S Corporation

Closely held businesses that operate in corporate form often are not much different in their economic character and operation than closely held businesses that operate as partnerships. Recognizing this, in 1953 President Eisenhower proposed that:

> Small businesses should be able to operate under whatever form of organization is desirable for their particular circumstances, without incurring unnecessary tax penalties. To secure this result, I recommend that corporations with a small number of active stockholders be given the option to be taxed as partnerships and that certain partnerships be given the option to be taxed as corporations.[3]

In drafting what was to become the Internal Revenue Code of 1954, the Senate Finance Committee accepted President Eisenhower's recommendation and proposed legislation that would allow small corporations that are essentially partnerships to enjoy the advantages of the corporate form of organization without being made subject to the tax disadvantages of the corporate form.[4] The House Ways and Means Committee rejected the proposal of the Senate Finance Committee, but the Conference Committee accepted it, and provisions allowing corporations to be taxed as partnerships and partnerships to be taxed as corporations were included in the 1954 Code.

The Technical Amendments Act of 1958 amended the Code by adding Subchapter S, which preserves the corporate character of corporations for tax purposes but permits certain small corporations to pass through their income to their shareholders so that their income will be taxed only at the shareholder level. Congress enacted Subchapter S to minimize the effect of federal income taxes on the choice of form of organization by business owners and to permit the incorporation and operation of certain small businesses without incurring a second level of taxation on business income.[5]

The Subchapter S Revision Act of 1982 modified and simplified the rules relating to eligibility for Subchapter S status and the operation of S corporations. Many of the tax rules for S corporations were modified to make them more like the rules that govern the taxation of partnerships. Congress adopted a partnership approach to the tax treatment of items of income because it believed that partnership-like rules provide a simpler and more rational taxing scheme than the modified corporate rules adopted by the Technical Amendments Act of 1958.[6]

---

[1] IRS Data Book, 2007, Table 2, at *www.irs.gov/taxstats/article/0,,id=102174,00.html*

[2] Code Sec. 1371(a).

[3] President Eisenhower's Budget Message of January 1953, Tax Recommendation § 16.

[4] Senate Finance Committee Report to Accompany H.R. 8300 (June 18, 1954).

[5] H.R. Rep. No. 97-826 (September 16, 1982), at 5.

[6] S. Rep. No. 97-640 (September 29, 1982), at 6.

¶ 1502 Advantages and Disadvantages of Operating a Business as an S Corporation

An **S corporation** gets its name because it is a corporation that has elected to be taxed under Subchapter S of Chapter 1 of the Code. An S corporation is a flow-through entity, but only corporations that satisfy certain requirements can elect to be taxed as S corporations. A **C corporation** is a corporation other than an S corporation. A C corporation gets its name because many of the provisions that apply specifically to these types of corporations are located in Subchapter C of Chapter 1 of the Code.

As with any business entity, there are tax and nontax advantages to operating a business as an S corporation, as well as tax and nontax disadvantages that must be considered before electing to be treated as an S corporation. For example, the biggest advantage of operating a business as an S corporation is that shareholders enjoy limited liability, while imposing a single layer of taxation on the taxable income of the corporation. Also, S corporations are not subject to many of the taxes that apply to C corporations, including the accumulated earnings tax, personal holding company tax, and alternative minimum tax.

The main disadvantage of operating a business as an S corporation is that several restrictions exist as to the type and number of shareholders that an S corporation may have in order to retain its S status. Also, S corporations that were previously C corporations are subject to LIFO recapture tax. They also may be subject to a tax on excess passive investment income and built-in gains. Finally, S corporation shareholders may be taxed on fringe benefits they receive from the corporation. These advantages and disadvantages of operating a business as an S corporation are summarized in Table 15-1.

Table 15-1 Advantages and Disadvantages of Operating a Business as an S Corporation

Advantages	Discussion
Limited liability	Similar to C corporations and LLCs.
Single level of taxation	Similar to partnerships, as well as LLCs that elect to be taxed as partnerships.
Corporate losses flow through to shareholders	Similar to partnerships, as well as LLCs that elect to be taxed as partnerships.
No accumulated earnings tax, personal holdings tax, or alternative minimum tax	These additional taxes are imposed on C corporations.
Free transferability of stock	Unless specifically prohibited from doing so in accordance with a binding agreement among the shareholders.
Distributive share of S corporation income is not subject to self-employment tax	Unlike a general partnership where both a partner's distributive share of profits and guaranteed payments for services are subject to self-employment tax, S shareholders who work for the corporation are employees, and as such only their wages are subject to employment taxes.

Disadvantages	Discussion
Limit on the number of shareholders	No such restriction exists for C corporations.
Restrictions on who can be a shareholder	No such restrictions exist for C corporations.
Can have only a single class of stock	No such restriction exists for C corporations.
Flow-through percentage is pro rata	Partnerships (and LLCs that elect to be taxed as partnerships) can allocate items as specified in the partnership agreement.
Tax on built-in gains and excess passive investment income	An S corporation that was once a C corporation may be required to pay tax on its recognized built-in gains and may be subject to tax on excessive amounts of passive investment income that it earns during the year.
LIFO recapture tax	A corporation that used the last-in, first-out (LIFO) method for its inventory before it elected S status is required to include its LIFO recapture amount in gross income in its final C tax year.
Tax on fringe benefits	Shareholders who own more than two percent of the corporation's outstanding stock are taxed on the fringe benefits they receive from the S corporation.

¶ 1503 Corporations That Can Elect S Status

A corporation is an S corporation if it is a small business corporation that elects to be treated as an S corporation.[7] A corporation is a "small business corporation" if it satisfies each of the following five requirements.[8]

1. It is a domestic corporation,

2. It is not an ineligible corporation,

3. It has no more than 100 shareholders,

4. It has only permitted shareholders, and

5. It has only one class of stock.

A domestic corporation is a corporation organized or created in the United States or under the laws of the United States or the District of Columbia.[9] Corporations that are ineligible for S status include financial institutions that use the reserve method of accounting for bad debts, insurance companies, corporations that have elected the Puerto Rico and possession tax credit, and Domestic International Sales Corporations (DISCs) or former DISCs.[10]

For tax years beginning before 1997, a corporation could not elect S status if it was a member of an affiliated group. However, an S corporation may now elect to treat a wholly owned subsidiary as a **qualified Subchapter S subsidiary (QSub)**.[11] A QSub is a domestic corporation that is not an ineligible corporation. A QSub is not treated as a separate corporation; instead, all of its assets, liabilities, and items of income, deduction, and credit are treated as assets, liabilities, and items of income, deduction, and credit of the S corporation.

---

[7] Code Sec. 1361(a).
[8] Code Sec. 1361(b).
[9] Code Sec. 7701(a)(4), (10).

[10] Code Sec. 1361(b)(2); Reg. § 1.1361-1(d).
[11] Code Sec. 1361(b)(3).

.01 Permitted Shareholders

Individuals other than nonresident aliens, along with estates, eligible trusts, and certain tax-exempt organizations are *permitted shareholders* of an S corporation.[12] A corporation cannot elect S status if it has as a shareholder a nonresident alien, corporation, partnership, LLC, LLP, or ineligible trust.[13] A **nonresident alien** is an individual who is not a U.S. citizen or resident.[14] A resident of the United States is not a U.S. citizen but for federal income tax purposes, U.S. citizens and residents are treated similarly because they both pay U.S. income tax on their worldwide income. Permanent resident aliens ("green card" holders) are considered U.S. residents, as are some foreign citizens who become U.S. residents for tax purposes due to their extended stays in the United States.[15]

Example 1: A corporation has three individuals (all U.S. citizens) and a partnership as its shareholders. Because the corporation has a partnership as a shareholder, it cannot elect to be taxed as an S corporation.

Example 2: A corporation has as one of its shareholders a citizen and resident of France. Because the company has a nonresident alien as a shareholder, it may not elect to be taxed as an S corporation.

If a shareholder's spouse is a nonresident alien and the spouse is treated as having an ownership interest in a corporation's stock either because of community property laws or the laws in effect in a foreign country, the corporation cannot qualify as an S corporation. However, a nonresident alien married to a U.S. citizen or resident can elect to be treated as a U.S. resident for federal income tax purposes.[16] This allows the spouse to be treated as a U.S. resident for purposes of determining whether a corporation can be an S corporation. However, as long as the election is in effect, the spouse will be required to pay U.S. income tax on all worldwide income earned during the year.

Example 3: Billy Renteria, a U.S. citizen, marries Anna, a nonresident alien. Billy is the sole shareholder of a C corporation. The Renterias decide to move to Anna's country of residence. Under the law of the foreign country where Billy and Anna live, the stock is considered jointly owned by Billy and Anna. Because Anna (a nonresident alien) is considered to own stock in Billy's company, the corporation does not qualify for S corporation status.

Example 4: Assume the same facts as in Example 3, except that Billy and Anna elect to treat Anna as a U.S. resident. Anna will be required to pay U.S. income taxes on her worldwide income, and the corporation may qualify as an S corporation.

An estate may be a shareholder of an S corporation while the estate is being administered.[17] When a person dies, all property owned at the time of death represents the decedent's estate. As mentioned in Chapter 1, after reducing the value of the estate by obligations of the estate and bequests made to the decedent's spouse and qualified charitable organizations, the remainder of the estate is subject to estate tax. Once the obligations of the estate have been settled (including any estate taxes owed), the estate can be finalized and any remaining property can be distributed to the decedent's heirs. The process of settling an estate can take time, and during the administration period, the income earned by the estate is subject to income tax. Accordingly, the income, deductions, and credits that flow through to the estate as a shareholder in an S corporation are taxed to the estate.

Trusts as S corporation shareholders. A **trust** is a legal arrangement in which a person (often referred to as the trustor or grantor) transfers legal title to property to an individual, institution, or organization (the trustee), who is responsible for managing and administering the

---

[12] Code Sec. 1361(b)(1), (c)(2)(A).

[13] Reg. § 1.1361-1(f).

[14] Code Sec. 1361(b)(1)(C); Reg. § 1.1361-1(g); Code Sec. 7701(b)(1)(B).

[15] Code Sec. 7701(b).

[16] Code Sec. 6013(g).

[17] Code Sec. 1361(b)(1)(B).

property for the benefit of others (the beneficiaries). An income beneficiary benefits from the income derived from trust assets during the existence of the trust. The principal beneficiary receives title to the trust assets once the trust is terminated. A trust can be established for a set number of years (for example, until the beneficiary reaches age 25) or for the duration of a person's lifetime. A trust can have more than one income beneficiary and more than one principal beneficiary; however, some trusts specifically limit the number of beneficiaries the trust can have.

Trusts are an important tool in tax planning, as they allow the grantor to designate the persons or organizations that will benefit from the property and to control the ultimate owner of the property. There are several types of trusts, each having its own intended purpose. For example, a revocable trust is a trust that can be rescinded at any time by its grantor. A revocable trust is one type of grantor trust, where the grantor is treated as the owner of the trust assets, and accordingly, taxable income generated from those assets is taxed currently to the grantor. The advantage of forming a revocable trust is that upon the grantor's death, the trust assets avoid probate, which is a court-supervised procedure whereby the decedent's assets are collected and distributed after the debts and other obligations of the decedent's estate have been settled. Thus, creating a revocable trust results in a more cost effective and quicker way to distribute assets to the decedent's beneficiaries.

Testamentary trusts are created from a decedent's will and come into existence upon the death of the grantor. The advantage of a testamentary trust is that it allows grantors control over the distribution of the assets in their estates. For example, a testamentary trust can be set up to pay for a child's education or delay possession of the trust assets until the child reaches a certain age. A testamentary trust also can be used to provide a surviving spouse with the right to the income from the trust assets during the spouse's lifetime, after which the trust assets will pass to the grantor's children. Other types of trusts commonly used for tax planning purposes include life insurance trusts, personal residence trusts, and charitable remainder trusts.

During its legal existence, the taxable income of a trust is generally taxed to the income beneficiary to the extent that such income is distributed currently to the beneficiary. Income that is retained by the trust is taxable to the trust. The income tax rates that apply to trusts are progressive, with rates ranging from 15 to 35 percent. In 2009, the highest tax rate applies to trust taxable income in excess of $11,150.

The provisions in Subchapter S allow the following five types of trusts to be shareholders of an S corporation.[18]

- Qualified Subchapter S trusts,
- Electing small business trusts,
- Qualified grantor trusts,
- Testamentary trusts, but only for the two-year period after the stock is transferred to the trust,[19] and
- Qualified voting trusts.

However, note that foreign trusts are not eligible S corporation shareholders.[20] A trust is a foreign trust unless one or more U.S. persons have authority to control all substantial decisions of the trust and a court within the United States can exercise primary supervision over administration of the trust.[21]

Qualified Subchapter S trust. A trust is a **qualified Subchapter S trust (QSST)** if all of its income is required to be distributed each year to its one income beneficiary who is a U.S. citizen or resident. Such beneficiary must make a timely election to have the trust treated as a QSST and the terms of the trust must stipulate that:[22]

---

[18] Code Sec. 1361(b)(1)(B), (c)(2), (d).
[19] Reg. § 1.1361-1(h)(1).
[20] Reg. § 1.1361-1(h)(2).

[21] Code Sec. 7701(a)(30)(E).
[22] Reg. § 1.1361-1(j)(1).

- There be only one income beneficiary of the trust during the life of the current income beneficiary,

- Any trust principal distributed during the life of the current income beneficiary be distributed only to the income beneficiary,

- The current income beneficiary's income interest in the trust terminates upon the earlier of the termination of the trust or upon the death of the income beneficiary, and

- All trust assets be distributed to the current income beneficiary if the trust terminates during that beneficiary's lifetime.

If a husband and wife are income beneficiaries of the same trust and they file a joint income tax return and they are both U.S. citizens or residents, then the spouses will be treated as one beneficiary.

Planning Pointer: QSSTs are useful in estate planning because they can manage S corporation stock gifted or bequeathed to someone who needs a trust to manage his or her property (such as a minor or disabled individual). A QSST election must be made within the 2½-month period beginning on the day that stock is transferred to the trust. An election, once made, may be revoked only with the IRS's consent.

Electing small business trust.   An **electing small business trust (ESBT)** may be a shareholder of an S corporation.[23] A trust cannot be an ESBT if it is a QSST, a tax-exempt trust, or a charitable remainder annuity trust or unitrust. Any other trust may qualify as an ESBT, but only if no interest in the trust was acquired by purchase and the trust makes a timely election to be treated as an ESBT.[24] In addition, the trust cannot have as a beneficiary any person other than:

- An individual,

- An estate,

- A charitable organization, or

- A state, the District of Columbia, a U.S. possession, or any political subdivision thereof, but only if such entity holds a contingent interest in the trust and is not a potential current beneficiary.

Example 5:   Valerie Marra contributed 100 shares of S corporation stock to a trust for the benefit of her three children. Income from the stock was to be accumulated for her children until they reached age 21. The trustee may elect to treat the trust as an ESBT.

Reason for the Rule: The Small Business Job Protection Act of 1996 added ESBTs to the list of permissible shareholders because Congress believed that a trust providing for income to be distributed to (or accumulated for) a class of individuals should be allowed to hold S corporation stock.[25]

Qualified grantor trust.   A grantor trust may be a shareholder of an S corporation, provided that the grantor is a U.S. citizen or resident.[26] As previously mentioned, the grantor is treated as the "deemed owner" of the trust assets, and as such is responsible for paying the taxes owed on the trust income. A grantor trust that continues to exist after its deemed owner's death can be a shareholder of an S corporation for two years after the date of the deemed owner's death.[27]

---

[23] Code Sec. 1361(b)(1)(B), (c)(2); Reg. § 1.1361-1(h)(1)(vi).
[24] Code Sec. 1361(e); Reg. § 1.1361-1(m).
[25] H.R. Rep. No. 104-586 (May 20, 1996), at 82.

[26] Code Sec. 1361(c)(2)(A)(i); Reg. § 1.1361-1(h)(1)(i).
[27] Code Sec. 1361(c)(2)(A)(ii); Reg. § 1.1361-1(h)(1)(ii).

Example 6:   Vivian Briggs, a U.S. citizen, created a grantor trust for her own benefit and transferred all of her shares of stock in an S corporation to the trust. Vivian retained the right to revoke the trust at any time and to reinvest trust assets herself. The trust is a grantor trust that can be a shareholder of the S corporation.

Example 7:   Assume the same facts as in Example 6, except that Vivian dies in 2009. The trust can remain a shareholder of the S corporation for two years after her death. This gives the personal representative of Vivian's estate time to transfer the S corporation stock held by the trust to someone that is a permitted shareholder of an S corporation.

Qualified voting trust. A trust created primarily to exercise the voting power of S corporation stock transferred to it can be an S corporation shareholder if the beneficial owners are treated as the owners of their respective portions of the trust under the grantor trust rules in the Code. In addition, the trust must have been created pursuant to a written trust agreement entered into by the shareholders that delegates to one or more trustees the right to vote; requires all distributions with respect to the stock to be paid to, or on behalf of, the beneficial owners of that stock; requires that title and possession of that stock be delivered to the beneficial owners when the trust terminates; and terminates, pursuant to its terms or state law, on or before a specific date or event.

.02 100 Shareholder Limit

A corporation that wants to elect and retain S corporation status can at no time have more than 100 shareholders. Accordingly, it is important to be able to determine who is considered a shareholder for purposes of this rule. Ordinarily, the person who is taxed on the dividends paid by the corporation will be considered a shareholder of the corporation.[28]

 Spotlight: Over the years, the number of permitted shareholders has increased. When the S corporation provisions originally were enacted, only corporations with 10 or fewer shareholders could elect S status. In the past 30 years, Congress has increased this limit several times, with the largest increase being to 75 shareholders with the passage of the Small Business Job Protection Act of 1996. By increasing the shareholder limit, Congress hoped it would facilitate corporate ownership by additional family members, employees, and capital investors.[29] This strategy seems to have worked, as the number of S corporation returns has risen from 724,749 in 1985 to 3,341,606 in 2003.[30] More recently, a provision in the American Jobs Creation Act of 2004 increased the number of permitted shareholders to 100.

Stock owned by a husband and wife is treated as owned by one shareholder. Stock held by an individual and the estate of the individual's spouse is also treated as being owned by one shareholder.[31]

Example 8:   Todd Rales and his wife each own stock in a corporation. The couple counts as one shareholder for purposes of determining the number of shareholders an S corporation has.

Example 9:   Larry Theriot and his wife each own stock in a corporation and count as one shareholder for purposes of calculating the number of the corporation's shareholders. Larry dies during 2010 and his shares of stock pass to his estate. The estate and Larry's surviving spouse count as one shareholder for purposes of determining the number of shareholders the S corporation has.

---

[28] Reg. § 1.1361-1(e)(1).

[29] H.R. Rep. No. 104-586 (May 20, 1996), at 82.

[30] "IRS Launches Study of S Corporation Reporting Compliance," IRS News Release, IR-2005-76, July 25, 2005; Kelly Luttrell,

"S Corporation Returns," 2003, *SOI Bulletin, Spring 2006, www.irs.gov/pub/irs-soi/03scorp.pdf.*

[31] Code Sec. 1361(c)(1)(A); Reg. § 1.1361-1(e)(2).

Members of a family. All members of a family are treated as one shareholder.[32] Members of a family must be within six generations of one another and all have the same *common ancestor.* Members of a family include the common ancestor, any lineal descendant of that common ancestor, and any spouse or former spouse of that common ancestor or any such lineal descendant.[33] For purposes of this rule, any legally adopted child, any child who is lawfully placed with an individual for legal adoption, and any eligible foster child of an individual are considered a child of the individual. An "eligible foster child" is an individual placed with the taxpayer by an authorized placement agency or by a judgment, decree, or other order of any court of competent jurisdiction.

Although an individual may be a member of more than one family, each family (not all of whose members are also members of the other family) will be treated as one shareholder. The estate, grantor trust, or testamentary trust of a deceased family member will be considered to be a family member during the period in which the estate or trust holds stock in the S corporation.

Example 10: Mattie and Mark Gourley own stock in an S corporation. Mark's father, as well as the Gourley's four children and nine grandchildren also own stock in the S corporation. These 16 individuals may elect to be treated as one shareholder for purposes of calculating the number of shareholders the corporation has, since they all have a common ancestor (Mark's father) and the members are not more than six generations apart.

Example 11: Jonathan and Martha Schindler adopted Lisa as their daughter. For purposes of determining who the members of Jonathan's family are, Lisa will be treated as a natural born child. Lisa's spouse and children will all be treated as members of Jonathan's family.

Special stock ownership rules. If stock is owned by joint tenants or tenants in common, each of the tenants is considered a shareholder. This rule does not apply to spouses that own stock as joint tenants or tenants in common, as the tax law specifically treats spouses as one shareholder. When a nominee, custodian, guardian, or agent holds stock in an S corporation, the person for whom stock is being held is considered the shareholder of the corporation.[34]

Example 12: Joan Wistrom and her daughter own stock in an S corporation as joint tenants. Both Joan and her daughter are treated as shareholders for purposes of determining whether a corporation has more than 100 shareholders.

Example 13: Dora Hardiman owns stock in a corporation on behalf of her son as his guardian. The son, not Dora, is considered a shareholder in the corporation.

Example 14: Lucretia Lemont holds stock for her son George under the Uniform Transfers to Minors Act. George, not Lucretia, is considered the shareholder.

When stock of an S corporation is owned by an eligible trust, the party treated as the shareholder depends on the type of trust.[35] In the case of a QSST, the income beneficiary is treated as the shareholder. For ESBTs, each potential current beneficiary is treated as a shareholder. If for any period there is no potential current beneficiary, the ESBT will be treated as the shareholder. A *potential current beneficiary* includes any person who at any time during the period is entitled to, or at the discretion of any person may receive, a distribution of trust principal or income. A person will not be treated as a potential current beneficiary solely because that person holds any future (contingent) interest in the trust.

If stock is held by a grantor trust, then the deemed owner of the trust is treated as the shareholder. When the deemed owner of a grantor trust dies, the estate of the deemed owner generally is treated as the shareholder starting on the day of the deemed owner's death. The estate ordinarily will cease to be treated as the shareholder when the stock is transferred to the

---

[32] Code Sec. 1361(c)(1)(B).

[33] Code Sec. 1361(c)(1)(B).

[34] Reg. § 1.1361-1(e)(1).

[35] Code Sec. 1361(c)(2); Reg. § 1.1361-1(h)(3).

beneficiary, or, if earlier, on the expiration of the two-year period beginning on the day of the deemed owner's death.

If stock is held by a testamentary trust, the estate is treated as the shareholder until the stock is transferred by the trust or on the expiration of the two-year period beginning on the day that stock is transferred or deemed distributed to the trust. If the stock is held by a qualified voting trust, then each beneficial owner of the stock is treated as a shareholder with respect to the owner's proportionate share of the stock held by the trust. The rules governing who is considered a shareholder when a trust owns stock in an S corporation are summarized in Table 15-2.

If stock is held by a decedent's estate, the decedent's estate, not the beneficiaries of the estate, is considered the shareholder.[36] If an IRA that is permitted to be a shareholder of an S corporation holds the stock, then the individual for whose benefit the IRA was created will be treated as a shareholder.

Table 15-2 Persons Treated as Shareholders of a Trust

Type of Trust	Person(s) Considered To Be Shareholders
QSST	The sole income beneficiary.
ESBT	Each potential current beneficiary.
Grantor trust	The deemed owner during the owner's lifetime. Upon the death of the deemed owner, the estate is generally considered to be a shareholder.
Testamentary trust	Estate of the testator for two years after the stock is transferred to the trust.
Qualified voting trust	Each beneficial owner of the stock.
Decedent's estate	The estate.

Example 15: Robert Riddick owns stock in an S corporation. Robert transfers some of his stock in the company to an ESBT and names his children, Gladys and Michael, as beneficiaries. Although the stock is held in trust, the stock is treated as owned by Gladys and Michael. Robert, Gladys, and Michael are members of a family, and as such, they are treated as one shareholder for purposes of determining the number of shareholders of the S corporation.

Example 16: S corporation stock is held in trust. Meri Eger is entitled to all of the income from the trust. Her friend, Chelsea, is entitled to all remaining trust assets after Meri dies. Chelsea also is entitled to receive distributions of trust principal at the discretion of the trustee. An election was made to treat the trust as an ESBT. Because both Meri and Chelsea are potential current beneficiaries of the trust, each is treated as a shareholder of the S corporation.

Example 17: Assume the same facts as in Example 16, except that Chelsea is not entitled to receive any distributions of trust principal. Chelsea is not a potential current beneficiary, and therefore, she is not considered a shareholder of the S corporation.

Example 18: Gerardo Hildenbrand dies and bequeaths his S corporation stock to his two children. Until such time that the stock is distributed to his two children, the estate is considered the shareholder of the S corporation.

---

[36] Reg. § 1.1361-1(e)(1).

A person will be counted as only one shareholder of a corporation even though that person may be treated as a shareholder by direct ownership and indirectly through one or more trusts permitted to be shareholders of an S corporation.[37]

Example 19: Rita Lyons owns stock in Tomei, Inc., an S corporation. She also is a potential current beneficiary of an ESBT that owns stock in Tomei. Rita counts as one shareholder of the S corporation.

Example 20: Damon Romain owns stock in R.W. Hoists, an S corporation. Damon's wife is a potential current beneficiary of an ESBT that owns stock in R.W. Hoists. Damon and his wife are considered one shareholder of the S corporation.

 Reason for the Rule: Due to the limitation on the number of shareholders an S corporation can have, Congress did not want taxpayers to be able to form trusts with multiple beneficiaries that would own stock in an S corporation in an attempt to circumvent the shareholder limit for S corporations. Accordingly, Congress specifically limits the types of trusts that can own stock in an S corporation and includes provisions in the tax law to be sure that each beneficiary counts as a shareholder.

.03 Single Class of Stock

A corporation cannot qualify as an S corporation if it has more than one class of stock.[38] As a general rule, a corporation will be treated as having only one class of stock if all of its outstanding shares of stock confer identical rights to distribution and liquidation proceeds. Differences in voting rights among shares of stock of a corporation are ignored for purposes of determining whether a corporation has more than one class of stock. Also, a corporation will not be considered to have more than one class of stock merely because there are differences in the timing of distributions.

Example 21: All of the outstanding shares of an S corporation give the owners identical rights to distribution and liquidation proceeds. However, some shares give their owner the right to vote on corporate matters, while others do not. Because all shares confer identical rights to distribution and liquidation proceeds, the corporation will be considered to have only one class of stock, even though some shares are voting and others are nonvoting.

Example 22: All of the outstanding shares of stock of an S corporation give the owners identical rights to distribution and liquidation proceeds. However, the corporation is required to withhold income tax from distributions made to some shareholders but not others. These differences will not cause the corporation to be treated as having more than one class of stock.

In an attempt to circumvent the single class of stock rule, S corporations may be tempted to disguise a second class of stock as debt. An instrument, obligation, or arrangement issued by a corporation, regardless whether it is designated as debt, will be considered as a second class of stock if both of the following requirements are satisfied.

1. The instrument, obligation, or arrangement constitutes equity or otherwise results in the holder being treated as the owner of stock under general principles of federal tax law, and

2. A principal purpose of issuing or entering into the instrument, obligation, or arrangement was to circumvent the rights to distribution or liquidation proceeds conferred by the outstanding shares of stock or to circumvent the limitation on eligible shareholders.

Example 23: Papuel Gaskets wants to elect S corporation status but currently has 101 shareholders. Papuel enters into an agreement to redeem for $10,000 all 500 shares of stock

---

[37] Reg. § 1.1361-1(m)(4)(vii).

[38] Code Sec. 1361(c)(4); Reg. § 1.1361-1(l).

owned by one of its shareholders, Alvin Seo. At the same time, Alvin agrees to loan the company $10,000. The terms of the loan do not set a schedule for repayment of the loan or require any security for the loan. Had Alvin continued as a shareholder, the company would have been obligated to pay Alvin $10,000 of dividends. Under these circumstances, the loan is equivalent to stock. If it can be established that a principal purpose of the loan was to circumvent the limit on shareholders, the loan will be treated as a second class of stock.

Straight debt will not be treated as a second class of stock, even though it is considered equity under general principles of federal tax law. **Straight debt** is a written, unconditional promise to pay a sum certain in money on demand or on a specified date, but only if it satisfies each of the following three requirements.

1. It does not provide for an interest rate or payment dates that are contingent on profits, the borrower's discretion, the payment of dividends with respect to common stock, or similar factors.

2. It cannot be converted (directly or indirectly) into stock or any other equity interest of the corporation.

3. It is held by an individual (other than a nonresident alien), estate, trust eligible to be an S corporation shareholder, or a person who is actively and regularly engaged in the business of lending money.

If the rate of interest is unreasonably high, an appropriate portion of the interest may be recharacterized as a payment that is not interest. However, such a recharacterization will not make the obligation a second class of stock.

¶ 1504 Electing S Corporation Status

In order to be treated as an S corporation, an eligible corporation must elect to be treated as such.[39] This election applies both to newly formed corporations as well as to existing C corporations that want to convert to S corporations. A corporation can make an election to be an S corporation by filing with Form 2553, *Election by a Small Business Corporation.* An election is not valid unless all of the corporation's shareholders at the time of the election consent to the election. A shareholder's consent may be made directly on Form 2553 or on a separate statement. Once a shareholder consents to an election, it is binding and cannot be withdrawn. The corporation does not need to obtain the consent of those who become shareholders after an election has been made, even if the effective date is not until the beginning of the subsequent tax year.

If an election is made by the 15th day of the third month of a tax year and is intended to be effective for that entire year, then each person who is a shareholder at the time of the election plus anyone who was a shareholder during the portion of the year prior to the election must consent to the election. If consent is not obtained, the election will be effective beginning on the first day of the following year.[40] If the election is to be effective for the following tax year, the consent is needed only from the shareholders at the time the election is made.

Example 24: A calendar year C corporation elects S corporation status on March 15, 2009. If the corporation wants the election to take effect retroactive to January 1, 2009, then it must obtain the written consent of each shareholder as of March 15, 2009, plus anyone who was a shareholder during the period from January 1, 2009, until March 14, 2009. If the corporation fails to obtain the consent of any shareholders who sold their shares during the first 2½ months of 2009, the election will take affect on January 1, 2010.

---

[39] Code Sec. 1362(a); Reg. § 1.1362-1(a).

[40] Code Sec. 1362(b); Reg. § 1.1362-6(a)(2).

Reason for the Rule: Items of income, gain, deduction, loss, and credit generated by an S corporation flow through to its shareholders on a pro rata basis. Income generated by a C corporation is taxed to the corporation and only taxed to the shareholders if distributed in the form of a dividend. Thus, beginning on the day that a corporation's S election becomes effective, its shareholders become responsible for the taxes owed on any income or gain the corporation generates. Accordingly, a corporation that files an S election during the first 2½ months of the tax year can have the election take retroactive effect to January 1 only if it obtains the consent of all who owned stock in the corporation during that year. By obtaining this consent, shareholders that sold their shares during the year up until the time of the election have agreed to pay tax on their respective shares of S corporation taxable income. Anyone who purchases stock after the election becomes effective will be aware of the corporation's intention to become an S corporation, and therefore, their purchasing the stock signifies their approval of election.

If stock is owned by spouses as community property or if the income from the stock is community property, each spouse must consent to the election. If stock is owned by tenants in common, joint tenants, or tenants by the entirety, each tenant must consent to the election. If stock is owned by a minor, the minor's consent must be made by the minor's legal representative (or by a parent of the minor if no legal representative has been appointed).

In the case of an ESBT, both the trustee and the owner must consent to the S corporation election. For all other trusts permitted to be shareholders of an S corporation, only the person treated as the shareholder must consent to the election. However, if spouses have a community interest in trust property, both spouses must consent to the election. In the case of an estate, consent must be obtained from the estate's executor or personal representative.

¶ 1505 Termination of S Status

An election of S status is effective for the entire tax year for which it is made and for all succeeding tax years until the election is terminated.[41] A corporation's S status can be terminated voluntarily or involuntarily. Normally if a corporation's S status is terminated, the corporation must wait at least five years before re-electing S status.[42] However, if the corporation can show that the termination was involuntary, the IRS may allow the corporation to retroactively reinstate its S status as if the terminating event never occurred.[43] (See ¶ 1505.02.)

.01 Voluntary Revocation of an S Election

A corporation may terminate its S status at anytime by revoking its election.[44] To revoke an S election, a corporation must file a statement with the IRS stating that it intends to revoke its S election and informing the IRS of the numbers of outstanding shares of S stock that it had at the time of the revocation.[45] An S election may be revoked only with the consent of the shareholders who own more than one-half of the number of outstanding shares of the corporation's stock at the time of the revocation.

Example 25: An S corporation decides to revoke its S election. The corporation has outstanding 60,000 shares of Class A voting common stock and 40,000 shares of Class B nonvoting common stock, for a total of 100,000 outstanding shares. Thus, to revoke its S election, shareholders owning at least 50,001 shares must consent to the revocation. If shareholders owning 25,000 shares of Class A stock and 26,000 shares of Class B stock consent to the revocation, the corporation will be able to revoke its S

---

[41] Reg. § 1.1362-1(b).
[42] Code Sec. 1362(d).
[43] Code Sec. 1362(f).

[44] Code Sec. 1362(d)(1); Reg. § 1.1362-2(a).
[45] Reg. § 1.1362-6(a)(3).

election, because shareholders owning more than 50 percent of the corporation's outstanding stock consent to the revocation.

A revocation may specify the date in the future for the revocation to become effective. If no such date is specified, a revocation will be effective retroactive to the first day of the tax year if the revocation is made within the first 2½ months of the tax year. If the revocation is made after the first 2½ months of the tax year and no future date is specified, then the revocation will be effective on the first day of the following tax year.

Example 26: On March 15, 2009, a calendar year S corporation files a statement with the IRS to revoke its S election. If the statement does not specify a future date on which the revocation is to take effect, the corporation's S status will be revoked retroactively to January 1, 2009.

Example 27: Assume the same facts as in Example 26, except that the corporation files the statement to revoke its S election on March 16, 2009. If the statement does not specify a future date on which the revocation is to take effect, the corporation's S status will be revoked effective January 1, 2010.

 Spotlight: To elect S status (and thus subject the corporation to a single layer of taxation), the tax laws require that all affected shareholders consent to the election. However, to revoke the corporation's S election (and thus subject the corporation to double taxation), only a majority of the corporation's shareholders must provide their consent.

A corporation may rescind a revocation at any time before it becomes effective. To rescind a revocation, a corporation must file a statement to the effect with the IRS service center where the revocation was made.[46] A rescission may be made only with the consent of each person who consented to the revocation and by each person who has become a shareholder of the corporation within the period beginning on the first day after the date that the revocation was made and ending on the date on which the rescission is made.

Example 28: Continuing with Example 27, anytime prior to January 1, 2010, the S corporation can rescind its revocation. However, to do so all shareholders who consented to the revocation plus any who purchased stock since March 16, 2009, must agree to rescind the revocation.

.02 Involuntary Revocation of an S Election

An S corporation may accidentally revoke its S status by either no longer qualifying as a small business corporation or by having excess passive investment income for three consecutive years. The latter situation only applies to corporations that were formerly C corporations that have undistributed accumulated earnings and profits (E&P) from those C corporation years.

Corporation ceases to be a small business corporation. A corporation's S election terminates if it ceases to be a small business corporation.[47] An S corporation ceases to be a small business corporation if a C corporation, partnership, nonresident alien, or other nonpermitted shareholder becomes a shareholder in the corporation. An S corporation also ceases to be a small business corporation if it issues a second class of stock, or if the number of shareholders exceeds 100. When an S corporation no longer qualifies as a small business corporation, its S corporation tax year closes on the day before the terminating event.

Example 29: On June 5, 2009, an S corporation ceased to be a small business corporation because the number of its shareholders increased to 101. The corporation's S status termi-

---

[46] Reg. § 1.1362-6(a)(4).   [47] Code Sec. 1362(d)(2); Reg. § 1.1362-2(b).

nates, and its S corporation tax year ends on June 4, 2009. The corporation reverts to a C corporation beginning on June 5, 2009.

Planning Pointer: If at anytime during its existence, a nonpermitted shareholder owns stock in an S corporation or if the number of shareholders of the S corporation exceeds 100, the corporation's S status is terminated and the corporation reverts back to being a C corporation. Thus, to avoid losing S status, shareholders of an S corporation should formally agree not to transfer shares of stock in their corporation to someone other than a permitted shareholder and not to transfer shares without the permission of the other shareholders.

Excessive passive investment income. A corporation's S election terminates if the corporation has accumulated E&P and reports excess passive investment income for three consecutive tax years. An S corporation can have accumulated E&P either from its years as a C corporation or because it acquired a C corporation with accumulated E&P. Excess passive investment income is defined as passive investment income that exceeds 25 percent of the corporation's gross receipts for the year.[48]

Gross receipts generally include the total amount a business receives or accrues (depending on the corporation's method of accounting). It is not reduced by returns and allowances, cost of goods sold, or any deductions. Gross receipts from dispositions of capital assets (other than stock and securities) are taken into account only to the extent of the capital gain net income from the dispositions. Gross receipts from the sale or exchange of stock or securities are taken into account only to the extent of the gains from the dispositions. **Passive investment income** includes gross receipts derived from royalties, rents, dividends, interest, and annuities.

The termination of a corporation's S status because of excessive passive investment income is effective on the first day of the tax year that begins after the third consecutive tax year in which the S corporation had excessive passive investment income.[49]

Example 30:   Eppini Real Estate Holdings is an S corporation that uses the calendar year as its tax year. Eppini has $100,000 in accumulated E&P from its years as a C corporation and from 2009–2011, it reports the following gross receipts and passive investment income.

Tax Year	Passive Investment Income (PII)	Gross Receipts	Percentage of Gross Receipts from PPI
2009	$115,000	$450,000	25.56%
2010	$105,000	$400,000	26.25%
2011	$140,000	$500,000	28.00%

Because Eppini's passive investment income exceeds 25 percent of its gross receipts for each of these three consecutive years, its S election terminates effective January 1, 2012.

Reason for the Rule: Accumulated E&P represent profits of a C corporation that have previously been taxed to the corporation, but have not been taxed at the shareholder level. When a C corporation with accumulated E&P elects to be taxed as an S corporation, its accumulated E&P avoid double taxation until the S corporation distributes these amounts to its shareholders. The excess passive investment income rule was enacted to prevent corporations with accumulated E&P from converting "a regular

---

[48] Code Sec. 1362(d)(3); Reg. § 1.1362-2(c).   [49] Code Sec. 1362(d)(3)(A).

> corporation's operating company into a holding company whose income is not subject to a corporate level tax, without the imposition of any shareholder tax on accumulated E&P as would occur if the corporation was liquidated."[50]

Petition to disregard inadvertent termination. A corporation may be treated as continuing as an S corporation during a period specified by the IRS even though its S status terminated because the corporation ceased to be a small business corporation or had excessive passive investment income. In order to receive this treatment, each of the following three requirements must be satisfied.

1. The IRS determines that the circumstances resulting in termination were inadvertent,

2. Within a reasonable period of time after the corporation discovered the circumstances resulting in termination, steps were taken to correct the problem, and

3. The corporation and each person who was a shareholder at any time during the period that the IRS permits the corporation to continue as an S corporation agree to make adjustments the IRS may require that are consistent with the treatment of the corporation as an S corporation.[51]

The IRS is more likely to accept an S corporation's request to disregard an inadvertent termination if it believes that the terminating event was not reasonably within the corporation's control and was not part of a plan to terminate the corporation's S status. If the terminating event took place without the corporation's knowledge, notwithstanding its due diligence to safeguard itself against such an event, it tends to establish that the termination was inadvertent.[52]

.03 Treatment of S Termination Year

In the year the S corporation terminates its S status, the portion of the tax year ending on the day before the effective date of the termination is treated as a short tax year for which the corporation was an S corporation (the "**S short year**"). Starting with the day of the terminating event, the remaining portion of the year is treated as a short tax year for which the corporation was a C corporation (the "**C short year**").[53] There is no S termination year when a corporation's S status is terminated because it had excessive passive investment income, as such termination is effective as of the first day of the corporation's tax year.

Computing short year taxable income. The amount of each item of income, gain, loss, deduction, and credit is allocated pro rata between the S short year and C short year on a daily basis unless the corporation elects otherwise. If the pro rata allocation rules do not apply, then the corporation must allocate its items of income, gain, deduction, loss, or credit on the basis of its normal tax accounting method. In these situations, the corporation's items are allocated to shareholders who owned stock in the corporation during the period that the items were generated. A corporation's election to allocate S termination year income on the basis of its normal tax accounting method may be made only with the consent of each person who is a shareholder at any time during the S short year and each person who is a shareholder on the first day of the C short year.[54]

Corporation's tax for its C short year. The corporation's tax for its C short year is the portion of the tax on annualized taxable income that relates to the period in which the business is taxed as a C corporation. This first step in this process involves annualizing the corporation's taxable income for the C short year. This can be accomplished by dividing taxable income for the C short year by the number of days in the C short year and multiplying this amount by the number of days in the year (365). Next, tax is computed on the annualized taxable income, and then multiplied by a percentage that represents the portion of the year that the corporation is taxed as a C corporation.[55]

---

[50] H.R. Rep. No. 97-826 (September 16, 1982), at 6.
[51] Code Sec. 1362(f).
[52] Reg. § 1.1362-4(b).

[53] Code Sec. 1362(e); Reg. § 1.1362-3(a).
[54] Reg. § 1.1362-3(b)(1).
[55] Code Sec. 1362(e)(5).

Example 31: On July 6, 2010, the number of shareholders of Freedberg Automotive increases to over 100. Freedberg, a calendar year corporation, has an S short year that ends on July 5, 2010, and a C short year that begins on July 6, 2010. Freedberg's taxable income for its C short year was $500,000. The first step in calculating its tax for its C short year is to annualize its taxable income for its C short year by dividing its taxable income for its C short year by the number of days in the C short year and then multiplying this amount by 365 (($500,000/179) × 365 = $1,019,553). Using the corporate income tax rates schedule, Freedberg's annual tax on that amount would be $346,648. Since the company is taxed as a C corporation for 179 days during 2010, its C short year tax liability is $170,000 ($346,648/365 × 179).

¶ 1506 Allocating S Corporation Items

S corporations, like partnerships, do not pay federal income tax on their taxable income.[56] Instead, an S corporation's shareholders are taxed on their pro rata share of the S corporation's income, gains, losses, deductions, and credits. S corporations are required to compute and report their taxable income on Form 1120S, *U.S. Income Tax Return for an S Corporation*. Since the activities of the S corporation flow through to its shareholders, some items of income, gain, deduction, loss, and credit must be separately stated from S corporation taxable income so that any limit that applies to the item at the shareholder-level can be applied on the shareholders' respective income tax returns.[57]

Most S corporations use a calendar year-end, but an S corporation may use a fiscal year if it establishes a business purpose for doing so. They also may select as their tax year a year end that does not defer recognition of income by their shareholders for more than three months, but only if the corporation agrees to pay an amount representing the tax on the deferral provided for its shareholders. This election under Code Sec. 444 is the same that applies to partnerships. (See ¶ 302.02 and ¶ 1404.01.)

No carryovers arising for a tax year for which a corporation is a C corporation may be carried to a tax year for which the corporation is an S corporation. However, if the S corporation reverts to C status before the end of the year carryover period, it may be able to utilize the carryovers on its C corporation income tax return.[58]

Example 32: In 2009, Folts Gutters and Downspouts, a C corporation, reported a $15,000 net operating loss, which would normally carry over to each of the following 20 tax years. If Folts elects S status, it will not be able to utilize any remaining net operating loss during its years as an S corporation. If Folts reverts back to a C corporation prior to 2030 (when its net operating loss expires), it may be able to utilize its net operating loss carryover.

S corporations make most of the elections affecting the computation of their taxable income and, consequently, the taxable income of their shareholders.[59] For example, they make elections regarding which accounting method and depreciation method to use, whether and how much to elect to expense under Code Sec. 179, and whether to deduct intangible drilling and development costs. The decision whether to reinvest the proceeds from an involuntary conversion in qualified replacement property to defer recognition of realized gain is also done at the entity level. However, the decision whether to deduct or take a credit for foreign income taxes paid or accrued by the S corporation is done at the shareholder level. Accordingly, the amount of foreign income taxes paid or accrued by the S corporation must be reported separately from other items on the S corporation's income tax return.

---

[56] Code Sec. 1363(a); Reg. § 1.1363-1(a)(1).
[57] Code Sec. 1363(b).

[58] Code Sec. 1371(b)(1).
[59] Code Sec. 1363(c)(1); Reg. § 1.1363-1(c)(1).

Spotlight: The S corporation rules required that items of income, gain, loss, deduction, and credit be allocated to shareholders on a pro rata basis. The ability to specially allocate these items is not an option as it is with partnerships and other entities that elect to be taxed as partnerships.

.01 Separately vs. Nonseparately-Stated Items

For the same reasons that a partnership is required to separately state certain items of income, gain, deduction, loss, or credit on its tax return, an S corporation must separately state certain items on Schedule K-1, *Shareholder's Share of Income, Deductions, Credits, etc.* of Form 1120S.[60] A list of items of income, gain, deduction, loss, or credit that an S corporation must separately state is provided in Table 15-3.

Table 15-3 Separately Stated Items of an S Corporation

Separately Stated Item	*Reason for Stating Separately*
Income or Loss:	
Net short-term capital gains and losses Net long-term capital gains and losses Net gains and losses from the sale of collectibles Unrecaptured Section 1250 gain Net Section 1231 gains and losses	For purposes of the netting process and computation of net capital gain taxed at a maximum 5-, 15-, 25-, or 28-percent tax rate. See ¶ 1306.01.
Taxable and tax-exempt interest income Qualified and nonqualified dividend income Investment expenses (other than interest)	For purposes of computing the investment interest expense limitation that applies to individual taxpayers. See ¶ 1304.03.
Net income or loss from rental real estate activities Net income or loss from other rental activities Royalty income	For purposes of computing the limitation on losses from passive activities. See IRS Publication 925.
Recoveries of tax benefit items	For purposes of determining whether the taxpayer benefited from deducting these items. See ¶ 313.
Deductions:	
Code Sec. 179 expenses	For purposes of applying the taxable income limitation. See ¶ 702.03.
Charitable contributions	For purposes of applying the 20-, 30-, and 50-percent limits that apply to individual taxpayers. See ¶ 1304.03.
Investment interest expense	For purposes of computing the investment interest expense limitation that applies to individual taxpayers. See ¶ 1304.03.

---

[60] Code Sec. 1366(a)(1).

Separately Stated Item	*Reason for Stating Separately*
Circulation expenditures, research and experimentation expenditures, intangible drilling costs, and mining exploration costs	Various tax preference items used in computing an individual's alternative minimum tax. See ¶ 1007, ¶ 1008, and ¶ 1307.
Post-1986 depreciation adjustment, adjusted gain or loss, depletion, gross income, and deductions from oil, gain and geothermal properties, and other AMT items	For purposes of computing tax adjustments necessary in computing an individual's alternative minimum taxable income. See ¶ 1011.01 and ¶ 1307.

Tax Credits:

Various business tax credits discussed in Chapter 11, including the low-income housing credit, work opportunity credit, and credit for increasing research activities, among others.	For purposes of computing the general business credit limitation on the shareholder's income tax return. See ¶ 1103.02.
Foreign taxes paid or accrued Gross income from foreign sources	For purposes of applying the formula for the foreign tax credit. See ¶ 1117.01.

Nonseparately stated items include the corporation's gross income from its business operations and its business deductions. Nonseparately stated items are those items of income, deduction, gain, or loss that are treated and taxed as ordinary income to all types of shareholders. Furthermore, nonseparately stated items are not subject to any limitations applied at the shareholder-level. The corporation's deductions are subtracted from its gross income from business operations, and the resulting ordinary income or loss is passed through to shareholders pro rata as one lump sum amount.

.02 Treatment of Organizational Expenditures

Recall from Chapter 5 that the tax law allows corporations to elect to deduct up to $5,000 of organizational expenditures for the tax year in which the corporation begins its business. The $5,000 amount is reduced dollar-for-dollar when the total organizational costs exceed $50,000. Thus, no current deduction is allowed to corporations that incur over $55,000 in organizational costs. At the taxpayer's election, any costs not currently expensed may be amortized ratably over a 180-month period, starting in the month in which the business begins.[61] If the election is not made, these expenses are capitalized and recovered in the year the corporation is liquidated (see ¶ 503). These rules apply equally to both C corporations and S corporations.

As with C corporations, organizational expenses are capital expenditures incident to the creation of a corporation. Examples include legal services to organize the corporation, accounting services, fees paid to the state of incorporation, expenses of temporary directors, and expenses for organizational meetings of directors and shareholders. Expenditures that do not qualify as organizational expenditures include commissions, professional fees, and printing costs to issue or sell stock or other securities, expenditures to transfer assets to a corporation, or expenses connected with the reorganization of a corporation.

As with other business entities, S corporations may make an election to amortize organizational expenses in a statement attached to their first tax return. The statement and return must be filed by the due date (including extensions) for filing that first tax return.

---

[61] Code Sec. 1363(b)(3).

Example 33: An S corporation incurs $18,000 in organizational expenses. Because these amounts do not exceed $50,000, the entire $18,000 can be deducted in arriving at taxable income in the first year of operations.

.03 Corporate Preference Items

If the S corporation was a C corporation for any of the three tax years immediately preceding its current tax year, it must adjust certain items before taking them into account in determining its taxable income. These adjustments result in the same amount of tax being collected as if the corporation had continued as a C corporation.

Gain on the disposition of Section 1250 property. Recall from Chapter 9 that when a corporation disposes of depreciable real property, 20 percent of the difference between the amount that would be treated as ordinary income if the property were Section 1245 property and the amount treated as ordinary income under Code Sec. 1250 is treated as ordinary income (see ¶ 905.02). When an individual sells Section 1250 property for a gain, the gain is treated as Section 1231 gain, assuming that the straight-line method was used to depreciate depreciable property. Consequently, when Section 1250 property is sold by an S corporation, the shareholders will include their pro rata shares of the gain on their tax return. Since no shareholders of an S corporation are C corporations, the portion of the gain that would have been taxed as ordinary income is now likely to be taxed as Section 1231 gain. Recall from Chapter 9 that for individual taxpayers, net Section 1231 gain often is treated as long-term capital gain, which is taxed at lower rates than ordinary income (see ¶ 901.02 and ¶ 904.01).

To prevent corporations from converting ordinary income into Section 1231 gain, if an S corporation sells such property during the first three years after converting from a C corporation, then the S corporation must characterize a portion of the gain as ordinary income using the same rules that would have applied if it were still a C corporation.[62] This ordinary income will be passed through and taxed as such to the S corporation's shareholders.

Example 34: Immediately after converting to S status, an S corporation sells an office building for $1 million. Its adjusted basis in the office building is $300,000, and it had depreciated the building using the straight-line method. Total depreciation deductions were $80,000. Accordingly, none of its $700,000 gain ($1,000,000 – $300,000) is recaptured as ordinary income under Code Sec. 1250. However, had the property sold been Section 1245 property, all $80,000 of depreciation taken would have been recaptured as ordinary income. Therefore, 20 percent of this amount, or $16,000, represents gain that flows through to shareholders as ordinary income. The remaining $64,000 of the gain ($80,000 – $16,000) flows through to the shareholders as Section 1231 gain.

Percentage depletion for iron ore and coal. A corporation's percentage depletion deduction for iron ore and coal is reduced by 20 percent of the difference between its percentage depletion deduction for the tax year and the adjusted basis (determined without regard to the depletion deduction for the tax year) of the property at the close of the tax year.

Amortization of pollution control facilities. An S corporation must reduce the amortizable basis of a certified pollution control facility by 20 percent before calculating its amortization deduction.

Mineral exploration and development costs. The S corporation may deduct only 70 percent of its domestic exploration costs. It capitalizes the remaining 30 percent of such costs and may amortize them over the 60-month period beginning with the month during which the costs were paid or incurred. The amount amortized is treated as additional depreciation and is subject to recapture as ordinary income when the corporation disposes of the property.

---

[62] Code Sec. 1363(b)(4).

¶ 1507 Tax Consequences to Shareholders

S corporation shareholders must report on their federal income tax returns their pro rata shares of each item of their corporation's separately stated income, gain, loss, deduction, and credit, regardless of the amounts distributed to them during the year.[63] They also must report their respective nonseparately computed income or loss, irrespective of any distributions made to them during the year. A shareholder's pro rata share of corporate items is reported to the shareholder on Schedule K-1, *Shareholder's Share of Income, Credits, Deductions, etc.,* for Form 1120S.

.01 Pro Rata Share

The tax laws normally require that S corporation income, gain, deduction, loss, and credit be allocated to shareholders on a pro rata basis. However, the pro rata allocation rules do not apply if at any time during the S termination year there is a change in ownership of 50 percent or more of the issued and outstanding shares of stock of the corporation.[64] A shareholder's pro rata share of any S corporation item for a tax year is determined by applying the following four steps:[65]

Step 1: Divide the amount of an item by the number of days in the corporation's tax year. This amount represents the per-day amount for that item.

Step 2: Divide the per-day amount by the number of outstanding shares on that day. This amount represents the per-share, per-day amount for that item.

Step 3: Multiply the number of the shareholder's shares on the per-day amount by the amount assigned to that day. Then multiply this amount by the number of days that the shareholder owned that exact number of shares.

Step 4: Repeat Step 3 for each different number of shares that the shareholder held during the year. When finished, the sum of these amounts equals the shareholder's pro rata share of the item.

If there is no change in a corporation's shareholders or their ownership interests during a year, a shareholder's pro rata share of an item may be calculated by multiplying the amount of the item by the shareholder's percentage ownership.

Example 35: Candida Rensch owns 15 percent of the shares of stock of an S corporation during the entire year. Her pro rata share of the corporation's $10,000 interest income for the year is $1,500 ($10,000 × 15%).

Example 36: William Reese owned 100 shares of stock in an S corporation from January 1, 2010, until May 24, 2010. This represented 10 percent of the 1,000 total shares of stock outstanding in the S corporation. On May 25, 2010, William purchased 275 additional shares and his ownership percentage increased to 25 percent of the 1,500 shares outstanding. William's pro rata share of the corporation's $30,000 dividend income for the year is $5,724.26.

Step 1: $30,000/365 = $82.19 (per-day amount)

Step 2: $82.19/1,000 shares = $.08219 (per-share, per-day amount from January 1, 2010–May 24, 2010)
$82.19/1,500 shares = $.05479 (per-share, per-day amount from May 25, 2010–December 31, 2010)

Step 3: $.08219 × 100 shares × 144 days = $1,183.54
$.05479 × 375 shares × 221 days = $4,540.72

Step 4: $1,183.54 + $4,540.72= $5,724.26

---

[63] Code Sec. 1366(a); Reg. § 1.1366-1(a)(1).
[64] Reg. § 1.1362-3(b).

[65] Code Sec. 1377(a)(1); Reg. § 1.1377-1(a)(1).

Election to terminate tax year following termination of shareholder's interest. If a shareholder's entire interest in an S corporation is terminated during the S corporation's tax year and the corporation and all affected shareholders agree, then the S corporation may elect to determine the shareholder's share of a corporation's separately and nonseparately stated items as if the corporation's tax year ended on the day that the shareholder's entire interest in the corporation terminated.[66] *Affected shareholders* are those shareholders whose interest is terminated and all shareholders to whom the shareholder has transferred shares during the tax year. If the shareholder has transferred shares to the corporation, affected shareholders include all persons who were shareholders during the tax year.[67]

Example 37: Archie Osaki, a shareholder of a calendar year S corporation, sells all of his shares of stock in the corporation on June 1. On September 1, the corporation disposes of a building and recognizes $1 million of gain. If all affected shareholders agreed to determine Archie's share of this gain as if the corporation's tax year ended on June 1, none of the gain from the sale of the building will be included in Archie's gross income.

Election to terminate tax year following qualifying disposition. If there is a qualifying disposition of stock, a corporation may elect to determine each shareholder's pro rata share of the corporation's separately and nonseparately stated items as if the corporation's tax year consisted of two separate tax years, the first of which ended at the close of the day on which the qualifying disposition occurred.[68] A "qualifying disposition" includes a shareholder's disposing of 20 percent or more of the outstanding stock of the corporation in one or more transactions during any 30-day period during the corporation's tax year. It also includes a redemption treated as an exchange under Code Secs. 302(a) or 303(a) of at least 20 percent of the corporation's outstanding stock from a shareholder in one or more transactions during any 30-day period during the corporation's tax year. Finally, it includes an issuance of an amount of stock of at least 25 percent of the previously outstanding stock to one or more new shareholders during any 30-day period during the corporation's tax year.

.02 When Income Must Be Reported

S corporation shareholders must include their pro rata shares of their corporation's items of income, gain, loss, deduction, and credit and their pro rata shares of their corporation's nonseparately computed gain or loss for their tax year with or within which their corporation's tax year ends.[69]

Example 38: Jayne Sloan is a shareholder of an S corporation. Jayne uses a calendar year-end; the corporation's tax year ends on September 30. For the fiscal year ending September 30, 2009, Jayne's pro rata share of the corporation's taxable income was $30,000. She must include that $30,000 in her taxable income for 2009, even though the corporation earned a portion of that amount during the last three months of 2008.

.03 Character of Items Constituting a Shareholder's Pro Rata Share

As a general rule, the character of any item of income, gain, loss, deduction, or credit included in a shareholder's pro rata share is determined at the entity level and retains that character in the shareholder's hands.[70] When it is necessary to determine the amount or character of a shareholder's gross income, the shareholder's gross income will include the shareholder's pro rata share of the corporation's gross income.[71]

Example 39: Robin Matus is a shareholder in an S corporation. Robin is an art dealer; the corporation is not. During the year, the corporation sells artwork held as an invest-

---

[66] Code Sec. 1377(a)(2); Reg. § 1.1377-1(b)(1).

[67] Reg. § 1.1377-1(b)(2).

[68] Reg. § 1.1368-1(g).

[69] Code Sec. 1366(a); Reg. § 1.1366-1(a)(1).

[70] Code Sec. 1366(b); Reg. § 1.1366-1(b)(1).

[71] Code Sec. 1366(c); Reg. § 1.1366-1(c)(1).

ment for a $1,000 gain. Robin's pro rata share of the corporation's gain from the sale of the artwork will be characterized as capital gain, even though Robin is a dealer in the property that was sold.

 Planning Pointer: Guaranteed payments a partnership makes to a partner are usually subject to self-employment tax, as are a general partner's distributive share of partnership income. In contrast, S corporation shareholders who also work for the corporation are treated as employees, and as such have FICA and income taxes withheld from their paychecks. Although the S corporation is responsible for the employer's share of FICA taxes on any wages paid to its employees plus unemployment taxes on its employees' wages, the shareholder's distributive share of the S corporation profits is not subject to employment taxes.[72]

.04 Limits on the Deductibility of Losses

An S corporation shareholder may deduct the shareholder's pro rata share of the corporation's items of loss and deduction only to the extent that the amount of those items does not exceed the sum of the adjusted basis of the shareholder's stock in the S corporation plus the adjusted basis of any S corporation indebtedness to the shareholder (see ¶ 1509).[73] A shareholder's aggregate amount of items of loss and deduction for a tax year in excess of the sum of the adjusted basis of the shareholder's stock in the S corporation and the adjusted basis of any indebtedness of the S corporation to the shareholder retains its character and is treated as incurred by the corporation in the next tax year (and subsequent tax years) with respect to the shareholder.[74]

Example 40: Suzan Resendes is a shareholder of an S corporation. Suzan's pro rata share of the corporation's loss for the tax year is $10,000. At the end of that year, Suzan's adjusted basis in her stock (before taking into account her share of the corporation's loss) is $6,000. She is not owed any money by the corporation. Suzan can deduct a $6,000 loss for the year, and her adjusted basis in the stock is reduced to zero. The remaining $4,000 ($10,000 – $6,000) of Suzan's loss is disallowed for the year.

Example 41: Continuing on with Example 40, in the next tax year, Suzan's pro rata share of the corporation's income increases her adjusted basis in her stock to $3,000 (before taking into account the $4,000 loss disallowed the previous year). Suzan may deduct $3,000 of the $4,000 loss carried over from the previous tax year. The loss once again reduces her adjusted basis in the stock to $0. She then carries over the $1,000 loss to the next tax year.

Example 42: Van Eisler is a shareholder of an S corporation. Van's pro rata share of the corporation's loss for the tax year is $20,000. At the end of that year, his adjusted basis in the stock (before taking into account his share of the corporation's loss) is $8,000. The corporation owes Van $15,000 from a loan he made the corporation in a previous tax year. Van can deduct a $20,000 loss for the year. The first $8,000 of loss reduces his adjusted basis in the stock to zero. The remaining $12,000 loss ($20,000 – $8,000) Van deducts reduces his basis in the indebtedness owed to him to $3,000 ($15,000 – $12,000).

If S corporation stock is transferred by a shareholder to the shareholder's spouse or to the shareholder's former spouse incident to their divorce, any suspended loss or deduction with respect to that stock carries over to the transferee and is treated as incurred by the corporation with respect to the transferee in the subsequent tax year.

---

[72] *A.R. Durando*, CA-9, 95-2 USTC ¶ 50,615, 70 F3d 548; Rev. Rul. 59-221, 1959-1 CB 225.

[73] Code Sec. 1366(d)(1); Reg. § 1.1366-2(a)(1).

[74] Code Sec. 1366(d)(2); Reg. § 1.1366-2(a)(2).

Passive activity losses. If an S corporation shareholder does not materially participate in the corporation's business activities, the shareholder may deduct the shareholder's pro rata share of losses only to the extent of the amount of the shareholder's passive activity income.[75] Passive activity income includes income other than from portfolio sources (interest, dividends, capital gains) or income from a business in which the taxpayer materially participates.

At-risk limitation. S corporation shareholders with sufficient adjusted basis to take advantage of their pro rata share of their corporation's loss nevertheless will be denied a deduction for the loss to the extent that the loss exceeds their amount at risk in a corporate activity.[76] An S corporation shareholder is considered at risk for all of the following amounts:

- The amount of money and the adjusted basis of other property contributed to the S corporation.

- The shareholder's share of net income retained by the S corporation.

- Amounts borrowed by the shareholder for use in the activity if the shareholder is personally liable for repayment of the amount borrowed or the amount borrowed is secured by the shareholder's property (other than property used in the activity). A shareholder's at-risk amount is also increased by the amount of qualified nonrecourse financing secured by real property used by the corporation.

¶ 1508 Adjustment of Shareholder's Basis in Stock

A shareholder's adjusted basis in stock of an S corporation determines the extent to which a distribution made by the corporation to the shareholder is taxable, as well as the amount of losses that shareholders may claim in a given year. A shareholder's adjusted basis in the stock is also used to determine the shareholder's realized gain or loss upon the disposition of the stock.

As discussed in previous chapters, the tax term "basis" is used to describe a taxpayer's investment in property that the taxpayer owns. With respect to stock, original basis is the basis of stock at the time it is acquired, and adjusted basis is the taxpayer's original basis adjusted for certain events that occur after the stock is acquired. A shareholder's original basis includes the amount the shareholder pays to acquire the stock. An S corporation shareholder may acquire stock from an S corporation in exchange for cash or property other than cash, or through other means, such as gift, inheritance, etc. For purposes of this introductory chapter on S corporations, we will assume that the shareholder acquired the S stock for cash from either the corporation itself or from another shareholder. Thus, the shareholder's original basis in the S corporation stock includes the amount of cash that the shareholder paid to acquire the stock. (See ¶ 1204 for discussion of special basis rules that apply to property acquired by means other than by purchase).

Once the shareholder's original basis from the acquisition of the S corporation stock has been determined, the shareholder's basis is adjusted to reflect a variety of transactions and events that occur with respect to the operations of the S corporation. For example, a shareholder's basis in S corporation stock is increased by the shareholder's pro rata share of income and gain (including tax-exempt interest), and is decreased by the shareholder's pro rata share of deductions, losses, excess depletion, and any noncapital, nondeductible expenses. A shareholder's basis in S corporation stock is also decreased by any distributions the corporation makes to the shareholder.

Example 43: During 20X0, Tammi Subaugh pays $5,000 for 100 shares of stock in an S corporation. During 20X0, Tammi is allocated a total of $1,000 of separately and non-separately stated income and gain. Her adjusted basis in her shares of stock increases by to $6,000 ($5,000 + $1,000).

---

[75] Code Sec. 469.   [76] Code Sec. 465.

> **Reason for the Rule:** A shareholder's adjusted basis in S corporation stock is increased by the shareholder's pro rata share of tax-exempt to ensure that shareholders are never taxed on any tax-exempt income that is earned by the S corporation and subsequently distributed to the shareholder. To illustrate this fact, take an S corporation with a single shareholder who contributes $10,000 to the corporation in exchange for his shares of S corporation stock. During the first year of operations, the only source of income earned by the corporation is $500 of tax-exempt income. This income is allocated to the shareholder and avoids tax at both the corporate- and shareholder-levels. If the shareholder's adjusted basis in the stock is not increased by the $500 of tax-exempt income, and if the corporation should liquidate, the shareholder will receive the $10,500 of cash, which will reduce his $10,000 adjusted basis to $0 and result in a $500 capital gain. Consequently, the $500 of tax-exempt income earned by the corporation eventually would be taxed to the shareholder.

After making all positive adjustments to a shareholder's basis, the basis in the S corporation stock decreases (but not below zero) by the following amounts in the following order:[77]

1. The amount of nontaxable distributions to the shareholder,

2. The shareholder's pro rata share of the corporation's noncapital, nondeductible expenses plus the corporation's deduction for depletion for any oil and gas property (to the extent that the deduction does not exceed the shareholder's proportionate share of the adjusted basis of such property),

3. The shareholder's pro rata share of the corporation's loss (if any) and any separately stated items of loss and deduction, and

4. Any amount of loss or deduction allowed at the end of the post-termination transition period.[78]

The decrease for a charitable contribution of property is the shareholder's pro rata share of the adjusted basis of the property. This rule does not apply to contributions made in tax years beginning after December 31, 2009.

Example 44: Jonas Sturman is a shareholder of an S corporation. At the beginning of the year, Jonas's adjusted basis in his stock was $2,000. On April 10, he receives a $1,300 distribution from the corporation. His pro rata share of the corporation's income for the year is $400, and his pro rata share of the corporation's separately stated items of loss and deduction for the year is $1,500. Jonas's basis in his stock is adjusted as follows.

Beginning basis in S stock	$2,000
Plus: Pro rata share of income	400
	$2,400
Less: Distribution	(1,300)
	$1,100
Less: Pro rata share of separately stated items of loss and deduction	(1,500)
Ending basis in S stock	$ 0

A shareholder's basis cannot be reduced below zero. Jonas's remaining $400 loss ($1,500 – $1,100) is treated as incurred the next tax year. If Jonas is able to increase his basis in the stock, either through additional contributions or his pro rata

---

[77] Code Sec. 1367(a)(2); Reg. §1.1367-1(c), (f).   [78] Code Sec. 1366(d)(3)(C).

shares of next year's S corporation income, he may be allowed to deduct the loss in that year.

 Spotlight: A distribution during the tax year reduces a shareholder's adjusted basis for purposes of determining the amount of loss that a shareholder may deduct.

Shareholders must reduce their adjusted basis in S corporation stock by their pro rata share of noncapital, nondeductible expenses. A corporation's noncapital, nondeductible expenses are those items for which no loss or deduction is allowable. The following are examples of noncapital, nondeductible expenses.[79]

- Illegal bribes, kickbacks, and other nondeductible payments (see ¶ 501.04).
- Nondeductible fines and penalties (see ¶ 501.04).
- Expenses and interest relating to tax-exempt income (see ¶ 505).
- Disallowed losses from transactions between related persons (see ¶ 804).
- The disallowed portion of meal and entertainment expenses (see ¶ 605).

An item for which a deduction is deferred to a later tax year is not a noncapital, nondeductible expense. For example, postponed losses resulting from like-kind exchanges do not reduce a shareholder's adjusted basis in S corporation stock.

¶ 1509 Adjustment to Basis of Indebtedness to Shareholder

Unlike partners, who increase their basis in their partnership interests by their allocable share of partnership liabilities, S corporation shareholders do not increase the adjusted basis of their stock by their share of the general liabilities of the corporation. However, S corporation shareholders keep track of their basis in any amounts they personally loan to the corporation. After the adjusted basis in their shares of S corporation stock has been reduced to zero, shareholders can use any basis they have in the corporation's debt to them to utilize any excess losses of the corporation that flow through to them.[80] The shareholder's original basis in an S corporation's indebtedness to the shareholder is the amount the shareholder loans to the corporation. This amount may be adjusted for the shareholder's pro rata share of the S corporation's losses, deductions, nondeductible expenses, and depletion to the extent such items exceed the shareholder's adjusted basis in the shareholder's S corporation stock at the time of allocation.

After making each of the adjustments that increase the adjusted basis in stock, basis reductions for any distributions are taken into consideration. After this, the shareholder's pro rata share of corporate deductions, losses, nondeductible expenses, and excess depletion are applied to the remaining adjusted basis of the shareholder's stock. If the shareholder's basis is reduced to zero, any excess corporate deductions, losses, nondeductible expenses, and excess depletion are applied to reduce (but not below zero) the shareholder's basis in any indebtedness of the corporation to the shareholder.[81] It is important to note that distributions do not reduce a shareholder's basis in indebtedness. Instead, these amounts reduce a shareholder's adjusted basis in the shareholder's S corporation stock to zero, and any excess is taxed as a capital gain.

Example 45: Barb Jendro is a shareholder of an S corporation. In April 2009, Barb loans the corporation $10,000. At the end of the corporation's 2008 tax year, Barb's adjusted basis in her stock in the corporation was $3,000, and her pro rata share of the corporation's losses, deductions, and nondeductible expenses for 2009 equals $3,500. The $3,500 reduces the adjusted basis of Barb's shares to $0, and the remaining $500 ($3,500 – $3,000) reduces her basis in the indebtedness to $9,500 ($10,000 – $500).

---

[79] Reg. § 1.1367-1(c)(2).

[80] Code Sec. 1367(b)(2)(A); Reg. § 1.1367-2(b).

[81] Code Sec. 1367(b)(2)(A); Reg. § 1.1367-2(b).

Barb is allowed to deduct on her 2009 tax return her entire pro rata share of losses and deductions because she has sufficient basis in her stock and indebtedness to absorb those losses.

If a shareholder's adjusted basis in the S corporation's indebtedness to the shareholder is decreased by corporate deductions, losses, nondeductible expenses, and excess depletion, any subsequent amounts of the shareholder's pro rata share of income and gain items will be applied first to increase the shareholder's basis in indebtedness owed the shareholder by the S corporation.[82] Once the shareholder's basis in the indebtedness is restored to the appropriate amount, any excess increases the shareholder's basis in the S corporation stock.

Example 46: Malcolm Caraveo is a shareholder of an S corporation. At the end of the corporation's 2009 tax year, Malcolm's adjusted basis in his S stock is reduced to $0, and his adjusted basis in indebtedness owed by the corporation to him is reduced from $5,000 to $2,000 due to S corporation losses and deductions allocated to him in 2009. At the end of the 2010 tax year, Malcolm's pro rata share of the corporation's taxable income equals $5,000. Malcolm's adjusted basis in the indebtedness is restored to the $5,000 that the corporation owes him, and the remaining $2,000 of Malcolm's pro rata share of the corporation's net income ($5,000 – $3,000) increases his adjusted basis in his shares of stock in the corporation to $2,000 ($0 + $2,000).

¶ 1510 Distributions to Shareholders

The tax consequences of distributions of property made by an S corporation to its shareholders depends on the adjusted basis of the shareholders' stock in the corporation and whether or not the S corporation has any accumulated E&P.[83] Shareholders who receive a distribution during the year must wait until the end of the year to determine how the amount they receive will be taxed.

.01 Accumulated Adjustments Account

An S corporation's accumulated E&P should be distinguished from its **accumulated adjustments account (AAA)**. The former represents the amount of the corporation's earnings as a C corporation that has only been taxed at the corporate level (see ¶ 1009.01 and ¶ 1207). The latter measures the accumulated undistributed net income of a corporation while it has been an S corporation.[84] Since the earnings of an S corporation are taxed each year to its shareholders, regardless of whether any of those earnings are distributed to the shareholders during the year, the amounts in the AAA represent undistributed, previously-taxed S corporation earnings. Normally, distributions from an S corporation are treated as first coming from AAA, and then from accumulated E&P. Consequently, the shareholders normally enjoy tax-free distribution of previously taxed earnings before receiving a dividend distribution from corporate accumulated E&P.

 Planning Pointer: S corporations with accumulated E&P must maintain an AAA to determine how distributions are taxed to its shareholders. Corporations without accumulated E&P are not required to maintain an AAA, but it is recommended that they do so because should they engage in a transaction (such as a merger with an S corporation that has accumulated E&P), they will know the balance in their AAA.

On the first day that a corporation is an S corporation, the balance of its AAA is zero. Subsequently, it is adjusted by the following amounts in the following order.[85] Through these adjustments, it is possible for a corporation's AAA to be reduced below zero.

---

[82] Code Sec. 1367(b)(2)(B); Reg. § 1.1367-2(c).
[83] Code Sec. 1368.

[84] Code Sec. 1368(e); Reg. § 1.1368-2(a).
[85] Code Sec. 1368(e); Reg. § 1.1368-2.

Step 1: AAA is first increased by the corporation's nonseparately and separately stated items of income and gain (other than tax-exempt income). It is also increased by the amount by which the corporation's deductions for depletion exceed the basis of its property (other than oil or gas property) subject to depletion.

Step 2: AAA is decreased, but only to the extent it is increased in Step 1, by the corporation's nonseparately and separately stated items of loss and deduction, including depletion on oil and gas property, and the amount of noncapital, nondeductible expenses, other than federal taxes attributable to any year in which the corporation was a C corporation and expenses related to tax-exempt income.

Step 3: AAA is then decreased (but not below zero) by the amount of distributions (other than dividend distributions) to shareholders made during the year.

Step 4: AAA is then decreased by the remaining amounts of loss and deduction items, nondeductible expenses (other than federal taxes attributable to when the corporation was a C corporation and expenses related to tax-exempt income), and shareholders' depletion deductions not already applied to decrease AAA in Step 2.

Step 5: Finally, AAA is adjusted (whether negative or positive) for distributions in redemption of shareholders' stock.

.02 S Corporations with No Accumulated E&P

If an S corporation has no accumulated E&P, its distribution of property to its shareholders with respect to their stock is a nontaxable distribution of previously-taxed S corporation earnings to the extent that the amount of the distribution does not exceed the adjusted basis of the shareholder's stock. Once the distribution reduces the shareholder's basis in the stock to $0, any additional distribution is treated as gain from the sale or exchange of property.[86] Since stock is a capital asset for most taxpayers, such gain will be taxed as capital gain. The length of time that the shareholder has owned the stock will determine whether the gain will be recognized as short-term or long-term capital gain.

Example 47: Quentin Sabino is a shareholder of an S corporation. Quentin's adjusted basis in his stock is $4,000. On June 1, the corporation distributes $5,000 to Quentin. The distribution is a nontaxable distribution to the extent that it does not exceed Quentin's $4,000 adjusted basis in his stock. The remaining $1,000 excess ($5,000 – $4,000) is treated as capital gain.

.03 S Corporations with Accumulated E&P

If an S corporation has accumulated E&P at the end of its tax year, a distribution made during the year by the corporation with respect to its shareholders is taxed as follows:[87]

1. The amount of a distribution that does not exceed the amount of the corporation's AAA is a nontaxable distribution of previously-taxed S corporation earnings. The distribution from AAA reduces the shareholder's adjusted basis in the stock accordingly.

2. The amount of a distribution that exceeds the amount of the corporation's AAA is treated as a dividend to the extent of the corporation's accumulated E&P. Any distribution from accumulated E&P does not affect the shareholder's adjusted basis in the stock.

3. Any remaining distribution is a nontaxable return of capital to the extent that it does not exceed the shareholder's adjusted basis in the shareholder's S corporation stock (after reducing it by the distribution from AAA in the first step). Any excess distribution is treated as capital gain.

Example 48: Rod Heldenbrand owns 25 percent of the shares of an S corporation that once was a C corporation. Rod's adjusted basis in those shares is $10,000. On April 1, the

---

[86] Code Sec. 1368(b); Reg. § 1.1368-1(c). [87] Code Sec. 1368(c); Reg. § 1.1368-1(d).

corporation distributes $48,000 to its shareholders. Rod's share of the distribution is $12,000 ($48,000 × 25%). The corporation has $14,000 of accumulated E&P carried over from its C corporation years. The balance in its AAA at the end of the tax year is $28,000.

Under the normal ordering rules, the first $28,000 of the distribution is deemed to come from AAA, and accordingly, the corporation's AAA is reduced to $0. Since this amount represents previously-taxed S corporation earnings, Rod's $7,000 share ($28,000 × 25%) of this amount is a tax-free distribution. This amount reduces Rod's basis in his S corporation stock to $3,000 ($10,000 – $7,000).

Of the remaining $20,000 distributed from the corporation ($48,000 – $28,000), $14,000 is deemed to come from accumulated E&P, which is taxed as a dividend to the shareholders. Rod includes his $3,500 share of this amount ($14,000 × 25%) as dividend income on his personal income tax return. Rod's basis in his S corporation stock is not affected by the dividend distribution. The remaining $1,500 distribution ($12,000 – $7,000 – $3,500) is not taxable to Rod and reduces his adjusted basis in the stock to $1,500 ($3,000 – $1,500).

Election to distribute accumulated E&P first. With the consent of all shareholders who receive a distribution during the tax year, an S corporation may elect to treat a distribution as coming first from its accumulated E&P and then from its AAA.[88] To the extent that the distribution comes from accumulated E&P, it is taxed as a dividend to the shareholders. Once accumulated E&P is reduced to zero, the distribution is then considered to come from the corporation's AAA. Amounts distributed from AAA are nontaxable distributions to shareholders of previously-taxed S corporation earnings. Any amount distributed after the corporation's accumulated E&P has been reduced to $0 is applied against the shareholder's adjusted basis in the S corporation stock. Any remaining distribution after the shareholder's basis in the S stock is reduced to zero is taxed as capital gain to the shareholder.

A corporation makes the election by attaching a statement to a timely filed original or amended Form 1120S. An election, which applies to all distributions made during the year for which it is made, is irrevocable and effective only for the tax year for which it is made. Therefore, if the amount of the distribution is not sufficient to eliminate the corporation's accumulated E&P, another election must be made in a subsequent tax year if the corporation wants to elect to distribute accumulated E&P prior to AAA.

 Planning Pointer: By making an election, a corporation can eliminate its accumulated E&P and avoid the tax on excessive passive investment income (see ¶ 1512). Furthermore, for S corporations that tend to have excessive amounts of passive investment income year-after-year, reducing the corporation's accumulated E&P to zero will prevent the corporation from involuntarily terminating its S election (see ¶ 1505.02).

Example 49: Dean Motta owns 20 percent of the shares of an S corporation that once was a C corporation. Dean's adjusted basis in those shares is $20,000. On June 11, the corporation distributes $50,000 to its shareholders. Dean's share of the distribution is $10,000 ($50,000 × 20%). The corporation has $24,000 of accumulated E&P carried over from its C corporation years. The balance in the corporation's AAA at the end of the tax year is $33,000. The shareholders of the S corporation elect to treat the $50,000 distribution as first having come from accumulated E&P.

The first $24,000 of the distribution is deemed to come from accumulated E&P, which is taxed as a dividend to the shareholders. Dean includes his $4,800 share of

---

[88] Code Sec. 1368(e)(3); Reg. § 1.1368-1(f)(2).

this amount ($24,000 × 20%) in his gross income on his personal income tax return. The remaining $26,000 of the distribution ($50,000 – $24,000) is deemed to come from AAA, which results in a tax-free distribution to shareholders. The AAA balance at the end of the year is reduced to $7,000 ($33,000 – $26,000).

Dean's adjusted basis in the shares is not affected by the $4,800 dividend distribution. However, his $5,200 share of the $26,000 distribution from AAA ($26,000 × 20%) reduces his basis to $14,800 ($20,000 – $5,200).

.04 Distributions of Property Other Than Cash

When an S corporation distributes property to its shareholders, the property is valued at its FMV, which becomes the shareholder's basis in the property. The corporation recognizes gain to the extent that the FMV of the property distributed exceeds the corporation's basis in the property, as it would if it sold the property for its FMV.[89] Accordingly, the gain recognized by the corporation flows through to the shareholders on a pro rata basis. The character of the gain (ordinary income, Section 1231 gain, or capital gain) depends on the asset being distributed.

The S corporation does not recognize loss on the distribution of property where the FMV is less than the corporation's adjusted basis in the property. The shareholder's basis in the distributed property is its (lesser) FMV. Thus, recognition of any loss is deferred until the shareholder subsequently sells the property.

 Reason for the Rule: If the basis to the shareholder of appreciated property equals its FMV, then any appreciation would escape tax entirely if the tax law did not require that the corporation pick up the gain and allocate it pro rata to its shareholders.

.05 Distributions During the Post-Termination Transition Period

If a corporation distributes cash (but not property) with respect to its stock during the post-termination transition period, the distribution will be a nontaxable distribution of previously taxed S corporation earnings to the extent of the balance in the corporation's AAA.[90] After the post-termination transition period ends, the AAA disappears and distributions are taxed under the rules applicable to C corporation distributions (i.e., distributions are taxed as dividends to the extent of the corporation's current and accumulated E&P).

The **post-termination transition period** is the period that begins on the day after the last day of the corporation's last tax year as an S corporation and generally ends one year later or (if later) on the due date for filing a tax return for the corporation's last year as an S corporation.

Instead of treating a distribution as coming first from the corporation's AAA, a corporation may elect to treat a distribution as coming first from the corporation's accumulated E&P (thus making the distribution taxable as a dividend to the extent of the corporation's accumulated E&P).[91] All shareholders to whom distributions are made during the post-termination transition period (whether or not the distribution is a cash distribution) must consent to the election for it to be valid.

Example 50: Saginaw Corporation, a calendar-year taxpayer, elects to terminate its Subchapter S status effective January 1, 20X0. As of that date, it has an AAA of $30,000. On December 31, 20X0, it has a total of $40,000 current and accumulated E&P. On March 1 of that year, it distributes $50,000 in cash to its shareholders. Of the $50,000 distribution, $30,000 is treated as coming from Saginaw's AAA; consequently, this portion of the distribution is not taxed to the shareholders and reduces each

---

[89] Code Secs. 311(b) and 1371(a).
[90] Code Sec. 1371(e)(1).

[91] Code Sec. 1371(e)(2); Reg. § 18.1371-1.

shareholder's respective basis in the Saginaw stock. The remaining $20,000 distribution is treated as a dividend and is taxable to the shareholders to the extent of Saginaw's current and accumulated E&P.

Example 51: Assume the same facts as in Example 50, except that Saginaw elects to treat distributions in its post-termination transition period as coming first from accumulated E&P. Under this scenario, $40,000 of the distribution will be taxable to the shareholders as dividend income, and $10,000 will not be taxable but will be applied to reduce the shareholders' basis in their stock.

 Planning Pointer: Shareholders can use the post-termination transition period to increase their basis in stock or debt so that they can claim losses and deductions that were suspended because they did not have sufficient basis in their stock or debt.

¶ 1511 Fringe Benefits for Shareholders

Unlike a C corporation, an S corporation cannot provide certain shareholder-employees with tax-free fringe benefits. Shareholders that own more than two-percent of the stock in an S corporation are treated like partners for purposes of determining how the fringe benefits that they receive are taxed.[92] Other shareholder-employees are treated as employees and can be provided tax-favored fringe benefits. A "two-percent shareholder" is a person who actually or constructively owns on any day during the corporation's tax year more than two percent of the corporation's outstanding stock or stock representing more than two percent of the total combined voting power of all of the corporation's stock.[93]

Employee fringe benefits paid or furnished by an S corporation to a two-percent shareholder-employee in consideration for services rendered are treated like partnership guaranteed payments.[94] They are deducted by an S corporation as a trade or business expense. Two-percent shareholders are treated as self-employed individuals and must include the value of fringe benefits in their gross income unless an exclusion is available to self-employed individuals. Two-percent shareholders may be entitled to a deduction for the amount included in their gross income (e.g., if the payment was for health care premiums).

Example 52: Pettway Heaters, Inc., an S corporation, paid $4,000 of Cesar Dole's health insurance premiums. Cesar owns 10 percent of the shares of Pettway. Because Cesar is a two-percent shareholder, Pettway deducts the $4,000 as a business expense. Cesar must include the $4,000 payment in his gross income but may offset that amount by taking a $4,000 deduction from AGI for his self-employed health insurance premiums.

¶ 1512 Corporate Tax on Excess Passive Investment Income

If an S corporation has accumulated E&P at the close of a tax year, and for three consecutive years more than 25 percent of its gross receipts comes from passive investment income, then the corporation is taxed at the top corporate tax rate (currently 35 percent) on its excess net passive income.[95]

 Reason for the Rule: This "sting tax" is similar to the personal holding company tax imposed on C corporations and is intended to prevent C corporations otherwise subject to the personal holding company tax from avoiding that tax by electing S corporation

---

[92] Code Sec. 1372(a).
[93] Code Sec. 1372(b).

[94] Rev. Rul. 91-26, 1991-1 CB 184.
[95] Code Sec. 1375(a).

> status. An S corporation is subject to this sting tax for having excess passive investment income until it distributes all of its accumulated E&P from its years as a C corporation.

Example 53: Hermon Toys is an S corporation with accumulated E&P from its years as a C corporation. In 2008, more than 25 percent of its gross receipts consisted of passive income, and its excess net passive income was $100,000. The corporation's tax on passive investment income equals $35,000 ($100,000 × 35%).

.01 Amounts Subject to Passive Investment Income Tax

The amount subject to the 35-percent passive income tax (excess net passive income) is the corporation's net passive income multiplied by the portion of passive investment income that represents excessive passive investment income.[96] The amount of an S corporation's excess net passive income for any tax year may not exceed the amount of the corporation's taxable income for that year (determined without regard to the dividends received or net operating loss deductions). A corporation's *net passive income* is its passive investment income reduced by deductions that are directly connected with the production of such income.[97] The amount of its "excess passive investment income" is the amount of passive investment income that exceeds 25 percent of the corporation's gross receipts. Thus, the amount subject to the passive investment income tax can be stated as:

$$\text{net passive income} \quad \times \quad \frac{\text{excess passive investment income}}{\text{passive investment income}}$$

where:

net passive income = passive investment income – deductions related to such income

excess passive investment income = passive investment income – 25% gross receipts

Example 54: McQuiller Elevators, Inc. is an S corporation with accumulated E&P. Its gross receipts for the year are $2 million, and its passive investment income is $625,000. McQuiller's deductions related to passive investment income equal $25,000, making net passive income $600,000. Its excess net passive income of $120,000 is computed as follows.

$$\$600,000 \quad \times \quad \frac{[\$625,000 - (0.25 \times \$2,000,000)]}{\$625,000} \quad = \quad \$120,000$$

McQuiller's excess passive investment income tax for the year equals $42,000 ($120,000 × 35%).

Passive investment income includes gross receipts derived from royalties, rents, dividends, interest, and annuities.[98] Passive investment income does not include interest on any obligation acquired in the ordinary course of the corporation's trade or business or from its sale of inventory. Passive investment income also does not include any recognized built-in gain or loss of the S corporation for any tax year during the recognition period.[99] (See ¶ 1513.)

Gross receipts generally include the total amount received or accrued under the method of accounting used by a corporation in computing its taxable income.[100] Gross receipts are not reduced by returns and allowances, cost of goods sold, or deductions. If capital assets (other than stock and securities) are disposed of, gross receipts from such dispositions are taken into account only to the

---

[96] Code Sec. 1375(b)(1).
[97] Code Sec. 1375(b)(2).
[98] Code Sec. 1375(b)(3).

[99] Code Sec. 1375(b)(4).
[100] Code Sec. 1375(b)(3).

extent of the corporation's capital gain net income from the disposition. Gross receipts from sales or exchanges of stock and securities are taken into account only to the extent of gains from such sales. Losses are not taken into consideration in computing gross receipts.

Waiver of the tax. The IRS may waive imposition of the tax on excess passive investment income if the S corporation establishes to the IRS's satisfaction that:[101]

- The corporation determined in good faith that it had no accumulated E&P at the close of the tax year, and

- During a reasonable period of time after it was determined that the corporation did, in fact, have accumulated E&P, the corporation distributed those amounts.

 Planning Pointer: Only S corporations with accumulated E&P are subject to the tax on excess passive investment income. Corporations that are subject to this tax for three consecutive years automatically lose their S election beginning with the next tax year (see ¶ 1505.02). S corporations that have been subject to the tax for two consecutive years can keep from losing their S status by making an election to treat distributions during the third year first from accumulated E&P and then distributing enough during the year to eliminate the balance in the accumulated E&P account.

.02 Deduction for the Tax

Each item of passive investment income that is allocated to shareholders is reduced by its proportionate share of the excess passive income tax. That amount is calculated by multiplying the amount of the tax by a fraction whose numerator is the net amount of the item and whose denominator is the corporation's total passive investment income for the tax year.[102] This reduction in amount taxed to shareholders is consistent with the amount of after-tax income that normally would increase a C corporation's earnings and profits for the year in which the income is earned.

Example 55: An S corporation generates $10,000 of interest income during the year. The corporation is subject to the tax on excess passive investment income, and the portion of the tax that relates to interest income is $55. When allocating the interest income to its shareholders at the end of the year, the corporation will allocate a total of $9,945 ($10,000 – $55).

¶ 1513 Corporate Tax on Built-In Gains

When a C corporation sells appreciated property, it normally recognizes gain, which is taxed accordingly to the corporation and is included in the corporation's accumulated E&P until distributed to the shareholders in the form of a dividend. Because the tax laws operate under the realization principle, where gain is not taxed on appreciated property until such time that the property is disposed of, any appreciation in the assets of a C corporation at the time it converts to an S corporation would avoid double taxation.

To prevent corporations from escaping tax at the entity-level for unrealized gains from periods during its C corporation years, S corporations that were once C corporations are taxed at the highest corporate tax rate (currently 35 percent) on any net recognized **built-in gain** for any tax year beginning during the recognition period.[103] The recognition period is the 10-year (120-month) period generally beginning with the first day of the first tax year for which a corporation was an S corporation.[104]

Special rule for 2009 and 2010. In the case of any tax year beginning in 2009 or 2010, the recognition period ends after the seventh preceding tax year.

---

[101] Code Sec. 1375(d).

[102] Code Sec. 1366(f)(3); Reg. § 1.1366-4(c).

[103] Code Sec. 1374(a), (b).

[104] Code Sec. 1374(d)(7); Reg. § 1.1374-1(d).

In addition to taxing the S corporation on its net recognized built-in gain, the recognized gain is allocated pro rata to its shareholders, thereby imposing a tax on the gain at the shareholder-level as well. However, each item subject to recognized built-in gain is reduced by its proportionate share of the built-in gains tax.[105] This is consistent with the amount of after-tax gain that normally would increase a C corporation's earnings and profits in the year of the sale.

 Reason for the Rule: This tax was enacted by the Tax Reform Act of 1986 to prevent C corporations from avoiding double taxation on sales and distributions of appreciated property by converting to an S corporation.[106]

Example 56: At the time a corporation elects S status, it has a capital asset with an adjusted basis of $100,000 that is currently worth $400,000. If the corporation had sold the asset as a C corporation, it would pay tax on the $300,000 of capital gain ($400,000 – $100,000) at the ordinary income rates. If the after-tax gain were distributed to the shareholders, that amount would be taxed to the shareholders as a dividend.

If the corporation waits until after it converts to an S corporation to sell the asset, without the built-in gains tax rules, the $300,000 gain would be allocated pro rata to its shareholders and taxed to them as capital gain (and perhaps long-term capital gain) on their respective income tax returns. The gain would increase the S corporation's AAA, and accordingly, when the $300,000 is distributed to the shareholders, it would be in the form of a tax-free distribution from previously-taxed S corporation earnings.

Because of the built-in gain tax rules, if within 10 years of electing S status the corporation sells appreciated property from its C corporation years, such appreciation is subject to built-in gains tax. Accordingly, when the S corporation sells the property, the $300,000 gain is subject to built-in gains tax equal to 35 percent of the gain ($300,000 × 35% = $105,000). The amount of gain that is allocated to the shareholders is reduced by the gain taxed to the corporation. Thus, the gain of $195,000 ($300,000 – $105,000) would be allocated pro rata to the shareholders. Accordingly, any appreciation resulting from the C corporation years is subject to tax at both the corporate and shareholder levels.

.01 Calculating the Built-In Gains Tax

Only amounts of appreciation generated during a corporation's existence as a C corporation are subject to the built-in gains tax. Accordingly, if property with an adjusted basis of $100,000 is sold for $500,000, any amount of gain resulting from appreciation while the corporation was an S corporation would not be subject to the built-in gains tax. Also, the built-in gains tax is limited to the amount of the corporation's taxable income assuming that the corporation was taxed as a C corporation. Thus, any built-in gain that is triggered during years in which the S corporation has little or no taxable income is carried over to tax years in which the S corporation produces higher levels of taxable income. Furthermore, even though net operating loss and capital loss carryovers from a corporation's C tax years cannot be utilized to offset taxable income generated by the S corporation, the tax laws allow these carryover amounts to offset the corporation's built-in gain.[107] The specific details of the calculation of these limits are beyond the scope of this chapter.

---

[105] Code Sec. 1366(f)(2); Reg. § 1.1366-4(b).

[106] Joint Committee on Taxation, *General Explanation of the Tax Reform Act of 1986*, (J.C.T. Rep. No. JCS-10-87), at 337.

[107] Code Sec. 1374.

Planning Pointer: By waiting 10 years before selling any appreciated assets it owned while it was a C corporation, an S corporation can avoid the tax on built-in gains altogether.

¶1514 Corporate Tax on LIFO Recapture Amount

In times of rising prices, the last-in, first-out (LIFO) method produces a higher deduction of cost of goods sold and lower basis in ending inventory. If a C corporation uses the LIFO method to determine which items of inventory were sold during the year before its S election became effective, the corporation must include the LIFO recapture amount in its gross income for its last tax year as a C corporation. If a C corporation transfers LIFO inventory assets to an S corporation in a nonrecognition transfer and the S corporation takes the C corporation's basis in the transferred inventory assets, the C corporation must include the LIFO recapture amount in its gross income for the year of the transfer.[108]

The *recapture date* is the day before the effective date of the S election if the tax was triggered by the S election. If the tax was triggered by a transfer of assets, the recapture date is the date of the transfer.[109] The recapture amount is determined as of the end of the recapture date if that date is the day before the effective date of the S election. The recapture amount is determined as of the moment before the transfer if the recapture date is the date of a transfer.

Reason for the Rule: Congress enacted this tax because it was concerned that corporations using the LIFO method could avoid the tax on built-in gains to the extent that they did not invade LIFO layers during the 10-year period following their conversion to S corporation status.[110]

The **LIFO recapture amount** is the difference between the amount of the corporation's inventory assets under the first-in, first-out (FIFO) method and the amount of the corporation's inventory assets under the LIFO method.[111] If a corporation uses the retail method to value its inventories, it must use that method to value its inventory assets. Otherwise, the corporation must use the lower of cost or FMV to value its inventory assets.[112]

Example 57: Lion Plastics, Inc. elects to become an S corporation beginning on January 1, 2010. Lion uses the calendar year and the LIFO method to value its inventory. Lion includes the LIFO recapture amount in its 2009 gross income on its final C income tax return. If the value of its inventory under the FIFO method is $1 million as of the end of 2009 and the value of its inventory under the LIFO method is $750,000, the LIFO recapture amount that it must include in its gross income for its 2009 tax year equals $250,000 ($1,000,000 – $750,000).

Any increase in a corporation's tax caused by including the LIFO recapture amount in the corporation's gross income is payable in four equal installments.[113] The IRS does not charge interest on these amounts as they are paid in installments.

Appropriate adjustments must be made to the basis of the corporation's inventory to reflect the amount included in the corporation's gross income.[114] Basis is adjusted by collapsing any LIFO layers and adding the LIFO recapture amount to the LIFO value of the ending inventory as of the end of the taxpayer's last tax year as a C corporation.[115]

---

[108] Code Sec. 1363(d)(1); Reg. § 1.1363-2(a).

[109] Reg. § 1.1363-2(c).

[110] H.R. Rep. No. 100-391 (October 26, 1987), at 1097-1098.

[111] Code Sec. 1363(d)(3).

[112] Code Sec. 1363(d)(4)(C).

[113] Code Sec. 1363(d)(2); Reg. § 1.1363-2(b).

[114] Code Sec. 1363(d)(1).

[115] Rev. Proc. 94-61, 1994-2 CB 775 (Q&A-2).

¶ 1515 Summary

Business owners have a variety of legal entities to choose from for operating their businesses. In deciding which form of entity to select, one of the factors they should consider is which entity will save them the most in taxes. Flow-through entities, which tax income earned by a business to its owners instead of to the business, are popular business entities. One type of flow-through business is the S corporation; however, only certain smaller businesses can elect S status.

The rules for distinguishing nonseparately and separately stated items are very similar to those studied in Chapter 14 that govern partnerships. However, unlike partnerships, which are allowed to specially allocate various items to their partners, all items from an S corporation are allocated to shareholders on a pro rata basis. Shareholders of an S corporation are shielded from the liabilities of the business, a protection which is generally otherwise afforded only to C corporation shareholders, limited partners in limited partnerships, and members of LLCs and LLPs.

S corporations continue to be more popular than C corporations. However, before electing S status, a C corporation needs to keep in mind the various taxes that may apply after it converts to an S corporation. Some of these taxes can be avoided if the corporation distributes its accumulated E&P prior to electing S status.

Glossary of Terms Introduced in This Chapter

Accumulated adjustments account (AAA). Measures the accumulated undistributed net income of a corporation while it has been an S corporation.

Built-in gains. All unrealized gain that arose on assets during the time that a corporation was taxed as a C corporation.

Built-in gains tax. A tax imposed on built-in gains that are recognized during an S corporation's first 10 years of existence after converting from a C corporation.

C corporation. A corporation other than an S corporation that is treated as a separate tax entity from its shareholders. The income of a C corporation is subject to two layers of taxation.

C short year. In the S termination year, the portion of the year beginning on the effective date of the termination of the corporation's S status.

Electing small business trust (ESBT). A trust that is eligible to be a shareholder of an S corporation at the trustee's election. Such a trust may have multiple beneficiaries, but no person or entity other than an individual, estate, or certain types of charitable organizations may be a beneficiary.

Excess passive investment income tax. A tax imposed on an S corporation with accumulated E&P if more than 25 percent of its gross receipts are derived from passive investment income.

Grantor trust. A trust whose income is taxed to its grantor under the grantor trust rules of Code Sec. 671 et. seq. One example of a grantor trust is a revocable trust, which is a trust that can be revoked by its grantor.

LIFO recapture amount. Used in computing the corporate tax on the last-in, first-out (LIFO) recapture amount. Equals the difference between the amount of the corporation's inventory assets under the first-in, first-out (FIFO) method and the amount of the corporation's inventory assets under the LIFO method.

Nonresident alien. An individual who is not a U.S. citizen or resident.

Passive investment income. Gross receipts derived from royalties, rents, dividends, interest, and annuities.

Post-termination transition period. Term relevant to S corporations. Generally the one year period that starts one day after the corporation ceases to be an S corporation.

Pro rata share. The portion (based on ownership percentage) of each item of an S corporation's taxable income that a shareholder is required to take into account when calculating the shareholder's taxable income.

Qualified Subchapter S subsidiary (QSub). A domestic corporation that is 100-percent owned by an S corporation that the S corporation has elected to treat as a QSub.

Qualified Subchapter S trust (QSST). One of the types of trusts that can be a shareholder of an S corporation if the beneficiary elects to qualify the trust as a shareholder. All of the income of the trust must be distributed to one individual, who must be a U.S. citizen or resident. Any trust principal distributed during the income beneficiary's lifetime can be distributed only to that income beneficiary.

S corporation. An S corporation is a flow-through entity, but only corporations that satisfy certain requirements can elect to be taxed as S corporations. An S corporation gets its name because it is a corporation that has elected to be taxed under Subchapter S of Chapter 1 of the Code.

S short year. In the S termination year, the portion of the year ending before the effective date of the termination of the corporation's S status.

S termination year. The year that a corporation's status as an S corporation terminates.

Straight debt. A written, unconditional promise to pay a sum certain in money on demand or on a specified date that provides for an interest rate or payment dates that are not contingent on profits, the borrower's discretion, the payment of dividends with respect to common stock, or similar factors. It also cannot be converted in any type of equity interest of the corporation and must be held by an individual (other than a nonresident alien), estate, trust eligible to be an S corporation shareholder, or a person who is actively and regularly engaged in the business of lending money.

Testamentary trusts. Trusts created from a decedent's will that come into existence upon the death of the grantor.

CHAPTER PROBLEMS

The following questions and problems relate to the discussion in Chapter 15, Flow-Through Entities: S Corporations, which begins at ¶ 1500 in *Part V: Business Entity Issues*.

Chapter 15 Discussion Questions

1. What is an S corporation?

2. What are the advantages of operating a business as an S corporation?

3. What corporations qualify as a small business corporation, and why is this status significant?

4. Who can be a shareholder of an S corporation?

5. Dominic Rutigliano, a U.S. citizen who lives in Freedonia, owns 100 shares of stock in a corporation. Dominic is married to a citizen of Freedonia, whose laws applicable to assets owned by married persons are similar to those of an American "community property state." Can the corporation elect S status? If not, is there anything that can be done to allow the corporation to elect S status?

6. When will a corporation be treated as having one class of stock?

7. Under what circumstances will debt be considered a second class of stock?

8. Under what circumstances may a corporation's S status terminate?

9. How can an S corporation revoke its S election?

10. Who pays tax on an S corporation's taxable income that is not distributed to shareholders?

11. What are the basic rules for computing an S corporation's taxable income?

12. Why is it important to determine a shareholder's adjusted basis in the stock of an S corporation?

13. What amounts increase or decrease a shareholder's basis in S corporation stock?

14. How is a shareholder's basis in an S corporation's indebtedness to the shareholder affected by the S corporation's income, gain, loss, deduction, and credit?

15. What is an accumulated adjustments account?

16. What happens to income previously taxed to shareholders after a corporation converts from an S corporation to a C corporation?

17. Under what circumstances may an S corporation be subject to the tax on excess passive investment income?

18. Under what circumstances may an S corporation have to pay the tax on built-in gains?

19. Under what circumstances may a corporation have to pay the LIFO recapture tax?

20. If a LIFO recapture tax has to be paid, when does it have to be paid, and who has to pay it?

Chapter 15 Problems

1. The stock in an S corporation is owned by 105 different persons. Among its shareholders are Bree Corlew, Bree's mother, Bree's two children, her brother, and one of her nephews. Based on these facts, how many shareholders does the corporation have for purposes of determining whether it can elect S status?

2. Deland Ice Cream has 103 shareholders. Two of the shareholders are Portia Merchant and her husband, Bassanio. A third shareholder is an electing small business trust (ESBT). The income beneficiaries of the ESBT are Samantha Beno and her husband, Joshua. The Benos's son is entitled to all remaining trust assets after his parents die and is entitled to distributions of trust principal at the trustee's election. Samantha, Joshua, and their son do not own any stock in the corporation except through the ESBT. How many shareholders does the corporation have for purposes of determining whether it can elect S status?

3. Kohen Pipe is eligible to be an S corporation and has decided that it wants to become an S corporation starting with its 2010 tax year. If the corporation uses the calendar year as its tax year, when can it make an election that will be effective for its 2010 tax year?

4. Robin Cottone, one of the shareholders of McCrady Sandals, Inc., wishes to have the corporation revoke its S election. Robin owns 100 shares of the corporation's voting stock. Kelvin Kotlone owns 50 shares of the corporation's voting stock and 150 shares of the corporation's nonvoting stock. Kelvin's wife, Amy, owns 50 shares of the corporation's voting stock and 50 shares of the corporation's nonvoting stock. The rest of the stock is owned by Alton Snide and his wife, Margaret, who each own 75 shares of the corporation's voting stock. How many other shareholders must Robin convince to consent to the revocation?

5. Booster Seats, Inc. is an S corporation using the calendar year as its tax year. In 2007, Booster had gross receipts of $500,000 and passive investment income of $200,000. In 2008, it had gross receipts of $550,000 and passive investment income of $137,500. In 2009, it had gross receipts of $600,000 and passive investment income of $155,000. For each of those years it had accumulated E&P. Can Booster continue to be an S corporation for 2010? Explain.

6. Alene Harledge's pro rata share of her S corporation's loss for the tax year was $10,000. Her adjusted basis in her shares of stock in the corporation was $6,500, and her adjusted basis in a loan she made to the corporation was $1,000. How much of her pro rata share of the loss may Alene deduct?

7. Machinery Slides, an S corporation, has $1 million of taxable income for its 2009 tax year, which began November 1, 2009, and ended October 31, 2010. Vernell Teachout is its sole shareholder. Machinery Slides earns $200,000 of its taxable income in November and December of 2009, $800,000 from January 1–October 31, 2010, and $300,000 from November 1, 2010–December 31, 2010. How much taxable income must Vernell include in his gross income on his 2010 tax return?

8. Shandra Flohr's adjusted basis in her shares of stock of an S corporation was $20,000 at the beginning of the year. Shandra's share of the corporation's separately and nonseparately computed income for the year was $25,000. She received a distribution of $20,000 during the year, and her share of separately stated items of loss and deduction was $10,000. What is Shandra's adjusted basis of her shares of stock at the end of the year?

9. Samantha Presley owns 1,000 shares of stock in an S corporation. At the beginning of the year, her adjusted basis in her shares of stock was $30,000. Her share of the corporation's income for the year is $10,000 (which includes $3,000 of tax-exempt interest). She received a distribution of $20,000 during the year, and her share of separately stated items of loss and deduction is $22,000. What is Samatha's adjusted basis of her share of stock at the end of the year?

10. Rina Heart owns 200 shares of stock in an S corporation. The adjusted basis in her shares was $25,000 at the beginning of the year. During the year, Rina's share of the corporation's income was $10,000, and she received an $8,000 distribution from the corporation. If Rina's share of the corporation's separately stated items of loss and deduction is $15,000, what is her adjusted basis of her shares at the end of the year?

11. Lena Susa owns 100 shares of stock in Algee Roofing Company, an S corporation. The adjusted basis in her shares was $5,000 at the beginning of 20X1. During 20X0, Lena had loaned $10,000 to the corporation, which still remains owed to Lena. Lena's share of the corporation's income for 20X1 was $20,000, and her share of the corporation's separately stated items of loss and deductions was $24,000. Also during 20X1, Lena received a distribution of $8,000 from the corporation. Compute Lena's adjusted basis of her stock and her indebtedness at the end of 20X1.

12. Assume the same facts as in Problem 11, except that in 20X2, Lena's share of the S corporation's income is $30,000, her share of separately stated items of loss and deduction is $25,000, and she receives a $6,000 distribution during the year. Compute Lena's adjusted basis of her stock and indebtedness at the end of 20X2.

13. An S corporation with no accumulated E&P distributes $10,000 to one of its shareholders, Darius Camelo. Darius's adjusted basis in his shares of stock in the corporation was $6,000 prior to the distribution. How will Darius be taxed on the distribution?

14. Marcel Morles is a shareholder of an S corporation. On August 10, the corporation distributes $20,000 to Marcel. Of this distribution, $5,000 came from the corporation's accumulated E&P. Marcel's adjusted basis in his shares is $10,000. What amount must Marcel include in his gross income, and how is it characterized?

15. An S corporation paid the health insurance premiums for two of its employees, Jonathon Tremmel and Sam Fussler. The premiums were $4,000 for Jonathon and $5,000 for Sam. Jonathon owns 100 of the corporation's 1,000 outstanding shares of stock; Sam owns 20 shares. How are the premium payments taxed to the corporation and its two employees?

16. An S corporation has accumulated E&P and therefore is subject to the tax on excess passive investment income. If its excess net passive income for the year is $50,000, how much excess passive investment income tax does it owe?

17. An S corporation has accumulated E&P and therefore is subject to the tax on excess passive investment income. If the corporation's gross receipts are $4 million, its passive investment income is $1,500,000, and deductions related to passive investment income are $300,000, how much tax will it pay on its excess net passive income?

18. Selsor Data Processing converted from a C corporation to an S corporation on January 1, 2010. At the time it converted to an S corporation, Selsor had $50,000 of accumulated E&P. On January 1, 2010, it owned a motor vehicle with a FMV of $10,000 and an adjusted basis of $5,000. On January 13, 2013, the company sold the motor vehicle for $6,000. At that time, the motor vehicle's adjusted basis was $0. What is the company's recognized built-in gain from the sale?

19. Coated Fabrics converted from a C corporation to an S corporation on January 1, 2011. At the time it converted to an S corporation, Coated Fabrics had $100,000 of accumulated E&P. On July 3, 2011, it sold a building that it had owned while it was a C corporation. The sale price was $300,000. On January 1, 2011, the FMV of the building was $280,000, and its adjusted basis was $100,000. Assuming that it has sufficient taxable income during 2011 and recognizes sufficient taxable gain on the sale, what amount of built-in gains tax can the corporation expect to pay?

20. Copper Tubing, Inc., a corporation that had been using the LIFO method to value its inventory, elects to be an S corporation, effective January 1, 2010. The value of its inventory under the FIFO method is $450,000 and $500,000, respectively at the beginning and end of 2009. The value of its inventory under the LIFO method is $150,000 and $200,000, respectively at the beginning and end of 2009. Compute Copper's LIFO recapture amount.

21. Shane Earhart and his spouse own shares of stock in an S corporation. Shane not only owns stock in his own name but also holds stock for his son George under the Uniform Transfers to Minors Act. Dustin Blakeslee and Dina Briant own stock as joint tenants. An ESBT with four potential current beneficiaries also holds stock in the corporation. How many shareholders is the S corporation treated as having?

22. Jillian McSweeney sold her 30-percent interest in an S corporation on April 30. The corporation, which uses the calendar year as its tax year, had $36,000 in income from business operations. Most of this income was earned in December. $5,475 of its gross income was earned before Jillian sold her shares. What is Jillian's pro rata share of the corporation's income from business operations?

23. Pocock Data Processing, Inc. is an S corporation with $2,000 of accumulated E&P and an AAA with a balance of $15,000. If the corporation makes a $3,000 distribution to Earl Pocock and elects to distribute accumulated E&P before AAA, how will the distribution be taxed?

24. Haycraft Housewares, Inc. terminated its S status. At the time that it terminated its S status, the corporation had $10,000 of accumulated E&P and $30,000 in its AAA. Two months after the effective date of its S status termination, Haycraft Housewares distributed $4,000 in cash and property with a fair market value of $5,000 to Ricardo Haycraft. How will those distributions be taxed?

25. Lemelle China, Inc. elected S status. While it was a C corporation, it used LIFO to value its inventory. On the day before the effective date of its S election, its inventory was valued at $80,000 under LIFO. If the company had used FIFO to value its inventory, its inventory would have been valued at $120,000. Before calculating the value of its inventory using FIFO, the corporation had determined that its taxable income for its last year as a C corporation was $260,000. How much additional federal income tax will the corporation have to pay?

Chapter 15 Review Problems

1. Cotterman Stains, Inc. converts from an S corporation to a C corporation, effective January 1, 2009. At the time of the conversion, it had an accumulated adjustments account (AAA) of

$30,000 and $10,000 of accumulated E&P. Cotterman retains the calendar year as its tax year. During 2009, the company had $300,000 of gross income from its business operations and $200,000 of deductions. It sold for $50,000 a capital asset with an adjusted basis of $20,000. Darius Baulch owns 25 percent of the shares of stock in the company. His shares have an adjusted basis of $40,000. During the year, the corporation distributes cash and property to its shareholders with respect to their stock. It distributes to Darius $57,500 in cash. Based on these facts, how are Darius and the corporation taxed for 2009?

2. Larita Goetze owned 25 percent (1,000 shares) of the stock of Sun Lamps, Inc., an S corporation. Her adjusted basis in the shares at the beginning of the year was $40,000. On March 31, she sold her shares for $60,000. The corporation's net income for the three months ending March 31 was $30,000. Its net income for the remainder of the year was $300,000 (including a gain of $200,000 on the sale of some property). None of the corporation's income was distributed to Larita during the year. Compare how Larita will be taxed if an election is made to calculate Larita's share of the corporation's income as if the corporation's tax year ended on March 31 and how Larita will be taxed if no such election is made.

Chapter 15 Research Question

An S corporation's election terminated because a shareholder transferred stock to a trust not qualifying as an eligible shareholder. Under what circumstances is it possible for the corporation to retain its S corporation status through the "inadvertent termination" procedures?

Appendix

TAX TERMS

This tax glossary defines the words and phrases most commonly used in talking about federal taxes. The language of federal taxation is the language of law, accounting and business. Many of the terms have precise, technical meanings as compared with their meanings in everyday use. These definitions are only adaptations of the full meanings prescribed by the law, regulations and rulings, which are discussed in the explanatory text.

12-month rule. A tax law that allows taxpayers to deduct as prepaid expense in full in the year it is paid provided that it creates (or facilitates the creation of) any right or benefit that does not extend beyond the *earlier* of (1) 12 months after the first date any right or benefit is realized or (2) the end of the tax year that follows the tax year in which the payment was made.

Abandoned spouse. A married individual who lives with a dependent child but had not lived with his or her spouse for the last six months of the year.

Abandonment. The situation in which the owner of property permanently and intentionally relinquishes any claim to the property without receiving any consideration in return.

Ability-to-pay concept. Taxes are imposed on taxpayers that are in the best position to pay the taxes by having them pay a greater share of their tax bases toward the tax burden.

Accountable plan. Requires that employees submit adequate documentation or receipts for any reimbursed expenses and that any advances in excess of substantiated expenses be returned to the employer.

Accrual method. Income is included in gross income when all events have occurred that fix the right to receive the item and its amount can be determined with reasonable accuracy. Expenses are deducted when all events have occurred that determine the liability exists, the amount of the liability can be determined with reasonable accuracy, and economic performance has occurred with respect to the liability.

Accumulated adjustments account (AAA). Measures the accumulated undistributed net income of a corporation while it has been an S corporation.

Accumulated earnings and profits. The amount of E&P a C corporation has generated over the years that has not been distributed as of the beginning of its current tax year.

Accumulated earnings credit. Used in the calculation of the accumulated earnings tax. A credit allowed a corporation in computing accumulated taxable income that represents the amount by which the *greater of* (1) the corporation's foreseeable reasonable financial needs or (2) $250,000 ($150,000 for personal service corporations) exceeds the corporation's accumulated E&P at the beginning of the year.

Accumulated earnings tax. A penalty tax imposed on C corporations formed or that continue to exist for the purpose of preventing individual shareholders from paying tax on the profits of the corporation by allowing E&P to accumulate.

Action on decision. An IRS pronouncement that informs the public as to whether the IRS issued an acquiescence or nonacquiescence to a decision by a court other than the Tax Court.

Ad valorem **tax.** A tax that uses the value of property as the tax base.

Adjusted basis. The tax equivalent to book value. Adjusted basis equals the initial cost basis of the asset (typically its cost in the case of an acquired asset) plus any postponed losses and improvements made to the asset, minus any postponed gains and capital recoveries (including accumulated depreciation) taken on the asset over the years.

Adjusted current earnings (ACE). An alternative minimum tax concept similar to current E&P. ACE differs from current E&P in that current E&P attempts to measure the corporation's capacity to pay dividends from current period earnings, while the ACE calculation is intended to measure pretax income before any distributions.

Adjusted gross income (AGI). An intermediate step between gross income and taxable income that individuals calculate. Only deductions for AGI are subtracted from gross income in computing AGI.

Administrative convenience. When a tax law is enacted because it reduces administrative costs or taxpayers' compliance costs.

All-events test. A test used to determine when an accrual method taxpayer has to report income and can deduct or capitalize an expense.

All-inclusive approach. The method used to define gross income. Under this approach, all income is subject to income tax unless a provision in the tax laws allows it not to be taxed.

Alternative depreciation system (ADS). An alternative to depreciating property under general MACRS when the recovery periods tend to be longer and use of the straight-line method is required.

Alternative minimum tax (AMT). Rules in the federal tax system enacted to enhance equity in the income tax system by ensuring that all taxpayers pay at least some minimum income taxes each year.

Alternative minimum taxable income (AMTI). Term used in the alternative minimum tax system. AMTI is determined by making certain adjustments to regular taxable income. *See also* Alternative minimum tax.

Amortizable Section 197 intangibles. Intangible assets for which amortization deductions may be taken under Code Sec. 197. Amortizable Section 197 intangibles are intangibles listed in Code Sec. 197 that are acquired by the taxpayer and held in connection with the conduct of a trade or business or for the production of income.

Amortization. The annual deduction taken to recover the cost of intangible assets over time.

Amount realized. The sum of the cash, other non-like-kind boot, FMV of property, and release of mortgage received in a sale or an exchange of property minus any selling expenses. Used in determining the realized gain or loss from the sale of property. *See also* Realized gain or loss.

AMT base. The tax base used in the AMT system; determined by subtracting the exemption amount from the alternative minimum taxable income. This amount is analogous to taxable income in the regular income tax system. *See also* Alternative minimum tax *and* Alternative minimum taxable income.

Annotated tax service. A tax service that is organized by Code section rather than by topic. CCH's *Standard Federal Tax Reporter* is an example of an annotated tax service.

Announcements. IRS pronouncements that inform the public as to matters of general interest. They may provide guidance as to both substantive and procedural matters.

Applicable federal rate (AFR). A statutory federal rate of interest that is adjusted monthly and is published by the IRS. The rates are based on the average market yield on outstanding marketable obligations of the United States during the one-month period ending on the 14th day of the preceding month.

Average tax rate. The total tax liability divided by the tax base. Used in determining the portion of the tax base that is paid in taxes.

Below market loan. A loan arrangement in which the interest charged by the lender is less than adequate (below the market rate of interest).

Blue book. An explanation of a tax act prepared by the staff of the Joint Committee on Taxation.

Book value. The financial accounting equivalent of adjusted basis, i.e., cost less accumulated depreciation.

Boot. A term tax practitioners use to describe nonlike-kind property involved in a like-kind exchange. Cash and other property added to an exchange to equalize the value of exchanged items. When made part of an otherwise nontaxable exchange, the portion of realized gain equal to the value of the boot will have to be recognized.

Built-in gains. All unrealized gain that arose on assets during the time that a corporation was taxed as a C corporation.

Built-in gains tax. A tax imposed on built-in gains that are recognized during an S corporation's first 10 years of existence after converting from a C corporation.

Business bad debt. A *bona fide* debt that is closely related to a taxpayer's trade or business. There must have been a business reason for entering into the debt arrangement.

Business tax credit. Tax credit used by governments to reward businesses for participating in certain types of activities by subsidizing a portion of the expenditures that they incur by participating in those activities.

C corporation. An incorporated business entity other than an S corporation that is treated as a separate tax entity from its shareholders. The income of a C corporation is subject to two layers of taxation.

C short year. In the S termination year, the portion of the year beginning on the effective date of the termination of the corporation's S status.

Calendar year. A tax year that begins January 1 and ends December 31.

Capital and profits interest. The term used to describe a partner's interest in a partnership when the partner has an interest in the future profits the partnership generates as well as an interest in the partnership's assets upon liquidation of the partner's interest or dissolution of the partnership.

Capital asset. An asset other than the property listed in Code Sec. 1221. In general, a capital asset is an asset held for investment or a personal use asset.

Capital expenditure. An expenditure that creates an asset expected to benefit a business for more than one year.

Capital recovery doctrine. When taxpayers dispose of property, in determining the amount of gain included in gross income (or loss deductible from gross income) they are allowed to recover their investment in the property.

Cash receipts and disbursements method. A method of accounting under which a business is required to recognize income when it is received and may deduct expenses when they are disbursed.

Court of Appeals. The court to which decisions made by the U.S. Tax Court, a U.S. district court, or the U.S. Court of Federal Claims may be appealed. There are 13 Courts of Appeals: 12 geographical (11 numbers and one named) plus the Federal Court of Appeals.

Circulation costs. Amounts paid or incurred to establish, maintain, or increase the circulation of a newspaper, magazine, or other periodical.

Claim of right doctrine. A rule that requires taxpayers that receive money or other property under a claim of right without restriction to include the amount received in gross income for the year of receipt, regardless of the taxpayer's method of accounting.

Closely-held corporations. Corporations whose stock is held by a small number of shareholders, typically from the same family or a related group of individuals.

Collateral. Property offered by the borrower that the lender can use to satisfy the debt in the event the borrower defaults on the loan.

Collectibles. Works of art, antiques, rugs, metals, gems, stamps, coins, and other similar items of tangible personal property.

Completed contract method. A special method of accounting for long-term contracts in which no income or expenses related to the contract are recognized until the contract is completed.

Condemnation. A legal action in which the government takes possession of property under the power of eminent domain.

Constructive dividend. A payment to or for the benefit of a shareholder that is treated as a dividend even though it may not be denoted as such by the corporation.

Constructive ownership. A rule under which a taxpayer may be treated as owning stock that is actually owned by another person or entity in which the taxpayer has an ownership interest.

Constructive receipt doctrine. A rule that requires cash method taxpayers to report gross income in the tax year during which amounts are credited to the business's account, set apart for the business, or otherwise made available without any substantial limitation or restriction. A business may be treated as having constructively received income even though it does not have actual possession of the income until after the end of the tax year.

Control. Persons control a corporation if they own stock possessing at least 80 percent of the total combined voting power of all classes of stock entitled to vote and at least 80 percent of the total number of shares of all other classes of stock of the corporation.

Cost depletion. One of two acceptable tax methods for expensing the costs of a natural resource. This method is similar to the units-of-production method of depreciation and is the only acceptable method of depletion for financial reporting.

Court of appeals. The court to which decisions made by the U.S. Tax Court, a U.S. district court, or the U.S. Court of Federal Claims may be appealed. There are 13 Circuit Courts of Appeals: 12 geographical (11 numbers and one named) plus the Federal Court of Appeals.

Current distributions. Distributions from a partnership to a partner that do not completely liquidate the partner's interest in the partnership.

Current earnings and profits. A C corporation's earnings and profits for its current tax year. A corporate tax concept that attempts to capture a corporation's capacity to pay dividends from its current year's earnings.

Deduction. Expenditure made by a taxpayer that the government allows the taxpayer to use to reduce taxable income.

Deficiency interest. The interest charged on tax deficiencies when taxpayers fail to pay the proper amount of taxes on their income tax returns.

Defined benefit plan. A type of retirement plan that promises participants specified benefits during retirement years and continuing until the death of the participant, and often until the death of the spouse of the participant.

Defined contribution plan. A type of retirement plan where the amounts are contributed to an employee's own account, and the amount available upon retirement depends on the performance of the investments in the account.

Depletion. The annual deduction taken to recover an investment in productive natural resources.

Depreciable cost. In financial accounting, it represents the portion of the cost of an asset that may be written off over the asset's useful life, i.e., the costs associated with the acquisition of the asset minus the estimated salvage value. *See also* Salvage value.

Depreciation. An annual deduction taken to recover the capitalized cost of business or income-producing property that is either tangible personal property or real property (other than land).

Determination letter. A written determination issued by an IRS District Director in response to a written request from a taxpayer or the taxpayer's authorized representative. A determination letter will be issued only when the question presented is specifically answered by a statute, a tax treaty, the regulations, a conclusion stated in a revenue ruling, or an opinion or court decision that represents the IRS's position.

Direct tax. A tax levied on the party who ultimately bears the burden of the tax.

Disabled access tax credit. A nonrefundable credit that eligible small businesses may take for amounts paid or incurred to enable them to comply with applicable requirements under the Americans with Disabilities Act of 1990.

Distributive share. A partner's allocated share of partnership income, gains, losses, deductions, and credits as specified in either the partnership agreement or in accordance with each partner's interest in the partnership.

District court. One of the trial courts to which taxpayers may appeal an IRS determination.

Dividend. A distribution of current and/or accumulated earnings and profits by a C corporation to its shareholders.

Dividends received deduction. The amount of dividend income received by a C corporation that is not subject to taxation. It can be 70, 80, or 100 percent of the dividend income.

Domestic production gross receipts (DPGR). The gross receipts the taxpayer derives from any lease, rental, license, sale, exchange, or other disposition of (1) qualifying production property, a significant part of which was manufactured, produced, grown, or extracted by the taxpayer within the United States; (2) any qualified film produced by the taxpayer; or (3) electricity, natural gas, or potable water produced by the taxpayer in the United States.

Dwelling unit. A house or apartment used to provide living accommodations; includes mobile homes and manufactured homes; does not include a unit in a hotel, motel, inn, or other establishment in which more than 50 percent of the units are used on a transient basis. *See also* Residential real property.

Earnings and profits (E&P). A tax term used to reflect a C corporation's economic capacity to make a distribution from corporate earnings that is not a return of a shareholder's capital. It is computed by making adjustments to the corporation's taxable income.

Electing small business trust (ESBT). A trust that is eligible to be a shareholder of an S corporation at the trustee's election. Such a trust may have multiple beneficiaries, but no person or entity other than an individual, estate, or certain types of charitable organizations may be a beneficiary.

Employer-provided child care credit. A nonrefundable income tax credit for employers who provide employees with child care and child care resource and referral services.

Employment tax. A tax imposed by the government on employee wages (FICA and FUTA) and on net earnings from a sole proprietorship (self-employment taxes).

Empowerment zone and renewal community employment credit. A nonrefundable tax credit for employers who hire individuals who both live *and* work in an empowerment zone or renewal community.

Empowerment zones and renewal communities. Specific geographic regions within the United States that the federal government has identified as being in need of revitalization.

Estate tax. A wealth transfer tax assessed on a decedent's taxable estate.

Estimated tax payments. Amounts that C corporations and individuals with taxable income not subject to withholding must pay during the year in order to avoid an underpayment of tax penalty.

Excess passive investment income tax. A tax imposed on an S corporation with accumulated E&P if more than 25 percent of its gross receipts are derived from passive investment income.

Exchange. A transaction in which two parties exchange property. Various types of boot (see definition above) may also constitute part of the proceeds.

Excise tax. A tax on the production or consumption of specific goods or services, like tobacco products, alcohol, and gasoline.

Exclusion. An item of income that according to the tax laws is not subject to taxation.

Externality. The positive or negative effect of a transaction that occurs to persons or businesses that are not part of that transaction.

Fair market value (FMV). The amount that would induce a willing seller to sell and a willing buyer to buy certain property.

Federal Insurance Contributions Act (FICA). A program enacted under the Federal Social Security Act that established a federal unemployment insurance program (Medicare) and a program to provide old-age, survivors, and disability benefits to employees (social security). Contributions to this plan are shared by employers and employees through FICA and self-employment taxes.

Federal Unemployment Tax Act (FUTA). FUTA was enacted by Congress to finance the federal unemployment program. Contributions to this plan are funded entirely by employers. The tax base is employee wages up to $7,000; the tax rate equals 6.2 percent.

Final regulation. A proposed regulation that has been adopted as a regulation having the full force and effect of law.

Financial accounting. Rules used to determine how information, including income and expenses, should be reported on a business's financial statements.

Fiscal year. A tax year that ends on the last day of any month other than December.

Flat tax. *See* Proportional tax.

Flexible spending account (FSA). This type of account is offered to employees to cover their dependent care costs and/or medical costs. Employees can set aside each year up to $5,000 of their pre-tax wages from which they can pay qualified health costs (in the case of Medical FSAs) or qualified child care costs (in the case of Dependent Care FSAs).

Flow-through entity. A business entity that does not pay taxes, but files a tax return reporting the amounts of gross income, deductions, and credits generated by the business during the year, and passes information along to its owners regarding their respective shares of such items. Examples include partnerships, S corporations, limited liability corporations, and limited liability partnerships.

Foreign tax credit (FTC). A nonrefundable income tax credit for income, war profits, and excess profits taxes paid or accrued to a foreign country or to a U.S. possession during the tax year.

Franchise tax. An annual tax on the privilege of doing business in the state.

GAAP (Generally Accepted Accounting Principles). The set of rules publicly-traded companies must adhere to when preparing financial statements.

General business credit. A combination of business credits, each of which is computed under its own set of rules.

General partnership. A business entity that arises from an agreement among two or more persons, all of whom have unlimited liability for the debts of the partnership, to operate a business for profit.

Gift tax. A wealth transfer tax the government imposes upon the transferor for transfers to nonspouses in excess of a certain amount each year.

Golsen **rule.** This rule provides that the U.S. Tax Court will follow a Court of Appeals decision that is squarely on point when appeal of the Tax Court's decision lies to that Court of Appeals and that court alone.

Grantor trust. A trust whose income is taxed to its grantor under the grantor trust rules of Code Sec. 671 et. seq. One example of a grantor trust is a revocable trust, which is a trust that can be revoked by its grantor.

Gross income. All income from whatever source derived, except as specifically excluded by a provision in the Internal Revenue Code or other tax law. Represents the income the government has chosen to tax. Equals income minus exclusions.

Gross receipts. The total amount of money and the fair market value of any other property received for selling property or performing services.

Gross sales. The total amount of sales at invoice prices, unreduced by any discounts, returns, or allowances.

Guaranteed payments. Amounts paid from the partnership to a partner that are determined *without regard* to the profits generated by the partnership during the year.

Half-year convention. Averaging convention used for tax depreciation in which any property put in service in a trade or business during a tax year is deemed to be placed in service in the middle of the year.

Head of household. A filing status available to taxpayers who are not married and do not qualify as a surviving spouse but maintain a household for more than half of the tax year in which a qualifying child of the taxpayer or any other person who is a dependent of the taxpayer lives.

Holding period. Time period that generally begins the day after a taxpayer acquires property and ends on the day the taxpayer disposes of the property. Used in determining the short-term versus long-term nature of a recognized gain or loss.

Hybrid method. A method of accounting that combines elements of the cash and accrual methods of accounting. *See also* Accrual method *and* Cash receipts and disbursements method.

Imputed interest. The "deemed" interest payments a borrower makes to a lender on a below market loan, including a loan involving original issue discount. *See also* Below market loan *and* Original issue discount.

Income. Broadly defined as increases in wealth that the taxpayer has realized.

Indirect tax. A tax levied on someone other than the one who ultimately bears the burden of the tax.

Inheritance tax. A tax levied on the beneficiary upon receipt of inherited property.

Installment method. A special method of accounting in which a taxpayer recognizes gain as the payments are received rather than at the time the sale occurs.

Installment sale. A sale or exchange of property in which the seller receives payments in more than one tax year.

Intangible property. Personal property that has no physical characteristics. Examples include goodwill, patents, copyrights, mutual funds, stocks, and bonds.

Internal Revenue Code. The primary statutory source of federal tax law. It is set forth in Title 26 of the United States Code.

Interpretive regulation. A regulation that interprets the Code. It is promulgated pursuant to the Secretary of the Treasury's general authority to issue regulations.

Involuntary conversion. An event caused by casualty, theft, or condemnation in which the taxpayer's property is damaged or destroyed.

Itemized deductions. A deduction from adjusted gross income that consists of various personal expenses that the federal government allows individuals to deduct in lieu of a standard deduction.

Least aggregate deferral of income rule. The last of three tests used to determine a partnership's required tax year. It involves performing a test using each of the year-ends of its partners and determining which of those year-ends, on average, will allow the government to collect taxes on the partnership income the most quickly. *See also* Majority partners rule *and* Principal partner rule.

Legislative regulation. A regulation that defines a statutory term or prescribes a method for implementing a Code provision. It is promulgated pursuant to a specific grant of authority by Congress.

LIFO recapture amount. Used in computing the corporate tax on the last-in, first-out (LIFO) recapture amount. Equals the difference between the amount of the corporation's inventory assets under the first-in, first-out (FIFO) method and the amount of the corporation's inventory assets under the LIFO method.

Limited liability. When an owner's liability with respect to the business is limited to the amount the owner has invested in the business.

Limited liability company (LLC). A business entity that can be treated as a partnership for tax purposes and whose owners enjoy limited liability.

Limited liability partnership (LLP). A business entity that can be treated as a partnership for tax purposes, but whose owners enjoy some aspects of limited liability.

Limited partnership. A business entity that arises from an agreement among two or more partners to operate a business for profit in which one or more of the partners has limited liability with respect to the debts of the partnership and at least one partner is responsible for the debts of the partnership.

Listed property. Certain personal property susceptible to both business and personal use. Examples include passenger automobiles, computers, and cellular telephones.

Long-term capital gain or loss. A capital gain or loss on a capital asset held for more than one year.

Low-income housing credit. A nonrefundable income tax credit for taxpayers who purchase or substantially rehabilitate residential rental property used for low-income housing.

Majority partners rule. The first of three tests used to determine a partnership's required tax year. It requires that a partnership adopt the year-end of the partner, or group of partners, that owns more than a 50-percent interest in partnership capital *and* profits. *See also* Least aggregate deferral of income rule *and* Principal partner rule.

Marginal tax rate. The rate of tax on the last dollar of taxable income or the amount of taxes saved on an additional dollar of deduction.

Medicare taxes. The hospital insurance (HI) portion of the FICA tax.

Method of accounting. The rules that govern when a business must recognize income and when it may deduct expenses. It refers not only to the overall method of accounting that a taxpayer uses but also to a taxpayer's accounting treatment of any particular item.

Mid-month convention. Averaging convention used for tax depreciation in which any property put in service in a trade or business during a month is deemed to be placed in service in the middle of the month.

Mid-quarter convention. Depreciation convention in which any property put in service in a trade or business during a quarter of a tax year is deemed to be placed in service in the middle of the quarter.

Minimum tax credit. A tax credit equal to the amount of alternative minimum tax paid in one year that is attributable to adjustments due to timing differences. The minimum tax credit can be carried forward and used to offset the regular tax liability of a subsequent year. *See also* Alternative minimum tax *and* Timing differences.

Modified Accelerated Cost Recovery System (MACRS). A system of recovering the cost of capital expenditures through periodic depreciation deductions. MACRS applies to depreciable tangible property placed in service after 1986.

Municipal interest. Interest from state and local government bonds (municipal bonds, or "muni" bonds for short) that is not subject to federal income tax.

Necessary expense. An expense that is appropriate or helpful to the continuation of the taxpayer's business.

Net capital gain. The excess of a net long-term capital gain over any net short-term capital loss. Relevant to individual taxpayers, as it represents the amount of capital gain subject to reduced tax rates.

Net earnings from self-employment. The amount from which self-employment taxes of a sole proprietor are based. It equals 92.35 percent of net profits reported on Schedule C.

Net income per books. The net income a corporation reports for financial accounting purposes.

Net income tax. Term used in the alternative minimum tax system. The sum of the net regular tax liability and any alternative minimum tax minus the same tax credits used in computing net regular tax liability.

Net long-term capital gain. The excess of long-term capital gains over long-term capital losses.

Net long-term capital loss. The excess of long-term capital losses over long-term capital gains.

Net operating loss deduction. The total of a taxpayer's net operating loss carryforwards and carrybacks to a tax year.

Net regular tax liability. Term used in the alternative minimum tax system. A taxpayer's regular tax liability minus certain tax credits, such as the foreign tax credit and personal tax credits.

Net short-term capital gain. The excess of short-term capital gains over short-term capital losses.

Net short-term capital loss. The excess of short-term capital losses over short-term capital gains.

New markets credit. A nonrefundable income tax credit for taxpayers who make a qualified equity investment in a qualified community development entity. See also *Qualified community development entity*.

News release. An IRS pronouncement issued to the media to announce items of general interest. They often are used to announce that an important new revenue ruling or revenue procedure is going to be released and set forth the text of that ruling or procedure.

Nonaccountable plan. Reimbursements paid through a system that does not meet the requirements for an accountable plan.

Nonbusiness bad debt. A *bona fide* debt that is not a business bad debt. *See also* Business bad debt.

Nonrecaptured net Section 1231 losses. Net Section 1231 losses recognized in the previous five tax years that have not previously caused a net Section 1231 gain to be treated as ordinary income.

Nonrecourse debt. The type of debt arrangement in which the lender has no recourse (no ability to collect the debt) directly from the borrower in the event the borrower defaults on the loan.

Nonrecourse liability. A liability for which the seller is not personally liable, but for which the creditor can only look to property specified in the loan agreement for satisfaction of the debt.

Nonrefundable tax credit. A tax credit that can only reduce a taxpayer's income tax liability.

Nonresident alien. An individual who is not a U.S. citizen or resident.

Notices. IRS pronouncements issued to the public to provide guidance involving substantive interpretations of the Code. They often are issued to provide taxpayers with guidance about recently enacted legislation or to alert taxpayers about pending regulations.

Ordinary expense. An expense that is customary and acceptable in the taxpayer's type of business.

Organizational costs. Certain costs incurred in the process of incorporating a business.

Original issue discount (OID). Additional interest income representing the difference between the issue price of indebtedness and the amount due at maturity (face value). It is a function of the difference between the face rate associated with the bond and the current market interest rate.

Originating difference. The initial difference that occurs in the year in which a timing difference is created. *See also* Reversing difference *and* Timing difference.

Partner's capital account. An account on the partnership books that keeps track of what a partner is entitled to receive upon the liquidation of the partner's interest or upon dissolution of the partnership.

Partnership. A flow-through entity that has at all times at least two owners, at least one of whom is responsible for the debts of the business.

Partnership agreement. A written or oral agreement among the partners in a partnership that provides, among other things, how the partners will share in the partnership's profits and losses and how the assets of the partnership will be divided upon dissolution of the partnership.

Passive investment income. Gross receipts derived from royalties, rents, dividends, interest, and annuities.

Patent. An intangible asset that gives its owner the exclusive right to commercially profit from a specified product or process for a limited number of years.

Per diem. Established amounts allowed by the IRS to be deducted in lieu of substantiation for an employee's lodging, meals, and incidental expenses or a sole proprietor's for meals and entertainment expenses.

Percentage depletion. One of two acceptable tax methods for expensing the costs of a natural resource. Because the expense is calculated as a percentage of gross profits generated by the resource, over time the costs expensed can exceed the income tax basis of the property.

Percentage of completion method (PCM). A special method of accounting that applies to long-term contracts for which the taxpayer reports in gross income each year a portion of the total contract price that corresponds to the portion of the total estimated contract costs actually incurred during the year.

Permanent difference. The condition that exists when items of income or expense are reported for financial accounting purposes but *never* for tax purposes, or vice versa.

Perquisites. Fringe benefits that represent privileges that businesses make available to their employees.

Personal and dependency exemptions. A deduction from adjusted gross income the government allows to individual taxpayers. A deduction is allowed for the taxpayer, the taxpayer's spouse (if filing a joint return), and the taxpayer's dependents.

Personal holding company (PHC). Any corporation for which (1) during the last half of the tax year, more than 50 percent of the corporation's stock is owned, *directly or indirectly*, by five or fewer individuals and (2) at least 60 percent of the corporation's adjusted ordinary income for the year is PHC income.

Personal holding company income. Eight specific types of ordinary income, including: (1) dividends, interest, and royalties; (2) rents; (3) mineral, oil, and gas royalties; (4) copyright royalties; (5) produced film rents; (6) amounts received by a corporation for the use of its property; (7) compensation under personal services contracts; and (8) estate or trust income.

Personal property. Property that is not real estate. *See* Tangible personal property *and* Intangible property.

Personal tax credit. A tax credit available only to individuals.

Points. Term used to describe the prepaid interest a lender charges in exchange for a lower interest rate to the borrower over the term of the loan.

Portfolio income. Income derived from investments, such as stocks, bonds, and mutual funds.

Post-termination transition period. Term relevant to S corporations. Generally the one year period that starts one day after the corporation ceases to be an S corporation.

Precedent. Refers to a principle in law of using the past decisions to assist in making current decisions.

Primary sources of authority. Part of the tax law. Examples of primary sources include legislative authority (e.g., the Code, tax treaties, and Congressional reports), administrative authority (e.g., Treasury regulations and IRS rulings), and judicial decisions.

Principal partner. A partner that has at least a five-percent interest in the profits *or* capital of the partnership.

Principal partner rule. The second of three tests used to determine a partnership's required tax year. If the majority interest rule does not apply, this rule requires that a partnership adopt the tax year of *all* of its principal partners. *See also* Least aggregate deferral of income rule *and* Majority partners rule.

Private activity bond. A bond issued by a state or other municipality from which more than 10 percent of the proceeds are used to finance private business activities. Interest paid on these bonds is exempt from regular income tax if the issuer has complied with certain limitations concerning the volume of the bonds issued and the use of the bond proceeds.

Private letter ruling. A written statement issued by the Associate Chief Counsel that interprets and applies the tax laws to a specific set of facts presented by a taxpayer. A letter ruling is issued at the request of a taxpayer and upon payment of a fee.

Private nonoperating foundation. A privately funded, tax-exempt, nonprofit organization that does not meet the requirements of a private operating foundation.

Private operating foundation. A privately funded organization that directly carries out its own activities and is required to spend at least 85 percent of its earnings carrying out its activities and to pass certain other tests.

Pro rata share. The portion (based on ownership percentage) of each item of an S corporation's taxable income that a shareholder is required to take into account when calculating the shareholder's taxable income.

Procedural regulation. A regulation that establishes procedure or practice requirements (such as prescribing how an election is made).

Profits-only interest. The term used to describe a partner's interest in a partnership when the partner is entitled to a share of future partnership profits but does not have an ownership interest in the capital of the partnership.

Progressive tax. A tax structure in which the average tax rate increases as the tax base increases.

Property tax. A tax assessed on property, including real property, tangible personal property, and intangible personal property.

Proportional tax. A tax structure in which the average tax rate does not change as the tax base changes (also referred to as flat tax).

Proposed regulation. A Treasury regulation that the Secretary of the Treasury proposes to issue.

Public charities. Charitable organizations such as churches, public universities, the Red Cross, and the United Way that receive their funding from the general public.

Public good. A government-provided good or service for which enjoyment of the good cannot be limited.

Publicly-held corporations. Corporations whose stock is traded on one of the U.S. stock exchanges, such as the American Stock Exchange, New York Stock Exchange, or NASDAQ.

Qualified charitable organization. A tax-exempt, nonprofit organization formed and operated exclusively for the purposes specified in Code Sec. 501(c)(3).

Qualified community development entity (qualified CDE). A domestic corporation or partnership whose primary mission is serving, or providing investment capital for, low-income communities or low-income persons.

Qualified dividends. Dividends that are taxed to individual taxpayers at a rate lower than the taxpayers' marginal tax rates. They represent dividends paid on stock of a U.S. corporation or a qualified foreign corporation that the individual held for 121 days surrounding the ex-dividend date.

Qualified personal service corporation (QPSC). A corporation engaged almost exclusively in performing services in the fields of health, law, engineering, architecture, accounting, actuarial science, performing arts, or consulting. At least 95 percent of the value of its stock is held, directly or indirectly, by its employees, by retired employees who performed services for the corporation, or by an estate or other person owning stock because of the death of such employees or retired employees.

Qualified rehabilitated building. A building that is a certified historic structure or a building that originally was placed in service before 1936 and with respect to which the taxpayer paid or incurred substantial rehabilitation expenditures.

Qualified Subchapter S subsidiary (QSub). A domestic corporation that is 100-percent owned by an S corporation that the S corporation has elected to treat as a QSub.

Qualified Subchapter S trust (QSST). One of the types of trusts that can be a shareholder of an S corporation if the beneficiary elects to qualify the trust as a shareholder. All of the income of the trust must be distributed to one individual, who must be a U.S. citizen or resident. Any trust principal distributed during the income beneficiary's lifetime can be distributed only to that income beneficiary.

Qualified zone employee. An employee who performs substantially all of his or her services for an employer within an empowerment zone or renewal community and whose principal residence while performing such services is located within an empowerment zone or renewal community.

Qualified zone wages. Wages paid or incurred by an employer for services performed by an employee while working as a qualified zone employee.

Real property. Land and buildings (also referred to as real estate).

Realization principle. Gains and losses on property are not reported on the tax return until the year in which property is disposed of in a taxable transaction.

Realized gain or loss. Measure of the taxpayer's true economic gain or loss resulting from the disposal of property in a sale, an exchange, or an abandonment.

Recapture of a tax credit. If a taxpayer ceases to use property for the purposes that qualified the property for a tax credit, all or a portion of the credit may have to be added to the taxpayer's tax liability for the year that the property ceased to be used for the qualified purpose.

Recognized gain or loss. The amount of the realized gain or loss that is reported on the tax return.

Recourse debt. The type of debt arrangement in which the lender can proceed directly against the borrower for any debt on which the borrower defaults.

Recourse liability. Liability for which the seller is personally liable.

Refundable tax credit. A credit that can reduce a taxpayer's tax liability to zero and produce a refund for any amount of the credit in excess of the taxpayer's tax liability.

Regressive tax. A tax structure in which the average tax rate decreases as the tax base increases.

Rehabilitation credit. A nonrefundable credit available for substantially rehabilitating a depreciable building that was placed in service before 1936 or that qualifies as a certified historic structure. *See also* Substantially rehabilitated *and* Qualified rehabilitated building.

Research activities credit. A nonrefundable income tax credit for conducting qualified research.

Residential real property. Rental property for which 80 percent or more of the gross rental income is derived from the rental of dwelling units. *See also* Dwelling unit.

Return of capital distribution. A distribution of cash or other property from a corporation that is not made from current or accumulated earnings and profits.

Revenue procedure. A ruling issued by the IRS that involves a procedural issue.

Revenue ruling. An official interpretation by the IRS as to the application of the tax laws to a specific set of facts.

Reversing difference. Timing difference that occurs in years subsequent to the year in which the originating difference occurs. *See also* Originating difference *and* Timing difference.

S corporation. A flow-through business entity that does not pay income taxes. An S corporation gets its name because it is a corporation that has elected to be taxed under Subchapter S of Chapter 1 of the Code. Only corporations that satisfy certain requirements can elect to be taxed as S corporations.

S short year. In the S termination year, the portion of the year ending before the effective date of the termination of the corporation's S status.

S termination year. The year that a corporation's status as an S corporation terminates.

Sales tax. A broad-based tax on the consumption of goods and services.

Salvage value. Term used in financial accounting. The amount for which the owner of an asset believes the asset could be sold at the end of its useful life.

Schedule M-1. Part of Form 1120, *U.S. Corporation Income Tax Return*; it requires corporations to reconcile their net income for financial accounting purposes with their taxable income. Must be filed by corporations with total receipts and/or total assets of at least $250,000 (but total assets less than $10 million).

Schedule M-2. Part of Form 1120, *U.S. Corporation Income Tax Return*; it requires corporations to explain changes during the year in their unappropriated retained earnings. Must be filed by corporations that file Schedule M-1 or Schedule M-3.

Schedule M-3. An expanded version of Schedule M-1. Must be filed by corporations with total receipts of at least $250,000 and total assets of at least $10 million.

Secondary sources of authority. A reference that explains, comments on, or updates primary sources of tax authority. Examples include topical and annotated tax services, treatises, journals, papers from tax institutes, newsletters, and citators.

Section 179 property. Property eligible for immediate expensing under Code Sec. 179. Section 179 property is tangible personal property that is depreciable under MACRS and is acquired by purchase for use in the active conduct of a trade or business.

Section 291 gain. Ordinary income recognized on the sale of depreciable real property sold by a C corporation.

Section 1231 gain. The gain on the sale, exchange, or condemnation of Section 1231 property other than ordinary gain due to depreciation recapture.

Section 1231 loss. A loss on the sale, exchange, or condemnation of Section 1231 property.

Section 1231 property. Land or depreciable property used in a business and held for more than one year.

Section 1244 stock. Stock issued by a domestic corporation in exchange for money or property at a time the corporation does not have more than $1 million in paid-in capital. The corporation must also meet an active business requirement unless it is a new corporation.

Section 1245 gain. The (ordinary income) gain that results from depreciation recapture on depreciable personal property held for more than one year. The amount of gain is equal to the *lesser* of the amount of the gain or the accumulated depreciation taken on the property.

Section 1250 gain. The (ordinary income) gain on the sale of depreciable real property that is recaptured as ordinary income. The amount recaptured is the *lesser* of the amount of the gain or the excess of the depreciation taken over the amount that would have been allowed under the straight-line method.

Self-employment tax. The employee and employer portions of FICA tax that are imposed on net earnings from self-employment.

Short tax year. A tax year lasting fewer than 12 months.

Short-term capital gain or loss. A capital gain or loss on a capital asset held for one year or less.

Social security taxes. The old-age, survivors, and disability insurance (OASDI) portion of the FICA tax.

Sole proprietor. The owner of an unincorporated business.

Standard deduction. A deduction from adjusted gross income that the federal government allows individual taxpayers to deduct in lieu of itemized deductions.

Start-up costs. Costs that normally would be currently deductible if they were incurred in connection with the operation of an existing trade or business and that are not organizational costs.

Stock dividend. A dividend payable in shares of the distributing corporation's own stock.

Straight debt. A written, unconditional promise to pay a sum certain in money on demand or on a specified date that provides for an interest rate or payment dates that are not contingent on profits, the borrower's discretion, the payment of dividends with respect to common stock, or similar factors. It also cannot be converted in any type of equity interest of the corporation and must be held by an individual (other than a nonresident alien), estate, trust eligible to be an S corporation shareholder, or a person who is actively and regularly engaged in the business of lending money.

Substantial authority. An objective standard that is less stringent than the "more-likely-than-not" standard, but more rigorous than the "reasonable basis" standard.

Substantial economic effect. The standard that must be met before allocations of partnership items can be made to the partners as specified in the partnership agreement.

Surviving spouse. A filing status available to taxpayers widowed during one of the two preceding tax years who have a dependent son or daughter living with them the entire year.

Tangible personal property. Property that has physical characteristics but is not real estate.

Tax accounting. Rules used to determine when income and expenses are recognized for tax purposes.

Tax authority. Established tax law that can be used to help in reaching a conclusion about a tax issue.

Tax avoidance. The art of reducing tax liability through legitimate means.

Tax base. Used in computing tax liability. It represents the amount subject to tax. The tax base is multiplied by the tax rate to determine the taxpayer's tax liability.

Tax benefit rule. A tax rule under which an amount recovered must be included in gross income for the year of the recovery if all or a portion of the expense deducted in a prior tax year is recovered in a subsequent tax year and if the deduction resulted in a tax benefit for the taxpayer.

Tax compliance research. The process of determining how an item of income already received, an expense already incurred, or a transaction already completed should be reported for tax purposes.

Tax credit. Amount that reduces a taxpayer's tax liability. Can be either refundable or nonrefundable.

Tax deferred. When income or gain is postponed to some future point in time but is eventually taxed.

Tax evasion. Understating taxes due to the government through unlawful means.

Tax planning research. The process of determining how best to plan for income not yet received, expenses not yet incurred, and transactions that have not yet occurred to achieve the most favorable tax consequences.

Tax preference. A deduction or exclusion allowed in the calculation of regular taxable income that the Internal Revenue Code specifically singles out as excessive and, therefore, not allowed in the calculation of alternative minimum taxable income.

Tax year. The period of time over which taxable income is reported to the government.

Taxable income. The difference between a taxpayer's gross income and the total deductions a taxpayer is allowed. The tax base used in the regular income tax system.

Taxable income limitation. A limitation that disallows any Section 179 expense from being deducted in the current year for amounts that exceed the aggregate of the taxpayer's taxable income derived from the active conduct of any trade or business.

Taxable income per return. A corporation's taxable income, as reported on the U.S. federal income tax return.

Technical advice memorandum (TAM). Written advice from the IRS on the interpretation and proper application of tax law, tax treaties, regulations, revenue rulings, notices, or other precedents to a specific set of facts. A TAM is requested by IRS personnel, not taxpayers. No fee is charged a taxpayer for a TAM.

Temporary regulation. A Treasury regulation issued to provide interim guidance to tax practitioners and the public until final regulations are issued. The rules contained in temporary regulations can be used as authority pending issuance of final regulations.

Testamentary trusts. Trusts created from a decedent's will and come into existence upon the death of the grantor.

Timing difference. Difference that results when income and expenses are reported in one year for financial accounting purposes and in a different year for tax purposes. In the alternative minimum tax system, a difference in the treatment of an item for determining regular taxable income and alternative minimum taxable income that reverses itself over time. *See also* Originating difference *and* Reversing difference.

Topical tax service. A tax service that is arranged by topic rather than by Code section. CCH's *Tax Research Consultant* is an example of a topical tax service.

Treasury regulations. The official interpretation of the Code by the Secretary of the Treasury.

U.S. Court of Federal Claims. One of the trial courts to which taxpayers may appeal an IRS determination.

U.S. Supreme Court. The last resort for those appealing a decision of a Circuit Court of Appeal and final authority as to what the Code means.

U.S. Tax Court. One of the trial courts to which taxpayers may appeal an IRS determination. Unlike the U.S. district court or U.S. Court of Federal Claims, there is no requirement that the taxpayer pay any alleged deficiency before the court will hear the taxpayer's appeal.

Undistributed personal holding company income. The amount subject to the personal holding company tax, determined by applying certain adjustments to the taxable income of the corporation.

Uniform capitalization (UNICAP) rules. The rules that require a taxpayer to capitalize certain costs as part of the cost of real or tangible personal property the taxpayer produces.

Unrealized gains and losses. The difference between the FMV of property and its adjusted basis at a time other than when the property has been disposed of. Sometimes referred to as paper gains and losses because they represent the appreciation or decline in value of property that has yet to be sold.

Unrealized receivable. Any right to income for services or goods that are not capital assets that have not been previously recorded in gross income under the taxpayer's method of accounting.

Unreasonable Position. A tax return preparer can be penalized for preparing a return or claim of refund that understates tax liability if the understatement is due to an unreasonable position. If a position (other than a position with respect to a tax shelter or reportable transaction to which Code Sec. 6662A applies) is adequately disclosed, it will be considered unreasonable unless the preparer had a reasonable basis for it (*reasonable basis standard*). If a position (other than a position with respect to a tax shelter or reportable transaction to which Code Sec. 6662A applies) is not adequately disclosed, it will be considered unreasonable unless there is or was substantial authority for it (*substantial authority standard*). If a position is with respect to a tax shelter or reportable transaction to which Code Sec. 6662A applies, it will be considered unreasonable unless it was reasonable for the preparer to believe that it would more likely than not be sustained on its merits (*more-likely-than-not standard*).

Unrecaptured Section 1250 gain. A term applicable only to individual taxpayers. The portion of the gain on the sale of depreciable realty that is taxed at a maximum 25-percent tax rate.

Use tax. A tax charged by states on the consumption, use, or storage of goods and services that are not subject to sales tax.

User fee. A tax charged to those that use a government-provided good or service.

Wash sale. A sale of securities (stocks and bonds) in which a taxpayer realizes a loss on the sale and then purchases the same or substantially identical securities within 30 days before or 30 days after the date of the sale; tax laws do not allow taxpayers to recognize losses that result from wash sales.

Wealth transfer tax. The tax a government imposes on transfers of wealth between two individuals. *See also* Estate tax, Gift tax, *and* Inheritance tax.

Wherewithal-to-pay concept. The principle that taxes income at the point at which the taxpayer has the greatest ability to pay the tax on realized income.

Work opportunity credit. A nonrefundable income tax credit for employing individuals from certain targeted groups.

Written determinations. IRS rulings issued specifically to taxpayers. *See* private letter ruling, technical advice memorandum, *and* determination letter.

2009 TAX RATE TABLES

Schedule X: Single

If taxable income is:	The tax is:
Not over $8,350	10% of the taxable income
Over $8,350 but not over $33,950	$835.00 + 15% of the amount over $8,350
Over $33,950 but not over $82,250	$4,675.00 + 25% of the amount over $33,950
Over $82,250 but not over $171,550	$16,750.00 + 28% of the amount over $82,250
Over $171,550 but not over $372,950	$41,754.00 + 33% of the amount over $171,550
Over $372,950	$108,216.00 + 35% of the amount over $372,950

Schedule Y-1: Married Filing Jointly/Qualifying Widow(er)

If taxable income is:	The tax is:
Not over $16,700	10% of the taxable income
Over $16,700 but not over $67,900	$1,670.00 + 15% of the amount over $16,700
Over $67,900 but not over $137,050	$9,350.00 + 25% of the amount over $67,900
Over $137,050 but not over $208,850	$26,637.50 + 28% of the amount over $137,050
Over $208,850 but not over $372,950	$46,741.50 + 33% of the amount over $208,850
Over $372,950	$100,894.50 + 35% of the amount over $372,950

Schedule Y-2: Married Filing Separately

If taxable income is:	The tax is:
Not over $8,350	10% of the taxable income
Over $8,350 but not over $33,950	$835.00 + 15% of the amount over $8,350
Over $33,950 but not over $68,525	$4,675.00 + 25% of the amount over $33,950
Over $68,525 but not over $104,425	$13,318.75 + 28% of the amount over $68,525
Over $104,425 but not over $186,475	$23,370.75 + 33% of the amount over $104,425
Over $186,475	$50,447.25 + 35% of the amount over $186,475

Schedule Z: Head of Household

If taxable income is:	The tax is:
Not over $11,950	10% of the taxable income
Over $11,950 but not over $45,500	$1,195.00 + 15% of the amount over $11,950
Over $45,500 but not over $117,450	$6,227.50 + 25% of the amount over $45,500
Over $117,450 but not over $190,200	$24,215.00 + 28% of the amount over $117,450
Over $190,200 but not over $372,950	$44,585.00 + 33% of the amount over $190,200
Over $372,950	$104,892.50 + 35% of the amount over $372,950

CCH TAX BRIEFING: AMERICAN RECOVERY AND REINVESTMENT ACT OF 2009

CCH Tax Briefing:

AMERICAN RECOVERY AND REINVESTMENT ACT OF 2009

◉.CCH
a Wolters Kluwer business

February 17, 2009

Special Report

Highlights:

✔ *New Making Work Pay Credit*

✔ *Enhanced Child Tax Credit*

✔ *American Opportunity Tax Credit for Education*

✔ *Expand Homebuyer Tax Credit*

✔ *Extended Bonus Depreciation and Code Sec. 179 Expensing*

✔ *Five-Year Carryback of NOLs*

✔ *Extensions/Increases of Many Energy Tax Incentives*

✔ *Recovery Zone Bonds and Related Relief*

Inside

President Signs Massive Stimulus Bill; Nearly $300 Billion in Tax Relief

The much-anticipated economic stimulus package, the American Recovery and Reinvestment Act of 2009 (P.L. 111-5), is now law. President Obama signed this historic measure on February 17. Moving through Congress in less than four weeks, the new law won House approval on February 13 by a 246-183 margin, followed by same-day Senate passage 60-38. The $787 billion new law, which contains nearly $300 billion in tax relief, sets in motion a wave of direct spending and tax incentives to jump start the U.S. economy out of recession.

The tax title in the new law — the *American Recovery and Reinvestment Tax Act of 2009*—is itself a massive piece of legislation. The tax provisions add many new tax breaks and significant enhancements to existing deductions and credits. Major provisions include a new Making Work Pay credit, enhancements to the child tax credit and first-time homebuyer credit, a 2009 alternative minimum tax (AMT) patch, taxpayer-friendly additions to many energy incentives, extensions of 2008 bonus depreciation and increased Code Sec. 179 expensing, along with a five-year net operating loss (NOL) carryback for small businesses, state and local government relief, and more. In all, the new law makes over 300 changes to the Internal Revenue Code.

Impact *The new law provides immediate relief to both individuals and businesses. Most of the tax incentives in the new law are retroactive to January 1, 2009. What's more, over $280 billion in tax relief is concentrated within the next two years.*

Caution *While the overall size of the new law remains massive, those who have been following the bill over the past month will note that some House and Senate provisions were pared back or otherwise modified in final negotiations. To win passage of the package, lawmakers reduced the Making Work Pay credit, placed a limit on the new five-year NOL carryback to small businesses, cut back on proposals to raise and extend the first-time homebuyers credit, as well as proposals to create a higher new car buyers deduction. Nevertheless, tax cuts remain a large part of the overall stimulus package, comprising over 35 percent of its final price tag.*

INDIVIDUAL INCENTIVES

Making Work Pay Credit

The new law includes President Obama's signature provision aimed at individual tax relief: the Making Work Pay credit. The

Making Work Pay credit allows a credit against income tax in an amount equal to the lesser of 6.2 percent of the individual's earned income or $400 ($800 for married couples filing jointly). The credit applies retroactively to the start of 2009 and will be repeated again in 2010.

The credit applies in full for individuals whose modified adjusted gross income (MAGI) does not exceed $75,000 or $150,000 in the case of married couples filing jointly. The credit is phased out at a two percent rate above that limit.

The employer's share of FICA, or its 6.2 percent equivalent to be more precise, would remain unchanged. Qualified taxpayers would take this credit through a reduction in wage withholding or in a lump sum when filing their returns for the tax year. Earnings from self-employment also qualify to the extent they are taken into account in computing taxable income. Individuals who do not provide a Social Security number on their returns, however, are ineligible.

Impact *Only individuals with earned income would qualify for the Making Work Pay credit, which would effectively offset an individual's share of FICA payroll taxes for the first $6,452 in earnings ($12,904 for couples).*

Comment *MAGI is equal to adjusted gross income increased by certain exclusions for income earned outside the U.S. Individuals in Puerto Rico and U.S. possessions would receive a mirror benefit.*

Caution *Excluded from the Making Work Pay credit are nonresident aliens, Code Sec. 151 dependents, and any estate or trust.*

$250 Economic Recovery Payment

The new law provides a one-time payment of $250–for 2009 only– to individuals on fixed incomes (primar-

ily Social Security recipients, railroad retirees, and disabled veterans). Retired government workers, who generally are ineligible for Social Security, also will receive one-time payments of $250. These payments will reduce any Making Work Pay credit to which the individual would otherwise be entitled.

Impact *The logistics for distributing the $250 checks have not yet been announced. The assumption, however, is that the IRS will follow a distribution plan similar to the 2008 stimulus payments.*

> The final stimulus package frontloads at least $280 billion in tax breaks within the first two years: 2009 and 2010. In all, more than 50 major provisions have been rolled up into this massive tax recovery package.

AMT Patch

The new law includes an alternative minimum tax (AMT) patch for 2009. The AMT patch for 2009 raises exemption amounts slightly above the 2008 patch levels. The 2009 AMT exemption amounts are: $70,950 for joint filers and surviving spouses (up from $69,950 in 2008); and $46,700 for singles and heads of households (up from $46,200).

Impact *The patch is designed to insulate approximately 26 million middle-income taxpayers from the reach of the AMT. The AMT patch costs roughly $70 billion.*

First-Time Homebuyer Tax Credit

The new law raises the current maximum $7,500 first-time homebuyer tax credit to $8,000, and extends it at that level through November 30, 2009. It also eliminates any required repayment to the IRS after 36 months in the home. These enhancements apply to purchases of a principal residence by a first-time homebuyer after December 31, 2008. Purchases on or after April 9, 2008, and before January 1, 2009, continue to be governed by the original first-time homebuyer credit enacted last year. The credit phase-outs that start for taxpayers with AGI in excess of $75,000 ($150,000 for joint filers) continue to apply to both years.

Comment *The effective date for the new law's no pay-back provision is keyed to "residences purchased after December 31, 2008." A purchase takes place when title closes rather than when a contract of sale is executed.*

Comment *The Senate had proposed raising the credit to $15,000 and making it applicable to all home purchasers and regardless of income level. Those enhancements were rejected during conference negotiations.*

New Car Deduction

A surprise provision arriving late in drafting the stimulus package allows purchasers of new vehicles for the rest of 2009 an above-the-line deduction for state and local sales taxes or excise taxes paid on the purchase. The new law puts two limits on this new deduction:

(1) Deductible sales or excise taxes cannot exceed the portion of the tax attributable to the first $49,500 of the purchase price of any one vehicle; and

(2) Any deduction will be phased out to the extent the purchaser has adjusted gross income exceeding $125,000 ($250,000 for joint returns).

Any newly purchased vehicle, including cars, SUVs, light trucks or motorcycles, first used by the taxpayer that weighs no more than 8,500 gross pounds generally qualifies. Motor homes also qualify.

Impact *Both domestic and foreign made vehicles qualify. However, sales taxes paid on a lease agreement are not included. Assuming a four percent sales tax on a $40,000 vehicle, the above-the-line deduction would equal $1,600.*

Caution *The new car deduction is effective only for purchases "on or after date of enactment," which takes place only when President Obama signs the legislation.*

Education Credit

The new law temporarily enhances the existing HOPE education credit–for 2009 and 2010 only– in amount (from a maximum $1,800 to $2,500 per year), in scope (extending it to all four years of college and adding course materials to qualifying expenses), and in phase-out level (to $80,000/$160,000 joint filers). The new law renames the credit the "American Opportunity Tax Credit" and makes 40 percent of the credit refundable. Under the new credit, the maximum $2,500 per year would be allowed on $4,000 in qualifying payments (100 percent of the first $2,000 and 25 percent of the next $2,000).

Comment *Although this credit would be made retroactive to January 1, 2009, it does not automatically apply to a college semester that begins in 2009. Tuition paid late in 2008 for an upcoming 2009 semester qualifies only for a 2008 credit under existing rules.*

Comment *The new law instructs the Treasury Department to study how to better coor-*

dinate the education credits with the federal Pell Grant program and the feasibility of requiring students to perform community service for purposes of the education credits.

Child Tax Credit

The new law increases the refundable portion of the child tax credit for 2009 and 2010. The agreement does so by setting the income threshold at $3,000.

Impact *The child tax credit currently gives individuals with dependent children under age 17 at the close of a calendar year a $1,000 per child credit through 2010. The Emergency Economic Stabilization Act of 2008 (EESA) enhanced the credit for 2008. Taxpayers in 2008 were eligible for a refundable credit equal to 15 percent of their earned income in excess of a $8,500 threshold up to the child credit amount if the total amount of their allowable credit exceeds their total tax liability (regular and AMT).*

Earned Income Tax Credit

The new law provides a temporary increase in the *Earned Income Tax Credit (EITC)* for 2009 and 2010. Prior to this change, the credit percentage for the EITC for a taxpayer with two or more qualifying children was 40 percent of the first $12,570 of earned income. The new law increases the percentage to 45 percent of the first $12,570 of earned income for taxpayers with three or more qualifying children. The EITC phase-out range has also been adjusted upward by $1,880 for joint filers to eliminate any marriage penalty.

Planning Tip *Eligible individuals may elect to receive advance payment of the EITC from their employer. This is handled through the withholding system.*

Unemployment Compensation

Currently, unemployment benefits are included in a recipient's gross income for federal income tax purposes. The new law temporarily excludes up to $2,400 of unemployment compensation from a recipient's gross income for 2009.

Caution *Amounts in excess of $2,400 remain fully taxable.*

Transit Benefits Parity

Qualified transportation fringe benefits, such as transit passes, van pooling and qualified parking, are not included in an employee's income up to specified dollar amounts. The new law increases the current $120 per month income exclusion amount for transit passes and van pooling to $230 per month for 2009 (starting in March 2009), and continues it through 2010 with an inflation adjustment.

Impact *The new law in effect equalizes the $230/month amount now permitted for parking, with similar inflation adjustments for 2010. These benefits are a tax-free fringe if provided by an employer. If paid for by the employee, they can qualify as a pretax deduction from wages provided a plan is in place. In either case, the employer must take the initiative by sponsoring a plan.*

Qualified Tuition Programs

Qualified tuition program (aka "529 plan") distributions used to pay a beneficiary's qualified education expenses are tax-free. Other distributions are included in the beneficiary's income and are subject to a penalty. For 2009 and 2010 the new law allows beneficiaries of qualified tuition programs to use tax-free distributions to pay for computers and computer technology, including internet access.

Impact *Laptops and computers are required for most first-year students at colleges, universi-*

TAX ★★★2009 Legislation Update

ties and other postsecondary education institutions so the change is very practical. As long as the student uses the technology, the new law allows other family members to use it without allocation.

BUSINESS INCENTIVES

The new law provides businesses with over $75 billion in tax benefits for 2009 and 2010 alone. It does so by extending bonus depreciation, increasing Code Sec. 179 expensing, allowing a five-year carryback of net operating losses (NOLs) to small businesses, and providing other business-related incentives.

Bonus Depreciation

The new law extends the 50-percent first-year bonus depreciation allowed under the *2008 Economic Stimulus Act* through December 31, 2009. The extension is retroactive to January 1, 2009. The new law also extends, through 2010, the additional year of bonus depreciation allowed under the *2008 Economic Stimulus Act* for property with a recovery period of 10 years or longer, for transportation property (tangible personal property used to transport people or property), and for certain aircraft.

> **Planning Tip** *50-percent bonus depreciation is taken on top of the regular depreciation reported for the year the property is placed in service. As with any accelerated depreciation, however, a large current depreciation deduction results in smaller future deductions.*

Higher Caps on Vehicle Depreciation.

Also extended for bonus depreciation purposes, the regular dollar cap for new vehicles placed in service in 2009 is raised again by $8,000, effective January 1, 2009. This increase mirrors the temporary 2008 cap increase. For 2008, the regular first-year depreciation dollar cap of $2,960 for autos was raised to $10,960

if bonus depreciation is elected ($11,160 for light trucks and vans).

Code Sec. 179 Expensing

The new law extends the increased 2008 Code Sec. 179 expensing (aka, small business expensing) amounts to 2009. The *2008 Economic Stimulus Act* increased the amount of Code Sec. 179 expensing for 2008 to $250,000 and increased the threshold for reducing the deduction to $800,000. Without the 2009 extension, businesses placing property in service in 2009 would have been limited to a $125,000 inflation adjusted maximum deduction with a $500,000 cap.

> **Impact** *Unlike bonus depreciation, Code Sec. 179 expensing is available on new or used property. However, the $800,000 qualifying property ceiling effectively limits Code Sec. 179 expensing to small businesses.*

NOL Carryback

The new law provides a five-year carryback of 2008 NOLs but only for qualified small businesses with average gross receipts of $15 million or less. The new law gives these businesses the choice to carry back NOLs three, four or five years. The new treatment will apply only to NOLs for any tax year beginning or ending in 2008. The normal NOL carryback period, which is two years for all businesses, returns for NOLs incurred in 2009.

> **Impact** *Earlier versions of the bill provided NOL relief to all businesses and covered both 2008 and 2009.*

> **Planning Tip** *As soon as a taxpayer has filed a 2008 return containing an NOL, it can begin the process of claiming a refund to get cash back into its pockets. The amount of the refund for a carryback year is computed on page 1 of Form 1045 in the case of an individual*

and on page 1 of Form 1139 in the case of a corporation. The NOL is computed by making specified modifications to taxable income.

Work Opportunity Tax Credit

The new law creates two new categories of targeted groups under the existing Work Opportunity Tax Credit (WOTC): unemployed veterans and disconnected youth. These new categories apply to individuals who are hired and begin work in 2009 or 2010.

> **Comment** *The WOTC is combined with the Welfare-to-Work credit for qualified individuals who begin working for an employer after December 31, 2006, and before September 1, 2011.*

Refundable Credits in Lieu of Bonus Depreciation

The new law allows businesses to monetize accumulated AMT and R&D credits in lieu of taking bonus depreciation. The election to accelerate these historic AMT and R&D credits originally applied only to 2008, but the new law extends this option to all property qualifying for bonus depreciation placed in service through 2009.

> **Comment** *Under the 2008 Economic Stimulus Act, and by extension under the new law, businesses eligible for 50-percent bonus depreciation may instead elect to claim additional research or minimum tax credits that are refundable. The research credit or minimum tax credit is increased by the bonus depreciation amount, which is 20 percent of the difference between depreciation claimed on eligible property with and without bonus depreciation. The bonus depreciation amount is limited to the lesser of (1) $30 million or (2) research and AMT credits accumulated for years before January 1, 2006.*

Impact *The new law also allows a business to change its election from 2008 to 2009, or to make an election in 2009 when no election was made in 2008. This is a sharp difference from recent regulatory guidance issued by the IRS that would make a 2008 election binding on the business for 2009.*

Cancellation of Indebtedness

The new law will allow certain businesses to elect to recognize cancellation of indebtedness income over five years, beginning in 2014, for specified types of business debt repurchased by the business after December 31, 2008, and before January 1, 2011. An applicable debt instrument under the new law means a bond, debenture, note, certificate, or any other instrument constituting indebtedness issued by a C corporation or any other "person" in connection with the conduct of a trade or business by such person.

Caution *Once made, the election is irrevocable. The new law further provides for acceleration of deferred items in triggering circumstances, such as the liquidation or sale of substantially all of the assets of the taxpayer or the cessation of business by the taxpayer.*

Comment *The new law also modifies the rules for original issue discount on certain high yield obligations.*

Qualified Small Business Stock

Under current law, investors may exclude 50 percent of the gain from the sale of certain small business stock acquired and held for more than five years. The new law increases the exclusion to 75 percent for stock acquired after the date of enactment and before January 1, 2011. A small business cannot have assets over $50 million and must conduct an active trade or business.

S Corp Built-In Gain Period

The new law temporarily shortens, from 10 to seven years, the holding period for assets subject to the built-in gains tax imposed after a C corp elects to become an S corp. This provision applies to S corps that recognize built-in gain in tax years beginning in 2009 and 2010.

Impact *The built-in gains tax prevents C corps from avoiding corporate level tax on the disposition of appreciated assets it acquired while a C corp by first converting to S status. However, these rules also discourage S conversions in situations in which the business may not survive under C corp rules. The new law will give shareholders more flexibility during the current economic crisis.*

NOL Limitations on Banks Reinstated

The new law repeals Notice 2008-83 effective for ownership changes after January 16, 2009, with respect to which there was no written agreement before that date. In Notice 2008-83, the IRS provided relief from the NOL limitations for corporations acquiring a financially-strapped bank. Consequently, the losses were not limited by the normal Code Sec. 382 loss limitations.

Impact *Many lawmakers had criticized the IRS for issuing Notice 2008-83 claiming that the agency over-stepped its authority without giving proper deference to Congress. The new law also clarifies application of Code Sec. 382 for any restructuring required by Treasury.*

Comment *The new law amends Code Sec. 382 favorably for certain struggling taxpayers. It does so by providing that the limitation under Code Sec. 382(a) generally will not apply in the case of an ownership change under a restructuring plan required by a loan agreement or line of credit entered into with the Treasury Department under the EESA.*

Estimated Taxes

The new law decreases required estimated tax payments for individuals whose incomes primarily come from a small business in 2009. Rather than being required to make quarterly estimated tax payments based on 100 percent of their 2008 returns, the new law allows computation based on 90 percent.

Comment *The individual's AGI must be less than $500,000 and he or she must certify that more than 50 percent of the gross income shown on his or her return for the prior tax year was income from a small business. Income from a small business generally means income from a trade or business with an average number of employees of 500 or fewer.*

New Markets Tax Credit

The new law increases the New Markets Tax Credit (NMTC) program by authorizing maximum allocations of $5 billion for 2008 and 2009.

COBRA Benefits

The new law allows an individual who is involuntarily separated from employment between September 1, 2008, and January 1, 2010, to elect to pay 35 percent of his/her COBRA coverage and have it treated as paying the full amount.

The former employer will be required to pay the remaining 65 percent but, in effect, will be reimbursed by crediting those amounts against income tax withholding and payroll taxes it is otherwise required to remit to the federal government. Income and other limitations on COBRA coverage apply.

6

TAX
★★★2009 Legislation Update

ENERGY INCENTIVES

The energy incentives in the new law are targeted to both individuals and businesses. President Obama has pledged to significantly expand the development and production of alternative sources of energy, such as biomass, solar and wind energy, in part to create new "green collar" jobs. The more significant incentives provided under the new law include:

Residential Energy Property Credit

The new law increases the Code Sec. 25C residential energy property tax credit from 10 percent to 30 percent, raises the maximum cap to a $1,500 aggregate amount for 2009 and 2010 installations, eliminates the $500 lifetime cap, and makes several other modifications. The changes are effective for eligible property placed in service after December 31, 2008, and before January 1, 2011.

> **Impact** *Higher energy costs should accelerate the "pay-back" period for qualifying home improvements. The credit was in effect in prior years through 2007, but Congress allowed it to lapse for 2008. Pre-2008 credits are not counted toward the new $1,500 maximum.*

> **Comment** *Improvements eligible for the Code Sec. 25C credit include insulation materials, exterior windows including skylights, exterior doors, central air conditioners, natural gas, propane or oil water heaters or furnaces, hot water boilers, electric heat pump water heaters, certain metal roofs and stoves, and advanced main air circulating fans.*

Residential Energy Efficient Property Credit

The new law removes the individual dollar caps under the Code Sec. 25D residential energy efficient property credit for solar hot water property, geothermal heat pumps and wind energy property. The new law, however, does place a $500 credit cap on qualified fuel cell property expenditures.

Alternative Fuel Pump Tax Credit

The new law increases the credit for alternative fuel vehicle refueling property for commercial and retail refueling stations for 2009 and 2010. The credit currently equals 30 percent of the cost of property placed in service at each location by the taxpayer during the tax year but is limited to $30,000. The agreement increases the credit to 50 percent (capped at $50,000) for property placed in service in 2009 and 2010. For individuals, the credit is also increased to 50 percent (capped at $2,000).

> **Comment** *Although the 30 percent credit continues to apply to hydrogen refueling property, the maximum credit for hydrogen refueling property jumps to $200,000.*

Renewable Electricity Production Credit

Code Sec. 45 provides a credit for electricity produced from renewable sources, such as wind. The new law extends (generally, through 2013; through 2012 for wind facilities) the placed-in-service dates for qualified wind and other facilities under Code Sec. 45.

Energy Investment Credit

The Economic Stimulus Act expanded the Code Sec. 48 energy investment credit to include qualified small wind energy property. The new law removes the credit cap for qualified small wind energy property. A 30 percent credit presently is available for qualified small wind energy property expenses made by the taxpayer during the tax year.

> **Comment** *The new law also removes the provision under Code Sec. 48(a)(4) that currently reduces the amount of the credit available for taxpayers financing their qualified facility with subsidized energy financing or proceeds from a private activity bond. This provision is effective for periods after December 31, 2008.*

Investment Credit Election

In lieu of producers taking the Code Sec. 45 production tax credit, the new law allows taxpayers to treat certain qualified alternative energy facilities as energy property eligible for a 30 percent investment credit under Code Sec. 48. Code Sec. 45 provides a credit for the production of electricity from alternative sources of energy at qualified facilities. The agreement limits the election for wind property placed in service in 2009-2012 and for other property placed in service in 2009-2013. The new law also coordinates Code Sec. 48 with renewable energy grants.

Plug-in Electric Vehicles

Although plug-in electric vehicles are not yet on the market, the new law modifies the existing credit for these environmentally-friendly vehicles. Separate treatment has also been carved out for low-speed vehicles. The base amount of the credit for qualified plug-in electric vehicles is $2,500. The full amount of the credit will be reduced once the manufacturer records its 200,000[th] sale.

> **Comment** *If a vehicle is eligible for the plug-in electric vehicle credit, it is not eligible for the Code Sec. 30B qualified hybrid vehicle credit. The new law allows the Code Sec. 30B credit as a personal credit against the alternative minimum tax (AMT) for tax years beginning after 2009.*

HELP FOR STATE/LOCAL GOVERNMENTS

The new law provides fiscal relief for states facing large budget deficits. The relief is designed to prevent cuts in health care, education, law enforcement and other programs, to avoid tax increases, and to increase spending on infrastructure improvements.

Bonds

The new law enhances existing bond programs and creates some new ones:

- *Recovery Zone bonds.* The new law creates a new category of tax credit bonds for 2009 and 2010 to be invested in economic recovery zones.
- *Industrial Development bonds.* The new law temporarily extends the scope of state and local government-issued industrial development bonds to facilities manufacturing intangible property.
- *Build America bonds.* The new law creates Build America bonds.

- *Qualified School Construction bonds.* The law provides for a new category of state and local government-issued tax-credit bond, known as a qualified school construction bond.
- *Qualified Zone Academy bonds (QZ-ABs).* The law increases the annual limit on QZABs and extends their availability at the heightened limit through 2010.
- *Tribal Economic Development bonds.* The new law authorizes Indian tribal governments to issue tax-exempt "tribal economic development bonds."
- *High-Speed Rail bonds.* The new law fine-tunes the maximum speed requirements for high-speed intercity rail facilities for purposes of high-speed rail bonds.
- *AMT limits on new private activity bonds.* Previously, Congress excluded interest on private activity bonds for hous-

ing from treatment as a tax-preference item subject to the individual alternative minimum tax (AMT). The new law expands the exclusion to all private activity bonds issued in 2009 and 2010.

- *Tax-exempt interest paid to financial institutions.* The new law creates a de minimis safe harbor for financial institutions deducting interest expense allocable to investments in tax-exempt municipal bonds issued in 2009 and 2010.

Low-Income Housing Credit

The new law allows states to receive a grant for low-income housing in lieu of low-income housing credit allocations for 2009.

Withholding On Government Contractors

The new law delays three-percent withholding on government contractors for one year, to December 31, 2011.

CASE TABLE

References are to paragraph (¶) numbers.

FINDING LIST

References are to paragraph (¶) numbers.

Proposed Regulations

Technical Advice Memoranda

Treasury Decisions

TOPICAL INDEX

References are to paragraph (¶) numbers.

References are to paragraph (¶) numbers.

References are to paragraph (¶) numbers.

References are to paragraph (¶) numbers.

References are to paragraph (¶) numbers.

References are to paragraph (¶) numbers.

References are to paragraph (¶) numbers.

References are to paragraph (¶) numbers.